Contents
For Statistics in the Workplace

CHAPTER 2   Marketing Application *24*
CHAPTER 4   Human Resources Application *96*
               Finance Application *108*
               Marketing Application *138*
               Accounting Application *138*
CHAPTER 6   Operations Management Application *184*
               Finance Application *208*
CHAPTER 7   Operations Management Application *251*
               Operations Management Application *252*
               Operations Management Application *253*
               Operations Management Application *258*
               Operations Management Application *259*
CHAPTER 9   Marketing Application *293*
               Operations Management Application *299*
CHAPTER 10   Operations Management Application *328*
CHAPTER 11   Operations Management Application *354*
               Finance Application *358*
               Operations Management Application *367*
               Marketing Application *375*
               Marketing Application *378*
CHAPTER 12   Operations Management Application *403*
               Operations Management Application *437*
               Marketing Application *440*
               Marketing Application: Market Segmentation *454*
CHAPTER 15   Market Segmentation *560*
               Market Segmentation *569*
CHAPTER 17   Human Resources Application *635*
               Human Resources Application *649*
CHAPTER 18   Operations Management Application *682*
               Human Resources Application *697*
               Economic Application *742*
CHAPTER 19   Operations Management Application *743*
               Accounting Application *753*
               Human Resources Application *754*

STATISTICS

for Management and Economics

STATISTICS

for Management and Economics

FIFTH EDITION

Gerald Keller

Wilfrid Laurier University

Brian Warrack

Wilfrid Laurier University

® Duxbury
Thomson Learning™

Pacific Grove • Albany • Belmont • Boston • Cincinnati • Detriot • Johannesburg • London •
Madrid • Melborune • Mexico City • New York • Scottsdale • Singapore • Tokyo • Toronto

Sponsoring Editor: *Curt Hinrichs*
Assistant Editor: *Bryon Granmo*
Marketing Team: *Laura Hubrich, Karin Sandberg, and Beth Kroenke*
Editorial Assistant: *Carrie Izant*
Production Coordinator: *Mary Anne Shahidi*
Editorial Project Management: *GTS Publishing Services*
Manuscript Editor: *Lorretta Palagi*
Permissions Editor: *Catherine Gingras*
Interior Design: *Rita Naughton and GTS Publishing Services*

Cover Design: *Laurie Albrecht*
Cover Photo/Illustration: *Yuji Tachibana/Photonica*
Interior Illustration: *GTS Graphics*
Photo Researcher: *Sue C. Howard*
Print Buyer: *Vena Dyer*
Composition: *GTS Graphics*
Cover Printing: *Phoenix*
Printing and Binding: *World Color–Versailles*

For more information about this or any other Duxbury products, contact:
DUXBURY
511 Forest Lodge Road
Pacific Grove, CA 93950 USA
www.duxbury.com
1-800-423-0563 (Thomson Learning Academic Resource Center)

Printed in United States of America

10   9   8   7   6   5

Library of Congress Cataloging-in-Publication Data

Keller, Gerald.
   Statistics for management and economics/Gerald Keller, Brian
Warrack. —5th ed.
          p.   cm.
   Includes bibliographical references and index.
   ISBN 0-534-36830-1
   1. Management—Statistical methods.   2. Economics—Statistical
methods.   I. Warrack, Brian.   II. Title.
HD30.215.K45   1999
658.4′033—dc21

99-30181
CIP

Brief Contents

1   What Is Statistics?   1

2   Graphical Descriptive Techniques   17

3   Art and Science of Graphical Presentations   73

4   Numerical Descriptive Measures   89

5   Data Collection and Sampling   147

6   Probability and Discrete Probability Distributions   165

7   Continuous Probability Distributions   235

8   Sampling Distributions   261

9   Introduction to Estimation   285

10   Introduction to Hypothesis Testing   311

11   Inference About the Description of a Single Population   347

12   Inference About the Comparison of Two Populations   393

REVIEW CHAPTER
13   Statistical Inference: A Review of Chapters 11 and 12   461

14   Analysis of Variance   480

15   Additional Test for Qualitative Data   543

16   Nonparametric Statistics   575

17   Simple Linear Regression and Correlation   625

18   Multiple Regression   679

19   Model Building   731

20   Time-Series Analysis and Forecasting   777

21   Statistical Process Control   833

REVIEW CHAPTER
22   Statistical Inference: Conclusion   867

Appendix A   Data File Sample Statistics   A-1

Appendix B   Tables   B-1

Appendix C   Answers to Selected Even-Numbered Exercises   C-1

Index   I-1

Guide to Statistical Techniques   Inside Front Cover (left)

Guide to Statistics in the Workplace   Inside Front Cover (right)

Index of Computer Instructions   Inside Back Cover (left)

Contents

1 WHAT IS STATISTICS? 1

1.1 Introduction to Statistics 2

1.2 Key Statistical Concepts 6

1.3 Statistical Applications in Business 7

1.4 Statistics and the Computer 14

1.5 World Wide Web and Learning Center 15

2 GRAPHICAL DESCRIPTIVE TECHNIQUES 17

2.1 Introduction 18

2.2 Types of Data 18

2.3 Graphical Techniques for Quantitative Data 23

2.4 Pie Charts, Bar Charts, and Line Charts 44

2.5 Scatter Diagrams 55

2.6 Summary 61

CASE 2.1 Pacific Salmon Catches 66

CASE 2.2 Bombardier, Inc. 66

CASE 2.3 The North American Free Trade Agreement (NAFTA) 67

APPENDIX 2.A Brief Introduction to Microsoft Excel 69

APPENDIX 2.B Brief Introduction to Minitab 70

3 ART AND SCIENCE OF GRAPHICAL PRESENTATIONS 73

3.1 Introduction 74

3.2 Graphical Excellence 74

3.3 Graphical Deception 82

3.4 Summary 87

CASE 3.1 Canadian Federal Budget 87

4 NUMERICAL DESCRIPTIVE MEASURES 89

4.1 Introduction 90

4.2 Measures of Central Location 90

4.3   Measures of Variability   102

4.4   Interpreting Standard Deviation   113

4.5   Measures of Relative Standing and Box Plots   117

4.6   Approximating Descriptive Measures for Grouped Data   124

4.7   Measures of Association   126

4.8   General Guidelines on the Exploration of Data   140

4.9   Summary   140

APPENDIX 4.A Summation Notation   144

5 DATA COLLECTION AND SAMPLING   147

5.1   Introduction   148

5.2   Sources of Data   148

5.3   Sampling   152

5.4   Sampling Plans   154

5.5   Errors Involved in Sampling   160

5.6   Use of Sampling in Auditing   161

5.7   Summary   162

6 PROBABILITY AND DISCRETE PROBABILITY DISTRIBUTIONS   165

6.1   Introduction   166

6.2   Assigning Probabilities to Events   166

6.3   Probability Rules and Trees   178

6.4   Random Variables and Probability Distributions   186

6.5   Expected Value and Variance   192

6.6   Bivariate Distributions   200

6.7   Finance Application: Investment Portfolio Diversification   205

6.8   Binomial Distribution   209

6.9   Poisson Distribution   219

6.10   Summary   225

CASE 6.1 Let's Make a Deal   231

CASE 6.2 Gains from Market Timing   231

CASE 6.3 Calculating Probabilities Associated with the Stock Market   232

CASE 6.4 To Bunt or Not to Bunt?   233

7 CONTINUOUS PROBABILITY DISTRIBUTIONS   235

7.1   Introduction   236

7.2   Continuous Probability Distributions   236

7.3   Normal Distribution   240

7.4   Exponential Distribution   254

7.5   Summary   259

8 SAMPLING DISTRIBUTIONS   261

8.1   Introduction   262

8.2   Sampling Distribution of the Mean   262

8.3   Creating the Sampling Distribution by Computer Simulation (Optional)   273

8.4   Sampling Distribution of a Proportion   276

8.5   Sampling Distribution of the Difference Between Two Means   280

8.6   From Here to Inference   282

8.7   Summary   284

9 INTRODUCTION TO ESTIMATION   285

9.1   Introduction   286

9.2   Concepts of Estimation   286

9.3   Estimating the Population Mean When the Population Standard Deviation Is Known   289

9.4   Selecting the Sample Size   302

9.5   Simulation Experiments (Optional)   305

9.6   Summary   308

10 INTRODUCTION TO HYPOTHESIS TESTING   311

10.1   Introduction   312

10.2   Concepts of Hypothesis Testing   313

10.3   Testing the Population Mean When the Population Standard Deviation Is Known   315

10.4   Calculating the Probability of a Type II Error   334

10.5   The Road Ahead   342

10.6   Summary   344

11 INFERENCE ABOUT THE DESCRIPTION OF A SINGLE POPULATION 347

11.1 Introduction 348

11.2 Inference About a Population Mean When the Population Standard Deviation Is Unknown 349

11.3 Inference About a Population Variance (Optional) 363

11.4 Inference About a Population Proportion 373

11.5 The Myth of the Law of Averages (Optional) 386

11.6 Summary 388

CASE 11.1 Pepsi's Exclusivity Agreement with a University 391

CASE 11.2 Pepsi's Exclusivity Agreement with a University: Coke's Side of the Equation 392

CASE 11.3 Number of Uninsured Motorists 392

12 INFERENCE ABOUT THE COMPARISON OF TWO POPULATIONS 393

12.1 Introduction 394

12.2 Inference About the Difference Between Two Means: Independent Samples 395

12.3 Observational and Experimental Data 413

12.4 Inference About the Difference Between Two Means: Matched Pairs Experiment 414

12.5 Inference About the Ratio of Two Variances (Optional) 425

12.6 Inference About the Difference Between Two Population Proportions 434

12.7 Marketing Application: Market Segmentation 447

12.8 Summary 449

CASE 12.1 Specialty Advertising Recall 454

CASE 12.2 Bonanza International 455

CASE 12.3 Accounting Course Exemptions 456

APPENDIX 12.A Excel Instructions 458

APPENDIX 12.B Minitab Instructions 459

13 REVIEW CHAPTER STATISTICAL INFERENCE: A REVIEW OF CHAPTERS 11 AND 12 461

13.1 Introduction 462

13.2 Guide to Identifying the Correct Technique: Chapters 11 and 12 462

CASE 13.1 Stock Market Returns After the Death of Key Executives 475

CASE 13.2 Quebec Separation: *Oui ou Non*? 476

CASE 13.3 Host Selling and Announcer Commercials 476

14 ANALYSIS OF VARIANCE 479

14.1 Introduction 480

14.2 Single-Factor (One-Way) Analysis of Variance: Independent Samples 481

14.3 Analysis of Variance Models 497

14.4 Single-Factor Analysis of Variance: Randomized Blocks 499

14.5 Two-Factor Analysis of Variance: Independent Samples 507

14.6 Operations Management Application: Finding and Reducing Variation 521

14.7 Multiple Comparisons (Optional) 526

14.8 Bartlett's Test (Optional) 533

14.9 Summary 536

CASE 14.1 Effects of Financial Planning 540

CASE 14.2 Diversification Strategy for Multinational Firms 541

15 ADDITIONAL TEST FOR QUALITATIVE DATA 543

15.1 Introduction 544

15.2 Chi-Squared Goodness-of-Fit Test 544

15.3 Chi-Squared Test of a Contingency Table 551

15.4 Summary of Tests on Qualitative Data 560

15.5 Chi-Squared Test for Normality (Optional) 562

15.6 Summary 566

CASE 15.1 Predicting the Outcomes of Basketball, Baseball, Football, and Hockey Games from Intermediate Results 569

CASE 15.2 Can Exposure to a Code of Professional Ethics Help Make Managers More Ethical? 570

CASE 15.3 Stock Return Distributions 571

APPENDIX 15.A Minitab Instructions 573

16 NONPARAMETRIC STATISTICS 575

16.1 Introduction 576

16.2 Wilcoxon Rank Sum Test for Independent Samples 577

16.3 Sign Test and Wilcoxon Signed Rank Sum Test for Matched Pairs 589

16.4   Kruskal-Wallis Test   602

16.5   Friedman Test   608

16.6   Testing for Normality   613

16.7   Summary   618

CASE 16.1 Capitalization Ratios in the United States and Japan   622

CASE 16.2 Bank of Commerce Customer Survey   623

17   SIMPLE LINEAR REGRESSION AND CORRELATION   625

17.1   Introduction   626

17.2   Model   627

17.3   Estimating the Coefficients   629

17.4   Error Variable: Required Conditions   636

17.5   Assessing the Model   638

17.6   Finance Application: Market Model   649

17.7   Using the Regression Equation   652

17.8   Coefficients of Correlation   657

17.9   Regression Diagnostics—I   664

17.10   Summary   673

CASE 17.1 Duxbury Press   676

CASE 17.2 Predicting University Grades from High School Grades   676

CASE 17.3 Insurance Compensation for Lost Revenues   677

18   MULTIPLE REGRESSION   679

18.1   Introduction   680

18.2   Model and Required Conditions   680

18.3   Estimating the Coefficients and Assessing the Model   681

18.4   Regression Diagnostics—II   699

18.5   Regression Diagnostics—III (Time Series)   714

18.6   Summary   725

CASE 18.1 Duxbury Press Revisited   729

CASE 18.2 Quebec Referendum Vote: Was There Electoral Fraud?   729

CASE 18.3 Quebec Referendum Vote: The Rebuttal   730

19 MODEL BUILDING 731

19.1   Introduction   732

19.2   Polynomial Models   732

19.3   Qualitative Independent Variables   745

19.4   Regression and the Analysis of Variance (Optional)   755

19.5   Stepwise Regression   758

19.6   Model Building   765

19.7   Human Resources Application: Pay Equity   766

19.8   Summary   772

CASE 19.1 Challenger Disaster   774

CASE 19.2 Track and Field Performance Forecasts   775

20 TIME-SERIES ANALYSIS AND FORECASTING 777

20.1   Introduction   778

20.2   Components of a Time Series   779

20.3   Smoothing Techniques   781

20.4   Trend Analysis   794

20.5   Measuring the Cyclical Effect   800

20.6   Measuring the Seasonal Effect   805

20.7   Introduction to Forecasting   811

20.8   Time-Series Forecasting with Exponential Smoothing   814

20.9   Time-Series Forecasting with Regression   819

20.10 Summary   829

21 STATISTICAL PROCESS CONTROL 833

21.1   Introduction   834

21.2   Process Variation   834

21.3   Control Charts for Variables: $\bar{x}$ and S Charts 840

21.4   Control Charts for Variables: $\bar{x}$ and R Charts (Optional)   853

21.5   Control Chart for Attributes: p Chart   860

21.6   Summary   865

22 REVIEW CHAPTER
STATISTICAL INFERENCE: CONCLUSION 867

22.1   Introduction   868

22.2   Identifying the Correct Techniques: Summary of Statistical Inference   868

CASE 22.1 Do Banks Discriminate Against Women Business Owners?—I   875

CASE 22.2 Do Banks Discriminate Against Women Business Owners?—II   879

22.3   The Last Word   885

CASE 22.3 Ambulance and Fire Department Response Interval Study   897

CASE 22.4 Underpricing in Initial Public Offerings   898

CASE 22.5 PC Magazine Survey   898

CASE 22.6 WLU Graduate Survey   899

CASE 22.7 Evaluation of a New Antidepressant Drug   900

CASE 22.8 Nutrition Education Programs   901

CASE 22.9 Do Banks Discriminate Against Women Business Owners?–III   901

Appendix A   Data File Sample Statistics   A-1

Appendix B   Tables   B-1

Appendix C   Answers to Selected Even-Numbered Exercises   C-1

Index   I-1

Guide to Statistical Techniques   Inside Front Cover (left)

Guide to Statistics in the Workplace   Inside Front Cover (right)

Index of Computer Instructions   Inside Back Cover (left)

Preface

This edition of *Statistics for Management and Economics* integrates statistics into business and economics curricula. We continue to emphasize real examples, exercises, and cases, and the use of computers and software including Microsoft Excel.

WHY WE WROTE THIS BOOK

The first edition of this book (1988) attempted to remedy a problem in the way applied statistics was taught: The existing literature stressed the arithmetic of statistical procedures. However, graduates need more than the ability to compute statistics—they also need the skill to select the appropriate method from the dozens of techniques taught in most introductory courses. And this skill must be taught.

Our approach teaches students how to recognize the correct procedure. As each technique is introduced, we demonstrate how to recognize when its use is appropriate and when it is not. Review chapters (13 and 22) that allow students to hone their technique-selection skills are also a feature of this approach. In each review chapter a flowchart develops the logical process for choosing the correct technique. In 1988, *Statistics for Management and Economics* was the only book with these features.

Our approach divides the solution of statistical problems into three parts: (1) *identify* the technique, (2) *solve,* or compute the required statistics, and (3) *interpret* the results. Our focus has been on the first and third parts because the statistics could be produced relatively easily with a computer. However, at the time of the first edition few students had easy access to a computer and statistical software, so we have continued teaching the how of statistical procedures through manual calculation.

Today most courses use the computer and statistical software or spreadsheets. Since most instructors do not want to teach how to use the software, we provide step-by-step instructions in the use of Microsoft Excel and Minitab for Windows. These instructions appear in the book with the printouts. Therefore, it is not necessary for students to purchase separate software manuals. Additionally, most examples, exercises, and cases feature raw data stored on the disk that accompanies this book, so students do not have to spend time inputting data.

For students without access to a computer and statistical software, we continue to teach how to calculate statistics manually (with the exception of the most complicated procedures), and most exercises can be solved in this way.

Because in practice a statistician often has access only to raw data and the correct procedure to employ is not obvious, our approach allows us to offer more realistic applications. In fact, many of the examples, exercises, and cases are based on real studies that have been reported in newspapers, magazines, and journals, and on television and at academic conferences. Several examples from our own consulting projects also have been included. Such applications can motivate students, who unfortunately often believe that statistics is not very relevant to their future careers. We believe that our approach changes these attitudes.

RATIONALE FOR THIS EDITION

This edition of *Statistics for Management and Economics* is devoted to the principle that statistics is a vital subject in business and economics programs. Accordingly, in this edition we have integrated statistics into all the functional areas of business and economics.

In teaching an applied statistics course it is important to demonstrate statistical techniques in the field of interest to the students in the course. However, in most undergraduate and graduate business programs, statistics is taught before students take courses in accounting, human resources, finance, marketing, and operations management. In many economics curricula statistics is taught in the first or second year. These schedules make it difficult for students to fully understand the business and economics applications. In this edition we have attempted to remedy the problem by providing brief introductions to each of the functional areas of business and economics in Chapter 1. Throughout the rest of the book we have scattered 35 "Statistics in the Workplace" boxes wherein we describe how statistical techniques are used in business and economics. Each is followed by an example or by exercises that demonstrate the application. For example, in Chapter 4 we briefly describe the accounting concepts *fixed* and *variable costs*. This presentation is followed by an example in which total costs and number of units are graphed in a scatter diagram. By interpreting the straight line drawn through the data points we show how scatter diagrams are used by accountants. This example is followed up by several exercises that appear in later chapters on the same subject but use other techniques.

Five topics in "Statistics in the Workplace" are so large or important that they merit their own section. These are Section 6.7, Investment Portfolio Diversification, Section 12.10, Market Segmentation, Section 14.6, Operations Management Application: Finding and Reducing Variation (including Taguchi loss functions), Section 17.10, Market Model, and Section 19.7, on Pay Equity.

In addition to the aforementioned topics we have boxes and sections that cover learning curves (operations management), human resources (absenteeism, aptitude testing, and turnover analysis), economics (demand curves), marketing (test marketing, advertising, and pricing).

KEY FEATURES OF OUR APPROACH

- **Teaches technique-identification skills.** Guides (see inside front cover), flowcharts, and review chapters develop this critical skill.

- **Offers review chapters.** Exercises and cases that appear at the end of chapters naturally require the use of the techniques introduced in those chapters. To help further develop technique-identification skills, two review chapters (13 and 22) contain exercises and cases that require the use of techniques previously introduced. Each review chapter features a flowchart that guides students in determining the correct problem-solving technique.

- **Uses Excel and Minitab.** Both software packages are used extensively throughout the book to compute solutions. It is possible to eliminate some, most, or all manual calculations, depending on instructor preference.

- **Presents computer instructions.** Detailed instructions for both Microsoft Excel and Minitab for Windows make it easy for both instructors and students to make use of the computer.

- **Provides Data Analysis Plus.**® Excel spreadsheet macros work as a statistical add-in to make the spreadsheet capable of using all of the techniques and solving the problems in the book.

- **Includes a CD that stores the data files** (in several formats, including Minitab,

Excel, SAS, and ASCII) rather than summary statistics for most examples, exercises, and cases. This increases student involvement and promotes active learning.

- **Uses real data in examples and exercises.** Using actual problems solved by statisticians demonstrates how statistics is practical and applies to every business and economics discipline.

- **Provides case studies.** More extended applications based on real data suggest the wide variety of problems that require statistical solutions.

NEW IN THIS EDITION

- "Statistics in the Workplace" boxes and sections as described previously.

- New Excel macros. These include Bartlett's test, chi-squared test for normality, Lilliefors test for normality, multiple comparisons (LSD, Bonferronni adjustment, and Tukey), prediction interval for regression (simple and multiple), and stepwise regression. We have also created the "Inference from Summary Statistics Workbook," which contains 18 worksheets that allow students to complete various statistical procedures from statistics (as opposed to raw data). For example, there is a worksheet that computes the interval estimate of the difference between two means, which requires the sample means, standard deviations, and sizes as inputs. One of the worksheets computes the probability of Type II errors (beta). These worksheets also allow students to perform "what-if" analyses to determine the effect of changing inputs. A number of exercises in Chapters 9 through 12 are designed to be answered either manually or by using this add-in.

- Nonparametric techniques are grouped together in one chapter.

- Simulation experiments using Excel and Minitab are introduced in Chapters 8 and 9. These experiments allow students to "discover" important statistical concepts that otherwise can only be taught using mathematical concepts. These experiments mesh perfectly with our overall approach—to teach applications and not mathematical derivations.

- More than 300 new exercises and cases. There are now approximately 1300 exercises and 41 cases. The cases are designed to be answered by students; they are not simple descriptions of what some analyst once did. They are based on real studies, some featuring real data.

- A larger number of data sets (from less than 500 to about 600). Many of the data sets are realistic and large. Students can easily access the files to answer the realistic questions posed in the examples, exercises, and cases.

- Appendix A, for students without computers who will solve most problems manually. This appendix provides summary statistics (e.g., means, variances, counts) for most of the exercises with data sets. This replaces the orange boxes that accompanied many exercises in the 4th edition.

- Least squares method introduced in Chapter 4.

- Geometric mean, approximating the mean and standard deviation from grouped data, and Chebycheff's Theorem.

- A section on the sampling distribution of a proportion (including a subsection on the normal approximation of the binomial).

- A section on the sampling distribution of the difference between two means.

- A section "From Here to Inference," which discusses the connection between sampling distributions and statistical inference.

- A subsection dealing with the width of a confidence interval and the amount of information provided.

- New nonstatistical (criminal trial) introduction to hypothesis testing.

- Earlier introduction of p-values and greater emphasis on them (we continue to use the rejection region method for manual calculations), including: a chart describing how to verbally interpret p-values, a subsection discussing the relationship between interval estimators and hypothesis testing, and a subsection of the proper way to ask statistical questions.

- A subsection on missing data.

- Multiple comparison methods including LSD, Bonferronni adjustment and Tukey (with new Excel macro), Bartlett's Test (used to test for equality of variances).

- A section on chi-squared test for normality (with Excel macro).

- A section on Lilliefors test for normality (with Excel macro).

- Improved regression diagnostics using chi-squared test for normality and Lilliefors test to check normality requirement.

- Expanded instructor and student resources. The Fifth Edition now offers the Instructor's Suite for Microsoft Office (see below), videos, and expanded Web resources.

TEACHING AIDS

Duxbury Press offers a complete collection of teaching tools.

Annotated Instructor's Edition

This valuable teaching tool contains answers to all exercises and cases, teaching hints and suggestions. A demo of this Instructor's Suite is packaged with the AIE. (ISBN: 0-534-36875-1)

Instructor's Suite for Microsoft Office

This full electronic resource includes solutions for every exercise and case study in Microsoft Word, a complete set of chapter-by-chapter PowerPoint slides, and test items in Microsoft Word. The PowerPoint slides, developed by Zvi Goldstein of California State University, Fullerton, also contain animations of concepts relating to in-text examples. This ancillary is available to adopters of the text only. (ISBN: 0-534-37148-5)

Instructor's Solutions Manual

This manual supplies complete solutions for every exercise and case study in the book. (ISBN: 0-534-37149-3)

Instructor's Resource Manual

In this manual we've included suggestions about teaching from the book, transparency masters, teaching notes for each case study, and supplementary topics that do not appear in the textbook. These topics are formatted for easy reproduction and distribution to students. (ISBN: 0-534-37150-7)

Test Bank

This is a print version of the test items, by Mohammed A. El-Saidi of Ferris State University, to accompany the text. The items are grouped by chapter and by difficulty. (ISBN: 0-534-36146-9)

Thomson Learning Testing Tools™

This is a fully integrated suite of test creation, delivery, and classroom management tools. It includes *World Class Test* and *Test Online* and *World Class Manager* software. *World Class Test* allows you to create dynamic, algorithmic questions that regenerate the values of variables and calculations among multiple versions of the same test. Tests, practice tests, quizzes, and tutorials created in *World Class Test* can be delivered via paper, diskette, local hard drive, local area network, or our Internet server. You can create a test from an existing bank of objective questions including multiple-choice, true/false, and matching questions. Both testing and tutorial results can then be integrated into a complete classroom management tool, *World Class Manager,* with scoring, gradebook, and reporting capabilities. (Macintosh ISBN: 0-534-37152-3; Windows ISBN: 0-534-37151-5)

www.duxbury.com

This Web site includes information about Duxbury Press as well as book-specific information. To reach Keller and Warrack's *Statistics for Management and Economics* home page, click "Online Book Companions" at this web site. Their home page contains additional exercises and case studies, updated information on software and the book, technical support, and more.

LEARNING AIDS

Duxbury Press offers a complete set of tools to help students master the course.

Data Analysis Plus® 2.12 and Data CD-ROM

This dual-platform CD-ROM includes Excel add-ins with statistical menu capability not contained in the standard Excel, plus more than 600 data sets for examples, exercises, and case studies in the text. It's packaged with every new copy of the text.

Video Applications

Also included on the accompanying CD-ROM are video segments linking important statistical concepts to real applications.

Thomson Learning Web Tutor™

Web Tutor™ offers students real-time access to a full array of study tools, including flashcards (with audio), practice quizzes and tests, online tutorials, exercises, discussion questions, web links, and a full glossary. Contact your Brooks/Cole-ITP representative for details about this exciting new product. (ISBN: 0-534-76358-8 and ISBN 0-534-76497-5)

Student Solutions Manual

In this helpful manual, students are furnished detailed solutions for the textbook's even-numbered exercises. This is for sale to students. (ISBN: 0-534-37145-0)

Study Guide

In this book, students will find more detailed Excel instructions, overviews of each text chapter, examples illustrating specific techniques, exercises and their solutions, and instructions for newcomers to Microsoft Excel. This is available for sale to students. (ISBN: 0-534-37147-7)

Cyber Stats*

CyberStats (by Cybergnostics) is an online web resource that includes case studies, tutorials, applications, and java-applets to help visualize statistical concepts. (Smart-Pak ISBN: 0-534-75712-X)

Succeeding in Statistics*

Succeeding in Statistics, by Ronald E. Shiffler and Arthur J. Adams, provides a review of math and of spreadsheet and calculator skills needed for statistics. Modular and keyed to the requirements of specific statistical concepts, this self-paced review is a must for any math-fearing students. A brief introduction to Excel is included. (Smart-Pak ISBN: 0-534-75721-9)

ACKNOWLEDGMENTS

We are grateful to Curt Hinrichs, editor of this book, whose guidance, advice, and encouragement were an integral part of the development of the last two editions. We appreciate the assistance of Jeffery Keller in creating Data Analysis Plus®, and Gita and Jonathan Keller in finding and develolping many of the examples, exercises, and cases. We would like to thank Zvi Goldstein of CSU Fullerton for the excellent PowerPoint slides and Mohammed El-Saidi of Ferris State University for developing test item files that are especially well suited to our approach. We would also like to thank the following reviewers for their helpful comments and suggestions: Sung K. Ahn, Washington State University; Randy J. Anderson, California State University, Fresno; Paul Baum, California State University, Northridge; Terry Dielman, Texas Christian University; Mark Eakin, University of Texas, Arlington; David W. Pentico, Duquesne University; Ivilina Popova, Purdue University; Amy V. Puelz, Southern Methodist University; Walter A. Rosenkrantz, University of Massachusetts; and John Wiorkowski, University of Texas, Dallas.

Gerald Keller
Brian Warrack

---

*Combine either of these products with *Statistics for Management and Economics, Fifth Edition* in a money-saving Smart-Pak! Contact your local representative for more information.

NEW AND KEY FEATURES OF THE FIFTH EDITION

In the Fifth Edition of *Statistics for Management and Economics,* Keller and Warrack have revised their highly successful text to make sure it is the best teaching and learning text available. They continue their practical approach to provide students with a framework to understand and apply statistics using actual data in almost every example, exercise, and case study.

In this edition, they apply their three-step problem-solving approach to every appropriate example. They fully integrate hand calculations and Excel and Minitab output and instructions in almost every example so instructors may choose which method to emphasize, and they relate pertinent information about its link to the workplace in their new "Statistics in the Workplace" feature. Also included is **Data Analysis Plus®️ 2.12** statistical add-ins for Excel!

RELEVANT, MODERN, AND FLEXIBLE

The success of this book is based on the popularity of its key features: relevance, modern coverage, and flexibility. With each new edition, the authors work to find and use actual problems and real data from varied business settings, to remain relevant, stay up-to-date with respect to technology, and to build in more flexibility for the instructors and the students. Here's a closer look at each of these features.

RELEVANT—STATISTICS IS VITAL TO BUSINESS AND ECONOMICS

Students often believe that statistics is not very relevant to their future careers. By including examples, exercises and cases from newspapers, journals, television, and academic conferences, the authors motivate the students and work toward changing their attitudes. This motivation is provided in several ways:

These applications keep students motivated.

- Statistics in the Workplace boxes describe how statistical techniques are used in business and economics and are related to future studies. Each box is followed by an example or exercise that demonstrates the application.

S TATISTICS IN THE W ORKPLACE

Finance Application

In this section on investment portfolio diversification, we have briefly introduced a procedure for computing the expected return and variance (risk) of a portfolio consisting of two stocks. This procedure assumes that we know the expected returns and variances of each of the two stocks, and the covariance between the two stocks. The question then arises: How do we come up with the values of the expected returns, variances, and covariances for individual stocks? (By the way, this question is rarely addressed in finance textbooks!) The most common pro-

cedure in practice is to *estimate* these values (population parameters) from historical data, using *sample* means, variances, and covariances. You will need to compute and use such estimates to answer the questions asked in Exercises 6.74 and 6.75.

• Important "Statistics in the Workplace" topics merit their own section.

These sections help students develop a better understanding of the important role of statistics in business and economics.

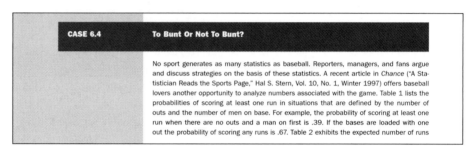

6.7 INVESTMENT PORTFOLIO DIVERSIFICATION (OPTIONAL)

Most investors are probably familiar with the notion that lowering your investment risk by diversification means "not putting all your eggs in one basket." This sensible notion was first analyzed carefully by Harry Markowitz in 1952, when he developed a model that clarified how risk reduction is achieved through diversification. His model forms the foundation of what has become known as modern portfolio theory (MPT), which is widely used by professional investors.

To illustrate the basics of portfolio diversification, consider an investor who forms a portfolio, consisting of only two stocks, by investing $4,000 in one stock and $6,000

• Cases present real business situations. Students are asked to apply the concept they have just learned and interpret the results.

These cases reinforce learning the process (identify, solve, interpret) and provide motivation.

CASE 6.4	To Bunt Or Not To Bunt?

No sport generates as many statistics as baseball. Reporters, managers, and fans argue and discuss strategies on the basis of these statistics. A recent article in *Chance* ("A Statistician Reads the Sports Page," Hal S. Stern, Vol. 10, No. 1, Winter 1997) offers baseball lovers another opportunity to analyze numbers associated with the game. Table 1 lists the probabilities of scoring at least one run in situations that are defined by the number of outs and the number of men on base. For example, the probability of scoring at least one run when there are no outs and a man on first is .39. If the bases are loaded with one out the probability of scoring any runs is .67. Table 2 exhibits the expected number of runs

MODERN—FOCUS ON THE PROCESS

The authors emphasize the complete process of data analysis and believe that students need to have more than just the ability to compute statistics. They want them to develop the skill to recognize the correct procedure to use and to interpret the results.

• A three-step process is integrated in appropriate examples.

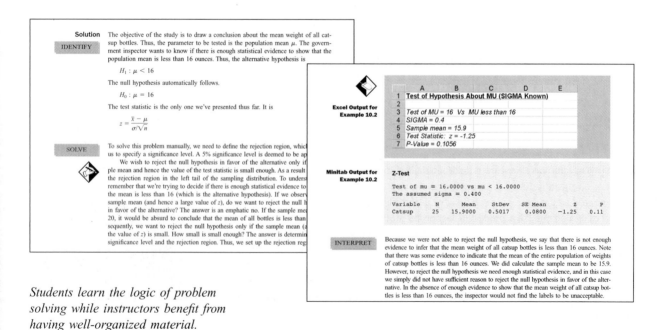

Students learn the logic of problem solving while instructors benefit from having well-organized material.

• Flowcharts in review chapters develop technique-selection skills.

These graphical representations develop the logical process for choosing the correct technique, reinforce learning the process, and provide easy review material for the students.

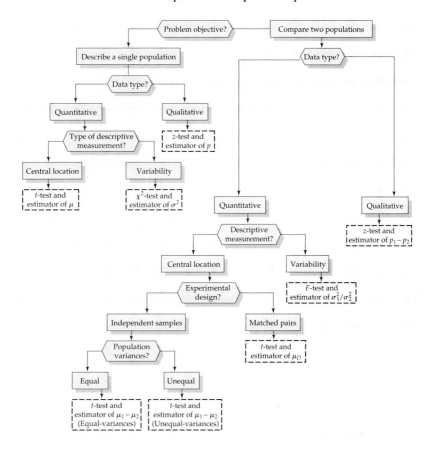

• Guides identify techniques.

Students will appreciate having these quick reference guides.

A GUIDE TO STATISTICAL TECHNIQUES

PROBLEM OBJECTIVES

		Describe a Single Population	Compare Two Populations	Compare Two or More Populations	Analyze the Relationship Between Two Variables	Analyze the Relationship Among Two or More Variables
DATA TYPES	Quantitative	Histogram **Section 2.3** Ogive **Section 2.3** Stem-and-leaf **Section 2.3** Dot plot **Section 2.3** Box plot **Section 4.5** Mean, median, and mode **Section 4.2** Geometric mean **Section 4.2** Range, variance, standard deviation, and coefficient of variation **Section 4.3** Percentiles and quartiles **Section 4.5** t-test and estimator of a mean **Section 11.2** Chi-squared test and estimator of a variance **Section 11.3**	Equal-variance t-test and estimator of the difference between two means (independent samples) **Section 12.2** Unequal-variance t-test and estimator of the difference between two means (independent samples) **Section 12.2** t-test and estimator of mean difference (matched pairs) **Section 12.4** F-test and estimator of the ratio of two variances **Section 12.5** Wilcoxon rank sum test **Section 16.2** Wilcoxon signed rank sum test **Section 16.3**	Analysis of variance: Independent samples single-factor **Section 14.2** Analysis of variance: independent samples two-factor **Section 14.5** Analysis of variance: Randomized blocks **Section 14.4** Kruskal-Wallis test **Section 16.4** Friedman test **Section 16.5** Tukey's multiple comparison method **Section 14.7** LSD multiple comparison method **Section 14.7** Bartlett's test **Section 14.8**	Scatter diagram **Section 2.5** Covariance **Section 4.7** Correlation **Section 4.7** t-test of correlation **Section 17.8** Simple linear regression **Chapter 17** Spearman rank correlation test **Section 17.8**	Multiple regression **Chapter 18 and 19**
	Qualitative	Pie chart **Section 2.4** Bar chart **Section 2.4** Line chart **Section 2.4** z-test and estimator of a proportion **Section 11.4** Chi-squared goodness-of-fit test **Section 15.2**	z-test and estimator of difference between two proportions **Section 12.6** Chi-squared test of a contingency table **Section 15.3**	Chi-squared test of a contingency table **Section 15.3**	Chi-squared test of a contingency table **Section 15.3**	Not covered
	Ranked	Box plot **Section 4.5** Median **Section 4.2** Percentiles and Quartiles **Section 4.5**	Wilcoxon rank sum Test **Section 16.2** Sign test **Section 16.3**	Kruskal-Wallis test **Section 16.4** Friedman test **Section 16.5**	Spearman rank correlation test **Section 17.8**	Not covered

- Simulation experiments focus on the process. By using Excel and Minitab in these experiments, students "discover" the statistical concept, not just the mathematical derivation.

These simulations develop understanding of the concept over just understanding of the mathematical calculation.

▼ **SIMULATION EXPERIMENT 9.4**

Excel Instructions   Repeat the first 6 steps of Simulation Experiment 8.4. At this point you should have the row means computed in column J.

   7 In column K calculate the lower confidence limit LCL = $\bar{x}$ − 13.71. In cell K1 type **=J1−13.71** and drag to fill the column.

   8 In column L calculate the upper confidence limit UCL = $\bar{x}$ + 13.71. In cell L1 type **=J1+13.71** and drag.

   9 In column M type **=AND(KI < 100, LI > 100)** and drag to fill the column.

If K1 (lower confidence limit) is less than 100 and L1 (upper confidence limit) is greater than 100, the word **TRUE** will be recorded in column M. If not, the word **FALSE** will be recorded.

   10 Click **f, Statistical, COUNTIF,** and **Next>**.

   11 Specify the range of the column where the words **TRUE** and **FALSE** are stored: **M1:M1000**.

   12 Specify the criteria: **TRUE**.

   13 Click **OK**.

Steps 9 through 13 count the number of times the word **TRUE** appears in the last column. Thus, it counts the number of intervals that include the true value of μ.

Minitab Instructions   Repeat the first 9 steps of Simulation Experiment 8.4, which will store the sample means in column 10.

   10 Click **Calc** and **Calculator . . . .**

   11 Type **C11 (Store results in variable:)**

   12 Hit **tab** and type **C10 − 13.71**. **Click OK**.

   13 Click **Calc** and **Calculator . . . .**

   14 Type **C12 (Store results in variable:)**

   15 Hit **tab** and type **C10 + 13.74**. **Click OK**.

   16 Click **Calc** and **Calculator . . . .**

   17 Type **C13 (Store results in variable:)**

   18 Hit **tab** and type **(C11 < 100) AND (C12 > 100)**. **Click OK**

   19 Click **Stat, Tables,** and **Tally . . . .**

   20 Type **C13** and use the cursor to specify **Percents**. Click **OK**.

Columns 11 and 12 contain the lower and upper confidence limits, respectively. Column 13 uses comparison and logical operators to count the number of interval estimates that are correct. If the value in column 11 (lower confidence limit) is less than 100 and the value in column 12 (upper confidence limit) is greater than 100, a 1 will be recorded in column 13. If not, a 0 will be recorded. Thus, a 1 in column 13 indicates an interval estimate that includes the true value of μ, which is 100. Minitab counts the number of 1s and 0s in column 13 and prints the percentages.

Report for Simulation Experiment 9.4   **1** What is the number of intervals containing the true population mean you anticipated seeing?

FLEXIBLE—A PRACTICAL APPROACH

It is now easier to assign the approach of your choice.

Keller and Warrack organize the text to be as flexible as possible to accommodate different teaching and learning styles. Instructors have the options to use hand calculations or to choose either Excel 5.0, '95, '97 or 2000 or Minitab 12 for calculations.

New icons and consistent use of color clearly identify the methods.

All but the most complicated techniques are solved manually, to help develop an understanding of the technique.

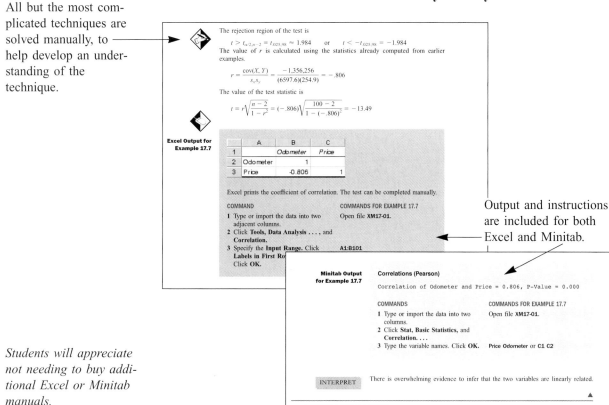

The rejection region of the test is

$$t > t_{\alpha/2, n-2} = t_{.025, 98} \approx 1.984 \quad \text{or} \quad t < -t_{.025, 98} = -1.984$$

The value of r is calculated using the statistics already computed from earlier examples.

$$r = \frac{\text{cov}(X, Y)}{s_x s_y} = \frac{-1,356,256}{(6597.6)(254.9)} = -.806$$

The value of the test statistic is

$$t = r\sqrt{\frac{n-2}{1-r^2}} = (-.806)\sqrt{\frac{100-2}{1-(-.806)^2}} = -13.49$$

Excel Output for Example 17.7

	A	B	C
1		Odometer	Price
2	Odometer	1	
3	Price	-0.806	1

Excel prints the coefficient of correlation. The test can be completed manually.

COMMAND	COMMANDS FOR EXAMPLE 17.7
1 Type or import the data into two adjacent columns.	Open file XM17-01.
2 Click **Tools, Data Analysis . . .**, and **Correlation.**	
3 Specify the **Input Range.** Click **Labels in First Row.** Click **OK.**	A1:B101

Minitab Output for Example 17.7

Correlations (Pearson)

Correlation of Odometer and Price = 0.806, P-Value = 0.000

COMMANDS	COMMANDS FOR EXAMPLE 17.7
1 Type or import the data into two columns.	Open file XM17-01.
2 Click **Stat, Basic Statistics,** and **Correlation. . . .**	
3 Type the variable names. Click **OK.**	Price Odometer or C1 C2

INTERPRET   There is overwhelming evidence to infer that the two variables are linearly related.

Output and instructions are included for both Excel and Minitab.

Students will appreciate not needing to buy additional Excel or Minitab manuals.

CD-ROM for students is practical, modern, and relevant.

CD-ROM for students makes learning statistics relevant. This dual-platform CD-ROM, included in every copy of the book, contains raw data for 600 problems and case studies throughout the book. The data sets are preformatted for Excel, Minitab, SPSS, JMP IN, SAS, and ASCII. Coupled with features mentioned earlier, students gain a greater understanding of how to apply statistics to raw data and become better prepared to handle problems in the real world.

- The CD includes *Data Analysis Plus*® *2.12* statistical add-ins for Excel.

These add-ins cover all techniques used in the course and now include advanced features such as stepwise regression and more.

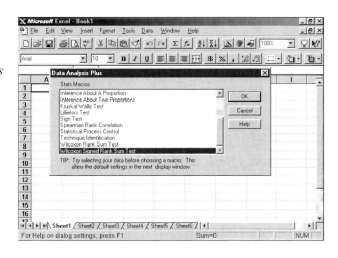

Chapter 1

What
Is
Statistics?

1.1 Introduction to Statistics

1.2 Key Statistical Concepts

1.3 Statistical Applications in Business

1.4 Statistics and the Computer

1.5 World Wide Web and Learning Center

1.1 INTRODUCTION TO STATISTICS

Statistics is a way to get information from data. That's it! Most of this textbook is devoted to describing how, when, and why managers conduct statistical procedures. You may ask, "If that's all there is to statistics, why is this book (and most other statistics books) so large?" The answer is that there are different kinds of information and data to which students of applied statistics should be exposed. We demonstrate some of these with four cases that are featured later in this book. (The numbering used here for these cases is the same as that used when the cases are featured later in this book. For example, Case 11.1 appears in Chapter 11.)

CASE 11.1: PEPSI'S EXCLUSIVITY AGREEMENT WITH A UNIVERSITY

In the last few years colleges and universities have signed exclusivity agreements with a variety of private companies. These agreements bind the university to sell that company's products exclusively on the campus. Many of the agreements involve food and beverage firms.

A large university with a total enrollment of about 50,000 students has offered Pepsi-Cola an exclusivity agreement, which would give Pepsi exclusive rights to sell their products at all university facilities for the next year and an option for future years. In return the university would receive 35% of the on-campus revenues and an additional lump sum of $100,000 per year. Pepsi has been given 2 weeks to respond.

The management at Pepsi quickly reviews what they know. The market for soft drinks is measured in terms of 12-ounce cans. Pepsi currently sells an average of 7,000 cans per week. The cans sell for an average of 75 cents each. The costs including labor amount to 20 cents per can. Pepsi is unsure of their market share but suspect it is considerably less than 50%. A quick analysis reveals that if their current market share were 25% then, with an exclusivity agreement, Pepsi would sell 28,000 cans per week or 1,456,000 cans per year. The gross revenue would be computed as follows.

$$1,456,000 \times \$.75 \text{ profit/can} = \$1,092,000$$

This figure must be multiplied by 65% since the university would rake in 35% of the gross. Thus,

$$65\% \times \$1,092,000 = \$709,800$$

The total cost of 20 cents per can (or $291,200) and the annual payment to the university of $100,000 is subtracted to obtain the net profit.

$$\text{Net profit} = \$709,800 - \$291,200 - \$100,000 = \$318,600$$

Their current annual profit is

$$52 \text{ weeks} \times 7,000 \text{ cans/week} \times \$.55 = \$200,200$$

If the current market share is 25% the potential gain from the agreement is

$$\$318,600 - \$200,200 = \$118,400$$

The only problem with this analysis is that Pepsi does not know how many soft drinks are sold weekly at the university. Coke is not likely to supply Pepsi with information about their sales, which together with Pepsi's line of products constitute virtually the entire market.

A recent graduate of a business program volunteers that a survey of the university's students can supply the missing information. Accordingly, she organizes a survey that asks 500 students to keep track of the number of soft drinks they purchase in the next 7 days. The responses are stored in a file on the disk that accompanies this book.

The data in this case are the numbers of cans of soft drinks consumed by students on the university campus. The information we would like to acquire is an estimate of annual profits from the exclusivity agreement. The question we need to address is how to extract the required information from the data. This is the function of **descriptive statistics.**

Descriptive statistics deals with methods of organizing, summarizing, and presenting data in a convenient and informative way. One form of descriptive statistics uses graphical techniques, which allow us to draw a picture that presents the data in such a way that we can easily see what numbers the students are reporting. Chapter 2 presents a variety of graphical methods used by statisticians to present data in ways that allow the reader to extract useful information.

Another form of descriptive statistics uses numerical techniques to summarize data. One such method that you have already used frequently is the average or mean. In the same way that you calculate the average age of the employees of a company, we can compute the mean number of soft drinks consumed by the 500 students in our survey. Chapter 4 introduces several numerical statistical measures that describe different features of the data. In Case 11.1, however, we are not so much interested in what the 500 students are reporting as we are in knowing the mean number of soft drinks consumed by all 50,000 students on campus. To accomplish this goal we need another branch of statistics—**inferential statistics.**

Inferential statistics is a body of methods used to draw conclusions or inferences about characteristics of populations based on sample data. The population in question in Case 11.1 is the university's 50,000 students' soft drink consumption. The cost of interviewing each would be prohibitive and extremely time consuming. Statistical techniques make such endeavors unnecessary. Instead, we can sample a much smaller number of students (in this case the sample size is 500) and infer from the data in the sample the mean number of soft drinks consumed by all 50,000 students. We can then estimate annual profits for Pepsi.

CASE 13.2: QUEBEC SEPARATION? *OUI OU NON?*

Since the 1960s there has been an ongoing campaign among Quebecers to separate from Canada and form an independent nation. Should Quebec separate, the ramifications for the rest of Canada, American states that border Quebec, the North American Free Trade Agreement and numerous multinational corporations would be enormous. In 1994, the ruling party in Quebec promised to hold a referendum on separation. As with most political issues, polling plays an important role in trying to influence voters and to predict the outcome of the referendum vote. Shortly after the 1993 federal election, *The Financial Post Magazine,* in cooperation with several polling companies, conducted a survey of Quebecers.

A total of 641 adult Quebecers were interviewed. They were asked the following questions. (Francophones were asked the questions in French.) The pollsters recorded the answer and also the language (English or French) in which the respondent answered.

If a referendum were held today on Quebec's sovereignty with the following question, "Do you want Quebec to separate from Canada and become an independent country?" would you vote yes or no?

2 Yes
1 No

The responses are stored on the data disk accompanying this book.

What conclusions can you draw from these results?

This case exemplifies one of the most common applications of statistical inference. The population we want to make inferences about is the approximately 7 million potential voters in the province of Quebec. The sample consists of the 641 Quebecers randomly selected by the polling company. The characteristic of the population that we would like to know is the proportion of the total electorate that supports separation. Specifically, we would like to know whether more than 50% of voters will vote for separation. It must be made clear that, because we will not ask every one of the 7 million potential voters how he or she will vote, we cannot predict the outcome with 100% certainty. This is a fact that statisticians and even students of statistics must understand. A sample that is only a small fraction of the size of the population can lead to correct inferences only a certain percentage of the time. You will find that statisticians can control that fraction and usually set it between 90 and 99%.

CASE 13.3: HOST SELLING AND ANNOUNCER COMMERCIALS*

A study was undertaken to compare the effects of host selling commercials and announcer commercials on children. Announcer commercials are straightforward commercials in which the announcer describes to viewers why they should buy a particular product. Host selling commercials feature a children's show personality or television character who extols the virtues of the product. In 1975, the National Association of Broadcasters prohibited the use of show characters to advertise products during the same program in which the characters appear. However, this prohibition was overturned in 1982 by a judge's decree.

The objective of the study was to determine whether the two types of advertisements have different effects on children watching them. Specifically, the researchers wanted to know whether children watching host selling commercials would remember more details about the commercial and be more likely to buy the advertised product than children watching announcer commercials. The experiment consisted of two groups of children ranging in age from 6 to 10. One group of 121 children watched a program in which two host selling commercials appeared. The commercials tried to sell Canary Crunch, a breakfast cereal. A second group of 121 children watched the same program but was exposed to two announcer commercials for the same product. Immediately after the show, the children were given a questionnaire that tested their memory concerning the commercials they had watched.

Each child was rated (on a scale of 10) on his or her ability to remember details of the commercial. In addition, each child was offered a free box of cereal. The children were shown four different brands of cereal—Froot Loops (FL), Boo Berries (BE), Kangaroo Hops (KH), and Canary Crunch (CC; the advertised cereal)—and asked to pick the one they wanted. The results are stored on the data disk provided with this book. (Some of the data are shown in Table 1.1.) Are there differences in memory test scores and cereal choices between the two groups of children?

In this case, we want to compare the population of children who watch host commercials with the population of children who watch announcer commercials. The experiment consists of drawing samples of 121 children from each population. For each child, researchers recorded two observations. The first was the score out of 10

---

*Adapted from J. H. Miller, "An Empirical Evaluation of the Host Selling Commercial and the Announcer Commercial When Used on Children," *Developments in Marketing Science* 9 (1985): 276–78.

Table 1.1 **Memory Test Scores and Cereal Choices**

Children Who Watch Host Selling Commercials		Children Who Watch Announcer Commercials	
Memory Test Scores	Cereal Choices	Memory Test Scores	Cereal Choices
6	FL	8	BB
9	CC	6	FL
7	KH	10	CC
7	CC	8	FL
.	.	.	.
.	.	.	.
.	.	.	.
8	BB	9	CC

the child received on a test to measure his or her memory about the commercial. The second was the brand the child chose from among the four brands of breakfast cereals. Notice that, contrary to what you probably believed, data are not necessarily numbers. The test scores, of course, are numbers; however, the cereal choices are not. In Chapter 2, we will discuss the different types of data you will encounter in statistical applications and how to deal with them. The information sought by the researchers is whether there are differences in the test scores and the cereal selections between the two populations of children. By applying the appropriate statistical techniques, the researchers may be able to infer which type of commercial is more effective.

CASE 17.1: DUXBURY PRESS

The academic book business is different from most other businesses because of the way the purchasing decision is made. The customer, who is usually a student taking a university or college course, buys a specific book because the instructor of the course adopts (chooses to use) that book. Sales representatives of publishers sell their products by persuading instructors to adopt their books. Unfortunately, judging the quality of textbooks is not easy. To help with the decision process, sales representatives give free examination copies to instructors so they can review the book and decide whether or not to adopt it. In many universities, several sections of the same course are taught, and book adoption committees meet to make the adoption decision.

Curt Hinrichs, an editor at Duxbury Press, was examining the latest data on the sales of three recently published statistics textbooks. He noted that the number of examination copies was quite large, which can be a serious problem given the high cost of producing books. Duxbury distributes review copies only of the books or editions that came out in the current year. He wondered whether his sales representatives were giving away too many free books or perhaps not enough. The data that he is examining contain a code that identifies the sales representative (of which there are 78), the gross revenues from the sales of the statistics books, and the number of free copies given to professors by that representative. These data are stored on the data disk. Curt would like to know whether there is a direct link between the number of free copies distributed and the gross revenues from new editions.

This case illustrates another statistical objective. The Pepsi-Cola case (Case 11.1) addressed the problem of estimating the number of soft drinks to be consumed by the university students. The objective of the problem described in the host selling commercial case (Case 13.3) was to compare two populations, the responses of children who watch two different types of television commercials. In this case, we need to analyze the relationship between two variables, the number of examination copies distributed and revenues from sales of these books. By applying the appropriate statistical technique, Curt will be able to determine whether the two variables are related, and if so, whether distributing more examination copies produces higher sales. As you will discover, the technique also permits statisticians to include other variables to determine whether they affect revenues.

1.2 KEY STATISTICAL CONCEPTS

As the preceding cases illustrate, statistical inference problems involve three key concepts: the population, the sample, and the statistical inference. We now discuss each of these concepts in more detail.

POPULATION

A **population** is the set of all items of interest in a statistical problem. It is frequently very large and may, in fact, be infinitely large. Unlike its meaning in everyday usage, the word *population* in statistics does not necessarily refer to a group of people. It may, for example, refer to the population of diameters of ball bearings produced at a large plant. Even in situations involving a population of people, the term *population* will generally refer to the population of data. For example, in the Pepsi-Cola case, the population of interest is the population of the number of soft drinks to be consumed by students. Thus, our population consists not of 50,000 students but instead of the 50,000 numbers of soft drinks to be consumed. Just imagine a giant container holding 50,000 slips of paper, each marked with a number equal to the number of soft drinks to be drunk by one particular student. This container is our population of interest.

A descriptive measure of a population is called a **parameter**. The parameter of interest in Case 11.1 is the mean number of soft drinks consumed by all the students at the university. The parameters in the Quebec case (Case 13.2) are the proportions of all of Quebec's voters who will vote for separation. In the host selling commercial case, the parameters are the differences in the mean scores on the memory test and the differences in the proportions of breakfast cereals selected by each population.

SAMPLE

A **sample** is a set of data drawn from the population. A descriptive measure of a sample is called a **statistic**. We use statistics to make inferences about parameters. In the Pepsi-Cola case, the statistic we would compute is the mean number of soft drinks consumed in the last week by the 500 students in the sample. We would then use the sample mean to infer the value of the population mean, which is the parameter of interest in this problem. In the Quebec separation case, we compute the proportion of the sample of 641 Quebecers who will vote for separation. The sample statistics are then used to make inferences about the population of Quebec's voters. That is, we predict the result of the referendum.

STATISTICAL INFERENCE

Statistical inference is the process of making an estimate, prediction, or decision about a population based on sample data. Because populations are almost always very large, investigating each member of the population would be impractical and expensive. It is far easier and cheaper to take a sample from the population of interest and draw conclusions or make estimates about the population on the basis of information provided by the sample. However, such conclusions and estimates are not always going to be correct. For this reason, we build into the statistical inference a measure of reliability. There are two such measures, the **confidence level** and the **significance level**. The confidence level is the proportion of times that an estimating procedure will be correct. For example, in the Pepsi-Cola case, we will produce an estimate of the average number of soft drinks to be consumed by all 50,000 students that has a confidence level of 95%. That means that, in the long run, estimates based on this form of statistical inference will be correct 95% of the time. When the purpose of the statistical inference is to draw a conclusion about a population, the significance level measures how frequently the conclusion will be wrong. For example, if the results of the analysis in the Quebec separation case lead us to conclude that *less* than 50% of the electorate will vote yes on the referendum, a significance level of 5% means that there is a 5% chance that, in fact, *more* than 50% of the electorate support separation.

1.3 STATISTICAL APPLICATIONS IN BUSINESS

We assume that most students taking their first statistics course have not taken courses in finance, marketing, and operations management. However, to understand fully how statistics is used in these and other subjects, it is necessary to know something about them. Naturally, we cannot teach all aspects of these subjects here, but in this chapter we introduce the topics where statistics can and does play a vital supporting role.

ORGANIZATIONAL FUNCTIONS

Companies are often organized on the basis of the kind of functions performed. This is often referred to as a *functional organization.* In this formulation organizations perform three primary functions: finance, marketing, and operations. In addition to these functions, organizations undertake several secondary functions. These include accounting, human resources, and information systems.

In this chapter we briefly introduce each of these functions and describe how statistics helps managers convert data into information and how that information plays a critical role in decision making.

FINANCIAL MANAGEMENT

Financial management (or simply finance) is the functional area of business that deals with the financial (money-related) decisions made by a firm in providing its products and services.

Every company must make decisions regarding what assets to acquire to produce its products, how to raise money to finance these assets, and how to manage the assets on an ongoing day-to-day basis. Corporate finance focuses on the financial aspects of these decisions.

Capital Budgeting

Capital budgeting is the process by which a firm generates, analyzes, and selects the projects that it will invest in and pursue. As we mention in the Operations Management section, the principal activity of every organization is the production and delivery of its products and services. The most important decision to be addressed, therefore, is the composition of the firm's product line. On which products, services, and markets should the company choose to focus?

Once an idea for a new product or project has been generated (often by the operations group), the financial feasibility of the project must be examined. Consideration must be given to estimating the cost of the *real assets* (such as land, buildings, and equipment) that must be purchased, and projections must be made of the revenues and operating costs associated with the project. The probability concepts to be introduced in Chapter 6 will be helpful in dealing with the uncertainty surrounding the projected values of these future cash flows.

Capital Structure

The two primary sources of funds for a company are long-term debt (such as bonds) and equity (i.e., common shares). A company's capital structure decision refers to its choice of the proportions of long-term debt and equity to be used for long-term financing. Determining the desired capital structure for a firm requires an understanding of the basics of stock and bond valuation, which we discuss later in this book.

Working Capital Management

Once management has chosen a project to invest in and arranged for its financing, it must turn its attention to the ongoing management of its *working capital,* which refers to a firm's current assets and current liabilities. The cash position must be carefully managed, accounts receivable must be collected and bad debt avoided, short-term sources of financing such as bank loans must be arranged, and accounts payable must be paid.

Stock and Bond Valuation

A basic understanding of how financial assets, such as stocks and bonds, are valued is critical to good financial management. Understanding the basics of valuation is necessary for the capital budgeting and capital structure decisions. Moreover, understanding the basics of valuing investments such as stocks and bonds is at the heart of the huge and growing discipline known as *investment management.*

As billions upon billions of dollars have flowed into mutual funds and the stock market generally during the past decade, investors have become increasingly aware of investment risks and returns. A central theme throughout all of finance, and the investment area in particular, is the positive relationship between risk and return. The more risky an investment, the higher should be the profit (or rate of return) one can expect to receive from the investment. (Loosely speaking, the rate of return on an investment is the profit divided by the amount of the investment.) While most of us intuitively feel that this positive relationship between risk and return should hold, a precise specification of this relationship is very difficult to state, to say the least. A model that is widely used for this analysis is the **market model,** which will be discussed in Chapter 17. This model relies heavily on the relationship between the return on an individual stock and the return on some major stock index, such as the Dow Jones Industrial Average. But before discussing this model, we must consider the measurement of risk. We begin doing so in Chapters 4 and 6.

Understanding Capital Markets

It is important for a financial manager to be familiar with the main characteristics of the capital markets where long-term financial assets such as stocks and bond trade. A well-functioning capital market provides managers with useful information concerning the appropriate prices and rates of return that are required for a variety of financial securities with differing levels of risk. Statistical methods can be used to analyze capital markets and summarize their characteristics, such as the shape of the distribution of stock or bond returns.

MARKETING MANAGEMENT

Traditionally, marketing has been defined in terms of the four P's: product, price, promotion, and place. *Marketing management* is the functional area of business that focuses on the development of a product, together with its pricing, promotion, and distribution. Decisions are made in these four areas with a view to satisfying the wants and needs of consumers, while also satisfying the firm's objective.

A more contemporary view of the philosophy of marketing management, while embracing the four P's, prefers to concentrate on enhancing service and customer satisfaction, while also meeting the firm's objective.

Market Segmentation

Mass marketing refers to the mass production and marketing by a company of a single product for the entire market. Mass marketing is especially effective for commodity goods such as gasoline, which are very difficult to differentiate from the competition, except through price and convenience of availability. But generally speaking, mass marketing has given way to *target marketing,* which focuses on satisfying the demands of a particular *segment* of the entire market.

As we discuss in Section 12.7, even the Coca-Cola Company has moved from the mass marketing of a single beverage to the production of several different beverages. Among the cola products, there is Coca-Cola Classic, Coke, Diet Coke, and Caffeine-Free Diet Coke. Each product is aimed at a different market segment. Statistical methods play an important role in identifying the segments of a market.

Because there is no single way to segment a market, managers must consider several different variables (or characteristics) that could be used to identify segments. Surveys of customers are used to gather data about various aspects of the market, and statistical techniques are applied to define the segments. Managers must then formulate a strategy to target these profitable segments, using the four elements of the marketing mix: product, pricing, promotion, and place.

Product

The term *product* can refer to a physical good (e.g., a computer), a service (e.g., a haircut), a person (e.g., Michael Jordan), a place (e.g., Niagara Falls), or an idea (e.g., total quality management). After a new product has been conceived and some initial development has been undertaken, perhaps in conjunction with the operations management group, a marketing product planner must address such questions as the desired quality level, the special options that can be made available, the appropriate type and design of packaging, and various *branding* issues such as an appropriate name and logo. The objective is to select an attractive mix of features that will provide a product that appeals to consumers and which can be differentiated from those of competitors. Test marketing, a statistical procedure, can be used on data provided by consumer surveys or other sources to test if one particular feature of the product is preferred over another by consumers in the target market.

Pricing

Another important decision in the overall marketing plan is the pricing decision, which needs to be addressed both for a new product, and from time to time for an existing product. Anyone buying a product such as a personal computer has been confronted with a wide variety of prices, accompanied by a corresponding wide variety of features. From a vendor's standpoint, establishing the appropriate price and corresponding set of attributes for a product is complicated, and must be done in the context of the overall marketing plan for the product. Here too, statistics plays a central role in the pricing decision.

Place

The third element of a product's marketing mix is *distribution,* otherwise known as placing the product. Having developed a product and packaged it, a manager must then make it available to potential buyers. The first decision is whether to sell directly to the consumer, as does Dell Computers with great success, or to resort to the more common approach of distributing the goods to various wholesalers and retailers. Distribution decisions involve deciding how to deliver the product to the market, including what mode of transportation to use and what use must be made of warehouses.

Promotion

The final component of the marketing mix is promotion, or marketing communication. Having produced a product, priced it, and decided how to make it available to the consumer, a company must next decide how to best promote the product. A company must communicate with consumers to inform them about the company itself and its products, and to interest them in purchasing its products. Promotional tools available to achieve these objectives include advertising, public relations, sales promotion (employing discount coupons or contests, for example), and personal selling. Statistical methods can be used to help assess how successful these tools have been in generating sales.

OPERATIONS MANAGEMENT

Operations management, production, or simply *operations* is the functional area of business that transforms inputs such as labor, material, and capital into outputs, such as products and services. This is the principal activity of every organization.

The tasks undertaken by the operations management function include designing the product (henceforth we will refer to a company's "product," which includes both products and *services*), choosing the production process, arranging the physical plant layout, designing jobs, monitoring quality, scheduling the work, managing inventories, and planning production.

Product Design

The process that is used to design new products or improve an existing product consists of several stages.

1 **Generating ideas.** Sources of new and improved products can come from the research and development (R&D) department, customers, suppliers, and competitors. Statistics plays an important role by analyzing surveys of customers that help determine what products a firm's customers want.

2 **Feasibility study.** The concepts developed in stage 1 are modified and developed, usually by the marketing function. A market analysis can include another survey of customers as well as focus groups, which entail a small group of consumers expressing their attitudes toward a new product. This stage also examines the potential costs and profits.

3 **Preliminary design.** The description of the product developed in the feasibility study is converted into technical specifications. From these a final design can be evolved.

4 **Functional design.** This stage involves examining the way a product performs, which includes the concepts of reliability and maintainability. Reliability is the probability that a product or component will function properly. Maintainability refers to the product's capacity to be maintained or repaired. In Chapter 6 we

will introduce probability and illustrate it with several examples dealing with reliability and maintainability.

5 **Form design.** This design addresses the appearance of the product. Decisions include the color, size, and shape. Marketers can analyze surveys to determine which factors are important in customers' decisions to buy or not buy.

6 **Production design.** This stage deals with the *how* of manufacturing the product. Statistical studies can be used to compare several different methods of production. The methods can be compared on the basis of cost, ease of construction, quality, reliability, and maintainability. In Chapter 12 we will provide several examples and exercises featuring this aspect of operations management. In Chapter 14 we will introduce a statistical method that is used to determine which factors most affect the quality of products. These are often referred to as the 4 M's: machines, material, methods, and manpower (the last factor has been altered to "personnel," a nonsexist term).

Process Planning

After designing or redesigning the product, management must decide how the product is to be made. The process plan converts the process design into working instructions for production. Decisions include whether the components are to be made or purchased and what equipment will be employed in the production process.

Facility Layout

Once management has determined how the product is to be produced, the next decision concerns how the manufacturing facility is to be laid out. The objective is to arrange machines and workers in such a way as to minimize costs, avoid bottlenecks, eliminate waste (of material and labor), and develop quality.

Location Analysis and Logistics

A critical decision for any firm is where to locate its production facility, storage center, or retail outlet. The circumstances that affect the location decision depend on the type of facility. For example, heavy industry requires a large amount of space so that construction and land costs must be low. The facility must be close to suppliers and distribution links such as highways and railroads must be easily accessible. Light industries usually are located where skilled labor is plentiful. Retail and service industries must be close to their customers. A variety of statistical techniques can be employed to help make this decision.

Aggregate Production Planning

The aggregate production plan (APP) determines the number of units to be produced over the next 6 to 18 months. The APP begins with a forecast of demand over the planning horizon time period. It then arranges for (usually) the lowest cost method of satisfying that demand.

Several strategies can be utilized.

1 **Level production.** With this strategy we produce the same amount each day, week, or month, building inventories for times when supply exceeds demand and drawing from inventory when demand exceeds the amount produced. The key costs here are storage.

2 **Chase strategy.** Hire and lay off workers so that each period's production matches the forecasted demand. Aside from the very negative effects this strategy has on a firm's workers, the economic costs include the cost of hiring and training new workers and the costs associated with laying off workers.

3 Overtime and undertime. Fluctuations in periodic demand are matched by planning overtime shifts or by assigning excess workers to other (perhaps) non-productive jobs. For example, when potential supply exceeds demand workers can be given tasks such as cleaning the facility or be sent for more training.

4 Subcontracting. Additional units can be produced by other companies.

5 Part-time workers. Part-time workers can be hired to meet demand when the regular workforce is overwhelmed.

6 Backordering. For some products it is possible to backorder to satisfy customer demands. For example, if a car dealer does not have a car with the features a customer desires the dealer can order that car from the manufacturer and deliver it at some future date to the customer.

There are a number of management science techniques that can be used as well as a trial-and-error approach. Statistical techniques are often used to provide information as inputs to the analysis that determines the optimum strategy. The process usually begins with a forecast, a statistical process that is covered in some detail in Chapter 20.

Inventory

Inventory models allow managers to determine the optimum number of units to produce in one production run. The models are usually based on balancing the costs of storage, ordering, and shortage. Probability concepts and methods are useful when making inventory decisions.

Queuing

Management scientists have developed a variety of probability-based tools to measure the lengths of waiting lines (called queues) and the number of people waiting for service. These techniques help managers make decisions about the size and number of service facilities (e.g., checkouts in a supermarket or tellers in a bank) and staffing. The Poisson and exponential distributions (Chapters 6 and 7) are useful in queuing analysis.

Project Management

PERT (project evaluation and review technique) and CPM (critical path method) are management science procedures that help control and plan large-scale projects (e.g., buildings, nuclear reactors, and shops). Probability distributions such as the normal distribution (Chapter 7) are applied in this topic.

ACCOUNTING

The functional areas of finance, operations, and marketing are directly involved with a company's production and delivery of goods and services to it customers. Although the accounting area is not directly involved in the financing, production, and marketing of a product, *accounting* is the functional area that collects, organizes, and provides information about a company's activities that helps these other areas to make decisions. Accounting information is provided both for internal use (such as for planning, control, decision making, and performance evaluation) and for external use (such as keeping investors informed). The terms *managerial accounting* and *financial accounting* are used to distinguish between the internal and external focuses, respectively, of a company's accounting activities.

The focus of managerial accounting is to provide information for internal use, to help managers make decisions regarding planning and control. For planning purposes, accountants prepare budgets, which include forecasts of sales revenues and the associated costs. The statistical forecasting methods described in Chapter 20 can be used to assist in preparing sales forecasts. Forecasting costs often make use of a cost function, which expresses the relationship between a cost and some measure of the level of activity (such as production) that creates that cost. Cost functions can be estimated using a statistical procedure described in Chapter 4. Applications involving the estimation of cost functions can be found in Chapters 4 and 17.

Financial accounting typically communicates its information in the form of financial statements. Publicly held corporations are required to obtain independent external audits of the financial statements to assess their validity. Statistical sampling plays an important role in selecting samples of units (such as accounts or invoices) for inspection by auditors. The samples must be chosen randomly, so that probabilistic inferences can be legitimately made about the entire population from which the sample was taken. Section 5.6 provides a brief description of the use of statistical sampling in auditing.

HUMAN RESOURCES MANAGEMENT

Human resources management is the functional area of business that deals with the people-related decisions made by a firm. Companies are not simply buildings filled with desks and equipment. Human resources, or people, are needed to finance, produce, and market the products and services offered by the company. In fact, management of human resources must be practiced by managers in each of these functional areas, and is not restricted to the human resources department.

Personal or human resources management involves such activities as recruitment, training, performance appraisal, compensation, and motivation. The human resources department must periodically forecast its needs, both in terms of number of employees needed and their required skills. If additional employees are required, the recruitment process begins. Following an initial interview, prospects are usually required to take written or manual tests to determine if their skills are suitable for the job. The firm must be prepared to provide evidence that these tests are *valid* selection instruments. In other words, higher scoring applicants must be more likely to perform well than lower scoring applicants. Statistical methods can be used to assess the validity of such tests.

Tests are often administered again at the end of a training program, to verify that an employee has benefited from the program. Once again, managers must ensure that the tests are valid measuring devices. Analysis of test results can also help to reveal deficiencies in the training program itself.

Periodic performance appraisal is necessary for the purpose of making decisions regarding retention, compensation, and promotion. Statistical methods can be used, for example, to assess the compensation program to determine whether it supports performance objectives. Statistical methods are also used to ensure that these decisions are taken without bias or discrimination. Recently, statistical procedures have been used by pay equity administrators, who attempt to judge which jobs are of "equal value" so that workers in these jobs receive equal pay.

Another aspect of compensation involves the development of severance packages for employees whose jobs become redundant as the result of a merger, or who simply lose their jobs because of a decision to reduce the size of the workforce (as happened at IBM in the late 1980s).

In the interest of raising productivity and reducing absenteeism and employee turnover, a company can use statistical methods to process the data gathered from employee interviews and surveys that seek to determine the level of employee satisfaction, as well as major areas of discontent in the workplace.

INFORMATION SYSTEMS

Information systems is often incorrectly defined to be the use of computers in the storage and movement of information. In fact, the term refers to any process by which information is created and used. By this definition everything we do in this book addresses information systems.

Throughout this book we describe a wide variety of statistical techniques whose goal is to provide information to financial analysts, accountants, and to marketing, operations, and human resources managers. The process starts with the demand for information. For example, in the Pepsi-Cola case described earlier, management needs to know the amount of soft drinks consumed by the university's students each week. A survey of students produces the data. Statistical procedures are employed to convert the data into information, which the manager can use to make decisions. This model will be used repeatedly in describing how statistical techniques are used in business and economics.

ECONOMICS

Broadly speaking, *economics* is the study of the use of scarce resources (such as natural resources, human resources, and financial resources) to produce goods and services to satisfy the wants of consumers. Because resources are scarce and wants are unlimited, *choices* must be made concerning production and consumption. This in turn necessitates consideration of *opportunity costs.* (Students choosing to attend university rather than working incur an opportunity cost: namely, the income that could have been earned if they had chosen to work.) Economists therefore study how producers choose to employ their limited resources, and how consumers choose to spend their income, giving consideration to opportunity costs.

It is conventional to view economics from two complementary perspectives: the "small picture" and the "big picture." *Microeconomics* (the "small picture") is the study of the behavior of individual economic decision makers (such as consumers and firms) and of the operation of individual markets (or industries). Economists working in this area routinely use statistical methods to provide business managers with forecasts of consumption, production, and pricing in various individual markets, such as the market for personal computers.

The focus of *macroeconomics* (the "big picture") is at a more aggregated level, concentrating on such topics as the level and growth rate in employment, income, and inflation. Economists use statistical methods to summarize and analyze the data they collect in these areas. They might, for example, use descriptive statistical methods to describe the distribution of all household incomes. Another well-known function of economists is to provide forecasts of the future level of economic variables. Economists frequently apply statistical methods to time series of data, such as the level of inflation or GDP (gross domestic product), in order to forecast their level next period. Statistical methods are also used to study *relationships* between variables, such as the relationship between mortgage rates and housing starts, or the relationship between consumption and disposable income. These and other applications of statistical methods in economics will be addressed throughout this book.

1.4 STATISTICS AND THE COMPUTER

In almost all practical applications of statistics, the statistician must deal with large amounts of data. For example, Case 11.1 involves 500 observations. To estimate annual profits, the statistician would have to perform computations on the data;

although the calculations do not require any great mathematical skill, the sheer amount of arithmetic makes this aspect of the statistical method time consuming and tedious. Fortunately, numerous commercially prepared computer programs are available to perform the arithmetic. In most of the examples used to illustrate statistical techniques in this book, we will provide three methods for answering the question.

1 **Solving by hand.** Except where doing so is prohibitively time consuming, we will show how to answer the question by using hand calculations (with only the aid of a calculator). It is useful for you to produce some solutions in this way, because by doing so you will gain some insights into statistical concepts.

2 **Using Microsoft Excel.** Many business students own a spreadsheet package, and university and college courses incorporate a spreadsheet into their curriculum. We have chosen to use Microsoft Excel because we believe that it is and will continue to be the most popular spreadsheet package. One of its drawbacks is that it offers relatively few of the statistical techniques we introduce in this book. Consequently, we created macros that can be loaded onto your computer to enable you to use Excel for almost all procedures. We provide detailed instructions for all techniques. We use the Office 97 version of Excel.

3 **Using Minitab.** The Minitab software package is one of the easiest packages to use. It is used by universities and businesses around the world. We will show the Minitab output for most examples and provide detailed instructions in its use. In addition, we created macros to augment Minitab's list of techniques. We use Release 12 for Windows.

We anticipate that most instructors will choose to use some combination (but not all three) of the methods described. For example, many instructors prefer to have students solve small-sample problems involving few calculations manually but turn to the computer for large-sample problems or more complicated techniques.

To allow as much flexibility as possible, most examples, exercises, and cases are accompanied by a set of data stored on the diskette supplied with this book. You can solve these problems using a software package. In addition, we have made it possible for students without access to a computer to solve these problems.

Ideally, students will solve the small-sample, relatively simple problems by hand and use the computer to solve the others. The approach we prefer to take is to minimize the time spent on manual computations and to focus instead on selecting the appropriate method for dealing with a problem and on interpreting the output after the computer has performed the necessary computations. In this way, we hope to demonstrate that statistics can be as interesting and practical as any other subject in your curriculum.

1.5 WORLD WIDE WEB AND LEARNING CENTER

To assist students in the various aspects of using the computer to learn statistics, we have created a web page. It offers useful information including additional exercises and cases, corrections to the different printings and supplements, and updates on the data sets and macros. Additionally, you can e-mail the authors to make comments and ask questions about the installation of the files stored on the diskettes. The site can be accessed from the publisher's home page

http://www.duxbury.com

Click **Online Book Companions**, which will take you to

http://www.duxbury.com/titles.htm

Find and click the cover of this book.

IMPORTANT TERMS

Descriptive statistics   *3*

Inferential statistics   *3*

Population   *6*

Parameter   *6*

Sample   *6*

Statistic   *6*

Satistical inference   *6*

Confidence level   *7*

Significance level   *7*

Market model   *8*

E X E R C I S E S

1.1 In your own words, define and give an example of each of the following statistical terms.

a population   **b** sample   **c** parameter   **d** statistic   **e** statistical inference

1.2 Briefly describe the difference between descriptive statistics and inferential statistics.

1.3 A politician who is running for the office of mayor of a city with 25,000 registered voters commissions a survey. In the survey, 48% of the 200 registered voters interviewed say they plan to vote for her.

a What is the population of interest?
b What is the sample?
c Is the value 48% a parameter or a statistic? Explain.

1.4 A manufacturer of computer chips claims that less than 10% of his products are defective. When 1,000 chips were drawn from a large production run, 7.5% were found to be defective.

a What is the population of interest?
b What is the sample?
c What is the parameter?
d What is the statistic?
e Does the value 10% refer to the parameter or to the statistic?
f Is the value 7.5% a parameter or a statistic?
g Explain briefly how the statistic can be used to make inferences about the parameter to test the claim.

1.5 Suppose you believe that, in general, graduates of business programs are offered higher salaries upon graduating than are graduates of arts and science programs. Describe a statistical experiment that could help test your belief.

1.6 You are shown a coin that its owner says is fair in the sense that it will produce the same number of heads and tails when flipped a very large number of times.

a Describe an experiment to test this claim.
b What is the population in your experiment?
c What is the sample?
d What is the parameter?
e What is the statistic?
f Describe briefly how statistical inference can be used to test the claim.

1.7 Suppose that in Exercise 1.6 you decide to flip the coin 100 times.

a What conclusion would you be likely to draw if you observed 95 heads?
b What conclusion would you be likely to draw if you observed 55 heads?
c Do you believe that, if you flip a perfectly fair coin 100 times, you will always observe exactly 50 heads? If you answered no, what numbers do you think are possible? If you answered yes, how many heads would you observe if you flipped the coin twice? Try it several times, and report the results.

1.8 The owner of a large fleet of taxis is trying to estimate his costs for next year's operations. One major cost is fuel purchases. To estimate fuel purchases, the owner needs to know the total distance his taxis will travel next year, the cost of a gallon of fuel, and the fuel mileage of his taxis. The owner has been provided with the first two figures (distance estimate and cost). However, because of the high cost of gasoline, the owner has recently converted his taxis to operate on propane. He measures the propane mileage (in miles per gallon) for 50 taxis. The results are stored in file XR01-08.

a What is the population of interest?
b What is the parameter the owner needs?
c What is the sample?
d What is the statistic?
e Describe briefly how the statistic will produce the kind of information the owner wants.

Chapter 2

Graphical

Descriptive

Techniques

2.1 Introduction

2.2 Types of Data

2.3 Graphical Techniques for Quantitative Data

2.4 Pie Charts, Bar Charts, and Line Charts

2.5 Scatter Diagrams

2.6 Summary

2.1 INTRODUCTION

In Chapter 1, we pointed out that statistics is divided into two basic areas: descriptive statistics and inferential statistics. The purpose of this chapter, together with the next two, is to present the principal methods that fall under the heading of descriptive statistics. In this chapter, we introduce graphical statistical methods that allow managers to summarize data visually to extract useful information. Chapter 3 presents a discussion on how to make interesting and informative use of these techniques. Another class of descriptive techniques, numerical methods, is introduced in Chapter 4.

Managers frequently have access to large masses of potentially useful data. But before the data can be used to support a decision, they must be organized and summarized. Consider, for example, the problems faced by managers who have access to the databases created by the use of debit cards. (Debit cards are like credit cards except that when purchases are made, the amount is immediately deducted from the customer's bank account.) The database consists of customer information taken from the bank account application (i.e., age, income, occupation, residence, and the like), plus a history of all purchases made using the debit card. Using these data, marketing managers can determine which segments of the market are buying their products and which are not. Specialized marketing campaigns can then be developed. However, before that can be done, the data must be summarized so that the relevant information can be extracted. The use of descriptive statistical methods is often the first step in the process.

Descriptive statistics, then, involves arranging, summarizing, and presenting a set of data in such a way that the meaningful essentials of the data can be extracted and interpreted easily. Its methods make use of graphical techniques and numerical descriptive measures (such as averages) to summarize and present the data to yield useful information, allowing managers to make decisions and recommendations. Although descriptive statistical methods are quite straightforward (and far less space is devoted to them than to inferential statistical methods), their importance should not be underestimated. Most business students will encounter numerous opportunities to make valuable use of graphical and numerical descriptive techniques when preparing reports and presentations in the workplace. According to a Wharton Business School study, top managers reach a consensus 25% more quickly when responding to a presentation in which graphics are used.

Review the distinction between a population and a sample. Recall from Chapter 1 that a **population** is the entire set of observations or measurements under study, whereas a **sample** is a set of observations selected from the population and is therefore only a part of the entire population. The descriptive methods presented in this chapter and in Chapter 3 apply equally well to data consisting of an entire population and to data consisting of a sample drawn from a population.

Before we present descriptive techniques, we need to discuss the different types of data. The type of data to be analyzed plays a critical role in determining the appropriate statistical method to apply.

2.2 TYPES OF DATA

To assist in our discussion we need to define two terms, one of which we've already used. They are *variable* and *data*. A **variable** is any characteristic of a population or sample that is of interest to us. For example, in Case 11.1 (introduced in Chapter 1), the variable in which we are interested is the number of soft drinks sold weekly at the university. In Case 13.3, there were two variables: memory test scores and cereal choices.

The term **data** refers to the actual values (measurements or observations) of variables. (Incidentally, the word *data* is plural for *datum;* datum refers to one single observation, and data refers to a group of observations.) The numbers and cereal abbreviations that appear in Table 1.1 on page 5 constitute some of the data in Case 13.3. Thus, *variable* is the word we use to describe the name of the characteristic of interest, and *data* is the word that describes the actual values or observations of the variable.

Data may be either **quantitative** (numerical) or **qualitative** (categorical). When you see the word *data,* you probably think of a group of numbers, such as incomes, sales, profits, and losses. The data in these examples are quantitative—they are real numbers and are said to have an *interval scale.* All types of statistical calculations are permitted on quantitative data.

Quantitative Data

Quantitative data are numerical observations.

If 75 managers are surveyed and asked to state their age and annual income, the numerical responses they give are quantitative data. If the managers are also asked to indicate their marital status (single, married, divorced, or widowed), their responses are nonnumerical, but each response can still be classified as falling into one of four categories. Observations that can be sorted into categories on the basis of qualitative attributes, such as marital status, race (Asian, Black, Caucasian, Hispanic, Other), sex, occupation, or type of dwelling inhabited, constitute qualitative data. The data in these examples are simply the names of possible classifications and are said to have a *nominal scale.*

Qualitative Data

Qualitative data are categorical observations.

All we can do with qualitative data is count the number of observations in each category and then calculate the proportion or percentage of all observations that fall into each category. It is important to realize that this is the case even if numbers are used to label the categories. For example, consider once again the survey questionnaire asking managers to indicate their marital status, with the possible responses being single, married, divorced, and widowed. To help record the responses (for example, when they are stored and processed by a computer), such data are often converted into numbers. But data produced in this way are still *qualitative,* because the numbers merely represent the name of the response; they have no real numerical meaning. As a result, any arithmetic calculations performed on qualitative data are also meaningless. For example, suppose that we recorded the responses to the marital-status question as follows:

Single	1	Divorced	3
Married	2	Widowed	4

Suppose further that the first 10 managers interviewed responded 1, 1, 3, 4, 1, 1, 2, 3, 1, 3. If we were to calculate the average of these numerical responses, we would find it to be 2. Does this mean that the average manager was married? Now suppose that four more managers were interviewed, of whom three were widowed and one divorced. After summing all 14 numerical responses and dividing by 14, we would find that the average numerical response turns out to be 2.5. Does this mean that the average manager was married but halfway toward being divorced? Obviously, the answer to both questions is no, and the reason is that arithmetic calculations, such as averages, performed on qualitative data provide meaningless results. All we can do when the data are qualitative is count the number of times each value has occurred and then calculate the proportion (in this case) of managers who fall into each marital-status category.

Knowing the type of data being measured is important, because it is one of the factors that determines which statistical technique should be used. Usually, identifying the data as being either quantitative or qualitative will be sufficient. But in a few situations (primarily in choosing the appropriate nonparametric technique in Chapter 16), it will be necessary to recognize whether or not the nonquantitative data under consideration can be ranked. If the categories for a set of nonquantitative data can be ordered or ranked, we refer to the data as being **ranked data.** The data are then said to have an **ordinal scale.**

This would be the case, for example, if each manager were asked to classify a particular hotel as excellent, good, fair, or poor, based on the quality of accommodation provided. Because the responses here are nonquantitative and categorical, the data appear to be nominal. Notice, however, that the responses are ranked in preferential order by the quality of accommodation. The first response (excellent) is the highest rating, the second response (good) is the second highest rating, and so on. Any numerical representation of the four answers should maintain the ranked ordering of the responses. Such a numerical system would form an *ordinal scale.* The only constraint on our choice of numbers for this scale is that they must represent the order of the responses; the actual values to be used are arbitrary. For example, we could record the responses as follows:

Excellent	4	Fair	2
Good	3	Poor	1

Another, equally valid representation of the ratings would be the following:

Excellent	9	Fair	2
Good	5	Poor	1

And we could simply reverse our original 4-3-2-1 ratings so that excellent = 1 and poor = 4, with no effect on the statistical technique to be used.

The only information provided by ranked data that is not provided by qualitative data is the ranked order of the responses. We still cannot interpret the difference between values for ranked data, because the actual numbers used are arbitrary. For example, the 4-3-2-1 rating implies that the difference between excellent and good ($4 - 3 = 1$) is equal to the difference between fair and poor ($2 - 1 = 1$), whereas the 9-5-2-1 rating implies that the difference between excellent and good ($9 - 5 = 4$) is four times as large as the difference between fair and poor ($2 - 1 = 1$). Since both numbering systems are valid (though arbitrary), no inferences can be drawn as to the differences between values of ranked variables. Thus, statistics such as averages are often misleading. To illustrate this point, suppose that of 10 people interviewed, 4 rated their hotel accommodation excellent, 3 good, and 3 poor. The average using the 4-3-2-1 system is 2.8, which suggests that the average hotel is between fair and good. Using the 9-5-2-1 system, the average is 5.4, which implies that the average hotel is between good and excellent.

It should be understood that the mean of ranked data does provide *some* useful information and certainly more than that provided by the mean of qualitative data (which provides *no* useful information). However, because of the arbitrary nature of ranked data, the most appropriate statistical techniques are ones that put the data in order. (In Chapter 4 we present the *median,* which is calculated by placing the numbers in order and selecting the observation that falls in the middle.) You will find that an ordering process is used throughout this book whenever the data are ranked.

The types of data can be ranked according to the valid calculations they permit. Qualitative data have the lowest rank, since no calculations (other than counting the number of observations) are permitted. Ranked data come next, since we may calculate statistics using an ordering procedure (as well as counting the number of times each value is observed). Then comes quantitative data, for which all calculations are valid. It is important to understand that we can treat higher ranked data as if they were lower ranked. We can treat quantitative data as ranked—or even qualitative, if it suits our purposes. For example, suppose that our data consist of the times taken for athletes to run a 100-meter race. These data, of course, are quantitative. If we wish, we can calculate the mean time for a particular runner. This statistic provides us with information that summarizes how fast he or she can run. Suppose that instead of measuring time, we record position in the race. These data are ranked. Calculating the mean would give us some information, but you can see how little information is provided by determining that the average finish of a runner is, say, 2.63. What does this number tell you about the athlete's ability? On the other hand, if you know that the runner's average time is 10.03 seconds (and the world record is around 9.85 seconds), you have much more information about the runner.

The type of data being analyzed plays a critical role in determining which statistical technique to use. Section 2.3 presents graphical methods to describe a set of quantitative data. Section 2.4 introduces techniques to describe qualitative data. In the rest of this book, we will stress the importance of the data type (as well as other factors) in determining the most appropriate statistical technique to use. Having said that, it will be sufficient (after this section) to identify data as either quantitative or qualitative until we reach Chapter 16, where we discuss ranked data more fully. We conclude our discussion of data types with the following summary.

Types of Data

- *Quantitative Data (Interval)*
  Values are real numbers.
  Arithmetic calculations are valid.

- *Qualitative Data (Nominal)*
  Categorical data.
  Values are the (arbitrary) names of possible categories.
  Valid computation: count of the number of observations in each category.

- *Ranked Data (Ordinal)*
  Categorical data.
  Values must represent the ranked order of responses.
  Valid computations: those based on an ordering process.

CROSS-SECTIONAL AND TIME-SERIES DATA

Data can also be classified according to whether the observations are measured at the same time **(cross-sectional data)** or whether they represent measurements at successive points in time **(time-series data).** Marketing surveys and political opinion polls are familiar methods of collecting cross-sectional data. The data from a marketing survey might include, for example, the preferences and demographic characteristics of a sample of 1,000 consumers at the same point in time. Statistical techniques could be applied to the data, such as testing for differences in preferences between men and women.

To give another example, consider a real estate consultant who feels that the selling price of a house is a function of its size, age, and lot size. To estimate the specific form of the function, she collects the sample data shown in the following table. The values in the table represent cross-sectional data, in that they all are observations at the same point in time. (You will learn how to estimate such a function from these data in Chapter 18.)

The real estate consultant is also working on a separate project to forecast the monthly housing starts in the northeastern United States over the next year. To do so, she collects the monthly housing starts in this region for each of the past five years (similar to the data shown in Example 20.10 in Chapter 20). These 60 values (housing starts) represent time-series data, because they are observations taken over time.

House	Selling Price ($1,000s) y	House Size (100 ft^2) x_1	Age (Years) x_2	Lot Size (1,000 ft^2) x_3
1	89.5	20.0	5	4.1
2	79.9	14.8	10	6.8
3	83.1	20.5	8	6.3
4	56.9	12.5	7	5.1
5	66.6	18.0	8	4.2
6	82.5	14.3	12	8.6
7	126.3	27.5	1	4.9
8	79.3	16.5	10	6.2
9	119.9	24.3	2	7.5
10	87.6	20.2	8	5.1
11	112.6	22.0	7	6.3
12	120.8	19.0	11	12.9
13	78.5	12.3	16	9.6
14	74.3	14.0	12	5.7
15	74.8	16.7	13	4.8

Generally speaking, cross-sectional data represent measurements at the micro level, such as preferences of individual consumers or prices of individual houses. Time-series data, on the other hand, frequently represent aggregated data such as housing starts, unemployment rates, or the values of the stock market index over time. Consequently, time-series data are often readily available from secondary sources, reducing the cost of their collection compared with cross-sectional data.

Although most of the data that we'll be working with in this book will be cross-sectional data, time-series data will be used somewhat in the regression chapters (Chapters 17–19) and extensively in the time-series analysis chapter (Chapter 20).

EXERCISES

2.1 Provide two examples each of qualitative, ranked, and quantitative data.

2.2 For each of the following examples of data, determine the type.

  a the starting salaries of graduates from an M.B.A. program

  b the months in which a firm's employees take their vacations

  c the final letter grades received by students in a statistics course

  d the number of miles driven annually by employees in company cars

2.3 For each of the following examples of data, determine the type.

  a the month of highest sales for each firm in a sample

  b the weekly closing price of gold throughout the year

  c the size of soft drink (small, medium, or large) ordered by a sample of Burger King customers

  d the amount of crude oil imported monthly by the United States for the past 10 years

  e the marks achieved by the students in a statistics course final exam in which there are 10 questions each worth 10 marks

2.4 Information concerning a magazine's readership is of interest both to the publisher and to the magazine's advertisers. A survey of 500 subscribers included the following questions. For each, determine the type of data.

  a What is your age?

  b What is your sex?

  c What is your marital status?

  d Is your annual income less than $20,000, between $20,000 and $40,000, or more than $40,000?

  e How many other magazine subscriptions do you have?

2.5 A random sample of 400 university professors was taken. Each was asked the following questions. Identify the type of data.

  a What is your rank (lecturer, assistant professor, associate professor, full professor)?

  b What is your annual salary?

  c By which faculty (Arts and Science, Business, Engineering, etc.) in the university are you employed?

  d How many years have you been a professor?

2.6 Baseball fans are regularly quizzed concerning their opinions about various aspects of the sport. A sample of 300 baseball fans was asked the following questions. Identify the data type for each.

  a How many games do you attend annually?

  b Would you rate the entertainment excellent, good, fair, or poor?

  c Do you have season tickets?

  d How much money on average do you spend at the food concession at each game?

  e Rate the food: edible, barely edible, or abominable.

2.3 GRAPHICAL TECHNIQUES FOR QUANTITATIVE DATA

In this section, we introduce several graphical methods that are used when the data are quantitative. Often, the first step taken toward summarizing a mass of numbers is to form what is known as a *frequency distribution*. This is a simple, effective method of organizing and presenting quantitative data so that one can get an overall picture of where the data are concentrated and how spread out they are. Before looking at an example, we briefly describe our first marketing application.

S TATISTICS IN THE W ORKPLACE

Marketing Application

Following deregulation of the provision of telephone services, several new companies were created to engage in a fierce battle for market share in the market for long-distance service. Effective **pricing** of long-distance service is essential to the success of these companies. As mentioned in the introduction to marketing management, pricing a service (or product) effectively in the face of strong competition is a very difficult task. Factors to be considered include supply, demand, price elasticity, and the expected response of competitors. Long-distance packages may employ per-minute charges, a fixed monthly rate, or some combination of the two. Determining the appropriate rate structure is facilitated by knowing something about the behavior of customers, in terms of the frequency of their long-distance calls, the duration of those calls, and the monthly amount spent on long-distance calls.

▼ EXAMPLE 2.1

In the last decade, a number of companies have been created to compete in the long-distance telephone business. Suppose, as part of a much larger study, one such company wanted to get some information concerning the monthly bills of new subscribers in the first month after signing on with the company. A survey of 200 new residential subscribers was undertaken, and the first month's bills were recorded. These data appear in Table 2.1 and are stored in file XM02-01. As a first step, a statistician wanted

Table 2.1   Long-Distance Telephone Bills (in Dollars)

42.19	15.30	49.24	9.44	2.67	4.69	41.38	45.77
38.45	29.23	89.35	118.04	110.46	0.00	72.88	83.05
95.73	103.15	94.52	26.84	93.93	90.26	72.78	101.38
104.80	74.01	56.01	39.21	48.54	93.31	104.88	30.61
22.57	63.70	104.84	6.45	16.47	89.50	13.36	44.16
92.97	99.56	92.62	78.89	87.71	93.57	0.00	75.71
88.62	99.50	85.00	0.00	8.41	70.48	92.88	3.20
115.50	2.42	1.08	76.69	13.62	88.51	55.99	12.24
119.63	23.31	11.05	8.37	7.18	11.07	1.47	26.40
13.26	21.13	95.03	29.04	5.42	77.21	72.47	0.00
5.64	6.48	6.95	19.60	8.11	9.01	84.77	1.62
91.10	10.88	30.62	100.05	26.97	15.43	29.25	1.88
16.44	109.08	2.45	21.97	17.12	19.70	6.93	10.05
99.03	29.24	15.21	28.77	9.12	118.75	0.00	13.95
14.34	79.52	2.72	9.63	21.34	104.40	2.88	65.90
20.55	3.43	10.44	21.36	24.42	95.52	6.72	35.32
117.69	106.84	8.40	90.04	3.85	91.56	10.13	5.72
33.69	115.78	0.98	19.45	0.00	27.21	89.27	14.49
92.17	21.00	106.59	13.90	9.22	109.94	10.70	0.00
11.27	72.02	7.74	5.04	33.40	6.95	6.48	11.64
83.26	15.42	24.49	89.13	111.14	92.64	53.90	114.67
27.57	64.78	45.81	56.04	20.39	31.77	94.67	44.32
3.69	19.34	13.54	18.89	1.57	0.00	5.20	2.80
5.10	3.03	9.16	15.30	75.49	68.69	35.00	9.12
18.49	84.12	13.68	20.84	100.04	112.94	20.12	53.21

to summarize the data in preparation for a presentation to the president of the company.

Solution   Very little knowledge about the monthly bills is acquired by casually reading through Table 2.1. You probably see that most of the bills are less than $100, but that is likely to be the extent of the information garnered by browsing through the data. If you examine the data more carefully, you'll discover that the smallest bill is $0 and the largest is $119.63. This simple exercise provides you with *some* information. However, the company president will not be impressed with your statistical skills if you do not reap additional information from the data. For example, how are the numbers distributed between $0 and $119.63? Are there many small bills and some large bills, or are most of the bills in the center of the range with very few extreme values?

To acquire more information, we construct a **frequency distribution**—an arrangement or table that groups data into nonoverlapping intervals called **classes** and records the number of observations in each class. Table 2.2 provides an illustration of how this is accomplished.

Table 2.2 was created by more or less arbitrarily deciding that we will use eight classes. (We will soon discuss how to determine the number of classes to be used to build a frequency distribution.) The class width is computed by taking the difference between the largest and smallest observations and then dividing by the number of classes. Thus,

$$\text{Approximate class width} = \frac{\text{Largest value} - \text{Smallest value}}{\text{Number of classes}}$$

$$= \frac{119.63 - 0}{8} = 14.95$$

For convenience, we round this number to 15, an acceptable action because there is no fixed rule about the number of class intervals, which ultimately determines the class width. The classes are the intervals 0 up to but not including 15, 15 up to but not including 30, and so on. Notice that the class intervals were created so that there was no overlap. For example, the value 15 was included in the second class but not in the first. We then count the number of observations that fall into each class interval (or more precisely, we let the computer count the observations). The counts, or frequencies, of observations are then listed next to their respective classes. The frequency distribution is then complete, as shown in Table 2.2. The next step in the information-mining process is to draw a picture of the data by constructing a histogram.

Table 2.2 **Frequency Distribution of Long-Distance Telephone Bills**

Class Limits	Frequency
0 up to 15*	71
15 up to 30	37
30 up to 45	13
45 up to 60	9
60 up to 75	10
75 up to 90	18
90 up to 105	28
105 up to 120	14
Total	200

*Class contains observations up to but not including 15. The other classes are defined similarly.

Histograms   The information in a frequency distribution is often grasped more easily—and the presentation is made more visually appealing—if the distribution is graphed. One very common graphical presentation is the **histogram,** which is created by drawing rectangles. The bases of the rectangles correspond to the class intervals, and the height of each rectangle equals the number of observations in that class. Figure 2.1 depicts the histogram created from the frequency distribution in Table 2.2. We call this diagram a **frequency histogram** because the numbers on the vertical axis represent the frequencies.

INTERPRET

The histogram gives us quite a clear view of the way the bills are distributed. About half of the monthly bills are small (between $0 and $30), there are few bills in the middle of the range ($30 to $75), and there are a relatively large number of long-distance bills at the high end of the range. It would appear from this sample of first-month long-distance bills that the company's customers are split unevenly between light and heavy users of long-distance telephone service. At this point, it is not clear what this means to the company. Further analysis might reveal more information about our customers.

Figure 2.1 was drawn by hand to show how histograms are created and interpreted. We now show how histograms are actually drawn in practice. We employ Excel and Minitab software to do the work for us.

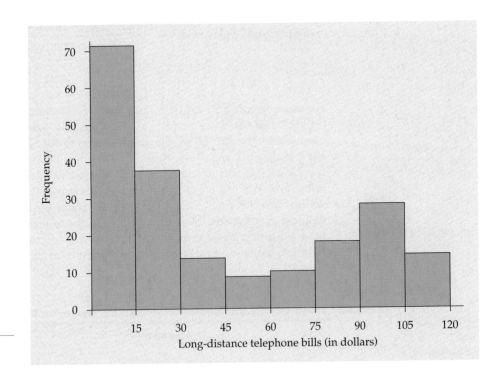

Figure 2.1

Histogram of long-distance telephone bills

As we promised in Chapter 1 (and the Preface), we will solve all examples in this book using three approaches (where feasible). We have already constructed the histogram by hand. We will now use Excel and Minitab to output the histogram for Example 2.1.

Appendix 2.A introduces Excel, provides some background information, and gives instructions for inputting data and printing results. Appendix 2.B provides a similar service for the Minitab package.

For each example, we present not only the output, but also the commands to produce it. For each of our software packages, we provide general instructions as well as instructions for the specific example. The Minitab instructions assume that you will be using the menu commands.

Excel Output for Example 2.1

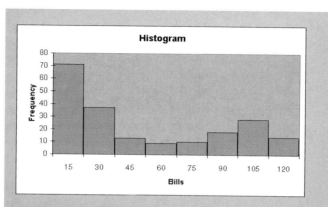

Note that the numbers that appear along the horizontal axis represent the upper limits of the class intervals even though they appear in the center of the classes on the histogram.

COMMANDS	COMMANDS FOR EXAMPLE 2.1
1 Type or import the data into column A. (See Appendix 2.A.)	Open file **XM02-01**.
2 Type **Bin** in cell B1. [If you don't wish to specify the bins (intervals), skip steps 2 and 3, in which case Excel will automatically construct its own set of bins from which the histogram will be drawn.]
3 In B2 type the upper limit of the first interval. In B3 type the upper limit of the second interval. Drag B2 and B3 to complete the listing of bins.	**15** **30** . . **120**
4 Click **Tools, Data Analysis . . . ,** and **Histogram.**
5 Type the location of the data (including cell containing name, if necessary).	**A1:A201**
6 If a variable name has been included with the data, use the cursor to specify **Labels.** (That is, click the box.)
7 Hit **tab** and type the location of the bins. If a variable name for the data has been included and you indicated that there are labels in the first row, include the cell where **Bin** is typed.	**B1:B9**

8 Move cursor to **Chart Output** and click. (That is, place a check mark in the box.) Click **OK.** This will produce a histogram with spaces between the rectangles. To remove these gaps, proceed as follows.

9 Use the left button on the mouse and click one of the bars. Click the right button.

10 Click (with the left button) **Format Data Series . . . .**

11 Click **Options** and move the pointer to **Gap Width:** and change the number to 0. Click **OK.**

12 To remove the "More" category, use the left button on the mouse and click the number of the line (10, in this example) where "More" appears. Click the right button. Click (with the left button) **Delete.**

13 To improve the appearance of the histogram, you may wish to type a new caption to replace **Bin.** If so, move pointer to the word **Bin** on the histogram and click. Type a new caption (e.g., **Bills** for Example 2.1).

Minitab Output for Example 2.1

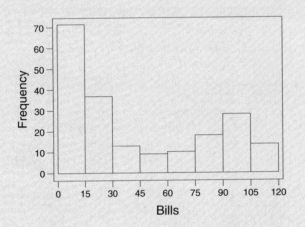

COMMANDS

1 Type or import the data into a column. (See Appendix 2.B.)

2 Click **Graph** and **Histogram . . . .**

3 Type the variable name in box 1 of **Graph variables.**

4 Use the cursor to choose the following under **Data display: Bar** (under **Display**) and **Graph** (under **For each**). Click **OK.**

COMMANDS FOR EXAMPLE 2.1

Open file **XM02-01**

Bills or **C1**

Minitab will produce a histogram using its own rules to select the classes. To choose your own classes, proceed with the following steps.

5 Before clicking **OK** click **Options . . . .**

6 Use the cursor to specify **Frequency** or **Percent** (relative frequency).

7 To specify midpoints, use the cursor to select **Midpoint.** Specify **Midpoint/cutpoint positions:,** hit **tab**, and type the midpoints you want.

8 To specify cutpoints, use the cursor to select **Cutpoint.** Specify the **Midpoint/cutpoint positions:,** hit **tab**, and type the cutpoints you want. (The first cutpoint specified must be the lower limit of the first interval. For Example 2.1, begin with **0.**) Click **OK** twice.

Excel Histogram

As noted earlier, the numbers along the horizontal axis of a histogram represent the upper limits of the interval they represent, even though they appear in the center of the classes on the histogram produced by Excel. Note also that, unlike Minitab and the authors, Excel counts observations equal to the upper limit of an interval as belonging to that interval. Thus, there will be a slight difference between the Excel and Minitab histograms if one or more values in the data set being summarized is equal to one of the upper limits. (This was not the case in the previous example, but does occur in Example 2.2.) If desired, you can avoid this slight difference with Excel by using upper limits of the form 29.99 instead of 30, for example.

Choosing the Number of Classes

Using the computer to draw histograms means that there is only one "job" for the statistician to perform (besides interpreting the results)—to choose the number of classes. As a general rule, we want to have a small number of classes when the number of observations is small and a large number of classes when the number of observations is large. Table 2.3 provides a rough guide for this decision.

Table 2.3 **Approximate Number of Classes in Frequency Distribution**

Number of Observations	Number of Classes
Less than 50	5–7
50–200	7–9
200–500	9–10
500–1,000	10–11
1,000–5,000	11–13
5,000–50,000	13–17
More than 50,000	17–20

To illustrate what happens when we have too few classes, we used both Excel and Minitab to create histograms for Example 2.1 with only five classes. Note that the smaller number of classes results in the loss of useful detail. It now appears that most of the bills are less than $25 and the rest of the bills are more or less evenly distributed between $25 and $125.

If, on the other hand, there is a small number of observations and a *large* number of classes, each class will contain few observations, which results in a histogram that yields little useful information. In Example 2.1, the number of classes would have to be quite large for that to happen.

Excel Output for
Example 2.1
(Five Classes)

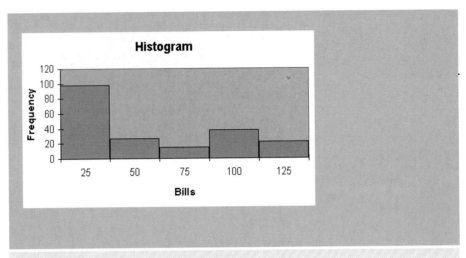

Minitab Output for
Example 2.1
(Five Classes)

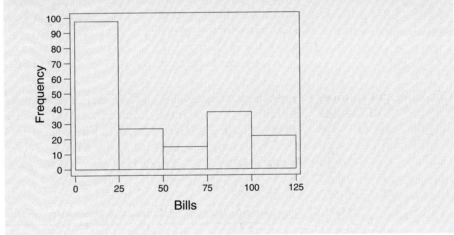

Relative Frequency
Histograms

Instead of showing the absolute frequency of observations in each class, it is often preferable to show the proportion (or percentage*) of observations falling into the various classes. To do this, we replace the class frequency by the **class relative frequency.**

$$\text{Class relative frequency} = \frac{\text{Class frequency}}{\text{Total number of observations}}$$

We can then talk about a **relative frequency distribution** (see Table 2.4) and a **relative frequency histogram** (see Figure 2.2). Notice that, in Figure 2.2, the area of any rectangle is proportional to the relative frequency, or proportion, of observations falling into that class. These relative frequencies are useful when you are dealing with a sample of data, because they provide insights into the corresponding relative frequencies for the population from which the sample was taken. Furthermore, relative frequencies should be used when you are comparing histograms or other graphical descriptions of two or more data sets. Relative frequencies permit a meaningful comparison of data sets even when the total numbers of observations in the data sets differ.

---

*Over the course of this book, we express relative frequencies (and later probabilities) variously as decimals, fractions, and percentages.

Table 2.4   Relative Frequency Distribution of Long-Distance Telephone Bills

Class Limits	Relative Frequency
0 up to 15*	71/200 = .355
15 up to 30	37/200 = .185
30 up to 45	13/200 = .065
45 up to 60	9/200 = .045
60 up to 75	10/200 = .050
75 up to 90	18/200 = .090
90 up to 105	28/200 = .140
105 up to 120	14/200 = .070
Total	200/200 = 1.000

*Class contains observations up to but not including 15. The other classes are defined similarly.

To facilitate interpretation, it is generally best to use equal class widths whenever possible. In some cases, however, *unequal class widths* are called for to avoid having to represent several classes with very low relative frequencies. For example, suppose that, instead of having 7% of the telephone bills falling between $105 and $120, we have 7% of the bills sparsely scattered between $105 and $165. This new situation might be best represented by the relative frequency histogram shown in Figure 2.3, where the uppermost four classes have been combined. It is important, however, that the height of the corresponding rectangle be adjusted (from .07 to .07/4) so that the area of the rectangle remains proportional to the relative frequency of all observations falling between $105 and $165.

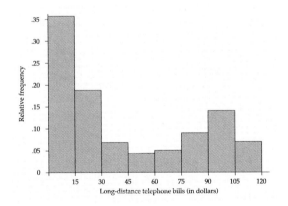

Figure 2.2

Relative frequency histogram of telephone bills

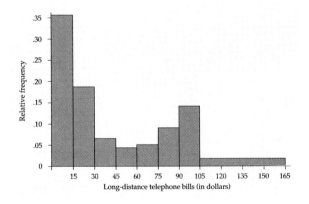

Figure 2.3

Relative frequency histogram with unequal class widths

The observations in the preceding example all fall within a fairly compact range. In some cases, however, observations may be sparsely scattered over a large range of values at either end of the distribution. If this situation arises, it may be necessary to use an **open-ended class** to account for the observations, as shown in the relative frequency distribution in Table 2.5. Because incomes ranging from $75,000 to millions of dollars are scattered fairly sparsely over a wide range of values, we use a single class with no specified upper limit to capture these incomes. Notice also that Table 2.5 makes use of unequal class widths, which were discussed in the preceding paragraph.

Table 2.5 **Percentage Distribution of American Family Income for 1992**

Class Limits ($1,000s)	Percentage
Under 5	3.7%
5 up to 10	5.8
10 up to 15	7.3
15 up to 25	15.5
25 up to 35	15.0
35 up to 50	19.2
50 up to 75	19.6
75 and over	13.9

Source: Statistical Abstract of the United States 1994.

SHAPES OF HISTOGRAMS

We often wish to describe the shape of histograms. We usually do so on the basis of the following four characteristics.

Symmetry

A histogram is said to be **symmetric** if, when we draw a line down the center of the histogram, the two sides have identical shapes. Figure 2.4 depicts three symmetric histograms.

Skewness

A skewed histogram is one that features a long tail extending either to the right or to the left. The former is called **positively skewed,** and the latter is called **negatively skewed.** Figure 2.5 depicts examples of both. Incomes of individuals working for large companies are usually positively skewed, since there is a large number of relatively low-paid workers and a small number of well-paid executives. The time taken by students to write exams is frequently negatively skewed; few students turn in their papers early, preferring to wait until the formal end of the test period.

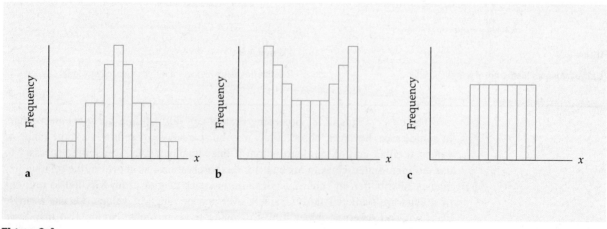

Figure 2.4

Symmetric histograms

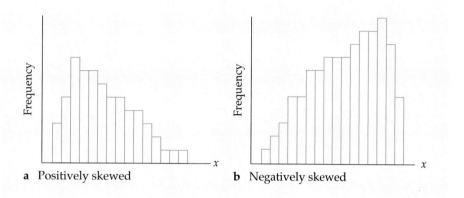

Figure 2.5

Skewed histograms

Number of Modal Classes

We will provide a definition of the mode in Chapter 4. However, we can explain here that a **modal class** is the one with the largest number of observations. Thus, a **unimodal** histogram is one with a single peak. The histograms in Figure 2.5 are unimodal. A **bimodal** histogram is one with two peaks, not necessarily equal in height. The histogram produced with eight classes in Figure 2.1 is bimodal. The final marks in the authors' statistics courses often appear to be bimodal. Figure 2.6 depicts one such histogram. We leave it to you to interpret the implications of this information. A **multimodal** histogram is one with two or more peaks.

Bell-Shaped Histogram

You will discover later in this book the importance of the normal distribution, which appears bell shaped when drawn. Figure 2.7 illustrates a bell-shaped histogram. Many statistical techniques require that the population be bell shaped, and we often draw the histogram to check that this requirement is satisfied.

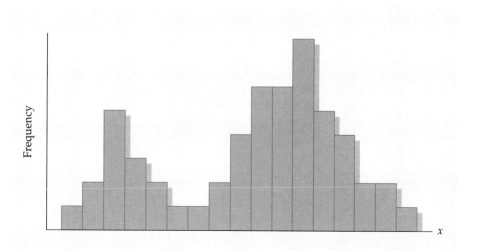

Figure 2.6

Bimodal histogram

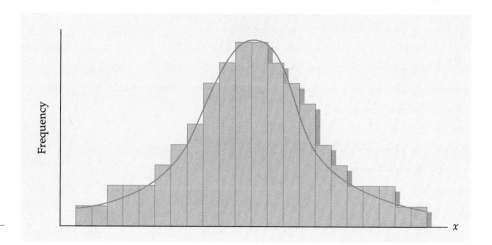

Figure 2.7

Bell-shaped histogram

OGIVES

Given a set of observations that have been grouped into classes, we've seen that the relative frequency distribution identifies the proportion of observations falling into each class. In some instances, however, our needs are better served by a cumulative relative frequency distribution. The **cumulative relative frequency** of a particular class is the proportion of observations that are less than the upper limit of that class. Table 2.6 displays the cumulative relative frequency distribution of the long-distance bills in Example 2.1.

From the cumulative relative frequency distribution, we can state, for example, that 54% of the bills were less than $30 and 70% were less than $75. Another way of presenting this information is the **ogive,** which is a graphical representation of the cumulative relative frequency distribution (see Figure 2.8).

The cumulative relative frequency of each class is plotted above the *upper limit* of the corresponding class, and the points representing the cumulative relative frequencies are then joined by straight lines. The ogive is closed at the lower end by extending a straight line to the lower limit of the first class. Once an ogive like the one shown in Figure 2.8 has been constructed, the approximate proportion of observations that are less than any given value on the horizontal axis can be read from the graph. Thus, for example, we can estimate from Figure 2.8 that the proportion of long-distance bills that are less than $25 is approximately 48%. The proportion of bills less than $50 is about 62%.

Table 2.6 Cumulative Relative Frequencies for Example 2.1

Classes	Frequency	Cumulative Frequency	Cumulative Relative Frequency
0 up to 15	71	71	71/200 = .355
15 up to 30	37	108	108/200 = .540
30 up to 45	13	121	121/200 = .605
45 up to 60	9	130	130/200 = .650
60 up to 75	10	140	140/200 = .700
75 up to 90	18	158	158/200 = .790
90 up to 105	28	186	186/200 = .930
105 up to 120	14	200	200/200 = 1.000

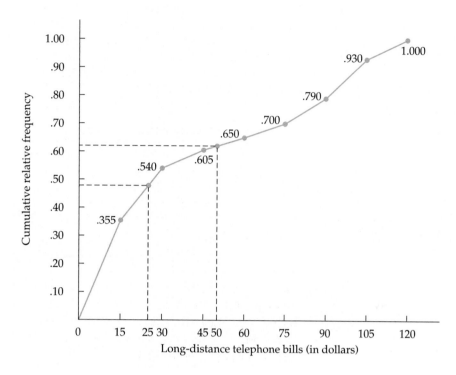

Figure 2.8

Ogive for telephone bills

Excel can be used to produce a cumulative frequency distribution and ogive as follows. Proceed through the first seven steps in constructing a histogram (see page 27). Then use the cursor to click **Cumulative Percentage, Chart Output,** and **OK.** Minitab does not produce an ogive.

STEM AND LEAF DISPLAYS

A statistician named John Tukey introduced a method of organizing interval-scaled data called the **stem and leaf display.** This display, which may be viewed as an alternative to the histogram, is most useful in preliminary analysis. In particular, it provides a useful first step in constructing a frequency distribution and histogram. The stem and leaf display is quite similar to the histogram. The main difference is that a stem and leaf display shows the values of the original observations, whereas the histogram "loses" them by classifying the observations. To illustrate, suppose that we had collected the 30 observations listed in Table 2.7 (and stored in file TAB02-07).

The first step in developing the display is to split each observation into two parts: a stem and a leaf. There are usually several alternatives. For example, the number 19.1 can be split so that its stem is 19 and its leaf is 1. Thus, using this definition, the **stem** consists of the digits to the left of the decimal and the **leaf** is the digit to the right of the decimal.

Table 2.7   Sample of 30 Observations

19.1	19.8	18.0	19.2	19.5	17.3	20.0	20.3
19.6	18.5	18.1	19.7	18.4	17.6	21.2	20.6
22.2	19.1	21.1	19.3	20.8	21.2	21.0	18.7
19.9	18.7	22.1	17.2	18.4	21.4		

Having determined what constitutes the stem and the leaf of an observation, we next list the stems in a column from smallest to largest, as shown in Table 2.8. After this has been done, we consider each observation in turn and place its leaf in the same row as its stem, in the second column. The resulting stem and leaf display presents the original observations in a more organized fashion. Table 2.8 presents the stem and leaf display for the data in Table 2.7.

Table 2.8 **Stem and Leaf Display for Data in Table 2.7**

Stem	Leaf	Stem	Leaf
17	623	20	0368
18	4705147	21	12204
19	198362751	22	12

The first line in Table 2.8, describing stem 17, has three leaves: 6, 2, and 3. The three observations represented in the first row are therefore 17.6, 17.2, and 17.3. Similarly, seven observations are represented in the second row. Whether to arrange the leaves in each row from smallest to largest or to keep them in order of occurrence is largely a matter of personal preference. The advantage of having the leaves arranged in order of magnitude is that, for example, you can then more easily determine the number of observations less than 19.5. The disadvantage is that it is more troublesome to do the arranging. Minitab constructs stem and leaf displays with the leaves in order. Excel does not produce stem and leaf displays. Minitab's stem and leaf display is shown below.

From the stem and leaf display in Table 2.8, we can quickly determine that the observations range from 17.2 to 22.2, that most observations fall between 18.0 and 20.0, and that the shape of the distribution is not symmetrical. A stem and leaf display is similar to a histogram turned on its side, but the display has the advantage of retaining the original observations. Moreover, because the stems are listed in order of size, the middle observation(s) can be determined fairly easily. In this example, the two middle observations are 19.5 and 19.6; splitting the difference, we can assert that half the observations are below 19.55 and half are above it. On the other hand, a histogram can readily accommodate a large number of observations, can display relative frequencies, and can be adapted more easily to changes in the classes used.

Minitab Stem and Leaf Display for Table 2.7

```
Character Stem-and-Leaf Display
Stem-and-Leaf of Observe    N = 30
Leaf Unit = 0.10

     3    17 236
    10    18 0144577
    (9)   19 112356789
    11    20 0368
     7    21 01224
     2    22 12
```

The numbers in the left column are called *depths*. Each depth counts the number of observations that are on its line or beyond. For example, the fifth depth, 7, reports that there are seven observations that are greater than or equal to 21, which is the lower limit of the fifth class. The sixth depth, 2, tells us that there are two observations that are greater than or equal to 22. Notice that the third depth, 9, is in parentheses. The parentheses indicate that the third class contains the observation that falls in the middle of the data, a statistic we call the *median* (which is discussed in Chapter 4). Its depth provides only the number of observations in that class. For classes below the median, the depth reports the number of observations that are less than the upper limit of that class. For example, there are 10 observations whose stems are less than 19.

The appropriate definitions of the stem and the leaf depend, in part, on the range of the observations. Suppose that the observations in Table 2.7 had ranged from 17.2 to 55.5. In such a case, it would be reasonable to define the stem as the first digit and the leaf as the remaining two digits. The number 19.1 would then have a stem 1 and leaf 9.1, and there would be five stems in all: 1, 2, 3, 4, and 5. Because each leaf would consist of more than a single digit, the leaves in any row should be separated by commas for clarity.

COMMANDS	COMMANDS FOR TABLE 2.7
1 Type or import the data into one column.	Open file **TAB02-07**.
2 Click **Graph, Character Graphs,** and **Stem-and-Leaf . . . .**	
3 Type the variable name.	**Observe** or **C1**
4 Use the cursor to type the value of the **increment.** (Increment is the distance between the smallest number on consecutive lines.) We chose 1 to produce the preceding output. Click **OK.**	

The output below shows Minitab's stem and leaf display for the data in Example 2.1 (using an increment of 10).

Minitab Stem and Leaf Display for Example 2.1

```
Character Stem-and-Leaf Display
Stem-and-Leaf of Bills    N = 200
Leaf Unit = 1.0

    52      0 000000000011111222222333334555555666666667788889999999
    85      1 0000011112333333344455555667889999
   (23)     2 00001111123446667789999
    92      3 001335589
    83      4 124445589
    75      5 33566
    70      6 3458
    66      7 022224556789
    54      8 334457889999
    42      9 00112222233344555999
    22     10 001344446699
    10     11 0124557889
```

The stem here is the "tens" digit; and the leaf is the "ones" digit. Hence, the first row represents bills that are less than $10. The second row represents bills that are between $10 and $19.99. The last entry in the last row represents the bill that is $119.63. The stem is 11, and the leaf is 9. Notice that in this display we do not show the part that is to the right of the decimal point (which is the cents part of the bill).

As you can see, the information we get from the stem and leaf display is similar to that obtained from the histogram.

DOT PLOTS

A dot plot is a graph that is similar to a histogram. One difference is that the horizontal axis is divided into more classes. In fact, ideally each observation would have its own position on the axis. The second difference is that the observations are represented by dots. Minitab's dot plot of the data in Example 2.1 is shown next. (Excel does not draw a dot plot.)

Minitab Dot Plot for Example 2.1

Character Dotplot

```
       :  . :
       :  : :         .
     : :  : :  .  :
     : : : : : :   :      .
     : : : : : :  : .  . :                      . :
     : : : : : : : : : :  : : .      :   :       : : :   .          : :   : : : .
     : : : : : : : : : : : : : . . : : . . . :   . : . . : : : : : : : : :   : : : : : . : : :
     +---------+---------+---------+---------+---------+-------Bills
     0        25        50        75       100       125
```

Notice that each $25 interval has 10 spaces on the *x*-axis. As a result, each space represents an interval that is $2.50 wide. The point representing 25 actually counts the number of bills between $25 - 1.25$ ($= 23.75$) and $25 + 1.25$ ($= 26.25$). Counting the dots at 25, we see that two bills fell between $23.75 and $26.25.

COMMANDS	COMMANDS FOR EXAMPLE 2.1
1 Type or import the data into a column.	Open file **XM02-01**.
2 Click **Graph, Character Graphs,** and **Dotplot . . . .**	
3 Type the variable name. Click **OK.**	**Bills** or **C1**

You can see that the dot plot, histogram, and stem and leaf display all yield very similar information. The choice of which to use is mostly a matter of personal preference. Generally, dot plots and stem and leaf displays are used with smaller data sets, and histograms are used for larger ones.

BOX PLOTS

Box plots are yet another method of graphing quantitative data. However, we will have to present this useful technique in Chapter 4, after we've discussed various statistics that are represented on the box plot.

We'll now summarize the techniques presented in this section with another example.

▼ **EXAMPLE 2.2**

In 1994 and 1995, the Barnes Exhibit toured major cities all over the world, with millions of people flocking to see it. Dr. Albert Barnes was a wealthy art collector who accumulated a large number of impressionist masterpieces; the total exceeds 800 paintings. When Dr. Barnes died in 1951, he willed that his collection not be allowed to tour. However, because of the deterioration of the exhibit's home near Philadelphia, a judge ruled that the collection could go on tour to raise enough money to renovate the building. Because of the size and value of the collection, it was predicted (correctly) that in each city a large number of people would come to view the paintings. Because space was limited, most galleries had to sell tickets that were valid at only one time (much like a play). In this way, they were able to control the number of visitors at any one time. To judge how many people to let in at any time, it was necessary to know the length of time people would spend at the exhibit; longer times would dictate smaller audiences, shorter times would allow for sale of more tickets. Suppose that in one city the amount of time (rounded to the nearest minute) taken to view the complete exhibit (which consisted of only 83 paintings) by each of 400 people was measured and recorded in file XM02-02. Draw the histogram, stem and leaf display, and dot plot of these data, and interpret the results.

Solution

We begin by producing the stem and leaf display.

**Minitab Stem and Leaf
Display for Example 2.2**

Character Stem-and-Leaf Display
```
Stem-and-Leaf of Times    N = 400
Leaf Unit = 1.0

    24     2  345677778888888889999999
    98     3  00000001111112222222222333333333333344444455555555666666677788888888+
  (115)    4  000000000001111111111111111222222222222222333333333333344444444444444+
   187     5  00000000000111112222222233333333344444444444455555666777777788888899+
   120     6  0000000111112222222233333333334444444445555666667778889
    69     7  000000000001111122334445788889
    38     8  01222345558889
    24     9  000111234888
    12    10  246779
     6    11  23
     4    12  15
     2    13  4
     1    14
     1    15  1
```

The stems are the "tens" digit and the leaves are the "ones." Notice that the number of leaves for stems 3, 4, and 5 have been truncated; there are too many leaves for Minitab to handle.

We draw the histogram using the stem and leaf display as our guide. We note that the smallest time was 23 minutes (stem 2 and leaf 3 on the first line), the largest time was 151 minutes, and there were 400 observations. We decided (for comparison purposes) to produce two different histograms, each having about 12 class intervals, using class widths of 15 for Excel and 10 for Minitab.

**Excel Histogram for
Example 2.2**

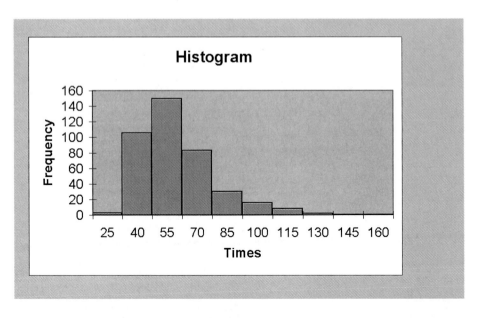

Minitab Histogram for Example 2.2

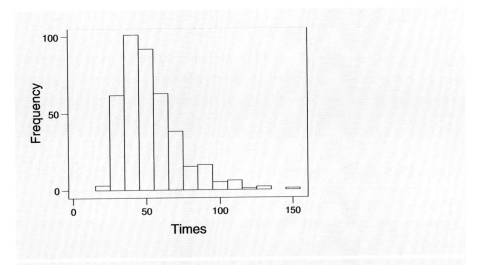

Minitab Dot Plot for Example 2.2

Character Dotplot

Each dot represents 2 points

(dot plot showing Time along horizontal axis with marks at 25, 50, 75, 100, 125, 150)

INTERPRET

Finally, we drew the dot plot letting minitab choose its own formats. All three graphical procedures tell us that the times are quite variable and the distribution is positively skewed. It appears that most visitors to the exhibit will leave within 1 hour, but there are many who will take an additional 30 minutes. Very few visitors stay longer than 1.5 hours. If we were to admit 400 people per hour, within a short time there would be far more people than the gallery could accommodate. Perhaps the admission of between 150 and 200 every 45 minutes would be a satisfactory plan.

▲

SAMPLE OR POPULATION?

Before proceeding, we should note that the descriptive methods in this chapter apply equally well to samples and to populations of data. If, for some reason, you are interested only in the long-distance telephone bills of 200 specific customers for some particular month, then the 200 observations in Table 2.1 can be considered a population, and your task simply is to summarize those 200 bills. On the other hand, if your primary interest is to obtain information concerning the distribution of the population of first-month long-distance bills of all new subscribers, the 200 bills represented in Table 2.1 may be treated as a sample, and you will want to make sure that the sample has been properly selected so that it can be used as a basis for statistical inference about the population.

> ### *Factors that Identify When to Use a Histogram or Ogive*
>
> **1** Problem objective: describe a single set of data
> **2** Data type: quantitative

EXERCISES

2.7 The number of items rejected daily by a manufacturer because of defects was recorded for the last 25 days. The results are as follows:

21 8 17 22 19 18 19 14 17 11 6 21 25
19 9 12 16 16 10 29 24 6 21 20 25

  a Construct a frequency distribution for these data. Use five class intervals, with the lower boundary of the first class being five items.
  b Construct a histogram for these data.
  c Construct a relative frequency distribution for these data.
  d What is the relationship between the areas under the histogram you have constructed and the relative frequencies of observations?

2.8 The grades on a statistics exam are as follows:

75 66 77 66 64 73 91 65 59 86 61 86 61 58 70
77 80 58 94 78 62 79 83 54 52 45 82 48 67 55

  a Construct a stem and leaf display for these data.
  b Construct a dot plot.
  c Construct a frequency distribution for these data, using six class intervals.
  d Construct a histogram for these data.
  e Briefly describe what the histogram and the stem and leaf display tell you about the data.
  f Construct a cumulative relative frequency distribution for the grades.
  g What proportion of the grades is less than 70? Greater than or equal to 70?

2.9 A large investment firm on Wall Street wants to review the distribution of the ages of its stockbrokers. The firm feels that this information will be useful in developing plans relating to recruitment and retirement options. The ages of a sample of 25 brokers are as follows:

50 64 32 55 41 44 24 46 58 47 36 52 54
44 66 47 59 51 61 57 49 28 42 38 45

  a Construct a stem and leaf display for the ages.
  b Construct a frequency distribution for the data, using five class intervals and the value 20 as the lower limit of the first class.

  c Construct a histogram for the data, using five class intervals and the value 20 as the lower limit of the first class.
  d Construct an ogive for the data.
  e What proportion of the total area under the histogram constructed in part (c) falls between 20 and 40?

2.10 The number of weekly sales calls by a sample of 25 salespersons for a dress manufacturer is shown below. Manually draw each of the following graphs.

  a a histogram with five classes
  b a histogram with 10 classes
  c a stem and leaf display
  d a dot plot
  e an ogive

24 56 43 35 37 27 29 44 34 28 33 28 46
31 38 41 48 38 27 29 37 33 31 40 50

2.11 The amount of time (in seconds) needed for assembly-line workers to complete a weld was recorded for 40 workers. Manually draw the following graphs.

  a a histogram with six classes
  b a histogram with 12 classes
  c a stem and leaf display
  d a dot plot
  e an ogive

69 60 75 74 68 66 73 76 63 67 69 73
65 61 73 72 72 65 69 70 64 61 74 76
72 74 65 63 69 73 75 70 60 62 68 74
71 73 68 67

The remaining exercises require the use of a computer and statistical software.

2.12 The annual income in thousands of dollars for a sample of 200 first-year accountants was recorded and stored in file XR02-12. Use a computer and software to perform the following techniques.

  a stem and leaf display (if your software allows it)
  b histogram
  c dot plot

2.13 Construct an ogive for the data in Exercise 2.12. Estimate the proportion of accountants who earn

    a less than $20,000

    b more than $35,000

    c between $25,000 and $40,000

2.14 Use any or all of the graphs drawn in Exercise 2.12 to describe the shape of the distribution of first-year incomes of accountants. Discuss what you have learned.

2.15 The final marks on a mathematics exam are stored in file XR02-15.

    a Construct a stem and leaf display (if your software allows it).

    b Construct a histogram.

    c Briefly describe what the histogram and stem and leaf display tell you about the data.

2.16 Construct a cumulative relative frequency distribution, and draw the ogive for the marks in Exercise 2.15.

    a Estimate the proportion of grades that are less than 70.

    b Estimate the proportion of grades that are less than 75.

2.17 The real estate board in a wealthy suburb wants to investigate the distribution of prices of homes sold during the past year. The prices are stored in the file XR02-17.

    a Construct a histogram (and a stem and leaf display if your software allows it).

    b What does the histogram (and stem and leaf display) tell you about the prices?

2.18 Refer to Exercise 2.17.

    a Construct an ogive for the house prices.

    b Estimate the proportion of prices that are less than $350,000.

    c Estimate the proportion of prices that are less than $325,000.

2.19 The president of a local consumer advocacy group is concerned about reports that similar generic drugs are being sold at widely differing prices at local drug stores. A survey of 100 stores produced the selling price of one popular generic drug. These data are stored in file XR02-19.

    a Construct a histogram.

    b What does the histogram tell you about the price?

2.20 The number of customers entering a bank during each hour of operation (10:00 A.M. to 3:00 P.M.) for each of the last 100 days was recorded and stored in file XR02-20 in the following way.

Column 1: number of arrivals between 10:00 A.M. and 11:00 A.M.
Column 2: number of arrivals between 11:00 A.M. and 12:00 P.M.
Column 3: number of arrivals between 12:00 P.M. and 1:00 P.M.

Column 4: number of arrivals between 1:00 P.M. and 2:00 P.M.
Column 5: number of arrivals between 2:00 P.M. and 3:00 P.M.

    a Use a bar chart to describe the number of customers arriving in each of the time periods.

    b For each of the time periods, construct a histogram to describe the distribution of the number of customers arriving during that hour.

    c Describe the shape of each time period's number of arrivals.

    d Discuss similarities and differences between time periods.

    e What are the implications of your findings?

2.21 The grades on a statistics exam are stored in file XR02-21. Fifty percent of the exam marks were allotted to questions that required only numerical calculations, while the remaining marks were allotted to questions that mostly involved understanding and interpretation of the results.

    a Construct a histogram using eight classes.

    b Describe the shape of the histogram in part (a).

    c Give a possible explanation for the shape of the histogram.

2.22 The average mortgage rates for each of the years 1951 to 1991 are stored in file XR02-22.

    a Construct a histogram using 8 classes.

    b Describe the shape of the histogram in part (a)

    c Give a possible explanation for the shape of the histogram.

2.23 The annual percentage rates of return on common stock* and on government bonds from 1960 to 1994 are stored in file XR02-23. (Column 1 stores the stock returns and column 2 stores the bond returns.)

    a Construct a histogram for the stock returns and a histogram for the bond returns. For each histogram, use eight class intervals and the value -30 as the lower limit of the first class.

    b Compare the shapes of the two histograms in part (a).

    c For which histogram are the returns more concentrated (that is, less scattered)?

    d On the basis of these two histograms, would you feel more certain about the return you would likely earn if you invested in stocks or in bonds? Explain your choice.

2.24 The length of time (in minutes) taken to service a random sample of customers at a certain restaurant is stored in file XR02-24.

*To understand the meaning of these rates of return, consider the 25.07% return that was realized on common stock in 1985. This means that $100 invested in common stocks at the beginning of 1985 would have yielded a profit (capital gain plus dividend) of $25.07 over the year.

a Construct a frequency distribution for these data.
b Construct a histogram using seven classes.
c Does the shape of the histogram appear to be reasonable? Briefly explain why or why not.

2.25 In Chapter 5 (Example 5.2), we illustrate how Excel and Minitab can be used to randomly select 50 numbers between 1 and 1,000. (In Example 5.2, these numbers are used to randomly select income tax returns to be audited.) The 50 numbers generated by Excel are stored in file XR02-25.

a Construct a histogram for these numbers, using five classes of equal size.
b Does the shape of the histogram appear to be reasonable? Briefly explain why or why not.

2.4 PIE CHARTS, BAR CHARTS, AND LINE CHARTS

Several types of commonly used graphical presentations are available besides those introduced in Section 2.3. The graphical presentations considered in this section are used primarily for *qualitative data.* The increasing availability of desktop computers with color graphics enables managers quickly to summon a bar chart showing sales in various regions, a pie chart displaying major causes of accidents within their firm, or a line chart depicting the trend in productivity over time. Although types of graphical presentations are numerous, only a few of the more popular ones are discussed here.

If the raw data to be summarized are quantitative and come from a single population, as was the case with the Barnes Exhibit data in Example 2.2, the descriptive methods presented in Section 2.3 (frequency distributions, histograms, stem and leaf displays, and dot plots) are useful and appropriate. These methods basically group the raw data into categories, which we call *classes,* and record the number of measurements that fall into each category. The categories are defined in a rather arbitrary manner, with the objective of conveying some idea of how the data are distributed. We now consider a situation in which the raw data can be naturally categorized in a more meaningful and less arbitrary manner.

PIE CHARTS

As we pointed out in Section 2.2, when the data are qualitative, all that statisticians can do to summarize samples and populations is count the number of times, and compute the proportion of times, each value occurs. The most popular graphical method for nominal data is the pie chart. To illustrate its application, consider the following example.

▼ **EXAMPLE 2.3**

The student placement office at a university conducted a survey of last year's business school graduates to determine the general areas in which the graduates found jobs. The placement office intended to use the data to help decide where to concentrate its efforts in attracting companies to campus to conduct job interviews. Each graduate was asked in which area he or she found a job. The areas of employment are Accounting (1), Finance (2), General Management (3), Marketing (4), and Other (5). The data are stored in file XM02-03 using the codes 1, 2, 3, 4, and 5. Create a pie chart of the data to summarize the data.

Solution The problem objective is to describe a single population of data. The data are qualitative because the "values" of the variable, area of employment, are the five categories. The numbers (1, 2, 3, 4, and 5) used to record the data in the file were assigned completely arbitrarily. The only legitimate statistical technique is to count the number of occurrences of each value and then to convert these counts into proportions. The results are shown below.

Area	Number of Graduates	Proportion of Graduates
Accounting	73	28.9%
Finance	52	20.6
General Management	36	14.2
Marketing	64	25.3
Other	28	11.1
Total	253	100

The graphical technique we choose to use, the pie chart, exhibits the proportion of each area. A **pie chart** is simply a circle subdivided into a number of slices that represent the various categories. It should be drawn so that the size of each slice is proportional to the percentage corresponding to that category. Because the entire circle corresponds to 360°, every 1% of the observations should correspond to $.01 \times 360 = 3.6°$. The angle between the lines demarcating the Accounting sector is therefore $28.9 \times 3.6 = 104°$. The angles of the pie chart for the other four categories are calculated similarly. They are as follows.

Finance	$20.6 \times 3.6 = 74.2°$
General Management	$14.2 \times 3.6 = 51.1°$
Marketing	$25.3 \times 3.6 = 91.1°$
Other	$11.1 \times 3.6 = 40.0°$

Figure 2.9 was drawn using these angles.

Now that you know how to construct a pie chart by hand, let's see how we actually draw such diagrams in practice.

Figure 2.9

Pie chart of employment areas

Excel Pie Chart for Example 2.3

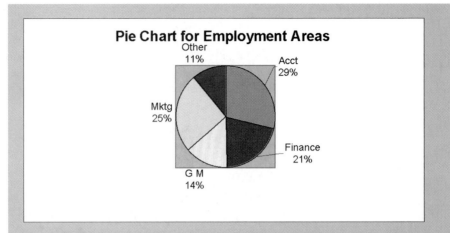

Each pie segment is denoted by its label and its percent.

COMMANDS	COMMANDS FOR EXAMPLE 2.3
1 If you have access only to the raw data, (e.g., as the data are in file **XM02-03**), proceed through the first eight steps in constructing a histogram (see page 27). (Use the codes representing the categories as the upper limits of the histogram intervals.)	Open file **XM02-03** Bin **1 2 3 4 5** (in cells B1 to B6)
2 Click once inside the boundaries of the histogram. Then click **Chart, Chart type . . .** , **Pie** and your choice of **chart subtype** (the first one is recommended). Click **OK.**	
3 To remove the "More" category, use the left button on the mouse and click the number of the line where "More" appears in the frequency distribution. Click the right button. Click (With the left button) **Delete.**	7
4 If you wish to add a title, click **Chart** and **Chart Options . . . .** Click **Titles** and fill in the **Chart title** box. Click **OK.**	**Pie Chart for Employment Areas**
5 If you wish to add the label and percent corresponding to each pie segment, click **Chart** and **Chart Options . . . .** Click **Data Labels** and use the cursor to specify **Show label and percent.** (That is, click the circle.) Click **OK.**	

If you already know the number of occurrences of each value, proceed as follows.

1 Type the number of occurrences of each value in a column (column A).	**73 52 36 64 28**
2 Click the **Chart Wizard** icon, **Pie,** and **Next>.**	
3 Type the block coordinates of the data and click **Next>.**	**A1:A5**
4 If you wish to add a title or labels, click **Titles** and/or **Data Labels** and proceed as in steps 4 and 5 above.	

Minitab Pie Chart for Example 2.3

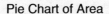
Pie Chart of Area

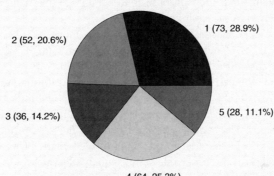

Minitab draws the first category starting at 3:00 and continues counterclockwise. Each pie segment is denoted by its code (1, 2, 3, 4, or 5), its frequency, and its relative frequency.

COMMANDS

COMMANDS FOR EXAMPLE 2.3

1 If we have the raw data (as the data are in file **XM02-03**), type or import the observations into one column.

Open file **XM02-03**.

2 Click **Graph** and **Pie Chart . . .**

3 Click **Chart data in:,** hit **tab,** and type the variable name.

Area or **C1**

If we already know the frequency with which each value occurs, the results should be recorded in two columns.

1 Store the codes in one column and the frequencies in a second column.

2 Click **Graph** and **Pie Chart . . .**

3 Click **Chart table.**

4 Use the cursor and type the column number where the categories are stored **(Categories in:)** and where the frequencies are stored **(Frequencies in:).** Click **OK.**

Other Applications of Pie Charts and Bar Charts

Pie charts (and bar charts—to be discussed next) are used widely in business and government reports, newspapers, and magazines. One of the reasons for this appeal is they are eye catching and can attract the reader's interest whereas a table of numbers might not. Perhaps no one understands this better than the newspaper *USA Today*, which typically has a colored graph on the front page and others inside. Graphical techniques are most useful for summarizing a large amount of data. As we point out in Chapter 3, small data sets can be presented in tabular form. But pie and bar charts are frequently used to simply present number (dollar amounts or percentages) associated with categories. The only reason to use a pie or bar chart in such a situation would be if the chart enhanced the reader's ability to grasp the substance of the data. It might, for example, allow the reader to more quickly recognize the relative sizes of the categories, as in the breakdown of a budget. Similarly, treasurers might use pie charts to show the breakdown of a firm's revenues by department, or business students might use pie charts to show the amount of time devoted to daily activities (e.g., eat, 10%; sleep, 30%; and study statistics, 60%). If you do use these charts, you should realize that their purpose is to summarize the data, and that they do not lend themselves to in-depth analysis.

Pie charts also can be used to compare two breakdowns. Figure 2.10 shows the sources of revenue for the conglomerate Gulf + Western Industries before and after it sold off a large portion of its operations.

We can represent yet another bit of information by varying the sizes of the pie charts. Gulf + Western's revenues before and after the sale were $4 billion and $3.1 billion, respectively. The pie charts in Figure 2.11 reflect the different levels of revenues. The charts were drawn so that the area in the "after sale" chart was 3.1/4 = 77.5% of the area in the "before sale" chart. [This was accomplished by letting the radius of the "after sale" circle equal .88 (which is $\sqrt{.775}$) of the radius of the "before sale" circle.] Pie charts with different radii must be hand-drawn; our computer software programs are not capable of this feat.

BAR CHARTS

Bar charts provide an alternative to pie charts. They graphically represent the frequency (or relative frequency) of each category as a bar rising vertically from the hor-

Figure 2.10

Pie charts of Gulf + Western's sources of revenue
Source: New York Times, 23 February 1986, p. 8F

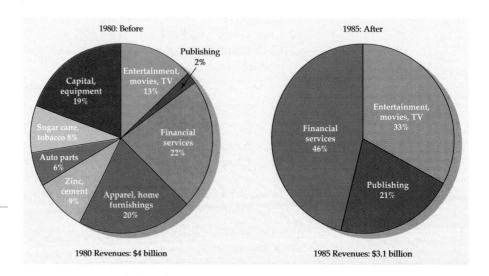

1980: Before

Publishing 2%
Capital, equipment 19%
Entertainment, movies, TV 13%
Sugar cane, tobacco 8%
Financial services 22%
Auto parts 6%
Zinc, cement 9%
Apparel, home furnishings 20%

1980 Revenues: $4 billion

1985: After

Entertainment, movies, TV 33%
Financial services 46%
Publishing 21%

1985 Revenues: $3.1 billion

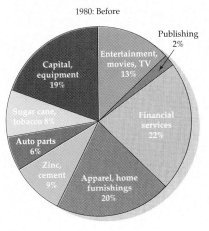

1980: Before

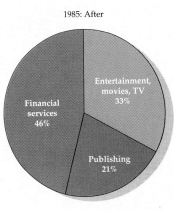

1985: After

1980 Revenues: $4 billion

1985 Revenues: $3.1 billion

Figure 2.11

Pie chart of Gulf + Western's
sources of revenue

izontal axis; the height of each bar is proportional to the frequency (or relative frequency) of the corresponding category. Because the bars correspond to categories or points, rather than to class intervals (as the rectangles of a histogram do), the widths assigned to the bars are arbitrary, although all must be equal. (The distorted impression that can be created by using unequal bar widths will be addressed in Chapter 3.) To improve clarity, a space is usually left between bars. Excel and Minitab were used to produce the bar chart for the employment data in Example 2.3.

**Excel Bar Chart for
Example 2.3**

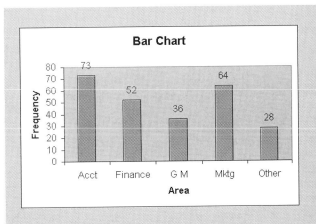

COMMANDS

Proceed as you did to create the pie chart (page 46) with the following change. Select **Column** from the **Galleries** list instead of **Pie** to obtain vertical bars. (Select **Bar** for horizontal bars.)

Minitab Bar Chart for Example 2.3

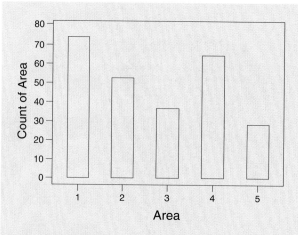

COMMANDS

1 If you have the raw data, type or import the data into a column.
2 Click **Graph** and **Chart** . . . .
3 Using the cursor specify **Function** and **Count.**
4 Use the cursor and type **C1** under **Y** and **C1** under **X.**
5 Using the cursor specify **Display** and **Bar.**
6 Click **OK.**

If we already know the frequency with which each value occurs, the results should be recorded in two columns. Column 1 contains the codes representing the categories, and column 2 contains the frequencies.

1 Click **Graph** and **Chart** . . . .
2 Use the cursor to specify **Function** and **Sum.**
3 Use the cursor and type **C2** under **Y** and **C1** under **X.**
4 Using the cursor specify **Display** and **Bar.** Click **OK.**

Bar charts are also used to present the frequencies of qualitative data, or categories, that should be presented in a particular order. For example, Figure 2.12 shows the total number of new products introduced in North America in the six years from 1989 to 1994. Because the horizontal axis implies an order (years 1989, 1990, . . ., 1994), bar charts are superior to pie charts for such applications.

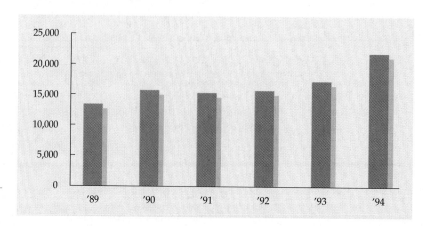

Figure 2.12

Number of new products introduced annually

Bar Chart or Pie Chart?

Since either a bar chart or a pie chart can be used to represent qualitative data graphically, which representation should be used? The answer depends on what you want to emphasize.

Although market shares are usually displayed graphically with a pie chart, professional chartists sometimes opt for the bar chart, as did a newspaper when it published the bar chart shown in Figure 2.13. This figure shows the share of U.S. prime-time television viewing enjoyed by each of the major television networks between September 1993 and April 1994. Figure 2.14 displays the conventional pie chart of the networks' market shares. But figure 2.13, which omits the very sizable "Other" category, is preferable if the objective is to emphasize CBS's leadership over the other networks.

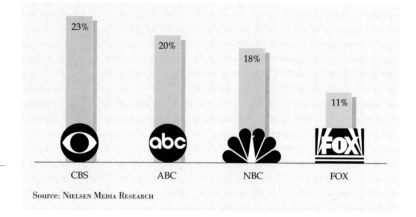

Figure 2.13

Share of U.S. prime-time television viewing (September 1993—April 1994)

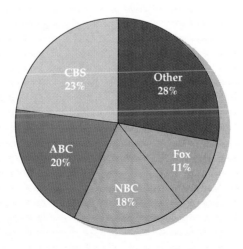

Figure 2.14

Pie chart of share of U.S. prime-time television viewing (September 1993—April 1994)

LINE CHARTS

The last graphical technique to be considered here is the line chart. A **line chart** is obtained by plotting the frequency of a category above the point on the horizontal axis representing that category and then joining the points with straight lines. A line chart is often used when the categories are points in time; such a chart is known alternatively as a **time-series chart.** An excellent example is the graph that plots the last few weeks or months of the daily values of the Dow Jones Industrial Average (DJIA), like the one shown in Figure 2.15. (We note that by early 1999, the DJIA exceeded 10,000!)

Line Charts or Bar Charts?

We can use either a line chart or a bar chart to present time-series data. In Figure 2.12, we displayed the number of new products introduced annually for 1989–1994 with a bar chart. Figure 2.16 exhibits the same data using a line chart. Which one is better? The answer depends on two factors: the objective of the graph and the number of periods. If the objective of the graph is to focus on the *trend* in the value over the year, a line chart is superior. If the goal is to emphasize the *relative sizes* of the total amounts in different years, a bar chart is recommended.

If there are a large number of periods (for example, a graph of the number of new products introduced monthly for five years), a line chart looks less cluttered and makes a clearer impression.

Pie charts, bar charts, and line charts are used extensively in reports compiled by businesses, governments, and the media. Variations on these and other pictorial representations of data abound, and their possibilities are limited only by their creators' imaginations. The objective of all such charts is to present a summary of the data clearly and in a form that allows the reader to grasp the relevant comparisons or trends quickly.

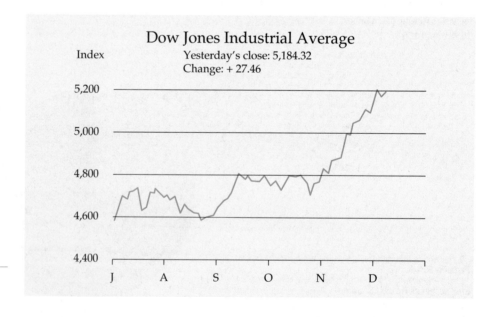

Figure 2.15

Dow Jones Industrial Average:
July–December 1994

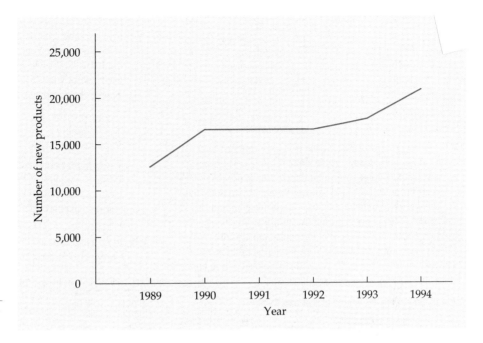

Figure 2.16

Line chart for the number of new products introduced annually

---

> ***Factors that Identify When to Use Pie Charts or Bar Charts***
>
> **1** Problem objective: describe a single set of data
>
> **2** Data type: qualitative

EXERCISES

2.26 Given the following four categories and the number of times each occurs, draw a pie chart by hand.

Category	Frequency	Category	Frequency
1	14	3	27
2	43	4	16

2.27 In a taste test, 250 people were asked which of five light beers they preferred. The beers were labeled 1, 2, 3, 4, and 5. The data are stored in file XR02-27. Use your software to create the pie chart of these data.

2.28 Repeat Exercise 2.26 using a bar chart instead.

2.29 Repeat Exercise 2.27 using a bar chart instead.

2.30 A breakdown of Hewlett-Packard's sales for the 6-month period November 1992 to April 1993 is as follows. (*Source:* Company reports.)

Computers and printers	$7,401,000,000
Test and measurement equipment	1,135,000,000
Medical equipment	553,000,000
Analytical instruments	349,000,000
Electronic components	262,000,000

Use a pie chart to describe the percentage breakdown of Hewlett-Packard's sales during the 6-month period.

2.31 Retirement savings plans are very popular in the United States and Canada because they are used to defer income tax. A survey conducted by the Caledon Institute of Social Policy (reported in the *Globe and Mail,* 5 February 1994) determined the percentage of different income groups that used retirement savings plans as a tax deduction in 1990. These statistics are listed below.

Income group	Percentage using retirement savings plans	Income group	Percentage using retirement savings plans
Less than $10,000	3%	50,000–79,999	51
10,000–19,999	13	80,000–99,999	57
20,000–29,999	28	100,000–250,000	63
30,000–39,999	40	Over 250,000	68
40,000–49,999	49		

Use a bar chart to present these figures.

2.32 A variety store's monthly sales (in thousands of dollars) for the last year were as follows:

Month	Sales	Month	Sales	Month	Sales
January	65	May	72	September	91
February	61	June	80	October	78
March	70	July	88	November	68
April	74	August	93	December	84

a Construct a relative frequency bar chart for these data.

b Construct a line chart for these data.

2.33 The city of North York is one of five boroughs which, together with the city of Toronto, comprise Metropolitan Toronto. Like Toronto and the other boroughs, it collects property tax to pay for local government activities as well as administrative costs. In its 1993 annual report, North York reported the administrative costs per person for each of the five boroughs and Toronto. It also described the percentage of its tax dollars that went to each of its activities. These statistics are shown in tables 1 and 2.

Table 1   Administrative Spending (Cost per Person)

City	Administrative cost per person	City	Administrative cost per person
Toronto	$292.00	East York	96.67
York	104.63	Scarborough	80.77
Etobicoke	96.71	North York	74.21

Table 2   Percent of Total Budget Spent on Government Activities

Activity	Percent of budget	Activity	Percent of budget
Public works	22.8%	Library	11.5
Fire	16.9	Corporate	8.2
Parks and recreation	16.3	Public health	6.6
Administration	14.9	Transportation	2.8

Use a bar chart and a pie chart to present the results shown in Tables 1 and 2, respectively.

2.34 The director of an M.B.A. program has asked you to provide a graphical summary of the gender, residence, work experience, and highest degree held by this year's successful applicants. The data are stored in file XR02-34 in the following way:

Column 1: gender (1 = male; 2 = female)
Column 2: residence (1 = in-state; 2 = out-of-state; 3 = out-of-country)
Column 3: full-time work experience (1 = none; 2 = at most 2 years; 3 = more than 2 years)
Column 4: highest degree held (1 = bachelor's; 2 = master's; 3 = Ph.D.)

a Identify the type of data stored in each column.

b Provide a graphical summary of these data for each of the four variables.

2.35 Perceptions of how well or poorly the economy will perform can sometimes result in self-fulfilling prophecies. As a result, executives, economists, and government officials are interested in the public's perceptions about the economy. Every year, 500 adults are surveyed in late December and asked "Compared with last year, do you think this coming year will be a year of economic prosperity, economic difficulty, or about the same as last year?" The responses are as follows:

1 = Prosperity
2 = Difficulty
3 = About the same

The responses (coded as 1, 2, and 3) for the years 1998, 1995, 1992, 1989, 1986, and 1983 are stored in columns 1 through 6 of file XR02-35. Use pie charts to summarize the data and briefly describe what the graphs tell you.

2.36 In an article about Chinese birth rates, *Newsweek* (November 1994) presented the following statistics.

Year	Population (billions)	Fertility rate (number of births per woman)
1950	.55	6.2
1960	.68	5.9
1970	.79	4.8
1980	.99	2.5
1990	1.17	2.2
1994	1.22	1.8
2000	1.26 (est.)	1.8 (est.)
2010	1.32 (est.)	1.8 (est.)
2020	1.45 (est.)	1.8 (est.)

Use two superimposed line graphs to present these numbers.

2.37 In 1994, a spate of small aircraft crashes made the safety of turboprop airplanes an issue. As part of an analysis of different types of accidents, Airjet Ltd. determined where accidents occurred for both turboprop airplanes and jets in the period 1984–1993. The data are stored in file XR02-37 using the following format.

When accidents happen	Code	When accidents happen	Code
Ground	1	Cruise	5
Takeoff	2	Descent	6
Initial climb	3	Approach	7
Climb	4	Landing	8

The results for turboprops are stored in column 1, and the results for jets are stored in column 2.

a Identify the type of data stored in each column.

b Use two pie charts to summarize these data.

c Does it appear that turboprop airplanes and jets have similar accident patterns?

2.38 Women own about 40% of Canadian small businesses, but there are large variations in the types of businesses owned by men and women. Suppose that a survey of female-owned and male-owned small businesses was conducted and the type of business each operated was recorded in the following format.

Business	Code	Business	Code
Services	1	Construction	5
Retail/Wholesale/Trade	2	Manufacturing	6
Finance/Insurance/Real Estate	3	Agriculture and primary	7
Transportation/Communication	4		

The responses of women and men are stored in columns 1 and 2, respectively, in file XR02-38.

a Identify the type of data stored in each column.

b Use two pie charts to summarize and present these data.

2.39 According to recent statistics, less than 1% of all personal income tax returns are audited by the IRS. Among those audited, about 75% are required to pay more tax. However, the possibility of being audited varies greatly by state. The tables below list the 10 most "dangerous" states and the 10 "safest" states, and the ratio of audited returns to the total number of returns in those states. Use two bar charts to present these results visually.

Table 1 Ten Most Dangerous States (Proportion of Audited Returns)

State	Ratio	State	Ratio
Utah	1 in 21	Texas	1 in 80
Nevada	1 in 60	Massachusetts	1 in 85
California	1 in 67	Alaska	1 in 89
Georgia	1 in 73	Montana	1 in 91
Missouri	1 in 76	Wyoming	1 in 91

Table 2 Ten Safest States (Proportion of Audited Returns)

State	Ratio	State	Ratio
Maine	1 in 227	Oregon	1 in 189
Wisconsin	1 in 227	South Carolina	1 in 185
Hawaii	1 in 222	Virginia	1 in 175
North Carolina	1 in 208	Michigan	1 in 175
New Jersey	1 in 204	West Virginia	1 in 169

Source: National Institute of Business Management and IRS

2.40 For the past few years, the U.S. government has been quite concerned with its trade imbalance with the rest of the world. To develop an understanding of the problem, a statistician determined the annual American trade deficit (the difference between what the United States sells to other countries and what the United States buys from others). These data are listed below.

Year	Trade deficit (billions of dollars)
1983	52
1984	107
1985	118
1986	138
1987	151
1988	119
1989	109
1990	102
1991	68
1992	85
1993	116

a Draw a line chart of the annual trade deficits.

b Draw a bar chart of the annual trade deficits.

2.5 SCATTER DIAGRAMS

The two previous sections presented a variety of graphical techniques for *describing* single sets of data. We now discuss how a scatter diagram can be used to begin investigating the *relationship* between two sets of data.

Statisticians frequently need to determine how two *quantitative* variables are related to one another. For example, economists are interested in the relationship between inflation rates and unemployment rates. Financial analysts need to understand how the returns of individual stocks are related to the behavior of the entire stock market. Company executives often try to determine the effect of a price increase on the demand for their firm's products. The graphical technique used to depict relationships is the **scatter diagram.**

To draw a scatter diagram we need a set of data for two variables. We'll label one variable *x* and the other *y*. Each pair of values of *x* and *y* constitutes a point on the graph. To illustrate, consider the following example.

S TATISTICS IN THE W ORKPLACE

Marketing Application

Advertising is one of the major promotional tools used by a company to inform customers about its products and services. In determining the size of the advertising budget, a manager must consider the expected effectiveness of the advertising campaign. Although this assessment of effectiveness is sometimes purely subjective, the manager's decision making can often be improved by looking at the historical relationship between sales and advertising expenditures. The data should reveal whether advertising expenditures are an important factor in the level of sales and, if so, what the marginal return on advertising expenditures is.

▼ EXAMPLE 2.4

A small business owner has experienced fairly uniform sales levels from month to month in previous years. This year, he decided to vary his advertising expenditures from month to month to see if that would have a significant impact on the sales level. To help assess the effect of advertising on sales level, he collected the data shown in the accompanying table. Construct a scatter diagram for these data, and describe the relationship between advertising expenditure and sales level.

Month	Advertising Expenditure x ($1,000s)	Sales Level y ($1,000s)
1	1	30
2	3	40
3	5	40
4	4	50
5	2	35
6	5	50
7	3	35
8	2	25

Solution In some cases we may feel that the value of one variable depends (to some degree) on the value of the other variable. When that is the case, the first variable is called the **dependent variable** and is plotted on the vertical axis. (Much more will be said about this in Chapter 17.) If we are concerned only with the relationship between two variables, and not whether the values of one depend on the values of the other, then the choice of variable to be plotted on the vertical axis is arbitrary. In this example, the monthly sales level is the dependent variable, labeled y.

The eight pairs of values for advertising expenditure (x) and monthly sales level (y) are plotted in Figure 2.17. The pattern of the resulting scatter diagram provides us with two pieces of information about the relationship between these two variables. We first observe that, generally speaking, sales level (y) tends to increase as advertising expenditure (x) increases. Whenever two variables such as these move

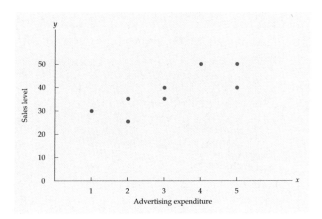

Figure 2.17

Scatter diagram for Example 2.4

together—that is, their values tend to increase together and decrease together—we say that there is a **positive relationship** between the two variables. The second observation is that the relationship between sales level and advertising expenditure appears to be *linear.* Although the eight points don't all lie on a straight line, we can imagine drawing a *straight line* through the scatter diagram that approximates the positive relationship between the two variables. Finding the straight line that "best fits" the scatter diagram will be addressed in Chapter 4.

The pattern of the scatter diagram provides us with information about the relationship between the two variables. Figure 2.17 depicts a relationship that is called **linear.** A **linear relationship** is one that can be graphed with a straight line. If the two variables generally move in unison—they both increase or both decrease together—we say that there is a **positive** linear relationship. If they move in opposite directions, and the scatter diagram is a straight line, we say that there is a **negative** linear relationship (see Figure 2.18). We can have **nonlinear relationships** (see Figures 2.19 and 2.20), as well as cases where the two variables are unrelated (see Figure 2.21). We will have a lot more to say about this subject in Section 4.6 and Chapters 17 through 19.

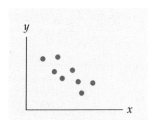

Figure 2.18

Negative linear relationship

Figure 2.19

Nonlinear relationship

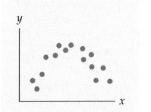

Figure 2.20

Nonlinear relationship

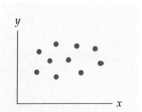

Figure 2.21

No relationship

**Excel Output for
Example 2.4**

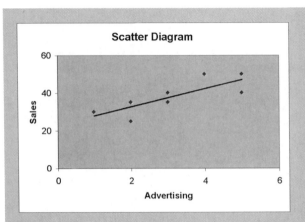

COMMANDS

1 Type or import the data into two
adjacent columns. The variable to
appear on the vertical axis must be in
the second column.
2 Click the **Chart Wizard** icon, select
XY (Scatter) from **chart type,** click
on the first **Chart sub-type,** and
click **Next>**.
3 Click **Data Range** (if necessary)
and type the block coordinates in
the **Data range** box. Click **Next>**.
4 If you wish to label the chart and
axes, you can click **Titles**
(if necessary) and fill in the boxes.

COMMANDS FOR EXAMPLE 2.4

Open file **XM02-04**

A1:B9
Chart title: **Example 2.4**
Value (X) Axis: **Advertising**
Value (Y) Axis: **Sales**

5 Check **Gridlines** and remove the check mark, to eliminate the horizontal
lines that will automatically appear on the scatter diagram. Click **Finish.**
6 If you wish to change the scale, double-click the *y*-axis, click **Scale,**
remove the check mark under **Auto,** and change the **Minimum, Maximum,**
and/or **Major** and **Minor Units.** Click **OK.** Repeat for the *x*-axis.
7 To draw a straight line through the points, click **Chart** and **Add Trendline.**
Specify **Linear** and click **OK.**

**Minitab Output for
Example 2.4**

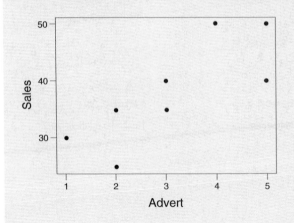

COMMANDS	COMMANDS FOR EXAMPLE 2.4
1 Type or import the data into two columns.	Open file **XM02-04**.
2 Click **Graph** and **Plot . . . .**	
3 Type the name of the variable to appear on the *y*-axis.	**Sales** or **C2**
4 Use the cursor and type the name of the variable to appear on the *x*-axis. Click **OK**.	**Advert** or **C1**

LEAST SQUARES LINE

It was mentioned earlier that we can imagine drawing a straight line through the scatter diagram (Figure 2.17) that approximates the positive relationship between the two variables. But how should this straight line be drawn? The simplest way is to draw it freehand, attempting to ensure that the line passes through the middle of the scatter of points in a way that best approximates the relationship between the two variables. Although this freehand approach is useful as a first approximation, it has the disadvantage of being subjective, meaning that different people will likely draw different lines. What we need is an objective method of determining the "best" line for a given sample of data.

The most popular method for fitting a line (or a curve) to a set of data is the **method of least squares,** which we will describe only briefly here. The **least squares line** that "best fits" the data will be written

$$\hat{y} = b_0 + b_1 x$$

where b_0 is the *y*-intercept, and b_1 is the slope of the line. The term $\hat{y}$ is the "fitted" value of *y;* that is, $\hat{y}$ is the value of *y* calculated from the equation of the line shown above.

Observed values of *y* can lie above or below the fitted line, with $(y_i - \hat{y}_i)$ representing the differences between an observed value y_i and the value $\hat{y}_i$ calculated from the equation of the line. The method of least squares determines the values of the constant term b_0 and the slope b_1 (and hence the "best" line) that will cause the sum of the squared differences to be minimized. That is, the least squares line will minimize

$$\sum_{i=1}^{n} (y_i - \hat{y}_i)^2$$

for the sample of *n* values y_i of the dependent variable. It is this least squares line that is produced when you ask Excel to draw a linear trendline through the points. The method of least squares is covered in considerably more detail in Section 4.6.

Factors that Identify When to Use a Scatter Diagram

1 Problem objective: describe relationship between two variables

2 Data type: quantitative

▲

EXERCISES

2.41 A real estate board has collected data to help determine how the number of house sales in its region is related to interest rate levels. The numbers of houses sold in the region and the average monthly mortgage rates for 12 randomly selected months are shown in the following table.

Mortgage rate (%)	Number of houses sold	Mortgage rate (%)	Number of houses sold
8.0	188	10.5	140
9.5	145	7.0	203
7.5	181	7.5	188
11.0	137	11.0	144
8.5	157	9.0	150
10.0	148	8.0	166

  a Draw a scatter diagram for these data with the number of houses sold on the vertical axis.
  b Describe the relationship between mortgage rate and number of homes sold.

2.42 A manufacturing firm has recorded its electrical power costs and the total number of hours of machine time for each of 12 months in the following table.

Machine time (thousands of hours)	Cost of power (dollars)	Machine time (thousands of hours)	Cost of power (dollars)
6	760	5	700
9	1,000	7	910
8	890	6	745
7	880	9	950
10	1,070	8	870
10	1,030	11	1,040

  a Draw a scatter diagram for these data with the cost of electrical power on the vertical axis.
  b Describe the relationship between electrical power cost and hours of machine usage.

2.43 A retailer, interested in the relationship between the firm's total selling expenses and total sales, has collected the data shown in the following table (and stored in file XR02-43).

Month	Total selling expenses ($1,000s)	Total sales ($1,000s)
J	14	20
F	16	40
M	18	60
A	17	50
M	17.5	50
J	17.5	55
J	18	60
A	20	70
S	19	70
O	22	95
N	20	80
D	19	65

  a Draw a scatter diagram for these data with total selling expenses on the vertical axis.
  b Describe the relationship between total selling expenses and total sales.

2.44 A certain manufacturing firm produces its products in batches using sophisticated machines and equipment. The firm has decided to investigate the relationship between direct labor costs and the number of units produced per batch. The data for 30 batches are stored in file XR02-44.

  a Draw a scatter diagram for these data with labor costs on the vertical axis.
  b Describe the relationship between labor costs and number of units per batch.

2.45 Because inflation reduces the purchasing power of the dollar, investors seek investments that will provide higher returns when inflation is higher. It is frequently stated that common stocks provide just such a hedge against inflation. The annual percentage rates of return on common stock* and the annual inflation rates (as measured by percentage changes in the Consumer Price Index) from 1985 through 1994 are shown in the accompanying table. (The data are also stored in file XR02-45. Column 1 stores the stock returns, and column 2 stores the inflation rates.)

Year	Common stock return (%)	Inflation rate (%)
1985	25.07	4.38
1986	8.95	4.19
1987	5.88	4.12
1988	11.08	3.96
1989	21.37	5.17
1990	−14.80	5.00
1991	12.02	3.78
1992	−1.43	2.14
1993	32.55	1.70
1994	−.18	.23

Source: *Report on Canadian Economic Statistics: 1924–1994* (Canadian Institute of Actuaries, 1995)

  a Construct a scatter diagram for these data with the stock returns on the vertical axis.
  b Describe the relationship between common stock returns and inflation rates over the period 1985 through 1994.
  c Does it appear that common stocks provide a good hedge against inflation?

*To understand the meaning of these rates of return, consider the 25.07% return that was realized on common stock in 1985. This means that $100 invested in common stocks at the beginning of 1985 would have yielded a profit (capital gain plus dividend) of $25.07 over the year.

Exercises 2.46–2.48 require the use of a computer and statistical software.

2.46 Refer to Exercise 2.45. The annual percentage rates of return on common stock and the annual inflation rates (as measured by percentage changes in the Consumer Price Index) from 1960 through 1994 are stored in file XR02-46. (Column 1 stores the stock returns, and column 2 stores the inflation rates.)

   a Construct a scatter diagram for these data with the stock returns on the vertical axis.

   b Describe the relationship between common stock returns and inflation rates over the period 1960 through 1994. How does your answer compare with part (b) of Exercise 2.45?

   c Does it appear that common stocks provide a good hedge against inflation?

2.47 Investment managers are often interested in the relationship between the monthly rate of return on an individual stock (R) and the monthly rate of return on the overall stock market (R_m). For practical purposes, R_m is taken to be the monthly rate of return on some major stock market index, such as the Dow Jones Industrial Average or the Toronto Stock Exchange 300 Index. The monthly rates of return on American Barrick Resources (North America's largest gold producer) and on the overall stock market (as measured by the TSE 300 Index) over a 5-year period are stored in file XR02-47. (Column 1 stores the monthly percentage return on American Barrick Resources, and column 2 stores the monthly percentage return on the TSE 300 Index.)

   a Construct a scatter diagram for these data with the returns for American Barrick Resources on the vertical axis.

   b Describe the relationship between the returns on the individual stock and the returns on the overall stock market.

2.48 The economics department of a national investment banking firm is conducting a study (similar to the one in Exercise 2.41) to determine how house sales are related to mortgage rate levels. The number of houses sold and the average monthly mortgage rate for 36 months are stored in file XR02-48.

   a Draw a scatter diagram for these data with number of houses sold on the vertical axis.

   b Describe the relationship between mortgage rates and number of homes sold.

2.6 SUMMARY

Descriptive statistics is concerned with methods of summarizing and presenting the essential information contained in a set of data. This chapter focused on graphical methods of summarizing and presenting data.

   A collection of **quantitative data** can be usefully summarized by grouping the observations to form a **frequency distribution.** Constructing a **stem and leaf display** is often helpful during preliminary analysis of the data. Either a **histogram** or a **relative frequency histogram** can be used to convey the shape of the distribution. Other graphical techniques include **pie charts, bar charts,** and **line charts. Scatter diagrams** describe the relationship between two quantitative variables.

IMPORTANT TERMS

Descriptive statistics   *18*
Population   *18*
Sample   *18*
Variable   *18*
Data   *19*
Quantitative (numerical) data   *19*
Qualitative (categorical) data   *19*
Ranked data   *20*
Ordinal Scale   *20*
Cross-sectional data   *22*
Time-series data   *22*
Frequency distribution   *25*

Classes   *25*
Histogram   *26*
Class relative frequency   *30*
Relative frequency distribution   *30*
Relative frequency histogram   *30*
Open-ended class   *31*
Symmetric   *32*
Positively skewed   *32*
Negatively skewed   *32*
Modal class   *33*
Unimodal   *33*
Bimodal   *33*

Multimodal	*33*	Time-series chart	*51*
Cumulative relative frequency	*34*	Scatter diagram	*55*
Ogive	*34*	Dependent variable	*56*
Stem and leaf display	*35*	Positive relationship	*57*
Stem	*35*	Linear relationship	*57*
Leaf	*35*	Negative relationship	*57*
Pie chart	*44*	Nonlinear relationship	*57*
Bar chart	*48*	Method of least squares	*59*
Line chart	*51*	Least squares line	*59*

SUPPLEMENTARY EXERCISES

2.49 The data from the survey referred to in Exercise 2.5 (page 23) were stored in file XR02-49 in the following way:

Column 1: rank (1 = lecturer; 2 = assistant professor; 3 = associate professor; 4 = full professor)
Column 2: annual salary
Column 3: university faculty (1 = Arts and Sciences; 2 = Engineering; 3 = Business; 4 = other)
Column 4: years of experience

  a Identify the type of data stored in each column.
  b Use histograms and pie charts, as appropriate, to describe the data.

2.50 The data from the survey in Exercise 2.6 (page 23) were stored in file XR02-50 in the following way:

Column 1: number of games attended annually
Column 2: entertainment rating (4 = excellent; 3 = good; 2 = fair; 1 = poor)
Column 3: season tickets (1 = yes; 2 = no)
Column 4: average amount of money spent at the food concession at each game
Column 5: food rating (12 = edible; 7 = barely edible; 1 = abominable)

  a Identify the type of data stored in each column.
  b Use pie charts or histograms, as appropriate, to describe the data.

2.51 The data from the survey referred to in Exercise 2.4 (page 23) have been stored in file XR02-51 using the following format:

Column 1: age
Column 2: sex (1 = female; 2 = male)
Column 3: marital status (1 = single; 2 = married; 3 = divorced; 4 = widowed)
Column 4: annual income (1 = less than $20,000; 2 = between $20,000 and $40,000; 3 = over $40,000)
Column 5: number of other magazine subscriptions

  a Identify the type of data stored in each column.
  b Use histograms and pie charts, as appropriate, to describe these data.

2.52 In an effort to track the increasing prices of homes in a large city, a statistician took a random sample of homes sold this year and another sample of homes sold 5 years ago. The data are stored in columns 1 (sale prices 5 years ago) and 2 (sale prices this year) in file XR02-52.

  a What is the data type?
  b Use graphical techniques to describe each of the sets of data.
  c Discuss similarities and differences between the two sets of data.

2.53 The head coach of an NFL football team is trying to decide among three candidates for the position of punter. The coach knows that longer punts are desirable, but so is consistency. As an avid student of statistics, the coach often uses his knowledge in that subject to help him make decisions. He has recorded the distance of the last 100 punts for each of the three candidates and stored them in columns 1 to 3 of file XR02-53. Use three graphs to display the data in the columns. Referring to these graphs, describe the data and provide the head coach with your recommendation.

2.54 In the last few years, regional airlines have come under scrutiny because of safety concerns. In response, the Regional Airline Association produced the results listed below (and stored in file XR02-54).

Year	Fatal accidents (per 100,000 departures)	Number of passengers (millions)
1983	.10	21
1984	.23	27
1985	.24	28
1986	.02	29
1987	.31	32
1988	.04	36
1989	.12	38
1990	.04	42
1991	.24	42
1992	.15	48
1993	.10	53
1994	.04 (est.)	58 (est.)

  a Use two superimposed line graphs to help make the association's argument.

b Construct a graph to depict the *relationship* between the number of passengers and fatal accidents.

c What do the graphs tell you about regional airline safety?

2.55 Mutual funds are becoming an increasingly popular investment alternative among small investors. To help investors decide on the particular fund to invest in, various publications regularly report the average annual rate of return achieved by each of more than 100 mutual funds during the past 10 years. [The annual rate of return of a mutual fund is given by $(P_1 - P_0)/P_0$, where P_0 and P_1 are the prices of the fund's shares at the beginning and end of the year, respectively. This definition assumes that no dividends are paid by the fund during the year.] Some publications also indicate each fund's level of risk by classifying the historical variability of each fund's rate of return as high, intermediate, or low. Suppose that the annual (percentage) rates of return over the past 10 years for five mutual funds are stored in columns 1 through 5 of file XR02-55. Use five bar charts to describe the five sets of data.

2.56 Airlines are rated on a number of dimensions, but for many passengers one of the most important is the frequency and magnitude of late arrivals and departures. Suppose that the amount of time that each departure was behind schedule was recorded for the last 250 departures for each of five airlines and was stored in columns 1 through 5 of file XR02-56.

a Use a bar chart to compare the percentage of late departures (defined as any time greater than 5 minutes behind schedule) for the five airlines.

b Which airline is best at adhering to its departure schedule?

2.57 Many economic analysts have predicted that North American pulp and paper mills are likely to continue to decline in the face of stiffer worldwide competition and rising costs. An analysis of the competitiveness of plants in different parts of North America reveals a wide divergence in terms of manufacturing costs. The following table lists the number of pulp mills in each of nine geographic regions that are above the average cost and below the average cost. Use a bar chart, consisting of nine pairs of contiguous bars, to present these figures.

Geographic region	Number of mills above average manufacturing cost	Number of mills below average manufacturing cost
U.S. South	5	37
U.S. Northeast	4	0
U.S. Central	0	1
U.S. Northwest	1	3
U.S. West	3	0
Ontario	9	2
Quebec	7	0
Western Canada	12	8
Atlantic Canada	3	1

2.58 Refer to Exercise 2.57. The following table lists the number of newsprint mills that are above and below average cost by region. Use two pie charts to describe these figures.

Geographic region	Number of mills above average manufacturing cost	Number of mills below average manufacturing cost
U.S. South	1	10
U.S. Northeast	3	4
U.S. Central	0	2
U.S. Northwest	1	1
U.S. West	0	2
Ontario	4	3
Quebec	15	1
Western Canada	3	6
Atlantic Canada	3	4

2.59 A hotly debated subject in the United States is universal health coverage for all Americans. Many people in the United States are urging Congress and the president to adopt a plan similar to the Canadian plan. However, critics point out that there are a variety of shortcomings in the Canadian plan. Foremost among them is the amount of time Canadians must wait for treatment. Table 1 provides the waiting time in each of the 10 provinces of Canada to see four types of specialists after a referral from a general practitioner. Table 2 lists the waiting time in each province for seven different treatments after an appointment with a specialist (*source:* Fraser Institute). (The data are also stored in file XR02-59, with Table 1 in cols. 1–4, and Table 2 in cols. 5–11.)

Table 1 Average 1992 Wait (in weeks) to See a Specialist After Referral from a General Practitioner

Province	Specialists			
	Neurosurgery	Orthopedics	Cardiovascular surgery	Internal medicine
British Columbia	7.5	11.6	6.7	5.5
Alberta	15.0	7.8	5.2	3.9
Saskatchewan	4.5	11.1	6.7	2.4
Manitoba	12.0	11.1	3.3	4.7
Ontario	11.2	9.9	3.9	7.0
Quebec	4.6	8.4	3.2	3.3
New Brunswick	4.0	7.1	3.0	2.2
Newfoundland	4.3	13.9	1.0	3.0
Nova Scotia	3.5	8.8	3.8	4.5
Prince Edward Island	4.2	6.0	2.8	4.5

Table 2 Average 1992 Patient Wait (in weeks) for Treatment After Appointment with Specialist

Province	Treatment						
	Hysterectomy	Cataract removal	Hernia repair	Breast biopsy	Disc surgery	Pin removal	Hip arthoplasty
British Columbia	10.4	15.4	8.0	2.5	8.1	12.2	25.1
Alberta	8.7	8.8	4.9	1.6	7.8	6.5	19.9

(continued)

Table 2   Average 1992 Patient Wait (in weeks) for Treatment After Appointment with Specialist *(continued)*

Province	Hysterectomy	Cataract removal	Hernia repair	Breast biopsy	Disc surgery	Pin removal	Hip arthoplasty
				Treatment			
Saskatchewan	10.7	26.9	9.8	1.9	4.0	9.0	18.8
Manitoba	13.0	21.6	7.9	1.9	8.0	17.3	58.6
Ontario	5.8	13.2	4.6	2.0	7.5	9.7	17.0
Quebec	5.4	15.7	7.1	2.6	25.1	11.2	15.4
New Brunswick	26.6	21.1	6.0	1.8	1.0	26.0	19.5
Newfoundland	5.1	3.7	12.7	1.6	4.2	15.3	16.7
Nova Scotia	11.0	20.6	7.6	2.1	9.0	6.8	32.0
Prince Edward Island	31.0	27.0	13.7	2.3	5.1	8.0	35.0

a To display the waiting times in Table 1, construct a bar chart using 10 groups of bars, with each group consisting of four contiguous bars (one bar for each of the types of specialists).

b For each of the seven treatments in Table 2, construct a bar chart showing the average wait in each of the 10 provinces.

2.60 Much progress has been made in the economic and political battles to create a more equitable society in the United States. Just how much can be measured using the statistics below. Use bar charts, employing contiguous pairs of bars corresponding to the two racial groups, to present the figures.

Education: Persons 25 Years and Older, with Four Years of College or More, by Percentage of Their Racial Group

Year	Blacks	Whites
1940	1%	5%
1971	5	12
1991	12	22

Source: U.S. Bureau of the Census

Occupation: Employed Civilians, 1992, by Percentage of Their Racial Group in Specific Jobs

	Blacks	Whites
Professional/managerial	17%	28%
Technical/sales/administrative	29	34
Service occupations	24	12
Construction/repairs	8	12
Laborers/operators	22	14

Source: U.S. Bureau of Labor Statistics

Family Income: Percentage of Racial Group by Total Income Using 1992 Dollars

		Blacks	Whites
$50,000 to 74,999	1982	9%	19%
	1992	11	21
$75,000 to 99,999	1982	2%	7%
	1992	3	8
$100,000 and over	1982	1%	5%
	1992	2	7

Source: U.S. Bureau of the Census

2.61 A growing concern at universities and colleges across North America is the number of professors who will retire in the next 5, 10, and 15 years. To examine the problem, a statistics professor took a random sample of 1,000 professors and recorded their ages. These data are stored in file XR02-61. What is the data type? Assuming that professors will retire at age 65, use a frequency distribution and histogram to help discuss the retirement problem facing universities during the next 15 years.

2.62 Credit scoring is a statistical technique used by banks to decide whether to approve applications for loans, credit cards, and other forms of credit. The technique works by assigning a weight to the responses in an application for credit. The total weight is then used to make decisions. Higher scores represent more desirable applicants, ones whose applications will likely be accepted. To judge the effectiveness of one such scoring method, a bank recorded the scores from a random sample of 200 applicants, all of whom were given a $1,000 loan. The scorecard recommended that only the top 125 applicants be given loans. After 2 years, the status of each loan was determined (there were two categories: loan paid in full and defaulted on loan or is behind in payments). The scores are stored in file XR02-62; the loans paid in full are stored in column 1; column 2 contains the scores of the defaulted or late-payment loans.

a Identify the types of data stored in the columns.

b Prepare a brief report on how well the scorecard works, supported by two graphs, to be presented to the bank's board of directors.

2.63 The 1993 annual report for the Thomson Corporation, which owns newspapers, travel agencies, and publishing companies, presented the following information.

Business segment	Sales by business segment		Operating profit by business segment		Assets by business segment	
	1993	1992	1993	1992	1993	1992
Thomson Information/ Publishing	46%	44%	60%	57%	56%	56%
Thomson Newspapers	19	19	24	28	24	26
Thomson Travel	35	37	16	15	20	18
Total (millions of U.S. dollars)	5,849	5,980	731	688	8,213	7,907

Geographic area	Sales by geographic area		Operating profit by geographic area	
	1993	1992	1993	1992
United States	42%	38%	59%	61%
United Kingdom	47	50	30	25
Canada	8	9	8	11
Other Countries	3	3	3	3
Total (millions of U.S. dollars)	5,849	5,980	731	688

a Use a bar chart, employing contiguous pairs of bars representing 1992 and 1993, to display total sales, profits, and assets in the 2 years.

b For each of 1992 and 1993 separately, use component bar charts to show the contribution to sales, profits, and assets by the business segments.

c Repeat part (b), showing the contribution by geographic area.

2.64 The ranks of the elderly are growing. This phenomenon has enormous implications for society because elderly people require more medical care than do younger people. The following table describes the percentages of the North American and European population that were over 65, over 75, and over 80 in 1990. Also listed are forecasts for 2010 and 2025.

	Percentage over 65		Percentage over 75		Percentage over 80	
Year	North America	Europe	North America	Europe	North America	Europe
1990	12.4%	13.2%	5.2%	5.8%	3.2%	3.2%
2010	14.1	17.7	7.0	8.2	4.5	4.8
2025	20.3	22.1	8.2	8.1	4.9	7.2

To display the percentages of elderly people, construct a bar chart using six groups of bars, with each group consisting of three contiguous bars (corresponding to the three age groups).

2.65 How does the level of an individual's education affect his or her income? An economist decided to examine this question. She took a random sample of 1,000 40- to 45-year-old people and recorded the highest education level each person achieved. The categories are

1 = did not complete primary education
2 = completed primary school
3 = completed high school
4 = received a bachelor's (or equivalent) degree
5 = received a master's or doctoral degree

The economist also recorded the annual income. These are stored in file XR02-65 using the following format.

Column 1: annual incomes of category 1
Column 2: annual incomes of category 2
Column 3: annual incomes of category 3
Column 4: annual incomes of category 4
Column 5: annual incomes of category 5

a Identify the type of data stored in each column.
b Perform whatever graphical analyses you deem necessary and report your findings (bearing in mind the purpose of collecting the data).

2.66 Exercises 2.45 and 2.46 addressed the issue of whether common stocks are a good hedge against inflation. To investigate the same issue for long-term bonds, the annual percentage rates of return on bonds and the annual inflation rates from 1985 through 1994 are shown in the accompanying table. (The data are also stored in file XR02-66. Column 1 stores the bond returns, and column 2 stores the inflation rates.)

Year	Bond return (%)	Inflation rate (%)
1985	25.26	4.38
1986	17.54	4.19
1987	.45	4.12
1988	10.45	3.96
1989	16.29	5.17
1990	3.34	5.00
1991	24.43	3.78
1992	13.07	2.14
1993	22.88	1.70
1994	−10.46	.23

Source: Report on Canadian Economic Statistics: 1924–1994 (Canadian Institute of Actuaries, 1995)

a Construct a scatter diagram for these data, with the bond returns on the vertical axis.
b Describe the relationship between bond returns and inflation rates from 1985 to 1994.
c Does it appear that bonds provide a good hedge against inflation?

2.67 Refer to Exercise 2.66. The annual percentage rates of return on bonds and the annual inflation rates from 1960 to 1994 are stored in file XR02-67. (Column 1 stores the bond returns, and column 2 stores the inflation rates.)

a Construct a scatter diagram for these data with the bond returns on the vertical axis.
b Describe the relationship between bond returns and inflation rates from 1960 to 1994. How does your answer compare with part (b) of Exercise 2.66?
c Does it appear that bonds provide a good hedge against inflation?

CASE 2.1   Pacific Salmon Catches*

A national publication has presented a detailed study about commercial salmon fishing in the United States, Canada, Japan, and the former U.S.S.R. These four nations account for the bulk of the total annual Pacific Rim catch of salmon, which can be worth as much as $5 billion. The total size of the salmon catch in 1987 for each of these countries is shown in the following table, together with a breakdown of their catches by species.

Develop an interesting and informative graphical descriptive method to exhibit the data. Your graphical presentation should emphasize the relative sizes of the total catches for the four countries, as well as the relative importance (according to size) of the species caught for each country.

1987 Salmon Catches (in Metric Tons)

Species	United States	Canada	Japan	Former U.S.S.R.
Sockeye	102,165	14,650	945	11,521
Pink	75,914	26,045	17,000	96,390
Chum	40,440	10,490	145,440	23,810
Coho	18,450	8,320	3,300	4,224
Chinook	18,444	5,607	—	2,304
Cherry	—	—	3,310	—
Total	255,413	65,112	169,995	138,249

CASE 2.2   Bombardier Inc.

Bombardier Inc. is an international manufacturer and distributor of transportation equipment (such as railcars for the English Channel Tunnel), motorized consumer products (such as Ski-Doo snowmobiles and Sea-Doo watercraft), and various types of aircraft. According to Bombardier's 1995 Annual Report, "Completion of the major Eurotunnel contract led to a reduction in the level of Bombardier Eurorail's production during the year, but was offset by higher volume in our North American facilities," as a result of "a return of consumer confidence in the economy, combined with heightened interest for personal watercraft and snowmobiles." The increase in deliveries of aircraft in 1995 also contributed to the outstanding growth in Bombardier's revenues in 1995.

It is January 1996, and you have been asked to summarize the financial data in the accompanying table, using graphical techniques, for presentation to the shareholders at Bombardier's upcoming annual meeting. Be prepared to explain your choice of graphs. In addition, prepare a sentence to accompany each graph that describes an important point being conveyed by that graph.

*Adapted from Jere Van Dyk, "Long Journey of the Pacific Salmon," *National Geographic* 178 (July 1990): 3–37.

Bombardier's Financial Statistics

	1995	1994	1993	1992	1991
Revenues	$5,943*	$4,769	$4,448	$3,059	$2,892
By Product					
Transportation Equipment	1,310	1,312	1,238	726	697
Aerospace	2,981	2,243	2,228	1,519	1,383
Motorized Consumer Products	1,111	791	556	392	398
Other	541	423	426	422	414
By Market					
North America	3,266	2,524	2,131	1,233	1,247
Europe	2,034	1,946	2,119	1,652	1,383
Other	643	299	198	174	262
Net Income	242	176	133	108	100
Before Tax Income	346	207	151	121	121
By Product					
Transportation Equipment	66	(24)	(73)	4	20
Aerospace	141	137	181	137	113
Motorized Consumer Products	117	76	29	(9)	(30)
Other	21	18	14	(10)	17
Share Price					
High	25.00	22.00	17.38	17.60	10.31
Low	8.00	9.63	10.63	8.38	7.25

Source: Bombardier Inc., Annual Reports, 1991–1995
*All figures are rounded to the nearest million dollars, except for share price.

CASE 2.3 **The North American Free Trade Agreement**

The North American Free Trade Agreement (NAFTA) recently was enacted by the governments of the United States, Canada, and Mexico. Its effect will be to increase trade among the three countries. It is informative to compare various aspects of the countries involved. Tables 1, 2, and 3 present several statistical comparisons for 1992. Table 1 lists economic figures, Table 2 describes the magnitude of current trade, and Table 3 describes household ownership of luxury items in the three countries (sources: OECD, IMF, Statistics Canada). Use graphical techniques to present the information contained in the tables.

Table 1 Economics

	United States	Canada	Mexico
Population (millions)	256	28.8	89.5
GDP (millions of U.S. dollars)	$8,000	$840	$488
Economic growth	2.6%	0.7%	2.7%
Inflation	2.6	1.5	14.5
Share of world exports	13.0	4.0	1.0

Table 2   Magnitude of Trade

	Exports (billions of dollars)	Percent of Total Exports
U.S. to Canada	$ 96.4	20%
Canada to U.S.	118.4	77
U.S. to Mexico	48.7	9
Mexico to U.S.	39.1	76
Canada to Mexico	0.8	0.5
Mexico to Canada	2.8	5

Table 3   What People Have

Item	Percentage of Households with Each Item		
	United States	Canada	Mexico
Domestic help	7%	10%	11%
Cable television	61	71	15
Videocassette recorder	61	74	63
Color television	93	97	83
Telephone	92	98	50
Compact disk player	30	25	23
Car	88	76	54
Auto insurance	79	76	26

Appendix 2.A

Brief Introduction To Microsoft Excel

We have chosen to use Microsoft Excel to produce statistical output because most students already know how to use the most popular spreadsheet on the market. Throughout this book we provide simple step-by-step instructions for using Excel. We assume that students are already familiar with their computers and with Excel in general. Our instructions deal specifically with statistical components of Excel. For readers who do not know how to use this spreadsheet, we recommend the Study Guide that is available from the publisher. Among other topics covered it explains the fundamentals of Microsoft Excel.

DATA ANALYSIS

To access the statistical tools that analyze data, click **Tools** and **Data Analysis . . . .** If **Data Analysis** is not in the **Tools** menu, install the **Analysis ToolPak.** To do so, click **Tools** and **Add-Ins.** Then click the **Analysis ToolPak** check box.

If **Analysis ToolPak** is not listed in the **Add-Ins** dialog box, click **Browse** and find the folder name and file name for the **Analysis ToolPak** add-in. It is probably in the **Library/Analysis** folder. If not found, the **Analysis ToolPak** was probably not included when Excel was installed. Run the setup program again.

USING THE ANALYSIS TOOLPAK

Click **Tools, Data Analysis . . . ,** and the statistical technique you want. In the dialog box, enter the information requested. Include the **Input Range:,** specify whether the range includes the name of the variable **(Label),** and select any options you need.

MACROS

Excel's menu does not include all the techniques covered in this book. So we have created several macros—sets of commands that are executed all at once—that are designed to perform many of the "missing" techniques. This will allow Excel users to avoid manual calculations. Instructions for their use are described throughout this book. The macros are stored on the CD that accompanies the book. Instructions for copying them to your computer are in the README file. After copying the macros to your computer, access them through the **Tools** menu. To use the macros, click **Tools, Data Analysis Plus^{TM},** and the technique you wish to use. The macros work in Excel 5.0, Office 95, and Office 97.

DATA RETRIEVAL

The CD that accompanies this book contains 595 data files occupying 17 MB. The instructions that copy the macros will also copy the data files to your computer. Instructions for opening these files appear throughout the book.

COMPUTER OUTPUT

To improve the readability of computer printouts for most of the examples used in this book, we have deleted portions of the output and moved some of the headings.

Appendix 2.B

Brief Introduction To Minitab

Minitab Release 12 for Windows 95 and NT is a statistical software package that is extremely easy to use and understand. This software features a wide variety of statistical methods; we will only use a fraction of Minitab's capabilities. Our goal in this appendix is to introduce you to the basics of Minitab. As we stated in Chapter 1 we will use Minitab to solve most of the examples presented in this book. When we exhibit the output we will also describe the commands that produced the printout.

Within Minitab you will find a number of different windows and tools. Here is brief description of each.

Minitab Environment

WINDOWS

The **Session window** displays the statistical output requested. Most of what you command Minitab to do will appear here.

The **Data window** shows the data in the worksheet you are conducting your analysis on. Each column represents a variable.

The **History window** keeps track of all the commands you have issued.

Graph windows exhibit the graphs you requested. The maximum number of graphs that can be open at any time is 15.

The **Info window** summarizes each open worksheet.

MENUS AND TOOLS

The **Menu bar** is the starting point for selecting commands.

The **Toolbar** displays buttons for functions that are used most frequently.

The **Status bar** shows an explanation when you point at a menu item.

Shortcut menus appear when you right click on a window.

COMMANDS

There are three ways to issue commands.

1 Click menu items.

2 Select from a toolbar.

3 Use session commands.

In this book we describe the menu items only. For example, to produce a histogram (see page 28) from the menu bar click **Graph.** From the list that appears click **Histogram . . . .** A dialog box will appear requesting you to identify the variable or variables you wish to describe as well as other information.

DIALOG BOXES

Among other things you will have to identify the variable from which you wish to compute statistics or graphs. Minitab displays the **variable list,** which contains all the variables, constants, or matrices in the current worksheet. (The current worksheet is the one associated with the active Data window. You activate a Data window by clicking on it.) If the variables have been named the names will appear in the list. If the variables are unnamed the column in which the variables is stored appears. To select a variable, type its name or column in the **Variables** box. Alternatively, click in the text box you wish to fill, highlight the variable in the variable list and click **Select.**

DATA INPUT

Activate the data window and start typing the data into a column starting in row 1. You can type the name of the variable in the cell immediately under the column number (e.g., C1). When finished you may issue commands.

IMPORTING DATA

Most of the examples, exercises, and cases in this book have data sets associated with them. To import the data you will have to install the Minitab files from the disk that accompanies this book. (Follow the instructions in the README file.)

To open a file, click **File** and **Open Worksheet . . . .** (Do not click the file symbol. The reasons are explained below.) Select the folder containing the data files. All the data files are saved in chapter subdirectories. To open a file in Chapter 2 click **CH02.** A complete list of files will appear. The files beginning with XM refer to files for examples. The data files associated with exercises begin with XR, and files connected to cases begin with C. For example, the get the data for Example 2.2 click **XM02-02.**

MINITAB PROJECTS AND WORKSHEETS

A Minitab project contains all the data, the output from any commands issued on the data set, and graphs. When you save the project all of this will be saved. You may have as many worksheets as you like in any project. For example, one worksheet can contain the data, another a graph, a third descriptive statistics, and so on. All the data files on the disk are worksheets. If you click the file symbol on the toolbar, Minitab will attempt to open a project. The only projects you will have are the ones you yourself previously created.

PREVIOUS RELEASES OF MINITAB

A number of new Minitab functions are provided in Release 12. Moreover, some of the commands are new. Users of earlier versions of Minitab can go to our web page (see page 15) and see the commands and macros for Releases 10 and 11.

MINITAB WEB SITE

For assistance you can go to Minitab's web page

http://www.minitab.com

You can get answers to frequently asked questions as well as other information.

Chapter 3

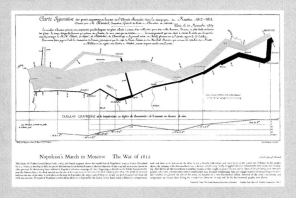

Napoleon's March to Moscow   The War of 1812

Art and Science

of Graphical

Presentations

3.1 Introduction

3.2 Graphical Excellence

3.3 Graphical Deception

3.4 Summary

3.1 INTRODUCTION

In Chapter 2, we introduced a number of graphical techniques. The emphasis was on how to construct each one manually and how to command the computer to draw them. In Chapter 3, we discuss how to use graphical techniques effectively. We introduce the concept of **graphical excellence,** which is a term we apply to techniques that are informative and concise and that impart the information clearly to their viewers. Section 3.2 discusses how to achieve excellence in the presentation of graphical methods. In Section 3.3, we discuss an equally important concept, graphical integrity. In that section, we learn about how charts are often used to mislead readers.

3.2 GRAPHICAL EXCELLENCE

Graphical excellence is achieved when the following characteristics apply.

1 *The graph presents large data sets concisely and coherently.* Graphical techniques were created to summarize and describe large data sets. Small data sets are easily summarized with a table. One or two numbers can best be presented in a sentence.

2 *The ideas and concepts the statistician wants to deliver are clearly understood by the viewer.* The chart is designed to describe what would otherwise be described in words. An excellent chart is one that can replace a thousand words and still be clearly comprehended by its readers.

3 *The graph encourages the viewer to compare two or more variables.* Graphs displaying only one variable provide very little information. Graphs are often best used to depict relationships between two or more variables or to explain how and why the observed results occurred.

4 *The display induces the viewer to address the substance of the data and not the form of the graph.* The form of the graph is supposed to help present the substance. If the form replaces the substance, the chart is not performing its function.

5 *There is no distortion of what the data reveal.* You *cannot* make statistical techniques say whatever you like. A knowledgeable reader will easily see through distortions and deception. This is such an important topic that we devote Section 3.3 to its discussion.

Edward Tufte, professor of statistics at Yale University, summarized graphical excellence this way:

Graphical excellence is the well-designed presentation of interesting data—a matter of substance, of statistics, and of design.

Graphical excellence is that which gives the viewer the greatest number of ideas in the shortest time with the least ink in the smallest space.

Graphical excellence is nearly always multivariate.

And graphical excellence requires telling the truth about the data.

In attempting to demonstrate what constitutes excellence, we searched through newspapers, magazines, and financial reports. Unfortunately, we found far more examples of bad statistical applications than excellent ones. Fortunately, we can learn just as much about the proper use of graphs by examining bad ones. Here are good and bad examples.

EXAMPLES

Graphical techniques should be used when there is a large amount of data. In general, small data sets can be presented in tabular form. Examine Figure 3.1, which is a bar chart depicting the number of visitors in 1994 to Disney theme parks around the world. Does the chart provide the reader with any more information than Table 3.1 does? From both you can see that Tokyo Disneyland drew the most visitors—about 16 million—while the others drew between 8 and 11.2 million. The bar chart is completely unnecessary for two reasons. First, there are only six numbers represented; a data set this small does not need a graphical display. Second, there is no analysis associated with the attendance figures to explain why Tokyo Disneyland outdrew the others or how these figures are related to other variables, such as profits or sales. This chart also fails to address why the reader would be interested in this "information." What concept is being imparted to the reader? None that we could see.

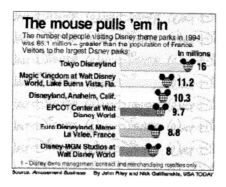

Figure 3.1

Table 3.1   **Number of People Visiting Disney Theme Parks in 1994**

Park	Number of Visitors (in millions)
Tokyo Disneyland	16.0
Walt Disney World, Florida	11.2
Disneyland, California	10.3
EPCOT Center, Florida	9.7
Euro Disneyland, France	8.8
Disney-MGM Studios, Florida	8.0

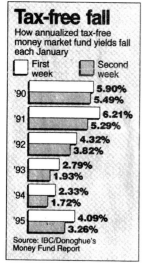

Figure 3.2

Compare the amount of information contained in Figure 3.1 with that of Figure 3.2, which describes the January effect on tax-free money funds. The January effect is a phenomenon that results in a drop in the yield of money funds during the second week of January. It is caused by investors paying their Christmas shopping bills by taking money out of their tax-free funds, which causes the yield to drop. In Figure 3.2, the concept the author wishes to describe is clear. For each of the years 1990 to 1995, the yield during the second week of January was less than the yield during the first week. However, because of the small amount of data (there are only 12 numbers shown), a table would provide at least as much information. In fact, by adding an extra column for the difference between the first-week yield and the second-week yield, Table 3.2 provides *more* information. We clearly can see the magnitude of the difference between the yields in weeks 1 and 2.

In an article about the uneven work distribution in Canada, Figure 3.3 was drawn. A large amount of data is summarized concisely. The number of hours specified in

Table 3.2   Yields of Tax-Free Funds for First and Second Weeks in January

Year	Yield: First Week	Yield: Second Week	Difference Between First and Second Weeks
1990	5.90%	5.49%	0.41%
1991	6.21	5.29	0.92
1992	4.32	3.82	0.50
1993	2.79	1.93	0.86
1994	2.33	1.72	0.61
1995	4.09	3.26	0.83

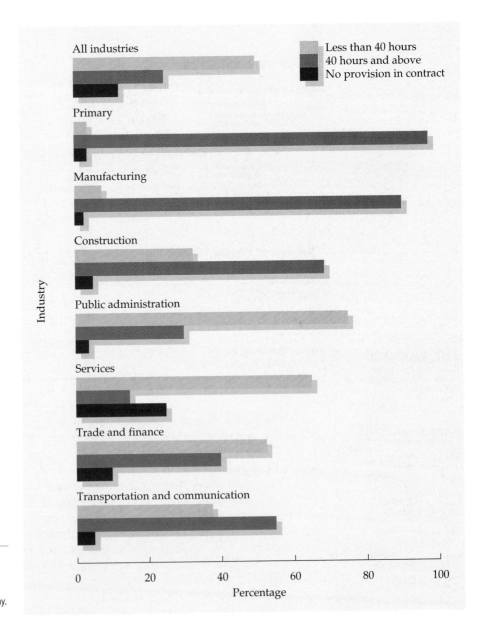

Figure 3.3

Number of working hours by industry (in major collective agreements)
Source: Creative Statistics Company.

many collective agreements had to be collected, recorded, and tabulated. The main point is clear: There is great variation in the work hours across different industries. Moreover, the reader is coaxed into analyzing the relationship between two variables: working hours and type of industry. On the negative side, a larger number of categories of working hours (e.g., 35–37.5, 37.5–40, 40–42.5, 42.5 and over) would be more useful. And, why don't the three percentages for "All Industries" add up to 100%?

The overwhelming majority of poorly executed charts can be attributed to the contempt most people have for statistics. It is generally believed that statistics can be manipulated to prove anything that the statistician wishes to prove. It would follow that statistics and graphs mean nothing and that there are no rules governing how they should be used. This is absolute nonsense! You cannot lie to a knowledgeable viewer. It is usually easy to detect deception in the application of statistical techniques.

It is also generally accepted that statistics are boring, and authors must resort to desperate measures to attract readers. This attitude is exemplified in Figure 3.4, which is a pie chart of the percentages of the uses of sports apparel. This is one of the worst examples of graphical techniques that we have encountered. It fails on every characteristic. It contains very little data, and hence a table would suffice. The idea that the author wants to deliver is not clear. Perhaps the creator of the chart had no ideas to impart. There is no analysis associated with the chart that would entail examining why these results were observed. Finally, because of the other shortcomings of the graph, the author was forced to enhance it by making the pie chart part of an illustration of a runner. Consequently, the viewer addresses the design rather than the substance. Statisticians refer to this type of graphical display as **chartjunk.** We make one request of our readers: If you ever create a chart like Figure 3.4, please don't tell anyone you learned statistics from this book.

Time lines representing time-series data are often seen in the financial sections of newspapers. However, they are often devoid of substance. For example, Figure 3.5 is a time line of the number of basis points by which Quebec 10-year bonds exceed 10-year Canadian bonds. Since the late 1960s, the province of Quebec has threatened to secede from Canada, which has made many investors nervous about investing in Quebec. The chart depicts the degree of concern among investors—the greater the

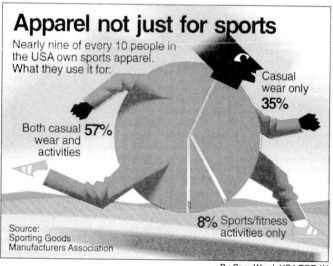

Figure 3.4

Source: USA Today (11 January, 1995).

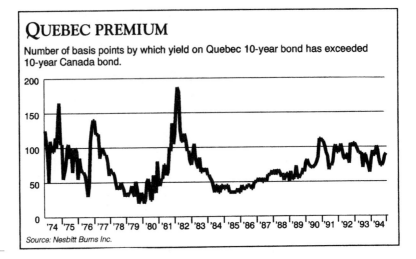

Figure 3.5

concern, the greater the premium that must be offered by the Quebec government. In its present form, the graph tells us very little. It could be improved by adding the time line of one or more related variables. Examples of related variables include Quebec's budget deficits, unemployment rates, and survey results showing support for separation. The authors could also indicate the dates of Quebec's provincial elections. They could also attempt to explain the spikes in 1975, 1977, and 1982 and the steady increase since 1984.

Contrast Figure 3.5 with Figure 3.6, which plots a consumer sentiment index in the United States from 1950 to 1994. The index measures how people feel about their financial prospects. The score in 1966 was arbitrarily set equal to 100. In addition to the scores, we also see the periods during which the U.S. economy underwent recessions. The years in which a new president was inaugurated as well as other key events also appear on the chart. Examining the chart provides rich details about the factors that affect Americans' perceptions of their financial circumstances. For example, recessionary periods mostly coincide with downturns in the index. From the early 1960s to 1980, there was a general downward drift. Historians would agree that this was a troubled time in the United States. The period started with the assassination of Pres-

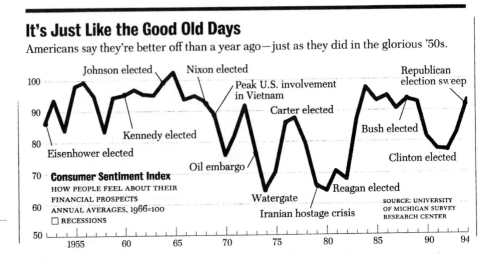

Figure 3.6

Source: Newsweek (30 January, 1995).

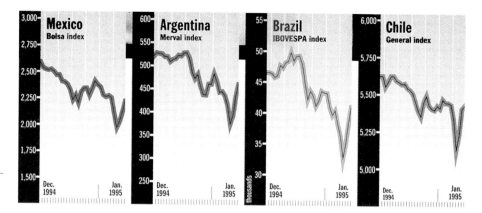

Figure 3.7

© 1995 *TIME Inc.* Reprinted by permission.

ident John Kennedy, followed by the Vietnam War, the rapid increase in the price of oil, gasoline shortages, the Watergate scandal, and the Iranian hostage crisis. The inauguration of Ronald Reagan as president in 1980 marked the end of the decline, and the sharpest increase in the index took place during his 8-year stint in office, during which the greatest boom in U.S. history occurred. This graph is more than just a graph; it's a short story.

In January 1995, a financial crisis in Mexico caused many foreign investors to sell their Mexican holdings. As a result, the Mexican stock market (as measured by the *Bolsa* Index) fell by 6.6% on one day (January 9). In a story about the widespread effect of this event, *Time* magazine published the graphs shown in Figure 3.7, which are time lines for the stock market indexes in Mexico, Argentina, Brazil, and Chile. The story is summarized concisely and clearly by the graphs. The shock to the Mexican stock market reverberated across South America with equally disastrous consequences.

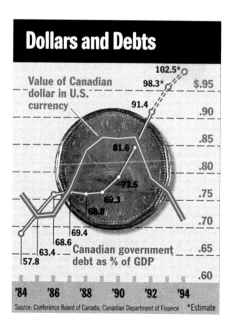

Figure 3.8

© 1995 *TIME Inc.* Reprinted by permission.

In the same section, *Time* also published an article about the fall of the Canadian dollar. Figure 3.8 depicts the time line showing the value of the Canadian dollar in U.S. dollars. It shows that in 1990 the Canadian dollar was worth about $0.86 U.S. but had dropped to about $0.71 in 1994. The article discussed several reasons for this decrease in value but pointed to Canada's rapidly increasing debt as the chief cause. The chart also included Canada's debt as a percentage of gross domestic product (GDP). As you can easily see, the debt/GDP ratio was constant between 1986 and 1989, but started a sharp increase in 1990. The argument is clear: The increasing debt produced a much lower value for the dollar.

Figures 3.6, 3.7, and 3.8 illustrate one of the determinants of graphical excellence. The graphs are well designed, presenting interesting data although the Canadian dollar is extraneous. It imparts ideas concisely because it presents several variables at the same time. And finally, it does not distort the data in any way.

EXERCISES

3.1 Geac is a computer company that has diversified its operations into financial services, construction, manufacturing, and hotels. In its 1994 annual report, the following tables were provided.

Region	Sales (millions of dollars) by region	
	1994	1993
United States	67.3	40.4
Canada	20.9	18.9
Europe	37.9	35.5
Australasia	26.2	10.3
Total	152.2	105.1

Division	Sales (millions of dollars) by division	
	1994	1993
Customer service	54.6	43.8
Library systems	49.3	30.5
Construction and property management	17.5	7.7
Manufacturing and distribution	15.4	8.9
Financial systems	9.4	10.9
Hotels and clubs	5.9	3.4

Create charts to present these data so that the differences between 1994 and 1993 are clear.

3.2 The following chart appeared in *USA Today* (11 January, 1995). Grade it A, B, C, D, or F. Explain why you graded it the way you did.

Foreign office rents

Non-U.S. cities with highest, lowest average office rents:

Cost per square foot[1]

$134.29 $129.26 $92.10

Highest — Hong Kong, Tokyo, Shanghai

Lowest — Edmonton, Alberta ($6.41), Sevilla, Spain ($8.88), Lima, Peru ($9.20)

Highest U.S. city — Washington $32.43

Lowest U.S. city — Houston $13.15

1 – Jan.-June, 1994

Source: Colliers International   By Web Bryant, USA TODAY

3.3 A line chart showing the value of the Canadian dollar in terms of the U.S. dollar from 1984 to 1994 is provided below.

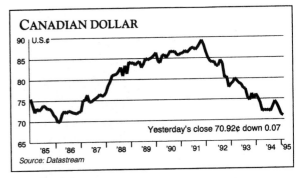

CANADIAN DOLLAR

U.S.¢

Yesterday's close 70.92¢ down 0.07

'85 '86 '87 '88 '89 '90 '91 '92 '93 '94 '95

Source: Datastream

Exercise 3.3

a Write as many sentences as you need to describe the chart.

b How would you judge the amount of information that can be extracted from the chart?

c Describe how the chart could be made more informative.

3.4 The U.S. Federal Reserve Board raises interest rates during economic booms to help control inflation and produce the so-called "soft landing" when the boom eventually ends. Signs that usually indicate that the economy is overheating and likely to result in inflation are the changes in the consumer price index and annual growth rates. In an article (*Globe and Mail,* 16 January, 1995) about increases in interest rates, the three charts shown appeared. Discuss the information that is imparted by the charts. Do the charts justify increases in the interest rate?

Exercise 3.2

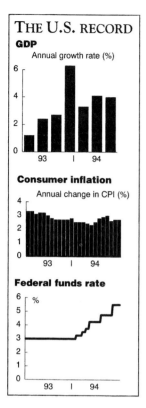

THE U.S. RECORD

GDP

Annual growth rate (%)

Consumer inflation

Annual change in CPI (%)

Federal funds rate

Exercise 3.4

Source: Globe and Mail (16 January, 1995).

3.5 The accompanying line chart graphs the number of hard-cover books that appeared on the top-50 bestseller list each week during 1994. Grade it A, B, C, D, or F, and justify your grade. What have you learned from the chart?

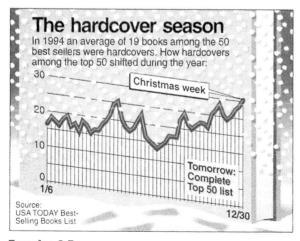

The hardcover season

In 1994 an average of 19 books among the 50 best sellers were hardcovers. How hardcovers among the top 50 shifted during the year:

Christmas week

Tomorrow:
Complete
Top 50 list

Source:
USA TODAY Best-
Selling Books List

Exercise 3.5

3.6 During 1993 and 1994, the Canadian government threatened cutbacks in university funding. Students and educa-tors protested, arguing that higher education is critical not only to the nation but to individual students as well. The following chart was produced (*Globe and Mail,* 6 October, 1994), showing the percent changes in the number of jobs for four groups with different educational attainment levels. Grade it A, B, C, D, or F, and explain your reasons for your grade assignment.

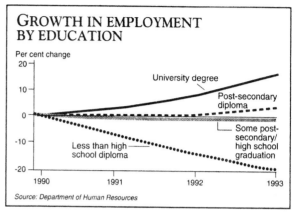

GROWTH IN EMPLOYMENT BY EDUCATION

Per cent change

University degree

Post-secondary diploma

Some post-secondary/ high school graduation

Less than high school diploma

Source: Department of Human Resources

Exercise 3.6

3.7 In 1987, the U.S. government established Sematech, a federally financed consortium to boost sales of semiconductors, a critical component of computers. Before 1987, the U.S. market share of semiconductors was decreasing while that of Japanese companies was increasing. The market shares of companies in the United States, Japan, and all other countries for the years 1981 to 1994 are listed below. Draw a time line of these data. Show the point at which Sematech was formed. How well does the graph describe the effect of Sematech? Grade the graph A, B, C, D, or F, and justify your grade.

Percent of Semiconductors Sold by American, Japanese, and Other Countries' Companies

Year	U.S.	Japan	All others
1981	73	19	8
1982	70	24	6
1983	68	28	4
1984	65	30	5
1985	61	34	5
1986	59	37	4
1987	56	39	5
1988	50	42	8
1989	48	45	7
1990	43	48	9
1991	46	45	9
1992	50	41	9
1993	52	40	8
1994	53	39	8

Source: Creative Statistics Company.

3.3 GRAPHICAL DECEPTION

The use of graphs and charts is pervasive in newspapers, magazines, business and economic reports, and seminars, in large part due to the increasing availability of computers and software that allow the storage, retrieval, manipulation, and summary of large masses of raw data. It is therefore more important than ever to be able to evaluate critically the information presented by means of graphical techniques. In the final analysis, graphical techniques merely create a visual impression, which is easy to distort. In fact, distortion is so easy and commonplace that in 1992 the Canadian Institute of Chartered Accountants found it necessary to begin setting guidelines for financial graphics, after a study of hundreds of the annual reports of major corporations found that 8% contained at least one misleading graph that covered up bad results. Although the heading for this section mentions deception, it is quite possible for an inexperienced person inadvertently to create distorted impressions with graphs. In any event, you should be aware of possible methods of **graphical deception.** This section illustrates a few of them.

The first thing to watch for is a graph without a scale on one axis. The time-series graph of a firm's sales in Figure 3.9 might represent a growth rate of 100% or 1% over the 5 years depicted, depending on the vertical scale. It is best simply to ignore such graphs.

A second trap to avoid is being influenced by a graph's caption. Your impression of the trend in interest rates might be different depending on whether you read a newspaper carrying caption (a) or caption (b) in Figure 3.10.

Perspective is often distorted if only absolute changes in value, rather than percentage changes, are reported. A $1 drop in the price of your $2 stock is relatively more distressing than a $1 drop in the price of your $100 stock. On January 9, 1986, newspapers throughout North America displayed graphs similar to the one shown in Figure 3.11 and reported that the stock market, as measured by the Dow Jones Industrial Average (DJIA), had suffered its worst 1-day loss ever on the previous day. The loss was 39 points, exceeding even the loss of Black Tuesday—October 28, 1929. While the loss was indeed a large one, many news reports failed to mention that the 1986 level of the DJIA was much higher than the 1929 level. A better perspective on the situation could be gained by noticing that the loss on January 8, 1986, represented a 2.5% decline, while the decline in 1929 was 12.8%. As a point of interest, we note

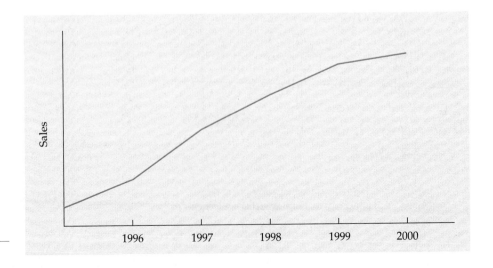

Figure 3.9

Graph without a vertical scale

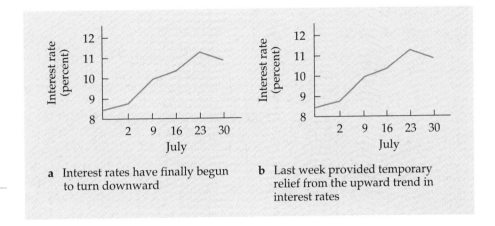

Figure 3.10

Different captions for the same graph

that the stock market was 12% higher within 2 months of this historic drop and 40% higher 1 year later. The worst 1-day loss ever, 22%, occurred on October 19, 1987.

We now turn to some rather subtle methods of creating distorted impressions with graphs. Consider the graph in Figure 3.12, which depicts the growth in a firm's quarterly sales during the past year, from $100 million to $110 million. This 10% growth in quarterly sales can be made to appear more dramatic by stretching the vertical axis—a technique that involves changing the scale on the vertical axis so that a given dollar amount is represented by a greater height than before. As a result, the rise in sales appears to be greater, because the slope of the graph is visually (but not numerically) steeper. The expanded scale is usually accommodated by employing a break in the vertical axis, as in Figure 3.13(a), or by truncating the vertical axis, as in Figure 3.13(b), so that the vertical scale begins at a point greater than zero. The effect of making slopes appear steeper can also be created by shrinking the horizontal axis, in which case points on the horizontal axis are moved closer together.

Just the opposite effect is obtained by stretching the horizontal axis; that is, spreading out the points on the horizontal axis to increase the distance between them so that slopes and trends will appear to be less steep. The graph of a firm's profits

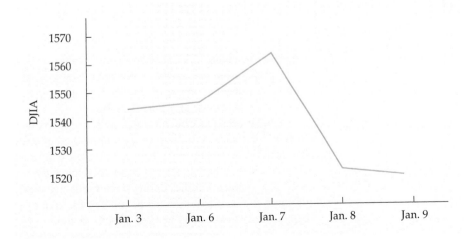

Figure 3.11

Historic drop in the DJIA, 1986

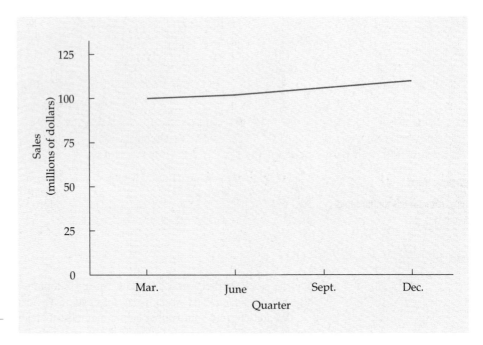

Figure 3.12

Quarterly sales for the past year

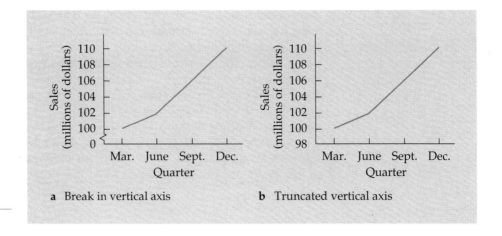

Figure 3.13

Stretching the vertical axis

presented in Figure 3.14(a) shows considerable swings, both upward and downward, in the profits from one quarter to the next. However, the firm could convey the impression of reasonable stability in profits from quarter to quarter by stretching the horizontal axis, as shown in Figure 3.14(b).

Similar illusions can be created with bar charts by stretching or shrinking the vertical or horizontal axis. Another popular method of creating distorted impressions with bar charts is to construct the bars so that their widths are proportional to their heights. The bar chart in Figure 3.15(a) correctly depicts the average weekly amount spent on food by Canadian families during three particular years. This chart correctly uses bars of equal width so that both the height and the area of each bar are proportional to the expenditures they represent. The growth in food expenditures is exaggerated in Figure 3.15(b), in which the widths of the bars increase with their heights. A quick glance

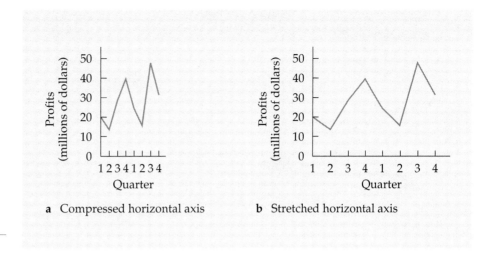

Figure 3.14

Quarterly profits over two years

at this bar chart might leave the viewer with the mistaken impression that food expenditures increased fourfold over the decade, since the 1990 bar is four times the size of the 1980 bar.

Size distortions should be watched for particularly in pictograms, which replace the bars with pictures of objects (such as bags of money, people, or animals) to enhance the visual appeal. Figure 3.16 displays the misuse of a pictogram—the snowman grows in width as well as height. The proper use of a pictogram is shown in Figure 3.17, which effectively uses pictures of Coca-Cola bottles.

The preceding examples of creating a distorted impression using graphs are not exhaustive, but they include some of the more popular methods. They should also serve to make the point that graphical techniques are used to create a visual impression, and the impression you obtain may be a distorted one unless you examine the graph with care. You are less likely to be misled if you focus your attention on the numerical values that the graph represents. Begin by carefully noting the scales on both axes; graphs with unmarked axes should be ignored completely.

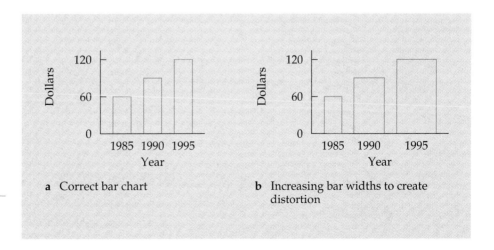

Figure 3.15

Average weekly food expenditures by Canadian families

Snowfall in Metro climbs relentlessly

Snowfall last winter was more than 50% greater than the previous winter, and more than double what fell four winters ago.

1988–89

79.8 cm

1991–92

95.2 cm

1992–93

163.6 cm

Figure 3.16

Incorrect pictogram
Source: Environment Canada, Metro Toronto Branch.

Shareholders Get More for Their Money

Return on Coca-Cola's shareholders' equity, in percent.

9.7%   15.3%   22.1%   29.5%

'85   '87   '91   '92

Figure 3.17

Correct pictogram
Source: Value Line Investment Survey (21 May, 1993).

EXERCISES

3.8 The U.S. seasonally adjusted unemployment rate from July 1993 to July 1994 is listed below.

   a Draw a bar chart of these data with 6.0% as the lowest point on the vertical axis.

   b Draw a bar chart of these data with 0.0% as the lowest point on the vertical axis.

   c Discuss the impression given by the two charts.

   d Which chart would you use? Explain.

	Month	Seasonally adjusted unemployment rate
1993	July	7.6%
	August	7.6
	September	7.5
	October	7.3
	November	7.3
	December	7.2
1994	January	7.0
	February	6.7
	March	6.4
	April	6.4
	May	6.3
	June	6.0
	July	6.1

Source: U.S. Department of Labor.

3.9 The following table lists family incomes (in thousands of 1991 dollars) and family size between 1971 and

1991. Draw time lines that describe how both variables have changed and how they appear to be related.

Year	Family income (in thousands of 1991 dollars)	Average family size
1971	39.8	3.68
1972	42.1	3.62
1973	43.5	3.60
1974	47.1	3.54
1975	48.3	3.47
1976	48.6	3.42
1977	48.2	3.40
1978	50.2	3.38
1979	50.4	3.34
1980	50.9	3.30
1981	49.2	3.27
1982	49.0	3.24
1983	48.4	3.21
1984	48.9	3.18
1985	50.2	3.17
1986	50.9	3.18
1987	52.2	3.16
1988	52.8	3.12
1989	54.2	3.10
1990	51.7	3.09
1991	51.1	3.08

Source: Creative Statistics Company.

3.10 Enerflex Systems, Inc., provides a full range of natural gas compression equipment by way of manufacturing and leasing services. In its 1993 annual report the following data were presented.

	1993	1992	1991	1990	1989
Sales (millions of dollars)	199	69	85	88	82
Net income (millions of dollars)	7.7	3.0	4.7	4.8	1.8
Return on equity (%)	32.9	13.6	24.4	31.7	12.0
Net income per common share ($)	1.02	0.36	0.57	0.56	0.15

a Use bar charts to present these data.

b Assume that you are an unscrupulous statistician and want to make the data appear more positive than they really are. Draw the bar charts accordingly.

3.4 SUMMARY

This chapter completes our discussion of graphical techniques, which began in Chapter 2. In Chapter 2, we showed how and when to construct the graphs. In this chapter, we provided guidelines for the application of graphical methods. We illustrated graphical excellence and graphical deception, and in so doing, we showed you what to do and what not to do.

IMPORTANT TERMS

Graphical excellence *74*
Chartjunk *77*
Graphical deception *82*

CASE 3.1	Canadian Federal Budget

The 1994–1995 federal budget estimates, showing where revenues are generated and where tax dollars are spent, are listed below.

		Revenues (billions of dollars)
Personal income tax		59.5
Deficit		30.2
Insurance premiums		19.3
Goods and services tax		16.5
Corporate income tax		10.3
Excise taxes and duties		10.1
Other revenues		8.2
Interest on the debt		41.0
Transfers to other levels of government		26.3
Health	6.7	
Postsecondary education	2.1	
Canada assistance plan	7.4	
Equalization	8.5	
Territories and municipalities	1.6	
Pensions		20.6
Old-age security	15.8	
Guaranteed income supplement	4.4	
Spouses allowance	0.4	
Government operations		20.5
Unemployment insurance benefits		18.3
Regular benefits	14.4	

(continued)

Revenues (billions of dollars) *(continued)*

Other	3.9	
Subsidies and other transfer payments		17.2
Grants to business	3.3	
Grants to farmers	2.3	
Grants to natives	3.8	
International assistance	2.6	
Infrastructure	0.7	
Other	4.5	
Defense		10.8
Crown corporations		4.6
Canada Mortgage and housing	2.1	
CBC	1.1	
Other	1.4	
Reserves		2.4
Veterans		1.9

Use any graphical techniques you deem necessary to present the figures above.

Chapter 4

Numerical

Descriptive

Measures

4.1 Introduction

4.2 Measures of Central Location

4.3 Measures of Variability

4.4 Interpreting Standard Deviation

4.5 Measures of Relative Standing and Box Plots

4.6 Approximating Descriptive Measures for Grouped Data

4.7 Measures of Association

4.8 General Guidelines on the Exploration of Data

4.9 Summary

4.1 INTRODUCTION

In this chapter, we continue to examine how to summarize a large set of raw data so that meaningful information can be extracted from it. Thus far, we have looked at how to group the data set into a more manageable form and how to construct various graphical representations of it. Faced with a set of observations like the telephone data in Table 2.1, we began by finding the smallest and largest values, and then we formed a frequency distribution and histogram. These revealed the approximate shape of the distribution and indicated where the observations were concentrated.

Although a frequency distribution is certainly useful in providing a general idea about how the data are distributed between the two extreme values, it is usually desirable to summarize the data even further by computing a few numerical descriptive measures. Numerical descriptive measures provide precise, objectively determined values that can easily be manipulated, interpreted, and compared with one another. In short, they permit a more careful analysis of the data than do the general impressions conveyed by tabular and graphical summaries. This is especially important when the data represent a sample from which inferences must be made concerning the entire population.

There are a variety of different types of descriptive measures. In Section 4.2, we introduce measures of central location, and Section 4.3 presents measures of variability. In Section 4.7, we present measures of association, which gauge the relationship between two variables. We conclude our presentation of graphical and numerical techniques for extracting information from data by discussing some general guidelines on their use.

4.2 MEASURES OF CENTRAL LOCATION

In computing numerical descriptive measures of the data, interest usually focuses on two measures: a measure of the central, or average, value of the data and a measure of the degree to which the observations are spread out about this average value. **Measures of central location** (averages) are discussed in this section, and measures of dispersion are discussed in Section 4.3. Of the various types of measures of central location, we will consider only three: the arithmetic mean, the median, and the mode.

ARITHMETIC MEAN

By far the most popular and useful measure of central location is the **arithmetic mean,** which we will refer to simply as the mean. Widely known in everyday usage as the average, the mean of a set of observations is defined as follows:

$$\text{Mean} = \frac{\text{Sum of the observations}}{\text{Number of observations}}$$

Before expressing this definition algebraically, we should introduce some notation.* If we are dealing with a population of observations, the total number of observations is denoted by N, and the mean is represented by μ (the lowercase Greek letter *mu*). If the set of measurements is a sample, the total number of measurements is denoted by n, and the sample mean is represented by $\bar{x}$ (referred to as *x*-**bar**). (If the observations under consideration are represented by a letter other than x, such as y, the sample mean is denoted by $\bar{y}$.) Because the observations in a sample are a subset of the observations in the parent population, $n \leq N$ if the parent population con-

---

*Students unfamiliar with summation notation should read Appendix 4.A for further background.

sists of N observations. In actual practice, you won't normally have access to all observations in a population, so you will most often calculate the sample mean. As we'll see in Chapter 9, the sample mean $\bar{x}$ is used to make inferences about μ (the mean of the population from which the sample was taken). In particular, the value of $\bar{x}$ is frequently used as an estimate of μ.

Sample Mean

The **mean of a sample** of n observations $x_1, x_2, \ldots, x_n$ is defined as

$$\bar{x} = \frac{\sum_{i=1}^{n} x_i}{n}$$

▼ **EXAMPLE 4.1**

The mean of the sample of six observations 7, 3, 9, -2, 4, and 6 is given by

$$\bar{x} = \frac{\sum_{i=1}^{n} x_i}{n} = \frac{7 + 3 + 9 - 2 + 4 + 6}{6} = 4.5$$

▲

The formula for calculating the mean of a population is the same as the formula for calculating the mean of a sample, differing only in the notation of the variables.

Population Mean

The **mean of a population** of N observations $x_1, x_2, \ldots, x_N$ is defined as

$$\mu = \frac{\sum_{i=1}^{N} x_i}{N}$$

▼ **EXAMPLE 4.2**

Suppose that the telephone bills in Table 2.1 (see page 24) represent a population of observations. Then the population mean is

$$\mu = \frac{\sum_{i=1}^{N} x_i}{N} = \frac{42.19 + 15.30 + \cdots + 53.21}{200} = 43.59$$

Referring to the histogram of telephone bills in Figure 2.1 (page 26), we see that the value 43.59 is located at *approximately* the center of the distribution. The reason for this mean value being somewhat to the left of center is that, rather than having a symmetrical distribution of telephone bills, there is a disproportionate number of small telephone bills.

▲

When many of the observations in a sample (or population) have the same value, the observations are often summarized in a frequency table. Suppose that the numbers of children in a sample of 16 employees' families were recorded as follows.

Number of Children	0	1	2	3
Number of Employees	3	4	7	2

Notice that we are dealing with a total of $n = 16$ observations here—one for each employee. To find the sample mean $\bar{x}$ of the number of children per employee, we divide the total number of children by the total number of employees. That is,

$$\bar{x} = \frac{\sum_{i=1}^{16} x_i}{n} = \frac{0 + 0 + 0 + 1 + \cdots + 2 + 3 + 3}{16}$$

$$= \frac{3(0) + 4(1) + 7(2) + 2(3)}{16}$$

$$= \frac{24}{16} = 1.5$$

Notice that we could find $\bar{x}$ by skipping directly to the next to the last line in this computation, where each distinct value of the observation (number of children) is multiplied by the frequency with which it occurs and the total is then divided by the total number of observations.

▲

The sum of deviations of individual observations from the mean is zero, or

$$\sum_{i=1}^{n} (x_i - \bar{x}) = 0$$

This property has an interesting physical interpretation. Imagine that the individual observations are marked off along a weightless bar and that a 1-lb weight is placed at each such mark, as depicted in the accompanying diagram (based on observations from Example 4.1). The bar will be in perfect balance if a support is placed at the mean; therefore, the arithmetic mean can be interpreted as the center of gravity, or the balance point.

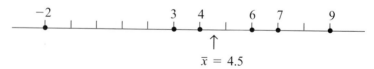

$$\bar{x} = 4.5$$

The mean is a popular measure because it is simple to compute and interpret and because it lends itself to mathematical manipulation. More important for decision makers, it is generally the best measure of central location for purposes of statistical inference. Its one serious drawback is that it is unduly influenced by extreme observations. For example, if the sample of six observations in Example 4.1 is enlarged to include a seventh observation that has a value of 22, the mean of the resulting sample of seven observations is $49/7 = 7$. Adding a single, relatively large value to the original sample of measurements substantially increases the value of the mean. This is one reason why we sometimes resort to another measure of central location, the median.

THE MEDIAN

> **Median**
>
> The **median** of a set of observations is the value that falls in the middle when the observations are arranged in order of magnitude.

When an even number of observations is involved, any number between the two middle values will satisfy the preceding definition of *median*. In such a case, however, it is conventional to take the midpoint between the two middle values as the median.

> **Calculating the Median**
>
> Given n observations arranged in order of magnitude,
>
> $$\text{Median} = \begin{cases} \text{Middle value, if } n \text{ is odd} \\ \text{Mean of the two middle values, if } n \text{ is even} \end{cases}$$

In the examples that follow, we have arbitrarily chosen to arrange the measurements in ascending order (from smallest to largest) as a preliminary step in locating the median. Arranging them in descending order would, of course, yield identical results. The median has intuitive appeal as a measure of central location: At most, half of the observations fall below the median, and at most half fall above. Because of the distorting effect of extreme observations on the mean, the median is often the preferred measure in such situations as salary negotiations.

▼ **EXAMPLE 4.4**

The annual salaries (in thousands of dollars) of the seven employees of a small government department are as follows.

28, 60, 26, 32, 30, 26, 29

To find the median salary, first arrange the salaries in ascending order: 26, 26, 28, 29, 30, 32, 60. The median salary is therefore $29,000, which is clearly more representative of a typical salary than is the mean value ($33,000).

Notice that if there had been an eighth employee with a salary of $31,000, the median would be 29.5—the midpoint between 29 and 30. For an even number of observations the convention is to locate the median at the midpoint between the two middle values.

▲

The median is the most appropriate measure of central location to use when the data under consideration are ranked qualitative data, rather than quantitative data. Such a situation arises whenever items are simply ranked—perhaps according to preference, degree of ability, or degree of difficulty. For example, if 11 statistical problems are ranked from 1 to 11 according to their degree of difficulty, problem 6 is the problem of median difficulty.

MODE

A third measure of central location is the mode, which indicates the most frequently occurring value in a series. The mode doesn't necessarily lie in the middle of the set of observations, although it often does; its claim to be a measure of central location is based on the fact that it indicates the location of greatest clustering or concentration of values (just as a population center describes a location of concentrated population).

Mode
The **mode** of a set of observations is the value that occurs most frequently.

Notice that, while a distribution can have only one mean and one median, it can have more than one mode (although Excel reports only one mode).

When the data have been organized into a histogram, we are often interested in knowing which class has the largest number of observations. We refer to that class as the modal class. In Chapter 2, we discussed modal classes in the context of describing the shape of a histogram.

▼ **EXAMPLE 4.5**

The manager of a men's store observes that the 10 pairs of trousers sold yesterday had the following waist sizes (in inches).

31, 34, 36, 33, 28, 34, 30, 34, 32, 40

The mode of these waist sizes is 34 in., and this fact is undoubtedly of more interest to the manager than are the facts that the mean waist size is 33.2 in. and the median waist size is 33.5 in.

▲

MEAN, MEDIAN, MODE: WHICH IS BEST?

As we've already pointed out, this textbook will emphasize the "when" of statistical analysis. This means that, for any given technique, we plan to outline the circumstances under which that technique should be employed. However, it is not always a clear-cut choice when there are several different methods available. A perfect case in point is the choice among the three measures of central location. The question arises: "Which measure should we use?" The mean is generally the measure of central location to be used unless there are valid reasons to use some other measure. However, one disadvantage of using the mean is that it is sensitive to extreme values; a large proportion of extremely large numbers, for example, would unduly influence the mean. In such cases, the median is considered to be a better measure of central location. For quantitative data, the mode is the least useful of the three measures of central location. The mode is most useful when an important aspect of describing the data involves determining the number of times each value occurs. In that case, we're interested in knowing which value occurs most frequently. Even then, the mode is really useful only for large data sets.

If the data are qualitative, such as the employment areas in Example 2.3 (page 44), using the mean or the median is senseless; the mode must be used. The modal value (or employment area) in that example is accounting, because that category contains the most students. On the other hand, if the measurement data are quantitative, all three measures of central tendency are meaningful. Because the mean is the best measure of central location for the purpose of statistical inference, it will be used extensively from Chapter 9 onward. But for descriptive purposes, it is usually best to report the values of all three measures, because each conveys somewhat different information. Moreover, the relative positions of the mean and the median provide some information about the shape of the distribution of the observations.

RELATIONSHIP AMONG MEAN, MEDIAN, AND MODE

The relationship among the three measures of central location can be observed from the smoothed relative frequency histograms shown in Figure 4.1.* If the distribution is symmetrical and unimodal, the three measures coincide, as in Figure 4.1(a). If a distribution is not symmetrical, it is said to be **skewed.** The distribution in Figure 4.1(b) is **skewed to the right,** or **positively skewed,** since it has a long tail extending off to the right (indicating the presence of a small proportion of relatively large extreme values) but only a short tail extending to the left. Distributions of incomes commonly exhibit such positive skewness. As mentioned earlier, these extreme values pull the mean to the right more than the median. A mean value that is greater than the median therefore provides some evidence of positive skewness.

The distribution in Figure 4.1(c) is **skewed to the left,** or **negatively skewed,** since it has a long tail to the left but a short tail to the right. Once again, the extreme

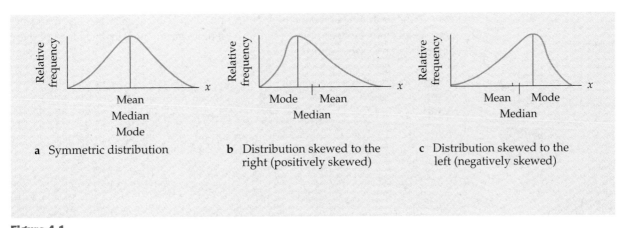

Figure 4.1

Relationship among mean, median, and mode

*The upper boundary of relative frequency histograms tends to look more and more like a smooth curve as the underlying data set gets larger and the class width is decreased.

Sᴛᴀᴛɪsᴛɪᴄs ɪɴ ᴛʜᴇ Wᴏʀᴋᴘʟᴀᴄᴇ

Human Resources Application

One of the important functions of the human resources department of a large corporation is the hiring and training of personnel. **Administering an aptitude or dexterity test** is often part of the hiring (or training) process. In addition to forming part of the initial screening process, such test results can form the first component of an ongoing process that tracks the progress of successful applicants during their years of tenure with the firm. These initial test results can be used later, for example, to assess how reliable they are as predictors of employee performance.

Faced with such a set of test marks, a manager finds it useful to review descriptive statistics summarizing the results: the "average" of the marks, their variability, and the shape of the distribution of the marks. These descriptive statistics are helpful in making comparisons with other groups of applicants, as well as for assessing the validity and reliability of the exam as a measurement tool.

values affect the mean more than they do the median, and the mean value is pulled more noticeably in the direction of the skewness. A mean value less than the median is an indication of negative skewness.

We now look at another example, for which we'll compute all three measures of central location, using the computer.

▼ **EXAMPLE 4.6**

As part of its recruiting process, the human resources department of a national marketing firm has administered an aptitude test to 100 job applicants. The test marks are shown below (and stored in file XM04-06). Find the mean, median, and mode of these data and describe what information they provide.

TEST MARKS OF 100 APPLICANTS

81	92	30	79	90	69	96	39	94	88	65	73	84	83	95	38	97	72	83
87	94	93	73	78	86	57	98	93	83	99	42	99	51	84	90	88	59	74
94	90	95	70	81	91	75	82	83	65	34	89	43	85	75	64	64	93	86
84	95	90	84	48	81	96	91	96	83	41	100	25	48	71	89	61	77	76
18	73	99	85	53	69	66	94	80	55	84	66	34	98	72	11	38	85	77
96	50	71	37	16														

Solution

We will use our statistical software to calculate the three measures of central location.

Excel Output for Example 4.6

	A	B
1	*Marks*	
2		
3	Mean	73.98
4	Standard Error	2.15
5	Median	81
6	Mode	84
7	Standard Deviation	21.50
8	Sample Variance	462.3
9	Kurtosis	0.394
10	Skewness	-1.073
11	Range	89
12	Minimum	11
13	Maximum	100
14	Sum	7398
15	Count	100
16	Largest(25)	90
17	Smallest(25)	64

Excel outputs all three measures of central location. The mean and the median are 73.98 and 81, respectively. Notice that Excel identifies only one mode: 84. Obviously, Excel is mistaken. In fact there are two: 83 and 84, both of which occur five times. Excel also outputs a variety of other statistics that we'll explain later.

COMMANDS	COMMANDS FOR EXAMPLE 4.6
1 Type or import the data.	Open file **XM04-06**.
2 Click **Tools, Data Analysis . . . ,** and **Descriptive Statistics.**	
3 Type input range. (Include the cell containing the variable name and click **Labels in First Row.**)	**A1:A101**
4 Click **Summary Statistics** and click **OK.** To improve the look of the output, widen the columns (by clicking **Format, Column,** and **AutoFit Selection**).	

Minitab Output for
Example 4.6

Descriptive Statistics

Variable	N	Mean	Median	TrMean	StDev	SE Mean
Marks	100	73.98	81.00	75.59	21.50	2.15

Variable	Minimum	Maximum	Q1	Q3
Marks	11.00	100.00	64.25	90.00

The mean and median are 73.98 and 81, respectively. Minitab does not print the mode. The rest of the output will be explained later.

COMMANDS	COMMANDS FOR EXAMPLE 4.6
1 Type or import the data into a column.	Open file **XM04-06**.
2 Click **Stat, Basic Statistics,** and **Descriptive Statistics . . . .**	
3 Type the variable name and click **OK**.	**Marks** or **C1**

INTERPRET

Most applicants would want to know the mean, which is generally interpreted as measuring the "average" applicant's performance. The median tells us that half of this group of applicants received a grade greater than 81% and the other half had grades below 81%. Which is the better measure? The answer depends on what we want to measure.

If we want an overall measure of how well the group performed, the mean should be used. Because the mean is computed by adding all the marks and dividing by the number of applicants, the mean provides a number based on the total marks of the group and thus provides a measure of the group performance. For example, the mean should be used to compare two or more groups who are taking the same test. The median, on the other hand, gives us a mark that truly represents the center of the data. Half the group was above the median and half the group was below it.

If the marks are classified by letter grade, where A = 80 to 100, B = 70 to 79, C = 60 to 69, D = 50 to 59, and F = 0 to 49, we can count the frequency of each grade. Because we're now interested in the number of each type of grade, the mode becomes a logical measure to compute. As we pointed out in Chapter 2, we designate the category or class with the largest number of observations as the **modal class.** As you can see, the modal class is A.

Regarding the shape of the grade distribution, the fact that the mean value is less than the median indicates that the distribution is skewed to the left, which is also clear from the following histograms.

Frequency of Marks Converted to Letter Grades

Grade	Frequency
A	53
B	16
C	9
D	6
F	16

Excel Histogram for Example 4.6

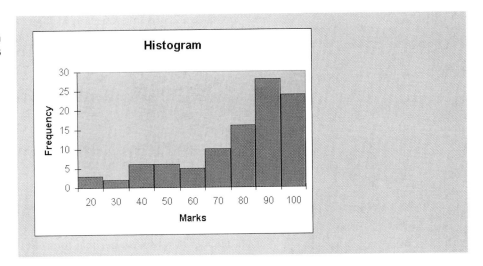

Recall that the numbers along the horizontal axis represent the upper limits of the intervals they represent. Note again that, unlike Minitab and the authors, Excel counts observations equal to the upper limit of an interval as belonging to that interval. This explains the slight difference between the Minitab and Excel histograms.

Minitab Histogram for Example 4.6

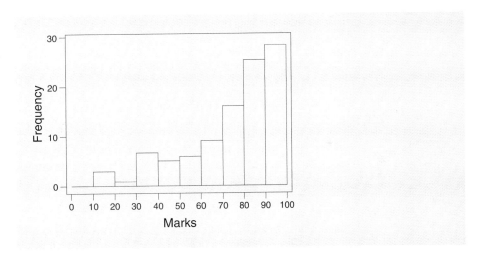

We remind you to be careful when interpreting histograms with unequal intervals. Only the heights of the rectangles are meaningful and not the areas when such histograms are produced by the computer.

▲

GEOMETRIC MEAN

We now introduce another very useful mean, but one that is not a measure of central location. The arithmetic mean, as mentioned earlier, is the single most popular and useful measure of central tendency, and will be used extensively throughout topics involving statistical inference. But it is not a good measure of the "average" growth rate, or rate of change, in a variable (such as the value of an investment) over time. This will become apparent from the following example.

Suppose you make a 2-year investment of $1,000, and it grows by 100% to $2,000 during the first year. During the second year, however, the investment declines by 50%, from $2,000 back to $1,000.* Letting R_1 and R_2 denote the returns in years 1 and 2, respectively, we compute the arithmetic mean return to be

$$\overline{R} = \frac{R_1 + R_2}{2} = \frac{100 + (-50)}{2} = 25\%$$

But this arithmetic mean return of 25% is misleading. Because there was no change in the value of the investment at the end of the two periods, the "average" *compounded* return over the two periods was actually 0%. This is the value obtained when we compute the geometric mean.

Geometric Mean

Let R_i denote the rate of return (in decimal form) in period i ($i = 1, \ldots, n$). The **geometric mean** of the returns $R_1, R_2, \ldots, R_n$ is the constant return R_g that produces the same terminal wealth at the end of period n as do the actual returns for the n periods. That is,

$$\left(1 + R_g\right)^n = \left(1 + R_1\right)\left(1 + R_2\right) \cdots \left(1 + R_n\right)$$

or

$$R_g = \sqrt[n]{(1 + R_1) \cdots (1 + R_n)} - 1$$

Computing the geometric mean for the preceding example, where $R_1 = 100\% = 1.00$ and $R_2 = -50\% = -.50$, we obtain

$$R_g = \sqrt[2]{(1 + 1)(1 - .50)} - 1$$
$$= 1 - 1 = 0$$

The geometric mean return is therefore 0%. This is the single "average" return that allows us to compute the ending value of the investment (after two periods) from the beginning value of $1,000, as follows:

$$1,000(1 + R_g)^2 = 1,000(1 + 0)^2 = 1,000$$

The geometric mean is relevant whenever we wish to find the "average" growth rate, or rate of change, in a variable *over time*. For example, this variable could be the value of an investment, the dividend paid on a stock, or the level of sales for a company.

We stress, however, that the arithmetic mean of n returns (or growth rates) is the appropriate mean to use if you wish to estimate the expected mean return (or growth rate) for any *single* year in the future.

▼ **EXAMPLE 4.7**

Suppose that a firm's sales were $1,000,000 three years ago, and sales have grown annually by 20%, 10%, and -5% since that time. What was the geometric mean growth rate in sales during the past 3 years?

---

*The *rate of change* (R) or *growth rate* in the value of a variable V over one period is obtained by subtracting 1 from the ending value (V_e) divided by the beginning value (V_b): $R = (V_e / V_b) - 1$. If V is the value of an investment, then R is called the **(rate of) return** on the investment. In this example, the return on the investment during the second year is $R_2 = (1,000 / 2,000) - 1 = -.5$, or -50%.

Solution   If R_g is the geometric mean, then

$$(1 + R_g)^3 = (1 + .20)(1 + .10)(1 - .05) = 1.2540$$

Thus,

$$R_g = \sqrt[3]{1.2540} - 1 = .0784, \text{ or } 7.84\%$$

Notice that the geometric mean is less than the arithmetic mean of 8.33%. It will always be the case that the geometric mean is less than the arithmetic mean, unless all of the annual rates are equal.

Finally, if we know each of the annual growth rates, we can find the geometric mean as above. However, if we know only that sales were $1,000,000 three years ago and are $1,254,000 today, then we can solve

$$1,000,000(1 + R_g)^3 = 1,254,000$$

to (again) find that $R_g = .0784$.

▲

EXERCISES

4.1 Manually calculate the mean, median, and mode or modes for the following sample.

7, 4, 6, 2, 6, 7, 3, 5

4.2 Manually calculate the three measures of central location for the following sample.

$0, -3, 5, -2, -6, 4, 7, 9, 4, -3, 0, 2$

4.3 What are the characteristics of a set of data for which the mean, median, and mode are identical?

4.4 Given a set of qualitative (categorical) data, what measure of central location is always appropriate?

4.5 The ages of the employees of a fast-food outlet are as follows.

19, 19, 65, 20, 21, 18, 20

a Compute the mean, the median, and the mode of the ages.

b How would these three measures of central location be affected if the oldest employee retired?

4.6 When a certain professor left one university to teach at another, a student was heard to remark, "That move will surely raise the average IQ at both universities." Explain the meaning of the remark.

4.7 Twenty families were asked how many cars they owned. Their responses are summarized in the following table.

Number of cars	Number of families
0	3
1	10
2	4
3	2
4	1

Determine the mean, the median, and the mode of the number of cars owned per family.

The next eight exercises require the use of a computer and statistical software.

population

4.8 The amount of time needed to complete a telephone survey by 100 respondents is stored in file XR04-08. (Times are rounded to the nearest whole minute.)

a Use a software package to produce the mean, median, and mode.

b Describe briefly what each measure tells you about the data.

sample

4.9 A sample of 40 people was asked how much change they had in their pockets and wallets. Their responses (in cents) are stored in column 1 of file XR04-09.

a What are the mean, median, and mode of the data?

b Describe briefly what these measures tell you about the data.

4.10 Example 2.1 dealt with the problem of graphically summarizing the 200 long-distance bills. Recall that the data were stored in file XM02-01. Use your software to compute the mean, median, and mode of these data and interpret their values.

4.11 The summer incomes of a sample of 125 second-year business students are stored in file XR04-11.

a Calculate the mean and median of these data.

b What do the two measures of central location tell you about second-year business students' summer incomes?

c Which measure would you use to summarize the data? Explain.

4.12 Refer to Exercise 2.12, where the annual incomes of 200 first-year accountants were stored in file XR02-12.

   a Determine the mean and median of the sample.

   b Briefly describe what each statistic tells you.

4.13 Refer to Exercise 2.17, where the prices (in thousands of dollars) of homes in a wealthy suburb are stored in file XR02-17.

   a Determine the mean and median of this sample.

   b What information about the prices have you learned from the statistics in part (a)?

4.14 The owner of a hardware store that sells electrical wire by the meter is considering selling the wire in precut lengths to save on labor costs. A sample of wire sold over the course of 1 week was recorded and stored in file XR04-14.

   a Compute the mean, median, and mode.

   b For each measure of central location calculated in part (a), discuss the weaknesses in providing useful information to the owner.

   c How might the owner decide on the lengths to pre-cut?

4.15 The amount of time (in seconds) to perform a spot weld on a car under production was recorded for 50 workers. These times are stored in file XR04-15.

   a Compute the mean, median, and mode of these data.

   b Discuss what information you have discovered from the statistics computed in part (a).

4.16 The Standard and Poor's 500-stock index, the S&P 500 Index, is one of the most widely used measures of the performance of the stock market in the United States. The annual percentage changes (rates of return) in the S&P 500 Index for 6 years is shown in the table.

   a Find the geometric mean return over this period.

   b Find the arithmetic mean return over this period.

   c If you invested $1,000 at the beginning of 1989 and the investment grew at the same average rate as the S&P 500 Index, what would the investment be worth at the end of 1994?

   d Based on these data, what is your best estimate of what the return on the S&P 500 Index will be in 1995?

Year	Return (%)
1989	31.49
1990	−3.17
1991	30.55
1992	7.67
1993	10.00
1994	1.34

4.17 One of the most popular models used to value a firm's common stock requires an estimate of the future growth rate in the stock's dividends. One method of obtaining this estimate is to consider historic growth rates. Suppose that the dividends for the last 7 years are as shown in the table.

   a Compute the six annual growth rates in the dividends from 1993 to 1999.

   b Find the arithmetic mean of the annual percentage changes (growth rates) in the dividends.

   c Find the geometric mean growth rate in dividends over this period.

   d What growth rate would you recommend to be used in the stock valuation model?

   e What is your best estimate of the dividend to be paid in 2000?

Year	Dividend
1993	$2.00
1994	2.40
1995	2.20
1996	2.40
1997	2.60
1998	2.70
1999	2.80

4.3 MEASURES OF VARIABILITY

We are now able to compute three measures of central location, but these measures fail to tell the whole story about a distribution of measurements. For example, if you were told only that the average maximum temperature is 83.2°F in Honolulu and 79.4°F in Las Vegas, you might ask why Honolulu attracts significantly more sun-seekers in the winter months than does Las Vegas. A contributing factor might be that Honolulu's climate is much more temperate year-round. Honolulu's monthly average maximum temperatures vary only from 79°F to 87°F, while those of Las Vegas vary from 56°F to 104°F. Clearly, the average maximum temperature of 83.2° for Honolulu is far closer to the maximum monthly temperatures likely to be encountered than is Las Vegas's average maximum temperature.

Once we know the average value of a set of observations, our next question should be "How typical is the average value of all observations in the data set?" In other words, how spread out are the observations about their average value? Are the observations highly variable and widely dispersed about the average value, as depicted by the smoothed relative frequency histogram Figure 4.2(a), or do they exhibit low variability and cluster about the average value, as in Figure 4.2(b)?

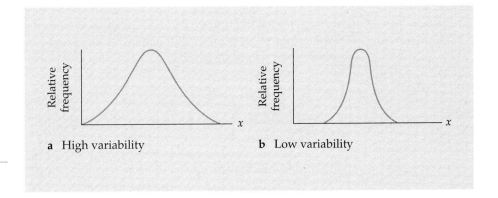

Figure 4.2

Smoothed relative frequency histograms

The importance of looking beyond the average value is borne out by the fact that many individuals make use of the concept of variability in everyday decision making, whether or not they compute a numerical measure of the dispersion. Consider the case of Tuffy Rocknee, a college football coach, who is agonizing over which player should be assigned punting duties in Saturday's big game. Tuffy has decided to base his decision on the results of 10 practice kicks by each player. The recorded yardages are as follows.

> *A:* 41, 55, 30, 38, 50, 42, 39, 25, 28, 52
> *B:* 39, 42, 38, 42, 44, 40, 41, 38, 36, 40

The mean number of yards punted by each player is 40 (which you should verify), but if Tuffy is looking for consistency, he will select player *B*. Without actually computing a measure of dispersion (and probably not caring to know how to), Tuffy will choose the player whose punts exhibit the least variability.

The concept of variability is of fundamental importance in statistical inference. It is therefore important that we, unlike Tuffy, be able to measure the degree of variability in a set of measurements.

RANGE

The first and simplest measure of variability is the range, which we already encountered when forming frequency distributions.

Range

The **range** of a set of observations is the numerical difference between the largest and smallest observations.

The usefulness of the range stems from the ease with which it can be computed and interpreted. The first observation we made concerning the telephone data in Table

2.1 was that the smallest and largest telephone bills were $0 and $119.63, respectively, which established that the range was $119.63 - 0 = 119.63$ dollars. We later computed the mean amount of the telephone bills as $43.59.

A major shortcoming of the range is that it provides us with no information about the dispersion of the values that fall between the smallest and largest observations. These intermediate values might all be clustered very closely about the mean value of $43.59, they might be dispersed fairly evenly across the range between the two extreme values, or they might be clumped in two groups near each extreme (resulting in a barbell-shaped distribution). A popular measure of the dispersion of these intermediate values is variance.

VARIANCE

Variance is one of the two most widely accepted measures of the variability of a set of quantitative data (the other is standard deviation). Closely related to one another, variance and standard deviation take into account all the data in a set and (as we will see in Chapter 8) are of fundamental importance in statistical inference.

Consider two very small populations, each consisting of five observations.

A: 8, 9, 10, 11, 12
B: 4, 7, 10, 13, 16

The mean of both population A and population B is 10, as you can easily verify. The population values are plotted along the horizontal x-axis in Figure 4.3. Visual inspection of these graphs indicates that the observations in population B are more widely dispersed than those in A. We are searching for a measure of a dispersion that confirms this notion and takes into account each observation in the population.

Consider the five observations in population A. To obtain a measure of their dispersion, we might begin by calculating the deviation of each value from the mean.

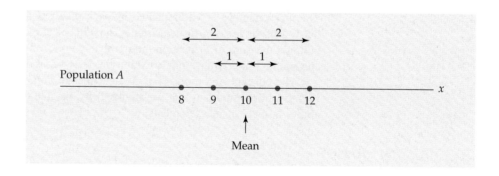

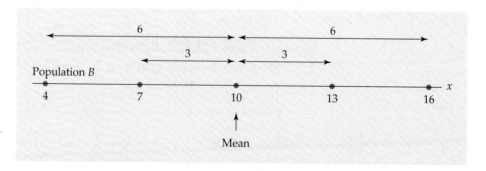

Figure 4.3

Deviations of measurements
from the mean

$$(8 - 10), (9 - 10), (10 - 10), (11 - 10), (12 - 10)$$

The four nonzero deviations are represented by the double-pointed arrows above the *x*-axis in Figure 4.3. It might at first seem reasonable to take the sum of these deviations as a measure of dispersion, but the sum of deviations from the mean is always zero. Although this difficulty could be overcome by summing the absolute values of the deviations from the mean, absolute values are somewhat difficult to work with mathematically. More mathematically tractable and more useful in statistical inference are the squares of the deviations from the mean. Thus, we might consider

$$(8 - 10)^2 + (9 - 10)^2 + (10 - 10)^2 + (11 - 10)^2 + (12 - 10)^2 = 10$$

as a measure of the variability of our observations in population *A*. The corresponding expression for a population of observations $x_1, x_2, \ldots, x_N$ would be

$$\sum_{i=1}^{N}(x_i - \mu)^2$$

Unfortunately, although this sum of squared deviations has the desirable property of being larger for sets of observations that have greater dispersion, it also increases in magnitude simply from an increase in the number of observations in the data set—even though the larger data set may have less dispersion than a smaller one. This is remedied by taking the *average* of the *squared* deviations as the required measure of dispersion. This measure of the dispersion, or variability, of a population of observations is called the **variance;** it is denoted by σ^2, where σ is the lowercase Greek letter *sigma.*

Letting σ_A^2 denote the variance of population *A,* we obtain

$$\sigma_A^2 = \frac{(8 - 10)^2 + (9 - 10)^2 + (10 - 10)^2 + (11 - 10)^2 + (12 - 10)^2}{5}$$

$$= \frac{(-2)^2 + (-1)^2 + 0^2 + 1^2 + 2^2}{5} = \frac{10}{5} = 2$$

Proceeding in an analogous manner for population *B,* we obtain

$$\sigma_B^2 = \frac{(4 - 10)^2 + (7 - 10)^2 + (10 - 10)^2 + (13 - 10)^2 + (16 - 10)^2}{5} = 18$$

The variance of *B* therefore exceeds the variance of *A,* consistent with our initial visual impression that the values in population *B* are more dispersed than those in population *A.*

Variance of a Population

The **variance of a population** of N observations $x_1, x_2, \ldots, x_N$ having mean μ is defined as

$$\sigma^2 = \frac{\sum_{i=1}^{N}(x_i - \mu)^2}{N}$$

We suggest that, rather than blindly memorizing this formula, you think of the variance as being the *mean squared deviation*—the mean of the squared deviations of the observations from their mean μ. This should help you both to remember and to interpret the formula for the variance.

Now suppose that you are working with a sample, rather than with a population. If you are given a sample of n observations, your interest in computing the variance of the sample (denoted by s^2) lies in obtaining a good estimate of the population variance (σ^2). While it would seem reasonable to define the sample variance s^2 as the average of the squared deviations of the sample measurements from their mean $\bar{x}$, doing so tends to underestimate the population variance σ^2. This problem can be rectified, however, by defining the sample variance s^2 as the sum of the squared deviations divided by $n - 1$, rather than by n. Further discussion of this point is provided in Chapter 9.

Variance of a Sample

The **variance of a sample** of n observations $x_1, x_2, \ldots, x_n$ having mean $\bar{x}$ is defined as

$$s^2 = \frac{\sum_{i=1}^{n}(x_i - \bar{x})^2}{n - 1}$$

Computing the variance of a large sample can be made less tedious by use of a shortcut formula derivable through simple algebraic manipulation of the formula just presented. The sample mean is usually calculated before the sample variance, in which case the value of the second summation in the shortcut formula is already known.

Shortcut Formula

The **shortcut formula** for the sample variance is

$$s^2 = \frac{1}{n - 1}\left[\sum_{i=1}^{n}x_i^2 - \frac{\left(\sum_{i=1}^{n}x_i\right)^2}{n}\right]$$

▼ **EXAMPLE 4.8**

Find the mean and the variance of the following sample of measurements (in years).

3.4, 2.5, 4.1, 1.2, 2.8, 3.7

Solution The mean of this sample of six measurements is

$$\bar{x} = \frac{\sum_{i=1}^{6} x_i}{6} = \frac{3.4 + 2.5 + 4.1 + 1.2 + 2.8 + 3.7}{6} = \frac{17.7}{6} = 2.95 \text{ years}$$

To find the sample variance by means of the shortcut formula, we first compute

$$\sum_{i=1}^{6} x_i^2 = (3.4)^2 + (2.5)^2 + (4.1)^2 + (1.2)^2 + (2.8)^2 + (3.7)^2 = 57.59$$

From the computation of the mean, we already know that

$$\sum_{i=1}^{6} x_i = 17.7$$

Therefore,

$$s^2 = \frac{1}{5}\left[\sum_{i=1}^{6} x_i^2 - \frac{\left(\sum_{i=1}^{6} x_i\right)^2}{6}\right] = \frac{1}{5}\left[57.59 - \frac{(17.7)^2}{6}\right] = 1.075 \text{ (years)}^2$$

Alternatively, we could compute s^2 directly, using the definition of sample variance.

$$s^2 = \frac{(3.4 - 2.95)^2 + (2.5 - 2.95)^2 + (4.1 - 2.95)^2 + (1.2 - 2.95)^2 + (2.8 - 2.95)^2 + (3.7 - 2.95)^2}{5}$$

$$= 1.075 \text{ (years)}^2$$

▲

STANDARD DEVIATION

Because calculating variance involves squaring the original observations, the unit attached to a variance is the square of the unit attached to the original observations. For example, if our original observations are expressed in minutes, the variance is expressed in minutes squared. While variance is a useful measure of the relative variability of two sets of observations, statisticians often want a measure of variability that is expressed in the same units as the original observations, as is the mean. Such a measure can be obtained simply by taking the square root of the variance.

Standard Deviation

The **standard deviation** of a set of observations is the positive square root of the variance of the observations.

Sample standard deviation: $s = \sqrt{s^2}$

Population standard deviation: $\sigma = \sqrt{\sigma^2}$

For example, the standard deviation of the sample of observations in Example 4.8 is

$$s = \sqrt{s^2} = \sqrt{1.075} = 1.037 \text{ years}$$

One important application of variance (or, alternatively, of standard deviation) arises in finance, where variance is the most popular numerical measure of risk. For example, we might be concerned with the variance of a firm's sales, profits, or return on investment. In all cases, the underlying assumption is that a larger variance corresponds to a higher level of risk. The next example illustrates this important application of variance.

Finance Application

A rising stock market is referred to as a *bull market*. One of the greatest bull markets that Wall Street has ever witnessed took place from 1991 to 1999, resulting in billions of dollars flowing into the stock market as investors attempted to profit from the ever-rising prices. A convenient way for small investors to participate in the stock market is to invest their money in *mutual funds*, which are professionally managed portfolios consisting of a large number of stocks and bonds. Proper measurement of the past performance of portfolios, such as mutual funds, is important. Not only do performance measurements inform investors about the return they have earned on their investments, they also provide investors with information to help them choose which mutual fund is best for them. Proper **portfolio performance measurement** involves consideration of the level of risk of the portfolio as well as the rate of return achieved.

▼ EXAMPLE 4.9

Mutual funds are becoming an increasingly popular investment alternative among small investors. To help investors decide on the particular fund to invest in, various publications regularly report the average annual rate of return achieved by each of more than 100 mutual funds during the past 10 years.* Some publications also indicate each fund's level of risk by classifying the historical variability of each fund's rate of return as high, intermediate, or low.

If the annual (percentage) rates of return over the past 10 years for two mutual funds are as follows, which fund would you classify as having the higher level of risk?

Fund *A:* 8.3, −6.2, 20.9, −2.7, 33.6, 42.9, 24.4, 5.2, 3.1, 30.5

Fund *B:* 12.1, −2.8, 6.4, 12.2, 27.8, 25.3, 18.2, 10.7, −1.3, 11.4

Solution

For each fund, we must find the variance of the sample of rates of return. To avoid having to compute several squared deviations of returns from their mean, we'll use the shortcut formula for calculating a sample variance. For Fund *A*, we have

$$\sum_{i=1}^{10} x_i = 8.3 - 6.2 + \cdots + 30.5 = 160.0$$

$$\sum_{i=1}^{10} x_i^2 = (8.3)^2 + (-6.2)^2 + \cdots + (30.5)^2 = 5{,}083.06$$

The variance for Fund *A* is therefore

$$s_A^2 = \frac{1}{9}\left[\sum_{i=1}^{10} x_i^2 - \frac{\left(\sum_{i=1}^{10} x_i\right)^2}{10}\right] = \frac{1}{9}\left[5{,}083.06 - \frac{(160.0)^2}{10}\right] = 280.34 \; (\%)^2$$

For Fund *B*, we have

---

*The annual rate of return of a mutual fund is given by $(P_1 - P_0) / P_0$, where P_0 and P_1 are the prices of the fund's shares at the beginning and end of the year, respectively. This definition assumes that no dividends are paid by the fund during the year.

$$\sum_{i=1}^{10} x_i = 12.1 - 2.8 + \cdots + 11.4 = 120.0$$

$$\sum_{i=1}^{10} x_i^2 = (12.1)^2 + (-2.8)^2 + \cdots + (11.4)^2 = 2,334.36$$

The variance for Fund B is therefore

$$s_B^2 = \frac{1}{9}\left[\sum_{i=1}^{10} x_i^2 - \frac{\left(\sum_{i=1}^{10} x_i\right)^2}{10}\right] = \frac{1}{9}\left[2,334.36 - \frac{(120.0)^2}{10}\right] = 99.37 \ (\%)^2$$

Notice that, because the calculation of s^2 involves squaring the original measurements, the sample variance is expressed in $(\%)^2$, which is the square of the unit (percent) used to express the original measurements of rate of return.

Excel Output for Example 4.9

	A	B	C	D
1	*Fund A*		*Fund B*	
2				
3	Mean	16	Mean	12
4	Standard Error	5.29	Standard Error	3.15
5	Median	14.60	Median	11.75
6	Mode	#N/A	Mode	#N/A
7	Standard Deviation	16.74	Standard Deviation	9.97
8	Sample Variance	280.3	Sample Variance	99.4
9	Kurtosis	-1.34	Kurtosis	-0.464
10	Skewness	0.217	Skewness	0.107
11	Range	49.1	Range	30.6
12	Minimum	-6.2	Minimum	-2.8
13	Maximum	42.9	Maximum	27.8
14	Sum	160	Sum	120
15	Count	10	Count	10

Use the commands described in Example 4.6 to produce descriptive statistics for the data. Excel prints the range, sample standard deviation, and sample variance, as well as a variety of other statistics, some of which we'll present in this book.

Minitab Output for Example 4.9

Descriptive Statistics

Variable	N	Mean	Median	TrMean	StDev	SEMean
Fund A	10	16.00	14.60	15.41	16.74	5.29
Fund B	10	12.00	11.75	11.88	9.97	3.15

Variable	Min	Max	Q1	Q3
Fund A	-6.20	42.90	1.65	31.28
Fund B	-2.80	27.80	4.47	19.98

Use the commands described in Example 4.6 to produce descriptive statistics for the data. Minitab outputs the sample standard deviation, the minimum and maximum observations (allowing you to compute the range), quartiles, as well as the measures of central location and other statistics that we'll eventually discuss.

From the sample data, we conclude that Fund A has the higher level of risk as measured by variance, because the variance of its rates of return exceeds that of Fund B's rates of return. Notice that Fund A has also enjoyed a higher average rate of return during the past 10 years. Specifically, the mean rates of return for Funds A and B were

$$\bar{x}_A = \frac{160.0}{10} = 16\% \quad \text{and} \quad \bar{x}_B = \frac{120.0}{10} = 12\%$$

This result is in keeping with our intuitive notion that an investment that involves a higher level of risk should produce a higher average rate of return.*

Notice that, alternatively, we could have used standard deviation as our measure of variability. For instance, the standard deviations of the samples of rates of return for Funds A and B are

$$s_A = \sqrt{s_A^2} = \sqrt{280.3} = 16.74\%$$

and

$$s_B = \sqrt{s_B^2} = \sqrt{99.4} = 9.97\%$$

As you can see, the measurements in sample A are more variable than those in sample B, whether we use variance or standard deviation as our measure of variability. But standard deviation is the more useful measure of variability in situations where the measure is to be used in conjunction with the mean to make a statement about a single population, as we will see in the next section.

▲

COEFFICIENT OF VARIATION

Would you worry more about losing $5 if you had invested $100 or $500? You probably answered "if I had invested $100," because the $5 loss then represents a greater *proportionate* change in the value of your investment. In a similar manner, we sometimes adjust the standard deviation (our measure of variability) of a data set by dividing it by the data set's mean to obtain a *relative* measure of variability. This measure, called the coefficient of variation, allows us to compare the *relative* variabilities of the two data sets, because it adjusts for differences in the magnitudes of the means of the data sets.

Coefficient of Variation

The **coefficient of variation** of a set of measurements is the standard deviation of the measurements divided by their mean.

Sample coefficient of variation: $cv = \dfrac{s}{\bar{x}}$

Population coefficient of variation: $CV = \dfrac{\sigma}{\mu}$

For instance, the coefficients of variation of the sample rates of return for Funds A and B in Example 4.9 are

---

*Students of finance will realize that, strictly speaking, the mutual funds must be well diversified for this statement to hold when variance is used as the measure of risk.

$$cv_A = \frac{s_A}{\bar{x}_A} = \frac{16.74}{16} = 1.05 \quad \text{and} \quad cv_B = \frac{s_B}{\bar{x}_B} = \frac{9.97}{12} = .83$$

In this particular case, comparing coefficients of variation and comparing standard deviations lead to the same conclusion: The measurements in sample A are more variable. But if the mean return for Fund A in Example 4.9 was 21% with the same standard deviation of $s_A = 16.74\%$, the coefficient of variation of the returns for Fund A would then be

$$cv_A = \frac{16.74}{21} = .80$$

In this case, Fund A would have relatively less variability than Fund B (9.97/12 = .83).

The coefficient of variation is sometimes multiplied by 100 and reported as a percentage, which effectively expresses the standard deviation as a percentage of the mean. Thus, for the Fund A returns in Example 4.9, the coefficient of variation is 105%.

EXERCISES

4.18 Is it possible for a standard deviation to be negative? Explain.

4.19 Is it possible for the standard deviation of a data set to be larger than its variance? Explain.

4.20 Compute the mean, range, variance, and standard deviation for the following sample of data.

5, 7, 12, 14, 15, 15, 17, 20, 21, 24

4.21 Refer to the sample of data in Exercise 4.20. Try to answer each of the following questions without performing any calculations. Then verify your answers by performing the necessary calculations.

  a If we drop the largest value from the sample, what will happen to the mean and variance?

  b If each value is increased by 2, what will happen to the mean and variance?

  c If each value is multiplied by 3, what will happen to the mean and variance?

4.22 Calculate $\bar{x}$, s^2, and s for the following sample of data.

3, −2, −4, 1, 0, −1, 2

4.23 Calculate $\bar{x}$, s^2, and s for each of the following samples of data.

  a 14, 7, 8, 11, 5
  b −3, −2, −1, 0, 1, 2, 3
  c 4, 4, 8, 8
  d 5, 5, 5, 5

4.24 Treating each of the four sets of data in Exercise 4.23 as populations, calculate μ, σ^2, and σ for each of the four populations.

4.25 Examine the three samples shown below. Without performing any calculations, indicate which sample has the largest amount of variability and which sample has the least amount of variability. Explain why.

  a 27, 39, 22, 36, 31
  b 32, 28, 33, 30, 27
  c 34, 47, 16, 49, 39

4.26 Calculate the variance and standard deviation of the three samples listed in Exercise 4.25.

4.27 Calculate $\sum (x_i - \bar{x})$ for the three samples in Exercise 4.25. What can you infer about this calculation in general?

4.28 Create a sample of size 4 whose mean is 10 and whose variance is zero.

4.29 The number of hours a student spent studying over the past 7 days was recorded as follows.

2, 5, 6, 1, 4, 0, 3

Compute the range, $\bar{x}$, s, and s^2 for these data. Express each answer in appropriate units.

4.30 Given a set of quantitative data, what is the most popular measure of central location? What is the best measure of variability? Explain both answers.

4.31 The 15 stocks in your portfolio had the following percentage changes in value over the past year.

3, 0, 6, −5, −2, 5, −18, 20, 14, 18, −10, 10, 50, −20, 14

  a Compute μ^2, σ^2, and σ for this population of data. Express each answer in appropriate units.
  b Compute the range and median for these data.

4.32 Consider once again the two mutual funds, A and B, in Example 4.9. For convenience, their annual percentage rates of return over the past 10 years are repeated here.

For each of the 10 years, consider the portfolio obtained by investing equal amounts of money in each of the two funds. Over the first year of your investment, Fund *A* had an 8.3% return, while Fund *B* had a 12.1% return. The rate of return you would have earned on the portfolio over the first year would then have been 0.5(8.3) + 0.5(12.1) = 10.2%.

Fund *A:* 8.3, −6.2, 20.9, −2.7, 33.6, 42.9, 24.4, 5.2, 3.1, 30.5

Fund *B:* 12.1, −2.8, 6.4, 12.2, 27.8, 25.3, 18.2, 10.7, −1.3, 11.4

a Compute the rate of return earned on the portfolio for each of the 10 years.

b Find the mean return on the portfolio over the past 10 years.

c Find the standard deviation of the portfolio returns over the past 10 years.

d Rank the three possible investments (Fund *A*, Fund *B*, and the portfolio) according to their average returns and according to their riskiness (as measured by standard deviation) over the past 10 years.

The next seven questions require the use of a computer and statistical software.

4.33 The annual total rates of return on Canadian common stocks and long-term government bonds, for each of 30 years, are shown in Table E4.33. (The data are also stored in file XR04-33. Column 1 stores the stock returns, and column 2 stores the bond returns.) To understand the meaning of these returns, consider the 15.56% return that was realized on common stocks in 1963. This means that $100 invested in common stocks at the beginning of 1963 would have yielded a profit of $15.56 over the year, leaving a total of $115.56 at year's end.

Table E4.33   Annual Total Rates of Return (in %)

Years	Common stocks					Long-term government bonds				
1960–64	1.66	32.54	−7.52	15.56	25.30	7.10	9.78	3.05	4.60	6.59
1965–69	6.54	−7.10	18.00	22.36	−0.96	0.96	1.55	−2.20	−0.52	−2.31
1970–74	−3.60	8.07	27.31	−0.42	−26.61	−21.98	11.55	1.11	1.71	−1.69
1975–79	19.70	10.94	9.93	29.22	44.38	2.82	19.02	5.97	1.29	−2.62
1980–84	29.93	−10.29	5.51	34.84	−2.44	2.06	−3.02	42.98	9.60	15.09
1985–89	25.07	8.95	5.88	11.08	21.37	25.26	17.54	0.45	10.45	16.29

Source: Report on Canadian Economic Statistics: 1924–1991 (Canadian Institute of Actuaries, April 1992), p. 18.

a Find the mean, the median, the range, and the standard deviation of this sample of common-stock returns.

b Repeat part (a) for the bond returns.

c Which type of investment (common stocks or bonds) appears to have the higher level of risk? The higher average return?

d To help support his contention that investors in common stocks rarely lose money over the long run, an investment advisor claims that the average stock return for each of the six 5-year periods tabulated here is positive. For which average is his claim correct: the arithmetic mean or the geometric mean?

e Which average mentioned in part (d) is more relevant to the advisor's contention regarding the long run?

4.34 Refer to Exercise 4.8, where the amount of time needed to complete a telephone survey by 100 respondents is stored in column 1 of file XR04-08.

a Use a software package to calculate the variance and the standard deviation.

b Use a software package to draw the histogram.

4.35 Example 2.1 dealt with the problem of graphically summarizing the 200 long-distance bills. Recall that the data were stored in XM02-01. Use your software to compute several measures of dispersion.

4.36 Refer to Example 2.2, where a sample of 400 Barnes Exhibit visitors was timed to determine how long each took to view the exhibit. Suppose that, in fact, three samples of size 400 were taken: one in the morning, the second in the afternoon, and the third in the evening. These data are stored in columns 1, 2, and 3, respectively, of file XR04-36. (Column 2 contains the same data as in XM02-02.)

a Determine the mean and the median of each sample.

b Determine the range, variance, and standard deviation of each sample.

c Discuss the similarities and differences among the three samples.

d What are the implications of your findings?

4.37 Refer to Exercise 2.20. Recall that the number of customers entering a bank during each hour of operation for the last 100 days was recorded in columns 1 through 5 of file XR02-20.

a For each hour of operation, determine the mean and standard deviation.

b Briefly describe what the statistics in part (a) tell you.

4.38 The relationship between the monthly rates of return on American Barrick Resources and on the TSE 300 Index over a 5-year period was considered in Exercise 2.47. (Column 1 of file XR02-47 stores the monthly percentage returns on American Barrick Resources, and column 2 stores the monthly percentage returns on the TSE 300 Index.)

a Without performing any computations, would you expect American Barrick Resources (North America's largest gold producer) or the TSE 300-stock Index to have the higher mean return? The higher standard deviation? Explain your answers.

b Compute the mean and standard deviation of the returns of both American Barrick Resources and the TSE 300 Index. Compare the results with your answer to part (a).

4.39 The annual percentage rates of return on common stocks and on bonds from 1960 through 1994 are stored in file XR02-23. (Column 1 stores the stock returns, and column 2 stores the bond returns.)

    a Without performing any computations, would you expect the stock returns or the bond returns to have the higher mean? The higher standard deviation? Explain your answers.

    b Compute the mean and standard deviation of both the stock returns and the bond returns. Compare the results with your answer to part (a).

4.4 INTERPRETING STANDARD DEVIATION

By now, you probably understand how variance and standard deviation can be used as relative measures of variability. If you are comparing two sets of data, the one with the larger standard deviation has the greater amount of variability. Given the standard deviation of a single set of observations, however, you would likely have difficulty interpreting that value intuitively. The standard deviation would be more useful if it could be used to make a statement about the proportion of observations that fall into various intervals of values.

The purpose of this section is to illustrate how the standard deviation of a *single* set of data can be useful. Both the Empirical Rule and Chebyshev's theorem make use of the standard deviation of a data set to make statements about the percentage of observations in the data set that lie within a certain number of standard deviations of the mean of that data set. The objective is to help us get a feel for how standard deviation can be used to express either how tightly clustered or how spread out the observations are about their mean. Although we will usually use samples in our discussion, the statements are equally valid for populations.

For example, suppose you are told that the average (mean) of the final marks in an accounting course is 70, with a standard deviation of 6. The professor could convey useful information regarding the dispersion of the marks about the mean of 70 by announcing the percentage of marks that fall, for example, within 1 standard deviation of the mean; that is, within the interval

$$(\bar{x} - s, \bar{x} + s) = (70 - 6, 70 + 6) = (64, 76)$$

Similarly, the professor could count and announce the percentage of marks that fall within 2 standard deviations of the mean: within the interval (58, 82).

In many real-world applications, the sample of data is so large that determining the percentage of observations lying within a particular interval by counting them would be impractical. A very good estimate of this percentage is available, however, if the distribution of the data is mound shaped (or bell shaped). An example of a mound-shaped distribution is shown in Figure 4.4, which displays a relative frequency histogram of the 30 telephone call durations in Table 4.1. (A smoothed outline of the histogram would resemble a mound.)

A rule of thumb, called the **Empirical Rule,** has evolved from empirical studies that have produced data sets possessing mound-shaped distributions. There is no theoretical justification for the Empirical Rule. It has simply been observed that it is approximately correct for data sets—both populations and (large) samples—that have mound-shaped distributions. For a sample (or population) of observations with a mound-shaped distribution, the Empirical Rule states the approximate percentage of the observations in that sample (or population) that fall within 1, 2, or 3 standard deviations of the mean.

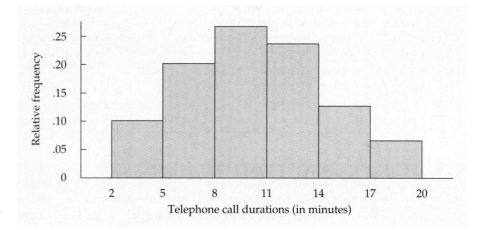

Figure 4.4

Mound-shaped histogram

Empirical Rule

If a sample of observations has a mound-shaped distribution, the interval

$(\bar{x} - s, \bar{x} + s)$ contains approximately 68% of the observations

$(\bar{x} - 2s, \bar{x} + 2s)$ contains approximately 95% of the observations

$(\bar{x} - 3s, \bar{x} + 3s)$ contains virtually all of the observations

---

▼ **EXAMPLE 4.10**

The durations of a sample of 30 long-distance telephone calls placed by a firm in a given week are recorded in Table 4.1.* It can be shown that this sample of 30 durations has a mean of $\bar{x} = 10.26$ and a standard deviation of $s = 4.29$. Moreover, the durations have an approximately mound-shaped distribution (see Figure 4.4). Consequently, according to the Empirical Rule, approximately 68% of the 30 durations lie in the interval

$$(\bar{x} - s, \bar{x} + s) = (10.26 - 4.29, 10.26 + 4.29)$$
$$= (5.97, 14.55)$$

You can check this result by counting the actual contents of the specified interval. In fact, this interval contains 70% (21 out of 30) of the durations—a percentage that comes very close to the Empirical Rule's approximation.

Similarly, the Empirical Rule states that approximately 95% of the durations lie in the interval

$$(\bar{x} - 2s, \bar{x} + 2s) = (10.26 - 2[4.29], 10.26 + 2[4.29])$$
$$= (1.68, 18.84)$$

In fact, all but the largest of the 30 durations fall within this interval; that is, the interval actually contains 96.7% of the telephone call durations—a percentage that comes very close to the Empirical Rule's approximation.

---

*We use a small sample size of 30 here to enable us to easily count the number of observations in various intervals for illustrative purposes.

Table 4.1   **Duration of Long-Distance Calls (in minutes)**

11.8	3.6	16.6	13.5	4.8	8.3
8.9	9.1	7.7	2.3	12.1	6.1
10.2	8.0	11.4	6.8	9.6	19.5
15.3	12.3	8.5	15.9	18.7	11.7
6.2	11.2	10.4	7.2	5.5	14.5

▲

Example 4.10 may also be used to anticipate an idea that will be expanded on in Chapter 7, when we deal with a particular mound-shaped distribution called the *normal distribution*. We noted in Section 2.2 that the area of any rectangle erected as part of a histogram is proportional to the percentage of the measurements that fall into the class it describes. As we've just observed, the Empirical Rule states that about 95% of the telephone call durations fall in the interval between 1.68 and 18.84 minutes. Therefore, approximately 95% of the area under the mound-shaped histogram in Figure 4.4 lies between 1.68 and 18.84. More generally, approximately 95% of the area under any mound-shaped histogram lies between $\bar{x} - 2s$ and $\bar{x} + 2s$.

As a final point, we note that the Empirical Rule forms the basis for a crude method of approximating the standard deviation of a sample of observations that has a mound-shaped distribution. Because most of the sample observations (about 95%) fall within 2 standard deviations of the mean, the range of the observations is approximately equal to $4s$. After we have found the range of the observations, we can approximate the sample standard deviation by

$$s \simeq \text{Range}/4$$

This **range approximation of** s is useful as a quick check to ensure that our computed value of s is reasonable, or "in the ballpark." For example, the range of the telephone call durations is 17.2, so $17.2/4 = 4.3$ is an approximation of s. In this case, the range approximation is very close to 4.29, our computed value of s. Such accuracy isn't generally to be expected. More will be said about this approximation in Chapter 9.

CHEBYSHEV'S THEOREM

The Empirical Rule states the approximate percentage of observations in a data set that fall within a specified number of standard deviations of the mean, providing that the data set has a mound-shaped distribution. If a data set does *not* have a mound-shaped distribution, we must resort to a theorem first proved by Russian mathematician Pavroty Chebyshev.

Chebyshev's Theorem

Given any set of observations and a number $k \geq 1$, the fraction of these observations that lie within k standard deviations of their mean is at least $1 - 1/k^2$.

Because this famous theorem is valid for any set of observations, it holds both for a sample and for a population. Although we have chosen to use the notation for a sample in the discussion that follows, population notation would serve equally well.

The thrust of the theorem is to provide a minimum value for the fraction of observations falling within an interval of the form $(\bar{x} - ks, \bar{x} + ks)$, where $\bar{x}$ and s are the mean and standard deviation of a sample of observations and k is some number greater than 1.*

For example, Chebyshev's theorem states that (with $k = 2$) at least $1 - 1/2^2 = 3/4$ of the observations lie in the interval $(\bar{x} - 2s, \bar{x} + 2s)$. Similarly (with $k = 3$), at least 8/9 of the observations lie in the interval $(\bar{x} - 3s, \bar{x} + 3s)$. These statements are summarized in Table 4.2, together with the corresponding statements using the Empirical Rule, which assumes the data have a mound-shaped distribution. Figure 4.5 illustrates Chebyshev's theorem graphically for $k = 2$, where $\bar{x}$ and s are the mean and the standard deviation of a sample of observations x_i.

Table 4.2 **Percentage of Observations in Intervals**

k	Interval	Chebyshev Percentage	Empirical Rule Percentage
2	$(\bar{x} - 2s, \bar{x} + 2s)$	At least 75% (or 3/4)	Approximately 95%
3	$(\bar{x} - 3s, \bar{x} + 3s)$	At least 89% (or 8/9)	Approximately 100%

The importance of Chebyshev's theorem stems from the fact that it applies to *any* set of observations, regardless of their distribution. Consequently, $1 - 1/k^2$ is necessarily a conservative lower bound on the fraction of observations in the interval $(\bar{x} - ks, \bar{x} + ks)$. In other words, because the fraction of observations in the interval $(\bar{x} - ks, \bar{x} + ks)$ varies from one set of data to another, the best we can do is specify a minimum value for this fraction—a value that is correct for any set of observations. For a particular set of data, the actual fraction of observations lying in the interval may in fact be much larger.

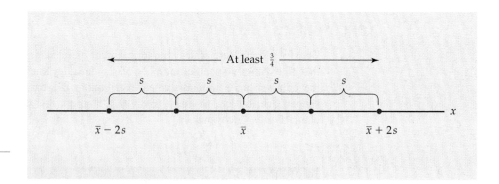

Figure 4.5

Chebyshev's theorem for $k = 2$

*Strictly speaking, for the purpose of applying Chebyshev's theorem to a sample of data, we should compute the variance (and hence standard deviation) by dividing the sum of squared deviations by n instead of the usual $(n-1)$. Use of the *sample* standard deviation in Chebyshev's theorem will result in an interval that is slightly larger than necessary, resulting in a somewhat weaker statement than otherwise. But samples in most practical applications are large enough that the difference is negligible.

EXERCISES

4.40 The mean and the standard deviation of the grades of 500 students who took an economics exam were 69 and 7, respectively.

  a What are the numerical values of the endpoints of the intervals $(\bar{x} - s, \bar{x} + s)$, $(\bar{x} - 2s, \bar{x} + 2s)$, and $(\bar{x} - 3s, \bar{x} + 3s)$?

  b If the grades have a mound-shaped distribution, approximately how many students received a grade in each of the three intervals specified in part (a)?

4.41 The mean and standard deviation of the wages of 1,000 factory workers are \$25,600 and \$2,200, respectively. If the wages have a mound-shaped distribution, how many workers receive wages of between \$23,400 and \$27,800? Between \$21,200 and \$30,000? Between \$19,000 and \$32,200?

4.42 The following 20 values represent the number of seconds required to complete one spot weld by a sample of 20 automated welders on a company's production line.

  2.1, 2.7, 2.6, 2.8, 2.3, 2.5, 2.6, 2.4, 2.6, 2.7
  2.4, 2.6, 2.8, 2.5, 2.6, 2.4, 2.9, 2.4, 2.7, 2.3

  a Calculate the variance and the standard deviation for this sample of 20 measurements.

  b Use the range approximation of s to check your calculations in part (a). What assumption must you make in order to use this approximation?

4.43 A bookstore has determined that weekly sales of *Newsweek* have an approximately mound-shaped distribution, with a mean of 85 and a standard deviation of 6.

  a For what percentage of the time can we expect weekly sales to fall in the intervals $\bar{x} \pm s$ and $\bar{x} \pm 3s$?

  b For what percentage of the time can we expect weekly sales to have a value that is more than 2 standard deviations from the mean?

  c If the bookstore stocks 97 copies of *Newsweek* each week, for what percentage of weeks will there be an insufficient number of copies to meet the demand? (HINT: A mound-shaped distribution is symmetrical.)

4.44 Last year, the rates of return on the common stocks in a large portfolio had an approximately mound-shaped distribution, with a mean of 20% and a standard deviation of 10%.

  a What proportion of the stocks had a return of between 10% and 30%? Between −10% and 50%?

  b What proportion of the stocks had a return that was either less than 10% or more than 30%?

  c What proportion of the stocks had a positive return? (HINT: A mound-shaped distribution is symmetrical.)

4.45 Refer to Exercise 4.33, which deals with stock and bond returns.

  a Compute the standard deviation of both the common-stock returns and the bond returns.

  b Use the range approximation of s to check your answers to part (a).

4.46 Consider the following sample of house prices (in thousands of dollars).

  274 429 229 435 260 222 292 419 242 202 235
  215 390 359 409 375 209 265 440 365 319 338
  414 249 279

  a Calculate the variance and the standard deviation of this sample of prices.

  b Compare the range approximation of s to the true value of s. Explain why you would or would not expect the approximation to be a good one for this sample.

4.47 Refer to Exercise 4.40.

  a If the grades do not have a mound-shaped distribution, how many students received a grade in the interval $(x - 3s, x + 3s)$?

  b How does your answer compare with how you would answer if the grades were mound shaped?

4.48 Refer to Exercise 4.41.

  a If the wages do not have a mound-shaped distribution, how many workers receive wages between \$21,200 and \$30,000? Between \$19,000 and \$32,200?

  b How does your answer compare with how you would answer if the wages were mound shaped?

4.49 Refer to Exercise 4.46.

  a Using Chebyshev's theorem, what can you say about the fraction of observations falling within 2 standard deviations of the mean of the 25 prices?

  b How does you answer to part (a) compare with the actual fraction of observations falling within 2 standard deviations of the mean?

4.5 MEASURES OF RELATIVE STANDING AND BOX PLOTS

The measures of central location (Section 4.2) and measures of variability (Section 4.3) provide the statistician with useful information about the location and dispersion of a set of observations. The measures in this section describe another aspect of the shape of the distribution of data, and also provide information about the relative standing of particular observations. For example, a high score on the Graduate Management Admission Test (GMAT) is one of the requirements to enter an M.B.A. program. The scores range from 200 to 800 with a mean of about 460. Suppose that you have just been told that your GMAT exam score is 600. Because entry into most programs is highly competitive, you need to know how well you did relative to the other people who have taken the test. To extract this information we need to compute percentiles.

Percentile

The pth **percentile** of a set of observations is the value for which *at most p%* of the observations are less than that value and *at most* $(100 - p)$% of the observations are greater than that value.

For example, if the 78th percentile of GMAT scores is 600, this means that 78% of the population that took the test scored below 600; 22% scored 600 or better.

The pth percentile is defined in much the same manner as is the median, which divides a series of observations in such a way that at most 50% of the observations are smaller than the median and at most 50% of the observations are greater. In fact, the median is simply the 50th percentile. Just as we have a special name for the percentile that divides the ordered set of observations in half, we have special names for percentiles that divide the ordered set of observations into quarters and into tenths: **quartiles*** and **deciles.** The following list identifies some of the more commonly used percentiles, together with notation for the quartiles.

$$
\begin{aligned}
&\text{First (lower) decile} && = \text{10th percentile} \\
Q_1 = \ &\text{First (lower) quartile} && = \text{25th percentile} \\
Q_2 = \ &\text{Second (middle) quartile} && = \text{Median (50th percentile)} \\
Q_3 = \ &\text{Third (upper) quartile} && = \text{75th percentile} \\
&\text{Ninth (upper) decile} && = \text{90th percentile}
\end{aligned}
$$

▼ EXAMPLE 4.11

To find the quartiles for the set of measurements

$$7, 18, 12, 17, 29, 18, 4, 27, 30, 2, 4, 10, 21, 5, 8$$

we must first arrange the measurements in ascending order.

$$2, 4, 4, 5, 7, 8, 10, 12, 17, 18, 18, 21, 27, 29, 30$$

      ↑   ↑   ↑

   lower   median   upper

  quartile   quartile

The lower quartile is the value for which at most $.25 \times 15 = 3.75$ of the observations are smaller and at most $.75 \times 15 = 11.25$ of the observations are larger. The only

---

*Quartiles are dividers—values that divide the entire range of measurements into four equal quarters. In practice, however, the word *quartile* is sometimes used to refer to one of these quarters. A measurement "in the first quartile" is in the bottom 25% of the measurements, whereas a measurement "in the upper quartile" is among the top 25%.

observation satisfying these criteria is 5, so 5 is the first quartile. The median is 12—the middle value. The upper quartile is the value for which at most $.75 \times 15 = 11.25$ of the observations are smaller and at most $.25 \times 15 = 3.75$ of the observations are larger. The only observation satisfying these criteria is 21, so 21 is the third quartile.

▲

Occasionally, you will find that the percentile you are seeking falls between two of the observations in the data set. When this happens, to avoid becoming unnecessarily pedantic, simply choose the midpoint between the two observations involved. This value will usually provide an adequate approximation of the required percentile. To illustrate this convention, suppose we want to find the 20th percentile of the observations in Example 4.11. The 20th percentile would be the value for which at most 3 of the observations are smaller and at most 12 of the observations are larger. Because any number between the observations 4 and 5 (inclusive) satisfies this criterion, we choose 4.5—the midpoint between 4 and 5—as the 20th percentile.

Measures of relative standing can be used in several ways to describe the shape of the distribution. For example, if the first decile is close to the median whereas the ninth decile is relatively far from the median, we may infer that the histogram is positively skewed. If the first and third quartiles are about the same distance from the median, it is quite probable that the histogram is approximately symmetric. Of course, we can *know* the shape by drawing the histogram, stem and leaf display, or dot plot.

We can also use quartiles to produce yet another measure of dispersion. It is called the **interquartile range** (IQR), defined as the difference between the third and first quartile. That is,

$$IQR = Q_3 - Q_1$$

The interquartile range measures the spread of the middle 50% of a data set. This measure is most useful when the data are ranked. It is also used on quantitative data to produce a measure of dispersion that is not sensitive to extreme values.

BOX PLOTS

When you are faced with the problem of summarizing the essential characteristics of a set of quantitative data, we have suggested that you begin by noting the smallest and largest values and then construct a histogram or stem and leaf display. We have also discussed the importance of numerical measures to describe the central location and dispersion of the data.

A **box plot,** alternatively called a **box-and-whisker plot,** is a clever pictorial display that indicates what the two extreme values of a data set are, where the data are centered, and how spread out the data are.* It does this by providing a graphic, five-number summary of the data. The five values plotted are the following:

Smallest	(S)
Lower quartile	(Q_1)
Median	(Q_2)
Upper quartile	(Q_3)
Largest	(L)

---

*The idea of a box plot was developed fairly recently by John Tukey.

The director of an M.B.A. program (known for its high admission requirements) wishes to construct a box plot of the scores obtained on the GMAT by this year's 200 applicants. The scores are stored in file XM04-12.

Solution

If you are creating a box plot by hand, the first step is to rank the data and note the smallest and largest values ($S = 449$ and $L = 788$).

The next step is to identify the other three values to be displayed. The median score (Q_2) is 537, because at most 50% of the scores are smaller than 537 and at most 50% are larger. The lower quartile (Q_1) is 512, because at most 25% of the scores are smaller and at most 75% of the scores are larger. Similarly, the upper quartile (Q_3) is 575, because at most 75% of the scores are smaller and at most 25% of the scores are larger..

The five values of interest are plotted in Figure 4.6. In this plot, a box with endpoints Q_1 and Q_3 is used to represent the middle half of the data. Notice that about a quarter of the data fall along the line (or **whisker**) to the left of the box, and about a quarter of the data fall along the whisker to the right of the box. The location of the median is indicated by the vertical line inside the box. The scores corresponding to some of the plotted values are also identified. The length of the box is given by the **interquartile range:**

$$\text{IQR} = Q_3 - Q_1$$
$$= 575 - 512 = 63$$

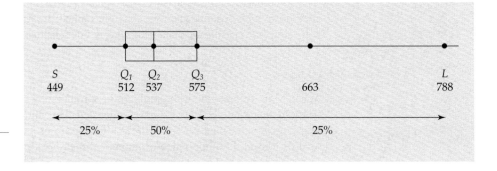

Figure 4.6

Display of five summary values for GMAT scores

Strictly speaking, Figure 4.6 is not a box plot, although it is close to being one. One small adjustment to the whiskers is needed, which involves the concept of an *outlier,* the name given to unusually large or small values in a data set. For our purposes here, we will define an **outlier** to be a value located at a distance of more than 1.5(IQR) from the box. In our GMAT scores example, 1.5(IQR) = 1.5(63) = 94.5. Therefore, an outlier is any value outside the interval (512 − 94.5, 575 + 94.5) = (417.5, 669.5).* In this example, there are 12 outliers, ranging from 675 up to 788.

The lines, or whiskers, emanating from each end of the box in a box plot should extend to the most extreme value that is not an outlier; in this case, to the extreme

---

*The endpoints of this interval are called *fences,* outside of which all values are outliers. We will not need this terminology, however.

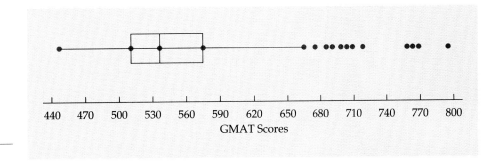

Figure 4.7

Box plot for GMAT scores

lower score of 449 and the extreme higher score of 663. The resulting box plot is shown in Figure 4.7.

Although the statistics in a box plot can be calculated manually and the box plot can also be drawn by hand, it is far easier to let the computer do the work. To show how the computer outputs box plots, we've used both Excel and Minitab (as usual) to print the box plot for the data in file XM04-12.

Incidentally, you can instruct Excel to include the quartiles in the list of descriptive statistics for a data set. Begin by clicking **Tools, Data Analysis . . . ,** and **Descriptive Statistics.** To produce the quartiles (calculated for relatively large sample sizes), use the cursor to put an **x** in the boxes indicating **Kth largest** and **Kth smallest.** Specify a number equal to the sample size divided by 4. (Round to nearest integer if necessary.)

Excel Output for Example 4.12

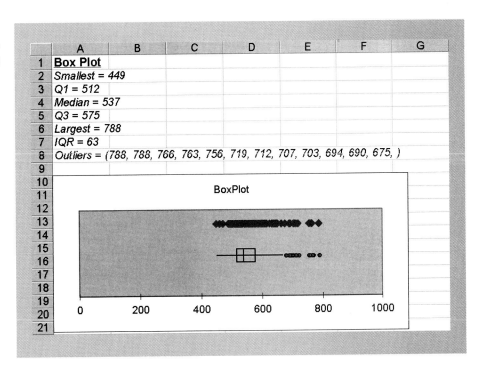

COMMANDS	COMMANDS FOR EXAMPLE 4.12
1 Type or import the data into one column.	Open file **XM04-12.**
2 Click **Tools, Data Analysis Plus,** and **Box Plot.**	
3 Specify the coordinates of the data. (Do not include cell containing variable name.)	**A2:A201**

Minitab Output for Example 4.12

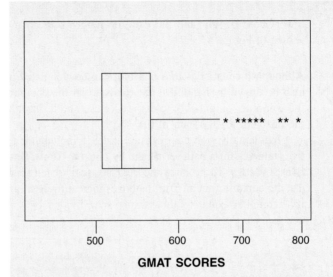

GMAT SCORES

COMMANDS	COMMANDS FOR EXAMPLE 4.12
1 Type or import the data into a column.	Open file **XM04-12.**
2 Click **Graph** and **Box Plot . . . .**	**GMAT Scores** or **C1**
3 Type the name of the variable and click **OK.**	

Minitab will print the box plot lying on its side. To put it right side up (as shown here), proceed as follows.

4 Before clicking **OK,** click **Options . . .** and click **Transpose X and Y.** Click **OK.**

INTERPRET

From the box plot in Figure 4.7, we can quickly grasp several points concerning the distribution of the GMAT scores. The scores range from 449 to 788, with about half being smaller than 537 and about half larger than 537. About half the scores lie between 512 and 575, with about a quarter below 512 and a quarter above 575. The distribution is considerably skewed to the right, as the right whisker is much longer than the left whisker. A possible explanation for this positive skewness is that applicants with low GMAT scores do not apply, knowing that this M.B.A. program has high admission standards.

Notice that the shape of a box plot is not heavily influenced by a few extreme observations, because the median and the other quartiles are not unduly influenced by extreme observations, in contrast to the situation with means and variances.

Before proceeding with a decision, the M.B.A. director will want to investigate the 12 outliers and confirm their validity.

OUTLIERS

In our discussion of box plots, we introduced the notion of an outlier: an unusually large or small value in a sample. Because an outlier is considerably removed from the main body of a sample, its validity is suspect and some investigation is needed to check that it is not the result of an error in measuring, recording, or transcribing the value. As well as providing a graphical summary of a data set, a box plot is useful for identifying outliers before performing further statistical analysis on a data set.

EXERCISES

4.50 What are the special names for the 25th, 50th, and 75th percentiles?

4.51 Refer to Exercise 4.31, which gives the percentage changes in value for 15 stocks. Compute the 20th percentile and 60th percentile for these data.

4.52 Refer to Exercise 4.33.

   a Find the upper and lower quartiles of the common-stock returns.

   b Find the upper and lower quartiles of the bond returns.

4.53 Consider a set of data with

$Q_1 = 50$
$Q_2 = 90$
$Q_3 = 110$

   a What do these statistics tell you about the shape of the distribution?

   b What can you say about the relative position of each of these observations?

     i   40

     ii 92

     iii 109

   c Calculate the interquartile range.

   d What does the interquartile range tell you about the data?

4.54 Suppose that an analysis of incomes in a large company reveals the following.

$Q_1 = \$23{,}000$
$Q_2 = \$31{,}000$
$Q_3 = \$46{,}000$

   a What do these statistics reveal about the distribution of incomes?

   b Suppose that your income is $48,000. What can you say about your income relative to the incomes of others in the company?

   c Calculate the interquartile range.

   d Interpret the value of the interquartile range.

4.55 A box plot can be described as a five-number summary of a data set in the form of a graph. What five numbers are plotted?

4.56 Define what is meant by the terms *interquartile range* and *outlier.*

4.57 Refer to Example 4.9.

   a Draw the box plot for each sample (fund).

   b Discuss the similarities and differences between the returns for Fund *A* and Fund *B.*

4.58 A sample of 100 observations is stored in column 1 of file XR04-58.

   a Use a software package to draw the box plot.

   b What are the values of the quartiles?

   c What information can you extract from the box plot?

4.59 Refer to Example 4.6, for which the 100 test marks are stored in file XM04-06.

   a Draw the box plot.

   b What are the quartiles?

   c Are there any outliers?

   d What does the box plot tell you about the marks on the statistics exam?

4.60 Refer to Exercise 2.22, where the number of customers entering a bank during each hour of operation for the last 100 days was stored in columns 1 through 5 of file XR02-22.

   a Draw the box plot for each hour of operation.

b What are the quartiles, and what do they tell you about the number of customers arriving each hour?

4.61 Refer to Exercise 4.33, for which the common-stock and bond returns are stored in file XR04-33.

    a Construct box plots for both the common-stock returns and the bond returns.

b Compare the locations and shapes of the distributions of the two sets of returns based on your box plots.

c Which type of investment (common stocks or bonds) appears to have the higher level of risk? The higher average return?

4.6 APPROXIMATING DESCRIPTIVE MEASURES FOR GROUPED DATA

The two most important descriptive measures are the mean and the variance (or alternatively, the standard deviation). This section looks briefly at how to approximate these two measures for data that have been grouped into a frequency distribution.

You will find that the approximations given here are useful in two types of situations. The first is when you are confronted with a large set of ungrouped data. Although you could calculate the mean and the variance precisely with the aid of a computer, you might decide that approximations of these measures suffice to meet your needs. In this case, you might find it faster and cheaper simply to group the data into a frequency distribution and use the methods described here. The second situation, which arises frequently in practice, is when you rely on secondary data sources such as government publications. Data collected by others are usually presented in the form of a frequency distribution, and you do not have access to the ungrouped data. In this case, you have no choice but to approximate the descriptive measures.

Consider a sample of n observations that have been grouped into k classes. If f_i denotes the frequency of class i (for $i = 1, 2, \ldots, k$), then $n = f_1 + f_2 + \cdots + f_k$. A good approximation of the sample mean $\bar{x}$ can be obtained by making the assumption that the midpoint m_i of each class i closely approximates the mean of the observations in class i. This assumption is reasonable whenever the observations in a class are dispersed fairly symmetrically about the midpoint. The sum of the observations in class i is then approximately equal to $f_i m_i$.

The approximation of the sample variance is obtained by approximating the short-cut formula for the sample variance of ungrouped data, which was given in Section 4.3. The approximation of the sample variance actually requires a stronger assumption than the assumption of symmetry mentioned above—each observation in a class is assumed to be equal to the midpoint of that class. The more accurate this assumption is, the better the approximation to the sample variance will be. If the grouped data represent a population of n observations, the formula for approximating σ^2 is $(n - 1)/n$ times the formula used to approximate s^2.

Approximate Mean and Variance for Grouped Data

$$\bar{x} \cong \frac{\sum_{i=1}^{k} f_i m_i}{n}$$

$$s^2 \cong \frac{1}{n-1} \left[\sum_{i=1}^{k} f_i m_i^2 - \frac{\left(\sum_{i=1}^{k} f_i m_i \right)^2}{n} \right]$$

▼ **EXAMPLE 4.13**

In Section 4.4 we constructed a histogram (Figure 4.4) for the sample of telephone call durations given in Table 4.1 (page 115). The corresponding frequency distribution for this sample of 30 telephone call durations is shown in Table 4.3. Three additional columns have been included in the table to record the information required by the formulas for approximating the mean and the variance of the durations from these grouped data. The sample mean and variance of the 30 telephone call durations are approximated as follows.

$$\bar{x} \cong \frac{\sum_{i=1}^{6} f_i \, m_i}{30} = \frac{312.0}{30} = 10.4$$

$$s^2 \cong \frac{1}{29}\left[\sum_{i=1}^{6} f_i \, m_i^2 - \frac{\left(\sum_{i=1}^{6} f_i \, m_i\right)^2}{30}\right] = \frac{1}{29}\left[3{,}751.5 - \frac{(312)^2}{30}\right] = 17.47$$

These approximations match the true values of $\bar{x} = 10.26$ and $s^2 = 18.40$ reasonably well.

Table 4.3 **Extended Frequency Distribution of Telephone Call Durations**

Class i	Class Limits	Frequency f_i	Midpoint m_i	$f_i m_i$	$f_i m_i^2$
1	2 up to 5	3	3.5	10.5	36.75
2	5 up to 8	6	6.5	39.0	253.50
3	8 up to 11	8	9.5	76.0	722.00
4	11 up to 14	7	12.5	87.5	1,093.75
5	14 up to 17	4	15.5	62.0	961.00
6	17 up to 20	2	18.5	37.0	684.50
Total		$n = 30$		312.0	3,751.50

▲

E X E R C I S E S

4.62 a Approximate the mean and the variance of the sample of data presented in the accompanying frequency distribution.

Class	Frequency
0 up to 16	50
16 up to 32	160
32 up to 48	110
48 up to 64	80

b Use the range approximation of s to check your approximation of the variance in part (a).

4.63 a Approximate the mean and the variance of the sample of data presented in the accompanying frequency distribution.

Class	Frequency
-20 up to -10	8
-10 up to 0	21
0 up to 10	43
10 up to 20	48
20 up to 30	25
30 up to 40	15

b Use the range approximation of s to check your approximation of the variance in part (a).

4.64 a Approximate the mean and the variance of the sample of data presented in the accompanying frequency distribution.

Class	Frequency
0 up to 10	90
10 up to 20	50
20 up to 30	40
30 up to 40	120

b Use the range approximation of s to check your approximation of the variance in part (a). Comment on the degree to which these two approximations differ from each other.

4.65 The gross hourly earnings of a group of workers randomly selected from the payroll list of a large industrial concern were organized into the following frequency distribution.

Hourly earnings	Number of workers
$8 up to $10	11
$10 up to $12	17
$12 up to $14	32
$14 up to $16	27
$16 up to $18	13

a Approximate the mean and the standard deviation of hourly earnings for this sample of workers.

b Your answers to part (a) only approximate the true values of $\bar{x}$ and s for this group's earnings. Explain why this is so.

4.66 A national car-rental agency recently bought 1,000 identical new compact cars from a major car manufacturer. After the customary 1,000-mile break-in period, it selected 100 cars randomly and obtained the following mileage data on them.

Gasoline mileage (miles per gallon)	Number of cars
24 up to 28	9
28 up to 32	13
32 up to 36	24
36 up to 40	38
40 up to 44	16

Approximate the average gasoline consumption and the standard deviation of consumption for this sample.

4.7 MEASURES OF ASSOCIATION

In Chapter 2, we presented scatter diagrams, which graphically depict how two variables are related. In this section, we present two numerical measures of the **linear** relationship depicted in a scatter diagram. The two measures are the **covariance** and the **coefficient of correlation.**

COVARIANCE

If we have all the observations that constitute a population, we can compute the population covariance. It is defined as follows.

$$\textbf{Population covariance} = \text{COV}(X,\ Y) = \frac{\sum(x_i - \mu_x)(y_i - \mu_y)}{N}$$

where μ_x is the population mean of the first variable, X; μ_y is the population mean of the second variable, Y; and N is the size of the population. The sample covariance is defined similarly, where n is the number of pairs of observations in the sample.

$$\textbf{Sample covariance} = \text{cov}(X,\ Y) = \frac{\sum(x_i - \bar{x})(y_i - \bar{y})}{n - 1}$$

For convenience, we label the population covariance $\text{COV}(X, Y)$ and the sample covariance $\text{cov}(X, Y)$. To illustrate how covariance measures association, consider the following three sets of sample data.

	x	y	$(x_i - \bar{x})$	$(y_i - \bar{y})$	$(x_i - \bar{x})(y_i - \bar{y})$
	2	13	-3	-7	21
Set 1	6	20	1	0	0
	7	27	2	7	14
	$\bar{x} = 5$	$\bar{y} = 20$			$17.5 = \text{cov}(X, Y)$

	x	y	$(x_i - \bar{x})$	$(y_i - \bar{y})$	$(x_i - \bar{x})(y_i - \bar{y})$
	2	27	-3	7	-21
Set 2	6	20	1	0	0
	7	13	2	-7	-14
	$\bar{x} = 5$	$\bar{y} = 20$			$-17.5 = \text{cov}(X, Y)$

	x	y	$(x_i - \bar{x})$	$(y_i - \bar{y})$	$(x_i - \bar{x})(y_i - \bar{y})$
	2	20	-3	0	0
Set 3	6	27	1	7	7
	7	13	2	-7	-14
	$\bar{x} = 5$	$\bar{y} = 20$			$-3.5 = \text{cov}(X, Y)$

In set 1, as x increases, so does y. In this case, when x is larger than its mean, y is at least as large as its mean. Thus $(x_i - \bar{x})$ and $(y_i - \bar{y})$ have the same sign or zero, which means that the product is either positive or zero. Consequently, the covariance is a positive number. In general, if two variables move in the same direction (both increase or both decrease), the covariance will be a large positive number. Figure 4.8(a) depicts a scatter diagram of one such case.

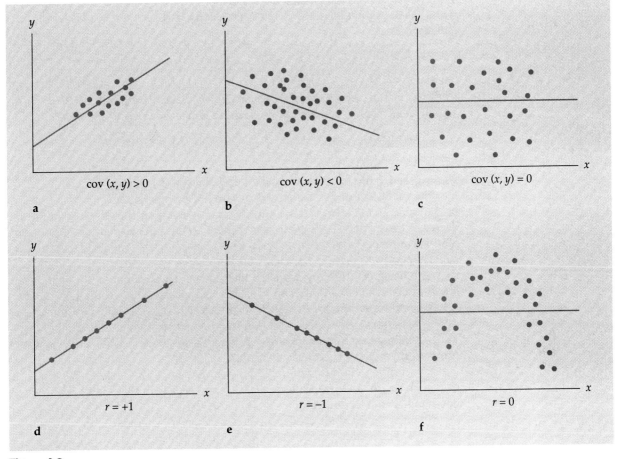

Figure 4.8

Covariance and correlation for various scatter diagrams

Next, consider set 2. As x increases, y decreases. Thus, the signs of $(x_i - \bar{x})$ and $(y_i - \bar{y})$ are opposite. As a result, the covariance is a negative number. If, as one variable increases, the other generally decreases, the covariance will be a large negative number. See Figure 4.8(b) for an illustrative scatter diagram.

Now consider set 3. As x increases, y exhibits no particular pattern. One product is positive, one is negative, and the third is zero. Consequently, the covariance is a small number. Generally speaking, if the two variables are unrelated (as one increases, the other shows no pattern), the covariance will be close to zero (either positive or negative). Figure 4.8(c) describes the movement of two unrelated variables.

As a measure of association, covariance suffers from a major drawback. It is usually difficult to judge the strength of the relationship from the covariance. For example, suppose that you have been told that the covariance of two variables is 250. What does this tell you about the relationship between the two variables? The sign, which is positive, tells you that as one increases, the other also generally increases. However, the degree to which the two variables move together is difficult to ascertain because we don't know whether 250 is a large number. To overcome this shortcoming, statisticians have produced another measure of association, which is based on the covariance. It is called the coefficient of correlation.

COEFFICIENT OF CORRELATION

The **coefficient of correlation** is the covariance divided by the standard deviations of X and Y. The **population** coefficient of **correlation** is labeled ρ (Greek letter rho) and is defined as

$$\rho = \frac{COV(X, Y)}{\sigma_x \sigma_y}$$

where σ_x and σ_y are the standard deviations of X and Y, respectively. We label the **sample** coefficient of **correlation** r, which we define as

$$r = \frac{cov(X, Y)}{s_x s_y}$$

where s_x and s_y are the sample standard deviations of X and Y, respectively.

The coefficient of correlation will always lie between -1 and $+1$. The sign will be the same as the sign of the covariance and is interpreted in the same way. The degree of association is gauged by the value of ρ (for a population) or r (for a sample). For example, a correlation close to $+1$ indicates two variables that are very strongly positively related. The closer the correlation is to 1, the closer the relationship is to being described by a straight line sloping upward from left to right. Figure 4.8(d) exhibits the behavior of two variables whose correlation coefficient is $+1$.

A correlation close to -1 tells us that there is a strong negative relationship—as one variable increases, the other decreases. A perfect straight line sloping downward would produce a correlation of -1. Figure 4.8(e) describes a scatter diagram of two perfectly negatively correlated variables.

A correlation close to zero indicates that no straight line relationship exists. It may mean no pattern, such as the scatter diagram depicted in Figure 4.8(c), or a relationship that is not a straight line, as in Figure 4.8(f).

All other values of the coefficient of correlation are interpreted in relation to $+1$, 0, and -1. For example, a correlation of $+.3$ means that there is weak positive association between the two variables. A correlation of $-.9$ means that there is a strong negative relationship.

▼ **EXAMPLE 4.14**

In Example 2.4, we constructed a scatter diagram to assess the relationship between advertising expenditure and sales level for a small business. The data are shown again below and stored in file XM02-04. Compute the covariance and coefficient of correlation to measure how the two variables are related.

Month	Advertising Expenditure X ($1,000s)	Sales Level Y ($1,000s)
1	1	30
2	3	40
3	5	40
4	4	50
5	2	35
6	5	50
7	3	35
8	2	25

Solution

We begin by providing two shortcut formulas that are useful when computing covariance and coefficient of correlation by hand. These two shortcut formulas represent, respectively, the numerators in the formulas for sample covariance and for sample variance.

Shortcut Formulas

$$\sum_{i=1}^{n}(x_i - \bar{x})(y_i - \bar{y}) = \sum_{i=1}^{n} x_i y_i - \frac{\sum_{i=1}^{n} x_i \sum_{i=1}^{n} y_i}{n}$$

$$\sum_{i=1}^{n}(x_i - \bar{x})^2 = \sum_{i=1}^{n} x_i^2 - \frac{\left(\sum_{i=1}^{n} x_i\right)^2}{n}$$

The required summations can be obtained from the following table.

Month	x	y	xy	x^2	y^2
1	1	30	30	1	900
2	3	40	120	9	1,600
3	5	40	200	25	1,600
4	4	50	200	16	2,500
5	2	35	70	4	1,225
6	5	50	250	25	2,500
7	3	35	105	9	1,225
8	2	25	50	4	625
Totals	25	305	1,025	93	12,175

Thus,

$$\text{cov}(X, Y) = \frac{\sum(x_i - \bar{x})(y_i - \bar{y})}{n - 1}$$

$$= \frac{1}{n - 1}\left[\sum x_i y_i - \frac{\sum x_i \sum y_i}{n}\right]$$

$$= \frac{1}{7}\left[1,025 - \frac{(25)(305)}{8}\right]$$

$$= 10.268$$

Using the second shortcut formula given earlier, we obtain

$$s_x^2 = \frac{\sum(x_i - \bar{x})^2}{n - 1} = \frac{1}{n - 1}\left[\sum x_i^2 - \frac{(\sum x_i)^2}{n}\right]$$

$$= \frac{1}{7}\left[93 - \frac{(25)^2}{8}\right] = 2.125$$

and

$$s_y^2 = \frac{1}{n - 1}\left[\sum y_i^2 - \frac{(\sum y_i)^2}{n}\right] = \frac{1}{7}\left[12,175 - \frac{(305)^2}{8}\right] = 78.125$$

Taking square roots, we obtain $s_x = 1.458$ and $s_y = 8.839$. The coefficient of correlation is therefore

$$r = \frac{\text{cov}(x, y)}{s_x s_y}$$

$$= \frac{10.268}{(1.458)(8.839)} = .797$$

Excel Output for Example 4.14

	A	B	C
1		Advert	Sales
2	Advert	2.125	
3	Sales	10.268	78.125

Excel prints the sample covariance and variances. Thus, the sample covariance is cov $(X, Y) = 10.268$, $s_x^2 = 2.125$ and $s_y^2 = 78.125$.

COMMANDS	COMMANDS FOR EXAMPLE 4.14
1 Type or import the data into two columns.	Open file **XM02-04**.
2 Click **Tools, Data Analysis . . .** , and **Covariance**.	
3 Specify the coordinates of the data.	**A1:B9**

	A	B	C
1		*Advert*	*Sales*
2	Advert		1	
3	Sales	0.7969	1

From the output, we observe that $r = .7969$.

COMMANDS

Repeat the steps above, except click **Correlation** instead of **Covariance.**

Minitab Output for Example 4.14

Covariances

	Advert	Sales
Advert	2.125	
Sales	10.268	78.125

Correlations (Pearson)
Correlation of Advert and Sales = 0.797, P-Value = 0.018

Minitab prints the sample covariance and variances. Thus, the sample covariance is $cov(X, Y) = 10.268$ $s_x = 2.125$ and $s_y = 78.125$. The correlation between X and Y is .797.

COMMANDS

1 Type or import the data into two columns.
2 Click **Stat, Basic Statistics,** and **Covariance . . . .**
3 Type the variable names. Click **OK.**
4 Repeat steps 2 and 3 using **Correlation . . .** instead of **Covariance . . . .**

COMMANDS FOR EXAMPLE 4.14

Open file **XM04-14**.

Advert and **Sales** or **C1** and **C2**

LEAST SQUARES METHOD

In Section 2.5, we discussed the use of a scatter diagram to depict graphically the relationship between two quantitative variables, such as advertising expenditure and sales level. We then briefly introduced the least squares lines as the line that provides the *best possible fit,* with the line being written as

$$\hat{y} = b_0 + b_1 x$$

where b_0 is the y-intercept, and b_1 is the slope of the line.

We can define what we mean by *best* in various ways. For example, we can draw the line that minimizes the sum of the differences between the line and the points. Because some of the differences will be positive (points above the line), and others will be negative (points below the line), a canceling effect might produce a straight line that does not fit the data at all. To eliminate having positive and negative differences, we will draw the line that minimizes the sum of *squared* differences.

That is, we want to determine the line that minimizes

$$\sum_{i=1}^{n} (y_i - \hat{y}_i)^2$$

where y_i represents an observed value of y, and $\hat{y}_i$ represents the value of y calculated from the equation of the line. That is,

$$\hat{y}_i = b_0 + b_1 x_i$$

The technique that produces this line is called the **least squares method.** The line itself is called the **least squares line,** the **fitted line,** or the **regression line.** The coefficients b_0 and b_1 can be computed from the sample data.

By using calculus, we can produce formulas for b_0 and b_1. Although we're sure that you are keenly interested in the calculus derivation of the formulas, we will not provide them, because we promised to keep the mathematics to a minimum. Instead, we offer the following, which were derived by calculus.

Calculation of b_0 and b_1

$$b_1 = \frac{\sum_{i=1}^{n} (x_i - \bar{x})(y_i - \bar{y})}{\sum_{i=1}^{n} (x_i - \bar{x})^2}$$

$$b_0 = \bar{y} - b_1 \bar{x}$$

where

$$\bar{y} = \frac{\sum_{i=1}^{n} y_i}{n} \quad \text{and} \quad \bar{x} = \frac{\sum_{i=1}^{n} x_i}{n}$$

The denominator in the formula for b_1 should look familiar; it is the numerator in the calculation of sample variance s^2. The numerator in the formula for b_1 also should look familiar; it is the numerator in the calculation of covariance (introduced earlier in this section). Thus, by dividing both the numerator and the denominator in the formula for b_1 by $(n - 1)$, we obtain the following relationship between b_1 (the slope of the least squares line) and the covariance between X and Y.

$$b_1 = \frac{\sum_{i=1}^{n} (x_i - \bar{x})(y_i - \bar{y})/(n - 1)}{\sum_{i=1}^{n} (x_i - \bar{x})^2/(n - 1)}$$

$$= \frac{\text{cov}(X, Y)}{s_x^2}$$

As was the case with covariance and the coefficient of correlation, calculating the least squares statistics manually in any realistic example is extremely time consuming. Naturally, we recommend the use of statistical software to produce the statistics we need. However, it may be worthwhile to perform the calculations manually for several small-sample problems. Such efforts may provide you with insights into the working of least squares analysis. To that end, you may find it helpful to use the two shortcut formulas provided earlier in this section (page 129). The first formula provides a shortcut for calculating the numerator of b_1, while the second formula provides a shortcut for calculating the denominator of b_1.

Shortcut Formula for b_1

$$b_1 = \frac{\sum x_i y_i - \dfrac{\sum x_i \sum y_i}{n}}{\sum x_i^2 - \dfrac{(\sum x_i)^2}{n}}$$

As you can see from the shortcut formulas, to estimate the least squares coefficients by hand, we need to determine the following summations.

Sum of x: $\sum x_i$

Sum of y: $\sum y_i$

Sum of x-squared: $\sum x_i^2$

Sum of x times y: $\sum x_i y_i$

Returning to Example 4.14, we find

$$\sum x_i = 25$$
$$\sum y_i = 305$$
$$\sum x_i^2 = 93$$
$$\sum x_i y_i = 1,025$$

Using these summations in our shortcut formulas, we find

$$\sum x_i^2 - \frac{(\sum x_i)^2}{n} = 93 - \frac{(25)^2}{8} = 14.875$$

and

$$\sum x_i y_i - \frac{\sum x_i \sum y_i}{n} = 1,025 - \frac{(25)(305)}{8} = 71.875$$

Dividing this last shortcut formula by the previous one, we calculate

$$b_1 = \frac{71.875}{14.875} = 4.832$$

and

$$b_0 = \bar{y} - b_1 \bar{x} = \frac{305}{8} - 4.832 \left(\frac{25}{8} \right) = 23.025$$

Thus, the least squares line is

$$\hat{y} = 23.025 + 4.832x$$

Figure 4.9 depicts the least squares (or regression) line. As you can see, the line fits the data quite well. We can measure how well by computing the value of the minimized sum of squared differences. The differences between the actual data points and the line are called **residuals,** denoted r_i. That is,

$$r_i = y_i - \hat{y}_i$$

The least squares line has been constructed to minimize the sum of the squared residuals.

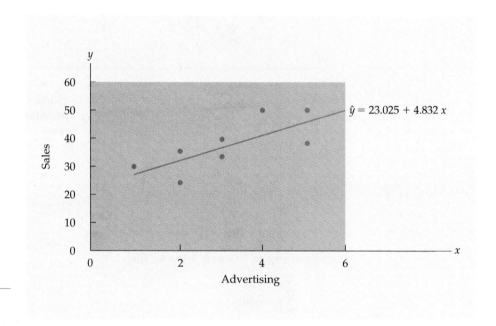

Figure 4.9

Scatter diagram with least squares line: Example 4.14

The residuals are the observed values of the error variable. Consequently, the minimized sum of squared differences is called the **sum of squares for error,** denoted SSE.

Sum of Squares for Error

$$SSE = \sum(y_i - \hat{y}_i)^2$$

The calculation of the residuals in this example is shown in Figure 4.10. Notice that we compute $\hat{y}_i$ by substituting x_i into the formula for the regression line. The residuals are the differences between the observed values y_i and the computed values $\hat{y}_i$. The following table describes the calculation of SSE.

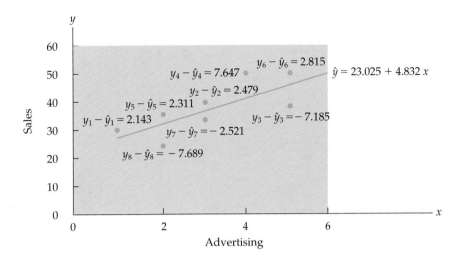

Figure 4.10

Calculation of residuals:
Example 4.14

i	x_i	y_i	$\hat{y}_i = 23.025 + 4.832x_i$	Residual $y_i - \hat{y}_i$	Residual Squared $(y_i - \hat{y}_i)^2$
1	1	30	27.857	2.143	4.592
2	3	40	37.521	2.479	6.145
3	5	40	47.185	−7.185	51.624
4	4	50	42.353	7.647	58.477
5	2	35	32.689	2.311	5.341
6	5	50	47.185	2.815	7.924
7	3	35	37.521	−2.521	6.355
8	2	25	32.689	−7.689	59.121

$$\sum(y_i - \hat{y}_i)^2 = 199.579$$

Thus, SSE = 199.579. No other straight line will produce a sum of squared errors as small as 199.579. In that sense, the regression line fits the data best. The sum of squares for error is an important statistic because it is the basis for other statistics that assess how well the linear model fits the data. We will introduce these statistics later, in Chapter 17.

As mentioned earlier, the use of statistical software is recommended to determine the coefficients b_0 and b_1 for the least squares line (as well as other statistics that we'll discuss in Chapter 17.) For this reason, we next provide the Excel and Minitab commands that produce these coefficients. We show only a portion of the printouts here, however, because the printouts include many more (regression) statistics than we need right now. Regression will be discussed in detail in Chapter 17.

Excel Output for Example 4.14

	A	B	C	D	E
1	SUMMARY OUTPUT				
2					
3	*Regression Statistics*				
4	Multiple R	0.7969			
5	R Square	0.6351			
6	Adjusted R Square	0.5742			
7	Standard Error	5.77			
8	Observations	8			
9					
10		*Coefficients*	*Standard Error*	*t Stat*	*P-value*
11	Intercept	23.025	5.10	4.52	0.0040
12	Advertising	4.832	1.50	3.23	0.0179

COMMANDS

1 Type or import the data into two columns.
2 Click **Tools, Data Analysis . . . ,** and **Regression.**
3 Specify **Input Y Range.**
4 Specify **Input X Range.** Click **OK.** Click **Labels** (if necessary).
5 To draw the scatter diagram click **Line Fit Plots** before clicking **OK.**

COMMANDS FOR EXAMPLE 4.14

Open file **XM02-04.**

B1:B9

A1:A9

(You can also draw the scatter diagram using the commands described in Chapter 2.)

Minitab Output for Example 4.14

Regression Analysis.
```
The regression equation is
Sales = 23.025 + 4.832 Advert

Predictor      Coef      StDev        T          P
Constant     23.025     5.099      4.52      0.004
Advert        4.832     1.495      3.23      0.018

S = 5.767   R-Sq = 63.5%   R-Sq(adj) = 57.4%
```

COMMANDS

1 Type or import the data into two columns.
2 Click **Stat, Regression,** and **Regression . . .**
3 Type the name of the dependent (**Response**) variable.
4 Hit **tab,** and type the name of the independent (**Predictors**) variable. Click **OK.**

COMMANDS FOR EXAMPLE 4.14

Open file **XM02-04.**

Sales or **C2**

Advert or **C1**

INTERPRET

The coefficient b_i is 4.832, which means that for each additional $1,000 spent on advertising, sales will increase by an average of $4,832.

The intercept is $b_0 = 23.025$. Technically, the intercept is the point at which the least squares line and the y-axis intersect. This means that when $x = 0$ (i.e., nothing at all was spent on advertising) the sales level is $23,025. We might be tempted to interpret this number as the sales level when nothing is spent on advertising. However, this intercept value may not be meaningful. Because our sample did not include any months with zero dollars spent on advertising, we have no sound basis for interpreting b_0. As a general rule, we cannot determine the value of y for a value of x that is far outside the range of the sample values of x. In this example, the smallest and largest values of x are $1,000 and $5,000, respectively. Because $x = 0$ is not in this interval, we cannot safely interpret the value of y when $x = 0$.

Notice that the R-square value is .635, which is the square of the correlation coefficient $r = .797$, as we observed earlier on page 130.

▲

EXERCISES

4.67 For the following sample, manually calculate the covariance and the coefficient of correlation.

x	3	6	5	9	4
y	9	12	13	16	11

4.68 Given the following six observations of variable x and y, determine manually the straight line that fits these data.

x	2	4	8	10	13	16
y	2	7	25	26	38	50

4.69 Given the following six points:

x	−5	−2	0	3	4	7
y	15	9	7	6	4	1

a Draw the scatter diagram.
b Determine the least squares line.

4.70 Given the following data:

x	115	220	86	99	50	110
y	1.0	1.3	0.6	0.8	0.5	0.7

a Draw the scatter diagram.
b Determine the least squares line.
c Calculate the covariance and the correlation coefficient, and comment on the relationship between x and y.

4.71 The observation of two variables was recorded as shown below.

x	1	2	3	4	5	6	7	8	9
y	5	28	17	14	27	33	39	26	30

a Draw the scatter diagram.
b Find the least squares line.
c Calculate the covariance and the coefficient of correlation, and comment on the relationship between x and y.

4.72 The weekly returns of two stocks are recorded for a 13-week period. These data are stored in file XR04-72 and listed below.

Week	Stock 1	Stock 2
1	−7	6
2	−4	6
3	−7	−4
4	−3	9
5	2	3
6	−10	−3
7	−10	7
8	5	−3
9	1	4
10	−4	7
11	2	9
12	6	5
13	−13	−7

a Draw the scatter diagram.
b Calculate the correlation coefficient.
c What does the correlation tell you about the relationship between the returns of these two stocks?

STATISTICS IN THE WORKPLACE

Marketing Application

As mentioned in the introduction to marketing management, **pricing** a product (or service) effectively is a difficult task. Supply and demand conditions must first be analyzed, and the current state of the economy must be considered. Pricing an entirely new type of product is the most difficult of all, because meaningful comparisons with other products are not available. Some companies rely on consumer surveys to gather information regarding consumers' attitudes toward a new product and its suggested price. In the case of an existing product such as a house or car, however, historical data may be used to assess the relationship between a characteristic of a product (such as house size or car odometer reading) and its selling price. In Chapter 18, we extend this type of analysis to consider the relationship between selling price and a set of two or more characteristics of the product.

4.73 A real estate agent wanted to know to what extent the selling price of a house is related to the number of square feet in the house. He took a sample of 15 homes that had recently sold, recording the price and size. These data are listed here and stored in file XR04-73.

a Compute the covariance and coefficient of correlation to measure how the two variables are related, and comment on the relationship.

b Draw the scatter diagram and plot the least squares line.

House size (100 ft^2)	Selling price ($1,000s)
20.0	219
14.8	190

House size (100 ft^2)	Selling price ($1,000s)
20.5	199
12.5	121
18.0	150
14.3	198
24.9	334
16.5	188
24.3	310
20.2	213
22.0	288
19.0	312
12.3	186
14.0	173
16.7	174

STATISTICS IN THE WORKPLACE

Accounting Application

A firm's operating costs can be classified as fixed, variable, or mixed. *Variable* costs (such as sales commissions) are those costs that vary in direct proportion to changes in the level of activity (such as production). *Fixed* costs (such as managerial salaries) are those costs that do not change with changes in the level of activity. Costs for items such as telephone, electrical power, and maintenance are often *mixed* costs, meaning they have both a fixed cost and variable cost component.

For planning purposes, companies prepare budgets, which include forecasts of future sales revenues. The associated costs are often estimated by a cost *function*, which expresses the relationship between a cost and some measure of the level of activity creating that cost. A total cost function is estimated from historical data and is assumed to take the linear form $y = b_0 + b_1x$. The coefficient b_0 estimates the fixed cost and b_1x the variable cost over the relevant range of activity (namely, the range of sample values for x). The following three exercises illustrate the estimation of a cost function.

The following exercises require the use of a computer and statistical software.

4.74 Refer to Exercise 2.42 (page 60), which considers the relationship between a manufacturing firm's cost of electrical power (Y) and hours of machine time (X). The monthly data are stored in file XR02-42.

  a Compute cov(X, Y) and r, and describe what these statistics tell you about the relationship between X and Y.

  b Determine the least squares line.

  c Use the line from part (b) to estimate the monthly fixed cost of power and the variable cost of power per thousand hours of machine time.

4.75 Refer to Exercise 2.43 (page 60), which considers the relationship between a firm's total selling expenses (Y) and total sales (X). The monthly data are stored in file XR02-43.

  a Compute cov(X, Y) and r, and describe what these statistics tell you about the relationship between X and Y.

  b Determine the least squares line.

  c Use the line from part (b) to estimate the monthly fixed selling expense and the variable selling expense per thousand dollars of sales.

4.76 Refer to Exercise 2.44 (page 60), which considers the relationship between direct labor costs (Y) and the number of units produced per batch (X). The data for 30 batches are stored in file XR02-44.

  a Compute cov(X, Y) and r, and describe what these statistics tell you about the relationship between X and Y.

  b Determine the least squares line.

  c Use the line from part (b) to estimate the fixed labor cost and variable cost per units per batch.

4.77 The data for 50 observations of variables X and Y are stored in columns 1 and 2, respectively, in file XR04-77. Determine the covariance and the correlation coefficient between X and Y, and interpret their meaning.

4.78 In television's early years, most commercials were 60 seconds long. Now, however, commercials can be any length. The objective of commercials remains the same—to have as many viewers as possible remember the product in a favorable way and eventually buy it. In an experiment to determine how the length of a commercial affects people's memory of it, 60 randomly selected people were asked to watch a 1-hour television program. In the middle of the show, a commercial advertising a brand of toothpaste appeared. Each viewer watched a commercial whose length varied between 20 and 60 seconds. The essential content of the commercials was the same. After the show, each person was given a test to measure how much he or she remembered about the product. The commercial times and test scores (on a 30-point test) are stored in file XR04-78. Some of the data are shown below.

  a Draw a scatter diagram of the data to determine whether a linear model appears to be appropriate.

  b Compute the covariance and correlation coefficient, and comment on the relationship between the variables.

  c Interpret the coefficients.

Respondent	Length of commercial	Memory test score
1	52	24
2	40	20
3	36	16
.	.	.
.	.	.
.	.	.
60	48	21

4.79 Refer to Exercise 2.45, which considers the relationship between common-stock returns (Y) and inflation (X). The annual common-stock returns and the annual inflation rates from 1985 to 1994 were stored in columns 1 and 2, respectively, in file XR02-45.

  a Compute cov(X, Y) and r.

  b What do these statistics tell you about the relationship between common-stock returns and inflation?

4.80 Refer to Exercise 2.46, where the annual common-stock returns (Y) and the annual inflation rates (X) from 1960 to 1994 were stored in columns 1 and 2, respectively, in file XR02-46.

  a Compute cov(X, Y) and r.

  b What do these statistics tell you about the relationship between common-stock returns and inflation over this long period?

  c Does it appear that common stocks provide a good hedge against inflation?

4.81 Refer to Exercise 2.47, which considered the relationship between the monthly returns on an individual stock (R) and the monthly returns on the overall stock market (R_m). The monthly returns on American Barrick Resources and on the overall stock market were stored in columns 1 and 2, respectively, in file XR02-47.

  a Compute cov(R, R_m) and r.

  b What do these statistics tell you about the relationship between returns on American Barrick Resources and returns on the overall stock market?

4.82 Refer to Exercise 2.48. Based on the data in file XR02-48, what can you say about the relationship between house sales and mortgage rates over that 3-year period?

4.8 GENERAL GUIDELINES ON THE EXPLORATION OF DATA

The purpose of applying graphical and numerical techniques is to describe and summarize data. Statisticians usually apply graphical techniques as a first step because we need to know the shape of the distribution. The shape of the distribution helps answer the following questions.

1 Where is the approximate center of the distribution?
2 Are the observations close to one another, or are they widely dispersed?
3 Is the distribution unimodal, bimodal, or multimodal? If there is more than one mode, where are the peaks, and where are the valleys?
4 Is the distribution symmetric? If not, is it skewed? If symmetric, is it bell shaped?

Histograms, stem and leaf displays, dot plots, and box plots provide most of the answers. We can frequently make several inferences about the nature of the data from the shape. For example, we can assess the relative risk of investments by noting their spreads. We can attempt to improve the teaching of a course by examining whether the distribution of final grades is bimodal or skewed.

The shape can also provide some guidance on which numerical techniques to use. As we noted in this chapter, the central location of highly skewed data may be more appropriately measured by the median. We may also choose to use the interquartile range instead of the standard deviation to describe the spread of skewed data.

When we have an understanding of the structure of the data, we may proceed to further analysis. For example, we often want to determine how one variable, or several variables, affects another. Scatter diagrams, covariance, and the coefficient of correlation are useful techniques for detecting relationships between variables. A number of techniques to be introduced later in this book will help uncover the nature of these associations.

4.9 SUMMARY

This chapter extended our discussion of **descriptive statistics,** which deals with methods of summarizing and presenting the essential information contained in a set of data. After constructing a frequency distribution to obtain a general idea about the distribution of a data set, we can use numerical measures to describe the central location and the dispersion of the data. Three popular measures of central location, or averages, are the **mean,** the **median,** and the **mode.** Taken by themselves, these measures provide an inadequate description of the data because they say nothing about the extent to which the data are dispersed about their central value. Information regarding the dispersion, or variability, of the data is conveyed by such numerical measures as the **range,** the **interquartile range, variance, standard deviation,** and **coefficient of variation.**

For the special case in which a sample of measurements has a mound-shaped distribution, the **Empirical Rule** provides a good approximation of the percentages of measurements that fall within 1, 2, or 3 standard deviations of the mean. Beginning in Chapter 9, you will learn how these two important descriptive measures (mean and standard deviation), computed for a sample of measurements, can be combined to support inferences about the mean and the standard deviation of the population from which the sample was taken.

This chapter also included an introduction to **box plots,** as well as to **covariance** and the **coefficient of correlation,** which are used to measure the relationship between two variables.

IMPORTANT TERMS

Measures of central location   *90*
Mean   *91*
Median   *93*
Mode   *94*
Skewed   *95*
Modal class   *98*
Geometric mean   *100*
Rate of return   *100*
Measures of variability   *102*
Range   *103*
Variance   *105*
Standard deviation   *107*
Coefficient of variation   *110*
Empirical Rule   *113*
Range approximation   *115*

Chebyshev's theorem   *115*
Percentiles   *118*
Quartiles   *118*
Deciles   *118*
Interquartile range   *119*
Box plots   *119*
Outlier   *120, 123*
Measures of association   *126*
Covariance   *126*
Coefficient of correlation   *126*
Least squares method   *132*
Least squares (regression) line   *132*
Residuals   *134*
Sum of squares for error   *134*

SUMMARY OF FORMULAS

Population mean: $\mu = \dfrac{\sum_{i=1}^{N} x_i}{N}$

Sample mean: $\bar{x} = \dfrac{\sum_{i=1}^{n} x_i}{n}$

Population variance: $\sigma^2 = \dfrac{\sum_{i=1}^{N}(x_i - \mu)^2}{N}$

Sample variance: $s^2 = \dfrac{\sum_{i=1}^{n} (x_i - \bar{x})^2}{n - 1}$

Population standard deviation: $\sigma = \sqrt{\sigma^2}$

Sample standard deviation: $s = \sqrt{s^2}$

Population coefficient of variation: $CV = \dfrac{\sigma}{\mu}$

Sample coefficient of variation: $cv = \dfrac{s}{\bar{x}}$

Population covariance: $COV(X,Y) = \dfrac{\sum(x_i - \mu_x)(y_i - \mu_y)}{N}$

Sample covariance: $cov(X, Y) = \dfrac{\sum(x_i - \bar{x})(y_i - \bar{y})}{n - 1}$

$$\text{Population coefficient of correlation: } \rho = \frac{COV(X, Y)}{\sigma_x \sigma_y}$$

$$\text{Sample coefficient of correlation: } r = \frac{cov(X, Y)}{s_x s_y}$$

SUPPLEMENTARY EXERCISES

4.83 Determine the mean, the median, and the standard deviation of the following sample of data.

43 46 44 55 59 48 44 50 40 54 52 42

4.84 Consider the following population of measurements.

11 −1 5 2 8 7 12 4 −6 −10 1 5

  a Find the mean, the median, and the standard deviation of this population of measurements.
  b Find the upper and lower quartiles of these measurements.

4.85 The number of items rejected daily by a manufacturer because of defects was recorded for the last 25 days. The results are as follows.

21 8 17 22 19 18 19 14 17 11 6
21 25 19 9 12 16 16 10 29 24 6 21
20 25

Find the median, the mode, $\bar{x}$, s^2, and s for these data.

4.86 Refer to Exercise 4.85.

  a Construct a frequency distribution for these data. Use five class intervals, with the lower boundary of the first class being five items.
  b What proportion of items falls into the interval $\bar{x} \pm 2s$?
  c Does it appear that the population from which this sample was taken has a mound-shaped distribution?
  d Compare the actual proportions of items falling into the intervals $(\bar{x} - s, \bar{x} + s)$ and $(\bar{x} - 2s, \bar{x} + 2s)$ with the proportions suggested by the Empirical Rule.

4.87 The ages of a sample of 25 brokers were recorded as follows.

50 64 32 55 41 44 24 46 58 47
36 52 54 44 66 47 59 51 61 57 49
28 42 38 45

  a Construct a stem and leaf display for the ages.
  b Find the median age.
  c Find the lower quartile of the ages.
  d Find the upper quartile of the ages.
  e Find the 80th percentile of the ages.
  f Does this firm have reason to be concerned about the distribution of ages of its brokers?

4.88 Refer to Exercise 4.87.

  a Compute the mean of the sample of data.
  b Compute the variance of the sample of data.
  c Compute the standard deviation of the sample of data.

4.89 Refer to Exercise 4.87.

  a Compute the range of the data.
  b Compute the range approximation to the standard deviation of the data.

4.90 Refer to Exercise 4.87.

  a Construct a histogram for the data, using five class intervals and the value 20 as the lower limit of the first class.
  b Locate the interval $\bar{x} \pm s$ on the histogram, and find the proportion of ages that fall in this interval. How does this proportion compare with the Empirical Rule approximation?

4.91 Refer to Exercise 4.87.

  a Construct a box plot for the brokers' ages.
  b Does the distribution of the ages appear to be symmetric or skewed? Explain.

4.92 In the last few years, North American car makers have significantly improved the quality of their products. To determine the degree of improvement, a survey of 200 new cars was undertaken. The number of minor flaws (e.g., slightly misaligned doors, improperly directed headlights) was recorded. These data and the data from a similar survey 5 years ago are stored in column 1 and column 2, respectively, in file XR04-92.

  a Use a graphical technique of your choosing to compare the two sets of data.
  b Use numerical techniques of your choosing to compare the two sets of data.
  c Briefly describe what you've learned from your statistical analysis.

4.93 Refer to Exercise 2.53, where the head coach of an NFL football team was trying to decide between three candidates for the position of punter. He has recorded the distances of the last 100 punts for each of the three candidates and stored them in columns 1 to 3 of file XR02-53.

  a Use numerical statistical techniques to describe each sample.
  b Using the statistics produced in part (a), provide the head coach with your recommendation.

4.94 Refer to Exercise 2.55, which dealt with the returns on five mutual funds stored in file XR02-55.

  a Use numerical statistical techniques to describe the five samples.
  b Briefly discuss the ways in which you would judge the "best" fund.

4.95 Slow play on golf courses frustrates most golfers and costs owners thousands of dollars annually. To find ways to speed up the game, the manager of one course undertook a study. The amount of time to complete a round of golf taken by samples of four different groups of golf foursomes was observed and recorded in file XR04-95 using the following format.

Column 1: time taken by four men without electric carts
Column 2: time taken by four men with electric carts
Column 3: time taken by four women without electric carts
Column 4: time taken by four women with electric carts

a For each sample, perform the following analyses.
  i Draw the histogram.
  ii Calculate the mean and median.
  iii Calculate the standard deviation.
  iv Draw the box plot.
b Interpret your findings, and describe the similarities and differences among the four groups.

4.96 A growing concern for educators in the United States is the number of teenagers who have part-time jobs while they attend high school. It is generally believed that the amount of time teenagers spend working is deducted from the amount of time devoted to schoolwork. To investigate this problem, a school guidance counselor took a random sample of 200 fifteen-year-old high school students and asked how many hours per week each worked at a part-time job. The results were recorded and stored in file XR04-96.

a Calculate whatever descriptive numerical measures you think necessary to describe the data in the sample.
b Interpret each numerical measure produced.

4.97 Refer to Exercise 2.56, where the amount of time behind schedule was recorded for the last 250 departures for each of five airlines and stored in columns 1 through 5 of file XR02-56.

a Use numerical descriptive measures to describe the behind-schedule times for each airline.
b Briefly discuss what each numerical measure tells you.
c Which airline is best at adhering to its schedule? Explain.

4.98 Refer to Exercise 2.62, where the credit scores for good and bad loans were recorded in file XR02-62. Use numerical descriptive measures and box plots to help present a report to the bank's board of directors who asked you to discuss how well the scorecard works.

4.99 The relationship between the level of an individual's education and his or her income was considered in Exercise 2.65. The incomes of 1,000 people are stored in file XR02-65 using the following format: Column i contains the incomes of those belonging to education category i (i=1, . . . , 5), where the 5 categories are described in Exercise 2.65.

a Without performing any computations, which category would you expect to have the highest mean income? The highest standard deviation? Explain your answers.
b Compute the mean and standard deviation of the incomes for each category. Compare the results with your answer to part (a).

4.100 Refer to Exercise 2.41, which considered the relationship between the number of houses sold *(Y)* and the mortgage rate *(X)*. The values of X and Y for each of 12 months (as shown in Exercise 2.41) are stored in columns 1 and 2, respectively, in file XR02-41.

a Compute cov*(X, Y)* and r.
b What do these statistics tell you about the relationship between the level of house sales and mortgage rates based on these data?

4.101 The annual percentage rates of return earned on money invested in a certain mutual fund for each of seven years is shown in the table.

a Find the geometric mean return over this period. (Round your answer to one decimal place.)
b Find the arithmetic mean return over this period.
c If you had invested $10,000 in this fund at the beginning of 1993, what would the investment be worth at the end of 1999?
d Based on these data, what is your best estimate of what the return on this fund will be in 2000?

Year	Return (%)
1993	9.6
1994	−2.4
1995	14.0
1996	24.6
1997	12.7
1998	−6.3
1999	−3.2

4.102 According to the *National Post* (28 October 1998), the average salaries (in U. S. dollars) of players in the National Hockey League (NHL) for seven seasons were as shown in the table.

a Compute the percentage increase in the average salary over the previous year for each of the seven seasons from 1991–92 to 1997–98. (Round answers to one decimal place.)
b Find the arithmetic mean of the annual percentage changes in the average salary.
c Find the geometric mean of the annual percentage changes in the average salary.
d What is your best estimate of the average salary for the 1998–99 season?
e Consider an NHL player whose salary was $200,000 for the 1990–91 season and $1,000,000 for the 1997–98 season. Find the average annual growth rate in this player's salary, and compare it to the growth rate in the average salary over this period.

Season	Average salary ($)
1990–91	271,000
1991–92	368,000
1992–93	467,000
1993–94	572,161
1994–95	733,000
1995–96	892,000
1996–97	984,500
1997–98	1,167,713

Appendix 4.A

Summation Notation

This appendix offers an introduction to the use of summation notation. Because summation notation is used extensively throughout statistics, you should review this appendix even if you've had previous exposure to summation notation. Our coverage of the topic begins with an introduction to the necessary terminology and notation, follows with some examples, and concludes with four rules that are useful in applying summation notation.

Consider n numbers $x_1, x_2, \ldots, x_n$. A concise way of representing their sum is

$$\sum_{i=1}^{n} x_i$$

That is,

$$\sum_{i=1}^{n} x_i = x_1 + x_2 + \cdots + x_n$$

NOTATION AND TERMINOLOGY

1 The symbol $\sum$ is the capital Greek letter sigma and means "the sum of."

2 The letter i is called the *index of summation*. The letter chosen to represent the index of summation is arbitrary.

3 The expression $\sum_{i=1}^{n} x_i$ is read "the sum of the terms x_i, where i assumes the values from 1 to n inclusive."

4 The numbers 1 and n are called the *lower* and the *upper limits of summation*, respectively.

Summation notation is best illustrated by means of examples.

▼ **EXAMPLES**

1 Suppose $x_1 = 5$, $x_2 = 6$, $x_3 = 8$, and $x_4 = 10$.

a $\displaystyle\sum_{i=1}^{4} x_i = x_1 + x_2 + x_3 + x_4 = 5 + 6 + 8 + 10 = 29$

b $\displaystyle\sum_{i=3}^{4} x_i = x_3 + x_4 = 8 + 10 = 18$

c $\displaystyle\sum_{i=1}^{2} x_i(x_i - 1) = x_1(x_1 - 1) + x_2(x_2 - 1)$
$$= 5(5 - 1) + 6(6 - 1)$$
$$= 50$$

d $\sum_{i=1}^{3} f(x_i) = f(x_1) + f(x_2) + f(x_3)$

$$= f(5) + f(6) + f(8)$$

2 Suppose $x_1 = 2$, $x_2 = 3$, $x_3 = 4$, $y_1 = 8$, $y_2 = 9$, and $y_3 = 13$.

a $\sum_{i=1}^{3} x_i y_i = x_1 y_1 + x_2 y_2 + x_3 y_3$

$$= 2(8) + 3(9) + 4(13)$$

$$= 95$$

b $\sum_{i=2}^{3} x_i y_i^2 = x_2 y_2^2 + x_3 y_3^2$

$$= 3(9^2) + 4(13^2)$$

$$= 919$$

c $\sum_{i=1}^{2} (x_i - y_i) = (x_1 - y_1) + (x_2 - y_2)$

$$= (2 - 8) + (3 - 9)$$

$$= -12$$

It is not necessary that the index of summation be a subscript, as the following examples demonstrate.

▲

Examples

1 $\sum_{x=0}^{4} x = 0 + 1 + 2 + 3 + 4 = 10$

2 $\sum_{x=1}^{3} (x^2 - x) = (1^2 - 1) + (2^2 - 2) + (3^2 - 3) = 8$

3 $\sum_{x=1}^{2} 5x = 5(1) + 5(2) = 15$

4 $\sum_{x=0}^{3} f(x) = f(0) + f(1) + f(2) + f(3)$

5 $\sum_{x=1}^{2} f(x, y) = f(1, y) + f(2, y)$

6 $\sum_{y=3}^{5} f(x, y^2) = f(x, 3^2) + f(x, 4^2) + f(x, 5^2)$

▲

RULES OF SUMMATION NOTATION

1 If c is a constant, then

$$\sum_{i=1}^{n} c x_i = c \sum_{i=1}^{n} x_i$$

2 If c is a constant, then

$$\sum_{x=1}^{n} c = nc$$

3 If a and b are constants, then

$$\sum_{i=1}^{n} (ax_i + by_i) = a \sum_{i=1}^{n} x_i + b \sum_{i=1}^{n} y_i$$

4 If c is a constant, then

$$\sum_{i=1}^{n} (x_i + c) = \sum_{i=1}^{n} x_i + nc$$

Notice that

$$\sum_{i=1}^{n} x_i^2 \neq \left(\sum_{i=1}^{n} x_i \right)^2$$

To verify this, observe that

$$\sum_{i=1}^{n} x_i^2 = x_1^2 + x_2^2 + \cdots + x_n^2$$

while

$$\left(\sum_{i=1}^{n} x_i \right)^2 = (x_1 + x_2 + \cdots + x_n)^2$$

EXERCISES

1 Evaluate $\displaystyle\sum_{i=1}^{5} (i^2 + 2i)$.

2 Evaluate $\displaystyle\sum_{x=0}^{2} (x^3 + 2x)$.

3 Using the accompanying set of measurements, evaluate the following sums.

a $\displaystyle\sum_{i=1}^{13} x_i$

b $\displaystyle\sum_{i=1}^{13} (2x_i + 5)$

c $\displaystyle\sum_{i=1}^{6} (x_i - 5)^2$

i	1	2	3	4	5	6	7	8	9	10	11	12	13
x_i	3	12	10	−6	0	11	2	−9	−5	8	−7	4	−5

Chapter **5**

Data Collection

and Sampling

5.1 Introduction

5.2 Sources of Data

5.3 Sampling

5.4 Sampling Plans

5.5 Errors Involved in Sampling

5.6 Use of Sampling in Auditing (Optional)

5.7 Summary

5.1 INTRODUCTION

In Chapter 1, we briefly introduced the concept of statistical inference—the process of inferring information about a population from a sample. Because information about populations can usually be described by parameters, the statistical technique used generally deals with drawing inferences about population parameters from sample statistics. (Recall that a parameter is a measurement about a population, and a statistic is a measurement about a sample.)

Working within the covers of a statistics textbook, we can assume that population parameters are known. In real life, however, calculating parameters becomes prohibitive because populations tend to be quite large. As a result, most population parameters are unknown. For example, in order to determine the mean annual income of North American blue-collar workers, we would have to ask each North American blue-collar worker what his or her income is and then calculate the mean of all the responses. Because this population consists of several million people, the task is both expensive and impractical. If we are willing to accept less than 100% accuracy, we can use statistical inference to obtain an estimate.

Rather than investigating the entire population, we select a sample of workers, determine the annual income of the workers in this group, and calculate the sample mean. While there is very little chance that the sample mean and the population mean are identical, we would expect them to be quite close. However, for the purposes of statistical inference, we need to be able to measure how close the sample mean is likely to be to the population mean. We postpone our discussion about how to do that until Chapters 8 and 9, after we have covered probability. In this chapter, however, we will discuss the basic concepts and techniques of sampling itself. But first we take a look at various sources for collecting data.

5.2 SOURCES OF DATA

The validity of the results of a statistical analysis clearly depends on the reliability and accuracy of the data used. Whether you are actually involved in collecting the data, performing a statistical analysis on the data, or simply reviewing the results of such an analysis, it is important to realize that the reliability and accuracy of the data depend on the method of collection. Three of the most popular sources of statistical data are published data, data collected from observational studies, and data collected from experimental studies.

PUBLISHED DATA

The use of published data is often preferred due to its convenience, relatively low cost, and reliability (assuming that it has been collected by a reputable organization). An enormous amount of published data is produced by government agencies and private organizations, available in printed form, on data tapes and disks, and increasingly on the Internet. Data published by the same organization that collected them are called **primary data.** An example of primary data would be the data published by the United States Bureau of the Census, which collects data on numerous industries as well as conducts the census of the population every 10 years. Statistics Canada is the central statistical agency in Canada, collecting data on almost every aspect of social and economic life in the country. These primary sources of information are invaluable to decision makers in both the government and private sectors.

Secondary data refers to data that are published by an organization different from the one that originally collected and published the data. A popular source of secondary data is *The Statistical Abstract of the United States,* which compiles data from several primary government sources and is updated annually. Another example of a secondary data source is Compustat, which sells a variety of financial data tapes that contain data compiled from such primary sources as the New York Stock Exchange. Care should be taken when using secondary data, because errors may have been introduced as a result of the transcription or due to misinterpretation of the original terminology and definitions employed.

An interesting example of the importance of knowing how data collection agencies define their terms appeared in an article in *The Globe and Mail* (12 February, 1996). The United States and Canada had similar unemployment rates up until the 1980s, at which time Canada's rate started to edge higher than the U.S. rate. By February 1996, the gap had grown to almost four percentage points (9.6% in Canada compared with 5.8% in the United States). Economists from the United States and Canada met for 2 days to compare research results and discuss possible reasons for this puzzling gap in jobless rates. The conference organizer explained that solving this mystery matters because "we have to understand the nature of unemployment to design policies to combat it." An Ohio State University economist was the first to notice a difference in how officials from the two countries define unemployment. "If jobless people say they are searching for work, but do nothing more than read job advertisements in the newspaper, Canada counts them as unemployed. U.S. officials dismiss such 'passive' job hunters and count them as being out of the labour force altogether, so they are not counted among the jobless." Statistics Canada reported that this difference in definitions accounted for almost one-fifth of the difference between the Canadian and U.S. unemployment rates.

OBSERVATIONAL AND EXPERIMENTAL STUDIES

If relevant data are not available from published sources, it may be necessary to generate the data by conducting a study. This will especially be the case when data are needed concerning a specific company or situation. The difference between two important types of studies—observational and experimental—is best illustrated by means of an example.

▼ **EXAMPLE 5.1**

Six months ago, the director of human resources for a large mutual fund company announced that the company had arranged for its salespeople to use a nearby fitness center free of charge. The director believes that fitter salespeople have more energy and an improved appearance, resulting in higher productivity. Interest and participation in the fitness initiative were high initially, but after a few months had passed, several employees stopped participating. Those who continued to exercise were committed to maintaining a good level of fitness, using the fitness center about three times per week on average.

The director recently conducted an **observational study** and determined that the average sales level achieved by those who regularly used the fitness center exceeded that of those who did not use the center. The director was tempted to use the difference in productivity levels to justify the cost to the company of making the fitness center available to employees. But the vice president of finance pointed out that the fitness initiative was not necessarily the cause of the difference in productivity levels. Because the salespeople who exercised were self-selected—they determined themselves whether or not to make use of the fitness center—it is quite likely that the salespeople who used the center were those who were more ambitious and disciplined. These people would probably have had higher levels of fitness and productivity even without the fitness initiative. We therefore cannot necessarily conclude that fitness center usage led to higher productivity. It may be that other factors, such as ambition and discipline, were responsible both for higher fitness center usage and higher productivity.

The director and vice president then discussed the possibility of conducting an **experimental study,** designed to control which salespeople made regular use of the fitness center. The director would randomly select 60 salespeople to participate in the study. Thirty of these would be randomly selected and persuaded to use the fitness center on a regular basis for 6 months. The other 30 salespeople selected would not be approached, but simply would have their sales performances monitored along with those using the fitness center regularly. Because these two groups were selected at random, we would expect them to be fairly similar in terms of original average fitness level, ambition, discipline, age, and other factors that might affect performance. From this experimental study, we would be more confident that any significantly higher level of productivity by the group using the fitness center regularly would be due to the fitness initiative rather than other factors.

▲

The point of the preceding example is to illustrate the difference between an observational study and an experimental (or controlled) study. In the observational study, a survey simply was conducted to observe and record the average sales level for each group, without attempting to control any of the factors that might influence the sales levels. In the experimental study, the director controlled one factor (regular use of the fitness center) by randomly selecting who would be persuaded to use the center regularly, thereby reducing the influence of other factors on the difference between the sales levels of the two groups.

Although experimental studies make it easier to establish a cause-and-effect relationship between two variables, observational studies are used predominantly in business and economics. More often than not, surveys are conducted to collect business and economic data (such as consumer preferences or unemployment statistics), with no attempt to control any factors that might affect the variable of interest.

More will be said about observational and experimental data in Chapter 11. The design and analysis of various experimental studies will be considered in Chapters 12 through 14.

SURVEYS

One of the most familiar methods of collecting primary data is the survey, which solicits information from people concerning such things as their income, family size, and opinions on various issues. We're all familiar, for example, with opinion polls that accompany each political election. The Gallup Poll and the Harris Survey are two well-known surveys of public opinion whose results are often reported by the media. But the majority of surveys are conducted for private use. Private surveys are used extensively by market researchers to determine the preferences and attitudes of consumers and voters. The results can be used for a variety of purposes, from helping to determine the target market for an advertising campaign to modifying a candidate's platform in an election campaign. As an illustration, consider a television network that has hired a market research firm to provide the network with a profile of owners of luxury automobiles, including what they watch on television and at what times. The network could then use this information to develop a package of recommended time slots for Cadillac commercials, including costs, that it would present to General Motors. It is quite likely that many students reading this book will one day be marketing executives who will "live and die" by such market research data.

Many researchers feel that the best way to survey people is by means of a **personal interview,** which involves an interviewer soliciting information from a respondent by asking prepared questions. A personal interview has the advantage of having a higher expected response rate than other methods of data collection. In addition, there will probably be fewer incorrect responses resulting from respondents misunderstanding some questions, because the interviewer can clarify misunderstandings when asked to. But the interviewer must also be careful not to say too much, for fear of biasing the response. To avoid introducing such biases, as well as to reap the potential benefits of a personal interview, the interviewer must be well trained in proper interviewing techniques and well informed on the purpose of the study. The main disadvantage of personal interviews is that they are expensive, especially when travel is involved. A **telephone interview** is usually less expensive, but it is also less personal and has a lower expected response rate. A third popular method of data collection is the **self-administered questionnaire,** which is usually mailed to a sample of people selected to be surveyed. This is a relatively inexpensive method of conducting a survey and is therefore attractive when the number of people to be surveyed is large. But self-administered questionnaires usually have a low response rate and may have a relatively high number of incorrect responses due to respondents misunderstanding some questions.

Whether a questionnaire is self-administered or completed by an interviewer, it must be well designed. Proper questionnaire design takes knowledge, experience, time, and money. Some basic points to consider regarding **questionnaire design** follow.

1 First and foremost, the questionnaire should be kept as short as possible to encourage respondents to complete it. Most people are unwilling to spend much time filling out a questionnaire.

2 The questions themselves should also be short, as well as simply and clearly worded, to enable respondents to answer quickly, correctly, and without ambiguity. Even familiar terms, such as "unemployed" and "family," must be defined carefully because several interpretations are possible.

3 Questionnaires often begin with simple demographic questions to help respondents get started and become comfortable quickly.

4 Dichotomous questions (questions with only two possible responses, such as "yes" and "no") and multiple-choice questions are useful and popular because of their simplicity, but they, too, have possible shortcomings. For example, a respondent's choice of *yes* or *no* to a question may depend on certain assumptions not stated in the question. In the case of a multiple-choice question, a respondent may feel that none of the choices offered is suitable.

5 Open-ended questions provide an opportunity for respondents to express opinions more fully, but they are time consuming and more difficult to tabulate and analyze.

6 Avoid using leading questions, such as "Wouldn't you agree that the statistics exam was too difficult?" These types of questions tend to lead the respondent to a particular answer.

7 Time permitting, it is useful to pretest a questionnaire on a small number of people in order to uncover potential problems, such as ambiguous wording.

8 Finally, when preparing the questions, think about how you intend to tabulate and analyze the responses. First determine whether you are soliciting values (i.e., responses) for a quantitative variable or a qualitative variable. Then consider which type of statistical techniques—descriptive or inferential—you intend to apply to the data to be collected, and note the requirements of the specific techniques to be used. Thinking about these questions will help to ensure that the questionnaire is designed to collect the data you need.

Whatever method is used to collect primary data, we need to know something about sampling, the subject of the next section.

EXERCISES

5.1 Briefly describe the difference between primary data and secondary data.

5.2a **American Version:** For each of the following data sources, determine the frequency of publication and write down two specific pieces of information contained in the latest issue.

   a *The Statistical Abstract of the United States*
   b *Survey of Current Business*
   c *Federal Reserve Bulletin*

5.2b **Canadian Version:** For each of the following data sources, determine the frequency of publication and write down two specific pieces of information contained in the latest issue.

   a *Canadian Economic Observer, Statistical Summary, Statistics Canada*
   b *Bank of Canada Review*
   c *Toronto Stock Exchange Review*

5.3 Describe the difference between an observational study and an experimental study.

5.4 A soft-drink manufacturer has been supplying its cola drink in bottles to grocery stores and in cans to small convenience stores. The company is analyzing sales of this cola drink to determine which type of packaging is preferred by consumers.

   a Is this study observational or experimental? Explain your answer.
   b Outline a better method for determining whether a store will be supplied with cola in bottles or in cans, so that future sales data will be more helpful in assessing the preferred type of packaging.

5.5 **a** Briefly describe how you might design a study to investigate the relationship between smoking and lung cancer.
   b Is your study in part (a) observational or experimental? Explain why.

5.6 **a** List three methods of conducting a survey of people.
   b Give an important advantage and disadvantage of each of the methods listed in part (a).

5.7 List five important points to consider when designing a questionnaire.

5.3 SAMPLING

The chief motive for examining a sample rather than a population is cost. Statistical inference permits us to draw conclusions about a population parameter based on a sample that is quite small in comparison to the size of the population. For example, television executives want to know the proportion of television viewers who watch a network's programs. Because 100 million people may be watching television in the United States on a given evening, determining the actual proportion of the population that is watching certain programs is impractical and prohibitively expensive. The Nielsen ratings provide approximations of the desired information by observing what is watched by a sample of 1,000 television viewers. The proportion of households watching a particular program can be calculated for the households in the Nielsen sample. This sample proportion is then used as an **estimate** of the proportion of all households (the population proportion) that watched the program.

Another illustration of sampling can be taken from the field of quality control. To ensure that a production process is operating properly, the operations manager needs to know what proportion of items being produced is defective. If the quality-control technician must destroy the item in order to determine whether it is defective, then there is no alternative to sampling: a complete inspection of the product population would destroy the entire output of the production process.

We know that the sample proportion of television viewers or of defective items is probably not exactly equal to the population proportion we want to estimate. Nonetheless, the sample statistic can come quite close to the parameter it is designed to estimate if the **target population** (the population about which we want to draw inferences) and the **sampled population** (the actual population from which the sample has been taken) are the same. In practice, these may not be the same, as the following example illustrates.

THE NIELSEN RATINGS

The Nielsen ratings are supposed to provide information about the television shows that all Americans are watching. Hence, the target population is the television viewers of the United States. If the sample of 1,000 viewers was drawn exclusively from the state of New York, however, the sampled population would be the television viewers of New York. In this case, the target population and the sampled population are not the same, and no valid inferences about the target population can be drawn. To allow proper estimation of the proportion of all American television viewers watching a specific program, the sample should contain men and women of varying ages, incomes, occupations, and residences in a pattern similar to that of the target population. The importance of sampling from the target population cannot be overestimated; the consequences of drawing conclusions from improperly selected samples can be costly. One of the most spectacular examples of how not to conduct a survey was the *Literary Digest* poll of 1936.

THE *LITERARY DIGEST* POLL

The *Literary Digest* was a popular magazine of the 1920s and 1930s that had correctly predicted the outcomes of several presidential elections. In 1936, the *Digest* predicted that the Republican candidate, Alfred Landon, would defeat the Democratic incumbent, Franklin D. Roosevelt, by a 3 to 2 margin. But in that election, Roosevelt defeated Landon in a landslide victory, garnering the support of 62% of the electorate. The source of this blunder was the sampling procedure, and there were two distinct mistakes. First, the *Digest* sent out 10 million sample ballots to prospective voters. However, most of the names of these people were taken from the *Digest's* subscription list and from telephone directories. Subscribers to the magazine and people who owned telephones tended to be wealthier than average, and such people then, as today, tended to vote Republican. Additionally, only 2.3 million ballots were returned, resulting in a self-selected sample.

Self-selected samples are almost always biased, because the individuals who participate in them are more keenly interested in the issue than are the other members of the population. You often find similar surveys conducted today when radio and television stations ask people to call and give their opinion on an issue of interest. Again, only listeners who are concerned about the topic and have enough patience to get through to the station will be included in the sample. Hence, the sampled population is comprised entirely of people who are interested in the issue, whereas the target population is made up of all the people within the listening radius of the radio station. As a result, the conclusions drawn from such surveys are frequently wrong.

An excellent example of this phenomenon occurred on ABC's "Nightline" in 1984. Viewers were given a 900 number (cost: 50 cents) and asked to phone in their responses to the question of whether the United Nations should continue to be located in the United States. More than 186,000 people called, with 67% responding "no". At the same time, a (more scientific) market research poll of 500 people revealed that 72% wanted the United Nations to remain in the United States. In general, because the true value of the parameter being estimated is never known, these surveys give the impression of providing useful information. In fact, the results of such surveys are likely to be no more accurate than the results of the 1936 *Literary Digest* poll* or "Nightline's" phone-in show. Statisticians have coined two terms to describe these polls: SLOP (self-selected opinion poll) and "oy vey" (from the Yiddish lament), both of which convey the contempt that statisticians have for such data-gathering processes.

EXERCISES

5.8 For each of the following sampling plans, indicate why the target population and the sampled population are not the same.

   a To determine the opinions and attitudes of customers who regularly shop at a particular mall, a surveyor stands outside a large department store in the mall and randomly selects people to participate in the survey.

   b A library wants to estimate the proportion of its books that has been damaged. The librarians decide to select one book per shelf as a sample by measuring 12 inches from the left edge of each shelf and selecting the book in that location.

   c Political surveyors visit 200 residences during one afternoon to ask eligible voters present in the house at the time whom they intend to vote for.

5.9 **a** Describe why the *Literary Digest* poll of 1936 has become infamous.

   b What caused this poll to be so wrong?

5.10 **a** What is meant by a self-selected sample?

   b Give an example of a recent poll that involved a self-selected sample.

   c Why are self-selected samples not desirable?

5.4 SAMPLING PLANS

Our objective in this section is to introduce three different sampling plans: simple random sampling, stratified random sampling, and cluster sampling. We begin our presentation with the most basic design.

SIMPLE RANDOM SAMPLING

> **Simple Random Sample**
>
> A **simple random sample** is a sample selected in such a way that every possible sample with the same number of observations is equally likely to be chosen.

---

*Many statisticians ascribe the *Literary Digest's* statistical debacle to the wrong causes. For a better understanding of what really happened, read Maurice C. Bryson, "The *Literary Digest* Poll: Making of a Statistical Myth," *American Statistician* 30(4) (November 1976): 184–85.

One way to conduct a simple random sample is to assign a number to each element in the population, write these numbers on individual slips of paper, toss them into a hat, and draw the required number of slips (the sample size, *n*) from the hat. This is the kind of procedure that occurs in raffles, when all the ticket stubs go into a large, rotating drum from which the winners are selected.

Sometimes the elements of the population are already numbered. For example, virtually all adults have Social Security numbers (in the United States) or Social Insurance numbers (in Canada); all employees of large corporations have employee numbers; many people have driver's license numbers, medical plan numbers, student numbers, and so on. In such cases, choosing which sampling procedure to use is simply a matter of deciding how to select from among these numbers.

In other cases, the existing form of numbering has built-in flaws that make it inappropriate as a source of samples. Not everyone has a phone number, for example, so the telephone book does not list all the people in a given area. Many households have two (or more) adults, but only one phone listing. Couples often list the phone number under the man's name, so telephone listings are likely to be disproportionately male. Some people do not have phones, some have unlisted phone numbers, and some have more than one phone; these differences mean that each element of the population does not have an equal probability of being selected.

After each element of the chosen population has been assigned a unique number, sample numbers can be selected at random. A random number table can be used to select these sample numbers. (See, for example, *CRC Standard Management Tables,* W. H. Beyer, Ed., Boca Raton: CRC Press.) Alternatively, we can employ a software package to generate random numbers. Both Minitab and Excel have this capability.

▼ EXAMPLE 5.2

A government income tax auditor has been given responsibility for 1,000 tax returns. A computer is used to check the arithmetic of each return. However, to determine if the returns have been completed honestly, the auditor must check each entry and confirm its veracity. Because it takes, on average, 1 hour to completely audit a return and she has only 1 week to complete the task, the auditor has decided to randomly select 40 returns. The returns are numbered from 1 to 1,000. Use a computer random number generator to select the sample for the auditor.

Solution

Several software packages can produce the random numbers we need. Minitab and Excel are two of these.

Excel Output for Example 5.2

165	78	120	987	705	827	725	466	759	361
504	545	578	820	147	276	237	764	85	528
160	357	44	971	269	517	711	721	192	926
832	661	426	173	909	973	856	813	152	915
544	622	830	382	198	830	700	256	210	621

We generated 50 numbers between 1 and 1,000 and stored them in column 1. Although we needed only 40 random numbers, we generated 50 numbers because it is likely that some of them will be duplicates. We will use the first 40 unique random numbers to select our sample.

COMMANDS	COMMANDS FOR EXAMPLE 5.2
1 Click **Tools, Data Analysis . . . ,** and **Random Number Generation.**	
2 Type the **Number of Variables.**	1
3 Hit **tab** and type the **Number of Random Numbers.**	50
4 Use the cursor to select the **Uniform Distribution.**	
5 Use the cursor to specify the range of the uniform distribution **(Parameters).** Click **OK.** Column A will fill with 50 numbers that range between 0 and 1.	0 and 1
6 Multiply column A by 1,000 and store the products in column B.	
7 Make cell C1 active, click **f**$_x$, **Math & Trig, ROUNDUP,** and **Next>.**	
8 Specify the first number to be rounded.	B1
9 Hit **tab** and type the **number of digits** (decimal places). Click **Finish.** Complete column C.	0

The first five steps command Excel to generate 50 uniformly distributed random numbers between 0 and 1 to be stored in column A. Steps 6 through 9 convert these random numbers to integers between 1 and 1,000. Each number has the same probability (1/1,000 = .001) of being selected. Thus, each member of the population is equally likely to be included in the sample.

Minitab Output for Example 5.2

173	184	953	896	82	388	232	962	391	95
259	544	588	754	870	700	893	690	320	28
312	183	271	587	922	759	929	526	112	43
811	480	984	991	100	367	655	877	59	642
654	859	478	633	157	470	615	32	258	887

We generated 50 numbers between 1 and 1,000 and stored them in column 1. Although we needed only 40 random numbers, we generated 50 numbers because it is likely that some of them will be duplicates. We will use the first 40 unique random numbers to select our sample.

COMMANDS	COMMANDS FOR EXAMPLE 5.2
1 Click **Calc, Random Data,** and **Integer . . . .**	
2 Type the number of random numbers to be generated.	50
3 Hit **tab** and type the column where the numbers are to be stored.	C1

4 Hit **tab** and type the **Minimum**   **1**
   value.

5 Hit **tab** and type the **Maximum**   **1,000**
   value. Click **OK.** Print the column
   of stored numbers.

These commands generate 50 random numbers that lie between 1 and 1,000. Each number has the same probability $(1/1,000 = .001)$ of being selected. Thus, each member of the population is equally likely to be included in the sample.

INTERPRET

The auditor would examine the tax returns selected by the computer. Using the Minitab output, she would pick returns numbered 173, 184, 953, . . . , 877, 59, and 642 (the first 40 unique numbers). Each of these would be audited to determine if they were fraudulent. If the objective is to audit these 40 returns, no statistical procedure would be employed. However, if the objective is to estimate the proportion of all 1,000 returns that were dishonest, she would use one of the inferential techniques presented later in this book.

▲

STRATIFIED RANDOM SAMPLING

In making inferences about a population, we attempt to extract as much information as possible from a sample. The basic sampling plan, simple random sampling, often accomplishes this goal at low cost. Other methods, however, can be used to increase the amount of information about the population. One such procedure is stratified random sampling.

> **Stratified Random Sample**
>
> A **stratified random sample** is obtained by separating the population into mutually exclusive sets, or strata, and then drawing simple random samples from each stratum.

Examples of criteria for separating a population into strata (and of the strata themselves) follow.

1 Sex

   male

   female

2 Age

   under 20

   20–30

   31–40

41–50

51–60

over 60

3 Occupation

professional

clerical

blue-collar

other

4 Household income

under $15,000

$15,000–$29,999

$30,000–$50,000

over $50,000

To illustrate, suppose a public opinion survey is to be conducted in order to determine how many people favor a tax increase. A stratified random sample could be obtained by selecting a random sample of people from each of the four income groups described above. We usually stratify in a way that enables us to obtain particular kinds of information. In this example, we would like to know if people in the different income categories differ in their opinions about the proposed tax increase, since the tax increase will affect the strata differently. We avoid stratifying when there is no connection between the survey and the strata. For example, little purpose is served in trying to determine if people within religious strata have divergent opinions about the tax increase.

One advantage of stratification is that, besides acquiring information about the entire population, we can also make inferences within each stratum or compare strata. For instance, we can estimate what proportion of the lowest income group favors the tax increase, or we can compare the highest and lowest income groups to determine if they differ in their support of the tax increase.

Any stratification must be done in such a way that the strata are mutually exclusive: Each member of the population must be assigned to exactly one stratum. After the population has been stratified in this way, we can employ simple random sampling to generate the complete sample. There are several ways to do this. For example, we can draw random samples from each of the four income groups according to their proportions in the population. Thus, if in the population the relative frequencies of the four groups are as listed below, our sample will be stratified in the same proportions. If a total sample of 1,000 is to be drawn, we will randomly select 250 from stratum 1, 400 from stratum 2, 300 from stratum 3, and 50 from stratum 4.

Stratum	Income Categories	Population Proportions
1	under $15,000	25%
2	15,000–29,999	40
3	30,000–50,000	30
4	over 50,000	5

The problem with this approach, however, is that if we want to make inferences about the last stratum, a sample of 50 may be too small to produce useful information. In such cases, we usually increase the sample size of the smallest stratum (or strata) to ensure that the sample data provide enough information for our purposes. An adjustment must then be made before we attempt to draw inferences about the entire population. This procedure is beyond the level of this book. We recommend that anyone planning such a survey consult an expert statistician or a reference book on the subject. Better still, become an expert statistician yourself by taking additional statistics courses.

CLUSTER SAMPLING

> **Cluster Sample**
>
> A **cluster sample** is a simple random sample of groups or clusters of elements.

Cluster sampling is particularly useful when it is difficult or costly to develop a complete list of the population members (making it difficult and costly to generate a simple random sample). It is also useful whenever the population elements are widely dispersed geographically. For example, suppose we wanted to estimate the average annual household income in a large city. To use simple random sampling, we would need a complete list of households in the city from which to sample. To use stratified random sampling, we would need the list of households, and we would also need to have each household categorized by some other variable (such as age of household head) in order to develop the strata. A less expensive alternative would be to let each block within the city represent a cluster. A sample of clusters could then be randomly selected, and every household within these clusters could be questioned to determine income. By reducing the distances the surveyor must cover to gather data, cluster sampling reduces the cost.

But cluster sampling also increases sampling error (see Section 5.5), because households belonging to the same cluster are likely to be similar in many respects, including household income. This can be partially offset by using some of the cost savings to choose a larger sample than would be used for a simple random sample.

SAMPLE SIZE

Whichever type of sampling plan you select, you still have to decide what size of sample to use. Determining the appropriate sample size will be addressed in detail in Chapter 9. Until then, we can rely on our intuition, which tells us that the larger the sample size is, the more accurate we can expect the sample estimates to be.

E X E R C I S E S

5.11 A statistician would like to conduct a survey to ask people their views on a proposed new shopping mall in their community. According to the latest census, there are 800 households in the community. The statistician has numbered each household (from 1 to 800), and she would like to randomly select 25 of these households to participate in the study. Use a software package to generate the sample.

5.12 A safety expert wants to determine the proportion of cars in his state with worn tire treads. The state license plate contains six digits. Use a software package to generate a sample of 20 cars to be examined.

5.13 The operations manager of a large plant with four departments wants to estimate the person-hours lost per month due to accidents. Describe a sampling plan that would be suitable for estimating the plant-wide loss and for comparing departments.

5.14 A statistician wants to estimate the mean age of children in his city. Unfortunately, he does not have a complete list of households. Describe a sampling plan that would be suitable for his purposes.

5.5 ERRORS INVOLVED IN SAMPLING

Two major types of errors can arise when a sample of observations is taken from a population: sampling error and nonsampling error. Managers reviewing the results of sample surveys and studies, as well as researchers who conduct the surveys and studies, should understand the sources of these errors.

SAMPLING ERROR

Sampling error refers to differences between the sample and the population that exist only because of the observations that happened to be selected for the sample. Sampling error is an error that we expect to occur when we make a statement about a population that is based only on the observations contained in a sample taken from the population. To illustrate, consider again the example described in Section 5.1 in which we wish to determine the mean annual income of North American blue-collar workers. As was stated there, we can use statistical inference to estimate the mean income (μ) of the population if we are willing to accept less than 100% accuracy. If we record the incomes of a sample of the workers and find the mean ($\bar{x}$) of this sample of incomes, this sample mean is an estimate of the desired population mean. But the value of $\bar{x}$ will deviate from the population mean (μ) simply by chance, because the value of the sample mean depends on which incomes just happened to be selected for the sample. The difference between the true (unknown) value of the population mean (μ) and its sample estimate ($\bar{x}$) is the sampling error. The size of this deviation may be large simply due to bad luck—bad luck that a particularly unrepresentative sample happened to be selected. The only way we can reduce the expected size of this error is to take a larger sample.

Given a fixed sample size, the best we can do is to state the probability that the sampling error is less than a certain amount (as we will discuss in Chapter 8). It is common today for such a statement to accompany the results of an opinion poll. If an opinion poll states that, based on sample results, Candidate Kreem has the support of 54% of eligible voters in an upcoming election, that statement may be accompanied by the following explanatory note: This percentage is correct to within three percentage points, 19 times out of 20. This statement means that we have a certain level of confidence (95%) that the actual level of support for Candidate Kreem is between 51% and 57%.

NONSAMPLING ERROR

Nonsampling error is more serious than sampling error, because taking a larger sample won't diminish the size, or the possibility of occurrence, of this error. Even a census can (and probably will) contain nonsampling errors. **Nonsampling errors** are due to mistakes made in the acquisition of data or due to the sample observations being selected improperly.

THREE TYPES OF NONSAMPLING ERRORS

1 *Errors in data acquisition.* These types of errors arise from the recording of incorrect responses. This may be the result of incorrect measurements being taken because of faulty equipment, mistakes made during transcription from primary sources, inaccurate recording of data due to misinterpretation of terms, or inaccurate responses to questions concerning sensitive issues such as sexual activity or possible tax evasion.

2 *Nonresponse error.* **Nonresponse error** refers to error (or **bias**) introduced when responses are not obtained from some members of the sample. When this happens, the sample observations that are collected may not be representative of the target population, resulting in biased results (as was discussed in Section 5.3). Nonresponse can occur for a number of reasons. An interviewer may be unable to contact a person listed in the sample, or the sampled person may refuse to respond for some reason. In either case, responses are not obtained from a sampled person, and bias is introduced. The problem of nonresponse is even greater when self-administered questionnaires are used rather than an interviewer, who can attempt to reduce the nonresponse rate by means of callbacks. As noted earlier, the *Literary Digest* fiasco was largely due to a high nonresponse rate, resulting in a biased, self-selected sample.

3 *Selection bias.* **Selection bias** occurs when the sampling plan is such that some members of the target population cannot possibly be selected for inclusion in the sample. Together with nonresponse error, selection bias played a role in the *Literary Digest* poll being so wrong, as voters without telephones or without a subscription to *Literary Digest* were excluded from possible inclusion in the sample taken.

E X E R C I S E S

5.15 a Explain the difference between sampling error and nonsampling error.
b Which type of error in part (a) is more serious? Why?

5.16 Briefly describe three types of nonsampling errors.

5.17 Is it possible for a sample to yield better results than a census? Explain.

5.6 USE OF SAMPLING IN AUDITING (OPTIONAL*)

The accounting profession in its role as external auditor of financial statements may be one of the principal users of a probability distribution called the Poisson distribution (covered in Chapter 6). Auditors make statistical inferences about the existence of errors and/or fraud in the accounting records in order to express an opinion on the fairness of published financial statements. The audit is divided into two phases. Phase one looks at the adequacy of the control environment. Here, *attribute sampling* is employed to estimate the **rate** of errors in the population. On the basis of these sample results, phase two of the audit employs *variable sampling* to estimate the magnitude of errors and/or defalcation caused by inadequacies in the control environment.

*This section can be omitted without loss of continuity. In any case, the reader may wish to read (or reread) this section after the Poisson distribution has been covered in Chapter 6. The authors are grateful to Professor Brian Gaber, York University, for his assistance in preparing this section.

Historically, *classical variable sampling* (mean per unit, difference, and ratio estimation), requiring an estimate of the population standard deviation, was employed. Classical variable sampling turned out to be unsuitable, especially in the detection of fraud, because frequency of occurrence is so small (often less than one occurrence per million). Required sample sizes were often so large that the statistical inference was economically nonviable, and auditors turned back to heuristic methods using nonstatistical inference.

Fortunately, the Poisson distribution (which we will soon study) allowed auditors to escape from this dilemma. When auditors noticed that the Poisson distribution was ideally suited for populations where the occurrence rate was extremely low, they developed a specialized statistical approach called PPS (probability proportionate to size) or sometimes referred to as DUS (dollar unit sampling), which is based on the Poisson distribution. In PPS, the individual dollar, rather than the account balance or an invoice, is defined as the sampling unit. Each dollar in the population has an equal chance of being selected, and, once selected, acts as a hook to draw in the invoice, account, etc., of which it is a part. The result is that the probability of selection into the sample becomes proportionate to size; for example, a one-million-dollar invoice is one million times more likely to be drawn for examination than a one-dollar invoice. By starting with an assumption that the underlying rate of error in the population is zero, PPS results in sample sizes that are far smaller than those suggested by classical variable sampling. Accordingly, PPS has become almost universally adopted in auditing.

The mean of the Poisson distribution is given by the expression $\mu = np$, where μ is the mean, n is the sample size (number of trials), and p is the probability of occurrence for one trial. The Poisson distribution allows the auditor to state, with a specified risk, the tolerable error per sample size n of the population when the sample contains x errors. The procedure is too lengthy to describe here and requires the use of specialized tables derived from the Poisson distribution. A detailed discussion of the theory can be found in the *Audit Sampling Guide,* by the Statistical Sampling Subcommittee of the American Institute of Certified Public Accountants, AICPA, New York, 1983, and the procedures for PPS are described in most auditing textbooks.

5.7 SUMMARY

Because most populations are very large, it is extremely costly and impractical to investigate each member of the population to determine the values of the parameters. As a practical alternative, we take a sample from the population and use the sample statistics to draw inferences about the parameters. Care must be taken to ensure that the sampled population is the same as the target population.

We can choose from among several different sampling plans, including simple random sampling, stratified random sampling, and cluster sampling. Whatever sampling plan is used, it is important to realize that both sampling error and nonsampling error will occur, and to understand what the sources of these errors are.

IMPORTANT TERMS

Primary data   *148*
Secondary data   *149*
Observational study   *149*
Experimental study   *150*

Personal interview   *151*
Telephone interview   *151*
Self-administered questionnaire   *151*
Questionnaire design   *151*

Estimate   *152*
Target population   *153*
Sampled population   *153*
Self-selected sample   *153*
Simple random sample   *154*
Stratified random sample   *157*

Cluster sample   *159*
Sampling error   *160*
Nonsampling errors   *160*
Nonresponse error (bias)   *161*
Selection bias   *161*

Chapter 6

Probability and Discrete Probability Distributions

6.1 Introduction

6.2 Assigning Probabilities to Events

6.3 Probability Rules and Trees

6.4 Random Variables and Probability Distributions

6.5 Expected Value and Variance

6.6 Bivariate Distributions

6.7 Investment Portfolio Diversification (Optional)

6.8 Binomial Distribution

6.9 Poisson Distribution

6.10 Summary

6.1 INTRODUCTION

Probability theory is an integral part of all statistics; in particular, it is essential to the theory of statistical inference. Statistical inference provides the decision maker—perhaps a businessperson or an economist—with a body of methods that aid in decision making under uncertainty. The uncertainty arises because, in real-life situations, we rarely have perfect information regarding various inputs to a decision. Whether our uncertainty relates to the future demand for our product, the future level of interest rates, the possibility of a labor strike, or the proportion of defective widgets in the next production run, probability theory can be used to measure the degree of uncertainty involved. Probability theory allows us to go beyond ignoring uncertainty or considering it in a haphazard fashion by giving us a foundation for dealing with uncertainty in a consistent, rational manner.

In the next two sections, we provide a fairly brief introduction to the basics of probability. We then introduce the concept of a random variable, which allows us to summarize the results of an experiment in terms of numerical-valued outcomes. For example, if the experiment consists of selecting five items from a production run and observing how many are defective, the appropriate random variable is defined as "the number of defective items." This random variable enables us to focus solely on the number of defective items observed rather than having to concern ourselves with exactly which of the items selected are defective, the nature of the defects, and other such nonessential details.

After introducing random variables, we consider probability distributions, which summarize the probabilities of observing the various numerical observations. Two descriptive measures of a random variable and its probability distribution—expected value and variance—are covered next. Having considered the probability distribution of a single random variable, we next introduce the bivariate (or joint) probability distribution, which is needed to analyze the relationship between *two* random variables. We first considered the relationship between two variables back in Chapter 2, where we introduced the scatter diagram to graphically depict a bivariate relationship. The remainder of this chapter looks in detail at two specific, commonly used probability distributions: the binomial and Poisson distributions.

6.2 ASSIGNING PROBABILITIES TO EVENTS

RANDOM EXPERIMENT

A logical development of probability begins with considering a random experiment, because this process generates the uncertain outcomes to which we will assign probabilities. Random experiments are of interest because they provide the raw data for statistical analysis.

> **Random Experiment**
>
> A **random experiment** is a process or course of action that results in one of a number of possible outcomes. The outcome that occurs cannot be predicted with certainty.

Following is a list of some random experiments, together with their possible outcomes:

1 Experiment: Flip a coin.
　Outcomes: heads, tails

2 Experiment: Roll a die.
　Outcomes: 1, 2, 3, 4, 5, 6

3 Experiment: Roll a die.
　Outcomes: even number, odd number

4 Experiment: Observe the unit sales of a product for one day.
　Outcomes: 0, 1, 2, 3, . . .

5 Experiment: Solicit a consumer's preference between product *A* and product *B.*
　Outcomes: prefer *A,* prefer *B,* indifferent

6 Experiment: Observe change in IBM share price over 1 week.
　Outcomes: increase, decrease, no change

An important feature of a random experiment is that the actual outcome cannot be determined in advance. That is, the outcome of a random experiment may change if the experiment is repeated. The best we can do is talk about the probability that a particular outcome will occur.

In order to determine, in advance of an experiment, the probabilities that various outcomes will occur, we first have to know what outcomes are possible. The first step in finding the probabilities, then, is to list the possible outcomes, as we did for the foregoing six examples of random experiments. For any such listing to suit our needs, the listed outcomes must be **exhaustive;** that is, each trial of the random experiment must result in some outcome on the list. Furthermore, the listed outcomes must be **mutually exclusive;** that is, no two outcomes on the list can both occur on any one trial of the experiment. Such a listing of the possible outcomes is called a *sample space,* denoted by *S.*

Sample Space

A **sample space** of a random experiment is a list of all possible outcomes of the experiment. The outcomes listed must be mutually exclusive and exhaustive.

Stated another way, the set of possible outcomes constituting a sample space must be defined in such a way that each trial of the experiment results in exactly one outcome in the sample space. In each of the foregoing six examples of random experiments, the accompanying list of possible outcomes is a sample space for that experiment.

The individual outcomes in a sample space are called **simple events.** In assigning probabilities, you should *define simple events in such a way that they cannot be broken down, or decomposed, into two or more constituent outcomes.* For example, in the foregoing die-tossing experiment, the outcome "an even number is observed" should not be used as a simple event in a sample space, because it can be further decomposed into three outcomes: 2, 4, and 6. An outcome such as "an even number is observed," which comprises a collection of simple events, is called an *event.*

> ## Event
>
> An **event** is any collection of one or more simple events.

Events are denoted by capital letters and can be defined either in words or by a list of their component simple events. For example, the event "an even number is observed" can be described alternatively as $A = \{2, 4, 6\}$, where { } is read "the set consisting of." It is conventional, when using letters to list the simple events that form a sample space, to use E_i to denote the ith simple event in the list.

Ultimately, we want to find the probability that an event A will occur, which is denoted $P(A)$. You undoubtedly have some idea of what is meant by the word *probability,* but now let's look more closely at its meaning.

THREE APPROACHES TO ASSIGNING PROBABILITIES

Beginning students of probability are usually disconcerted when they learn that the word *probability* has no precise definition. Any attempt to define it leads you around a circular series of statements consisting of such synonymous terms as *likelihood, chance,* and *odds.* There are, however, three distinct interpretations of probability that offer three approaches to determining the probability that a particular outcome will occur.

The **classical approach** attempts to deduce the probability of an outcome logically from the symmetric nature of the experiment. If a perfectly balanced coin is flipped, for example, it is logical to expect that the outcome heads and the outcome tails are equally likely. Hence, we assert that the probability of observing an occurrence of heads is $\frac{1}{2}$. More generally, if an experiment has n possible outcomes, each of which is equally likely, the probability of any particular outcome's occurrence is $1/n$. The classical approach can often be used effectively in games of chance. Our development of probability frequently uses examples from this area to illustrate a point, because these examples are easy to relate to. More practical situations, however, do not lend themselves to the classical, deductive approach. A businessperson will usually use either the relative frequency approach or the subjective approach.

The **relative frequency approach** expresses an outcome's probability as its long-run relative frequency of occurrence. Suppose a random experiment is repeated n times, where n is a large number. If x represents the number of times a particular outcome occurred in those n trials, the proportion x/n provides an estimate of the probability that that particular outcome will occur. For example, if 600 out of the last 1,000 customers entering a store have made purchases, the probability that any given customer entering the store will make a purchase is approximately .6. The larger n is, the better will be the estimate of the desired probability, which may be thought of as the limiting value of x/n as n becomes infinitely large. Using the relative frequency approach, then, means determining empirically the probability that a particular outcome will occur.

In many practical situations, the experimental outcomes are not equally likely, and there is no history of repetitions of the experiment. Such might be the case, for example, if you wanted to estimate the probability of striking oil at a new offshore drilling site or the likelihood of your firm's sales reaching $1 million this year. In such situations, we resort to the **subjective approach,** under which the probability assigned to an outcome simply reflects the degree to which we believe that the outcome will occur. The probability assigned to a particular outcome thus reflects a personal evaluation of the situation and may be based simply on intuition.

In many cases, however, a businessperson's intuition or subjective evaluation has probably been influenced by outcomes in similar situations, so the relative frequency approach often plays a role in the formation of the subjective probabilities. Consider, for example, a producer about to launch a new Broadway musical. The producer's subjective estimate of the probability that the show will return a profit to investors will be based on several factors, such as the reputation of the musical's principals, the quality of other Broadway shows currently running, and the state of the economy; but the producer will also be mindful of the fact that only about 25% of all Broadway musicals are profitable—a fact based on the relative frequency approach.

ASSIGNING PROBABILITIES

Having reviewed much of the necessary terminology, we now turn to the matter of assigning probabilities to outcomes and events. To each simple event E_i in a sample space, we want to attach a number $P(E_i)$—called the *probability of E_i*—representing the likelihood that that particular outcome will occur. Whichever of the three ways of assigning probabilities (classical, relative frequency, or subjective) is used, the probabilities assigned to simple events must satisfy the two conditions specified in the following box. Keep in mind, too, that the simple events E_i that form a sample space must be mutually exclusive and exhaustive.

Requirements of Probabilities

Given a sample space $S = \{E_1, E_2, \ldots, E_n\}$, the probabilities assigned to the simple events E_i must satisfy two basic requirements:

1 $0 \leq P(E_i) \leq 1$ for each i

2 $\displaystyle\sum_{i=1}^{n} P(E_i) = 1$

Suppose that probabilities have been assigned to all the simple events. We still need a method for finding the probabilities of an event that is not a simple one. Recall that an event A is just a collection of simple events; therefore, its probability can be determined in the manner described in the following box.

Probability of an Event

The probability of an event A is equal to the sum of the probabilities assigned to the simple events contained in A.

It follows from the two basic requirements that the probability of an event that is certain to occur is 1, because such an event must contain all the simple events in the sample space and the sum of all simple event probabilities must be 1. On the other hand, the probability of an event that cannot possibly occur is 0.

The two basic requirements tell us nothing about how to assign probabilities; they simply state conditions that must be met by probabilities once they have been assigned. In practice, a business manager or economist will usually resort to either the relative frequency approach or the subjective approach in assigning probabilities to events. For example, a promoter choosing a week during which to hold a 2-day, outdoor rock concert might consult meteorological records. If a particular week has been rain free for 35 of the past 50 years, then $\frac{35}{50} = .7$ would be a relative frequency estimate of the probability of that week being rain free this year. In many decision-making situations, however, a history of comparable circumstances is not available, and a businessperson must rely on an educated guess (that is, on the subjective approach). Such is the case with a bank manager who must estimate the probability of loan default by a country whose repayment ability has been impaired by declining oil prices.

Despite the prevalence of the relative frequency approach and the subjective approach, the examples that follow illustrate the assignment of probabilities to events using the classical approach. Not only will this be helpful in situations that do call for the classical approach, but it will also help clarify basic principles underlying the formulation of a sample space and the assignment of probabilities using any approach.

PROBABILITY TREES

One very useful method of calculating probabilities is to use a **probability tree,** in which the various possible events of an experiment are represented by lines or branches of the tree. When you want to construct a sample space for an experiment, a probability tree is a useful device for ensuring that you have identified all simple events and have assigned the associated probabilities.

The mechanics of using a probability tree can be illustrated by reference to the random experiment consisting of flipping a coin twice. A sample space for this experiment is

$$S = \{HH, HT, TH, TT\}$$

where the first letter of each pair denotes the result of the first flip. A probability tree for this experiment is shown in Figure 6.1.

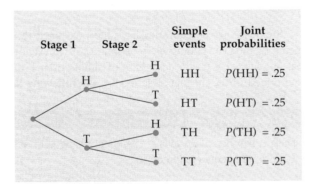

Figure 6.1

Probability tree for coin example

Whenever you can break down the process of observing the result of an experiment into stages, with a different aspect of the results observed at each stage, you can represent the various possible sequences of observations with a probability tree. In the coin example, stage 1 involves the outcome of the first flip, while stage 2 involves the outcome of the second flip. The heavy dots in Figure 6.1 are called *nodes,* and the branches emerging from a particular node represent the alternative outcomes that can occur at that point.

The initial (unlabelled) node is called the *origin*. Any path through the tree from the origin to a terminal node corresponds to one possible simple event. For example, if we follow along the top branches of the tree, we observe the simple event HH. Altogether, then, we have four simple events, each of which is equally likely. Hence,

$$P(HH) = P(HT) = P(TH) = P(TT) = .25$$

Having established the probabilities of the four simple events, we are now in a position to find the probabilities of other events we might want to consider. For example, suppose that A denotes the event of getting at least one head, and we want to find $P(A)$. Event A occurs if we arrive at the end of any one of the top three paths in Figure 6.1. Summing the probabilities assigned to the simple events contained in A, we obtain

$$P(A) = P(HH) + P(HT) + P(TH) = .75$$

PROBABILITIES OF COMBINATIONS OF EVENTS

After determining the probabilities of some of the basic outcomes and events, we often want to compute the probabilities of more complex, related events. The notation for the probabilities of these compound events is as follows, where A and B are any two events.

$P(A \text{ or } B) = P(A \text{ occurs } or \ B \text{ occurs } or \text{ both occur})$

$P(A \text{ and } B) = P(A \ and \ B \text{ both occur})$

$P(\overline{A}) = P(A \text{ does } not \text{ occur})$

$P(A \mid B). = P(A \text{ occurs } given \ that \ B \text{ has occurred})$

This last probability is called the *conditional probability* that A will occur, given that B has occurred. The event $\overline{A}$, called the **complement** of A, is the set of all outcomes that do not belong to A.

▼ EXAMPLE 6.1

The number of spots turning up when a six-sided die is tossed is observed. Consider the following events.

A: The number observed is at most 2.

B: The number observed is an even number.

C: The number 4 turns up.

a Define a sample space for this random experiment and assign probabilities to the simple events.

b Find $P(A)$.

c Find $P(\overline{A})$.

d Are events A and C mutually exclusive?

e Find $P(A \text{ or } C)$.

f Find $P(A \text{ and } B)$.

g Find $P(A \text{ or } B)$.

h Find $P(C \mid B)$.

Solution

a A sample space is $S = \{1, 2, 3, 4, 5, 6\}$. Because each of the six simple events is equally likely to occur,

$$P(1) = P(2) = P(3) = P(4) = P(5) = P(6) = \frac{1}{6}$$

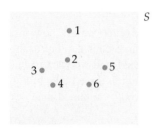

Figure 6.2

Venn diagram for Example 6.1

A useful geometrical representation of this sample space, called a **Venn diagram,** is presented in Figure 6.2. In a Venn diagram, the entire sample space S is represented by a rectangle; points inside the rectangle represent the individual outcomes, or simple events, in S.

b The event $A = \{1, 2\}$ is represented in a Venn diagram by a closed region containing the simple events that belong to A, as shown in Figure 6.3. Because the probability of an event A is equal to the sum of the probabilities assigned to the simple events contained in A,

$$P(A) = P(1) + P(2) = \frac{1}{6} + \frac{1}{6} = \frac{2}{6}$$

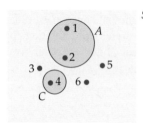

Figure 6.3

Venn diagram depicting events *A* and *C*

c The complement of event A is $\overline{A} = \{3, 4, 5, 6\}$. Therefore,

$$P(\overline{A}) = P(3) + P(4) + P(5) + P(6) = \frac{4}{6}$$

The four simple events in $\overline{A}$ are represented in Figure 6.3 by the points lying outside the region describing event A.

d Two events A and C are mutually exclusive if the occurrence of one precludes the occurrence of the other—that is, if the event (A and C) contains no outcomes. The events A and C defined in this example are mutually exclusive because they cannot both occur. (The regions representing A and C in Figure 6.3 do not overlap.) If the number observed is 4, it is not 1 or 2.

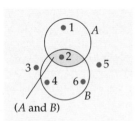

(*A* and *B*)

Figure 6.4

Venn diagram depicting
(*A* and *B*)

e Because $A = \{1, 2\}$ and $C = \{4\}$, either A or C occurs if the number observed is 1, 2, or 4. The event (A or C) $= \{1, 2, 4\}$ is depicted by the total shaded area in Figure 6.3, and

$$P(A \text{ or } C) = P(1) + P(2) + P(4) = \frac{3}{6}$$

Because A and C are mutually exclusive, we could also write

$$P(A \text{ or } C) = P(A) + P(C) = \frac{2}{6} + \frac{1}{6} = \frac{3}{6}$$

But the above equality only holds for mutually exclusive events, as is evident from part (g) below.

f Both A and B occur only if the number observed is 2. Therefore,

$$P(A \text{ and } B) = P(2) = \frac{1}{6}$$

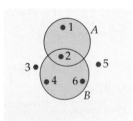

Figure 6.5

Venn diagram depicting
(*A* or *B*)

The event (A and B) is depicted by the shaded are in Figure 6.4.

g Because $A = \{1, 2\}$ and $B = \{2, 4, 6\}$, either A or B occurs if the number observed is 1, 2, 4, or 6. the event (A or B) $= \{1, 2, 4, 6\}$ is depicted by the shaded area in Figure 6.5, and

$$P(A \text{ or } B) = P(1) + P(2) + P(4) + P(6) = \frac{4}{6}$$

Note that in this case we can't find $P(A \text{ or } B)$ by simply adding $P(A)$ and $P(B)$, for we would then get $\frac{5}{6}$. This is incorrect because we have double counted the outcome 2, as can be seen from Figure 6.5. To correct for this, we must subtract $P(A \text{ and } B)$.

$$P(A \text{ or } B) = P(A) + P(B) - P(A \text{ and } B) = \frac{2}{6} + \frac{3}{6} - \frac{1}{6} = \frac{4}{6}$$

h We wish to find the probability that the number 4 turns up, given that the number turning up is even. If an even number turns up, we know the number is 2, 4, or 6. The information that the observed number is even has reduced our attention to these three numbers belonging to B. Of the three numbers comprising event B, only one is in $C = \{4\}$, so the required conditional probability is

$$P(C \mid B) = P(\text{number is } 4 \mid \text{number is even}) = \frac{1}{3}$$

▲

CONDITIONAL PROBABILITY

When finding the probability of an event, we can sometimes make use of partial knowledge about the outcome of the experiment. Consider, for example, the probability that a new product developed by our research department will be a success. Given no information about consumers' interest in the product, we might subjectively estimate the probability of success to be only .20. However, if we subsequently hear that the product has been test marketed and the results are positive, we would likely revise upward our estimate of the probability of success. In light of the new information, we can talk about the *conditional probability* that the new product will be successful, given that the test-market results were positive.

We saw an illustration of the computation of a conditional probability in part (h) of Example 6.1. In that example, we are informed that, when a single die is tossed, an even number turns up (event B). We then want to find the probability that the number 4 turns up (event C), making use of our knowledge that the number is even. In other words, we are seeking the **conditional probability** that C will occur, given that B has occurred; this is written $P(C \mid B)$. (The vertical stroke $\mid$ is read "given that"; it is followed by the event that has occurred.) To find this probability, we first note that knowing the information that an even number turned up restricts our inquiry to event B. That is, the new information has reduced the size of the relevant sample space to three possible outcomes. Of these three outcomes in the *reduced sample space*, only one belongs to event C. Hence, the desired conditional probability is

$$P(C \mid B) = \frac{1}{3}$$

which differs from the **unconditional probability** $P(C) = \frac{1}{6}$.

Notice that we computed the conditional probability $P(C \mid B)$ by dividing the number of outcomes belonging to both C and B by the number of outcomes in B. Alternatively, we can compute $P(C \mid B)$ as the ratio of the two probabilities $P(C \text{ and } B)$ and $P(B)$.

$$P(C \mid B) = \frac{1}{3} = \frac{1/6}{3/6} = \frac{P(C \text{ and } B)}{P(B)}$$

Having worked through the calculation of a particular conditional probability, we now present the general formula for a conditional probability.

Conditional Probability

Let A and B be two events such that $P(B) > 0$. The **conditional probability** that A occurs, given that B has occurred, is

$$P(A \mid B) = \frac{P(A \text{ and } B)}{P(B)}$$

In the preceding example, we saw that $P(C) = \frac{1}{6}$ and $P(C \mid B) = \frac{1}{3}$, so $P(C) \neq P(C \mid B)$. That is, the fact that event B occurred changes the probability that C will occur. Such events C and B are called **dependent events.**

On the other hand, if the occurrence of one event does not change the probability of occurrence of the other event, the two events are said to be **independent events.** Such is the case with events $A = \{1, 2\}$ and $B = \{2, 4, 6\}$ in Example 6.1. These events A and B are independent, because it can be shown that

$$P(A \mid B) = \frac{1}{3} = P(A) \quad \text{and} \quad P(B \mid A) = \frac{1}{2} = P(B)$$

Try to compute these probabilities on your own (see also Exercise 6.7). Just as important, ensure that you understand the difference in meaning between $P(A \mid B)$ and $P(B \mid A)$ for this example.

Independent and Dependent Events

Two events A and B are said to be **independent** if

$$P(A \mid B) = P(A) \quad \text{or} \quad P(B \mid A) = P(B)$$

Otherwise, the events are **dependent.**

If one equality in the preceding definition holds, so does the other. The concept of independence is illustrated in the following example.

▼ **EXAMPLE 6.2**

A group of female managers working for an insurance company has lodged a complaint with the personnel department. While the women agree that the company has increased the number of female managers, they assert that women tend to remain in lower level management positions when promotions are handed out. They have supported their argument by noting that, during the past 3 years, only 8 of the 54 promotions awarded went to women. The personnel department has responded by claiming that these numbers are misleading on two counts: First, there are far fewer female managers than male managers; second, many of the female managers have been hired during the past year, and employees are virtually never promoted during their first year at the managerial level. The personnel department has compiled the data shown in Table 6.1, in which managers who have been employed for at least 1 year are clas-

Table 6.1 **Classification of Managers**

Manager	Promoted	Not Promoted	Total
Male	46	184	230
Female	8	32	40
Total	54	216	270

sified according to gender and to promotion record. The department claims that the decision to promote a manager (or not) is independent of the manager's gender. Would you agree?

Solution   The events of interest are as follows.

M: A manager is male.

$\overline{M}$: A manager is female.

A: A manager is promoted.

$\overline{A}$: A manager is not promoted.

To show that the decision about whether or not to promote a manager is independent of the manager's gender, we must verify that

$$P(A \mid M) = P(A)$$

If this equality holds, the probability that a man is promoted is no different from the probability that any manager is promoted. Given no information other than the data in Table 6.1, the probability that a manager is promoted is

$$P(A) = \frac{54}{270} = .20$$

If we now consider only male managers, we restrict our attention to the first row of Table 6.1. Given that a manager is male, the probability that he is promoted is

$$P(A \mid M) = \frac{46}{230} = .20$$

Note the distinction between this conditional probability and the **joint probability** that a manager is both male and promoted, which is $P(A \text{ and } M) = 46/270 = .17$. In any case, we have verified that $P(A) = P(A \mid M)$, so the events A and M are independent. From the data in Table 6.1, we must conclude that there is no discrimination in awarding promotions.

As indicated in the definition of independent events, an alternative way of showing that A and M are independent events is to verify that $P(M \mid A) = P(M)$. The probability that a manager is male is $P(M) = 230/270 = 46/54$, which equals $P(M \mid A)$, the probability that a manager who is promoted is male. Thus, we again conclude that events A and M are independent.

Before concluding this section, we draw your attention to a common misconception. Students often think that independent events and mutually exclusive events are the same thing. They are not. For example, events A and M in the preceding example are independent events, but they are not mutually exclusive, since the event (A and M) contains 46 simple events. In fact, it can be shown that *any two independent events A and B that occur with nonzero probabilities cannot be mutually exclusive.* If A and

B were mutually exclusive, we would have $P(A$ and $B) = 0$ and $P(A \mid B) = 0$; but since A occurs with nonzero probability, $P(A) \neq P(A \mid B)$, so A and B cannot be independent events.

▲

EXERCISES

6.1 Explain what is meant by the statement "The simple events that constitute a sample space are mutually exclusive and exhaustive."

6.2 Specify a sample space S for each of the following random experiments by listing the simple events in S.

a The results of three flips of a coin are observed.

b The time required to complete an assembly is recorded to the nearest minute.

c The marital status of a loan applicant is solicited.

d Two six-sided dice are tossed, and the sum of the spots turning up is noted.

e The number of customers served by a restaurant on a particular day is recorded.

f After 20 shoppers are asked if they are satisfied with parking accessibility, the number of positive responses is recorded.

6.3 A contractor has submitted a bid on each of three separate contracts. The probability of winning each contract is .5, independent of whether the other two contracts are won or lost. Find the probability of the following.

a The contractor will win all three contracts.

b The contractor will win exactly one contract.

c The contractor will win at least two contracts.

6.4 A store that sells personal computers and related supplies is concerned that it may be overstocking surge suppressors. The store has tabulated the number of surge suppressors sold weekly for each of the last 80 weeks. The results are summarized in the following table.

Number of suppressors sold	Number of weeks
0	36
1	28
2	12
3	2
4	2

The store intends to use the tabulated data as a basis for forecasting surge suppressor sales in any given week.

a Define the random experiment of interest to the store.

b List the simple events in the sample space.

c Assign probabilities to the simple events.

d What approach have you used in determining the probabilities in part (c)?

e Find the probability of selling at least three surge suppressors in any given week.

6.5 The trustee of a company's pension plan has solicited the employees' feelings toward a proposed revision in the plan. A breakdown of the responses is shown in the accompanying table. Suppose that an employee is selected at random.

Decision	Blue-collar	White-collar workers	Managers
For	67	32	11
Against	63	18	9

Find the probability that the employee selected is

a a blue-collar worker.

b against the proposed revision.

c not a manager.

6.6 During a recent promotion, a bank offered mortgages with terms of 1, 2, and 3 years at a reduced interest rate. Customers could also choose between open and closed mortgages. Suppose that 300 mortgage applications were approved and that the numbers of mortgages of each type were as shown in the following table. The manager selects one mortgage application at random, and the relevant events are defined as follows.

L: The application selected is for a 1-year mortgage.
M: The application selected is for a 2-year mortgage.
N: The application selected is for a 3-year mortgage.
C: The application selected is for a closed mortgage.

Type of mortgage	Term of mortgage (in years) 1	2	3
Open	32	36	60
Closed	80	48	44

a Find $P(L)$, $P(M)$, $P(N)$, $P(C)$, and $P(\overline{C})$.

b Find the probability that the term of the mortgage selected is longer than 1 year.

6.7 The random experiment in Example 6.1 was to observe the number of spots turning up when a six-sided die is tossed. The events $A = \{1, 2\}$ and $B = \{2, 4, 6\}$ were considered there.

a Find $P(A \mid B)$.

b Find $P(B \mid A)$.

c Are A and B independent events? Explain.

6.8 An ordinary deck of playing cards has 13 cards of each suit. Suppose a card is selected at random from the deck.

a What is the probability that the card selected is an ace?

b Given that the card selected is a spade, what is the probability that the card is an ace?

c Are "an ace is selected" and "a spade is selected" independent events?

6.9 Suppose A and B are two mutually exclusive events. Do A and B represent independent events? Explain.

6.10 Of a company's employees, 30% are women and 6% are married women. Suppose an employee is selected at random. If the employee selected is a woman, what is the probability that she is married?

6.11 A firm classifies its customers' accounts in two ways: according to the balance outstanding and according to whether or not the account is overdue. The accompanying table gives the proportion of accounts falling into various categories. One account is selected at random.

Account balance	Overdue	Not overdue
Under $100	.08	.42
$100–$500	.08	.22
Over $500	.04	.16

a If the account selected is overdue, what is the probability that its balance is under $100?

b If the balance of the account selected is over $500, what is the probability that it is overdue?

c If the balance of the account selected is $500 or less, what is the probability that it is overdue?

6.12 A department store manager wants to investigate whether the method of payment chosen by customers is related to the size of the purchases. The manager has cross-classified a sample of 250 customer purchases, as shown in the following table. One of these 250 customers is selected at random.

| | Method of payment | |
Size of purchase	cash	credit card
Under $20	51	31
$20 or more	65	103

a What is the probability that the customer selected paid by credit card?

b What is the probability that the customer selected made a purchase of under $20?

c Are the events "payment by cash" and "purchase of under $20" mutually exclusive? Explain.

d Are the events "payment by cash" and "purchase of under $20" independent? Explain.

6.13 A personnel manager has cross-classified the 400 employees of a firm according to their record of absenteeism last year and according to whether or not they were smokers, as shown in the accompanying table. One of these employees is selected at random.

Number of days absent	Smoker	Nonsmoker
Less than 10	34	260
10 or more	78	28

a What is the probability that the employee selected was a nonsmoker?

b What is the probability that the employee selected was absent for 10 or more days?

c Are the events "nonsmoker" and "absent less than 10 days" mutually exclusive? Explain.

d Determine whether an employee's being absent for 10 or more days last year was independent of the employee's being a smoker.

6.14 Refer to Exercise 6.4. Find the probability that the store sells exactly two surge suppressors in a week, given that it sells at least one that week.

6.15 Insurance companies rely heavily on probability theory when they compute the premiums to be charged for various life insurance and annuity products. Probabilities are often computed on the basis of life tables like the accompanying table, which tabulates the average number of American males per 100,000 who will die during various age intervals. For example, out of 100,000 male babies born alive, 1,527 will die before their first birthday, and 29,721 will live to the age of 80. Answer the following questions based on this life table.

a What is the probability that a newborn male will reach the age of 50? The age of 70?

b What is the probability that an American male will reach the age of 70, given that he has just turned 50?

c What is the probability that an American male will reach the age of 70, given that he has just turned 60?

Number of Deaths at Various Ages out of 100,000 American Males Born Alive

Age interval*	Number of deaths
0–1	1,527
1–10	495
10–20	927
20–30	1,901
30–40	2,105
40–50	4,502
50–60	10,330
60–70	19,954
70–80	28,538
80 and over	29,721
Total:	100,000

*Interval contains all ages from lower limit up to but not including upper limit.

Source: *Life Tables, Vital Statistics of the United States* (1978). U.S. Department of Health and Human Services.

6.3 PROBABILITY RULES AND TREES

After determining some of the simpler probabilities of experimental outcomes and events, we can use various rules of probability to compute the probabilities of more complex, related events. Consider, for example, an aerospace company that has submitted bids on two separate federal defense contracts, A and B. Suppose the company has estimated $P(A)$ and $P(B)$, the probabilities of winning each of the contracts, as well as $P(A \mid B)$, the probability of winning contract A given that it wins contract B. Using the rules of probability, the company can then readily calculate various related probabilities such as $P(\overline{A})$, the probability of failing to win contract A; $P(A \text{ and } B)$, the probability of winning both contracts; and $P(A \text{ or } B)$, the probability of winning at least one of the two contracts.

Following is a summary of the rules of probability, many of which were anticipated in the solution to Example 6.1.

COMPLEMENT RULE

The first rule of probability follows easily from the basic requirement that the sum of the probabilities assigned to the simple events in a sample space must be 1. Given any event A and its complement $\overline{A}$, each simple event must belong to either A or $\overline{A}$. We therefore must have

$$P(A) + P(\overline{A}) = 1$$

The complement rule is obtained by subtracting $P(\overline{A})$ from each side of the equality.

Complement Rule

$$P(A) = 1 - P(\overline{A})$$

for any event A.

Despite its simplicity, the complement rule can be very useful. The task of finding the probability that an event will not occur and then subtracting this probability from 1 is often easier than the task of directly computing the probability that it will occur.

ADDITION RULE

The second rule of probability enables us to find the probability of the union of two events from the probabilities of other events.

Addition Rule

$$P(A \text{ or } B) = P(A) + P(B) - P(A \text{ and } B)$$

where A and B are any two events.

If A and B are mutually exclusive, we have $P(A \text{ and } B) = 0$, and the addition rule simplifies to $P(A \text{ or } B) = P(A) + P(B)$. You will probably find that, more often than not, the two events of interest in practical situations will be mutually exclusive, and you will use this special form of the addition rule.

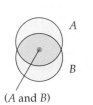

S

A

B

$(A \text{ and } B)$

Figure 6.6

Entire shaded area is event $(A \text{ or } B)$

Addition Rule for Mutually Exclusive Events

$$P(A \text{ or } B) = P(A) + P(B)$$

for any two mutually exclusive events A and B.

In general, however, we must subtract the joint probability $P(A \text{ and } B)$ in order to avoid double-counting a simple event that belongs to both A and B. This is apparent from the Venn diagram in Figure 6.6, in which $(A \text{ or } B)$ is represented by the entire shaded area. When finding the probability $P(A \text{ or } B)$ by summing $P(A)$ and $P(B)$, we must subtract $P(A \text{ and } B)$ to avoid double-counting the probability of event $(A \text{ and } B)$, which belongs to both A and B.

MULTIPLICATION RULE

The third rule of probability, which is used to find the probability of a joint event, is simply a rearrangement of the definition of conditional probability. Because

$$P(A \mid B) = \frac{P(A \text{ and } B)}{P(B)} \qquad \text{and} \qquad P(B \mid A) = \frac{P(A \text{ and } B)}{P(A)}$$

we obtain the following rule for computing the joint probability $P(A \text{ and } B)$.

Multiplication Rule

$$P(A \text{ and } B) = P(A) \cdot P(B \mid A)$$
$$= P(B) \cdot P(A \mid B)$$

for any two events A and B.

Notice that the two expressions for using the multiplication rule to find a joint probability are equivalent. Which expression to use in a particular situation depends on the information given.

For the special case in which A and B are independent events, we have $P(B \mid A) = P(B)$, so we can simply write $P(A \text{ and } B) = P(A) \cdot P(B)$.

Multiplication Rule for Independent Events

$$P(A \text{ and } B) = P(A) \cdot P(B)$$

for any two independent events A and B.

▼ **EXAMPLE 6.3**

Mutual fund management companies are companies that manage a family of mutual funds. Many such companies are listed on a stock exchange. They derive much of their earnings from annual management expense fees, which are calculated as a percentage of total assets under management. Both a rising stock market and increased contributions (dollars invested) by investors will therefore benefit earnings. A stock market analyst feels that the probability that a certain mutual fund company will receive increased contributions this year is .6. The probability of increased contributions rises to .9 if the stock market goes up this year, but will fall below .6 if the market drops. The analyst suggests there is a 50–50 chance of the stock market rising this year. Define the following events:

A: The stock market rises.

B: The company receives increased contributions.

The analyst wishes to find

a the probability that both *A* and *B* will occur, in which case earnings will increase sharply; and

b the probability that either *A* or *B* will occur, in which case earnings will at least increase moderately.

Solution   Summarizing the given information, we know that

$$P(A) = .5$$
$$P(B) = .6$$
$$P(B \mid A) = .9$$

a Applying the multiplication rule, we conclude that the probability that the stock market will rise and the company will receive increased contributions this year is

$$P(A \text{ and } B) = P(A) \cdot P(B \mid A) = (.5)(.9) = .45$$

b Notice that $P(A \text{ or } B)$ can be determined only after $P(A \text{ and } B)$ has been calculated. The probability that either the stock market will rise or that the company will receive increased contributions this year is

$$P(A \text{ or } B) = P(A) + P(B) - P(A \text{ and } B) = .5 + .6 - .45 = .65$$

Thus, the probability that either *A* or *B* will occur is .65. That is, the probability that *at least* one of these two favorable events will occur is .65.

▲

PROBABILITY TREES REVISITED

Having explored the meaning of conditional probability and various rules of probability, we can become a bit more precise about the notation used for probabilities on a probability tree. Consider once again the random experiment consisting of flipping a coin twice. Earlier, we expressed the sample space for this experiment as follows.

$$S = \{HH, HT, TH, TT\}$$

where the first letter of each pair denotes the result of the first flip. An alternative representation of S, differing only in the notation used, is

$$S = \{H_1 \text{ and } H_2, H_1 \text{ and } T_2, T_1 \text{ and } H_2, T_1 \text{ and } T_2\}$$

where the events are defined as follows.

    H_1: Heads is observed on the first flip.

    H_2: Heads is observed on the second flip.

    T_1: Tails is observed on the first flip.

    T_2: Tails is observed on the second flip.

The probability tree for this experiment is repeated in Figure 6.7, using new notation.

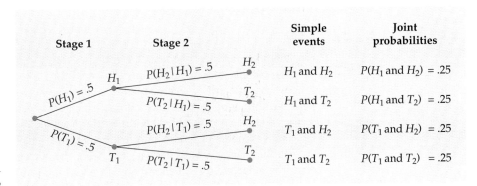

Figure 6.7

Probability tree for coin example

    Recall that the branches emerging from a particular node represent the alternative outcomes that may occur at that point. The probability attached to each branch is the conditional probability that that branch outcome will occur, given that the outcomes represented by preceding branches have all occurred. For example, the probability attached to the top branch at stage 2 is $P(H_2 \mid H_1) = .5$—the probability of obtaining a result of heads on the second flip, given that a result of heads was obtained on the first flip. Because the branches emerging from any particular node represent all possible outcomes that may occur at that point, the sum of the probabilities on those branches must equal 1.

    Since any path through the tree from the origin to a terminal node corresponds to one possible simple event, the probability of that event is the product of the probabilities attached to the branches forming the path. For example, if we follow along the top branches of the tree, we observe the simple event (H_1 and H_2), which (according to the multiplication rule) has the probability

$$P(H_1 \text{ and } H_2) = P(H_1) \cdot P(H_2 \mid H_1) = (.5) \cdot (.5) = .25$$

    You might be wondering why we went to all the trouble of using a probability tree to determine that each of the four possible simple events occurs with a probability of $\frac{1}{4}$, because this may have been obvious to you from the beginning. The main point of this example was to introduce the mechanics of probability trees; the next example illustrates the advantages of using probability trees. In Example 6.4, the probability tree helps sort out the given information and clarifies what has to be calculated to reach a solution. In other situations, you may find a probability tree to be useful in identifying the possible simple events and their associated probabilities.

Suppose we are interested in the condition of a machine that produces a particular item. Let A designate the event "the machine is in good operating condition"; then $\overline{A}$ represents "the machine is not in good operating condition." We might know from experience that the machine is in good condition 90% of the time. That is, the initial or **prior probabilities** regarding the machine's condition are $P(A) = .9$ and $P(\overline{A}) = .1$. Given the machine's condition, we might also know the probability that a defective item will be produced (event B). Suppose that, when the machine is in good condition, only 1% of the items produced are defective, while 10% are defective when the machine is in poor condition. We therefore have the following conditional probabilities.

$$P(B \mid A) = .01$$
$$P(B \mid \overline{A}) = .10$$

The situation just described can be treated as a two-stage experiment and represented by a probability tree, as in Figure 6.8.

We are primarily concerned with the machine's condition, and we know from historical information that there is a 90% chance of its being in good condition. We can get a better idea of the likelihood that the machine is in good condition right now, however, by obtaining more information. Suppose that, without knowing the condition of the machine, we select an item from the current production run and observe that it is defective. It is then possible to revise the prior probability that the machine is in good condition (event A) in light of the new information that event B has occurred. That is, we can find the revised or **posterior probability.**

$$P(A \mid B) = \frac{P(A \text{ and } B)}{P(B)}$$

The value of the numerator is obtained easily from the probability tree.

$$P(A \text{ and } B) = P(A) \cdot P(B \mid A)$$
$$= (.9)(.01)$$
$$= .009$$

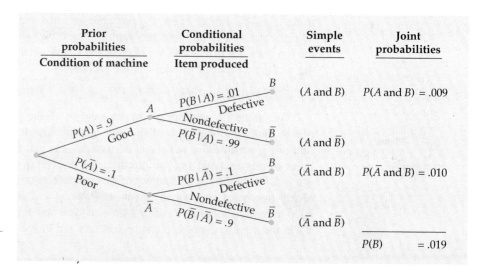

Figure 6.8

Probability tree for machine producing items

We next note that event B occurs only if one of two simple events, (A and B) or ($\overline{A}$ and B), occurs. The denominator is therefore

$$P(B) = P(A \text{ and } B) + P(\overline{A} \text{ and } B)$$
$$= .009 + .010$$
$$= .019$$

By using the rules of probability or simply by reading from the probability tree, we obtain

$$P(A \mid B) = \frac{P(A \text{ and } B)}{P(B)}$$
$$= \frac{P(A \text{ and } B)}{P(A \text{ and } B) + P(\overline{A} \text{ and } B)}$$
$$= \frac{.009}{.019} = .47$$

In light of the sample information, we have revised drastically downward—from .9 to .47—the probability that the machine is currently in good condition. Based on this posterior (after sampling) probability of .47, it is likely worth paying a mechanic to check and repair the machine.

▲

Take a moment to notice what we have done in the previous example. We were given $P(A)$ and the two conditional probabilities $P(B \mid A)$ and $P(B \mid \overline{A})$. Using the probability tree, we were able to find the related "reverse" conditional probability: $P(A \mid B)$. (Here we use "reverse" in the sense that the event given to have occurred is reversed.) This would not be nearly as easy to accomplish without the clarity provided by the probability tree. Some readers may recognize that we have essentially applied the formula provided by Bayes' theorem, which we do not discuss here. So important and widely used is Bayes' theorem in helping to establish decision strategies, there is an entire field called *Bayesian decision analysis*. The interested reader is encouraged to learn more about this area.

EXERCISES

6.16 A fair coin is flipped three times. Use a probability tree to find the probability of observing the following.

   a No heads.   **b** Exactly one heads.
   c Exactly two heads.   **d** At least one tails.

6.17 An aerospace company has submitted bids on two separate federal government defense contracts, A and B. The company feels that it has a 50% chance of winning contract A and a 40% chance of winning contract B. Furthermore, it believes that winning contract A is independent of winning contract B.

   a What is the probability that the company will win both contracts?

   b What is the probability that the company will win at least one of the two contracts?

6.18 Suppose the aerospace company in Exercise 6.17 feels that it has a 60% chance of winning contract A and a 30% chance of winning contract B. Given that it wins contract B, the company believes it has an 80% chance of winning contract A.

   a What is the probability that the company will win both contracts?

   b What is the probability that the company will win at least one of the two contracts?

   c If the company wins contract B, what is the probability that it will not win contract A?

S TATISTICS IN THE W ORKPLACE

Operations Management Application

In the introduction to operations management we pointed out that functional design concerns itself with how the product performs. Does the product work as it is supposed to for a reasonable period of time? A well-designed and manufactured product tries to meet the specifications created by marketing. One characteristic of the specification is the *reliability* of the product. Reliability is the probability that a product will function properly for a specified period of time. There are two aspects to the calculation of this type of probability. The first is the probability that a product will simply function, and the second is the probability that the product will perform as required for at least a minimum period of time.

We will postpone discussion of this second aspect until Chapter 7, and briefly discuss the first aspect now.

The probability that a product will work properly is a function of the probabilities that its components will work. Some products require that *all* parts work in order for them to function. In others there are system backups that allow for the failure of one or more parts. The next two exercises illustrate how probability techniques can be used to measure the reliability of a product.

6.19 The controls of an airplane have several backup systems or redundancies, so that if one fails the plane will continue to operate. Suppose that the mechanism that controls the flaps has two backups. If the probability that the main control fails is .00001 and that each of the backups fails is .0001, what is the probability that the plane will crash? What have you assumed?

6.20 A four-cylinder car has four spark plugs, each of which must work or the car will idle roughly and gas will be wasted. The supplier of spark plugs notes that the failure rate of a newly installed spark plug is .00001.

  a What is the probability that when a new car is started all the spark plugs work?

  b What is the probability that the car will idle roughly and waste gas (assuming at least one plug must work for the car to idle)?

  c What assumptions have you made in answering this question?

6.21 A sporting goods store estimates that 20% of the students at a nearby university ski downhill and 15% ski cross-country. Of those who ski downhill, 40% also ski cross-country.

  a What percentage of these students ski both downhill and cross-country?

  b What percentage of the students do not ski at all?

6.22 A union's executive conducted a survey of its members to determine what the members felt were the important issues to be discussed during upcoming negotiations with management. Results showed that 74% felt that job security was an important issue, while 65% felt that pension benefits were an important issue. Of those who felt that pension benefits were an important issue, 60% also felt that job security was an important issue.

  a What percentage of the members felt that both job security and pension benefits were important?

  b What percentage of the members felt that at least one of these two issues was important?

6.23 Two six-sided dice are rolled, and the number of spots turning up on each is observed. Determine the probability of observing four spots on at least one of the dice. (HINT: Use the complement rule.)

6.24 A certain city has one morning newspaper and one evening newspaper. It is estimated that 20% of the city's households subscribe to the morning paper and 60% subscribe to the evening paper. Of those who subscribe to the morning paper, 80% also subscribe to the evening paper. What proportion of households does the following?

  a Subscribes to both papers.

  b Subscribes to at most one of the papers.

  c Subscribes to neither paper.

6.25 Individuals who want to pursue a career in investment analysis are often encouraged to obtain the professional designation of Chartered Financial Analyst (CFA). A candidate must pass three exams to obtain this designation and can take only one exam in a given year. The results of the exams held in 1993, reported by the Institute of Chartered Financial Analysis in *The CFA Study Guide* (1994), are summarized in the accompanying table. One candidate is selected at random from those who took a CFA exam in 1993.

Exam	Number of candidates writing	Percentage who passed
I	6,588	55%
II	3,679	56
III	2,542	76

a What is the probability that the selected candidate passed?

b What is the probability that the selected candidate took Exam I and passed?

c If the selected candidate passed, what is the probability that the candidate took Exam III?

6.26 An assembler has been supplied with 10 electronic components, of which 3 are defective. If 2 components are selected at random, what is the probability that neither component is defective?

6.27 Approximately three out of every four Americans who filed a 1995 tax return received a refund. If three individuals are chosen at random from among those who filed a 1995 tax return, find the probabilities of the following events.

a All three received a refund.

b None of the three received a refund.

c Exactly one received a refund.

6.28 A door-to-door saleswoman sells rug shampoo in three tube sizes: small, large, and giant. The probability of finding a person at home is .6. If the saleswoman does find someone at home, the probabilities are .5 that she will make no sale, .2 that she will sell a small tube, .2 that she will sell a large tube, and .1 that she will sell a giant tube. The probability of selling more than one tube of rug shampoo at a house is 0.

a Find the probability that, in one call, she will not sell any shampoo.

b Find the probability that, in one call, she will sell either a large tube or a giant tube.

6.29 To determine who pays for coffee, three students each toss a coin and the odd person pays. If all coins show heads or all show tails, the students toss again. What is the probability that a decision will be reached in five or fewer tosses?

6.30 Of 20,000 small businesses surveyed, "about 82% said they employed women in some capacity." Of those that employed women, 19.5% employed no female supervisors, 50% employed only one female supervisor, and the remainder employed more than one female supervisor (*Globe and Mail*, October 1995).

a How many of the businesses surveyed employed no women?

b What proportion of businesses surveyed employed exactly one female supervisor?

c What proportion of businesses surveyed employed no female supervisors?

d Given that a firm employed women, what is the probability that it employed at least one female supervisor?

6.31 All printed circuit boards (PCBs) that are manufactured at a certain plant are inspected for flaws. Experience has shown that 50% of the PCBs produced are flawed in some way. Of the flawed PCBs, 60% are repairable, while the remainder are seriously flawed and must be discarded. A newly manufactured PCB is selected before undergoing inspection. What is the probability that it will not have to be discarded?

6.32 A foreman for an injection molding firm admits that, on 10% of his shifts, he forgets to shut off the injection machine on his line. This causes the machine to overheat and increases the chance that a defective molding will be produced during the early morning run from .5% to 5%. If the plant manager randomly selects a molding from the morning run and finds it to be defective, what is the probability that the foreman forgot to shut off the machine the previous night?

6.33 When a test is conducted to determine whether or not someone is infected with a particular virus, an incorrect test result can occur in two ways: An infected person may test negative, or a noninfected person may test positive. The latter is called a *false positive* test. It has been pointed out that the social consequences of false positive tests for the AIDS virus are particularly serious.* Such a false positive test will unnecessarily "stigmatize and frighten many healthy people," because "most people consider a positive AIDS test to be a sentence to ghastly suffering and death." Meyer and Pauker therefore assert that it is important that a patient who tests positive for the AIDS virus have a high probability of really being infected. In order to focus on the false positive rate of the test, assume throughout this question that we are dealing with a test that properly identifies all persons who really are infected with the AIDS virus.

a Assume that 5% of a population to be tested for the AIDS virus really is infected and that the test has a false positive rate of .5%. Find the probability that a person who tests positive really is infected.

b Would your answer to part (a) be higher or lower if more than 5% of the population to be tested were actually infected? Answer the question by referring to the formula for conditional probability without performing any calculations.

c Assume now that a low-risk population is to be tested. Specifically, assume that .01% of the population to be tested is actually infected with the AIDS virus and that the test has a false positive rate of .005% (which is unusually low). Find the probability that a person who tests positive really is infected.

d What would your answer to part (c) be if you assumed a false positive rate of .5%?

*Klemens Meyer and Stephen Pauker, "Screening for HIV: Can We Afford the False Positive Rate?" *New England Journal of Medicine* (1987): 238–41.

e Summarize the implications of your findings in parts (a) through (d).

6.34 A study by the Correctional Service of Canada has found that a new law designed to keep dangerous offenders behind bars longer has failed. The law created a special category of inmates based on whether they had committed crimes involving violence or drugs. Such criminals are subject to detention if the Correctional Service judges them to be highly likely to reoffend. Prisoners who are not so detained are automatically paroled after serving two-thirds of their sentence. Those detained under this law serve an average of 415 additional days in prison. Recent statistics reveal that 37% of those not detained reoffend within 2 years. However, only 16% of those detained reoffend within 2 years of their release.

a Suppose that 50% of all prisoners are detained under the new law. What is the probability that a criminal who has reoffended within 2 years of his release from prison was paroled after serving two-thirds of his sentence?

b Recalculate the probability above assuming that 90% of all prisoners are released after serving two-thirds of their sentence.

6.4 RANDOM VARIABLES AND PROBABILITY DISTRIBUTIONS

In most random experiments, we're interested only in a certain aspect of the experimental outcomes. The instrument we use to focus our attention on this particular aspect of an outcome (and to assign a numerical value to the outcome accordingly) is called a random variable. Consider once again the experiment consisting of flipping a coin twice. Recall that a sample space for this experiment is $S = \{HH, HT, TH, TT\}$. Suppose that we're interested in the total number of heads that turn up. If X denotes the total number of heads turning up, the value that X takes on will vary randomly from one trial of the experiment to the next, and X is called a **random variable.** In fact, X is a function that assigns a numerical value to each simple event in the sample space S, with the possible values of X being 0, 1, and 2, as shown in Figure 6.9.

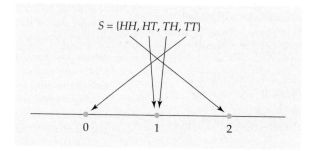

Figure 6.9

Random variable *X* assigning values to simple events

A formal definition of a random variable might read as follows.

Random Variable

A **random variable** is a function that assigns a numerical value to each simple event in a sample space.

Less formally, we might simply state that *a random variable is a variable whose numerical value is determined by the outcome of a random experiment.* Throughout this chapter, we stress the distinction between a random variable and the values it can assume by following the convention of using capital letters such as X and Y to denote random variables and using lowercase letters such as x and y to denote their values. Although many people consider this distinction in notation unnecessary, we believe it is a useful one to maintain while you are becoming familiar with the notion of a random variable. The notational distinction is dropped in subsequent chapters, however, because the interpretation of x is usually clear from the context in which it is used.

There are two types of random variables—discrete and continuous—distinguished from one another by the number of possible values that they can assume. A **discrete random variable** has a *countable* number of possible values. Put simply, this means that a variable is discrete if we can identify the first value, the second value, and all subsequent values of the random variable. In most practical situations, a discrete random variable counts the number of times a particular attribute is observed. Examples of discrete random variables include the number of defective items in a production batch, the number of telephone calls received in a given hour, and the number of shoppers surveyed who prefer a particular product. If X denotes the number of respondents, in a survey of 400 shoppers, who state a preference for a particular product, then X can take any one of the values $x = 0, 1, 2, \ldots, 400$.

Note that countable does not necessarily mean finite. It is possible to count the values of a random variable with no upper limit. One such variable is the one defined as the number of flips of a balanced coin until the first heads is observed. This random variable could equal 1 (first flip produces heads), 2 (first flip is tails and the second flip is heads), and so on. It is extremely unlikely that the value of this random variable is large [for example, we calculated the probability that 100 flips ($x = 100$) are required to produce the first heads to be 7.89×10^{-31}, which is a decimal point followed by 30 zeros and 789]; nevertheless there is no upper limit on its value. Because it is countable (we can identify all possible values), it is discrete.

Discrete and Continuous Random Variables

A random variable is **discrete** if it can assume only a countable number of possible values. A random variable that can assume an uncountable number of values is **continuous.**

A continuous random variable has an uncountably infinite number of possible values; that is, it can take on any value in one or more intervals of values. Continuous random variables typically record the value of a measurement such as time, weight, or length. For example, suppose that we measure the amount of time workers on an assembly line take to complete a particular task. Suppose further that the fastest time possible is 60 seconds. What is the next possible value? Is it 61 seconds, or 60.1 seconds, or 60.01 seconds? It is impossible to specify the next value because there is an infinite number of values starting with 60. Because we cannot specify the second value or the third, or fourth, we cannot count the number of values this random variable can equal. Hence, it is a continuous random variable. We will discuss this type of random variable later.

For the time being, we will restrict our attention to discrete random variables. Having considered the values of a random variable, we now turn to the probabilities associated with those values. When we know the possible values of a random variable and the probabilities associated with those values, we have the **probability distribution** of the random variable—our main object of interest.

> ### Discrete Probability Distribution
>
> A table, formula, or graph that lists all possible values a discrete random variable can assume, together with their associated probabilities, is called a **discrete probability distribution.**

The probability associated with a particular value of a random variable is determined in a manner you can probably anticipate. If x is a value of a random variable X, then the probability that X assumes the value x, denoted either by $P(X = x)$ or by $p(x)$, is the sum of the probabilities associated with the simple events for which X assumes the value x.

Let's apply this rule to the experiment involving two flips of a coin. If the random variable X represents the number of heads turning up, then X can assume any one of the values 0, 1, or 2. Probabilities can be assigned to the values of X with the help of Table 6.2, which records each simple event, its probability, and the corresponding value of X. (Recall that the simple event probabilities shown in Table 6.2 were calculated in Figure 6.1 with the help of a probability tree.) For example, X takes the value 1 if either simple event HT or TH occurs, so

$$P(X = 1) = P(HT) + P(TH) = \frac{1}{4} + \frac{1}{4} = \frac{1}{2}$$

Table 6.2 Values of X Corresponding to Simple Events

Simple Event	x	Probability
HH	2	1/4
HT	1	1/4
TH	1	1/4
TT	0	1/4

The distinct values of X and their associated probabilities are summarized in Table 6.3, which gives the probability distribution of X. The probability distribution of X can be presented in the tabular form shown in Table 6.3, in the graphical form of Figure 6.10, or in terms of the following formula.

$$p(x) = \begin{cases} \dfrac{1}{4} & \text{if } x = 0 \text{ or } 2 \\ \dfrac{1}{2} & \text{if } x = 1 \end{cases}$$

Table 6.3 Probability Distribution of X

x	p(x)
0	1/4
1	1/2
2	1/4

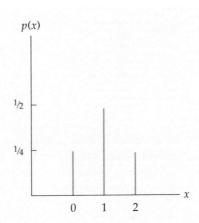

Figure 6.10

Graphical presentation of
probability distribution

In an example such as this one, where the formula is rather cumbersome, the tabular representation of the probability distribution of X is most convenient. Whichever representation is used, a discrete probability distribution must satisfy two conditions, which follow from the basic requirements for probabilities outlined in Section 6.2.

Requirements of Discrete Probability Distribution

If a random variable X can take values x_i, then the following must be true:

1. $0 \leq p(x_i) \leq 1$ for all x_i

2. $\displaystyle\sum_{\text{all } x_i} p(x_i) = 1$

After a probability distribution has been defined for a random variable X, we can talk about the probability that X takes a value in some range of values. The probability that X takes a value between a and b, inclusive, denoted by $P(a \leq X \leq b)$, is obtained by summing the probabilities $p(x)$ for all values of x such that $a \leq x \leq b$. In the preceding example, we would have

$$P(1 \leq X \leq 2) = p(1) + p(2) = \frac{1}{2} + \frac{1}{4} = \frac{3}{4}$$

In other words, the probability that the total number of heads turning up is either 1 or 2 is $\frac{3}{4}$, or .75.

PROBABILITIES AS RELATIVE FREQUENCIES

The probabilities in the coin-tossing example were assigned using the classical approach. In practice, probabilities assigned to values of a random variable are often estimated from relative frequencies. For example, suppose that we're interested in the number of cars a dealer sells daily. The sales manager observes the results of the last 100 days, which are displayed on the following page.

Daily Sales (X)	Frequency
0	5
1	15
2	35
3	25
4	20
	100

We can use the frequencies to estimate the probability of occurrence of each value of the random variable. Since the probabilities must sum to 1, we estimate the probabilities by dividing each frequency by the total number of days observed, which is 100. The estimated probability distribution is shown below.

Daily Sales (X)	Probability
0	5/100 = .05
1	15/100 = .15
2	35/100 = .35
3	25/100 = .25
4	20/100 = .20
	100/100 = 1.00

If we assume that the relative frequencies calculated above are accurate estimates of the true probabilities, we can say for example that, in the long run, on 5% of the days the dealer will sell no cars and on 35% of the days the dealer will sell 2 cars. We can also state that the probability of selling more than 2 cars on any single day is the sum of the probabilities of the values of X that are greater than 2. Hence $P(X > 2) = p(3) + p(4) = .25 + .20 = .45$, which means that in the long run 45% of the days will result in sales of more than 2 cars.

EXERCISES

6.35 The number of accidents that occur annually on a busy stretch of highway is a random variable.

a What are the possible values of this random variable?
b Are the values countable? Explain.
c Is there a finite number of values? Explain.
d Is the random variable discrete or continuous? Explain.

6.36 The distance a car travels on one tank of gasoline is a random variable.

a What are the possible values of this random variable?
b Are the values countable? Explain.
c Is there a finite number of values? Explain.
d Is the random variable discrete or continuous? Explain.

6.37 The average mark (out of 100) on a statistics test is a random variable.

a What are the possible values of this random variable?
b Are the values countable? Explain.
c Is there a finite number of values? Explain.
d Is the random variable discrete or continuous? Explain.

6.38 Consider a random variable X with the following probability distribution.

x	−4	0	1	2
$p(x)$	.2	.3	.4	.1

Find the following probabilities.

a $P(X > 0)$ **b** $P(X \geq 0)$ **c** $P(0 \leq X \leq 1)$
d $P(X = -4)$ **e** $P(X = -2)$ **f** $P(X < 2)$

6.39 Consider a random variable X with the following probability distribution.
$p(x) = .1x$, where $x = 1, 2, 3,$ or 4

Express the probability distribution in tabular form, and use it to find the following probabilities.

a $P(X \geq 1)$ **b** $P(X > 1)$ **c** $P(2 \leq X \leq 3)$
d $P(X = 4)$ **e** $P(X = 3.5)$

6.40 Determine which of the following are not valid probability distributions, and explain why not.

a

x	1	2	3	4
p(x)	.2	.2	.3	.4

b

x	0	2	4	5
p(x)	−.1	.2	.3	.4

c

x	−2	−1	1	2
p(x)	.1	.1	.1	.7

6.41 Let X be the number of spots that turn up when a six-sided die is tossed.

  a Express the probability distribution of X in tabular form.
  b Express the probability distribution of X in graphical form.

6.42 Let X be the number of heads that are observed when a fair coin is flipped three times.

  a Express the probability distribution of X in tabular form.
  b Express the probability distribution of X in graphical form.

6.43 Let X represent the number of children under 18 years old in an American family. According to the *Statistical Abstract of the United States: 1993,* the probability distribution of X is as follows.

x	0	1	2	3	4	5
p(x)	.49	.21	.19	.08	.02	.01

  a What proportion of American households have 2 or fewer children under 18?
  b What proportion of American households have more than 3 children under 18?
  c What proportion of American households have between 1 and 3 (inclusive) children under 18?

6.44 Let X represent the number of people in an American household. According to the *Statistical Abstract of the United States: 1993,* the probability distribution of X is as follows (rounded to two decimal places).

x	1	2	3	4	5	6	7
p(x)	.24	.31	.17	.16	.07	.03	.02

  a What is the probability of a randomly selected household having fewer than 4 people?
  b What is the probability of a randomly selected household having between 2 and 5 (inclusive) people?
  c What is the probability of a randomly selected household having more than 6 people?

6.45 Using historical data, the personnel manager of a plant has determined that the probability distribution of X, the number of employees absent on any given day, is as follows.

x	0	1	2	3	4	5	6	7
p(x)	.005	.025	.310	.340	.220	.080	.019	.001

Find the following.

  a $P(2 \leq X \leq 4)$
  b $P(X > 5)$
  c $P(X \leq 6)$

6.46 A mutual fund saleswoman has arranged to call on three households tomorrow. Based on past experience, she feels that there is a 20% chance of closing a sale on each call and that the outcome of each call is independent of the others. Let X represent the number of sales she closes tomorrow.

  a Find the probability distribution of X.
  b Express the probability distribution of X graphically.
  c What is the probability that more than one sale will be closed tomorrow?

6.47 Second-year business students at a certain university are required to take 10 one-semester courses. Suppose that the number of courses in which a student will receive a grade of A has a **discrete uniform distribution** (that is, each possible number has the same probability of occurrence).

  a What are the possible values of the random variable and their probabilities?
  b What is the probability that a second-year business student receives an A in exactly three courses?
  c What is the probability that a second-year business student receives an A in more than 10 courses?
  d What is the probability that a second-year business student's highest grade is a B?

6.5 EXPECTED VALUE AND VARIANCE

As stated previously, probability is the link between a sample and the population from which it is taken. This is so because a probability distribution is the distribution of a population. Consider, for example, the probability distribution shown in Table 6.4, where the random variable X represents the payoff (in dollars) from a proposed investment of $25.

We can conceive of the underlying population in the following way: Imagine a barrel containing infinitely many chips, of which one-half are labeled 20, one-quarter are labeled 40, and one-quarter are labeled 60. If X denotes the label on a chip that is randomly selected from the population of chips, the probability distribution of X is as shown in Table 6.4.

Table 6.4   **Probability Distribution of X**

x	$p(x)$
20	1/2
40	1/4
60	1/4

Now consider the population of labels on all chips. We might want to find the mean of this population, just as we did with the populations encountered back in Chapter 4, where we defined the *mean of a population* of N values of x to be

$$\mu = \frac{\sum_{i=1}^{N} x_i}{N} = \sum_{i=1}^{N} x_i \cdot \frac{1}{N}$$

For the infinitely large population of labels, however, we must replace $1/N$ with the probability, or relative frequency, with which x_i occurs. The mean of such a population, called the **mean value** of X, is therefore given by

$$\mu = \sum x \cdot p(x)$$

where the sum is taken over all values of X. This value is also referred to as the **expected value** of X, written $E(X)$. Hence, the expected value of the payoff from the $25 investment is

$$E(X) = \mu$$

$$= 20\left(\frac{1}{2}\right) + 40\left(\frac{1}{4}\right) + 60\left(\frac{1}{4}\right) = \$35$$

In general, we have the following definition.

Expected Value

Given a discrete random variable X with values x_i that occur with probabilities $p(x_i)$, the expected value of X is

$$E(X) = \sum_{\text{all } x_i} x_i \cdot p(x_i)$$

The expected value of a random variable X is the weighted average of the possible values it can assume, where the weights are the probabilities of occurrence of those values. The expected value of X should be interpreted simply as a weighted average of the possible values of X, rather than as a value that X is expected to assume. In fact, as the preceding example illustrates, $E(X)$ might not even be a possible value of X.

An alternative interpretation of the expected value of X employs the long-run relative frequency approach to probability described in Section 6.2. If the investment in the foregoing example were undertaken repeatedly a large number of times, the expected value of X, \$35, would be a good approximation to the average payoff resulting from the many investments.

LAWS OF EXPECTED VALUE

Various algebraic identities or laws are available to help simplify the calculation of an expected value. Although the proofs are not difficult, the laws are stated here without proof. Exercises 6.59 and 6.60 provide you with opportunities to verify these laws.

If X and Y are random variables and c is any constant, the following identities hold.

1 $E(c) = c$

2 $E(cX) = cE(X)$

3 $E(X + Y) = E(X) + E(Y)$

$\quad E(X - Y) = E(X) - E(Y)$

4 $E(XY) = E(X)E(Y)$, if X and Y are independent random variables*

The utility of these laws derives from the fact that, given a function of one or more random variables, the expected value of the terms the function comprises may already be known or may be easier to compute than the expected value of the function itself. For example, if the random variable X is the number of units of an item that are produced daily, a is the variable cost of production per unit, and b is the daily fixed cost of production, the total daily production cost is $Y = aX + b$. The expected daily production cost is $E(Y) = aE(X) + b$. Calculating $E(X)$ and then using the formula is normally easier than finding $E(Y)$ directly.

VARIANCE

The expected value of a random variable X is a weighted average of the values of X; it therefore provides us with a measure of the central location of the distribution of X. It does not tell us, however, whether the values of X are clustered closely about the expected value or are widely scattered. That is, the mean, or expected value, of a random variable does not by itself adequately describe the random variable. Just as in Chapter 4, we need a measure of dispersion.

---

*Although beginning students of statistics will not normally find occasion to use this law, it is included for completeness. Two random variables X and Y are said to be *independent* if the value assumed by one variable in no way affects the probability of a particular value's being assumed by the other. That is, X and Y are independent if $P(X = x \mid Y = y_0) = P(X = x)$ or, equivalently, if $P(Y = y \mid X = x_0) = P(Y = y)$, for all x_0 and y_0.

Recall that a popular measure of the dispersion of a population of N measurements $x_1, \ldots, x_N$ is the variance, given by

$$\sigma^2 = \frac{\sum_{i=1}^{N} (x_i - \mu)^2}{N} = \sum_{i=1}^{N} (x_i - \mu)^2 \cdot \frac{1}{N}$$

The variance of a random variable X is defined in a similar manner, with $1/N$ being replaced by $p(x_i)$. We can then describe the variance of a random variable X as the weighted average of the squared deviations of the values of X from their mean μ, with the weight attached to $(x_i - \mu)^2$ being $p(x_i)$—the probability with which that squared deviation occurs. In other words, the variance of X is the expected value of the random variable $(X - \mu)^2$.

Variance

Let X be a discrete random variable with possible values x_i that occur with probabilities $p(x_i)$, and let $E(X) = \mu$. The variance of X is defined to be

$$\sigma^2 = E[(X - \mu)^2] = \sum_{\text{all } x_i} (x_i - \mu)^2 \, p(x_i)$$

Notice that a variance is always nonnegative, since each item in the summation is nonnegative. Alternative notations for the variance of X are σ_X^2 and $V(X)$, both of which are useful ways to indicate the random variable in question.

To illustrate the computation of variance, we consider once again the probability distribution (Table 6.4) for X, the payoff from an investment of $25. The variance of the payoff is

$$\sigma_X^2 = (20 - 35)^2 \left(\frac{1}{2}\right) + (40 - 35)^2 \left(\frac{1}{4}\right) + (60 - 35)^2 \left(\frac{1}{4}\right) = 275 \text{ (dollars)}^2$$

A variance, considered by itself, is somewhat difficult to interpret. The notion of variance is therefore chiefly used to compare the variabilities of different distributions, which might, for example, represent the possible outcomes of alternative courses of action under consideration. One important application arises in finance, where variance is the most popular numerical measure of risk; the underlying assumption is that a larger variance corresponds to a higher level of risk.

Let Y represent the payoff from a second proposed investment of $25. The possible payoffs in this case are $10, $40, and $80, occurring with probabilities $\frac{1}{2}, \frac{1}{4}$, and $\frac{1}{4}$, respectively. The expected value of Y can be shown to be $35—the same as the expected value of X—but the variance of Y is 825 (dollars)^2, as you can verify. If the riskiness of the investments is measured by the variance of their payoffs, the second proposed investment is riskier than the first, since $\sigma_Y^2 > \sigma_X^2$. This risk assessment is probably consistent with the intuitive impression you would obtain from a casual comparison of the distributions of X and Y.

The variance of X is defined to be $E[(X - \mu)^2]$. By expanding $(X - \mu)^2$ and applying the laws of expected value, we can identify an alternative formulation of the variance of X.

$$\sigma_X^2 = E(X^2) - \mu^2$$

This **shortcut for computing the variance** is useful because the calculation of $E(X^2)$ is often simpler than the direct computation of σ_X^2, which involves squared deviations. Like that of any other random variable, the expected value of X^2 is obtained by taking the weighted average of its possible values.

$$E(X^2) = \sum_{i=1}^{n} x_i^2 p(x_i)$$

As was the case in Chapter 4 with a set of measurement data, we might want to express the variability of X in terms of a measure having the same units as X. Once again, this is accomplished by taking the positive square root of the variance.

Standard Deviation

The **standard deviation** of a random variable X, denoted σ, is the positive square root of the variance of X.

For instance, the standard deviation of X, the payoff from the first proposed investment, is

$$\sigma_X = \sqrt{275} = \$16.58$$

▼ EXAMPLE 6.5

Now that the new models are available, a car dealership has lowered the prices on last year's models in order to clear its holdover inventory. With prices slashed, a young and aggressive salesman estimates the following probability distribution of X, the total number of cars that he'll sell next week.

x	0	1	2	3	4
$p(x)$	.05	.15	.35	.25	.20

Determine the expected value and the standard deviation of X.

Solution The expected value, variance, and standard deviation of X can be calculated directly from their definitions.

$$E(X) = \mu = \sum_{i=1}^{5} x_i p(x_i)$$
$$= 0(.05) + 1(.15) + 2(.35) + 3(.25) + 4(.20)$$
$$= 2.40$$

$$V(X) = \sigma^2 = \sum_{i=1}^{5} (x_i - 2.4)^2 p(x_i)$$
$$= (0 - 2.4)^2(.05) + (1 - 2.4)^2(.15) + (2 - 2.4)^2(.35)$$
$$+ (3 - 2.4)^2(.25) + (4 - 2.4)^2(.20)$$
$$= 1.24$$
$$\sigma = \sqrt{1.24}$$
$$= 1.11$$

The expected number of cars that the salesman will sell next week is 2.4, with a standard deviation of 1.11.

A convenient alternative for computational purposes is to record the probability distribution of X (and subsequent computations) in a table such as Table 6.5. Rather than having a column for $(x - \mu)^2$, we have chosen to use the shortcut formula for variance, which entails finding the expected value of X^2. Therefore, from Table 6.5,

$$E(X) = \mu = 2.4$$
$$V(X) = E(X^2) - \mu^2 = 7 - (2.4)^2 = 1.24$$
$$\sigma = \sqrt{1.24} = 1.11$$

Table 6.5   Computations for $E(X)$ and $E(X^2)$

x	$p(x)$	$xp(x)$	x^2	$x^2 p(x)$
0	.05	0	0	0
1	.15	.15	1	.15
2	.35	.70	4	1.40
3	.25	.75	9	2.25
4	.20	.80	16	3.20
Total		2.40 = $E(X)$		7.00 = $E(X^2)$

▲

LAWS OF VARIANCE

Just as with the calculation of expected value, various laws help simplify the calculation of variance; they are stated here without proof.

If X and Y are random variables and c is a constant, the following identities hold.

1 $V(c) = 0$

2 $V(cX) = c^2 V(X)$

3 $V(X + c) = V(X)$

4 $V(X + Y) = V(X) + V(Y)$, and
   $V(X - Y) = V(X) + V(Y)$, if X and Y are independent

▼ **EXAMPLE 6.6**

In Example 6.5, the young salesman estimated the probability distribution of X (the total number of cars he would sell next week) to be as follows.

x	0	1	2	3	4
$p(x)$	.05	.15	.35	.25	.20

Subsequent calculations revealed that $E(X) = 2.4$ and $V(X) = 1.24$. Now suppose that this salesman earns a fixed weekly wage of $150 plus a $200 commission for each car sold. His weekly wage is therefore $Y = 200X + 150$. What is his expected wage for next week? What is the variance of Y?

Solution   The probability distribution of Y and the computations for $E(Y)$ and $E(Y^2)$ are shown in Table 6.6. From the table, we know that $E(Y) = 630$ and that $V(Y) = E(Y^2) - \mu^2 = 446,500 - (630)^2 = 49,600$. Rather than performing the mind-numbing calculations in Table 6.6, we could simply use the laws of expected value and variance.

$$
\begin{aligned}
E(Y) &= E(200X + 150) & V(Y) &= V(200X + 150) \\
&= 200E(X) + 150 & &= (200)^2 V(X) \\
&= 200(2.4) + 150 & &= (200)^2(1.24) \\
&= 630 & &= 49,600
\end{aligned}
$$

The young salesman's expected wage for next week is therefore \$630, with a variance of 49,600 (dollars)^2.

Table 6.6   Computations for $E(Y)$ and $E(Y^2)$

y	$p(y)$	$yp(y)$	y^2	$y^2p(y)$
150	.05	7.5	22,500	1,125
350	.15	52.5	122,500	18,375
550	.35	192.5	302,500	105,875
750	.25	187.5	562,500	140,625
950	.20	190.0	902,500	180,500
Total		$630.0 = E(Y)$		$446,500 = E(Y^2)$

▲

EXERCISES

6.48 Let X be a random variable with the following probability distribution.

x	1	2	3	4
$p(x)$	.4	.3	.2	.1

a Find $E(X)$ and $V(X)$.
b Is $E(X)$ a possible value of X?

6.49 Let X be a random variable with the following probability distribution.

x	−4	0	1	2
$p(x)$	.2	.3	.4	.1

a Find μ and σ.
b Is μ a possible value of X?
c Find $E(X^2)$ and $E(3X^2 + 2)$.

6.50 Let X be a random variable with the following probability distribution.

x	5	10	15	20	25
$p(x)$	.05	.30	.25	.25	.15

a Find the expected value and variance of X.
b Find the expected value and variance of $Y = 4X - 3$.

6.51 Let X be a random variable with the following probability distribution.

x	−10	−5	0	5	10
$p(x)$	.10	.20	.20	.20	.30

a Find the mean and standard deviation of X.
b Find the mean and standard deviation of $2X$.
c Find the mean and standard deviation of $2X + 5$.

6.52 Let X be a random variable with the following probability distribution.

x	0	5	10	20
p(x)	.2	.3	.3	.2

a Find the mean and standard deviation of X.
b Find $E(X^2)$.
c Find $E(5X^2)$.

6.53 Let X represent the number of times a student visits a nearby pizza parlor in a 1-month period. Assume that the following table is the probability distribution of X.

x	0	1	2	3
p(x)	.1	.3	.4	.2

a Find the mean (μ) and the standard deviation (σ) of this distribution.
b What is the probability that the student visits the pizza parlor at least twice in a month?
c Find $P(X \geq 1.5)$.
d Construct a graph of the probability distribution, and locate μ and the interval $\mu \pm \sigma$ on the graph.

6.54 The owner of a small firm has just purchased a personal computer, which she expects will serve her for the next 2 years. The owner has been told that she "must" buy a surge suppressor to provide protection for her new hardware against possible surges or variations in the electrical current. Her son David, a recent university graduate, advises that an inexpensive suppressor could be purchased that would provide protection against one surge only. He notes that the amount of damage without a suppressor would depend on the extent of the surge. David conservatively estimates that, during the next 2 years, there is a 1% chance of incurring $400 damage and a 2% chance of incurring $200 damage. But the probability of incurring $100 damage is .1.

a How much should the owner be willing to pay for a surge suppressor?
b Determine the standard deviation of the possible amount of damage.

6.55 In Exercise 6.15, it was noted that insurance companies rely heavily on probability theory when they compute the premiums to charge for various life insurance and annuity products. Suppose a 40-year-old male purchases a $100,000 10-year term life policy from an insurance company, meaning that the insurance company must pay out $100,000 if the insured male dies within the next 10 years.

a Use the accompanying life table to determine the insurance company's expected payout on this policy.
b What would the expected payout be if the same policy were taken out by a 50-year-old male?

Number of Deaths at Various Ages out of 100,000 American Males Born Alive

Age interval*	Number of deaths
0–1	1,527
1–10	495
10–20	927
20–30	1,901
30–40	2,105
40–50	4,502
50–60	10,330
60–70	19,954
70–80	28,538
80 and over	29,721
Total	100,000

*Interval contains all ages from lower limit up to but not including upper limit.

Source: *Life Tables, Vital Statistics of the United States* (1978). U.S. Department of Health and Human Services.

6.56 Suppose you have the choice of receiving $500 in cash or receiving a gold coin that has a face value of $100. The actual value of the gold coin depends on its gold content. You are told that the coin has a 40% chance of being worth $400, a 30% chance of being worth $900, and a 30% chance of being worth its face value. If you base your decision on expected value, which should you choose?

6.57 To examine the effectiveness of its four annual advertising promotions, a mail-order company has sent a questionnaire to each of its customers, asking how many of the previous year's promotions prompted orders that otherwise would not have been made. The following table summarizes the data received, where the random variable X is the number of promotions indicated in the customers' responses.

x	0	1	2	3	4
p(x)	.10	.25	.40	.20	.05

a Assuming that the responses received were accurate evaluations of individual effectiveness and that customer behavior in the coming year will not change, what is the expected number of promotions that each customer will take advantage of next year by ordering goods that otherwise would not be purchased?
b What is the variance of X?
c A previous analysis of historical data found that the mean value of orders for promotional goods is $12.50, with the company earning a gross profit of 20% on each order. The fixed cost of conducting the four promotions next year is estimated to be $15,000, with a variable cost of $3.00 per customer for mailing and handling costs. Assuming that the survey results can be used as an accurate predictor of behavior for existing and potential customers, how large a customer base must the company have in order to cover the cost of promotions?

6.58 Let X be a random variable with mean μ and standard deviation σ. Consider a new random variable Z, obtained by subtracting the constant μ from X and dividing the result by the constant σ: $Z = (X - \mu)/\sigma$. The variable Z is called a **standardized random variable.** Use the laws of expected value and variance to show the following.

a $E(Z) = 0$ **b** $V(Z) = 1$

6.59 Let X and Y be two independent random variables with the following probability distributions.

x	p(x)	y	p(y)
2	.3	0	.2
4	.5	1	.6
6	.2	2	.2

To illustrate the laws of expected value and variance, verify the following equalities by separately evaluating the two sides of each.

a $E(3X) = 3E(X)$

$V(3X) = 9V(X)$

b $E(Y + 4) = E(Y) + 4$

$V(Y + 4) = V(Y)$

c $E(X + Y) = E(X) + E(Y)$

$V(X + Y) = V(X) + V(Y)$

d $E(X - Y) = E(X) - E(Y)$

$V(X - Y) = V(X) + V(Y)$

6.60 Refer to Exercise 6.59. Since X and Y are independent random variables, the probability $p(xy)$ is given by $P(X = x \text{ and } Y = y) = p(x)p(y)$.

a Verify that the probability distribution of the random variable XY is given by the following table.

xy	0	2	4	6	8	12
p(xy)	.20	.18	.36	.12	.10	.04

b Verify that $E(XY) = E(X)E(Y)$ by separately evaluating each side of the equality.

6.61a **Canadian Version:** You are planning a December break trip to Miami Beach. You are told that the mean daytime temperature at that time of year is 74°F with a standard deviation of 5°F. Being a Canadian, you are familiar only with the centigrade temperature scale. The relationship between the two temperature scales is represented by the formula

$$C = \left(\frac{5}{9}\right) \times (F - 32)$$

Find the mean and standard deviation of the daytime temperatures using the centigrade scale.

6.61b **American Version:** You are planning a December ski trip to Quebec City. You are told that the mean daytime temperature at that time of year is $-10°C$ (centigrade) with a standard deviation of 3°C. Being an American,

you are familiar only with the Fahrenheit temperature scale. The relationship between the two temperature scales is represented by the formula

$$F = \left(\frac{9}{5}\right)C + 32$$

Find the mean and standard deviation of the daytime temperatures using the Fahrenheit scale.

6.62 Suppose that you and a friend have contributed equally to a portfolio of $10,000 invested in a risky venture. The income (X) that will be earned on this portfolio during the next year has the following probability distribution.

x	$500	1,000	2,000
p(x)	.5	.3	.2

a Determine the expected value and the variance of the income earned on this portfolio.

b Determine the expected value and the variance of your share (one-half) of the income. Answer the question first by computing the expected value and the variance directly from the probability distribution of the income you will receive. Then check your answer using the laws of expected value and variance.

6.63 A company is trying to decide which of two product lines to select, both of which require the same dollar investment. The probabilities of market acceptance and the corresponding profits are shown in the following table.

Market acceptance	Probability	Line 1	Line 2
Poor	.05	$3,000	$2,250
Below average	.15	7,500	3,700
Average	.60	24,000	25,500
Above average	.15	40,500	44,250
Excellent	.05	45,000	48,750

a Draw a graph of the probability distribution of the profits for each line. Which line appears to have the higher expected profit? The higher risk?

b Compute the expected value and the variance of the profits for each line. Which line has the higher expected profit? The higher risk?

c Which line would you select based on the coefficient of variation?

6.64 A company is in the process of building a new power plant. There is some uncertainty regarding the size of the plant to be built. If the community that the plant will service attracts a large number of industries, the demand for electricity will be high. If commercial establishments (offices and retail stores) are attracted, demand will be moderate. If neither industries nor commercial stores locate in the community, the electricity demand will be low. The company can build a small, medium, or large plant, but if the plant is too small, the company will incur extra costs. The total costs (in $millions) of all options are shown in the accompanying table.

Demand for electricity	Size of plant		
	Small	Medium	Large
Low	220	300	350
Moderate	330	320	350
High	440	390	350

The following probabilities are assigned to the electricity demand.

Demand	P(Demand)
Low	.15
Moderate	.55
High	.30

What size of plant has the lowest expected cost?

6.6 BIVARIATE DISTRIBUTIONS

Thus far, we have considered the distribution of a *single* variable. The frequency distribution of a single variable was discussed in Chapter 2, and the probability distribution of a single variable was introduced earlier in this chapter. When we want to consider the relationship between two variables, however, the **bivariate** (or **joint**) **distribution** of the variables is needed.

BIVARIATE PROBABILITY DISTRIBUTIONS

If X and Y are discrete random variables, the **joint probability** that X will assume the value x and Y will assume the value y is denoted $p(x,y)$.

$$p(x,y) = P(X = x \text{ and } Y = y)$$

The joint probabilities must satisfy the two conditions:

1 $0 \leq p(x,y) \leq 1$ for all pairs of values (x,y)

2 $\displaystyle\sum_{\text{all } x} \sum_{\text{all } y} p(x,y) = 1$

A **bivariate** (or **joint**) **probability distribution** of X and Y is a table that gives the joint probabilities $p(x,y)$ for all pairs of values (x,y).

▼ **EXAMPLE 6.7**

Xavier and Yvette are two real estate agents. Let X denote the number of houses that Xavier will sell in a week, and let Y denote the number of houses that Yvette will sell in a week. Suppose that the joint probability distribution of X and Y is as shown in Table 6.7.

The nine probabilities in the interior of Table 6.7 are the joint probabilities $p(x,y)$. For example,

$$p(0, 0) = P(X = 0 \text{ and } Y = 0) = .12$$
$$p(0, 1) = P(X = 0 \text{ and } Y = 1) = .21$$
$$p(0, 2) = P(X = 0 \text{ and } Y = 2) = .07$$

Summing these three probabilities, we obtain the **marginal probability** $P(X = 0) = .40$ (so named because it appears in the margin of the table). Summing the prob-

Table 6.7   **Bivariate Probability Distribution of X and Y**

Y	X 0	X 1	X 2	p(y)
0	.12	.42	.06	.60
1	.21	.06	.03	.30
2	.07	.02	.01	.10
p(x)	.40	.50	.10	1.00

abilities in each of the other columns and rows, we obtain the other marginal probabilities.

$$p(x) = \sum_y p(x,y)$$

$$p(y) = \sum_x p(x,y)$$

Thus, the marginal probability distributions of X and Y are

x	p(x)	y	p(y)
0	.4	0	.6
1	.5	1	.3
2	.1	2	.1

These represent the probability distributions of X and Y with no consideration given to the value being assumed by the other random variable. It can be shown that $E(X) = .7$, $V(X) = .41$, $E(Y) = .5$, and $V(Y) = .45$. We will make use of these values later. ▲

CONDITIONAL PROBABILITY

Conditional probabilities are also defined and computed just as they were earlier in this chapter. The **conditional probability** that X will assume the value x given that Y assumes the value y is

$$P(X = x \mid Y = y) = \frac{P(X = x \text{ and } Y = y)}{P(Y = y)}$$

For example, the probability that Xavier will sell no houses given that Yvette sells one house is

$$P(X = 0 \mid Y = 1) = \frac{P(X = 0 \text{ and } Y = 1)}{P(Y = 1)} = \frac{.21}{.30} = .7$$

Similarly,

$$P(X = 1 \mid Y = 1) = \frac{P(X = 1 \text{ and } Y = 1)}{P(Y = 1)} = \frac{.06}{.30} = .2$$

$$P(X = 2 \mid Y = 1) = \frac{P(X = 2 \text{ and } Y = 1)}{P(Y = 1)} = \frac{.03}{.30} = .1$$

Notice that the sum of the three conditional probabilities of X given $Y = 1$ is 1.0. This will always be the case. The sum of all the conditional probabilities of one variable given a specific value of the other variable will always be 1.0.

Notice that the conditional probability $P(X = 0 \mid Y = 1) = .7$ differs from the (unconditional or marginal) probability $P(X = 0) = .4$. This implies that X and Y are dependent random variables.

Two random variables X and Y are said to be *independent* if the value assumed by one variable in no way affects the probability of a particular value being assumed by the other. That is, X and Y are **independent random variables** if

$$P(X = x \mid Y = y) = P(X = x) \qquad \text{for all pairs of values } (x,y)$$

Recall that if A and B are independent events, their joint probability is given by $P(A \text{ and } B) = P(A) \cdot P(B)$. Similarly, if X and Y are independent random variables, their joint probabilities are given by

$$P(X = x \text{ and } Y = y) = P(X = x) \cdot P(Y = y)$$

THE SUM OF TWO RANDOM VARIABLES

Many applied situations require that we consider the sum of two random variables. Referring back to Example 6.7, the random variable $X + Y$ represents the total number of houses that the two real estate agents will sell next week. The possible values that $X + Y$ can assume are 0, 1, 2, 3, and 4. The probability that $X + Y$ will assume the value 2, for example, is obtained by summing the joint probabilities of all pairs of values (x,y) for which $x + y = 2$.

$$P(X + Y = 2) = p(0,2) + p(1,1) + p(2,0)$$
$$= .07 + .06 + .06$$
$$= .19$$

After computing the probabilities corresponding to the other four possible values in a similar manner, we obtain the probability distribution of $X + Y$.

$x + y$	0	1	2	3	4
$p(x + y)$	.12	.63	.19	.05	.01

Using the formulas for expected value and variance, it can be shown that $E(X + Y) = 1.2$ and $V(X + Y) = .56$.

We were able to construct the foregoing distribution of $X + Y$ since we knew the joint distribution of X and Y. In practice, the precise form of this distribution may be unknown. Frequently, however, we know (or have good estimates of) the expected values and variances of X and Y. If that is the case, we can still determine the expected value and variance of a linear combination $aX + bY$, where a and b are constants and X and Y are independent. From the laws of expected value and variance, we can write

$$E(aX + bY) = aE(X) + bE(Y)$$
$$V(aX + bY) = a^2V(X) + b^2V(Y) \qquad \text{if } X \text{ and } Y \text{ are independent}$$

To enable us to find the variance of a linear combination of X and Y when X and Y are not independent, we need to reconsider the concept of covariance (discussed in Chapter 4) in the context of random variables.

COVARIANCE

Covariance is a statistical measure of the strength of the *linear* relationship between two random variables; it measures the degree to which the two variables tend to move together. If μ_X and μ_Y are the respective means (or expected values) of two random variables X and Y, the **covariance** of X and Y is given by

$$\text{COV}(X,Y) = \sum_{\text{all } (x,y)} (x - \mu_x)(y - \mu_y) \cdot P(X = x \text{ and } Y = y)$$
$$= E\left[(X - \mu_X)(Y - \mu_Y)\right]$$
$$= E(XY) - \mu_X\mu_Y$$

The last expression for covariance is often preferable for computational purposes. Recall (from Chapter 4) that the **coefficient of correlation** can now be found by dividing the covariance by the product of the standard deviations of X and Y.

$$\rho = \frac{\text{COV}(X,Y)}{\sigma_x \sigma_y}$$

As a numerical illustration, we will compute the covariance of the random variables X and Y in Example 6.7. The means of X and Y are

$$\mu_x = \sum x_i p(x_i) = 0(.4) + 1(.5) + 2(.1) = .7$$

$$\mu_y = \sum y_i p(y_i) = 0(.6) + 1(.3) + 2(.1) = .5$$

Hence

$$\text{COV}(X,Y) = \sum_{\text{all } (x,y)} (x - \mu_x)(y - \mu_y) \cdot P(X = x \text{ and } Y = y)$$
$$= (0 - .7)(0 - .5)(.12) + (0 - .7)(1 - .5)(.21) + (0 - .7)(2 - .5)(.07)$$
$$+ (1 - .7)(0 - .5)(.42) + (1 - .7)(1 - .5)(.06) + (1 - .7)(2 - .5)(.02)$$
$$+ (2 - .7)(0 - .5)(.06) + (2 - .7)(1 - .5)(.03) + (2 - .7)(2 - .5)(.01)$$
$$= -.15$$

This value simply tells us that there is a negative relationship between X and Y. To get an idea of the strength of that relationship, we compute the coefficient of correlation.

To compute the correlation we must first find the standard deviations of X and Y, which are calculated from the marginal probability distributions.

$$V(X) = \sum (x_i - \mu_x)^2 p(x_i)$$
$$= (0 - .7)^2(.4) + (1 - .7)^2(.5) + (2 - .7)^2(.1) = .41$$
$$\sigma_x = \sqrt{.41} = .64$$

$$V(Y) = \sum (y_i - \mu_y)^2 p(y_i)$$
$$= (0 - .5)^2(.6) + (1 - .5)^2(.3) + (2 - .5)^2(.1) = .45$$
$$\sigma_y = \sqrt{.45} = .67$$

Therefore,

$$\rho = \frac{\text{COV}(X,Y)}{\sigma_x \, \sigma_y} = \frac{-.15}{(.64)(.67)} = -.35$$

The value of this correlation indicates a relatively weak negative relationship between X and Y.

Loosely speaking, if X tends to assume large values when Y assumes large values and X tends to assume small values when Y assumes small values, then COV(X,Y) is positive. The greater is this tendency, the larger will be the covariance. On the other hand, if X tends to assume large values when Y assumes small values, and vice versa, then COV(X,Y) is negative. The covariance of X and Y will be close to zero if X and Y have little tendency to move together. In particular, if X and Y are independent random variables, COV(X,Y) = 0. This follows from the definition of covariance, together with the law of expected value (from the preceding section) that states

$$E(XY) = E(X)E(Y) \qquad \text{if } X \text{ and } Y \text{ are independent}$$

An expression for computing the variance of a linear combination $aX + bY$ must take into account the tendency of X and Y to move together. The measure that takes this tendency into account is COV(X,Y). We now state, without proof, expressions for computing the expected value and variance of $aX + bY$ as functions of the expected value and variance of X and Y, and their covariance.

$$E(aX + bY) = aE(X) + bE(Y)$$
$$V(aX + bY) = a^2 V(X) + b^2 V(Y) + 2ab \, \text{COV}(X,Y)$$
$$= a^2 V(X) + b^2 V(Y) + 2ab\rho\sigma_x \, \sigma_y$$

This last equality makes use of the basic relationship between the covariance and the correlation coefficient (ρ):

$$\text{COV}(X,Y) = \rho\sigma_x \, \sigma_y$$

One of the most important applications of these formulas is in the field of financial analysis. When we introduced variance and standard deviation, we pointed out that these measures are often used to assess the risk associated with investments. Financial analysts have shown that risk can be reduced by diversifying investments. Diversification is achieved by combining investments whose correlation is small. The following section discusses this principle.

EXERCISES

6.65 The table below lists the joint probabilities of X and Y.

	x	
y	1	2
1	.5	.1
2	.1	.3

a Find the marginal probabilities.
b Determine the mean, variance, and standard deviation for X and for Y.
c Calculate the conditional probabilities.
d Compute the covariance and the coefficient of correlation.
e Are X and Y independent? Explain.

6.66 Show that X and Y are independent given the following bivariate distribution.

	x	
y	1	2
1	.28	.42
2	.12	.18

6.67 A statistics professor developed the bivariate distribution (shown below) of the grades achieved by business students in accounting and statistics. (The corresponding grade points are shown in parentheses.)

a Find the marginal probabilities.

b Determine the mean and variance of the grade points in accounting and in statistics.

c Calculate the covariance and the coefficient of correlation.

d Are the grades in accounting and statistics independent?

Accounting grades	Statistics grades				
	A	B	C	D	F
A (= 4)	.05	.07	.08	.02	.00
B (= 3)	.02	.05	.09	.04	.01
C (= 2)	.02	.03	.08	.09	.03
D (= 1)	.01	.02	.06	.04	.05
F (= 0)	.00	.00	.04	.04	.06

6.68 The joint probability distribution of X and Y is shown in the accompanying table.

y	x		
	0	1	2
0	.42	.12	.06
1	.21	.06	.03
2	.07	.02	.01

a Determine the (marginal) probability distributions of X and Y.

b Are X and Y independent? Explain.

c Find $P(Y = 1 \mid X = 2)$.

d Find the probability distribution of $X + Y$.

e Find $E(XY)$.

f Find $COV(X, Y)$.

6.69 Several reasons have been suggested to explain why two companies (A and B) decide to merge. One of the most popular is the synergy argument, which suggests that the combination of the assets and managerial talent of the two firms combined is worth more than the sum of the values of the two firms standing alone, because of benefits such as economies of scale. Others have sug- gested that there are financial benefits to mergers even in the absences of synergistic operating benefits. A well-known research study* considered the example of two firms (A and B, each faced with the same probability distribution of annual cash flows as shown below. Assume that X_A and X_B, which denote the respective cash flows of the two firms, are statistically independent. (That is, they are uncorrelated.)

X_A	100	250	500
Probability	.1	.2	.7

X_B	100	250	500
Probability	.1	.2	.7

a Suppose that each firm has borrowed money to finance operations, and that each firm faces a contractual obligation to pay $240 annually to service this debt. Assuming the cash flows (X_A and X_B) of the two firms are independent, what is the probability that either A or B (or both) will default on their obligation?

b Construct the bivariate probability distribution of the cash flows of the two firms. (HINT: Construct a 3 × 3 table showing the probabilities associated with the 9 combinations of values for X_A and X_B. For example, the joint probability that $X_A = 100$ and $X_B = 20$ is $(.1)(.1) = .02$).

c Now suppose that the two firms merge. Find the probability distribution of $X_A + X_B$, the combined cash flow of the merged firms. For example, from the bivariate distribution constructed in part (b), $P(X_A + X_B = 200) = .01$.

d The merged firms have a contractual obligation to pay $480 annually. What is the probability that the merged firms will default on this obligation?

e Does there appear to be a financial benefit to this merger? Explain.

6.7 INVESTMENT PORTFOLIO DIVERSIFICATION (OPTIONAL)

Most investors are probably familiar with the notion that lowering your investment risk by diversification means "not putting all your eggs in one basket." This sensible notion was first analyzed carefully by Harry Markowitz in 1952, when he developed a model that clarified how risk reduction is achieved through diversification. His model forms the foundation of what has become known as modern portfolio theory (MPT), which is widely used by professional investors.

To illustrate the basics of portfolio diversification, consider an investor who forms a portfolio, consisting of only two stocks, by investing $4,000 in one stock and $6,000

---

*Wilbur G. Lewellen, "A Pure Financial Rationale for the Conglomerate Merger," *Journal of Finance*, 1971.

Table 6.8   **One-Year Results of Investment**

Stock	Initial Investment	Value of Investment After One Year	Rate of Return on Investment	
1	$4,000	$5,000	$R_1 = .25$	(25%)
2	$6,000	$5,400	$R_2 = -.10$	(−10%)
Total	$10,000	$10,400	$R_p = .04$	(4%)

in a second stock. Suppose that the one-year results of this investment are as summarized in Table 6.8.

From Table 6.8, we observe that the value of the investment in stock 1 rose to $5,000 after 1 year. The rate of return *realized* on the investment in stock 1 was therefore

$$R_1 = \frac{5,000 - 4,000}{4,000} = .25 \quad \text{(or 25\%)}$$

The value of the investment in stock 2 declined to $5,400, so that the rate of return realized on stock 2 was

$$R_2 = \frac{5,400 - 6,000}{6,000} = -.10 \quad \text{(or} -10\%)$$

The rate of return on the entire portfolio was therefore

$$R_p = \frac{10,400 - 10,000}{10,000} = .04 \quad \text{(or 4\%)}$$

Another way of calculating the portfolio return R_p is to compute the weighted average of the individual stock returns R_1 and R_2, where the portfolio weights w_1 and w_2 are the proportions of the initial $10,000 invested in stock 1 and stock 2, respectively. In this example, $w_1 = .4$ and $w_2 = .6$. (Observe that w_1 and w_2 must always sum to 1, because the two stocks constitute the entire investment.) That is,

$$R_p = w_1 R_1 + w_2 R_2$$
$$= (.4)(.25) + (.6)(-.10) = .04$$

This is how portfolio returns are usually calculated in portfolio theory.

Notice that, *when the investment is initially undertaken,* the three returns in the expression

$$R_p = w_1 R_1 + w_2 R_2$$

can be viewed as random variables, since what their values will be at the end of the year is unknown. Applying the laws of expected value and variance to this expression we obtain

$$E(R_p) = w_1 E(R_1) + w_2 E(R_2)$$
$$V(R_p) \equiv \sigma_p^2 = V(w_1 R_1 + w_2 R_2)$$
$$= w_1^2 \sigma_1^2 + w_2^2 \sigma_2^2 + 2w_1 w_2 \, \text{COV}(R_1, R_2)$$
$$= w_1^2 \sigma_1^2 + w_2^2 \sigma_2^2 + 2w_1 w_2 \rho \sigma_1 \sigma_2$$

where ρ is the correlation between the returns R_1 and R_2.

Portfolio theory uses equations like these to find characteristics of a portfolio (such as its expected value or variance) from characteristics of the component stocks in the portfolio. The following example illustrates how portfolio theory can be used to provide insight into the notion of diversification.

▼ **EXAMPLE 6.8**

An investor has decided to form a portfolio by putting equal amounts of money into each of two investments. Both investments are quite risky because the possible returns are highly variable. Investment 1 has a mean return of 15% with a standard deviation of 25%. Investment 2 is expected to return 27%, and its standard deviation is 40%.

    a Find the expected return on the portfolio.
    b If the two investments' returns are perfectly positively correlated (that is, $\rho = 1$), find the standard deviation of the return on the portfolio.
    c What is the portfolio's standard deviation if $\rho = .5$?
    d What is the portfolio's standard deviation if $\rho = 0$?

Solution

a Since equal amounts are allocated to each investment, the portfolio weights are $w_1 = w_2 = .5$. The return on the portfolio can therefore be expressed as

$$R_p = .5R_1 + .5R_2$$

Thus,

$$E(R_p) = .5E(R_1) + .5E(R_2)$$
$$= .5(.15) + .5(.27) = 21$$

The expected return on the portfolio is therefore 21%.

b The variance of the portfolio's return is

$$V(R_1 + R_2) = w_1^2\sigma_1^2 + w_2^2\sigma_2^2 + 2w_1w_2\rho\sigma_1\sigma_2$$
$$= (.5)^2(.25)^2 + (.5)^2(.40)^2 + 2(.5)(.5)(1)(.25)(.40)$$
$$= .1056$$

The standard deviation of the portfolio return when $\rho = 1$ is therefore $\sigma_p = .3250$.

c The variance of the portfolio return is

$$V(R_p) = w_1^2\sigma_1^2 + w_2^2\sigma_2^2 + 2w_1w_2\rho\sigma_1\sigma_2$$
$$= (.5)^2(.25)^2 + (.5)^2(.40)^2 + 2(.5)(.5)(.5)(.25)(.40)$$
$$= .0806$$

The standard deviation of the portfolio return when $\rho = .5$ is therefore $\sigma_p = .2839$.

d The variance of the portfolio return is

$$V(R_p) = w_1^2\sigma_1^2 + w_2^2\sigma_2^2 + 2w_1w_2\rho\sigma_1\sigma_2$$
$$= (.5)^2(.25)^2 + (.5)^2(.40)^2 + 2(.5)(.5)(0)(.25)(.40)$$
$$= .0556$$

The standard deviation of the portfolio return when $\rho = 0$ is therefore $\sigma_p = .2358$.

Notice that the standard deviations of the portfolio returns have decreased as the correlation between the two investment returns has decreased. This illustrates the diversification effect. When the correlation ρ is less than 1, the prices of the two investments do not fluctuate up and down together. Often, one goes up in price when the other goes down, dampening the swings in the price (and the return) and thereby lowering the standard deviation.

Observe that the expected value is not affected by the correlation and that the variance and standard deviation of the portfolio's returns decrease as the correlation coefficient decreases. This means that investors can reduce their risk by finding investments whose returns are independent, or at least weakly correlated.

▲

EXERCISES

6.70 The concept of covariance has important applications in modern portfolio theory. Suppose we wish to form a portfolio consisting of two investments. Let X_1 and X_2 be the percentage rates of return that will be realized over the coming year on the two investments, respectively. Suppose that $E(X_1) = 20\%$, $\sigma_1 = 8\%$, $E(X_2) = 15\%$, $\sigma_2 = 5\%$, and $\text{COV}(X_1, X_2) = 4(\%)^2$. If we invest 40% of our money in the first investment and the remainder in the second investment, the rate of return on our portfolio will be $.4X_1 + .6X_2$.

a Find the expected value and variance of the rates of return on our portfolio.

b Which investment has the lowest risk as measured by the variance of its return: the first investment, the second investment, or the portfolio?

6.71 An analysis of the stock market produces the following information about the returns of two stocks.

	Stocks	
	1	2
Expected returns	12%	17%
Standard deviations	25	38

a Assuming that the returns are perfectly positively correlated, find the mean and standard deviation of the return on a portfolio consisting of an equal investment in each of the two stocks.

b Repeat part (a), assuming that $\rho = .7$.

c Repeat part (a), assuming that the returns are uncorrelated.

6.72 Suppose that you wish to invest $1 million. After careful consideration of investment opportunities, you reduce the number of choices to two. The means and standard deviations of the two investments are listed in the following table. The returns are highly correlated with $\rho = .8$. Discuss whether you should put all your money in investment 1, investment 2, or a portfolio composed of an equal amount of investments 1 and 2.

	Investments	
	1	2
Expected returns	12%	17%
Standard deviations	25	38

6.73 Repeat Exercise 6.72, assuming that $\rho = 0$.

6.74 Motorola and Coca-Cola are two of the best managed companies listed on the New York Stock Exchange. The 48 monthly rates of return (for the years 1993 to 1996) for each of these companies are stored in files XR17-31 and XR17-36. (The returns are stored in decimal form, so that 2% would appear as .02.)

  a Compute the mean and variance of the sample of returns for Motorola and for Coca-Cola, and compare the results for the two companies.

  b Compute the sample covariance between the returns of these two companies.

  c Consider the portfolio formed by using 20% of your

investable funds to purchase Motorola stock and the other 80% to purchase Coca-Cola stock. Calculate the expected value and the variance of the returns for this portfolio.

  d Compare and discuss the results in parts (a) and (c).

6.75 Intel Corporation and General Electric are two very profitable firms that are world leaders in their respective fields. The 48 monthly rates of return (for the years 1993 to 1996) for each of these companies are stored in files XR17-30 and XR17-34. (The returns are stored in decimal form, so that 2% would appear as .02.)

  a Compute the mean and variance of the sample of returns for Intel and for General Electric, and compare the results for the two companies.

  b Compute the sample covariance between the returns of these two companies.

  c Consider the portfolio formed by placing 30% of your investable funds in Intel stock and the other 70% in General Electric stock. Calculate the expected value and variance of the returns for this portfolio.

  d Compare and discuss the results in parts (a) and (c).

6.8   BINOMIAL DISTRIBUTION

Having considered the basic properties of probability distributions in general, we now consider in detail the binomial distribution—the first of four important specific probability distributions we will consider. The binomial distribution is probably the single most important discrete distribution. An important characteristic of the underlying binomial random experiment is that there are only two possible outcomes. Experiments with such a dichotomy of outcomes are numerous: A coin flip results in heads or tails, an election candidate is favored or not, a product is defective or nondefective, an employee is male or female, and an invoice being audited is correct or incorrect. It is conventional to apply the generic labels **success** and **failure** to the two possible outcomes. Binomial experiments of interest usually involve several repetitions or trials of the basic experiment; these trials must satisfy the conditions outlined below in the definition of a binomial experiment.

Binomial Experiment

A **binomial experiment** possesses the following properties.

  1 The experiment consists of a fixed number n of trials.

  2 The result of each trial can be classified into one of two categories: success or failure.

  3 The probability p of a success remains constant for each trial.

  4 Each trial of the experiment is independent of the other trials.

An example of a binomial experiment is to flip a coin 10 times and observe the result of each flip. Which of the two possible outcomes of each trial (flip) is designated a success is arbitrary. We will designate the appearance of heads as a success.

Assuming the coin is fair, the probability of a success is $p = .5$ for each of the 10 trials. Clearly, each trial is independent of the others. Our main interest in a binomial experiment such as this is the number of successes (heads) observed in the 10 trials. The random variable that records the number of successes (heads) observed in the $n = 10$ trials is called the **binomial random variable.**

Here are two more examples of a binomial experiment.

1 Test 500 randomly selected computer chips produced at a manufacturing facility and determine whether each is defective. The number of trials is 500. There are two outcomes per trial: The product is either defective or nondefective. Assuming the defective rate is 1% and labeling the occurrence of a defective to be a success, then $p = .01$ and $(1 - p) = .99$. If the computer chips are selected at random for testing, the trials are independent.

2 Ask 1,500 people whether they prefer the taste of Coca-Cola over that of other colas. The number of trials is 1,500. There are two possible outcomes per trial: The respondent prefers Coca-Cola or does not. If we assume that 20% of the population prefers Coca-Cola, $p = .2$ and $(1 - p) = .8$. The trials are independent.

Notice that in each example we made an assumption that allowed us to assign a value to p. Also note that we need to define what we mean by a success. In general, a success is defined arbitrarily and is not necessarily something we want to happen. When selecting computer chips, we defined success as finding a defective. The random variable of interest in these experiments is the number of successes, and is called the binomial random variable.

Binomial Random Variable

The **binomial random variable** indicates the number of successes in n trials of a binomial experiment.

A binomial random variable is therefore a discrete random variable that can take on any one of the values 0, 1, 2, . . . , n. The probability distribution of this random variable, called the **binomial probability distribution,** gives us the probability that a success will occur x times in the n trials, for $x = 0, 1, 2, \ldots, n$. Rather than working out binomial probabilities from scratch each time, we would do better to have a general formula for calculating the probabilities associated with any binomial experiment. As a first step toward developing this formula, let's look at another binomial experiment.

Consider a binomial experiment consisting of $n = 3$ trials, with the two possible outcomes of each trial designated S (success) and F (failure). The binomial random variable X indicates the number of successes in the three trials. Let p denote the probability of a success in any trial, and let $(1 - p)$ denote the probability of a failure. The possible outcomes of any binomial experiment can be represented by a probability tree, with the stages corresponding to the trials of the experiment. The probability tree for this experiment is shown in Figure 6.11.

Recall from Section 6.3 that the probability attached to a branch of the tree is the conditional probability of that branch's outcome occurring. But because the trials of a binomial experiment are independent, the conditional probability that any branch outcome will occur is the same as the unconditional probability that it will occur. The simple event probabilities are obtained by applying the multiplication rule for inde-

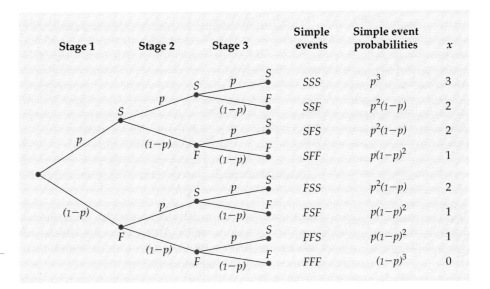

Figure 6.11

Probability Tree for Three Trials of a Binomial Experiment

pendent events. As an example, the probability that SSF will occur is $p \cdot p \cdot (1 - p) = p^2(1 - p)$.

Once all the simple event probabilities are found, the binomial probabilities appearing in Table 6.9 can be determined by summing the (simple event) probabilities associated with a given value x. For example, there is only one simple event (FFF) for which $x = 0$, and its probability is $(1 - p)^3$. Hence, $p(0) = (1 - p)^3$. But there are three simple events with exactly $x = 1$ success: SFF, FSF, and FFS. Because each of these simple events occurs with probability $p(1 - p)^2$, the probability of exactly one success is $p(1) = 3p(1 - p)^2$. The probabilities $p(2)$ and $p(3)$ are obtained in a similar manner. The complete probability distribution of X is shown in Table 6.9.

It is impractical to resort to a probability tree each time we want to find a binomial probability distribution. Instead, we need a general formula for the probability $p(x)$ of obtaining x successes in the n trials, when the probability of a success is p. To this end, notice that we will observe exactly x successes in the n trials whenever we observe a simple event with a total of x S's and $(n - x)$ F's. One such simple event is

$$\underbrace{SS \quad \cdots \quad SFF}_{x \text{ times}} \underbrace{\quad \cdots \quad F}_{(n - x) \text{ times}}$$

Applying the multiplication rule for independent events, we see that the probability that any such simple event will occur is $p^x(1 - p)^{n-x}$, since p is the probability of a success and $(1 - p)$ is the probability of failure. We must now multiply this probability by the number of simple events having exactly x successes. But the number of

Table 6.9 **Binomial Distribution for *n* = 3**

x	$p(x)$
0	$(1 - p)^3$
1	$3p(1 - p)^2$
2	$3p^2(1 - p)$
3	p^3

Table 6.10 **Binomial Coefficients ($n = 3$)**

x	C_x^3
0	$C_0^3 = \dfrac{3!}{0!(3-0)!} = \dfrac{3!}{0!3!} = \dfrac{3 \cdot 2 \cdot 1}{(1)(3 \cdot 2 \cdot 1)} = 1$
1	$C_1^3 = \dfrac{3!}{1!(3-1)!} = \dfrac{3!}{1!2!} = \dfrac{3 \cdot 2 \cdot 1}{(1)(2 \cdot 1)} = 3$
2	$C_2^3 = \dfrac{3!}{2!(3-2)!} = \dfrac{3!}{2!1!} = \dfrac{3 \cdot 2 \cdot 1}{(2 \cdot 1)(1)} = 3$
3	$C_3^3 = \dfrac{3!}{3!(3-3)!} = \dfrac{3!}{3!0!} = \dfrac{3 \cdot 2 \cdot 1}{(3 \cdot 2 \cdot 1)(1)} = 1$

simple events with exactly x successes is the same as the number of ways of choosing the x stages at which a success occurs. This number is found by using the following well-known **counting rule:** The number of different ways of choosing x objects from a total of n objects is

$$C_x^n = \frac{n!}{x!(n-x)!}$$

where $n! = n(n-1)(n-2) \cdots (2)(1)$ and 0! is defined to be 1.

Let's use this counting rule to determine the number of simple events that have exactly x successes (for $x = 0, 1, 2,$ and 3) in the $n = 3$ trials of the experiment depicted by the probability tree in Figure 6.11. The four values to be calculated (called binomial coefficients, with values recorded in Table 6.10) can be checked against the values that were previously determined by counting the simple events at the end of the probability tree in Figure 6.11. The binomial probabilities $p(x)$ in Table 6.10 are now obtained by multiplying these four (binomial) coefficients by the corresponding probabilities $p^x(1-p)^{n-x}$, for $x = 0, 1, 2,$ and 3.

We are now in a position to give the general formulation of the binomial probability distribution.

Probability Distribution of a Binomial Experiment

If the random variable X is the number of successes in the n trials of a binomial experiment that has probability p of a success on any given trial, the probability distribution of X is given by

$$P(X = x) = p(x) = C_x^n p^x (1-p)^{n-x}$$

$$= \left(\frac{n!}{x!(n-x)!}\right) p^x (1-p)^{n-x} \qquad x = 0, 1, \ldots, n$$

Each pair of values (n, p) determines a distinct binomial distribution. Graphical representations of three binomial distributions are shown in Figure 6.12. Each of the $(n + 1)$ possible values of a binomial random variable X has a positive probability of occurring. The fact that some possible values of X do not have a vertical line above them in Figure 6.12 simply means that the probability that those values will occur is too small to be displayed on the graph. A binomial distribution is symmetrical whenever $p = .5$, and it is asymmetrical otherwise.

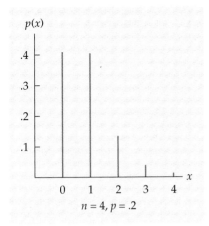 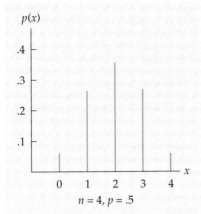 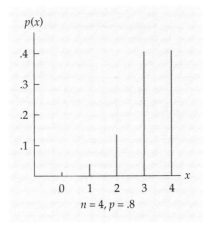

Figure 6.12

Graphs of three binomial distributions

▼ EXAMPLE 6.9

The quality-control department of a manufacturer has determined that 5% of the catalytic converters produced by the company will be defective until an expensive overhaul is undertaken 2 weeks from now. If a sample of three converters is randomly selected from next week's production, what is the probability distribution of the number of defective converters in the sample?

Solution   The first thing to do is to make sure that the conditions for a binomial experiment are satisfied. The experiment consists of a fixed number of $n = 3$ trials, with each trial resulting in one of two possible outcomes: a defective converter (success) or a nondefective converter (failure). The probability p of selecting a defective converter is .05 for each trial. The binomial model therefore applies in this situation.

Let X be the binomial random variable indicating the number of defective converters in the sample of three. We can then compute probabilities as follows:

$$P(X = 0) = p(0) = \frac{3!}{0!3!}(.05)^0(.95)^3 = .8574$$

$$P(X = 1) = p(1) = \frac{3!}{1!2!}(.05)^1(.95)^2 = .1354$$

$$P(X = 2) = p(2) = \frac{3!}{2!1!}(.05)^2(.95)^1 = .0071$$

$$P(X = 3) = p(3) = \frac{3!}{3!0!}(.05)^3(.95)^0 = .0001$$

We thereby obtain the probability distribution of the number of defective converters in the sample of three, as shown in Table 6.11.

Table 6.11 **Binomial Distribution ($n = 3$, $p = .05$)**

x	p(x)
0	.8574
1	.1354
2	.0071
3	.0001

▲

USING THE BINOMIAL TABLES

An alternative way of presenting the binomial distribution ($n = 3$, $p = .05$) in Table 6.11 is depicted in Table 6.12. The difference here is that the probabilities in Table 6.12 are **cumulative probabilities** that represent the sum of binomial probabilities from $x = 0$ to $x = k$. If $k = 1$, for example, we have

$$P(X \le 1) = \sum_{x=0}^{1} p(x) = p(0) + p(1)$$
$$= .8574 + .1354$$
$$= .9928$$

Table 6.12 **Cumulative Binomial Distribution ($n = 3$, $p = .05$)**

k	$\sum_{x=0}^{k} p(x)$
0	.8574
1	.9928
2	.9999
3	1.0000

The advantage of working with a table of cumulative binomial probabilities is that it enables us to find more quickly the probability that X will assume some value within a range of values.

Individual binomial probabilities are obtained from Table 6.12 by subtraction. For example, the probability of exactly two successes is

$$p(2) = P(X \le 2) - P(X \le 1)$$
$$= \sum_{x=0}^{2} p(x) - \sum_{x=0}^{1} p(x)$$
$$= .9999 - .9928$$
$$= .0071$$

Calculating binomial probabilities by means of the formula, as in Example 6.9, is time consuming and tiresome when n is large. Fortunately, tables identifying these probabilities are available. One such table is Table 1 in Appendix B at the back of this book, which presents cumulative binomial distributions for various values of n and p. (Although the probabilities in the preceding example were computed to four decimal places, the binomial probabilities provided by Table 1 are rounded to three decimal places.) A partial reproduction of this table, for $n = 5$, is shown in

Table 6.13. The 15 columns in Table 6.13, corresponding to 15 different values of p, represent 15 distinct binomial distributions. Individual tabulated values are of the form

$$P(X \leq k) = \sum_{x=0}^{k} p(x)$$

To find the probability of at most three successes in $n = 5$ trials of a binomial experiment with $p = .2$, we locate the entry corresponding to $k = 3$ and $p = .2$.

$$P(X \leq 3) = \sum_{x=0}^{3} p(x)$$
$$= p(0) + p(1) + p(2) + p(3)$$
$$= .993$$

Table 6.13 **Partial Reproduction of Table 1: Binomial Probabilities for $n = 5$***

k	.01	.05	.10	.20	.25	.30	.40	.50
0	.951	.774	.590	.328	.237	.168	.078	.031
1	.999	.977	.919	.737	.633	.528	.337	.187
2	1.000	.999	.991	.942	.896	.837	.683	.500
3	1.000	1.000	1.000	.993	.984	.969	.913	.812
4	1.000	1.000	1.000	1.000	.999	.998	.990	.969

k	.60	.70	.75	.80	.90	.95	.99
0	.010	.002	.001	.000	.000	.000	.000
1	.087	.031	.016	.007	.000	.000	.000
2	.317	.163	.104	.058	.009	.001	.000
3	.663	.472	.367	.263	.081	.023	.001
4	.922	.832	.763	.672	.410	.226	.049

*Tabulated values are $P(X \leq k) = \sum_{x=0}^{k} p(x)$. (Entries are rounded to three decimal places.)

Notice that the final probability in each column (distribution) of the table—reading horizontally, the row corresponding to $k = n$—has been omitted. This probability will always be equal to 1, since, for $k = n$,

$$P(X \leq k) = P(X \leq n) = 1$$

We have just seen how to use Table 1 in Appendix B to save time in finding binomial probabilities. There is also a time-saving procedure for finding the mean and the variance of a binomial random variable. While these two parameters could be calculated in the usual time-consuming way—using the definitional formulas involving summations—it can be shown that the mean and the variance of a binomial random variable are given by the following pair of formulas.

Mean and Variance of Binomial Random Variables

If X is a binomial random variable, the mean and the variance of X are

$$E(X) = \mu = np$$
$$V(X) = \sigma^2 = np(1 - p)$$

where n is the number of trials, p is the probability of success on any trial, and $(1 - p)$ is the probability of failure on any trial.

▼ **EXAMPLE 6.10**

A shoe store's records show that 30% of customers making a purchase use a credit card to make payment. This morning, 20 customers purchased shoes from the store.

a Using Table 1 of Appendix B, find the probability that at least 12 of the customers used a credit card.

b What is the probability that at least 3 customers, but not more than 6, used a credit card?

c What is the expected number of customers who used a credit card?

d Find the probability that exactly 14 customers did not use a credit card.

e Find the probability that at least 9 customers did not use a credit card.

Solution   If making a payment with a credit card is designated a success, we have a binomial experiment with $n = 20$ and $p = .3$. Let X denote the number of customers who used a credit card.

a We must first express the probability we seek in the form $P(X \leq k)$, since this is the form in which probabilities are tabulated in Table 1.

$$P(X \geq 12) = P(X = 12) + P(X = 13) + \cdot \cdot \cdot + P(X = 20)$$
$$= P(X \leq 20) - P(X \leq 11)$$

Because the probabilities in a binomial distribution must sum to 1, $P(X \leq 20) = 1$. From Table 1, $P(X \leq 11) = .995$. Therefore,

$$P(X \geq 12) = 1 - .995 = .005$$

The probability that at least 12 customers used a credit card is .005.

b Expressing the probability we seek in the form used for the probabilities tabulated in Table 1, we have

$$P(3 \leq X \leq 6) = P(X = 3) + P(X = 4) + P(X = 5) + P(X = 6)$$
$$= P(X \leq 6) - P(X \leq 2)$$
$$= .608 - .035 = .573$$

The probability that between 3 and 6 customers used a credit card is .573.

c The expected number of customers who used a credit card is

$$E(X) = np = 20(.3) = 6$$

d Let Y denote the number of customers who did not use a credit card. The probability that a customer did not use a credit card is $(1 - .3) = .7$. This part of the example can be solved in either of two ways.

i You can interchange the designations of success and failure and work with $p = .7$.

ii You can express the required probability in terms of the number of customers who did not use a credit card, and proceed with $p = .3$.

Method (i) is probably easier to use with the tables in the text. In many cases, however, binomial tables with p values above .5 are not available, and method (ii) must be used.

Using method (i), we begin by recognizing that, since the original assignment of the designations *success* and *failure* was arbitrary, we can interchange them. If not using a credit card is designated as a success, then $p = .7$. From Table 1, we find that

$$P(Y = 14) = P(Y \le 14) - P(Y \le 13)$$
$$= .584 - .392$$
$$= .192$$

In method (ii), we retain the original designation, according to which using a credit card is a success and $p = .3$. If 14 customers did not use a credit card, the number of customers who did use one is $(20 - 14) = 6$. Hence,

$$P(Y = 14) = P(X = 6)$$
$$= P(X \le 6) - P(X \le 5)$$
$$= .608 - .416$$
$$= .192$$

Using either method, we find that the probability that exactly 14 customers did not use a credit card is .192.

e Again, let Y denote the number of customers who did not use a credit card. If not using a credit card is designated a success, then $p = .7$. Expressing the required probability in terms of values tabulated in Table 1, we have

$$P(Y \ge 9) = 1 - P(Y \le 8)$$
$$= 1 - .005$$
$$= .995$$

The probability that at least 9 customers did not use a credit card is .995.

▲

USING THE COMPUTER TO FIND BINOMIAL PROBABILITIES

There are a few software packages that compute probabilities in addition to their more traditional duties involving statistical procedures. Excel and Minitab are two of these, allowing us to easily produce the probability distributions for various random variables. We now describe the Excel and Minitab commands that output $p(x)$ and $P(X \le x)$ for any value of x, where X is a binomial random variable.

Excel Instructions

1 Click f_x, **Function Category: Statistical,** and **Function Name: BINOMDIST.** Click **Next >.**

2 Use the cursor and type the value of x **(number_s),** the number of n **(trials),** the probability of success p **(probability),** and true **(cumulative).** Click **Finish.** This will produce $P(X \le x)$. If you type false **(cumulative),** Excel will compute $P(X = x)$.

Minitab Instructions

1 Click **Calc, Probability Distributions,** and **Binomial . . . .**

2 Use the cursor to specify either **Probability** [to compute $p(x)$] or **Cumulative probability** [to compute $P(X \leq x)$].

3 Hit **tab** and type the value of n **(Number of trials:).**

4 Hit **tab** and type the value of p **(Probability of success:).**

5 Click **Input column,** hit **tab,** and type the value of x. Click **OK.**

If you have several values of x, store them in a column (say, column 1) and proceed as above, except at step 5, click **Input column,** hit **tab,** and type the column number (**C1**). Click **OK.**

EXERCISES

6.76 Evaluate the following binomial coefficients.

a C_2^5 **b** C_2^6 **c** C_4^6
d C_0^7 **e** C_7^7

6.77 Consider a binomial random variable X with $n = 4$ and $p = .6$.

a Find the probability distribution of X, and graph it.

b Find $P(X \leq 2)$.

c Find the mean and the variance of X.

6.78 Let X be a binomial random variable. Use the formula to compute the following probabilities.

a $P(X = 2)$, if $n = 8$ and $p = .1$
b $P(X = 5)$, if $n = 9$ and $p = .5$
c $P(X = 9)$, if $n = 10$ and $p = .95$

6.79 Use Table 1 in Appendix B to check your answers to Exercise 6.78.

6.80 Let X be a binomial random variable. Use the formula to compute the following probabilities.

a $P(X = 3)$, if $n = 5$ and $p = .2$
b $P(X = 2)$, if $n = 6$ and $p = .3$
c $P(X = 5)$, if $n = 7$ and $p = .75$

6.81 Use Table 1 in Appendix B to check your answers to Exercise 6.80.

6.82 Given a binomial random variable X with $n = 15$ and $p = .3$, find the following probabilities, using Table 1 in Appendix B.

a $P(X \leq 2)$ **b** $P(X \geq 7)$ **c** $P(X = 6)$
d $P(4 \leq X \leq 8)$ **e** $P(X \geq 12)$ **f** $P(7 < X < 10)$

6.83 Given a binomial random variable X with $n = 25$ and $p = .6$, find the following probabilities, using Table 1 in Appendix B.

a $P(X \leq 10)$ **b** $P(X \geq 12)$ **c** $P(X = 15)$
d $P(18 \leq X \leq 21)$ **e** $P(18 < X < 21)$

6.84 A sign on the gas pumps of a certain chain of gasoline stations encourages customers to have their oil checked, claiming that one out of every four cars should have its oil topped up.

a What is the probability that exactly 3 of the next 10 cars entering a station should have their oil topped up?

b What is the probability that at least half of the next 10 cars entering a station should have their oil topped up? At least half of the next 20 cars?

6.85 A multiple-choice quiz has 15 questions. Each question has five possible answers, of which only one is correct.

a What is the probability that sheer guesswork will yield at least seven correct answers?

b What is the expected number of correct answers by sheer guesswork?

6.86 A student majoring in accounting is trying to decide on the number of firms to which she should apply. Given her work experience, grades, and extracurricular activities, she has been told by a placement counselor that she can expect to receive a job offer from 80% of the firms to which she applies. Wanting to save time, the student applies to only five firms. Assuming the counselor's estimate is correct, find the probability that the student receives the following.

a No offers.
b At most two offers.
c Between two and four offers (inclusive).
d Five offers.

6.87 An auditor is preparing for a physical count of inventory as a means of verifying its value. Items counted are reconciled with a list prepared by the storeroom supervisor. Normally, 20% of the items counted cannot be reconciled without reviewing invoices. The auditor selects 10 items.

a Find the probability of each of the following.

i Up to 4 items cannot be reconciled.

ii At least 6 items cannot be reconciled.

iii Between 4 and 6 items (inclusive) cannot be reconciled.

b If it normally takes 20 minutes to review the invoice for an item that cannot be reconciled and 1 hour for the balance of the count, how long should the auditor expect the physical count to take?

6.88 When Earth traveled through the storm of meteorites trailing the comet Tempel-Tuttle on November 17, 1998, the storm was 1,000 times more intense than the average meteor shower. Before the comet arrived, governments and telecommunications companies worried about the potential damage that might be inflicted on the approximately 650 satellites in orbit. It was estimated that each satellite had a 1% chance of being hit, causing damage to the satellite's electronic system. A certain company had three communications satellites orbiting Earth at that time. Find the probability distribution of the number of satellites owned by this company that would be damaged.

6.89 Flight delays at major American airports are an increasing source of exasperation to executives, who may miss important appointments as a result. About 190,000 flights were delayed by more than 15 minutes during the first 6 months of 1984, with many of the delays lasting hours (*Fortune,* 1 October, 1984). During this period, 13% of all arrivals and departures at New York's LaGuardia Airport experienced delays of at least 15 minutes. The corresponding level of delays at Denver's Stapleton Airport was about 5%. Suppose an executive made three round trips from Denver and New York during this period.

a Find the probability that the executive experienced at least four delays of 15 minutes or more at Stapleton Airport during arrival or departure.

b Find the probability that the executive experienced no delays of 15 minutes or more upon arrival at or departure from LaGuardia Airport during the three trips.

c Find the probability that the executive experienced no delays of 15 minutes or more during the three round trips.

d What assumptions have you made in solving the first three parts of this exercise?

6.9 POISSON DISTRIBUTION

A second important discrete distribution is the Poisson distribution. While a binomial random variable counts the number of successes that occur in a fixed number of trials, a Poisson random variable counts the number of rare events (successes) that occur in a specified time interval or a specified region. Activities to which the Poisson distribution can be successfully applied include counting the number of telephone calls received by a switchboard in a specified time period, counting the number of arrivals at a service location (such as a service station, tollbooth, or grocery checkout counter) in a given time period, and counting the number of bacteria in a specified culture. In order for the Poisson distribution to be appropriately applied to situations such as these, three conditions must be satisfied, as enumerated in the accompanying box. In the following description of a Poisson experiment, *success* refers to the occurrence of the event of interest, and *interval* refers to either an interval of time or an interval of space (such as an area or region).

Poisson Experiment

A **Poisson experiment** possesses the following properties.

1 The number of successes that occur in any interval is independent of the number of successes that occur in any other interval.

2 The probability that a success will occur in an interval is the same for all intervals of equal size and is proportional to the size of the interval.

3 The probability that two or more successes will occur in an interval approaches zero as the interval becomes smaller.

The Poisson model thus is applicable when the events of interest occur *randomly, independently* of one another, and *rarely,* as specified by the preceding conditions. In particular, condition 3 specifies what is meant by *rarely.* The arrival of individual diners at a restaurant, for example, would not fit the Poisson model because diners usually arrive with companions, violating the independence condition.

Poisson Random Variable

The **Poisson random variable** indicates the number of successes that occur during a given time interval or in a specified region in a Poisson experiment.

Probability Distribution of Poisson Random Variables

If X is a Poisson random variable, the probability distribution of X is given by

$$P(X = x) = p(x) = \frac{e^{-\mu}\mu^x}{x!} \qquad x = 0, 1, 2, \ldots$$

where μ is the average number of successes occurring in the given time interval or region, and $e = 2.71828\ldots$ is the base of the natural logarithms.

Notice that, since μ (the average number of successes occurring in a specified interval) appears in the formula for the Poisson probability $p(x)$, we must obtain an estimate of μ—usually from historical data—before we can apply the Poisson distribution. Care must be taken to ensure that the intervals specified in the definitions of X and μ are the same size and that the same units are used for each.

Although the formula can be used to compute a Poisson probability, it requires us to calculate $e^{-\mu}$. If your calculator will not perform this calculation, you must resort to tabulated values of $e^{-\mu}$, but this becomes impractical when you want to find the probability that a Poisson random variable will assume any one of a large number of specified values. Fortunately, there is an easier method. To ease the computation of Poisson probabilities, we have included tabulated values of cumulative Poisson probabilities in Table 2 of Appendix B.

There is no limit to the number of values a Poisson random variable can assume. The Poisson random variable is a discrete random variable with infinitely many possible values—unlike the binomial random variable, which has only a finite number of possible values. If X is a Poisson random variable for which μ is the average number of successes that occur in a specified interval, the expected value and the variance of X have the same value.

$$E(X) = V(X) = \mu$$

The graphs of three specific Poisson distributions are shown in Figure 6.13.

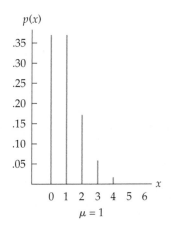

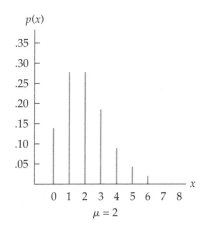

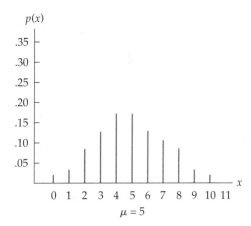

Figure 6.13

Graphs of three Poisson distributions

▼ **EXAMPLE 6.11**

A tollbooth operator has observed that cars arrive randomly at an average rate of 360 cars per hour.

    a Using the formula, calculate the probability that only two cars will arrive during a specified 1-minute period.

    b Using Table 2 of Appendix B, find the probability that only two cars will arrive during a specified 1-minute period.

    c Using Table 2, find the probability that at least four cars will arrive during a specified 1-minute period.

Solution Let X denote the number of arrivals during the 1-minute period. Then the mean value of X is $\mu = 360/60 = 6$ cars per minute. Notice that we have defined both X and μ in terms of the same time interval, 1 minute.

    a According to the formula for a Poisson probability, the probability of exactly two arrivals is

$$P(X = 2) = \frac{(e^{-6})(6^2)}{2!}$$

$$= \frac{(.00248)(36)}{2 \cdot 1}$$

$$= .0446$$

The value of e^{-6} was obtained by using a calculator.

b According to the cumulative Poisson probabilities in Table 2, the probability of exactly two arrivals is

$$P(X = 2) = P(X \leq 2) - P(X \leq 1)$$

$$= .062 - .017$$

$$= .045$$

c The probability of at least four arrivals is

$$P(X \geq 4) = 1 - P(X \leq 3)$$

$$= 1 - .151$$

$$= .849$$

▲

USING THE COMPUTER TO FIND POISSON PROBABILITIES

Excel and Minitab can be used to calculate Poisson probabilities. We now describe the commands that will output $p(x)$ and $P(X \leq x)$ for any value of x from any Poisson distribution.

Excel Instructions

To compute Poisson probabilities click **POISSON** instead of **BINOMDIST** in step 1 on page 217.

Minitab Instructions

To compute Poisson probabilities click **Poisson . . .** instead of **Binomial . . .** in step 1 on page 218.

POISSON APPROXIMATION OF THE BINOMIAL

Although binomial and Poisson random variables have distinct distributions, the two distributions are related. If we imagine a Poisson random variable whose interval has been subdivided into n (where n is large) very small subintervals, the probability of a success in any subinterval is approximately $p = \mu/n$, and we have an approximate binomial random variable. Similarly, a binomial distribution for which the number of trials n is large and the probability p of a success is very small can be approximated by a Poisson distribution. This approximation is useful because for large values of *n,* binomial probability tables are often unavailable.

The appropriate Poisson distribution to use for the approximation will have $\mu =$ *np,* the mean for the binomial distribution. In order for the approximation to be a good one, *p* should be very small. It is conventional to suggest that at the least, we should have $p < .05$.

▼ EXAMPLE 6.12

A warehouse engages in **acceptance sampling** to determine if it will accept or reject incoming lots of designer sunglasses, some of which invariably are defective. Specifically, the warehouse has a policy of examining a sample of 50 sunglasses from each lot and accepting the lot only if the sample contains no more than two defective pairs. What is the probability of a lot's being accepted if, in fact, 2% of the sunglasses in the lot are defective?

Solution

We are dealing with a binomial experiment for which $n = 50$ and $p = .02$. The required probability cannot be found by using the binomial tables in this text because *n* is too large. But since $p < .05$ and the expected number of defective sunglasses in the sample is $np = 50(.02) = 1$, the required probability can be approximated by using the Poisson distribution with $\mu = 1$. From Table 2 of Appendix B, we find that the probability that a sample contains at most two defective pairs of sunglasses is .920.

For purposes of illustrating how well the Poisson distribution approximates the binomial distribution in this example, we have reproduced the two distributions in Table 6.14. Probabilities corresponding to values of *x* greater than 6 are omitted because they consist entirely of zeros to three decimal places. Summing the first three probabilities in the table, we see that the true (binomial) probability of accepting a lot containing 2% defective sunglasses is .922, while the Poisson approximation to this probability is .920. The Poisson approximation to the binomial distribution in this example is excellent.

Table 6.14 Comparison of Binomial and Poisson Probabilities

x	Binomial Probability ($n = 50, p = .02$)	Poisson Probability ($\mu = np = 1$)
0	.364	.368
1	.372	.368
2	.186	.184
3	.061	.061
4	.014	.015
5	.003	.003
6	.000	.001

EXERCISES

6.90 Compute the following Poisson probabilities, using the formula.

    a $P(X = 4)$, if $\mu = 1$
    b $P(X \leq 1)$, if $\mu = 1.5$
    c $P(X \geq 2)$, if $\mu = 2$

6.91 Repeat Exercise 6.90 using Table 2 of Appendix B.

6.92 Let X be a Poisson random variable with $\mu = 5$. Use Table 2 to find the following probabilities.

    a $P(X \leq 5)$ **b** $P(X = 5)$ **c** $P(X \geq 7)$

6.93 Suppose X is a Poisson random variable whose distribution has a mean of 2.5. Use Table 2 to find the following probabilities.

    a $P(X \leq 3)$ **b** $P(X = 6)$
    c $P(X \geq 2)$ **d** $P(X > 2)$

6.94 Graph the probability distribution of a Poisson random variable with $\mu = .5$.

6.95 Let X be a binomial random variable with $n = 25$ and $p = .01$.

    a Use Table 1 in Appendix B to find $P(X = 0)$, $P(X = 1)$, and $P(X = 2)$.
    b Approximate the three probabilities in part (a) using the appropriate Poisson distribution. (You will need a calculator.) Compare your approximations with the exact probabilities found in part (a).

6.96 Let X be a binomial random variable with $n = 25$ and $p = .05$.

    a Use Table 1 in Appendix B to find $P(X = 0)$, $P(X = 1)$, and $P(X = 2)$.
    b Approximate the three probabilities in part (a) using the appropriate Poisson distribution. (You will need a calculator.) Compare your approximations with the exact probabilities found in part (a).

6.97 The number of calls received by a switchboard operator between 9 and 10 A.M. has a Poisson distribution with a mean of 12. Find the probability that the operator received at least five calls during the following periods.

    a between 9 and 10 A.M.
    b between 9 and 9:30 A.M.
    c between 9 and 9:15 A.M.

6.98 The marketing manager of a company has noted that she usually receives 10 complaint calls from customers during a week (consisting of 5 working days) and that the calls occur at random. Find the probability of her receiving exactly 5 such calls in a single day.

6.99 The numbers of accidents that occur on an assembly line have a Poisson distribution, with an average of three accidents a week.

    a Find the probability that a particular week will be accident free.

b Find the probability that at least three accidents will occur in a week.
c Find the probability that exactly five accidents will occur in a week.
d If the accidents occurring in different weeks are independent of one another, find the expected number of accidents in a year.

6.100 During the summer months (June to August, inclusive), an average of 5 marriages per month take place in a small city. Assuming that these marriages occur randomly and independently of one another, find the probability of the following.

    a Fewer than 4 marriages will occur in June.
    b At least 14 but not more than 18 marriages will occur during the entire 3 months of summer.
    c Exactly 10 marriages will occur during the 2 months of July and August.

6.101 The number of arrivals at a service counter between 1:00 and 3:00 P.M. has a Poisson distribution with a mean of 14.

    a Find the probability that the number of arrivals between 1:00 and 3:00 P.M. is at least 8.
    b Find the probability that the number of arrivals between 1:30 and 2:00 P.M. is at least 8.
    c Find the probability of there being exactly 1 arrival between 2:00 and 3:00 P.M.

6.102 A snow-removal company bills its customers on a per-snowfall basis, rather than at a flat monthly rate. Based on the fee it charges per snowfall, the company will just break even in a month that has exactly six snowfalls. Suppose that the average number of snowfalls per month (during the winter) is eight.

    a What is the probability that the company will just break even in a given winter month?
    b What is the probability that the company will make a profit in a given winter month?

6.103 A biologist knows that about 1% of a certain breed of frogs mutate. Given a random sample of 50 developing frogs, what is the probability that the sample will contain at least 1 mutated frog?

6.104 A paper manufacturer claims that fewer than 1 in 100 of its reels (two-ton rolls) of paper is flawed. A customer has just received a large shipment of these reels and proceeds to check a random sample of 600 of them for flaws. Of this sample, 14 reels are found to be flawed.

    a What was the probability of finding at least 14 flawed reels in this sample?
    b Based on your answer to part (a), what would you conclude about the manufacturer's claim?

6.9 SUMMARY

Gamblers, businesspeople, and economists frequently find themselves in decision-making situations involving uncertain events. Probability is the basic tool they use to make rational judgments in such situations. The first step in assigning probabilities to uncertain events is to form a **sample space**—a listing of all the simple events that can result from a random experiment. A **probability** (number between 0 and 1) is then assigned to each simple event, measuring the likelihood of occurrence of that outcome. The use of a **probability tree** often facilitates both the formation of a sample space and the assignment of probabilities to its simple events. Probabilities can then be computed for more complex events in accordance with rules of probability. The notion of **conditional probability** allows us to express the probability that a particular event will occur when some partial knowledge of the experimental outcome is available.

The concept of a random variable permits us to summarize the results of an experiment in terms of numerical-valued events. Specifically, a **random variable** assigns a numerical value to each simple event of an experiment. A random variable is **discrete** if it can assume at most a countably infinite number of values; it is **continuous** if it can take any of infinitely many values within some interval of values. Once the **probability distribution** of a random variable is known, we can determine its **expected value,** its **variance,** and the probability that it will assume various values. These abilities will stand us in good stead when we reach the study of statistical inference, where we will want to determine the probability that any particular sample will be selected from a population over which the random variable is defined.

After the basic concepts of probability were introduced, including an introduction to **bivariate probability distributions,** a special section devoted to *investment portfolio diversification* served to illustrate an important application of probability and statistics in the workplace.

Two discrete random variables that frequently arise in real-world applications are the **binomial** and the **Poisson.** We described the characteristics of random experiments that give rise to each of these random variables and gave the formulas for their probability distributions.

IMPORTANT TERMS

Random experiment   *166*
Exhaustive   *167*
Mutually exclusive   *167*
Sample space   *167*
Simple event   *167*
Event   *168*
Classical approach   *168*
Relative frequency approach   *168*
Subjective approach   *168*
Probability of an event   *169*
Probability tree   *170*
Complement of an event   *171*
Venn diagram   *172*
Conditional probability   *173*
Independent events   *174*

Joint probability   *175*
Prior probability   *182*
Posterior probability   *182*
Random variable   *186*
Discrete random variable   *187*
Continuous random variable   *187*
Discrete probability distribution   *188*
Expected value of a discrete random variable   *192*
Variance of a discrete random variable   *194*
Standard deviation of a random variable   *195*
Bivariate (or joint) distribution   *200*
Marginal probability   *200*
Covariance   *203*

Coefficient of correlation   *203*   Poisson experiment   *219*
Binomial experiment   *209*   Poisson random variable   *220*
Binomial random variable   *210*   Poisson probability distribution   *220*
Binomial probability   Acceptance sampling   *223*
    distribution   *212*

SUMMARY OF FORMULAS

$$P(A \mid B) = \frac{P(A \text{ and } B)}{P(B)}$$

$$P(A) = 1 - P(\overline{A})$$

$$P(A \text{ or } B) = P(A) + P(B) - P(A \text{ and } B)$$

$$P(A \text{ and } B) = P(A) \cdot P(B \mid A)$$

$$= P(B) \cdot P(A \mid B)$$

$$\mu = E(X) = \sum_{i=1}^{N} x_i \cdot p(x_i)$$

$$\sigma^2 = \sum_{i=1}^{N} (x_i - \mu)^2 \cdot p(x_i)$$

$$= E(X^2) - \mu^2, \text{ where } E(X^2) = \sum x_i^2 \cdot p(x_i)$$

Bivariate

$$p(x,y) = P(X = x \text{ and } Y = y)$$

$$P(X = x \mid Y = y) = \frac{P(X = x \text{ and } Y = y)}{P(Y = y)}$$

$$\text{COV}(X,Y) = \sum_{\text{all } (x,y)} (X - \mu_x)(y - \mu_y) \cdot P(X = x \text{ and } Y = y)$$

$$\rho = \frac{\text{COV}(X,Y)}{\sigma_x \sigma_y}$$

Binomial

$$P(X = x) = p(x) = C_x^n \cdot p^x \cdot (1 - p)^{n-x}$$

$$= \left(\frac{n!}{x!(n - x)!}\right) p^x \cdot (1 - p)^{n-x}, \qquad x = 0, 1, \ldots, n$$

$$E(X) = \mu = np$$

$$V(X) = \sigma^2 = np(1 - p)$$

Poisson

$$P(X = x) = p(x) = \frac{e^{-\mu} \cdot \mu^x}{x!}, \qquad x = 0, 1, 2, \ldots$$

$$E(X) = V(X) = \mu$$

SUPPLEMENTARY EXERCISES

6.105 There are three approaches to determining the probability that an outcome will occur: classical, relative frequency, and subjective. Which approach is appropriate in determining each of the following probabilities?

a It will rain tomorrow.

b A coin toss will result in heads.

c A Michelin tire will last more than 40,000 miles.

d When a single card is selected from a well-shuffled deck, it will be a diamond.

e An automobile will pass quality-control inspection.

f A firm's sales will grow by at least 10% next year.

6.106 Two six-sided dice are rolled, and the number of spots turning up on each is observed. Find the probability of each of the following.

a Observing three spots on one die and five spots on the other.

b Observing exactly one die that has two spots showing.

c Observing that the sum of the spots showing is 7.

d Observing that the sum of the spots showing is 8.

e Observing that the sum of the spots showing is an even number.

f Observing that the sum of the spots showing is 8, given that the sum is an even number.

6.107 Referring to Exercise 6.106, define the following events.

A: The sum of the spots showing is 2, 3, or 12.

B: The sum of the spots showing is an even number.

Are A and B independent events? Explain.

6.108 Exactly 100 employees of a firm have each purchased one ticket in a lottery, with the draw to be held at the firm's annual party. Of the 80 men who purchased tickets, 25 are single. Only 4 of the women who purchased tickets are single.

a Find the probability that the lottery winner is married.

b Find the probability that the lottery winner is a married woman.

c If the winner is a man, what is the probability that he is married?

6.109 A customer service supervisor regularly conducts a survey of customer satisfaction as part of a management control system. The results of his latest survey show that 5% of those surveyed are not satisfied with the service they receive. While only 30% of those surveyed are in arrears, 80% of the dissatisfied customers are in arrears. If the report on one customer surveyed is selected at random, find the probability that this customer has the following characteristics.

a In arrears and dissatisfied.

b Either in arrears or dissatisfied or both.

6.110 As input into his pricing policy, the owner of an appliance store is interested in the relationship between the price at which an item is sold (regular or sale price) and the customer's decision on whether or not to purchase an extended warranty. The owner has constructed the accompanying table of probabilities, based on a study of 2,000 sales invoices. Suppose one sales invoice is selected at random, with the relevant events being defined as follows.

A: Item is purchased at regular price.

B: Item is purchased at sale price.

C: Extended warranty is purchased.

D: Extended warranty is not purchased.

	Extended warranty	
	Purchased	Not purchased
Regular price	.21	.57
Sale price	.14	.08

Express each of the following probabilities in words, and find its value.

a $P(A)$ **b** $P(\overline{A})$ **c** $P(C)$ **d** $P(C \mid A)$

e $P(C \mid B)$ **f** $P(D \mid B)$ **g** $P(B \mid D)$ **h** $P(C \mid D)$

i $P(A \text{ or } B)$ **j** $P(A \text{ and } D)$

6.111 The director of an insurance company's computing center estimates that the company's computer has a 20% chance of "catching" a computer virus. However, she feels that there is only a 6% chance of the computer's "catching" a virus that will completely disable its operating system. If the company's computer should "catch" a virus, what is the probability that the operating system will be completely disabled?

6.112 It is known that 3% of the tickets in a certain scratch-and-win game are winners, in the sense that the purchaser of such a ticket will receive a prize. If three tickets are purchased at random, what is the probability of each of the following?

a All three tickets are winners.

b Exactly one of the tickets is a winner.

c At least one of the tickets is a winner.

6.113 A financial analyst estimates that a certain mutual fund has a 60% chance of rising in value by more than 15% over the coming year. She also predicts that the stock market in general, as measured by the S&P 500 Index, has only a 20% chance of rising more than 15%. But if the Index does so, she feels that the mutual fund has a 95% chance of rising by more than 15%.

a Find the probability that both the S&P 500 Index and the mutual fund will rise in value by more than 15%.

b Find the probability that either the Index or the mutual fund, or both, will rise by more than 15%.

6.114 Because the likelihood of an event's occurring is sometimes expressed in terms of betting *odds* rather than probability, it is useful to be able to convert odds into probabilities, and vice versa. If the odds of an event's occurring are a to b, then the probability that the event will occur is $a/(a + b)$. The probability that the event will not occur is therefore $b/(a + b)$. Find the probability that an event A will occur, if the odds that A will occur are as follows.

a 4 to 1   **b** 3 to 2   **c** 3 to 5

6.115 Many authors have developed models, based on financial ratios, that predict whether or not a company will go bankrupt in the next year. In a test of one such model, the model correctly predicted the bankruptcy of 85% of firms that in fact did fail, and it correctly predicted nonbankruptcy for 82% of firms that did not fail.* Suppose the model maintains the same reliability when applied to a new group of 100 firms, of which 4 fail in the year following the time at which the model makes its predictions.

a Determine the number of firms for which the model's prediction will prove to be correct.

b Find the probability that one of these firms will go bankrupt, given that the model has predicted it will do so.

6.116 A gas plant in Texas is equipped with a standby generator that automatically starts up if the main power fails. It is estimated that, on any given day, there is a 1.5% chance that the main power supply will fail. The standby generator is 95% reliable; should it fail, there is also a battery-driven utility power system (UPS) available. The UPS consists of six batteries connected in parallel so that power is supplied by the UPS if any one of the six batteries is properly charged. The UPS can supply sufficient power for n hours, where n is the number of batteries properly charged. For each of the six batteries, there is a probability of .1 that it is not properly charged.

a Find the probability that all three power sources will fail at the same time.

b Find the probability that the UPS can supply power for at least 2 hours.

6.117 A novelty shop sells coins that come up heads two-thirds of the time. The result of flipping two of these coins is observed.

a Define a sample space for this experiment.

b Assign probabilities to the simple events.

c Find the probability of observing exactly one head.

6.118 A modern version of Russian roulette was invented recently on a small southern Ontario campus by three students (Able, Baker, and Carter): Line up six identical cars, two of which have had the master brake cylinder secretly removed by participating sweethearts.

Each player then randomly selects one car, and one by one (in alphabetical order) they drive at high speed toward the edge of the cliff. At the cliff, they slam on the brakes in time to stop. The first player over the cliff loses, and the game stops. Before they will agree to play the game, however, the students want to understand the odds better, so they have posed the following two questions.

a What is each player's probability of losing?

b What is the probability that there will be no loser?

If it were your job to advise them, how would you answer each of these probing questions?

6.119 Rachel has reached the finals of her tennis club's annual tournament, but she must await the outcome of a match between Linda and Tina before knowing who her opponent will be. Observers feel that Rachel has a 50% chance of winning if she plays Linda and a 75% chance of winning if she plays Tina. They also believe the probability that Linda will reach the finals is .8. After the final match is played, you are told that Rachel won. What is the probability that she played Linda?

6.120 Consider a roulette wheel that is divided into 36 equal segments, numbered from 1 to 36. The wheel has stopped at an even number on each of the last 16 spins. On the next spin of the wheel, would you bet on an even number or an odd number? Explain your answer.

6.121 Bill and Irma are planning to take a 2-week vacation in Hawaii, but they can't decide whether to spend 1 week on each of the islands of Maui and Oahu, 2 weeks on Maui, or 2 weeks on Oahu. Agreeing to leave the decision to chance, Bill places two Maui brochures in one envelope, two Oahu brochures in a second envelope, and a brochure from each of the two islands in a third envelope. Irma is to select one envelope, and they will spend 2 weeks on Maui if it contains 2 Maui brochures, and so on. After selecting one envelope at random, Irma removes one brochure from the envelope and notes that it is a Maui brochure. What is the probability that the other brochure in the envelope is a Maui brochure? (HINT: Proceed with caution!)

6.122 Let X be a random variable with the following probability distribution.

x	0	2	4	6	8
$p(x)$	.10	.20	.25	.30	.15

a Find the expected value and the standard deviation of X.

b Find $E(X^2)$.

c Find $E(4X^2 - 5)$.

d Find the expected value and the standard deviation of $3X + 7$.

6.123 Two coins are selected from a box containing four coins: a nickel, two dimes, and a quarter. Let X be the number of dimes selected.

a Express the probability distribution of X in tabular form.

b Express the probability distribution of X in graphical form.

6.124 A large manufacturer has purchased an insurance policy for $500,000 per year to insure itself against four specific types of losses. The cost associated with each type of loss and its probability are listed in the following table.

Cost	Probability	Cost	Probability
$100,000	.15	$1,500,000	.08
800,000	.10	2,500,000	.04

Of the total cost of the policy, 20% goes to cover administrative expenses.

a What is the expected *profit* to the insurance company on this policy?

b What is the standard deviation of the profits to the insurance company?

6.125 Let X, Y, and W be the three random variables with the following probability distribution.

x	p(x)	y	p(y)	w	p(w)
2	1/4	2	1/8	1	1/4
4	1/4	4	3/8	4	1/4
6	1/4	6	3/8	6	1/4
8	1/4	8	1/8	9	1/4

a Determine the means of X, Y, and W simply by inspection.

b Verify your answers to part (a) by calculating the means.

c Without performing any calculations, determine which of the three distributions has the smallest variance and which has the largest. Explain your reasoning. (HINT: Compare X with Y and X with W.)

d Verify your answer to part (c) by computing the variances.

6.126 An investor intends to place one-quarter of his funds in a real estate venture and the remaining three-quarters in a portfolio of common stocks. The real estate venture has an expected return of 28% with a standard deviation of 20%, while the stock portfolio has an expected return of 12% with a standard deviation of 6%. Assume that the returns on these two investments are independent.

a What are the expected value and the standard deviation of the return on the total amount of funds invested? (HINT: Let X be the return on the real estate venture, let Y be the return on the stock portfolio, and express the return on the total funds invested as a function of X and Y.)

b Using the variance of the possible returns on an investment as a measure of its relative riskiness, rank the real estate venture, the stock portfolio, and the combination of the two in order of increasing riskiness.

6.127 Exercise 6.43 gave the probability distribution of the number of children in American families, as shown in the accompanying table. Use the data in this table to find the probability distribution of the number of children in families having at least one child. (This is called a **conditional probability distribution.**)

x	0	1	2	3	4	5
p(x)	.49	.21	.19	.08	.02	.01

6.128 Let X be a binomial random variable with $n = 20$ and $p = .4$. Use Table 1 of Appendix B to find the following probabilities.

a $P(X \leq 3)$ **b** $P(X = 3)$ **c** $P(X \geq 6)$

d $P(X > 9)$ **e** $P(4 < X \leq 8)$ **f** $P(7 \leq X \leq 9)$

6.129 The BDW car dealership sells one sports model, the FX500. Of the customers who buy this model, 50% choose fire-engine red as the color, 30% choose snow white, and 20% choose jet black.

a What is the probability that at least 6 of the next 10 customers who buy an FX500 model will choose red cars?

b On average, a customer who buys a red FX500 orders options worth $3,000. Customers who buy white FX500 models buy only $2,000 worth of options, and those who buy black FX500 models buy $1,500 worth of options. What is the expected value of the options bought by the next 10 customers who buy an FX500?

6.130 Financing acquisitions often takes the form of putting together a leveraged buyout (LBO), in which a substantial portion of the purchase price is financed by debt. Bankers look at a number of factors when evaluating an LBO proposal. In the United States, an estimated 70% of all LBO proposals are not accepted by bankers (*Canadian Business,* August 1985). If 25 LBO proposals are randomly selected for consideration by a bank, find the probability that each of the following occurs.

a Not more than 8 are accepted.

b Exactly 8 are accepted.

c More than 8 are accepted.

d At least 5 but fewer than 12 are accepted.

6.131 What assumptions did you make in answering Exercise 6.130?

6.132 ACME Plumbing Supply has just received a shipment of 5,000 stainless steel valves that are designed to be used in chemical plants producing acidic chemicals that corrode regular steel valves. Minutes after receiving the valves, the supplier calls to inform ACME that one of its employees inadvertently included 100 regular steel valves in the shipment. Unfortunately, there is no way to distinguish the regular valves from the stainless ones without extensive testing. At about the same time, ACME receives an emergency order for 5 of the stainless steel valves from one of its largest customers.

a If ACME decides to fill the order for 5 stainless steel valves, what is the probability that 1 or more will be regular steel valves?

b If ACME explains its predicament to the customer and ships 6 valves, which the customer is to test prior to use, what is the probability that at least 5 of them will be stainless steel?

6.133 Suppose a machine breaks down occasionally as a result of a particular part that wears out, and suppose these breakdowns occur randomly and independently. The average number of breakdowns per 8-hour day is four, and the distribution of breakdowns is stable within the 8-hour day.

a Find the probability that no breakdowns will occur during a given day.

b Find the probability that at most two breakdowns will occur during the first hour of the day.

c What is the minimum number of spare parts that management should have on hand on a given day if it wants to be at least 90% sure that the machine will not be idle at any time during the day because of a lack of parts?

6.134 The MacTell Toy Company produces toy fire trucks. Suppose that records kept on the imperfections per fire truck show that the imperfections observed arise independently of one another and are unpredictable in nature. That is, the distribution of the number of imperfections approximates a Poisson distribution. The records also indicate that the fire trucks are produced with a mean imperfection rate of .5 per truck.

An order for 1,000 toy fire trucks has been received. The cost department must estimate the total cost of repairing the trucks before the work begins. Past experience indicates that the first imperfection on each fire truck costs 20¢ to repair, while each subsequent imperfection on a fire truck costs 10¢ to repair. (Thus, a truck with three imperfections costs 40¢ to repair.) Find the total expected repair cost involved in supplying the order for 1,000 fire trucks.

6.135 In 1986, the Bank of Canada made some changes in the design and coloring of its $5 bills. Users of banks' automated teller machines soon discovered that the machines would sometimes make a mistake, due to the coloring, and would issue two $5 bills when only one was called for. The manufacturer of the machines claims that remedying the problem isn't worth the cost, because the chance that a mistake will be made on any one transaction is only 1 in 500. If one of these machines handles 250 transactions on a given day, what is the probability that the machine will make more than two mistakes that day?

6.136 The sales manager for a national women's apparel distributor claims that 20% of the company's orders are for a low-end line of apparel, 70% are for a medium line, and 10% are for a high-end line.

a If the next 5 orders are independent of one another, what is the probability that at least 3 of them will be for a medium line of apparel?

b If the next 15 orders are independent of one another, what is the probability that at most 8 of them will be for a low-end line of apparel?

c Suppose that 30% of orders for a low-end line of apparel include an order for some accessories (such as hats or jewelry), 50% of orders for a medium line include an order for accessories, and 40% of orders for a high-end line include an order for accessories. What is the probability that an order for accessories will be included in the next order for an apparel line?

6.137 A boat broker in Florida receives an average of 26 orders per year for an exotic model of cruiser. Assuming that the demand for this model is uniform throughout the year, what is the probability that the boat broker will receive the following?

a Exactly 1 order for this model in a given week.

b Exactly 2 orders for this model over a given 2-week period.

c Exactly 4 orders for this model over a given 4-week period.

6.138 A maintenance worker in a large paper-manufacturing plant knows that, on average, the main pulper (which beats solid materials to a pulp) breaks down six times per 30-day month. Find the probability that, on a given day, she will have to repair the pulper the following number of times.

a Exactly once.

b At least once.

c At least once but not more than twice.

6.139 The scheduling manager for a certain hydropower utility company knows that there are an average of 12 emergency calls regarding power failures per month. Assume that a month consists of 30 days.

a Find the probability that the company will receive at least 12 emergency calls during a specified month.

b Suppose the utility company can handle a maximum of 3 emergency calls per day. What is the probability that there will be more emergency calls than the company can handle on a given day?

CASE 6.1   Let's Make a Deal

A number of years ago, there was a popular television game show called "Let's Make a Deal." The host, Monty Hall, would randomly select contestants from the audience and, as the title suggests, he would make deals for prizes. Contestants would be given relatively modest prizes and then would be offered the opportunity to risk that prize to win better ones.

Suppose you are a contestant on this show. Monty has just given you a free trip worth $500 to a locale that is of little interest to you. He now offers you a trade: Give up the trip in exchange for a gamble. On the stage are three curtains, A, B, and C. Behind one of them is a brand new car worth $20,000. Behind the other two curtains, the stage is empty. You decide to gamble and you select Curtain A. In an attempt to make things more interesting, Monty then exposes an empty stage by opening Curtain C (he knows that there is nothing behind Curtain C). He then offers you the free trip again if you now quit or, if you like, propose another deal (i.e., you can choose Curtain A or B). What do you do?

CASE 6.2   Gains from Market Timing

Many investment managers employ a strategy called *market timing*, which involves forecasting the direction of the overall stock market and adjusting one's investment holdings accordingly. A study conducted by Sharpe* provides insight into how accurate a manager's forecasts must be in order to make a market-timing strategy worthwhile.

Sharpe considers the case of a manager who, at the beginning of each year, either invests all funds in stocks for the entire year (if a good year is forecast) or places all funds in cash equivalents for the entire year (if a bad year is forecast). A good year is defined as one in which the rate of return on stocks (as represented by the Standard and Poor's Composite Index) is higher than the rate of return on cash equivalents (as represented by U.S. Treasury bills). A bad year is one that is not good. The average annual returns for the period from 1934 to 1972 on stocks and on cash equivalents, both for good years and for bad years, are shown in the accompanying table. Two-thirds of the years from 1934 to 1972 were good years.

    a Suppose a manager decides to remain fully invested in the stock market at all times rather than employing market timing. What annual rate of return can this manager expect?

    b Suppose a market timer accurately predicts a good year 80% of the time and accurately predicts a bad year 80% of the time. What is the probability that this manager will predict a good year? What annual rate of return can this manager expect?

    c What is the expected rate of return for a manager who has perfect foresight?

    d Consider a market timer who has no predictive ability whatsoever, but who recognizes that a good year will occur two-thirds of the time. Following Sharpe's

*William F. Sharpe, "Likely Gains from Market Timing," *Financial Analysts' Journal 31* (1975): 60–69.

description, imagine this manager "throwing a die every year, then predicting a good year if numbers 1 through 4 turn up, and a bad year if number 5 or 6 turns up." What is the probability that this manager will make a correct prediction in any given year? What annual rate of return can this manager expect?

Type of Year	Average Annual Returns	
	Stocks	Cash Equivalents
Good year	22.99%	2.27%
Bad year	−7.70	2.68

CASE 6.3   Calculating Probabilities Associated with the Stock Market

The Value Line Investment Survey is a stock market advisory service that is well known for its fine performance record. Value Line follows 1,700 stocks. Every week it assigns each stock a ranking of from 1 (best) to 5 (worst) indicating the stock's timeliness for purchase. There are always 100 stocks in the (top) Rank 1 group.

Suppose that, at the beginning of a calendar year, a portfolio (called the passive Rank 1 portfolio) consisting of the 100 Rank 1 stocks is formed and is held, unchanged, for 1 year. At the end of the year, the rate of return on this passive Rank 1 portfolio is compared to the return on the market portfolio, which consists of all 1,700 stocks. Holloway observed that the passive Rank 1 portfolio outperformed the market portfolio in each of the 14 years from 1965 to 1978, with the exception of 1970.* The probability that this would occur by chance is .00085. After noting that the performances of the two portfolios were almost identical in two of the years (1975 and 1976), Holloway stated: "Even if we count these two years as failures, the probability of obtaining the Value Line results by *chance* is only .0286." Subsequently, Gregory took exception to this statement and wrote: "That observation is a misuse of statistics."† He pointed out that, while the probability of .0286 would be correct if applied to an advisory service selected at random, Value Line was selected *because* of its fine performance record. Gregory then noted that "out of a population of, say, 20 investment advisory services, the probability of finding at least one with 3 [or fewer] bad years out of 14 is .44." In other words, it isn't all that surprising to find one advisory service with such a good performance record.

Holloway also examined an active portfolio strategy, in which the Rank 1 portfolio was "updated weekly to consist always of the 100 Rank 1 stocks." This strategy "outperformed the market in each of the 14 consecutive years" from 1965 to 1978, neglecting the brokerage commission incurred whenever a stock was bought or sold. Although the probability of achieving this performance by chance is only .000061, analysis of results that included brokerage commissions indicated that performance under this active strategy was not significantly superior to the performance of the passive Rank 1 portfolio.

In another phase of Holloway's study, the 100 Rank 1 stocks were partitioned into five subportfolios. Holloway monitored the performance of each of the five subportfolios over

*Clark Holloway, "A Note on Testing an Aggressive Investment Strategy Using Value Line Ranks," *Journal of Finance* 36(3) (1981): 711–19.
†N. A. Gregory, "Testing an Aggressive Investment Strategy Using Value Line Ranks: A Comment," *Journal of Finance* 38(1) (1983): 257–70.

the 4 years from 1974 to 1977, thereby observing 20 returns. These were compared with the 20 corresponding returns from a passive (buy-and-hold) strategy. The active strategy performed better than the passive strategy in 17 of these 20 cases when brokerage commissions were not considered, but it was superior in only 12 of these cases when brokerage costs were included. Are either of these two results significantly different from what could be expected to happen simply by chance?

Verify the values of the four different probabilities mentioned in this case.

CASE 6.4　　　　　**To Bunt Or Not To Bunt?**

No sport generates as many statistics as baseball. Reporters, managers, and fans argue and discuss strategies on the basis of these statistics. A recent article in *Chance* ("A Statistician Reads the Sports Page," Hal S. Stern, Vol. 10, No. 1, Winter 1997) offers baseball lovers another opportunity to analyze numbers associated with the game. Table 1 lists the probabilities of scoring at least one run in situations that are defined by the number of outs and the number of men on base. For example, the probability of scoring at least one run when there are no outs and a man on first is .39. If the bases are loaded with one out the probability of scoring any runs is .67. Table 2 exhibits the expected number of runs

Table 1　Probability of Scoring Any Runs

Bases Occupied	0 Out	1 Out	2 Outs
0	.26	.16	.07
1	.39	.26	.13
2	.57	.42	.24
3	.72	.55	.28
1 & 2	.59	.45	.24
1 & 3	.76	.61	.37
2 & 3	.83	.74	.37
1, 2, & 3	.81	.67	.43

Table 2　Expected Number of Runs Scored

Bases Occupied	0 Out	1 Out	2 Outs
0	.49	.27	.10
1	.85	.52	.23
2	1.06	.69	.34
3	1.21	.82	.38
1 & 2	1.46	1.00	.48
1 & 3	1.65	1.10	.51
2 & 3	1.94	1.50	.62
1, 2, & 3	2.31	1.62	.82

scored in those situations. (Probabilities and expected values are based on results from the American League during the 1989 season. The results for the National League are shown in the article and are similar.) These tables allow us to determine the best strategy in a variety of circumstances. This case will concentrate on the strategy of sacrifice bunting.

The purpose of the sacrifice bunt is to sacrifice the batter to move base runners to the next base. It can be employed when there are less than two out and men on base. Ignoring the suicide squeeze, four outcomes can occur.

1. The bunt is successful. The runner (or runners) advances one base and the batter is out.

2. The batter is out but fails to advance the runner.

3. The batter bunts into a double play.

4. The batter is safe (hit or error) and the runner advances.

Suppose you are a major league manager. The score is tied in the middle of a game and there is a runner on first base with no one out. Given the following probabilities of the four outcomes of a bunt for the batter at the plate, should you bunt?

P(outcome 1) = .75

P(outcome 2) = .10

P(outcome 3) = .10

P(outcome 4) = .05

(We will assume for simplicity that after the hit or error in outcome 4 there will be men on first and second and no one out.)

Chapter 7

Continuous

Probability

Distributions

7.1   Introduction

7.2   Continuous Probability Distributions

7.3   Normal Distribution

7.4   Exponential Distribution

7.5   Summary

7.1 INTRODUCTION

This chapter continues our discussion of probability distributions. We begin by describing continuous probability distributions in general, and then we take a detailed look at the normal distribution, which is the most important specific continuous distribution. The normal distribution will be used extensively when we cover statistical inference. We conclude with a discussion of yet another important specific continuous distribution: the exponential distribution.

7.2 CONTINUOUS PROBABILITY DISTRIBUTIONS

Up to this point, we have focused our attention on discrete distributions—distributions of random variables that have either a finite number of possible values (for example, $x = 0, 1, 2, \ldots, n$) or a countably infinite number of values ($x = 0, 1, 2, \ldots$). In contrast, a continuous random variable has an uncountably infinite number of possible values and can assume any value in the interval between two points a and b ($a < x < b$). Whereas discrete random variables typically involve counting, continuous random variables typically involve measurement attributes such as length, weight, time, and temperature.

One major distinction between a continuous and a discrete random variable relates to the numerical events of interest. We can list all possible values of a discrete random variable, and it is meaningful to consider the probability that a particular individual value will be assumed. On the other hand, we cannot list all the values of a continuous random variable—because there is always another possible value between any two of its values—so the only meaningful events for a continuous random variable are intervals. *The probability that a continuous random variable X will assume any particular value is zero.* While this may appear strange at first, it becomes reasonable when you consider that you could not possibly assign a positive probability to each of the (uncountably) infinitely many values of X and still have the probabilities sum to 1. This situation is analogous to the fact that, while a line segment has a positive length, no single point on the line segment does. For a continuous random variable X, then, it is meaningful only to talk only about the probability that the value assumed by X will fall within some interval of values.

We first encountered continuous data in Chapter 2, when we considered the distribution of long-distance telephone bills. We encountered continuous distributions again in Chapter 4, when we discussed the Empirical Rule. In particular, we illustrated the application of the Empirical Rule using the distribution of a sample of telephone call durations. The relative frequency histogram for these telephone call durations (Figure 4.4) is reproduced in Figure 7.1, with one slight alteration: The heights of the rectangles have been scaled down so that the total area under the histogram is equal to 1. The area under a rectangle now represents the proportion of measurements falling into that class. For example, the area under the first rectangle is 3(3/90) = 3/30, which is the proportion of telephone call durations falling between 2 and 5 minutes. If we had taken a very large sample of measurements, the resulting relative frequency distribution would closely approximate the relative frequency distribution of the entire population of telephone call durations, and the proportion represented by the area of a rectangle would be a very good approximation of the true probability of obtaining a measurement in the class interval corresponding to that rectangle. Experience has shown that, as the size of the sample of measurements becomes larger and as the class width is reduced, the outline of the relative frequency distribution tends toward a smooth curve. That is, the shape of the relative frequency polygon (adjusted

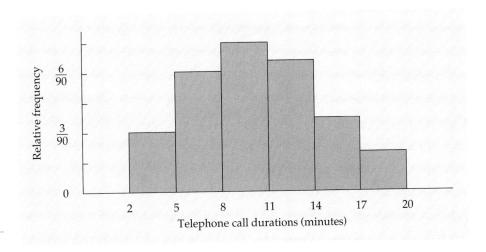

Figure 7.1

Relative frequency histogram

to have a total area equal to 1) for the entire population of measurements progressively approaches a smooth curve.

When dealing with continuous data, we attempt to find a function $f(x)$, called a **probability density function,** whose graph approximates the relative frequency polygon for the population. A probability density function f(x) must satisfy two conditions:

1 $f(x)$ is nonnegative.

2 The total area under the curve representing $f(x)$ equals 1.

It is important to note that $f(x)$ is not a probability. That is, $f(x) \neq P(X = x)$. As previously mentioned, the probability that X will take any specific value is zero: $P(X = x) = 0$. Given a probability density function $f(x)$, the area under the graph of $f(x)$ between the two values a and b is the probability that X will take a value between a and b.* This area is the shaded area in Figure 7.2.

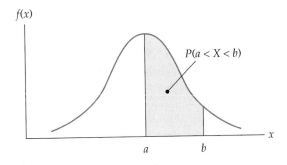

Figure 7.2

Probability density function $f(x)$
[shaded area is $P(a < X < b)$]

*Students who have taken calculus will recognize that

$$P(a < X < b) = \int_a^b f(x)\, dx$$

The two conditions to be satisfied by a probability density function $f(x)$ are $f(x) \geq 0$ and

$$\int_{-\infty}^{\infty} f(x)\, dx = 1$$

A continuous random variable X has an expected value and a variance, just as a discrete variable does. In Chapter 6, we saw how to compute the expected value and the variance of any discrete random variable; we also saw that when dealing with a well-known discrete distribution such as the binomial or Poisson, we need not calculate the expected value and the variance from their definitions, because these parameters are well known. Similarly, most continuous distributions used in practice are well-known distributions with expected values and variances that are also well known and therefore need not be computed.*

UNIFORM DISTRIBUTION

A continuous distribution that possesses appealing descriptive simplicity but unfortunately has limited practical application (except as a theoretical tool) is the **uniform distribution.** The domain of a uniform random variable X consists of all values within some interval $a \leq x \leq b$.

Uniform Distribution

A random variable X, defined over an interval $a \leq x \leq b$, is uniformly distributed if its probability density function is given by

$$f(x) = \frac{1}{b - a} \qquad a \leq x \leq b$$

It can be shown that the expected value and the variance of a uniform random variable X are as follows.

$$E(X) = \frac{a + b}{2}$$

$$V(X) = \frac{(b - a)^2}{12}$$

Note that the expected value of X is simply the midpoint of the domain of X, which should appeal to your intuition, given the symmetrical shape of the probability density function of X. As is evident from Figure 7.3, the values of a uniform random variable X are distributed evenly, or uniformly, across the domain of X. In other words, intervals of equal size within the domain of X are equally likely to contain the value that the variable X will assume.

---

*For students who are interested and know calculus, the expected value and the variance of a continuous random variable X with probability density function $f(x)$ are given by

$$E(X) = \mu = \int_{-\infty}^{\infty} x f(x)\, dx$$

$$V(X) = \sigma^2 = \int_{-\infty}^{\infty} (x - \mu)^2 f(x)\ dx$$

These expressions are the same as those for the discrete case, except that summation is replaced by integration.

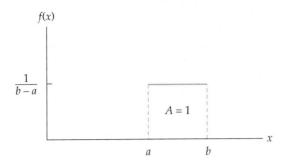

Figure 7.3

Uniform distribution

Notice that the total area A under the uniform density function $f(x)$ equals 1, as is required for any probability function. The area A of the rectangle under $f(x)$ is the height of the rectangle, $1/(b - a)$, times its base.

$$A = \left(\frac{1}{b - a}\right) \cdot (b - a) = 1$$

The probability that X will take a value within any given interval is found in a similar manner by multiplying $1/(b - a)$ by the width of the interval in question. Thus, the probability the X will take a value between x_1 and x_2 is

$$P(x_1 \leq X \leq x_2) = \left(\frac{1}{b - a}\right) \cdot (x_2 - x_1)$$

▼ **EXAMPLE 7.1**

A manufacturer has observed that the time that elapses between the placement of an order with a just-in-time supplier and the delivery of the parts is uniformly distributed between 100 and 180 minutes.

a Define and graph the density function.
b What proportion of orders takes between 2 and 2.5 hours to be delivered?

Solution **a** If X denotes the number of minutes that elapse between the placement and delivery of the order, then X can take any value in the interval $100 \leq x \leq 180$. Because the width of the interval is 80, the height of the density function must be 1/80, in order for the total area under the density function to equal 1. That is, the density function is

$$f(x) = 1/80, \quad 100 \leq x \leq 180$$

The graph of this function is shown in Figure 7.4.

b The required probability, which is represented by the shaded area in Figure 7.4, is

$$P(120 \leq X \leq 150) = (\text{Base})(\text{Height}) = (150 - 120)(1/80) = .375$$

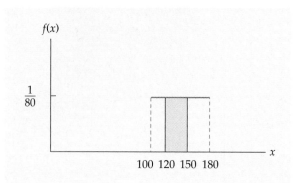

Figure 7.4

Shaded area is
$P(120 \le X \le 150)$

EXERCISES

7.1 Consider a random variable X with a probability density function described by

$$f(x) = -.5x + 1, \quad 0 \le x \le 2$$

a Graph the density function $f(x)$.
b Verify that $f(x)$ is a probability density function.
c Find $P(X \ge 1)$.
d Find $P(X \le .5)$.
e Find $P(X = 1.5)$

7.2 Consider a random variable X having the uniform density function $f(x)$, with $a = 20$ and $b = 30$.

a Define and graph the density function $f(x)$.
b Verify that $f(x)$ is a probability density function.
c Find $P(22 \le x \le 30)$.
d Find $P(X = 25)$.
e Find $P(X \le 25)$.

7.3 Consider a random variable X with a probability density function described by

$$f(x) = \begin{cases} .2 + .04x, & -5 \le x \le 0 \\ .2 - .04x, & 0 \le x \le 5 \end{cases}$$

a Graph the density function $f(x)$.
b Verify that $f(x)$ is a probability density function.
c Find $P(X \ge -2)$.
d Find $P(X \le 3)$.
e Find $P(3 \le X \le 5)$.

7.4 A hospital receives a pharmaceutical delivery each morning at a time that varies uniformly between 7:00 and 8:00 A.M.

a Find the probability that the delivery on a given morning will occur between 7:15 and 7:30 A.M.
b What is the expected time of delivery?
c Find the probability that the time of delivery will be within 1 standard deviation of the expected time—that is, within the interval $\mu - \sigma \le x \le \mu + \sigma$.

7.3 NORMAL DISTRIBUTION

The **normal distribution** is the most important specific continuous distribution that we will consider in some detail. Other important continuous distributions (most of which we will encounter in later chapters) include the exponential distribution, the Student t distribution, the chi-squared distribution, and the F distribution. The graph of the normal distribution is the familiar symmetrical, bell-shaped curve shown in Figure 7.5. One reason for the importance of the normal distribution is that it usefully models or describes the distributions of numerous random variables that arise in practice, such as the heights or weights of a group of people, the total annual sales of a firm, the grades of a class of students, and the measurement errors that arise in the performance of an experiment. In examples such as these, the observed measurements tend to cluster in a symmetrical fashion about the central value, giving rise to a bell-shaped distribution curve.

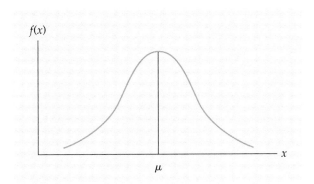

Figure 7.5

Symmetrical, bell-shaped
normal distribution

A second reason for the normal distribution's importance is that this distribution provides a useful approximation to many other distributions, including discrete ones such as the binomial distribution. Finally, as we will see in Chapter 9, the normal distribution is the cornerstone distribution of statistical inference, representing the distribution of the possible estimates of a population parameter that may arise from different samples. This last point, in fact, is the main reason for the importance of the normal distribution.

A random variable that is normally distributed is called a **normal random variable.** A normal random variable can take on any real value from $-\infty$ to $+\infty$, and the

---

Normal Distribution

A random variable X with mean μ and variance σ^2 is normally distributed if its probability density function is given by

$$f(x) = \left(\frac{1}{\sigma\sqrt{2\pi}}\right)e^{-(1/2)[(x-\mu)/\sigma]^2}, \qquad -\infty < x < \infty$$

where $\pi = 3.14159\ldots$ and $e = 2.71828.\ldots$

---

normal probability density function $f(x)$ is continuous and has a positive value for all values of x. As is the case with any other probability density function, the value of $f(x)$ here is not the probability that X assumes the value x, but an expression of the height of the curve at the value x. Moreover, the entire area under the curve depicting $f(x)$ must equal 1.

It is apparent from the formula for the probability density function that a normal distribution is completely determined once the parameters μ and σ^2 are specified. That is, a whole family of different normal distributions exists, but one differs from another only in the location of its mean μ and in the variance σ^2 of its values; all normal distributions have the same symmetrical, bell-shaped appearance. Figure 7.6 depicts three normal distributions with the same variance but different means, while Figure 7.7 shows three normal distributions with the same mean but different variances. Notice that the shape of the distribution becomes flatter and more spread out as the variance becomes larger.

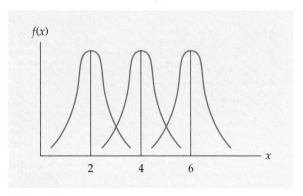

Figure 7.6

Normal distributions with the same variance but different means

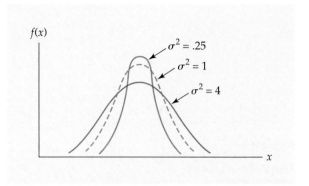

Figure 7.7

Normal distributions with the same Mean but different variances

FINDING NORMAL PROBABILITIES

After we determine that a situation can be modeled appropriately by using a normal distribution, we'll want to find various normal probabilities, which are represented by areas under the normal curve. The procedure for finding normal probabilities is illustrated in the following example.

Suppose that the length of time students take in writing a standard entrance examination is known to be normally distributed, with a mean of 60 minutes and a standard deviation of 8 minutes. If we observe the time taken by a particular student, what is the probability that the student's time will be between 60 and 70 minutes?

Given that X denotes the time taken to write the entrance examination, the probability we are seeking is written $P(60 < X < 70)$.* This probability is given by the area under the normal curve between 60 and 70, depicted by the shaded region in Figure 7.8(a). The actual calculation of such an area (probability) is difficult, however, so we will resort to the tabulated areas provided by Table 3 in Appendix B.†

Because each pair of values for the parameters μ and σ^2 gives rise to a different normal distribution, there are infinitely many possible normal distributions, making it impossible to provide a table of areas for each one. Fortunately, we can make do with just one table.

The particular normal distribution for which Table 3 in Appendix B has been constructed is the normal distribution with $\mu = 0$ and $\sigma = 1$, called the **standard normal distribution.** The corresponding normal random variable, with a mean of 0 and a standard deviation of 1, is called the **standard normal random variable** and is denoted Z. Thus, before using Table 3, we must convert or transform our normal random variable X into the standard normal random variable Z. We accomplish this by applying the following transformation.

---

*Recall that the probability that a continuous random variable X will assume any particular value is zero. Hence, $P(60 \leq X \leq 70) = P(60 < X < 70)$. These two forms for expressing a normal probability will therefore be used interchangeably.

†For students familiar with calculus, the probability that X takes a value between a and b is given by

$$P(a < X < b) = \int_a^b \left(\frac{1}{\sigma\sqrt{2\pi}}\right) e^{-(1/2)[(x-\mu)/\sigma]^2} \, dx$$

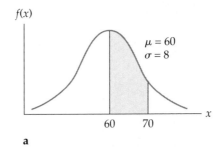
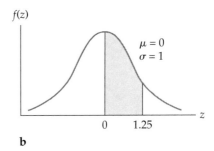

Figure 7.8

Shaded area is $P(60 < X < 70)$
$= P(0 < Z < 1.25)$

Standard Normal Random Variable
$$Z = \frac{X - \mu}{\sigma}$$

For our example, we obtain

$$Z = \frac{X - 60}{8}$$

We can easily verify, using the laws of expected value and of variance, that we have created a random variable Z with a mean of 0 and a standard deviation of 1 (see Exercise 6.58). Moreover, it can be shown that Z is normally distributed. The interpretation of Z is most important. A value of Z equals the distance from the corresponding value of X to μ, measured in standard deviations of X.

To find the desired probability, $P(60 < X < 70)$, we must first determine the interval of z-values corresponding to the interval of x-values of interest: $60 < x < 70$. Using elementary algebra, we know that $60 < x < 70$ holds whenever

$$\frac{60 - 60}{8} < \frac{x - 60}{8} < \frac{70 - 60}{8}$$

or

$$0 < z < 1.25$$

We therefore obtain

$$P(60 < X < 70) = P(0 < Z < 1.25)$$

Thus, we can find the required area (probability) by finding the corresponding area under the standard normal curve, which is depicted by the shaded area in Figure 7.8(b). Areas like this that correspond to probabilities of the form $P(0 < Z < z_0)$ are tabulated in Table 3 in Appendix B. Table 3 is reproduced here as Table 7.1.

In Table 3 (and in Table 7.1), a value of z that is correct to the first decimal place is found in the left-hand column; the second decimal place is located across the top row. We need to find $P(0 < Z < 1.25)$, which is represented by the area over the interval from 0 to 1.25. To find this area corresponding to $z = 1.25$, first locate 1.2 in the left-hand column and then move across the row until you reach the column with .05 at the top. The area corresponding to $z = 1.25$ is .3944, so

$$P(60 < X < 70) = P(0 < Z < 1.25)$$
$$= .3944$$

Table 7.1 Reproduction of Table 3: Standard Normal Curve Areas

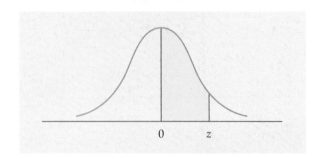

z	.00	.01	.02	.03	.04	.05	.06	.07	.08	.09
0.0	.0000	.0040	.0080	.0120	.0160	.0199	.0239	.0279	.0319	.0359
0.1	.0398	.0438	.0478	.0517	.0557	.0596	.0636	.0675	.0714	.0753
0.2	.0793	.0832	.0871	.0910	.0948	.0987	.1026	.1064	.1103	.1141
0.3	.1179	.1217	.1255	.1293	.1331	.1368	.1406	.1443	.1480	.1517
0.4	.1554	.1591	.1628	.1664	.1700	.1736	.1722	.1808	.1844	.1879
0.5	.1915	.1950	.1985	.2019	.2054	.2088	.2123	.2157	.2190	.2224
0.6	.2257	.2291	.2324	.2357	.2389	.2422	.2454	.2486	.2517	.2549
0.7	.2580	.2611	.2642	.2673	.2704	.2734	.2764	.2794	.2823	.2852
0.8	.2881	.2910	.2939	.2967	.2995	.3023	.3051	.3078	.3106	.3133
0.9	.3159	.3186	.3212	.3238	.3264	.3289	.3315	.3340	.3365	.3389
1.0	.3413	.3438	.3461	.3485	.3508	.3531	.3554	.3577	.3599	.3621
1.1	.3643	.3665	.3686	.3708	.3729	.3749	.3770	.3790	.3810	.3830
1.2	.3849	.3869	.3888	.3907	.3925	.3944	.3962	.3980	.3997	.4015
1.3	.4032	.4049	.4066	.4082	.4099	.4115	.4131	.4147	.4162	.4177
1.4	.4192	.4207	.4222	.4236	.4251	.4265	.4279	.4292	.4306	.4319
1.5	.4332	.4345	.4357	.4370	.4382	.4394	.4406	.4418	.4429	.4441
1.6	.4452	.4463	.4474	.4484	.4495	.4505	.4515	.4525	.4535	.4545
1.7	.4554	.4564	.4573	.4582	.4591	.4599	.4608	.4616	.4625	.4633
1.8	.4641	.4649	.4656	.4664	.4671	.4678	.4686	.4693	.4699	.4706
1.9	.4713	.4719	.4726	.4732	.4738	.4744	.4750	.4756	.4761	.4767
2.0	.4772	.4778	.4783	.4488	.4793	.4798	.4803	.4808	.4812	.4817
2.1	.4821	.4826	.4830	.4834	.4838	.4842	.4846	.4850	.4854	.4857
2.2	.4861	.4864	.4868	.4871	.4875	.4878	.4881	.4884	.4887	.4890
2.3	.4893	.4896	.4898	.4901	.4904	.4906	.4909	.4911	.4913	.4916
2.4	.4918	.4920	.4922	.4925	.4927	.4929	.4931	.4932	.4934	.4936
2.5	.4938	.4940	.4941	.4943	.4945	.4946	.4948	.4949	.4951	.4952
2.6	.4953	.4955	.4956	.4957	.4959	.4960	.4961	.4962	.4963	.4964
2.7	.4965	.4966	.4967	.4968	.4969	.4970	.4971	.4972	.4973	.4974
2.8	.4974	.4975	.4976	.4977	.4977	.4978	.4979	.4979	.4980	.4981
2.9	.4981	.4982	.4982	.4983	.4984	.4984	.4985	.4985	.4986	.4986
3.0	.4987	.4987	.4987	.4988	.4988	.4989	.4989	.4989	.4990	.4990

Source: Abridged from Table 1 of A. Hald, *Statistical Tables and Formulas* (New York: John Wiley & Sons, 1952). Reproduced by permission.

The probability that a particular student will take between 60 and 70 minutes to write the entrance exam is therefore .3944.

We repeat that the z-value corresponding to a given value x_0 has an important interpretation. Because $(x_0 - \mu)$ expresses how far x_0 is from the mean, the corresponding z-value

$$z_0 = \frac{x_0 - \mu}{\sigma}$$

tells us how many standard deviations x_0 is from the mean. Moreover, if z_0 is positive, then x_0 lies to the right of the mean; conversely, if z_0 is negative, then x_0 lies to the left of the mean. Thus, in the preceding example, the value 70 lies 1.25 standard deviations to the right of the mean value of 60; that is, $70 = 60 + 1.25(8)$.

As we have just seen, we can obtain desired probabilities for any normal distribution from probabilities tabulated for the standard normal distribution. A table of probabilities for just one normal distribution supplies us with all the information we need, because normal distributions differ from one another only in their means and variances. The probability that the variable will assume a value within z_0 standard deviations of the mean remains constant from one normal random variable to the next. In other words, if X is any normal random variable with mean μ and standard deviation σ, then

$$P(\mu - z_0\sigma < X < \mu + z_0\sigma) = P(-z_0 < Z < z_0)$$

We first caught a glimpse of this concept when we took up the Empirical Rule in Chapter 4. According to this rule, about 68% of the values from a mound-shaped distribution (such as the normal distribution) lie within 1 standard deviation of the mean, about 95% of the values lie within 2 standard deviations of the mean, and almost 100% of the values lie within 3 standard deviations.*

Therefore, probabilities of the form $P(-z_0 < Z < z_0)$ need only be tabulated for one normal distribution, because they are the same for all others. In fact, because a normal distribution is symmetrical, it suffices to tabulate probabilities of the form $P(0 \leq Z \leq z_0)$. The probabilities found in Table 3 in Appendix B, then, are of the form $P(0 \leq Z \leq z_0)$, for values of z_0 from .00 to 3.09. Given that the total area under the normal curve equals 1, any desired probability can be obtained by adding and subtracting probabilities of this form.

▼ EXAMPLE 7.2

Determine the following probabilities.
a $P(Z \geq 1.47)$
b $P(-2.25 \leq Z \leq 1.85)$
c $P(.65 \leq Z \leq 1.36)$

Solution   **a** It is always advisable to begin by sketching a diagram and indicating the area of interest under the normal curve, as shown in Figure 7.9. Area A_1 corresponds to the required probability, and area A_2 is the area between $z = 0$ and $z = 1.47$. Because the entire area under the normal curve equals 1, and because the curve is symmetrical about $z = 0$, the entire area to the right of $z = 0$ is .5. Therefore,

---

*For the special mound-shaped distribution called the *normal distribution,* Table 3 in Appendix B identifies the precise percentages as 68.26, 95.44, and 99.74, respectively.

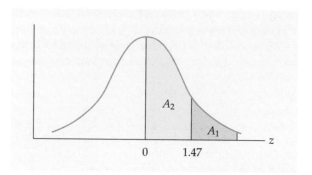

Figure 7.9

Shaded areas are
$P(0 < Z < 1.47)$ and
$P(Z \geq 1.47)$
in Example 7.2(a)

$$A_1 + A_2 = .5$$

Area A_2 is of the form that can be found in Table 3. Locating $z = 1.47$ in Table 3, we find that area A_2 is .4292, so $P(0 \leq Z \leq 1.47) = .4292$. The required probability is therefore

$$
\begin{aligned}
P(Z \geq 1.47) &= A_1 \\
&= .5 - A_2 \\
&= .5 - .4292 \\
&= .0708
\end{aligned}
$$

b Whenever the area of interest straddles the mean, as in this situation, we must express it as the sum of the portions to the left and to the right of the mean. The required probability $P(-2.25 \leq Z \leq 1.85)$ corresponds to the sum of the areas A_1 and A_2 in Figure 7.10. That is,

$$P(-2.25 \leq Z \leq 1.85) = A_1 + A_2$$

From Table 3, we find that $A_2 = .4678$. Because the normal distribution is symmetrical, we can write

$$A_1 = P(-2.25 \leq Z \leq 0) = P(0 \leq Z \leq 2.25)$$

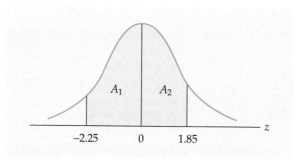

Figure 7.10

Shaded area is
$P(-2.25 \leq Z \leq 1.85)$
in Example 7.2(b)

Locating $z = 2.25$ in Table 3, we find that $A_1 = .4878$. Therefore, the required probability is

$$
\begin{aligned}
P(-2.25 \leq Z \leq 1.85) &= A_1 + A_2 \\
&= .4878 + .4678 \\
&= .9556
\end{aligned}
$$

c $P(.65 \leq Z \leq 1.36)$ corresponds to the shaded area A in Figure 7.11. Since Table 3 only provides areas from zero up to some positive value of Z, we must express A as the difference between two such areas. If A_1 is the area between $z = 0$ and $z = 1.36$, then $A_1 = .4131$ (from Table 3). Similarly, if A_2 is the area between $z = 0$ and $z = .65$, then $A_2 = .2422$. Therefore,

$$P(.65 \leq Z \leq 1.36) = A$$
$$= A_1 - A_2$$
$$= P(0 \leq Z \leq 1.36) - P(0 \leq Z \leq .65)$$
$$= .4131 - .2422$$
$$= .1709$$

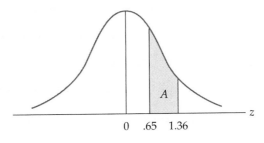

Figure 7.11

Shaded area is
$P(0.65 \leq Z \leq 1.36)$
in Example 7.2(c)

▼ **EXAMPLE 7.3**

A venture capital company feels that the rate of return (X) on a proposed investment is approximately normally distributed, with a mean of 30% and a standard deviation of 10%.

a Find the probability that the return will exceed 55%.
b Find the probability that the return will be less than 22%.

Solution   **a** Figure 7.12 shows the required area A_1, together with values of Z corresponding to selected values of X. The value of Z corresponding to $x = 55$ is

$$z = \frac{x - \mu}{\sigma} = \frac{55 - 30}{10} = 2.5$$

Therefore,

$$P(X > 55) = A_1$$
$$= P(Z > 2.5)$$
$$= .5 - P(0 \leq Z \leq 2.5)$$
$$= .5 - .4938$$
$$= .0062$$

The probability that the return will exceed 55% is .0062.

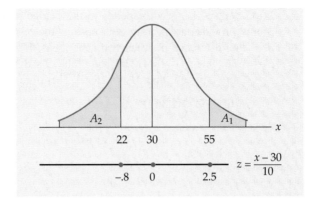

Figure 7.12

Corresponding values of X and Z
for Example 7.3

b Figure 7.12 shows the required area A_2. By the same logic as that used in part (a),

$$P(X < 22) = A_2$$
$$= P\left(Z < \frac{22 - 30}{10}\right)$$
$$= P(Z < -.8) = P(Z > .8)$$
$$= .5 - P(0 \le Z \le .8) = P(Z > .8)$$
$$= .5 - P(0 \le Z \le .8)$$
$$= .5 - .2881$$
$$= .2119$$

The probability that the return will be less than 22% is .2119.

On page 250, we describe how Excel and Minitab can be employed to solve these problems.

As we progress throughout this book, we will have need to use the normal table "backwards." That is, we will have a probability, and we will have to find the z-value associated with that probability. Here is an example.

▼ EXAMPLE 7.4

If Z is a standard normal variable, determine the value z for which $P(Z \le z) = .6331$.

Solution Because the area to the left of 0 is .5 in Figure 7.13, z must be a positive number. Since the area between 0 and z is $P(0 \le Z \le z)$,

$$.6331 = .5 + P(0 \le Z \le z)$$

Therefore,

$$P(0 \le Z \le z) = .6331 - .5 = .1331$$

Locating the area .1331 in the body of Table 3, we find that the corresponding value of z is .34. Therefore,

$$P(Z \le .34) = .6331$$

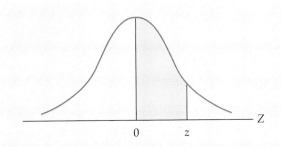

Figure 7.13

Shaded area is $P(0 \leq Z \leq z)$ in Example 7.4

▼ **EXAMPLE 7.5**

This example introduces some notation that you will use frequently in statistical inference, beginning in Chapter 9. If Z is a standard normal random variable and A is any probability, then z_A represents that value for which the area under the standard normal curve to the right of z_A is A. In other words,

$$P(Z > z_A) = A$$

Thus, because the normal distribution is symmetrical, $-z_A$ represents that value for which the area under the standard normal curve to the left of $-z_A$ is A. Determine $z_{.025}$.

Solution   Since the area in Figure 7.14 between $z = 0$ and $z_{.025}$ is given by $P(0 \leq Z \leq z_{.025})$, the desired value $z_{.025}$ is the z-value in Table 3 corresponding to the area $P(0 \leq Z \leq z_{.025})$. But the area under the curve to the right of $z_{.025}$ is .025, so

$$P(0 \leq Z \leq z_{.025}) = .5 - .025 = .475$$

From Table 3, the z-value corresponding to the area .475 is

$$z_{.025} = 1.96$$

so

$$P(Z > 1.96) = .025$$

From symmetry, the area to the left of $z = -1.96$ is also .025. That is,

$$P(Z < -1.96) = .025$$

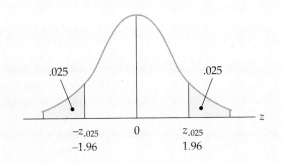

Figure 7.14

Locating $z_{.025}$ in Example 7.5

FUNCTIONS OF NORMAL RANDOM VARIABLES

In Section 6.6, we considered the sum of two random variables and provided (without proof) the following expressions for computing the expected value and variance of $aX + bY$, where a and b are constants.

$$E(aX + bY) = aE(X) + bE(Y)$$

$$V(aX + bY) = aV(X) + bV(Y) + 2ab\,COV(X,Y)$$

If X is a normal random variable and a is a constant, then the variables $X + a$, $X - a$, and aX are all normally distributed.

In the special case for which X and Y are *independent* normal random variables, it can be shown that the random variables $X + Y$ and $X - Y$ are also normally distributed. These properties of functions of two random variables will be useful in Chapter 8, which introduces sampling distributions, and in Chapter 12, which addresses the problem of comparing two populations.

USING THE COMPUTER TO FIND NORMAL PROBABILITIES

We now describe how to command Excel and Minitab to calculate normal probabilities. The probability that is produced is of the form $P(X < x)$, which means that the output is the probability that a normal random variable with a given mean and standard deviation falls between $-\infty$ and x. That is, the computer will print $P(-\infty < X < x)$ for any value of x. Note that the normal table (Table 3 in Appendix B) lists the probabilities of the form $P(0 < Z < z)$.

Excel Instructions

To calculate $P(X < x)$ when X is normally distributed, follow the procedure described below.

COMMANDS

1 Click **f$_x$**, **Function Category: Statistical,** and **Function Name: NORMDIST.** Click **Next>.**
2 Use the cursor and type the value of x **(x)**, the mean of the distribution **(mean)**, the standard deviation of the distribution **(standard_dev)**, and true **(cumulative)**. Click **Finish.** [Typing false will produce $f(x)$, which is merely the value of the normal function at x, a value that has little meaning for you.]

Minitab Instructions

To calculate $P(X < x)$ when X is normally distributed, follow the procedure below.

1 Click **Calc, Probability Distributions,** and **Normal . . . .**
2 Use the cursor to specify **Cumulative probability.** (If you specify **Probability density,** you will compute the value of the normal function at x, a value that has little meaning for you.)
3 Hit **tab** and type the value of the **Mean.**
4 Hit **tab** and type the value of the **Standard deviation.**
5 Click **Input column,** hit **tab,** and type the value of x. Click **OK.**

If you have several values of x, store them in a column (say, column 1) and proceed as above, except at step 5, click **Input column,** hit **tab**, and type the value of x. Click **OK.**

EXERCISES

7.5 Use Table 3 of Appendix B to find the area under the standard normal curve between the following values.

  a $z = 0$ and $z = 2.3$
  b $z = 0$ and $z = 1.68$
  c $z = .24$ and $z = .33$
  d $z = -2.575$ and $z = 0$
  e $z = -2.81$ and $z = -1.35$
  f $z = -1.73$ and $z = .49$

7.6 Use Table 3 to find the following probabilities.

  a $P(Z \geq 1.7)$ **b** $P(Z \geq -.95)$ **c** $P(Z \leq -1.96)$
  d $P(Z \leq 2.43)$ **e** $P(-2.97 \leq Z \leq -1.38)$
  f $P(-1.14 \leq Z \leq 1.55)$

7.7 Use Table 3 to find the value of z for each of the following.

  a $P(0 \leq Z \leq z) = .41$
  b $P(Z \geq z) = .025$
  c $P(Z \geq z) = .9$
  d $P(Z \leq z) = .95$
  e $P(Z \leq z) = .2$
  f $P(-z \leq Z \leq z) = .88$

7.8 Determine z_A and locate its value on a graph of the standard normal distribution for each of the following values of A.

  a .005 **b** .01   **c** .05

7.9 Let X be a normal random variable with a mean of 50 and a standard deviation of 8. Find the following probabilities.

  a $P(X \geq 52)$ **b** $P(X < 40)$ **c** $P(X = 40)$
  d $P(X > 40)$ **e** $P(35 < X \leq 64)$
  f $P(32 \leq X \leq 37)$

7.10 If X is a normal random variable with a mean of 50 and a standard deviation of 8, how many standard deviations away from the mean is each of the following values of X?

  a $x = 52$ **b** $x = 40$ **c** $x = 35$
  d $x = 64$ **e** $x = 32$ **f** $x = 37$

7.11 The time required to assemble an electronic component is normally distributed, with a mean of 12 minutes and a standard deviation of $1\frac{1}{2}$ minutes. Find the probability that a particular assembly takes the following length of time.

  a More than 14 minutes.
  b More than 8 minutes.
  c Less than 14 minutes.
  d Less than 10 minutes.
  e Between 10 and 15 minutes.

7.12 The lifetime of a certain brand of tires is approximately normally distributed, with a mean of 45,000 miles and a standard deviation of 4,000 miles. The tires carry a warranty for 35,000 miles.

  a What proportion of the tires will fail before the warranty expires?
  b At what mileage should warranty life be set so that fewer than 5% of tires must be replaced under warranty?

7.13 A certain type of lightbulb is advertised to have an average lifetime of 1,000 hours. Assume the lifetimes of these lightbulbs are approximately normally distributed with a standard deviation of 250 hours.

  a Find the proportion of lightbulbs that will fail during their first 250 hours of use.

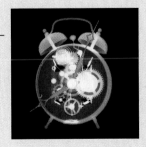

b Find the proportion of lightbulbs that will fail within 125 hours of their average lifetime, and compare your answer to that obtained in part (a). (Just as in part (a), we are considering a total period of 250 hours during which the bulbs might fail.)

c Based on your answers to parts (a) and (b), what can you say about the failure rate of these bulbs?

d At what number of hours should the warranty lifetime be set so that fewer than 2% of bulbs must be replaced under warranty?

7.14 A firm's marketing manager believes that total sales for the firm next year can be modeled by using a normal distribution, with a mean of $2.5 million and a standard deviation of $300,000.

a What is the probability that the firm's sales will exceed $3 million?

b What is the probability that the firm's sales will fall within $150,000 of the expected level of sales?

c To cover fixed costs, the firm's sales must exceed the break-even level of $1.8 million. What is the probability that sales will exceed the break-even level?

d Determine the sales level that has only a 9% chance of being exceeded next year.

7.15 Empirical studies have provided support for the belief that a common stock's annual rate of return is approximately normally distributed. Suppose you have invested in the stock of a company for which the annual return has an expected value of 16% and a standard deviation of 10%.

a Find the probability that your 1-year return will exceed 30%.

b Find the probability that your 1-year return will be negative.

c Suppose this company embarks on a new high-risk, but potentially highly profitable venture. As a result, the return on the stock now has an expected value of 25% and a standard deviation of 20%. Answer parts (a) and (b) in light of the revised estimates regarding the stock's return.

d As an investor, would you approve of the company's decision to embark on the new venture?

7.16 A steel fabricator produces pipes with a diameter that is approximately normally distributed, with a mean of 10 cm and a variance of .01 cm^2.

a Suppose the tolerance limit for these pipes is .2 cm, so pipes with a diameter falling within the interval $10 \pm .2$ cm are acceptable. What proportion of the pipes produced will be acceptable?

b Suppose that pipes with too small a diameter can be reworked, but that pipes with too large a diameter must be scrapped. Suppose also that the tolerance has been reduced to .1 cm. What proportion of the pipes must be scrapped?

7.17 Mensa is an organization whose members possess IQs in the top 2% of the population.

a If IQs are normally distributed, with a mean of 100 and a standard deviation of 16, what is the minimum IQ necessary for admission?

b If three individuals are chosen at random from the general population, what is the probability that all three satisfy the minimum requirement for admission to Mensa?

7.18 Universities throughout the United States and Canada are concerned about the aging of their faculty members, as the average age of professors is at a historic high. A

STATISTICS IN THE WORKPLACE

Operations Management Application

Every organization maintains some **inventory,** which is defined as a stock of items. For example, grocery stores hold inventories of almost all the products they sell. When the total number of a product drops to a specified level, the manager arranges for the delivery of more of that product. An automobile repair shop keeps an inventory of a large number of replacement parts. A school keeps a stock of items that it uses regularly, including chalk, pens, envelopes, file folders, and paper clips. There are costs associated with inventories. These include cost of capital, losses (theft and obsolescence), warehouse storage, as well as maintenance and record keeping. Management scientists have developed several models to help determine the optimum inventory level

that balances the cost of inventory with the cost of shortages and the

cost of making small orders. Several of these models are deterministic, which assume that the demand for the product is constant. However, in almost all applications demand is a random variable. One commonly used probabilistic model assumes that the demand during lead time is a normally distributed random variable. Lead time is defined as the amount of time between the order being made and the delivery of the product. Exercises 7.20 and 7.21 involve inventory.

very large number of faculty members will retire within the next decade, making it difficult to find adequate replacements to fill all the positions that will become available. Suppose that North American professors have a median age of 46.4 years, and 36% of them are at least 50 years of age. Assume that the ages of these professors are normally distributed.

a Determine the standard deviation of the ages.

b Assume that there are currently 40,000 professors at North American universities and that the mandatory retirement age is 65. What is the minimum number of professors who will retire during the next decade?

7.19 The maintenance department of a city's electric power company finds that it is cost-efficient to replace all streetlight bulbs at once, rather than replacing the bulbs individually as they burn out. Assume that the lifetime of a bulb is normally distributed, with a mean of 3,000 hours and a standard deviation of 200 hours.

a If the department wants no more than 1% of the bulbs to burn out before they are replaced, after how many hours should all the bulbs be replaced?

b If two bulbs are selected at random from among those that have been replaced, what is the probability that at least one of them has burned out?

7.20 The owner of a convenience store has newspapers delivered early each morning. The demand for the newspaper is normally distributed, with a mean of 75 and a standard deviation of 16.

a What is the probability that the newspapers will sell out on a given day if the owner orders 65 copies? If 80 are ordered?

b How many copies should be ordered so that the probability of selling out is at most 10%?

7.21 A retailer of computing products sells an average of 200 printers per week. *Lead time* for a new order of printers is 1 week, meaning it takes 1 week for the order to arrive after it has been placed. If the demand for printers was a constant level of 200 per week, the retailer could wait until inventory fell to 200 before placing a new order, thereby saving on inventory costs. (The inventory level when a new order should be placed is called the *reorder point,* which would be 200 in the case of constant demand.) But weekly demand for these printers is variable and is approximately normally distributed with a standard deviation of 30, meaning that the reorder point must be set at a level above 200 to avoid a stockout.

a Determine the reorder point if the retailer wants to be 90% certain of avoiding a stockout. (This is sometimes called a 90% service level.)

b Determine the reorder point for each of the following service levels: 95%, 96%, 97%, 98%, 99%, and 99.9%.

c Graph the relationship between the reorder point and service level. What do you observe?

7.22 A contractor is planning the construction of a new office building, and has identified three major critical activities involved in the project. He estimates that excavating and foundation work will take an expected time of 2 weeks with a variance of .10, framing will take an expected 3 weeks with a variance of .15, and finishing will take an expected 5 weeks with a variance of .90. Assume that the completion times for these three

STATISTICS IN THE WORKPLACE

Operations Management Application

PERT (Project Evaluation and Review Technique) and **CPM** (Critical Path Method) are related management science techniques that help operations managers control the activities and the amount of time it takes to complete a project. Both techniques are based on the order in which the activities must be performed. For example, in building a house the excavation for the foundation must precede the pouring of the foundation, which in turn precedes the framing. The difference between CPM and PERT is that under CPM the estimates of the amount of time to complete each activity are assumed to be a fixed value. In PERT we have three time estimates (most likely, pessimistic, and optimistic) that en-

able us to estimate the mean and variance of the time for each activity. In both techniques  we assume that the total time to complete the project (called the critical path time) is a normally distributed random variable whose mean and variance are calculated from the mean and variance of the activity times. From this distribution we can compute the probability that a project will be completed by a certain time and any related events. Exercises 7.22 and 7.23 provide illustrations of this concept.

activities are statistically independent, and that the total time to complete the project is normally distributed.

a Find the variance of the total time to complete the project.

b Find the probability that the project will take at most 12 weeks to complete.

c The contractor will receive a bonus if the project is completed in less than 9 weeks. Find the probability that a bonus will be paid.

7.23 Hardkey Software Company has been hired to develop a software package for a corporate client. The firm has identified four major critical activities, with the expected value and standard deviation of the time to complete each activity summarized in the table. The activities must be undertaken in the order shown, and each activity must be completed before the next one can begin.

	Completion time (days)	
Activity	Expected	Standard deviation
Consultations to understand client's needs	5	1.6
Designing the system	8	3
Coding the software	10	3.3
Testing the software	6	2.2

a What is the probability that the project will take at most 30 days to complete? At most 20 days?

b Hardkey's contract stipulates that a penalty will be imposed if the software is not delivered within 40 days. Find the probability that the penalty will be imposed.

7.4 EXPONENTIAL DISTRIBUTION

Another important continuous distribution, the **exponential distribution,** is closely related to the Poisson distribution, even though the latter distribution is discrete. Recall that a Poisson random variable counts the number of occurrences of an event during a given time interval. In contrast, an **exponential random variable,** X, can be used to measure the time that elapses before the first occurrence of an event, where occurrences of the event follow a Poisson distribution. Equivalently, an exponential random variable can be used to measure the time that elapses between occurrences of an event. For example, the exponential distribution can be used to model the length of time before the first telephone call is received by a switchboard or the length of time between arrivals at a service location (such as a service station, tollbooth, or grocery checkout counter). It has been used with considerable success in applications involving waiting times, and it can also be used to model the length of life of various electronic components, such as tubes and transistors.

Exponential Distribution

A random variable X is exponentially distributed if its probability density function is given by

$$f(x) = \lambda e^{-\lambda x}, \qquad x \geq 0$$

where $e = 2.71828\ldots$ and λ is the parameter of the distribution ($\lambda > 0$).

It can be shown that the mean and the standard deviation of an exponential probability distribution are equal to each other.

$$\mu = \sigma = 1/\lambda$$

Recall that the normal distribution is a two-parameter distribution: The distribution is completely specified once the values of the two parameters μ and σ are known. In contrast, the exponential distribution is a one-parameter distribution: The distribution is completely specified once the value of the parameter λ is known. If X is an exponential random variable that measures the time that elapses before the first occurrence

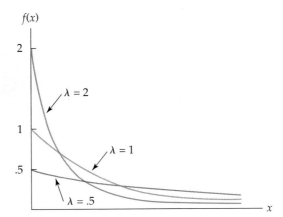

Figure 7.15

Graphs of three exponential distributions

of an event, where occurrences of the event follow a Poisson distribution, then λ is the average number of occurrences of the event per unit of time.

The graphs of three exponential distributions, corresponding to three different values of λ, are shown in Figure 7.15. Notice that, for any exponential density function $f(x)$, $f(0) = \lambda$ and $f(x)$ approaches zero as x approaches infinity.

Recall that, for a continuous random variable, probabilities are represented by areas under the graph of the probability density function $f(x)$. In the case of an exponential random variable X, it can be shown that the probability that X will take a value greater than a specified nonnegative number a is $e^{-\lambda a}$.*

Probability that an Exponential Variable Exceeds the Number a

If X is an exponential variable,

$$P(X \geq a) = e^{-\lambda a}$$

The value of $e^{-\lambda a}$ can be obtained with the aid of a calculator. Since the total area under the graph of $f(x)$ must equal 1,

$$P(X \leq a) = 1 - e^{-\lambda a}$$

for any nonnegative number a.

The probability that X will take a value between two numbers a and b can now be obtained by subtraction.

$$P(a \leq X \leq b) = P(X \leq b) - P(X \leq a)$$
$$= e^{-\lambda a} - e^{-\lambda b}$$

As an illustration of the relationship between the exponential and Poisson distributions, let us consider once again the situation described in Example 6.11.

---

*For students familiar with calculus,

$$P(X \geq a) = \int_a^\infty \lambda e^{-\lambda x}\, dx = -e^{-\lambda x}\Big|_a^\infty = e^{-\lambda a}$$

▼ **Example 7.6**

A tollbooth operator has observed that cars arrive randomly and independently at an average rate of 360 cars per hour.

a Use the exponential distribution to find the probability that the next car will *not* arrive within half a minute.

b Use the Poisson distribution to find the probability required in part (a).

Solution **a** Let X denote the time *in minutes* that will elapse before the next car arrives. It is important that X and λ be defined in terms of the same units. Thus, λ is the average number of cars arriving per minute: $\lambda = 360/60 = 6$. According to the formula for exponential probabilities, the probability that at least half a minute will elapse before the next car arrives is

$$P(X \geq .5) = e^{-6(.5)} = e^{-3}$$
$$= .0498$$

This probability is represented by the shaded area in Figure 7.16.

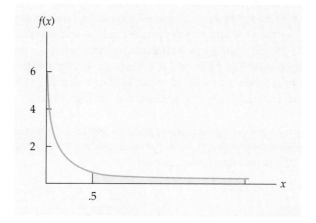

Figure 7.16

Shaded area is $P(X \geq .5)$ in Example 7.6

b Let Y be the number of cars that will arrive in the next half minute. Then Y is a Poisson random variable, with $\mu = .5(\lambda) = 3$ cars per half minute. We want to find the probability that no cars will arrive within the next half minute. Using the formula for a Poisson probability, we find

$$P(Y = 0 | \mu = 3) = \frac{(e^{-3})(3^0)}{0!}$$
$$= .0498$$

▲

▼ **EXAMPLE 7.7**

The lifetime of a transistor is exponentially distributed, with a mean of 1,000 hours. Find the probability that such a transistor will last between 1,000 and 1,500 hours.

Solution   Let X denote the lifetime (in hours) of a transistor. Since the mean lifetime is 1,000 hours, $\lambda = 1/\mu = 1/1{,}000 = .001$. The required probability is therefore

$$P(1{,}000 \le X \le 1{,}500) = e^{-.001(1000)} - e^{-.001(1500)}$$
$$= e^{-1} - e^{-1.5}$$
$$= .3679 - .2231$$
$$= .1448$$

▲

USING THE COMPUTER TO FIND EXPONENTIAL PROBABILITIES

We now provide you with Excel and Minitab instructions to allow you to calculate exponential probabilities. The output is the probability that an exponential random variable with a given mean is less than x. That is, the computer prints $P(X < x)$.

Excel Instructions

Refer to the instructions on page 250 for calculating normal probabilities.

To compute exponential probabilities click **EXPONDIST** instead of **NORMDIST** in step 1. type the value of x, λ (lambda), and true (cumulative) at step 2.

Minitab Instructions

Refer to the instructions on page 250 for calculating normal probabilities.

To compute exponential probabilities click **Exponential . . .** instead of **Normal . . .** in step 1.

EXERCISES

7.24 Let X be an exponential random variable with $\lambda = 3$. Sketch the graph of the distribution of X by plotting and connecting the points representing $f(x)$ for $x = 0$, .5, 1, 1.5, and 2.

7.25 Let X be an exponential random variable with $\lambda = 1$. Sketch the graph of the distribution of X by plotting and connecting the points representing $f(x)$ for $x = 0$, .5, 1, 1.5, and 2.

7.26 Let X be an exponential random variable with a mean of .5. Find the following probabilities.

    a $P(X \ge 1)$ **b** $P(X \ge 2)$
    c $P(X \le .5)$ **d** $P(X \le .4)$

7.27 Let X be an exponential random variable with $\lambda = 1.5$. Find the following probabilities.

    a $P(X \ge 1)$ **b** $P(X \le 3)$
    c $P(2 \le X \le 4)$ **d** $P(X \ge .5)$

7.28 Let X be an exponential random variable with $\lambda = 3$. Find the following probabilities.

    a $P(X \ge 2)$ **b** $P(X \le 4)$
    c $P(1 \le X \le 3)$ **d** $P(X = 2)$

7.29 Let X be an exponential random variable with $\lambda = 2$. Find the probability that X will take a value within 1.5 standard deviations of its mean.

7.30 Let X be an exponential random variable with $\lambda = 4$. Find the probability that X will take a value within 1.2 standard deviations of its mean.

7.31 The expected value of an exponential random variable, X, is $1/\lambda$. Find the probability that X will take a value that is less than its expected value.

7.32 Suppose that customers arrive at a checkout counter at an average rate of two customers per minute and that their arrivals follow the Poisson model.

S TATISTICS IN THE W ORKPLACE

Operations Management Application

Waiting in line is a most common experience. We wait in line in restaurants, supermarkets, and movie theaters. We also experience **waiting lines** in many business activities. For example, trucks often have to wait to be loaded or unloaded, and airplanes often must wait before taking off and landing. For most of us waiting is merely annoying but not costly. Unfortunately, the same cannot be said for many businesses. When trucks wait to be loaded or unloaded, or are tied up in traffic, the costs (including the cost of the trucks and the hourly wages of the driver) add up quickly. Measuring and controlling waiting line costs is another function of operations managers.

Several management science models are employed to keep track of the time and the cost of waiting. Many of these models assume that the number units (e.g., trucks) arriving for service in a given time period follow a Poisson distribution and the service times are exponentially distributed. See Exercises 7.32 and 7.33.

a Sketch a graph of the (exponential) distribution of the time that will elapse before the next customer arrives by plotting and joining the points representing $f(t)$ for $t = 0, .5, 1, 1.5,$ and 2.

b Use the appropriate exponential distribution to find the probability that the next customer will arrive within 1 minute; within 2 minutes.

c Use the exponential distribution to find the probability that the next customer will not arrive within the next 1.5 minutes.

d Use the appropriate Poisson distribution to answer part (c).

7.33 Airplanes arrive at an airport according to the Poisson model, with a mean time between arrivals of 5 minutes.

a Find the probability that a plane will arrive within the next 5 minutes.

b Find the probability that no planes will arrive during a given 30-minute period.

c Find the probability that no more than one plane will arrive during a given 30-minute period.

7.34 A specific type of transistor is known to have a mean time to failure of 10,000 hours. The lifetimes of these transistors can be assumed to be exponentially distributed.

a What is the probability that the lifetime of a transistor will exceed the mean lifetime? (Notice that this probability can be interpreted as the proportion of transistors that will survive longer than the mean lifetime.)

b Comment on the symmetry or skewness of the distribution of lifetimes, with reference to part (a).

c What is the probability that a transistor will fail within the first 1,000 hours of use?

d What is the probability that the lifetime of a transistor will be between 1,000 and 1,100 hours?

e Consider only those transistors that are still operating after 10,000 hours. Their *failure rate** over the next 1,000 hours is the answer to part (d) divided by the answer to part (a). What do you observe when you compare this failure rate to the answer to part (c)?

7.35 The length of life of a certain type of electronic tube is exponentially distributed, with a mean of 4,000 hours.

a Find the probability that a tube will last more than 1,000 hours.

b Find the probability that a tube will fail within the first 200 hours.

c Find the probability that the length of life of a tube will be between 600 and 800 hours.

d At what length should the warranty life be set such that at most 5% of the tubes will fail under warranty?

---

*The *failure rate* during a specified time period is the (conditional) probability of failure during that time period *given that* the transistor has survived up until that time period. In other words, the failure rate during a specified time period is the number of transistors that fail during that time period divided by the number of transistors that are still operating at the beginning of that period.

S TATISTICS IN THE W ORKPLACE

Operations Management Application

Exercises 7.12 and 7.13 illustrated the use of the normal distribution in calculating the probability that a product will fail before the warranty expires. We noted that the normal distribution provides an adequate approximation for the length of life for a number of products. However, there are other products for which the exponential distribution provides the best approximation for their lifetimes. For example, it is generally accepted that the lifetimes of electronic products can often be approxi-

mated by an exponential distribution. The failure rate of such products remains constant over time, whereas the failure rate of products whose lifetimes are normally distributed increases over time. See Exercises 7.34 and 7.35 for illustrations.

7.5 SUMMARY

This chapter was devoted to a discussion of continuous random variables and their probability distributions. A random variable is **continuous** if it can take any of infinitely many values within some interval of values.

The **normal probability distribution** is the most important continuous distribution. Besides approximating the distribution of numerous random variables that arise in practice, the normal distribution is the cornerstone distribution of statistical inference. Finally, we considered the **exponential distribution,** a continuous distribution that is especially useful in applications involving waiting lines, or queuing.

IMPORTANT TERMS

Probability density function   *237*
Uniform distribution   *238*
Normal distribution   *241*
Normal random variable   *241*
Standard normal distribution   *242*

Standard normal random variable   *242*
Exponential distribution   *254*
Exponential random variable   *254*

SUMMARY OF FORMULAS

Standard Normal Random Variable

$$Z = \frac{X - \mu}{\sigma}$$

Exponential Probability

$$P(X \geq a) = e^{\lambda a}$$

SUPPLEMENTARY EXERCISES

7.36 Use Table 3 of Appendix B to find the following probabilities.

   a $P(Z > 1.64)$
   b $P(1.23 \le Z \le 2.71)$
   c $P(Z < .52)$
   d $P(-.68 < Z \le 2.42)$

7.37 Use Table 3 of Appendix B to find the following probabilities, where X has a normal distribution with $\mu = 24$ and $\sigma = 4$.

   a $P(X > 30)$ **b** $P(25 < X < 27)$
   c $P(X \le 26)$ **d** $P(18 \le X \le 23)$

7.38 Suppose that the actual amount of instant coffee a filling machine puts into 6-ounce cans varies from can to can and that the actual fill may be considered a random variable having a normal distribution, with a standard deviation of .04 ounces. If only 2 out of every 100 cans contain less than 6 ounces of coffee, what must be the mean fill of these cans?

7.39 A soft-drink bottling plant uses a machine that fills bottles with drink mixture. The contents of the bottles filled are normally distributed, with a mean of 16 ounces and a variance of 4 (ounces)^2.

   a Determine the weight exceeded by only the heaviest 10% of the filled bottles.
   b Determine the probability that the combined weight of two of these bottles is less than 30 ounces. (HINT:

If X_1 and X_2 are normally disributed variables, then $Y = X_1 + X_2$ is also normally distributed.)

7.40 Consumer advocates frequently complain about the large variation in the prices charged by different pharmacies for the same prescription. A survey of pharmacies in Chicago by one such advocate revealed that the prices charged for 100 tablets of Tylenol 3 were normally distributed, with about 90% of the prices ranging between $8.25 and $11.25. The mean price charged was $9.75. What proportion of the pharmacies charged more than $10.25 for the prescription?

7.41 Suppose that men's heights are normally distributed, with a mean of 5 feet 9 inches and a standard deviation of 2 inches. Find the minimum ceiling height of an airplane in which at most 2% of the men walking down the aisle will have to duck their heads.

7.42 A firm has monitored the duration of long-distance telephone calls placed by its employees to help it decide which long-distance package to purchase. The duration of calls was found to be exponentially distributed, with a mean of 5 minutes.

   a What proportion of calls lasts more than 2 minutes?
   b What proportion of calls lasts more than 5 minutes?
   c What proportion of calls is shorter than 10 minutes?

Chapter 8

Sampling

Distributions

8.1 Introduction

8.2 Sampling Distribution of the Mean

8.3 Creating the Sampling Distribution by Computer Simulation (Optional)

8.4 Sampling Distribution of a Proportion

8.5 Sampling Distribution of the Difference Between Two Means

8.6 From Here to Inference

8.7 Summary

8.1 INTRODUCTION

In Chapter 1, we briefly introduced the concept of statistical inference—the process of inferring information about a population from a sample. Because information about populations can usually be described by parameters, the statistical technique used generally deals with drawing inferences about population parameters from sample statistics. Recall that a parameter is a measurement about a population, and a statistic is a measurement about a sample.

Working within the covers of a statistics textbook, we can assume that population parameters are known. In real life, however, calculating parameters becomes prohibitive because populations tend to be quite large. As a result, most population parameters are unknown. For example, in order to determine the mean annual income of North American blue-collar workers, we would have to ask each North American blue-collar worker what his or her income is and then calculate the mean of all the responses. Because this population consists of several million people, the task is both expensive and impractical. If we are willing to accept less than 100% accuracy, we can use statistical inference to obtain an estimate.

Rather than investigating the entire population, we take a sample, determine the annual income of the workers in this group, and calculate the sample mean. While there is very little chance that the sample mean and the population mean are identical, we would expect them to be quite close. However, for the purposes of statistical inference, we need to be able to measure how close the sample mean is likely to be to the population mean. The **sampling distribution** provides this service. It plays a critical role in statistics, because the measure of proximity it provides is the key to statistical inference. In this chapter, we discuss the sampling distribution of the sample mean, as well as other sampling distributions needed throughout this book.

8.2 SAMPLING DISTRIBUTION OF THE MEAN

The following problem illustrates the importance of the sampling distribution in statistical inference. The management of a large oil company is trying to assess the effectiveness of its periodic sales campaigns. During a campaign, customers who buy at least 5 gallons of gasoline are given free coupons that can be used to get discounts in local restaurants. Because of the advertising, printing, and other costs involved, management is willing to continue to schedule the campaigns only if it is satisfied that mean daily sales of gasoline during the sales push are at least 18,000 gallons per station. In a random sample of 100 stations during the last campaign, mean daily sales was 18,200 gallons. On the basis of this statistic, should the oil company continue the coupon giveaways?

Before we attempt to answer the question, let's make sure that the issues are clear. The parameter of interest is μ, the mean daily sales during the campaign (the population mean) by all the stations owned by the company. If management were satisfied that mean daily sales exceeded 18,000 gallons, it would approve of the campaign. The only statistic available, however, is the sample mean, $\bar{x}$, of 100 stations. Our initial reaction is that, since the sample mean (which equals 18,200) exceeds 18,000, the population mean exceeds 18,000; however, this is not necessarily correct. The conclusion that can be drawn about the population mean very much depends on how close $\bar{x}$ is expected to be to μ. If management believes that $\bar{x}$ is close to μ, it will be confident that the population mean is greater than 18,000. Conversely, if $\bar{x}$ can be quite different from μ, the population mean actually may be less than 18,000. Unfortunately, from the information provided, we cannot determine the expected proximity of $\bar{x}$ and

μ. That is the function of the sampling distribution, which we discuss next. When we have completed our discussion of the sampling distribution, we will return to this problem and answer the question.

To grasp the idea of a sampling distribution, consider the population created by throwing a fair die infinitely many times, with the random variable x indicating the number of spots showing on any one throw. The probability distribution of the random variable x is as follows.

x	1	2	3	4	5	6
$p(x)$	$\frac{1}{6}$	$\frac{1}{6}$	$\frac{1}{6}$	$\frac{1}{6}$	$\frac{1}{6}$	$\frac{1}{6}$

The population is infinitely large, since we can throw the die infinitely many times (or at least imagine doing so). From the definitions of expectation and variance, we calculate the population mean to be

$$\begin{aligned} \mu &= E(X) \\ &= \sum x \cdot p(x) \\ &= 1\left(\frac{1}{6}\right) + 2\left(\frac{1}{6}\right) + \cdots + 6\left(\frac{1}{6}\right) \\ &= 3.5 \end{aligned}$$

and the population variance to be

$$\begin{aligned} \sigma^2 &= V(X) \\ &= \sum (x - \mu)^2 \cdot p(x) \\ &= (1 - 3.5)^2\left(\frac{1}{6}\right) + (2 - 3.5)^2\left(\frac{1}{6}\right) + \cdots + (6 - 3.5)^2\left(\frac{1}{6}\right) \\ &= 2.92 \end{aligned}$$

Now suppose that μ is unknown and that we want to estimate its value by using the sample mean $\bar{x}$, calculated from a sample of size $n = 2$. In actual practice, only one sample would be drawn, and hence there would be only one value of $\bar{x}$; but to assess how closely $\bar{x}$ estimates the value of μ, we will develop the sampling distribution of $\bar{x}$ by evaluating every possible sample of size 2.

Consider all the possible different samples of size 2 that could be drawn from the parent population. Figure 8.1 depicts this process. For each sample, we compute the mean as shown in Table 8.1. Because the value of the sample mean varies randomly from sample to sample, we can regard $\bar{x}$ as a new random variable created by sampling. Table 8.1 lists all the possible samples and their corresponding values of $\bar{x}$.

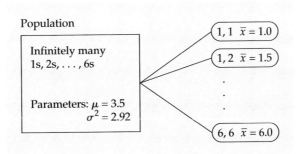

Figure 8.1

Drawing samples of size 2 from a population

Table 8.1 All Samples of Size 2 and Their Means

Sample	$\bar{x}$	Sample	$\bar{x}$	Sample	$\bar{x}$
1, 1	1.0	3, 1	2.0	5, 1	3.0
1, 2	1.5	3, 2	2.5	5, 2	3.5
1, 3	2.0	3, 3	3.0	5, 3	4.0
1, 4	2.5	3, 4	3.5	5, 4	4.5
1, 5	3.0	3, 5	4.0	5, 5	5.0
1, 6	3.5	3, 6	4.5	5, 6	5.5
2, 1	1.5	4, 1	2.5	6, 1	3.5
2, 2	2.0	4, 2	3.0	6, 2	4.0
2, 3	2.5	4, 3	3.5	6, 3	4.5
2, 4	3.0	4, 4	4.0	6, 4	5.0
2, 5	3.5	4, 5	4.5	6, 5	5.5
2, 6	4.0	4, 6	5.0	6, 6	6.0

There are 36 different possible samples of size 2; since each sample is equally likely, the probability of any one sample being selected is $\frac{1}{36}$. However, $\bar{x}$ can assume only 11 different possible values: 1.0, 1.5, 2.0, . . . , 6.0, with certain values of $\bar{x}$ occurring more frequently than others. The value $\bar{x} = 1.0$ occurs only once, so its probability is $\frac{1}{36}$. The value $\bar{x} = 1.5$ can occur in two ways; hence, $p(1.5) = \frac{2}{36}$. The probabilities of the other values of $\bar{x}$ are determined in similar fashion, and the sampling distribution of $\bar{x}$ that results is shown in Table 8.2.

The most interesting aspect of the sampling distribution of $\bar{x}$ is how different it is from the distribution of x, as can be seen in Figure 8.2.

Table 8.2 Sampling Distribution of $\bar{x}$

$\bar{x}$	$p(\bar{x})$	$\bar{x}$	$p(\bar{x})$	$\bar{x}$	$p(\bar{x})$
1.0	$\frac{1}{36}$	3.0	$\frac{5}{36}$	5.0	$\frac{3}{36}$
1.5	$\frac{2}{36}$	3.5	$\frac{6}{36}$	5.5	$\frac{2}{36}$
2.0	$\frac{3}{36}$	4.0	$\frac{5}{36}$	6.0	$\frac{1}{36}$
2.5	$\frac{4}{36}$	4.5	$\frac{4}{36}$		

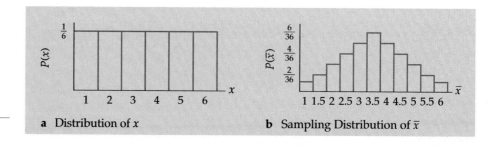

a Distribution of x

b Sampling Distribution of $\bar{x}$

Figure 8.2

Distributions of x and $\bar{x}$

We can also compute the mean and variance of the sampling distribution. Using our definition of expectation and variance, we determine the mean of $\bar{x}$,

$$\mu_{\bar{x}} = E(\bar{X})$$
$$= \sum \bar{x} \cdot p(\bar{x})$$
$$= 1.0\left(\frac{1}{36}\right) + 1.5\left(\frac{2}{36}\right) + \cdots + 6.0\left(\frac{1}{36}\right)$$
$$= 3.5$$

and the variance of $\bar{x}$,

$$\sigma_{\bar{x}}^2 = V(\bar{X})$$
$$= \sum (\bar{x} - \mu_{\bar{x}})^2 \cdot p(\bar{x})$$
$$= (1.0 - 3.5)^2\left(\frac{1}{36}\right) + (1.5 - 3.5)^2\left(\frac{2}{36}\right) + \cdots + (6.0 - 3.5)^2\left(\frac{1}{36}\right)$$
$$= 1.46$$

It is important to recognize that the distribution of $\bar{x}$ is different from the distribution of x. Figure 8.2 shows that the shapes of the two distributions differ. From our previous calculations, we know that the mean of the sampling distribution of $\bar{x}$ is equal to the mean of the distribution of x; that is, $\mu_{\bar{x}} = \mu$. However, the variance of $\bar{x}$ is not equal to the variance of x; we calculated $\sigma^2 = 2.92$, while $\sigma_{\bar{x}}^2 = 1.46$. It is no coincidence that the variance of $\bar{x}$ is exactly half the variance of x, as we will see shortly.

Don't get lost in the terminology and notation. Remember that μ and σ^2 are the parameters of the population of x. To create the sampling distribution of $\bar{x}$, we repeatedly drew samples of size 2 from the population and calculated $\bar{x}$ for each sample. Thus, we treat $\bar{x}$ as a brand-new random variable, with its own distribution, mean, and variance. The mean is denoted $\mu_{\bar{x}}$, and the variance is denoted $\sigma_{\bar{x}}^2$.

If we now repeat the sampling process with the same population but with other values of n, we produce somewhat different sampling distributions of $\bar{x}$. Figure 8.3 shows the sampling distributions of $\bar{x}$ when $n = 5$, 10, and 25. As n grows larger, the

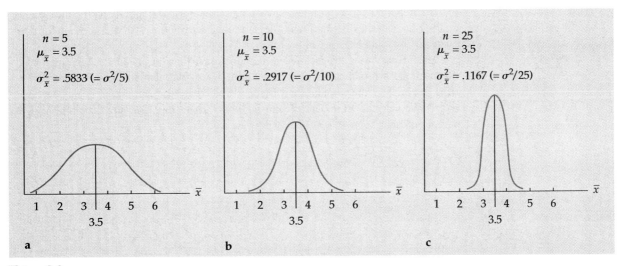

Figure 8.3

Sampling distributions of $\bar{x}$ when $n = 5$, 10, and 25 number of possible values of $\bar{x}$ also grows larger; consequently, the distributions depicted in Figure 8.3 have been smoothed (to avoid drawing a large number of rectangles). Observe that in each case $\mu_{\bar{x}} = \mu$ and $\sigma_{\bar{x}}^2 = \sigma^2/n$.

Notice that in each case the variance of the sampling distribution is less than that of the parent population; that is, $\sigma_{\bar{x}}^2 < \sigma^2$. Given that $\sigma_{\bar{x}}^2 < \sigma^2$, a randomly selected value of $\bar{x}$ (the mean of the number of spots observed in, say, five throws of the die) is likely to be closer to the mean value of 3.5 than is a randomly selected value of x (the number of spots observed in one throw). Indeed, this is what you would expect, because in five throws of the die you are likely to get some 5s and 6s and some 1s and 2s, which will tend to offset one another in the averaging process and produce a sample mean reasonably close to 3.5. As the number of throws of the die increases, the likelihood that the sample mean will be close to 3.5 also increases. Thus, we observe in Figure 8.3 that the sampling distribution of $\bar{x}$ becomes narrower (or more concentrated about the mean) as n increases.

Another thing that happens as n gets larger is that the sampling distribution of $\bar{x}$ becomes increasingly bell shaped. This phenomenon is summarized in the **central limit theorem.**

Central Limit Theorem

If a random sample is drawn from any population, the sampling distribution of the sample mean is approximately normal for a sufficiently large sample size. The larger the sample size, the more closely the sampling distribution of $\bar{x}$ will resemble a normal distribution.

The accuracy of the approximation alluded to in the central limit theorem depends on the probability distribution of the parent population and on the sample size. If the population is normal, then $\bar{x}$ is normally distributed for all values of n. If the population is nonnormal, then $\bar{x}$ is approximately normal only for larger values of n. In many practical situations, a sample size of $n > 30$ may be sufficiently large to allow us to use the normal distribution as an approximation for the sampling distribution of $\bar{x}$. We urge you, however, to be cautious about the sample size. If a population is extremely nonnormal (examples of extremely nonnormal populations include bimodal and highly skewed distributions), the sampling distribution will also be nonnormal—even for moderately large values of n.

In our previous discussion, we demonstrated that the mean of $\bar{x}$ is equal to the mean of the original population. That is, $\mu_{\bar{x}} = \mu$. We also showed that the variance of $\bar{x}$ is equal to the population variance divided by the sample size. That is, $\sigma_{\bar{x}}^2 = \sigma^2/n$.* We can now summarize what we know about the sampling distribution of the sample mean.

---

*The variance of $\bar{x}$ is σ^2/n if the population from which we are sampling is infinitely large. If the population is finite, the variance of $\bar{x}$ is

$$\sigma_{\bar{x}}^2 = \left(\frac{\sigma^2}{n}\right)\left(\frac{N-n}{N-1}\right)$$

where N is the population size and $(N - n)/(N - 1)$ is the finite population correction factor. In most practical situations (including all examples and exercises in this book), the target population is finite but very large relative to the sample size (e.g., the population of television viewers in North America). In such cases, the finite population correction factor is so close to 1 that we can ignore it. As a general rule, include the finite population correction factor only if the sample size is greater than 1% of the population size.

Sampling Distribution of the Sample Mean

1 $\mu_{\bar{x}} = \mu$

2 $\sigma_{\bar{x}}^2 = \sigma^2/n$, or $\sigma_{\bar{x}} = \sigma/\sqrt{n}$ (The standard deviation of $\bar{x}$ is called the **standard error of the mean.**)

3 If x is normal, $\bar{x}$ is normal. If x is nonnormal, $\bar{x}$ is approximately normally distributed for sufficiently large sample sizes.

CREATING THE SAMPLING DISTRIBUTION EMPIRICALLY

In the analysis above, we created the sampling distribution of the mean theoretically. We did so by listing *all* of the possible samples of size 2 and their probabilities. (They were all equally likely with probability $\frac{1}{36}$.) From this distribution, we produced the sampling distribution. We could also create the distribution empirically by actually tossing two fair dice repeatedly, calculating the sample mean for each sample, counting the number of times each value of $\bar{x}$ occurs, and computing the relative frequencies to estimate the theoretical probabilities. If we toss the two dice a large enough number of times, the relative frequencies and theoretical probabilities (computed above) will be similar. Try it yourself. Toss two dice 500 times, count the number of times each sample mean occurs, and construct the sampling distribution. Obviously, this approach is far from ideal because of the excessive amount of time required to toss the dice enough times to make the relative frequencies good approximations for the theoretical probabilities. However, we can use the computer to quickly "simulate" tossing dice many times.

In Section 8.3, we introduce simulation experiments, which will enable students to create sampling distributions. We show how to use Excel and Minitab to generate a large number of samples to construct sampling distributions empirically. The experiments will deal with the effect of the population distribution and the sample size on the sampling distribution of the mean. Other simulation experiments will let students discover for themselves some of the key statistical concepts that we discuss in this textbook.

▼ **EXAMPLE 8.1**

The foreman of a bottling plant has observed that the amount of soda pop in each "32-ounce" bottle is actually a normally distributed random variable, with a mean of 32.2 ounces and a standard deviation of .3 ounces.

a Find the probability that if a customer buys one bottle, that bottle will contain more than 32 ounces.

b Find the probability that if a customer buys a carton of four bottles the mean of the four will be greater than 32 ounces.

Solution

a Because the random variable is the amount of soda in one bottle, we want to find $P(X > 32)$, where X is normally distributed, $\mu = 32.2$, and $\sigma = .3$. Hence,

$$P(X > 32) = P\left(\frac{X - \mu}{\sigma} > \frac{32 - 32.2}{.3}\right)$$

$$= P(Z > -.67)$$

$$= .7486$$

b Now we want to find the probability that the mean of four filled bottles exceeds 32 ounces. That is, we want $P(\bar{X} > 32)$. From our previous analysis and from the central limit theorem, we know the following.

1 $\bar{X}$ is normally distributed.

2 $\mu_{\bar{x}} = \mu = 32.2$

3 $\sigma_{\bar{x}} = \sigma/\sqrt{n} = .3/\sqrt{4} = .15$

Hence,

$$P(\bar{X} > 32) = P\left(\frac{\bar{X} - \mu_{\bar{x}}}{\sigma_{\bar{x}}} > \frac{32 - 32.2}{.15}\right)$$
$$= P(Z > -1.33)$$
$$= .9082$$

Figure 8.4 illustrates the distributions used in this example.

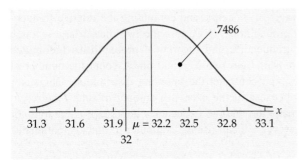
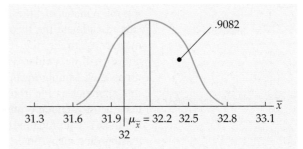

Figure 8.4

Distribution of x and sampling distribution of x̄ in Example 8.1

In Example 8.1(b), we began with the assumption that both μ and σ were known. Then, using the sampling distribution, we made a probability statement about $\bar{X}$. Unfortunately, the values of μ and σ are not usually known, so an analysis such as that in Example 8.1 cannot usually be conducted. However, we can use the sampling distribution to infer something about an unknown value of μ on the basis of a sample mean.

▼ **EXAMPLE 8.2**

The dean of a business school claims that the average weekly income of graduates of his school 1 year after graduation is $600.

a If the dean's claim is correct, and if the distribution of weekly incomes has a standard deviation of $100, what is the probability that 25 randomly selected graduates have an average weekly income of less than $550?

b If a random sample of 25 graduates had an average weekly income of $550, what would you conclude about the validity of the dean's claim?

Solution

a We want to find $P(\bar{X} < 550)$. The distribution of X, the weekly income, is likely positively skewed, but not sufficiently so to make the distribution of $\bar{X}$

nonnormal. As a result, the central limit theorem tells us that $\overline{X}$ is approximately normally distributed. We also know that $\mu_{\bar{x}} = 600$ and $\sigma_{\bar{x}} = 100/\sqrt{25} = 20$. Thus,

$$P(\overline{X} < 550) = P\left(\frac{\overline{X} - \mu_{\bar{x}}}{\sigma_{\bar{x}}} < \frac{550 - 600}{20}\right)$$
$$= P(Z < -2.5)$$
$$= .0062$$

b The probability of observing a sample mean as low as \$550 when the population mean is \$600 is extremely small, as Figure 8.5 indicates. Because this event is quite rare and thus quite unlikely, we would have to conclude that the dean's claim is probably unjustified.

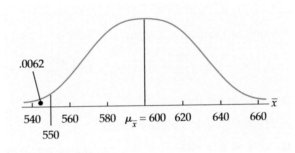

Figure 8.5

Sampling distribution of $\bar{x}$ for Example 8.2

USING THE SAMPLING DISTRIBUTION FOR INFERENCE

Our conclusion in Example 8.2(b) illustrates how the sampling distribution can be used to make inferences about population parameters. The first form of inference is **estimation,** which we introduce in the next chapter. In preparation for this momentous occasion we'll present another way of expressing the probability associated with the sampling distribution.

Recall the notation introduced in Chapter 7 (see page 249). We defined z_A to be the value of z such that the area to the right of z_A under the standard normal curve is equal to A. We also showed that $z_{.025} = 1.96$. Because the standard normal distribution is symmetric about 0, the area to the left of -1.96 is also .025. The area between -1.96 and 1.96 is .95. Figure 8.6 depicts this notation. We can express the notation algebraically as

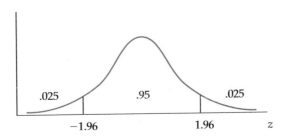

Figure 8.6

Standard normal distribution

$$P(-1.96 < Z < 1.96) = .95$$

In this section we established that

$$Z = \frac{\bar{X} - \mu}{\sigma/\sqrt{n}}$$

is standard normally distributed. Substituting this form of Z into the probability statement above we produce

$$P\left(-1.96 < \frac{\bar{X} - \mu}{\sigma/\sqrt{n}} < 1.96\right) = .95$$

With a little algebraic manipulation (multiply all three terms by $\sigma/\sqrt{n}$ and add μ to all three terms), we determine

$$P\left(\mu - 1.96\frac{\sigma}{\sqrt{n}} < \bar{X} < \mu + 1.96\frac{\sigma}{\sqrt{n}}\right) = .95$$

Returning to Example 8.2 where $\mu = 600$, $\sigma = 100$, and $n = 25$, we compute

$$P\left(600 - 1.96\frac{100}{\sqrt{25}} < \bar{X} < 600 + 1.96\frac{100}{\sqrt{25}}\right) = .95$$

Thus, we can say that

$$P(560.8 < \bar{X} < 639.2) = .95$$

This tells us that there is a 95% probability that a sample mean will fall between 560.8 and 639.2. Because the sample mean was computed to be \$550 we would have to conclude that the dean's claim is not supported by the statistic.

Changing the probability from .95 to .90 changes the probability statement to

$$P\left(\mu - 1.645\frac{\sigma}{\sqrt{n}} < \bar{X} < \mu + 1.645\frac{\sigma}{\sqrt{n}}\right) = .90$$

We can also produce a general form of this statement.

$$P\left(\mu - z_{\alpha/2}\frac{\sigma}{\sqrt{n}} < \bar{X} < \mu + z_{\alpha/2}\frac{\sigma}{\sqrt{n}}\right) = 1 - \alpha$$

In this formula α (Greek letter *alpha*) is the probability that $\bar{X}$ does not fall into the interval. To apply this formula all we need do is substitute the values for μ, σ, n, and α. For example with $\mu = 600$, $\sigma = 100$, $n = 25$ and $\alpha = .01$, we produce

$$P\left(\mu - z_{.005}\frac{\sigma}{\sqrt{n}} < \bar{X} < \mu + z_{.005}\frac{\sigma}{\sqrt{n}}\right) = 1 - .01$$

$$= P\left(600 - 2.575\frac{100}{\sqrt{25}} < \bar{X} < 600 + 2.575\frac{100}{\sqrt{25}}\right) = .99$$

$$= P(548.5 < \bar{X} < 651.5) = .99$$

which is another probability statement about $\bar{X}$. In Section 9.3 we will use a similar type of probability statement to derive the first estimator.

Let's now return to the problem introduced at the beginning of this section and see how the sampling distribution allows us to answer the question. Recall the issue: Does a sample of 100 gas stations showing a mean daily sale of 18,200 gallons give management a basis for confidently concluding that the mean sale of all gas stations exceeds 18,000 gallons?

Suppose the population standard deviation of daily sales is known to be 8,000 gallons. From the discussion in this section, we know the following.

1 $\bar{x}$ is approximately normally distributed.

2 $\mu_{\bar{x}} = \mu$

3 $\sigma_{\bar{x}} = \dfrac{\sigma}{\sqrt{n}} = \dfrac{8,000}{\sqrt{100}} = 800$

If we assume that the mean daily sale of all gas stations during the campaign is only 18,000, then

$$\mu_{\bar{x}} = \mu = 18,000$$

We can then calculate

$$P(\bar{X} > 18,200) = P\left(\frac{\bar{X} - \mu}{\sigma_{\bar{x}}} > \frac{18,200 - 18,000}{800}\right)$$
$$= P(Z > .25)$$
$$= .4013$$

This means that there is a fairly large probability that $\bar{x}$ can be 18,200 or more when, in fact, μ is equal to 18,000. As a result, management would not have reason to be very confident that the coupons are effective.

To put this result in perspective, suppose the population standard deviation is 1,000 gallons, instead of 8,000 gallons. Now,

$$\sigma_{\bar{x}} = \frac{\sigma}{\sqrt{n}} = \frac{1,000}{\sqrt{100}} = 100$$

and

$$P(\bar{X} > 18,200) = P\left(\frac{\bar{X} - \mu_{\bar{x}}}{\sigma_{\bar{x}}} > \frac{18,200 - 18,000}{100}\right)$$
$$= P(Z > 2.0)$$
$$= .0228$$

This indicates that we would be quite unlikely to observe a value of $\bar{x}$ as large as 18,200 from a population whose mean is only 18,000. Hence, in this case, management would be justified in concluding that μ is actually larger than 18,000 and that the campaigns are successful.

DEVELOPING AN UNDERSTANDING OF STATISTICAL CONCEPTS

Understanding how the sampling distribution is created and used may be the most important factor in learning about statistics. Several critical concepts were developed in this section. First, the sampling distribution is the distribution of a sample statistic, which is created by repeated sampling from a given population. Second, the parameters (mean and standard deviation) of the sampling distribution are related to the parameters of the original population. Third, the connection between the sampling distribution and the original population is at the heart of statistical inference. Understanding the contents of this section will go a long way toward developing an understanding of statistics.

EXERCISES

8.1 A normally distributed population has a mean of $\mu = 40$ and a standard deviation of 12. What does the central limit theorem say about the sampling distribution of the mean if samples of size 100 are drawn from this population?

8.2 Refer to Exercise 8.1. Suppose that the population is not normally distributed. Does this change your answer? Explain.

8.3 A sample of $n = 100$ observations is drawn from a normal population, with $\mu = 1,000$ and $\sigma = 200$. Find the following.

    a $P(\overline{X} > 1,050)$ **b** $P(\overline{X} < 960)$ **c** $P(\overline{X} > 1,100)$

8.4 Suppose the sample size in Exercise 8.3 was 16. Find the following.

    a $P(\overline{X} > 1,050)$ **b** $P(\overline{X} < 960)$ **c** $P(\overline{X} > 1,100)$

8.5 Given a normal population whose mean is 50 and whose standard deviation is 5,

    a Find the probability that a random sample of 4 has a mean between 49 and 52.

    b Find the probability that a random sample of 16 has a mean between 49 and 52.

    c Find the probability that a random sample of 25 has a mean between 49 and 52.

8.6 Repeat Exercise 8.5 for a standard deviation of 10.

8.7 The heights of North American women are normally distributed with a mean of 64 inches and a standard deviation of 2 inches.

    a What is the probability that a randomly selected woman is taller than 66 inches?

    b A random sample of four women is selected. What is the probability that the sample mean is greater than 66 inches?

    c What is the probability that the mean height of a random sample of 100 women is greater than 66 inches?

8.8 Refer to Exercise 8.7. If the population of women's heights is *not* normally distributed, which, if any, of the questions can you answer? Explain.

8.9 An automatic machine in a manufacturing process is operating properly if the lengths of an important subcomponent are normally distributed, with mean $\mu = 117$ cm and standard deviation $\sigma = 5.2$ cm.

    a Find the probability that one randomly selected unit has a length greater than 120 cm.

    b Find the probability that, if four units are randomly selected, their mean length exceeds 120 cm.

    c Find the probability that, if four units are randomly selected, all four have lengths that exceed 120 cm.

8.10 The mean and standard deviation of the number of customers (which is normally distributed) who enter a supermarket each hour are 600 and 200, respectively. The supermarket is open 16 hours per day. What is the probability that the total number of customers who enter the store in one day is greater than 10,000? (HINT: Calculate the average hourly number of customers to achieve 10,000 in one 16-hour day.)

8.11 The marks on a statistics midterm test are normally distributed with a mean of 75 and a standard deviation of 6.

    a What proportion of the class has a midterm test mark that is less than 70?

    b What is the probability that a class of 50 has an average midterm test mark that is less than 70?

8.12 The amount of time spent by North American adults watching television per day is normally distributed with a mean of 6 hours and a standard deviation of 1.5 hours.

    a What is the probability that a randomly selected North American adult watches television for more than 7 hours per day?

    b What is the probability that the average number of hours spent watching television by a random sample of five adults is more than 7 hours?

    c What is the probability that in a random sample of five adults all watch television for more than 7 hours per day?

8.13 The manufacturer of cans of salmon that are supposed to have a net weight of 6 ounces tells you that the net weight is actually a normal random variable with a mean of 6.05 ounces and a standard deviation of .18 ounce. Suppose you take a random sample of 36 cans.

    a Find the probability that the mean weight of the sample is less than 5.97 ounces.

    b Suppose your random sample of 36 cans of salmon produces a mean weight that is less than 5.97 ounces. Comment on the statement made by the manufacturer.

8.14 The sign on the elevator in the Peters Building, which houses the School of Business and Economics at Wilfrid Laurier University, states, "Maximum Capacity 1,140 Kilograms (2,500 pounds) or 16 Persons." A professor of business statistics wonders what the probability is that 16 people would weigh more than 1,140 kilograms. Discuss what the professor needs (besides the ability to calculate probabilities) in order to satisfy his curiosity.

8.15 Refer to Exercise 8.14. Suppose that the professor discovers that people who use the elevator weigh on average 75 kilograms with a standard deviation of 10 kilograms and that their weights are normally distributed. Calculate the probability that the professor seeks.

8.3 CREATING THE SAMPLING DISTRIBUTION BY COMPUTER SIMULATION (OPTIONAL)

In Section 8.2 we created the sampling distribution of the mean theoretically by listing *all* of the possible samples of size 2 and their probabilities. In each sample we computed the sample mean, and collecting like values and their probabilities we constructed the sampling distribution. Mathematicians can create sampling distributions by using calculus, a method we will do you the favor of not presenting. However, there is another way of at least approximating the sampling distribution that may appeal to students of applied statistics.

We can create the sampling distribution of the mean of two dice by tossing two balanced dice repeatedly. For each toss we would record the mean and determine the frequency distribution of these means. You should realize, however, that the frequency distribution so produced would only approximate the theoretical distribution. That's because the theoretical distribution is based on throwing the dice an infinite number of times. (Recall that probability is defined as relative frequency over an infinite number of experiments.) If we toss the dice, say, 100 times the approximation is likely to be relatively poor. If we toss them 1,000 times the frequency distribution will be closer to the theoretical, yet not a perfect match. Obviously, we can never throw the dice enough times to achieve perfection. Moreover, even 1,000 tosses would be very time consuming, not to mention mind numbing. Fortunately, there is a way to generate the empirical frequency distribution more quickly—by computer simulation.

Both Excel and Minitab possess random number generators that can produce data from a variety of distributions. In Chapter 5, we discussed how to generate random numbers from a discrete uniform distribution to help select a random sample. We use this feature here to simulate repeated sampling to illustrate how sampling distributions are created.

We'll begin with the dice-tossing experiment described in Section 8.2. Below we describe the commands that will create two columns of 1,000 numbers where the numbers are drawn from a discrete uniform distribution whose integers fall between 1 and 6 (just like the toss of a balanced die). Both Excel and Minitab will be instructed to treat each *row* of the array as a sample of size 2. We then compute the row means and store them in a third column. We can examine the resulting sampling distribution by drawing the histogram and calculating the mean and standard deviation.

▼ **SIMULATION EXPERIMENT 8.1**

Excel Instructions

1 In column A store the numbers 1, 2, 3, 4, 5, 6.

2 In cell B1 type =**1/6** and drag to fill cells B2 through B6. (Do not type .1667 or any other versions of 1/6 since the sum of the probabilities will not equal 1 causing Excel to issue an error warning.)

3 Click **Tools, Data Analysis . . . ,** and **Random Number Generation.**

4 Type **2** to specify the **Number of Variables** and **1000** to specify the **Number of Random Variables.** This will create an array of two columns and 1,000 rows. (If Excel responds **"Selection too large. Continue without undo?"** click **OK.**)

5 Click **Discrete** distribution. In the parameters box type **A1:B6** to specify the **Value and Probability Input Range.**

6 Specify **New Worksheet Ply** (the default). Click **OK.** Columns A and B of a new worksheet will fill with the random numbers.

7 Move to Cell C1 and type **=AVERAGE(A1:B1)**.

8 Drag to fill the rest of column C. Column C will now contain the values of the sample means.

9 Draw the histogram using bins 1.0, 1.5, 2.0, ... , 6.0.

10 Calculate the mean and the standard deviation of the sample means in column C. In cells D1 and D2, respectively, type **=AVERAGE(C1:C1000)** and **=STDEV(C1:C1000)**.

Minitab Instructions

1 Click **Calc, Random Data,** and **Integer ...**

2 Type **1000 (rows of data)**.

3 Hit **tab** and type **C1 C2 (Store in column(s))**.

4 Hit **tab** and type **1 (Minimum value)**.

5 Hit **tab** and type **6 (Maximum value)**. Click **OK.**

6 Click **Calc** and **Row Statistics ....**

7 Use the cursor to select **Mean.**

8 Hit **tab** and type **C1 C2 (Input variables)**.

9 Hit **tab** and type **C3** to **Store results in** column 3. Click **OK.**

10 Calculate the descriptive statistics for column C3.

11 Draw the histogram of C3 with midpoints 1, 1.5, 2, ... , 6.

We suggest that you write a brief report of the results of the simulation experiment.

Report for Simulation Experiment 8.1

1 Compare the histogram that was drawn to the theoretical sampling distribution. Are they similar?

2 What did you anticipate seeing when the computer printed the mean and standard deviation of the sampling distribution of the mean? What did the computer print?

3 Discuss the significance of your experiment.

▲

INCREASING THE SAMPLE SIZE

To examine the effect of increasing the sample size repeat the experiment with $n = 5$, 10, and 25.

▼ **SIMULATION EXPERIMENT 8.2**

Excel Instructions   In step 4 of Excel Instructions for Simulation Experiment 8.1, type **5** (for $n = 5$), **10**, or **25**. Change the instructions in steps 7, 8, and 10 to store the sample (row) means in the next available column.

Minitab Instructions   In step 3 of Minitab Instructions for Simulation Experiment 8.1, type **C1-C5** (for $n = 5$), **C1-C10**, or **C1-C25**.

In steps 8, 9, and 10, change the instructions so that the sample (row) means are stored in the next available column.

Write a report for each sample size providing the information you gave in Simulation Experiment 8.1.

▲

SAMPLING FROM A NORMAL POPULATION

The central limit theorem states that the sampling distribution of the mean is normal when the population is normal. The following experiment is designed to confirm this part of the theorem.

▼ **SIMULATION EXPERIMENT 8.3**

In this experiment we sample from a normal population whose mean is 100 and whose standard deviation is 25. We use a sample size of 4.

Excel Instructions

1 Click **Tools, Data Analysis . . .** , and **Random Number Generation.**
2 Type **4** to specify the **Number of Variables** and **1000** to specify the **Number of Random Variables.**
3 Click **Normal** distribution. Specify **Mean** 100 and **Standard deviation** 25.
4 Specify **New Worksheet Ply** (the default). Click **OK.**
5 Move to cell E1 and type **=AVERAGE(A1:D1)**.
6 Drag to fill the rest of column E.
7 Draw the histogram and calculate the mean and standard deviation of the sample means in column E.

Minitab Instructions

1 Click **Calc, Random Data,** and **Normal . . . .**
2 Type **1000 (rows of data).**
3 Hit **tab** and type **C1-C4 (Store in column(s)).**
4 Hit **tab** and type **100 (Mean).**
5 Hit **tab** and type **25 (Standard deviation).** Click **OK.**
6 Click **Calc** and **Row Statistics . . . .**
7 Use the cursor to select **Mean.**
8 Hit **tab** and type **C1-C4 (Input variables).**
9 Hit **tab** and type **C5** to **Store results in** column 5. Click **OK.**
10 Calculate the descriptive statistics and the histogram for column C5.

Report for Simulation Experiment 8.3

1 Does it appear that the sampling distribution is normal?

2 What did you anticipate seeing when the computer printed the mean and standard deviation of the sampling distribution of the mean? What did the computer print?

3 Discuss the significance of your experiment.

▲

▼ **SIMULATION EXPERIMENT 8.4**

Repeat Simulation Experiment 8.3 using a sample size of 9. Write a report describing your results.

▲

▼ **SIMULATION EXPERIMENT 8.5**

Repeat Simulation Experiment 8.3 using a sample size of 25. Write a report describing your results.

▲

8.4 SAMPLING DISTRIBUTION OF A PROPORTION

When the data that we're dealing with in a particular problem are qualitative, the parameter of interest is the proportion of times a particular outcome occurs. Using the terminology developed in Chapter 6 we call these outcomes *successes*. The estimator of a population proportion of successes is the sample proportion. That is, we count the number of successes in a sample and compute

$$\hat{p} = \frac{X}{n}$$

($\hat{p}$ is read as *p-hat*) where X is the number of successes and n is the sample size. Recall that X is binomially distributed and thus the probability of any value of $\hat{p}$ can be calculated from its value of x. For example, suppose that we have a binomial experiment with $n = 20$ and $p = .5$. To find the probability that the sample proportion $\hat{p}$ is less than or equal to .60 we find the probability that X is less than or equal to 12 (since $12/20 = .60$). From Table 1 in Appendix B we find with $n = 20$ and $p = .5$

$$P(\hat{p} \leq .60) = P(X \leq 12) = .868$$

Discrete distributions like the binomial do not lend themselves easily to the kinds of calculation needed for inference. And inference is the reason we need sampling distributions. Fortunately, we can approximate the binomial distribution using the normal distribution.

NORMAL APPROXIMATION OF THE BINOMIAL

The normal distribution can be used to approximate a number of probability distributions including the binomial. The **normal approximation of the binomial distrib-**

ution works best when the number of experiments (sample size) is large and when the binomial distribution is symmetrical (like the normal). The binomial distribution is symmetrical when the probability of a success equals 50% ($p = .5$). The farther p is from .5, the larger n must be in order for a good approximation to result. The value of n must be sufficiently large so that np and $n(1 - p)$ are both greater than 5.

To see how the approximation works, consider a binomial random variable with $n = 20$ and $p = .5$, the graph of which is shown in Figure 8.7. We approximate the binomial probabilities using a normal distribution whose mean and standard deviation are equal to the mean and standard deviation of the binomial. Recall that the mean and standard deviation of a binomial random variable are np and $\sqrt{np(1 - p)}$ (see page 215). For $n = 20$ and $p = .5$, we calculate

$$\mu = np = 20(.5) = 10$$
$$\sigma = \sqrt{np(1 - p)} = \sqrt{20(.5)(1 - .5)} = \sqrt{5} = 2.24$$

Suppose we wish to determine the probability that $X = 10$. We can compute the exact binomial distribution using the binomial formula or Table 1 from Appendix B. Both yield

$$P(X = 10) = .176.$$

To use the normal approximation we draw (or imagine drawing) the binomial distribution and we fit a normal curve over it. See Figure 8.8. The area in the rectangle whose base is the interval 9.5 to 10.5 is the exact binomial probability. Notice that to draw a binomial distribution, which is discrete it was necessary to draw rectangles whose base is constructed by adding and subtracting 0.5 to the values of X. The 0.5 is called the *continuity correction factor.*

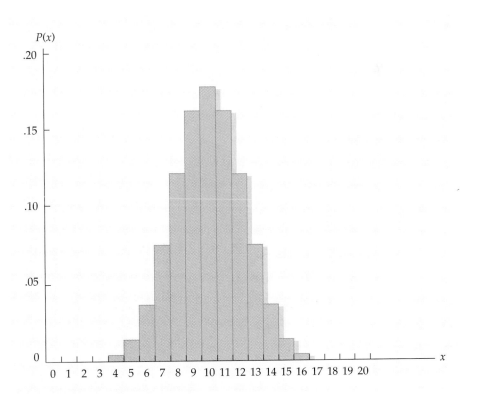

Figure 8.7

Binomial distribution with
$n = 20$ and $p = .5$

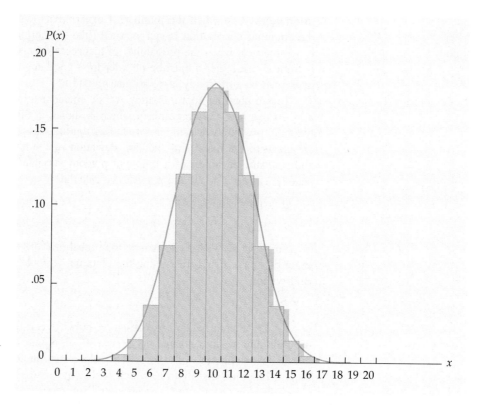

Figure 8.8

Binomial distribution with
$n = 20$ and $p = .5$ and normal
approximation

To calculate the probability that $X = 10$ using the normal distribution requires that we find the area under the normal curve between 9.5 and 10.5. That is,

$$P(X = 10) \approx P(9.5 < Y < 10.5)$$

where Y is a normal random variable approximating the binomial random variable X. We standardize Y (by subtracting its mean and dividing by its standard deviation) and employ Table 3 of Appendix B.

$$P(9.5 < Y < 10.5) = P\left(\frac{9.5 - 10}{2.24} < \frac{Y - \mu}{\sigma} < \frac{10.5 - 10}{2.24}\right)$$
$$= P(-.22 < Z < .22) = 2(.0871) = .1742$$

As you can see the actual value of $P(X = 10)$ is .176 and the normal approximation is .1742.

The approximation for any other value of X would proceed in the same manner. In general, the binomial probability $P(X = x)$ is approximated by the area under a normal curve between $x - .5$ and $x + .5$. To find the binomial probability $P(X \leq x)$, we calculate the area under the normal curve to the left of $x + .5$. For the same binomial random variable the probability that its value is less than or equal to 8 is $P(X \leq 8) = .252$. The normal approximation is

$$P(X \leq 8) \approx P(Y < 8.5) = P\left(\frac{Y - \mu}{\sigma} < \frac{8.5 - 10}{2.24}\right) = P(Z < -.67) = .2514$$

We find the area under the normal curve to the right of $x - .5$ to determine the binomial probability $P(X \geq x)$. To illustrate, the probability that the binomial random variable is greater than or equal to 14 is $P(X \geq 14) = .058$. The normal approximation is

$$P(X \geq 14) \approx P(Y > 13.5) = P\left(\frac{Y - \mu}{\sigma} > \frac{13.5 - 10}{2.24}\right) = P(Z > 1.56) = .0594$$

For large values of n the effect of the continuity correction factor is negligible (since each rectangle representing the binomial distribution is quite small) and effectively can be omitted. When we use the normal approximation of the binomial in inferential statistics the values of n will be large enough to ignore the correction factor.

APPROXIMATE SAMPLING DISTRIBUTION OF A SAMPLE PROPORTION

We have established that for sufficiently large n a binomial distribution can be approximated by a normal distribution. Thus, the number of successes in n identical independent trials X is approximately normally distributed with mean np and standard deviation $\sqrt{np(1 - p)}$. We now turn our attention to the **approximate sampling distribution of a sample proportion** of successes $\hat{p}$.

Using the laws of expected value and variance (for a review turn to pages 193 and 196), we can determine the mean, variance, and standard deviation of $\hat{p}$. (The standard deviation of $\hat{p}$ is called the standard error or $\hat{p}$.) That is,

$$E(\hat{p}) = E\left(\frac{X}{n}\right) = \frac{E(X)}{n} = \frac{np}{n} = p$$

$$V(\hat{p}) = \sigma_{\hat{p}}^2 = V\left(\frac{X}{n}\right) = \frac{V(X)}{n^2} = \frac{np(1 - p)}{n^2} = \frac{p(1 - p)}{n}$$

$$\sigma_{\hat{p}} = \sqrt{p(1 - p)/n}$$

If np and $n(1 - p)$ are both greater than 5, the variable

$$Z = \frac{\hat{p} - p}{\sqrt{p(1 - p)/n}}$$

is approximately standard normally distributed.

▼ EXAMPLE 8.3

The Laurier Company's brand has a market share of 30%. Suppose that in a survey, 1,000 consumers of the product are asked which brand they prefer. What is the probability that more than 32% of the respondents will say they prefer the Laurier brand?

Solution The number of respondents who prefer the Laurier brand is a binomial random variable with $n = 1,000$ and $p = .30$. We want to determine the probability that the sample proportion is greater than 32%. That is, we want to find $P(\hat{p} > .32)$.

We now know that the sample proportion $\hat{p}$ is approximately normally distributed with mean $p = .30$ and standard deviation $= \sqrt{p(1 - p)/n} = \sqrt{(.30)(.70)/1,000} = .0145$. Thus we calculate

$$P(\hat{p} > .32) = P\left(\frac{\hat{p} - p}{\sqrt{p(1 - p)/n}} > \frac{.32 - .30}{.0145}\right) = P(Z > 1.38) = .0838$$

There is an 8.38% probability that more than 32% of 1,000 respondents will say they prefer the Laurier brand.

EXERCISES

8.16 Given a binomial random variable with $n = 25$ and $p = .3$, find the (exact) probabilities of the following events and their normal approximations.

   a $X = 9$
   b $X \geq 5$
   c $X \leq 11$

8.17 A binomial experiment was performed with 15 identical trials and the probability of success equal to .5. Find the following binomial probabilities and their normal approximations.

   a $P(X = 10)$
   b $P(X \leq 6)$
   c $P(X \geq 11)$

8.18 Use Excel or Minitab to find the (exact) probabilities and their normal approximations of the following binomial random variables.

   a $X \leq 225, n = 1200, p = .18$
   b $X \leq 130, n = 600, p = .20$
   c $X \geq 150, n = 400, p = .4$
   d $X \geq 220, n = 700, p = .3$
   e $X = 240, n = 500, p = .5$

Use the normal approximation (without the correction factor) to find the probabilities in the following exercises.

8.19 The probability of success any trial of a binomial experiment is 25%. Find the probability that the proportion of successes in a sample of 500 is less than 22%.

8.20 Repeat Exercise 8.19 given $n = 800$.

8.21 Repeat Exercise 8.19 given $n = 1,000$.

8.22 The proportion of eligible voters in the next election who will vote for the incumbent is assumed to be 55%. What is the probability that in a random sample of 500 voters, less than 49% will say they will vote for the incumbent?

8.23 The assembly line that produces an electronic component of a missile system has historically experienced a 2% defective rate. A random sample of 800 components is drawn. What is the probability that the defective rate is greater than 4%? Suppose that in the random sample the defective rate is 4%. What does that suggest about the assembly line defective rate?

8.24 The manufacturer of aspirin claims that the proportion of headache sufferers who get relief with just two aspirins is 53%. What is the probability that in a random sample of 400 headache sufferers, less than 50% obtain relief? If 50% of the sample actually obtained relief what does this suggest about the manufacturer's claim?

8.25 Repeat Exercise 8.24 using a sample of 1,000.

8.26 A commercial for a household appliances manufacturer claims that less than 5% of all of its products require a service call in the first year. A consumer protection association wants to check the claim by surveying 400 households that recently purchased one of the company's appliances. What is the probability that more than 10% require a service call within the first year? What would you say about the commercial's honesty if in a random sample of 400 households 10% reports at least one service call?

8.5 SAMPLING DISTRIBUTION OF THE DIFFERENCE BETWEEN TWO MEANS

Another sampling distribution that you will soon encounter is that of the difference between two sample means. The sampling plan calls for independent random samples drawn from each of two normal populations. The samples are said to be independent if the selection of the members of one sample is independent of the selection of the members of the second sample. We will expand on this discussion in Chapter 12. We are interested in the **sampling distribution of the difference between two sample means.**

In Section 8.2 we introduced the central limit theorem, which stated that in repeated sampling from a normal population whose mean is μ and whose standard deviation is σ the sampling distribution of the sample mean is normal with mean μ and standard deviation $\sigma/\sqrt{n}$. In Chapter 7 we pointed out that the difference between two normal random variables is also normally distributed. Thus, the statistic $\bar{X}_1 - \bar{X}_2$ is normally distributed if both populations are normal.

In Chapter 6 we presented the laws of expected value and variance where we asserted the following.

$$E(X - Y) = E(X) - E(Y)$$

and

$$V(X - Y) = V(X) + V(Y) \qquad \text{if } X \text{ and } Y \text{ are independent}$$

Applying these two laws we determine the mean and variance of $\bar{X}_1 - \bar{X}_2$.

$$E(\bar{X}_1 - \bar{X}_2) = E(\bar{X}_1) - E(\bar{X}_2) = \mu_1 - \mu_2$$

and

$$V(\bar{X}_1 - \bar{X}_2) = V(\bar{X}_1) + V(\bar{X}_2) = \frac{\sigma_1^2}{n_1} + \frac{\sigma_2^2}{n_2}$$

Thus, it follows that in repeated independent sampling from two normal populations with means μ_1 and μ_2, and standard deviations σ_1 and σ_2, respectively, the sampling distribution of $\bar{X}_1 - \bar{X}_2$ is normal with mean $\mu - \mu_2$ and standard deviation (standard error)

$$\sqrt{\frac{\sigma_1^2}{n_1} + \frac{\sigma_2^2}{n_2}}$$

If the populations are nonnormal then the sampling distribution is only approximately normal for large sample sizes. The required sample sizes depend on the extent of nonnormality. However, for most populations, sample sizes of 30 or more are sufficient.

Figure 8.9 depicts the sampling distribution of the difference between two means.

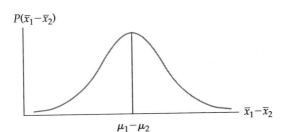

Figure 8.9

Sampling distribution of $\bar{X}_1 - \bar{X}_2$

▼ **EXAMPLE 8.4**

Suppose that the starting salaries of M.B.A.s at Wilfrid Laurier University (WLU) are normally distributed with a mean of $62,000 and a standard deviation of $14,500. The starting salaries of M.B.A.s at the University of Western Ontario (UWO) are normally distributed with a mean of $60,000 and a standard deviation of $18,300. If a random sample of 50 WLU M.B.A.s and a random sample of 60 UWO M.B.A.s are selected, what is the probability that the sample mean of WLU graduates will exceed that of the UWO graduates?

Solution We want to determine $P(\bar{X}_1 - \bar{X}_2 > 0)$. We know that $\bar{X}_1 - \bar{X}_2$ is normally distributed with mean $\mu - \mu_2 = 62,000 - 60,000 = 2,000$ and standard deviation

$$\sqrt{\frac{\sigma_1^2}{n_1} + \frac{\sigma_2^2}{n_2}} = \sqrt{\frac{14,500^2}{50} + \frac{18,300^2}{60}} = 3,128$$

We can standardize the variable and refer to Table 3 in Appendix B.

$$P(\bar{X}_1 - \bar{X}_2 > 0) = P\left(\frac{(\bar{X}_1 - \bar{X}_2) - (\mu_1 - \mu_2)}{\sqrt{\dfrac{\sigma_1^2}{n_1} + \dfrac{\sigma_2^2}{n_2}}} > \frac{0 - 2{,}000}{3{,}128}\right)$$

$$= P(Z > -.64) = .7389$$

There is a 73.89% probability that, in drawing a sample of size of 50 WLU graduates and a sample of size 60 of UWO graduates, the sample mean of WLU graduates will exceed the sample mean of UWO graduates. Note that this means that, even though the population mean of WLU graduates is $2,000 more than that of the UWO graduates, there is a 26.11% probability (calculated from $1 - .7389$) that the sample mean of UWO graduates would be greater than the sample mean of WLU graduates.

EXERCISES

8.27 Independent random samples of 10 observations each are drawn from normal populations. The parameters of these populations are

Population 1: $\mu_1 = 280$ $\sigma_1 = 25$

Population 2: $\mu_2 = 270$ $\sigma_2 = 30$

Find the probability that the mean of sample 1 is greater than the mean of sample 2 by more than 25.

8.28 Repeat Exercise 8.27 with samples of size 50.

8.29 Repeat Exercise 8.27 with samples of size 100.

8.30 A widget factory's worker productivity is normally distributed. One worker produces an average of 75 widgets per day with a standard deviation of 20. Another worker produces at an average rate of 65 per day with a standard deviation of 21.

a What is the probability that in any single day worker 1 will outproduce worker 2?

b What is the probability that during 1 week (5 working days) worker 1 will outproduce worker 2?

8.31 A professor of statistics noticed that the grades in his course are normally distributed. He has also noticed that his morning classes average 73% with a standard devia-

tion of 12% on their final exams. His afternoon classes average 77% with a standard deviation of 10%.

a What is the probability that a randomly selected student in the morning class has a higher final exam mark than a randomly selected student from an afternoon class?

b What is the probability that the mean grade of four randomly selected students from a morning class is greater than the average grade of four randomly selected students from an afternoon class?

8.32 The manager of a restaurant believes that waiters and waitresses who introduce themselves by telling customers their names will get larger tips than those who don't. In fact, she claims that the average tip for the former group is 18% while that of the latter is only 15%. If tips are normally distributed with a standard deviation of 3%, what is the probability that, in a random sample of 10 tips recorded from waiters and waitresses who introduce themselves and 10 tips from waiters and waitresses who don't do so, the mean of the former will exceed that of the latter?

8.6 FROM HERE TO INFERENCE

The primary function of the sampling distribution is statistical inference. To see how the sampling distribution contributes to the development of inferential methods we need to briefly review how we got to this point.

In Chapters 6 and 7 we introduced probability distributions, which allow us to make probability statements about values of the random variable. A prerequisite of this calculation is knowledge of the distribution and the relevant parameters. In Example 6.10, we needed to know that the proportion of successes was 30% and that the number of successes in 20 trials is a binomial random variable. We then could compute the probability of any number of successes. In Example 7.3 we needed to know that the rate of return was normally distributed with mean 30% and standard deviation 10%. These three bits of information allowed us to calculate the probability of various values of the random variable.

Figure 8.10 symbolically represents the use of probability distributions. Simply put, knowledge of the population and its parameter(s) allows us to use the probability distribution to make probability statements about individual members of the population.

Figure 8.10

Probability distribution

$$\dfrac{Population}{\& \ Parameter(s)} \ \text{──────} \ Probability\ distribution \ \text{──────▶} \ Individual$$

In this chapter we developed the sampling distribution, wherein knowledge of the parameter(s) and some information about the distribution allows us to make probability statements about a sample statistic. In Example 8.2 knowing the population mean and standard deviation and assuming that the population is not extremely nonnormal enabled us to calculate a probability statement about a sample mean. Figure 8.11 describes the application of sampling distributions.

Figure 8.11

Sampling distribution

$$\dfrac{Population}{\& \ Parameter(s)} \ \text{──────} \ Sampling\ distribution \ \text{──────▶} \ Statistic$$

Notice that in applying both probability distributions and sampling distributions, we need to know the value of the relevant parameters, a highly unlikely circumstance. In the real world, parameters are almost always unknown because they represent descriptive measurements about extremely large populations. Statistical inference addresses this problem. It does so by reversing the direction of the flow of knowledge in Figure 8.11. In Figure 8.12 we display the character of statistical inference. Starting in Chapter 9, we will assume that most population parameters are unknown, but that sample statistics are known. The sampling distribution will enable us to draw inferences about the parameter(s) from the statistic(s).

Figure 8.12

Sampling distribution in inference

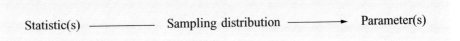

Statistic(s) ────── Sampling distribution ──────▶ Parameter(s)

You may be surprised to learn that by and large that is all we do in the remainder of this book. Why then do we need another 14 chapters? Because there are many more parameter/sampling distribution combinations that define the inferential procedures that we plan to cover. However, they all work in the same way. If you understand how one procedure is evolved you are likely to understand all of them. Our task in the next two chapters is to ensure that you understand the first inferential method. Your job is identical.

8.7 SUMMARY

The sampling distribution of a statistic is created by repeated sampling from one population. In this chapter we introduced the sampling distribution of the mean, the proportion, and the difference between two means. We described how these distributions are created theoretically and empirically.

IMPORTANT TERMS

Sampling distribution   *262*
Central limit theorem   *266*
Sampling distribution of the
  sample mean   *267*
Standard error of the mean   *267*
Estimation   *269*
Normal approximation of the
  binomial distribution   *276*

Sampling distribution of a sample
  proportion   *279*
Sampling distribution of the
  difference between two sample
  means   *280*

SUMMARY OF FORMULAS

$$E(\bar{X}) = \mu_{\bar{x}} = \mu$$

$$V(\bar{X}) = \sigma_{\bar{x}}^2 = \frac{\sigma^2}{n}$$

$$\sigma_{\bar{x}} = \frac{\sigma}{\sqrt{n}}$$

$$Z = \frac{\bar{X} - \mu}{\sigma/\sqrt{n}}$$

$$E(\hat{p}) = \mu_{\hat{p}} = p$$

$$V(\hat{p}) = \sigma_{\hat{p}}^2 = \frac{p(1-p)}{n}$$

$$\sigma_{\hat{p}} = \sqrt{\frac{p(1-p)}{n}}$$

$$Z = \frac{\hat{p} - p}{\sqrt{p(1-p)/n}}$$

$$E(\bar{X}_1 - \bar{X}_2) = \mu_{\bar{x}_1 - \bar{x}_2} = \mu_1 - \mu_2$$

$$V(\bar{X}_1 - \bar{X}_2) = \sigma_{\bar{x}_1 - \bar{x}_2}^2 = \frac{\sigma_1^2}{n_1} + \frac{\sigma_2^2}{n_2}$$

$$\sigma_{\bar{x}_1 - \bar{x}_2} = \sqrt{\frac{\sigma_1^2}{n_1} + \frac{\sigma_2^2}{n_2}}$$

$$Z = \frac{(\bar{X}_1 - \bar{X}_2) - (\mu_1 - \mu_2)}{\sqrt{\frac{\sigma_1^2}{n_1} + \frac{\sigma_2^2}{n_2}}}$$

Chapter 9

Introduction to
Estimation

9.1 Introduction

9.2 Concepts of Estimation

9.3 Estimating the Population Mean When the Population Standard Deviation Is Known

9.4 Selecting the Sample Size

9.5 Simulation Experiments (Optional)

9.6 Summary

9.1 INTRODUCTION

Having discussed descriptive statistics (Chapter 4), probability distributions (Chapter 6 and 7), and sampling distributions (Chapter 8), we are ready to tackle statistical inference. As we explained in Chapter 1, statistical inference is the process by which we acquire information and draw conclusions about populations from samples. There are two general procedures for making inferences about populations: estimation and hypothesis testing. In this chapter, we introduce the concepts and foundations of estimation and demonstrate them with simple examples. In Chapter 10, we describe the fundamentals of hypothesis testing. Because most of what we do in the remainder of this book applies the concepts of estimation and hypothesis testing, understanding Chapters 9 and 10 is vital to your development as a statistician.

9.2 CONCEPTS OF ESTIMATION

As its name suggests, the objective of estimation is to determine the approximate value of a population parameter on the basis of a sample statistic. For example, the sample mean is employed to estimate the population mean. We refer to the sample mean as the estimator of the population mean. Once the sample mean has been computed, its value is called the **estimate**.

POINT AND INTERVAL ESTIMATORS

We can use sample data to estimate a population parameter in two ways. First, we can compute the value of the estimator and consider that value as the estimate of the parameter. Such an estimator is called a **point estimator.**

> **Point Estimator**
>
> A **point estimator** draws inferences about a population by estimating the value of an unknown parameter using a single value or point.

In drawing inferences about a population, it is intuitively reasonable to expect that a large sample will produce more accurate results, because it contains more information than a smaller sample does. But point estimators don't have the capacity to reflect the effects of larger sample sizes. The second way of estimating a population parameter is to use an **interval estimator.**

> **Interval Estimator**
>
> An **interval estimator** draws inferences about a population by estimating the value of an unknown parameter using an interval.

As you will see, the interval estimator is affected by the sample size; because it possesses this feature, we will deal mostly with interval estimators in this text.

To illustrate the difference between point and interval estimators, suppose that a statistics professor wants to estimate the mean summer income of his second-year business students. Selecting 25 students at random, he calculates the sample mean weekly income to be $400. The point estimate is the sample mean. That is, he estimates the mean weekly summer income of all second-year business students to be $400. Using the technique described below, he may instead use an interval estimate, in which he estimates that the average second-year business student earns between $350 and $450 per week during the summer.

Numerous applications of estimation occur in the real world. For example, television network executives want to know the proportion of television viewers who are tuned in to their networks; an economist wants to know the mean income of university graduates. In each of these cases, in order to accomplish the objective exactly, the interested party would have to examine each member of the population and then calculate the parameter of interest. For instance, network executives would have to ask each person in the country what he or she is watching to determine the proportion of people who are watching their shows. Since there are millions of television viewers, the task is both impractical and prohibitively expensive. An alternative would be to take a random sample from this population, calculate the sample proportion, and use that as an estimator of the population proportion. The use of the sample proportion to estimate the population proportion seems logical. The selection of the sample statistic to be used as an estimator, however, depends on the characteristics of that statistic. Naturally, we want to use the statistic with the most desirable qualities for our purposes.

One desirable quality of an estimator is *unbiasedness.*

Unbiased Estimator

An **unbiased estimator** of a population parameter is an estimator whose expected value is equal to that parameter.

This means that, if you were to take an infinite number of samples, calculate the value of the estimator in each sample, the average value of the estimators would equal the parameter. This amounts to saying that, on average, the sample statistic is equal to the parameter.

We know that the sample mean $\bar{X}$ is an unbiased estimator of the population mean μ. In presenting the sampling distribution of $\bar{X}$ in Chapter 8 we demonstrated that $E(\bar{X}) = \mu$. We also know that the sample proportion is an unbiased estimator of the population proportion since $E(\hat{p}) = p$ and that the difference between two sample means is an unbiased estimator of the difference between two population means because $E(\bar{X}_1 - \bar{X}_2) = \mu_1 - \mu_2$.

Recall that in Chapter 4 we defined the sample variance as

$$s^2 = \sum \frac{(x_i - \bar{x})^2}{n-1}$$

At the time, it seemed odd that we divided by $n - 1$ rather than by n. The reason for choosing $n - 1$ was to make $E(S^2) = \sigma^2$ so that this definition makes the sample variance an unbiased estimator of the population variance. (The proof of this statement requires about a page of algebraic manipulation, which is more than we would be comfortable in presenting here. Later in this chapter we describe a simulation experiment that demonstrates this point.) Had we defined the sample variance using n in the denominator the resulting statistic would be a biased estimator of the population variance, one whose expected value is less than the parameter.

Knowing that an estimator is unbiased merely assures us that its expected value equals the parameter; it does not tell us how close the estimator is to the parameter. Another desirable quality is that as the sample size grows larger, the sample statistic should come closer to the population parameter. This quality is called **consistency.**

Consistency

An unbiased estimator is said to be consistent if the difference between the estimator and the parameter grows smaller as the sample size grows larger.

The measure we use to gauge closeness is the variance (or the standard deviation). Thus, $\bar{X}$ is a consistent estimator of μ, because the variance of $\bar{X}$ is σ^2/n. This implies that as n grows larger, the variance of $\bar{X}$ grows smaller. As a consequence, an increasing proportion of sample means falls close to μ.

Figure 9.1 depicts two sampling distributions of $\bar{X}$ when samples are drawn from a population whose mean is 0 and whose standard deviation is 10. One sampling distribution is based on samples of size 25, and the other is based on samples of size 100. The former is more spread out than the latter.

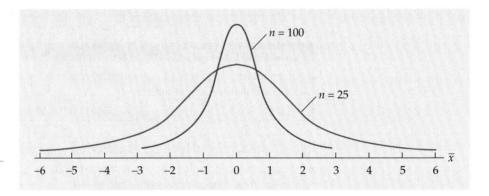

Figure 9.1

Sampling distributions of $\bar{x}$ with $n = 25$ and $n = 100$

Similarly, $\hat{p}$ is a consistent estimator of p because it is unbiased and the variance of $\hat{p}$ is $\sqrt{p(1-p)/n}$, which grows smaller as n grows larger.

A third desirable quality is **relative efficiency,** which compares two unbiased estimators of a parameter.

Relative Efficiency

If there are two unbiased estimators of a parameter, the one whose variance is smaller is said to be relatively efficient.

We have already seen that the sample mean is an unbiased estimator of the population mean and that its variance is σ^2/n. Statisticians have established that (sampling from a normal population) the sample median is also an unbiased estimator of the population mean, but that its variance is $1.57\sigma^2/n$. Consequently, we say that the sample mean is relatively more efficient than the sample median. Not surprisingly, the sample mean will be our first choice for drawing inferences about a population mean.

In the remaining chapters of this book, we will present the statistical inference of a number of different population parameters. In each case, we will select a sample statistic that is unbiased and consistent, and where there is more than one such statistic we will choose the one that is relatively efficient to serve as the estimator.

DEVELOPING AN UNDERSTANDING OF STATISTICAL CONCEPTS

We just described three desirable characteristics of estimators: unbiasedness, consistency, and relative efficiency. An understanding of statistics requires you to understand that there are several potential estimators for each parameter, but that we choose the estimators used in this book because they possess these desirable characteristics.

E X E R C I S E S

9.1 Define unbiasedness.

9.2 Draw a diagram depicting the sampling distribution of an unbiased estimator.

9.3 Draw a diagram depicting the sampling distribution of a biased estimator.

9.4 Define consistency.

9.5 Is the sample median a consistent estimator of the population mean? Explain.

9.6 Draw diagrams representing what happens to the sampling distribution of a consistent estimator when the sample size increases.

9.7 Define relative efficiency.

9.8 Draw a diagram representing the sampling distribution of two unbiased estimators, one of which is relatively efficient.

9.3 ESTIMATING THE POPULATION MEAN WHEN THE POPULATION STANDARD DEVIATION IS KNOWN

We now describe how an interval estimator is produced from a sampling distribution. We choose to demonstrate estimation with an example that in general is unrealistic. However, this liability is offset by the example's simplicity. When you understand more about estimation, you will be able to apply the technique to more realistic situations.

Suppose we have a population with mean μ and standard deviation σ. The population mean is assumed to be unknown, and our task is to estimate its value. As we just discussed, the estimation procedure requires the statistician to draw a random sample of size n and calculate the sample mean $\bar{x}$.

In Chapter 8, we saw that $\bar{X}$ is normally distributed (if X is normally distributed) or approximately normally distributed (if X is nonnormal and n is sufficiently large*). This means that the variable

$$Z = \frac{\bar{X} - \mu}{\sigma/\sqrt{n}}$$

is standard normally distributed (or approximately so). In Section 8.2 (page 270) we developed the following probability statement associated with the sampling distribution of the mean.

---

*The value of n required to make the approximation valid depends on the extent of nonnormality.

$$P\left(\mu - z_{\alpha/2}\frac{\sigma}{\sqrt{n}} < \bar{X} < \mu + z_{\alpha/2}\frac{\sigma}{\sqrt{n}}\right) = 1 - \alpha$$

which was derived from

$$P\left(-z_{\alpha/2} < \frac{\bar{X} - \mu}{\sigma/\sqrt{n}} < z_{\alpha/2}\right) = 1 - \alpha$$

Using a similar algebraic manipulation we can express the probability in a slightly different form. That is,

$$P\left(\bar{X} - z_{\alpha/2}\frac{\sigma}{\sqrt{n}} < \mu < \bar{X} + z_{\alpha/2}\frac{\sigma}{\sqrt{n}}\right) = 1 - \alpha$$

Notice that in this form the population mean is in the center of the interval created by adding and subtracting $z_{\alpha/2}$ standard errors to the sample mean. It is important for you to understand that this is merely another form of probability statement about the sample mean. This equation says that, with repeated sampling from this population, the proportion of values of $\bar{X}$ for which the interval

$$\bar{X} - z_{\alpha/2}\,\sigma/\sqrt{n}, \quad \bar{X} + z_{\alpha/2}\,\sigma/\sqrt{n}$$

includes the population mean μ is equal to $1 - \alpha$. However, this form of probability statement is very useful to us because it is the **interval estimator of μ.**

Interval Estimator of μ*

$$\bar{x} - z_{\alpha/2}\,\sigma/\sqrt{n}, \quad \bar{x} + z_{\alpha/2}\,\sigma/\sqrt{n}$$

The probability $1 - \alpha$ is called the **confidence level.**
$\bar{x} - z_{\alpha/2}\,\sigma/\sqrt{n}$ is called the **lower confidence limit (LCL).**
$\bar{x} + z_{\alpha/2}\,\sigma/\sqrt{n}$ is called the **upper confidence limit (UCL).**
We often represent the interval estimator as

$$\bar{x} \pm z_{\alpha/2}\,\sigma/\sqrt{n}$$

where the minus sign defines the lower confidence limit and the plus sign defines the upper confidence limit.

To apply this formula we specify the confidence level $1 - \alpha$, from which we determine α, $\alpha/2$, and $z_{\alpha/2}$ (from Table 3 in Appendix B). Because the confidence level is the probability that the interval includes the actual value of μ, we generally set $1 - \alpha$ close to 1 (usually between 90% and 99%).

---

*Since Chapter 6 we've been using the convention whereby an uppercase letter (usually X) represents a random variable and a lowercase letter (usually x) represents one of its values. However, in the formulas used in statistical inference, the distinction between the variable and its value becomes blurred. Accordingly, we will discontinue the notational convention and simply use lowercase letters.

In Table 9.1, we list four commonly used confidence levels and their associated values of $z_{\alpha/2}$. For example, if the confidence level is 95%, then $1 - \alpha = .95$, $\alpha = .05$, $\alpha/2 = .025$, and $z_{\alpha/2} = z_{.025} = 1.96$. The resulting interval estimator is then called the **95% confidence interval estimator of μ.**

Table 9.1 **Four Commonly Used Confidence Levels and $z_{\alpha/2}$**

Confidence Level

$1 - \alpha$	α	$\alpha/2$	$z_{\alpha/2}$
.90	.10	.05	$z_{.05} = 1.645$
.95	.05	.025	$z_{.025} = 1.96$
.98	.02	.01	$z_{.01} = 2.33$
.99	.01	.005	$z_{.005} = 2.575$

As an illustration, suppose we want to estimate the mean value of the distribution resulting from the throw of a fair die. Because we know the distribution, we also know that $\mu = 3.5$ and $\sigma = 1.71$. Pretend now that we know only that $\sigma = 1.71$, that μ is unknown, and that we want to estimate its value. To estimate μ, we draw a sample of size $n = 100$ and calculate $\bar{x}$. The interval estimator of μ is

$$\bar{x} \pm z_{\alpha/2} \frac{\sigma}{\sqrt{n}}$$

The 90% confidence interval estimator is

$$\bar{x} \pm z_{\alpha/2} \frac{\sigma}{\sqrt{n}} = \bar{x} \pm 1.645 \frac{1.71}{\sqrt{100}} = \bar{x} \pm .28$$

This notation means that, if we repeatedly draw samples of size 100 from this population, 90% of the values of $\bar{x}$ will be such that μ would lie somewhere between $\bar{x} - .28$ and $\bar{x} + .28$, and 10% of the values of $\bar{x}$ will produce intervals that would not include μ. To illustrate this point, imagine that we draw 40 samples of 100 observations each. The values of $\bar{x}$ and the resulting interval estimates of μ are shown in Table 9.2. Notice that not all the intervals include the true value of the parameter. Samples 5, 16, 22, and 34 produce values of $\bar{x}$ that in turn produce intervals that exclude μ.

Students often react to this situation by asking "What went wrong with samples 5, 16, 22, and 34?" The answer is *nothing*. Statistics does not promise 100% certainty. In fact, in this illustration, we expected 90% of the intervals to include μ and 10% to exclude μ. Since we produced 40 intervals, we expected that 4.0 (10% of 40) intervals would not contain $\mu = 3.5$.* It is important to understand that, even when the statistician performs experiments properly, a certain proportion (in this example, 10%) of the experiments will produce incorrect estimates by random chance.

---

*In this illustration, exactly 10% of the 40 sample means produced interval estimates that excluded the value of μ, but this will not always be the case. Remember, we expect 10% of the sample means in the long run to result in intervals excluding μ. This group of 40 sample means does not constitute "the long run."

Table 9.2 **90% Confidence Interval Estimates of μ**

Sample	$\bar{x}$	LCL = $\bar{x}$ − .28	UCL = $\bar{x}$ + .28	Does Interval Include μ = 3.5?
1	3.55	3.27	3.83	Yes
2	3.61	3.33	3.89	Yes
3	3.47	3.19	3.75	Yes
4	3.48	3.20	3.76	Yes
5	3.80	3.52	4.08	No
6	3.37	3.09	3.65	Yes
7	3.48	3.20	3.76	Yes
8	3.52	3.24	3.80	Yes
9	3.74	3.46	4.02	Yes
10	3.51	3.23	3.79	Yes
11	3.23	2.95	3.51	Yes
12	3.45	3.17	3.73	Yes
13	3.57	3.29	3.85	Yes
14	3.77	3.49	4.05	Yes
15	3.31	3.03	3.59	Yes
16	3.10	2.82	3.38	No
17	3.50	3.22	3.78	Yes
18	3.55	3.27	3.83	Yes
19	3.65	3.37	3.93	Yes
20	3.28	3.00	3.56	Yes
21	3.40	3.12	3.68	Yes
22	3.88	3.60	4.16	No
23	3.76	3.48	4.04	Yes
24	3.40	3.12	3.68	Yes
25	3.34	3.06	3.62	Yes
26	3.65	3.37	3.93	Yes
27	3.45	3.17	3.73	Yes
28	3.47	3.19	3.75	Yes
29	3.58	3.30	3.86	Yes
30	3.36	3.08	3.64	Yes
31	3.71	3.43	3.99	Yes
32	3.51	3.23	3.79	Yes
33	3.42	3.14	3.70	Yes
34	3.11	2.83	3.39	No
35	3.29	3.01	3.57	Yes
36	3.64	3.36	3.92	Yes
37	3.39	3.11	3.67	Yes
38	3.75	3.47	4.03	Yes
39	3.26	2.98	3.54	Yes
40	3.54	3.26	3.82	Yes

We can improve the confidence associated with the interval estimate. If we let the confidence level $1 - \alpha$ equal .95, the interval estimator is

$$\bar{x} \pm z_{\alpha/2} \frac{\sigma}{\sqrt{n}} = \bar{x} \pm 1.96 \frac{1.71}{\sqrt{100}} = \bar{x} \pm .34$$

Because this interval is wider, it is more likely to include the value of μ. If you redo Table 9.2, this time using a 95% confidence interval estimator, only samples 16, 22, and 34 will produce intervals that do not include μ. (Notice that we expected 5% of the intervals to exclude μ and that we actually observed $3/40 = 7.5\%$.) The 99% confidence interval estimate is

$$\bar{x} \pm z_{\alpha/2} \frac{\sigma}{\sqrt{n}} = \bar{x} \pm 2.575 \frac{1.71}{\sqrt{100}} = \bar{x} \pm .44$$

Applying this interval estimate to the sample means listed in Table 9.2 would result in having all 40 interval estimates include the population mean $\mu = 3.5$. (We expected 1% of the intervals to exclude μ; we observed $0/40 = 0\%$.)

In actual practice, only one sample will be drawn, and thus only one value of $\bar{x}$ will be calculated. The resulting interval estimate will either correctly include the parameter or incorrectly exclude it. Unfortunately, statisticians do not know whether in each case they are correct; they know only that, in the long run, they will incorrectly estimate the parameter some of the time. Statisticians accept that as a fact of life, as should anyone who uses statistical results.

The following example illustrates how estimation techniques are applied. It also illustrates how we intend to solve problems in the rest of this book. The solution process that we advocate and use throughout this book is by and large the same one that statisticians use to apply their trade in the real world. The process is divided into three stages. The first step is to identify the correct statistical technique. Of course, for this example you will have no difficulty identifying the technique, since at this point you only know one.

The second step is to perform the calculations. We will do this in three ways. To illustrate how the computations are completed, we will do the arithmetic manually with the assistance of a calculator. Solving problems by hand often provides insights into the statistical inference technique. We will also use Excel and Minitab. The choice of which one to use is left to the instructor and student.

In the third and last step of the solution, we intend to interpret the results and deal with the question that began the problem. This may be more difficult than it appears, because to be capable of properly interpreting statistical results one needs to have an understanding of the fundamental principles underlying statistical inference. This last step will emphasize this understanding.

STATISTICS IN THE WORKPLACE

Marketing Application

As mentioned in the introduction to marketing management in Chapter 1, one of the major tools in the promotion mix is advertising. One of the many important decisions to be made by the advertising manager is how to allocate the company's total advertising budget among the various competing media types, including television, radio, and newspapers. Ultimately, the manager wants to know, for example, which television programs are most watched by potential customers, and how effective it is to sponsor these programs through advertising. But first the manager must assess the size of the audience, part of which involves estimating the amount of exposure potential customers have to the various media types, such as television.

▼ EXAMPLE 9.1

The sponsors of television shows targeted at the children's market wanted to know the amount of time children spend watching television, since the types and number of programs and commercials are greatly influenced by this information. As a result, the decision was made to survey 100 North American children and ask them to keep track of the number of hours of television they watch each week. The data were recorded and appear below. (They are also stored on the data disk in file XM09-01.) From past experience, it is known that the population standard deviation of the weekly amount of television watched is $\sigma = 8.0$ hours. The television sponsors want an estimate of the amount of television watched by the average North American child. A confidence level of 95% is judged to be appropriate.

AMOUNT OF TIME SPENT WATCHING TELEVISION EACH WEEK

39.7	21.5	40.6	15.5	43.9	33.0	21.0	15.8	27.1	23.8	18.3	23.4	20.6
28.4	29.8	41.3	36.8	35.5	27.2	21.0	19.7	22.8	30.0	22.1	30.8	34.7
15.0	23.6	38.9	29.1	28.7	29.3	20.3	36.1	21.6	15.1	43.8	29.0	30.2
26.5	20.5	24.1	29.3	14.7	13.9	37.1	32.5	24.4	22.9	24.5	19.5	29.9
46.4	31.6	20.6	38.0	21.8	23.2	22.0	35.3	17.0	24.4	34.9	24.0	32.9
15.1	23.4	19.5	26.5	42.4	38.6	23.4	37.8	26.5	22.7	27.0	16.4	39.4
38.7	9.5	20.6	21.3	33.5	23.0	35.7	23.4	30.8	27.7	25.2	50.3	31.3
28.9	31.2	15.6	32.8	17.0	11.3	26.9	26.9	21.9				

Solution

IDENTIFY

The parameter to be estimated is μ, the mean amount of television watched by all North American children. At this point, we have described only one estimator. Thus, the interval estimator that we intend to employ is

$$\bar{x} \pm z_{\alpha/2} \frac{\sigma}{\sqrt{n}}$$

SOLVE

The next step is to perform the computations. As we discussed above, we will perform the calculations in three ways: manually, using Excel, and using Minitab.

We need four values to construct the interval estimate of μ. These are

$$\bar{x}, z_{\alpha/2}, \sigma, \text{ and } n$$

Using our calculator, we determine the summation $\Sigma x_i = 2,719.1$. From this, we find

$$\bar{x} = \frac{\sum x_i}{n} = \frac{2,719.1}{100} = 27.191$$

The confidence level is represented by $1 - \alpha$. For this problem, we want a 95% confidence level, which means that $1 - \alpha = .95$. Thus, $\alpha = .05$ and $\alpha/2 = .025$. Using Table 3 in Appendix B or, more simply, Table 9.1, we find

$$z_{\alpha/2} = z_{.025} = 1.96$$

We are told that the population standard deviation is $\sigma = 8.0$. Finally, the sample size is $n = 100$. Substituting $\bar{x}, z_{\alpha/2}, \sigma,$ and n into the interval estimator described above, we produce

$$\bar{x} \pm z_{\alpha/2} \frac{\sigma}{\sqrt{n}} = 27.191 \pm z_{.025} \frac{8.0}{\sqrt{100}} = 27.191 \pm 1.96 \frac{8.0}{\sqrt{100}} = 27.191 \pm 1.568$$

Thus, the lower confidence limit is 25.623 and the upper confidence limit is 28.759.

**Excel Output for
Example 9.1**

	A	B	C	D	E
1	0.95 Confidence Interval Estimate of MU (SIGMA Known)				
2					
3	Sample mean = 27.191				
4	SIGMA = 8				
5	Lower confidence limit = 25.623				
6	Upper confidence limit = 28.759				

The 95% confidence interval estimate is the interval 25.623 to 28.759. (Note that we have altered the printout by omitting the data that are printed.)

COMMANDS	COMMANDS FOR EXAMPLE 9.1
1 Type or import the data into one column.	Open file **XM09-01.**
2 Click **Tools, Data Analysis Plus,** and **Inference About a Mean (SIGMA Known).**	
3 Specify the input range. (Either highlight the data before clicking **Tools** or type the block coordinates.) Do not include the cell containing the variable name.	**A2:A101**
4 Click **Interval Estimate.**	
5 Type the value of the population standard deviation.	**8.0**
6 Specify the confidence level. The default is .95. Click **OK.**	**.95**

There is another way to produce the interval estimate for this problem. If you (or someone else) have calculated the sample mean and know the sample size and population standard deviation you need not employ the data set and the macro described above. Instead click **Data Analysis Plus** and **Inference from Summary Statistics (Workbook).** This workbook contains 18 sheets, each showing the solution to an example in the book. Find the sheet titled **z-Estimate of a Mean.** The worksheet that will be opened represents the solution to Example 9.1. We typed the values of $\bar{x}$ **(27.191)**, σ **(8)**, and n **(100)** in cells B3, B4, and B5, respectively, and the confidence level in cell B7 **(0.95)**. The lower and upper confidence limits are calculated in cells B9 and B10, respectively. The complete output is shown below.

	A	B
1	**z-Estimate of a Mean**	
2		
3	Sample mean	27.191
4	Population standard deviation	8
5	Sample size	100
6		
7	Confidence level	0.95
8		
9	Lower confidence limit	25.6230
10	Upper confidence limit	28.7590

There are two ways to use this sheet. First, to solve other problems simply type in the new values of $\bar{x}$, σ, n, and $1 - \alpha$ in cells B3, B4, B5, and B7, respectively. Do not change any other cells. We recommend you *not* save any of these files in order to avoid altering the calculations in cells B9 and B10.

Second, you can perform a "what-if" analysis. That is, this worksheet provides you the opportunity to observe how changing some of the inputs affects the estimate. For example, type **0.99** in cell B7 to see what happens to the size of the interval when you increase the confidence level. Type **1000** in cell B5 to examine the effect of increasing the sample size. Type **1** in cell B4 and see what happens when the population standard deviation is smaller.

In the next two chapters we will describe the other 17 sheets in this workbook. They are all designed in the same way. They can complete the calculation of various techniques from summary statistics and perform what-if analyses.

NOTE: You must click the **Exit** button to shut the workbook.

Minitab Output for Example 9.1

Z Confidence Intervals

```
The assumed sigma = 8.00

Variable      N    Mean   StDev   SE Mean      95.0 % CI
Time        100  27.191   8.373     0.800  (  25.623,  28.759)
```

The output includes the value of σ **(The assumed sigma),** the sample size **(N),** the sample mean **(Mean),** and the sample standard deviation **(StDev = 8.373,** which is not needed for this interval estimate). Also printed are the standard error **SE Mean** $= \sigma/\sqrt{n} = 0.800$) and last, but not least, the 95% confidence interval estimate of the population mean. To produce this output, see the commands below.

COMMANDS

1 Type or import the data into one column.

2 Click **Stat, Basic Statistics,** and **1-Sample Z . . . .**

COMMANDS FOR EXAMPLE 9.1

Open file **XM09-01.**

3 Type the variable name.	**Time** or **C1**
4 Use the cursor to select **Confidence interval.**	
5 Hit **tab** and type the confidence **Level.**	**95.0**
6 Hit **tab** and type the value of the population standard deviation σ (**Sigma:**). Click **OK.**	**8.0**

INTERPRET

We estimate that the average number of hours children spend watching television each week lies somewhere between

LCL = 25.623 hours   and   UCL = 28.759 hours.

From this estimate, a network executive may decide (for example) that since the average child watches at least 25.623 hours of television per week, the number of commercials children see is sufficiently high to satisfy the program's sponsors. A number of other decisions may follow from that one.

Of course, the point estimate ($\bar{x} = 27.191$ hours per week) alone would not provide enough information to the executive. He would also need to know how low the population mean is likely to be; and for other decisions, he might need to know how high the population mean is likely to be. An interval estimate gives him that information.

▲

INTERPRETING THE INTERVAL ESTIMATE

In Example 9.1, we found the 95% confidence interval estimate of the mean number of hours that children watch television per week to be LCL = 25.623 and UCL = 28.759. Some people erroneously interpret this interval to mean that there is a 95% probability that the population mean lies between 25.623 and 28.759. This interpretation is wrong because it implies that the population mean is a variable about which we can make probability statements. In fact, the population mean is a fixed but unknown quantity. Consequently, we cannot interpret the confidence interval estimate of μ as a probability statement about μ.

To translate the interval estimate properly, we must remember that the interval estimator was derived from the sampling distribution of the mean. In Chapter 8, we showed that the sample mean is a random variable with mean μ and standard deviation $\sigma/\sqrt{n}$. It follows that the lower confidence limit and the upper confidence limit are themselves random variables. That is,

$$\text{LCL} = \bar{x} - z_{\alpha/2}\frac{\sigma}{\sqrt{n}}$$

is approximately normally distributed with mean $\mu - z_{\alpha/2}\sigma/\sqrt{n}$ and standard deviation $\sigma/\sqrt{n}$, and

$$\text{UCL} = \bar{x} + z_{\alpha/2}\frac{\sigma}{\sqrt{n}}$$

is approximately normally distributed with mean $\mu + z_{\alpha/2}\sigma/\sqrt{n}$ and standard deviation $\sigma/\sqrt{n}$. Figure 9.2 depicts the sampling distributions of LCL and UCL.

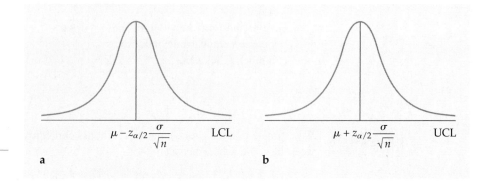

Figure 9.2

Sampling distributions of LCL and UCL

To elaborate further, let's return to the die-tossing illustration we used earlier. The mean and standard deviation of the population of die tosses is $\mu = 3.5$ and $\sigma = 1.71$, respectively. With $n = 100$ and $1 - \alpha = .90$, the following statements are equivalent.

1 $\bar{x}$ is approximately normally distributed with mean $\mu = 3.5$ and standard deviation $\sigma/\sqrt{n} = 1.71/\sqrt{100} = .171$.

2 $LCL = \bar{x} - z_{\alpha/2}\sigma/\sqrt{n} = \bar{x} - 1.645 \times 1.71/\sqrt{100} = \bar{x} - .28$, which is approximately normally distributed with mean $3.5 - .28 = 3.22$ and standard deviation $\sigma/\sqrt{100} = .171$.

3 $UCL = \bar{x} + z_{\alpha/2}\sigma/\sqrt{n} = \bar{x} + 1.645 \times 1.71/\sqrt{100} = \bar{x} + .28$, which is approximately normally distributed with mean $3.5 + .28 = 3.78$ and standard deviation $\sigma/\sqrt{100} = .171$.

Figure 9.3 describes the sampling distributions of the confidence limits.

It must be understood that LCL and UCL are related since both are based on the value of the sample mean. Thus, if LCL lies between 2.94 $(3.22 - .28)$ and 3.5, UCL will lie between 3.5 and 4.06 $(3.78 + .28)$. In that case, the interval estimate is correct. This will occur for 90% of the sample means. That is, 90% of the sample means will produce an LCL that is less than 3.5 and a UCL that is greater than 3.5.

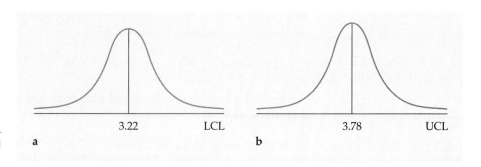

Figure 9.3

Sampling distribution of LCL and UCL (die tossing)

STATISTICS IN THE WORKPLACE

Operations Management Application

Operations managers use inventory models to determine the stock level that minimizes total costs. In Chapter 7 we showed how the probabilistic model is used to make the inventory level decision. (See page 252.) One component of that model is the mean demand during lead time. Recall that lead time refers to the interval between the time an order is received and when it is delivered. Demand during lead time is a random variable that is often assumed to be normally distributed. There are several ways to determine mean demand during lead time, but the simplest is to estimate that quantity from a sample.

▼ **EXAMPLE 9.2**

The Doll Computer Company makes its own computers and delivers them directly to customers who order them via the Internet. Doll competes primarily on price and speed of delivery. To achieve its objective of speed, Doll makes each of their five most popular computers and transports them to storage warehouses across the country, from which it generally takes 1 day to deliver a computer to the customer. This strategy requires high levels of inventory that add considerably to the cost. To lower these costs, the operations manager wants to employ an inventory model. He notes that both daily demand and lead time are random variables. He concludes that demand during lead time is normally distributed and he needs to know the mean in order to compute the optimum inventory level. He observes 60 lead time periods and records the demand during each period. These data are stored in file XM09-02 and listed below. The manager would like a 95% confidence interval estimate of the mean demand during lead time. Assume that the manager knows that the standard deviation is 50 computers.

DEMAND DURING LEAD TIME

514	493	497	638	514	504	456	460	429	505
525	519	510	476	457	484	512	476	514	529
509	500	490	497	479	555	543	510	510	471
423	474	575	507	505	464	561	556	505	548
441	414	486	490	516	481	392	555	554	479
452	480	481	518	598	505	496	491	486	476

Solution

IDENTIFY

To ultimately determine the optimum inventory level the manager needs to know the mean demand during lead time. Thus, the parameter to be estimated is μ and the interval estimator is

$$\bar{x} \pm z_{\alpha/2} \frac{\sigma}{\sqrt{n}}$$

Using a calculator, we determine the summation $\Sigma x_i = 29,985$. From this we find

$$\bar{x} = \frac{\Sigma x_i}{n} = \frac{29,985}{60} = 499.75$$

The confidence level is set at 95%; thus $1 - \alpha = .95$, $\alpha = .05$, and $\alpha/2 = .025$. From Table 3 in Appendix B or from Table 9.1 we find

$$z_{\alpha/2} = z_{.025} = 1.96$$

The population standard deviation is $\sigma = 50$, and the sample size is 60. Substituting $\bar{x}$, $z_{\alpha/2}$, σ, and n into the confidence interval estimator, we find

SOLVE

$$\bar{x} \pm z_{\alpha/2}\frac{\sigma}{\sqrt{n}} = 499.75 \pm 1.96\frac{50}{\sqrt{60}} = 499.75 \pm 12.65$$

The lower and upper confidence limits are 487.1 and 512.4, respectively.

Excel Output for Example 9.2

	A	B	C	D	E
1	0.95 Confidence Interval Estimate of MU (SIGMA Known)				
2					
3	Sample mean = 499.75				
4	SIGMA = 50				
5	Lower confidence limit = 487.0985				
6	Upper confidence limit = 512.4015				

Minitab Output for Example 9.2

Z Confidence Intervals

The assumed sigma = 50.0

Variable	N	Mean	StDev	SE Mean	95.0 % CI
Demand	60	499.75	42.52	6.45	(487.10, 512.40)

INTERPRET

We estimate that the mean demand during lead time lies between 487.1 and 512.4. From this estimate we can develop a range of inventory levels from which we can choose the one most likely to minimize inventory costs.

▲

INFORMATION AND THE WIDTH OF THE INTERVAL

Interval estimation like all other statistical techniques is designed to convert data into information. However, a wide interval provides little information. For example, suppose that as a result of a statistical study we estimate with 95% confidence that the average starting salary of an accountant lies between $15,000 and $100,000. This interval is so wide that very little information was derived from the data. Suppose, however, that the interval estimate was $42,000 to $45,000. This interval is much narrower, and thus provides accounting students with more precise information about the average starting salary.

The width of the interval estimate is a function of the population standard deviation, the confidence level, and the sample size. Consider Example 9.1 where σ was assumed to be 8.0. The interval estimate was 27.191 ± 1.568. Had σ equaled 16.0 the estimate would change to 27.191 ± 3.136. Thus doubling the population standard deviation has the effect of doubling the width of the interval estimate. This result is quite logical. If there is a great deal of variation in the random variable (reflected by a large standard deviation), it is more difficult to estimate the population mean accurately. That difficulty is translated into a wider interval.

Although we have no control over the value of σ we do have the power to select values for the other two elements. In example 9.1 we chose a 95% confidence level. Had we chosen 99% instead, the interval estimate would be 27.191 ± 2.060. A 90% confidence level results in the interval 27.191 ± 1.316. Decreasing the confidence level will narrow the interval; increasing it widens the interval. A large confidence level, however, is generally desirable since that means a larger proportion of interval estimates that will be correct in the long run. There is a direct relationship between the width of the interval and the confidence level. This is because in order to be more confident in the estimate we need to widen the interval. (The analogy is that to be more likely to capture a butterfly we need a larger butterfly net.) The trade-off between increased confidence and the resulting wider interval estimates must be resolved by the manager. As a general rule, however, 95% confidence is considered "standard."

The third element is the sample size. Had the sample size been 400 instead of 100 the interval would have been $27.191 \pm .784$. Increasing the sample size fourfold decreases the width of the interval by half. A larger sample size provides more potential information. The increased amount of information is reflected in a narrower interval. However, there is another trade-off; increasing the sample size increases the sampling cost. We will discuss these issues when we present sample size selection in Section 9.4.

DEVELOPING AN UNDERSTANDING OF STATISTICAL CONCEPTS

The interval estimator is derived directly from the sampling distribution, an algebraic manipulation that will be repeated throughout this book. In Chapter 8, we used the sampling distribution to make probability statements about the sample mean. Although the form has changed, the interval estimator is also a probability statement about the sample mean. It states that there is $1 - \alpha$ probability that the sample mean will be equal to a value such that the interval $\bar{x} - z_{\alpha/2}\sigma/\sqrt{n}$ to $\bar{x} + z_{\alpha/2}\sigma/\sqrt{n}$ will include the population mean. Once the sample mean is computed, the interval acts as the lower and upper limits of the interval estimate of the population mean.

EXERCISES

*Exercises 9.9–9.16 are "what-if" analyses designed to determine what happens to the interval estimate when the confidence level, sample size, and standard deviation change. These problems can be solved manually or using Excel's **Inference from Summary Statistics (Workbook)** option.*

9.9 Suppose that the amount of time teenagers spend working at part-time jobs is normally distributed with a standard deviation of 20 minutes. A random sample of 100 observations is drawn and the sample mean computed as 125 minutes. Determine the 95% interval estimate of the population mean.

9.10 Repeat Exercise 9.9 using a 90% confidence level.

9.11 Repeat Exercise 9.9 using a 99% confidence level.

9.12 Repeat Exercise 9.9 changing the population standard deviation to 10.

9.13 Repeat Exercise 9.9 changing the population standard deviation to 40.

9.14 Repeat Exercise 9.9 assuming a sample size of 25.

9.15 Repeat Exercise 9.9 assuming a sample size of 400.

9.16 Summarize Exercises 9.9–9.15 by describing what happens to the width of the interval estimate when each of the following happens.

a The confidence level increases.

b The standard deviation decreases.

c The sample size increases.

9.17 The number of cars sold annually by used car salespeople is normally distributed with a standard deviation of 15. A random sample of 400 salespeople was taken and the mean number of cars sold annually was found to be 75. Find the 95% confidence interval estimate of the population mean. Interpret what the interval estimate tells you.

9.18 It is known that the amount of time needed to change the oil on a car is normally distributed with a standard deviation of 5 minutes. A random sample of 100 oil changes yielded a sample mean of 22 minutes. Compute the 99% confidence interval estimate of the mean of the population.

9.19 The following data represent a random sample of 9 marks (out of 10) on a statistics quiz. The marks are normally distributed with a standard deviation of 2. Estimate the population mean with 90% confidence.

7, 9, 7, 5, 4, 8, 3, 10, 9

9.20 The following observations are the ages of a random sample of eight men in a bar. It is known that the ages are normally distributed with a standard deviation of 10. Determine the 95% confidence interval estimate of the population mean. Interpret what the interval estimate tells you.

52, 68, 22, 35, 30, 56, 39, 48

The following exercises require the use of a computer and software. The answers may be calculated manually. See Appendix A for the sample statistics.

9.21 A survey of 400 statistics professors was undertaken. Each was asked how much time was devoted to teaching graphical techniques. We believe that the times are normally distributed with a standard deviation of 30 minutes. The data are stored in file XR09-21. Estimate the population mean with 95% confidence.

9.22 In a survey conducted to determine, among other things, the cost of vacations, 64 individuals were randomly sampled. Each person was asked to compute the cost of her or his most recent vacation. The data are stored in file XR09-22. Assuming that the standard deviation is $400, estimate with 95% confidence the average cost of all vacations.

9.23 In an article about *disinflation,* various investments were examined. The investments included stocks, bonds, and real estate. Suppose that a random sample of 200 rates of return on real estate investments were computed and stored in file XR09-23. Assuming that the standard deviation of all rates of return on real estate investments is 2.1%, estimate the mean rate of return on all real estate investments with 90% confidence. Interpret the estimate.

9.24 A statistics professor is in the process of investigating how many classes university students miss each semester. To help answer this question, she took a random sample of 100 university students and asked each to report how many classes he or she had missed in the previous semester. These data are stored in file XR09-24. Estimate the mean number of classes missed by all students at the university. Use a 99% confidence level and assume that the population standard deviation is known to be 2.2 classes.

9.25 As part of a project to develop better lawn fertilizers, a research chemist wanted to determine the mean weekly growth rate of Kentucky bluegrass, a common type of grass. A sample of 250 blades of grass was measured, and the amount of growth in 1 week was recorded. These data are stored in file XR09-25. Assuming that weekly growth is normally distributed with a standard deviation of .10 inches, estimate with 99% confidence the mean weekly growth of Kentucky bluegrass. Briefly interpret what the interval estimate tells you about the growth of Kentucky bluegrass.

9.26 A time study of a large production facility was undertaken to determine the mean time required to assemble a widget. A random sample of the times to assemble 50 widgets was recorded and stored in file XR09-26. An analysis of the assembly times reveals that they are normally distributed with a standard deviation of 1.3 minutes. Estimate with 95% confidence the mean assembly time for all widgets. What do your results tell you about the assembly times?

9.4 SELECTING THE SAMPLE SIZE

As we discussed in the previous section if the interval estimate is too wide it provides little information. In Example 9.2 the interval estimate was 487.1 to 512.4. If the manager is to use this estimate as input for an inventory model, he needs greater precision. Fortunately, statisticians can control the width of the interval by determining the sample size necessary to produce narrow intervals. Suppose that before gathering the data the manager decided that he needed to estimate the mean demand to within 5 units of the true value. The phrase "to within 5 units" means that the interval estimate is

$$\bar{x} \pm 5$$

That is, the manager has specified the quantity following the plus/minus sign to be 5. The formula for the interval estimate of μ is

$$\bar{x} \pm z_{\alpha/2} \frac{\sigma}{\sqrt{n}}$$

It follows, therefore, that

$$z_{\alpha/2} \frac{\sigma}{\sqrt{n}} = 5$$

After some algebra the equation becomes

$$n = \left(\frac{z_{\alpha/2}\sigma}{5} \right)^2$$

We have specified the confidence level to be 95%, thus $z_{\alpha/2} = 1.96$. The value of σ is 50. Thus,

$$n = \left(\frac{(1.96)(50)}{5} \right)^2 = 384$$

To produce the 95% confidence interval estimate of the mean $\bar{x} \pm 5$ we need to sample 384 lead time periods. Notice that all that is left to be done is to take the sample and calculate the sample mean. If the sample mean is, say, 510 the interval estimate becomes 510 ± 5.

To derive a general formula for the sample size needed to estimate a population mean, let W represent the quantity following the $\pm$ sign. With the same algebraic performance we derive the formula for the sample size.

Sample Size to Estimate a Mean

To produce an interval estimator $\bar{x} \pm W$ with $1 - \alpha$ confidence we need a sample size of

$$n = \left(\frac{z_{\alpha/2}\sigma}{W} \right)^2$$

In this chapter we have assumed that we know the value of the population standard deviation. In practice, this is seldom the case. (In Chapter 11 we introduce a more realistic interval estimator of the population mean.) To use the formula above it is frequently necessary to "guesstimate" the value of σ. That is, we must use our knowledge of the variable with which we're dealing to assign some value to σ. Unfortunately, we cannot be very precise in this guess. However, in guesstimating the value of σ we prefer to err on the high side. To understand why consider the following example.

▼ **EXAMPLE 9.3**

Lumber companies need to be able to estimate the amount of lumber that they can harvest in a tract of land to determine whether the effort will be profitable. To do so, they must estimate the mean diameter of the trees. The company decides to estimate that parameter to within 1 inch with 99% confidence. A forester familiar with the territory guesses that the diameters of the trees are normally distributed with a standard deviation of 6 inches. How large a sample should be taken?

Solution The confidence level is 99% ($1 - \alpha = .99$). Thus $\alpha = .01$ and $\alpha/2 = .005$. It follows that $z_{\alpha/2} = 2.575$. Substituting this quantity, $W = 1$, and $\sigma = 6$, we compute

$$n = \left(\frac{z_{\alpha/2}\sigma}{W}\right)^2 = \left(\frac{2.575 \times 6}{1}\right)^2 = 239$$

To estimate with 99% confidence the mean of a normal population whose standard deviation is assumed to be 6 requires a random sample of 239 trees. From the data the sample mean will be computed and ultimately the interval estimator will be produced. If the standard deviation is actually 6 inches, the interval estimate will be $\bar{x} \pm 1$.

However, if the standard deviation is actually a number larger than 6, the interval estimator will be wider than planned and thus less precise and useful. To illustrate, suppose that after sampling the trees we discover that σ is actually 12 inches. The interval estimator becomes

$$\bar{x} \pm z_{\alpha/2}\frac{\sigma}{\sqrt{n}} = \bar{x} \pm 2.575\frac{12}{\sqrt{239}} = \bar{x} \pm 2$$

which is twice the width we had planned.

If we discover that the standard deviation is less than we assumed when we determined the sample size, the interval estimator will be narrower and, therefore, more precise. In the example above, if σ is actually 3 inches the interval estimator becomes

$$\bar{x} \pm z_{\alpha/2}\frac{\sigma}{\sqrt{n}} = \bar{x} \pm 2.575\frac{3}{\sqrt{239}} = \bar{x} \pm 0.5$$

Although this means that we have sampled more trees than needed the additional cost is relatively low when compared to the value of the information derived.

▲

EXERCISES

9.27 Determine the sample size that is required to estimate a population mean to within 0.2 units with 90% confidence when the standard deviation is 1.0.

9.28 Find n, given that we want to estimate μ to within 10 units, with 95% confidence, and assuming that $\sigma = 100$.

9.29 Determine the sample size necessary to estimate a population mean to within 5 units, with 99% confidence. We believe that the population standard deviation is 50 units.

9.30 Refer to Exercise 9.29. Suppose that the mean of the sample taken is 100.

   a Determine the 99% confidence interval estimate of the mean.

   b You should have answered part (a) in less than 5 seconds. Why?

9.31 Refer to Exercise 9.29. Suppose that after taking the

sample you find that σ is 70 and that $\bar{x} = 100$. Find the 99% confidence interval estimate.

9.32 Refer to Exercise 9.29. Suppose that after taking the sample you find that σ is 20 and that $\bar{x} = 100$. Find the confidence interval estimate.

9.33 A medical statistician wants to estimate the average weight loss of people who are on a new diet plan. In a preliminary study, he guesses that the standard deviation of the population of weight losses is about 10 pounds. How large a sample should he take to estimate the mean weight loss to within 2 pounds, with 90% confidence?

9.34 The operations manager of a large production plant would like to estimate the average amount of time needed by a worker to assemble a new electronic component. After observing a number of workers assembling similar devices, she guesses that the standard deviation is 6 minutes. How large a sample of workers should she take if she wishes to estimate the mean assembly time to within 20 seconds? Assume that the confidence level is to be 99%.

9.35 A statistics professor wants to compare today's students with those 25 years ago. All of his current students' marks are stored on a computer so that he can easily determine the population mean. However, the marks 25 years ago reside only in his musty files. He does not want to retrieve all the marks and will be satisfied with a 95% confidence interval estimate of the mean mark 25 years ago. If he assumes that the population standard deviation is 12, how large a sample should he take to estimate the mean to within 2 marks?

9.36 A medical researcher wants to investigate the amount of time it takes for patients' headache pain to be relieved after taking a new prescription painkiller. She plans to use statistical methods to estimate the mean of the population of relief times. She believes that the population is normally distributed with a standard deviation of 20 minutes. How large a sample should she take to achieve 90% confidence to within 1 minute?

9.5 SIMULATION EXPERIMENTS (OPTIONAL)

The simulation experiments in this section are designed to reinforce some of the concepts introduced earlier in this chapter. We begin by recycling some of the experiments described in Chapter 8.

UNBIASEDNESS

▼ SIMULATION EXPERIMENT 9.1

You can demonstrate that the sample mean is an unbiased estimator of the population mean by repeating Simulation Experiment 8.4 and noting the average value of the sample means.

Report for Simulation Experiment 9.1

1 What is the mean of the population you have sampled?

2 If the sample mean is an unbiased estimator of the population mean, what value did you expect as output when you computed the mean of the sample means?

3 What conclusion can you draw form this experiment?

▲

▼ SIMULATION EXPERIMENT 9.2

To demonstrate that the sample variance is an unbiased estimator of the population variance repeat Simulation Experiment 8.4 but calculate the row variances instead of the row means. In Excel at step 5 type

= VAR(A1:I1)

to calculate the variance of samples of size 9. Don't draw the histogram—simply output the mean of the sample variances.

Minitab does not compute row variances, but does calculate row standard deviations. Using the menu commands at step 7 type **Standard deviation** instead of **Mean**. Square the standard deviations to produce the variances. Calculate the mean of the sample variances.

1 What is the variance of the population you have sampled?

2 If the sample variance is an unbiased estimator of the population variance, what value did you expect as output when you computed the mean of the sample variances?

3 What conclusion can you draw from this experiment?

▲

RELATIVE EFFICIENCY

▼ SIMULATION EXPERIMENT 9.3

In discussing relative efficiency we pointed out that the median is an unbiased estimator of the population mean. Repeat Simulation Experiment 8.4 again but compute the median instead of the mean or variance. In Excel type

= MEDIAN(A1:I1)

In Minitab type **Median** instead of **Mean**.

**Report for Simulation
Experiment 9.3**

1 Does it appear that the sampling distribution of the median is normal?

2 What are the mean and standard deviation of the sampling distribution of the median?

3 Compare the mean and standard deviation of the sampling distribution of the median with the mean and standard deviation of the sampling distribution of the mean (Simulation Experiment 8.4).

4 What does this experiment tell you about the relationship between the sampling distribution of the mean and the sampling distribution of the median when sampling from the same normal population and identical sample sizes?

▲

INTERVAL ESTIMATES

One of the fundamental concepts of statistical inference is that the interval estimate does not always include the value of the parameter we're trying to estimate. That means, for example, that the process that produces 95% confidence intervals will produce intervals that contain the true value of the parameter 95% of the time. The remaining 5% of the time, the interval estimate will be incorrect. The objective of the next experiment is to demonstrate 90% confidence interval estimates.

We will generate 1,000 samples of 9 observations from a normal population with mean 100 and standard deviation 25. For each sample we will compute the 90% confidence interval estimator, which is

$$\bar{x} \pm 1.645\frac{\sigma}{\sqrt{n}} = \bar{x} \pm 1.645\frac{25}{\sqrt{9}} = \bar{x} \pm 13.71$$

The computer will then be instructed to count the number of intervals that include the true value of the population mean, which is $\mu = 100$.

▼ SIMULATION EXPERIMENT 9.4

Excel Instructions   Repeat the first 6 steps of Simulation Experiment 8.4. At this point you should have the row means computed in column J.

7 In column K calculate the lower confidence limit LCL = $\bar{x}$ − 13.71. In cell K1 type **=J1−13.71** and drag to fill the column.

8 In column L calculate the upper confidence limit UCL = $\bar{x}$ + 13.71. In cell L1 type **=J1+13.71** and drag.

9 In column M type **=AND(KI < 100, LI > 100)** and drag to fill the column.

If K1 (lower confidence limit) is less than 100 and L1 (upper confidence limit) is greater than 100, the word **TRUE** will be recorded in column M. If not, the word **FALSE** will be recorded.

10 Click **f, Statistical, COUNTIF,** and **Next>.**

11 Specify the range of the column where the words **TRUE** and **FALSE** are stored: **M1:M1000**.

12 Specify the criteria: **TRUE.**

13 Click **OK.**

Steps 9 through 13 count the number of times the word **TRUE** appears in the last column. Thus, it counts the number of intervals that include the true value of μ.

Minitab Instructions   Repeat the first 9 steps of Simulation Experiment 8.4, which will store the sample means in column 10.

10 Click **Calc** and **Calculator . . . .**

11 Type **C11 (Store results in variable:)**

12 Hit **tab** and type **C10 − 13.71. Click OK.**

13 Click **Calc** and **Calculator . . . .**

14 Type **C12 (Store results in variable:)**

15 Hit **tab** and type **C10 + 13.74. Click OK.**

16 Click **Calc** and **Calculator . . . .**

17 Type **C13 (Store results in variable:)**

18 Hit **tab** and type **(C11 < 100) AND (C12 > 100). Click OK**

19 Click **Stat, Tables,** and **Tally . . . .**

20 Type **C13** and use the cursor to specify **Percents.** Click **OK.**

Columns 11 and 12 contain the lower and upper confidence limits, respectively. Column 13 uses comparison and logical operators to count the number of interval estimates that are correct. If the value in column 11 (lower confidence limit) is less than 100 and the value in column 12 (upper confidence limit) is greater than 100, a 1 will be recorded in column 13. If not, a 0 will be recorded. Thus, a 1 in column 13 indicates an interval estimate that includes the true value of μ, which is 100. Minitab counts the number of 1s and 0s in column 13 and prints the percentages.

Report for Simulation Experiment 9.4

1 What is the number of intervals containing the true population mean you anticipated seeing?

2 What is the number of intervals containing the true population mean observed in this experiment?

3 What conclusions can you draw from this experiment?

▲

▼ **SIMULATION EXPERIMENT 9.5**

Repeat Simulation Experiment 9.4 using a confidence level of 95%. The 95% confidence interval estimator is

$$\bar{x} \pm 1.96\frac{\sigma}{\sqrt{n}} = \bar{x} \pm 1.96\frac{25}{\sqrt{9}} = \bar{x} \pm 16.33$$

Write a brief report describing your findings.

▲

9.6 SUMMARY

This chapter introduced the concepts of estimation and the estimator of a population mean when the population variance is known. It also presented a formula to calculate the sample size necessary to estimate a population mean. Both formulas are shown below.

IMPORTANT TERMS

Estimate   *286*

Point estimator   *286*

Interval estimator   *286*

Unbiased estimator   *287*

Consistency   *288*

Relative efficiency   *288*

Interval estimator of μ *290*

Confidence level   *290*

Lower confidence limit (LCL)   *290*

Upper confidence limit (UCL)   *290*

95% Confidence interval estimator
 of μ *291*

Sample size to estimate a mean   *303*

SUMMARY OF FORMULAS

Interval Estimator of μ and the Formula to Determine the Sample Size to Estimate μ

Interval estimator of μ: $\bar{x} \pm z_{\alpha/2}\dfrac{\sigma}{\sqrt{n}}$

Sample size to estimate μ: $n = \left(\dfrac{z_{\alpha/2}\sigma}{W}\right)^2$

SUPPLEMENTARY EXERCISES

The following exercises require the use of a computer and software. The answers may be calculated manually. See Appendix A for the sample statistics.

9.37 The image of the Japanese manager is that of a workaholic with little or no leisure time. In a survey, a random sample of 250 Japanese middle managers was asked how many hours per week they spent in leisure activities (e.g., sports, movies, television). The results of the survey are stored in file XR09-37. Assuming that the population standard deviation is 6 hours, estimate with 90% confidence the mean leisure time per week for all Japanese middle managers. What do these results tell you?

9.38 One measure of physical fitness is the amount of time it takes for the pulse rate to return to normal after exercise. A random sample of 100 women aged 40–50 exercised on stationary bicycles for 30 minutes. The amount of time for their pulse rates to return to pre-exercise levels was measured and recorded. The data are stored in file XR09-38. If the times are normally distributed with a standard deviation of 2.3 minutes, estimate with 99% confidence the true mean pulse-recovery time for all 40- to 50-year-old women. Interpret the results.

9.39 A survey of 20 randomly selected companies asked them to report the annual income of their presidents. These data are stored in file XR09-39. Assuming that incomes are normally distributed with a standard deviation of $30,000, determine the 90% confidence interval estimate of the mean annual income of all company presidents. Interpret the statistical results.

9.40 The operations manager of a plant making cellular telephones has proposed rearranging the production process to make it more efficient. She wants to estimate the time to assemble the telephone using the new arrangement. She believes that the population standard deviation is 15 seconds. How large a sample of workers should she take to estimate the mean assembly time to within 2 seconds with 95% confidence?

9.41 A random sample of 300 business executives was asked how many vacation days they take annually. The results are stored in file XR09-41. Estimate with 95% confidence the mean number of vacation days all business executives take annually if the population standard deviation is known to be 5 days. What do the statistics tell you about the population in question?

9.42 To help make a decision about expansion plans, the president of a music company needs to know how many compact discs teenagers buy annually. Accordingly, he commissions a survey of 250 teenagers. Each is asked to report how many CDs he or she purchased in the previous 12 months. The responses are stored in file XR09-42. Estimate with 90% confidence the mean annual number of CDs purchased by all teenagers. Assume that the population standard deviation is three CDs.

9.43 The label on 1-gallon cans of paint states that the amount of paint in the can is sufficient to paint 400 square feet. However, this number is quite variable. In fact, the amount of coverage is known to be approximately normally distributed with standard deviation of 25 square feet. How large a sample should be taken to estimate the true mean coverage of all 1-gallon cans to within 5 square feet with 95% confidence.

9.44 Refer to Exercise 9.43. Suppose that a random sample of one hundred 1-gallon cans of paint was drawn and used to paint walls. The amount of coverage for each can was recorded and stored in file XR09-44. Estimate the mean coverage with 95% confidence.

Chapter **10**

Introduction to

Hypothesis

Testing

10.1 Introduction

10.2 Concepts of Hypothesis Testing

10.3 Testing the Population Mean When the Population Standard Deviation Is Known

10.4 Calculating the Probability of a Type II Error

10.5 The Road Ahead

10.6 Summary

10.1 INTRODUCTION

In Chapter 9, we introduced estimation and showed how it is used. Now we're going to present the second general procedure of making inferences about a population—hypothesis testing. The purpose of this type of inference is to determine whether enough statistical evidence exists to enable us to conclude that a belief or hypothesis about a parameter is reasonable. Examples of hypothesis testing include the following.

Example 1   Thousands of new products are developed every year. For a variety of reasons, most never reach the market. Products that reach the final stages are evaluated by marketing managers who attempt to predict how well the product will sell. Statistics in general, and hypothesis testing specifically, often help in this assessment. Suppose that a company has developed a new product that it hopes will be very successful. After a complete financial analysis, the company's directors have determined that if more than 12% of potential customers buy the product, the company will make a profit. A random sample of potential customers is asked whether they would buy the product. The sampling procedure and data collection would be as described in Chapter 5. Statistical techniques would convert the raw data into information that would permit the marketing manager to decide whether to proceed. The parameter is the proportion of customers who would buy the product. The hypothesis to test is that the proportion is greater than 12%. In Chapter 11, we present the technique that would be used in this example.

Example 2   Scientific and medical discoveries are tested to determine whether they are improvements over current technology. When a new drug is developed, it is usually tested to determine whether it is effective. The test is conducted by selecting a random sample of patients suffering from the disease that the drug is intended to cure. Half the sample is given the new drug and the other half is given a placebo, which looks like a drug but contains no medication. The experiment is called a "double-blind" experiment because neither the patients nor the doctors know which patients are taking the drug and which the placebo. The effectiveness of each is then measured. We can measure the degree of improvement and compute means or we can count the number of patients cured and determine proportions. In either case, we compare the two samples, and using methods presented in Chapter 12, we can infer whether the new drug works.

Example 3   Forecasting is one of the most important topics in statistics. Managers often need forecasts of product demand, commodity prices, and general economic activity to help make decisions. Economists and statisticians create equations called mathematical models that are designed to forecast. Hypothesis testing is used extensively in evaluating how well the model is likely to perform. Suppose that a stock analyst wants to predict the return on a particular investment. The analyst would collect data for a variety of variables that she thinks are related to return on investment. Using techniques introduced in Chapters 17, 18, and 19, she would develop the model. She would conduct various tests of hypotheses to determine whether the model is likely to produce accurate forecasts.

In the next section, we will introduce the concepts of hypothesis testing, and in Section 10.3 we will develop the method employed to test a hypothesis about a population mean when the population standard deviation is known. The rest of the chapter deals with related topics.

10.2 CONCEPTS OF HYPOTHESIS TESTING

In Chapter 9 we introduced estimation, the first form of statistical inference. In this chapter we present the second form, **hypothesis testing.** This term may be new to most readers, but the concepts underlying hypothesis testing are quite familiar. Various nonstatistical applications use hypothesis testing, the best known of which is a criminal trial.

When a person is accused of a crime, he or she faces a trial. The prosecution presents its case and a jury must make a decision on the basis of the evidence presented. In fact, the jury conducts a hypothesis test; actually, two hypotheses are tested. The first is called the **null hypothesis** represented by H_0. It is

H_0: The defendant is innocent

The second is called the **alternative** or **research hypothesis** denoted by H_1. In a criminal trial it is

H_1: The defendant is guilty

Of course, the jury does not know which hypothesis is correct. They must make a decision on the basis of evidence presented by both the prosecution and defense. There are only two possible decisions: Convict or acquit the defendant. In statistical parlance convicting the defendant is equivalent to *rejecting; the null hypothesis in favor of the alternative.* When a jury acquits a defendant, a statistician says that we *don't reject the null hypothesis.* Notice that we do not say that we accept the null hypothesis. In a criminal trial that would be interpreted as finding the defendant innocent. Our justice system does not allow this decision.

When testing hypotheses there are two possible errors. A **Type I error** occurs when we reject a true null hypothesis. A **Type II error** is defined as not rejecting a false null hypothesis. In the criminal trial, a Type I error is made when an innocent person is wrongly convicted. A Type II errors occurs when a guilty defendant is acquitted. The probability of a Type I error is denoted by α, which is called the *significance level.* The probability of a Type II error is denoted by β (Greek *beta*). α and β are inversely related, meaning that any attempt to reduce one will increase the other.

In our justice system Type I errors are regarded as more serious. As a consequence the system is set up so that the probability of a Type I error is small. This is arranged by placing the burden of proof on the prosecution (the prosecution must prove guilt—the defense need not prove anything) and by having judges instruct the jury to find the defendant guilty only if there is "evidence beyond a reasonable doubt." In the absence of enough evidence, the jury must acquit even though there may be some evidence of guilt. The consequence of this arrangement is that the probability of acquitting guilty people is relatively large. Oliver Wendell Holmes, a U.S. Supreme Court justice, once phrased the relationship between the probabilities of Type I and Type II errors in the following way. "Better to acquit a hundred guilty men than convict one innocent one." In Justice Holmes's opinion the probability of a Type I error should be 1/100 of the probability of a Type II error.

The critical concepts are these.

1 There are two hypotheses. One is called the null hypothesis and the other the alternative or research hypothesis.

2 The testing procedure assumes that the null hypothesis is true.

3 The goal of the process is to determine whether there is enough evidence to infer that the alternative hypothesis is true.

4 There are two possible decisions:

> Reject the null hypothesis in favor of the alternative.
> Do not reject the null hypothesis in favor of the alternative.

5 Two possible errors can be made in any test. Type I errors occur when we reject a true null hypothesis and Type II errors occur when we don't reject a false null hypothesis.

Let's extend these concepts to statistical hypothesis testing.

In statistics we frequently test hypotheses about parameters. (It is too early in the pedagogy to discuss variations that do not involve parameters.) The hypotheses we test are generated by questions that managers need to answer. To illustrate, suppose that in Example 9.1 the marketing manager did not want to estimate the mean amount of time spent watching television, but instead wanted to know whether the mean exceeds 25 hours, which may be the point at which the child sees some critical number of commercials. That is, the manager wants to determine whether he can infer that $\mu > 25$. As was the case with the criminal trial, whatever we're investigating is specified as the alternative (research) hypothesis. Thus,

$$H_1 : \mu > 25$$

Had the manager wanted to determine whether the mean is *less than* 25 he would have set up the alternative hypothesis as

$$H_1 : \mu < 25$$

If he wanted to know whether the mean *differs from* 25 the alternative hypothesis would be

$$H_1 : \mu \neq 25$$

To test the alternative hypothesis we employ the sampling distribution of the mean. We do so by assuming that the mean television time is equal to 25. (In the criminal trial we assume that the defendant is innocent.) This is represented by the null hypothesis. That is,

$$H_0 : \mu = 25$$

Why do we need the null hypothesis if we want to know whether the alternative hypothesis is true? Because the sampling distribution requires us to assume that μ is a specific value. In this case we will assume its value is 25.

The next element in the procedure is to randomly sample the population and calculate the sample mean. This is called the **test statistic.** The test statistic is the criterion on which we base our decision about the hypotheses. (In the criminal trial analogy this is equivalent to the evidence presented in the case.) The test statistic is based on the best estimator of the parameter. In Chapter 9 we stated that the best estimator of a population mean is the sample mean.

If the test statistic's value is inconsistent with the null hypothesis we reject it and infer that the alternative hypothesis is true. For example, if we're trying to decide whether the mean is greater than 25, a large value of $\bar{x}$ (say, 35) would provide evidence that the null hypothesis is false and that the alternative is true. If the test statistic value is consistent with the null hypothesis, we do not reject the null. For instance, if $\bar{x}$ is close to 25 (say, 25.4) we could not say that this provides a great deal of evidence to infer that the mean is greater than 25. In the absence of sufficient evidence we do not reject the null hypothesis in favor of the alternative. (In the absence of sufficient evidence of guilt a jury finds the defendant not guilty.)

In a criminal trial "sufficient evidence" is defined as "evidence beyond a reasonable doubt." In statistics we need to use the test statistic's sampling distribution to define "sufficient evidence." We do so in the next section.

10.3 TESTING THE POPULATION MEAN WHEN THE POPULATION STANDARD DEVIATION IS KNOWN

To illustrate the process, consider the following example.

▼ EXAMPLE 10.1

The manager of a department store is thinking about establishing a new billing system for the store's credit customers. After a thorough financial analysis, she determines that the new system will be cost effective only if the mean monthly account is more than $170. A random sample of 400 monthly accounts is drawn for which the sample mean is $178. (The data are stored in file XM10-01.) The manager knows that the accounts are approximately normally distributed with a standard deviation of $65. Can the manager conclude from this that the new system will be cost effective?

Solution

IDENTIFY

This example deals with the population of the credit accounts at the store. To conclude that the system will be cost effective requires the manager to show that the mean account for all customers is greater than $170. Consequently, we set up the alternative hypothesis to express this circumstance.

$$H_1 : \mu > 170$$

The null hypothesis must specify a single value for the parameter. Thus the null hypothesis is

$$H_0 : \mu = 170$$

As we pointed out earlier, the test statistic is the best estimator of the parameter. In Chapter 8, we used the sample mean to estimate the population mean. To conduct this test we ask and answer the following question: "Is a sample mean of 178 sufficiently greater than 170 to allow us to confidently infer that the population mean is greater than 170?"

There are two approaches to answering this question. The first is called the *rejection region method*. It can be used in conjunction with the computer but it is mandatory for those computing statistics manually. The second is the *p-value approach*, which in general can only be employed in conjunction with a computer and statistical software. We recommend, however, that users of statistical software be familiar with both approaches.

REJECTION REGION METHOD

It seems reasonable to reject the null hypothesis if the value of the sample mean is large relative to 170. If we had calculated the sample mean to be, say, 500, it would be quite apparent that the null hypothesis is false and we would reject it. On the other hand, values of $\bar{x}$ close to 170, such as 171 do not allow us to reject the null hypothesis because it is entirely possible to observe a sample mean of 171 from a population whose mean is 170. Unfortunately, the decision is not always so obvious. In this example, the sample mean was calculated to be 178, a value apparently neither very far away from nor very close to 170. In order to make a decision about this sample mean we set up the **rejection region.**

Rejection Region

The **rejection region** is a range of values such that if the test statistic falls into that range, we decide to reject the null hypothesis in favor of the alternative hypothesis.

Suppose we define the value of the sample mean that is just large enough to reject the null hypothesis as $\bar{x}_L$. ($\bar{x}_L$ is called the *critical value* of $\bar{x}$.) The rejection region is

$$\bar{x} > \bar{x}_L$$

Since a Type I error is defined as rejecting a true null hypothesis, and the probability of committing a Type I error is α, it follows that

$$\alpha = P(\text{rejecting } H_0 \text{ given that } H_0 \text{ is true})$$
$$= P(\bar{x} > \bar{x}_L \text{ given that } \mu = 170)$$

Figure 10.1 depicts the sampling distribution and the rejection region.

From Section 8.2, we know that the sampling distribution of $\bar{x}$ is normal or approximately normal, with mean μ, and standard deviation $\sigma/\sqrt{n}$. As a result, we can standardize $\bar{x}$ and obtain the following probability:

$$P\left(\frac{\bar{x} - \mu}{\sigma/\sqrt{n}} > \frac{\bar{x}_L - \mu}{\sigma/\sqrt{n}}\right) = P\left(Z > \frac{\bar{x}_L - \mu}{\sigma/\sqrt{n}}\right) = \alpha$$

From Section 7.3, we have

$$P(Z > z_\alpha) = \alpha$$

Since both probability statements involve the same distribution (standard normal) and the same probability (α), it follows that the limits are identical. Thus,

$$\frac{\bar{x}_L - \mu}{\sigma/\sqrt{n}} = z_\alpha$$

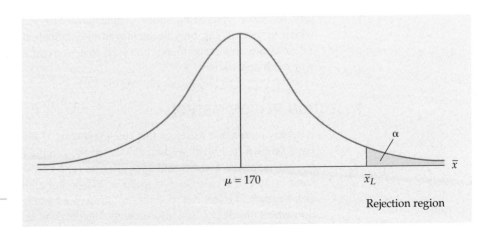

Figure 10.1

Sampling distribution for Example 10.1

SOLVE

We know that $\sigma = 65$ and $n = 400$. Because the probabilities defined above are conditional on the null hypothesis being true, we have $\mu = 170$. To calculate the rejection region, we need a value of α. Suppose that the supervisor chose α to be 5%. It follows that $z_\alpha = z_{.05} = 1.645$. We can now find the value $\bar{x}_L$.

$$\frac{\bar{x}_L - \mu}{\sigma/\sqrt{n}} = z_\alpha$$

$$\frac{\bar{x}_L - 170}{65/\sqrt{400}} = 1.645$$

$$\bar{x}_L = 175.34$$

Therefore, the rejection region is

$$\bar{x} > 175.34$$

The sample mean was computed to be 178. Since the test statistic (sample mean) is in the rejection region (it is greater than 175.34), we reject the null hypothesis. Thus, there is sufficient evidence to infer that the mean monthly account is greater than 170.

Our calculations determined that any value of $\bar{x}$ above 175.34 represents an event that is quite unlikely when sampling from a population whose mean is 170. This suggests that the assumption that the null hypothesis is true is incorrect, and in that case we reject the null hypothesis.

THE STANDARDIZED TEST STATISTIC

The preceding test used the test statistic $\bar{x}$. As a result, the rejection region had to be set up in terms of $\bar{x}$. An easier method to use specifies that the test statistic be the standardized value of $\bar{x}$. That is, we use the **standardized test statistic**

$$z = \frac{\bar{x} - \mu}{\sigma/\sqrt{n}}$$

and the rejection region consists of all values of z that are greater than z_α. Algebraically, the rejection region is

$$z > z_\alpha$$

We can redo Example 10.1 using the standardized test statistic.

$H_0 : \mu = 170$

$H_1 : \mu > 170$

Test statistic: $z = \dfrac{\bar{x} - \mu}{\sigma/\sqrt{n}}$

Rejection region: $z > z_\alpha = z_{.05} = 1.645$

Value of the test statistic: $z = \dfrac{\bar{x} - \mu}{\sigma/\sqrt{n}} = \dfrac{178 - 170}{65/\sqrt{400}} = 2.46$

Conclusion: Since 2.46 is greater than 1.645, reject the null hypothesis and conclude that there is enough evidence to infer that the mean monthly account is greater than $170.

As you can see, the conclusions we draw from using the test statistic $\bar{x}$ and the standardized test statistic z are identical. Figures 10.2 and 10.3 depict the two sampling distributions, highlighting the equivalence of the two tests.

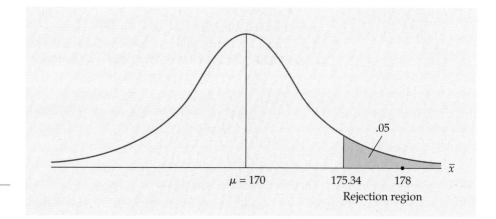

Figure 10.2

Sampling distribution of $\bar{x}$ for Example 10.1

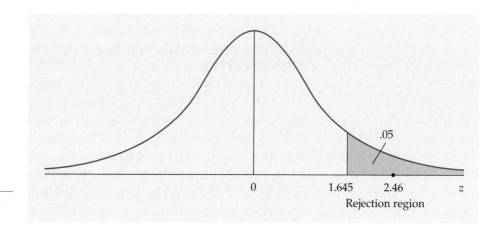

Figure 10.3

Sampling distribution of z, for Example 10.1

Because of its convenience and because statistical software packages employ them, the standardized test statistic will be used throughout this book. For simplicity we will refer to the *standardized test statistic* simply as the *test statistic.*

Incidentally, when a null hypothesis is rejected, the test is said to be *statistically significant* at whatever significance level the test was conducted at. Summarizing Example 10.1 we would say that the test was significant at the 5% significance level.

p-VALUE METHOD

There are several drawbacks to the rejection region method. Foremost among them is the type of information provided by the result of the test. The rejection region method produces a "yes" or "no" response to the question "Is there sufficient statistical evidence to infer that the alternative hypothesis is true?" The implication is that the result of the test of hypothesis will be converted automatically into one of two possible courses of action: one action as a result of rejecting the null hypothesis in favor of the alternative, and another as a result of not rejecting the null hypothesis in favor of the alternative. In Example 10.1 the rejection of the null hypothesis seems to imply that the new billing system will be installed.

In fact, this is not the way in which the result of a statistical analysis is utilized. The statistical procedure is only one of several factors considered by a manager when making a decision. In Example 10.1 the manager discovered that there was enough statistical evidence to conclude that the mean monthly account is greater than 170. However, before taking any action the manager would probably consider a number of factors including the cost and feasibility of restructuring the billing system and the possibility of making an error, in this case a Type I error.

What is needed to take full advantage of the information available from the test result and make a better decision is a measure of the amount of statistical evidence supporting the alternative hypothesis so that it can be weighed in relation to the other factors, especially the economic ones. The **p-value of a test** provides this measure.

---

p-Value

The **p-value of a test** is the probability of observing a test statistic at least as extreme as the one computed given that the null hypothesis is true.

In Example 10.1 the p-value is the probability of observing a sample mean at least as large as 178 when the population mean is 170. Thus,

$$p\text{-value} = P(\bar{X} > 178) = P\left(\frac{\bar{X} - \mu}{\sigma/\sqrt{n}} > \frac{178 - 170}{65/\sqrt{400}}\right) = P(Z > 2.46) = .0069$$

Figure 10.4 describes this calculation.

INTERPRETING THE p-VALUE

To interpret the results of an inferential procedure properly, you must remember that the technique is based on the sampling distribution—and the sampling distribution allows us to make probability statements about a sample statistic assuming knowledge of the population parameter. Thus, the probability of observing a sample mean at least as large as 178 from a population whose mean is 170 is .0069, which is very small. In other words, we have just observed an unlikely event, an event so unlikely that we must doubt the assumption that began the process. Recall that we assume that the null

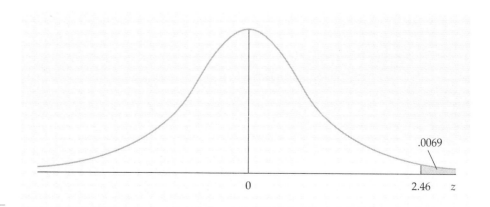

Figure 10.4

p-value for Example 10.1

hypothesis is true in order to calculate the value of the test statistic. Consequently, we have reason to reject the null hypothesis and support the alternative hypothesis.

Students may be tempted to simplify the interpretation by stating that the p-value is the probability that the null hypothesis is true. Don't! As was the case with interpreting the interval estimator, you cannot make a probability statement about a parameter. It is not a random variable.

The p-value of a test provides valuable information because it measures the amount of statistical evidence that supports the alternative hypothesis. To understand this interpretation fully, refer to Table 10.1 where we list several values of $\bar{x}$, their z-statistics, and p-values for Example 10.1. Notice that the closer $\bar{x}$ is to the hypothesized mean 170, the larger the p-value. The farther $\bar{x}$ is above 170, the smaller the p-value. Values of $\bar{x}$ far above 170 tend to indicate that the alternative hypothesis is true. Thus, the smaller the p-value, the more statistical evidence exists to support the alternative hypothesis. Figure 10.5 graphically depicts the information in Table 10.1.

Table 10.1   Test Statistics and p-Values for Example 10.1

Sample Mean $\bar{x}$	Test Statistic $z = \dfrac{\bar{x} - \mu}{\sigma/\sqrt{n}} = \dfrac{\bar{x} - 170}{65/\sqrt{400}}$	p-Value
170	0	.5000
171	0.3077	.3792
172	0.6154	.2692
173	0.9231	.1780
174	1.2308	.1092
175	1.5385	.0620
176	1.8462	.0324
177	2.1538	.0156
178	2.4615	.0069
179	2.7692	.0028
180	3.0769	.0010

This raises the question "How small does the p-value have to be to infer that the alternative hypothesis is true?" In general, the answer depends on a number of factors, including the costs of making Type I and Type II errors. In Example 10.1 a Type I error would occur if the manager adopts the new billing system when it is not cost effective. If the cost of this action is high we attempt to minimize its probability. In the rejection region method we do so by setting the significance level quite low, say, 1%. Using the p-value method we would insist that the p-value be quite small, providing sufficient evidence to infer that the mean monthly account is greater than 170 before proceeding with the new billing system.

DESCRIBING THE p-VALUE

Statisticians can translate p-values into several different descriptive terms.

If the p-value is less than 1%, we say that there is *overwhelming* evidence to infer that the alternative hypothesis is true. We also say that the test is *highly significant*.

If the p-value lies between 1% and 5%, there is *strong* evidence to infer that the alternative hypothesis is true. The result is deemed to be *significant*.

If the p-value is between 5% and 10%, we say that there is *weak* evidence to indicate that the alternative hypothesis is true. When the p-value is greater than 5%, we say that the result is not statistically significant.

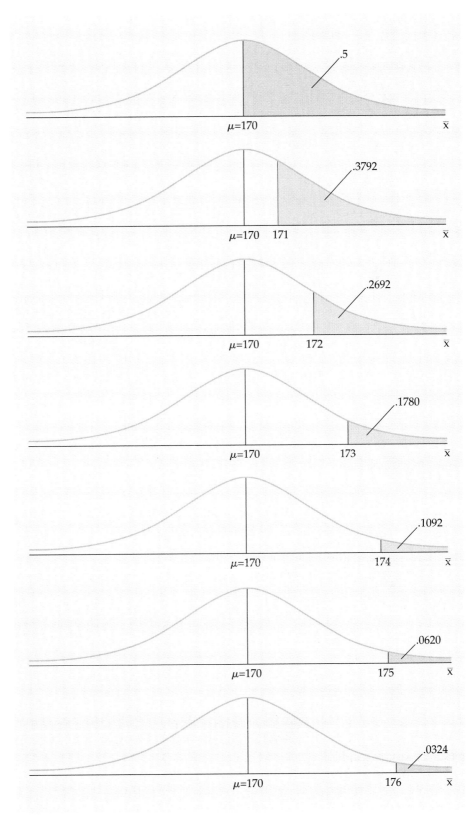

Figure 10.5

p-values for Example 10.1

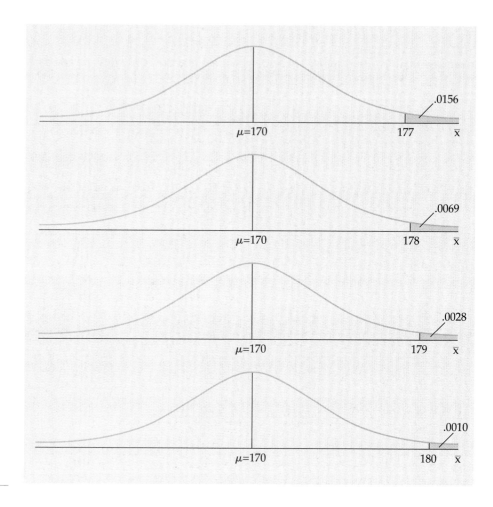

Figure 10.5 (continued)

When the *p*-value exceeds 10%, we say that there is no evidence to infer that the alternative hypothesis is true.

Figure 10.6 summarizes these terms.

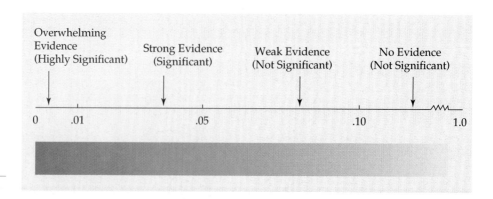

Figure 10.6

Describing the *p*-value of a test

THE *p*-VALUE AND REJECTION REGION METHODS

IDENTIFY

If we so choose we can use the *p*-value to make the same type of decisions we make in the rejection region method. The rejection region method requires the decision maker to select a significance level from which the rejection region is constructed. We then decide to reject or not reject the null hypothesis. Another way of making that type of decision is to compare the *p*-value with the selected value of the significance level. If the *p*-value is less than α we judge the *p*-value to be small enough to reject the null hypothesis. If the *p*-value is greater than α, we do not reject the null hypothesis.

Solving by Hand, Using Excel, and Using Minitab

SOLVE

As you have already seen we offer three ways to solve statistical problems. When we perform the calculations manually we will use the rejection region approach. We will set up the rejection region using the test statistic's sampling distribution and associated probability table (in Appendix B). The calculations will be performed manually and a reject/don't reject decision will be made. In this chapter it is possible to compute the *p*-value of the test manually. However, in later chapters we will be using test statistics that are not normally distributed making it impossible to calculate the *p*-values precisely. (They can be approximated using linear interpolation.) In these instances manual calculations require the decision to be made via the rejection region method only.

Most software packages used to compute statistics, including the two used in this book, Excel and Minitab, print the *p*-value of the test. When we employ the computer we will not set up a rejection region. Instead we will focus on the interpretation of the *p*-value.

Excel Output for Example 10.1

	A	B	C	D	E
1	**Test of Hypothesis About MU (SIGMA Known)**				
2					
3	*Test of MU = 170 Vs MU greater than 170*				
4	*SIGMA = 65*				
5	*Sample mean = 177.9965*				
6	*Test Statistic: z = 2.4605*				
7	*P-Value = 0.0069*				

COMMANDS	COMMANDS FOR EXAMPLE 10.1
1 Type or import the data.	Open file **XM10-01.**
2 Click **Tools, Data Analysis Plus,** and **Inference About a Mean (SIGMA Known).**
3 Specify the input range. Do not include cell containing the variable name.	**A2:A401**
4 Click **Test of Hypothesis.**
5 Specify σ **(SIGMA).**	**65**
6 Specify the value of μ under the null hypothesis.	**170**
7 Click the appropriate alternative hypothesis.	**MU greater than 170**

The printout above was produced from the raw data. That is, we input the 400 observations in the data set and the computer calculated the value of the test statistic and the *p*-value. As was the case with estimation, we can use Excel in another way. Click **Data Analysis Plus** and **Inference from Summary Statistics (Workbook).** Find the sheet **z-Test of a Mean.** You can input the components of the test $\bar{x}$, σ, n and the hypothesized value of μ. The value of z and the two-tail *p*-value (discussed below) will be output. We can also conduct a what-if analysis. Try changing any of the inputs to discover their effects.

Note: Don't forget to click the **Exit** button.

Minitab Output for Example 10.1

Z-Test

```
Test of mu = 170.00 vs mu > 170.00
The assumed sigma = 65.0

Variable      N      Mean    StDev    SE Mean       Z        P
Accounts    400    178.00    68.37       3.25    2.46   0.0070
```

COMMANDS	COMMANDS FOR EXAMPLE 10.1
1 Type or import the data.	Open file **XM10-01.**
2 Click **Stat, Basic Statistics,** and **1-Sample Z . . . .**	
3 Type the variable name **(Variables).**	**Accounts**
4 Use the cursor to choose **Test mean:.**	
5 Hit **tab,** type the value of μ under the null hypothesis.	**170**
6 Use the cursor to select **Alternative:.**	**greater than**
7 Hit **tab** and type the value of σ **(Sigma:). Click OK.**	**65**

INTERPRET

In Example 10.1, we rejected the null hypothesis. Does this prove that the alternative hypothesis is true? The answer is no; because our conclusion is based on sample data (and not on the entire population), we can never prove anything by using statistical inference. Consequently, we summarize the test by stating that there is enough statistical evidence to infer that the null hypothesis is false and that the alternative hypothesis is true.

Now suppose that $\bar{x}$ had equaled 174 instead of 178. We would then have calculated $z = 1.23$ (*p*-value = .1093), which is not in the rejection region. Could we conclude on this basis that there is enough statistical evidence to infer that the null hypothesis is true and hence that $\mu = 170$? Again the answer is no because it is absurd to suggest that a sample mean of 174 provides enough evidence to infer that the population mean is 170. Because we're testing a single value of the parameter under the null hypothesis, we can never have enough statistical evidence to establish that the null hypothesis is true (unless we sample the entire population).

Consequently, if the value of the test statistic does not fall into the rejection region (or the *p*-value is large), rather than say we accept the null hypothesis (which implies that we're stating that the null hypothesis is true) we state that we do not reject the null hypothesis, and we conclude that not enough evidence exists to show that the alternative hypothesis is true. While it may appear that we're being overly technical, such is not the case. Your ability to set up tests of hypotheses properly and to interpret their results correctly very much depends on your understanding of this point. The point is that the conclusion is based on the alternative hypothesis. In the final analysis, there are only two possible conclusions of a hypothesis test.

Conclusions of a Test of Hypothesis

If we reject the null hypothesis, we conclude that there is enough statistical evidence to infer that the alternative hypothesis is true.

If we do not reject the null hypothesis, we conclude that there is not enough statistical evidence to infer that the alternative hypothesis is true.

Observe that, the alternative hypothesis is the more important one. It represents what we are investigating. That is why it is also called the research hypothesis. Whatever you're trying to show statistically must be represented by the alternative hypothesis (bearing in mind that you have only three choices for the alternative hypothesis—the parameter is greater than, less than, or not equal to the value specified in the null hypothesis).

When we introduced statistical inference in Chapter 9, we pointed out that the first step in the solution is to identify the technique. Part of this process when the problem involves hypothesis testing is the specification of the hypotheses. Because the alternative hypothesis represents the condition we're researching, we will identify it first. The null hypothesis automatically follows because the null hypothesis must specify equality. However, by tradition, when we list the two hypotheses, the null hypothesis comes first, followed by the alternative hypothesis. All examples in this book will follow that format.

▼ **EXAMPLE 10.2**

A variety of government agencies are devoted to ensuring that food producers package their products in such a way that the weight or volume of the contents listed on the label is correct. For example, bottles of catsup, whose labels state that the contents have a net weight of 16 ounces, must have a net weight of at least 16 ounces. However, it is impossible to check all packages sold in the country. As a result, statistical techniques are used. A random sample of the product is selected and its contents measured. If the mean of the sample provides sufficient evidence to infer that the mean weight of all bottles is less than 16 ounces, the product label is deemed to be unacceptable. Suppose that a government inspector weighs the contents of a random sample of 25 bottles of catsup labeled "Net weight: 16 ounces" and records the measurements below. (The data are also stored on the data disk in file XM10-02.) The inspector knows from previous experiments that the weights of all catsup bottles are normally distributed with a standard deviation of 0.4 ounces. Can the inspector conclude that the product label is unacceptable?

NET WEIGHT OF "16-OUNCE" CATSUP BOTTLES

15.8	16.0	16.2	15.7	15.4	16.1	16.2	17.3	15.0
16.8	15.6	15.9	16.0	16.2	15.6	16.0	16.8	15.7
15.6	15.3	15.7	15.8	15.6	15.5	15.7		

Solution

The objective of the study is to draw a conclusion about the mean weight of all catsup bottles. Thus, the parameter to be tested is the population mean μ. The government inspector wants to know if there is enough statistical evidence to show that the population mean is less than 16 ounces. Thus, the alternative hypothesis is

$$H_1 : \mu < 16$$

The null hypothesis automatically follows.

$$H_0 : \mu = 16$$

The test statistic is the only one we've presented thus far. It is

$$z = \frac{\bar{x} - \mu}{\sigma/\sqrt{n}}$$

To solve this problem manually, we need to define the rejection region, which requires us to specify a significance level. A 5% significance level is deemed to be appropriate.

We wish to reject the null hypothesis in favor of the alternative only if the sample mean and hence the value of the test statistic is small enough. As a result we locate the rejection region in the left tail of the sampling distribution. To understand why, remember that we're trying to decide if there is enough statistical evidence to infer that the mean is less than 16 (which is the alternative hypothesis). If we observe a large sample mean (and hence a large value of z), do we want to reject the null hypothesis in favor of the alternative? The answer is an emphatic no. If the sample mean is, say, 20, it would be absurd to conclude that the mean of all bottles is less than 16. Consequently, we want to reject the null hypothesis only if the sample mean (and hence the value of z) is small. How small is small enough? The answer is determined by the significance level and the rejection region. Thus, we set up the rejection region as

$$z < -z_\alpha = -z_{.05} = -1.645$$

Note that the direction of the inequality in the rejection region ($z < -z_\alpha$) matches the direction of the inequality in the alternative hypothesis ($\mu < 16$). Also note the negative sign, since the rejection region is in the left tail (containing values of z less than zero) of the sampling distribution.

From the data, we compute the sample mean. It is

$$\bar{x} = 15.90$$

Since the population standard deviation is known to be $\sigma = 0.4$, the sample size is $n = 25$, and the value of μ is hypothesized to be 16, we compute the value of the test statistic as

$$z = \frac{x - \mu}{\sigma/\sqrt{n}} = \frac{15.90 - 16}{0.4/\sqrt{25}} = -1.25$$

Because the value of the test statistic, $z = -1.25$, is not less than -1.645, we do not reject the null hypothesis in favor of the alternative hypothesis. There is insufficient evidence to infer that the mean is less than 16 ounces.

We can determine the p-value of the test. It is

$$p\text{-value} = P(Z < -1.25) = .1056$$

In this type of test of hypothesis we calculate the p-value as $P(Z < z)$ where z is the actual value of the test statistic. Figure 10.7 depicts the sampling distribution, rejection region, and p-value.

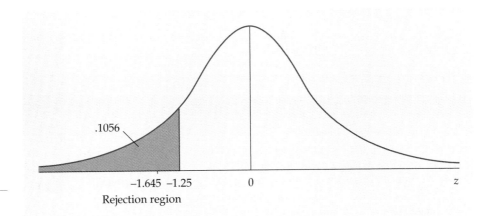

Figure 10.7

Sampling distribution for
Example 10.2

**Excel Output for
Example 10.2**

	A	B	C	D	E
1	**Test of Hypothesis About MU (SIGMA Known)**				
2					
3	*Test of MU = 16 Vs MU less than 16*				
4	*SIGMA = 0.4*				
5	*Sample mean = 15.9*				
6	*Test Statistic: z = -1.25*				
7	*P-Value = 0.1056*				

**Minitab Output for
Example 10.2**

Z-Test

Test of mu = 16.0000 vs mu < 16.0000
The assumed sigma = 0.400

Variable	N	Mean	StDev	SE Mean	Z	P
Catsup	25	15.9000	0.5017	0.0800	−1.25	0.11

INTERPRET

Because we were not able to reject the null hypothesis, we say that there is not enough evidence to infer that the mean weight of all catsup bottles is less than 16 ounces. Note that there was some evidence to indicate that the mean of the entire population of weights of catsup bottles is less than 16 ounces. We did calculate the sample mean to be 15.9. However, to reject the null hypothesis we need enough statistical evidence, and in this case we simply did not have sufficient reason to reject the null hypothesis in favor of the alternative. In the absence of enough evidence to show that the mean weight of all catsup bottles is less than 16 ounces, the inspector would not find the labels to be unacceptable.

The statistical tests conducted in Examples 10.1 and 10.2 are called **one-tail tests** because the rejection region is located in only one tail of the sampling distribution. The right tail in Example 10.1 is the important one because the alternative hypothesis specifies that the mean is *greater than* 170. In Example 10.2 the left tail is critical because the alternative hypothesis specifies that the mean is *less than* 16.

We'll now present an example that requires a **two-tail test.**

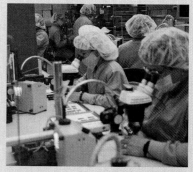

Statistics in the Workplace

Operations Management Application

An important operations management function is line balancing of an assembly line. This ensures that operations at different stations take approximately the same amount of time. If the line is not balanced, at some points operators will be idle, and at other points bottlenecks will occur. This results in the product piling up at the operation that is more time consuming than at least one other operation that precedes it. Assembly lines are often set up using a variety of management science tools and it may become necessary to examine the assumptions that went into the management scientists' decisions.

▼ EXAMPLE 10.3

The supervisor of a production line that assembles computer keyboards has been experiencing problems since a new process was instituted. He notes that there has been an increase in the number of defective units and occasional backlogs when the output of one station does not match other stations' productivity. Upon reviewing the process, the supervisor discovered that the management scientists who developed the production process assumed that the amount of time to complete a critical part of the process is normally distributed with a mean of 130 seconds and a standard deviation of 15 seconds. He is satisfied that the process times are normally distributed with a standard deviation of 15 seconds, but he is unsure about the mean assembly time. To determine what, if any, adjustments should be made to the line, he measures the times for 100 randomly selected assemblies of the critical part. (These data are listed below and stored in file XM10-03.) Can the supervisor conclude that the management scientists' belief that the mean assembly time is 130 seconds is incorrect?

TIMES TO COMPLETE CRITICAL PART

145	126	142	147	96	130	135	152	130	107
128	129	129	132	103	138	140	120	117	131
153	106	115	112	119	113	134	144	99	130
141	118	147	133	141	104	141	117	106	140
119	122	148	126	130	116	131	142	121	121
101	133	139	114	127	132	133	134	114	140
136	124	108	136	130	136	126	125	121	134
104	146	147	112	148	149	133	130	120	157
154	136	141	127	125	105	126	120	107	103
106	113	132	116	138	104	111	138	117	106

Solution

IDENTIFY

In this problem we want to know whether the mean assembly time μ is different from 130 seconds. Consequently, we set up the alternative hypothesis to express this condition.

$$H_1 : \mu \neq 130$$

The null hypothesis specifies that the mean is equal to the value specified under the alternative hypothesis. Hence,

$$H_0 : \mu = 130$$

SOLVE

To set up the rejection region, we need to realize that we can reject the null hypothesis when the test statistic is large or when it is small. That is, we must set up a *two-tail rejection region*. Because the total area in the rejection region must be α we divide this probability by 2. Thus, the rejection region* is

$$z < -z_{\alpha/2} \quad \text{or} \quad z > z_{\alpha/2}$$

For $\alpha = .05$, $\alpha/2 = .025$, and $z_{\alpha/2} = z_{.025} = 1.96$. It follows that the rejection region is

$$z < -1.96 \quad \text{or} \quad z > 1.96$$

From the data we compute

$$\bar{x} = 126.8$$

The value of the test statistic is

$$z = \frac{\bar{x} - \mu}{\sigma/\sqrt{n}} = \frac{126.8 - 130}{15/\sqrt{100}} = -2.13$$

Since -2.13 is less than -1.96 we reject the null hypothesis.

We can also calculate the *p*-value of the test. Because it is a two-tail test we determine the *p*-value by finding the area in both tails. That is,

$$p\text{-value} = P(Z < -2.13) + P(Z > 2.13) = .0166 + .0166 = .0332$$

Or, more simply multiply the probability in one tail by 2.

In general, the *p*-value in a two-tail test is determined by

$$p\text{-value} = 2P(Z > |z|)$$

where z is the actual value of the test statistic and $|z|$ is its absolute value. Figure 10.8 exhibits the test statistic's sampling distribution.

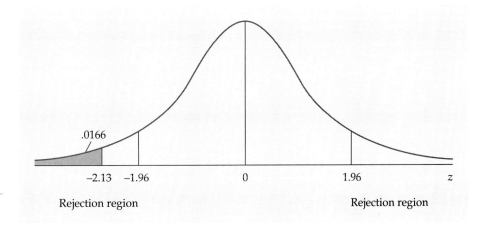

Figure 10.8

Sampling distribution for Example 10.3

---

*Statisticians often represent this rejection region as $|z| > z_{\alpha/2}$, which reads, the *absolute* value of z is greater than $z_{\alpha/2}$. We prefer our method because it is clear that we are performing a two-tail test.

Excel Output for Example 10.3

	A	B	C	D	E
1	**Test of Hypothesis About MU (SIGMA Known)**				
2					
3	*Test of MU = 130 Vs MU not equal to 130*				
4	*SIGMA = 15*				
5	*Sample mean = 126.8*				
6	*Test Statistic: z = -2.1333*				
7	*P-Value = 0.0329*				

Minitab Output for Example 10.3

Z-Test

```
Test of mu = 130.00 vs mu not = 130.00
The assumed sigma = 15.0
```

Variable	N	Mean	StDev	SE Mean	Z	P
Time	100	126.80	14.48	1.50	−2.13	0.033

INTERPRET   There is evidence to infer that the mean time to complete this stage of the production process is not equal to 130 seconds. The operations manager will have to juggle several issues in deciding how to proceed. First, how likely is it that the mean time is actually some other value than 130 seconds? The *p*-value indicates that there is statistical evidence, but it is hardly overwhelming. Second, the problem of bottlenecks and increased defects may be attributable to some other cause or causes. Third, even if the problems are isolated to this stage of the production process, it may not be possible or financially feasible to correct the process. It is clear that more investigating is necessary. However, the statistical analysis allows the manager to start the search for a solution.

▲

TESTING HYPOTHESES AND INTERVAL ESTIMATORS

As you've seen, the test statistic and the interval estimator are both derived from the sampling distribution. It shouldn't be a surprise then that we can use the interval estimator to test hypotheses. To illustrate, consider Example 10.3. The 95% confidence interval estimate of the population mean is

$$\bar{x} \pm z_{\alpha/2} \frac{\sigma}{\sqrt{n}} = 126.8 \pm 1.96 \frac{15}{\sqrt{100}} = 126.8 \pm 2.94$$

$$\text{LCL} = 123.86 \quad \text{and} \quad \text{UCL} = 129.74$$

We estimate that μ lies between 123.86 and 129.74. Because the interval does not include 130, we can conclude that there is sufficient evidence to infer that the population mean differs from 130.

The 95% confidence interval estimator for Example 10.2 is LCL = 15.74 and UCL = 16.06. Since this interval includes 16 we cannot infer that the labels are unacceptable.

In Example 10.1 the 95% confidence interval estimate is LCL = 171.63 and UCL = 184.37. The interval estimate excludes 170, allowing us to conclude that the population mean account is not equal to $170.

As you can see the interval estimator can be employed to conduct tests of hypotheses. This process is equivalent to the rejection region approach. But, instead of finding the critical values of the rejection region and determining whether the test statistic falls into the rejection region, we compute the interval estimate and determine whether the hypothesized value of the mean falls into the interval.

Using the interval estimator to test hypotheses has the advantage of simplicity. Apparently, we don't need the formula for the test statistic; we only need the interval estimator. However, there are two serious drawbacks.

First, when conducting a one-tail test our conclusion may not answer the question. In Example 10.1 we wanted to know whether there was enough evidence to infer that the mean is *greater than* 170. The estimate concludes that the mean *differs from* 170. You may be tempted to say that since the entire interval is greater than 170 that there is enough statistical evidence to infer that the population mean is greater than 170. However, in attempting to draw this conclusion we run into the problem of determining the procedure's significance level. Is it 5% or is it 2.5%? We may be able to overcome this problem through the use of **one-sided interval estimators.** However, if the purpose of using interval estimators instead of test statistics is simplicity, one-sided estimators are a contradiction.

Second, the interval estimator does not yield a *p*-value, which we have argued is the better way to draw inferences about a parameter. Using the interval estimator to test hypotheses forces the decision maker into making a reject/don't reject decision rather than providing information about how much statistical evidence exists to be judged with other factors in the decision process. Furthermore, we only postpone the point in time when a test of hypothesis must be used. In later chapters we will present problems where only a test produces the information we need to make decisions.

DEVELOPING AN UNDERSTANDING OF STATISTICAL CONCEPTS

As is the case with the interval estimator, the test of hypothesis is based on the sampling distribution of the sample statistic. The result of a test of hypothesis is a probability statement about the sample statistic. We assume that the population mean is specified by the null hypothesis. We then compute the test statistic and determine how likely it is to observe this large (or small) a value when the null hypothesis is true. If the probability is small, we conclude that the assumption that the null hypothesis is true is unfounded and we reject it.

EXERCISES

Exercises 10.1–10.5 feature nonstatistical applications of hypothesis testing. For each exercise identify the hypotheses, define Type I and Type II errors, and discuss the consequences of each error. In setting up the hypotheses you will have to consider where to place the "burden of proof."

10.1 It is the responsibility of the federal government to judge the safety and effectiveness of new drugs. There are two possible decisions: Approve the drug or disapprove the drug.

10.2 You are contemplating a Ph.D. in business or economics. If you succeed, a life of fame, fortune, and happiness awaits you. If you fail you've wasted 5 years of your life. Should you go for it?

10.3 You are the centerfielder of the New York Yankees. It is the bottom of the ninth inning of the seventh game of the World Series. The Yanks lead by 2 with 2 out and men on second and third. The batter is known to hit for high average, runs very well, but with mediocre power. A single will tie the game and a hit over your head will likely result in the Yanks losing. Do you play shallow?

10.4 You are faced with two investments. One is very risky but the potential returns are high. The other is safe but the potential is quite limited. Pick one.

10.5 (At the time this edition was being prepared, Swissair Flight 111 had just crashed off the coast of Nova Scotia after the plane caught on fire.) You are the pilot of a jumbo jet. You smell smoke in the cockpit. The nearest airport is less than 5 minutes away. Should you land the plane immediately?

10.6 Several years ago in a high-profile case, a defendant was acquitted in a double-murder trial but was subsequently found responsible for the deaths in a civil trial. (Guess the name of the defendant—the answer is in Appendix C.) In a civil trial the plaintiff (the victims' relatives) are required only to show that the preponderance of evidence points to the guilt of the defendant. Aside from the other issues in the cases discuss why these results are logical.

For Exercises 10.7–10.12, calculate the value of the test statistic, set up the rejection region, determine the p-value, and interpret the result.

10.7 $H_0 : \mu = 1{,}000$
$H_1 : \mu \neq 1{,}000$
$\sigma = 200, n = 100, \bar{x} = 980, \alpha = .01$

10.8 $H_0 : \mu = 50$
$H_1 : \mu > 50$
$\sigma = 5, n = 9, \bar{x} = 51, \alpha = .03$

10.9 $H_0 : \mu = 15$
$H_1 : \mu < 15$
$\sigma = 2, n = 25, \bar{x} = 14.3, \alpha = .10$

10.10 $H_0 : \mu = 100$
$H_1 : \mu \neq 100$
$\sigma = 10, n = 100, \bar{x} = 100, \alpha = .05$

10.11 $H_0 : \mu = 70$
$H_1 : \mu > 70$
$\sigma = 20, n = 100, \bar{x} = 80, \alpha = .01$

10.12 $H_0 : \mu = 50$
$H_1 : \mu < 50$
$\sigma = 15, n = 100, \bar{x} = 52, \alpha = .05$

*Exercises 10.13–10.30 are "what-if" analyses designed to determine what happens to the test statistic and p-value when the sample size, standard deviation, and sample mean change. These problems can be solved manually or using Excel's **Inference from Summary Statistics (Workbook)** option.*

10.13 A random sample of 50 young adult men (20–30 years old) was sampled. Each person was asked how many minutes of sports they watch on television daily. The sample mean was found to be $\bar{x} = 64$. Suppose that $\sigma = 20$. Test to determine at the 5% significance level whether there is enough statistical evidence to infer that the mean amount of television watched by all young adult men is greater than 60 minutes.

10.14 Repeat Exercise 10.13 with $n = 25$.

10.15 Repeat Exercise 10.13 with $n = 100$.

10.16 Repeat Exercise 10.13 with $\sigma = 10$.

10.17 Repeat Exercise 10.13 with $\sigma = 40$.

10.18 Repeat Exercise 10.13 with $\bar{x} = 62$.

10.19 Repeat Exercise 10.13 with $\bar{x} = 68$.

10.20 Summarize Exercises 10.13 to 10.19 by describing what happens to the value of the test statistic when each of the following happens.

  a The sample size increases.
  b The standard deviation decreases.
  c The value of $\bar{x}$ increases.

10.21 A random sample of 50 second-year university students enrolled in a business statistics course was drawn. At the course's completion each student was asked how many hours he or she spent doing homework in statistics. The sample mean was computed to be $\bar{x} = 33$. It is known that the population standard deviation is $\sigma = 8.0$. The instructor has recommended that students devote 3 hours per week for the duration of the 12-week semester, which totals to 36 hours. Test to determine whether there is evidence that the average student spent less than the recommended amount of time. Compute the *p*-value of the test.

10.22 Repeat Exercise 10.21 with $n = 25$.

10.23 Repeat Exercise 10.21 with $n = 100$.

10.24 Repeat Exercise 10.21 with $\sigma = 5$.

10.25 Repeat Exercise 10.21 with $\sigma = 12$.

10.26 Repeat Exercise 10.21 with $\bar{x} = 30$.

10.27 Repeat Exercise 10.21 with $\bar{x} = 35$.

10.28 Summarize Exercises 10.21 to 10.27 by describing what happens to the *p*-value of the test when each of the following happens.

  a The sample size increases.
  b The standard deviation decreases.
  c The value of $\bar{x}$ decreases.

10.29 Perform a what-if analysis on Example 10.1. Change each of the following and determine the effect.

  a Sample size becomes 100.
  b The standard deviation is 100.
  c The value of the sample mean is 176.

10.30 Perform a what-if analysis on Example 10.2. Change each of the following and determine the effect.

  a Sample size becomes 100.
  b The standard deviation is 1.
  c The value of the sample mean is 15.8.

10.31 Determine if there is enough statistical evidence at the 1% significance level to infer from the following information that the population mean is less than 250.

$$\bar{x} = 247, \ \sigma = 40, \ n = 400$$

10.32 A random sample of 200 observations from a normal population whose standard deviation is 100 produced a mean of 150. Does this statistic provide sufficient evidence at the 5% significance level to infer that the population mean is less than 160?

10.33 Determine if there is enough statistical evidence at the 10% significance level to infer that the population mean is not equal to 50, given that $\bar{x} = 56$, $\sigma = 10$, and $n = 25$.

10.34 Suppose that the following observations were drawn from a normal population whose standard deviation is 10. Test with $\alpha = .10$ to determine whether there is enough evidence to conclude that the population mean differs from 25.

21 37 33 47 28 16 29 37 41 20

10.35 Given the following data drawn from a population whose standard deviation is known to be 1, test to determine if there is enough evidence at the 5% significance level to infer that the population mean is greater than 5.

9 8 4 8 7 8 5 9 7 4 8 5 6 3 9 4 7 4 6 3 9

10.36 A machine that produces ball bearings is set so that the average diameter is .50 inch. In a sample of 100 ball bearings, it was found that $\bar{x} = .51$ inch. Assuming that the standard deviation is .05 inch, can we conclude at the 5% significance level that the mean diameter is not .50 inch?

Exercises 10.37–10.41 require the use of a computer and software. The answers may be calculated manually. See Appendix A for the sample statistics.

10.37 A manufacturer of light bulbs advertises that, on average, its long-life bulb will last more than 5,000 hours. To test the claim, a statistician took a random sample of 100 bulbs and measured the amount of time until each bulb burned out. The data are stored in file XR10-37. If we assume that the lifetime of this type of bulb has a standard deviation of 400 hours, can we conclude at the 5% significance level that the claim is true?

10.38 In the midst of labor–management negotiations, the president of a company argues that the company's blue-collar workers, who are paid an average of $30,000 per year, are well paid because the mean annual income of all blue-collar workers in the country is less than $30,000. That figure is disputed by the union, which does not believe that the mean blue-collar income is less than $30,000. To test the company president's belief, an arbitrator draws a random sample of 350 blue-collar workers from across the country and asks each to report his or her annual income. The results are stored in file XR10-38. If the arbitrator assumes that the blue-collar incomes are distributed with a standard deviation of $8,000, can it be inferred at the 5% significance level that the company president is correct?

10.39 A dean of a business school claims that the GMAT scores of applicants to the school's M.B.A. program have increased during the past 5 years. Five years ago, the mean and standard deviation of GMAT scores of M.B.A. applicants were 560 and 50, respectively. Twenty applications for this year's program were randomly selected and the GMAT scores recorded. These are stored in file XR10-39. If we assume that the distribution of GMAT scores of this year's applicants is the same as that of 5 years ago, with the possible exception of the mean, can we conclude at the 5% significance level that the dean's claim is true?

10.40 A study in the *Academy of Management Journal* (D.R. Woods and R. L. LaForge, "The Impact of Comprehensive Planning on Financial Performance," *Academy of Management Journal* 22(3) (1979): 516–26) reported that the average annual return on investment for American banks was 10.2% with a standard deviation of 0.8%. The article hypothesized that banks that exercised comprehensive planning would outperform the average bank. A random sample of 26 banks that exercised comprehensive planning was drawn, and the return on investment for each was calculated and stored in file XR10-40. Assuming that the return on investment is normally distributed with a standard deviation of 0.8%, can we conclude at the 10% significance level that the article's hypothesis is correct?

10.41 Past experience indicates that the monthly long-distance telephone bill is normally distributed with a mean of $17.85 and a standard deviation of $3.87. After an advertising campaign aimed at increasing long-distance telephone usage, a random sample of 25 household bills was taken. The results are stored in file XR10-41.

a Do the data allow us to infer at the 10% significance level that the campaign was successful?

b What assumption must you make to answer part (a)?

10.4 CALCULATING THE PROBABILITY OF A TYPE II ERROR

To properly interpret the results of a test of hypothesis requires that you be able to specify an appropriate significance level or to judge the p-value of a test. However, it also requires that you have an understanding of the relationship between Type I and Type II errors. In this section, we describe how the probability of a Type II error is computed and interpreted.

Recall Example 10.1, where we conducted the test using the sample mean as the test statistic and we computed the rejection region (with $\alpha = .05$) as

$$\bar{x} > 175.34$$

A Type II Error occurs when a false null hypothesis is not rejected. Thus, in Example 10.1, if $\bar{x}$ is less than 175.34 we will not reject the null hypothesis. If we do not reject the null hypothesis we will not install the new billing system. Thus, the consequence of a Type II error in this example is that we will not install the new system when it would be cost effective. The probability of this occurring is the probability of a Type II error. It is defined as

$$\beta = P(\bar{X} < 175.34 \text{ given that the null hypothesis is false})$$

The condition that the null hypothesis is false only tells us that the population mean is not equal to 170. If we want to compute β, we need to specify a value for μ. Suppose that when the mean account is at least \$180, the new billing system's savings become so attractive that the manager would hate to make the mistake of not installing it. As a result she would like to determine the probability of not installing the new system when it would produce large cost savings. Because calculating sampling distribution (approximately normal) probabilities requires us to substitute one value of μ (as well as σ and n) we will calculate the probability of not installing the new system when μ is *equal* to 180.

$$\beta = P(\bar{X} < 175.34, \text{ given that } \mu = 180)$$

We know that $\bar{X}$ is approximately normally distributed with mean μ and standard deviation $\sigma/\sqrt{n}$. To proceed we standardize $\bar{X}$ and use the standard normal table (Table 3 in Appendix B).

$$\beta = P\left(\frac{\bar{X} - \mu}{\sigma/\sqrt{n}} < \frac{175.34 - 180}{65/\sqrt{400}}\right) = P(Z < -1.43) = .0764$$

This tells us that when the mean account is actually \$180, the probability of incorrectly not rejecting the null hypothesis is .0764. Figure 10.9 graphically depicts how the calculation was performed. Notice that in order to calculate the probability of a Type II error, we had to express the rejection region in terms of the unstandardized test statistic $\bar{x}$, and we had to specify a value for μ other than the one shown in the null hypothesis. In this illustration the value of μ used was based on a financial analysis indicating that when μ is at least \$180 the cost savings would be very attractive.

EFFECT ON β OF CHANGING α

Suppose that in the illustration above we had used a significance level of 1% instead of 5%. The rejection region expressed in terms of the standardized test statistic would be

$$z > z_{.01} = 2.33$$

or

$$\frac{\bar{x} - 170}{65/\sqrt{400}} > 2.33$$

Solving for $\bar{x}$ we find the rejection region in terms of the unstandardized test statistic.

$$\bar{x} > 177.57$$

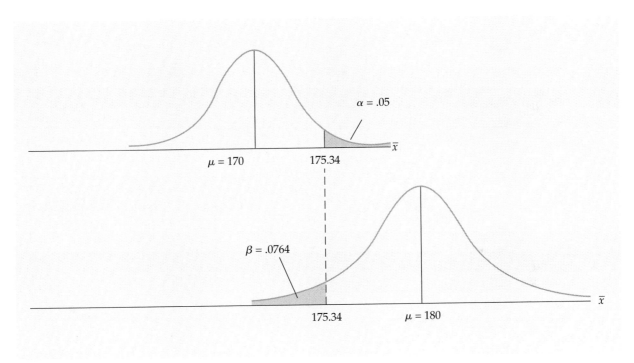

Figure 10.9

Calculating β for $\mu = 180$, $\alpha = .05$, and $n = 400$

The probability of a Type II error when $\mu = 180$ is

$$\beta = P\left(\frac{\bar{x} - \mu}{\sigma/\sqrt{n}} < \frac{177.57 - 180}{65/\sqrt{400}}\right) = P(Z < -.74) = .2296$$

Figure 10.10 depicts this calculation. Compare this figure with Figure 10.9. As you can see, by decreasing the significance level from 5% to 1% we have shifted the critical value of the rejection region to the right and thus enlarged the area where the null hypothesis is not rejected. The probability of a Type II error increases from .0764 to .2296.

This calculation illustrates the inverse relationship between the probabilities of Type I and Type II errors alluded to in Section 10.2. It is important to understand this relationship. From a practical point of view it tells us that if you want to decrease the probability of a Type I error (by specifying a small value of α) you increase the probability of a Type II error.

In applications where the cost of a Type I error is considerably larger than the cost of a Type II error, this is appropriate. In fact, a significance level of 1% or less is probably justified. However, when the cost of a Type II error is relatively large, a significance level of 5% or more may be appropriate.

Unfortunately, there is no simple formula to determine what the significance level should be. It is necessary for the manager to consider the costs of both mistakes in deciding what to do. Judgment and knowledge of the factors in the decision are critical.

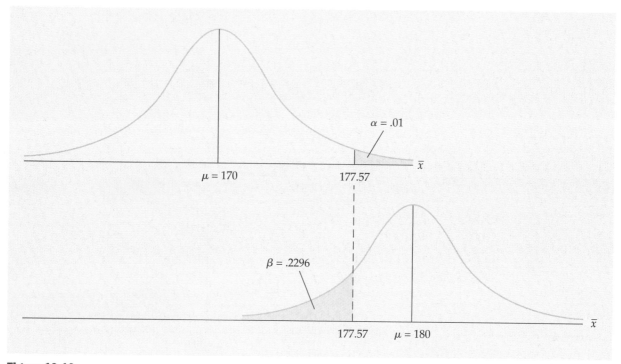

Figure 10.10

Calculating β for $\mu = 180$, $\alpha = .01$, and $n = 400$

JUDGING THE TEST

There is another important concept to be derived from this section. A statistical test of hypothesis is effectively defined by the significance level and the sample size, both of which are selected by the manager. We can judge how well the test functions by calculating the probability of a Type II error at some value of the parameter. To illustrate, in Example 10.1 the manager chose a sample size of 400 and a 5% significance level on which to base her decision. With those selections we found β to be .0764 when the actual mean is 180. If we believe that the cost of a Type II error is high and thus that the probability is too large we have two ways to reduce the probability. We can increase the value of α. However, this would result in an increase in the chances of making a Type I error, which is very costly. Instead, we can increase the sample size.

Suppose that the manager chose a sample size of 1,000. We'll now recalculate β with $n = 1,000$ (and $\alpha = .05$). The rejection region is

$$z > z_{.05} = 1.645$$

or

$$\frac{\bar{x} - 170}{65/\sqrt{1,000}} > 1.645$$

which yields

$$\bar{x} > 173.38$$

The probability of a Type II error is

$$\beta = P\left(\frac{\bar{x} - \mu}{\sigma/\sqrt{n}} < \frac{173.38 - 180}{65/\sqrt{1,000}}\right) = P(Z < -3.22) = 0 \text{ (approximately)}$$

In this case we left $\alpha = .05$ but we reduced the probability of not installing the system when the actual mean account is \$180 to virtually zero.

DEVELOPING AN UNDERSTANDING OF STATISTICAL CONCEPTS: LARGER SAMPLE SIZE EQUALS MORE INFORMATION EQUALS BETTER DECISIONS

Figure 10.11 displays the calculation above. Compared to Figure 10.9, we can see that the sampling distribution of the mean is narrower because the standard error of the mean $\sigma/\sqrt{n}$ becomes smaller as n increases. Narrower distributions represent more information. The increased information is reflected in a smaller probability of a Type II error.

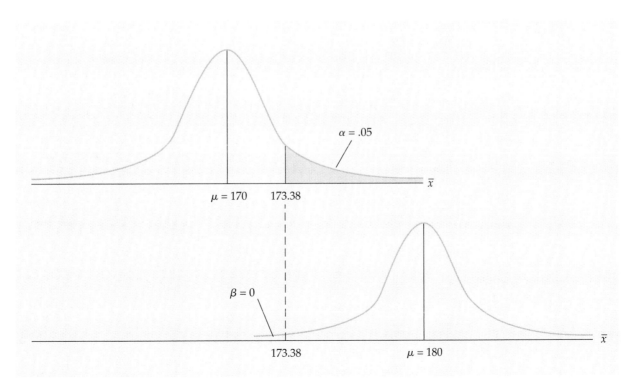

Figure 10.11

Calculating β for $\mu = 180$, $\alpha = .05$, and $n = 1,000$

The calculation of the probability of a Type II error for $n = 400$ and for $n = 1{,}000$ illustrates a concept whose importance cannot be overstated. By increasing the sample size we reduce the probability of a Type II error. By reducing the probability of a Type II error we make this type of error less frequently. Hence, we make better decisions in the long run. This finding lies at the heart of applied statistical analysis and reinforces the book's first sentence, "Statistics is a way to get information from data."

Throughout this book we introduce a variety of applications in finance, marketing, operations management, human resources, and economics. In all such applications the manager must make a decision, which involves converting data into information. The more information, the better the decision. Without such information decisions must be based on guesswork, instinct, and luck. A famous statistician, W. Edwards Deming, said it best. "Without data you're just another person with an opinion."

POWER OF A TEST

Another way of expressing how well a test performs is to report its *power*—the probability of its leading us to rejecting the null hypothesis when it is false. Thus, the power of a test is $1 - \beta$.

When more than one test can be performed in a given situation, we would naturally prefer to use the test that is correct more frequently. If (given the same alternative hypothesis, sample size, and significance level) one test has a higher power than a second test, the first test is said to be more powerful.

Excel

We have made it possible to utilize Excel to calculate β for any test of hypothesis. To do so follow these instructions.

Click **Tools, Data Analysis Plus,** and **Inference from Summary Statistics (Workbook).** Find the worksheet titled **Beta.** In this worksheet we have calculated the probability of a Type II error for three different tests. Column B performs a one-tail (right-tail) test, column C, a one-tail (left-tail) test, and column D, a two-tail test. The worksheet shows the value of β for Example 10.1 (with $\mu = 180$), Example 10.2 (with $\mu = 15.8$), and Example 10.3 (with $\mu = 135$). To use the worksheet go to the column representing the test you are conducting and substitute new values for μ under the null hypothesis, σ, n, α, and the value of μ under the alternative hypothesis in rows 5 through 9, respectively. In row 11 Excel computes the critical value of the rejection region for the two one-tail tests and rows 11 and 12 for the two-tail test. Rows 14 and 16 list the value of β and the power of the test. (*Remember:* Click **Exit.**)

The current form of the worksheet follows.

	A	B	C	D
1	**Probability of a Type II error**			
2				
3		**Right-tail Test**	**Left-tail Test**	**Two-tail Test**
4				
5	H0: MU	170	16	130
6	SIGMA	65	0.4	15
7	Sample size	400	25	100
8	ALPHA	0.05	0.05	0.05
9	H1: MU	180	15.8	135
10				
11	Critical value(s)	175.35	15.87	127.06
12				132.94
13				
14	Prob(Type II error)	0.0761	0.1962	0.0848
15				
16	Power of the test	0.9239	0.8038	0.9152

In column C Excel computes the probability of a Type II error for Example 10.2 when the mean weight of all catsup bottles is actually 15.8 ounces. The probability of not finding the labels unacceptable when the mean weight is 15.8 is .1962. If regulators decide that this probability is too large they would have to change the test. If we increase the significance level, we would increase the percentage of tests where we erroneously conclude that the labels are unacceptable when in fact they are acceptable. We can also increase the sample size. (See Exercise 10.42.)

Column D shows the calculation of β for Example 10.3 when $\mu = 135$. Note that in a two-tail test there are two critical values that define the rejection region. The probability of a Type II error is the area between these two values assuming that population mean is 135 (in this illustration).

Minitab

Minitab computes the power of the test.

COMMANDS

1 Click **Stat, Power and Sample Size,** and **1-Sample Z . . . .**
2 Use the cursor to select **Calculate power for each sample size.**
3 Hit **tab** and type the value or values of the **Sample sizes:.** (You can specify more than one value of n. Minitab will compute the power for each value.)
4 Hit **tab** and type the **Difference:** between the hypothesized value of μ under the null hypothesis and the actual value of μ.
5 Hit **tab** and type the value of **sigma:.**
6 Click **Options . . .** and specify the **Alternative Hypothesis** and the **Significance level. Click OK.**

For Example 10.1 we typed **400** to select the **Sample sizes:,** the **Difference:** was **10** (= **180 − 170**), **Sigma:** was **65,** the **Alternative Hypothesis** was Greater than, and the **Significance level** was **0.05.** The output follows.

Minitab Output for the Power of the Test: Example 10.1	**Power and Sample Size**
	
	`1-Sample Z Test`
	
	`Testing mean = null (versus > null)`
	`Calculating power for mean = null + 10`
	`Alpha = 0.05  Sigma = 65`
	
	`Sample`
	` Size   Power`
	`  400  0.9239`

Minitab Output for the Power of the Test: Example 10.2	**Power and Sample Size**
	
	`1-Sample Z Test`
	
	`Testing mean = null (versus < null)`
	`Calculating power for mean = null − 0.2`
	`Alpha = 0.05 Sigma = 0.4`
	
	`Sample`
	` Size   Power`
	`   25  0.8038`

Minitab Output for the Power of the Test: Example 10.3	**Power and Sample Size**
	
	`1-Sample Z Test`
	
	`Testing mean = null (versus not = null)`
	`Calculating power for mean = null + 5`
	`Alpha = 0.05  Sigma = 15`
	
	`Sample`
	` Size   Power`
	`  100  0.9152`

SETTING UP THE ALTERNATIVE HYPOTHESIS TO DEFINE TYPE I AND TYPE II ERRORS

We've already discussed how the alternative hypothesis is set up. It represents the condition we're investigating. In Example 10.2 we wanted to know whether there was sufficient statistical evidence to infer that the labels are unacceptable. That is, that the mean of all catsup bottles is less than 16 ounces. In this textbook you will encounter many problems using similar phraseology. Your job will be to conduct the test that answers the question.

In real life, however, the manager (that's you 5 years from now) will be asking and answering the question. In general, you will find that the question can be posed in two ways. In Example 10.2 we asked whether there was evidence to conclude that the labels are unacceptable. Another way of investigating the issue is to determine whether there is sufficient evidence to infer that the labels are acceptable. We remind you of the criminal trial analogy. In a criminal trial the burden of proof falls on the prosecution to prove that the defendant is guilty. In other countries with less emphasis on individual rights the defendant is required to prove his or her innocence. In the United States and Canada (and in other countries) we chose the former because we consider the conviction of an innocent defendant to be the greater error. Thus the test is set up with the null and alternative hypotheses as described in Section 10.2.

In a statistical test where we are responsible for asking the question, as well as answering it, we must ask the question so that we directly control the error that is more costly. As you have already seen, we control the probability of a Type I error by specifying its value (the significance level). Consider Example 10.2 once again. There are two possible errors: Conclude that the labels are unacceptable when they are correct and conclude that the labels are acceptable when they are not correct. Which error is more costly? If the government regulators conclude that the labels are unacceptable the catsup manufacturer will have to take some remedial action. If, in reality, the labels are correct the company will incur a high cost for no valid reason. On the other hand, if the regulators conclude that the labels are correct (by not taking any action) but in reality they are not, consumers will receive less catsup than they are entitled. The cost to individual consumers is small. Consequently, the error we wish to avoid is the erroneous conclusion that the labels are unacceptable. We define this as a Type I error. As a result the "burden of proof" is placed on government regulators to deliver sufficient statistical evidence that the mean net weight is less than 16 ounces. The alternative hypothesis is formulated accordingly.

EXERCISES

10.42 Calculate the probability of a Type II error in Example 10.2 when $\mu = 15.80$ and the sample size is 100.

10.43 Calculate the probability of a Type II error in Example 10.2 if the true mean weight of all catsup bottles is 15.7 ounces.

10.44 Find the probability of a Type II error in Example 10.3 if $\mu = 132$.

10.45 Draw a figure similar to Figure 10.9 depicting the calculation in Exercise 10.43.

10.46 Draw a figure similar to Figure 10.9 depicting the calculation in Exercise 10.44.

10.47 Calculate the probability of a Type II error for the following test of hypothesis, given that $\mu = 203$.

$$H_0 : \mu = 200$$
$$H_1 : \mu \neq 200$$
$$\alpha = .05, \sigma = 10, n = 100$$

10.48 Find the probability of a Type II error for the following test of hypothesis, given that $\mu = 1,050$.

$$H_0 : \mu = 1,000$$
$$H_1 : \mu > 1,000$$
$$\alpha = .01, \sigma = 50, n = 25$$

10.49 Determine β for the following test of hypothesis, given that $\mu = 48$.

$$H_0 : \mu = 50.$$
$$H_1 : \mu < 50$$
$$\alpha = .05, \sigma = 10, n = 40$$

10.50 For the test of hypothesis

$$H_0 : \mu = 1,000$$
$$H_1 : \mu \neq 1,000$$
$$\alpha = .05, \sigma = 200, n = 100$$

find β when $\mu = 900, 940, 980, 1,020, 1,060,$ and $1,100$.

10.51 For Exercise 10.50, graph μ (on the horizontal axis) versus β (on the vertical axis). If necessary, calculate β for additional values of μ. The resulting graph is called the *operating characteristic (OC) curve*.

10.52 For Exercise 10.50, graph μ versus $1 - \beta$. Recall that $1 - \beta$ is called the *power of the test;* as a consequence, the graph is called the *power curve*.

10.53 Repeat Exercises 10.50–10.52 with $n = 25$.

10.54 What do you notice about the graphs in Exercises 10.52 and 10.53? What are the implications of your observations?

10.55 Refer to Exercise 10.39. Find the probability of erroneously concluding that there is not enough evidence to support the claim when, in fact, the true mean GMAT score is 600.

10.56 Suppose that in Example 10.1 we wanted to determine whether there was sufficient evidence to conclude that the new system would *not* be cost effective. Set up the null and alternative hypotheses and discuss the consequences of Type I and Type II errors. Conduct the test. Is your conclusion the same one reached in Example 10.1? Explain.

10.57 A school board administrator believes that the average number of days absent per year among students is less than 10 days. From past experience, he knows that the population standard deviation is 3 days. In testing to determine whether his belief is true, he could use either of the following plans.

i $n = 100, \alpha = .01$
ii $n = 75, \alpha = .05$
iii $n = 50, \alpha = .10$

Which plan has the lower probability of a Type II error, given that the true population average is 9 days?

10.5 THE ROAD AHEAD

We had two principal goals to accomplish in Chapters 9 and 10. First, we wanted to present the concepts of estimation and hypothesis testing. Second, we wanted to show how to produce interval estimates and conduct tests of hypotheses. The importance of both of these goals should not be underestimated. Almost everything that follows this chapter will involve either estimating a parameter or testing a set of hypotheses. Consequently, Sections 9.3 and 10.3 set the pattern for the way in which statistical techniques are applied. It is no exaggeration to state that if you understand how to produce and use interval estimates and how to conduct and interpret hypothesis tests, then you are well on your way to the ultimate goal of being competent at analyzing, interpreting, and presenting data. It is fair for you to ask what more you must accomplish to achieve this goal. The answer, simply put, is much more of the same.

In the chapters that follow, we plan to present about three dozen different statistical techniques that can be (and frequently are) employed by decision makers. To calculate the value of test statistics or interval estimates requires nothing more than the ability to add, subtract, multiply, divide, and compute square roots. If you intend to use the computer, all you need to know are the commands. The key, then, to applying statistics is knowing which formula to calculate or which set of commands to issue. Thus, the real challenge of the subject lies in being able to define the problem and identify which statistical method is the most appropriate one to use.

Most students have some difficulty recognizing the particular kind of statistical problem they are addressing unless, of course, the problem appears among the exercises at the end of a section that just introduced the technique needed. Unfortunately, in practice, statistical problems do not appear already so identified. Consequently, we have adopted an approach to teaching statistics that is designed to help identify the statistical technique.

A number of factors determine which statistical method should be used, but two are especially important: the type of data and the purpose of the statistical inference. In Chapter 2, we pointed out that there are effectively three types of data—qualitative, ranked, and quantitative. Recall that qualitative data represent categories such as marital status, occupation, and gender. Statisticians often record qualitative data by assigning numbers to the responses (e.g., 1 = single; 2 = married; 3 = divorced; 4 = widowed). Because these numbers are assigned completely arbitrarily, any calculations performed on them are meaningless. All that we can do with qualitative data is count the number of times each category is observed. Ranked data are obtained from questions whose answers represent a rating or ranking system. For example, if students are asked to rate a university professor, the responses may be *excellent, good, fair,* or *poor.* To draw inferences about such data, we convert the responses to numbers. Any numbering system is valid as long as the order of the responses is preserved. Thus "4 = excellent; 3 = good; 2 = fair; 1 = poor" is just as valid as "10 = excellent; 5 = good; 2 = fair; 1 = poor." Because of this feature, the most appropriate statistical procedures for ranked data are ones based on a ranking process.

Quantitative data are real numbers such as those representing income, age, height, weight, and volume. Computation of means and variances is permissible.

The second key factor in determining the statistical technique is the purpose of doing the work. Every statistical method has some specific objective. There are five such objectives addressed in this book.

PROBLEM OBJECTIVES

1 **Describe a single population.** Our objective here is to describe some property of a population of interest. The decision about which property to describe is generally dictated by the type of data. For example, suppose the population of interest consists of all purchasers of home computers. If we are interested in the purchasers' incomes (for which the data are quantitative), we may calculate the mean or the variance to describe that aspect of the population. But if we are interested in the brand of computer that has been bought (for which the data are qualitative), all we can do is compute the proportion of the population that purchases each brand.

2 **Compare two populations.** In this case, our goal is to compare a property of one population with a corresponding property of a second population. For example, suppose the populations of interest are male and female purchasers of computers. We could compare the means of their incomes, or we could compare the proportion of each population that purchases a certain brand. Once again, the data type generally determines what kinds of properties we compare.

3 **Compare two or more populations.** We might want to compare the average income in each of several locations in order (for example) to decide where to build a new shopping center. Or we might want to compare the proportions of defective items in a number of production lines in order to determine which line is the best. In each case, the problem objective involves comparing two or more populations.

4 **Analyze the relationship between two variables.** There are numerous situations in which we want to know how one variable is related to another. Governments need to know what effect rising interest rates have on the unemployment rate. Companies want to investigate how the sizes of their advertising budgets influence sales volume. In most of the problems in this introductory text, the two variables to be analyzed will be of the same type; we will not attempt to cover the fairly large body of statistical techniques that has been developed to deal with two variables of different types.

5 **Analyze the relationship among two or more variables.** Our objective here is usually to forecast one variable (called the **dependent variable**) on the basis of several other variables (called **independent variables**). We will deal with this problem only in situations in which all variables are quantitative.

Table 10.2 lists the types of data and the five problem objectives. For each combination, the table specifies the chapter and/or section where the appropriate statistical technique is presented. For your convenience, a more detailed version of this table is reproduced inside the front cover of this book.

A BRIEF COMMENT ABOUT DERIVATIONS

Because this book is about statistical applications, we assume that our readers have little interest in the mathematical derivations of the techniques described. However, it might be helpful for you to have some understanding about the process that produces the formulas.

As described above, factors such as the problem objective and the type of data determine the parameter to be estimated and tested. For each parameter, statisticians have determined which statistic to use. That statistic has a sampling distribution that can usually be expressed as a formula. For example, in this chapter, the parameter of interest was the population mean μ, whose best estimator is the sample mean $\bar{x}$. Assuming that the population standard deviation σ is known, the sampling distribution of $\bar{x}$ is normal (or approximately so) with mean μ and standard deviation $\sigma/\sqrt{n}$. The sampling distribution can be described by the formula

$$z = \frac{\bar{x} - \mu}{\sigma/\sqrt{n}}$$

This formula also describes the test statistic for μ with σ known. With a little algebra, we were able to derive (in Section 9.3) the interval estimator of μ.

In future chapters, we will repeat this process, which in several cases involves the introduction of a new sampling distribution. While its shape and formula will differ from the sampling distribution used in this chapter, the pattern will be the same. In general, the formula that expresses the sampling distribution will describe the test statistic. Then some algebraic manipulation (which we will not show) produces the interval estimator. Consequently, we will reverse the order of presentation of the two techniques. That is, we will present the test of hypothesis first, followed by the interval estimator.

Table 10.2   Guide to Statistical Inference Showing Where Each Technique Is Introduced

Problem Objective	Data Type		
	Qualitative	Ranked	Quantitative
Describe a single population	Sec 11.4, 15.2	Not covered	Sec 11.2, 11.3
Compare two populations	Sec 12.6 Sec. 15.3	Sec 16.2, 16.3	Sec 12.2, 12.4, 12.5, 16.2, 16.3
Compare two or more populations	Sec 15.3	Sec 16.4, 16.5	Chapter 14, Sec 16.4, 16.5
Analyze the relationship between two variables	Sec 15.3	Sec 17.8	Chapter 17
Analyze the relationship among two or more variables	Not covered	Not covered	Chapters 18, 19

10.6 SUMMARY

In this chapter, we introduced the concepts of hypothesis testing and applied them to testing hypotheses about a population mean. We showed how to specify the null and alternative hypotheses, set up the rejection region, compute the value of the test statistic, and finally, to make a decision. Equally as important, we discussed how to interpret the test results. This chapter also demonstrated another way to make decisions—by calculating and using the p-value of the test. To help interpret test results, we showed how to calculate the probability of a Type II error. Finally, we provided a road map of how we plan to present statistical techniques. We complete this summary by listing the formulas described in this chapter.

IMPORTANT TERMS

Hypothesis testing *313*	Standardized test statistic *317*
Null hypothesis *313*	*p*-value of a test *319*
Alternative hypothesis *313*	One-tail test *327*
Type I error *313*	Two-tail test *327*
Type II error *313*	One-sided interval estimator *331*
Test statistic *314*	Problem objective *343*
Rejection region *316*	

SUMMARY OF FORMULAS

Test statistic

$$z = \frac{\bar{x} - \mu}{\sigma/\sqrt{n}}$$

p-value of the test

$P(Z > z)$ if H_1: $\mu > \mu_0$

$P(Z < z)$ if H_1: $\mu < \mu_0$

$2P(Z > |z|)$ if H_1: $\mu \neq \mu_0$

Probability of a Type II error

$\beta = P(\bar{x}_S < \bar{x} < \bar{x}_L$ given that μ = other than that specified under the null hypothesis)

SUPPLEMENTARY EXERCISES

The following exercises require the use of a computer and software. The answers may be calculated manually. See Appendix A for the sample statistics.

10.58 In an attempt to reduce the number of person-hours lost as a result of industrial accidents, a large production plant installed new safety equipment. In a test of the effectiveness of the equipment, a random sample of 50 departments was chosen. The number of person-hours lost in the month prior to and the month after the installation of the safety equipment was recorded. The percentage change was calculated, and the data stored in file XR10-58. Assume that the population standard deviation is $\sigma = 5$. What conclusion can you draw using a 10% significance level?

10.59 A highway patrol officer believes that the average speed of cars traveling over a certain stretch of highway exceeds the posted limit of 55 mph. The speeds of a random sample of 200 cars were recorded and stored in file XR10-59. Do these data provide sufficient evidence at the 1% significance level to support the offi-

cer's belief? What is the *p*-value of the test? (Assume that the standard deviation is known to be 5.)

10.60 An automotive expert claims that the large number of self-serve gasoline stations has resulted in poor automobile maintenance, and that the average tire pressure is more than 4 psi (pounds per square inch) below its manufacturer's specification. As a quick test, 50 tires were examined, and the number of psi each tire is below specification was recorded and stored in file XR10-60. If we assume that tire pressure is normally distributed with $\sigma = 1.5$ psi, can we infer at the 10% significance level that the expert is correct? What is the *p*-value?

10.61 For the past few years, the number of customers of a drive-up bank in New York has averaged 20 per hour, with a standard deviation of 3 per hour. This year, another bank 1 mile away opened a drive-up window. The manager of the first bank believes that this will result in a decrease in the number of customers. The number of customers who arrived during 36 randomly selected hours was recorded and stored in file XR10-61. Can we conclude at the 5% significance level that the manager is correct? What is the p-value?

10.62 A fast-food franchiser is considering building a restaurant at a certain location. Based on financial analyses, a site is acceptable only if the number of pedestrians passing the location averages more than 100 per hour. The number of pedestrians observed for each of 40 hours was recorded and stored in file XR10-62. Assuming that the population standard deviation is known to be 12, can we conclude that the site is acceptable? (Set your own significance level.)

10.63 In recent years, a number of companies have been formed that offer competition to AT&T in long distance calls. All advertise that their rates are lower than AT&T's, and as a result their bills will be lower. AT&T has responded by arguing that for the average consumer there will be no difference in billing. Suppose that a statistician working for AT&T determines that the mean and standard deviation of monthly long distance bills for all its residential customers are $17.85 and $3.87, respectively. He then takes a random sample of 100 customers and recalculates their last month's bills using the rates quoted by a leading competitor. These data are stored in file XR10-63. Assuming that the standard deviation of this population is the same as for AT&T, can we conclude at the 5% significance level that there is a difference between AT&T's bills and those of the leading competitor?

Chapter 11

Inference About the Description of a Single Population

11.1 Introduction

11.2 Inference About a Population Mean When the Population Standard Deviation Is Unknown

11.3 Inference About a Population Variance (Optional)

11.4 Inference About a Population Proportion

11.5 The Myth of the Law of Averages (Optional)

11.6 Summary

11.1 INTRODUCTION

In the previous two chapters, we introduced the concepts of statistical inference and showed how to estimate and test a population mean. However, the illustration we chose is unrealistic because the techniques require us to use the population standard deviation σ, which, in general, is unknown. The purpose, then, of Chapters 9 and 10 was to set the pattern for the way in which we plan to present other statistical techniques. That is, we will begin by identifying the parameter to be estimated or tested. We will then specify the parameter's estimator (each parameter has an estimator chosen because of the characteristics we discussed at the beginning of Chapter 9) and its sampling distribution. Using simple mathematics, statisticians have derived the interval estimator and the test statistic. This pattern will be used repeatedly as we introduce new techniques.

In Section 10.5, we described the five problem objectives addressed in this book, and we laid out the order of presentation of the statistical methods. In this chapter, we will present techniques employed when the problem objective is to describe a single population. When the data are quantitative, the parameters of interest are the population mean μ and the population variance σ^2. In Section 11.2, we describe how to make inferences about the population mean under the more realistic assumption that the population standard deviation is unknown. In Section 11.3, we continue to deal with quantitative data, but our parameter of interest becomes the population variance.

In Chapter 2 and in Section 10.5, we pointed out that when the data are qualitative, the only computation that makes sense is determining the proportion of times each value occurs. Section 11.4 discusses inference about the proportion p.

Here are three examples of inference about the description of a single population.

Example 1   The number of automatic teller machines (ATMs) has grown dramatically in the last several years. It has been estimated that for each transaction performed by an ATM instead of a teller, a bank saves more than $1. However, because of the cost of installation and maintenance, the number and placement of ATMs must be carefully planned. To help determine potential savings and thus whether a particular site should have an ATM, a bank conducted a survey to estimate the frequency with which each of several thousand potential ATM users will actually use the ATM annually. The problem objective is to describe the population of potential ATM users. The data are quantitative, because the bank intends to determine how many times per year each person will use the ATM. The parameter to be estimated is the mean frequency of use annually per person. From this statistic, the bank can estimate annual savings to decide whether to install an ATM.

Example 2   Bottlenecks in a production line can occur for a variety of reasons. For example, if the amount of time taken to complete a certain task is always greater than some others on an assembly line, several workers and/or machines will be idle while others will be overworked. In designing the way in which products will be produced, managers must consider a number of factors in order to avoid bottlenecks. Suppose that in an experiment to measure the amount of time required to complete a task on an assembly line, a random sample of workers' times is measured. The problem objective is to describe the population of workers' times—data that are quantitative. The managers would like to draw inferences about the central location of the times, in which case the parameter to be estimated or tested is the population mean. Equally important in this scenario is the variability of the times, because a great deal of variation can cause bottleneck problems even when the mean assembly times of different tasks are identical. Consequently, management will also draw inferences about the population variance. Several different production designs will be examined before a final decision is made.

Example 3 The profits of television networks depend greatly on the number of viewers who are tuned into each network. In most North American cities, viewers can choose from among the major networks and an assortment of independent stations, cable, and pay TV. Because the population of television viewers is so large (more than 100 million in the United States and more than 10 million in Canada), statistical techniques are used to draw inferences about it. In North America, this service is provided by several firms, including A. C. Nielsen, and the results are known as the Nielsen ratings. The problem objective is to describe the population of television viewers. Each respondent would be asked (among other things) which programs he or she watches at particular times. The data are qualitative. Consequently, the parameter of interest is the proportion of viewers who watch each program.

11.2 INFERENCE ABOUT A POPULATION MEAN WHEN THE POPULATION STANDARD DEVIATION IS UNKNOWN

In Sections 9.3 and 10.3, we demonstrated how to estimate and test the population mean when the population standard deviation is known. The interval estimator and the test statistic were derived from the sampling distribution of the sample mean with σ known, expressed as

$$z = \frac{\bar{x} - \mu}{\sigma/\sqrt{n}}$$

In this section, we assume that σ is unknown. Consequently, the sampling distribution above cannot be used. Instead, we substitute the sample standard deviation s in place of the unknown population standard deviation σ. The result is called a *t*-statistic because that is what mathematician William S. Gosset called it. In 1908, Gosset showed that the *t*-statistic defined as

$$t = \frac{\bar{x} - \mu}{s/\sqrt{n}}$$

is Student *t* distributed when the sampled population is normally distributed. (Gosset published his findings under the pseudonym "Student," hence the **Student *t* distribution.**)

Student *t* Distribution

Figure 11.1 depicts a **Student *t* distribution.** As you can see, the Student *t* distribution is similar to the standard normal distribution. Like the standard normal distribution, the Student *t* distribution is symmetrical about zero. It is also mound shaped, whereas the normal distribution is bell shaped. Figure 11.2 shows both a Student *t* and a standard normal distribution. The former is more widely dispersed than the latter. The extent to which the Student *t* distribution is more spread out than the standard normal distribution is determined by a function of the sample size called the **degrees of freedom** (abbreviated d.f.), which varies by the *t*-statistic. (This application is only the first of several different statistics that are Student *t* distributed.) For this application, the number of degrees of freedom equals the sample size minus 1. That is, d.f. = $n - 1$. Figure 11.3 depicts Student *t* distributions with several different degrees of freedom. Notice that as the degrees of freedom grow larger, the Student *t* distribution's dispersion gets smaller.

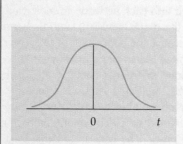

Figure 11.1

Student *t* distribution

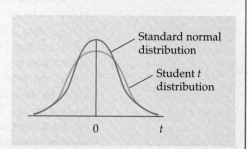

Figure 11.2

Student *t* and standard normal distribution

For the purpose of computing interval estimates and setting up rejection regions for tests of hypothesis, we need to be able to determine critical values. Table 4 in Appendix B specifies values of t_A, where t_A equals the value of t for which the area to its right under the Student t curve is equal to A. (See Figure 11.4.) This table is reproduced as Table 11.1.

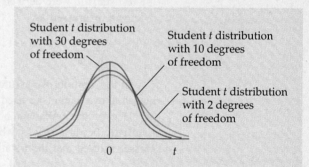

Figure 11.3

Student *t* distributions

Observe that t_A is provided for degrees of freedom ranging from 1 to 200 and ∞. To read this table, simply identify the degrees of freedom and find that value or the closest number to it. Then locate the column representing the t_A value you want. We denote this value $t_{A,df}$. For example, if we want the value of t such that the area under the Student t curve is .05 and the number of degrees of freedom is 10, we locate 10 in the first column and move across this row until we locate the value under the heading $t_{.05}$. We find (see Table 11.2)

$$t_{.05,10} = 1.812$$

Figure 11.4

Student *t* value such that the area to its right under the curve is *A*

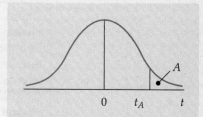

Table 11.1 **Critical Values of the Student t Distribution**

Degrees of Freedom	$t_{.10}$	$t_{.05}$	$t_{.025}$	$t_{.01}$	$t_{.005}$
1	3.078	6.314	12.706	31.821	63.657
2	1.886	2.920	4.303	6.965	9.925
3	1.638	2.353	3.182	4.541	5.841
4	1.533	2.132	2.776	3.747	4.604
5	1.476	2.015	2.571	3.365	4.032
6	1.440	1.943	2.447	3.143	3.707
7	1.415	1.895	2.365	2.998	3.499
8	1.397	1.860	2.306	2.896	3.355
9	1.383	1.833	2.262	2.821	3.250
10	1.372	1.812	2.228	2.764	3.169
11	1.363	1.796	2.201	2.718	3.106
12	1.356	1.782	2.179	2.681	3.055
13	1.350	1.771	2.160	2.650	3.012
14	1.345	1.761	2.145	2.624	2.977
15	1.341	1.753	2.131	2.602	2.947
16	1.337	1.746	2.120	2.583	2.921
17	1.333	1.740	2.110	2.567	2.898
18	1.330	1.734	2.101	2.552	2.878
19	1.328	1.729	2.093	2.539	2.861
20	1.325	1.725	2.086	2.528	2.845
21	1.323	1.721	2.080	2.518	2.831
22	1.321	1.717	2.074	2.508	2.819
23	1.319	1.714	2.069	2.500	2.807
24	1.318	1.711	2.064	2.492	2.797
25	1.316	1.708	2.060	2.485	2.787
26	1.315	1.706	2.056	2.479	2.779
27	1.314	1.703	2.052	2.473	2.771
28	1.313	1.701	2.048	2.467	2.763
29	1.311	1.699	2.045	2.462	2.756
30	1.310	1.697	2.042	2.457	2.750
35	1.306	1.690	2.030	2.438	2.724
40	1.303	1.684	2.021	2.423	2.705
45	1.301	1.679	2.014	2.412	2.690
50	1.299	1.676	2.009	2.403	2.678
60	1.296	1.671	2.000	2.390	2.660
70	1.294	1.667	1.994	2.381	2.648
80	1.292	1.664	1.990	2.374	2.639
90	1.291	1.662	1.987	2.369	2.632
100	1.290	1.660	1.984	2.364	2.626
120	1.289	1.658	1.980	2.358	2.617
140	1.288	1.656	1.977	2.353	2.611
160	1.287	1.654	1.975	2.350	2.607
180	1.286	1.653	1.973	2.347	2.603
200	1.286	1.653	1.972	2.345	2.601
∞	1.282	1.645	1.960	2.326	2.576

Source: From M. Merrington, "Table of Percentage Points of the *t*-Distribution," *Biometrika 32* (1941): 300. Reproduced by permission of the Biometrika trustees.

Table 11.2 **Finding $t_{.05,10}$**

Degrees of Freedom	$t_{.10}$	$t_{.05}$	$t_{.025}$	$t_{.01}$	$t_{.005}$
1	3.078	6.314	12.706	31.821	63.657
2	1.886	2.920	4.303	6.965	9.925
3	1.638	2.353	3.182	4.541	5.841
4	1.533	2.132	2.776	3.747	4.604
5	1.476	2.015	2.571	3.365	4.032
6	1.440	1.943	2.447	3.143	3.707
7	1.415	1.895	2.365	2.998	3.499
8	1.397	1.860	2.306	2.896	3.355
9	1.383	1.833	2.262	2.821	3.250
10	1.372	1.812	2.228	2.764	3.169
11	1.363	1.796	2.201	2.718	3.106
12	1.356	1.782	2.179	2.681	3.055

If the number of degrees of freedom is 25, we find (see Table 11.3)

$$t_{.05,25} = 1.708$$

Table 11.3 **Finding $t_{.05,25}$**

Degrees of Freedom	$t_{.10}$	$t_{.05}$	$t_{.025}$	$t_{.01}$	$t_{.005}$
1	3.078	6.314	12.706	31.821	63.657
2	1.886	2.920	4.303	6.965	9.925
3	1.638	2.353	3.182	4.541	5.841
4	1.533	2.132	2.776	3.747	4.604
5	1.476	2.015	2.571	3.365	4.032
.					
.					
.					
21	1.323	1.721	2.080	2.518	2.831
22	1.321	1.717	2.074	2.508	2.819
23	1.319	1.714	2.069	2.500	2.807
24	1.318	1.711	2.064	2.492	2.797
25	1.316	1.708	2.060	2.485	2.787
26	1.315	1.706	2.056	2.479	2.779

If the number of degrees of freedom is 74, we find the number of degrees of freedom closest to 74 listed in the table, which is 70. (See Table 11.4.)

$$t_{.05,74} \approx t_{.05,70} = 1.667$$

Table 11.4 **Finding** $t_{.05,70}$

Degrees of Freedom	$t_{.10}$	$t_{.05}$	$t_{.025}$	$t_{.01}$	$t_{.005}$
1	3.078	6.314	12.706	31.821	63.657
2	1.886	2.920	4.303	6.965	9.925
3	1.638	2.353	3.182	4.541	5.841
4	1.533	2.132	2.776	3.747	4.604
5	1.476	2.015	2.571	3.365	4.032
			.		
			.		
			.		
45	1.301	1.679	2.014	2.412	2.690
50	1.299	1.676	2.009	2.403	2.678
60	1.296	1.671	2.000	2.390	2.660
70	1.294	1.667	1.994	2.381	2.648
80	1.292	1.664	1.990	2.374	2.639
90	1.291	1.662	1.987	2.369	2.632
100	1.290	1.660	1.984	2.364	2.626
120	1.289	1.658	1.980	2.358	2.617
140	1.288	1.656	1.977	2.353	2.611
160	1.287	1.654	1.975	2.350	2.607
180	1.286	1.653	1.973	2.347	2.603
200	1.286	1.653	1.972	2.345	2.601
∞	1.282	1.645	1.960	2.326	2.576

In his 1908 article, Gosset showed that when the number of degrees of freedom is infinitely large, t_A is equal to z_A. (As the sample size increases, s approaches σ, and hence t approaches z.) That is, the Student t distribution is identical to the standard normal distribution. As you can see, the last row in the Student t table shows values of t_A with d.f. $= \infty$ that are equal to the z_A values we used in the previous chapter. (They do not appear equal except for $t_{.05,\infty} = z_{.05} = 1.96$ because we had only two decimal places to measure z_A, whereas the t_A values have three decimal places.) Notice the similarity between the values of t_A with 200 degrees of freedom and those with an infinite number of degrees of freedom. Consequently, when we have a Student t distribution with degrees of freedom greater than 200, we will approximate it by a Student t distribution with an infinite number of degrees of freedom (which is the same as the standard normal distribution).

Note that the statistic $(\bar{x} - \mu)/(s/\sqrt{n})$ has the Student t distribution only if the sample is drawn from a normal population. However, this application of the t distribution is said to be **robust;** this means that the t distribution also provides an adequate approximate sampling distribution of the t-statistic for moderately nonnormal populations. Thus, the statistical inference techniques that follow are valid except when applied to distinctly nonnormal populations.

In actual practice, some statisticians ignore the preceding requirement or blindly assume that the population is normal or only somewhat nonnormal. We urge you not to be one of them. Because we seldom get to know the true value of the parameter in question, our only way of knowing whether the statistical technique is valid is to be certain that the requirements underlying the technique are satisfied. At the very least, you should draw the histogram of any random variable that you are assuming is normal to ensure that the assumption is not badly violated.

TESTING THE POPULATION MEAN WHEN THE POPULATION STANDARD DEVIATION IS UNKNOWN

With exactly the same logic used to develop the test statistic in Section 10.3, we derive the following test statistic.

Test Statistic for μ when σ Is Unknown

When the population standard deviation is unknown and the population is normally distributed, the test statistic for testing hypotheses about μ is

$$t = \frac{\bar{x} - \mu}{s/\sqrt{n}}$$

which has a Student t distribution with $n - 1$ degrees of freedom.

Note that we have now presented two different test statistics for testing the population mean. In Section 10.3, we tested μ under the assumption that the population standard deviation σ was known. In that case we employed the test statistic

$$z = \frac{\bar{x} - \mu}{\sigma/\sqrt{n}}$$

However, as we've already discussed, the application of this statistic is quite rare in practice. Consequently, henceforth when we test hypotheses about a population mean we will use the test statistic

$$t = \frac{\bar{x} - \mu}{s/\sqrt{n}}$$

because the population standard deviation is unknown.

STATISTICS IN THE WORKPLACE

Operations Management Application

In Chapter 1 we discussed the operations management function of aggregate production planning. We pointed out that several strategies can be used to meet the demand for a company's product. These include level production, chase strategy, scheduling overtime and undertime, subcontracting, hiring part-time workers, and backordering when demand exceeds supply.

Using the chase strategy we hire and lay off workers so that each period's production matches the forecasted demand. However, the productivity of new workers tends to be quite variable making it difficult for managers to know how many units they will produce. One way to get the information managers require is to employ statistical analyses.

▼ EXAMPLE 11.1

Couriers like UPS and FedEx compete on service and price. One way to reduce costs is to keep labor costs low by hiring and laying off workers to meet demand. This strategy requires managers to hire and train new workers. But newly hired and trained workers are not as productive as more experienced ones. Thus, determining the number of workers required and the work schedule is difficult. The current work schedule is based on the belief that trainees will achieve more than 90% of the level of experienced workers within 1 week of hiring. To determine the accuracy of this number an operations manager conducted an experiment. Fifty trainees were observed for 1 hour and the number of packages processed and routed were recorded. These data appear below and are stored in file XM11-01. It is known that experienced workers process an average of 500 packages per hour. The manager is concerned that if he concludes that the mean is greater than 450 when it isn't the result will be many late deliveries, a disaster for a courier. Can the manager conclude from the data that the belief is correct?

NUMBER OF PACKAGES

505	467	480	537	487	427	482	488	409	475
400	551	466	484	373	509	442	508	501	470
499	444	477	418	416	410	465	432	440	485
415	481	445	465	424	515	449	405	444	469
418	429	413	496	471	435	523	440	485	450

Solution

IDENTIFY

The problem objective is to describe the population of the number of packages processed in 1 hour by trainees. The data are quantitative, indicating that the parameter to be tested is the population mean. Because the manager wants to know whether the belief that trainees' productivity is more than 90% of experienced workers who process an average of 500 packages per hour the alternative hypothesis is

$$H_1 : \mu > 450$$

The null hypothesis automatically follows.

$$H_0 : \mu = 450$$

The test statistic is

$$t = \frac{\bar{x} - \mu}{s/\sqrt{n}} \quad \text{d.f.} = n - 1$$

SOLVE

The manager believes that the cost of a Type I error (concluding that the mean is greater than 450 when it isn't) is not excessively high. Consequently, he sets the significance level at 5%. The rejection region is

$$t > t_{\alpha,n-1} = t_{.05,49} \approx t_{.05,50} = 1.676$$

To calculate the value of the test statistic we need to calculate the sample mean $\bar{x}$ and the sample standard deviation s. From the data we determine

$$\sum x_i = 23{,}019 \quad \text{and} \quad \sum x_i^2 = 10{,}671{,}357$$

Thus,

$$\bar{x} = \frac{\sum x_i}{n} = \frac{23{,}019}{50} = 460.38$$

and

$$s^2 = \frac{\sum x_i^2 - \frac{(\sum x_i)^2}{n}}{n-1} = \frac{10,671,357 - \frac{(23,019)^2}{50}}{50-1} = 1,507.55$$

Thus

$$s = \sqrt{s^2} = \sqrt{1,507.55} = 38.83$$

The value of μ is found in the null hypothesis. It is 450. The value of the test statistic is

$$t = \frac{\bar{x} - \mu}{s/\sqrt{n}} = \frac{460.38 - 450}{38.83/\sqrt{50}} = 1.89$$

Because 1.89 is greater than 1.676 we reject the null hypothesis in favor of the alternative. See Figure 11.5 below.

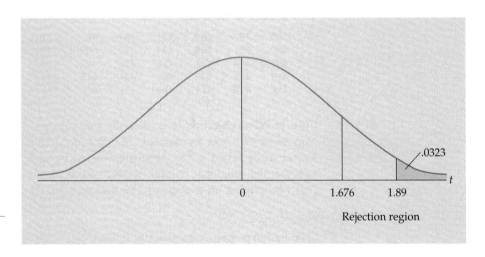

Figure 11.5

Sampling distribution for Example 11.1

Excel Output for Example 11.1

	A	B	C	D	E
1	**Test of Hypothesis About MU (SIGMA Unknown)**				
2					
3	Test of MU = 450 Vs MU greater than 450				
4	Sample standard deviation = 38.8271				
5	Sample mean = 460.38				
6	Test Statistic: t = 1.8904				
7	P-Value = 0.0323				

COMMANDS

1 Type or import the data.
2 Click **Tools, Data Analysis Plus,** and **Inference About a Mean (SIGMA Unknown).**

COMMANDS FOR EXAMPLE 11.1

Open file **XM11-01.**

3 Specify the input range. Do not include cell containing the variable name. **A2:A51**

4 Click **Test of Hypothesis.**

5 Specify the value of μ under the null hypothesis. **450**

6 Click the appropriate alternative hypothesis. **MU greater than 450**

To conduct this test from statistics or perform a what-if analysis click **Tools, Data Analysis Plus,** and **Inference from Summary Statistics (Workbook).** Activate the worksheet **t-Test of a Mean.**

Minitab Output for Example 11.1

T-Test of the Mean

```
Test of mu = 450.00 vs mu > 450.00

Variable     N      Mean    StDev    SE Mean      T       P
Packages    50    460.38    38.83       5.49    1.89   0.032
```

COMMANDS

1 Type or import the data into one column.

2 Click **Stat, Basic Statistics,** and **1-Sample t . . . .**

3 Type the variable name.

4 Use the cursor to choose **Test mean.**

5 Hit **tab** and type the value of μ under the null hypothesis.

6 Use the cursor to select **less than, not equal,** or **greater than.** Click **OK.**

COMMANDS FOR EXAMPLE 11.1

Open file **XM11-01.**

Packages or C1

450

greater than

INTERPRET

There is enough evidence to infer that the mean number of parcels processed by trainees is more than 90% of that of experienced workers. Thus, the number of workers hired to meet demand under the chase strategy should be valid and the resulting aggregate production plan satisfactory.

▲

ESTIMATING THE POPULATION MEAN WHEN THE POPULATION STANDARD DEVIATION IS UNKNOWN

Using the identical algebraic manipulation we employed to produce the interval estimator of the population mean when the population standard deviation is known (see Section 9.3), we develop the following estimator.

Interval Estimator of μ When σ Is Unknown

$$\bar{x} \pm t_{\alpha/2}\frac{s}{\sqrt{n}} \qquad \text{d.f.} = n - 1$$

As was the case with testing a population mean, we have two different interval estimators of μ. In practice, we use the one presented here because it is almost always the case that the population standard deviation is unknown.

STATISTICS IN THE WORKPLACE

Finance Application

In Chapter 4 we defined return on investment and pointed out that investors often look at this variable to make decisions about which stocks to buy. Investors are always looking for ways to identify stocks and other investments that are likely to have high returns. They recognize that return on investment is a random variable often with a large standard deviation, which measures the risk. Investors would like to know the mean return on investment for the entire population of returns. However, we can only estimate these parameters.

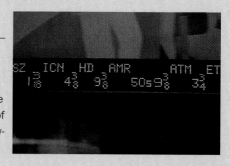

▼ EXAMPLE 11.2

During the last decade a number of institutions dedicated to improving the quality of products and services in the United States have been formed. Many of these groups give annual awards to companies that produce high-quality goods and services. An investor believes that publicly traded companies that win awards are likely to outperform companies that do not win such awards. To help determine his return on investment in such companies, he took a random sample of 50 firms that won quality awards the previous year and computed the annual return had he invested. These data are listed below and stored in file XM11-02. The investor would like an estimate of the returns he can expect. A 95% confidence interval is deemed appropriate.

RETURNS

18.58	17.27	26.28	15.58	5.14	7.88	13.53	0.56	19.12	19.04
10.35	24.16	14.53	20.6	2.34	16.51	2.07	27.05	14.93	16.78
22.41	22.33	17.71	2.21	14.89	6.9	5.2	20.91	11.97	20.09
4.51	19.83	20.25	17.1	26	12.43	19.83	20.6	4.19	6.56
5.4	18.85	25.1	21.5	32.14	22.74	11.27	12.46	−1.49	1.42

Solution

IDENTIFY

The problem objective is to describe the population of annual returns from buying shares of quality-award winners. The data are quantitative and, hence, the parameter to be estimated is the population mean μ whose interval estimator is

$$\bar{x} \pm t_{\alpha/2}\frac{s}{\sqrt{n}}$$

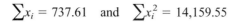

SOLVE

From the data we determine

$$\sum x_i = 737.61 \quad \text{and} \quad \sum x_i^2 = 14{,}159.55$$

Thus,

$$\bar{x} = \frac{\sum x_i}{n} = \frac{737.61}{50} = 14.75$$

and

$$s^2 = \frac{\sum x_i^2 - \frac{(\sum x_i)^2}{n}}{n - 1} = \frac{14{,}159.55 - \frac{(737.61)^2}{50}}{50 - 1} = 66.90$$

Thus,

$$s = \sqrt{s^2} = \sqrt{66.90} = 8.18$$

Because we want a 95% confidence interval estimate, $1 - \alpha = .95$, $\alpha = .05$, $\alpha/2 = .025$, and $t_{\alpha/2,n-1} = t_{.025,49} \approx t_{.025,50} = 2.009$. Thus, the 95% confidence interval estimate of μ is

$$\bar{x} \pm t_{\alpha/2} \frac{s}{\sqrt{n}} = 14.75 \pm 2.009 \frac{8.18}{\sqrt{50}} = 14.75 \pm 2.32$$

$$\text{LCL} = 12.43 \quad \text{UCL} = 17.07$$

Excel Output for Example 11.2

	A	B	C	D	E	F
1	**0.95 Confidence Interval Estimate of MU (SIGMA Unknown)**					
2						
3	*Sample mean = 14.7522*					
4	*Sample standard deviation = 8.1793*					
5	*Lower confidence limit = 12.4277*					
6	*Upper confidence limit = 17.0767*					

COMMANDS

COMMANDS FOR EXAMPLE 11.2

1 Type or import the data into one column.

Open file **XM11-02**.

2 Click **Tools, Data Analysis Plus,** and **Inference About a Mean (SIGMA Unknown).**

3 Specify the **Input Range:**. Do not include the cell containing the variable name.

A2:A51

4 Click **Interval Estimate.**

5 Specify the confidence level.

.95

To compute the interval estimate from the sample mean and standard deviation or perform a what-if analysis, click **Tools, Data Analysis Plus,** and **Inference from Summary Statistics (Workbook).** Activate the worksheet **t-Estimate of a Mean.** Click **Exit** when finished.

Minitab Output for Example 11.2

T Confidence Intervals

Variable	N	Mean	StDev	SE Mean	95.0 % CI
Returns	50	14.75	8.18	1.16	(12.43, 17.08)

COMMANDS	COMMANDS FOR EXAMPLE 11.2
1 Type or import the data into one column.	Open file **XM11-02.**
2 Click **Stat, Basic Statistics,** and **1-Sample t . . . .**	
3 Type the variable name.	**Returns** or **C1**
4 Use the cursor to select **Confidence interval.**	
5 Hit **tab** and type the confidence level. Click **OK.**	.95

INTERPRET

We estimate that the mean return lies between 12.43% and 17.08%. We can use this estimate to help decide whether to invest in quality-award winners and if so, what return on investment we can expect.

▲

CHECKING THE REQUIRED CONDITIONS

When we introduced the Student t distribution, we pointed out that the t-statistic is Student t distributed only if the population from which we've sampled is normal. We also noted that the techniques introduced in this section are robust, meaning that if the population is nonnormal, the techniques are still valid provided that the population is not *extremely* nonnormal. Later in this book we will introduce two statistical methods that test for normality, but at this point we recommend drawing the histogram to examine the shape of the distribution. Our two software packages can be used for this purpose. Figures 11.6 and 11.7 depict the Excel histograms for Examples 11.1 and 11.2, respectively. (The Minitab histograms are similar.) Both histograms suggest that the variables may be normal or at least not extremely nonnormal.

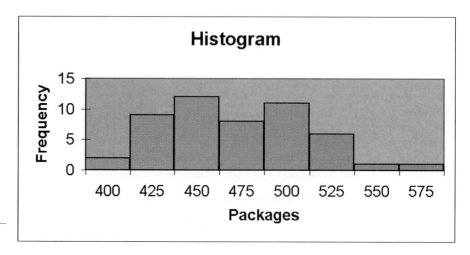

Figure 11.6

Histogram for Example 11.1

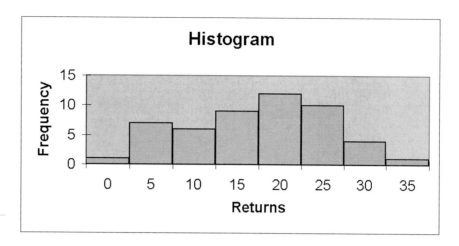

Figure 11.7

Histogram for Example 11.2

DEVELOPING AN UNDERSTANDING OF THE STATISTICAL CONCEPTS

In Chapters 9 and 10, we introduced the procedures used to estimate and test parameters. The examples we chose to illustrate the process were unrealistic, requiring that the population standard deviation be known when the population mean is not. We chose those examples because of their linkage to Chapter 8 (sampling distribution of the mean) and Chapter 7 (normal distribution). The concept developed in this section is that to expand the application to more realistic situations, we must use another sampling distribution. The Student t distribution was derived by W. S. Gosset for this purpose.

Another important development in this section is the use of the term "degrees of freedom." We will encounter this term many times in this book, so a brief discussion of its meaning is warranted.

The Student t distribution is based on using the sample variance to estimate the unknown population variance. The sample variance is defined as

$$s^2 = \frac{\sum(x_i - \bar{x})^2}{n - 1}$$

To compute s^2, we must first determine $\bar{x}$. Recall that sampling distributions are derived by repeated sampling of size n from the same population. To repeatedly take samples to compute s^2, we can choose any numbers for the first $n - 1$ observations in the sample. However, we have no choice on the nth value because the sample mean must be calculated first. To illustrate, suppose that $n = 3$ and we find $\bar{x} = 10$. We can have x_1 and x_2 assume any values without restriction. However, x_3 must be such that $\bar{x} = 10$. For example, if $x_1 = 6$ and $x_2 = 8$, then x_3 must equal 16. Therefore, there are only two degrees of freedom in our selection of the sample. We say that we lose one degree of freedom because we had to calculate $\bar{x}$.

Notice that the denominator in the calculation of s^2 is equal to the number of degrees of freedom. This is not a coincidence and will be repeated throughout this book.

Let's complete this section with a review of how we identify this technique.

Factors that Identify the t-Test and Estimator of μ

1 Problem objective: describe a single population

2 Data type: quantitative

3 Descriptive measurement: central location

EXERCISES

*Exercises 11.1–11.25 are "what-if" analyses designed to determine what happens to the test statistics and interval estimates when elements of the statistical inference change. These problems can be solved manually or using Excel's **Inference from Summary Statistics (Workbook)** option.*

11.1 A random sample of 50 was drawn from a normal population. The sample mean and standard deviation are $\bar{x} = 510$ and $s = 125$. Estimate μ with 95% confidence.

11.2 Repeat Exercise 11.1 with $n = 100$.

11.3 Repeat Exercise 11.1 with $n = 25$.

11.4 Repeat Exercise 11.1 with $s = 200$.

11.5 Repeat Exercise 11.1 with $s = 75$.

11.6 Repeat Exercise 11.1 with a 90% confidence level.

11.7 Repeat Exercise 11.1 with a 99% confidence level.

11.8 Review the results of Exercises 11.1–11.7.

    a What is the effect of decreasing the sample size?
    b What is the effect of increasing s?
    c What is the effect of increasing the confidence level?

11.9 The sample mean and standard deviation from a random sample of 20 observations from a normal population were computed as $\bar{x} = 23$ and $s = 9$. Can we infer at the 5% significance level that the population mean is greater than 20?

11.10 Repeat Exercise 11.9 with $n = 10$.

11.11 Repeat Exercise 11.9 with $n = 50$.

11.12 Repeat Exercise 11.9 with $s = 5$.

11.13 Repeat Exercise 11.9 with $s = 20$.

11.14 Repeat Exercise 11.9 with $\bar{x} = 21$.

11.15 Repeat Exercise 11.9 with $\bar{x} = 26$.

11.16 Review the results of Exercises 11.9–11.15.

    a What is the effect of decreasing the sample size?
    b What is the effect of increasing s?
    c What is the effect of increasing $\bar{x}$?

11.17 A random sample of 10 observations was drawn from a normal population. The sample mean and standard deviation are $\bar{x} = 50$ and $s = 15$. Estimate the population mean with 95% confidence.

11.18 Repeat Exercise 11.17 assuming that you know that the population standard deviation is $\sigma = 15$.

11.19 Review Exercises 11.17 and 11.18. Explain why the interval estimate produced in Exercise 11.18 is narrower than that in Exercise 11.17.

11.20 A random sample of 8 observations was taken from a normal population. The sample mean and standard deviation are $\bar{x} = 75$ and $s = 50$. Can we infer at the 10% significance level that the population mean is less than 100?

11.21 Repeat Exercise 11.20 assuming that you know that the population standard deviation is $\sigma = 50$.

11.22 Review Exercises 11.20 and 11.21. Explain why the test statistics differed.

11.23 After sampling 1,000 members of a normal population you find $\bar{x} = 15,500$ and $s = 9,950$. Estimate the population mean with 90% confidence.

11.24 Repeat Exercise 11.23 assuming that you know that the population standard deviation is $\sigma = 9,950$.

11.25 Review Exercises 11.23 and 11.24. Explain why the interval estimates were virtually identical.

11.26 A random sample of 11 observations was drawn from a normal population. These are

7   1   2   8   4   9   3   4   9   5   2

Estimate the population mean with 90% confidence.

11.27 Given the following observations, test at the 10% significance level to determine whether the mean differs from 15.

12   23   11   25   28   7   16   27   11   8   4   14

Exercises 11.28–11.35 require the use of a computer and software. The answers may be calculated manually. See Appendix C for the sample statistics.

11.28 The following observations were drawn from a normal population (The data are also stored in file XR11-28.)

22   18   25   28   19   20   24   26   19   26   27
22   23   25   25   18   20   26   18   26   27   24
20   19   18

a Estimate the population mean with 95% confidence.

b Test to determine if we can infer at the 10% significance level that the population mean is greater than 20.

c What is the required condition of the techniques used in parts (a) and (b)? Use a graphical technique to check to see if that required condition is satisfied.

11.29 A random sample of 75 observations from a normal population is stored in file XR11-29. Test to determine whether we can conclude at the 5% significance level that the population mean is not equal to 103.

11.30 A growing concern for educators in the United States is the number of teenagers who have part-time jobs while they attend high school. It is generally believed that the amount of time teenagers spend working is deducted from the amount of time devoted to schoolwork. To investigate this problem, a school guidance counselor took a random sample of two hundred high school students who reported that they have part-time jobs and asked how many hours per week each worked. The results were recorded (to the nearest hour) and stored in file XR11-30. Estimate with 95% confidence the mean amount of time all high school students who have part-time jobs devote per week to their jobs.

11.31 A federal agency responsible for enforcing laws governing weights and measures routinely inspects packages to determine if the weight of the contents is at least as great as that advertised on the package. A random sample of 50 containers whose packaging states that the contents weigh 8 ounces was drawn. The contents were weighed and the results (to the nearest tenth) are stored in file XR11-31. Estimate the mean weight of all the containers with 99% confidence.

11.32 A diet doctor claims that the average North American is more than 20 pounds overweight. To test his claim, a random sample of 100 North Americans was weighed, and the difference between their actual weight and their ideal weight was calculated. The data are stored in file XR11-32. Do these data allow us to infer at the 5% significance level that the doctor's claim is true?

11.33 A courier service advertises that its average delivery time is less than 6 hours for local deliveries. A random sample of times for 50 deliveries to an address across town is stored in file XR11-33.

a Is this sufficient evidence to support the courier's advertisement at the 5% level of significance?

b What assumption must be made in order to answer part (a)? Use whatever graphical technique you deem appropriate to confirm that the required condition is satisfied.

11.34 A manufacturer of a brand of designer jeans has pitched her advertising to develop an expensive and classy image. The suggested retail price is $75. However, she is concerned that retailers are undermining her image by offering the jeans at discount prices. To better understand what is happening, she randomly samples 30 retailers who sell her product and determines the price. The results are stored in file XR11-34. She would like an estimate of the mean selling price of the jeans at all retail stores.

a Determine the 95% confidence interval estimate.

b What assumption must be made to be sure that the estimate produced in part (a) is valid? Use a graphical technique to check the required condition.

11.35 Ecologists have long advocated recycling newspapers as a way of saving trees and reducing landfills. In recent years a number of companies have gone into the business of collecting used newspapers from households and recycling them. A financial analyst for one such company has recently computed that the firm would make a profit if the mean weekly newspaper collection from each household exceeded 2 pounds. In a study to determine the feasibility of a recycling plant, a random sample of 100 households was drawn, and the weekly weight of newspapers discarded for recycling by each household was recorded and stored in file XR11-35. Do these data provide sufficient evidence at the 1% significance level to allow the analyst to conclude that a recycling plant would be profitable?

11.3 INFERENCE ABOUT A POPULATION VARIANCE (OPTIONAL)

In Section 11.2, where we presented the inferential methods about a population mean, we were interested in acquiring information about the central location of the population. As a result, we tested and estimated the population mean. If we are interested instead in making an inference about the variability, the parameter we need to investigate is the population variance σ^2. Inference about the variance can be used to make decisions in a variety of problems. For example, quality-control engineers must ensure that their company's products meet specifications. One way of judging the consistency of a production process is to compute the variance of the size, weight, or volume of the product. That is, if the variation in product size, weight, or volume is large, it is likely that an unsatisfactorily large number of products will lie outside the specifications for that product. Another example comes from the subject area of finance. Investors use the variance of the returns on a portfolio of stocks, bonds, or other investments as a measure of the uncertainty and risk inherent in that portfolio. Investors often go to great lengths to avoid risky investments.

The task of deriving the test statistic and the interval estimator provides us with another opportunity to show how statistical techniques in general are developed. We begin by identifying the best estimator. That estimator has a sampling distribution, from which we produce the test statistic and the interval estimator.

POINT ESTIMATOR

The point estimator for σ^2 is the sample variance introduced in Section 4.3 and used repeatedly, most recently in the section above to test and estimate μ. The statistic s^2 has the desirable characteristics presented in Section 9.2; that is, s^2 is an unbiased, consistent estimator of σ^2.

SAMPLING DISTRIBUTION OF s²

To create the sampling distribution of the sample variance, we repeatedly take samples of size n from a normal population whose variance is σ^2, calculate s^2 for each sample, and then draw the histogram. The result would appear similar to Figure 11.8. The actual shape would vary according to the sample size and the value of σ^2, However, regardless of the sample size or the value of σ^2, the sampling distribution would be positively skewed.

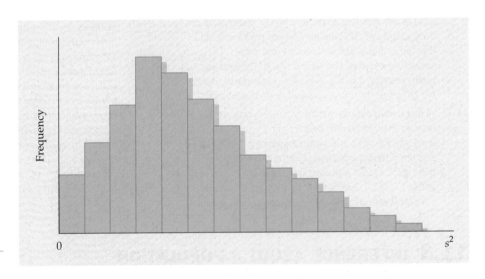

Figure 11.8

Histogram of s²

Mathematicians have shown that the sum of squared differences $\sum(x_i - \bar{x})^2$ [which is equal to $(n - 1)s^2$] divided by the population variance is distributed according to what is called the **chi-squared distribution** provided that the sampled population is normal. The statistic

$$\chi^2 = \frac{(n - 1)s^2}{\sigma^2}$$

is called the **chi-squared statistic (χ^2-statistic)** and is denoted by the Greek letter *chi* squared.

Chi-Squared Distribution

The **chi-squared distribution** is positively skewed ranging between 0 and ∞. Like that of the Student t distribution, its shape depends on its number of degrees of freedom. Figure 11.9 depicts several chi-squared distributions with different numbers of degrees of freedom.

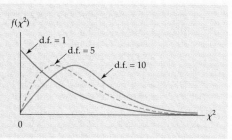

Figure 11.9

Chi-squared distributions

The value of χ^2 such that the area to its right under the chi-squared curve is equal to A is denoted χ^2_A. We cannot use $-\chi^2_A$ to represent the point such that the area to its *left* is A (as we did with z and t) because the χ^2-statistic is always greater than 0. To represent the left-tail critical values, we note that if the area to the left of a point is A, the area to its right must be $1 - A$ since the entire area under the chi-squared curve (as well as all continuous distributions) must equal 1. Thus, χ^2_{1-A} denotes the point such that the area to its *left* is A. Figure 11.10 depicts a chi-squared distribution with χ^2_A and χ^2_{1-A}. Table 5 in Appendix B, reproduced here as Table 11.5, lists the critical values of the chi-squared distribution for degrees of freedom equal to 1 to 30, 40, 50, 60, 70, 80, 90, and 100. For example, to find the point in a chi-squared distribution with eight degrees of freedom such that the area to its right is .05, locate eight degrees of freedom in the left column and $\chi^2_{.050}$ across the top row. The intersection of the row and column contains the value we seek as shown in Table 11.6. That is,

$$\chi^2_{.050,8} = 15.5073$$

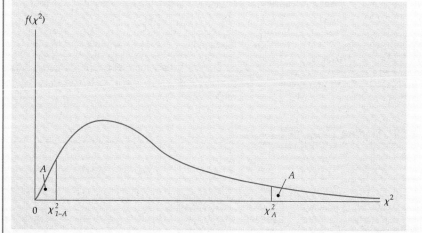

Figure 11.10

χ^2_A and χ^2_{1-A}

To find the point in the same distribution such that the area to its *left* is .05, find the point such that the area to its *right* is .95. Locate $\chi^2_{.950}$ across the top row and eight degrees of freedom down the side (also shown in Table 11.6). You should see that

$$\chi^2_{.950,8} = 2.73264$$

Table 11.5 Critical Values of χ^2

Degrees of Freedom	$\chi^2_{.995}$	$\chi^2_{.990}$	$\chi^2_{.975}$	$\chi^2_{.950}$	$\chi^2_{.900}$	$\chi^2_{.100}$	$\chi^2_{.050}$	$\chi^2_{.025}$	$\chi^2_{.010}$	$\chi^2_{.005}$
1	0.0000393	0.0001571	0.0009821	0.0039321	0.0157908	2.70554	3.84146	5.02389	6.63490	7.87944
2	0.0100251	0.0201007	0.0506356	0.102587	0.210720	4.60517	5.99147	7.37776	9.21034	10.5966
3	0.0717212	0.114832	0.215795	0.351846	0.584375	6.25139	7.81473	9.34840	11.3449	12.8381
4	0.206990	0.297110	0.484419	0.710721	1.063623	7.77944	9.48773	11.1433	13.2767	14.8602
5	0.411740	0.55430	0.831211	1.145476	1.61031	9.23635	11.0705	12.8325	15.0863	16.7496
6	0.675727	0.872085	1.237347	1.63539	2.20413	10.6446	12.5916	14.4494	16.8119	18.5476
7	0.989265	1.239043	1.68987	2.16735	2.83311	12.0170	14.0671	16.0128	18.4753	20.2777
8	1.344419	1.646482	2.17973	2.73264	3.48954	13.3616	15.5073	17.5346	20.0902	21.9550
9	1.734926	2.087912	2.70039	3.32511	4.16816	14.6837	16.9190	19.0228	21.6660	23.5893
10	2.15585	2.55821	3.24697	3.94030	4.86518	15.9871	18.3070	20.4831	23.2093	25.1882
11	2.60321	3.05347	3.81575	4.57481	5.57779	17.2750	19.6751	21.9200	24.7250	26.7569
12	3.07382	3.57056	4.40379	5.22603	6.30380	18.5494	21.0261	23.3367	26.2170	28.2995
13	3.56503	4.10691	5.00874	5.89186	7.04150	19.8119	22.3621	24.7356	27.6883	29.8194
14	4.07468	4.66043	5.62872	6.57063	7.78953	21.0642	23.6848	26.1190	29.1413	31.3193
15	4.60094	5.22935	6.26214	7.26094	8.54675	22.3072	24.9958	27.4884	30.5779	32.8013
16	5.14224	5.81221	6.90766	7.96164	9.31223	23.5418	26.2962	28.8454	31.9999	34.2672
17	5.69724	6.40776	7.56418	8.67176	10.0852	24.7690	27.5871	30.1910	33.4087	35.7185
18	6.26481	7.01491	8.23075	9.39046	10.8649	25.9894	28.8693	31.5264	34.8053	37.1564
19	6.84398	7.63273	8.90655	10.1170	11.6509	27.2036	30.1435	32.8523	36.1908	38.5822
20	7.43386	8.26040	9.59083	10.8508	12.4426	28.4120	31.4104	34.1696	37.5662	39.9968
21	8.03366	8.89720	10.28293	11.5913	13.2396	29.6151	32.6705	35.4789	38.9321	41.4010
22	8.64272	9.54249	10.9823	12.3380	14.0415	30.8133	33.9244	36.7807	40.2894	42.7956
23	9.26042	10.19567	11.6885	13.0905	14.8479	32.0069	35.1725	38.0757	41.6384	44.1813
24	9.88623	10.8564	12.4011	13.8484	15.6587	33.1963	36.4151	39.3641	42.9798	45.5585
25	10.5197	11.5240	13.1197	14.6114	16.4734	34.3816	37.6525	40.6465	44.3141	46.9278
26	11.1603	12.1981	13.8439	15.3791	17.2919	35.5631	38.8852	41.9232	45.6417	48.2899
27	11.8076	12.8786	14.5733	16.1513	18.1138	36.7412	40.1133	43.1944	46.9630	49.6449
28	12.4613	13.5648	15.3079	16.9279	18.9392	37.9159	41.3372	44.4607	48.2782	50.9933
29	13.1211	14.2565	16.0471	17.7083	19.7677	39.0875	42.5569	45.7222	49.5879	52.3356
30	13.7867	14.9535	16.7908	18.4926	20.5992	40.2560	43.7729	46.9792	50.8922	53.6720
40	20.7065	22.1643	24.4331	26.5093	29.0505	51.8050	55.7585	59.3417	63.6907	66.7659
50	27.9907	29.7067	32.3574	34.7642	37.6886	63.1671	67.5048	71.4202	76.1539	79.4900
60	35.5346	37.4848	40.4817	43.1879	46.4589	74.3970	79.0819	83.2976	88.3794	91.9517
70	43.2752	45.4418	48.7576	51.7393	55.3290	85.5271	90.5312	95.0231	100.425	104.215
80	51.1720	53.5400	57.1532	60.3915	64.2778	96.5782	101.879	106.629	112.329	116.321
90	59.1963	61.7541	65.6466	69.1260	73.2912	107.565	113.145	118.136	124.116	128.299
100	67.3276	70.0648	74.2219	77.9295	82.3581	118.498	124.342	129.561	135.807	140.169

Source: From C. M. Thompson, "Tables of the Percentage Points of the χ^2-Distribution," *Biometrika 32* (1941): 188–89. Reproduced by permission of the Biometrika trustees.

Table 11.6 Finding $\chi^2_{.050,8}$ and $\chi^2_{.950,8}$

Degrees of Freedom	$\chi^2_{.995}$	$\chi^2_{.990}$	$\chi^2_{.975}$	$\chi^2_{.950}$	$\chi^2_{.900}$	$\chi^2_{.100}$	$\chi^2_{.050}$	$\chi^2_{.025}$	$\chi^2_{.010}$	$\chi^2_{.005}$
1	0.0000393	0.0001571	0.0009821	0.0039321	0.0157908	2.70554	3.84146	5.02389	6.63490	7.87944
2	0.0100251	0.0201007	0.0506356	0.102587	0.210721	4.60517	5.99147	7.37776	9.21034	10.5966
3	0.0717212	0.114832	0.215795	0.351846	0.584375	6.25139	7.81473	9.34840	11.3449	12.8381
4	0.206990	0.297110	0.484419	0.710721	1.063623	7.77944	9.48773	11.1433	13.2767	14.8602
5	0.411740	0.554300	0.831211	1.145476	1.61031	9.23635	11.0705	12.8325	15.0863	16.7496
6	0.675727	0.872085	1.237347	1.63539	2.20413	10.6446	12.5916	14.4494	16.8119	18.5476
7	0.989265	1.239043	1.68987	2.16735	2.83311	12.0170	14.0671	16.0128	18.4753	20.2777
8	1.344419	1.646482	2.17973	2.73264	3.48954	13.3616	15.5073	17.5346	20.0902	21.9550
9	1.734926	2.087912	2.70039	3.32511	4.16816	14.6837	16.9190	19.0228	21.6660	23.5893
10	2.15585	2.55821	3.24697	3.94030	4.86518	15.9871	18.3070	20.4831	23.2093	25.1882
11	2.60321	3.05347	3.81575	4.57481	5.57779	17.2750	19.6751	21.9200	24.7250	26.7569

TESTING THE POPULATION VARIANCE

As we discussed in Section 10.5, the formula that describes the sampling distribution is the formula of the test statistic.

Test Statistic for σ^2

The test statistic used to test hypotheses about σ^2 is

$$\chi^2 = \frac{(n-1)s^2}{\sigma^2}$$

which is chi-squared distributed with $(n-1)$ degrees of freedom when the population random variable is normally distributed with variance equal to σ^2.

STATISTICS IN THE WORKPLACE

Operations Management Application

A critical aspect of production is quality. The quality of a final product is a function of the quality of the product's components. If the components don't fit, the product will not function as planned and is likely to cease functioning before its customers expect it to. For example, if a car door is not made to specifications it will not fit. As a result the door will leak both water and air.

Operations managers attempt to maintain and improve the quality of products by ensuring that all components are made so that there is as little variation as possible. As you have already seen, statisticians measure variation by computing the variance.

Incidentally, an entire chapter (Chapter 21) is devoted to the topic of quality.

▼ **EXAMPLE 11.3**

Container-filling machines are used to package a variety of liquids, including milk, soft drinks, and paint. Ideally, the amount of liquid should vary only slightly, since large variations will cause some containers to be underfilled (cheating the customer) and some to be overfilled (resulting in costly waste). The president of a company that developed a new type of machine boasts that this machine can fill 1-liter (1,000-cm^3) containers so consistently that the variance of the fills will be less than 1 cm^3. To examine the veracity of the claim, a random sample of twenty-five 1-liter fills was taken and the results recorded. To avoid rounding problems, the results were coded by subtracting 1,000. These data are listed below and also stored in file XM11-03. Do these data allow the president to make this claim at the 5% significance level?

SAMPLE OF TWENTY-FIVE "1-LITER" FILLS (IN CM³ MINUS 1,000)

0.3	−0.3	−1.3	−0.6	−0.5	−0.4	−1.5	0.7	0.7
1.0	−0.7	0.6	1.0	−1.5	−0.2	1.4	−0.9	
−0.5	−0.2	−0.6	−0.6	1.3	0.0	−1.9	1.1	

Solution

IDENTIFY

The problem objective is to describe the population of 1-liter fills from this machine. The data are quantitative, and we're interested in the variability of the fills. It follows that the parameter of interest is the population variance. Because we want to determine whether there is enough evidence to support the claim, the alternative hypothesis is

$$H_1: \sigma^2 < 1$$

The null hypothesis automatically follows as

$$H_0: \sigma^2 = 1$$

The complete test is shown below.

$$H_0: \sigma^2 = 1$$
$$H_1: \sigma^2 < 1$$

Test statistic:

$$\chi^2 = \frac{(n-1)s^2}{\sigma^2}$$

Rejection region:

$$\chi^2 < \chi^2_{1-\alpha,n-1} = \chi^2_{.95,24} = 13.8484$$

SOLVE

The test statistic is

$$\chi^2 = \frac{(n-1)s^2}{\sigma^2}$$

The numerator is $(n-1)s^2$, which is equal to $\sum(x_i - \bar{x})^2$, which in turn equals $\sum x_i^2 - [(\sum x_i)^2/n]$. From the data we find

$$\sum x_i = -3.6$$
$$\sum x_i^2 = 21.3$$

Thus,

$$\sum x_i^2 - \frac{(\sum x_i)^2}{n} = 21.3 - \frac{(-3.6)^2}{25} = -20.8$$

As usual, the value of the parameter is taken from the null hypothesis, $\sigma^2 = 1$. The value of the test statistic is

$$\chi^2 = \frac{(n-1)s^2}{\sigma^2} = \frac{\sum(x_i - \bar{x})^2}{\sigma^2} = \frac{20.8}{1} = 20.8$$

Conclusion: Do not reject the null hypothesis. See Figure 11.11.

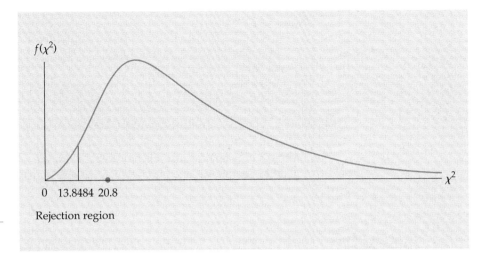

Figure 11.11

Sampling distribution for
Example 11.3

**Excel Output for
Example 11.3**

	A	B	C
1	**Chi-squared Test of a Variance**		
2			
3	**Sample variance**	0.8659	
4	**Sample size**	25	
5			
6	**Hypothesized variance**	1	
7			
8	**Chi-squared Stat**	20.7816	
9	**Two-tail p-value**	0.6969	

The value of the test statistic is 20.782. The two-tail p-value is .6969, which we
halve to yield the one-tail p-value .3485.

For this type of problem we use a worksheet rather than an add-in. To utilize the worksheet requires you to first calculate the sample variance.

COMMANDS	COMMANDS FOR EXAMPLE 11.3
1 Type or import the data into one column.	Open file **XM11-03.**
2 Compute the sample variance.	**=VAR(A2:A26)**
3 Click **Tools, Data Analysis Plus,** and **Inference from Summary Statistics (Workbook).** Find the worksheet **Chi-sq Test of a Variance.**	

> 4 In cells B3, B4, and B6 type in
>   the sample variance, sample size,
>   and value of σ^2 under the null
>   hypothesis.   .8659
>   25
>   1
> 5 Click **Exit**.

Minitab does not conduct this procedure. However, you can use Minitab to compute the sample variance from which the test statistic can be determined.

INTERPRET

There is not enough evidence to infer that the claim is true. As we discussed before, the result does not say that the variance is greater than 1; it merely states that we are unable to show that the variance is less than 1. The χ^2-test of σ^2 is somewhat more sensitive to violations of the normality requirement than the t-test of μ. Consequently, we must be more careful to ensure that the fills are normally distributed.

▲

ESTIMATING THE POPULATION VARIANCE

Using the notation developed above, we can make the following probability statement.

$$P(\chi^2_{1-\alpha/2} < \chi^2 < \chi^2_{\alpha/2}) = 1 - \alpha$$

Substituting

$$\chi^2 = \frac{(n-1)s^2}{\sigma^2}$$

and performing a little algebra we have the following.

Interval Estimator of σ^2

$$\text{Lower confidence limit (LCL)} = \frac{(n-1)s^2}{\chi^2_{\alpha/2}}$$

$$\text{Upper confidence limit (UCL)} = \frac{(n-1)s^2}{\chi^2_{1-\alpha/2}}$$

▼ **EXAMPLE 11.4**

Estimate with 99% confidence the variance of fills in Example 11.3.

Solution   In the solution to Example 11.3, we found $(n-1)s^2$ to be 20.8. From Table 5 in Appendix B we find

SOLVE

$$\chi^2_{\alpha/2,n-1} = \chi^2_{.005,24} = 45.5585$$
$$\chi^2_{1-\alpha/2,n-1} = \chi^2_{.995,24} = 9.88623$$

Thus,

$$\text{LCL} = \frac{(n-1)s^2}{\chi^2_{\alpha/2}} = \frac{20.8}{45.5585} = .46$$

$$\text{UCL} = \frac{(n-1)s^2}{\chi^2_{1-\alpha/2}} = \frac{20.8}{9.88623} = 2.10$$

We estimate that the variance of the fills is a number that lies between .46 and 2.10.

Excel Output for Example 11.4

	A	B	C
1	**Chi-squared Estimate of a Variance**		
2			
3	Sample variance	0.8659	
4	Sample size	25	
5			
6	Confidence level	0.99	
7			
8	Lower confidence limit	0.4562	
9	Upper confidence limit	2.1021	

COMMANDS

1 Type or import the data into one column.

2 Calculate the sample variance.

3 Click **Tools, Data Analysis Plus,** and **Inference from Summary Statistics (Workbook).** Find the worksheet **Chi-sq Estimate of a Variance.**

4 In cells B3, B4, and B6 type the values of the sample variance, sample size, and confidence level.

5 Click **Exit.**

COMMANDS FOR EXAMPLE 11.4

Open file **XM11-03.**

=Var(A2:A26)

.8659
25
.99

Minitab does not compute the interval estimator of a variance. But, as was the case with the test statistic, the sample variance can be output and the interval estimate produced manually.

INTERPRET

In Example 11.3, we saw that there was insufficient evidence to infer that the population variance is less than 1. Here we can see that σ^2 is estimated to lie between .46 and 2.10. (Part of the interval is above 1, which tells us that the variance may be larger than 1, confirming the conclusion we reached in Example 11.3.) We may be able to use the estimate to predict the percentage of overfilled and underfilled bottles. This may allow us to choose among competing machines.

▲

A BRIEF DISCUSSION OF THE DERIVATION OF THE CHI-SQUARED DISTRIBUTION (OPTIONAL)

The chi-squared distribution is derived by squaring a standard normal random variable. Thus, z^2 is chi-squared distributed with one degree of freedom. If we add n independent chi-squared random variables each with one degree of freedom, the sum is chi-squared distributed with n degrees of freedom. Mathematicians can show that

$$\frac{(n-1)s^2}{\sigma^2}$$

is equal to

$$\sum_{i=1}^{n}\left(\frac{x_i - \mu}{\sigma}\right)^2 - \left(\frac{\bar{x} - \mu}{\sigma/\sqrt{n}}\right)^2$$

The first term is chi-squared distributed with n degrees of freedom, and the second term is chi-squared distributed with one degree of freedom. Thus,

$$\frac{(n-1)s^2}{\sigma^2}$$

is chi-squared distributed with $n - 1$ degrees of freedom. As with the Student t distribution, we "lose" one degree of freedom because we must use the sample mean to calculate s^2. Once again, the denominator in the calculation of s^2 defines the number of degrees of freedom.

Let's review how we recognize when to use the techniques introduced in this section.

Factors that Identify the Chi-Squared Test and Estimator of σ^2

1 Problem objective: describe a single population

2 Data type: quantitative

3 Descriptive measurement: variability

EXERCISES

11.36 A random sample of 100 observations was drawn from a normal population. The sample variance was calculated to be $s^2 = 220$. Test with $\alpha = .05$ to determine whether we can infer that the population variance differs from 300.

11.37 Repeat Exercise 11.36 changing the sample size to 50.

11.38 The sample variance of a random sample of 50 observations from a normal population was found to be $s^2 = 80$. Can we infer at the 1% significance level that σ^2 is less than 100?

11.39 Estimate σ^2 with 90% confidence given that $n = 15$ and $s^2 = 12$.

11.40 Can we conclude at the 10% significance level that σ^2 is greater than 50 if a random sample of 25 yields $s^2 = 58$?

11.41 Test the hypotheses below at the 5% significance level.

$$H_0: \sigma^2 = 100$$
$$H_1: \sigma^2 > 100$$

given the data:

85   59   66   81   35   57   55   63   66

11.42 The following data were drawn from a normal population.

92   93   54   58   74   53   63   83   64   51   103

At the 1% significance level, test to determine if there is enough evidence to conclude that the population variance is less than 500.

11.43 A random sample of 100 observations was taken from a normal population. The sample variance was computed to be $s^2 = 29.76$. Estimate the population variance with 90% confidence.

11.44 Given the following sample, estimate the population variance with 95% confidence.

4 5 6 5 5 6 5 6

11.45 The following observations were drawn from a normal population.

497 511 498 494 479 526 510 515 489
488 491

Estimate the population variance with 90% confidence.

Exercises 11.46–11.49 require the use of a computer and software. The answers may be calculated manually. See Appendix C for the sample statistics.

11.46 One important factor in inventory control is the variance of the daily demand for the product. A management scientist has developed the optimal order quantity and reorder point, assuming that the variance is equal to 250. Recently, the company has experienced some inventory problems, which induced the operations manager to doubt the assumption. To examine the problem, the manager took a sample of 25 daily demands and stored them in file XR11-46. Do these data provide sufficient evidence at the 5% significance level to infer that the management scientist's assumption about the variance is wrong?

11.47 Refer to Example 11.46. What are the smallest and largest values that σ^2 is likely to assume? (Define "likely" as 95% confidence.)

11.48 Some traffic experts believe that the major cause of highway collisions is the differing speeds of cars. That is, when some cars are driven slowly while others are driven at speeds well in excess of the speed limit, cars tend to congregate in bunches increasing the probability of accidents. Thus, the greater the variation in speeds, the greater the number of collisions that occur. Suppose that one expert believes that when the variance exceeds 18 $(mph)^2$, the number of accidents will be unacceptably high. A random sample of the speeds of 245 cars on a highway with one of the highest accident rates in the country was taken. These data are stored in file XR11-48. Can we conclude at the 10% significance level that the variance in speeds exceeds 18 $(mph)^2$?

11.49 One problem facing the manager of maintenance departments is when to change the bulbs in streetlamps. If bulbs are changed only when they burn out, it is quite costly to send crews out to change only one bulb at a time. This method also requires someone to report the problem, and in the meantime, the light is off. If each bulb lasts approximately the same amount of time, they can all be replaced periodically, producing significant cost savings in maintenance. Suppose that a financial analysis of the lights at Yankee stadium has concluded that it will pay to replace all of the lightbulbs at the same time if the variance of the lives of the bulbs is less than 200 $(hours)^2$. The length of life of the last 100 bulbs was recorded and stored in file XR11-49. What conclusion can be drawn from these data? (Use a 5% significance level.)

11.4 INFERENCE ABOUT A POPULATION PROPORTION

In this section, we continue to address the problem of describing a single population. However, we shift our attention to populations of qualitative data, which means that the population consists of qualitative or categorical values. For example, in a brand-preference survey where the statistician asks consumers of a particular product which brand they purchase, the values of the random variable are the brands. If there are five brands the values could be represented by their names, letters (A, B, C, D, and E), or by numbers (1, 2, 3, 4, and 5). When numbers are used it should be understood that the numbers merely represent the name of the brand, are completely arbitrarily assigned, and cannot be treated as real numbers. That is, we cannot calculate means and variances.

PARAMETER

Recall our earlier discussion in Chapter 2. When the data are qualitative all that we are permitted to do to describe the population or sample is count the number of occurrences of each value. From the counts we calculate proportions. Thus, the parameter of interest in describing a single population of qualitative data is the population proportion p. In Chapter 6 this parameter was used to calculate probabilities based on the binomial experiment. One of the characteristics of the binomial experiment is that there are only two possible outcomes per trial. Most practical applications of inference about p involve more than two outcomes. However, in most cases we're interested in only one outcome, which we label a success. All other outcomes are labeled as failures. For example, in brand-preference surveys we are interested in our company's brand. In political surveys we wish to estimate or test the proportion of voters who will vote for one particular candidate—probably the one who has paid for the survey.

STATISTIC AND SAMPLING DISTRIBUTION

The logical statistic employed to estimate and test the population proportion is the sample proportion defined as

$$\hat{p} = \frac{x}{n}$$

where x is the number of successes in the sample and n is the sample size. In Chapter 8 we presented the approximate sampling distribution of $\hat{p}$. (The actual distribution is based on the binomial distribution, which does not lend itself to statistical inference.) The sampling distribution of $\hat{p}$ is approximately normal with mean p and standard deviation $\sqrt{p(1-p)/n}$ (provided that np and $n(1-p)$ are greater than 5). We express this sampling distribution as

$$z = \frac{\hat{p} - p}{\sqrt{p(1-p)/n}}$$

As you have already seen the formula that summarizes the sampling distribution also represents the test statistic.

Test Statistic for p

$$z = \frac{\hat{p} - p}{\sqrt{p(1-p)/n}}$$

which is approximately normal for np and $n(1-p)$ greater than 5.

Using the same algebra employed in Sections 9.3 and 11.2, we attempt to derive the interval estimator of p from the sampling distribution. The result is

$$\hat{p} \pm z_{\alpha/2}\sqrt{p(1-p)/n}$$

This formula, although technically correct is useless. To understand why, examine the standard error of the sampling distribution $\sqrt{p(1-p)/n}$. To produce the interval estimate, we must compute the standard error, which requires us to know the value of p, which is the parameter we wish to estimate. This is the first of several statistical techniques where we face the same problem, how to determine the value of the standard error. In this application the problem is easily and logically solved, simply estimate the value of p with $\hat{p}$. Thus, we estimate the standard error with $\sqrt{\hat{p}(1-\hat{p})/n}$. The interval estimator follows.

> ### Interval Estimator of p
>
> $$\hat{p} \pm z_{\alpha/2}\sqrt{\hat{p}(1 - \hat{p})/n}$$
>
> which is valid provided that $n\hat{p}$ and $n(1 - \hat{p})$ are greater than 5.

STATISTICS IN THE WORKPLACE

Marketing Application

Consumer surveys are used extensively by marketing managers to assess the attitudes of consumers toward various characteristics of a product, such as its convenience, quality, and price. While information obtained from a survey is very useful to managers contemplating changes to an existing product, such information is absolutely invaluable to managers about to introduce a new, untested product to the market. Of utmost importance is whether the new product will capture sufficient market share to reach the break-even level of profitability within a reasonable period of time.

▼ EXAMPLE 11.5

In the fall of 1998, a newspaper publisher launched a new "national" newspaper in Canada. It was believed that the new newspaper would have to capture at least 12% of the Toronto market in order to be financially viable. During the planning stages of this new newspaper, a market survey was conducted of a sample of 400 Toronto readers. After providing a brief description of the proposed newspaper, one question asked if the survey participant would subscribe to the newspaper if the cost did not exceed $20 per month. If 58 participants said that they would subscribe, can the publisher conclude that the proposed newspaper will be financially viable?

Solution

IDENTIFY

The problem objective is to describe the population of newspaper readers in Toronto. The responses to the survey are "I would subscribe to the new newspaper" and "I would not subscribe to the new newspaper." These responses are qualitative. The combination of problem objective and data type makes the parameter to be tested the proportion of the entire population that would subscribe to the newspaper.

Because we want to determine whether the proportion would exceed 12% the alternative hypothesis is

$$H_1: p > .12$$

which makes the null hypothesis

$$H_0: p = .12$$

and the test statistic

$$z = \frac{\hat{p} - p}{\sqrt{p(1 - p)/n}}$$

SOLVE

It is likely that at this early stage we are concerned about both Type I and Type II errors and as a result we would set the significance level at 10%.

The rejection region is

$$z > z_\alpha = z_{.10} = 1.28$$

The sample proportion is

$$\hat{p} = \frac{58}{400} = .145$$

The value of the test statistic is

$$z = \frac{\hat{p} - p}{\sqrt{p(1 - p)/n}} = \frac{.145 - .12}{\sqrt{.12(1 - .12)/400}} = 1.54$$

Since the test statistic is (approximately) normally distributed we can determine the *p*-value. It is

$$p\text{-value} = P(Z > 1.54) = .0618$$

In this example the number of people who responded that they would subscribe has been determined. In most practical applications however, the statistician has access to the raw data only. Just as was the case with inference about a mean, no one except you is responsible for summarizing the data.

Suppose that the responses have been stored in file XM11-05 using the following codes. (Codes are necessary because the data are qualitative.)

1 = I would not subscribe to the newspaper.
2 = I would subscribe to the newspaper.

Excel Output for Example 11.5

	A	B	C	D
1	**Test of Hypothesis About p**			
2				
3	*Test of p = 0.12 Vs p greater than 0.12*			
4	*Sample Proportion = 0.145*			
5	*Test Statistic = 1.5386*			
6	P-Value = 0.0619			

COMMANDS

1 Type or import the data.
2 Click **Tools, Data Analysis Plus,** and **Inference About a Proportion.**
3 Specify the input range. Do not include the cell containing the variable name.
4 Specify the code representing a success.
5 Click **Test of Hypothesis.**

COMMANDS FOR EXAMPLE 11.5

Open file **XM11-05.**

A2:A401

2

6 Type the value of p under the null hypothesis.   **.12**

7 Click the appropriate alternative hypothesis.   **p greater than .12**

To complete the technique from the sample proportion or to conduct a what-if analysis, click **Tools, Data Analysis Plus,** and **Inference from Summary Statistics (Workbook).** Activate the **z-Test of a Proportion** worksheet. Click **Exit** when finished.

Minitab Output for Example 11.5

The data must represent successes and failures. The codes can be numbers or text. There can be only two kinds of entries, one representing success and the other representing failure. If numbers are used Minitab will interpret the larger one as a success.

Test and Confidence Interval for One Proportion

```
Test of p = 0.12 vs p > 0.12

Success = 2

Variable   X    N Sample p       95.0 % CI        Z-Value P-Value
Subcribe? 58  400 0.145000 (0.110495, 0.179505)    1.54    0.062
```

The value of the test statistic is $z = 1.54$ with a p-value of .062. Notice that Minitab also prints the interval estimate.

COMMANDS	COMMANDS FOR EXAMPLE 11.5
1 Type or import the data.	Open file **XM11-05.**
2 Click **Stat, Basic Statistics,** and **1 Proportion . . . .**	
3 Use the cursor to select **Samples in columns:** and type the name of the variable.	**Subscribe?** or **C1**
4 Click **Options . . .** and **Test proportion.** Type the value of p under the null hypothesis.	**.12**
5 Specify the **Alternative:** hypothesis.	**greater than**
6 To use the normal approximation of the binomial, specify **Use test and interval based on normal approximation.**	
7 Click **OK.**	

There are two variations on the instructions above.

1 If, instead of the raw data, you know the number of successes (and the sample size) you can specify **Summarized data:** (at step 3 above) and type the **Number of trials:** and the **Number of successes:.**

2 You can use the exact distribution (binomial) of the number of successes instead of the normal distribution. Simply omit step 6 above. For a discussion of the use of the binomial distribution, go to page 384.

INTERPRET   The *p*-value is .0619, which represents sufficient evidence to support the alternative hypothesis. This result is based on a preliminary survey so that any final decision about whether to launch the newspaper must take into consideration a variety of factors besides the statistical analysis. However, it does look promising. There is some evidence that the proportion of Toronto newspaper readers that will subscribe will exceed the break-even mark. And this outcome was achieved with little or no advertising.

▲

STATISTICS IN THE WORKPLACE

Marketing Application

Statistical techniques play a vital role in helping advertisers determine how many viewers watch the shows that they sponsor. There are several companies that sample television viewers to determine what shows they watch, the best known of which is the A.C. Nielsen firm. The Nielson ratings are based on a sample of 1,000 randomly selected families. A device attached to the family television keeps track of the channels the television receives. The ratings then produce the proportions of each show from which sponsors can determine the number of viewers and the potential value of any commercials.

▼ **EXAMPLE 11.6**

Suppose that the results of a survey of 2,000 television viewers at 11:40 P.M. on Monday September 28, 1998, were stored in file XM11-06 using the following codes.

1 = *Tonight Show* with Jay Leno (NBC)
2 = *The Late Show* with David Letterman (CBS)
3 = *Nightline* (ABC)
4 = Other
5 = Television turned off

If there are 100 million potential television sets in the population, estimate with 95% confidence the number of televisions tuned to the *Tonight Show.*

Solution

IDENTIFY   The problem objective is to describe the population of television viewers and the data are qualitative. The parameter to be estimated is the proportion of televisions tuned to the *Tonight Show.* The interval estimator is

$$\hat{p} \pm z_{\alpha/2}\sqrt{\frac{\hat{p}(1-\hat{p})}{n}}$$

SOLVE   To solve manually we count the number of ones in the file. We find this value to be 226. Thus,

$$\hat{p} = \frac{x}{n} = \frac{226}{2,000} = .113$$

The confidence level is $1 - \alpha = .95$. It follows that $\alpha = .05$, $\alpha/2 = .025$, and $z_{\alpha/2} = z_{.025} = 1.96$. The 95% confidence interval estimate of p is

$$\hat{p} \pm z_{\alpha/2}\sqrt{\frac{\hat{p}(1-\hat{p})}{n}} = .113 \pm 1.96 \sqrt{\frac{(.113)(.887)}{2,000}} = .113 \pm .014$$

If there were 100 million potential television sets, we estimate that the number tuned to the *Tonight Show* lies between

LCL $= .099 \times 100$ million $= 9.9$ million   and
UCL $= .127 \times 100$ million $= 12.7$ million

Excel Output for Example 11.6

	A	B	C	D
1	**0.95 Confidence Interval Estimate of p**			
2				
3	Sample proportion = 0.113			
4	Lower confidence limit = 0.0991			
5	Upper confidence limit = 0.1269			

COMMANDS

COMMANDS FOR EXAMPLE 11.6

1 Type or import the data into one column.

Open file **XM11-06.**

2 Click **Tools, Data Analysis Plus,** and **Inference about a Proportion.**

3 Specify the **Input Range:**. Do not include the cell containing the variable name.

A2:A2001

4 Specify the code representing a success.

1

5 Click **Interval Estimate.**

6 Specify the confidence level. Click **OK.**

.95

To complete the technique from the sample proportion or to conduct a what-if analysis, click **Tools, Data Analysis Plus,** and **Inference from Summary Statistics (Workbook).** Activate the **z-Estimate of a Proportion** worksheet. Click **Exit** when finished.

Minitab Output for Example 11.6

Minitab requires that there be only two possible codes. Therefore the data must be recoded so that $1 = $ *Tonight Show* and $0 = $ other. (See the subsection below.)

Test and Confidence Interval for One Proportion

```
Test of p = 0.5 vs p not = 0.5

Success = 1

Variable X      N   Sample p      95.0 % CI         Z-Value P-Value
Viewers   226 2000 0.113000  (0.099125, 0.126875)  -34.61   0.000
```

> Minitab performs both a test of hypothesis and computes the interval estimate. Ignore the test output.
>
> **COMMANDS**
>
> Follow the instructions on page 377 to test a proportion. After clicking **Options** . . . , type the confidence level.

INTERPRET   We estimate that between 9.9% and 12.7% of all television sets had received the *Tonight Show*. If we multiply these figures by the total number of televisions, 100 million, we produce an interval estimate of the number of televisions tuned to the *Tonight Show*. That is, we estimate that figure to lie between 9.9 million and 12.7 million. Sponsoring companies can then determine the value of any commercials that appeared on the show.

▲

MISSING DATA

When statisticians conduct experiments to collect data, they often encounter nonresponses. This is quite common in political surveys where we ask voters for whom they intend to vote in the next election. Some people will answer that they haven't decided or they refuse to answer. This is a troublesome issue for statisticians. We can't force people to answer our questions. However, if the number of nonresponses is high the results of our analysis may be invalid because the sample is no longer truly random. To understand why, suppose that people who are in the top quarter of household incomes regularly refuse to answer questions about their incomes. The estimate of the population household income mean will be lower than the actual value.

There are several ways to compensate for nonresponses. The simplest method is simply to eliminate the nonresponses. To illustrate, suppose that in a political survey respondents are asked for whom they intend to vote in a two-candidate race. Surveyors record the results as 1 = Candidate A, 2 = Candidate B, 3 = "Don't know," and 4 = "Refuse to say." If we wish to infer something about the proportion of decided voters who will vote for Candidate A, we can simply omit codes 3 and 4. If we're doing the work manually, we will count the number of voters who prefer Candidate A and the number who prefer Candidate B. The sum of these two numbers is the total sample size.

In the language of statistical software nonresponses that we wish to eliminate are collectively called "missing data." Each software deals with missing data in different ways.

Excel

Excel recognizes blank cells as missing data. However, the macros in **Data Analysis Plus** do not. For these techniques the easiest way to omit missing data is simply to delete the cells containing the missing data. Sort the data (Click **Data** and **Sort . . .**) in order, highlight the cells you wish to delete, and with one keystroke delete the missing data.

Minitab

Minitab treats an asterisk as missing data. You can record the data in this way. However, in most cases you will have to recode the data. We describe how to do so below.

RECODING DATA

Excel

To recode data we employ a logical function. Click **f$_x$, Logical (Function category:),** and **IF (Function name:).** To illustrate, suppose that in column A you have stored data consisting of codes 1 through 6 and you wish to convert all 4s, 5s, and 6s to 9s. Activate cell B1 and type

= IF(A1>=4,9,A1)

This logical function determines whether the value in cell A1 is greater than or equal to 4. If so, Excel places a 9 in cell B1. If A1 is less than 4, B1 = A1. Dragging to fill in column B converts all 4s, 5s, and 6s to 9s and stores the results in column B.

If 4s, 5s, and 6s represent nonresponses you can replace these codes with a blank. Type in cell B1

=IF(A1>=4," ",A1)

Minitab

To recode data in Minitab follow these instructions.

1 Click **Manip** and **Code.**
2 Specify **Numeric to Numeric . . . .**
3 Type the variable name of the **Code data from columns:.**
4 Type variable name where the new codes are to be placed **(Into columns:).**
5 Specify the **Original values:** you wish to recode and their **New:** values. Click **OK.**

SELECTING THE SAMPLE SIZE TO ESTIMATE THE PROPORTION

When we introduced the sample size selection method to estimate a mean in Section 9.4, we pointed out that the sample size depends on the confidence level and the size of the interval the statistician wants to produce. When the parameter to be estimated is a proportion the interval estimator is

$$\hat{p} \pm z_{\alpha/2}\sqrt{\frac{\hat{p}(1-\hat{p})}{n}}$$

When we specify the confidence level, we can determine the value of $z_{\alpha/2}$. The width of the interval is determined by the value of the quantity that follows the plus/minus sign. Thus, if we wish to estimate a proportion to within W we need to solve the following equation to find the sample size.

$$W = z_{\alpha/2}\sqrt{\frac{\hat{p}(1-\hat{p})}{n}}$$

Solving for n we produce:

Sample Size to Estimate a Proportion

To produce an interval estimator $\hat{p} \pm W$, we need a sample of size

$$n = \left(\frac{z_{\alpha/2} \sqrt{\hat{p}(1 - \hat{p})}}{W} \right)^2$$

To illustrate the use of this formula suppose that in a brand-preference survey we want to estimate the proportion of consumers who prefer our company's brand to within .03 with 95% confidence. This means that when the sample is taken and the calculations completed the interval estimate is to be $\hat{p} \pm .03$. Thus, $W = .03$. Since $1 - \alpha = .95$, $\alpha = .05$, $\alpha/2 = .025$, and $z_{\alpha/2} = z_{.025} = 1.96$. Therefore,

$$n = \left(\frac{1.96 \sqrt{\hat{p}(1 - \hat{p})}}{.03} \right)^2$$

To solve for n, we need to know $\hat{p}$. Unfortunately, this value is unknown, because the sample has not yet been taken. At this point, we can use either of two methods to solve for n.

Method 1

If we have no knowledge of even the approximate values of $\hat{p}$, we let $\hat{p} = .5$. We choose $\hat{p} = .5$ because the product $\hat{p}(1 - \hat{p})$ equals its maximum value at $\hat{p} = .5$. (Figure 11.12 illustrates this point.) This, in turn, results in a conservative value of n and, as a result, the confidence interval will be no wider than the interval $\hat{p} \pm .03$. If, when the sample is drawn, $\hat{p}$ does not equal .5, the interval estimate will be better (that is, narrower) than planned. Thus,

$$n = \left(\frac{1.96 \sqrt{(.5)(.5)}}{.03} \right)^2 = (32.67)^2 = 1,067$$

If it turns out that if $\hat{p} = .5$, the interval estimate is $.5 \pm .03$. If it turns out that, for example, $\hat{p} = .2$, the interval estimate is $.2 \pm .024$, which is better than we had planned.

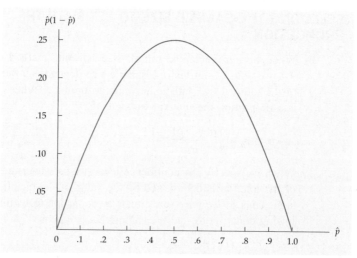

Figure 11.12

$\hat{p}$ versus $\hat{p}(1 - \hat{p})$

Method 2

If we have some idea about the value of $\hat{p}$, we can use that quantity to determine n. For example, if we believe that $\hat{p}$ will turn out to be approximately .2, we can solve for n as follows.

$$n = \left(\frac{1.96\sqrt{(.2)(.8)}}{.03}\right)^2 = (26.13)^2 = 683$$

Notice that this produces a smaller value of n (thus reducing sampling costs) than does method 1. If $\hat{p}$ actually lies between .2 and .8, however, the estimate will not be as good as we wanted, because the interval will be wider than desired.

Method 1 is often used to determine the sample size used in public opinion surveys reported by newspapers, magazines, television, and radio. These polls usually estimate proportions to within 3%, with 95% confidence. (The media often state the confidence level as "19 times out of 20.") If you've ever wondered why opinion polls almost always estimate proportions to within 3%, consider the sample size required to estimate a proportion to within 1%.

$$n = \left(\frac{1.96\sqrt{(.5)(.5)}}{.01}\right)^2 = (98)^2 = 9{,}604$$

The sample size 9,604 is 9 times the sample size needed to estimate a proportion to within 3%. Thus, to divide the width of the interval by 3 requires multiplying the sample size by 9. The cost would also increase considerably. For most applications, the increase in accuracy (created by decreasing the width of the interval estimate) does not overcome the increased cost. Interval estimates with 5% or 10% bounds (sample sizes 384 and 96, respectively) are generally considered too wide to be useful. Thus, 3% is the happy compromise between cost and accuracy.

TESTING HYPOTHESES ABOUT PROPORTIONS USING THE BINOMIAL DISTRIBUTION (OPTIONAL)

As we've noted several times, the actual distribution of $\hat{p}$ is related to the binomial distribution. But we use the normal approximation of $\hat{p}$ because the binomial is a discrete random variable and discrete distributions make it difficult for us to determine the critical values of an interval estimator and the rejection region and p-value of a test of hypothesis. However, when we use the computer to perform the calculations we can use the exact binomial distribution. Excel users can produce the p-value of the test, but they cannot find the interval estimate using the binomial distribution. Minitab users can employ the binomial distribution for both a test and an interval estimator.

Excel

To illustrate how Excel can produce the p-value refer to Example 11.5 where we wanted to know whether there was sufficient evidence to infer that the proportion of people who would buy the newspaper is greater than 12%. In a sample of 400, we found $x = 58$ people who said they would buy the newspaper. The exact (binomial) p-value of the test is

$P(X \geq 58$, given that $n = 400$ and $p = .12)$

Note that the p-value is the probability that the number of successes is greater than or equal to the actual number of successes in the sample, the sample size is 400, and under the null hypothesis the probability of success is .12. For smaller values of n, the binomial formula or table (Table 1 in Appendix B) may be used. For larger values of n, we must use the computer.

To find the p-value we need to calculate the cumulative probability

$P(X \leq 57$, given that $n = 400$ and $p = .12)$

which we compute to be .9254. thus the exact p-value is $1 - .9254 = .0746$. Note that the approximate p-value (based on the normal distribution) was found to be .0619. (See the Excel output on page 376.)

For Excel instructions on producing binomial distribution probabilities, see page 217.

Minitab

The version of Minitab that we employ in this book allows you to specify the use of the binomial distribution for both the interval estimator and the p-value of the test. The Minitab outputs for Examples 11.5 and 11.6 used the normal approximation to be consistent with the manual calculations.

Here are the printouts for both examples when we specify the use of the binomial distribution.

Minitab Output for Example 11.5 (Binomial Distribution)

Test and Confidence Interval for One Proportion

```
Test of p = 0.12 vs p > 0.12

Success = 2

                                                     Exact
Variable     X    N   Sample p        95.0 % CI      P-Value
Subscribe?  58  400   0.145000  (0.111981, 0.183378)  0.075
```

The approximate p-value was computed to be .062. (See the Minitab printout on page 377.)

Minitab Output for Example 11.6 (Binomial Distribution)

Test and Confidence Interval for One Proportion

```
Test of p = 0.5 vs p not = 0.5

Success = 1

                                                     Exact
Variable    X     N   Sample p        95.0 % CI      P-Value
Viewers   226  2000   0.113000  (0.099450, 0.127696)  0.000
```

The interval estimator based on the normal approximation was (.099125, .126875). (See the Minitab printout on page 379.) Because the sample size is so large there is little difference between the two estimates.

Note that earlier versions of Minitab can determine the exact p-values by finding the cumulative binomial probabilities. (See page 218.)

We complete this section by reviewing the factors that tell us when to test and estimate a population proportion.

Factors that Identify the z-Test and Interval Estimator of p

1 Problem objective: describe a single population

2 Data type: qualitative

EXERCISES

*Exercises 11.50–11.55 are "what-if" analyses designed to determine what happens to the test statistics and interval estimates when elements of the statistical inference change. These problems can be solved manually or using Excel's **Inference from Summary Statistics (Workbook)** option.*

11.50 In a random sample of 500 observations we found the proportion of successes to be 48%. Estimate with 95% confidence the population proportion of successes.

11.51 Repeat Exercise 11.50 with $n = 200$.

11.52 Repeat Exercise 11.50 with $n = 1,000$.

11.53 Repeat Exercise 11.50 with $\hat{p} = 33\%$.

11.54 Repeat Exercise 11.50 with $\hat{p} = 10\%$.

11.55 Review Exercises 11.50–11.54.

    a Discuss the effect on the width of the interval estimate of reducing the sample size.

    b Discuss the effect on the width of the interval estimate of reducing the sample proportion.

11.56 Given that $\hat{p} = .84$ and $n = 600$, estimate p with 90% confidence.

11.57 In a random sample of 250, we found 75 successes. Estimate the population proportion of success, with 99% confidence.

11.58 If $\hat{p} = .59$ and $n = 100$, can we conclude at the 5% level of significance that the population proportion p is greater than .50?

11.59 Suppose that, in a sample of 200, we observe 140 successes. Is this sufficient evidence at the 1% significance level to indicate that the population proportion of successes is greater than 65%?

11.60 Find the *p*-value of the test in Exercise 11.59.

11.61 Determine the sample size necessary to estimate a population proportion to within .03 with 90% confidence assuming you have no knowledge of the approximate value of the sample proportion.

11.62 Suppose that you used the sample size calculated in Exercise 11.61 and found $\hat{p} = .5$.

    a Estimate the population proportion with 90% confidence.

    b Is this the result you expected? Explain.

11.63 Suppose that you used the sample size calculated in Exercise 11.61 and found $\hat{p} = .75$.

    a Estimate the population proportion with 90% confidence.

    b Is this the result you expected? Explain.

    c If you were hired to conduct this analysis would the person who hired you be satisfied with the interval estimate you produced? Explain.

11.64 Redo Exercise 11.61 assuming that you know that the sample proportion will be no less than .75.

11.65 Suppose that you used the sample size calculated in Exercise 11.64 and found $\hat{p} = .75$.

    a Estimate the population proportion with 90% confidence.

    b Is this the result you expected? Explain.

11.66 Suppose that you used the sample size calculated in Exercise 11.64 and found $\hat{p} = .92$.

    a Estimate the population proportion with 90% confidence.

    b Is this the result you expected? Explain.

    c If you were hired to conduct this analysis would the person who hired you be satisfied with the interval estimate you produced? Explain.

11.67 Suppose that you used the sample size calculated in Exercise 11.64 and found $\hat{p} = .5$.

    a Estimate the population proportion with 90% confidence.

    b Is this the result you expected? Explain.

    c If you were hired to conduct this analysis would the person who hired you be satisfied with the interval estimate you produced? Explain.

Exercises 11.68–11.71 require the use of a computer and software. The answers may be calculated manually. See Appendix A for the sample statistics.

11.68 In a television commercial, the manufacturer of a toothpaste claims that more than four out of five dentists recommend the ingredients in his product. To test that claim, a consumer-protection group randomly samples 400 dentists and asks each one whether he or she would recommend toothpaste that contained the ingredients. The responses are 1 = No and 2 = Yes. The responses are stored in file XR11-68. At the 5% significance level, can the consumer group infer that the claim is true?

11.69 A professor of business statistics recently adopted a new textbook. At the completion of the course, 100 randomly selected students were asked to assess the book. The responses are as follows.

Excellent (1), Good (2), Adequate (3), Poor (4)

The results are stored in file XR11-69 using the codes in parentheses.

    a Do these results allow us to conclude at the 5% significance level that more than 50% of all business students would rate it as excellent?

    b Do these results allow us to conclude at the 5% significance level that more than 90% of all business students would rate it as at least adequate?

11.70 Refer to Example 11.6. Estimate with 95% confidence the number of televisions that had watched *The Late Show* with David Letterman.

11.71 The wine industry is an important part of the economy of western New York State and of Southern Ontario. During the winter some of the grape vines die from the extreme cold that is common in this part of the continent. In the spring the vines are pruned. If the vine is brown, it means that the plant is dead; green indicates a healthy vine. To test how well a vineyard has survived the winter, a random sample of vines is selected. The results of the latest pruning are stored in file XR11-71 (2 = Dead and 1 = Alive). Estimate with 90% confidence the degree of winter kill for this vine.

11.5 THE MYTH OF THE LAW OF AVERAGES (OPTIONAL)

Josh Billings, the U.S. humorist who provided Will Rogers with some of his best lines, once remarked that "Ignorance ain't what folks don't know, it's the stuff folks know that ain't so." There are no statistical topics that exemplify this description more than the "law of averages." Let's be clear on this: There is no law of averages. There is something called the law of large numbers, which states that, given a binomial experiment with p greater than zero, the sample proportion $\hat{p}$ approaches the theoretical probability p as n increases. This can be seen by examining the sampling distribution presented in Section 11.4. That is, $\hat{p}$ is approximately normally distributed with mean p and standard deviation $\sqrt{p(1-p)/n}$. As a result, as n increases, the standard deviation decreases, which means that the probability that $\hat{p}$ and p differ by a given amount increases as n increases.

To illustrate, suppose that our experiment consists of flipping a balanced coin. The probability that the sample proportion differs from $p = .5$ by less than .01 can be computed for any value of n. For $n = 100$, we find

$$P(.49 < \hat{p} < .51) = P\left(\frac{.49 - .5}{\sqrt{(.5)(.5)/100}} < \frac{\hat{p} - p}{\sqrt{p(1-p)/n}} < \frac{.51 - .5}{\sqrt{(.5)(.5)/100}}\right)$$

$$= P(-.2 < z < .2)$$

$$= .1586$$

With $n = 400$, $P(.49 < \hat{p} < .51) = .3108$.
With $n = 10,000$, $P(.49 < \hat{p} < .51) = .9544$.
With $n = 1,000,000$, $P(.49 < \hat{p} < .51) = 1$.

As you can see, the probability that $\hat{p}$ differs from .5 by less than .01 approaches 1 as n increases. In ordinary English, the law of large numbers means that in the long run the sample proportion will be quite close to the population proportion.

Unfortunately, among the statistically uneducated, the words *long run* are usually omitted. Thus, for these people, the law of averages means the law of *small numbers*. The usual interpretation is that after a small number of successes, the law of averages dictates that a failure is due on the next trial. Consider these examples taken from *Chance* magazine, Volume 8, No. 2, Spring 1995.

The first example refers to an announcer discussing the likelihood of basketball player Sam Parker of the Los Angeles Lakers making the seventh consecutive free throw in a game against the Golden State Warriors.

As Los Angeles Laker Sam Parker comes up for a seventh free throw, announcer Chick Hearn notes that Parker had made the last six out of six free throws and concludes that "the law of averages starts working for Golden State" (15 December 1990).

There are several problems with Mr. Hearn's statement. First, the law of large numbers refers to *future* trials, which means that the results of the previous six free throws have nothing whatever to do with the free throws that follow. That is, if Sam Parker's long-term success percentage is, say, 90%, the probability of making the next free throw is 90%, regardless of what happened on the previous 6, 60, or 600 free throws. Mr. Hearn's comment is equivalent to saying that after six tosses of a balanced coin that resulted in heads, the probability of heads on the seventh toss is something other than 50%. Second, if we wanted to comment on the probability that Sam Parker will make all of the next seven free throws we will need to know the probability of success on each trial.

While sportscasters are among the worst offenders, there are many uninformed in all walks of life. Here is one from a person who knows that the law of averages is mythical.

> "What I think is our best determination is it will be a colder than normal winter," said Pamela Naber Knox, a Wisconsin state climatologist. "I'm basing that on a couple of different things. First, in looking at the past few winters, there has been a lack of really cold weather. Even though we are not supposed to use the law of averages, we are due," said Naber Knox, an instructor in meteorology at the University of Wisconsin-Madison (Associated Press, Fall 1992).

Just because we have not observed a success in several consecutive trials does not mean that the probability of success increases in subsequent trials.

Another variation of the mistakes above applies the law of averages so that if we've observed a larger than expected number of successes in the past, we should observe a larger number of failures in the future. In other words, the law of averages acts as a balancer in all aspects of our lives. Consider this example.

> "The law of averages is what baseball is all about," says [Ralph] Kiner. "It is the leveling influence of the long season. A .250-hitter may hit .200 or .300 for a given period. But he will eventually level off at .250. The same is true of pitchers. Illnesses, sore arms, good and bad clubs are all part of it. But the law is inflexible. A player will average out to his true ability." What this means in Seaver's case is that he is now paying for his 1969 season in which he had a 25–7 record . . . ("Baseball Law of Averages Taking Toll on Seaver." *New Haven Register,* 2 June 1974. Quoted by Gary Smith (1985) in *Statistical Reasoning,* Boston: Allyn and Bacon, p. 175).

In this quote, Hall-of-Fame pitcher Tom Seaver was required to have a season with a larger number of losses than average because in 1969 he had a smaller number of losses than average. The problem with this "reasoning" is that we don't know an individual player's batting average or a pitcher's won–lost percentage until his career is over. The law of large numbers states that a baseball player's batting average over an increasing number of at-bats will more closely approximate his career average. Unfortunately, we don't know what that average is while the player is active.

Here is probably the worst example in the aforementioned *Chance* article. This was taken from a literary review of actor Marlon Brando's autobiography where he discussed, among other things, his very active love life.

> Brando has had so many lovers, it would be surprising if they were all of one gender; the law of averages alone would make him bisexual (*Los Angeles Times,* 18 September 1994, Book Reviews, p. 13).

This reference to the law of averages states that when n is very large, we are certain to observe at least one success even if $p = 0$. This is equivalent to flipping a two-headed coin thousands of times and expecting eventually to observe tails.

Unfortunately, there is no shortage of egregious illustrations of the mythical law of averages. We hope that none of our readers will be so quoted in the future.

11.6 SUMMARY

The inferential methods presented in this chapter address the problem of describing a single population. When the data are quantitative, the parameters of interest are the population mean μ and the population variance σ^2. The Student t distribution is used to test and estimate the mean when the population standard deviation is unknown. The chi-squared distribution is used to make inferences about a population variance. When the data are qualitative, the parameter to be tested and estimated is the population proportion p. The sample proportion follows an approximate normal distribution, which produces the test statistic and the interval estimator. We also discussed how to determine the sample size required to estimate a population proportion. Table 11.7 summarizes the formulas used in this chapter. We completed this chapter by pointing out that there is no law of averages despite its ubiquitous use.

IMPORTANT TERMS

t-Statistic   *349*
Student t distribution   *349*
Degrees of freedom   *349*
χ^2-statistic   *364*
Chi-squared (χ^2-squared) distribution   *365*

SUMMARY OF FORMULAS TO DESCRIBE A SINGLE POPULATION

Parameters	Test Statistic	Estimator	Required Condition
μ	$t = \dfrac{\bar{x} - \mu}{s/\sqrt{n}}$	$\bar{x} \pm t_{\alpha/2}\dfrac{s}{\sqrt{n}}$	x is normally distributed.
σ^2	$\chi^2 = \dfrac{(n-1)s^2}{\sigma^2}$	$LCL = \dfrac{(n-1)s^2}{\chi^2_{\alpha/2}}$	x is normally distributed.
		$UCL = \dfrac{(n-1)s^2}{\chi^2_{1-\alpha/2}}$	
p	$z = \dfrac{\hat{p} - p}{\sqrt{p(1-p)/n}}$	$\hat{p} \pm z_{\alpha/2}\sqrt{\dfrac{\hat{p}(1-\hat{p})}{n}}$	np and $n(1-\hat{p}) \geq 5$ (for test)
			$n\hat{p}$ and $n(1-\hat{p}) \geq 5$ (for estimation)

SUPPLEMENTARY EXERCISES

Exercises 11.72–11.90 require the use of a computer and software. The answers may be calculated manually. See Appendix A for the sample statistics.

11.72 One of the issues that came up in a recent municipal election was the high cost of housing. A candidate seeking to unseat an incumbent claimed that the average family spends more than 30% of its annual income on housing. A housing expert was asked to investigate the claim. A random sample of 125 households was drawn, and each household was asked to report the percentage of household income spent on housing costs. The data are stored in file XR11-72.

a Is there enough evidence at the 5% significance level to infer that the candidate is correct?

b Using a confidence level of 95%, estimate the mean percentage spent on housing by all households.

c What is the required condition for the techniques used in parts (a) and (b)? Use a graphical technique to check whether it is satisfied.

11.73 To help forecast the winner in a Democratic senate primary, a survey was conducted. A random sample of 681 registered Democrats was asked for whom they intended to vote in the primary to be held the following day. The results are stored in file XR11-73 using the following codes.

Barbara Jones (1), Bill Smith (2), Pat Jackson (3)

a Estimate with 90% confidence the proportion of all voters who will vote for Barbara Jones.

b Can we conclude at the 10% significance level that Bill Smith will receive more than 20% of the vote?

11.74 The "just-in-time" policy of inventory control (developed by the Japanese) is growing in popularity. For example, General Motors recently spent $2 billion on its Oshawa, Ontario, plant so that it will be less than 1 hour from most suppliers. Suppose that an automobile parts supplier claims to deliver parts to any manufacturer in an average time of less than 1 hour. In an effort to test the claim, a manufacturer recorded the times (in minutes) of 24 deliveries from this supplier. These data are stored in file XR11-74. Can we conclude at the 5% level of significance that the supplier's assertion is correct?

11.75 Robots are being used with increasing frequency on production lines to perform monotonous tasks. To determine whether a robot welder should replace human welders in producing automobiles, an experiment was performed. The time for the robot to complete a series of welds was found to be 38 seconds. A random sample of 20 workers was taken, and the time for each worker to complete the welds was measured and stored in file XR11-75. The mean was calculated to be 38 seconds, the same as the robot's time. However, the robot's time did not vary, whereas there was variation among the workers' times. An analysis of the production line revealed that if the variance exceeds 17 seconds^2, there will be problems. Perform an analysis of the data, and determine whether problems using human welders are likely. (Use a 10% significance level.)

11.76 The television networks often compete on the evening of an election day to be the first to identify the winner of the election correctly. One commonly used technique is the random sampling of voters as they exit the polling booths. Suppose that, in a two-candidate race, 500 voters were asked for whom they voted. The results are stored in file XR11-76 using the code 1 = Democrat and 2 = Republican. Can we conclude at the 5% level of significance that the Republican candidate will win?

11.77 Suppose that, in a large state university (with numerous campuses), the marks in an introductory statistics course are normally distributed with a mean of 68%. To determine the effect of requiring students to pass a calculus test (which at present is not a prerequisite), a random sample of 50 students who have taken calculus is given a statistics course. The marks out of 100 are stored in file XR11-77.

a Estimate with 95% confidence the mean statistics mark for all students who have taken calculus.

b Do these data provide evidence at the 5% significance level to infer that students with a calculus background would perform better in statistics than students with no calculus?

11.78 Duplicate bridge is a game in which players compete for master points. When a player receives 300 master points, he or she becomes a life master. Since that title comes with a year's free subscription to the American Contract Bridge League's (ACBL) monthly bulletin, the ACBL is interested in knowing the status of non-life masters. Suppose that a random sample of 80 non-life masters was asked how many master points they have. The results are stored in file XR11-78. The ACBL would like an estimate of the mean number of master points held by all non-life masters. A confidence level of 90% is considered adequate in this case.

11.79 A national health care system was an issue in the 1992 presidential election campaign and is likely to be a subject of debate for many years. The issue arose because of the large number of Americans who have no health insurance. Under the present system, free health care is available to poor people, while relatively well-off Americans buy their own health insurance. Those who are considered working poor and who are in the lower middle class economic stratum appear to be most unlikely to have adequate medical insurance. To investigate this problem, a statistician surveyed 250 families whose gross income last year was between $10,000 and $15,000. Family heads were asked whether they have medical insurance coverage. The answers are stored in file XR11-79 (2 = Has medical insurance and 1 = Doesn't have medical insurance). The statistician wanted an estimate of the fraction of all families whose incomes are in the range of $10,000 to $15,000 who have medical insurance. Perform the necessary calculations to produce an interval estimate with 90% confidence.

11.80 The routes of postal deliverers are carefully planned so that each deliverer works between 7 and 7.5 hours per shift. The planned routes assume an average walking speed of 2 miles per hour and no shortcuts across lawns. In an experiment to examine the amount of time deliverers actually spend completing their shifts, a random sample of 75 postal deliverers was secretly timed. The data from the survey are stored in file XR11-80.

a Estimate with 99% confidence the mean shift time for all postal deliverers.

b Check to determine if the required condition for this statistical inference is satisfied.

c Is there enough evidence at the 10% significance level to conclude that postal workers are on average spending less than 7 hours per day doing their jobs?

11.81 As you can easily appreciate, the number of Internet users is rapidly increasingly. A recent survey reveals that there are about 30 million Internet users in North America. Suppose that a survey of 200 of these people asked them to report the number of hours they spent on the Internet last week. The results are stored in file XR11-81. Estimate with 95% confidence the annual total amount of time spent by all North Americans on the Internet.

11.82 The manager of a branch of a major bank wants to improve service. She is thinking about giving $1 to any customer who waits in line for a period of time that is considered excessive. (The bank ultimately decided that more than 8 minutes is excessive.) However, to get a better idea about the level of current service, she undertakes a survey of customers. A student is hired to measure the time spent waiting in line by a random sample of 50 customers. Using a stopwatch, the student determined the amount of time between the time the customer joined the line and the time he or she reached the teller. The times were recorded and are stored in file XR11-82. Construct a 90% confidence interval estimate of the mean waiting time for all the bank's customers.

11.83 In an examination of consumer loyalty in the travel business, 72 first-time visitors to a tourist attraction were asked whether they planned to return. The responses are stored in file XR11-83 where 2 = Yes and 1 = No. Estimate with 95% confidence the proportion of all first-time visitors who planned to return to the same destination.

11.84 Engineers who are in charge of the production of springs used to make car seats are concerned about the variability of the springs. The springs are designed to be 500 mm long. When the springs are too long they will loosen and fall out. When they are too short they will not fit into the frames. The springs that are too long and too short must be reworked at considerable additional cost. The engineers have calculated that a standard deviation of 2 mm will result in an acceptable number of springs that must be reworked. A random sample of 100 springs was measured. The data are stored in file XR11-84. Can we infer at the 5% significance level that the number of springs requiring reworking is unacceptably large?

11.85 Refer to Exercise 11.84. Suppose the engineers recoded the data so that springs that were the correct length were recorded as 1, springs that were too long were recorded as 2, and springs that were too short were recorded as 3. These data are stored in file XR11-85. Can we infer at the 5% significance level that less than 90% of the springs are the correct length?

11.86 An advertisement for a major home appliance manufacturer claims that its repair personnel are the loneliest in the world because its appliances require the smallest number of service calls. To examine this claim, a researcher drew a random sample of 100 owners of 5-year-old washing machines. The number of service calls made in the 5-year period were recorded and stored in file XR11-86. Find the 90% confidence interval estimate of the mean number of service calls for all 5-year-old washing machines.

11.87 An oil company sends out monthly statements to its customers who purchased gasoline and other items using the company's credit card. Until now, the company has not included a preaddressed envelope for returning payments. The average and the standard deviation of the number of days before payment is received are 9.8 and 3.2, respectively. As an experiment to determine whether enclosing preaddressed envelopes speeds up payment, 150 customers selected at random were sent preaddressed envelopes with their bills. The number of days to payment was recorded and stored in file XR11-87.

a Do the data provide sufficient evidence at the 5% level of significance to establish that enclosure of preaddressed envelopes improves the average speed of payments?

b Can we conclude at the 5% significance level that the variability in payment speeds decreases when a preaddressed envelope is sent?

11.88 A rock promoter is in the process of deciding whether to book a new band for a rock concert. He knows that this band appeals almost exclusively to teenagers. According to the latest census, there are 400,000 teenagers in the area. The promoter decides to do a survey to try to estimate the proportion of teenagers who will attend the concert. How large a sample should be taken in order to estimate the proportion to within .02 with 95% confidence?

11.89 In Exercise 11.88, suppose that the promoter decided to draw a sample of size 600 (because of financial considerations). Each teenager was asked whether he or she would attend the concert. The answers are stored in file XR11-89 using the following codes: 2 = Yes, I will attend; 1 = No, I will not attend. Estimate with 95% confidence the number of teenagers who will attend the concert.

11.90 The owner of a downtown parking lot suspects that the person she hired to run the lot is stealing some money. The receipts as provided by the employee indicate that the average number of cars parked in the lot is 125 per day and that, on average, each car is parked for 3.5 hours. To determine whether the employee is stealing, the owner watches the lot for 5 days. On those days, the number of cars parked is as follows.

120   130   124   127   128

The time spent on the lot for the 629 cars that the owner observed during the 5 days is stored in file XR11-90. Can the owner conclude at the 5% level of significance that the employee is stealing? (HINT: Since there are two ways to steal two tests should be performed.)

Case 11.1   Pepsi's Exclusivity Agreement with a University

In the last few years colleges and universities have signed exclusivity agreements with a variety of private companies. These agreements bind the university to sell that company's products exclusively on the campus. Many of the agreements involve food and beverage firms.

A large university with a total enrollment of about 50,000 students has offered Pepsi-Cola an exclusivity agreement, which would give Pepsi exclusive rights to sell their products at all university facilities for the next year and an option for future years. In return the university would receive 35% of the on-campus revenues and an additional lump sum of $200,000 per year. Pepsi has been given 2 weeks to respond.

The management at Pepsi quickly reviews what they know. The market for soft drinks is measured in terms of the equivalent of 10-ounce cans. Pepsi currently sells an average of 22,000 cans or their equivalents per week (over the 40 weeks of the year that the university operates). The cans sell for an average of 75 cents each. The costs including labor amount to 20 cents per can. Pepsi is unsure of their market share but suspect it is considerably less than 50%. A quick analysis reveals that if their current market share were 25% then with an exclusivity agreement Pepsi would sell 88,000 cans per week. Thus, annual sales would be 3,520,000 cans per year (calculated as 88,000 cans per week $\times$ 40 weeks). The gross revenue would be computed as follows.

    Gross revenue = 3,520,000 cans $\times$ \$.75 revenue/can = \$2,640,000

This figure must be multiplied by 65% since the university would rake in 35% of the gross. Thus,

    65% $\times$ \$2,640,000 = \$1,716,000

The total cost of 20 cents per can (or $704,000) and the annual payment to the university of $200,000 is subtracted to obtain the net profit.

    Net profit = \$1,716,000 − \$704,000 − \$200,000 = \$812,000

Their current annual profit is

    Current profit = 40 weeks $\times$ 22,000 cans/week $\times$ \$.55/can = \$484,000

If the current market share is 25% the potential gain from the agreement is

    \$812,000 − \$484,000 = \$328,000

The only problem with this analysis is that Pepsi does not know how many soft drinks are sold weekly at the university. Coke is not likely to supply Pepsi with information about their sales, which together with Pepsi's line of products constitutes virtually the entire market.

A recent graduate of a business program volunteers that a survey of the university's students can supply the missing information. Accordingly, she organizes a survey that asks 500 students to keep track of the number of soft drinks they purchase on campus over the next 7 days. The responses are stored in file C11-01.

Perform a statistical analysis to extract the needed information from the data. Estimate with 95% confidence the parameter that is at the core of the decision problem. Use the estimate to compute estimates of the annual profit. Assume that Coke and Pepsi drinkers would be willing to buy either product in the absence of their first choice.

On the basis of maximizing profits from sales of soft drinks at the university, should Pepsi agree to the exclusivity agreement?

Case 11.2	Pepsi's Exclusivity Agreement with a University: The Coke Side of the Equation

While the executives of Pepsi Cola are trying to decide what to do, the university informs them that a similar offer has gone out to the Coca-Cola company. Furthermore, if both companies want exclusive rights then a bidding war will take place. The executives at Pepsi would like to know how likely is it that Coke will want exclusive rights under the conditions outlined by the university.

Perform a similar analysis to the one you did in Case 11.1, but this time Pepsi's management wants to determine Coke's profit from the exclusivity agreement.

Is it likely that Coke will want to conclude an exclusivity agreement with the university? Discuss the reasons for your conclusions.

Case 11.3	Number of Uninsured Motorists*

A number of years ago the Michigan legislature passed a law requiring insurance for all drivers. Prior to this event drivers did not have to be covered by insurance. The law was challenged on the grounds that it discriminated against poor people who would not be able legally to drive. At issue at the trial was the number of Michigan motorists who would be coerced by the law into buying insurance. To do so, it was necessary to count the number of uninsured motorists. (These would be the people who would be forced by law to buy insurance.) There were a total of 4,505,665 license plates for passenger vehicles registered in Michigan at the time. An investigation of each one of these to determine whether they had insurance coverage would be prohibitively expensive and time consuming. It was decided that the state would draw a random sample of motorists and estimate the number of Michigan's driving population who were uninsured from the sample data. A random sample of 249 license plates was drawn using statistically sound sampling methods. Each was investigated to determine its insurance status. The license plates sampled were placed in one of three categories. The categories and the codes on the disk are as follows.

    1 = Insured

    2 = Not insured

    3 = Missing

(License plates that were drawn for the sample but where investigators were unable to find the car or its owner were classified as missing.) The data are stored in column 1 of file C11-03.

Your job is to estimate the proportion of all Michigan passenger vehicles that are not insured. Provide two methods for dealing with the missing data. From each method determine the upper and lower limits for the estimated number of motorists who would have been forced by law to buy insurance. Discuss which method is more reasonable.

---

*Adapted from L. Katz, "Presentation of a Confidence Interval Estimate as Evidence in a Legal Proceeding," Department of Statistics, Michigan State University (1974).

Chapter 12

Inference About the Comparison of Two Populations

12.1 Introduction

12.2 Inference About the Difference Between Two Means: Independent Samples

12.3 Observational and Experimental Data

12.4 Inference About the Difference Between Two Means: Matched Pairs Experiment

12.5 Inference About the Ratio of Two Variances (Optional)

12.6 Inference About the Difference Between Two Population Proportions

12.7 Market Segmentation (Optional)

12.8 Summary

12.1 INTRODUCTION

We can compare learning how to employ statistical techniques to learning how to drive a car. We began by describing what you are going to do in this course (Chapter 1), followed by a presentation of the essential background material (Chapters 2 through 8). Learning the concepts of statistical inference and applying them the way we did in Chapters 9 and 10 is akin to driving a car in an empty parking lot. You're driving, but it's not a realistic experience. Learning Chapter 11 is like driving on a quiet side street with little traffic. The experience represents real driving, but much of the difficulties have been postponed. In this chapter, you begin to drive for real, with many of the actual problems faced by licensed drivers, and the experience prepares you to tackle the next difficulty.

In this chapter, we present a variety of techniques whose objective is to compare two populations. In Sections 12.2 and 12.4, we deal with quantitative variables; the parameter of interest is the difference between two means. The difference between these two sections introduces yet another factor that determines the correct statistical method—the design of the experiment used to gather the data. In Section 12.2, the samples are independently drawn, whereas in Section 12.4 the samples are taken from a matched pairs experiment. In Section 12.3, we discuss the difference between observational and experimental data, a distinction that is critical to the way in which we interpret statistical results.

Section 12.5 presents the procedures employed to infer whether two population variances differ. The parameter is the ratio σ_1^2/σ_2^2. (When comparing two variances, we use the ratio rather than the difference because of the nature of the sampling distribution.)

Section 12.6 addresses the problem of comparing two populations of qualitative data. The parameter to be tested and estimated is the difference between two proportions.

The following examples illustrate situations in which the problem objective is to compare two populations.

Example 1 Operations managers of production facilities are always looking for ways to improve productivity in their plants. This can be accomplished by rearranging sequences of operations, acquiring new technology, or improving the training of workers. When one or more such changes are made, their effect on the operation of the entire plant is of interest. The manager can measure the effect by comparing productivity after the innovation with productivity before the innovation. Because productivity is often measured by the mean number of units produced per hour, the parameter of interest is the difference between two means $\mu_1 - \mu_2$. We may also be interested in comparing the consistency before and after the innovation; the parameter to be tested or estimated is σ_1^2/σ_2^2.

Example 2 Market managers and advertisers are eager to know which segments of the population are buying their products. If they can determine these groups, they can target their advertising messages and tailor their products to these customers. For example, if advertisers determine that the decision to purchase a particular household product is made more frequently by men than by women, the interests and concerns of men will be the focus of most commercial messages. The advertising media also depend on whether the product is of greater interest to men or to women. The most common way of measuring this factor is to find the difference in the proportions of men and women buying the product. In these situations, the parameter to be tested or estimated is the difference between two proportions $p_1 - p_2$.

Example 3 Medical scientists are involved in various research projects. A number of projects are examining ways to reduce cholesterol levels, because high levels of cholesterol are linked to heart attacks and strokes. One method of testing the effectiveness of a new drug is to give the drug to one group of people and a placebo (a pill with no medicine) to another group of people. To judge how well the drug works, the reduction in cholesterol would be measured for each person. The mean reduction for those taking the drug could be compared with the mean reduction for those taking the placebo. The objective is to test to see if the former is greater than the latter. The parameter is the difference between two means $\mu_1 - \mu_2$.

Example 4 Politicians are constantly concerned about how the voting public perceives their actions and behaviors. Politicians are particularly concerned with the extent to which constituents approve of their behavior and the ways in which that approval changes over time. As a result, they frequently poll the public to determine the proportion of voters who support them and whether that support has changed since the previous survey. The parameter of interest to them is the difference between two proportions $p_1 - p_2$, where p_1 is the proportion of support at present, and p_2 is the proportion of support at the time of the previous survey.

12.2 INFERENCE ABOUT THE DIFFERENCE BETWEEN TWO MEANS: INDEPENDENT SAMPLES

To test and estimate the difference between two population means, the statistician draws random samples from each of two populations. In this section, we discuss independent samples. In Section 12.4, where we present the matched pairs experiment, the distinction between independent samples and matched pairs will be made clear. For now, we define independent samples as samples completely unrelated to one another.

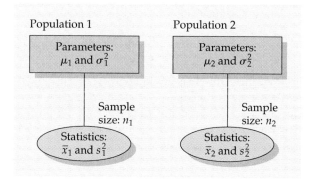

Figure 12.1

Independent samples from two populations

Figure 12.1 depicts the sampling process. Observe that we draw a sample of size n_1 from population 1 and a sample of size n_2 from population 2. For each sample, we compute the sample means and sample variances.

The best estimator of the difference between two population means $\mu_1 - \mu_2$ is the difference between two sample means $\bar{x}_1 - \bar{x}_2$. In Chapter 8 we presented the sampling distribution of $\bar{x}_1 - \bar{x}_2$.

> ### Sampling Distribution of $\bar{x}_1 - \bar{x}_2$
>
> 1 $\bar{x}_1 - \bar{x}_2$ is normally distributed if the populations are normal and approximately normal if the populations are nonnormal and the sample sizes are large.
>
> 2 The expected value of $\bar{x}_1 - \bar{x}_2$ is
>
> $$E(\bar{x}_1 - \bar{x}_2) = \mu_1 - \mu_2$$
>
> 3 The variance of $\bar{x}_1 - \bar{x}_2$ is
>
> $$V(\bar{x}_1 - \bar{x}_2) = \frac{\sigma_1^2}{n_1} + \frac{\sigma_2^2}{n_2}$$
>
> The standard error of $\bar{x}_1 - \bar{x}_2$ is
>
> $$\sqrt{\frac{\sigma_1^2}{n_1} + \frac{\sigma_2^2}{n_2}}$$

Thus,

$$z = \frac{(\bar{x}_1 - \bar{x}_2) - (\mu_1 - \mu_2)}{\sqrt{\dfrac{\sigma_1^2}{n_1} + \dfrac{\sigma_2^2}{n_2}}}$$

is a standard normal (or approximately normal) random variable. It follows that the test statistic is

$$z = \frac{(\bar{x}_1 - \bar{x}_2) - (\mu_1 - \mu_2)}{\sqrt{\dfrac{\sigma_1^2}{n_1} + \dfrac{\sigma_2^2}{n_2}}}$$

The interval estimator is

$$(\bar{x}_1 - \bar{x}_2) \pm z_{\alpha/2} \sqrt{\frac{\sigma_1^2}{n_1} + \frac{\sigma_2^2}{n_2}}$$

However, these formulas are rarely used because the population variances σ_1^2 and σ_2^2 are almost always unknown. Consequently, it is necessary to estimate the standard error of the sampling distribution. The way to do this depends on whether the two unknown population variances are equal. When they are equal, the test statistic and confidence interval estimator are as follows.

> ### Test Statistic for $\mu_1 - \mu_2$ when $\sigma_1^2 = \sigma_2^2$
>
> $$t = \frac{(\bar{x}_1 - \bar{x}_2) - (\mu_1 - \mu_2)}{\sqrt{s_p^2\left(\dfrac{1}{n_1} + \dfrac{1}{n_2}\right)}} \qquad \text{d.f.} = n_1 + n_2 - 2$$
>
> where
>
> $$s_p^2 = \frac{(n_1 - 1)s_1^2 + (n_2 - 1)s_2^2}{n_1 + n_2 - 2}$$

The quantity s_p^2 is called the **pooled variance estimate** of the common variance. It is the weighted average of the two sample variances. The requirement that the population variances be equal makes this calculation feasible, since we need only one estimate of the common value of σ_1^2 and σ_2^2. It makes sense for us to use the pooled variance estimate because, in combining both samples, we produce a better estimate.

The test statistic is Student t distributed, with $n_1 + n_2 - 2$ degrees of freedom, provided that the two populations are normal. The interval estimator is derived by mathematics that by now has become routine.

Interval Estimator of $\mu_1 - \mu_2$ when $\sigma_1^2 = \sigma_2^2$

$$(\bar{x}_1 - \bar{x}_2) \pm t_{\alpha/2}\sqrt{s_p^2\left(\frac{1}{n_1} + \frac{1}{n_2}\right)}$$

We will refer to the above formulas as the **equal-variances test statistic** and **interval estimator,** respectively.

The question naturally arises of "How do we know when the population variances are equal?" The answer is that since σ_1^2 and σ_2^2 are unknown, we can't know for certain whether they're equal. However, we can use the sample variances s_1^2 and s_2^2 to make inferences about the population variances. In Section 12.5, we will present a statistical technique that will allow us to test for equality. However, for now we will simply examine the sample variances and informally judge their relative values to determine whether we can assume that the population variances are equal.

When the population variances are unequal, we cannot use the pooled variance estimate. Instead, we estimate each population variance with its sample variance. Unfortunately, the sampling distribution of the resulting statistic

$$\frac{(\bar{x}_1 - \bar{x}_2) - (\mu_1 - \mu_2)}{\sqrt{\dfrac{s_1^2}{n_1} + \dfrac{s_2^2}{n_2}}}$$

is neither normal nor Student t. However, it can be approximated by a Student t distribution with degrees of freedom equal to

$$\text{d.f.} = \frac{(s_1^2/n_1 + s_2^2/n_2)^2}{\left(\dfrac{(s_1^2/n_1)^2}{n_1 - 1} + \dfrac{(s_2^2/n_2)^2}{n_2 - 1}\right)}$$

The test statistic and interval estimator are easily derived from the sampling distribution.

Test Statistic for $\mu_1 - \mu_2$ when $\sigma_1^2 \neq \sigma_2^2$

$$t = \frac{(\bar{x}_1 - \bar{x}_2) - (\mu_1 - \mu_2)}{\sqrt{\dfrac{s_1^2}{n_1} + \dfrac{s_2^2}{n_2}}} \qquad \text{d.f.} = \frac{(s_1^2/n_1 + s_2^2/n_2)^2}{\left(\dfrac{(s_1^2/n_1)^2}{n_1 - 1} + \dfrac{(s_2^2/n_2)^2}{n_2 - 1}\right)}$$

Interval Estimator of $\mu_1 - \mu_2$ when $\sigma_1^2 \neq \sigma_2^2$

$$(\bar{x}_1 - \bar{x}_2) \pm t_{\alpha/2} \sqrt{\frac{s_1^2}{n_1} + \frac{s_2^2}{n_2}}$$

We will refer to the above formulas as the **unequal-variances test statistic** and **interval estimator,** respectively.

▼ **EXAMPLE 12.1**

Despite some controversy, scientists generally agree that high-fiber cereals reduce the likelihood of various forms of cancer. However, one scientist claims that people who eat high-fiber cereal for breakfast will consume, on average, fewer calories for lunch than people who don't eat high-fiber cereal for breakfast (*Toronto Star,* 2 July, 1991). If this is true, high-fiber cereal manufacturers will be able to claim another advantage of eating their product—potential weight reduction for dieters. As a preliminary test of the claim, 150 people were randomly selected and asked what they regularly eat for breakfast and lunch. Each person was identified as either a consumer or a non-consumer of high-fiber cereal, and the number of calories consumed at lunch was measured and recorded. These data are listed below and stored in columns 1 and 2 of file XM12-01. Can the scientist conclude at the 5% significance level that his belief is correct?

CALORIES CONSUMED AT LUNCH

Consumers of High-Fiber Cereal

568	646	607	555	530	714	593	647	650
498	636	529	565	566	639	551	580	629
589	739	637	568	687	693	683	532	651
681	539	617	584	694	556	667	467	
540	596	633	607	566	473	649	622	

Nonconsumers of High-Fiber Cereal

705	754	740	569	593	637	563	421	514	536
819	741	688	547	723	553	733	812	580	833
706	628	539	710	730	620	664	547	624	644
509	537	725	679	701	679	625	643	566	594
613	748	711	674	672	599	655	693	709	596
582	663	607	505	685	566	466	624	518	750
601	526	816	527	800	484	462	549	554	582
608	541	426	679	663	739	603	726	623	788
787	462	773	830	369	717	646	645	747	
573	719	480	602	596	642	588	794	583	
428	754	632	765	758	663	476	490	573	

Solution

IDENTIFY

To assess the claim, the scientist needs to compare the population of consumers of high-fiber cereal to the population of nonconsumers. The data are quantitative (obviously, we've recorded real numbers). This problem objective–data type combination tells us that the parameter to be tested is the difference between two means $\mu_1 - \mu_2$. The claim to be tested is that the mean caloric intake of consumers (μ_1) is less than that of nonconsumers (μ_2). Hence, the alternative hypothesis is

$$H_1: (\mu_1 - \mu_2) < 0$$

To identify the test statistic, the scientist instructs the computer to output the sample standard deviations. They are

$$s_1 = 64.05 \quad \text{and} \quad s_2 = 103.29$$

There is reason to believe that the population variances are unequal. Thus, we use the unequal-variances test statistic.

$$t = \frac{(\bar{x}_1 - \bar{x}_2) - (\mu_1 - \mu_2)}{\sqrt{\dfrac{s_1^2}{n_1} + \dfrac{s_2^2}{n_2}}} \qquad \text{d.f.} = \frac{(s_1^2/n_1 + s_2^2/n_2)^2}{\left(\dfrac{(s_1^2/n_1)^2}{n_1 - 1} + \dfrac{(s_2^2/n_2)^2}{n_2 - 1}\right)}$$

The complete test follows.

$$H_0: (\mu_1 - \mu_2) = 0$$
$$H_1: (\mu_1 - \mu_2) < 0$$

Test statistic: $t = \dfrac{(\bar{x}_1 - \bar{x}_2) - (\mu_1 - \mu_2)}{\sqrt{\dfrac{s_1^2}{n_1} + \dfrac{s_2^2}{n_2}}}$

SOLVE

From the data we calculated the following statistics.

$$\bar{x}_1 = 604.02$$
$$\bar{x}_2 = 633.23$$
$$s_1 = 64.05$$
$$s_2 = 103.29$$

The number of degrees of freedom of the test statistic is

$$\text{d.f.} = \frac{(s_1^2/n_1 + s_2^2/n_2)^2}{\left(\dfrac{(s_1^2/n_1)^2}{n_1 - 1} + \dfrac{(s_2^2/n_2)^2}{n_2 - 1}\right)}$$

$$= \frac{[(64.05)^2/43 + (103.29)^2/107]^2}{\left(\dfrac{[(64.05)^2/43]^2}{43 - 1} + \dfrac{[(103.29)^2/107]^2}{107 - 1}\right)}$$

$$= 122.60 \ (\approx 123)$$

The rejection region is

$$t < -t_{\alpha,\text{d.f.}} = -t_{.05,123} \approx -1.658$$

The value of the test statistic is

$$t = \frac{(\bar{x}_1 - \bar{x}_2) - (\mu_1 - \mu_2)}{\sqrt{\dfrac{s_1^2}{n_1} + \dfrac{s_2^2}{n_2}}}$$

$$= \frac{(604.02 - 633.23) - 0}{\sqrt{\dfrac{(64.05)^2}{43} + \dfrac{(103.29)^2}{107}}}$$

$$= -2.09$$

Conclusion: Reject the null hypothesis.

Excel Output for Example 12.1

	A	B	C
1	t-Test: Two-Sample Assuming Unequal Variances		
2			
3		Consumers	Nonconsumers
4	Mean	604.0	633.2
5	Variance	4103	10670
6	Observations	43	107
7	Hypothesized Mean Difference	0	
8	df	123	
9	t Stat	-2.09	
10	P(T<=t) one-tail	0.0193	
11	t Critical one-tail	1.657	
12	P(T<=t) two-tail	0.0386	
13	t Critical two-tail	1.979	

The value of the test statistic (**t Stat**) is -2.09. The one-tail *p*-value (**P(T <=t) one-tail**) is .0193. Excel prints the two-tail *p*-value (**P(T<=t) two-tail**) since Excel does not "know" the alternative hypothesis. It also prints the critical values of the one-tail and two-tail rejection regions.

COMMANDS	COMMANDS FOR EXAMPLE 12.1
1 Type or import the data into two columns.	Open file **XM12-01.**
2 Click **Tools, Data Analysis . . . . ,** and **t-Test: Two-Sample Assuming Unequal Variances.**	
3 Specify the **Variable 1 Range.**	A1:A44
4 Specify the **Variable 2 Range.**	B1:B108
5 Type the value of the **Hypothesized Mean Difference** and click **Labels** (if necessary). Click **OK.**	0

To conduct this test from means and standard deviations or to perform a what-if analysis activate the **t-Test of 2 Means (Uneq-Var)** worksheet in the **Inference from Summary Statistics (Workbook)** option.

Minitab Output for Example 12.1

Two Sample T-Test and Confidence Interval

Test sample T for Consumers vs Nonconsumers

	N	Mean	StDev	SE Mean
Consumer	43	604.0	64.1	9.8
Nonconsu	107	633	103	10

95% CI for mu Consumer - mu Nonconsu: (-56.9, -2)
T-Test mu Consumer = mu Nonconsu (vs <): T = -2.09 P = 0.019
                                    DF = 122

The value of the test statistic is $t = -2.09$ with a p-value of .019.

COMMANDS	COMMANDS FOR EXAMPLE 12.1
1 Type or import the data.	Open file **XM12-01**.
2 Click **Stat, Basic Statistics,** and **2-Sample t. . . .**	
3 Use the cursor to select **Samples in one column** (stacked data) or **Samples in different columns** (unstacked data). (See the "Manipulating Data" subsection in Appendix 12.B for a discussion of stacked and unstacked data.)	Samples in different columns
4 Select the variable names or columns.	Consumers Nonconsumers or **C1 C2**
5 Use the cursor to select one of **less than, not equal,** or **greater than.**	less than
6 Use the cursor to indicate that the population variances are not equal. (Leave the box empty.) Click **OK.**	

INTERPRET

The p-value of the test is small (and the test statistic falls into the rejection region). As a result we conclude that there is sufficient evidence to infer that consumers of high-fiber cereal do eat fewer calories at lunch than do nonconsumers. However, there are two reasons to be cautious about concluding that high-fiber cereals constitute an effective contribution to weight loss. First, the data were likely self-reported, which means that each person determined the number of calories recorded that he or she consumed. Such data are often unreliable. Ideally, a less subjective method of counting calories should be used. Second, the way in which the experiment was performed may lead to several contradictory interpretations of the data. We will discuss this important issue in the next section.

In addition to testing to determine whether a difference exists, we can estimate the difference in mean caloric intake.

SOLVE

The confidence interval estimator of the difference between two means with unequal population variances is

$$(\bar{x}_1 - \bar{x}_2) \pm t_{\alpha/2} \sqrt{\frac{s_1^2}{n_1} + \frac{s_2^2}{n_2}}$$

The 95% confidence interval estimate of the difference between the mean caloric intake of those who do eat and those who do not eat high-fiber cereal for breakfast is

$$(\bar{x}_1 - \bar{x}_2) \pm t_{\alpha/2} \sqrt{\frac{s_1^2}{n_1} + \frac{s_2^2}{n_2}} = (604.02 - 633.23) \pm 1.980 \sqrt{\frac{(64.05)^2}{43} + \frac{(103.29)^2}{107}}$$

$$= -29.21 \pm 27.65$$

The lower and upper limits are -56.86 and -1.56.

Excel Output

The Excel output does not include the interval estimator. However, you can use the **t-Estimate of 2 Means (Uneq-Var)** worksheet (described above). Simply plug in the values of the sample means, sample standard deviations, and sample sizes, as well as the confidence level. We found the 95% confidence interval estimate to be

	A	B	C	D	E	F
1	t-Estimate of the Difference Between Two Means (Unequal-Variances)					
2						
3	**Sample 1**					
4	Sample mean	604.0				
5	Sample standard deviation	64.05				
6	Sample size	43				
7						
8	**Sample 2**					
9	Sample mean	633.2				
10	Sample standard deviation	103.3				
11	Sample size	107				
12						
13	Confidence level	0.95				
14						
15	Degrees of freedom	122.6				
16						
17	Lower confidence limit	-56.86				
18	Upper confidence limit	-1.56				

Minitab Output

The Minitab output includes the 95% confidence interval estimate.

```
95% CI for mu Consumer - mu Nonconsu:  ( -56.9,  -2)
```

INTERPRET

We estimate that nonconsumers of high-fiber cereal eat on average between 1.56 and 56.86 calories more than do consumers.

STATISTICS IN THE WORKPLACE

Operations Management Application

In Chapter 1 we discussed production design wherein an operations manager determines how a product is to be manufactured. The objective is to produce the highest quality product at a reasonable cost. This objective is achieved by choosing the machines, materials, methods, and "manpower" (personnel), the so-called 4 Ms. The manager can often employ statistical tools to help make this decision. Various experiments can be conducted to determine the lowest cost or fastest production schedule. The experiments use different materials, machines, methods, or personnel. There are several ways to judge differences in processes.

The manager can determine whether differences in quality exist, or differences in cost. If no differences exist, the manager may decide on the basis of some other criteria, such as the process that requires the least new training of workers.

▼ EXAMPLE 12.2

The plant manager of a company that manufactures office equipment is attempting to determine the process that will be used to assemble a new ergonomic chair. The material, machines, and workforce have already been decided. However, two methods of assembly are under consideration. The methods differ by the order in which the separate operations are performed. To help decide which should be used, an experiment was performed. Twenty-five randomly selected workers each assembled the chair using method A, and 25 workers each assembled the chair using method B. The assembly times in minutes were recorded and are exhibited below and stored in file XM12-02. The plant manager would like to know whether the assembly times of the two methods differ. A 5% significance level is judged to be appropriate.

ASSEMBLY TIMES

Method A

6.8	5.0	7.9	5.2	7.6	5.0	5.9	5.2	6.5	7.4	6.1
6.2	7.1	4.6	6.0	7.1	6.1	5.0	6.3	7.0	6.4	6.1
6.6	7.7	6.4

Method B

5.2	6.7	5.7	6.6	8.5	6.5	5.9	6.7	6.6	4.2	4.2
4.5	5.3	7.9	7.0	5.9	7.1	5.8	7.0	5.7	5.9	4.9
5.3	4.2	7.1

Solution

IDENTIFY

The data are quantitative, and the objective of the experiment is to compare the two populations of assembly times. The parameter of interest is the difference between two population means $\mu_1 - \mu_2$. The plant manager wants to determine whether a difference between the two methods exists. As a result, the alternative hypothesis is

$$H_1: (\mu_1 - \mu_2) \neq 0$$

To identify the correct test statistic, we need to calculate the sample standard deviations. They are

$$s_1 = .921 \quad \text{and} \quad s_2 = 1.142$$

Because s_1 is approximately equal to s_2, we can infer that the population variances are approximately equal. Thus, we employ the equal-variances test statistic.

$$t = \frac{(\bar{x}_1 - \bar{x}_2) - (\mu_1 - \mu_2)}{\sqrt{s_p^2\left(\dfrac{1}{n_1} + \dfrac{1}{n_2}\right)}}$$

The complete test is shown below.

$H_0: (\mu_1 - \mu_2) = 0$

$H_1: (\mu_1 - \mu_2) \neq 0$

Test statistic: $t = \dfrac{(\bar{x}_1 - \bar{x}_2) - (\mu_1 - \mu_2)}{\sqrt{s_p^2\left(\dfrac{1}{n_1} + \dfrac{1}{n_2}\right)}}$

SOLVE

The number of degrees of freedom is

$$\text{d.f.} = n_1 + n_2 - 2 = 25 + 25 - 2 = 48$$

The rejection region is

$$t < -t_{\alpha/2,\text{d.f.}} = -t_{.025,48} \approx -2.009 \quad \text{or}$$

$$t > t_{\alpha/2,\text{d.f.}} = t_{.025,48} \approx 2.009$$

We determined the following statistics.

$\bar{x}_1 = 6.288$

$\bar{x}_2 = 6.016$

$s_1 = .921$

$s_2 = 1.142$

$s_p^2 = \dfrac{(n_1 - 1)s_1^2 + (n_2 - 1)s_2^2}{n_1 + n_2 - 2}$

$\quad = \dfrac{(25 - 1)(.921)^2 + (25 - 1)(1.142)^2}{25 + 25 - 2}$

$\quad = 1.076$

The value of the test statistic is

$$t = \frac{(\bar{x}_1 - \bar{x}_2) - (\mu_1 - \mu_2)}{\sqrt{s_p^2\left(\dfrac{1}{n_1} + \dfrac{1}{n_2}\right)}}$$

$$= \frac{(6.288 - 6.016) - 0}{\sqrt{1.076\left(\dfrac{1}{25} + \dfrac{1}{25}\right)}}$$

$$= .93$$

Conclusion: Do not reject the null hypothesis.

**Excel Output for
Example 12.2**

	A	B	C
1	t-Test: Two-Sample Assuming Equal Variances		
2			
3		*Method A*	*Method B*
4	Mean	6.29	6.02
5	Variance	0.848	1.303
6	Observations	25	25
7	Pooled Variance	1.075	
8	Hypothesized Mean Difference	0	
9	df	48	
10	t Stat	0.93	
11	P(T<=t) one-tail	0.1792	
12	t Critical one-tail	1.677	
13	P(T<=t) two-tail	0.3584	
14	t Critical two-tail	2.011	

The value of the test statistic is .93 and the *p*-value is .3584.

COMMANDS	COMMANDS FOR EXAMPLE 12.2
1 Type or import the data into two columns.	Open file **XM12-02**.
2 Click **Tools, Data Analysis . . . ,** and **t-Test: Two-Sample Assuming Equal Variances.**	
3 Specify **Variable 1 Range.**	A1:A26
4 Specify **Variable 2 Range.**	B1:B26
5 Type the value of the **Hypothesized Mean Difference** and click **Labels** (if necessary). Click **OK.**	0

Use the **t-Test of 2 Means (Eq-Var)** worksheet to complete this test from the sample statistics and to perform a what-if analysis.

To estimate the difference between two means with equal population variances, activate the **t-Estimate of 2 Means (Eq-Var)** worksheet and substitute the sample statistics and confidence level. We produced the following output.

	A	B	C	D	E	F
1	t-Estimate of the Difference Between Two Means (Equal-Variances)					
2						
3	Sample 1					
4	Sample mean	6.29				
5	Sample standard deviation	0.921				
6	Sample size	25				
7						
8	Sample 2					
9	Sample mean	6.02				
10	Sample standard deviation	1.140				
11	Sample size	25				
12						
13	Confidence level	0.95				
14						
15	Pooled Variance estimate	1.074				
16						
17	Lower confidence limit	-0.32				
18	Upper confidence limit	0.86				

Minitab Output for Example 12.2

Two Sample T-Test and Confidence Interval

```
Two sample T for Method A vs Method B

            N    Mean    StDev   SE Mean
Method A   25    6.288   0.921    0.18
Method B   25    6.02    1.14     0.23

95% CI for mu Method A - mu Method B: ( -0.32,  0.86)
T-Test mu Method A = mu Method B (vs not =): T = 0.93  P = 0.36 DF = 48
Both use Pooled StDev = 1.04
```

The value of the test statistic is $t = .93$ with a p-value of .36. The 95% confidence interval estimate of the difference between the two means is $(-.32, .86)$.

COMMANDS	COMMANDS FOR EXAMPLE 12.2
1 Type or import the data.	Open file **XM12-02.**
2 Click **Stat, Basic Statistics,** and **2-Sample t. . . .**	
3 Use the cursor to select **Samples in one column** (stacked data) or **Samples in different columns.**	**Samples in different columns**
4 Select the variable names or columns.	**Method A Method B** or **C1 C2**
5 Use the cursor to select one of **less than, not equal,** or **greater than.**	**not equal**
6 Use the cursor to indicate that the population variances are equal. Click **OK.**	

INTERPRET

We conclude that there is no evidence to infer that the mean times differ. Once again, the manager should determine that all of the required conditions are satisfied (see the following subsection) and that there are no other factors that need to be considered. For example, is the quality of the finished product identical using the two designs? Is it possible that one method is better than another, but this experiment failed to demonstrate it because it takes longer to adapt to the new production design than this experiment allowed? If the conclusion stands, however, the manager should choose the design using some other criterion, such as worker preference.

▲

CHECKING THE REQUIRED CONDITION

Both the equal-variances and unequal-variances techniques require that the populations be normally distributed. As before, we can check to see if the requirement is satisfied by drawing the histograms of the data. To illustrate, we used Excel (Minitab histograms are almost identical) to create the histograms for Examples 12.1 (Figures 12.2 and 12.3) and 12.2 (Figures 12.4 and 12.5). Although the histograms are not bell-shaped, it appears that the assembly times are at least approximately normal. Because this technique is robust, we can be confident in the validity of the results.

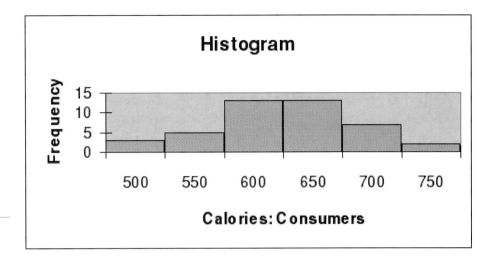

Figure 12.2

Histogram of consumers in Example 12.1

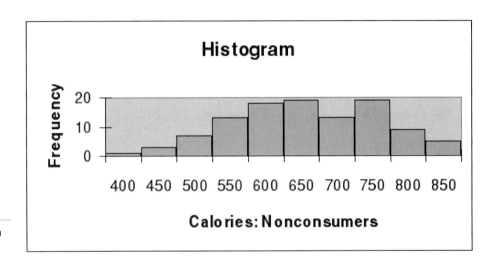

Figure 12.3

Histogram of nonconsumers in Example 12.1

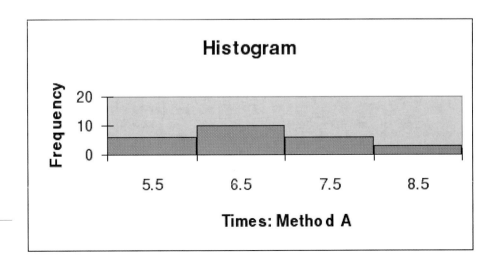

Figure 12.4

Histogram for method A in Example 12.2

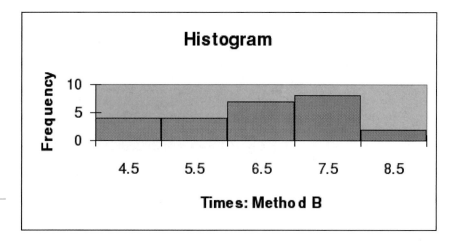

Figure 12.5

Histogram for method B in
Example 12.2

VIOLATION OF THE REQUIRED CONDITION

When the normality requirement is unsatisfied, we can use a nonparametric technique—the Wilcoxon rank sum test for independent samples (Chapter 16)—to replace
the equal-variances test of $\mu_1 - \mu_2$. We have no alternative to the unequal-variances
test of $\mu_1 - \mu_2$ when the populations are very nonnormal.

MANIPULATING DATA

There are two ways in which the data associated with the problems presented in this
section may be stored. As we discuss in Appendixes 12.C and 12.B, we can store the
observations of one sample in one column and the observations of the second sample in another column. When the data are stored in this manner, we say that the data
are *unstacked.* Alternatively, we can *stack* the data by storing all the observations from
both samples in one column and use a second column to store codes identifying the
sample from which the observation is drawn. Here is an example of unstacked data.

Column 1 (Sample 1)	Column 2 (Sample 2)
12	18
19	23
13	25

Here are the same data in stacked form.

Column 1	Column 2
12	1
19	1
13	1
18	2
23	2
25	2

It should be understood that the data need not be in order. Hence, they could have
been stored in this way.

Column 1	Column 2
18	2
25	2
13	1
12	1
23	2
19	1

If there are two populations to compare and only one variable, it is probably better to record the data in unstacked form. However, it is frequently the case that we want to observe several variables and compare them. For example, suppose that we survey male and female M.B.A.s and ask each to report his or her income, number of years of education, and number of years of experience. These data are usually stored in stacked form using the following format.

Column 1: code identifying female (1) and male (2)

Column 2: income

Column 3: years of education

Column 4: years of experience

To compare incomes, we would use columns 1 and 2. Columns 1 and 3 are used to compare education and columns 1 and 4 are used to compare experience levels.

Most statistical software requires one form or the other. Excel demands that the data must be unstacked. Some of Minitab's procedures allow either format, while others specify only one. Fortunately, both of our software packages allow the statistician to alter the format. (See Appendixes 12.C and 12.B for details.) We say "fortunately" because this allowed us to store the data in either form on the data disk provided with this book. In fact, we've used both forms to allow you to practice your ability to manipulate the data as necessary. You will need this ability to perform statistical techniques in this and other chapters in this book.

DEVELOPING AN UNDERSTANDING OF STATISTICAL CONCEPTS

The method we use to compute the standard deviation of the sampling distribution of $\bar{x}_1 - \bar{x}_2$ depends on whether the population variances are equal. When they are equal we calculate and use the pooled variance estimate s_p^2. An important principle is being applied here and will be again in this chapter (Section 12.6) and in later chapters. The principle can be loosely stated as follows: Where possible, it is advantageous to pool sample data to estimate the sampling distribution standard deviation. In the application above, we are able to pool because we assume that the two samples were drawn from populations with a common variance. Combining both samples increases the accuracy of the estimate. Thus, s_p^2 is a better estimator of the common variance than either s_1^2 or s_2^2 separately.

When the two population variances are unequal, we cannot pool the data and produce a common estimator. We must compute s_1^2 and s_2^2 and use them to estimate σ_1^2 and σ_2^2, respectively.

Here is a summary of how we recognize the techniques presented in this section.

Factors that Identify the Equal-Variances t-Test and Estimator of
$\mu_1 - \mu_2$

1 Problem objective: compare two populations

2 Data type: quantitative

3 Descriptive measurement: central location

4 Experimental design: independent samples

5 Population variances: equal

Factors that Identify the Unequal-Variances t-Test and Estimator of
$\mu_1 - \mu_2$

1 Problem objective: compare two populations

2 Data type: quantitative

3 Descriptive measurement: central location

4 Experimental design: independent samples

5 Population variances: not equal

EXERCISES

Exercises 12.1–12.18 are "what-if analyses" designed to determine what happens to the test statistics and interval estimates when elements of the statistical inference change. These problems can be solved manually or using Excel's **Inference from Summary Statistics (Workbook).**

12.1 In random samples of 25 from each of two normal populations we found the following statistics.

$$\bar{x}_1 = 524 \quad s_1 = 129 \quad \bar{x}_2 = 469 \quad s_2 = 150$$

a Test with $\alpha = .05$ to determine whether we can infer that the population means differ.

b Estimate the difference between the two population means with 95% confidence.

12.2 Repeat Exercise 12.1, increasing the standard deviations to $s_1 = 255$ and $s_2 = 307$.

12.3 Review Exercises 12.1 and 12.2. Describe what happens when the sample standard deviations get larger.

12.4 Repeat Exercise 12.1 with samples of size 100.

12.5 Review Exercises 12.1 and 12.4. Discuss the effects of increasing the sample size.

12.6 Random sampling from two normal populations produced the following results.:

$$\bar{x}_1 = 63 \quad s_1 = 8 \quad n_1 = 50$$
$$\bar{x}_2 = 60 \quad s_2 = 7 \quad n_2 = 45$$

a Can we infer at the 5% significance level that μ_1 is greater than μ_2?

b Estimate with 90% confidence the difference between the two population means.

12.7 Repeat Exercise 12.6 changing the sample standard deviations to 25 and 22, respectively.

12.8 Review Exercises 12.6 and 12.7. What happens when the sample standard deviations increase?

12.9 Repeat Exercise 12.6, doubling the sample sizes.

12.10 Review Exercises 12.6 and 12.9. Describe the effects of increasing the sample sizes.

12.11 After drawing random samples from two normal populations, a statistician produced the following statistics.

$$\bar{x}_1 = 884 \quad s_1 = 302 \quad n_1 = 38$$
$$\bar{x}_2 = 963 \quad s_2 = 49 \quad n_2 = 24$$

a Can we infer at the 10% significance level that μ_1 is less than μ_2?

b Estimate with 95% confidence the difference in population means.

12.12 Repeat Exercise 12.11, increasing the sample standard deviations to 588 and 103, respectively.

12.13 Review Exercises 12.11 and 12.12. Discuss the effect of increasing the sample standard deviations.

12.14 Repeat Exercise 12.11 increasing the sample sizes to 80 and 75, respectively.

12.15 Review Exercises 12.11 and 12.14. Describe what happens when the sample sizes increase.

12.16 Repeat Exercise 12.11, changing $\bar{x}_1$ to 850.

12.17 Repeat Exercise 12.11, changing $\bar{x}_1$ to 900.

12.18 Review Exercises 12.11, 12.16, and 12.17. Discuss the effect of increasing and decreasing $\bar{x}_1$.

Exercises 12.19–12.30 require the use of a computer and software. The answers may be calculated manually. See Appendix A for the sample statistics.

12.19 The data obtained from sampling two populations are stored in columns 1 and 2, respectively, in file XR12-19.

  a Conduct a test to determine whether the population means differ. Use a 5% significance level.
  b Estimate the difference in population means with 95% confidence.
  c What is the required condition(s) of the techniques employed in parts (a) and (b)?
  d Check to ensure that the required condition(s) is satisfied.

12.20 Random samples were drawn from each of two populations. The data are stored in columns 1 and 2, respectively, in file XR12-20.

  a Is there sufficient evidence at the 5% significance level to infer that the mean of population 1 is greater than the mean of population 2?
  b Estimate with 90% confidence the difference between the two population means.
  c What is the required condition(s) of the techniques employed in parts (a) and (b)?
  d Check to ensure that the required conditions(s) is satisfied.

12.21 Two samples of 40 observations from each of two populations were taken. The data are stored in columns 1 (all observations) and 2 (code specifying the sample) in file XR12-21. Do these data provide sufficient evidence at the 1% significance level to infer that the mean of population 2 is greater than the mean of population 1?

12.22 A statistician gathered data from two populations and stored them in columns 1 (sample 1) and 2 (sample 2) in file XR12-22. Can the statistician infer at the 10% significance level that the mean of population 1 is less than the mean of population 2?

12.23 The president of Tastee Inc., a baby-food producer, claims that his company's product is superior to that of his leading competitor, because babies gain weight faster with his product. (This is a good thing for babies.) To test the claim, a survey was undertaken. Mothers of newborn babies were asked which baby food they intended to feed their babies. Those who responded Tastee or the leading competitor were asked to keep track of their babies' weight gains over the next 2 months. There were 15 mothers who indicated that they would feed their babies Tastee and 25 who responded that they would feed their babies the product of the leading competitor. Each baby's weight gain (in ounces) was recorded and stored in column 1 (Tastee) and column 2 (leading competitor) in file XR12-23.

  a Can we conclude that, using weight gain as our criterion, Tastee baby food is indeed superior? (Conduct the test using a 5% significance level.)
  b Estimate with 95% confidence the difference between the mean weight gains of the two products.
  c Check to ensure that the required conditions(s) is satisfied.

12.24 Medical experts advocate the use of vitamin and mineral supplements to help fight infections. A study, undertaken by Dr. Ranjit Schneider of Memorial University (reported in the British journal *Lancet,* November 1992), recruited 96 men and women age 65 and older, one-half of them received daily supplements of vitamins and minerals, while the other half received placebos. The supplements contained the daily recommended amounts of 18 vitamins and minerals. These included vitamins B-6, B-12, C, D, and E, thiamine, riboflavin, niacin, calcium, copper, iodine, iron, selenium, magnesium, and zinc. The doses of vitamins A and E were slightly less than the daily requirements. The supplements included four times the amount of beta-carotene that the average person ingests daily. The number of days of illness from infections (ranging from colds to pneumonia) was recorded for each person. The data are stored in stacked form in file XR12-24 (code 1 = supplements and code 2 = placebo). Can we infer at the 5% significance level that taking vitamin and mineral supplements daily increases the body's immune system response?

12.25 Automobile insurance companies take many factors into consideration when setting rates. These factors include age, marital status, and miles driven per year. To determine the effect of gender, 100 male and 100 female drivers were surveyed. Each was asked how many miles he or she drove in the past year. The distances (in thousands of miles) are stored in stacked format (code 1 = male and code 2 = female) in file XR12-25.

  a Can we conclude at the 5% significance level that male and female drivers differ in the number of miles driven per year?
  b Estimate with 95% confidence the difference in mean distance driven by male and female drivers.
  c Check to ensure that the required condition(s) of the techniques used in parts (a) and (b) is satisfied.

12.26 The president of a company that manufactures automobile air conditioners is considering switching his supplier of condensers. Supplier A, the current producer of condensers for the manufacturer, prices its product 5% higher than Supplier B does. Since the president wants to maintain his company's reputation for quality, he wants to be sure that Supplier B's condensers last at least as long as Supplier A's. After a careful analysis, the president decided to retain Supplier A if there is sufficient statistical evidence that Supplier A's condensers last longer on average than Supplier B's condensers. In an experiment, 30 midsize cars were equipped with air conditioners using type A condensers while another 30 midsize cars were equipped with type B condensers. The number of miles (in thousands) driven by each car before the condenser broke down was recorded, and the data stored in unstacked format (column 1 = Supplier A and column 2 = Supplier B) in file XR12-26. Should the President retain Supplier A? (Use a 10% significance level.)

12.27 High blood pressure is a leading cause of strokes. Medical researchers are constantly seeking ways to treat patients suffering from this condition. A specialist in hypertension claims that regular aerobic exercise can reduce high blood pressure just as successfully as drugs, with none of the adverse side effects. To test the claim, 50 patients who suffer from high blood pressure were chosen to participate in an experiment. For 60 days, half the sample exercised three times per week for 1 hour; the other half took the standard medication. The percentage reduction in blood pressure was recorded for each individual, and the resulting data are stored (column 1 = exercise and column 2 = drug) in file XR12-27.

a Can we conclude at the 5% significance level that exercise is more effective than medication in reducing hypertension?

b Estimate with 95% confidence the difference in mean percentage reduction in blood pressure between drugs and exercise programs.

c Check to ensure that the required conditions(s) of the techniques used in parts (a) and (b) is satisfied.

12.28 In assessing the value of radio advertisements, sponsors not only measure the total number of listeners, but also record their ages. The 18-to-34 age group is considered to spend the most money. To examine the issue, the manager of an FM station commissioned a survey. One objective was to measure the difference in listening habits between the 18-to-34 and 35-to-50 age groups. The survey asked 250 people in each age category how much time they spent listening to FM radio per day. The results (in minutes) were recorded and stored in file XR12-28 (column 1 = listening times and column 2 identifies the age group: 1 = 18-to-34 and 2 = 35-to-50).

a Can we conclude at the 5% significance level that a difference exists between the two groups?

b Estimate with 95% confidence the difference in mean time listening to FM radio between the two age groups.

c Are the required conditions satisfied for the techniques you used in parts (a) and (b)?

12.29 A statistics professor is about to select a statistical software package for her course. One of the most important features, according to the professor, is the ease with which students learn to use the software. She has narrowed the selection to two possibilities: Software A, a menu-driven statistical package with some high-powered techniques, and Software B, a spreadsheet that has the capability of performing most techniques. To help make her decision, she asks 40 statistics students selected at random to choose one of the two packages. She gives each student a statistics problem to solve by computer and the appropriate manual. The amount of time (in minutes) each student needs to complete the assignment was recorded and stored in unstacked format (column 1 = package A and column 2 = package B) in file XR12-29.

a Can the professor conclude from these data that the two software packages differ in the amount of time needed to learn how to use them? (Use a 1% significance level.)

b Estimate with 95% confidence the difference in the mean amount of time needed to learn to use the two packages.

c What are the required conditions for the techniques used in parts (a) and (b)?

d Check to see if the required conditions are satisfied.

12.30 One factor in low productivity is the amount of time wasted by workers. Wasted time includes time spent cleaning up mistakes, waiting for more material and equipment, and performing any other activity not related to production. In a project designed to examine the problem, an operations management consultant surveyed 200 workers in companies that were classified as successful (on the basis of their latest annual profits) and another 200 workers from unsuccessful companies. The amount of time (in hours) wasted during a standard 40-hour workweek was recorded for each worker. These data are stored in columns 1 (successful companies) and 2 (unsuccessful companies) in file XR12-30.

a Do these data provide enough evidence at the 1% significance level to infer that the amount of time wasted in unsuccessful firms exceeds that of successful ones?

b Estimate with 95% confidence how much more time is wasted in unsuccessful firms than in successful ones.

12.3 OBSERVATIONAL AND EXPERIMENTAL DATA

As we've pointed out several times, the ability to properly interpret the results of a statistical technique is a critical skill for students to develop. This ability is dependent on your understanding of Type I and Type II errors and the fundamental concepts that are part of statistical inference. However, there is another component that needs to be understood: the difference between **observational data** and **experimental data.** To explain this difference, we will reexamine Examples 12.1 and 12.2 and analyze the way the data were obtained in each example.

In Example 12.1, we randomly selected 150 people and, on the basis of *their* responses, assigned them to one of two groups: high-fiber consumers and nonconsumers. We then recorded the number of calories consumed at lunch for the members of each group. Such data are called *observational.* Now examine Example 12.2, where the data were gathered by randomly assigning 25 workers to assemble chairs using method A and 25 workers to assemble chairs using method B. Data produced in this manner are said to be *experimental* or *controlled.* The statistical technique to be applied is not affected by whether the data are observational or experimental. However, the interpretation of the results may be affected.

In Example 12.1, we found that there was evidence to infer that people who eat high-fiber cereal for breakfast consume fewer calories at lunch than do nonconsumers of high-fiber cereal. From this result, we're inclined to believe that eating a high-fiber cereal at breakfast may be a way to reduce weight. However, other interpretations are possible. For example, people who eat fewer calories are probably more health conscious, and such people are more likely to eat high-fiber cereal as part of a healthy breakfast. In this interpretation, high-fiber cereals do not necessarily lead to fewer calories at lunch. Instead another factor, general health consciousness, leads to both fewer calories at lunch *and* high-fiber cereal for breakfast. Notice that the conclusion of the statistical procedure is unchanged. On average, people who eat high-fiber cereal consume fewer calories at lunch. However, because of the way the data were gathered, we have more difficulty interpreting this result.

Suppose that we redo Example 12.1 using the experimental approach. We randomly select 150 people to participate in the experiment. We randomly assign 75 (or 43, as we had in the original experiment) to eat high-fiber cereal for breakfast and the other 75 to eat something else. We then record the number of calories each person consumes at lunch. Ideally, in this experiment both groups will be similar in all other dimensions, including health consciousness. (Larger sample sizes increase the likelihood that the two groups will be similar.) If the statistical result is about the same as in Example 12.1, we may have some valid reason to believe that high-fiber cereal leads to a decrease in caloric intake.

Experimental data are usually more expensive to obtain because of the planning required to set up the experiment; observational data usually require less work to gather. Furthermore, in many situations it is impossible to conduct a controlled experiment. For example, suppose that we want to determine if engineering students outperform arts students in M.B.A. programs. In a controlled experiment we would randomly assign some students to achieve a degree in engineering and other students to obtain an arts degree. We would then make them sign up for an M.B.A. program where we would record their grades. Unfortunately for statistical despots (and fortunately for the rest of us), we live in a democratic society, which makes the coercion necessary to perform this controlled experiment impossible.

To answer our question about the relative performance of engineering and arts students, we have no choice but to obtain our data by observational methods. We would take a random sample of engineering students and arts students who have already entered M.B.A. programs and record their grades. If we find that engineering students do better, we may tend to conclude that an engineering background better prepares students for an M.B.A. program. However, it may be true that better students tend to choose engineering as their undergraduate major, and that better students achieve higher grades in all programs, including the M.B.A. program.

Although we've discussed observational and experimental data in the context of the test of the difference between two means, you should be aware that the issue of how the data are obtained is relevant to the interpretation of all the techniques that follow.

EXERCISES

12.31 Examine Exercises 12.23 to 12.30. Which of the data sets were obtained by observational methods and which were obtained through controlled experiments? Explain the reasons for your choices.

12.32 Provide two interpretations of the results you produced in Exercise 12.23.

12.33 Discuss how the data in Exercise 12.23 could have been obtained through a controlled experiment.

12.34 Suppose that you are analyzing one of the hundreds of statistical studies linking smoking with lung cancer. The study analyzed thousands of randomly selected people, some of whom had lung cancer. The statistics indicate that those who have lung cancer smoked on average significantly more than those who did not have lung cancer.

a Explain how you know that the data are observational.

b Is there another interpretation of the statistics besides the obvious one that smoking causes lung cancer? If so, what is it? (Students who produce the best answers will be eligible for a job in the public relations department of a tobacco company.)

c Is it possible to conduct a controlled experiment to produce data that addresses the question of the relationship between smoking and lung cancer? If so, describe the experiment.

12.4 INFERENCE ABOUT THE DIFFERENCE BETWEEN TWO MEANS: MATCHED PAIRS EXPERIMENT

We continue our presentation of statistical techniques that address the problem of comparing two populations of quantitative data. In Section 12.2, the parameter of interest was the difference between two population means, where the data were generated from independent samples. In this section, the data are gathered from a matched pairs experiment. To illustrate why matched pairs experiments are needed and how we deal with data produced in this way, consider the following example.

▼ **EXAMPLE 12.3**

Tire manufacturers are constantly researching ways to produce tires that last longer. New innovations are tested by professional drivers on race tracks. However, any promising inventions are also test-driven by ordinary drivers. The latter tests are closer to what the tire company's customers will actually experience. Suppose that to determine whether a new steel-belted radial tire lasts longer than the company's current model, two new-design tires were installed on the rear wheels of 20 randomly selected cars and two existing-design tires were installed on the rear wheels of another 20 cars. All drivers were told to drive in their usual way until the tires wore out. The number of miles driven by each driver was recorded and is shown below, as well as being stored in file XM12-03. Can the company infer that the new tire will last on average longer than the existing tire?

Distance (in thousands of miles) Until Wear-Out

New-Design Tire										Existing-Design Tire									
70	83	78	46	74	56	74	52	99	57	47	65	59	61	75	65	73	85	97	84
77	84	72	98	81	63	88	69	54	97	72	39	72	91	64	63	79	74	76	43

Solution

IDENTIFY

The objective is to compare two populations of quantitative data. The parameter is the difference between two means $\mu_1 - \mu_2$. (μ_1 = mean distance to wear-out for the new-design tire, and μ_2 = mean distance to wear-out for the existing-design tire.) Because we want to determine whether the new tire lasts longer, the alternative hypothesis will specify that μ_1 is greater than μ_2. Calculation of the sample variances allows us to use the equal-variances test statistic.

$$H_0: (\mu_1 - \mu_2) = 0$$
$$H_1: (\mu_1 - \mu_2) > 0$$

SOLVE

Test statistic: $t = \dfrac{(\bar{x}_1 - \bar{x}_2) - (\mu_1 - \mu_2)}{\sqrt{s_p^2\left(\dfrac{1}{n_1} + \dfrac{1}{n_2}\right)}}$

Excel Output for Example 12.3

	A	B	C
1	t-Test: Two-Sample Assuming Equal Variances		
2			
3		New-Dsn	Exst-Dsn
4	Mean	73.6	69.2
5	Variance	243.4	226.8
6	Observations	20	20
7	Pooled Variance	235.1	
8	Hypothesized Mean Difference	0	
9	df	38	
10	t Stat	0.907	
11	P(T<=t) one-tail	0.1849	
12	t Critical one-tail	1.686	
13	P(T<=t) two-tail	0.3699	
14	t Critical two-tail	2.024	

Minitab Output for Example 12.3

Two Sample T-Test and Confidence Interval

```
Testsample T for New-Dsn vs Exst-Dsn
                 N      Mean     StDev    SE Mean
New-Dsn         20      73.6     15.6        3.5
Exst-Dsn        20      69.2     15.1        3.4

95% C.I.  for mu New-Dsn - mu Exst-Dsn: ( -5.4,  14.2)
T-Test mu  New-Dsn = mu Exst-Dsn (vs >): T= 0.91  P=0.18  DF=  38
Both use   Pooled StDev = 15.3
```

INTERPRET

The value of the test statistic ($t = .907$) and its p-value (.1849) indicate that there is very little evidence to support the hypothesis that the new-design tire lasts longer on average than the existing-design tire.

▲

As was the case with some earlier examples, we have some evidence to support the alternative hypothesis, but not enough. Note that the difference in sample means is $(\bar{x}_1 - \bar{x}_2) = (73.6 - 69.2) = 4.4$. However, we judge the difference in sample means in relation to the standard deviation of the sampling distribution. As you can easily calculate,

$$s_p^2 = 235.1$$

and

$$\sqrt{s_p^2 \left(\frac{1}{n_1} + \frac{1}{n_2} \right)} = 4.85$$

Consequently, the value of the test statistic is $t = 4.4/4.85 = .91$, a value that does not allow us to reject the null hypothesis. We can see that although the difference between the sample means was quite large, the variability of the data, as measured by s_p^2, was also large, resulting in a small test statistic value.

▼ EXAMPLE 12.4

Suppose now we redo the experiment in the following way. On 20 randomly selected cars, one of each type of tire is installed on the rear wheels and, as above, the cars are driven until the tires wear out. The number of miles until wear-out occurred is shown below and stored in file XM12-04. Can we conclude from *these* data that the new tire is superior?

Distance (in thousands of miles) Until Wear-Out

Car	New-Design Tires	Existing-Design Tires
1	57	48
2	64	50
3	102	89
4	62	56
5	81	78
6	87	75
7	61	50
8	62	49
9	74	70
10	62	66
11	100	98
12	90	86
13	83	78
14	84	90
15	86	98
16	62	58
17	67	58
18	40	41
19	71	61
20	77	82

Solution The experiment described in Example 12.3 is one where the samples are independent. That is, there was no relationship between the observations in one sample and the observations in the second sample. However, in this example the experiment was designed in such a way that each observation in one sample is matched with an observation in the other sample. The matching is conducted by using the same set of cars for each sample. Thus, it is logical to compare the distance until wear-out for both types of tires for *each* car. This type of experiment is called **matched pairs.** Here is how we conduct the test.

For each car, we calculate the matched pairs difference between the distances obtained with each type of tire.

Matched Pairs Differences

Car	Difference	Car	Difference
1	9	11	2
2	14	12	4
3	13	13	5
4	6	14	−6
5	3	15	−12
6	12	16	4
7	11	17	9
8	13	18	−1
9	4	19	10
10	−4	20	−5

The experimental design tells us that the parameter of interest is the **mean of the population of differences**, which we label μ_D. Note that $\mu_1 - \mu_2 = \mu_D$, but that we test μ_D because of the way the experiment was performed. The hypotheses to be tested are

H_0: $\mu_D = 0$

H_1: $\mu_D > 0$

We have already presented inferential techniques about a population mean. Recall that in Chapter 11 we introduced the *t*-test of μ. Thus, to test hypotheses about μ_D, we use the test statistic

$$t = \frac{\bar{x}_D - \mu_D}{s_D/\sqrt{n_D}}$$

which is Student *t* distributed with $n_D - 1$ degrees of freedom, provided that the differences are normally distributed. (Aside from the subscript D, this test statistic is identical to the one presented in Chapter 11.) We conduct the test in the usual way.

SOLVE

Rejection region:

$$t > t_{\alpha,n_{D-1}} = t_{.05,19} = 1.729$$

Using the differences computed above, we found the following statistics.

$\bar{x}_D = 4.55$

$s_D = 7.22$

Value of the test statistic:

$$t = \frac{\bar{x}_D - \mu_D}{s_D/\sqrt{n_D}} = \frac{4.55 - 0}{7.22/\sqrt{20}} = 2.82$$

Conclusion: Reject the null hypothesis.

**Excel Output for
Example 12.4**

	A	B	C
1	t-Test: Paired Two Sample for Means		
2			
3		*New-Dsn*	*Exst-Dsn*
4	Mean	73.6	69.1
5	Variance	242.8	316.4
6	Observations	20	20
7	Pearson Correlation	0.9147	
8	Hypothesized Mean Difference	0	
9	df	19	
10	t Stat	2.82	
11	P(T<=t) one-tail	0.0055	
12	t Critical one-tail	1.729	
13	P(T<=t) two-tail	0.0110	
14	t Critical two-tail	2.093	

The value of the test statistic is $t = 2.82$ with a *p*-value of .0055.

COMMANDS	COMMANDS FOR EXAMPLE 12.4
1 Type or import the data into two columns.	Open file **XM12-04**.
2 Click **Tools, Data Analysis . . . ,** and **t-Test: Paired Two-Sample for Means.**	
3 Specify the **Variable 1 Range.**	**A1:A21**
4 Specify the **Variable 2 Range.**	**B1:B21**
5 Type the value of the **Hypothesized Mean Difference** and click **Labels** (if necessary). Click **OK.**	**0**

**Minitab Output for
Example 12.4**

Paired T-Test and Confidence Interval

Paired T for New-Dsn - Exst-Dsn

```
                   N     Mean    StDev   SE Mean
New-Dsn           20    73.60    15.58      3.48
Exst-Dsn          20    69.05    17.79      3.98
Difference        20     4.55     7.22      1.61

95% CI for mean difference: (1.17, 7.93)
T-Test of mean difference = 0 (vs > 0): T-Value = 2.82 P-Value = 0.005
```

The test statistic is 2.82 and its *p*-value is .005.

COMMANDS	COMMANDS FOR EXAMPLE 12.4
1 Type or import the data.	Open file **XM12-04**.
2 Click **Stat, Basic Statistics,** and **Paired t. . . .**	
3 Select the variable names of the **First sample:.**	**New Design** or **C1**
4 Select the variable name of the **Second sample:.**	**Existing Design** or **C2**
5 Click **Options. . . .**	
6 Use the cursor to specify **Test mean** and type the hypothesized paired difference.	0
7 Specify the **Alternative** as **less than, not equal,** or **greater than.** Click **OK.**	**greater than**

INTERPRET

There is now overwhelming evidence to infer that the new-design tire lasts longer on average than the existing design. By redoing the experiment as matched pairs we were able to extract this information from the data.

▲

ESTIMATING THE MEAN DIFFERENCE

Applying the usual algebra we derive the interval estimator of μ_D.

Interval Estimator of μ_D

$$\bar{x}_D \pm t_{\alpha/2}\frac{s_D}{\sqrt{n_D}}$$

The 95% confidence interval estimate of the mean difference for Example 12.4 is

$$\bar{x}_D \pm t_{\alpha/2}\frac{s_D}{\sqrt{n_D}} = 4.55 \pm 2.093\frac{7.22}{\sqrt{20}} = 4.55 \pm 3.38$$

We estimate that the new-design tires last on average between 1.17 and 7.93 thousand miles more than the existing design.

Excel

To estimate the mean difference calculate the paired differences and use the *t*-estimate of a population mean. (See Section 11.2.)

Minitab

Minitab prints the interval estimate (You can specify the confidence level.) The 95% confidence interval estimate of μ_D is (1.17, 7.93) in thousands of miles.

INDEPENDENT SAMPLES OR MATCHED PAIRS: WHICH EXPERIMENTAL DESIGN IS BETTER?

Examples 12.3 and 12.4 demonstrated that the experimental design is an important factor in statistical inference. However, these two examples raise several questions about experimental designs.

1 Why does the matched pairs experiment result in rejecting the null hypothesis, whereas the independent samples experiment could not?

2 Should we always use the matched pairs experiment? In particular, are there disadvantages to its use?

3 How do we recognize when a matched pairs experiment has been performed?

Here are our answers.

1 The matched pairs experiment worked in Example 12.4 by reducing the variation in the data. To understand this point, examine the statistics from both examples. In Example 12.3, we found $\bar{x}_1 - \bar{x}_2 = 4.4$. In Example 12.4, we computed $\bar{x}_D = 4.55$. Thus, the numerators of the two test statistics were almost identical. However, the reason that the test statistic in Example 12.3 was so much smaller than in Example 12.4 was because of the standard deviations of the sampling distributions. In Example 12.3, we calculated

$$s_p^2 = 235.1 \qquad \text{and} \qquad \sqrt{s_p^2\left(\frac{1}{n_1} + \frac{1}{n_2}\right)} = 4.85$$

Example 12.4 produced

$$s_D^2 = 52.16 \qquad \text{and} \qquad \frac{s_D}{\sqrt{n_D}} = 1.615$$

As you see, the difference in the test statistics was caused not by the numerator but by the denominator. This raises another question. Why was the variation in the data of Example 12.3 so much greater than the variation in the data of Example 12.4? If you examine the data and statistics from Example 12.3, you will find that there was a great deal of variation *between* the cars. That is, some drivers drove in a way that extended the life of the tires, while others drove faster and braked harder, resulting in shorter tire lives. This high level of variation made the difference between the sample means appear to be small. As a result, we could not reject the null hypothesis.

Looking at the data from Example 12.4, we see that there is very little variation among the paired differences. Now the variation caused by different driving habits has been markedly decreased. The smaller variation causes the value of the test statistic to be larger. Consequently, we reject the null hypothesis.

2 Will the matched pairs experiment always produce a larger test statistic than the independent samples experiment? The answer is not necessarily. Suppose that in our example we found that most drivers drove in about the same way and that there was very little difference among drivers in the distances until tire wear-out. In such circumstances, the matched pairs experiment would result in no significant decrease in variation when compared to independent samples. It is possible that the matched pairs experiment may be *less* likely to reject the null hypothesis than the independent samples experiment. The reason can be seen by calculating the degrees of freedom. In Example 12.3, the number of degrees of freedom was 38, whereas in Example 12.4, it was 19. Even though we had the same number of observations (20 in each sample), the matched pairs experiment had half the number of degrees of freedom as the equivalent independent samples experiment. For exactly the same value of the test statistic, a smaller number of degrees of freedom in a Student t distributed test statistic yields a larger p-value. What this means is that if there is little reduction in variation to be achieved by the matched pairs experiment, the statistician should choose instead to conduct the experiment with independent samples.

3 As you've seen, in this book we deal with questions arising from experiments that have already been conducted. Thus, one of your tasks is to determine the appropriate test statistic. In the case of comparing two populations of quantitative data, you must decide whether the samples are independent (in which case the parameter is $\mu_1 - \mu_2$) or matched pairs (in which case the parameter is μ_D) in order to select the correct test statistic. To help you do so, we suggest you ask and answer the following question: "Does some natural relationship exist between *each pair* of observations that provides a logical reason to compare the first observation of sample 1 with the first observation of sample 2, the second observation of sample 1 with the second observation of sample 2, and so on?" If so, the experiment was conducted by matched pairs. If not, it was conducted using independent samples.

OBSERVATIONAL AND EXPERIMENTAL DATA

The points we made in Section 12.3 are also valid in this section. That is, we can design a matched pairs experiment where the data are gathered using a controlled experiment or by observation. The data in Examples 12.3 and 12.4 are experimental, which means the statistician randomly assigned the tires to the cars. As a consequence, when we established that the new-design tire lasted longer, we were able to conclude that the new tire is indeed superior. Because very few cars would be equipped with different brands of tires on their rear wheels, in this type of problem only experimental data are available.

In most applications of the matched pairs experiment, the data are experimental because of the control required to conduct such experimental designs.

CHECKING THE REQUIRED CONDITION

The validity of the results of the t-test of μ_D depends on the normality of the differences. The Excel histogram (Figure 12.6) confirms that assuming normality in this example is reasonable.

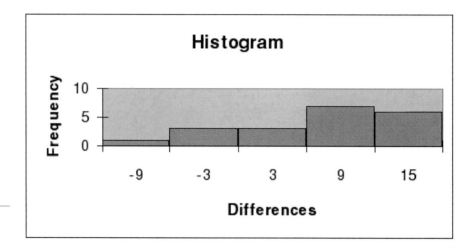

Figure 12.6

Histogram of matched pairs differences in Example 12.4

VIOLATION OF THE REQUIRED CONDITION

If the differences are very nonnormal, we cannot use the t-test of μ_D. We can, however, employ a nonparametric technique—the Wilcoxon signed rank sum test for matched pairs, which we present in Chapter 16.

DEVELOPING AN UNDERSTANDING OF STATISTICAL CONCEPTS

Two of the most important principles in statistics were applied in this section. The first is the concept of analyzing sources of variation. In Examples 12.3 and 12.4, we showed that by reducing the variation among drivers we were able to detect a real difference between tire designs. This was an application of the more general procedure of analyzing data and attributing some fraction of the variation to several sources. In Example 12.4, the two sources of variation were the car drivers and the tire designs. However, we were not interested in the variation among drivers because we weren't interested in determining whether drivers actually differ. Instead, we merely wanted to eliminate that source of variation, making it easier to determine if tire designs represented a real source of variation, and thus that one tire design is superior to another tire design.

In Chapter 14, we will introduce a technique called the *analysis of variance,* which does what its name suggests; it analyzes sources of variation in an attempt to detect real differences. In most applications of this procedure, we will be interested in each source of variation and not simply in reducing one source. We refer to the process as *explaining* the variation. The concept of explaining variation also will be applied in Chapters 17, 18, and 19.

The second principle demonstrated in this section is that statisticians can design data-gathering procedures in such a way that we can analyze sources of variation. Before conducting the experiment in Example 12.4, the statistician suspected that there were large differences among drivers in the way they wear tires out. Consequently he (or she) set up the experiment so that the effects of those differences were mostly eliminated. It is also possible to design experiments that allow for easy detection of real differences and minimize the costs of data gathering. Unfortunately, we will not present this topic. However, you should understand that the entire subject of the design of experiments is an important one, because managers often need to be able to analyze data to detect differences, and the cost is almost always a factor.

Here is a summary of the test statistic, interval estimator, and how we determine when to use the inferential techniques about the matched pairs experiment.

Test Statistic for μ_D

$$t = \frac{\bar{x}_D - \mu_D}{s_D/\sqrt{n_D}} \qquad \text{d.f.} = n_D - 1$$

Interval Estimator of μ_D

$$\bar{x}_D \pm t_{\alpha/2} \frac{s_D}{\sqrt{n_D}}$$

Factors that Identify the t-Test and Estimator of μ_D

1 Problem objective: compare two populations

2 Data type: quantitative

3 Descriptive measurement: central location

4 Experimental design: matched pairs

EXERCISES

12.35 Given the following data generated from a matched pairs experiment, test to determine if we can infer that the mean of population 1 exceeds the mean of population 2. (Use $\alpha = .01$.)

Pair:	1	2	3	4	5
Sample 1:	20	23	15	18	19
Sample 2:	17	16	9	19	15

12.36 The data below and stored in file XR12-36 were produced from a matched pairs experiment. Determine whether these data are sufficient to infer at the 10% significance level that the two population means differ.

Pair:	1	2	3	4	5	6	7	8	9	10
Sample 1:	7	12	19	17	22	18	30	33	40	48
Sample 2:	10	13	18	21	25	19	31	31	44	47

12.37 The following data were generated from a matched pairs experiment. (The data are stored in columns 1 and 2 of file XR12-37.)

Pair:	1	2	3	4	5	6	7	8	9	10
Sample 1:	3	12	15	10	17	14	10	9	16	8
Sample 2:	7	13	14	14	23	13	12	12	18	9

a Estimate with 90% confidence the mean difference.

b Briefly describe what the interval estimate in part (a) tells you.

12.38 Samples of size 12 were drawn independently from two normal populations. These data are listed below and stored in columns 1 and 2 of file XR12-38. A matched pairs experiment was then conducted; 12 pairs of observations were drawn from the same populations. These data are also shown below and stored in columns 3 and 4 of file XR12-38.

INDEPENDENT SAMPLES

Sample 1: 66 19 88 72 61 32 75 61 71 54 79 40
Sample 2: 69 37 66 59 27 18 47 67 83 61 32 37

MATCHED PAIRS

Pair:	1	2	3	4	5	6	7	8	9	10	11	12
Sample 1:	55	45	52	87	78	42	62	90	23	60	67	53
Sample 2:	48	37	43	75	78	35	45	79	12	53	59	37

a Using the data taken from independent samples, test to determine whether the means of the two populations differ. (Use $\alpha = .05$.)

b Using the data taken from independent samples, estimate with 95% confidence the difference between the two population means.

c Repeat part (a) using the matched pairs data.

d Repeat part (b) using the matched pairs data.

e Describe the differences between parts (a) and (c) and between (b) and (d). Discuss why these differences occurred.

12.39 Repeat Exercise 12.38 using the data below, which are stored in columns 1 through 4 of file XR12-39.

INDEPENDENT SAMPLES

Sample 1:	199	261	295	183	161	104
	199	248	105	197	249	218
Sample 2:	286	211	121	134	210	68
	166	157	258	184	116	203

MATCHED PAIRS

Pair:	1	2	3	4	5	6
Sample 1:	218	144	286	208	234	256
Sample 2:	154	160	239	198	211	241

Pair:	7	8	9	10	11	12
Sample 1:	133	87	224	212	256	133
Sample 2:	136	39	192	183	215	117

12.40 Repeat Exercise 12.38 using the data below, which are stored in columns 1 through 4 of file XR12-40.

INDEPENDENT SAMPLES

Sample 1:	103	86	101	112	111	100
	97	105	119	89	104	99
Sample 2:	71	86	100	89	92	105
	85	85	97	98	107	96

MATCHED PAIRS

Pair:	1	2	3	4	5	6
Sample 1:	91	120	97	94	107	107
Sample 2:	88	75	108	84	97	92

Pair:	7	8	9	10	11	12
Sample 1:	91	118	94	101	87	102
Sample 2:	92	76	86	97	107	98

12.41 Discuss what you have discovered from Exercises 12.38–12.40.

12.42 In an effort to determine whether or not a new type of fertilizer is more effective than the type currently in use, researchers took twelve 2-acre plots of land scattered throughout the county. Each plot was divided into two equal-sized subplots, one of which was treated with the current fertilizer and the other of which was treated with the new fertilizer. Wheat was planted, and the crop yields were measured. These data are stored in file XR12-42 and listed below.

Plot:	1	2	3	4	5	6
Current:	56	45	68	72	61	69
New:	60	49	66	73	59	77

Plot:	7	8	9	10	11	12
Current:	57	55	60	72	75	66
New:	61	60	58	75	72	71

a Can we conclude at the 5% significance level that the new fertilizer is more effective than the current one?

b Estimate with 95% confidence the difference in mean crop yields between the two fertilizers.

c What is the required conditions(s) for the validity of the results obtained in parts (a) and (b)?

d Is the required condition(s) satisfied?

e Are these data experimental or observational? Explain.

f How should the experiment be conducted if the researchers believe that the land throughout the county is pretty much the same?

12.43 The president of a large company is in the process of deciding whether to adopt a lunchtime exercise program. The purpose of such programs is to improve the health of workers and, in so doing, reduce medical expenses. To get more information, she instituted an exercise program for the employees in one office. The president knows that during the winter months medical expenses are relatively high because of the incidence of colds and flu. Consequently, she decides to use a matched pairs design by recording medical expenses for the 12 months before the program and for 12 months after the program. The "before" and "after" expenses (in thousands of dollars) are compared on a month-to-month basis and shown below. (These data are stored in columns 1 and 2 of file XR12-43.)

Month:	Jan	Feb	Mar	Apr	May	Jun
Before program:	68	44	30	58	35	33
After program:	59	42	20	62	25	30

Month:	Jul	Aug	Sep	Oct	Nov	Dec
Before program:	52	69	23	69	48	30
After program:	56	62	25	75	40	26

a Do the data indicate that exercise programs reduce medical expenses? (Test with $\alpha = .05$.)

b Estimate with 95% confidence the mean savings produced by exercise programs.

c Was it appropriate to conduct a matched pairs experiment? Explain.

Exercises 12.44–12.46 require the use of a computer and software. The answers may be calculated manually. See Appendix A for the sample statistics.

12.44 Do waiters or waitresses earn larger tips? To answer this question, a restaurant consultant undertook a preliminary study. The study involved measuring the percentage of the total bill left as a tip for one randomly selected waiter and one randomly selected waitress in each of 20 restaurants during a 1-week period. The data are stored in columns 1 and 2 of file XR12-44. Can we infer at the 5% significance level that waiters and waitresses earn different size tips?

12.45 To determine the effect of advertising in the Yellow Pages, Bell Telephone took a sample of 40 retail stores that did not advertise in the Yellow Pages last year but did so this year. The annual sales (in thousands of dollars) for each store in both years were recorded and stored in file XR12-45.

a Estimate with 90% confidence the improvement in sales between the 2 years.

b Can we infer at the 5% significance level that advertising in the Yellow Pages improves sales?

c Check to ensure that the required condition(s) of the techniques above is satisfied.

d Would it be advantageous to perform this experiment with independent samples? Explain why or why not.

12.46 Research scientists at a pharmaceutical company have recently developed a new nonprescription sleeping pill. They decide to test its effectiveness by measuring the time it takes for people to fall asleep after taking the pill. Preliminary analysis indicates that the time to fall asleep varies considerably from person to another. Consequently, they organize the experiment in the following way. A random sample of 50 volunteers who regularly suffer from insomnia is chosen. Each person is given one pill containing the newly developed drug and one placebo. (A placebo is a pill that contains absolutely no medication.) Participants are told to take one pill one night and the second pill one night a week later. (They do not know whether the pill they are taking is the placebo or the real thing, and the order of use is random.) Each participant is fitted with a device that measures the time until sleep occurs. The data are stored in columns 1 (new drug) and 2 (placebo) of file XR12-46. Can we conclude that the new drug is effective? (Use a 5% significance level.)

12.5 INFERENCE ABOUT THE RATIO OF TWO VARIANCES (OPTIONAL)

In Sections 12.2 and 12.4, we dealt with statistical inference concerning the difference between two population means. The problem objective in each case was to compare two populations of quantitative data, and our interest was in comparing measures of central location. This section discusses the statistical techniques to use when the problem objective and the data type are the same as in Sections 12.2 and 12.4, but our interest is in comparing variability. Here we will study the ratio of two population variances σ_1^2/σ_2^2. We make inferences about the *ratio* because the sampling distribution features ratios rather than differences.

In the previous chapter, we presented the procedures used to draw inferences about a single population variance. We pointed out that variance can be used to address problems where we need to know the variance in order to judge the consistency of a production process. We also use variance to measure the risk associated with a portfolio of investments. In this section we compare two variances, enabling us to compare the consistency of two production processes. We can also compare the relative risks of two sets of investments.

There is one other important use of the statistical methods to be presented in this section. One of the factors that determine the correct technique when testing or estimating the difference between two means from independent samples is whether the two unknown population variances are equal. Statisticians often test for the equality of σ_1^2 and σ_2^2 before deciding which of the two procedures introduced in Section 12.2 is to be used.

We will proceed in a manner that is probably becoming quite familiar.

PARAMETER

As you will see shortly, we compare two population variances by determining the ratio. Consequently, the parameter of interest is σ_1^2/σ_2^2.

POINT ESTIMATOR OF σ_1^2/σ_2^2

We have previously noted that the sample variance (defined in Chapter 4) is an unbiased and consistent estimator of the population variance. Not surprisingly, the estimator of the parameter σ_1^2/σ_2^2 is the ratio of the two sample variances drawn from their respective populations. The point estimator is s_1^2/s_2^2.

SAMPLING DISTRIBUTION OF s_1^2/s_1^2

The sampling distribution of s_1^2/s_2^2 is said to be F distributed provided that we have independently sampled from two normal populations. (The **F distribution** is presented below.)

Statisticians have shown that the ratio of two independent chi-squared variables divided by their degrees of freedom is F distributed. The degrees of freedom of the F distribution are identical to the degrees of freedom for the two chi-squared distributions. In Section 11.3, we pointed out that $(n-1)s^2/\sigma^2$ is chi-squared distributed provided that the sampled population is normal. If we have independent samples drawn from two normal populations, then both $(n_1-1)s_1^2/\sigma_1^2$ and $(n_2-1)s_2^2/\sigma_2^2$ are chi-squared distributed. If we divide each by their respective numbers of degrees of freedom and take the ratio, we produce

$$\frac{\dfrac{(n_1-1)s_1^2/\sigma_1^2}{(n_1-1)}}{\dfrac{(n_2-1)s_2^2/\sigma_2^2}{(n_2-1)}}$$

which simplifies to

$$\frac{s_1^2/\sigma_1^2}{s_2^2/\sigma_2^2}$$

This statistic is F distributed with $\nu_1 = n_1 - 1$ and $\nu_2 = n_2 - 1$ degrees of freedom.

F Distribution

Variables that are F distributed range from 0 to ∞. The approximate shape of the distribution is depicted in Figure 12.7. The exact shape is determined by two numbers of degrees of freedom. Because the statistic is a ratio, the number of degrees of freedom is labeled as either the *numerator degrees of freedom,* denoted ν_1 (Greek letter nu), or the *denominator degrees of freedom,* denoted ν_2. Table 6 in Appendix B provides the critical values for the F distribution. It lists values of F_{A,ν_1,ν_2}, where F_{A,ν_1,ν_2} is the value of F with ν_1 and ν_2 degrees of freedom such that the area to its right under the F distribution is A. That is,

$$P(F > F_{A,\nu_1,\nu_2}) = A$$

Another property of the F distribution is

$$F_{1-A,\nu_1,\nu_2} = \frac{1}{F_{A,\nu_2,\nu_1}}$$

Part of Table 6 (for $A = .05$) is reproduced here as Table 12.1. To determine any critical value, find the numerator degrees of freedom ν_1 across the top row and the denominator degrees of freedom ν_2 down the first column. The intersection of that row and that column shows the critical value. To illustrate, suppose that we want to find $F_{.05,5,7}$. Table 6 in Appendix B provides the critical values for three values of A: .05, .025, and .01. (Table 12.1 lists some of the critical values for $A = .05$.) The numerator number of degrees of freedom is 5, which we find across the top row, and the denominator number of degrees of freedom is 7, which we locate in the first column. The intersection is 3.97. Thus, $F_{.05,5,7} = 3.97$. (See Table 12.2.)

Note that the order in which the degrees of freedom appear is important. To find $F_{.05,7,5}$ (numerator degrees of freedom = 7 and denominator degrees of freedom = 5), we locate 7 across the top row and 5 down the first column. The number in the intersection is $F_{.05,7,5} = 4.88$.

Table 6 provides only values of F_A, which are the values of F that are in the right tail of the F distribution. The left-tail values, which we label F_{1-A} (as we did to denote the left-tail values of the chi-squared distribution), are not listed. They are not provided because we can easily determine the values of F_{1-A} from the values of F_A. Mathematicians have derived the following formula.

$$F_{1-A,v_1,v_2} = \frac{1}{F_{A,v_2,v_1}}$$

For example,

$$F_{.95,4,8} = \frac{1}{F_{.05,8,4}} = \frac{1}{6.04} = .166$$

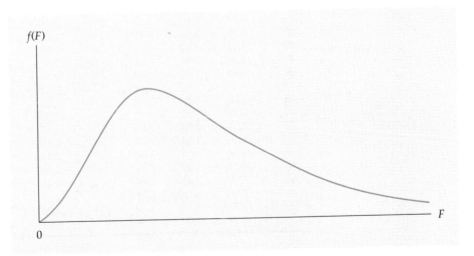

Figure 12.7

F distribution

Table 12.1 Percentile Points of the *F* Distribution *A* = .05

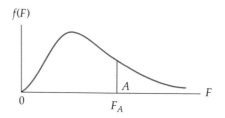

ν_2	Numerator Degrees of Freedom								
	1	**2**	**3**	**4**	**5**	**6**	**7**	**8**	**9**
1	161.4	199.5	215.7	224.6	230.2	234.0	236.8	238.9	240.5
2	18.51	19.00	19.16	19.25	19.30	19.33	19.35	19.37	19.38
3	10.13	9.55	9.28	9.12	9.01	8.94	8.89	8.85	8.81
4	7.71	6.94	6.59	6.39	6.26	6.16	6.09	6.04	6.00
5	6.61	5.79	5.41	5.19	5.05	4.95	4.88	4.82	4.77
6	5.99	5.14	4.76	4.53	4.39	4.28	4.21	4.15	4.10
7	5.59	4.74	4.35	4.12	3.97	3.87	3.79	3.73	3.68
8	5.32	4.46	4.07	3.84	3.69	3.58	3.50	3.44	3.39
9	5.12	4.26	3.86	3.63	3.48	3.37	3.29	3.23	3.18
10	4.96	4.10	3.71	3.48	3.33	3.22	3.14	3.07	3.02
11	4.84	3.98	3.59	3.36	3.20	3.09	3.01	2.95	2.90
12	4.75	3.89	3.49	3.26	3.11	3.00	2.91	2.85	2.80
13	4.67	3.81	3.41	3.18	3.03	2.92	2.83	2.77	2.71
14	4.60	3.74	3.34	3.11	2.96	2.85	2.76	2.70	2.65
15	4.54	3.68	3.29	3.06	2.90	2.79	2.71	2.64	2.59
16	4.49	3.63	3.24	3.01	2.85	2.74	2.66	2.59	2.54
17	4.45	3.59	3.20	2.96	2.81	2.70	2.61	2.55	2.49
18	4.41	3.55	3.16	2.93	2.77	2.66	2.58	2.51	2.46
19	4.38	3.52	3.13	2.90	2.74	2.63	2.54	2.48	2.42
20	4.35	3.49	3.10	2.87	2.71	2.60	2.51	2.45	2.39
21	4.32	3.47	3.07	2.84	2.68	2.57	2.49	2.42	2.37
22	4.30	3.44	3.05	2.82	2.66	2.55	2.46	2.40	2.34
23	4.28	3.42	3.03	2.80	2.64	2.53	2.44	2.37	2.32
24	4.26	3.40	3.01	2.78	2.62	2.51	2.42	2.36	2.30
25	4.24	3.39	2.99	2.76	2.60	2.49	2.40	2.34	2.28
26	4.23	3.37	2.98	2.74	2.59	2.47	2.39	2.32	2.27
27	4.21	3.35	2.96	2.73	2.57	2.46	2.37	2.31	2.25
28	4.20	3.34	2.95	2.71	2.56	2.45	2.36	2.29	2.24
29	4.18	3.33	2.93	2.70	2.55	2.43	2.35	2.28	2.22
30	4.17	3.32	2.92	2.69	2.53	2.42	2.33	2.27	2.21
40	4.08	3.23	2.84	2.61	2.45	2.34	2.25	2.18	2.12
60	4.00	3.15	2.76	2.53	2.37	2.25	2.17	2.10	2.04
120	3.92	3.07	2.68	2.45	2.29	2.17	2.09	2.02	1.96
∞	3.84	3.00	2.60	2.37	2.21	2.10	2.01	1.94	1.88

Denominator Degrees of Freedom

Source: From M. Merrington and C. M. Thompson, "Tables of Percentage Points of the Inverted Beta (*F*)-Distribution," *Biometrika* 33 (1943): 73–88. Reproduced by permission of the Biometrika trustees.

Table 12.2 Finding $F_{.05,5,7}$

ν_2 \ ν_1	Numerator Degrees of Freedom								
	1	**2**	**3**	**4**	**5**	**6**	**7**	**8**	**9**
1	161.4	199.5	215.7	224.6	230.2	234.0	236.8	238.9	240.5
2	18.51	19.00	19.16	19.25	19.30	19.33	19.35	19.37	19.38
3	10.13	9.55	9.28	9.12	9.01	8.94	8.89	8.85	8.81
4	7.71	6.94	6.59	6.39	6.26	6.16	6.09	6.04	6.00
5	6.61	5.79	5.41	5.19	5.05	4.95	4.88	4.82	4.77
6	5.99	5.14	4.76	4.53	4.39	4.28	4.21	4.15	4.10
7	5.59	4.74	4.35	4.12	3.97	3.87	3.79	3.73	3.68
8	5.32	4.46	4.07	3.84	3.69	3.58	3.50	3.44	3.39
9	5.12	4.26	3.86	3.63	3.48	3.37	3.29	3.23	3.18
10	4.96	4.10	3.71	3.48	3.33	3.22	3.14	3.07	3.02
11	4.84	3.98	3.59	3.36	3.20	3.09	3.01	2.95	2.90
12	4.75	3.89	3.49	3.26	3.11	3.00	2.91	2.85	2.80
13	4.67	3.81	3.41	3.18	3.03	2.92	2.83	2.77	2.71
14	4.60	3.74	3.34	3.11	2.96	2.85	2.76	2.70	2.65
15	4.54	3.68	3.29	3.06	2.90	2.79	2.71	2.64	2.59

Denominator Degrees of Freedom

TESTING σ_1^2/σ_2^2

In this book, our null hypothesis will *always* specify that the two variances are equal. As a result, the ratio will equal 1. Thus, the null hypothesis will always be expressed as

$$H_0: \sigma_1^2/\sigma_2^2 = 1$$

The alternative hypothesis can state that the ratio is either not equal to 1, greater than 1, or less than 1. Technically, the test statistic is

$$F = \frac{s_1^2/\sigma_1^2}{s_2^2/\sigma_2^2}$$

However, under the null hypothesis, which states that $\sigma_1^2/\sigma_2^2 = 1$, the test statistic becomes as follows.

Test Statistic for σ_1^2/σ_2^2

The test statistic employed to test hypotheses about σ_1^2/σ_2^2 is

$$F = s_1^2/s_2^2$$

which is F distributed with $\nu_1 = n_1 - 1$ and $\nu_2 = n_2 - 1$ degrees of freedom provided that the populations are normal.

▼ **EXAMPLE 12.5**

In Example 12.1, we applied the unequal-variances t-test of $\mu_1 - \mu_2$. We chose that test statistic after computing the variance of the sample of consumers of high-fiber cereal to be 4102.98 and the variance of the sample of nonconsumers of high-fiber cereal to be 10,669.77. The difference between the two sample variances appears to indicate that the population variances differ. Test to determine whether that decision was correct.

Solution

We need to conduct the F-test of σ_1^2/σ_2^2 to determine whether the two population variances differ. The test proceeds as follows.

H_0: $\sigma_1^2/\sigma_2^2 = 1$

H_1: $\sigma_1^2/\sigma_2^2 \neq 1$

The rejection region (assuming that $\alpha = .05$) is

$$F > F_{\alpha/2, \nu_1, \nu_2} = F_{.025, 42, 106} \approx F_{.025, 40, 120} = 1.61$$

or

$$F < F_{1-\alpha/2, \nu_1, \nu_2} = F_{.975, 42, 106} = \frac{1}{F_{.025, 106, 42}} \approx \frac{1}{F_{.025, 120, 40}} = \frac{1}{1.72} = .58$$

The value of the test statistic is

$$F = \frac{s_1^2}{s_2^2} = \frac{4102.98}{10669.77} = .3845$$

Since the value of the test statistic is less than .58, we reject the null hypothesis.

Excel Output for Example 12.5

	A	B	C
1	F-Test Two-Sample for Variances		
2			
3		Consumers	Nonconsumers
4	Mean	604.0	633.2
5	Variance	4103	10670
6	Observations	43	107
7	df	42	106
8	F	0.38	
9	P(F <=f) one-tail	0.0004	
10	F Critical one-tail	0.637	

The value of the test statistic is $F = .38$. Excel outputs the one-tail p-value. Because we're conducting a two-tail test, we double that value. Thus, the p-value of the test we're conducting is $2 \times .0004 = .0008$.

COMMANDS	COMMANDS FOR EXAMPLE 12.5
1 Type or import the data into two columns.	Open file **XM12-01**.
2 Click **Tools, Data Analysis . . . ,** and **F-Test Two-Sample for Variances.**	
3 Specify the **Variable 1 Range:**.	A1:A44
4 Specify the **Variable 2 Range:**.	B1:B108
5 Click **Labels** (if necessary) and click **OK.**	

Use the **F-Test of 2 Variances** worksheet to complete this test from the sample variances and to perform a what-if analysis.

Minitab Output for Example 12.5

Homogeneity of Variance

```
F-Test (normal distribution)

Test Statistic: 2.600
P-Value      : 0.001
```

Minitab's F-statistic is the ratio of the larger sample variance divided by the smaller sample variance. Thus the value of the test statistic is $F = 10669.77/4102.98 = 2.60$. The p-value is .001. (*Note:* Some of the printout has been omitted.)

COMMANDS	COMMANDS FOR EXAMPLE 12.5
1 Type or import the data into stacked format.	Open file **XM12-01**. Columns 1 and 2 are stacked in column 3. The subscripts are stored in column 4.
2 Click **Stat, ANOVA,** and **Homogeneity of Variance. . . .**	
3 Specify the variable name of the data (**Responses:**).	C3
4 Specify the name of the codes (**Factor:**). Click **OK**.	C4

The commands above employ Bartlett's test, a statistical technique designed to test two or more variances. When there are only two variances to be tested, Minitab uses the F-test. (Bartlett's test will be presented in Chapter 14.)

INTERPRET

There is sufficient evidence to infer that the population variances differ. It follows that we were justified in using the unequal-variances t-test in Example 12.1. We're confident that the normality requirement for this test is satisfied. It is the same requirement for the t-test, which we checked when we drew the histograms. (See Figures 12.2 and 12.3.)

▲

ESTIMATING THE RATIO OF TWO POPULATION VARIANCES

Another way of expressing the notation associated with the F distribution is

$$P(F_{1-\alpha/2} < F < F_{\alpha/2}) = 1 - \alpha$$

This states that the probability that an F distributed random variable falls between $F_{1-\alpha/2}$ and $F_{\alpha/2}$ is $1 - \alpha$. If we substitute the F statistic

$$F = \frac{s_1^2/\sigma_1^2}{s_2^2/\sigma_2^2}$$

into the equation, we produce

$$P\left(F_{1-\alpha/2} < \frac{s_1^2/\sigma_1^2}{s_2^2/\sigma_2^2} < F_{\alpha/2}\right) = 1 - \alpha$$

Applying algebra, we isolate σ_1^2/σ_2^2 in the center of the probability statement. Incorporating the formula

$$F_{1-\alpha/2,\nu_1,\nu_2} = \frac{1}{F_{\alpha/2,\nu_2,\nu_1}}$$

we get the following.

Interval Estimator of σ_1^2/σ_2^2

$$\text{LCL} = \left(\frac{s_1^2}{s_2^2}\right)\frac{1}{F_{\alpha/2,\nu_1,\nu_2}}$$

$$\text{UCL} = \left(\frac{s_1^2}{s_2^2}\right)F_{\alpha/2,\nu_2,\nu_1}$$

where $\nu_1 = n_1 - 1$ and $\nu_2 = n_2 - 1$

▼ **EXAMPLE 12.6**

Determine the 95% confidence interval estimate of the ratio of the two population variances in Example 12.1

Solution We find

SOLVE

$$F_{\alpha/2,\nu_1,\nu_2} = F_{.025,42,106} \approx F_{.025,40,120} = 1.61$$

and

$$F_{\alpha/2,\nu_2,\nu_1} = F_{.025,106,42} \approx F_{.025,120,40} = 1.72$$

Thus,

$$\text{LCL} = \left(\frac{s_1^2}{s_2^2}\right)\frac{1}{F_{\alpha/2,\nu_1,\nu_2}} = \left(\frac{4102.98}{10{,}669.77}\right)\frac{1}{1.61} = .2388$$

$$\text{UCL} = \left(\frac{s_1^2}{s_2^2}\right)F_{\alpha/2,\nu_2,\nu_1} = \left(\frac{4102.98}{10{,}669.77}\right)1.72 = .6614$$

We infer that σ_1^2/σ_2^2 lies between .2388 and .6614.

Excel Output for Example 12.6

	A	B	C
1	**F-Estimate of the Ratio of Two Variances**		
2			
3	**Sample 1**		
4	Sample variance	4103	
5	Sample size	43	
6			
7	**Sample 2**		
8	Sample variance	10670	
9	Sample size	107	
10			
11	Confidence level	0.95	
12			
13	Lower confidence limit	0.2374	
14	Upper confidence limit	0.6594	

COMMANDS   **COMMANDS FOR EXAMPLE 12.6**

1 Calculate the sample variances.
2 Click **Tools, Data Analysis Plus,** and **Inference from Summary Statistics (Workbook).** Find the worksheet **F-Estimate of 2 Variances.**
3 In cells B4, B5, B8, B9 and B11   4103   43   10670   107   .95
type the values of s_1^2, n_1, s_2^2, n_2, and $1 - \alpha$, respectively

Minitab does not compute the estimate of the ratio of two variances.

INTERPRET

As we pointed out in Chapter 10, we can often use an interval estimator to test hypotheses. In this example the interval estimate excludes the value of 1. Consequently, we can draw the same conclusion as we did in Example 12.5: The appropriate technique to test the data in Example 12.1 was the unequal-variances t-test of $\mu_1 - \mu_2$.

▲

Factors that Identify the F-Test and Estimator of σ_1^2/σ_2^2

1 Problem objective: compare two populations
2 Data type: quantitative
3 Descriptive measurement: variability

EXERCISES

12.47 Random samples from two normal populations produced the following statistics.

$$s_1^2 = 350 \quad n_1 = 30 \quad s_2^2 = 700 \quad n_2 = 30$$

Can we infer at the 5% significance level that the two population variances differ?

12.48 Refer to Exercise 12.47. Estimate with 95% confidence the ratio of the two population variances.

12.49 Given the following statistics, test to determine whether the variance of population 1 is larger than the variance of population 2. (Use $\alpha = .05$.)

$$s_1^2 = 60 \quad n_1 = 20 \quad s_2^2 = 25 \quad n_2 = 20$$

12.50 Given the data below, test the following hypotheses with $\alpha = .10$.

$$H_0: \sigma_1^2/\sigma_2^2 = 1$$
$$H_1: \sigma_1^2/\sigma_2^2 \neq 1$$

Sample 1:   7 4   9 12 8 6   9 14
Sample 2:   10 7 13 18 4 8 21 20 5 8

12.51 Random samples from two normal populations produced the following results. Is there enough evidence at the 5% significance level to infer that the population variances differ?

Sample 1:   27 52 41 20 33 59 41 28 29 51
Sample 2:   18 15 19 31 49 12 48 29 45 50

Exercises 12.52–12.58 require the use of a computer and software. The answers may be calculated manually. See Appendix A for the sample statistics.

12.52 Can we conclude at the 1% significance level from the data stored in columns 1 and 2 of file XR12-52 that the variance of population 1 is less than that of population 2?

12.53 Refer to Exercise 12.52. Estimate the ratio of population variances with 95% confidence.

12.54 Test at the 5% significance level to determine whether the t-test of $\mu_1 - \mu_2$ you applied in Exercise 12.23 was justified.

12.55 Determine whether the test you used to answer Exercise 12.24 was appropriate. Conduct a test with $\alpha = .10$.

12.56 Did you use the correct technique when you answered the question posed in Exercise 12.30? Answer by conducting a test with $\alpha = .05$.

12.57 The weekly returns of two portfolios were recorded for 1 year with the results stored in columns 1 and 2 of file XR12-57. Can we conclude at the 5% significance level that portfolio 2 is riskier than portfolio 1?

12.58 An important statistical measurement in service facilities (such as restaurants and banks) is the variability in service times. As an experiment, two bank tellers were observed, and the service times for each of 100 customers were recorded and stored in columns 1 and 2 of file XR12-58. Do these data allow us to infer at the 10% significance level that the variance in service times differs between the two tellers?

12.6 INFERENCE ABOUT THE DIFFERENCE BETWEEN TWO POPULATION PROPORTIONS

In this section, we present the procedures for drawing inferences about the difference between populations whose data are qualitative. When data are qualitative, the only meaningful computation is to count the number of occurrences of each type of outcome and calculate proportions. Consequently, the parameter to be tested and estimated in this section is the difference between two population proportions, $p_1 - p_2$.

To draw inferences about $p_1 - p_2$, we take a sample of size n_1 from population 1 and a sample of size n_2 from population 2 (Figure 12.8 depicts the sampling process). For each sample, we count the number of successes (recall that we call anything we're looking for a success) in each sample, which we label x_1 and x_2, respectively. The sample proportions are then computed.

$$\hat{p}_1 = \frac{x_1}{n_1} \quad \text{and} \quad \hat{p}_2 = \frac{x_2}{n_2}$$

Statisticians have proved that the statistic $\hat{p}_1 - \hat{p}_2$ is an unbiased consistent estimator of the parameter $p_1 - p_2$.

$$\hat{p}_1 - \hat{p}_2$$

...mathematics as in Chapter 11 to derive the sampling distribution of ...ple proportion $\hat{p}$, we determine the sampling distribution of the difference ...tween two sample proportions.

Sampling Distribution of $\hat{p}_1 - \hat{p}_2$

1 The statistic $\hat{p}_1 - \hat{p}_2$ is approximately normally distributed provided the sample sizes are large enough so that n_1p_1, $n_1(1 - p_1)$, n_2p_2, and $n_2(1 - p_2)$ are all greater than or equal to 5. (Since p_1 and p_2 are unknown, we express the sample size requirement as $n_1\hat{p}_1$, $n_1(1 - \hat{p}_1)$, $n_2\hat{p}_2$, and $n_2(1 - \hat{p}_2) \geq 5$.)

2 The mean of $\hat{p}_1 - \hat{p}_2$ is

$$E(\hat{p}_1 - \hat{p}_2) = p_1 - p_2$$

3 The variance of $\hat{p}_1 - \hat{p}_2$ is

$$V(\hat{p}_1 - \hat{p}_2) = \frac{p_1(1 - p_1)}{n_1} + \frac{p_2(1 - p_2)}{n_2}$$

The standard deviation is

$$\sigma_{\hat{p}_1 - \hat{p}_2} = \sqrt{\frac{p_1(1 - p_1)}{n_1} + \frac{p_2(1 - p_2)}{n_2}}$$

Thus, the variable

$$z = \frac{(\hat{p}_1 - \hat{p}_2) - (p_1 - p_2)}{\sqrt{\dfrac{p_1(1 - p_1)}{n_1} + \dfrac{p_2(1 - p_2)}{n_2}}}$$

is approximately standard normally distributed.

$$\sqrt{\hat{p}(1 - \quad \quad n_1 \quad n_2)}$$

where $\hat{p}$ is the **pooled proportion est**

$$\hat{p} = \frac{x_1 + x_2}{n_1 + n_2}$$

The principle used in estimating the standard deviation of $\hat{p}_1 - \hat{p}_2$ is a
that applied in Section 12.2 to produce the pooled variance estimate s_p^2, which
to test $\mu_1 - \mu_2$ with σ_1^2 and σ_2^2 unknown but equal. That principle roughly state
where possible, pooling data from two samples produces a better estimate of the s
dard deviation. Here, pooling is made possible by hypothesizing (under the nu
hypothesis) that $p_1 = p_2$. (In Section 12.2, we used the pooled variance estimate
because we assumed that $\sigma_1^2 = \sigma_2^2$) We will call this application *Case 1*.

Test Statistic for $p_1 - p_2$: Case 1

If the null hypothesis specifies

$$H_0: (p_1 - p_2) = 0$$

the test statistic is

$$z = \frac{(\hat{p}_1 - \hat{p}_2) - (p_1 - p_2)}{\sqrt{\hat{p}(1 - \hat{p})\left(\dfrac{1}{n_1} + \dfrac{1}{n_2}\right)}}$$

Because we hypothesize $p_1 - p_2 = 0$, we simplify the test statistic to

$$z = \frac{(\hat{p}_1 - \hat{p}_2)}{\sqrt{\hat{p}(1 - \hat{p})\left(\dfrac{1}{n_1} + \dfrac{1}{n_2}\right)}}$$

The second case applies when, under the null hypothesis, we state that $H_0: (p_1 - p_2)$
$= D$, where D is some value *other than zero*. Under such circumstances, we cannot
pool the sample data to estimate the standard deviation of $\hat{p}_1 - \hat{p}_2$. The appropriate
test statistic is described next as *Case 2*.

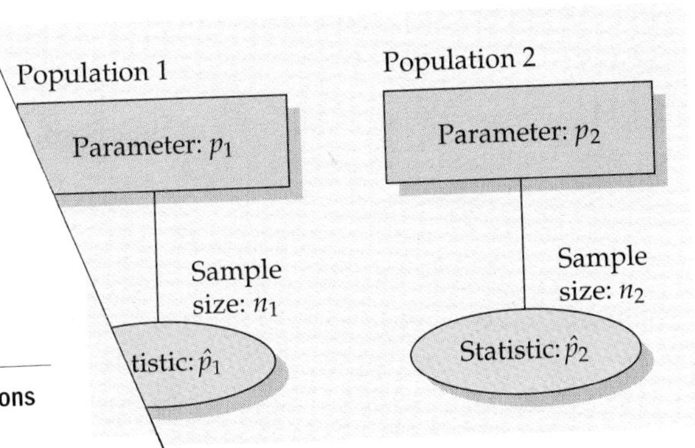

Population 1

Parameter: p_1

Population 2

Parameter: p_2

Sample size: n_1

Sample size: n_2

tistic: $\hat{p}_1$

Statistic: $\hat{p}_2$

Figure 12.8

Sampling from two populations of qualitative data

SAMPLING DISTION OF $\hat{p}$

Using the same ~~mathen....~~ as in Chapter 11 to derive the sampling distribution of the sample proportion $\hat{p}$, we determine the sampling distribution of the difference between two sample proportions.

Sampling Distribution of $\hat{p}_1 - \hat{p}_2$

1 The statistic $\hat{p}_1 - \hat{p}_2$ is approximately normally distributed provided the sample sizes are large enough so that $n_1 p_1$, $n_1(1 - p_1)$, $n_2 p_2$, and $n_2(1 - p_2)$ are all greater than or equal to 5. (Since p_1 and p_2 are unknown, we express the sample size requirement as $n_1 \hat{p}_1$, $n_1(1 - \hat{p}_1)$, $n_2 \hat{p}_2$, and $n_2(1 - \hat{p}_2) \geq 5$.)

2 The mean of $\hat{p}_1 - \hat{p}_2$ is

$$E(\hat{p}_1 - \hat{p}_2) = p_1 - p_2$$

3 The variance of $\hat{p}_1 - \hat{p}_2$ is

$$V(\hat{p}_1 - \hat{p}_2) = \frac{p_1(1 - p_1)}{n_1} + \frac{p_2(1 - p_2)}{n_2}$$

The standard deviation is

$$\sigma_{\hat{p}_1 - \hat{p}_2} = \sqrt{\frac{p_1(1 - p_1)}{n_1} + \frac{p_2(1 - p_2)}{n_2}}$$

Thus, the variable

$$z = \frac{(\hat{p}_1 - \hat{p}_2) - (p_1 - p_2)}{\sqrt{\dfrac{p_1(1 - p_1)}{n_1} + \dfrac{p_2(1 - p_2)}{n_2}}}$$

is approximately standard normally distributed.

TESTING THE DIFFERENCE BETWEEN TWO POPULATION PROPORTIONS

We would like to use the z-statistic just described est statistic; however, the standard deviation of $\hat{p}_1 - \hat{p}_2$, which is

$$\sigma_{\hat{p}_1 - \hat{p}_2} = \sqrt{\frac{p_1(1 - p_1)}{n_1} + \frac{p_2(1 - p_2)}{n_2}}$$

is unknown, since both p_1 and p_2 are unkn a result, the standard error of $\hat{p}_1 - \hat{p}_2$ must be estimated from the sample here are two different estimators of this quantity, and the determination of wh to use depends on the null hypothesis. If the null hypothesis states that p_1 0, the hypothesized equality of the two population proportions allows us to data from the two samples. Thus, the estimated standard error of $\hat{p}_1 - \hat{p}$

$$\sqrt{\hat{p}(1 - \quad n_1 \quad n_2)} \quad 1$$

where $\hat{p}$ is the **pooled proportion est** defined as

$$\hat{p} = \frac{x_1 + x_2}{n_1 + n_2}$$

The principle used in estimating the standard deviation of $\hat{p}_1 - \hat{p}_2$ is a that applied in Section 12.2 to produce the pooled variance estimate s_p^2, which analogous to to test $\mu_1 - \mu_2$ with σ_1^2 and σ_2^2 unknown but equal. That principle roughly stat is used where possible, pooling data from two samples produces a better estimate of the ss that, dard deviation. Here, pooling is made possible by hypothesizing (under the n an-hypothesis) that $p_1 = p_2$. (In Section 12.2, we used the pooled variance estimate ll because we assumed that $\sigma_1^2 = \sigma_2^2$.) We will call this application *Case 1*.

Test Statistic for $p_1 - p_2$: Case 1

If the null hypothesis specifies

$H_0: (p_1 - p_2) = 0$

the test statistic is

$$z = \frac{(\hat{p}_1 - \hat{p}_2) - (p_1 - p_2)}{\sqrt{\hat{p}(1 - \hat{p})\left(\dfrac{1}{n_1} + \dfrac{1}{n_2}\right)}}$$

Because we hypothesize $p_1 - p_2 = 0$, we simplify the test statistic to

$$z = \frac{(\hat{p}_1 - \hat{p}_2)}{\sqrt{\hat{p}(1 - \hat{p})\left(\dfrac{1}{n_1} + \dfrac{1}{n_2}\right)}}$$

The second case applies when, under the null hypothesis, we state that $H_0: (p_1 - p_2) = D$, where D is some value *other than zero*. Under such circumstances, we cannot pool the sample data to estimate the standard deviation of $\hat{p}_1 - \hat{p}_2$. The appropriate test statistic is described next as *Case 2*.

> ### Test Statistic for $p_1 - p_2$: Case 2
>
> If the null hypothesis specifies
>
> $$H_0: (p_1 - p_2) = D \qquad (D \neq 0)$$
>
> the test statistic is
>
> $$z = \frac{(\hat{p}_1 - \hat{p}_2) - (p_1 - p_2)}{\sqrt{\dfrac{\hat{p}_1(1 - \hat{p}_1)}{n_1} + \dfrac{\hat{p}_2(1 - \hat{p}_2)}{n_2}}}$$

Notice that this test statistic is determined by simply substituting the sample statistics $\hat{p}_1$ and $\hat{p}_2$ in the standard deviation of the sampling distribution.

You will find that, in most practical applications (including the exercises and cases in this book), Case 1 applies—in most problems, we want to know if the two population proportions differ; that is,

$$H_1: (p_1 - p_2) \neq 0$$

or if one proportion exceeds the other; that is,

$$H_1: (p_1 - p_2) > 0 \qquad \text{or} \qquad H_1: (p_1 - p_2) < 0$$

In some problems, however, the objective is to determine if one proportion exceeds the other by a specific nonzero quantity. In such situations, Case 2 applies.

STATISTICS IN THE WORKPLACE

Operations Management Application

When new products are developed they are tested in several ways. First, does the new product work? Second, is it better than the existing product? Third, will customers buy it at a price that is profitable? Performing a customer survey or some other experiment that yields the information needed often tests the last question. This experiment is usually the domain of the marketing manager.

The other two questions are dealt with by the developers of the new product, which usually means the research department or the operations manager. When the product is a new drug, the data are gathered in particular ways. The sample is divided into two groups. One group is assigned the new drug and the other is assigned a placebo, a pill that contains no medication. The experiment is often called "double-blind" because neither the subjects who take the drug nor the physician/scientist who provides the drug know which individual is taking the drug or the placebo. At the end of the experiment the data are produced that allow the statisticians to do their work.

▼ EXAMPLE 12.7

In a study that was highly publicized, doctors discovered that aspirin seems to help prevent heart attacks. The research project, which was scheduled to last for 5 years, employed 22,000 American physicians (all male). Half took an aspirin tablet three times per week, while the other half took a placebo on the same schedule. After 3 years, researchers determined that 104 of those who took aspirin and 189 of those who took the placebo had had heart attacks. Determine whether these results indicate that aspirin is effective in reducing the incidence of heart attacks.

Solution

IDENTIFY

The problem objective is to compare two populations. The first is the population of men who take aspirin regularly, and the second is the population of men who do not regularly take aspirin. The data are qualitative because there are only two possible observations: "The man suffered a heart attack" and "The man did not suffer a heart attack." These two factors tell us that the parameter to be tested is the difference between two population proportions $p_1 - p_2$ (where p_1 = proportion of all men who regularly take aspirin who suffer a heart attack, and p_2 = proportion of all men who do not take aspirin who suffer a heart attack). Because we want to know if aspirin is effective in reducing heart attacks, the alternative hypothesis is

$$H_1: (p_1 - p_2) < 0$$

The null hypothesis must be

$$H_0: (p_1 - p_2) = 0$$

which tells us that this is an application of Case 1. Thus, the test statistic is

$$z = \frac{(\hat{p}_1 - \hat{p}_2)}{\sqrt{\hat{p}(1 - \hat{p})\left(\frac{1}{n_1} + \frac{1}{n_2}\right)}}$$

SOLVE

A 5% significance level seems to be appropriate. Thus, the rejection region is

$$z < -z_\alpha = -z_{.05} = -1.645$$

The sample proportions are

$$\hat{p}_1 = \frac{104}{11,000} = .009455$$

and

$$\hat{p}_2 = \frac{189}{11,000} = .01718$$

The pooled proportion is

$$\hat{p} = \frac{104 + 189}{11,000 + 11,000} = \frac{293}{22,000} = .01332$$

The value of the test statistic follows.

$$z = \frac{(\hat{p}_1 - \hat{p}_2)}{\sqrt{\hat{p}(1 - \hat{p})\left(\frac{1}{n_1} + \frac{1}{n_2}\right)}} = \frac{(.009455 - .01718)}{\sqrt{(.01332)(.98668)\left(\frac{1}{11,000} + \frac{1}{11,000}\right)}} = -5.02$$

The value of the test statistic easily falls into the rejection region.

 As was the case with the inferential techniques for one proportion we will assume that the codes representing the qualitative data have been recorded and stored. In this example 2 = Suffered a heart attack and 1 = Did not suffer a heart attack. Column 1 stores the data for the group of physicians who took aspirin and column 2 contains the data for the group taking a placebo.

Excel Output for Example 12.7

	A	B	C	D
1	Test of Hypothesis About P1-P2			
2				
3	Test of P1-P2 = 0 Vs P1-P2 less than 0			
4	Sample 1 proportion = 0.0095			
5	Sample 2 proportion = 0.0172			
6	Test Statistic = -4.9992			
7	P-Value = 0			

COMMANDS

1 Type or import the data into two adjacent columns.
2 Click **Tools, Data Analysis Plus,** and **Inference about Two Proportions.**
3 Specify the **Input Range:.** Do not include the cells containing the variable names.
4 Type the code representing a success.
5 Click **Test of Hypothesis (Case 1).**
6 Click the appropriate alternative hypothesis.

COMMANDS FOR EXAMPLE 12.7

Open file **XM12-07.**

A2:B11001

2

P1—P2 less than zero

To conduct this procedure from the sample proportions or to perform a what-if analysis activate the **z-Test of 2 Proportions (Case 1)** in the **Inference from Summary Statistics (Workbook)** option.

Minitab Output for Example 12.7

Test and Confidence Interval for Two Proportions

```
Success = 2

Variable         X       N   Sample p
Aspirin        104   11000   0.009455
Placebo        189   11000   0.017182

Estimate for p(Aspirin) - p(Placebo):  -0.00772727
95% CI for p(Aspirin) - p(Placebo):  (-0.0107551, -0.00469945)
Test for p(Aspirin) - p(Placebo) = 0(vs < 0):Z = -5.00   P-Value = 0.000
```

COMMANDS

1 Type or import the data into two columns
2 Click **Stat, Basic Statistics,** and **2 Proportions. . . .**
3 Use the cursor to specify **Samples in different columns.**
4 Type the name of the **First:** and **Second:** variables.
5 Click **Options . . .** and type the value of the **Test difference:.**
6 Specify the **Alternative:** hypothesis.
7 Click **Use pooled estimate of p for test.** Click **OK.**

COMMANDS FOR EXAMPLE 12.7

Open file **XM12-07.**

Aspirin Placebo or **C1 C2**

0

less than

The data may also be input in stacked format. If so, at step 3 specify **Samples in one column:,** where the data are located **(Samples:),** and where the codes identifying the sample are stored **(Subscripts:).**

The test can also be completed from statistics. At step 3 click **Summarized data:,** specify the sample sizes **(Trials:)** and the number of **Successes:** for the **First sample:** and the **Second sample:.**

INTERPRET

There is overwhelming evidence to infer that aspirin reduces the incidence of heart attacks among men. In fact, the evidence was so strong that the experiment, which was originally scheduled to run for 5 years, was cut short after only 3 years so that the results could be made public. The effect on aspirin sales around the world was quite impressive.

One of the flaws in the aspirin study is that all of the subjects were male physicians. Consequently, the effect of taking aspirin regularly on women is unknown. Moreover, to claim that aspirin reduces the frequency of heart attacks among all men is based on the assumption that male physicians are similar to all men, a contention that is easily disputed. Nevertheless, medical researchers appear to be satisfied in advising middle-aged people who are not adversely affected by aspirin to take aspirin regularly.

▲

Sᴛᴀᴛɪsᴛɪᴄs ɪɴ ᴛʜᴇ Wᴏʀᴋᴘʟᴀᴄᴇ

Marketing Application

Marketing managers frequently make use of test marketing to assess consumer reaction to a change in a characteristic (such as price or packaging) of an existing product, or to assess consumers' preferences regarding a proposed new product. **Test marketing** involves experimenting with changes to the marketing mix in a small,

limited test market and assessing consumers' reaction in the test market before undertaking costly changes in production and distribution for the entire market.

▼ **EXAMPLE 12.8**

A soap manufacturer is hoping to improve sales with the introduction of more attractive packaging, but can't decide which of two new designs to adopt. Having decided to conduct an experiment to collect data to help make his decision, the marketing manager selects two communities known to be similar in terms of sales and preferences. Soap packaged with the new Design A is distributed to one community, and soap packaged with the new Design B is distributed to the other community. In each community, soap in the old packaging will continue to be available, and will be placed next to the soap packaged with one of the new designs. The number of purchases of each type of packaging during the trial period is shown below. Because Design A is considerably more costly than Design B management has decided that Design A will have to outsell Design B by more than 3% to be financially viable. Using a significance level of 1%, conduct a test to help management decide which type of packaging to use.

| | Packaging | |
	New	Old
Community 1	580	324
Community 2	604	442

Solution

IDENTIFY

The problem objective is to compare two populations, each population consisting of the values "Consumer purchased product in the new packaging" and "Consumer purchased product in the old packaging." The data are obviously qualitative, making the parameter to be tested the difference between two population proportions $p_1 - p_2$, where p_1 is the proportion of consumers (in community 1) who purchased product with new Design A and p_2 is the proportion of consumers (in community 2) who purchased the product with new Design B.

We want to determine whether we can infer that p_1 is more than 3% larger than p_2. Hence we set up the alternative hypothesis accordingly.

$$H_1: p_1 - p_2 > .03$$

The null hypothesis meekly follows.

$$H_0: p_1 - p_2 = .03$$

Because the null hypothesis specifies a value for the parameter that is not zero, we identify this procedure as case 2. The test statistic is

$$z = \frac{(\hat{p}_1 - \hat{p}_2) - (p_1 - p_2)}{\sqrt{\dfrac{\hat{p}_1(1 - \hat{p}_1)}{n_1} + \dfrac{\hat{p}_2(1 - \hat{p}_2)}{n_2}}}$$

SOLVE

The rejection region is

$$z > z_\alpha = z_{.01} = 2.33$$

The sample proportions are

$$\hat{p}_1 = \frac{x_1}{n_1} = \frac{580}{580 + 324} = \frac{580}{904} = .642$$

$$\hat{p}_2 = \frac{x_2}{n_2} = \frac{604}{604 + 442} = \frac{604}{1046} = .577$$

The value of the test statistic is

$$z = \frac{(\hat{p}_1 - \hat{p}_2) - (p_1 - p_2)}{\sqrt{\dfrac{\hat{p}_1(1 - \hat{p}_1)}{n_1} + \dfrac{\hat{p}_2(1 - \hat{p}_2)}{n_2}}} = \frac{(.642 - .577) - (.03)}{\sqrt{\dfrac{.642(1 - .642)}{904} + \dfrac{.577(1 - .577)}{1046}}} = 1.58$$

As we have done previously, we assume that the statistician has only the raw data with which to work. In file XM12-08 we have stored two columns of data representing the outcomes from communities 1 and 2, respectively, where 2 = Purchased product with new design and 1 = Purchased product with old design.

Excel Output for Example 12.8

	A	B	C	D
1	Test of Hypothesis About P1-P2			
2				
3	Test of P1-P2 = 0.03 Vs P1-P2 greater than 0.03			
4	Sample 1 proportion = 0.6416			
5	Sample 2 proportion = 0.5774			
6	Test Statistic = 1.5467			
7	P-Value = 0.061			

COMMANDS

Follow the first four steps of the instructions provided for Example 12.7.

5 Click **Test of Hypothesis (Case 2).**
6 Specify the value of **'P1-P2'** under the null hypothesis.
7 Click the appropriate alternative hypothesis.

COMMANDS FOR EXAMPLE 12.8

.03

P1-P2 greater than .03

As was the case with previous Excel computations starting in Chapter 9 we can complete the test using sample proportions as well as what-if analyses. Activate the worksheet **z-Test of 2 Proportions (Case 2)** and substitute the sample statistics.

Minitab Output for Example 12.8

Test and Confidence Interval for Two Proportions

```
Success = 2

Variable        X       N   Sample p
Design A      580     904   0.641593
Design B      604    1046   0.577438

Estimate for p(Design A) - p(Design B):  0.0641551
95% CI for p(Design A) - p(Design B):  (0.0208738, 0.107436)
Test for p(Design A) - p(Design B) = 0.03 (vs > 0.03):
   Z = 1.55  P-Value =  0.061
```

COMMANDS	COMMANDS FOR EXAMPLE 12.8

Follow the first four steps of the
instructions provided for Example 12.7.

5 Click **Options . . .** and type the .03
value of the **Test difference:**.
6 Specify the **Alternative:** hypothesis. greater than
7 Do not click **Use pooled estimate
of p for test.** Click **OK.**

INTERPRET

There is not enough evidence to infer that the proportion of customers who buy the product with the Design A packaging is more than 3% higher than the proportion of customers who buy the product with the Design B packaging. In the absence of sufficient evidence the analysis suggests that the product should be packaged using Design B.

▲

ESTIMATING THE DIFFERENCE BETWEEN TWO POPULATION PROPORTIONS

The interval estimator of $p_1 - p_2$ can very easily be derived from the sampling distribution of $\hat{p}_1 - \hat{p}_2$.

Interval Estimator of $p_1 - p_2$

$$(\hat{p}_1 - \hat{p}_2) \pm z_{\alpha/2}\sqrt{\frac{\hat{p}_1(1-\hat{p}_1)}{n_1} + \frac{\hat{p}_2(1-\hat{p}_2)}{n_2}}$$

This formula is valid when $n_1\hat{p}_1$, $n_1(1-\hat{p}_1)$, $n_2\hat{p}_2$, and $n_2(1-\hat{p}_2)$ exceed 5. Notice that the standard deviation of $\hat{p}_1 - \hat{p}_2$ is estimated using $\hat{p}_1$ and $\hat{p}_2$. In this application, we cannot use the pooled proportion estimate because we cannot assume that $p_1 = p_2$.

▼ **EXAMPLE 12.9**

Estimate with 95% confidence the proportion of men who would avoid a heart attack if they started taking aspirin regularly. If 100 million men adopt the practice of the regular use of aspirin, estimate the number of men who would avoid heart attacks.

Solution

IDENTIFY

We already know that the parameter of interest is $p_1 - p_2$. The confidence interval estimator is

$$(\hat{p}_1 - \hat{p}_2) \pm z_{\alpha/2}\sqrt{\frac{\hat{p}_1(1-\hat{p}_1)}{n_1} + \frac{\hat{p}_2(1-\hat{p}_2)}{n_2}}$$

Recall that

p_1 = proportion of all men who take aspirin who suffer a heart attack

p_2 = proportion of all men who do not take aspirin who suffer a heart attack

and that

$$\hat{p}_1 = \frac{104}{11,000} = .009455$$

and

$$\hat{p}_2 = \frac{189}{11,000} = .01718$$

SOLVE

The 95% confidence interval estimate of $p_1 - p_2$ is

$$(\hat{p}_1 - \hat{p}_2) \pm z_{\alpha/2}\sqrt{\frac{\hat{p}_1(1 - \hat{p}_1)}{n_1} + \frac{\hat{p}_2(1 - \hat{p}_2)}{n_2}}$$

$$= (.009455 - .01718) \pm 1.96\sqrt{\frac{(.009455)(.990545)}{11,000} + \frac{(.01718)(.98282)}{11,000}}$$

$$= -.007725 \pm .003028$$

The 95% confidence interval estimate is $(-.010753, -.004697)$.

Excel Output for Example 12.9

	A	B	C	D
1	0.95 Confidence Interval Estimate of P1-P2			
2				
3	Sample 1 proportion = 0.0095			
4	Sample 2 proportion = 0.0172			
5	Lower confidence limit = -0.0108			
6	Upper confidence limit = -0.0047			

COMMANDS

Proceed through the first four steps of the instructions for Example 12.7. At step 5 click **Interval Estimate** and type the confidence level.

Minitab Output for Example 12.9

```
Estimate for p(Aspirin) - p(Placebo):  -0.00772727
95% CI for p(Aspirin) - p(Placebo):  (-0.0107551, -0.00469945)
```

This printout appeared as part of the output for Example 12.7.

COMMANDS

Use the instructions for Example 12.7. After clicking **Options ...** type the confidence level.

INTERPRET

We estimate that the proportion of men who suffer a heart attack is between .47% and 1.08% less for men who take aspirin than for those who do not. If 100 million men start taking aspirin, between 470,000 and 1,080,000 of them will avoid heart attacks.

▲

The test statistics, interval estimator, and the critical factors that identify their use are listed below.

Test Statistics for $p_1 - p_2$

Case 1: $z = \dfrac{(\hat{p}_1 - \hat{p}_2)}{\sqrt{\hat{p}(1-\hat{p})\left(\dfrac{1}{n_1} + \dfrac{1}{n_2}\right)}}$

Case 2: $z = \dfrac{(\hat{p}_1 - \hat{p}_2) - (p_1 - p_2)}{\sqrt{\dfrac{\hat{p}_1(1-\hat{p}_1)}{n_1} + \dfrac{\hat{p}_2(1-\hat{p}_2)}{n_2}}}$

Interval Estimator of $p_1 - p_2$

$(\hat{p}_1 - \hat{p}_2) \pm z_{\alpha/2}\sqrt{\dfrac{\hat{p}_1(1-\hat{p}_1)}{n_1} + \dfrac{\hat{p}_2(1-\hat{p}_2)}{n_2}}$

Factors that Identify the z-Test and Estimator of $p_1 - p_2$

1 Problem objective: compare two populations

2 Data type: qualitative

EXERCISES

12.59 Random samples from two binomial populations yielded the following statistics

$\hat{p}_1 = .45 \quad n_1 = 100 \quad \hat{p}_2 = .39 \quad n_2 = 100$

Test with $\alpha = .10$ to determine whether we can infer that the population proportions differ.

12.60 Compute the *p*-value of the test in Exercise 12.59.

12.61 Refer to Exercise 12.59. Estimate the difference between the two population proportions with 95% confidence.

12.62 Repeat Exercises 12.59–12.61 increasing the sample sizes to 400.

12.63 Review Exercises 12.59–12.62. Describe what happens when the sample sizes increase.

12.64 After sampling from two binomial populations we found the following.

$\hat{p}_1 = .368 \quad n_1 = 1000 \quad \hat{p}_2 = .275 \quad n_2 = 1000$

Can we infer at the 5% significance level that p_1 is greater than p_2 by more than 5%?

12.65 Refer to Exercise 12.64. Estimate the difference in population proportions. Use a confidence level of 90%.

12.66 The following statistics were calculated.

$\hat{p}_1 = .12 \quad n_1 = 400 \quad \hat{p}_2 = .16 \quad n_2 = 400$

Test with $\alpha = .10$ to determine whether p_1 is less than p_2.

12.67 Refer to Exercise 12.65. Estimate with 95% confidence the difference between the two population proportions.

12.68 Repeat Exercises 12.66 and 12.67 increasing the sample proportions to .42 and .46, respectively.

12.69 Review Exercises 12.66–12.68. Describe the effects of increasing the sample proportions.

12.70 Cold and allergy medicines have been available for a number of years. One serious side effect of these medications is that they cause drowsiness, which makes them dangerous for industrial workers. In recent years, a nondrowsy cold and allergy medicine has been developed. One such product, Hismanal, is claimed by its manufacturer to be the first, once-a-day nondrowsy allergy medicine. The nondrowsy part of the claim is based on a clinical experiment in which 1,604 patients were given Hismanal and 1,109 patients were given a placebo; 7.1% of the first group and 6.4% of the second group reported drowsiness. Do these results allow us to infer at the 5% significance level that Hismanal's claim is false?

12.71 Surveys have been widely used by politicians around the world as a way of monitoring the opinions of the electorate. Six months ago, a survey was undertaken to determine the degree of support for a national party leader. Of a sample of 1,100, 56% indicated that they would vote for this politician. This month, another survey of 800 voters revealed that 46% now support the leader.

　a At the 5% significance level, can we infer that the nation leader's popularity has decreased?

　b At the 5% significance level, can we infer that the national leader's popularity has decreased by more than 5%?

　c Estimate with 95% confidence the decrease in percentage support between now and 6 months ago.

12.72 The process that is used to produce a complex component used in medical instruments typically results in defective rates in the 40% range. Recently, two innovative processes have been developed to replace the existing process. Process 1 appears to be more promising, but it is considerably more expensive to purchase and operate than process 2. After a thorough analysis of the costs, management decides that it will adopt process 1 only if the proportion of defective components it produces is more than 8% smaller than that produced by process 2. In a test to guide the decision, both processes were used to produce 300 components. Of the 300 components produced by process 1, 33 were found to be defective, while 84 out of the 300 produced by process 2 were defective. Using a significance level of 1%, conduct a test to help management make a decision.

12.73 Refer to Example 12.7. A not-so-widely-publicized British study attempted to replicate the American research plan; however, it used 5,000 men (2,500 took aspirin, and 2,500 took the placebo). Suppose that the respective proportions of men who suffered heart attacks were exactly the same as in the American study. Do such results allow us to draw the same conclusion?

Exercises 12.74–12.77 require the use of a computer and software. The answers may be calculated manually. See Appendix A for the sample statistics.

12.74 A random sample of $n_1 = 1,000$ from population 1 and a random sample of $n_2 = 600$ from population 2 produced the data in columns 1 and 2, respectively, in file XR12-74. The results are either success (2) or failure (1).

　a Test at the 1% significance level to determine whether we can infer that the two population proportions of success differ.

　b Estimate $p_1 - p_2$ with 99% confidence.

12.75 The data stored in columns 1 and 2 in file XR12-75 were drawn from random samples from two populations of qualitative data where 2 = success and 1 = failure.

　a Do these data allow us to infer at the 1% significance level that p_1 is greater than p_2?

　b Do these data allow us to infer at the 1% significance level that p_1 exceeds p_2 by more than 3%?

　c Estimate $p_1 - p_2$ with 95% confidence.

12.76 An insurance company is thinking about offering discounts on its life insurance policies to nonsmokers. As part of its analysis, it randomly selects 200 men who are 60 years old and asks them if they smoke at least one pack of cigarettes per day and if they have ever suffered from heart disease. The results are stored in file XR12-76 using the following format.

Column 1: sample of smokers: 2 = suffer from heart disease; 1 = do not suffer from heart disease

Column 2: sample of nonsmokers: 2 = suffer from heart disease; 1 = do not suffer from heart disease

　a Can the company conclude at the 5% significance level that smokers have a higher incidence of heart disease than nonsmokers?

　b Estimate with 90% confidence the difference in the fraction of men suffering from heart disease between smokers and nonsmokers.

12.77 The impact of the accumulation of carbon dioxide in the atmosphere caused by burning fossil fuels such as oil, coal, and natural gas has been hotly debated for more than a decade. Some environmentalists and scientists have predicted that the excess carbon dioxide will increase the earth's temperature during the next 50 to 100 years with disastrous consequences. This belief is often called the "greenhouse effect." Other scientists claim that we don't know what the effect will be, and yet others believe that the earth's temperature is likely to decrease. Given the debate among scientists, it is not surprising that the general population is confused. To gauge the public's opinion on the subject, 2 years ago a random sample of 400 people was asked if they believed in the greenhouse effect. This year, 500 people were asked the same question. The results are stored in file XR12-77 using the following format.

Column 1: results 2 years ago: 2 = believe greenhouse effect; 1 = do not believe greenhouse effect

Column 2: results this year: 2 = believe greenhouse effect; 1 = do not believe greenhouse effect

a Can we infer at the 5% significance level that there has been a decrease in belief in the greenhouse effect?

b Estimate the real change in the public's opinion about the subject. Use a 90% confidence level.

12.7 MARKET SEGMENTATION (OPTIONAL)

Marketing managers will frequently perform a statistical analysis to determine what differences exist between buyers and nonbuyers of a company's products. This analysis is called *market segmentation,* which was briefly described in Chapter 1. Markets are segmented to develop products and services for particular groups of customers. For example, soft-drink manufacturers feature a variety of products. Each product has a particular target group that it attempts to satisfy. For example, the Coca-Cola Company produces Coke Classic, Diet Coke, Caffeine-Free Coke, and several other types of drinks. Coke Classic is aimed at cola drinkers who are older than 30 since many of these consumers started to drink this product before there were many other choices. Diet Coke is purchased by people concerned with their weight and Caffeine-Free Coke is consumed by individuals who are at least somewhat health conscious.

To segment the cola market the marketing manager first had to determine that there were differences among consumers. There are several segmentation variables that managers can use to test for differences. These variables include geographic (e.g., state, provinces, counties, cities), demographic (e.g., age, sex, occupation, income, marital status, religion), psychographic (e.g., social class, lifestyle, personality), and behavioristic (e.g., brand loyalty, usage, benefits sought).

Consumer surveys are generally employed by marketing researchers to determine what, if any, differences exist. For example, cola drinkers could be asked to identify which cola product they generally consume and then report some of the segmentation variables described above. Census data and surveys are used to measure the size of the segments and whether it is profitable to satisfy some or all of the segments.

Statistics plays a vital role in market segmentation. First, surveys are used to gather the relevant data. Second, statistical tests are used to differentiate among several segments. Third, sales and profit estimates are derived from the segments and census data.

In this chapter we have introduced several statistical techniques, all of which are used to determine whether differences exist between two populations. The example below will feature these techniques. In later chapters we will present examples of market segmentation where we have more than two populations.

▼ EXAMPLE 12.10

During the 1930s, 1940s, 1950s, 1960s, and 1970s, car owners brought their cars to the dealer from which they purchased their cars or to local service stations to have their oil and filters changed. One usually needed an appointment and the service frequently required the owner to leave his or her car for the better part of a day or overnight for the service to be completed. During the last 25 years, however, a number of service centers offering no-wait oil and filter changes have appeared. A new company in the market wanted to launch their new service by advertising extensively.

To help make decisions about where to advertise and the size of the budget, a market researcher was employed. She took a random sample of 1,000 car owners and asked them to report whether or not they used one of several no-wait service centers and various characteristics of their lives including their age. The data are stored in file XM12-10 in the following way.

Column 1: Ages of customers who use a no-wait service

Column 2: Ages of customers who use some other facility

The researcher would like to know whether differences in age exist between customers of no-wait service centers and customers of other types of facilities.

Solution

IDENTIFY

The problem objective is to compare two populations. Population 1 is composed of the customers of a no-wait service center and population 2 is customers of other facilities. Age is a quantitative variable. The characteristic of these populations that we wish to compare is their location. The data were gathered as independent samples. The combination of problem objective, data type, descriptive measure, and experimental design tells the market researcher that the parameter to be tested is the difference between the population means. Because she wants to know whether the ages differ the alternative hypothesis is

$$H_1: \mu_1 - \mu_2 \neq 0$$

and the null hypothesis is

$$H_0: \mu_1 - \mu_2 = 0$$

All that is left to identify is which of the two test statistics to use, the equal-variances or unequal-variances t-test of $\mu_1 - \mu_2$. The easiest way to make this decision is to conduct the F-test of σ_1^2/σ_2^2. the printouts below of this procedure tell the market researcher that there is enough evidence to infer that the population variances differ. (The F-statistic equals 1.284 and its two-tail p-value is .0076.) As a result the appropriate technique is the unequal-variances t-test of $\mu_1 - \mu_2$.

SOLVE

A sample of 1,000 is too large to even pretend we could complete the calculation manually.

Excel Outputs for Example 12.10

	A	B	C
1	F-Test Two-Sample for Variances		
2			
3		No-Wait	Other
4	Mean	47.78	44.03
5	Variance	77.17	60.10
6	Observations	623	377
7	df	622	376
8	F	1.284	
9	P(F<=f) one-tail	0.0038	
10	F Critical one-tail	1.201	

	A	B	C
1	t-Test: Two-Sample Assuming Unequal Variances		
2			
3		No-Wait	Other
4	Mean	47.78	44.03
5	Variance	77.17	60.10
6	Observations	623	377
7	Hypothesized Mean Difference	0	
8	df	870	
9	t Stat	7.043	
10	P(T<=t) one-tail	0.0000	
11	t Critical one-tail	1.647	
12	P(T<=t) two-tail	0.0000	
13	t Critical two-tail	1.963	

Minitab Outputs for Example 12.10

Homogeneity of Variance

F-Test (normal distribution)

Test Statistic: 1.284
P-Value   : 0.008

Two Sample T-Test and Confidence Interval

Two sample T for No-Wait vs Other

```
           N    Mean   StDev  SE Mean
No-Wait  623   47.78    8.78     0.35
Other    377   44.03    7.75     0.40
```

95% CI for mu No-Wait - mu Other: (2.70, 4.79)
T-Test mu No-Wait = mu Other (vs not =): T = 7.04   P = 0.0000   DF = 869

INTERPRET

There is overwhelming evidence to infer that mean age of customers of no-wait oil change facilities differs from the mean age of customers who use other facilities. This suggests that different kinds of advertising should be designed for the two different age groups. Advertising that encourages customers of other no-wait companies to switch to the new firm should be aimed at older people. Advertising that encourages car owners who use other type of facilities to switch to a no-wait facility in general, and to this company in particular, should be directed at younger car owners.

▲

12.8 SUMMARY

In this chapter, we presented a variety of techniques that allow statisticians to compare two populations. When the data are quantitative and we are interested in measures of central location, we encountered two more factors that must be considered when choosing the appropriate technique. When the samples are independent, we can use either the equal-variances or unequal-variances formulas. When the samples are matched pairs, we have only one set of formulas. We introduced the F distribution, which is used to make inferences about two population variances. When the data are qualitative, the parameter of interest is the difference between two proportions. For this parameter we had two test statistics and one interval estimator. All these techniques are summarized in the following table. Finally, we discussed observational and experimental data, important concepts in attempting to interpret statistical findings.

SUMMARY OF INFERENCE ABOUT COMPARING TWO POPULATIONS

Parameter	Test Statistic	Interval Estimator	Required Conditions
$\mu_1 - \mu_2$	$t = \dfrac{(\bar{x}_1 - \bar{x}_2) - (\mu_1 - \mu_2)}{\sqrt{s_p^2\left(\dfrac{1}{n_1} + \dfrac{1}{n_2}\right)}}$ d.f. $= n_1 + n_2 - 2$	$(\bar{x}_1 - \bar{x}_2) \pm t_{\alpha/2}\sqrt{s_p^2\left(\dfrac{1}{n_1} + \dfrac{1}{n_2}\right)}$	Samples are independent; populations are normal; $\sigma_1^2 = \sigma_2^2$.
$\mu_1 - \mu_2$	$t = \dfrac{(\bar{x}_1 - \bar{x}_2) - (\mu_1 - \mu_2)}{\sqrt{\dfrac{s_1^2}{n_1} + \dfrac{s_2^2}{n_2}}}$ d.f. $= \dfrac{(s_1^2/n_1 + s_2^2/n_2)^2}{\left(\dfrac{(s_1^2/n_1)^2}{n_1 - 1} + \dfrac{(s_2^2/n_2)^2}{n_2 - 1}\right)}$	$(\bar{x}_1 - \bar{x}_2) \pm t_{\alpha/2}\sqrt{\dfrac{s_1^2}{n_1} + \dfrac{s_2^2}{n_2}}$	Samples are independent; populations are normal; $\sigma_1^2 \neq \sigma_2^2$.
μ_D	$t = \dfrac{\bar{x}_D - \mu_D}{s_D/\sqrt{n_D}}$ d.f. $= n_D - 1$	$\bar{x}_D \pm t_{\alpha/2}\dfrac{s_D}{\sqrt{n_D}}$	Samples are matched pairs; differences are normal.
σ_1^2/σ_2^2	$F = s_1^2/s_2^2$ $\mu_1 = n_1 - 1$ $\mu_2 = n_2 - 1$	$\text{LCL} = \left(\dfrac{s_1^2}{s_2^2}\right)\dfrac{1}{F_{\alpha/2,\nu_1,\nu_2}}$ $\text{UCL} = \left(\dfrac{s_1^2}{s_2^2}\right)F_{\alpha/2,\nu_2,\nu_1}$	Populations are normal.
$p_1 - p_2$	Case 1: $H_0: (p_1 - p_2) = 0$ $z = \dfrac{(\hat{p}_1 - \hat{p}_2)}{\sqrt{\hat{p}(1 - \hat{p})\left(\dfrac{1}{n_1} + \dfrac{1}{n_2}\right)}}$ Case 2: $H_0: (p_1 - p_2) = D$ $(D \neq 0)$ $z = \dfrac{(\hat{p}_1 - \hat{p}_2) - (p_1 - p_2)}{\sqrt{\dfrac{\hat{p}_1(1 - \hat{p}_1)}{n_1} + \dfrac{\hat{p}_2(1 - \hat{p}_2)}{n_2}}}$	$(\hat{p}_1 - \hat{p}_2) \pm z_{\alpha/2}\sqrt{\dfrac{\hat{p}_1(1 - \hat{p}_1)}{n_1} + \dfrac{\hat{p}_2(1 - \hat{p}_2)}{n_2}}$	$n_1\hat{p}_1, n_1(1 - \hat{p}_1), n_2\hat{p}_2, n_2(1 - \hat{p}_2) \geq 5$

IMPORTANT TERMS

Pooled variance estimate   *397*
Equal-variances test statistic and
   interval estimator   *397*

Unequal-variances test statistic and
   interval estimator   *398*
Observational data   *413*

Experimental data   *413*

Matched pairs experiment   *414*

Mean of the population of
    differences   *417*

F distribution   *426*

F-statistic   *426*

Pooled proportion estimate   *436*

S U P P L E M E N T A R Y   E X E R C I S E S

The following exercises require the use of a computer and software. The answers may be calculated manually. See Appendix A for the sample statistics or list of raw data.

12.78 Is eating oat bran an effective way to reduce cholesterol? Early studies indicated that eating oat bran daily reduced cholesterol levels by 5 to 10%. Reports of this study resulted in the introduction of many new breakfast cereals with various percentages of oat bran as an ingredient. However, a January 1990 experiment performed by medical researchers in Boston, Massachusetts, cast doubt on the effectiveness of oat bran. In that study, 120 volunteers ate oat bran for breakfast, and another 120 volunteers ate another grain cereal for breakfast. At the end of 6 weeks, the percentage of cholesterol reduction was computed for both groups. These data are stored in columns 1 (% cholesterol reduction with oat bran) and 2 (% cholesterol reduction with other cereal) in file XR12-78. Can we infer at the 5% significance level that oat bran is different from other cereals in terms of cholesterol reduction?

12.79 A restaurant located in an office building decides to adopt a new strategy for attracting customers to the restaurant. Every week it advertises in the city newspaper. To measure how well the advertising is working, the restaurant owner recorded the weekly gross sales for the 15 weeks after the campaign began and the weekly gross sales for the 24 weeks immediately prior to the campaign. These data are stored in columns 1 (during campaign) and 2 (before campaign) in file XR12-79.

a Can the restaurateur conclude at the 5% significance level that the advertising campaign is successful?

b Assume that the profit is 20% of the gross. If the ads cost $50 per week, can the restaurateur conclude that the ads are profitable?

12.80 Because of the high cost of energy, home owners in northern climates need to find ways to cut their heating costs. A building contractor wanted to investigate the effect on heating costs of increasing the insulation. As an experiment, he located a large subdevelopment built around 1970 with minimal insulation. His plan was to insulate some of the houses and compare the heating costs in the insulated homes with those that remained uninsulated. However, it was clear to him that the size of the house was a critical factor in determining heating costs. Consequently, he found 15 pairs of identical-sized houses ranging from 1,200 to 2,800 square feet. He insulated one house in each pair (levels of R20 in the walls and R32 in the attic) and left the other house unchanged. The heating cost for the following winter season was recorded for each house. The data are stored in file XR12-80. (Column 1 = size of the house, column 2 = heating cost of uninsulated house, column 3 = heating cost of insulated house.)

a Do these data allow the contractor to infer at the 5% significance level that the heating cost for the insulated house is less than that for the uninsulated one?

b Estimate with 95% confidence the mean savings due to insulating the house.

c What is the required condition for the use of the techniques in parts (a) and (b)?

12.81 An inspector for the Atlantic City Gaming Commission suspects that a particular blackjack dealer may be cheating when he deals at expensive tables. To test her belief, she observed 500 hands each at the $100-limit table and the $3,000-limit table. For each hand, she recorded whether the dealer won (code = 2) or lost (code = 1). When a tie occurs there is no winner or loser. These data are stored in file XR12-81. (Column 1 stores the outcomes for the $100-limit table, and column 2 stores the outcomes for the $3,000-limit table.) Can the inspector conclude at the 10% significance level that the dealer is cheating at the more expensive table?

12.82 In recent years, a number of state governments have passed mandatory seat-belt laws. Although the use of seat belts is known to save lives and reduce serious injuries, compliance with seat-belt laws is not universal. In an effort to increase the use of seat belts, a government agency sponsored a 2-year study. Among its objectives was to determine if there was enough evidence to infer that seat-belt usage increased between last year and this year. To test this belief, random samples of drivers last year and this year were asked whether they always used their seat belts. The responses were stored in file XR12-82 in the following way.

Column 1: last year's survey responses, 2 = wear seat belt; 1 = do not wear seat belt

Column 2: this year's survey responses, 2 = wear seat belt; 1 = do not wear seat belt

What conclusions can be drawn from the results? (Use a 5% significance level.)

12.83 In designing advertising campaigns to sell magazines, it is important to know how much time each of a number of demographic groups spends reading magazines. In a preliminary study, 40 people were randomly selected. Each was asked how much time per week he or she spent reading magazines; additionally, each was categorized by sex and by income level (high or low). The data are stored in file XR12-83 in the following way: column 1 = time spent reading magazines per week in minutes for all respondents; column 2 = gender (1 = male and 2 = female); column 3 = income level (1 = low and 2 = high).

a Is there sufficient evidence at the 5% significance level to conclude that men and women differ in the amount of time spent reading magazines?

b Is there sufficient evidence at the 5% significance level to conclude that high-income individuals devote more time to reading magazines than low-income people?

12.84 An important component of the cost of living is the amount of money spent on housing. Housing costs include rent (for tenants), mortgage payments and property tax (for home owners), heating, electricity, and water. An economist undertook a 5-year study to determine how housing costs have changed. Five years ago, he took a random sample of 200 households and recorded the percentage of total income spent on housing. This year, he took another sample of 200 households. The data are stored in columns 1 (five years ago) and 2 (this year) in file XR12-84.

a Conduct a test (with $\alpha = .10$) to determine whether the economist can infer that housing cost as a percentage of total income has increased over the last 5 years.

b Use whatever statistical method you deem appropriate to check the required condition(s) of the test used in part (a).

12.85 In a study to determine whether gender affects salary offers for graduating M.B.A. students, 25 pairs of students were selected. Each pair consisted of a female and a male student who were matched according to their grade-point averages, courses taken, ages, and previous work experience. The highest salary offered (in thousands of dollars) to each graduate was recorded and stored in file XR12-85. (Column 1 = salary offer for females and column 2 = salary offer for males.)

a Is there enough evidence at the 10% significance level to infer that gender is a factor in salary offers?

b Discuss why the experiment was organized in the way it was.

c Is the required condition for the test in part (a) satisfied?

12.86 Have North Americans grown to distrust television and newspaper journalists? A survey was conducted this year to compare what Americans currently thought of the press versus what they said three years ago. The survey asked respondents whether they agreed that press tends to favor one side when reporting on political and social issues. A random sample of people were asked to participate in this year's survey. The results of a survey of another random sample taken 3 years ago is also available. The responses are stored in file XR12-86 using the following format.

Column 1: this year's survey response: 2 = agree; 1 = disagree

Column 2: 3 years ago survey response: 2 = agree; 1 = disagree

Can we conclude at the 5% significance level that Americans have become more distrustful of television and newspaper reporting this year than they were 3 years ago?

12.87 Before deciding which of two types of stamping machines should be purchased, the plant manager of an automotive parts manufacturer wants to determine the number of units that each produces. The two machines differ in cost, reliability, and productivity. The firm's accountant has calculated that Machine A must produce 25 more nondefective units per hour than Machine B to warrant buying Machine A. To help decide, both machines were operated for 24 hours. The total number of units and the number of nondefective units produced by each machine per hour were recorded. These data are stored in file XR12-87 (column 1 = total number of units produced by machine A; column 2 = number of defectives produced by Machine A; column 3 = total number of units produced by Machine B; column 4 = number of defectives produced by Machine B). Determine which machine should be purchased. (Use a 5% significance level.)

12.88 Refer to Exercise 12.87. Can we conclude at the 5% significance level that the defective rate differs between the two machines?

12.89 The growing use of bicycles to commute to work has caused many cities to create exclusive bicycle lanes. These lanes are usually created by disallowing parking on streets that formerly allowed curbside parking. Merchants on such streets complain that the removal of parking will cause their businesses to suffer. To examine this problem, the mayor of a large city decided to launch an experiment on one busy street that had 1-hour parking meters. The meters were removed and a bicycle lane was created. The mayor asked the three businesses (a dry cleaner, a doughnut shop, and a convenience store) in one block to record daily sales for two complete weeks (Sunday to Saturday) prior to the change and two complete weeks after the change. The data are stored in file XR12-89 (column 1 = day of the week, column 2 = sales before change for dry cleaner, column 3 = sales after change for dry cleaner, column 4 = sales before change for doughnut shop, column 5 = sales after change for doughnut shop, column 6 = sales before change for convenience store, and column 7 = sales after change for convenience store). What conclusions can you draw from these data? Use $\alpha = .05$.

12.90 There may be a new health concern—too much iron in our bodies. An article in the *Wall Street Journal* (17 January, 1992) reported that some scientists have implicated iron as a factor in various diseases, including cancer. Part of the problem, it is believed, is that iron builds up in the body over many years. To examine the issue, a random sample of 20-year-old men and women and 40-year-old men and women was drawn. The amount of iron in their bodies was measured and recorded. The results are stored in file XR12-90 in the following way: column 1 shows the amount of stored iron in men (in milligrams); column 2 indicates the men's ages; column 3 shows the amount of stored iron in women; column 4 lists the women's ages.

   a Conduct a test at the 5% significance level to determine whether we can infer that 40-year-old men have more iron in their bodies than do 20-year-old men.

   b Repeat part (a) for women.

12.91 It is known that clinical depression is linked to several other diseases. Scientists at Johns Hopkins University undertook a study to determine whether heart disease is one of these. A group of 1,190 male medical students were tracked over a 40-year period. Of these 132 had suffered clinically diagnosed depression. For each student the scientists recorded whether the student died of a heart attack (code = 2) or did not (code = 1). These data are stored in columns 1 (clinically depressed) and 2 (not clinically depressed) in file XR12-91.

   a Can we infer at the 5% significance level that men who are clinically depressed are more likely to die from heart diseases?

   b If the answer to part (a) is yes, can you interpret this to mean that depression causes heart disease? Explain.

12.92 Most English professors complain that students don't write very well. In particular they point out that students often confuse quality and quantity. A study at the University of Texas examined this claim. In the study undergraduate students were asked to compare the cost benefits of Japanese and American cars. All wrote their analyses on computers. Unbeknownst to the students the computers were rigged so that some students would have to type twice as many words to fill a single page. The number of words used by each student was recorded and stored in file XR12-92. (Column 1 contains the number of words written by students who were allotted a small space and column 2 contains the number of words written by students who were allotted a large space.) Can we conclude at the 10% significance level that students write in such a way as to fill the allotted space?

12.93 Approximately 20 million Americans work for themselves. Most run single-person businesses out of their homes. One-quarter of these individuals use personal computers in their businesses. A market research firm, Computer Intelligence InfoCorp, wanted to know whether single-person businesses that use personal computers are more successful than those with no computer. They surveyed 150 single-person firms and recorded their annual incomes. These data are stored in file XR12-93. (Column 1 stores the incomes of businesses that use a computer and column 2 stores the incomes of businesses that do not.) Can we infer at the 5% significance level that single-person businesses that use a personal computer earn more than those that do not?

12.94 Many small retailers advertise in their neighborhoods by sending out flyers. People who deliver flyers are paid according to the number of flyers delivered. Each deliverer is given several streets whose homes become their responsibility. One of the ways retailers use to check the performance of deliverers is to randomly sample some of the homes and ask the homeowner whether he or she received the flyer. Recently university students started a new delivery service. They have promised better service at a competitive price. A retailer wanted to know whether the new company's delivery rate is better than that of the existing firm. She had both companies deliver her flyers. Random samples of homes were drawn and each was asked whether he or she received the flyer (2 = yes and 1 = no). These data are stored in columns 1 (new company) and 2 (older company) in file XR12-94. Can the retailer conclude that the new company is better? (Test with $\alpha = .10$.)

12.95 A study in a journal published by the *American Academy of Pediatrics* (as reported in the *Miami Herald* 14 January, 1997) seems to suggest that preschoolers who drink more than a cup and half of fruit juice tend to be heavier and shorter than children who do not. The study involved 168 healthy youngsters of whom 59 drank on average more than 12 ounces of fruit juice per day. Each child was weighed and measured. These measurements were converted to percentage of normal height and weight for a child of that age and gender. For example, a weight percentage of 1.1 indicates that that child is 10% heavier than average. The data are stored in columns 1, 2, and 3 in file XR12-95. Column 1 indicates whether the child drank more than 12 ounces of fruit juice per day (1) or not (2). Column 2 stores the weight percentages and column 3 contains the height percentages.

a Can we conclude at the 1% significance level that children who drink more than 12 ounces of fruit juice per day are heavier than those who do not?

b Can we conclude at the 1% significance level that children who drink more than 12 ounces of fruit juice per day are shorter than those who do not?

c Are these data experimental or observational?

d If the answers to questions 1 and 2 are affirmative, does this indicate that drinking too much fruit juice causes the preschoolers to be heavier and shorter? Explain. Is there another explanation for your results?

Sᴛᴀᴛɪꜱᴛɪᴄꜱ ɪɴ ᴛʜᴇ Wᴏʀᴋᴘʟᴀᴄᴇ

Marketing Application: Market Segmentation

The following exercises address the problem of segmenting a market. See Section 12.7 for a discussion of the technique.

12.96 Toyota manufactures a variety of cars over a wide range of prices. At the low end the company makes Tercels and Corollas. At the high end they make Avalons and Solaras. The prevailing view of the marketing managers is that as a general rule buyers of Tercels are younger than buyers of Avalons. To determine whether the belief is correct, the company randomly sampled 100 owners of Tercels and 100 Avalons bought within the past month. The ages of each buyer were recorded and stored in columns 1 and 2, respectively, in file XR12-96. Is there sufficient evidence to conclude at the 5% significance level that buyers of Avalons are older than buyers of Tercels?

12.97 Refer to Exercise 12.96. As part of the survey respondents were also asked to report their annual household incomes. These data (in $1,000s) are stored in columns 1 (incomes of Tercel buyers) and 2 (incomes of Avalon buyers) in file XR12-97. Can we conclude at the 5% significance level that Avalon owners have higher household incomes than do Tercel buyers?

Case 12.1   Specialty Advertising Recall*

Advertisers are extremely interested not only in having customers hear about their products but also in having consumers remember the product and its name. It is generally believed that if an advertisement is seen only once, the amount of recall diminishes over time. In an experiment to study the amount of recall in specialty advertising, 355 people were randomly selected. Each received by mail three specialty items with imprinted advertising: a ballpoint pen with the name American Airlines printed on it, a key ring with the

*Adapted from A. Raj, C. R. Stoner, and R. A. Schreiber, "Advertising Specialties: A Note on Recall," *Developments in Marketing Science* 8 (1985): 308–11.

letters TIW on it, and a note pad with the name General Electric imprinted on the cover. One week later, 164 of these people were asked if they remembered the products received and if they could also recall the products' sponsors. One month after the products were received, the remaining 191 people were asked the same questions. The numbers of those who could recall the products and the sponsors' names are shown in Tables 1 and 2.

For each product and for each sponsor, determine whether we can infer that the level of recall about these specialty items and their sponsors decreases over time.

Table 1: Number Who Recalled Product

Product	One Week	One Month
Ballpoint pen	140	159
Key ring	141	125
Note pad	149	150

Table 2: Number Who Recalled Sponsor's Name

Sponsor's Name	One Week	One Month
American Airlines	74	63
TIW	45	36
General Electric	74	58

Case 12.2   Bonanza International*

Bonanza International is one of the top 15 fast-food franchisers in the United States. Like McDonald's, Burger King, and most others, Bonanza uses a menu board to inform customers about its products. One of Bonanza's bright young executives believes that not all positions on the board are equal; specifically, that the position of the menu item on the board influences sales. If this hypothesis is true, Bonanza would be well advised to place its high-profit items in the positions that produce the highest sales.

After watching the eye movements of several people, the executive determined that customers first look at the upper right-hand corner, then cross the top row toward the left-hand side, then move down to the lower left-hand corner, and finally scan across the bottom toward the right.

This analysis suggests that items listed in the upper right-hand corner may achieve higher sales than items listed in the lower left-hand corner. To test this hypothesis, 10 stores with similar characteristics were selected as test restaurants, and two moderately popular items were selected as test menu items. During weeks 1 and 3 (of a 4-week study), item A was placed in the upper right-hand corner, and item B was placed in the lower left-hand corner. During weeks 2 and 4, the positions were reversed. The number of sales of each item was recorded, and the results are summarized in Tables 1 and 2. These data are also stored in columns 1 through 4 of file C12-02.

On the basis of the data, what can you conclude regarding the executive's belief?

*Adapted from M. G. Sobol and T. E. Barry, "Item Positioning for Profits: Menu Boards at Bonanza International," *Interfaces* (February): 55–60.

Table 1   Sales of Item A

Store	Sales with Item A in Upper Right-Hand Corner	Sales with Item A in Lower Left-Hand Corner
1	642	485
2	912	681
3	221	138
4	312	237
5	295	258
6	775	725
7	511	553
8	726	524
9	476	384
10	570	529

Table 2   Sales of Item B

Store	Sales with Item B in Upper Right-Hand Corner	Sales with Item B in Lower Left-Hand Corner
1	372	351
2	334	312
3	160	136
4	285	305
5	271	289
6	464	430
7	327	310
8	642	557
9	213	215
10	493	446

Case 12.3   Accounting Course Exemptions*

One of the problems encountered in teaching accounting in a business program is the issue of what to do with students who have taken one or more accounting courses in high school. Should these students be exempted from the introductory accounting course usually offered in the first or second year of the business program? Some professors have argued that high school courses do not have the breadth or depth of university courses, and that as a consequence, high school accounting students should not be exempted. Others think that the high school accounting course coverage is sufficiently close to that of the university course, and that forcing students with high school accounting to "retake" the course is a waste of time and resources.

To examine the problem, students who were enrolled in the third year of the Bachelor of Commerce program at St. Mary's University were sampled. In the third year of this program, two introductory accounting half-credits are required: ACT 241 and ACT 242. Of the 638 students enrolled in ACT 241 in the fall semester, 374 were selected because of the similarities in their educational backgrounds (excluding high school accounting). Student files were examined for all 374 students, of whom 275 continued on to ACT 242 in the

*Adapted from E. Morass, G. Walsh, and N. M. Young, "Accounting for Performance: An Analysis of the Relationship Between Success in Introductory Accounting in University and Prior Study of Accounting in High School," *Proceedings of the 14th Annual Atlantic Schools of Business Conference* (1984): 13–44.

winter semester. For each student, researchers recorded the grade in ACT 241 and the grade in ACT 242 (if it was taken), as well as the number of high school accounting courses (either 0, 1, or 2). The results are stored in the file C12-03 on the data disk, using the following format.

Columns 1, 2, and 3: grades in ACT 241 (4 = A, 3 = B, 2 = C, 1 = D, 0 = F) for students who have taken 0, 1, and 2 high school accounting courses, respectively.

Columns 4, 5, 6: grades in ACT 242 (4 = A, 3 = B, 2 = C, 1 = D, 0 = F) for students who have taken 0, 1, and 2 high school accounting courses, respectively.

The researchers would like to know for each of ACT 241 and ACT 242 whether students with one high school accounting course outperform those with no high school accounting and whether students with two high school accounting courses outperform those with no high school accounting. What exemption policy should be adopted?

Appendix 12.A

Excel Instructions

MANIPULATING DATA

To use Excel to test $\mu_1 - \mu_2$, the data must be unstacked. Suppose that the data are stacked in the following way: Column A stores the observations, and column B stores the indexes. If the data are scrambled (not in order), proceed with steps 1, 2, and 3 below. Otherwise, go to step 4.

1 Highlight columns A and B.

2 Click **Data** and **Sort. . . .**

3 Specify column B and **Ascending.** Click **OK.**

The data will now be unscrambled—all the observations from the first sample will occupy the top rows of column A, and the observations from the second sample will occupy the bottom rows of column A. To unstack, issue the following commands. (The following commands assume that there are only two samples.)

4 Highlight the rows of column A that were taken from sample 2.

5 Click **Edit** and **Cut.**

6 Make cell C1 active.

7 Click **Edit** and **Paste.**

8 Delete column B.

Columns A and B will now store the unstacked data.

If the data are unstacked and you wish to stack them in column A proceed as follows.

1 Highlight the cells in column B.

2 Click **Edit** and **Cut.**

3 Make the first empty cell in column A active. Click **Edit** and **Paste.**

4 Type the codes in column B.

Columns A and B will now contain the stacked data—all the observations in column A and the codes identifying the sample in column B.

Appendix 12.B

Minitab Instructions

MANIPULATING DATA

Minitab can draw inferences about $\mu_1 - \mu_2$ when the data are stacked or unstacked. The commands for either format are described in the Minitab Output for Example 12.1. However, other techniques require one format only. In this appendix, we discuss how to change the format of the data.

To stack the unstacked data:

1 Click **Manip, Stack/Unstack,** and **Stack Columns. . . .**
2 Specify the variables to be stacked **(Stack the following columns:).**
3 Specify the variable where the data are to be stored **(Store the stacked data in:).**
4 Specify where the codes are to be stored **(Store subscripts in:).**

To unstack stacked data:

1 Click **Manip, Stack/Unstack,** and **Unstack One Column. . . .**
2 Specify the variable to be unstacked **(Unstack the data in:).**
3 Specify the variables where the data are to be stored **(Store the unstacked data in:).**
4 Specify where the codes are stored **(Using subscripts in:).**

DESCRIPTIVE STATISTICS AND GRAPHS FOR STACKED DATA

When the data are stacked, you can unstack the data before instructing Minitab to calculate the descriptive statistics or draw various graphs. Alternatively, you can use the following commands.

1 Click **Stat, Basic Statistics,** and **Display Descriptive Statistics. . . .**
2 Specify the **Variables:** to be described.
3 Use the cursor to click **By variable:** and specify the codes.

To draw histograms and stem and leaf displays, proceed as above.

1 Click **Graph, Character Graphs,** and any one of **Histogram . . . , Box-plot . . . , Dotplot . . . ,** or **Stem-and-Leaf. . . .**
2 Specify the **Variables:** to be described.
3 Use the cursor to click **By variable:** and specify the codes.

Chapter **13**

Statistical Inference:

A Review of

Chapters 11 and 12

13.1 Introduction

13.2 Guide to Identifying the Correct Technique: Chapters 11 and 12

13.1 INTRODUCTION

This chapter is more than just a review of the previous two chapters. It is a critical part of your development as a statistician. When you solved problems at the end of each section in the preceding chapters (You *have* been solving problems at the end of each section covered, haven't you?), you probably had no great difficulty identifying the correct technique to use. You used the statistical technique introduced in that section. While those exercises provided practice in setting up hypotheses, calculating test statistics or interval estimates, or producing computer output and interpreting the results, you did not address a fundamental question faced by statisticians: which technique to use. If you still do not appreciate the dimension of this problem, consider the following, which lists all the inferential methods covered thus far.

t-test and estimator of μ

χ^2-test and estimator of σ^2

z-test and estimator of p

t-test and estimator of $\mu_1 - \mu_2$ (equal variances formulas)

t-test and estimator of $\mu_1 - \mu_2$ (unequal variances formulas)

t-test and estimator of μ_D

F-test and estimator of σ_1^2/σ_2^2

z-test (cases 1 and 2) and estimator of $p_1 - p_2$

Counting tests and interval estimators of a parameter as two different techniques, a total of 17 statistical procedures have been presented thus far, and there is much left to be done. Faced with statistical problems that require the use of some of these techniques (such as in real-world applications or on a midterm test), most students need some assistance in identifying the appropriate method. In the next section we discuss in greater detail how to make this decision. At the end of this chapter you will have the opportunity to practice your decision skills; we've provided exercises and cases that cumulatively require all of the inferential techniques introduced in Chapters 11 and 12. Solving these problems will require you to do what statisticians must do. You must analyze the problem, identify the technique or techniques, calculate the test statistics or interval estimates, or employ statistical software and a computer to yield the required statistics and interpret the results.

13.2 GUIDE TO IDENTIFYING THE CORRECT TECHNIQUE: CHAPTERS 11 AND 12

As you've probably already discovered, the two most important factors in determining the correct statistical technique are the problem objective and the data type. In some situations, once these have been recognized, the technique automatically follows. In other cases, however, several additional factors must be identified before you can proceed. For example, when the problem objective is to compare two populations and the data are quantitative, three other significant issues must be addressed: the descriptive measurement (central location or variability), whether the samples are independently drawn, and if so, whether the unknown population variances are equal.

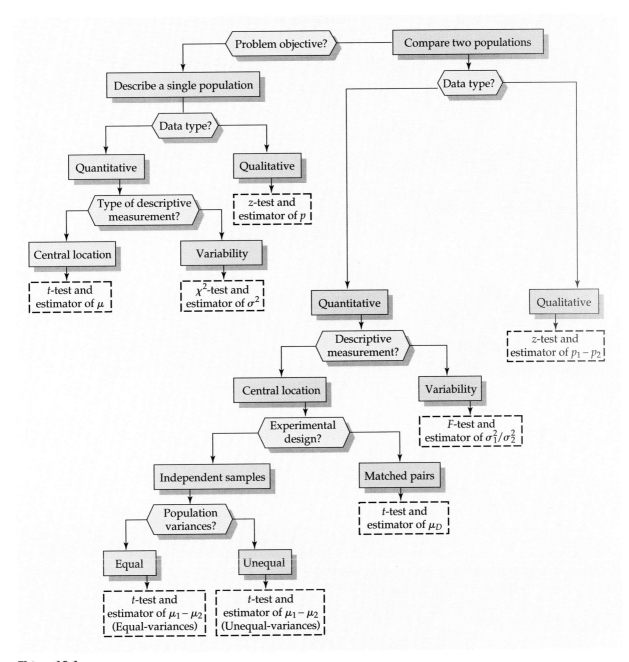

Figure 13.1

Flowchart of techniques: Chapters 11 and 12

The flowchart in Figure 13.1 represents the logical process that leads to the identification of the appropriate method. We've also included a more detailed guide to the statistical techniques that lists the formulas of the test statistics, the interval estimators, and required conditions (see Table 13.1).

Table 13.1   Summary of Statistical Inference: Chapters 11 and 12

Problem objective: Describe a single population.

Data type: Quantitative

Descriptive measurement: Central location

Parameter: μ

Test statistic: $t = \dfrac{\bar{x} - \mu}{s/\sqrt{n}}$

Interval estimator: $\bar{x} \pm t_{\alpha/2} \dfrac{s}{\sqrt{n}}$

Required condition: Population is normal.

Descriptive measurement: Variability

Parameter: σ^2

Test statistic: $\chi^2 = \dfrac{(n-1)s^2}{\sigma^2}$

Interval estimator: $\text{LCL} = \dfrac{(n-1)s^2}{\chi^2_{\alpha/2}}$ $\text{UCL} = \dfrac{(n-1)s^2}{\chi^2_{1-\alpha/2}}$

Required condition: Population is normal.

Data type: Qualitative

Parameter: p

Test statistic: $z = \dfrac{\hat{p} - p}{\sqrt{p(1-p)/n}}$

Interval estimator: $\hat{p} \pm z_{\alpha/2} \sqrt{\dfrac{\hat{p}(1-\hat{p})}{n}}$

Required condition: $np \geq 5$ and $n(1-p) \geq 5$ (for test)

$\qquad\qquad\qquad\quad n\hat{p} \geq 5$ and $n(1-\hat{p}) \geq 5$ (for estimate)

Problem objective: Compare two populations.

Data type: Quantitative

Descriptive measurement: Central location

Experimental design: Independent samples

Population variances: $\sigma_1^2 = \sigma_2^2$

Parameter: $\mu_1 - \mu_2$

Test statistic: $t = \dfrac{(\bar{x}_1 - \bar{x}_2) - (\mu_1 - \mu_2)}{\sqrt{s_p^2\left(\dfrac{1}{n_1} + \dfrac{1}{n_2}\right)}}$

Interval estimator: $(\bar{x} - \bar{x}_2) \pm t_{\alpha/2} \sqrt{s_p^2\left(\dfrac{1}{n_1} + \dfrac{1}{n_2}\right)}$

Required condition: Populations are normal.

Population variances: $\sigma_1^2 \neq \sigma_2^2$

Parameter: $\mu_1 - \mu_2$

Test statistic: $t = \dfrac{(\bar{x}_1 - \bar{x}_2) - (\mu_1 - \mu_2)}{\sqrt{\dfrac{s_1^2}{n_1} + \dfrac{s_2^2}{n_2}}}$

Interval estimator: $(\bar{x}_1 - \bar{x}_2) \pm t_{\alpha/2} \sqrt{\dfrac{s_1^2}{n_1} + \dfrac{s_2^2}{n_2}}$

Required condition: Populations are normal.

Experimental design: Matched pairs

Parameter: μ_D

Test statistic: $t = \dfrac{\bar{x}_D - \mu_D}{s_D/\sqrt{n_D}}$

Interval estimator: $\bar{x}_D \pm t_{\alpha/2}\dfrac{s_D}{\sqrt{n_D}}$

Required condition: Differences are normal.

Descriptive measurement: Variability

Parameter: σ_1^2/σ_2^2

Test statistic: $F = s_1^2/s_2^2$

Interval estimator: $\text{LCL} = \left(\dfrac{s_1^2}{s_2^2}\right)\dfrac{1}{F_{\alpha/2,\nu_1,\nu_2}}$

$\text{UCL} = \left(\dfrac{s_1^2}{s_2^2}\right)F_{\alpha/2,\nu_2,\nu_1}$

Required condition: Populations are normal.

Data type: Qualitative

Parameter: $p_1 - p_2$

Test statistic:

Case 1: $H_0: (p_1 - p_2) = 0$

$$z = \dfrac{(\hat{p}_1 - \hat{p}_2)}{\sqrt{\hat{p}(1 - \hat{p})\left(\dfrac{1}{n_1} + \dfrac{1}{n_2}\right)}}$$

Case 2: $H_0: (p_1 - p_2) = D \quad (D \neq 0)$

$$z = \dfrac{(\hat{p}_1 - \hat{p}_2) - (p_1 - p_2)}{\sqrt{\dfrac{\hat{p}_1(1 - \hat{p}_1)}{n_1} + \dfrac{\hat{p}_2(1 - \hat{p}_2)}{n_2}}}$$

Interval estimator: $(\hat{p}_1 - \hat{p}_2) \pm z_{\alpha/2}\sqrt{\dfrac{\hat{p}_1(1 - \hat{p}_1)}{n_1} + \dfrac{\hat{p}_2(1 - \hat{p}_2)}{n_2}}$

Required conditions: $n_1\hat{p}_1$, $n_1(1 - \hat{p}_1)$, $n_2\hat{p}_2$, and $n_2(1 - \hat{p}_2) \geq 5$

▼ EXAMPLE 13.1

Is the antilock braking system (ABS), now available as a standard feature on many cars, really effective? The ABS works by automatically pumping brakes extremely quickly on slippery surfaces so the brakes do not lock, avoiding an uncontrollable skid. If ABS is effective, we would expect that cars equipped with ABS would have fewer accidents, and the costs of repairs for the accidents that do occur would be smaller. To investigate the effectiveness of ABS, the Highway Loss Data Institute gathered data on a random sample of 500 1991 General Motors cars that did not have ABS and 500 1992 GM cars that were equipped with ABS. For each year, the institute recorded whether the car was involved in an accident and, if so, the cost of making repairs. Forty-two 1991 cars and 38 1992 cars were involved in accidents. The cost of repairs were stored in columns 1 (1991 cars) and 2 (1992 cars) in file XM13-01. Using frequency of accidents and cost of repairs as measures of effectiveness, can we conclude that ABS is effective? If so, estimate how much better are cars equipped with ABS compared to cars without ABS.

Solution This is a typical illustration of the work that statisticians perform and the way they do it. The Highway Loss Data Institute wants to determine whether ABS is effective. Even before the data are gathered, the statistician must decide which techniques to apply. To do so requires the statistician to frame the questions so that tests of hypotheses or interval estimators can be specified. Simply asking whether ABS works is not sufficiently well defined. Because there are several ways to measure the effectiveness of ABS, the following questions were posed.

a Is there sufficient evidence to infer that the accident rate is lower in ABS-equipped cars than in cars without ABS? (If ABS is effective, we would expect a lower accident rate in ABS-equipped cars.)

b Is there sufficient evidence to infer that the cost of repairing accident damage in ABS-equipped cars is less than that of cars without ABS? (When accidents do occur we expect the severity of accidents to be lower in ABS-equipped cars, assuming that ABS is effective.)

c Assuming that we discover that ABS-equipped cars suffer less damage in accidents, estimate how much cheaper they are to repair on average than cars without ABS.

These questions allow the statistician to select the appropriate techniques. We will proceed through the flowchart to illustrate how this is done. When the data are gathered and stored in the computer, the statistician executes the commands to output the results. The results are interpreted to answer the central question: Is ABS effective?

Because we wish to emphasize technique recognition and interpretation of the results, we will answer the questions using only Excel and Minitab.

QUESTION (a)

IDENTIFY

The first factor to identify in the flowchart is the problem objective. In Question (a), the problem objective is to compare two populations: 1991 model results and 1992 model results. Next, we're asked to determine the data type. The data are qualitative. (The values of the random variable are "accident occurred" and "no accident occurred.") The flowchart (Figure 13.1) identifies the technique as the z-test and estimator of $p_1 - p_2$. To answer this question, we conduct the z-test of $p_1 - p_2$. Let

p_1 = proportion of 1991 model cars without ABS involved in an accident

p_2 = proportion of 1992 model cars with ABS involved in an accident

Because we want to know whether ABS brakes are effective in reducing accidents, we specify the alternative hypothesis as

$$H_1: (p_1 - p_2) > 0$$

The null hypothesis automatically becomes

$$H_0: (p_1 - p_2) = 0,$$

which indicates the use of the case 1 test statistic.

Test statistic: $z = \dfrac{(\hat{p}_1 - \hat{p}_2)}{\sqrt{\hat{p}(1 - \hat{p})\left(\dfrac{1}{n_1} + \dfrac{1}{n_2}\right)}}$

**Excel Output for
Example 13.1(a)**

The sample proportion of accidents for 1991 cars is

$$\hat{p}_1 = \frac{42}{500} = .084$$

The accident rate for 1992 cars is

$$\hat{p}_2 = \frac{38}{500} = .076$$

The sample proportions and sample sizes were input into the **z-Test of the Difference Between Two Proportions (Case 1)** worksheet of the **Inference from Summary Statistics (Workbook)** with the resulting printout shown below.

	A	B	C	D	E
1	z-Test of the Difference Between Two Proportions (Case 1)				
2					
3	Sample 1				
4	Sample proportion	0.084			
5	Sample size	500			
6					
7	Sample 2				
8	Sample proportion	0.076			
9	Sample size	500			
10					
11	z Stat	0.47			
12	Two-tail p-value	0.6410			

The one-tail p-value is .6410/2 = .3205.

**Minitab Output for
Example 13.1(a)**

Test and Confidence Interval for Two Proportions

```
Sample       X       N   Sample p
1           42     500   0.084000
2           38     500   0.076000

Estimate for p(1) - p(2):   0.008
95% CI for p(1) - p(2):   (-0.0256256, 0.0416256)
Test for p(1) - p(2) = 0 (vs > 0):   z = 0.47   P-Value = 0.321
```

There is not enough evidence to infer that ABS-equipped cars have fewer accidents than cars without ABS.

QUESTION (b)

IDENTIFY

The problem objective is to compare two populations. The data are quantitative because we measure the cost of repairs, which is a real number. The flowchart now asks about the descriptive measurement, which we identify as central location. (We want to know whether one population mean is larger than another.) The next question asks us to identify the experimental design. Because there is no relationship between the two samples, we know that the samples are independent. The next factor we need to specify is whether the population variances are equal. To make this decision we apply the F-test of σ_1^2/σ_2^2. The result, $F = 1.256$ indicates that there is not enough evidence to infer that the variances differ. Putting all the factors together we identify the equal-variances t-test of $\mu_1 - \mu_2$.

μ_1 = mean cost of repairing 1991 model cars without ABS damaged in accidents

μ_2 = mean cost of repairing 1992 model cars with ABS damaged in accidents

Because we want to know whether μ_1 is greater than μ_2 we specify the alternative hypothesis as

$$H_1: (\mu_1 - \mu_2) > 0$$

and the null hypothesis is

$$H_0: (\mu_1 - \mu_2) = 0$$

The test statistic is

SOLVE

$$z = \frac{(\bar{x}_1 - \bar{x}_2) - (\mu_1 - \mu_2)}{\sqrt{s_p^2\left(\dfrac{1}{n_1} + \dfrac{1}{n_2}\right)}}$$

Excel Output for the F-Test of σ_1^2/σ_2^2

	A	B	C
1	F-Test Two-Sample for Variances		
2			
3		cost1991	cost1992
4	Mean	2035.9	1707.6
5	Variance	512898	408221
6	Observations	42	38
7	df	41	37
8	F	1.26	
9	P(F<=f) one-tail	0.2421	
10	F Critical one-tail	1.713	

Excel Output for the Equal-Variances t-Test of $\mu_1 - \mu_2$

	A	B	C
1	t-Test: Two-Sample Assuming Equal Variances		
2			
3		cost1991	cost1992
4	Mean	2035.9	1707.6
5	Variance	512898	408221
6	Observations	42	38
7	Pooled Variance	463244	
8	Hypothesized Mean Difference	0	
9	df	78	
10	t Stat	2.15	
11	P(T<=t) one-tail	0.0171	
12	t Critical one-tail	1.665	
13	P(T<=t) two-tail	0.0343	
14	t Critical two-tail	1.991	

Minitab Output for the F-Test of σ_1^2/σ_2^2

Homogeneity of Variance

```
F-Test (normal distribution)


Test Statistic: 1.256
P-Value        : 0.484
```

Minitab Output for the Equal-Variances t-Test of $\mu_1 - \mu_2$

Two Sample T-Test and Confidence Interval

```
Two sample T for Cost1991 vs Cost1992

            N      Mean    StDev   SE Mean
Cost1991   42      2036      716      111
Cost1992   38      1708      639      104

95% CI for mu Cost1991 - mu Cost1992: ( 25,   632)
T-Test mu Cost1991 = mu Cost1992 (vs >): T = 2.15  P = 0.017  DF = 78
Both use Pooled StDev = 681
```

Conclusion: The t-test of $\mu_1 - \mu_2$ indicates that the cost of repairs is less for ABS-equipped cars than cars without ABS.

QUESTION (c)

IDENTIFY

To measure how much better off a car owner is with ABS, we determine the 95% confidence interval estimate of the difference between the two mean costs. The interval estimator is

$$(\bar{x}_1 - \bar{x}_2) \pm t_{\alpha/2}\sqrt{s_p^2\left(\frac{1}{n} + \frac{1}{n_2}\right)}$$

The Minitab output for part (b) exhibits the interval estimate. We used the Excel worksheet **t-Estimate of 2 Means (Eq-Var)** with the result shown next.

**Excel Output for
the *t*-Estimate of
2 Means (Eq-Var)**

	A	B	C	D	E
1	t-Estimate of the Difference Between Two Means (Equal-Variances)				
2					
3	**Sample 1**				
4	Sample mean	2035.9			
5	Sample standard deviation	716.2			
6	Sample size	42			
7					
8	**Sample 2**				
9	Sample mean	1707.6			
10	Sample standard deviation	638.9			
11	Sample size	38			
12					
13	Confidence level	0.95			
14					
15	Pooled Variance estimate	463243			
16					
17	Lower confidence limit	24.95			
18	Upper confidence limit	631.69			

Conclusion: The 95% confidence interval estimate of $\mu_1 - \mu_2$ is

$$LCL = 25 \text{ and } UCL = 632.$$

INTERPRETING ALL OF THE STATISTICAL RESULTS

The data indicate that the accident rate in ABS-equipped cars may be no lower than that of cars without ABS. However, the cost of repairing the accident damage is less for the former group. We estimate that the average repair bill for an ABS-equipped car is between $25 and $632 less than a car not equipped with ABS. Can we now say conclusively that ABS is effective? Unfortunately, this is only one interpretation of the results.

Because the experiment uses observational data, we must be careful about the meaning of the tests. It is possible that poor drivers will buy ABS-equipped cars and better drivers will not. If so, the results would tend to indicate that ABS is either ineffective, as in part (a), or not as effective as it appears as in parts (b) and (c). Experimental data may have been able to overcome this problem. Experimental data could be gathered by randomly selecting people to drive either ABS-equipped cars or cars without ABS for 1 year and recording the data. In this way the drivers in both groups should be quite similar, making the comparison more definitive.

Another problem in interpreting the results to proclaim that ABS is effective is that it is possible that driving ABS-equipped cars changes the behavior of the drivers. They may drive more dangerously in the mistaken belief that ABS will save them. It may be possible to remedy this problem by not telling the drivers which type of car they have been assigned to drive. However, most drivers will likely know from the feel and performance of the brakes. Another experiment can be undertaken to determine whether driving behavior is indeed altered by ABS. (See Exercise 13.23.)

Yet another difficulty arose because the experiment was performed using different model years. The ABS-equipped cars were all 1992 models, and the cars without ABS were all 1991 models. The results we observed may be due to differences either in the repair costs or the performance of the models between 1991 and 1992 cars. Undoubtedly, it would have been better to compare 1992 cars with and without ABS. (Note that we are merely reporting the way the Highway Loss Data Institute actually conducted the study; we are not endorsing their methods. We may have gathered the data in a different way.)

Besides teaching you how to identify the appropriate statistical technique, this example also highlights the issues that must be considered when interpreting the results.

EXERCISES

The purpose of the exercises that follow is twofold. First, the exercises provide you with practice in the critical skill of identifying the correct technique. Second, they allow you to improve your ability to determine the statistics needed to answer the question and interpret the results. We believe that the first skill is underdeveloped, because up to now you have had little practice. The exercises you've worked on have appeared at the end of sections and chapters where the correct techniques have just been presented. Determining the correct technique should not have been difficult. Because the exercises that follow were selected from the types that you have already encountered at the ends of Chapters 11 and 12, they will help you develop your technique-identification skills.

We suggest that you take a two-step approach to the exercises. The first step is to identify the parameter, set up the hypotheses, and specify the test statistic (for a test of hypothesis), or specify the interval estimator. To make the problems realistic, we provide only the raw data in the same way that most statisticians encounter it. We do not provide summarized statistics (e.g., mean, variance, or frequency distribution) as we've done in previous exercises. (By doing so, we would be indirectly telling you which technique to use.) As a consequence, students who do not have access to a computer and statistical software cannot calculate the value of the test statistic or interval estimator. Such students should nevertheless perform the first step—identify the technique that should be used and specify the hypotheses or estimator. Students with a computer and statistical software should perform both steps.

Remember, knowing how to conduct tests of hypothesis and interval estimation does not in itself make you a statistician. You must be capable of identifying the correct procedure to use in addition to the capability of interpreting the results.

You will note that in the exercises that require a test of hypothesis we do not specify a significance level. We have left this decision to you. The computer will usually print the p-value. (If it doesn't, you can calculate it from the value of the test statistic.) After analyzing the issues raised in the exercise, use your own judgment to determine whether the p-value is small enough to reject the null hypothesis.

13.1 Shopping malls are more than places where we buy things. We go to malls to watch movies; buy breakfast, lunch, and dinner; exercise; meet friends; and, in general, to socialize. Thus, the financial well-being of malls concerns us all. In a study of malls, a random sample of 100 mall shoppers was asked a variety of questions concerning their shopping behavior. This survey was first conducted 3 years ago with another sample of 100 shoppers. The results of the following questions asked this year and 3 years ago are stored in file XR13-01.

a How many hours do you spend in malls during an average week?

b How many stores do you visit during an average week?

c How many trips to malls do you make in an average month?

The results are stored in columns 1, 2, and 3. Column 4 contains a code indicating the year the survey was done (1 = this year; 2 = 3 years ago). Can we conclude that the owners of stores in the mall should be worried about changing shopping behaviors?

13.2 It is often useful for retailers to determine why their potential customers chose to visit their store. Possible reasons include advertising, advice from a friend, or previous experience. To determine the effect of full-page advertisements in the local newspaper, the owner of an electronic-equipment store asked 200 randomly selected people who visited the store whether they had seen the ad. He also determined whether the customers had bought anything, and if so, how much they spent. There were 113 respondents who saw the ad. Of these, 49 made a purchase. Of the 87 respondents who did not see the ad, 21 made a purchase. The amounts spent were stored in file XR13-02 in the following way.

Column 1 = amount spent at store among purchasers who saw the advertisement
Column 2 = amount spent at store among purchasers who did not see the advertisement

a Can the owner conclude that customers who see the ad are more likely to make a purchase than those who do not see the ad?

b Can the owner conclude that customers who see the ad spend more than those who do not see the ad (among those who make a purchase)?

c Estimate with 95% confidence the proportion of all customers who see the ad who then make a purchase.

d Estimate with 95% confidence the mean amount spent by customers who see the ad and make a purchase.

13.3 In an attempt to reduce the number of person-hours lost as a result of industrial accidents, a large multiplant corporation installed new safety equipment in all departments and all plants. To test the effectiveness of the equipment, a random sample of 25 plants was drawn. The number of person-hours lost in the month prior to installation of the safety equipment and in the month after installation were recorded. The results are stored in columns 1 (plant number), 2 (number of person-hours lost before installation), and 3 (number of person-hours lost after installation) of file XR13-03. Can we conclude that the equipment is effective?

13.4   The United States Postal Service (USPS) offers a service called Priority Mail that promises 2-day delivery. It costs about $3.00 to send a letter by Priority Mail within the United States. A spokesperson for the USPS claims that it has a success rate of more than 95% in delivering letters within the 2-day deadline. Station WARY in Miami (as reported in their newscast of December 24, 1992) decided to conduct an experiment to determine whether the $3.00 cost is worthwhile. Letters were sent by Priority Mail and by ordinary mail (at that time, a 29¢ stamp) from New York City to Cleveland, Ohio. Letters that arrived within the deadline were recorded with a 2; letters that were late were recorded with a 1. The data are stored in file XR13-04. (Column 1 stores the results of Priority Mail; column 2 stores the data for ordinary mail.)

   a   Do these data provide sufficient evidence to support the spokesperson's claim?
   b   Do these data provide sufficient evidence to infer that Priority Mail delivers letters within 2 days more frequently than does ordinary mail?

13.5   The electric company is considering an incentive plan to encourage its customers to pay their bills promptly. The plan is to discount the bills 1% if the customer pays within 5 days, as opposed to the usual 25 days. As an experiment, 50 customers are offered the discount on their September bill. The amount of time each takes to pay his or her bill is recorded. The amount of time a random sample of 50 customers not offered the discount takes to pay their bills is also recorded. Both sets of data are stored in file XR13-05. (Column 1 represents the first set of customers; column 2 represents the second set.) Do these data allow us to infer that the discount plan works?

13.6   Traffic experts are always looking for ways to control automobile speeds. Some communities have experimented with "traffic-calming" techniques. These include speed bumps and various obstructions that force cars to slow down or to drive around them. Critics point out that the techniques are counterproductive because they cause drivers to speed on other parts of these roads. In an analysis of the effectiveness of speed bumps a statistician organized a study over a 1-mile stretch of city road that had 10 stop signs. He then took a random sample of 100 cars and recorded their average speed (the speed limit was 30 mph.) and the number of proper stops at the stop signs. He repeated the observations for another sample of 100 cars after speed bumps were placed on the road. These data were stored in columns 1 and 2 (average speeds before and after the speed bumps) and columns 3 and 4 (number of proper stops before and after the speed bumps) in file XR13-06. Do

these data allow the statistician to conclude that the speed bumps are effective?

13.7   The proliferation of self-serve pumps at gas stations has generally resulted in poorer automobile maintenance. One feature of poor maintenance is low tire pressure, which results in shorter tire life and higher gasoline consumption. To examine this problem, an automotive expert took a random sample of cars across the country and measured the tire pressure. The difference between the recommended tire pressure and the observed tire pressure was recorded and stored in file XR13-07. [A recording of 8 means that that tire is 8 pounds per square inch (psi) less than the amount recommended by the tire manufacturer.] Suppose that for each psi below recommendation, tire life decreases by 100 miles and gasoline consumption increases by 0.1 gallons per mile. Estimate with 95% confidence the effect on tire life and gasoline consumption.

13.8   Many North American cities encourage the use of bicycles as a way to reduce pollution and traffic congestion. So many people now regularly use the bicycle to get to work and for exercise that some jurisdictions have enacted bicycle helmet laws, which specify that all bicycle riders must wear helmets to protect against head injuries. Critics of these laws complain that it is a violation of individual freedom and that helmet laws tend to discourage bicycle usage. To examine this issue, a researcher randomly sampled 50 bicycle users and asked each to record the number of miles he or she rode weekly. Several weeks later the helmet law was enacted. The number of miles each of the 50 bicycle riders rode weekly was recorded for the week after the law was passed. These data are stored in columns 1 (rider number), 2 (miles ridden before law), and 3 (miles ridden after law) in file XR13-08. Can we infer from these data that the law discourages bicycle usage?

13.9   Cardizem CD is a prescription drug that is used to treat high blood pressure and angina. One common side effect of such drugs is the occurrence of headaches and dizziness. To determine whether Cardizem CD has the same side effects the drug's manufacturer, Marion Merrell Dow Inc., undertook a study. A random sample of 908 high blood pressure sufferers was recruited; 607 took Cardizem CD and 301 took a placebo. Each reported whether they suffered from headaches and/or dizziness (2 = yes; 1 = no). The responses were recorded in columns 1 (Cardizem users) and 2 (placebo) in file XR13-09. Can the pharmaceutical company scientist infer that Cardizem CD users are more likely to suffer headache and dizziness side effects than nonusers?

13.10   A fast-food franchiser is considering building a restaurant at a downtown location. Based on a financial analysis, a site is acceptable only if the number of pedestrians passing the location during the workday averages more than 200 per hour. To help decide whether to build on the site, a statistician observes the number of pedestrians that pass the site each hour over a 40-hour workweek. These data are stored in file XR13-10. Should the franchiser build on this site?

13.11 There has been much debate about the effects of second-hand smoke. A recent U.S. government study (*Globe and Mail,* 20 June, 1991) observed samples of households with children living with at least one smoker and households with children living with no smokers. Each child's health was measured. The data from this study are stored in file XR13-11 in the following way.

Column 1: children living with at least one smoker; 2 = child is in fair to poor health; 1 = child is healthy
Column 2: children living with no smokers; 2 = child is in fair to poor health; 1 = child is healthy

a Can we infer that children in smoke-free households are less likely to be in fair to poor health than children in households with smokers?

b Assuming that there are 10 million children living in homes with at least one smoker, estimate with 95% confidence the number of children who are in fair to poor health living in a home with at least one smoker.

13.12 An actual U.S. government-funded study surveyed people to determine how they eat spaghetti. The study recorded whether respondents consume spaghetti by winding it on a fork or cutting the noodles into small pieces. Not included in the study, evidently, are those who slurp the noodles directly from their plates without using dining implements at all. The responses are stored in file XR13-12 (2 = wind the strands; 1 = cut the strands). Can we conclude that more Americans eat their spaghetti by winding on a fork than by cutting the strands?

13.13 Most automobile repair shops now charge according to a schedule that is claimed to be based on average times. This means that instead of determining the actual time to make a repair and multiplying this value by their hourly rate, repair shops determine the cost from a schedule that is calculated from average times. A critic of this policy is examining how closely this schedule adheres to the actual time to complete a job. He randomly selects five jobs. According to the schedule these jobs should take 45 minutes, 60 minutes, 80 minutes, 100 minutes, and 125 minutes, respectively. The critic then takes a random sample of repair shops and records the actual times for each of 20 cars for each job. The times are stored in columns 1 through 5, respectively, in file XR13-13. For each job, can we infer that the time specified by the schedule is greater than the actual time needed to complete the repair?

13.14 Most people who quit smoking cigarettes do so for health reasons. However, some quitters find that they gain weight after quitting, and scientists estimate that the health risks of smoking two packs of cigarettes per day and of carrying 65 extra pounds of weight are about equivalent. In an attempt to learn more about the effects of quitting smoking, the U.S. Centers for Disease Control conducted a study (reported in *Time,* 25 March, 1991). A sample of 1,885 smokers was taken. During the course of the experiment, some of the smokers quit their habit. The amount of weight gained by all of the subjects was recorded and stored in file XR13-14. The file is organized in the following way.

Column 1: weight gain of smokers who quit in the study
Column 2: weight gain of smokers who continued smoking in the study

Do these data allow us to conclude that quitting smoking results in weight gains?

13.15 Golf-equipment manufacturers compete against one another by offering a bewildering array of new products and innovations. Oversized clubs, square grooves, and graphite shafts are examples of such innovations. The effect of these new products on the average golfer is, however, much in doubt. One product, a perimeter-weighted iron, was designed to increase the consistency of distance and accuracy. The most important aspect of irons is consistency, which means that ideally there should be no variation in distance from shot to shot. To examine the relative merits of two brands of perimeter-weighted irons, an average golfer used the 7-iron, hitting 100 shots using each of two brands. The distance in yards was recorded and stored in columns 1 (Brand A) and 2 (Brand B) in file XR13-15. Can the golfer conclude that Brand B is superior to Brand A?

13.16 No one disputes the value of physical exercise. Regular exercise has been proven to prolong life and decrease the incidence of certain diseases. But what about exercise of the mind? Are there ways in which one can exercise one's intellect without resorting to the mental equivalent of boring calisthenics? The answer may lie in the game of bridge. In a study undertaken at Scripps College in California, researchers tested 50 bridge players and 50 nonplayers aged between 55 and 91 (as reported in the *ACBL Bulletin,* July 1992). The test measured working memory, reasoning, reaction time, and vocabulary. The results of the tests are stored in file XR13-16 (column 1 = working memory; column 2 = reasoning; column 3 = reaction time; column 4 = vocabulary; column 5 = code, where 1 = bridge player and 2 = nonplayer). Bearing in mind that the game of bridge places demands on memory and reasoning, but requires only 15 words and can be played quite slowly, can we infer that playing bridge improves one's memory and reasoning but does not affect one's reaction time and vocabulary?

13.17 Advertising is critical in the residential real estate industry. Agents are always seeking ways to increase sales through improved advertising methods. A particular agent believes that he can increase the number of inquiries (and thus the probability of making a sale) by describing the house for sale without indicating its asking price. To support his belief, he conducted an experiment in which 100 houses for sale were advertised in two ways—with and without the asking price. The number of inquiries for each house was recorded as well as whether the customer saw the ad with or without the asking price shown. The number of inquiries for each house is stored in file XR13-17 in the following way.

Column 1: house number (1 to 100)
Column 2: number of inquiries from customers who saw ad with the asking price shown
Column 3: number of inquiries from customers who saw ad without the asking price shown

Do these data allow the real estate agent to infer that ads with no price shown are more effective in generating interest in a house?

13.18 In most offices, the copier is the most frequently used and abused machine. Consequently, buyers of copiers need to know how frequently service will be required before a decision to buy is made. Prior to making a major purchase, the general manager of a large company asks 150 recent buyers of this copier if they required maintenance in the first year and, if so, how frequently. The number of service calls is stored in file XR13-18. If the president plans to buy 1,000 copiers, estimate with 95% confidence the number of service calls he expects in the first year.

13.19 Throughout the day a number of exercise shows appear on television. These usually feature attractive and fit men and women performing various exercises who urge viewers to duplicate the activity at home. Some viewers are exercisers. However, some people like to watch the shows without exercising (which explains why they use attractive people as demonstrators). Various companies sponsor the shows and there are commercial breaks. One sponsor wanted to determine whether there are differences between exercisers and nonexercisers in terms of how well they remember the sponsor's name. A random sample of viewers was selected and called after the exercise show was over. Each was asked to report whether they exercised or only watched. They were also asked to name the sponsor's brand name (2 = yes, they could; 1 = no, they couldn't). These results are stored in columns 1 (exercisers) and 2 (watchers), respectively, in file XR13-19. Can the sponsor conclude that exercisers are less likely to remember the sponsor's brand name than those who do not exercise?

13.20 A professor of statistics hands back his graded midterms in class by calling out the name of each student and personally handing the exam over to its owner. At the end of the process he notes that there are several exams left over, the result of students missing that class. He forms the theory that the absence is caused by a poor performance by those students on the test. If the theory is correct, the leftover papers will have a lower mark than those papers handed back. He records the mark (out of 100) for the leftover papers in column 1 and the marks of the returned papers in column 2. The data are stored in file XR13-20. Do the data support the professor's theory?

13.21 Periodically, coupons that can be used to purchase products at discount prices appear in newspapers. The goal is to persuade shoppers to take advantage of the coupon to visit the store and buy other products. The manager of a supermarket chain wonders whether the coupons actually work. As part of her analysis, she places 25-cent coupons for bread in the newspaper. Over the next two days, she randomly samples 500 shoppers and determines whether they used the coupon and how much they spent on groceries, not including bread. These data are stored in file XR13-21 (column 1 = amount spent when using the coupon; column 2 = amount spent without coupon). Can the manager conclude that coupon users spend more money on groceries than do non–coupon users?

13.22 According to the latest census, the number of households in a large metropolitan area is 425,000. The home delivery department of the local newspaper reports that there are 104,320 households that receive daily home delivery. To increase home delivery sales, the marketing department launches an expensive advertising campaign. A financial analyst tells the publisher that for the campaign to be successful, home delivery sales must increase to more than 110,000 households. Anxious to see if the campaign is working, the publisher authorizes a telephone survey of 400 households within 1 week of the beginning of the campaign to ask each household head whether or not he or she has the newspaper delivered. The responses are stored in file XR13-22 (2 = yes; 1 = no).

 a Do these data indicate that the campaign will increase home delivery sales?
 b Do these data allow the publisher to conclude that the campaign will be successful?

13.23 Does driving an ABS-equipped car change the behavior of drivers? To help answer this question the following experiment was undertaken. A random sample of 200 drivers who currently operate cars without ABS was selected. Each person was given an identical car to drive for 1 year. Half the sample were given cars that had ABS, and the other half were given cars with standard-equipment brakes. Computers on the cars recorded the average speed (in miles per hour) during the year. These data are stored in file XR13-23. Column 1 contains the average speeds of the drivers who were given ABS-equipped cars, and column 2 stores the speeds of the drivers who were given cars with standard brakes. Can we infer that operating an ABS-equipped car changes the behavior of the driver?

CASE 13.1   **Stock Market Returns After the Death of Key Executives***

How does the death of a key executive affect a company? Two researchers addressed this question. In particular, they wanted to know how the stock market would react to the deaths of the chief executive officer and/or the chairman of the board of companies whose stock trades over the counter. A sample of 21 companies whose CEO or chairman died during a 17-year period from 1966 to 1982 was selected. For each company, the weekly stock returns were recorded for each of 6 weeks starting with the week in which the key executive died. A market model (see Section 17.6) was used to determine expected returns, and the difference between the actual and expected returns was calculated. These are called *abnormal returns.* The abnormal returns for each company for the 6 weeks are shown in the accompanying table. ($t = 0$ represents the week of the death; $t = 1$ represents the first week after the death, etc.) The data are also stored in file C13-01 (columns 1 to 6).

Under stable conditions, the average abnormal return should equal zero. During the weeks before the deaths the abnormal returns would indicate stable conditions. However, after the deaths they would exhibit the effects of bad news—the abnormal returns are expected to be negative.

For each of the 6 weeks of abnormal returns, determine whether the stock market reflects the bad news with negative expected returns. How could an investor in possession of the information generated from your statistical analysis make money?

Abnormal Returns (in %)

Company	0	1	2	3	4	5
1	2.50%	−11.63%	5.59%	−4.53%	−2.09%	−2.65%
2	7.97	−4.37	1.63	−0.98	4.14	2.31
3	−7.17	−1.01	−1.51	−4.97	−1.48	0.27
4	−0.45	−0.32	6.91	−2.19	3.12	−1.62
5	−0.02	−1.52	−2.36	−5.16	−8.31	1.45
6	−5.04	−1.26	0.03	3.05	−4.10	4.01
7	−5.32	−4.14	−4.45	−5.97	11.54	3.67
8	−0.59	−0.11	−4.93	2.12	−1.59	1.89
9	−0.22	5.71	−3.63	−1.01	0.65	−4.54
10	−1.90	−0.83	8.51	−1.80	0.73	−1.75
11	−0.73	−3.10	−3.31	6.05	−3.89	−0.27
12	−2.48	3.42	4.54	4.33	−0.44	3.66
13	−0.62	−0.66	0.08	3.57	6.79	1.91
14	−1.33	−0.85	0.66	−4.72	−2.49	0.84
15	3.08	−0.68	−2.71	9.19	0.14	0.98
16	−3.19	−10.91	8.11	3.99	4.27	−0.68
17	−5.53	−2.13	−0.49	0.55	1.49	−3.80
18	−7.46	−0.66	0.14	1.35	1.44	−2.35
19	−7.51	1.19	−2.67	−0.67	−0.13	−1.85
20	−5.33	−2.38	−7.56	1.10	1.21	0.26
21	−0.75	1.77	−1.96	5.99	−1.64	−2.32

*Adapted from D. L. Warnell and W. N. Davidson, III, "The Death of Key Executives in Small Firms: Effects on Investor Wealth," *Journal of Small Business Management 27*(2) (April 1989): 10–16.

CASE 13.2　　Quebec Separation? *Oui ou Non?*

Since the 1960s there has been an ongoing campaign among Quebecers to separate from Canada and form an independent nation. Should Quebec separate, the ramifications for the rest of Canada, American states that border Quebec, the North American Free Trade Agreement, and numerous multinational corporations would be enormous. In the 1993 federal election, the pro-sovereigntist Bloc Quebecois won 54 of Quebec's 75 seats in the House of Commons. In 1994, the separatist Parti Quebecois formed the provincial government in Quebec and promised to hold a referendum on separation. Like most political issues, polling plays an important role in trying to influence voters and to predict the outcome of the referendum vote. Shortly after the 1993 federal election, *The Financial Post Magazine,* in cooperation with several polling companies, conducted a survey of Quebecers.

A total of 641 adult Quebecers were interviewed. They were asked the following question. (Francophones were asked the questions in French.) The pollsters recorded the answer and also the language (English or French) in which the respondent answered.

> **1** If a referendum were held today on Quebec's sovereignty with the following question, "Do you want Quebec to separate from Canada and become an independent country?" would you vote yes or no?
>
> 2　Yes
>
> 1　No

The responses are stored in columns 1 (planned referendum vote) and 2 (language: French = 1; English = 2) in file C13-02.

Infer from the data:

a If the referendum were held on the day of the survey, would Quebec vote to remain in Canada?

b Estimate with 95% confidence the difference between French- and English-speaking Quebecers in their support for separation.

CASE 13.3　　Host Selling and Announcer Commercials*

A study was undertaken to compare the effects of host selling commercials and announcer commercials on children. Announcer commercials are straightforward commercials in which the announcer describes to viewers why they should buy a particular product. Host selling commercials feature a children's show personality or television character who extols the virtues of the product. In 1975, the National Association of Broadcasters prohibited the use of show characters to advertise products during the same program in which the characters appear. However, this prohibition was overturned in 1982 by a judge's decree.

The objective of the study was to determine whether the two types of advertisements have different effects on children watching them. Specifically, the researchers wanted to know whether children watching host selling commercials would remember more details about the commercial and be more likely to buy the advertised product than children watch-

*Adapted from J. H. Miller, "An Emprical Evaluation of the Host Selling Commercial and the Announcer Commercial When Used on Children," *Developments in Marketing Science* 8 (1985): 276–78.

ing announcer commercials. The experiment consisted of two groups of children ranging in age from 6 to 10. One group of 121 children watched a program in which two host selling commercials appeared. The commercials tried to sell Canary Crunch, a breakfast cereal. A second group of 121 children watched the same program but was exposed to two announcer commercials for the same product. Immediately after the show, the children were given a questionnaire that tested their memory concerning the commercials they had watched.

Each child was rated (on a scale of 10) on his or her ability to remember details of the commercial. In addition, each child was offered a free box of cereal. The children were shown four different brands of cereal—Froot Loops (FL), Boo Berries (BE), Kangaroo Hops (KH), and Canary Crunch (CC; the advertised cereal)—and asked to pick the one they wanted. The results are stored in file C13-03 in the following way.

Column 1: recall test score for the children who watched the host commercial

Column 2: recall test score for the children who watched the announcer commercial

Column 3: children's choice of cereal where 1 = Froot Loops, 2 = Boo Berries, 3 = Kangaroo Hops, and 4 = Canary Crunch for children who watched the host commercial

Column 4: children's choice of cereal for children who watched the announcer commercial

Are there differences in memory test scores and children's choice of advertised cereal between the two groups of children?

Chapter 14

Analysis of
Variance

14.1 Introduction

14.2 Single-Factor (One-Way) Analysis of Variance: Independent Samples

14.3 Analysis of Variance Models

14.4 Single-Factor Analysis of Variance: Randomized Blocks

14.5 Two-Factor Analysis of Variance: Independent Samples

14.6 Operations Management Application: Finding and Reducing Variation

14.7 Multiple Comparisons (Optional)

14.8 Bartlett's Test (Optional)

14.9 Summary

14.1 INTRODUCTION

The technique presented in this chapter allows statisticians to compare two or more populations of quantitative data. The technique is called the **analysis of variance** and it is an extremely powerful and commonly used procedure. The analysis of variance allows statisticians to determine whether differences exist among population means. Ironically, the procedure works by analyzing the sample variance, hence the name. We will examine several different forms of the technique. Examples of problems where the statistical methods introduced in this chapter would be applied follow.

Example 1   A supermarket chain store executive needs to determine whether or not the sales of a new product are affected by the aisle in which the product is stored. If there are 10 aisles in the store, the experiment would consist of locating the product in a different aisle in each of 10 weeks and recording the daily sales. The executive would conduct an analysis of variance, which tests to determine if differences exist among mean daily sales. The parameters are $\mu_1, \mu_2, \ldots, \mu_{10}$ (mean daily sales for each aisle).

Example 2   A farm products manufacturer wants to determine if the yields of a crop differ when the soil is treated with various fertilizers. Similar plots of land are planted with the same type of seed but are fertilized differently. At the end of the growing season, the crop yields from the different plots are recorded. The analysis of variance procedure is applied, and the mean yields for each fertilizer are computed. Historically, this type of experiment was one of the first to employ the analysis of variance, and the terminology of the original experiment is still used. No matter what the experiment, the test is designed to determine whether there are significant differences among the **treatment means.**

Example 3   Golf equipment manufacturers are constantly researching new designs and materials with the goal of producing golf clubs that are capable of hitting longer distances. When new products are produced, they are tested in several ways. In one experiment, average golfers hit golf balls with the new clubs and with their older clubs. Suppose that 100 golfers are asked to use their own drivers and two newly designed ones. The distances that the balls travel are recorded. The analysis of variance technique is applied to determine whether there are differences among the mean distances for each of the three drivers. If differences exist, further research is conducted to determine which designs and/or materials are best.

In each of the examples above we are able to classify the populations using only one criterion or **factor.** Each population is called a factor **level.** In Example 1, the factor that defines the populations is the aisle where the product is stored, and there are 10 levels. The type of fertilizer is the factor in Example 2. In Example 3, the factor is the design of the golf club, and there are three levels of this factor.

To illustrate a problem where there are two factors that describe the populations, suppose that in Example 1 we could place the product on one of three shelves (bottom, middle, or top) in each aisle. In this case, there are two factors. Factor 1 is the aisle, which has 10 levels, and factor 2 is the shelf, which has 3 levels. In all there are 30 populations.

In Section 14.2, we introduce the **single-factor analysis of variance,** which is also called the **one-way analysis of variance.** In Section 14.3, we briefly describe some of the other analysis of variance techniques that are available to the statistician. In Sections 14.4 and 14.5, we introduce two of these.

14.2 SINGLE-FACTOR (ONE-WAY) ANALYSIS OF VARIANCE: INDEPENDENT SAMPLES

The analysis of variance is a procedure that tests to determine whether differences exist among two or more population means. The name of the technique derives from the way in which the calculations are performed. That is, the technique analyzes the variance of the data to determine whether we can infer that the population means differ. As in Chapter 12, the experimental design is a determinant in identifying the proper method to use. In this section, we describe the procedure to apply when the samples are independently drawn. In Section 14.4, we introduce the single-factor model when the experiment is designed so that the samples are matched.

Figure 14.1 depicts the sampling process for drawing independent samples. The mean and variance of population j ($j = 1, 2, \ldots , k$) are labeled μ_j and σ_j^2, respectively. Both parameters are unknown. For each population, we draw independent random samples. For each sample, we can compute the mean $\bar{x}_j$ and the variance s_j^2.

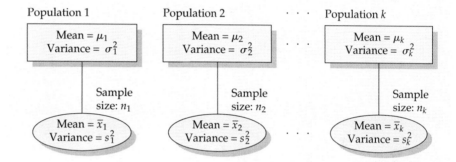

Figure 14.1

Sampling scheme for independent samples

STATISTICS IN THE WORKPLACE

Marketing Application

In Chapter 12 we described test marketing, which is often used to assess consumer reaction to changes in one or more elements of the marketing mix. Marketing managers will conduct experiments to determine whether differences in sales exist among different prices for the product, different package designs, or different advertising approaches. Some of these experiments are carried out in small communities where it is easy to vary particular elements that the manager wishes to investigate.

▼ **EXAMPLE 14.1**

An apple juice manufacturer has developed a new product—a liquid concentrate that, when mixed with water, produces 1 liter of apple juice. The product has several attractive features. First, it is more convenient than canned apple juice, which is the way apple juice is currently sold. Second, because the apple juice that is sold in cans is actually made from concentrate, the quality of the new product is at least as high as canned apple juice. Third, the cost of the new product is slightly lower than canned apple juice. The marketing manager has to decide how to market the new product. She can create advertising that emphasizes convenience, quality, or price. To facilitate a decision, she conducts an experiment. In three different small cities, she launches the product with advertising stressing the convenience of the liquid concentrate (e.g., easy to carry from store to home and takes up less room in the freezer) in one city. In the second city, the advertisements emphasize the quality of the product ("average" shoppers are depicted discussing how good the apple juice tastes). Advertising that highlighted the relatively low cost of the liquid concentrate is used in the third city. The number of packages sold weekly is recorded for the 20 weeks following the beginning of the campaign. These data are stored in file XM14-01 and are listed in the accompanying table. The marketing manager wants to know if differences in sales exist among the three advertising strategies. (We will assume that except for the type of advertising, the three cities are identical.)

Weekly Sales in the Three Cities

City 1 (Convenience)	City 2 (Quality)	City 3 (Price)
529	804	672
658	630	531
793	774	443
514	717	596
663	679	602
719	604	502
711	620	659
606	697	689
461	706	675
529	615	512
498	492	691
663	719	733
604	787	698
495	699	776
485	572	561
557	523	572
353	584	469
557	634	581
542	580	679
614	624	532

Solution   You should confirm that the data are quantitative and that the problem objective is to compare three populations (sales of the liquid concentrate in the three cities).

Following the pattern that we have used repeatedly in this book, we introduce the statistical technique by specifying the null and alternative hypotheses. The null hypothesis will state that there are no differences among the population means. Hence,

$$H_0: \mu_1 = \mu_2 = \mu_3$$

The analysis of variance determines whether there is enough statistical evidence to show that the null hypothesis is false. Consequently, the alternative hypothesis will always specify the following.

H_1: At least two means differ.

The next step is to determine the test statistic, which is somewhat more involved than the test statistics we have introduced thus far. The process of performing the analysis of variance is facilitated by the notation in Table 14.1.

Table 14.1 **Notation for the Single-Factor Analysis of Variance: Independent Samples**

Independent Samples From k Populations (Treatments)

Treatment			
1	**2**	**j**	**k**
x_{11}	x_{12}	x_{1j}	x_{1k}
x_{21}	x_{22}	x_{2j}	x_{2k}
.	.	. . .	.
.	.	. . .	.
.	.	. . .	.
$x_{n_1 1}$	$x_{n_2 2}$	$x_{n_j j}$	$x_{n_k k}$

For Each Treatment (Column)

Sample Size	n_1	n_2	n_j	n_k
Sample Mean	$\bar{x}_1$	$\bar{x}_2$	$\bar{x}_j$	$\bar{x}_k$

x_{ij} = ith observation of the jth sample

n_j = number of observations in the sample taken from the jth population

$\bar{x}_j$ = mean of the jth sample = $\dfrac{\sum_{i=1}^{nj} x_{ij}}{n_j}$

$\bar{\bar{x}}$ = grand mean of all the observations = $\dfrac{\sum_{j=1}^{k} \sum_{i=1}^{nj} x_{ij}}{n}$

where $n = n_1 + n_2 + \cdots + n_k$ and k is the number of populations. Notice that we allow the sample sizes to be different.

The variable x is called the **response variable,** and its values are called **responses.** The unit that we measure is called an **experimental unit.** In this example, the response variable is weekly sales, and the experimental units are the weeks in the three cities when we record sales figures. The sales figures are the responses. As you can see, there is only one factor, advertising approach, that defines the populations, and there are three levels of this factor. They are advertising that emphasizes convenience, advertising that emphasizes quality, and advertising that emphasizes price.

Test Statistic The test statistic is computed in accordance with the following rationale. If the null hypothesis is true, the population means would all be equal. We would then expect that the sample means would be close to one another. If the alternative hypothesis is true, however, there would be large differences between some of the sample means. The statistic that measures the proximity of the sample means to each other is called the **between-treatments variation,** denoted SST, which stands for **sum of squares for treatments.**

> **Sum of Squares for Treatments**
>
> $$\text{SST} = \sum_{j=1}^{k} n_j (\bar{x}_j - \bar{\bar{x}})^2$$

As you can deduce from this formula, if the sample means are close to each other, all of the sample means would be close to the grand mean, and as a result, SST would be small. In fact, SST achieves its smallest value (zero) when all the sample means are equal. That is, if

$$\bar{x}_1 = \bar{x}_2 = \cdots = \bar{x}_k$$

then

$$SST = 0$$

It follows that a small value of SST supports the null hypothesis.

In this example, we compute the sample means and the grand mean as

$$\bar{x}_1 = 577.55$$
$$\bar{x}_2 = 653.00$$
$$\bar{x}_3 = 608.65$$
$$\bar{\bar{x}} = 613.07$$

Then

$$SST = \sum_{j=1}^{k} n_j(\bar{x}_j - \bar{\bar{x}})^2$$
$$= 20(577.55 - 613.07)^2 + 20(653.00 - 613.07)^2 + 20(608.65 - 613.07)^2$$
$$= 57,512.23$$

If large differences exist among the sample means, at least some sample means differ considerably from the grand mean, producing a large value of SST. It is then reasonable to reject the null hypothesis in favor of the alternative hypothesis. The key question to be answered in this test (as in all other statistical tests) is "How large does the statistic have to be for us to justify rejecting the null hypothesis?" In our example, SST = 57,512.23. Is this value large enough to indicate that the population means differ? To answer this question, we need to know how much variation exists in the weekly sales, which is measured by the **within-treatments variation,** which is denoted by SSE **(sum of squares for error).** The within-treatments variation provides a measure of the amount of variation we can expect from the random variable we've observed.

Sum of Squares for Error

$$SSE = \sum_{j=1}^{k} \sum_{i=1}^{nj} (x_{ij} - \bar{x}_j)^2$$

To understand this concept, examine Tables 14.2 and 14.3 and Figures 14.2 and 14.3. Table 14.2 and Figure 14.2 describe an example in which, because the variation within each sample is quite small, SST is judged to be a large number. That is, this random variable displays very little variation. Consequently, the differences among the sample means appear to be caused by real differences among the population means. Contrast this example with the one depicted in Table 14.3. The value of SST in Table 14.3 is equal to that in Table 14.2. However, the variation within the samples is large, which tells us that this random variable features a great deal of variation. By comparison, SST is small, and we would conclude that the differences among the sample means do not allow us to infer that the population means differ.

Table 14.2   Relatively Large Variation Between Samples

	Treatment	
1	**2**	**3**
10	15	20
10	16	20
11	14	20
10	16	20
9	14	20
$\bar{x}_1 = 10$	$\bar{x}_2 = 15$	$\bar{x}_3 = 20$

Table 14.3   Relatively Small Variation Between Samples

	Treatment	
1	**2**	**3**
1	19	5
12	31	33
20	4	20
10	9	12
7	12	30
$\bar{x}_1 = 10$	$\bar{x}_2 = 15$	$\bar{x}_3 = 20$

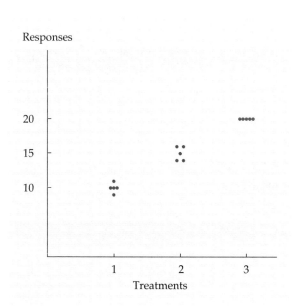

Figure 14.2

Relatively large variation between samples

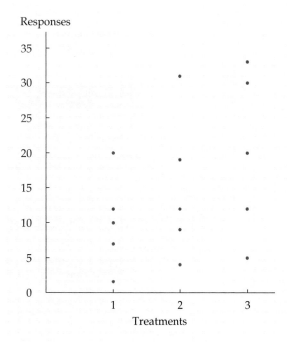

Figure 14.3

Relatively small variation between samples

When SSE is partially expanded, we get

$$SSE = \sum_{i=1}^{n_1}(x_{i1} - \bar{x}_1)^2 + \sum_{i=1}^{n_2}(x_{i2} - \bar{x}_2)^2 + \cdots + \sum_{i=1}^{n_k}(x_{ik} - \bar{x}_k)^2$$

If you examine each of the k components of SSE, you'll see that each is a measure of the variability of that sample. If we divide each component by $n_j - 1$, we compute the sample variances. We can express this by rewriting SSE as

$$SSE = (n_1 - 1)s_1^2 + (n_2 - 1)s_2^2 + \cdots + (n_k - 1)s_k^2 = \sum_{j=1}^{k}(n_j - 1)s_j^2$$

where s_j^2 is the sample variance of sample j. SSE is thus the combined or *pooled* variation of the k samples. This is an extension of a calculation we made in Section 12.2, where we tested and estimated the difference between two means using the pooled estimate of the common population variance (denoted s_p^2). One of the required conditions for that statistical technique is that the population variances are equal. That same condition is now necessary for us to use SSE. That is, we require that

$$\sigma_1^2 = \sigma_2^2 = \cdots = \sigma_k^2$$

Returning to our example, we calculate the sample variances as follows.

$$s_1^2 = 10{,}774.44$$
$$s_2^2 = 7{,}238.61$$
$$s_3^2 = 8{,}669.47$$

Thus,

$$\begin{aligned}
SSE &= (n_1 - 1)s_1^2 + (n_2 - 1)s_2^2 + (n_3 - 1)s_3^2 \\
&= 19(10{,}774.44) + 19(7{,}238.61) + 19(8{,}669.47) \\
&= 506{,}967.88
\end{aligned}$$

The next step is to compute quantities called the **mean squares.** The **mean square for treatments** is computed by dividing SST by the number of treatments minus 1.

Mean Square for Treatments

$$MST = \frac{SST}{k - 1}$$

The **mean square for error** is determined by dividing SSE by the total sample size (labeled n) minus the number of treatments.

Mean Square for Error

$$MSE = \frac{SSE}{n - k}$$

Finally, the test statistic is defined as the ratio of the two mean squares.

Test Statistic

$$F = \frac{\text{MST}}{\text{MSE}}$$

Sampling Distribution of the Test Statistic

The test statistic is F-distributed with $k - 1$ and $n - k$ degrees of freedom provided that the response variable is normally distributed. In Section 12.5, we introduced the F distribution and used it to test and estimate the ratio of two population variances. [If you did not cover Section 12.5 (or if you did, but need a review) turn to pages 426 to 428 for an introduction to the F distribution.] The test statistic in that application was the ratio of two sample variances s_1^2 and s_2^2.

If you examine the definitions of SST and SSE, you will see that both measure variation similar to the numerator in the formula used to calculate the sample variance s^2 used throughout this book. When we divide SST by $k - 1$ and SSE by $n - k$ to calculate MST and MSE, respectively, we're actually computing variance estimators. Thus, the ratio $F = \text{MST}/\text{MSE}$ is the ratio of two sample variances. The degrees of freedom for this application are the denominators in the mean squares. That is, $\nu_1 = k - 1$, and $\nu_2 = n - k$. For Example 14.1, the degrees of freedom are

$$\nu_1 = k - 1 = 3 - 1 = 2$$

and

$$\nu_2 = n - k = 60 - 3 = 57$$

In our example, we found

$$\text{MST} = \frac{\text{SST}}{k - 1} = \frac{57,512.23}{2} = 28,756.12$$

$$\text{MSE} = \frac{\text{SSE}}{n - k} = \frac{506,967.88}{57} = 8,894.17$$

$$F = \frac{\text{MST}}{\text{MSE}} = \frac{28,756.12}{8,894.17} = 3.23$$

Rejection Region

The purpose of calculating the F-statistic is to determine whether or not the value of SST is large enough to reject the null hypothesis. As you can see, if SST is large, F will be large. Hence, we reject the null hypothesis only if

$$F > F_{\alpha,k-1,n-k}$$

If we let $\alpha = .05$, the rejection region for Example 14.1 is

$$F > F_{\alpha,k-1,n-k} = F_{.05,2,57} \approx 3.15$$

We found the value of the test statistic to be $F = 3.23$. Thus, there is enough evidence to infer that the mean weekly sales differ among the three cities. The p-value of this test is

$$p\text{-value} = P(F > 3.23)$$

Figure 14.4 depicts the sampling distribution for Example 14.1.

The results of the analysis of variance are usually reported in an **analysis of variance (ANOVA) table.** Table 14.4 shows the general organization of the ANOVA table, while Table 14.5 shows the ANOVA table for Example 14.1.

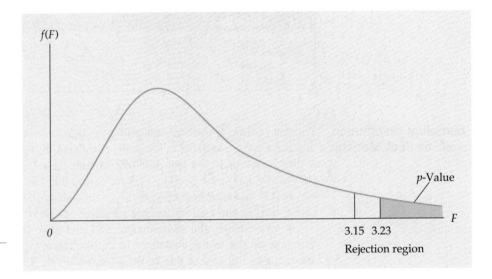

Figure 14.4

Sampling distribution for
Example 14.1

Table 14.4 **ANOVA Table for the Single-Factor Analysis of Variance: Independent Samples**

Source of Variation	Degrees of Freedom	Sums of Squares	Mean Squares	F-Statistic
Treatments	$k - 1$	SST	$MST = \dfrac{SST}{(k - 1)}$	$F = \dfrac{MST}{MSE}$
Error	$n - k$	SSE	$MSE = \dfrac{SSE}{(n - k)}$	
Total	$n - 1$	SS(Total)		

Table 14.5 **ANOVA Table for Example 14.1**

Source of Variation	Degrees of Freedom	Sums of Squares	Mean Squares	F-Statisitc
Treatments	2	57,512.23	28,756.12	$F = 3.23$
Error	57	506,967.88	8,894.17	
Total	59	564,480.11		

The terminology used in the ANOVA table (and, for that matter, in the test itself) is based on the **partitioning of the sum of squares.** Such partitioning is derived from the following equation (whose validity can be demonstrated by using the rules of summation).

$$\sum_{j=1}^{k}\sum_{i=1}^{nj}(x_{ij} - \bar{\bar{x}})^2 = \sum_{j=1}^{k}n_j(\bar{x}_j - \bar{\bar{x}})^2 + \sum_{j=1}^{k}\sum_{i=1}^{nj}(x_{ij} - \bar{x}_j)^2$$

The term on the left represents the total variation of all the data. This expression is denoted **SS(Total).** If we divide SS(Total) by the total sample size minus 1 (that is, by $n - 1$), we would compute the sample variance (assuming that the null hypothesis is true). The first term on the right of the equal sign is SST, and the second term is SSE. As you can see, the total variation SS(Total) is partitioned into two sources of variation. The sum of squares for treatments (SST) is the variation attributed to the differences among the treatment means, while the sum of squares for error (SSE) measures the amount of variation within the samples. The preceding equation can be restated as

$$SS(\text{Total}) = SST + SSE$$

The test is then based on the comparison of SST and SSE.

Recall that in discussing the advantages and disadvantages of the matched pairs experiment in Section 12.4, we pointed out that statisticians frequently seek ways to reduce or explain the variation in a random variable. In the analysis of variance introduced in this section, the sum of squares for treatments explains some of the variation. The sum of squares for error measures the amount of variation that is unexplained. If SST explains a significant portion of total variation, we conclude that the population means differ. In Sections 14.4 and 14.5, we will introduce other experimental designs of the analysis of variance, ones that attempt to reduce or explain even more of the variation.

If you've felt some appreciation for the computer and statistical software sparing you from the need to manually perform the statistical techniques in earlier chapters, your appreciation should now grow, because the computer will allow you to avoid the incredibly time-consuming and boring task of performing the analysis of variance by hand. As usual, we've solved Example 14.1 using Excel and Minitab, whose outputs are shown below.

Excel Output for Example 14.1

	A	B	C	D	E	F
1	Anova: Single Factor					
2						
3	SUMMARY					
4	*Groups*	*Count*	*Sum*	*Average*	*Variance*	
5	Convnce	20	11551	577.55	10775.00	
6	Quality	20	13060	653.00	7238.11	
7	Price	20	12173	608.65	8670.24	
8						
9						
10	ANOVA					
11	*Source of Variation*	*SS*	*df*	*MS*	*F*	*P-value*
12	Between Groups	57512	2	28756	3.23	0.0468
13	Within Groups	506984	57	8894		
14						
15	Total	564496	59			

The value of the test statistic is $F = 3.23$. The p-value is .0468.

COMMANDS

1 Type or import the data into adjacent columns. The data must be unstacked.

2 Click **Tools, Data Analysis . . .** , and **Anova: Single Factor.**

3 Specify the **Input Range:.** Click **Labels in First Row** (if necessary). Click **OK.**

COMMANDS FOR EXAMPLE 14.1

Open file **XM14-01.**

A1:C21

Minitab Output for Example 14.1

One-Way Analysis of Variance

```
Analysis of Variance
Source    DF      SS       MS       F       P
Factor     2    57512    28756    3.23    0.047
Error     57   506984     8894
Total     59   564496
                                  Individual 95% CIs For Mean
                                  Based on Pooled StDev
 Level    N    Mean    StDev    ---+---------+---------+---------+---
Convnce   20  577.55  103.80    (--------*-------)
Quality   20  653.00   85.08                (--------*-------)
Price     20  608.65   93.11        (--------*-------)
                                  ---+---------+---------+---------+---
Pooled StDev =  94.31             550       600       650       700
```

The first half of the printout gives us the ANOVA table, including the *p*-value, which is equal to .047. The second half lists the sample sizes, sample means, and sample standard deviations. It also graphically depicts the interval estimates of the population means, using a technique presented later in this chapter. The graphs provide some information about whether the means differ, and if so, how. You can see that the interval of the second mean is almost completely to the right of the interval representing the first mean. This confirms what the test statistic told us. That is, that there is evidence to infer that the population means differ.

COMMANDS

1 Type or import the data.

If the data are unstacked:

2 Click **Stat, ANOVA,** and **Oneway (unstacked)** . . . .
3 Type the variable names of the treatments. Click **OK.**

If the data are stacked:

2 Click **Stat, ANOVA,** and **Oneway** . . . .
3 Type the variable name of the response variable and the variable name of the factor. Click **OK.**

COMMANDS FOR EXAMPLE 14.1

Open file **XM14-01.**

Convnce, Quality, and **Price** or **C1, C2,** and **C3.**

INTERPRET

The *p*-value is .047, which means there is evidence to infer that mean weekly sales of the apple juice concentrate are different in at least two of the cities. Can we conclude that the effects of the advertising approaches differ? Recall that it is easier to answer this type of question when the data are obtained through a controlled experiment. In this example, the marketing manager randomly assigned an advertising approach to each city. Thus, the data are experimental. As a result, we are quite confident that the approach used to advertise the product will produce different sales figures.

Incidentally, when the data are obtained through a controlled experiment in the single-factor analysis of variance, we call the experimental design the **completely randomized design of the analysis of variance.**

▲

CHECKING THE REQUIRED CONDITIONS

The F-test of the analysis of variance requires that the random variable be normally distributed with equal variances. The normality requirement is easily checked graphically by producing the histograms for each sample. From the Excel histograms of Figures 14.5, 14.6, and 14.7, we can see that there is no reason to believe that the requirement is not satisfied.

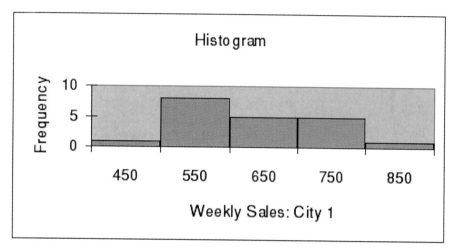

Figure 14.5

Histogram of weekly sales in City 1

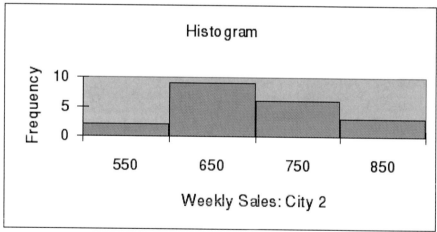

Figure 14.6

Histogram of weekly sales in City 2

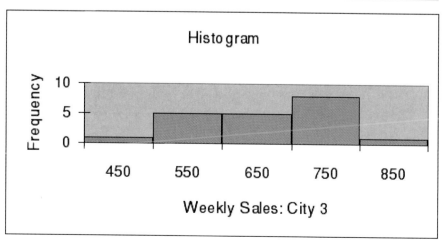

Figure 14.7

Histogram of weekly sales in City 3

The equality of variances is examined by printing the sample standard deviations or variances. Excel output includes the variances, and Minitab calculates the standard deviations. The similarity of sample variances allows us to assume that the population variances are equal. In Section 14.8 we present Bartlett's test, a statistical procedure designed to test for the equality of variances.

VIOLATION OF THE REQUIRED CONDITIONS

If the data are not normally distributed, we can replace the independent samples single-factor model of the analysis of variance with its nonparametric counterpart, which is the Kruskal–Wallis test. (See Section 16.4.) If the population variances are unequal, we can use several methods to correct the problem. However, these corrective measures are beyond the level of this book.

CAN WE USE *t*-TESTS OF THE DIFFERENCE BETWEEN TWO MEANS INSTEAD OF THE ANALYSIS OF VARIANCE?

The analysis of variance tests to determine whether there are differences among two or more population means. The *t*-test of $\mu_1 - \mu_2$ determines whether there is a difference between two population means. The question arises: Can we use *t*-tests instead of the analysis of variance? That is, instead of testing all the means in one test as in the analysis of variance, why not test each pair of means? In Example 14.1, we would test $\mu_1 - \mu_2$, $\mu_1 - \mu_3$, and $\mu_2 - \mu_3$. If we found no evidence of a difference in each test, we would conclude that none of the means differ. If there was evidence of a difference in at least one test, we would conclude that some of the means differ.

There are two reasons why we don't use multiple *t*-tests instead of one *F*-test. First, we would have to perform many more calculations. Even with a computer, this extra work is tedious. Second, and more importantly, conducting multiple tests increases the probability of making Type I errors. To understand why, consider a problem where we want to compare six populations, all of which are identical. If we conduct an analysis of variance where we set the significance level at 5%, there is a 5% chance that we would reject the true null hypothesis. That is, there is a 5% chance that we would conclude that differences exist when in fact they don't.

To replace the *F*-test, we would perform 15 *t*-tests. (This number is derived from the number of combinations of pairs of means to test, which is $C_2^6 = 6 \times \frac{5}{2} = 15$.) Each test would have a 5% probability of erroneously rejecting the null hypothesis. The probability of committing one or more Type I errors is about 54%.*

One remedy for this problem is to decrease the significance level. In this illustration, we would perform the *t*-tests with $\alpha = .05/15$, which is equal to .0033. (We will use this procedure in Section 14.7 when we discuss multiple comparisons.) Unfortunately, this would increase the probability of a Type II error. Regardless of the significance level, performing multiple *t*-tests increases the likelihood of making mistakes. Consequently, when we want to compare more than two populations of quantitative data, we use the analysis of variance.

Now that we've argued that the *t*-tests cannot replace the analysis of variance, we need to argue that the analysis of variance cannot replace the *t*-test.

---

*The probability of committing at least one Type I error is computed from a binomial distribution with $n = 15$ and $p = .05$. Thus

$$P(X \geq 1) = 1 - P(X = 0) = 1 - .463 = .537$$

CAN WE USE THE ANALYSIS OF VARIANCE INSTEAD OF THE t-TEST OF $\mu_1 - \mu_2$?

The analysis of variance is the first of several techniques that allow us to compare two or more populations. Most of the examples and exercises deal with more than two populations. However, it should be noted that like all other techniques whose objective is to compare two or more populations, we can use the analysis of variance to compare only two populations. If that's the case, why do we need techniques to compare exactly two populations? Specifically, why do we need the t-test of $\mu_1 - \mu_2$ when the analysis of variance can be used to test two population means?

To understand why we still need the t-test to make inferences about $\mu_1 - \mu_2$, suppose that we plan to use the analysis of variance to test two population means. The null and alternative hypotheses are

$H_0: \mu_1 = \mu_2$

$H_1:$ At least two means differ.

Of course, the alternative hypothesis specifies that $\mu_1 \neq \mu_2$. However, if we want to determine whether μ_1 is greater than μ_2 (or vice versa), we cannot use the analysis of variance because this technique only allows us to test for a difference. Thus, if we want to test to determine if one population mean exceeds the other, we must use the t-test of $\mu_1 - \mu_2$ (with $\sigma_1^2 = \sigma_2^2$). Moreover, the analysis of variance requires that the population variances are equal. If they are not, we must use the unequal variances test statistic.

RELATIONSHIP BETWEEN THE F-STATISTIC AND THE t-STATISTIC

It is probably useful for you to understand the relationship between the t-statistic and the F-statistic. The test statistic for testing hypotheses about $\mu_1 - \mu_2$ with equal variances is

$$t = \frac{(\bar{x}_1 - \bar{x}_2) - (\mu_1 - \mu_2)}{\sqrt{s_p^2\left(\frac{1}{n_1} + \frac{1}{n_2}\right)}}$$

If we square this quantity, the result is the F-statistic. That is, $F = t^2$. To illustrate this point, we'll redo Example 12.2 using the analysis of variance. If you reexamine Example 12.2, you'll see that the null and alternative hypotheses were

$H_0: \mu_1 = \mu_2$

$H_1: \mu_1 \neq \mu_2$

Because we were able to assume that the population variances were equal, the test statistic was as follows.

$$t = \frac{(\bar{x}_1 - \bar{x}_2) - (\mu_1 - \mu_2)}{\sqrt{s_p^2\left(\frac{1}{n_1} + \frac{1}{n_2}\right)}}$$

The value of the test statistic was $t = .93$ with a p-value of .36. Using the analysis of variance (the Excel output is shown below; Minitab's is similar), we find that the value of the test statistic is $F = .860$, which is $(.93)^2$, and that the p-value is .3584. Thus, we draw exactly the same conclusion using the analysis of variance as we did when we applied the t-test of $\mu_1 - \mu_2$.

Excel Analysis of Variance Output for Example 12.2

	A	B	C	D	E	F
1	Anova: Single Factor					
2						
3	SUMMARY					
4	Groups	Count	Sum	Average	Variance	
5	Method A	25	157.2	6.29	0.848	
6	Method B	25	150.4	6.02	1.303	
7						
8						
9	ANOVA					
10	Source of Variation	SS	df	MS	F	P-value
11	Between Groups	0.925	1	0.925	0.86	0.3584
12	Within Groups	51.62	48	1.075		
13						
14	Total	52.54	49			

DEVELOPING AN UNDERSTANDING
OF STATISTICAL CONCEPTS

Conceptually and mathematically, the F-test of the independent samples single-factor analysis of variance is an extension of the t-test of $\mu_1 - \mu_2$. Moreover, as we discussed above, if we simply want to determine if a difference between two means exists, we can use the analysis of variance. The advantage of using the analysis of variance is that we can partition the total sum of squares, which enables us to measure how much variation is attributable to differences *among* populations and how much variation is attributable to differences *within* populations. As we pointed out in Section 12.4, explaining the variation is an extremely important topic, one that will be seen again in other models of the analysis of variance and in regression analysis (Chapters 17, 18, and 19).

Let's review how we recognize the need to use this model of the analysis of variance.

Factors that Identify the Independent Samples
Single-Factor Analysis of Variance

1 Problem objective: compare two or more populations

2 Data type: quantitative

3 Experimental design: independent samples

EXERCISES

14.1 Provide an example with $k = 4$ where SST $= 0$.

14.2 Provide an example with $k = 4$ where SSE $= 0$.

14.3 A statistician calculated the following statistics. Complete the ANOVA table.

| | Treatment | | | |
Statistic	1	2	3	4
n	16	16	16	16
$\bar{x}$	158.6	149.2	151.3	157.6
s	9.76	10.10	9.84	9.95

14.4 The following statistics were calculated. Determine the ANOVA table.

| | Treatment | | |
Statistic	1	2	3
n	10	14	11
$\bar{x}$	14.7	11.6	19.3
s	5.3	7.1	6.8

14.5 Using the following statistics, test to determine whether differences exist among the population means. Use $\alpha = .01$.

$n_1 = 49$ $n_2 = 45$ $n_3 = 29$
$\bar{x}_1 = 8.36$ $\bar{x}_2 = 7.91$ $\bar{x}_3 = 9.02$
$s_1 = 2.98$ $s_2 = 3.15$ $s_3 = 3.62$

14.6 Test to discover whether differences exist among the population means given the statistics below. Use $\alpha = .05$.

$n_1 = 9$ $n_2 = 13$ $n_3 = 8$ $n_4 = 12$
$\bar{x}_1 = 35.0$ $\bar{x}_2 = 47.3$ $\bar{x}_3 = 39.2$ $\bar{x}_4 = 40.1$
$s_1 = 8.3$ $s_2 = 6.4$ $s_3 = 7.7$ $s_4 = 7.1$

The following exercises require the use of a computer and software. Some answers may be calculated manually. See Appendix A for the sample statistics.

14.7 Random samples of 25 were taken from each of three populations. The data are stored in columns 1 to 3, respectively, in file XR14-07.

a Can we infer at the 5% significance level that the three population means differ?

b What are the required conditions for the test in part (a)?

c Use whatever techniques you deem necessary to check the required conditions.

14.8 The data in file XR14-08 were generated by drawing random samples from five populations. (Columns 1 through 5 are used.)

a Is there sufficient evidence at the 1% significance level to infer that differences exist among the population means?

b What are the required conditions for the technique used in part (a)?

c Are the conditions satisfied?

14.9 Because there are no national or regional standards, it is difficult for university admission committees to compare graduates of different high schools. University administrators have noted that an 80% average at a high school with low standards may be equivalent to a 70% average at another school with higher standards of grading. In an effort to more equitably compare applications, a pilot study was initiated. Random samples of students who were admitted the previous year were drawn. All of the students entered the business program with averages between 74% and 76% from a random sample of four local high schools. Their average grades in the first year at the university were computed and stored in columns 1 through 4 of file XR14-09.

a Can the university admissions officer conclude at the 5% significance level that there are differences in grading standards among the four high schools?

b What are the required conditions for the test conducted in part (a)?

c Does it appear that the required conditions of the test in part (a) are satisfied?

14.10 The friendly folks at the Internal Revenue Service (IRS) are always looking for ways to improve the wording and format of its tax return forms. Three new forms have been developed recently. To determine which, if any, are superior to the current form, 120 individuals were asked to participate in an experiment. Each of the three new forms and the currently used form were filled out by 30 different people. The amount of time (in minutes) taken by each person to complete the task was recorded and stored in columns 1 through 4 (forms 1 through 4, respectively) in file XR14-10.

a What conclusions can be drawn from these data? (Use $\alpha = .05$.)

b What are the required conditions for the test conducted in part (a)?

c Does it appear that the required conditions of the test in part (a) are satisfied?

14.11 A manufacturer of outdoor brass lamps and mailboxes has received numerous complaints about premature corrosion. The manufacturer has identified the cause of the problem as being the low-quality lacquer used to coat the brass. He decides to replace his current lacquer supplier with one of five possible alternatives. In order to judge which is best, he uses each of the five lacquers to coat 25 brass mailboxes and puts all 125 mailboxes outside. He records, for each, the number of days until the first sign of corrosion is observed. The results are stored in columns 1 through 5 of file XR14-11.

a Is there sufficient evidence at the 5% significance level to allow the manufacturer to conclude that differences exist among the five lacquers?

b What are the required conditions for the test conducted in part (a)?

c Does it appear that the required conditions of the test in part (a) are satisfied?

14.12 A study performed by a Columbia University professor (described in *Report on Business,* August 1991) counted the number of times per minute professors from three different departments said "uh" or "ah" during lectures to fill gaps between words. The data derived from observing 100 minutes from each of the three departments are stored in file XR14-12 of the data disk. (Column 1 contains all the data for the English department, column 2 stores the data for the mathematics department, and column 3 stores the data for the political science department.) If we assume that the more frequent use of "uh" and "ah" results in more boring lectures, can we conclude at the 5% significance level that some departments' professors are more boring than others?

14.13 In the introduction to this chapter we mentioned that the first use of the analysis of variance was in the 1920s. It was employed to determine whether different amounts of fertilizer yielded different amounts of crop. Suppose that a scientist at an agricultural college wanted to redo the original experiment using three different types of fertilizer. Accordingly, he applied fertilizer A to 20 one-acre plots of land, fertilizer B to another 20 plots, and fertilizer C to yet another 20 plots of land. At the end of the growing season the crop yields were recorded and stored in columns 1 through 3, respectively, in file XR14-13. Can the scientist infer at the 1% significance level that differences exist among the crop yields?

14.14 In 1994 the chief executive officers of the major tobacco companies testified before a Senate subcommittee. One of the accusations made was that tobacco firms added nicotine to their cigarettes, which made them even more addictive to smokers. Company scientists argued that the amount of nicotine in cigarettes is independent of the size of the tobacco leaf. That is, during poor growing seasons the tobacco leaves would be smaller than in normal or good growing seasons. However, since the amount of nicotine in a leaf is a fixed quantity, smaller leaves would result in cigarettes having more nicotine (since a greater fraction of the leaf would be used to make a cigarette). To examine the issue, a university chemist took random samples of tobacco leaves that were grown in greenhouses where the amount of water was allowed to vary. Three different groups of tobacco leaves were grown. Group 1 leaves were grown with about an average season's rainfall. Group 2 leaves were given about 67% of group 1's water, and group 3 leaves were given 33% of group 1's water. The size of the leaf (in grams) and the amount of nicotine in each leaf were measured and stored in file XR14-14. Column 1 contains the leaf size, column 2 contains the amount of nicotine (in milligrams), and column 3 stores the group number.

a Test to determine whether the leaf sizes differ among the three groups. Use $\alpha = .01$.

b Test to determine whether the amounts of nicotine differ in the three groups. Use $\alpha = .01$.

c What conclusions about the scientists' claim can you draw from these data?

STATISTICS IN THE WORKPLACE

Marketing Application

Recall that in Chapter 12 we introduced the marketing application market segmentation, wherein managers attempt to identify distinct differences among consumers. In Chapter 12 we applied the procedure to two populations of quantitative data. The analysis of variance can be used to differentiate among more than two groups.

14.15 There is a bewildering number of breakfast cereals on the market. Each company produces several different products in the belief that there are distinct markets. For example, there is the market composed primarily of children, the market for diet-conscious adults, and that for health-conscious adults. Each cereal the companies produce has at least one market as its target. However, consumers make their own decisions, which may or may not match the target predicted by the cereal maker. In an attempt to distinguish among consumers a survey of adults between the ages of 25 and 65 was undertaken. Each was asked several questions including age, income, and years of education, as well as which brand of cereal they consumed most frequently. The cereal choices are

1 Sugar Smacks, a children's cereal

2 Special K, a cereal aimed at dieters

3 Fiber One, a cereal that is designed and advertised as healthy

4 Cheerios, a combination of healthy and tasty

The results of the survey are stored in file XR14-15 using the following format.

Column 1: cereal choice

Column 2: age of respondent

Column 3: annual household income

Column 4: years of education

a Determine whether there are differences among the ages of the respondents. Use $\alpha = .05$.

b Determine whether there are differences among the incomes of the respondents. Use $\alpha = .05$.

c Determine whether there are differences among the educational levels of the respondents. Use $\alpha = .05$.

d Summarize your findings in parts (a) through (c) and prepare a report describing the differences among the four groups of cereal consumers.

S TATISTICS IN THE W ORKPLACE

Marketing Application

In Example 14.1 we illustrated test marketing, which allows us to determine whether changing some of the elements of the marketing mix yields different sales. The technique was applied to determine whether there were differences in the advertising approaches. We can also apply the technique to discover the effect of different prices.

14.16 A manufacturer of novelty items is undecided about the price to charge for a new product. The marketing manager knows that it should sell for about $10, but is unsure of whether sales will vary significantly if it is priced at either $9 or $11. To conduct a pricing experiment, she distributes the new product to a sample of 60 stores belonging to a certain chain of variety stores. These 60 stores are all located in similar neighborhoods. The manager randomly selects 20 stores in which to sell the item at $9, 20 stores to sell it at $10, and the remaining 20 stores are to sell it at $11. Sales at the end of the trial period are stored in columns 1 ($9 price), 2 ($10 price), and 3 ($11 price) in file XR14-16. What should the manager conclude? Conduct a test with $\alpha = .05$.

14.3 ANALYSIS OF VARIANCE MODELS

Since we introduced the matched pairs experiment in Section 12.4, the experimental design has been one of the factors that determines which technique we use. As we pointed out in that section, statisticians often design experiments to help extract the information they need to assist them in making decisions. The independent samples single-factor analysis of variance is only one of many different experimental designs of the analysis of variance. For each design, we can describe the behavior of the response variable using a mathematical expression or model. Although we will not exhibit the mathematical expressions (we introduce models in Chapter 17) in this chapter, we think it is useful for you to be aware of the elements that distinguish one model or experimental design from another. In this section, we present some of these elements, and, in so doing, we introduce two of the models that will be presented later in this chapter.

SINGLE-FACTOR AND MULTIFACTOR MODELS

As we pointed out, the group of treatments or populations is called a factor. The model described in Section 14.2 is a single-factor analysis of variance, because it addresses the problem of comparing two or more populations defined on the basis of only one factor. A **multifactor** model is one where there are two or more factors that define the treatments. The technique employed to address Example 14.1 is a single-factor model because the treatments were the three advertising approaches. That is, the factor is the advertising approach, and the three levels are advertising that emphasizes convenience, advertising that emphasizes quality, and advertising that emphasizes price.

Suppose that in another study, the medium used to advertise also varied: We can advertise on television or in newspapers. We would then develop a **two-factor** analysis of variance model where the first factor, advertising approach, has three levels and the second factor, advertising medium, has two levels. We will discuss two-factor models in Section 14.5.

INDEPENDENT SAMPLES AND BLOCKS

In Section 12.4, we introduced statistical techniques where the data were gathered from a matched pairs experiment. As we pointed out in Section 12.4, this type of experimental design reduces the variation within the samples, making it easier to detect differences between the two populations. When the problem objective is to compare more than two populations, the experimental design that is the counterpart of the matched pairs experiment is called the **randomized block design.** The term *block* refers to a matched group of observations from each population. Here is an example.

To determine whether incentive pay plans are effective, a statistician selected three groups of five workers who assemble electronic equipment. Each group will be offered a different incentive plan. The treatments are the incentive plans, the response variable is the number of units produced in one day, and the experimental units are the workers. If we obtain data from independent samples, we may not be able to detect differences among the pay plans because of variation among workers. If there are differences among workers, we need to identify the source of the differences. Suppose, for example, that we know that more experienced workers produce more units no matter what the pay plan. We could improve the experiment if we were to block the workers into five groups of three according to their experience. The three workers with the most experience will represent block 1, the next three will constitute block 2, and so on. As a result, the workers in each block will have approximately the same amount of experience. By designing the experiment in this way, the statistician removes the effect of different amounts of experience on the response variable. By doing so, we improve the chances of detecting real differences among pay incentives.

We can also perform a blocked experiment by using the same subject (person, plant, store) for each treatment. For example, we can determine whether sleeping pills are effective by giving three brands of pills to the same group of people to measure the effects. Such applications are called **repeated measures designs.** Technically, this is a different design than the randomized block. However, the single-factor model is analyzed in the same way for both designs. Hence, we will treat repeated measures designs as randomized block designs.

In Section 14.4, we introduce the technique used to calculate the test statistic for this type of experiment.

FIXED- AND RANDOM-EFFECTS MODELS

If our analysis includes *all* possible levels of a factor, the technique is called a **fixed-effects** model of the analysis of variance. If the levels included in the study represent a random sample of all the levels that exist, the technique is called a **random-effects** model. In Example 14.1, there were only three possible advertising approaches. Consequently, the study is a fixed-effects experiment. However, if there were other advertising approaches besides the three described in the example, and we wanted to know whether there were differences in sales among all the advertising approaches, the application would be a random-effects model. Here's another example.

To determine if there is a difference in the number of units produced by the machines in a large factory, 4 machines out of 50 in the plant are randomly selected for study. The number of units each produces per day for 10 days will be recorded. This experiment is a random-effects experiment because the statistical results will allow us to determine whether there are differences among the 50 machines.

In some models, there are no differences in calculations of the test statistic between fixed and random effects. However, in others, including the two-factor model presented in Section 14.5, the calculations are different.

14.4 SINGLE-FACTOR ANALYSIS OF VARIANCE: RANDOMIZED BLOCKS

The purpose of designing a randomized block experiment is to reduce the within-treatments variation to more easily detect differences among the treatment means. In the independent samples single-factor analysis of variance, we partitioned the total variation into the between-treatments and the within-treatments variation. That is

$$SS(Total) = SST + SSE$$

In the randomized block design of the analysis of variance, we partition the total variation into three sources of variation.

$$SS(Total) = SST + SSB + SSE$$

where **SSB, the sum of squares for blocks,** measures the variation among the blocks. When the variation associated with the blocks is removed, SSE is reduced, making it easier to determine if differences exist among the treatment means.

At this point in our presentation of statistical inference, we will deviate from our usual procedure of solving examples in three ways: manually, using Excel, and using Minitab. The calculations for this model and for the model presented in the next section are so time consuming that solving them by hand is pointless. Consequently, while we will continue to present the concepts by discussing how the statistics are calculated, we will solve the problems only by computer.

To help you understand the formulas, we will use the following notation.

$\bar{x}[T]_j$ = mean of the observations in the jth treatment

$\bar{x}[B]_i$ = mean of the observations in the ith block

b = number of blocks

Table 14.6 summarizes the notation we use in this model.

Table 14.6 **Notation for the Randomized Block Design of the Analysis of Variance**

	Blocked Samples from k Populations (Treatments)				
	Treatment				
Block	**1**	**2**		**k**	**Block Mean**
1	x_{11}	x_{12}	$\cdots$	x_{1k}	$\bar{x}[B]_1$
2	x_{21}	x_{22}	$\cdots$	x_{2k}	$\bar{x}[B]_2$
.	.	.	$\cdots$	.	.
.	.	.	$\cdots$	.	.
.	.	.	$\cdots$	.	.
b	x_{b1}	x_{b2}	$\cdots$	x_{bk}	$\bar{x}[B]_b$
Treatment mean	$\bar{x}[T]_1$	$\bar{x}[T]_2$	$\cdots$	$\bar{x}[T]_k$	

The definitions of SS(Total) and SST in the randomized block design are identical to those in the independent samples design. SSE in the independent samples design is equal to the sum of SSB and SSE in the randomized block design.

Sums of Squares in the Randomized Block Design

$$SS(\text{Total}) = \sum_{j=1}^{k} \sum_{i=1}^{b} (x_{ij} - \bar{\bar{x}})^2$$

$$SST = \sum_{j=1}^{k} b(\bar{x}[T]_j - \bar{\bar{x}})^2$$

$$SSB = \sum_{i=1}^{b} k(\bar{x}[B]_i - \bar{\bar{x}})^2$$

$$SSE = \sum_{j=1}^{k} \sum_{i=1}^{b} (x_{ij} - \bar{x}[T]_j - \bar{x}[B]_i + \bar{\bar{x}})^2$$

The test is conducted by determining the mean squares, which are computed by dividing the sums of squares by their respective degrees of freedom.

Mean Squares for the Randomized Block Design

$$MST = \frac{SST}{k-1}$$

$$MSB = \frac{SSB}{b-1}$$

$$MSE = \frac{SSE}{n-k-b+1}$$

Finally, the test statistic is

> ### Test Statistic for the Randomized Block Design
>
> $$F = \frac{MST}{MSE}$$
>
> which is F-distributed with $k - 1$ and $n - k - b + 1$ degrees of freedom

An interesting, and sometimes useful, by-product of the test of the treatment means is that we can also test to determine if the block means differ. This will allow us to determine whether the experiment *should* have been conducted as a randomized block design. (If there are no differences among the blocks, the randomized block design is *less* likely to detect real differences among the treatment means.) Such a discovery could be useful in future similar experiments. The test of the block means is almost identical to that of the treatment means except the test statistic is

$$F = \frac{MSB}{MSE}$$

which is F-distributed with $b - 1$ and $n - k - b + 1$ degrees of freedom.

Like the independent samples design, the statistics generated in the randomized block design are summarized in an ANOVA table, whose general form is exhibited in Table 14.7.

Table 14.7 **ANOVA Table for the Randomized Block Design**

Source of Variation	Degrees of Freedom	Sums of Squares	Mean Squares	F-Statistics
Treatments	$k - 1$	SST	$MST = \dfrac{SST}{(k-1)}$	$F = \dfrac{MST}{MSE}$
Blocks	$b - 1$	SSB	$MSB = \dfrac{SSB}{(b-1)}$	$F = \dfrac{MSB}{MSE}$
Error	$n - k - b + 1$	SSE	$MSE = \dfrac{SSE}{(n-k-b+1)}$	
Total	$n - 1$	SS(Total)		

▼ EXAMPLE 14.2

The advertising revenues commanded by a radio station depend on the number of listeners it has. The manager of a station that plays mostly hard rock music wants to learn more about its listeners—mostly teenagers and young adults. In particular, he wants to know if the amount of time they spend listening to radio music varies by the day of the week. If the manager discovers that the mean time per day is about the same, he will schedule the most popular music evenly throughout the week. Otherwise, the top hits will be played mostly on the days that attract the greatest audience. An opinion survey company is hired, and it randomly selects 200 teenagers and asks them to record the amount of time spent listening to music on the radio for each day of the previous week. The data are stored in file XM14-02 (column 1 contains the teenagers' identification codes and column 2 through 8 store the listening times for Sunday through Saturday). Some of the data are shown below. What can the manager conclude from these data?

	Time Spent Listening to Radio Music (in minutes)						
Teenager	Sunday	Monday	Tuesday	Wednesday	Thursday	Friday	Saturday
1	65	40	32	48	60	75	110
2	90	85	75	90	78	120	100
3	30	30	20	25	30	60	70
.	.	.	.	.	.	.	.
.	.	.	.	.	.	.	.
.	.	.	.	.	.	.	.
200	80	95	90	80	80	120	120

Solution

IDENTIFY

The problem objective is to compare seven populations, and the data are quantitative. Because the survey company recorded the listening times for each day of the week for each teenager, we identify the experimental design as randomized block. The response variable is the amount of time listening to FM radio, the treatments are the days of the week, and the blocks are the 200 teenagers. The complete test is as follows.

$H_0: \mu_1 = \mu_2 = \cdots = \mu_7$

H_1: At least two means differ.

SOLVE

Test statistic: $F = \dfrac{\text{MST}}{\text{MSE}}$

Excel Output for Example 14.2

	A	B	C	D	E	F
1	ANOVA					
2	Source of Variation	SS	df	MS	F	P-value
3	Rows	209835	199	1054.4	2.63	0.0000
4	Columns	28674	6	4779.0	11.91	0.0000
5	Error	479125	1194	401.3		
6						
7	Total	717633	1399			

The output includes block and treatment statistics (sums, averages, and variances, which are not shown here) and the ANOVA table. The F-statistic to determine if differences exist among the days of the week **(Columns)** is 11.91. Its p-value is 0. The other F-statistic, which is 2.63, indicates that there are differences among the teenagers **(Rows).**

COMMANDS

1 Type or import the data into adjacent columns (unstacked format)
2 Click **Tools, Data Analysis . . . ,** and **Anova: Two-Factor Without Replication.**
3 Specify the **Input Range:.** Click **Labels** if necessary. If you do both, the treatments and blocks must be labeled (as in this example). Click **OK.**

COMMANDS FOR EXAMPLE 14.2

Open file **XM14-02.**

A1:H201

Minitab Output for Example 14.2

Two-way Analysis of Variance

```
Analysis of Variance for Times
Source        DF        SS       MS        F        P
Day            6     28674     4779    11.91    0.000
Teenager     199    209835     1054     2.63    0.000
Error       1194    479125      401
Total       1399    717633
```

The F-statistic for **Day** is 11.91 with a p-value of 0. The F-statistic for the blocks (**Teenager**) is 2.63, also with a p-value of 0.

COMMANDS	COMMANDS FOR EXAMPLE 14.2
1 Type or import the data in stacked format in three columns. One column contains the responses, another contains codes for the treatments, and a third column contains codes for the teenagers.	Open file **XM14-02.** Stack the data in C1, C2, and C3.
2 Click **Stat, ANOVA,** and **Twoway . . . .**	
3 Specify the **Responses:, Row factor:,** and **Column factor:.** Click **OK.**	**Times** or **C1** **Day** or **C2** **Teenager** or **C3**

INTERPRET

There is very strong evidence to infer that on certain days the mean listening time is greater than on other days. An examination of the results reveals that on Fridays and Saturdays, teenagers usually spend more time listening to radio music. The top hits should be played more frequently on those days.

▲

CHECKING THE REQUIRED CONDITIONS

The F-test of the randomized block design of the analysis of variance has the same requirements as the independent samples design. That is, the random variable must be normally distributed, and the population variances must be equal. The histograms (not shown) appear to support the validity of our results; the listening times appear to be normal. The equality of variances requirement also appears to be met.

VIOLATION OF THE REQUIRED CONDITIONS

When the random variable is not normally distributed, we can replace the randomized block model of the analysis of variance with the Friedman test, which is introduced in Section 16.5.

CRITERIA FOR BLOCKING

In Section 12.4, we listed the advantages and disadvantages of performing a matched pairs experiment. The same comments are valid when we discuss performing a blocked experiment. The purpose of blocking is to reduce the variation caused by differences among the experimental units. By grouping the experimental units into homogeneous blocks with respect to the response variable, the statistician increases the chances of detecting actual differences among the treatment means. Hence, we need to find criteria for blocking that significantly affect the response variable. For example, suppose that a statistician wants to determine which of four methods of teaching statistics is best. In an independent samples design he might take four samples of 10 students, teach each sample by a different method, grade the students at the end of the course, and perform an F-test to determine if differences exist. However, it is likely that there are very large differences among students *within* each class that may hide differences *between* classes. To reduce this variation, the statistician needs to identify variables that are linked to a student's grade in statistics. For example, overall ability of the student, completion of mathematics courses, and exposure to other statistics courses are all related to performance in a statistics course.

The experiment could be performed in the following way. The statistician selects four students at random whose average grade before statistics is 95–100. He then randomly assigns the students to one of the four classes. He repeats the process with students whose average is 90–95, 85–90, . . . , and 50–55. The final grades would be used to test for differences among the classes.

Any characteristics that are related to the experimental units are potential blocking criteria. For example, if the experimental units are people, we may block according to age, gender, income, work experience, intelligence, residence (country, county, or city), weight, or height. If the experimental unit is a factory and we're measuring number of units produced hourly, blocking criteria include workforce experience, age of the plant, and quality of suppliers.

DEVELOPING AN UNDERSTANDING OF STATISTICAL CONCEPTS

As we explained above, the randomized block experiment is an extension of the matched pairs experiment discussed in Section 12.4. In the matched pairs experiment, we simply remove the effect of the variation caused by differences among the experimental units. The effect of this removal is seen in the decrease in the value of the standard error (compared to the standard error in the test statistic produced from independent samples) and the increase in the value of the t-statistic. In the randomized block design of the analysis of variance, we actually measure the variation among the blocks by computing SSB. The sum of squares for error is reduced by SSB, making it easier to detect differences among the treatments. Additionally, we can test to determine whether the blocks differ—a procedure we were unable to perform in the matched pairs experiment.

To illustrate, let's return to Examples 12.3 and 12.4, which were experiments to determine whether there was a difference between two tire designs. (In fact, we tested to determine whether the new-design tires outlast the existing-design tires. However, the analysis of variance can only test for differences.) In Example 12.3 (independent samples), there was insufficient evidence to infer a difference between the two types of tires. In Example 12.4 (matched pairs experiment), there was enough evidence to infer a difference. As we pointed out in Section 12.4, matching cars allowed us to more easily discern a difference between the two types of tires. If we repeat Examples 12.3 and 12.4 using the analysis of variance, we come to the same conclusion. The Excel outputs are shown below. (Minitab's printouts are similar.)

Excel Analysis of Variance Output for Example 12.3

	A	B	C	D	E	F
1	ANOVA					
2	Source of Variation	SS	df	MS	F	P-value
3	Between Groups	193.6	1	193.6	0.82	0.3699
4	Within Groups	8934	38	235.1		
5						
6	Total	9127.6	39			

Excel Analysis of Variance Output for Example 12.4

	A	B	C	D	E	F
1	ANOVA					
2	Source of Variation	SS	df	MS	F	P-value
3	Rows	10128.3	19	533.1	20.44	0.0000
4	Columns	207.0	1	207.0	7.94	0.0110
5	Error	495.5	19	26.1		
6						
7	Total	10830.8	39			

In Example 12.3, we partition the total sum of squares [SS(Total) = 9,127.6] into two sources of variation: SST = 193.6 and SSE = 8,934. In Example 12.4, the total sum of squares is SS(Total) = 10,830.8, SST (sum of squares for tires) = 207.0, SSB (sum of squares for cars) = 10,128.3, and SSE = 495.5. As you can see, the total sums of squares for both examples are about the same (9,127.6 and 10,830.8), and the sums of squares for treatments are also approximately equal (193.6 and 207.0). However, where the two calculations differ is in the sums of squares for error. SSE in Example 12.4 is much smaller than SSE in Example 12.3 because the randomized block experiment allows us to measure and remove the effect of the variation among cars. The sum of squares for blocks (sum of squares for cars) is 10,128.3, a statistic that measures how much variation exists among the cars. As a result of removing this variation, SSE is small. Thus, we conclude in Example 12.4 that the tires differ whereas there was not enough evidence in Example 12.3 to draw the same conclusion.

We'll complete this section by listing the factors that we need to recognize to use this model of the analysis of variance.

Factors that Identify the Randomized Block Design of the Analysis of Variance

1 Problem objective: compare two or more populations

2 Data type: quantitative

3 Experimental design: blocked samples

EXERCISES

14.17 The following statistics were generated from a randomized block experiment with $k = 3$ and $b = 7$.

$$\text{SST} = 100 \quad \text{SSB} = 50 \quad \text{SSE} = 25$$

a Test to determine whether the treatment means differ. (Use $\alpha = .05$.)

b Test to determine whether the block means differ. (Use $\alpha = .05$.)

14.18 A randomized block experiment produced the following statistics.

$$k = 5 \quad b = 12 \quad \text{SST} = 1,500 \quad \text{SSB} = 1,000$$
$$\text{SS(Total)} = 3,500$$

a Test to determine whether the treatment means differ. (Use $\alpha = .01$.)

b Test to determine whether the block means differ. (Use $\alpha = .01$.)

14.19 Suppose the following statistics were calculated from data gathered from a randomized block experiment with $k = 4$ and $b = 10$.

$$\text{SS(Total)} = 1,210 \quad \text{SST} = 275 \quad \text{SSB} = 625$$

a Can we conclude from these statistics that the treatment means differ? (Use $\alpha = .01$.)

b Can we conclude from these statistics that the block means differ? (Use $\alpha = .01$.)

14.20 The following data were generated from a randomized block experiment.

a Test at the 5% significance level to determine whether the treatment means differ.

b Test at the 5% significance level to determine whether the block means differ.

	Treatment		
Block	1	2	3
1	7	12	8
2	10	8	9
3	12	16	13
4	9	13	6
5	12	10	11

14.21. A randomized block experiment produced the data below.

a Can we infer at the 5% significance level that the treatment means differ?

b Can we infer at the 5% significance level that the block means differ?

	Treatment			
Block	1	2	3	4
1	6	5	4	4
2	8	5	5	6
3	7	6	5	6

The following exercises require the use of a computer and software. The answers may be calculated manually. See Appendix C for the sample statistics.

14.22 Data from a randomized block experiment (three treatments and 10 blocks) are stored in file XR14-22 in columns 2 to 4. Column 1 stores the block numbers. Can we conclude that the treatment means differ? (Use $\alpha = .01$.)

14.23 The data from a randomized block experiment with $k = 4$ and $b = 25$ are stored in file XR14-23 in columns 2 to 5. Column 1 contains the block codes.

a Can we conclude that the treatment means differ? (Use $\alpha = .05$.)

b Is there enough evidence to infer that the block means differ?

c What are the required conditions for the procedure used in part (a)?

14.24 Repeat Exercise 12.44. Do you draw the same conclusion?

14.25 Refer to Exercise 14.13. Despite failing to show that differences in the three types of fertilizer exist, the scientist continued to believe that there were differences, and that the differences were masked by the variation among the plots of land. Accordingly, he conducted another experiment. In the second experiment he found 20 three-acre plots of land scattered across the county. He divided each into three plots and applied the three types of fertilizer on each of the 1-acre plots. The crop yields were recorded and stored in columns 2 through 4 of file XR14-25. Column 1 contains the plot numbers.

a Can the scientist infer at the 1% significance level that there are differences among the three types of fertilizer?

b What do these test results reveal about the variation among the plots?

14.26 In recent years, lack of confidence in the Postal Service has led many companies to send all of their correspondence by private courier. A large company is in the process of selecting one of three possible couriers to act as its sole delivery method. To help in making the decision, an experiment was performed whereby letters were sent using each of the three couriers at 12 different times of the day to a delivery point across town. The number of minutes required for delivery was recorded and stored in file XR14-26 (columns 2 through 4 list the delivery times of couriers 1, 2, and 3, respectively, and column 1 contains codes representing the time of day).

a Can we conclude at the 5% significance level that there are differences in delivery times among the three couriers?

b Did the statistician choose the correct design? Explain.

14.27 Exercise 14.10 described an experiment that involved comparing the completion times associated with four different income tax forms. Suppose the experiment is redone in the following way. Thirty people are asked to fill out all four forms. The completion times (in minutes) are recorded and stored in columns 2 through 5 of file XR14-27. Column 1 stores the taxpayer number.

a Is there sufficient evidence at the 1% significance level to infer that differences in the completion times exist among the four forms?

b Comment on the suitability of this experimental design in this problem.

14.28 A recruiter for a computer company would like to determine whether there are differences in sales ability among business, arts, and science graduates. She takes a random sample of 20 business graduates who have been working for the company for the past 2 years. Each is then matched with an arts graduate and a science graduate with similar educational and working experience. The commission earned by each (in thousands of dollars) in the last year was recorded and stored in columns 2, 3, and 4, respectively, of file XR14-28 with column 1 containing the block number.

a Is there sufficient evidence at the 5% significance level to allow the recruiter to conclude that there are differences in sales ability among the holders of the three types of degrees?

b Conduct a test to determine whether an independent samples design would have been a better choice.

c What are the required conditions for the test in part (a)?

14.29 Many North Americans suffer from high levels of cholesterol, which can lead to heart attacks. For those with very high levels (over 280), doctors prescribe drugs to reduce cholesterol levels. A pharmaceutical company has recently developed three such drugs. To determine if any differences exist in their benefits, an experiment was organized. The company selected 25 groups of three men, each of whom had levels in excess of 280. In each group, the men were matched according to age and weight. The drugs were administered over a 2-month period, and the reduction in cholesterol was recorded. The data are stored in columns 2 to 4 of file XR14-29. (Column 1 stores the code representing the group number.)

a Do these results allow the company to conclude at the 5% significance level that differences exist among the three new drugs?

b Test to determine whether an independent samples experiment would have been better.

14.5 TWO-FACTOR ANALYSIS OF VARIANCE: INDEPENDENT SAMPLES

In Section 14.2, we addressed problems where the data were generated from single-factor studies. In Example 14.1, the treatments were the three different marketing approaches. Thus, there were three levels of the factor advertising approach. In this section, we address the problem where the experiment features two factors. The general term for such data-gathering procedures is **factorial experiments.** In factorial experiments, we can examine the effect on the random variable of two or more factors, although we address the problem of only two factors in this book. We can use the analysis of variance to determine whether the levels of each factor are different from one another.

We will present the technique for the fixed-effects model. That means we will address problems where all the levels of the factors are included in the experiment.

As was the case with the randomized block design, calculation of the test statistic in this model is quite time consuming. As a result, we will use Excel and Minitab to produce our statistics.

▼ **EXAMPLE 14.3**

Suppose that in Example 14.1, in addition to varying the marketing approach, the manufacturer also decided to advertise in one of the two media that are available: television and newspapers. As a consequence, the experiment was repeated in the following way. Six different small cities were selected. In City 1, the marketing emphasized convenience, and all the advertising was conducted on television. In City 2, marketing also emphasized convenience, but all the advertising was conducted in the daily newspaper. Quality was emphasized in Cities 3 and 4. City 3 learned about the product from television commercials, and City 4 saw newspaper advertising. Price was the marketing emphasis in Cities 5 and 6. City 5 saw television commercials, and City 6 saw newspaper advertisements. In each city, the weekly sales for each of 10 weeks were recorded. These data are listed in the accompanying table and in file XM14-03 (columns 1 to 6 store the 10 observations for each of the cities). What conclusions can be drawn from these results? (As we did in Example 14.1 we assume that except for the advertising the cities are identical.)

Weekly Sales of Apple Juice Concentrate

		Cities			
1	**2**	**3**	**4**	**5**	**6**
491	464	677	689	575	803
712	559	627	650	614	584
558	759	590	704	706	525
447	557	632	652	484	498
479	528	683	576	478	812
624	670	760	836	650	565
546	534	690	628	583	708
444	657	548	798	536	546
582	557	579	497	579	616
672	474	644	841	795	587

Solution

IDENTIFY

Notice that there are six treatments. However, the treatments are defined by two different factors. One factor is the marketing approach, which has three levels (convenience, quality, and price). The second factor is the advertising medium, which has two levels (television and newspaper). If we assume that there are only three advertising approaches and only two advertising media, we identify this experiment as a fixed-effects design. We can proceed to solve this problem in the same way we did in Section 14.2. That is, we test the following hypotheses.

H_0: $\mu_1 = \mu_2 = \mu_3 = \mu_4 = \mu_5 = \mu_6$
H_1: At least two means differ.

SOLVE

Excel Output for Example 14.3

	A	B	C	D	E	F
1	ANOVA					
2	Source of Variation	SS	df	MS	F	P-value
3	Between Groups	113620	5	22724	2.45	0.0452
4	Within Groups	501137	54	9280		
5						
6	Total	614757	59			

Minitab Output for Example 14.3

One-way Analysis of Variance

```
Analysis of Variance
Source      DF        SS        MS        F        P
Factor       5    113620     22724     2.45    0.045
Error       54    501137      9280
Total       59    614757

                                    Individual 95% CIs For Mean
                                    Based on Pooled StDev
Level        N      Mean     StDev   ----------+---------+---------+------
City-1      10    555.50     92.96    (-------*--------)
City-2      10    575.90     92.44      (-------*--------)
City-3      10    643.00     62.33               (--------*---------)
City-4      10    687.10    112.06                  (--------*--------)
City-5      10    600.00     97.61      (--------*-------)
City-6      10    624.40    111.91        (--------*--------)

                                    ----------+---------+---------+------
Pooled StDev =    96.33                    560       630       700
```

INTERPRET

The value of the test statistic is $F = 2.45$ with a p-value of .045. This statistical result raises more questions. Namely, can we conclude that the differences in weekly sales among the cities are caused by differences among the marketing approaches? Or are they caused by differences between television and newspaper advertising? Or, perhaps, are there combinations of marketing approach and advertising medium that result in especially high or low sales? To show how we test for each type of difference, we need to develop some terminology.

Complete Factorial Experiment

A complete factorial experiment is an experiment in which the data for all possible combinations of the levels of the factors are gathered.

That means that in Example 14.3 we measured the sales for all six combinations. This experiment is called a **complete 3 × 2 factorial experiment.** Had we omitted gathering sales figures for (say) emphasizing price and advertising on television, we would not have a complete factorial experiment.

In general, we will refer to one of the factors as factor A (arbitrarily chosen). The number of levels of this factor will be denoted by a. The other factor is called factor B, and its number of levels is denoted by b. This terminology becomes clearer when we present the data from Example 14.3 in another format. Table 14.8 depicts the layout for a **two-way classification,** which is another name for the complete factorial experiment. The number of observations for each combination is called a **replicate.** The number of replicates is denoted by r. In this book, we only address problems in which the number of replicates is the same for each treatment. Such a design is called **balanced.**

Thus, we use a complete factorial experiment where the number of treatments is ab with r replicates per treatment. In Example 14.3, $a = 3$, $b = 2$, and $r = 10$. As a result, we have 10 observations for each of the six treatments.

Table 14.8 Two-Way Classification for Example 14.3

Weekly Sales of Apple Juice Concentrate			
Factor B:	**Factor A: Marketing Approach**		
Advertising Medium	**Convenience**	**Quality**	**Price**
Television	491	677	575
	712	627	614
	558	590	706
	447	632	484
	479	683	478
	624	760	650
	546	690	583
	444	548	536
	582	579	579
	672	644	795
Newspaper	464	689	803
	559	650	584
	759	704	525
	557	652	498
	528	576	812
	670	836	565
	534	628	708
	657	798	546
	557	497	616
	474	841	587

If there are differences among the treatment means, we would like to know if both factors affect the response. That is, are there differences among the levels of A and differences among the levels of B? If only one factor affects the response, is it A or is it B? If both A and B affect the response, do they do so independently, or do they interact, which means that some combinations of levels of factors A and B result in higher responses and some result in lower responses.

Figures 14.8 to 14.11 graphically depict the possible differences.

Figure 14.8 graphs the mean weekly sale when there are differences among the levels of A as well as differences among the levels of B. However, the factors affect sales independently, which means there is no interaction. Figure 14.9 describes the case where there are differences among the levels of A, but no difference among the levels of B. Figure 14.10 depicts differences among the levels of B but no differences among the levels of A. Figure 14.11 shows the levels of A and B interacting.

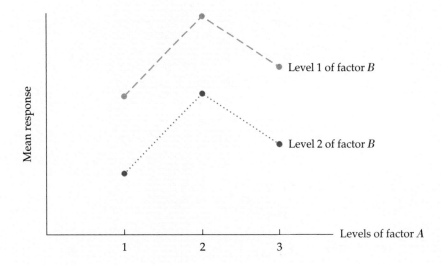

Figure 14.8

Differences among the levels of factor *A* and differences among the levels of factor *B*; no interaction

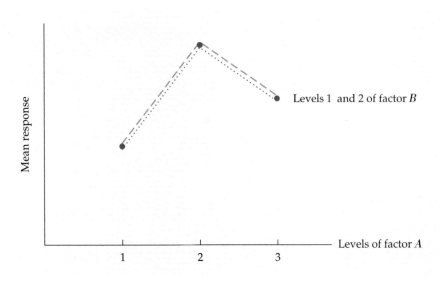

Figure 14.9

Differences among the levels of factor *A* and no difference among the levels of factor *B*

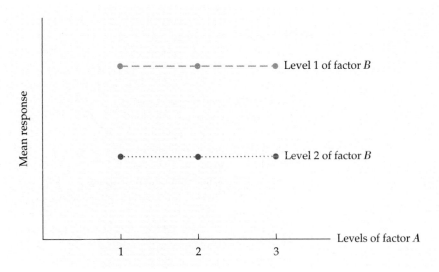

Figure 14.10

No differences among the levels of factor *A* and Differences among the levels of factor *B*

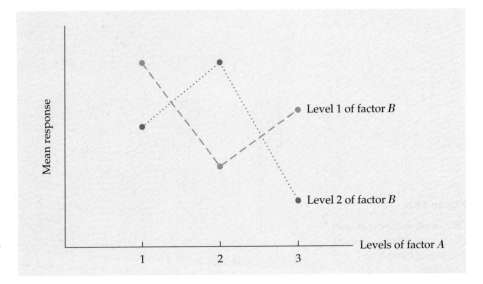

Figure 14.11

Interaction between factors *A* and *B*

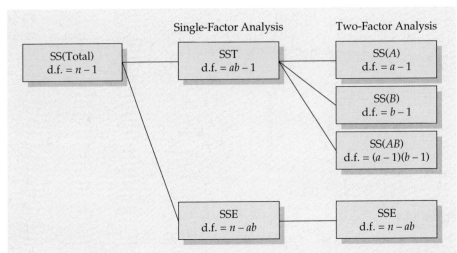

Figure 14.12

Partitioning SS(Total) in single-factor and two-factor analyses of variance

To test for each possibility, we conduct several *F*-tests similar to the one performed in Section 14.2. Figure 14.12 illustrates the partitioning of the total sum of squares that leads to the *F*-tests. We've included in this figure the partitioning used in the single-factor study. This part of the analysis of variance has already been performed in Example 14.3. When the single-factor analysis of variance allows us to infer that differences among the treatment means exist, we continue our analysis by partitioning the treatment sum of squares into three sources of variation. The first is sum of squares for factor *A*, which we label SS(*A*), which measures the variation among the levels of factor *A*. Its degrees of freedom are $a - 1$. The second is the sum of squares for factor *B*, whose degrees of freedom are $b - 1$. SS(*B*) is the variation among the levels of factor *B*. The interaction sum of squares is labeled SS(*AB*), which is a measure of the amount of variation among the combinations of factors *A* and *B*. Its degrees of freedom are $(a - 1) \times (b - 1)$. The sum of squares for error is SSE, and its degrees of freedom are $n - ab$. (Recall that *n* is the total sample size, which in this experiment is $n = abr$.) Notice that SSE and its number of degrees of freedom are identical in both partitions. As in the previous model, SSE is the variation within the treatments.

For those whose mathematical confidence is high, we have provided a listing of the notation and the definitions of the sums of squares below. (See Table 14.9.) Learning how the sums of squares are calculated is useful but hardly essential to your ability to conduct the tests.

We then perform three F-tests to determine whether the differences among the treatment means are caused by differences among levels of A, levels of B, or interaction. We call this analysis the **two-factor** or **two-way** analysis of variance. These tests are summarized below.

Notation And Definitions Of The Sums Of Squares For The Two-Factor Model (Optional)

To help you understand the formulas, we will use the following notation.

$\bar{x}[AB]_{ij}$ = mean of the responses variable in the ijth treatment (mean of the treatment when the factor A level is i and the factor B level is j)

$\bar{x}[A]_i$ = mean of the observations when the factor A level is i

$\bar{x}[B]_j$ = mean of the observations when the factor B level is j

$\bar{\bar{x}}$ = mean of all the observations

a = number of factor A levels

b = number of factor B levels

r = number of replicates

In this notation, $\bar{x}[AB]_{11}$ is the mean of the responses for factor A level 1 and factor B level 1. The mean of the responses for factor A level 1 is $\bar{x}[A]_1$. The mean of the responses for factor B level 1 is $\bar{x}[B]_1$. The sums of squares are defined as follows.

Table 14.9   Notation For Two-Factor Model

Factor B	Factor A					
	1	2	$\cdots$	a		
1	x_{111} x_{112} . . . x_{11r} $\bar{x}[AB]_{11}$	x_{211} x_{212} . . . x_{21r} $\bar{x}[AB]_{21}$		x_{a11} x_{a12} . . . x_{a1r} $\bar{x}[AB]_{a1}$	$\bar{x}[B]_1$	
2	x_{121} x_{122} . . . x_{12r} $\bar{x}[AB]_{12}$	x_{221} x_{222} . . . x_{22r} $\bar{x}[AB]_{22}$		x_{a21} x_{a22} . . . x_{a2r} $\bar{x}[AB]_{a2}$	$\bar{x}[B]_2$	
. . .						
b	x_{1b1} x_{1b2} . . . x_{1br} $\bar{x}[AB]_{1b}$	x_{2b1} x_{2b2} . . . x_{2br} $\bar{x}[AB]_{2b}$		x_{ab1} x_{ab2} . . . x_{abr} $\bar{x}[AB]_{ab}$	$\bar{x}[B]_b$	
	$\bar{x}[A]_1$	$\bar{x}[A]_2$		$\bar{x}[A]_a$	$\bar{\bar{x}}$	

Sums of Squares in the Two-Factor Analysis of Variance

$$SS(Total) = \sum_{i=1}^{a}\sum_{j=1}^{b}\sum_{k=1}^{r}(x_{ijk} - \bar{\bar{x}})^2$$

$$SS(A) = rb\sum_{i=1}^{a}(\bar{x}[A]_i - \bar{\bar{x}})^2$$

$$SS(B) = ra\sum_{j=1}^{b}(\bar{x}[B]_j - \bar{\bar{x}})^2$$

$$SS(AB) = r\sum_{i=1}^{a}\sum_{j=1}^{b}(\bar{x}[AB]_{ij} - \bar{x}[A]_i - \bar{x}[B]_j + \bar{\bar{x}})^2$$

$$SSE = \sum_{i=1}^{a}\sum_{j=1}^{b}\sum_{k=1}^{r}(x_{ijk} - \bar{x}[AB]_{ij})^2$$

To compute SS*(A)*, we calculate the sum of the squared differences between the factor *A* level means, which are denoted $\bar{x}[A]_i$, and the grand mean $\bar{\bar{x}}$. The sum of squares for factor *B* SS*(B)* is defined similarly. The interaction sum of squares SS*(AB)* is calculated by taking each treatment mean (a treatment consists of a combination of a level of factor *A* and a level of factor *B*), subtracting the factor *A* level mean, subtracting the factor *B* level mean, adding the grand mean, squaring this quantity, and adding. The sum of squares for error SSE is calculated by subtracting the treatment means from the observations, squaring, and adding.

F-Tests Conducted In Two-FactorAnalysis Of Variance

Test For Differences Among The Levels of Factor *A*

H_0: no difference among the means of the *a* levels of factor *A*

H_1: At least two means differ.

Test statistic: $F = \dfrac{MS(A)}{MSE}$

Test For Differences Among The Levels Of Factor *B*

H_0: no difference among the means of the *b* levels of factor *B*

H_1: At least two means differ.

Test statistic: $F = \dfrac{MS(B)}{MSE}$

Test For Interaction Between Factors *A* And *B*

H_0: Factors *A* and *B* do not interact to affect the mean response.

H_1: Factors *A* and *B* do interact to affect the mean response.

Test statistic: $F = \dfrac{MS(AB)}{MSE}$

Required Conditions

1 The distribution of the response is normally distributed.

2 The variance for each treatment is identical.

3 The samples are independent.

As in the two previous analysis of variance models, we summarize the results in an ANOVA table. Table 14.10 depicts the general form of the table for the complete factorial experiment.

We'll illustrate the techniques using the data in Example 14.3. All calculations will be performed by Excel and Minitab.

Table 14.10   **ANOVA Table for the Two-Factor Factorial Experiment with Fixed Effects and Independent Samples**

Source of Variability	Degrees of Freedom	Sums of Squares	Mean Squares	F-Ratios
Factor A	$a - 1$	SS(A)	$\text{MS}(A) = \dfrac{\text{SS}(A)}{(a - 1)}$	$F = \dfrac{\text{MS}(A)}{\text{MSE}}$
Factor B	$b - 1$	SS(B)	$\text{MS}(B) = \dfrac{\text{SS}(B)}{(b - 1)}$	$F = \dfrac{\text{MS}(B)}{\text{MSE}}$
Interaction	$(a - 1)(b - 1)$	SS(AB)	$\text{MS}(AB) = \dfrac{\text{SS}(AB)}{(a - 1)(b - 1)}$	$F = \dfrac{\text{MS}(AB)}{\text{MSE}}$
Error	$n - ab$	SSE	$\text{MSE} = \dfrac{\text{SSE}}{(n - ab)}$	
Total	$n - 1$	SS(Total)		

Test Of Differences In Mean Weekly Sales Among Three Marketing Approaches

H_0: no difference between the means of the 3 levels of factor A

H_1: At least two means differ.

Test statistic: $F = \dfrac{\text{MS}(A)}{\text{MSE}}$

Value of the test statistic: From the computer output on the following page, we have MS(A) = 49,419, MSE = 9,280, and F = 49,419/9,280 = 5.33 (p-value = .0077).

There is evidence at the 5% significance level to infer that differences in weekly sales exist among the different marketing approaches.

Test Of Differences In Mean Weekly Sales Between Two Advertising Media

H_0: no difference among the means of the 2 levels of factor B

H_1: At least two means differ.

Test statistic: $F = \dfrac{\text{MS}(B)}{\text{MSE}}$

Value of the test statistic: From the computer output below, we find MS*(B)* = 13,172 and MSE = 9,280. Thus, F = 13,172/9,280 = 1.42 (*p*-value = .2387).

There is insufficient evidence at the 5% significance level to infer that differences in weekly sales exist between television and newspaper advertising.

Test For Interaction Between Factors *A* And *B*

H_0: Factors *A* and *B* do not interact to affect the mean weekly sales.

H_1: Factors *A* and *B* do interact to affect the mean weekly sales.

Test statistic: $F = \dfrac{\text{MS}(AB)}{\text{MSE}}$

Value of the test statistic: From the printouts below MS*(AB)* = 805, MSE = 9,280, and F = 805/9,280 = .087 (*p*-value = .9171).

There is not enough evidence to conclude that there is an interaction between marketing approach and advertising medium that affects mean weekly sales.

SOLVE

Excel Output for Example 14.3

	A	B	C	D	E	F
1	ANOVA					
2	*Source of Variation*	SS	df	MS	F	P-value
3	Sample	13172	1	13172	1.42	0.2387
4	Columns	98839	2	49419	5.33	0.0077
5	Interaction	1610	2	805	0.087	0.9171
6	Within	501137	54	9280		
7						
8	Total	614757	59			

The actual output includes a variety of statistics, which we have omitted. In the ANOVA table **Sample** refers to factor *B* (medium) and **Columns** refers to factor *A* (advertising approach). Thus, MS(*B*) = 13,172., MS(*A*) = 49,419., MS(*AB*) = 805, and MSE = 9,280. The *F*-statistics are 1.42 (medium), 5.33 (advertising approach), and .087 (interaction).

COMMANDS	COMMANDS FOR EXAMPLE 14.3
1 Type or import the data. (See Table 14.9 for the correct format.)	Open file **XM14-03**.
2 Click **Tools, Data Analysis ...**, and **Anova: Two-Factor with Replication.**	
3 Specify the **Input Range:**.	**A1:D21**
4 Hit **tab** and type the number of replications *r* **(Rows per sample:)**. Click **OK**.	**10**

Minitab Output for Example 14.3

Two-way Analysis of Variance

Analysis of Variance for Sales

Source	DF	SS	MS	F	P
Mrkting	2	98839	49419	5.33	0.008
Medium	1	13172	13172	1.42	0.239
Interaction	2	1610	805	0.09	0.917
Error	54	501137	9280		
Total	59	614757			

The *F*-statistics are 5.33 for the advertising approach, 1.42 for the medium, and .09 for interaction.

COMMANDS	COMMANDS FOR EXAMPLE 14.3
1 Type or import the data in stacked format in three columns. One column contains the responses, another contains codes for the levels of factor *A,* and a third column contains codes for the levels of factor *B.*	Open file **XM14-03.** Stack the data in C1, C2, and C3.
2 Click **Stat, ANOVA,** and **Twoway . . . .**	
3 Specify the **Responses:, Row factor:,** and **Column factor:.** Click **OK.**	**Sales** or **C1** **Mrkting** or **C2** **Medium** or **C3**

INTERPRET

Figure 14.13 graphs the mean sales for each factor. As you can see, there are differences among the levels of factor *A,* no difference between the levels of factor *B,* and no interaction is apparent. These results indicate that emphasizing quality produces the highest sales and that television and newspaper are equally effective.

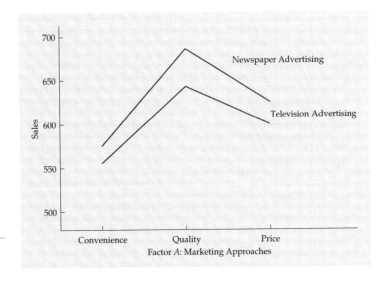

Figure 14.13

Mean responses for factors *A* and *B:* Example 14.3

CONDUCTING THE ANALYSIS OF VARIANCE FOR THE COMPLETE FACTORIAL EXPERIMENT

In addressing the problem outlined in Example 14.3, we began by conducting a single-factor analysis of variance to determine if differences existed among the six treatment means. This was done primarily for pedagogical reasons to enable you to see that when the treatment means differ we need to analyze the reasons for the differences. However, in practice, we generally do not conduct this test in the complete factorial experiment (although it should be noted that some statisticians prefer this "two-stage" approach). We recommend that you proceed directly to the two-factor analysis of variance.

You should also note the order in which we conducted the three F-tests in the two-factor analysis of variance. The order of the tests that we performed above in this part of the analysis was based on the way that most software (including Excel and Minitab) output the results of the tests. That is, the computer lists factors A and B as the first two sources of variation. Interaction is shown as the third source of variation. However, the test for interaction should be conducted first. To understand why, examine Figure 14.11, which depicts A and B interacting. When factors A and B interact, certain combinations of the levels of A and levels of B result in different mean responses. In most of these cases the F-test of the differences among the levels of A and/or the levels of B will yield statistically significant results. However, this inference may be wrong because the only differences among the levels of A and/or B may be due to the interaction. Thus, we first test to determine if there is interaction between factors A and B. If evidence to that effect exists, we do not perform the other two tests. If no interaction is evident, we test to determine if there are differences among the levels of A and if there are differences among the levels of B.

DEVELOPING AN UNDERSTANDING OF STATISTICAL CONCEPTS

You may have noticed that there are similarities between the independent samples two-factor model and the randomized block design (Section 14.4). In fact, when the number of replicates is one, the calculations are identical. (Minitab uses the same command.) This raises the question: What is the difference between a factor in a multifactor study and a block in a randomized block experiment? In general, the difference between the two designs is that in the randomized block experiment, blocking is performed specifically to reduce variation, whereas in the two-factor model the effect of the factors on the response variable is of interest to the statistician. The criteria that define the blocks are always characteristics of the experimental units. Consequently, factors that are characteristics of the experimental units will be treated not as factors in a multifactor study but as blocks in a randomized block experiment.

Let's review how we recognize the need to use this model of the analysis of variance.

> ### Factors that Identify the Independent Samples Two-Factor Analysis of Variance
>
> 1 Problem objective: compare two or more populations (populations are defined as combinations of levels of two factors)
> 2 Data type: quantitative
> 3 Experimental design: independent samples

E X E R C I S E S

14.30 A two-factor analysis of variance experiment was performed with $a = 3$, $b = 4$, and $r = 20$. The following sums of squares were computed.

$$SS(\text{Total}) = 42,450 \quad SS(A) = 1,560$$
$$SS(B) = 2,880 \quad SS(AB) = 7,605$$

a Test at the 1% significance level to determine whether differences exist among the levels of factor A.

b Test at the 1% significance level to determine whether differences exist among the levels of factor B.

c Test at the 1% significance level to determine whether factors A and B interact.

14.31 The following data were generated from a 2×2 factorial experiment with three replicates.

Factor A	Factor B	
	1	2
1	6	12
	9	10
	7	11
2	9	15
	10	14
	5	10

a Test at the 5% significance level to determine if factors A and B interact.

b Test at the 5% significance level to determine if differences exist among the levels of factor A.

c Test at the 5% significance level to determine if differences exist among the levels of factor B.

14.32 The data shown below were taken from a 2×3 factorial experiment with 4 replicates.

Factor A	Factor B	
	1	2
1	23	20
	18	17
	17	16
	20	19
2	27	29
	23	23
	21	27
	28	25
3	23	27
	21	19
	24	20
	16	22

a Test at the 5% significance level to determine if factors A and B interact.

b Test at the 5% significance level to determine if differences exist among the levels of factor A.

c Test at the 5% significance level to determine if differences exist among the levels of factor B.

14.33 Headaches are one of the most common, but least understood, ailments. Most people get headaches several times per month; over-the-counter medication is usually sufficient to eliminate their pain. However, for a significant proportion of people, headaches are debilitating and make their lives almost unbearable. Many such people have investigated a wide spectrum of possible treatments, including narcotic drugs, hypnosis, biofeedback, and acupuncture, with little or no success. In the last few years, a promising new treatment has been developed. Simply described, the treatment involves a series of injections of a local anesthetic to the occipital nerve (located in the back of the neck). The current treatment procedure is to schedule the injections once a week for 4 weeks. However, it has been suggested that another procedure may be better, one that features one injection every other day for a total of four injections. Additionally, some physicians recommend other combinations of drugs that may increase the effectiveness of the injections. To analyze the problem, an experiment was organized. It was decided to test for a difference between the two schedules of injection and to determine whether there are differences among four drug mixtures. Because of the possibility of an interaction between the schedule and the drug, a complete factorial experiment was chosen. Five headache patients were randomly selected for each combination of schedule and drug. Forty patients were treated and each was asked to report the frequency, duration, and severity of his or her headache prior to treatment and for the 30 days following the last injection. An index ranging from 0 to 100 was constructed for each patient, where 0 indicates no headache pain and 100 specifies the worst headache pain. The improvement in the headache index for each patient was recorded and reproduced in the accompanying table. (A negative value indicates a worsening condition.) (The authors are grateful to Dr. Lorne Greenspan for his help in writing this example.)

Improvement in Headache Index

Schedule	Drug mixture			
	1	2	3	4
One injection	17	24	14	10
every week	6	15	9	−1
(four weeks)	10	10	12	0
	12	16	0	3
	14	14	6	−1
One injection	18	−2	20	−2
every two days	9	0	16	7
(four days)	17	17	12	10
	21	2	17	6
	15	6	18	7

a What are the factors in this experiment?
b What is the response variable?
c Identify the levels of each factor.
d Can we conclude at the 1% significance level that differences exist between the two schedules?
e Can we conclude at the 1% significance level that differences exist among the four drug mixtures?
f Before answering the questions in parts (d) and (e), what test must you conduct?
g What is the result of the test referred to in part (f)? What does this test tell you?

14.34 Most college instructors prefer to have their students participate actively in class. Ideally, students will ask their professor questions and answer their professor's questions, making the classroom experience more interesting and useful. Many professors seek ways to encourage their students to participate in class. A statistics professor at a community college in upper New York state believes that there are a number of external factors that affect student participation. He believes that the time of day and the configuration of seats are two such factors. Consequently, he organized the following experiment. Six classes of about 60 students each were scheduled for one semester. Two classes were scheduled at 9:00 A.M., two at 1:00 P.M., and two at 4:00 P.M. At each of the three times, one of the classes was assigned to a room where the seats were arranged in rows of 10 seats. The other class was a U-shaped, tiered room, where students not only face the instructor, but face their fellow students as well. In each of the six classrooms, over 5 days, student participation was measured by counting the number of times students asked and answered questions. These data are displayed in the accompanying table and stored in file XR14-34 in exactly the same format as the table.

Class configuration	Time		
	9:00 A.M.	1:00 P.M.	4:00 P.M.
Rows	10	9	7
	7	12	12
	9	12	9
	6	14	20
	8	8	7
U-Shape	15	4	7
	18	4	4
	11	7	9
	13	4	8
	13	6	7

a How many factors are there in this experiment? What are they?
b What is the response variable?
c Identify the levels of each factor.
d What conclusions can the professor draw from these data at the 5% significance level?

The following exercises require the use of a computer and software.

14.35 Detergent manufacturers frequently make claims about the effectiveness of their products. A consumer-protection service decided to test the five best-selling brands of detergent, each of whose manufacturers claims that its product produces the "whitest whites" in all water temperatures. The experiment was conducted in the following way. One hundred fifty white sheets were equally soiled. Thirty sheets were washed in each brand—10 with cold water, 10 with lukewarm water, and 10 with hot water. After washing, the "whiteness" scores for each sheet were measured with laser equipment. The results are stored in file XR14-35 using the following format.

> Column 1: water temperature category
>
> Column 2: scores for detergent 1 (first 10 rows = cold water, middle 10 rows = lukewarm, and last 10 rows = hot)
>
> Column 3: scores for detergent 2 (same format as column 2)
>
> Column 4: scores for detergent 3 (same format as column 2)
>
> Column 5: scores for detergent 4 (same format as column 2)
>
> Column 6: scores for detergent 5 (same format as column 2)

a What are the factors in this experiment?
b What is the response variable?
c Identify the levels of each factor.
d Can we conclude at the 5% significance level that differences exist among the five detergents?
e Can we conclude at the 5% significance level that differences exist among the three water temperatures?
f Before answering the questions in parts (d) and (e), what test must you conduct?
g What is the result of the test referred to in part (f)? What does this test tell you?

14.36 Refer to Exercise 14.10. Suppose that the experiment is redone in the following way. Thirty taxpayers fill out each of the four forms. However, 10 taxpayers in each group are in the low income bracket, 10 are in the next income bracket, and the remaining 10 are in the highest bracket. The amount of time needed to complete the returns is recorded and stored in file XR14-36 using the following format.

> Column 1: group number
>
> Column 2: times to complete form 1 (first 10 rows = low income, next 10 rows = next income bracket, and last 10 rows = highest bracket)
>
> Column 3: times to complete form 2 (same format as column 2)
>
> Column 4: times to complete form 3 (same format as column 2)
>
> Column 5: times to complete form 4 (same format as column 2)

a How many treatments are there in this experiment?
b How many factors are there? What are they?
c What are the levels of each factor?
d Can we conclude at the 5% significance level that differences exist among the four forms?
e Can we conclude at the 5% significance level that taxpayers in different brackets require different amounts of time to complete their tax forms?
f What test must be conducted before answering the questions in parts (d) and (e)?
g What is the result of the test referred to in part (f)? What does this test tell you?

14.6 OPERATIONS MANAGEMENT APPLICATION: FINDING AND REDUCING VARIATION

In the introduction to Example 11.3, we pointed out that variation in the size, weight, or volume of a product's components cause the product to fail or not function properly. Unfortunately, it is impossible to eliminate all variation. Designers of products and the processes that make the products understand this phenomenon. Consequently, when they specify the length, weight, or some other measurable characteristic of the product they allow for some variation, called the *tolerance*. For example, a machined part of an engine may be designed to have a diameter of 55 millimeters (mm) with a tolerance of 0.25 mm. That is, the product will function provided that the diameter is between $55 - 0.25$ and $55 + 0.25$. Historically, operations managers applied the "goalpost" philosophy, a name derived from the game of football. If the ball is kicked *anywhere* between the goalposts, the kick is equally as successful as one that barely slips in beside one goalpost. Figure 14.14 describes the goalpost syndrome. Using this philosophy, the company sustains a loss only when the product falls outside the goalposts (point A). Products that lie between the goalposts (point B) suffer no financial loss. However, this philosophy is now outdated. It has been replaced by the Taguchi loss function (named for Genichi Taguchi, a Japanese statistician whose ideas and techniques permeate any discussion of statistical applications in quality management).

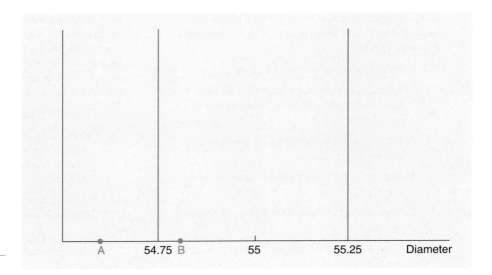

Figure 14.14

Goalpost philosophy of quality

TAGUCHI LOSS FUNCTION

Products whose length or weight fall within the tolerances of their specifications do not all function in exactly the same way. There is a difference between a product that barely falls between the goalposts and ones that are in the exact center. The Taguchi loss function recognizes that any deviation from the specification results in a financial loss. And, the further the product's variable is from the specification, the greater the loss. The machined part described above is specified to be exactly 55 mm, an amount specified by the manufacturer to work at the optimum level. Any deviation will cause that, and perhaps other parts, to wear out prematurely. Although customers will not know the reason for the problem, they will know that the unit had to be replaced. The greater the deviation, the more quickly the part will wear and need replacing. If the part is under warranty the company will incur a loss in replacing it. If the warranty has expired, customers will have to pay to replace the unit, causing some degree of displeasure, which may cause them to buy another company's product in the future. In either case, the company loses money. Figure 14.15 depicts the

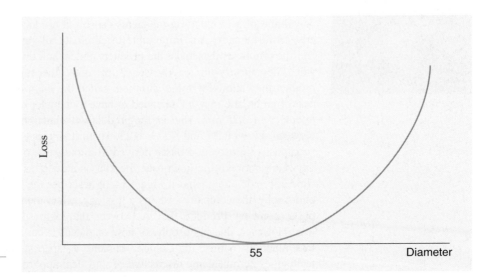

Figure 14.15

Taguchi loss function

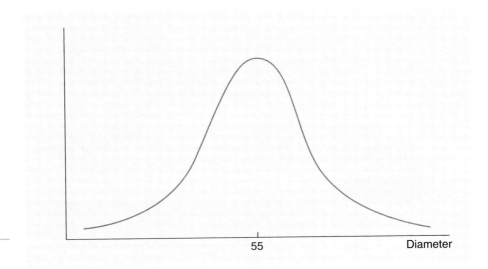

Figure 14.16

Distribution of diameter of machined part

55   Diameter

loss function. As you can see, any deviation from the specification results in some loss, with large deviations resulting in larger losses.

Management scientists have shown that the loss function can be expressed as a function of the production process mean and variance. In Figure 14.16 we describe a normal distribution of the diameter of the machined part specified to be 55 mm. When the mean of the distribution is 55, any loss is caused by the variance. The statistical techniques introduced in Chapter 21 are usually employed to center the distribution at its specification. However, reducing the variance is considerably more difficult. To reduce variation it is necessary to first find the sources of variation. We do so by conducting experiments. The principles are quite straightforward, drawing on the concepts developed in the previous section.

There are several factors that can affect the final product. In the introduction to operations management (see page 10) we discussed the four Ms: machines, materials, methods, and personnel (manpower). By altering some or all of these elements, the operations manager can alter the size, weight, or volume and ultimately, the quality of the product.

The following example illustrates this approach. Because we have limited our discussion to the two-factor model, the example will feature this experimental design. It should be understood, however, more complicated models are needed to fully investigate sources of variation.

▼ **EXAMPLE 14.4**

A critical component in an aircraft engine is a steel rod that must be 41.387 cm long. The operations manager has noted that there has been some variation in the lengths. In some cases the steel rods had to be discarded or reworked because they were either too short or too long. The operations manager feels that some of the variation is caused by the way the production process has been designed. Specifically, he believes that the rods vary from machine to machine and from operator to operator. To help unravel the truth he organizes an experiment. Each of the three operators produces five rods on each of the four machines. The lengths are measured and recorded in the following way. Columns 1 through 4 store the data for machines 1 to 4, respectively. In each column the first five rows represent operator 1, the next five rows are from operator 2, and the last five rows are the data for operator 3. The data have been transformed to ease the calculations. The data are calculated as the actual length minus 41.387 multiplied by 1,000. The transformed data are stored in file XM14-04. Perform a two-factor analysis of variance to determine whether the machines and/or the operators are indeed sources of variation.

Solution

IDENTIFY

The two factors are the operators and the machines. There are three levels of operators and four levels of machines. The model we employ is the two-factor model with interaction. The computer output is shown below.

SOLVE

Excel Output for Example 14.4

	A	B	C	D	E	F
1	ANOVA					
2	Source of Variation	SS	df	MS	F	P-value
3	Sample	15133	2	7566	6.98	0.0022
4	Columns	3363	3	1121	1.04	0.3856
5	Interaction	4646	6	774	0.71	0.6394
6	Within	51995	48	1083		
7						
8	Total	75137	59			

Minitab Output for Example 14.4

Two-way Analysis of Variance

```
Analysis of Variance for Rods
Source          DF          SS          MS          F          P
Machines         3        3363        1121       1.04      0.386
Operator         2       15133        7566       6.98      0.002
Interaction      6        4646         774       0.71      0.639
Error           48       51995        1083
Total           59       75137
```

We first test for interaction. The F-statistic for interaction is .71 and its p-value is .6394. There is no evidence to infer that there is interaction between the machines and the operators. Next, we test to determine whether there are differences among the levels of each factor. The F-statistic for the operator factor (Sample) is 6.98 (p-value $= .0022$). The F-statistics for the machine factor (Columns) is 1.04 (p-value $= .3856$).

INTERPRET

We conclude that there are differences only among the levels of the operators. Thus, the only source of variation here is the different operators. The operations manager can now focus on reducing or eliminating this variation. For example, the manager may use only one operator in the future or investigate why the operators differ.

▲

DESIGN OF EXPERIMENTS AND TAGUCHI METHODS

In Example 14.4 above the experiment employed only two factors. In practice there are frequently many more factors. The problem is that the total number of treatments or combinations can be quite high making any experimentation both time-consuming and expensive. For example, if there are 10 factors each with 2 levels the number of treatments is $2^{10} = 1{,}024$. If we measure each treatment with 10 replicates the number of observations, 10,240, makes this experiment prohibitive. Fortunately, it is possible to reduce this number considerably. Through the use of *orthogonal arrays* we can conduct *fractional factorial* experiments that can produce useful results at a small fraction of the cost. The experimental designs and statistical analyses are beyond the level of this book. Interested readers can find a variety of books at different levels of mathematical and statistical sophistication to learn more about this application.

EXERCISES

The following exercises require the use of a computer and software. Conduct all tests at the 5% significance level.

14.37 The headrests on a car's front seats are designed to protect the driver and front-seat passenger from whiplash when the car is hit from behind. The frame of the headrest is made from metal rods. A machine is used to bend the rod into a U-shape exactly 440 millimeters wide. The width is critical; too wide or too narrow and it won't fit into the holes drilled into the car seat frame. The company has experimented with two different metal alloys in the hope of finding a material that will result in more headrest frames that fit. Another possible source of variation is the machines used. To learn more about the process, the operations manager conducts an experiment. Both of the machines are used to produce 10 headrests from each of the two metal alloys now being used. Each frame is measured and the data (in millimeters) stored in file XR14-37 using the following format.

> Column 2: Machine 1, rows 1 to 10 alloy A, rows 11–20, alloy B
>
> Column 3: Machine 2, rows 1 to 10 alloy A, rows 11–20, alloy B

Analyze the data to determine whether the alloys, machines, or both are sources of variation.

14.38 A paint manufacturer is attempting to improve the process that fills its 1-gallon containers. The foreperson has suggested that the nozzle can be made from several different alloys. Furthermore, the way that the process "knows" when to stop the flow of paint can be accomplished in two ways—by setting a predetermined amount or by measuring the amount of paint already in the can. To determine what factors lead to variation, an experiment is conducted. For each of the four alloys that could be used to make the nozzles and the two measuring devices, five cans are filled. The

amount of paint in each container is precisely measured. The data in liters are stored in file XR14-38 in the following way.

> Column 2: Device 1, rows 1 to 5 alloy A, rows 6 to 10 alloy B, etc.
>
> Column 3: Device 2, rows 1 to 5 alloy A, rows 6 to 10 alloy B, etc.

Can we infer that the alloys, the measuring devices, or both are sources of variation?

14.39 In Example 12.2, the operations manager wanted to know whether the two methods used to assemble a new ergonomic computer desk were different with respect to the amount of time taken to assemble the desk. The manager was now faced with another problem. The marketing department of the firm has ascertained that there is a growing market for a specialized desk that houses the various parts of a computer system. The operations manager is summoned to put together a plan that will produce high-quality desks at low cost. The characteristics of the desk have been dictated by the marketing department, which in turn has specified the material from which the desk will be made and the machines used to produce the parts. However, two methods can be utilized. Moreover, because of the complexity of the operation the manager realizes that it is possible that different skill levels of the workers will yield different results. Accordingly, he organized an experiment. Workers from each of three skill levels were chosen. These groups were further divided into two subgroups. Each subgroup assembled the desks using Methods A and B. The amount of time taken to assemble each of eight desks was recorded and stored in file XR14-39. (Columns 2 and 3 contain the times for Methods A and B; rows 1 to 8, 9 to 16, and 17 to 24 store the times for the three skill levels.) What can we infer from these data?

14.7 MULTIPLE COMPARISONS (OPTIONAL)

When the null hypothesis in the analysis of variance is rejected, it is often desirable to know which treatment means are responsible for the difference among population means. For example, if an experiment is undertaken to determine whether different locations within a store produce different mean sales, the manager would be keenly interested in determining which locations result in higher sales and which locations result in lower sales. Similarly, a stockbroker would like to know which one of several mutual funds outperforms the others, and a television executive would like to know which television commercials hold the viewers' attention and which are ignored.

While it may appear that all we need to do is examine the sample means and identify the largest or the smallest to determine which population means are largest or smallest, this is not the case. To illustrate, suppose that in a five-treatment analysis of variance, we discover that differences exist. The sample means are calculated as follows.

$$\bar{x}_1 = 20 \qquad \bar{x}_2 = 19 \qquad \bar{x}_3 = 25 \qquad \bar{x}_4 = 22 \qquad \bar{x}_5 = 17$$

The statistician wants to know which of the following conclusions are valid.

1 μ_3 is larger than the other means.

2 μ_3 and μ_4 are larger than the other means.

3 μ_5 is smaller than the other means.

4 μ_5 and μ_2 are smaller than the other means.

5 μ_3 is larger than the other means, and μ_5 is smaller than the other means.

From the information we have, it is impossible to determine which, if any, of the statements are true. We need a statistical method to make this determination.

Several statistical inference procedures deal with this problem. We will present three methods that allow us to determine which population means differ. All three methods apply to the independent samples single-factor model.

FISHER'S LEAST SIGNIFICANT DIFFERENCE (LSD) METHOD

Fisher's least significant difference (LSD) method was briefly introduced in section 14.2 (page 492). To determine which population means differ, we could perform a series of t-tests of the difference between two means on all pairs of population means to determine which are significantly different. In Chapter 12 we introduced the equal-variances t-test of the difference between two means. The test statistic and interval estimator are, respectively,

$$t = \frac{(\bar{x}_1 - \bar{x}_2) - (\mu_1 - \mu_2)}{\sqrt{s_p^2\left(\dfrac{1}{n_1} + \dfrac{1}{n_2}\right)}}$$

$$(\bar{x}_1 - \bar{x}_2) \pm t_{\alpha/2}\sqrt{s_p^2\left(\dfrac{1}{n_1} + \dfrac{1}{n_2}\right)}$$

with d.f. $= n_1 + n_2 - 2$.

Recall that s_p^2 is the pooled variance estimate, which is an unbiased estimator of the variance of the two populations. (Recall that in using these formulas we assume that the population variances are equal.) In this section we modify the test statistic and interval estimator.

Earlier in this chapter we pointed out that MSE is an unbiased estimator of the common variance of the populations we're testing. Because MSE is based on all the observations in the k samples, it will be a better estimator than s_p^2 (which is based on only two samples). Thus, we could draw inferences about every pair of means by substituting MSE in place of s_p^2 in the test statistic and interval estimator above. The number of degrees of freedom would also change to $n - k$ (where n is the total sample size). The test statistic to determine whether μ_i and μ_j differ is

$$t = \frac{(\bar{x}_i - \bar{x}_j) - (\mu_i - \mu_j)}{\sqrt{\text{MSE}\left(\dfrac{1}{n_i} + \dfrac{1}{n_j}\right)}}$$

The interval estimator is

$$(\bar{x}_i - \bar{x}_j) \pm t_{\alpha/2}\sqrt{\text{MSE}\left(\dfrac{1}{n_i} + \dfrac{1}{n_j}\right)}$$

and d.f. $= n - k$.

A simple way of determining whether differences exist between each pair of population means is to compare the absolute value of the difference between two sample means and

$$t_{\alpha/2}\sqrt{\text{MSE}\left(\dfrac{1}{n_i} + \dfrac{1}{n_j}\right)}$$

If we define the least significant difference (LSD) as

$$\text{LSD} = t_{\alpha/2}\sqrt{\text{MSE}\left(\dfrac{1}{n_i} + \dfrac{1}{n_j}\right)}$$

we conclude that μ_i and μ_j differ if

$$|\bar{x}_i - \bar{x}_j| > \text{LSD}$$

LSD will be the same for all pairs of means if all k sample sizes are equal. If some sample sizes differ, LSD must be calculated for each combination.

In Section 14.2 we argued that this method is flawed because it will increase the probability of committing a Type I error. That is, it is more likely to conclude that a difference exists in some of the population means when in fact none differ. On page 492 we calculated that if $k = 6$ and all population means are equal, the probability of erroneously inferring at the 5% significance level that at least two means differ is about 54%. The 5% figure is now referred to as the **comparisonwise Type I error rate.** The true probability of making at least one Type I error is called the **experimentwise Type I error rate,** denoted α_E. The experimentwise Type I error rate can be calculated as

$$\alpha_E = 1 - (1 - \alpha)^C$$

where C is the number of pairwise comparisons. That is, $C = k(k - 1)/2$. Mathematicians have proven that

$$\alpha_E \leq C\alpha$$

which means that if we want the probability of making at least one Type I error to be no more than α_E, we simply specify $\alpha = \alpha_E/C$. the resulting procedure is called the *Bonferroni adjustment.*

BONFERRONI ADJUSTMENT

The **Bonferroni adjustment** is made by dividing the specified experimentwise Type I error rate by the number of combinations of pairs of population means. For example, if $k = 6$, then

$$C = \frac{k(k-1)}{2} = \frac{6(5)}{2} = 15$$

If we want the true probability of a Type I error to be no more than 5% we divide this probability by C. Thus,

$$\alpha = \alpha_E/C = .05/15 = .0033$$

To illustrate Fisher's LSD method and the Bonferroni adjustment, consider Example 14.1 where we tested to determine whether three population means differ using a 5% significance level. The three sample means are 577.55, 653.0, and 608.65. The pairwise absolute differences are

$$|\bar{x}_1 - \bar{x}_2| = |577.55 - 653.0| = |-75.45| = 75.45$$
$$|\bar{x}_1 - \bar{x}_3| = |577.55 - 608.65| = |-31.10| = 31.10$$
$$|\bar{x}_2 - \bar{x}_2| = |653.0 - 608.65| = |44.35| = 44.35$$

If we conduct the LSD procedure with $\alpha = .05$ we find $t_{\alpha/2, n-k} = t_{.025,57} = 2.002$. (This figure was determined from Excel. If you find the critical value manually from Table 4 in Appendix B you will have to approximate the degrees of freedom with 60 and find $t_{.025,57} \approx t_{.025,60} = 2.000$.) Thus,

$$t_{\alpha/2}\sqrt{\text{MSE}\left(\frac{1}{n_i} + \frac{1}{n_j}\right)} = 2.002\sqrt{8,894\left(\frac{1}{20} + \frac{1}{20}\right)} = 59.71$$

We can see that only one pair of sample means differs by more than 59.71. That is, $|\bar{x}_1 - \bar{x}_2| = 75.45$, the other two differences are less than LSD. Consequently, we conclude that only μ_1 and μ_2 differ.

If we perform the LSD procedure with the Bonferroni adjustment, the number of pairwise comparisons is 3 [calculated as $C = k(k-1)/2 = 3(2)/2$]. We set $\alpha = .05/3 = .0167$. Thus, $t_{\alpha/2} = 2.467$ (available from Excel and difficult to approximate manually) and

$$t_{\alpha/2}\sqrt{\text{MSE}\left(\frac{1}{n_i} + \frac{1}{n_j}\right)} = 2.467\sqrt{8,894\left(\frac{1}{20} + \frac{1}{20}\right)} = 73.54$$

Again we conclude that only μ_1 and μ_2 differ. Notice, however, in the second calculation that LSD is larger, reflecting the higher hurdle dictated by the smaller probability.

The drawback to LSD is that we increase the probability of at least one Type I error. The Bonferroni adjustment corrects this problem. However, recall that the probabilities of Type I and Type II errors are inversely related. The Bonferroni adjustment uses a smaller value of α, which results in an increased probability of a Type II error. A Type II error occurs when a difference between population means exists yet we cannot detect it. The next multiple comparison method addresses this problem.

TUKEY'S MULTIPLE COMPARISON METHOD

A more powerful test is **Tukey's multiple comparison method.** This technique determines a critical number such that, if any pair of sample means has a difference greater than this critical number, we conclude that the pair's two corresponding population means are different.

The test is based on the Studentized range, which is defined as the variable

$$q = \frac{\bar{x}_{\max} - \bar{x}_{\min}}{s/\sqrt{n}}$$

where $\bar{x}_{\max}$ and $\bar{x}_{\min}$ are the largest and smallest sample means, respectively, assuming that there are no differences among the population means. We can find a critical number ω (Greek letter *omega*) such that if the difference between any pair of sample means exceeds ω, we can take this as sufficient evidence that the pair's corresponding population means differ. We define the number ω as follows.

Critical Number ω

$$\omega = q_\alpha(k, \nu)\sqrt{\frac{\text{MSE}}{n_g}}$$

where

n = number of observations ($n = n_1 + n_2 + \cdots + n_k$)

ν = number of degrees of freedom associated with MSE = $n - k$

n_g = number of observations in each of k samples

α = significance level

$q_\alpha(k,\nu)$ = critical value of the Studentized range

Table 7 in Appendix B provides values of $q_\alpha(k,\nu)$ for a variety of values of k and ν and for $\alpha = .01$ and $.05$. To illustrate the table's use, suppose that $k = 3$, $\nu = 15$, and $\alpha = .05$. From the table we find $q_{.05}(3,15) = 3.67$.

Theoretically, this procedure requires that all sample sizes be equal. However, if the sample sizes are different we can still use this technique provided that the sample sizes are at least similar. The value of n_g used above is the *harmonic mean* of the sample sizes. That is,

$$n_g = \frac{k}{\dfrac{1}{n_1} + \dfrac{1}{n_2} + \cdots + \dfrac{1}{n_k}}$$

Applying Tukey's method to Example 14.1 we find

$k = 3$

$n_1 = n_2 = n_3 = n_g = 20$

$\nu = n - k = 60 - 3 = 57$

$\text{MSE} = 8,894$

Thus,

$$\omega = q_\alpha(k,\nu)\sqrt{\frac{\text{MSE}}{n_g}} = q_{.05}(3,57)\sqrt{\frac{8,894}{20}} = 3.40 \times 21.09 = 71.70$$

[We approximated $q_{.05}(3,57)$ with $q_{.05}(3,60)$.]

Tukey's and Fisher's LSD method ($\alpha = .05$):

	A	B	C	D
1	**Multiple Comparisons**			
2	*Omega = 71.70*			
3	*Variable*	*Variable*	*Difference*	*LSD*
4	1	2	-75.45	59.72
5		3	-31.1	59.72
6	2	3	44.35	59.72

Tukey's and Fisher's LSD with the Bonferroni adjustment ($\alpha = .05/3 = .0167$):

	A	B	C	D
1	**Multiple Comparisons**			
2	*Omega = 71.70*			
3	*Variable*	*Variable*	*Difference*	*LSD*
4	1	2	-75.45	73.54
5		3	-31.1	73.54
6	2	3	44.35	73.54

The printout includes ω (Tukey's method), the differences between sample means for each combination of populations, and Fisher's LSD. (The Bonferroni adjustment is made by specifying another value for α.)

COMMANDS	COMMANDS FOR EXAMPLE 14.1
1 Type or import the data into adjacent columns.	Open file **XM14-01.**
2 Click **Tools, Data Analysis Plus,** and **Multiple Comparisons.**
3 Specify the **Input Range:**. Do not include cells containing the variable names.	**A2:C21**
4 Type the value of α. To use the Bonferroni adjustment divide α by $C = k(k-1)/2$. For Tukey, Excel computes ω only for $\alpha = .05$.	**.05** (for Fisher's LSD) and **.0167** for Bonferroni

Minitab Output for Example 14.1

One-Way Analysis of Variance

```
Analysis of Variance for Sales
Source     DF        SS        MS         F       P
City        2     57512     28756      3.23    0.047
Error      57    506984      8894
Total      59    564496
                                    Individual 95% CIs For Mean
                                    Based on Pooled StDev
Level       N      Mean     StDev   ---+---------+---------+---------+--
-
1          20    577.55    103.80   (--------*-------)
2          20    653.00     85.08                  (--------*-------)
3          20    608.65     93.11         (--------*-------)
                                    ---+---------+---------+---------+--
-
Pooled StDev =    94.31            550       600       650       700
```

```
Tukey's pairwise comparisons

      Family error rate = 0.0500
  Individual error rate = 0.0194

Critical value = 3.40

Intervals for (column level mean) - (row level mean)

                   1          2
      2        -147.2
                 -3.7

      3        -102.8      -27.4
                 40.6      116.1
```

```
Fisher's pairwise comparisons

      Family error rate = 0.121
  Individual error rate = 0.0500

Critical value = 2.002

Intervals for (column level mean) - (row level mean)

                   1          2
      2        -135.2
                -15.7

      3         -90.8      -15.4
                 28.6      104.1
```

The printout includes the ANOVA table and the multiple comparison statistics. For Tukey's method Minitab prints the critical value $q_\alpha(k, \nu) = 3.40$ from which you may calculate ω. (We calculated $\omega = 71.70$.) You need not do so, however, since Minitab prints the difference between each pair of sample means $\pm \omega$. For example, to determine whether μ_1 and μ_2 differ, Minitab prints

$$(\bar{x}_1 - \bar{x}_2) \pm \omega = (577.55 - 653.00) \pm 71.70$$
$$= -75.45 \pm 71.70 = (-147.2, -3.7)$$

We estimate that $\mu_1 - \mu_2$ falls between -147.2 and -3.7. Because this interval excludes zero, we infer that there is a difference between μ_1 and μ_2. Notice

(continued)

that the other two intervals $(-102.8, 40.6)$ and $(-27.4, 116.1)$, include zero indicating that μ_1 and μ_3 and μ_2 and μ_3 may not differ.

For Fisher's LSD, Minitab prints the difference between each pair of sample means $\pm$ LSD. The interpretation is the same as for Tukey's method. In the printout above we used $\alpha = .05$ for both Tukey's and Fisher's procedures.

COMMANDS	COMMANDS FOR EXAMPLE 14.1
1 Type or import the data. The data must be stacked. [We stacked the data into column 4 (Sales) and the subscript in column 5 (City).]	Open file **XM14-01.**
2 Click **Stat, ANOVA,** and **Oneway . . . .**	
3 Specify the **Response:.**	**Sales**
4 Specify the **Factor:.**	**City**
5 Click **Comparisons . . . .**	
6 Use the cursor to select Tukey's method and specify α.	**.05 or 5**
7 Use the cursor to select Fisher's method and specify α. For the Bonferroni adjustment divide α by $C = k(k - 1)/2$	**.05 or 5** **.0167 or 1.67**

INTERPRET

Using any of the three multiple comparison methods we discover that only μ_1 and μ_2 differ and no other pairs differ. This tells the marketing manager that advertising emphasizing quality (City 2) outsells advertising stressing convenience (City 1), and that there is no evidence to infer that advertising emphasizing price (City 3) is any different from the other two. It would appear that the company should launch an advertising campaign that features various ways of describing the high quality of the product. We may also advertise stressing the price of the product.

WHICH MULTIPLE COMPARISON METHOD TO USE

In Example 14.1 all three multiple comparison methods yielded the same results. This will not always be the case. When the results differ the statistician must choose which one to use. Bear in mind, as well, that there are other techniques besides the ones described here. Unfortunately, no one procedure works best in all types of problems. Most statisticians agree with the following guideline.

If you have identified two or three pairwise comparisons that you wish to make before conducting the analysis of variance, use the Bonferroni method. This means that if in a problem there are 10 populations but you're particularly interested in comparing, say, populations 3 and 7, and populations 5 and 9, use Bonferroni with $C = 2$.

If you plan on comparing all possible combinations, use Tukey.

When do we use Fisher's LSD? If the purpose of the analysis is to point to areas that should be investigated further, Fisher's LSD method is indicated.

Incidentally, to employ Fisher's LSD or the Bonferroni adjustment you must perform the analysis of variance first. Tukey's method can be employed instead of the analysis of variance.

EXERCISES

14.40 Use Fisher's LSD method with $\alpha = .05$ to determine which population means differ in the following problem.

$$k = 3 \quad n_1 = 10 \quad n_2 = 10 \quad n_3 = 10 \quad MSE = 700$$
$$\bar{x}_1 = 128.7 \quad \bar{x}_2 = 101.4 \quad \bar{x}_3 = 133.7$$

14.41 Repeat Exercise 14.40 using the Bonferroni adjustment.

14.42 Repeat Exercise 14.40 using Tukey's multiple comparison method.

14.43 Use Fisher's LSD procedure with $\alpha = .05$ to determine which population means differ given the following statistics.

$$k = 5 \quad n_1 = 5 \quad n_2 = 5 \quad n_3 = 5 \quad n_4 = 5$$
$$n_5 = 5 \quad MSE = 125 \quad \bar{x}_1 = 227 \quad \bar{x}_2 = 205$$
$$\bar{x}_3 = 219 \quad \bar{x}_4 = 248 \quad \bar{x}_5 = 202$$

14.44 Repeat Exercise 14.43 using the Bonferroni adjustment.

14.45 Repeat Exercise 14.43 using Tukey's multiple comparison method.

14.46 Apply Fisher's LSD method with the Bonferroni adjustment to determine which schools differ in Exercise 14.9. (Use $\alpha = .05$.)

14.47 Repeat Exercise 14.46 applying Tukey's method instead.

14.48 Apply Tukey's multiple comparison method to determine which forms differ in Exercise 14.10. (Use $\alpha = .05$.)

14.49 Repeat Exercise 14.48 applying the Bonferroni adjustment.

14.50 Use Tukey's multiple comparison method with $\alpha = .05$ to determine which lacquers differ in Exercise 14.11.

14.51 Repeat Exercise 14.50 using the Bonferroni adjustment with $\alpha = .10$.

The following exercises require a computer and software. The answers may be calculated manually. See Appendix B for the sample statistics.

14.52 Police cars, ambulances, and other emergency vehicles are required to carry road flares. One of the most important features of flares is their burning times. To help decide which of four brands on the market to use, a police laboratory technician measured the burning time for a random sample of 10 flares of each brand. The results, recorded to the nearest minute, are stored in columns 1 through 4 of file XR14-52.

   a Can we conclude at the 5% significance level that differences exist among the burning times of the four brands of flares?

   b Apply Fisher's LSD method with the Bonferroni adjustment to determine which flares are better.

   c Repeat part (b) using Tukey's method.

14.53 An engineering student who is about to graduate decided to survey various firms in Silicon Valley to see which offered the best chance for early promotion and career advancement. He surveyed 30 small firms (size level is based on gross revenues), 30 medium-sized firms, and 30 large firms and determined how much time must elapse before an average engineer can receive a promotion. These data are stored in columns 1 through 3 of file XR14-53.

   a Can the engineering student conclude at the 5% significance level that speed of promotion varies among the three sizes of engineering firms?

   b If differences exist, which of the following is true? Use Tukey's method.

      i Small firms differ from the other two.

      ii Midsized firms differ from the other two.

      iii Large firms differ from the other two.

      iv All three firms differ from one another.

      v Small firms differ from large firms.

14.8 BARTLETT'S TEST (OPTIONAL)

One of the required conditions for the F-test of the analysis of variance is that the population variances be equal. Informally, we can examine the sample variances or sample standard deviations (output by Excel and Minitab) and judge whether they are close enough to allow us to assume that the population variances are equal. Alternatively we can conduct a test similar to the F-test of σ_1^2/σ_2^2 we introduced in Chapter 12 to determine which t-test of $\mu_1 - \mu_2$ to use.

Several statistical tests are available for multiple variances. We introduce only one, **Bartlett's test,** which is applied to the independent samples single-factor model. The hypotheses we test are

$$H_0 : \sigma_1^2 = \sigma_2^2 = \cdots = \sigma_k^2$$
$$H_1 : \text{At least one variance differs.}$$

The test statistic is

$$B = \frac{1}{C}\left[(n - k)\ln(\text{MSE}) - \sum_{i=1}^{k}(n_i - 1)\ln(s_i^2)\right]$$

where

$$C = 1 + \frac{1}{3(k-1)}\left[\left(\sum_{i=1}^{k}\frac{1}{n_i - 1}\right) - \frac{1}{n - k}\right]$$

(*Note:* ln represents the natural logarithm.)

When the null hypothesis is true, $B = 0$. We reject the null hypothesis only when B is large. The critical value is determined from the sampling distribution, which is chi-squared distributed with $k - 1$ degrees of freedom. The required condition is the same as the condition for the analysis of variance; the populations must be normal. We illustrate Bartlett's test using Example 14.1.

SOLVE

The sample sizes are 20. Thus,

$$C = 1 + \frac{1}{3(k-1)}\left[\left(\sum_{i=1}^{k}\frac{1}{n_i - 1}\right) - \frac{1}{n - k}\right] = 1 + .167\left[\frac{1}{19} + \frac{1}{19} + \frac{1}{19} - \frac{1}{57}\right]$$

$$= 1.0234$$

The sample variances are 10,774, 7,239, and 8,669, respectively, and MSE $= 8,894$. Hence,

$$B = \frac{1}{C}\left[(n - k)\ln(\text{MSE}) - \sum_{i=1}^{k}(n_i - 1)\ln(s_i^2)\right]$$

$$= \frac{1}{1.0234} \times$$
$$\left[57 \times \ln(8,894) - \{19 \times \ln(10,77) + 19 \times \ln(7,239) + 19 \times \ln(8,669)\}\right]$$

$$= 0.7381$$

The rejection region is

$$B > \chi_{\alpha,k-1}^2 = \chi_{.05,2}^2 = 5.99147$$

Because B is less than 5.99147 we cannot reject the null hypothesis.

Excel Output for Example 14.1

	A	B	C	D
1	Bartlett's Test			
2		Variable 1	Variable 2	Variable 3
3	Variance	10775	7238	8670
4	B	0.7389		
5	df	2		
6	P-Value	0.6911		

COMMANDS	COMMANDS FOR EXAMPLE 14.1
1 Type or import the data into adjacent columns.	Open file **XM14-01**.
2 Click **Tools, Data Analysis Plus,** and **Bartlett's Test.**	
3 Specify the **Input Range:.** Do not include the cells containing the variable names.	**A2:C21**

Minitab Output for Example 14.1

Homogeneity of Variance

```
Bartlett's Test   (normal distribution)

Test Statistic:   0.739
P-Value       :   0.691
```

COMMANDS	COMMANDS FOR EXAMPLE 14.1
1 Type or import the data in stacked format.	Open file **XM14-01**.
2 Click **Stat, ANOVA,** and **Homogeneity of Variance . . . .**	
3 Specify the **Response:.**	**Sales**
4 Specify the **Factor:.**	**City**
5 Click **OK.**	

INTERPRET

There is not enough evidence to infer that the population variances differ. Earlier we showed that the data may be normally distributed. We're confident that the required conditions of the F-test of the analysis of variance are satisfied.

EXERCISES

The following exercises require the use of a computer and software.

14.54 Refer to Exercise 14.7. Test to determine whether the equality of variance requirement is satisfied. Use $\alpha = .10$.

14.55 Can we infer that variances are unequal in Exercise 14.8? Use $\alpha = .05$.

14.56 Is there sufficient evidence at the 5% significance level in Exercise 14.9 to infer that the population variances are unequal?

14.57 Test to determine whether the equality of variance requirement is satisfied in Exercise 14.10. Use $\alpha = .01$.

14.58 Refer to Exercise 14.11. Test to determine whether the equality of variance requirement is satisfied. Use $\alpha = .10$.

14.59 Conduct a test at the 1% significance level to determine whether the equality of variance requirement is satisfied in Exercise 14.12.

14.60 Can we infer that the equality of variances requirement is violated in Exercise 14.13? Use $\alpha = .05$.

14.9 SUMMARY

The analysis of variance allows us to test for differences among the populations when the data are quantitative. Three different models were introduced in this chapter. The first model is the independent samples single-factor model. In this model, the treatments are defined as the levels of one factor, and the experimental design specifies independent samples. The second model also defines the treatments on the basis of one factor. However, the randomized block design uses data gathered by observing the results of a matched or blocked experiment. The third model is the independent samples two-factor model wherein the treatments are defined as the combination of the levels of two factors. All models of the analysis of variance are based on partitioning the total sum of squares into sources of variation from which the mean squares and F-statistics are computed.

We introduced multiple comparison methods, which allow us to determine which means differ in the independent samples single-factor model. Finally, we presented Bartlett's test, which tests to determine whether the equal-variances requirement is satisfied.

IMPORTANT TERMS

Analysis of variance   *480*
Treatment means   *480*
Factor   *480*
Level   *480*
Single-factor analysis of
   variance   *480*
One-way analysis of variance   *480*
Response variable   *483*
Responses   *483*
Experimental units   *483*
Between-treatments variation   *483*
Sum of squares for treatments
   (SST)   *483*
Within-treatments variation   *484*
Sum of squares for error (SSE)   *484*
Mean squares   *486*
Mean square for treatments   *486*
Mean square for error   *486*
ANOVA table   *487*
Partitioning of the sum of
   squares   *488*
Total sum of squares SS(Total)   *488*
Completely randomized design   *490*
Multifactor   *498*

Two-factor   *498*
Randomized block design   *498*
Repeated measures design   *498*
Fixed effects   *499*
Random effects   *499*
Sum of squares for blocks
   (SSB)   *499*
Factorial experiment   *507*
Complete factorial experiment   *509*
Two-way classification   *509*
Replicate   *509*
Balanced   *509*
Taguchi Loss Function   *522*
Fisher's least significance
   difference (LSD) method   *526*
Comparisonwise Type I error
   rate   *527*
Experimentwise Type I error
   rate   *527*
Bonferroni adjustment   *528*
Tukey's multiple comparison
   method   *528*
Bartlett's test   *533*

SUPPLEMENTARY EXERCISES

The following exercises require the use of a computer and software. Conduct all tests at the 5% significance level.

14.61 The possible imposition of a residential property tax has been a sensitive political issue in a large city that consists of five boroughs. Currently, property tax is based on an assessment system that dates back to 1950. This system has produced numerous inequities whereby newer homes tend to be assessed at higher values than older homes. A new system based on the market value of the house has been proposed. Opponents of the plan argue that residents of some boroughs would have to pay considerably more on the average, while residents of other boroughs would pay less. As part of a study examining this issue, several homes in each borough were assessed under both plans. The percentage increase (a decrease is represented by a negative increase) in each case was recorded and stored in columns 1 through 5 of file XR14-61.

    a Can we conclude that there are differences in the effect the new assessment system would have on the five boroughs?

    b If differences exist, which boroughs differ? (Use Tukey's multiple comparison method.)

    c What are the required conditions for your conclusions to be valid?

    d Are required conditions satisfied?

14.62 The editor of the student newspaper was in the process of making some major changes in the newspaper's layout. He was also contemplating changing the typeface of the print used. To help himself make a decision, he set up an experiment in which 20 individuals were asked to read four newspaper pages, with each page printed in a different typeface. If the reading speed differed, then the typeface that was read fastest would be used. However, if there was not enough evidence to allow the editor to conclude that such differences existed, the current typeface would be continued. The times (in seconds) to completely read one page are stored in columns 1 to 4 of file XR14-62. What should the editor do?

14.63 Each year billions of dollars are lost because of worker injuries on the job. Costs can be decreased if injured workers can be rehabilitated quickly. As part of an analysis of the amount of time taken for workers to return to work, a sample of male blue-collar workers aged 35 to 45 who suffered a common wrist fracture was taken. The researchers believed that the mental and physical condition of the individual affects recovery time. Each man was given a questionnaire to complete, which measured whether he tended to be optimistic or pessimistic. Physical condition was also evaluated and categorized as very physically fit, average, or in poor condition. The number of days until the wrist returned to full function was measured for each individual. These data are stored in file XR14-63 in the following way.

    Column 2: time to recover for optimists (rows 1 to 10) = very fit, rows 11 to 20 = in average condition, rows 21 to 30 = poor condition

    Column 3: time to recover for pessimists (same format as column 2)

    a What are the factors in this experiment? What are the levels of each factor?

    b Can we conclude that pessimists and optimists differ in their recovery times?

    c Can we conclude that physical condition affects recovery times?

14.64 In the past decade, American companies have spent nearly $1 trillion on computer systems. However, productivity gains have been quite small. During the 1980s, productivity in U.S. service industries (where most computers are used) grew by only 0.7% annually. In the 1990s, this figure rose to 1.5%. (Source: *New York Times Service,* 22 February, 1995). The problem of small productivity increases may be caused by employee difficulty in learning how to use the computer. Suppose that in an experiment to examine the problem, 100 firms were studied. Each company had bought a new computer system 5 years ago. The companies reported their increase in productivity over the 5-year period and were also classified as offering extensive employee training, some employee training, little employee training, or no formal employee training in the use of computers. (There were 25 firms in each group.) The results are stored in columns 1 through 4 of file XR14-64.

    a Can we conclude that differences in productivity gain exist among the four groups of companies?

    b If there are differences, use Tukey's multiple comparison method to determine what they are.

14.65 The marketing manager of a large ski resort wants to advertise that his ski resort has the shortest lift lines of any resort in the area. To avoid the possibility of a false advertising liability suit, he collects data on the average wait in line at his resort and at each of two competing resorts on each of 15 days. These results are stored in columns 1 through 4 of file XR14-65. (Column 1 indicates the day, and columns 2 through 4 store the waiting times.) Can he conclude that there are differences in waiting times among the three resorts?

14.66 A popularly held belief about university professors is that they don't work very hard, and that the higher their rank, the less work they do. A statistics student decided to determine whether the belief is true. She took a random sample of 20 university instructors in each of the faculties of business, engineering, arts, and sciences. In each sample of 20, five were instructors, five were assistant professors, five were associate professors, and five were full professors. Each professor was surveyed and asked to report confidentially the number of weekly hours of work. These data are stored in file XR14-66 in the following way.

> Column 2: hours of work for business professors (first 5 rows = instructors, next 5 rows = assistant professors, next 5 rows = associate professors, and last 5 rows = full professors)
>
> Column 3: hours of work for engineering professors (same format as column 2)
>
> Column 4: hours of work for arts professors (same format as column 2)
>
> Column 5: hours of work for science professors (same format as column 2)

a What are the factors in this experiment? What are their levels?
b Are there differences among the four ranks of instructor?
c Are there differences among the four faculties?
d What test must be conducted before attempting to answer parts (b) and (c)?
e What is the result of the test described in part (d)? What does the test result tell you?

14.67 In marketing children's products, it's extremely important to produce television commercials that hold the attention of the children who view them. A psychologist hired by a marketing research firm wants to determine whether differences in attention span exist among children watching advertisements for different types of products. One hundred fifty children under 10 years of age were recruited for an experiment. One-third watched a 60-second commercial for a new computer game, one-third watched a commercial for a breakfast cereal, and another third watched a commercial for children's clothes. Their attention spans were measured. The results (in seconds) are stored in the first three columns of file XR14-67. Do these data provide enough evidence to conclude that there are differences in attention span among the three products advertised?

14.68 North American automobile manufacturers have become more concerned with quality because of foreign competition. One aspect of quality is the cost of repairing damage caused by accidents. A manufacturer is considering several new types of bumpers. To test how well they react to low-speed collisions, 40

bumpers of each of five different types were installed on midsize cars, which were then driven into a wall at 5 miles per hour. The cost of repairing the damage in each case was assessed, and the relevant data stored in columns 1 to 5 of file XR14-68.

a Is there sufficient evidence to infer that the bumpers differ in their reactions to low-speed collisions?
b If differences exist, use the Bonferroni adjustment to determine which bumpers differ.

14.69 It is important for salespeople to be knowledgeable about how people shop for certain products. Suppose that a new car salesman believes that the age and sex of a car shopper affects the way he or she makes an offer on a car. He records the initial offers made by a group of men and women shoppers on a $20,000 Mercury Sable. Besides the sex of the shopper, the salesman also notes the age category. The amount of money below the asking price that each person offered initially for the car was recorded and stored in file XR14-69 using the following format. Column 2 contains the data for the under 30 group; the first 25 rows store the results for female shoppers and the last 25 rows are the male shoppers. Columns 3 and 4 store the data for the 30–45 age category and over 45 category, respectively. What can we conclude from these data?

14.70 A study was undertaken to investigate whether different training programs and software packages offered by a business college were more effective than others. The study recorded the number of words per minute typed by six groups of 40 students who completed the training programs. The training program and software packages assigned to each group are as described below.

> Group 1: hands-on training/MS Word software
>
> Group 2: computer tutorial/MS Word software
>
> Group 3: hands-on training/WordPerfect software
>
> Group 4: computer tutorial/WordPerfect software
>
> Group 5: hands-on training/AmiPro software
>
> Group 6: computer tutorial/AmiPro software

The typing speeds for each student were recorded in columns 1 through 6 for groups 1 to 6, respectively, in file XR14-70. Can we conclude that the typing speeds differ among the six groups of students?

14.71 Refer to Exercise 14.70. Do the data allow us to infer that there are combinations of software packages and training programs that produce faster speeds than other combinations?

14.72 Many of you reading this page probably learned how to read using the whole-language method. This approach maintains that the natural and effective way is to be exposed to whole words in context. Students learn how to read by recognizing words they have seen before. In the past generation this has been the dominant teaching approach throughout North America. It replaced phonics, wherein children are taught to sound out the letters to form words. The whole-language method was instituted with little or no research and has been severely criticized in the past. A recent study may have resolved the question of which method should be employed. Barbara Foorman, an educational psychologist at the University of Houston, described the experiment at the annual meeting of the American Association for the Advancement of Science. The subjects were 375 low-achieving, poor, grade 1 students in Houston schools. The students were divided into three groups. One group was educated according to the whole-language philosophy, a second group was taught using a pure phonics approach, and the third was taught employing a mixed or embedded phonics technique. At the end of the term students were asked to read words on a list of 50 words. The number of words each child could read are stored in columns 1, 2, and 3 (whole-language, embedded phonics, and pure phonics, respectively) in file XR14-72.

a Can we infer that differences exist among the effects of the three teaching approaches?

b If differences exist, identify which method appears to be best. Use Tukey's multiple comparison method.

14.73 Are babies exposed to music before their birth smarter than those who are not? If so, what kind of music is best? Researchers at the University of Wisconsin conducted an experiment with rats. The researchers selected a random sample of pregnant rats and divided the sample into three groups. Mozart works were played to one group, a second group was exposed to white noise (a steady hum with no musical elements), and the third group listened to Philip Glass music, which consists of very simple compositions. The researchers then trained the young rats to run a maze in search of food. The amount of time for the rats to complete the maze was measured for all three groups. These data are stored in file XR14-73 (column 1 = time for "Mozart" rats, column 2 = "white noise" rates, and column 3 = time for "Glass" rats).

a Can we infer from these data that there are differences among the three groups?

b If there are differences, use Tukey's multiple comparison method to determine which group is best.

14.74 When the stock market has a large 1-day decline does it bounce back the next day or does the bad news endure? To answer this question, an economist examined a random sample of daily changes to the Toronto Stock Index (TSE). He recorded the percent change. He classified declines as

Down by less than 0.5%

Down by 0.5% to 1.5%

Down by 1.5% to 2.5%

Down by more than 2.5%

For each of these days he recorded the percent change the following day. These data are stored in columns 1 through 4 of file XR14-74. Do these data allow us to infer that there are differences in changes to the TSE depending on the loss the previous day? (This exercise is based on a study undertaken by Tim Whitehead, an economist for Left Bank Economics, a consulting firm near Paris, Ontario.)

14.75 Stock market investors are always seeking the "Holy Grail," a sign that tells them the market has bottomed out or achieved its highest level. There are several indicators: One is the buy signal developed by Gerald Appel. Appel says that a bottom has been reached when the difference between the weekly close of the NYSE index and the 10-week moving average (see Chapter 20) is −4.0 points or more. Another bottom indicator is based on identifying a certain pattern in the line chart of the stock market index. As an experiment a financial analyst randomly selected 100 weeks. For each week he determined whether there was an Appel buy, a chart buy, or no indication. For each type of week he recorded the percentage change over the next 4 weeks. These data are stored in columns 1 to 3, respectively, in file XR14-75. Can we infer that at least one buy indicator is useful?

CASE 14.1: Effects of Financial Planning*

In the United States, approximately one-half million small businesses fail annually. Many researchers have investigated small businesses in order to determine the factors distinguishing those that succeed from those that fail. One set of researchers suggested that a potential factor is the degree of planning. They identified three different levels of planning.

1 **Structured strategic planning.** This involves producing a formalized written description of long-term plans with a 3- to 15-year horizon.

2 **Structured operational planning.** This type of planning deals with short-term issues such as action plans for the current fiscal year.

3 **Unstructured planning.** This covers arrangements in which there is no formal or informal planning.

A random sample of 73 firms participated in the study. The mean age of the firms was 9.2 years, mean annual revenues were $4.25 million, and mean net income was $300,000. On average, 71 people were employed. These statistics suggest that the 73 participating companies are fairly representative of the population to be investigated.

The companies were analyzed over a 5-year period and the following four measures of performance were used.

1 **Revenue growth.** Average sales growth in percent over the 5 years.

2 **Net income growth.** Growth in percent average net income (before taxes) over the 5 years.

3 **Present value growth.** Average book value growth in percent over the 5 years.

4 **CEO cash compensation growth.** Percent average growth in the cash payments to chief executive officers over the 5 years.

The data are stored in file C14-01 using the following format.

Column 1: revenue growth for all companies

Column 2: income growth for all companies

Column 3: present value growth for all companies

Column 4: compensation growth for all companies

Column 5: index 1 = companies with structured strategic planning

2 = companies with structured operational planning

3 = companies with unstructured planning

Can we infer that for each of the performance measurements there are differences among firms at each planning level?

*Adapted from T. S. Bracker, B. W. Keats, and J. N. Pearson, "Planning and Financial Performance Among Small Firms in a Growth Industry," *Strategic Management Journal 9* (1988): 591–603.

CASE 14.2: Diversification Strategy for Multinational Firms*

One of the many goals of management researchers is to identify factors that differentiate between success and failure and among different levels of success in businesses. In this way, it may be possible to help more businesses become successful. Among multinational enterprises (MNEs), two factors to be examined are the degree of product diversification and the degree of internationalization. *Product diversification* refers to efforts by companies to increase the range and variety of the products they produce. The more unrelated the products are, the greater the degree of diversification created. *Internationalization* is a term that expresses geographic diversification. Companies that sell their products to many countries are said to employ a high degree of internationalization.

Three management researchers set out to examine these issues. In particular, they wanted to test two hypotheses.

1 MNEs employing strategies that result in more product diversification outperform those with less product diversification.

2 MNEs employing strategies that result in more internationalization outperform those with less internationalization.

Company performance was measured in two ways.

1 Profit-to-sales is the ratio of profit to total sales, expressed as a percentage.

2 Profit-to-assets is the ratio of profit to total assets, expressed as a percentage.

A random sample of 189 companies was selected. For each company, the profit-to-sales and profit-to-assets were measured. In addition, each company was judged to have a low (1), medium (2), or high (3) level of diversification. The degree of internationalization was measured on a five-point scale where 1 = lowest level and 5 = highest level.

The results are stored in file C14-02 on the data disk, using the following format.

Column 1: profit-to-sales ratio

Column 2: profit-to-assets ratio

Column 3: levels of diversification

Column 4: degrees of internationalism

What do these data tell you about the researchers' hypotheses?

---

*Adapted from J. M. Geringer, P. W. Beamish, and R. C. da Costa, "Diversification Strategy and Internationalization: Implication for MNE Performance," *Strategic Management Journal 10* (1989): 109–19.

Chapter 15

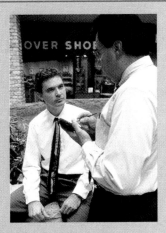

Additional

Tests for

Qualitative

Data

15.1 Introduction

15.2 Chi-Squared Goodness-of-Fit Test

15.3 Chi-Squared Test of a Contingency Table

15.4 Summary of Tests on Qualitative Data

15.5 Chi-Squared Test for Normality (Optional)

15.6 Summary

15.1 INTRODUCTION

This chapter develops two statistical techniques that involve qualitative data. The first is a goodness-of-fit test applied to data produced by a multinomial experiment, a generalization of a binomial experiment. The second uses data arranged in a table (called a contingency table) to determine whether or not two classifications of a population of qualitative data are statistically independent; this test can also be interpreted as a comparison of two or more populations. The sampling distribution of the test statistics in both tests is the chi-squared distribution introduced in Chapter 11. Two examples of situations follow in which chi-squared tests could be applied.

Example 1 Firms periodically estimate the proportion (or market share) of consumers who prefer their products, as well as the market shares of competitors. These market shares may change over time as a result of advertising campaigns or the introduction of new improved products. To determine whether the actual current market shares are in accord with its beliefs, a firm might sample several consumers and compute, for each of k competing companies, the proportion of consumers sampled who prefer that company's product. Such an experiment, in which each consumer is classified as preferring one of the k companies, is called a multinomial experiment. If only two companies were considered ($k = 2$), we would be dealing with the familiar binomial experiment. After computing the proportion of consumers preferring each of the k companies, a goodness-of-fit test could be conducted to determine whether the sample proportions (or market shares) differ significantly from those hypothesized by the firm. The problem objective is to describe the population of consumers, and the data are qualitative.

Example 2 For advertising and other purposes, it is important for a company to understand which segments of the market prefer which of its products. For example, it would be helpful for an automotive manufacturer to know if there is a relationship between the buyer preferences for its various models and the sex of the consumer. After conducting a survey to solicit consumers' preferences, the firm could classify each respondent according to two qualitative variables: model preferred and sex. A test could then be conducted to determine whether consumers' preferences are independent of their sex. Rather than interpreting this test as a test of the independence of two qualitative variables defined over a single population, we could view male and female consumers as representing two different populations. Then we could interpret the test as testing for differences in preferences between these two populations.

15.2 CHI-SQUARED GOODNESS-OF-FIT TEST

This section presents another test designed to describe a single population of qualitative data. The first such test was introduced in Section 11.4, where we discussed the statistical procedure employed to test hypotheses about a population proportion. In that case, the qualitative variable could assume one of only two possible values, success or failure. Our tests dealt with hypotheses about the proportion of successes in the entire population. Recall that the experiment that produces the data is called a binomial experiment. In this section, we introduce the **multinomial experiment,** which is an extension of the binomial experiment, wherein two or more outcomes per trial are possible.

> ### Multinomial Experiment
>
> A multinomial experiment is one possessing the following properties.
>
> **1** The experiment consists of a fixed number n of trials.
>
> **2** The outcome of each trial can be classified into one of k categories, called cells.
>
> **3** The probability p_i that the outcome will fall into cell i remains constant for each trial. Moreover, $p_1 + p_2 + \cdots + p_k = 1$.
>
> **4** Each trial of the experiment is independent of the other trials.

As you can see when $k = 2$, the multinomial experiment is identical to the binomial experiment. Just as we count the number of successes (recall that we label the number of successes x) and failures in a binomial experiment, we count the number of outcomes falling into each of the k cells in a multinomial experiment. In this way, we obtain a set of observed frequencies $f_1, f_2, \ldots, f_k$, where f_i is the observed frequency of outcomes falling into cell i, for $i = 1, 2, \ldots, k$. Because the experiment consists of n trials and an outcome must fall into some cell,

$$f_1 + f_2 + \cdots + f_k = n$$

Just as we used the number of successes x (by calculating the sample proportion p, which is equal to x/n) to draw inferences about p, so do we use the observed frequencies to draw inferences about the cell probabilities. We'll proceed in what by now has become a standard procedure. We will set up the hypotheses and develop the test statistic and its sampling distribution. We'll demonstrate the process with the following example.

▼ EXAMPLE 15.1

Two companies, A and B, have recently conducted aggressive advertising campaigns in order to maintain and possibly increase their respective shares of the market for fabric softener. These two companies enjoy a dominant position in the market. Before the advertising campaigns began, the market share of Company A was 45%, while Company B had 40% of the market. Other competitors accounted for the remaining 15%. To determine whether these market shares changed after the advertising campaigns, a marketing analyst solicited the preferences of a random sample of 200 customers of fabric softener. Of the 200 customers, 102 indicated a preference for Company A's product, 82 preferred Company B's fabric softener, and the remaining 16 preferred the products of one of the competitors. Can the analyst infer at the 5% significance level that customer preferences have changed from the levels they were at before the advertising campaigns were launched?

Solution

IDENTIFY

The population in question is composed of the brand preferences of the fabric softener customers. The data are qualitative because each respondent will choose one of three possible answers—prefer Company A's product, Company B's product, or another product. If there were only two categories, or if we were only interested in the proportion of one company's customers (which we would label as successes with the others labeled as failures), we would identify the technique as the z-test of p. However, in this problem we're interested in the proportions of all three categories. We recognize this experiment as a multinomial experiment, and we identify the technique as the chi-squared goodness-of-fit test.

Because we want to know if the market shares have changed, we specify those pre-campaign market shares in the null hypothesis.

$$H_0: p_1 = .45, p_2 = .40, p_3 = .15$$

The alternative hypothesis attempts to answer our question "Have the proportions changed?" Thus,

H_1: At least one p_i is not equal to its specified value

Test Statistic If the null hypothesis is true, we would expect the number of customers selecting Brand A, Brand B, and other to be 200 times the proportions specified under the null hypothesis. That is

$$e_1 = 200(.45) = 90$$
$$e_2 = 200(.40) = 80$$
$$e_3 = 200(.15) = 30$$

In general, the **expected frequency** for each cell is given by

$$e_i = np_i$$

This expression is derived from the formula for the expected value of a binomial random variable, first seen in Section 6.8.

If the expected frequencies e_i and the observed frequencies f_i are quite different, we would conclude that the null hypothesis is false, and we would reject it. However, if the expected and observed frequencies are similar, we would not reject the null hypothesis. The test statistic we employ to measure the similarity of the expected and observed frequencies is

$$\chi^2 = \sum_{i=1}^{k} \frac{(f_i - e_i)^2}{e_i}$$

The sampling distribution of the test statistic is approximately chi-squared with $k - 1$ degrees of freedom, provided that the sample size is large. We discuss this required condition later. (The chi-squared distribution was introduced in Section 11.4. See page 364 for a review or, perhaps, the introduction to this distribution and Table 5 in Appendix B.)

The following table demonstrates the calculation of the test statistic. Thus, the value $\chi^2 = 8.18$. As usual, we judge the size of this test statistic by specifying the rejection region or by determining the p-value.

Company	Observed Frequency f_i	Expected Frequency e_i	$(f_i - e_i)$	$\dfrac{(f_i - e_i)^2}{e_i}$
A	102	90	12	1.60
B	82	80	2	.05
Other	16	30	−14	6.53
Total	200	200		$\chi^2 = 8.18$

Rejection Region   When the null hypothesis is true, the observed and expected frequencies should be similar, in which case the test statistic

$$\chi^2 = \sum_{i=1}^{k} \frac{(f_i - e_i)^2}{e_i}$$

will be small. Thus, a small test statistic supports the null hypothesis. If the null hypothesis is untrue, some of the observed and expected frequencies will differ and the test statistic will be large. Consequently, we want to reject the null hypothesis when χ^2 is greater than $\chi^2_{\alpha, k-1}$. That is, the rejection region is

$$\chi^2 > \chi^2_{\alpha, k-1}$$

In Example 15.1, $k = 3$; the rejection region is

$$\chi^2 > \chi^2_{\alpha, k-1} = \chi^2_{.05, 2} = 5.99147$$

Since the test statistic is

$$\chi^2 = 8.18$$

we reject the null hypothesis.

The p-value of the test is

$$p\text{-value} = P(\chi^2 > 8.18)$$

Unfortunately Table 5 in Appendix B does not allow us to perform this calculation (except for approximation by interpolation). The p-value must be produced by computer.

 If we have the raw data representing the qualitative responses, we must first determine the frequency of each category (the observed values). The printout below was generated from the observed and expected values.

Excel Output for Example 15.1

Counting in Excel

Click f_x, **Statistical,** and **COUNTIF.** Specify the range of the data and the first code. The dialog box will show the frequency for that code. Repeat for each code.

	A	B
1	Observed	Expected
2	102	90
3	82	80
4	16	30
5		
6	0.016711	

The output from the commands listed below is the p-value of the test. It is .016711.

COMMANDS	COMMANDS FOR EXAMPLE 15.1
1 Type the observed values into one column and the expected values into another column. (If you wish you	102 90 82 80 16 30

can type the cell probabilities specified in the null hypothesis and let Excel convert these into expected values by multiplying by the sample size.)

2 Activate some empty cell and click f_x, **Statistical,** and **CHITEST.** Cell A5

3 Specify the range of the observed values (**Actual_range**). **A1:A3**

4 Specify the range of the expected values (**Expected_range**). Click **FINISH.** **B1:B3**

Counting in Minitab

Minitab does not conduct this procedure. However, it is relatively easy to program Minitab to do so. See Appendix 15.A for details.

INTERPRET There is sufficient evidence to infer that the proportions have changed since the advertising campaigns. If the sampling was conducted properly, we can be quite confident in our conclusion. This technique has only one required condition, which is satisfied. (See rule of five described below.) It is probably a worthwhile exercise to determine the nature and causes of the changes. The results of this analysis will determine the design and timing of other advertising campaigns.

▲

RULE OF FIVE

The test statistic used to compare the relative sizes of observed and expected frequencies is

$$\chi^2 = \sum_{i=1}^{k} \frac{(f_i - e_i)^2}{e_i}$$

We previously stated that this test statistic has an approximate chi-squared distribution. In fact, the actual distribution of this test statistic is discrete, but it can be approximated conveniently by using a continuous chi-squared distribution when the sample size n is large, just as we approximated the discrete binomial distribution by using the normal distribution. This approximation may be poor, however, if the expected cell frequencies are small. For the (discrete) distribution of the test statistic to be adequately approximated by the (continuous) chi-squared distribution, the conventional (and conservative) rule—known as the rule of five—is to require that the expected frequency for each cell be at least 5.* Where necessary, cells should be combined in order to satisfy this condition. The choice of cells to be combined should be made in such a way that meaningful categories result from the combination.

---

*To be on the safe side, this rule of thumb is somewhat conservative. A discussion of alternatives to the rule of five can be found in W. J. Conover, *Pratical Nonparametric Statistics* (New York: John Wiley, 1971), p. 152, and in S. Siegel, *Nonparametric Statistics for the Behavioral Sciences* (New York: McGraw-Hill, 1956), p. 178

Consider the following modification of Example 15.1. Suppose that three companies (A, B, and C) have recently conducted aggressive advertising campaigns; the market shares prior to the campaigns were $p_1 = .45$ for Company A, $p_2 = .40$ for Company B, $p_3 = .13$ for Company C, and $p_4 = .02$ for other competitors. In a test to see if market shares changed after the advertising campaigns, the null hypothesis would now be

$$H_0: p_1 = .45, p_2 = .40, p_3 = .13, p_4 = .02$$

Hence, if the preferences of a sample of 200 customers were solicited, the expected frequencies would be

$$e_1 = 90, \quad e_2 = 80, \quad e_3 = 26, \quad e_4 = 4$$

Since the expected cell frequency e_4 is less than 5, the rule of five requires that it be combined with one of the other expected frequencies (say, e_3) to obtain a combined cell frequency of (in this case) 30. Although e_4 could have been combined with e_1 or e_2, we have chosen to combine it with e_3 so that we still have a separate category representing each of the two dominant companies (A and B). After this combination is made, the null hypothesis reads

$$H_0: p_1 = .45, p_2 = .40, p_3 = .15$$

where p_3 now represents the market share of all competitors of companies A and B. Therefore, the appropriate number of degrees of freedom for the chi-squared test statistic would be $k - 1 = 3 - 1 = 2$, where k is the number of cells after some have been combined to satisfy the rule of five.

Let's summarize the factors that allow us to recognize when to use the chi-squared goodness-of-fit test for a multinomial experiment.

Factors that Identify the Chi-Squared Goodness-of-Fit Test

1 Problem objective: describe a single population

2 Data type: qualitative

3 Number of categories: 2 or more

EXERCISES

15.1 Consider a multinomial experiment involving $n = 200$ trials and $k = 5$ cells. The observed frequencies resulting from the experiment are shown in the following table, and the null hypothesis to be tested is as follows.

$$H_0: p_1 = .1, p_2 = .2, p_3 = .3, p_4 = .2, p_5 = .2$$

Cell	1	2	3	4	5
Frequency	28	56	48	36	32

Test the hypothesis at the 1% significance level.

15.2 Repeat Exercise 15.1 with the following frequencies.

Cell	1	2	3	4	5
Frequency	14	28	24	18	16

15.3 Repeat Exercise 15.1 with the following frequencies.

Cell	1	2	3	4	5
Frequency	7	14	12	9	8

15.4 Review the results of Exercises 15.1 to 15.3. What is the effect of decreasing the sample size?

15.5 Consider a multinomial experiment involving $n = 150$ trials and $k = 4$ cells. The observed frequencies resulting from the experiment are shown in the following table, and the null hypothesis to be tested is as follows.

$H_0: p_1 = .3, p_2 = .3, p_3 = .2, p_4 = .2$

Cell	1	2	3	4
Frequency	38	50	38	24

Test the hypotheses, using $\alpha = .05$.

15.6 For Exercise 15.5, retest the hypotheses, assuming that the experiment involved twice as many trials ($n = 300$) and that the observed frequencies were twice as high as before, as shown in the following table.

Cell	1	2	3	4
Frequency	76	100	76	48

The following exercises require the use of a computer and software. The answers may be calculated manually. See Appendix C for the sample statistics.

15.7 The results of a multinomial experiment with $k = 5$ are stored in file XR15-07. Each outcome is identified by the numbers 1 through 5 stored in column 1. Test to determine if there is enough evidence to infer that the proportion of each outcome is the same. (Use $\alpha = .10$.)

15.8 A multinomial experiment was conducted with $k = 4$. Each outcome is stored as an integer from 1 to 4 and the results of a survey are stored in file XR15-08. Test the following hypotheses with a 5% significance level.

$H_0: p_1 = .15, p_2 = .40, p_3 = .35, p_4 = .10$

H_1 : At least one p_i is not equal to its specified value

15.9 To determine whether a single die is balanced, or fair, the die was rolled 600 times. The outcomes are stored in file XR15-09. Is there sufficient evidence at the 5% significance level to allow you to conclude that the die is not fair?

15.10 Grades assigned by an economics instructor have historically followed a symmetrical distribution: 5% A's, 25% B's, 40% C's, 25% D's, and 5% F's. This year, a sample of 150 grades was drawn. The grades ($1 = A$, $2 = B, 3 = C, 4 = D$, and $5 = F$) are stored in file XR15-10. Can you conclude, at the 5% level of significance, that this year's grades are distributed differently from grades in the past?

15.11 Pat Statsdud is about to take a multiple-choice exam but as usual knows absolutely nothing. He plans to choose one of the five choices by guessing. Pat has been given one of the professor's previous exams with the correct answers marked. The correct choices are stored in file XR15-11 where $1 = $ (a), $2 = $ (b), $3 = $ (c), $4 = $ (d), and $5 = $ (e). Help Pat determine whether this professor does *not* randomly distribute the correct answer over the five choices. (Use a 10% significance level.) If this is true, how does it affect Pat's strategy?

15.12 Financial managers are interested in the speed with which customers who make purchases on credit pay their bills. In addition to calculating the average number of days that unpaid bills (called accounts receivable) remain outstanding, they often prepare an aging schedule. An aging schedule classifies outstanding accounts receivable according to the time that has elapsed since billing, and records the proportion of accounts receivable belonging to each classification. A large firm has determined its aging schedule for the past 5 years. These results are shown in the following table. During the past few months, however, the economy has taken a downturn. The company would like to know if the recession has affected the aging schedule. A random sample of 250 accounts receivable was drawn and each account was classified (and stored in file XR15-12) as follows.

1 = 0–14 days outstanding
2 = 15–29 days outstanding
3 = 30–59 days outstanding
4 = 60 or more days outstanding

Number of days outstanding	Proportion of accounts receivable past 5 years
0–14	.72
15–29	.15
30–59	.10
60 and over	.03

Determine whether the aging schedule has changed. (Use $\alpha = .05$)

15.13 License records in a county reveal that 15% of cars are subcompacts (1), 25% are compacts (2), 40% are midsize (3), and the rest are an assortment of other styles and models (4). A random sample of accidents involving cars licensed in the county was drawn. The type of car was stored in file XR15-13 using the codes in parentheses. Can we infer at the 5% significance level that certain sizes of cars are involved in a higher than expected percentage of accidents?

15.14 In an election held last year that was contested by three parties, Party A captured 31% of the vote, Party B garnered 51%, and Party C received the remaining votes. A survey of 1,200 voters asked each to identify the party that they would vote for in the next election. These results are stored in file XR15-14 where $1 = $ Party A, $2 = $ Party B, and $3 = $ Party C. Can we infer at the 10% significance level that voter support has changed since the election?

15.15 In a number of pharmaceutical studies volunteers who take placebos (but are told they have taken a cold remedy) report the following side effects.

Headache (1)	5%
Drowsiness (2)	7%

Stomach upset (3)   4%
No side effect (4)   84%

A random sample of 250 people who were given a placebo (but who thought they had taken an anti-inflammatory) reported whether they had experienced

each of the side effects. These data are stored in file XR15-15 using the codes in parentheses. Can we infer at the 5% significance level that the reported side effects of the placebo for an anti-inflammatory differ from that of a cold remedy?

15.3 CHI-SQUARED TEST OF A CONTINGENCY TABLE

In this section, we introduce another chi-squared test, this one designed to satisfy two different problem objectives. The **chi-squared test of a contingency table** is used to determine if there is enough evidence to infer that two qualitative variables are related and to infer that differences exist among two or more populations of qualitative variables. Completing both objectives entails classifying items according to two different criteria. To see how this is done, consider the following example.

▼ **EXAMPLE 15.2**

The M.B.A. program was experiencing problems scheduling their courses. The demand for the program's optional courses and majors was quite variable from one year to the next. In one year students seemed to want marketing courses and in other years accounting or finance were the rage. In desperation the dean of the business school turned to a statistics professor for assistance. The statistics professor believed that the problem could be the variability in the academic background of the students and that the undergraduate degree affects the choice of major. As a start he took a random sample of last year's M.B.A. students and recorded the undergraduate degree and the major selected in the graduate program. The undergraduate degrees were B.A., B.Eng., B.B.A., as well as several others. There are three possible majors for the M.B.A. students: accounting, finance, and marketing. The results were summarized in a table called a **contingency** or **cross-classification table,** shown below. Can the statistician conclude that the undergraduate degree affects the choice of major?

	M.B.A. Major		
Undergraduate Degree	Accounting	Finance	Marketing
B.A.	31	13	16
B.Eng.	8	16	7
B.B.A.	12	10	17
Other	10	5	7

Solution One way to solve the problem is to consider that there are two variables represented by the contingency table. The variables are the undergraduate degree and the M.B.A. major. Both are qualitative. The values of the undergraduate degree are B.A., B.Eng., B.B.A., and other. The values of M.B.A. majors are accounting, finance, and marketing. The problem objective is to analyze the relationship between the two variables. Specifically, we want to know whether one variable affects the other.

Another way of addressing the problem is to determine whether differences exist among B.A.'s, B.Eng.'s, B.B.A.'s, and others. In other words, we treat the earners of each undergraduate degree as a separate population. Each population has three possible values represented by the M.B.A. major. (We can also answer the question by treating the M.B.A. majors as populations and the undergraduate degrees as the values of the random variable.) Here the problem objective is to compare four populations.

As you will shortly discover both objectives lead to the same test. Consequently, we address both objectives at the same time. The null hypothesis will specify that there is no relationship between the two variables. We state this in the following way.

H_0: The two variables are independent

The alternative hypothesis specifies one variable affects the other, expressed as

H_1: The two variables are dependent

If the null hypothesis is true, undergraduate degree and M.B.A. major are independent of one another. This means that whether an M.B.A. student earned a B.A., B.Eng., B.B.A., or other degree does not affect his or her choice of major program in the M.B.A. Consequently, there is no difference in major choice among the graduates of the undergraduate programs. If the alternative hypothesis is true, undergraduate degree does affect the choice of M.B.A. major. Thus, there are differences among the four undergraduate degree categories.

Test Statistic The test statistic is the same as the one employed to test proportions in the goodness-of-fit-test. That is, the test statistic is

$$\chi^2 = \sum_{i=1}^{k} \frac{(f_i - e_i)^2}{e_i}$$

where k is the number of cells in the contingency table. If you examine the null hypothesis described in the goodness-of-fit test and the one described above, you will discover a major difference. In the goodness-of-fit test, the null hypothesis lists values for the probabilities p_i. The null hypothesis for the chi-squared test of a contingency table only states that the two variables are independent. However, we need the probabilities to compute the expected values e_i, which in turn are needed to calculate the value of the test statistic. (The entries in the table are the observed values f_i.) The question immediately arises: From where do we get the probabilities? The answer is that they must come from the data after we assume that the null hypothesis is true.

If we consider each undergraduate degree as a separate population, each row represents a multinomial experiment with three cells. If the null hypothesis is true, the four multinomial populations should have similar proportions in each cell. We can estimate the cell probabilities by calculating the total in each column and dividing by the sample size. Thus,

$$P(\text{Accounting}) = \frac{61}{152} = .401$$

$$P(\text{Finance}) = \frac{44}{152} = .289$$

$$P(\text{Marketing}) = \frac{47}{152} = .309$$

We can calculate the expected values for each cell in the four multinomial experiments by multiplying these probabilities by the total number of M.B.A. students from each undergraduate program. By adding across the each row, we find there were 60 B.A.'s, 31 B.Eng's, 39 B.B.A.'s, and 22 M.B.A. students with other undergraduate degrees.

Expected Number of M.B.A. Majors with B.A.'s

M.B.A. Major	Expected Value
Accounting	$60 \times \dfrac{61}{152} = 24.08$
Finance:	$60 \times \dfrac{44}{152} = 17.37$
Marketing	$60 \times \dfrac{47}{152} = 18.55$

Expected Number of M.B.A. Majors with B.Eng.'s

M.B.A. Major	Expected Value
Accounting	$31 \times \dfrac{61}{152} = 12.44$
Finance	$31 \times \dfrac{44}{152} = 8.97$
Marketing	$31 \times \dfrac{47}{152} = 9.59$

Expected Number of M.B.A. Majors with B.B.A.'s

M.B.A. Major	Expected Value
Accounting	$39 \times \dfrac{61}{152} = 15.65$
Finance	$39 \times \dfrac{44}{152} = 11.29$
Marketing	$39 \times \dfrac{47}{152} = 12.06$

Expected Number of M.B.A. Majors with Other Degrees

MBA Major	Expected Value
Accounting	$22 \times \dfrac{61}{152} = 8.83$
Finance	$22 \times \dfrac{44}{152} = 6.37$
Marketing	$22 \times \dfrac{47}{152} = 6.80$

Notice that the expected values are computed by multiplying the column total by the row total and dividing by the sample size.

> **Expected Frequencies for a Contingency Table**
>
> The expected frequency of the cell in column j and row i is
>
> $$e_{ij} = \frac{\text{Column } j \text{ total} \times \text{Row } i \text{ total}}{\text{Sample size}}$$

The expected cell frequencies are shown in parentheses in the following table. As in the case of the goodness-of-fit test, the expected cell frequencies should satisfy the rule of five.

Undergraduate Degree	M.B.A. Major		
	Accounting	Finance	Marketing
B.A.	31 (24.08)	13 (17.37)	16 (18.55)
B.Eng	8 (12.44)	16 (8.97)	7 (9.59)
B.B.A.	12 (15.65)	10 (11.29)	17 (12.06)
Other	10 (8.83)	5 (6.37)	7 (6.80)

We can now calculate the value of the test statistic.

$$\chi^2 = \sum_{i=1}^{k} \frac{(f_i - e_i)^2}{e_i}$$

$$= \frac{(31 - 24.08)^2}{24.08} + \frac{(13 - 17.37)^2}{17.37} + \frac{(16 - 18.55)^2}{18.55}$$

$$+ \frac{(8 - 12.44)^2}{12.44} + \frac{(16 - 8.97)^2}{8.97} + \frac{(7 - 9.59)^2}{9.59}$$

$$+ \frac{(12 - 15.65)^2}{15.65} + \frac{(10 - 11.29)^2}{11.29} + \frac{(17 - 12.06)^2}{12.06}$$

$$+ \frac{(10 - 8.83)^2}{8.83} + \frac{(5 - 6.37)^2}{6.37} + \frac{(7 - 6.80)^2}{6.80}$$

$$= 14.70$$

Notice that we continue to use a single subscript in the formula of the test statistic when we should use two subscripts, one for the rows and one for the columns. We feel that it is clear that for each cell, we need to calculate the squared difference between the observed and expected frequencies divided by the expected frequency. We don't believe that the satisfaction of using the mathematically correct notation overcomes the unnecessary complication.

Rejection Region   To determine the rejection region, we need to know the number of degrees of freedom associated with the chi-squared statistic. The number of degrees of freedom for a contingency table with r rows and c columns is

d.f. $= (r - 1)(c - 1)$

For this example the number of degrees of freedom is

d.f. $= (r - 1)(c - 1) = (4 - 1)(3 - 1) = 6$

If we employ a 5% significance level the rejection region is

$$\chi^2 > \chi^2_{\alpha, \text{d.f.}} = \chi^2_{.05,6} = 12.5916$$

Because $\chi^2 = 14.70$, we reject the null hypothesis and conclude that there is evidence of a relationship between undergraduate degree and M.B.A. major.

Excel and Minitab can produce the chi-squared statistic from either a contingency table whose frequencies have already been calculated or from raw data. The respective printouts are almost identical. We created file XM15-02, which contains the raw data using the following codes.

COLUMN 1 (UNDERGRADUATE DEGREE)	COLUMN 2 (M.B.A. MAJOR)
1 = B.A.	1 = Accounting
2 = B.Eng.	2 = Finance
3 = B.B.A.	3 = Marketing
4 = Other	

Excel Output for Example 15.2

A	B	C	D	E
Contingency Table				
	1	2	3	Total
1	31	13	16	60
2	8	16	7	31
3	12	10	17	39
4	10	5	7	22
Total	61	44	47	152
Test Statistic CHI-Squared = 14.7019				
P-Value = 0.0227				

COMMANDS (COMPLETED TABLE)

COMMANDS FOR EXAMPLE 15.2

1 Type the frequencies into adjacent columns.

2 Click **Tools, Data Analysis Plus,** and **CHI-Square Test of a Contingency Table.**

3 Specify the input range. Click **OK.**

```
31  13  16
 8  16   7
12  10  17
10   5   7
```

A1:C4

COMMANDS (RAW DATA)

COMMANDS FOR EXAMPLE 15.2

1 Type or import the data where one column represents the codes for one variable and a second column stores the codes for the second variable. The codes must be positive integers.

Open file **XM15-02.**

2 Click **Tools, Data Analysis Plus,** and **CHI-Square Test of a Contingency Table (Raw Data).**

3 Specify the input range. Do not include cells containing the variable names. Click **OK.**

A2:B153

Chi-Square Test

```
Expected counts are printed below observed counts
              C1          C2          C2      Total
    1         31          13          16         60
            24.08       17.37       18.55

    2          8          16           7         31
            12.44        8.97        9.59

    3         12          10          17         39
            15.65       11.29       12.06

    4         10           5           7         22
             8.83        6.37        6.80

Total         61          44          47        152

Chi-Sq =   1.989 +    1.099 +    0.351 +
           1.585 +    5.502 +    0.697 +
           0.852 +    0.147 +    2.024 +
           0.155 +    0.294 +    0.006 =   14.702
DF = 6, P-Value =    0.023
```

COMMANDS (COMPLETE TABLE)

1 Type the observed frequencies into adjacent columns.
2 Click **Stats, Tables,** and **Chisquare Test. . . .**
3 Type the names of the variables representing the columns. Click **OK.**

COMMANDS FOR EXAMPLE 15.2

```
31  13  16
 8  16   7
12  10  17
10   5   7
C1-C3
```

COMMANDS (RAW DATA)

1 Type or import the data where one column represents the codes for one variable and a second column stores the codes for the second variable. The codes must be positive integers.
2 Click **Stat, Tables,** and **Cross Classification. . . .**
3 Type the names of the variables.
4 Use the cursor to specify **Chisquare analysis** and **Above and expected count.** Click **OK.**

COMMANDS FOR EXAMPLE 15.2

Open file **XM15-02.**

Degree Major or **C1 C2**

INTERPRET

There is strong evidence to infer that the undergraduate degree and M.B.A. major are related. This suggests that the dean can predict the number of optional courses by counting the number of M.B.A. students with each type of undergraduate degree. We can see that B.A.'s favor accounting courses, B.Eng.'s prefer finance, B.B.A.'s drift to marketing, and others show no particular preference.

▲

RULE OF FIVE

In the previous section, we pointed out that the expected values should be at least five to ensure that the chi-squared distribution provides an adequate approximation of the sampling distribution. In a contingency table where one or more cells have expected values of less than 5, we need to combine rows or columns to satisfy the rule of five. To illustrate, suppose that we want to test for dependence in the following contingency table.

			Total
10	14	4	28
12	16	7	35
8	8	4	20
Total 30	38	15	83

The expected values are as follows.

10.1	12.8	5.1
12.7	16.0	6.3
7.2	9.2	3.6

The expected value of the cell in row 3 and column 3 is less than 5. To eliminate the problem, we can add column 3 to one of columns 1 and 2 or add row 3 to either row 1 or row 2. The combining of rows or columns should be done so that the combination forms a logical unit, if possible. For example, if the columns represent the age groups, young (under 40), middle-aged (40–65), and senior (over 65), it is logical to combine columns 2 and 3. The observed and expected values are combined to produce the following table (expected values in parentheses).

		Total
10 (10.1)	18 (17.9)	28
12 (12.6)	23 (22.3)	35
8 (7.2)	12 (12.8)	20
Total 30	53	83

The degrees of freedom must be changed as well. The number of degrees of freedom of the original contingency table is $(3 - 1) \times (3 - 1) = 4$. The number of degrees of freedom of the combined table is $(3 - 1) \times (2 - 1) = 2$. The rest of the procedure is unchanged.

Here is a summary of the factors that tell us when to apply the chi-squared test of a contingency table. Note that there are two problem objectives satisfied by this statistical procedure.

Factors that Identify the Chi-Squared Test of a Contingency Table

1 Problem objectives: analyze the relationship between two variables; compare two or more populations

2 Data type: qualitative

EXERCISES

15.16 Conduct a test to determine whether the two classifications L and M are dependent, using the data in the accompanying contingency table. (Use $\alpha = .05$.)

	M_1	M_2
L_1	28	68
L_2	56	36

15.17 Repeat Exercise 15.16 using the following table.

	M_1	M_2
L_1	14	34
L_2	28	18

15.18 Repeat Exercise 15.16 using the following table.

	M_1	M_2
L_1	7	17
L_2	14	9

15.19 Review the results of Exercises 15.16 to 15.18. What is the effect of decreasing the sample size?

15.20 Conduct a test to determine whether the two classifications R and C are dependent, using the data in the accompanying contingency table and $\alpha = .10$.

	C_1	C_2	C_3
R_1	40	32	48
R_2	30	48	52

15.21 The trustee of a company's pension plan has solicited the opinions of a sample of the company's employees about a proposed revision of the plan. A breakdown of the responses is shown in the accompanying table. Is there evidence at the 10% significance level to infer that the responses differ among the three groups of employees?

Responses	Blue-collar workers	White-collar workers	Managers
For	67	32	11
Against	63	18	9

15.22 The operations manager of a company that manufactures shirts wants to determine whether there are differences in the quality of workmanship among the three daily shifts. She randomly selects 600 recently made shirts and carefully inspects them. Each shirt is classified as either perfect or flawed, and the shift that produced it is also recorded. The accompanying table summarizes the number of shirts that fell into each cell. Do these data provide sufficient evidence at the 5% significance level to infer that there are differences in quality among the three shifts?

	Shift		
Shirt condition	1	2	3
Perfect	240	191	139
Flawed	10	9	11

15.23 One of the issues that came up in a recent national election (and is likely to arise in many future elections) is how to deal with a sluggish economy. Specifically, should governments cut spending, raise taxes, inflate the economy (by printing more money), or do none of the above and let the deficit rise? And like most issues, politicians need to know which parts of the electorate support these options. Suppose that a random sample of 1,000 people was asked which option they support and their political affiliations. The possible responses to the question about political affiliation were Democrat, Republican, and Independent (which included a variety of political persuasions). The responses are summarized in the table below. Do there results allow us to conclude at the 1% significance level that political affiliation affects support for the economic options?

	Political affiliation		
Economic options	Democrat	Republican	Independent
Cut spending	101	282	61
Raise taxes	38	67	25
Inflate the economy	131	88	31
Let deficit increase	61	90	25

The following exercises require the use of a computer and software. The answers may be calculated manually. See Appendix C for the sample statistics.

15.24 To determine if commercials viewed during happy television programs are more effective than those viewed during sad television programs, a study was conducted in which a random sample of students viewed an upbeat segment from "Real People" with commercials, while another random sample of students viewed a very sad segment from "Sixty Minutes" with commercials. The students were then asked what they were thinking during the final commercial. From their responses, they were categorized as thinking primarily about the commercial (1), thinking primarily about the program (2), or thinking about both (3). The results are stored in file XR15-24. (Column 1 lists the program, 1 = "Real People" and 2 = "Sixty Minutes," and column 2 lists the responses.) Do commercials viewed during happy television programs appear to have a different effect than those viewed during sad television programs? (Use $\alpha = .05$.) (Source: Marvin E. Goldberg and Gerald J. Gorn, "Happy and Sad TV Programs: How They Affect Reactions to Commercials," *Journal of Consumer Research 14* (1987): 387–403.)

15.25 Acute otitis media, an infection of the middle ear, is a very common childhood illness. Although it is normally treated with amoxicillin, emerging resistance to the antibiotic has promoted the search for an alternative. A recent article discussed the efficacy of one such alternative: trimethoprim-sulfamethoxazole. In this study, 203 "patients were randomly assigned to receive either amoxicillin (1) or trimethoprim-sulfamethoxazole (2) by means of a computer-generated table of random numbers." Each patient was judged to be cured (1), improved (2), or to have no improvement (3). The data are stored in columns 1 (drug) and 2 (outcome) of file XR15-25. Can we conclude from these data that there are differences in outcomes for children treated with amoxicillin and for children treated with trimethoprim-sulfamethoxazole? Use $\alpha = .10$.) (Source: William Feldman, Joanne Momy, and Corinne Dulberg, "Trimethoprim-Sulfamethoxazole v. Amoxicillin in the Treatment of Acute Otitis Media," *Canadian Medical Association Journal 139* (1988): 961–64.)

15.26 An antismoking group recently had a large advertisement published in local newspapers throughout Florida. Several statistical facts and medical details were included, in the hope that the ad would have a meaningful impact on smokers. The antismoking group is concerned, however, that smokers might have read less of the advertisement than did nonsmokers. This concern is based on the belief that a reader tends to spend more time reading articles that agree with his or her predisposition. The antismoking group has conducted a survey asking those who saw the advertisement if they read the headline only (1), some detail (2), or most of the advertisement (3). The questionnaire also asks respondents to identify themselves as either a heavy smoker—more than two packs per day (1), a moderate smoker—between one and two packs per day (2), a light smoker—less than one pack per day (3), or a nonsmoker (4). The results are stored in file XR15-26. (Column 1: type of smoker; column 2:

survey responses.) Do the data indicate that level of smoking affects how much one reads of an antismoking advertisement? (Use $\alpha = .05$.)

15.27 An investor who can correctly forecast the direction and size of changes in foreign currency exchange rates is able to reap huge profits in the international currency markets. A knowledgeable reader of *The Wall Street Journal* (in particular, of the currency futures market quotations) can determine the direction of change in various exchange rates that is predicted by all investors, viewed collectively. Predictions from 216 investors, together with the subsequent actual directions of change, are stored in file XR15-27. (Column 1: predicted change where 1 = positive and 2 = negative; column 2: actual change where 1 = positive and 2 = negative.)

a Test the hypothesis ($\alpha = .10$) that a relationship exists between the predicted and actual directions of change.

b To what extent would you make use of these predictions in formulating your forecasts of future exchange rate changes?

15.28 During the past decade many cigarette smokers have attempted to quit. Unfortunately, nicotine is highly addictive. Smokers employ a large number of different methods to help themselves quit. These include nicotine patches, hypnosis, and various forms of therapy. A researcher for the Addiction Research Council wanted to determine why some people are able to quit while others who attempted to quit failed. He surveyed 1,000 people who planned to quit smoking. He determined their educational level and whether, 1 year later, they continued to smoke. Educational level was recorded in the following way.

1 = did not finish high school
2 = high school graduate
3 = university or college graduate
4 = completed a postgraduate degree

A continuing smoker was recorded as 1; a quitter was recorded as 2. These data are stored in columns 1 (education level) and 2 (continuing smoker?) in file XR15-28. Can we infer at the 5% significance level that the amount of education is a factor in determining whether a smoker will quit?

Statistics in the Workplace

Market Segmentation

In Chapter 12 and again in Chapter 14 we discussed how marketing managers use statistical analysis to help identify distinct market groups. We can use the chi-squared test of a contingency table to determine whether there are differences in various qualitative variables among customers of different brands or products. The following exercises are such applications.

15.29 In Exercises 12.96 and 12.97 we applied the analysis of variance to help segment the market for Toyota cars on the basis of ages and incomes of customers, respectively. Suppose that as part of the survey in those exercises the questionnaire also asked about marital status. Recall that the study involved 100 customers of Tercels and 100 customers of Avalons. The responses to the question about marital status were recorded as

1 = single
2 = married
3 = divorced
4 = widowed

The results are stored in file XR15-29 where column 1 contains the responses about marital status and column 2 the type of car (1 = Tercel and 2 = Avalon). Can we infer at the 5% significance level that differences in marital status exist between the buyers of the two Toyotas?

15.30 After a thorough analysis of the market a publisher of business and economics statistics books has divided the market into three general approaches to teach applied statistics. These are (1) use of a computer and statistical software with no manual calculations, (2) traditional teaching of concepts and solution of problems by hand, and (3) mathematical approach with emphasis on derivations and proofs. The publisher wanted to know if this market could be segmented on the basis of the educational background of the instructor. As a result the statistics editor organized a survey that asked 195 professors of business and economics statistics to report their approach to teaching and which one of the following categories represents their highest degree.

1 = business (M.B.A. or Ph.D. in business)
2 = economics
3 = mathematics or engineering
4 = other

The responses are stored in columns 1 (teaching approach) and 2 (degree) in file XR15-30. Can the editor infer at the 1% significance level that there are differences in type of degree among the three teaching approaches? If so, how can the editor use this information?

15.4 SUMMARY OF TESTS ON QUALITATIVE DATA

At this point in the textbook, we've described four tests that are used when the data are qualitative. These are as follows.

1 z-test of p (Section 11.4)

2 z-test of $p_1 - p_2$ (Section 12.6)

3 Chi-squared test of a multinomial experiment (Section 15.2)

4 Chi-squared test of a contingency table (Section 15.3)

In the process of presenting these techniques, it was necessary to concentrate on one technique at a time and focus on the kinds of problems each addresses. However, this approach tends to conflict somewhat with our promised goal of emphasizing the "when" of statistical inference. In this section, we summarize the statistical tests on qualitative data to ensure that you are capable of selecting the correct method.

There are two critical factors in identifying the technique used when the data are qualitative. The first, of course, is the problem objective. The second is the number of categories that the qualitative variable can assume. Table 15.1 provides a guide to help select the correct technique.

Table 15.1   **Statistical Techniques for Qualitative Data**

Problem Objective	Number of Categories	Statistical Technique
Describe a single population	2	z-test of p or the chi-squared goodness-of-fit test
Describe a single population	2 or more	Chi-squared goodness-of-fit test
Compare two populations	2	z-test of $p_1 - p_2$ or the chi-squared test of a contingency table
Compare two populations	2 or more	Chi-squared test of a contingency table
Compare two or more populations	2 or more	Chi-squared test of a contingency table
Analyze the relationship between two variables	2 or more	Chi-squared test of a contingency table

Notice that when we describe a single population of qualitative data with exactly two categories, we can use either of two techniques. We can employ the z-test of p or the chi-squared goodness-of-fit test. These two tests are equivalent because if there are only two categories, the multinomial experiment is actually a binomial experiment (one of the categorical outcomes is labeled success and the other is labeled failure). Mathematical statisticians have established that if we square the value of z, the test statistic for the test of p, we produce the χ^2-statistic. That is, $z^2 = \chi^2$. Thus, if we want to conduct a two-tail test of a population proportion, we can employ either technique. However, the chi-squared test of a binomial experiment can only test to determine if the hypothesized values of p_1 (which we can label p) and p_2 (which we call $1 - p$) are not equal to their specified values. Consequently, to perform a one-tail test of a population proportion, we must use the z-test of p. (This issue was discussed in Chapter 14 when we pointed out that we can use either the t-test of $\mu_1 - \mu_2$ or the analysis of variance to conduct a test to determine if two population means differ.)

When we test for differences between two populations of qualitative data with two categories, we can also use either of two techniques: the z-test of $p_1 - p_2$ (case 1) or the chi-squared test of a contingency table. Once again, we can use either technique to perform a two-tail test about $p_1 - p_2$. (Squaring the value of the z-statistic yields the value of χ^2-statistic.) However, one-tail tests must be conducted by the z-test of $p_1 - p_2$. The rest of the table is quite straightforward. Notice that when we want to compare two populations when there are two or more categories, we use the chi-squared test of a contingency table.

Figure 15.1 offers another summary of the tests that deal with qualitative data introduced in this book. There are two groups of tests: ones that test hypotheses about single populations and ones that test either for differences or for independence. In the

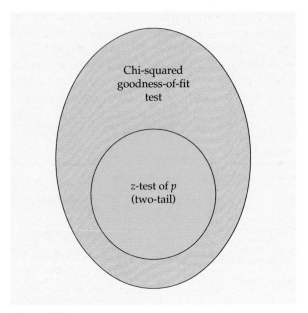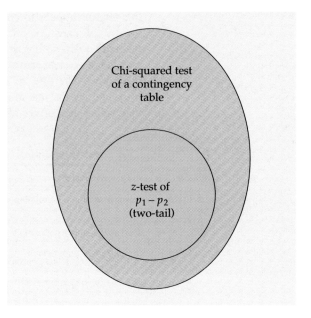

Figure 15.1

Tests on qualitative data

first set, we have the z-test of p, which can be replaced by the chi-squared goodness-of-fit test. The latter test is employed when there are more than two categories.

To test for differences between two proportions, we apply the z-test of $p_1 - p_2$. We can use instead the chi-squared test of a contingency table, which can be applied to a variety of other problems.

DEVELOPING AN UNDERSTANDING OF STATISTICAL CONCEPTS

Table 15.1 and Figure 15.1 summarize how we deal with qualitative data. We determine the frequency of each category and use these frequencies to compute test statistics. We can then compute proportions to calculate z-statistics or use the frequencies to calculate χ^2-statistics. Because squaring a standard normal random variable produces a chi-squared variable, we can employ either statistic to test for differences. As a consequence, when you encounter qualitative data in the problems described in this book (and other introductory applied statistics books), the most logical starting point in selecting the appropriate technique will be either a z-statistic or a χ^2-statistic. However, you should know that there are other statistical procedures that can be applied to qualitative data, techniques that are not included in this book.

15.5 CHI-SQUARED TEST FOR NORMALITY (OPTIONAL)

We can use the goodness-of-fit test presented in Section 15.2 in another way. We can test to determine whether data were drawn from any distribution. The most common application of this procedure is a test of normality.

In the examples and exercises shown in Section 15.2 the probabilities specified in the null hypothesis were derived from the question. In Example 15.1 the probabilities p_1, p_2, and p_3 were the market shares before the advertising campaign. To test for normality (or any other distribution) the probabilities must first be calculated using the hypothesized distribution. To illustrate consider Example 11.1 where we tested the mean productivity of new workers using the Student t distribution. The required condition for this procedure is that the data must be normally distributed. To determine whether the 50 observations in our sample were indeed taken from a normal distribution we must calculate the theoretical probabilities assuming a normal distribution. To do so we must first calculate the sample mean and standard deviation. They are $\bar{x} = 460.38$ and $s = 38.83$. Next we find the probabilities of an arbitrary number of intervals. For example, we can find the probabilities of the following intervals.

Interval 1: $X \leq 421.55$
Interval 2: $421.55 < X \leq 460.38$
Interval 3: $460.38 \leq X \leq 499.21$
Interval 4: $X > 499.21$

We will discuss the reasons for our choice of intervals later.

The probabilities are computed using the normal distribution and the values of $\bar{x}$ and s as estimators of μ and σ. Thus,

$$P(X \leq 421.55) = P\left(\frac{X - \mu}{\sigma} \leq \frac{421.55 - 460.38}{38.83}\right)$$
$$= P(Z \leq -1) = .1587$$

$$P(421.55 < X \leq 460.38) = P\left(\frac{421.55 - 460.38}{38.83} < \frac{X - \mu}{\sigma} \leq \frac{460.38 - 460.38}{38.83}\right)$$
$$= P(-1 < Z \leq 0) = .3413$$

$$P(460.38 < X \leq 499.21) = P\left(\frac{460.38 - 460.38}{38.83} < \frac{X - \mu}{\sigma} \leq \frac{499.21 - 460.38}{38.83}\right)$$
$$= P(0 < Z \leq 1) = .3413$$

$$P(X > 499.21) = P\left(\frac{X - \mu}{\sigma} > \frac{499.21 - 460.38}{38.83}\right)$$
$$= P(Z > 1) = .1587$$

To test for normality is to test the following hypotheses.

H_0: $p_1 = .1587$, $p_2 = .3413$, $p_3 = .3413$, $p_4 = .1587$
H_1: At least two proportions differ from their specified values

We complete the test as we did in Section 15.2 except that the number of degrees of freedom associated with the chi-squared statistic is the number of intervals minus 1 minus the number of parameters estimated, which in this illustration is 2. (We estimated the population mean μ and the population standard deviation σ.) Thus, in this case the number of degrees of freedom is $k - 1 - 2 = 1$.

The expected values are

$e_1 = np_1 = 50(.1587) = 7.94$
$e_2 = np_2 = 50(.3413) = 17.07$
$e_3 = np_3 = 50(.3413) = 17.07$
$e_4 = np_4 = 50(.1587) = 7.94$

The observed values are determined manually by counting the number of values in each interval. Thus,

$$f_1 = 10$$
$$f_2 = 13$$
$$f_3 = 19$$
$$f_4 = 8$$

The chi-squared statistic is

$$\chi^2 = \sum_{i=1}^{4} \frac{(f_i - e_i)^2}{e_i}$$

$$= \frac{(10 - 7.94)^2}{7.94} + \frac{(13 - 17.07)^2}{17.07} + \frac{(19 - 17.07)^2}{17.07} + \frac{(8 - 7.94)^2}{7.94}$$

$$= 1.72$$

The rejection region is

$$\chi^2 > \chi^2_{\alpha,k-3} = \chi^2_{.05,1} = 3.84146$$

There is no evidence to conclude that these data are not normally distributed.

CLASS INTERVALS

In practice you can use any intervals you like. We chose the intervals we did to facilitate the calculation of the normal probabilities. The *number* of intervals was chosen to comply with the rule of five, which requires that all expected values be at least equal to 5. Because the number of degrees of freedom is $k - 3$, the minimum number of intervals is $k = 4$.

Excel

We programmed Excel to calculate the value of the test statistic so that the expected values are at least five (where possible) and the minimum number of intervals is 4. Hence if the number of observations is more than 220, the intervals and probabilities are

Interval	Probability
$Z \leq -2$	.0228
$-2 < Z \leq -1$	.1359
$-1 < Z \leq 0$	.3413
$0 < Z \leq 1$	.3413
$1 < Z \leq 2$	.1359
$Z > 2$	.0228

If the sample size is less than or equal to 220 and greater than 80, the intervals are

Interval	Probability
$Z \leq -1.5$	.0668
$-1.5 < Z \leq -0.5$	.2417
$-0.5 < Z \leq 0.5$	.3829
$0.5 < Z \leq 1.5$	.2417
$Z > 1.5$	.0668

If the sample size is less than or equal to 80, we employ the minimum number of intervals 4. (When the sample size is less than 32 at least one expected value will be less than 5, making 32 the smallest sample size necessary for this procedure.) The intervals are

Interval	Probability
$Z \leq -1$	.1587
$-1 < Z \leq 0$	.3413
$0 < Z \leq 1$	.3413
$Z > 1$	.1587

Excel Output for the Test of Normality of the Data in Example 11.1

	A	B	C	D
1	Chi-Squared Test of Normality			
2				
3	Mean	460.38		
4	Standard deviation	38.83		
5	Observations	50		
6				
7	Intervals	Probability	Expected	Observed
8	(z <= -1)	0.1587	7.93	10
9	(-1 < z <= 0)	0.3413	17.07	13
10	(0 < z <= 1)	0.3413	17.07	19
11	(z > 1)	0.1587	7.93	8
12				
13				
14				
15	Chi-Squared Stat	1.73		
16	P-Value	0.1887		

COMMANDS

1 Type or import the data into one column

2 Click **Tools, Data Analysis Plus,** and **Chi-Squared Test of Normality.**

3 Specify the input range. Do not include the cells containing the variable name. Click **OK.**

COMMANDS FOR EXAMPLE 11.1

Open file **XM11-01.**

A2:A51

Minitab

Minitab does not conduct this procedure. However, you can use Minitab to perform several parts of the statistical procedure. See Appendix 15.C.

EXERCISES

15.31 Suppose that a random sample of 100 observations was drawn from a population. After calculating the mean and standard deviation each observation was standardized and the number of observations in each of the intervals below was counted. Can we infer at the 5% significance level that the data were not drawn from a normal population?

Interval	Frequency
$Z \leq -1.5$	10
$-1.5 < Z \leq -0.5$	18
$-0.5 < Z \leq 0.5$	48
$0.5 < Z \leq 1.5$	16
$Z > 1.5$	8

15.32 A random sample of 50 observations yielded the following frequencies for the standardized intervals.

Interval	Probability
$Z \leq -1$	6
$-1 < Z \leq 0$	27
$0 < Z \leq 1$	14
$Z > 1$	3

Can we infer that the data are not normal? (Use $\alpha = .10$.)

Exercises 15.33–15.36 require the use of a computer and software.

15.33 Refer to Exercise 11.32. Test at the 5% significance level to determine whether the amount overweight is normally distributed.

15.34 The test in Exercise 11.35 requires that the weight of discarded newspaper be normally distributed. Conduct a test with $\alpha = .05$ to determine whether the required condition is unsatisfied.

15.35 Exercise 12.30 required you to conduct a *t*-test of the difference between two means. Each sample's productivity data are required to be normally distributed. Is that required condition violated? Test with $\alpha = .05$.

15.36 In Exercise 12.46 you performed a test of the mean matched pairs difference. The test result depends on the requirement that the differences are normally distributed. Test with a 10% significance level to determine whether the requirement is violated.

15.6 SUMMARY

This chapter introduced three statistical techniques. The first is the chi-squared goodness-of-fit test, which is applied when the problem objective is to describe a single population of qualitative data with two or more categories. The second is the chi-squared test of a contingency table. There are two objectives of this test: to analyze the relationship between two qualitative variables and to compare two or more populations of qualitative data. The last procedure is designed to test for normality.

IMPORTANT TERMS

Multinomial experiment   *544*
Expected frequency   *546*
Chi-squared test of a contingency table   *551*
Contingency (cross-classification) table   *551*

SUMMARY OF FORMULAS

$$e_i = np_i$$

$$\chi^2 = \sum \frac{(f_i - e_i)^2}{e_i}$$

SUPPLEMENTARY EXERCISES

15.37 An organization dedicated to ensuring fairness in television game shows is investigating "Wheel of Fortune." In this show, three contestants are required to solve puzzles by selecting letters. Each contestant gets to select the first letter and continues selecting until he or she chooses a letter that is not in the hidden word, phrase, or name. The order of contestants is random. However, contestant 1 gets to start game 1, contestant 2 starts game 2, and so on. The contestant who wins the most money is declared the winner, and he or she is given an opportunity to win a grand prize. Usually, more than three games are played per show, and as a result it appears that contestant 1 has an advantage: Contestant 1 will start two games, whereas contestant 3 will usually start only one game. To see if this is the case, a random sample of 30 shows was taken and the starting position of the winning contestant for each show was recorded. These are shown in the following table.

Starting position	Number of winners
1	14
2	10
3	6

Do the tabulated results allow us to conclude at the 10% significance level that the game is unfair?

15.38 Econetics Research Corporation, a well-known Montreal-based consulting firm, wants to test how it can influence the proportion of questionnaires returned from surveys. Believing that the inclusion of an inducement to respond may be important, it sends out 1,000 questionnaires: 200 promise to send respondents a summary of the survey results, 300 indicate that 20 respondents (selected by lottery) will be awarded gifts, and 500 are accompanied by no inducements. Of these, 80 questionnaires promising a summary, 100 questionnaires offering gifts, and 120 questionnaires offering no inducements are returned. What can you conclude from these results? (Use $\alpha = .05$.) (HINT: The sample size is 1,000 and your analysis must include the complete sample.)

15.39 It has been estimated that employee absenteeism costs North American companies more than $100 billion per year. As a first step in addressing the rising cost of absenteeism, the personnel department of a large corporation recorded the weekdays during which individuals in a sample of 362 absentees were away over the past several months. Do these data suggest that absenteeism is higher on some days of the week than on others? (Use $\alpha = .05$.)

Day of the Week	M	T	W	T	F
Number Absent	87	62	71	68	74

15.40 Suppose that the personnel department in Exercise 15.39 continued its investigation by categorizing absentees according to the shift on which they worked, as shown in the following table. Is there sufficient evidence at the 10% significance level of a relationship between the days on which employees are absent and the shift on which the employees work?

	Day of week				
Shift	Monday	Tuesday	Wednesday	Thursday	Friday
Day	52	28	37	31	33
Evening	35	34	34	37	41

15.41 A management behavior analyst has been studying the relationship between male/female supervisory structures in the workplace and the level of employees' job satisfaction. The results of a recent survey are shown in the following table. Conduct a test with ($\alpha = .05$) to determine whether the level of job satisfaction depends on the boss/employee gender relationship.

	Boss/Employee			
Level of satisfaction	Female/Male	Female/Female	Male/Male	Male/Female
Satisfied	21	25	54	71
Neutral	39	49	50	38
Dissatisfied	31	48	10	11

The following exercises require the use of a computer and software. The answers may be calculated manually. See Appendix B for the sample statistics.

15.42 During the decade of the 1980s, professional baseball thrived in North America. Attendance rose continuously from 45 million in 1984 to 58 million in 1991. However, in 1992, attendance dropped about 2 million. In addition, the number of television viewers also decreased. To examine the popularity of baseball relative to other sports, surveys were performed. In 1985 and again in 1993, a Harris Poll asked a random sample of 500 people to name their favorite sport. The results, which were published in *The Wall Street Journal* (6 July, 1993), are stored in file XR15-42 in the following way.

Column 1: results from 1985 1 = professional football, 2 = baseball, 3 = professional basketball, 4 = college basketball, 5 = college football, and 6 = other

Column 2: results from 1993 using the same codes.

a Do these results indicate at the 5% significance level that North Americans changed their favorite sport between 1985 and 1993?

b Do these results indicate at the 5% significance level that the popularity of baseball has changed between 1985 and 1993?

15.43 According to NBC News (11 March, 1994) more than 3,000 Americans quit smoking each day. (Unfortunately, more than 3,000 Americans start smoking each day.) Because nicotine is one of the most addictive drugs, quitting smoking is a difficult and frustrating task. It usually takes several tries before success is achieved. There are various methods, including cold turkey, nicotine patch, hypnosis, and group therapy sessions. In an experiment to determine how these methods differ, a random sample of smokers who have decided to quit was selected. Each smoker chose one of the methods listed above. After 1 year the respondents reported whether they have quit (2 = yes and 1 = no) and which method they used (1 = cold turkey; 2 = nicotine patch; 3 = hypnosis; 4 = group therapy sessions). These data are stored in columns 1 and 2, respectively in file XR15-43. Is there sufficient evidence at the 5% significance level to conclude that the four methods differ in their success?

15.44 A newspaper publisher, trying to pinpoint his market's characteristics wondered whether the way people read a newspaper is related to the reader's educational level. A survey asked adult readers which section of the paper they read first and asked them to report their highest educational level. These data were recorded and stored in file XR15-44.

> Column 1: first section read where 1 = front page, 2 = sports, 3 = editorial, and 4 = other
>
> Column 2: educational level where 1 = did not complete high school, 2 = high school graduate, 3 = university or college graduate, and 4 = postgraduate degree

What do these data tell the publisher at the 1% significance level about how educational level affects the way adults read the newspaper?

15.45 Every week the Florida lottery draws 6 numbers between 1 and 49. Lottery ticket buyers are naturally interested in whether certain numbers are drawn more frequently than others. To assist players the *Sun-Sentinel* publishes the number of times each of the 49 numbers has been drawn in the past 52 weeks. The numbers and the frequency with which each occurred are stored in columns 1 and 2, respectively, in file XR15-45. These data are from the Sunday, 5 January, 1997, edition.

a If the numbers are drawn from a uniform distribution, what is the expected frequency for each number?

b Can we infer at the 5% significance level that the data were not generated from a uniform distribution?

15.46 Canadians have the option of investing income in registered retirement savings plans (RRSPs). Subject to limits calculated on the basis of income, employer retirement plans, and previous RRSPs, money invested in RRSPs is not taxable. (Money withdrawn from retirement plans is taxable.) Critics argue that RRSPs are a tax loophole for the rich because only wealthier people are in a position to take advantage of the tax provisions. In a study to determine who uses RRSPs, the Caledon Institute of Social Policy randomly sampled a variety of Canadians in different tax brackets. (Survey results were published in the *Globe and Mail*, 5 February, 1994.) For each respondent the researchers recorded the income bracket (1 = less than $20,000; 2 = $20–40,000; 3 = $40–$60,000; 4 = $60–100,000; 5 = over $100,000), and whether they invested in an RRSP this year (2 = yes; 1 = no). These data are stored in columns 1 and 2, respectively, in file XR15-46. Can we infer at the 1% significance level that there are differences in RRSP positions among the income groups?

15.47 *In Section 15.5 we showed how to test for normality. However, we can use the same process to test for any other distribution.* A scientist believes that the gender of a child is a binomial random variable with probability = .5 for a boy and .5 for a girl. To help test her belief she randomly samples 200 families with 5 children. She records the number of boys and stores the results in file XR15-47. Can the scientist infer at the 5% significance level that the number of boys in families with 5 children is not a binomial random variable with $p = .5$? (HINT: Find the probability of $X = 0$, 1, 2, 3, 4, and 5 from a binomial distribution with $n = 5$ and $p = .5$.)

15.48 The relationship between drug companies and medical researchers is under scrutiny because of possible conflict of interest. The issue that started the controversy was a 1995 case control study that suggested that the use of calcium-channel blockers to treat hypertension led to an increased risk of heart disease. This led to an intense debate both in technical journals and in the press. Researchers writing in the *New England Journal of Medicine* ("Conflict of Interest in the Debate over Calcium Channel Antagonists," 8 January, 1998, p. 101) looked at the 70 reports that appeared during 1996–1997, classifying them as favorable, neutral, or critical toward the drugs. The researchers then contacted the authors of the reports and questioned them about financial ties to drug companies. The results are stored in file XR15-48 in the following way.

> Column 1: results of the scientific study where 1 = favorable, 2 = neutral, 3 = critical

Column 2: 1 = financial ties to drug companies, 2 = no ties to drug companies

Do these data allow us to infer at the 5% significance level that the research findings for calcium-channel blockers are affected by whether the research is funded by drug companies?

15.49 The statistical analysis in Exercise 15.48 led to a further analysis. In addition to recording whether the study was favorable, neutral, or critical, researchers also recorded whether competing companies funded the research. The data for competing companies were stored in column 2 of file XR15-49 (Column 1 is identical to column 1 of file XR15-48.) Do these data allow us to infer at the 5% significance level that the research findings for calcium-channel blockers are affected by whether the research is funded by competing companies? (Note: Researchers can be funded by several companies.)

Sᴛᴀᴛɪsᴛɪᴄs ɪɴ ᴛʜᴇ Wᴏʀᴋᴘʟᴀᴄᴇ

Market Segmentation

Thus far in this book we have shown a number of exercises and examples where the objective is to segment a market for a particular product. Here is another illustration.

15.50 In Example 11.5 we described an application of marketing wherein a company surveyed newspaper readers to determine whether a new national newspaper is likely to succeed in the Canadian market. In October 1998 the *National Post* began operating across Canada. The biggest market in Canada is Toronto, which now has four daily newspapers. In addition to the *National Post*, there is the *Globe and Mail*, the *Sun*, and the *Toronto Star*. A marketing consultant wanted to determine the demographic characteristics of the readers of each newspaper. Accordingly he organized a survey that asked newspaper readers in Toronto which paper they regularly read and to indicate their occupation. The data were stored in file XR15-50 in the following way.

> Column 1: Newspaper, where 1 = *National Post*, 2 = *Globe and Mail*, 3 = *Sun*, 4 = *Toronto Star*

> Column 2: Occupation, where 1 = managerial, 2 = blue-collar, 3 = professional, 4 = other

Can we infer at the 5% significance level that the readerships of the four daily newspapers differ in terms of the occupations of their readers?

CASE 15.1	Predicting the Outcomes of Basketball, Baseball, Football, and Hockey Games from Intermediate Results*

Some basketball fans generally believe that it doesn't pay to watch an entire game because the outcome is determined in the last few minutes (some say the last 2 minutes) of the game. Is this really true and, if so, is basketball different in this respect from other professional sports played in North America? For example, is it true that the team that leads a baseball game after seven innings almost always wins the game? To address these questions, three researchers tracked basketball, baseball, football, and hockey games. The results of games during the 1990 season (for baseball and football) and during the 1990–1991 season (for basketball and hockey) were recorded. The numbers of games won by the early-game leader and by the late-game leader were recorded. Early-game leaders are defined as the teams that are ahead after one quarter of basketball and football, one

*Adapted from H. Cooper, K. M. DeNeve, and E. Mosteller, "Predicting Professional Sports Game Outcomes from Intermediate Game Scores," *Chance* 5, Nos. 3–4 (1992): 18–22.

period of hockey, or three innings of baseball. Late-game leaders are defined as the teams that are ahead after three quarters of basketball and football, two periods of hockey, or seven innings of baseball.

The data are stored in file C15-01 in the following way.

Columns 1–4: results of basketball, baseball, football, and hockey games, respectively, where 2 = early-game leader wins and 1 = early-game leader loses

Columns 5–8: results of basketball, baseball, football, and hockey games, respectively, where 2 = late-game leader wins and 1 = late-game leader loses

a Can we infer from these data that all four professional sports experience the same proportion of early-game leaders winning the game?

b Can we infer from these data that all four professional sports experience the same proportion of late-game leaders winning the game?

CASE 15.2 **Can Exposure to a Code of Professional Ethics Help Make Managers More Ethical?***

In many North American business schools, the issue of whether a course on ethics should be compulsory has been hotly debated. The empirical evidence appears to be far from consistent on the effects of such courses. To help shed more light on the issue, two researchers organized a study in which they took a random sample of 68 accounting students and 132 nonaccounting students. As part of their curriculum, the accounting students were exposed to the American Institute of Certified Public Accountants' code of professional ethics. The nonaccounting business students did not take any course that dealt with issues of ethical behavior.

All 200 students in the study were taking a required senior-level policy course. As part of the course, they were assigned to read the article "Crisis in Conscience at Quasar" by A. Fendrock (*Harvard Business Review,* March–April 1968, 112–20). In the case, Universal, the parent company, learned that the senior managers of one of its subsidiaries, Quasar, deliberately lied about financial conditions in their monthly report to corporate headquarters. Quasar's president, John Kane, and its controller, Hugh Kay, were forced to resign. Universal wanted to know why no one at Quasar provided any information about the true financial conditions, whether any other executives were accomplices to the phony reports, and what could be done to avert such occurrences in the future. Universal sent a fact finder to interview other executives at Quasar—George Kessler, vice president, manufacturing; William Heller, vice president, engineering; Peter Loomis, vice president, marketing; Donald Morgan, chief accountant; and Paul Brown, vice president, industrial relations.

After studying the case, students completed the questionnaire shown below. The results are stored in file C15-02. [The responses to questions 1 to 6 for all students are stored in columns 1 to 6; column 7 indicates whether the student was an accounting student (1) or a nonaccounting business student (2).

Does it appear that accounting students exposed to a code of ethics answer the questionnaire differently from nonaccounting business students not exposed to the same code?

*Adapted from W. E. Fulmer and B. R. Cargile, "Ethical Perceptions of Accounting Students: Does Exposure to a Code of Professional Ethics Help?" *Issues in Accounting Education* (Fall 1987): 207–19.

1 If you had been John Kane, president of Quasar, do you think you would have been tempted to withhold the bad news from corporate management at the parent company?

   2 Yes

   1 No

2 Do you think that under the circumstances you would have withheld the bad news?

   2 Yes

   1 No

3 Do you think you would have gone around the president and reported the bad news to corporate headquarters at Universal?

   2 Yes

   1 No

4 Do you think Kane's withholding the bad news was (check one) . . .

   _____ 1 practical?

   _____ 2 unethical?

   _____ 3 poor judgment?

5 Do you think the blame lies with (check just one) . . .

   _____ 1 Universal's corporate management?

   _____ 2 Quasar's president?

   _____ 3 Quasar's controller?

   _____ 4 Other?

6 Is the problem one of (check just one) . . .

   _____ 1 poor organization?

   _____ 2 lack of communication?

   _____ 3 excessive personal loyalty?

   _____ 4 inadequate supervision?

   _____ 5 other?

CASE 15.3   Stock Return Distributions*

When investors purchase common stock, the rate of return that they realize over the forthcoming period (which could be taken as a day, a week, a month, or a year) is a continuous random variable. Since the beginning of the 20th century, numerous studies of the stock market have hypothesized that stock returns are normally distributed.

In two well-known studies of stock price behavior, Eugene Fama observed both the daily returns and the monthly returns for the 30 stocks in the Dow Jones Industrial Average (DJIA)

---

*Adapted from the following sources: Eugene F. Fama, "Behavior of Stock Prices," *Journal of Business 38* (1965): 34–105; Eugene F. Fama, *Foundations of Finance* (New York: Basic Books, 1976), pp. 28–29; Lawrence Fisher and James H. Lorie, "Some Studies of Variability of Returns on Investments in Common Stocks," *Journal of Business 43* (1970): 99–117; Sheha M. Tinic and Richard R. West, *Investing in Securities: An Efficient Market Approach* (Cambridge, MA: Addison-Wesley, 1979), pp. 488–89.

over a 5-year period. Fama's results are summarized in Tables 1 and 2, which show the DJIA percentages of returns (for all 30 stocks in the index) that fell into various intervals constructed from the mean and standard deviation.

Conduct a test on the results in Tables 1 and 2 to determine whether the returns on the DJIA are normally distributed.

Table 1 Relative Frequency of 1,200 Daily Returns of DJIA Common Stocks

Intervals in Terms of Standardized Z-Values	Percentage of Observed Daily Returns
Less than −2.0	2.1%
−2.0 to −1.5	3.1
−1.5 to −1.0	7.4
−1.0 to −0.5	14.4
−0.5 to 0.5	46.7
0.5 to 1.0	13.6
1.0 to 1.5	6.4
1.5 to 2.0	3.2
Greater than 2.0	3.1

Table 2 Relative Frequency of 200 Monthly Returns of DJIA Common Stocks

Intervals in Terms of Standardized Z-Values	Percentage of Observed Daily Returns
Less than −2.0	1.6%
−2.0 to −1.5	3.7
−1.5 to −1.0	9.3
−1.0 to −0.5	15.9
−0.5 to 0.5	40.1
0.5 to 1.0	14.7
1.0 to 1.5	8.0
1.5 to 2.0	3.9
Greater than 2.0	2.8

Appendix 15.A

Minitab Instructions

CHI-SQUARED GOODNESS-OF-FIT TEST

In one column type the observed values and in a second column type the expected values. (If you wish you can type the cell probabilities specified in the null hypothesis and let Minitab convert these into expected values by multiplying by the sample size.) Suppose that the observed values are in column 1 and the expected values are in column 2. In the session window type

Let C3 = ((C1-C2)**2)/C2
SUM C3

The chi-squared statistic will be printed. Now type

CDF [SUM C3];
CHIS [DF].

where DF is the number of degrees of freedom, which in this application is the number of categories minus 1. The *p*-value of the test is 1 minus the probability printed. If you have only the raw data you will have to determine the observed values. To do so, click **Stat, Tables,** and **Tally.** Specify the column in which the data are stored and click **Counts.** The frequency for each code will be printed.

CHI-SQUARED TEST FOR NORMALITY

If you wish to use intervals different from the ones described above, refer to page 250 for instructions to print normal probabilities.

To calculate the normal probabilities proceed as follows.

1 Type the values of z that you wish to use in a column (e.g., $-2, -1, 0, 1, 2$).

2 Click **Calc, Probability Distributions,** and **Normal . . . .**

3 Use the cursor to select **Cumulative probability,** type the **Mean** (0.0), and the **Standard deviation** (1.0). Select **Input column** and type the name of the column containing the values of z. Click **OK.**

Minitab will print the cumulative probabilities from which you can calculate the probabilities of the intervals you plan to use.

To count the interval frequencies

1 Calculate the mean and standard deviation of the data.

2 Create a second column containing the standardized values. For example, if the data are in column 1 type

LET C2 = (C1−[mean])/[standard deviation]

3 Code data so that each standardized value is assigned a number. For example,

$$\text{CODE } (-99{:}{-}2) \ 1 \ (-2{:}{-}1) \ 2 \ (-1{:}0) \ 3 \ (0{:}1) \ 4 \ (1{:}2) \ 5 \ (2{:}99) \ 6 \ C2 \ C3$$

tells Minitab to code the data so that any value in column 2 between -99 and -2 is assigned a code of 1 in column 3. The other standardized values are similarly coded.

4 Count the number of 1's, 2's, etc., in column 3. Click **Stat, Tables,** and **Tally . . . .** Specify the column you wish to count. Click **OK.** The observed number for each interval will be printed. Use the instructions above to produce the chi-squared statistic and the p-value of the test.

Chapter 16

Nonparametric

Statistics

16.1 Introduction

16.2 Wilcoxon Rank Sum Test for Independent Samples

16.3 Sign Test and Wilcoxon Signed Rank Sum Test for Matched Pairs

16.4 Kruskal–Wallis Test

16.5 Friedman Test

16.6 Testing for Normality

16.7 Summary

16.1 INTRODUCTION

Throughout this book we have presented statistical techniques that are used when the data are either quantitative or qualitative. In this chapter, we introduce statistical techniques that deal with ranked data. We will introduce three methods that compare two populations, and two procedures used to compare two or more populations. As you've seen, when we compare two or more populations of quantitative data we measure the difference among means. However, as we discussed in Chapter 2, when the data are ranked, the mean is not the most appropriate measure of location. As a result, the methods in this chapter do not enable us to test the difference in population means; instead, we will test characteristics of populations without referring to specific parameters. For this reason, these techniques are called **nonparametric techniques.** Rather than testing to determine whether the population means differ, we will test to determine whether the **population locations** differ.

Although nonparametric methods are designed to test ranked data, they have another area of application. The statistical tests described in Sections 12.2 and 12.4 and Chapter 14 require that the populations be normally distributed. If the data are extremely nonnormal, the *t*-tests and *F*-test are invalid. Fortunately, nonparametric techniques can be used instead. For this reason, nonparametric procedures are often (perhaps more accurately) called **distribution-free statistics.** The techniques presented here can be used when the data are quantitative and the required condition of normality is unsatisfied. In such circumstances we will treat the quantitative data as if they were ranked. For this reason, even when the data are quantitative and the mean is the appropriate measure of location, we will choose instead to test population locations.

Figure 16.1 depicts the distributions of two populations when their locations are the same. Notice that, since we don't know (or care) anything about the shape of the distributions, we represent them as nonnormal. Figure 16.2 describes a circumstance when the location of population 1 is to the right of the location of population 2. The location of population 1 is to the left of the location of population 2 in Figure 16.3.

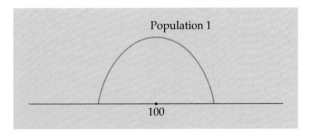

Figure 16.1

Population locations are the same

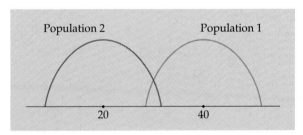

Figure 16.2

Location of population 1 to the right of the location of population 2

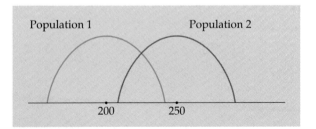

Figure 16.3

Location of population 1 to the left of the location of population 2

When the problem objective is to compare two populations the null hypothesis will state

H_0: The two population locations are the same

The alternative hypothesis can take on any one of the following three forms.

1 If we want to know whether there is sufficient evidence to infer that there is a difference between the two populations, the alternative hypothesis is

H_1: The location of population 1 is different from the location of population 2

2 If we want to know whether we can conclude that the random variable in population 1 is larger in general than the random variable in population 2 (see Figure 16.2), the alternative hypothesis is

H_1: The location of population 1 is to the right of the location of population 2

3 If we want to know whether we can conclude that the random variable in population 1 is smaller in general than the random variable in population 2 (see Figure 16.3), the alternative hypothesis is

H_1: The location of population 1 is to the left of the location of population 2

As usual, the alternative hypothesis specifies whatever we're investigating.

As you will see, nonparametric tests utilize a ranking procedure as an integral part of the calculations. You've actually dealt with such a process already in this book. In Chapter 4, we introduced the median as a measure of central location. The median is computed by placing the observations in order and selecting the observation that falls in the middle. Thus, the measure of central location of ranked data is the median, a statistic that is the product of a ranking process.

In the next section, we present the Wilcoxon rank sum test for independent samples. Section 16.3 introduces the sign test and the Wilcoxon signed rank sum test for matched pairs. Sections 16.4 and 16.5 introduce the Kruskal–Wallis test and the Friedman test, respectively, procedures that are employed when the objective is to compare two or more populations. Because the nonparametric methods are used to overcome the problem of nonnormality of quantitative data, we provide another test for normality in Section 16.6.

16.2 WILCOXON RANK SUM TEST FOR INDEPENDENT SAMPLES

The test we introduce in this section deals with problems with the following characteristics.

1 The problem objective is to compare two populations.

2 The data are either ranked or quantitative where the normality requirement necessary to perform the equal-variances t-test of $\mu_1 - \mu_2$ is unsatisfied.

3 The samples are independent.

To illustrate how to compute the test statistic for the **Wilcoxon rank sum test for independent samples,** we offer the following example.

Suppose that we want to determine whether the following observations drawn from two populations allow us to conclude at the 5% significance level that the location of population 1 is to the left of the location of population 2.

> Sample 1: 22   23   20
> Sample 2: 18   27   26

We want to test the following hypotheses.

> H_0: The two population locations are the same
>
> H_1: The location of population 1 is to the left of the location of population 2

Test statistic

The first step is to rank all six observations with rank 1 assigned to the smallest observation and rank 6 to the largest.

SAMPLE 1	RANK	SAMPLE 2	RANK
22	3	18	1
23	4	27	6
20	2	26	5
	$T_1 = 9$		$T_2 = 12$

Observe that 18 is the smallest number, so it receives a rank of 1; 20 is the second smallest number, and it receives a rank of 2. We continue until rank 6 is assigned to 27, which is the largest of the observations. In case of ties, we average the ranks of the tied observations. For example, if the observations are 18, 20, 20, 25, the ranks would be 1, 2.5, 2.5, 4, respectively. The second step is to calculate the sum of the ranks of each sample. The rank sum of sample 1, denoted T_1, is 9. The rank sum of sample 2, denoted T_2, is 12. (Note that T_1 plus T_2 must equal the sum of the integers from 1 to 6, which is 21.) We can use either rank sum as the test statistic. We arbitrarily select T_1 as the test statistic and label it T. Thus, the value of the test statistic in this example is $T = T_1 = 9$.

Sampling Distribution of the Test Statistic

A small value of T indicates that most of the smaller observations are in sample 1 and that most of the larger observations are in sample 2. This would imply that the location of population 1 is to the left of the location of population 2. Therefore, in order for us to conclude statistically that this is the case, we need to show that T is small. The definition of "small" comes from the sampling distribution of T. As we did in Chapter 8 when we derived the sampling distribution of the sample mean, we can derive the sampling distribution of T by listing all possible values of T. In Table 16.1 we show all possible rankings of two samples of size 3.

Table 16.1 All Possible Ranks and Rank Sums of Two Samples of Size 3

Ranks of 1	Rank Sum	Ranks of 2	Rank Sum
1, 2, 3	6	4, 5, 6	15
1, 2, 4	7	3, 5, 6	14
1, 2, 5	8	3, 4, 6	13
1, 2, 6	9	3, 4, 5	12
1, 3, 4	8	2, 5, 6	13
1, 3, 5	9	2, 4, 6	12
1, 3, 6	10	2, 4, 5	11
1, 4, 5	10	2, 3, 6	11
1, 4, 6	11	2, 3, 5	10
1, 5, 6	12	2, 3, 4	9
2, 3, 4	9	1, 5, 6	12
2, 3, 5	10	1, 4, 6	11
2, 3, 6	11	1, 4, 5	10
2, 4, 5	11	1, 3, 6	10
2, 4, 6	12	1, 3, 5	9
2, 5, 6	13	1, 3, 4	8
3, 4, 5	12	1, 2, 6	9
3, 4, 6	13	1, 2, 5	8
3, 5, 6	14	1, 2, 4	7
4, 5, 6	15	1, 2, 3	6

If the null hypothesis is true and the two population locations are identical, then it follows that each possible ranking is equally likely. Since there are 20 different possibilities, each value of T has the same probability, namely, 1/20. Notice that there is one value of 6, one value of 7, two values of 8, and so on. Table 16.2 summarizes the values of T and their probabilities, and Figure 16.4 depicts this sampling distribution.

Table 16.2 Sampling Distribution of *T* with Two Samples of Size 3

T	P(T)
6	1/20
7	1/20
8	2/20
9	3/20
10	3/20
11	3/20
12	3/20
13	2/20
14	1/20
15	1/20
Total	1

From this sampling distribution we can see that $P(T \leq 6) = .05$. Because we're trying to determine if the value of the test statistic is small enough for us to reject the null hypothesis at the 5% significance level, we specify the rejection region as $T \leq 6$. Since $T = 9$, we cannot reject the null hypothesis.

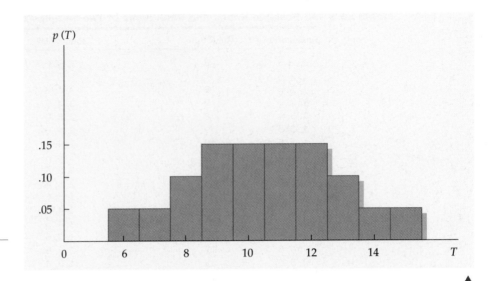

Figure 16.4

Sampling distribution of *T* with two samples of size 3

Mathematicians have generated the sampling distribution of T for various combinations of sample sizes. The critical values are provided in Table 8 in Appendix B and reproduced here as Table 16.3. Table 16.3 provides values of T_L and T_U for sample sizes between 3 and 10 (n_1 is the size of sample 1, and n_2 is the size of sample 2). The values of T_L and T_U in part (a) of the table are such that

$$P(T \leq T_L) = P(T \geq T_U) = .025$$

Table 16.3 **Critical Values of the Wilcoxon Rank Sum Test for Independent Samples**

(a) $\alpha = .025$ one-tail; $\alpha = .05$ two-tail

n_2 \ n_1	3		4		5		6		7		8		9		10	
	T_L	T_U	T_L	T_U	T_L	T_U	T_L	T_U	T_L	T_U	T_L	T_U	T_L	T_U	T_L	T_U
4	6	18	11	25	17	33	23	43	31	53	40	64	50	76	61	89
5	6	21	12	28	18	37	25	47	33	58	42	70	52	83	64	96
6	7	23	12	32	19	41	26	52	35	63	44	76	55	89	66	104
7	7	26	13	35	20	45	28	56	37	68	47	81	58	95	70	110
8	8	28	14	38	21	49	29	61	39	73	49	87	60	102	73	117
9	8	31	15	41	22	53	31	65	41	78	51	93	63	108	76	124
10	9	33	16	44	24	56	32	70	43	83	54	98	66	114	79	131

(b) $\alpha = .05$ one-tail; $\alpha = .10$ two-tail

n_2 \ n_1	3		4		5		6		7		8		9		10	
	T_L	T_U	T_L	T_U	T_L	T_U	T_L	T_U	T_L	T_U	T_L	T_U	T_L	T_U	T_L	T_U
3	6	15	11	21	16	29	23	37	31	46	39	57	49	68	60	80
4	7	17	12	24	18	32	25	41	33	51	42	62	52	74	63	87
5	7	20	13	27	19	36	26	46	35	56	45	67	55	80	66	94
6	8	22	14	30	20	40	28	50	37	61	47	73	57	87	69	101
7	9	24	15	33	22	43	30	54	39	66	49	79	60	93	73	107
8	9	27	16	36	24	46	32	58	41	71	52	84	63	99	76	114
9	10	29	17	39	25	50	33	63	43	76	54	90	66	105	79	121
10	22	31	18	42	26	54	35	67	46	80	57	95	69	111	83	127

Source: From F. Wilcoxon and R. A. Wilcox, "Some Rapid Approximate Statistical Procedures" (1964), p. 28. Reproduced with the permission of American Cyanamid Company.

The values of T_L and T_U in part (b) of the table are such that

$$P(T \leq T_L) = P(T \geq T_U) = .05$$

Part (a) is used either in a two-tail test with $\alpha = .05$ or in a one-tail test with $\alpha = .025$. Part (b) is employed either in a two-tail test with $\alpha = .10$ or in a one-tail test with $\alpha = .05$. Because no other values are provided, we are restricted to those values of α.

It is possible to derive the sampling distribution of the test statistic for any other sample sizes. This can be quite tedious. Fortunately, it is also unnecessary. Mathematicians have shown that when the sample sizes are larger than 10, the test statistic is approximately normally distributed with mean $E(T)$ and standard deviation σ_T where

$$E(T) = \frac{n_1(n_1 + n_2 + 1)}{2}$$

and

$$\sigma_T = \sqrt{\frac{n_1 n_2(n_1 + n_2 + 1)}{12}}$$

Thus, the standardized test statistic is

$$z = \frac{T - E(T)}{\sigma_T}$$

▼ EXAMPLE 16.2

A pharmaceutical company is planning to introduce a new painkiller. In a preliminary experiment to determine its effectiveness, 30 people were randomly selected, of whom 15 were given the new painkiller and 15 were given aspirin. All 30 were told to use the drug when headaches or other minor pains occurred and to indicate which of the following statements most accurately represented the effectiveness of the drug they took.

5 = The drug was extremely effective.
4 = The drug was quite effective.
3 = The drug was somewhat effective.
2 = The drug was slightly effective.
1 = The drug was not at all effective.

The responses are listed below using the codes. (The data are also stored in columns 1 and 2 in file XM16-02.) Can we conclude at the 5% significance level that the new painkiller is perceived to be more effective?

New painkiller: 3, 5, 4, 3, 2, 5, 1, 4, 5, 3, 3, 5, 5, 5, 4
Aspirin: 4, 1, 3, 2, 4, 1, 3, 4, 2, 2, 2, 4, 3, 4, 5

Solution

IDENTIFY

The objective is to compare two populations: the perceived effectiveness of the new painkiller and of aspirin. We recognize that the data are ranked, because except for the order of the codes, the numbers used to record the results are arbitrary. Finally, the samples are independent. These factors tell us that the appropriate technique is the Wilcoxon rank sum test for independent samples. We denote the effectiveness scores of the new painkiller as 1, and 2 represents the effectiveness scores of aspirin. Because we want to know whether the new painkiller is better than aspirin, the alternative hypothesis is

H_1: The location of population 1 is to the right of the location of population 2.

The complete test follows.

H_0: The two population locations are the same.

H_1: The location of population 1 is to the right of the location of population 2.

Test statistic: $z = \dfrac{T - E(T)}{\sigma_T}$

SOLVE

If the alternative hypothesis is true, the location of population 1 is to the right of the location of population 2. It follows that T and z would be large. Our job is to determine whether z is large enough to reject the null hypothesis in favor of the alternative hypothesis. Thus, the rejection region is

$z > z_\alpha = z_{.05} = 1.645$

We compute the test statistic by ranking all of the observations.

New Pain Killer	Rank	Aspirin	Rank
3	12	4	19.5
5	27	1	2
4	19.5	3	12
3	12	2	6
2	6	4	19.5
5	27	1	2
1	2	3	12
4	19.5	4	19.5
5	27	2	6
3	12	2	6
3	12	2	6
5	27	4	19.5
5	27	3	12
5	27	4	19.5
4	19.5	5	27
Rank Sums	$T_1 = 276.5$		$T_2 = 188.5$

Notice that there are three "ones" that occupy ranks 1, 2, and 3. The average is 2. Thus, each "one" is assigned a rank of 2. There are five "twos" whose ranks are 4, 5, 6, 7, and 8, the average of which is 6. We continue until all the observations have been similarly ranked. The rank sums are computed with $T_1 = 276.5$ and $T_2 = 188.5$. The unstandardized test statistic is $T = T_1 = 276.5$. To standardize, we determine $E(T)$ and σ_T.

$$E(T) = \frac{n_1(n_1 + n_2 + 1)}{2} = \frac{(15)(31)}{2} = 232.5$$

$$\sigma_T = \sqrt{\frac{n_1 n_2(n_1 + n_2 + 1)}{12}} = \sqrt{\frac{(15)(15)(31)}{12}} = 24.1$$

The standardized test statistic is

$$z = \frac{T - E(T)}{\sigma_T} = \frac{276.5 - 232.5}{24.1} = 1.83$$

p-value $= P(Z > 1.83) = .5 - .4664 = .0336.$

Excel Output for Example 16.2

	A	B	C	D	E	F
1	Wilcoxon Rank Sum Test					
2	Sample	RankSum	SampSize			
3	1	276.5	15	Large Sample Approximation		
4	2	188.5	15	Test Statistic Z = 1.825		
5				P-Value = 0.034		

COMMANDS

1 Type or import the data into two adjacent columns.
2 Click **Tools, Data Analysis Plus,** and **Wilcoxon Rank Sum Test.**
3 Specify the input range. Do not include the cells containing the variable names.
4 Click the appropriate alternative hypothesis.

COMMANDS FOR EXAMPLE 16.2

Open file **XM16-02.**

A2:B16

The location of Population 1 is right of Population 2

Minitab Output for Example 16.2

Mann-Whitney Confidence Interval and Test

```
New       N = 15      Median =      4.000
Aspirin   N = 15      Median =      3.000
Point estimate for ETA1-ETA2 is      1.000
95.4 Percent CI for ETA1-ETA2 is (0.001,2.000)
W = 276.5
Test of ETA1 = ETA2   vs  ETA1 > ETA2 is significant at 0.0356
The test is significant at 0.0321 (adjusted for ties)
```

Minitab performs the **Mann-Whitney test** rather than the Wilcoxon test. However, the tests are equivalent. In the output above, **ETA** represents the population median. The test statistic **W = 276.5,** is the value of the Wilcoxon rank sum statistic. That is $T = W = 276.5$. The output includes the *p*-value (**0.0356**) and another *p*-value calculated by making adjustments for tied observations (**0.0321**). We will report the first *p*-value only.

COMMANDS

1 Type or import the data into two columns.
2 Click **Stat, Nonparametrics,** and **Mann-Whitney . . . .**
3 Type the variable name for the **First Sample:.**
4 Type the variable name of the **Second Sample:.**
5 Specify one of **less than, not equal to,** or **greater than.** Click **OK.**

COMMANDS FOR EXAMPLE 16.2

Open file **XM16-02.**

New or **C1**

Aspirin or **C2**

greater than

INTERPRET

The data provide sufficient evidence to infer that the new painkiller is perceived to be more effective than aspirin. We note that the data were generated from a controlled experiment. That is, the subjects were assigned to take either the new painkiller or aspirin. (When subjects decide for themselves which medication to take, the data are observational.) This factor helps support the claim that the new painkiller is indeed more effective than aspirin. Factors that weaken the argument are small sample sizes and the inexactness of the responses. There may be methods to measure the effectiveness less subjectively. Additionally, a double-blind experiment should have been employed.

▲

As we pointed out in the introduction to this chapter, the Wilcoxon rank sum test is used to compare two populations when the data are either ranked or quantitative. Example 16.2 illustrated the use of the Wilcoxon rank sum test when the data are ranked. In the next example, we demonstrate its use when the data are quantitative.

▼ EXAMPLE 16.3

Because of the high cost of hiring and training new employees, employers would like to ensure that they retain highly qualified workers. To help develop a hiring program, the personnel manager of a large company wanted to compare how long business and nonbusiness university graduates worked for the company before quitting to accept a position elsewhere. The manager selected a random sample of 25 business and 20 nonbusiness graduates who had been hired 5 years ago. The number of months each had worked for the company was recorded. (Those who had not quit were recorded as having worked for 60 months.) The data are stored in column 1 (business graduates) and column 2 (nonbusiness graduates) in file XM16-03 and are listed below. Can the personnel manager conclude at the 5% significance level that a difference in duration of employment exists between business and nonbusiness graduates?

DURATION OF EMPLOYMENT OF BUSINESS GRADUATES (IN MONTHS)	DURATION OF EMPLOYMENT OF NONBUSINESS GRADUATES (IN MONTHS)
60, 11, 18, 19, 5, 25, 60, 7,	25, 60 22, 24, 23, 36, 39, 15,
8, 17, 37, 4, 8, 28, 27, 11,	35, 16, 28, 9, 60, 29 16, 22,
60, 25, 5, 13, 22, 11, 17, 9,	60, 17, 60, 32
4	

Solution

IDENTIFY

The problem objective is to compare two populations whose data are quantitative. The samples are independent. Thus, the appropriate parametric technique is the t-test of $\mu_1 - \mu_2$, which requires that the populations be normally distributed. However, when the histograms are drawn (see computer output on page 586), it becomes clear that this requirement is unsatisfied. It follows that the correct statistical procedure is the Wilcoxon rank sum test.

H_0: The two population locations are the same

H_1: The location of population 1 (business graduates) is different from the location of population 2 (nonbusiness graduates)

Test statistic: $z = \dfrac{T - E(T)}{\sigma_T}$

SOLVE

The rejection region is

$$z > z_{\alpha/2} = z_{.025} = 1.96 \quad \text{or} \quad z < -z_{\alpha/2} = -1.96$$

The data are ranked as follows:

Business (1)	Rank	Nonbusiness (2)	Rank
60	42	25	28
11	11	60	42
18	20	22	23
19	21	24	26
5	3.5	23	25
25	28	36	36
60	42	39	38
7	5	15	14
8	6.5	35	35
17	18	16	15.5
37	37	28	31.5
4	1.5	9	8.5
8	6.5	60	42
28	31.5	29	33
27	30	16	15.5
11	11	22	23
60	42	60	42
25	28	17	18
5	3.5	60	42
13	13	32	34
22	23		
11	11		
17	18		
9	8.5		
4	1.5		
Rank Sums	$T_1 = 463$		$T_2 = 572$

The unstandardized test statistic is $T = T_1 = 463$. To compute z, we first determine the mean and standard deviation of T. Note that $n_1 = 25$ and $n_2 = 20$.

$$E(T) = \frac{n_1(n_1 + n_2 + 1)}{2} = \frac{(25)(46)}{2} = 575$$

$$\sigma_T = \sqrt{\frac{n_1 n_2(n_1 + n_2 + 1)}{12}} = \sqrt{\frac{(25)(20)(46)}{12}} = 43.8$$

The standardized test statistic is

$$z = \frac{T - E(T)}{\sigma_T} = \frac{463 - 575}{43.8} = -2.56$$

p-value $= 2P(Z < -2.56) = 2(.5 - .4948) = .0104.$

Excel Output for
Example 16.3

	A	B	C	D	E	F
1	**Wilcoxon Rank Sum Test**					
2	*Sample*	*RankSum*	*SampSize*			
3	1	463	25	*Large Sample Approximation*		
4	2	572	20	*Test Statistic Z = -2.5583*		
5				*P-Value = 0.0105*		

Minitab Output for
Example 16.3

Mann-Whitney Confidence Interval and Test

```
Business    N = 25      Median =        17.00
Non-Bus     N = 20      Median =        26.50
Point estimate for ETA1-ETA2 is        -11.00
95.2 Percent CI for ETA1-ETA2 is (-19.00,-3.00)
W = 463.0
Test of ETA1 = ETA2  vs  ETA1 not = ETA2 is significant at 0.0109
The test is significant at 0.0107 (adjusted for ties)
```

The histograms (Figures 16.5 and 16.6, created in Excel) indicate that the number of months of employment is not a normally distributed random variable.

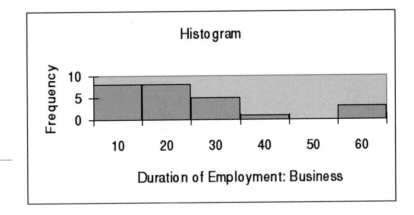

Figure 16.5

Histogram of length of employment of business graduates in Example 16.3

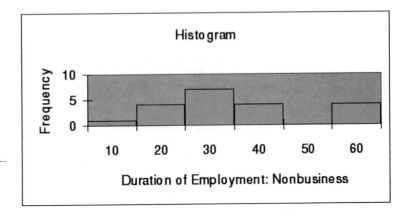

Figure 16.6

Histogram of length of employment of nonbusiness graduates in Example 16.3

INTERPRET   There is strong evidence to infer that the duration of employment is different for business and nonbusiness graduates. The data cannot tell us the cause of this conclusion. For example, we don't know whether business graduates are in greater demand, making it more likely that such employees will leave for better jobs, or that nonbusiness graduates are more satisfied with their jobs and thus remain longer. Moreover, we don't know what the results would have been had we surveyed employees 10 years after they were employed.

▲

REQUIRED CONDITIONS

The Wilcoxon rank sum test (like most of the nonparametric tests presented in this book) actually tests to determine whether the population distributions are identical. This means that it tests not only for identical locations, but for identical spreads (variances) and shapes (distributions) as well. Unfortunately, this means that the rejection of the null hypothesis may not necessarily signify a difference in population locations. The rejection of the null hypothesis may be due instead to a difference in distribution shapes and/or spreads. To avoid this problem, we will require that the two probability distributions be identical except with respect to location, which then becomes the sole focus of the test. This requirement is made for the tests introduced in the next three sections (sign test and Wilcoxon signed rank sum test, Kruskal–Wallis test, and Friedman test).

The histograms in Figures 16.5 and 16.6 appear to confirm that the required condition for the use of the Wilcoxon rank sum test is satisfied in Example 16.3.

DEVELOPING AN UNDERSTANDING OF STATISTICAL CONCEPTS

When applying nonparametric techniques, we do not perform any calculations using the original data. Instead, we perform computations only on the ranks. (We determine the rank sums and use them to make our decision.) As a result, we do not care about the actual distribution of the data (hence the name distribution-free techniques), and we do not specify parameters in the hypotheses (hence the name nonparametric techniques). Although there are other techniques that do not specify parameters in the hypotheses, we use the term *nonparametric* for procedures that feature these concepts.

Here is a summary of how to identify the Wilcoxon rank sum test.

Factors that Identify the Wilcoxon Rank Sum Test for Independent Samples

1 Problem objective: compare two populations

2 Data type: ranked or quantitative but nonnormal

3 Experimental design: independent samples

EXERCISES

16.1 Given the following statistics determine whether the population locations differ. Use a 5% significance level.

$$T_1 = 510 \quad n_1 = 25 \quad T_2 = 765 \quad n_2 = 25$$

16.2 From the following statistics test (with $\alpha = .01$) to determine whether the location of population 1 is to the right of the location of population 2.

$$T_1 = 1,205 \quad n_1 = 30 \quad T_2 = 1,280 \quad n_2 = 40$$

16.3 Use the following statistics to determine whether there is enough statistical evidence at the 10% significance level to infer that the location of population 1 is to the left of the location of population 2.

$$T_1 = 9,350 \quad n_1 = 100$$
$$T_2 = 10,750 \quad n_2 = 100$$

16.4 Use the Wilcoxon rank sum test on the data in the following table to determine whether the location of population 1 is to the left of the location of population 2. (Use $\alpha = .05$.)

Sample 1:   75   60   73 66   81

Sample 2:   90 72   103   82   78

16.5 Use the Wilcoxon rank sum test on the data below (which are also stored in file XR16-05) to determine whether the two population locations differ. (Column 1 contains sample 1, and column 2 contains sample 2.) (Use a 10% significance level.)

Sample 1:   15   7 22   20 32 18 26 17 23   30

Sample 2:   8 27 17 25   20 16 21 17 10 18

The following exercises require the use of a computer and software. The answers may be calculated manually. See Appendix A for the sample statistics.

16.6 In recent years, insurance companies offering medical coverage have given discounts to companies that are committed to improving the health of their employees. To help determine whether this policy is reasonable, the general manager of one large insurance company organized a study of a random sample of 30 workers who regularly participate in their company's lunchtime exercise program and 30 workers who do not. Over a 2-year period he observed the total dollar amount of medical expenses for each individual. These data are stored in columns 1 (exercisers) and 2 (nonexercisers) of file XR16-06. Can the manager conclude at the 5% significance level that companies that provide exercise programs should be given discounts? (Assume that expenses are not normally distributed.)

16.7 To producers of household products, the question of who does the housework is important because of the way advertising campaigns are designed. One of many issues affecting advertising campaigns is the extent to which women are doing less housework and men are doing more. Suppose that 58 women are asked how many hours of work around the home they perform weekly, and that these results are to be compared with the results of a similar survey taken 5 years ago that included 64 women. These data are stored in file XR16-07 (column 1 = hours of housework this year; column 2 = hours of housework 5 years ago). Can we conclude at the 10% significance level that women are doing less housework today than 5 years ago? (Assume that hours of housework is not normally distributed.)

16.8 The American public's support for the space program is important for the program's continuation and for the financial health of the aerospace industry. In a poll conducted by the Gallup organization last year, a random sample of 100 Americans was asked "Should the amount of money being spent on the space program be increased or kept at current levels (3), decreased (2), or ended altogether (1)?" The survey was conducted again this year. The results are stored in file XR16-08 using the codes in parentheses. (Column 1 = opinions last year; column 2 = opinions this year.) Can we conclude at the 10% significance level that public support decreased between this year and last year?

16.9 Certain drugs differ in their side effects depending on the gender of the patient. In a study to determine whether men or women suffer more serious side effects when taking a powerful penicillin substitute, 50 men and 50 women were given the drug. Each was asked to evaluate the level of stomach upset on a 4-point scale, where 4 = extremely upset, 3 = somewhat upset, 2 = not too upset, and 1 = not upset at all. The results are stored in file XR16-09 with column 1 = females' evaluation and column 2 = males' evaluation. Can we conclude at the 5% significance level that men and women experience different levels of stomach upset from the drug?

16.10 The president of Tastee Inc., a baby-food producer, claims that her company's product is superior to that of her leading competitor because babies gain weight faster with her product. As an experiment, 40 healthy newborn infants are randomly selected. For two months, 15 of the babies are fed Tastee baby food and the other 25 are fed the competitor's product. Each baby's weight gain (in ounces) is stored in columns 1 (Tastee) and 2 (leading competitor) in file XR16-10. Can we conclude at the 5% significance level that if we use weight gain as our criterion, Tastee baby food is indeed superior? It is known that weight gain is not normally distributed. This exercise is identical to Exercise 12.23 (except for the data).

16.11 Does the size of a woman's dress influence the ways that others judge her? This question was addressed by a researcher at Ohio State University (*Working Mother,* April 1992). The experiment consisted of asking women to rate how professional two women looked. One woman wore a size 6 dress and the other wore a size 14. Suppose that the researcher asked 20 women to rate the woman wearing the size 6 dress and another 20 to rate the woman wearing the size 14 dress. The ratings were as follows.

4 = highly professional
3 = somewhat professional

2 = not very professional
1 = not at all professional

The results are stored in columns 1 (size 6) and 2 (size 14) in file XR16-11. Do these data provide sufficient evidence at the 10% significance level to infer that women perceive another woman wearing a size 6 dress as more professional than one wearing a size 14 dress?

16.3 SIGN TEST AND WILCOXON SIGNED RANK SUM TEST FOR MATCHED PAIRS

In the preceding section, we discussed the nonparametric technique for comparing two populations of data that are either ranked or quantitative for which the data are independently drawn. In this section, the problem objective and data type remain as they were in Section 16.2, but we will be working with data generated from a matched pairs experiment. We have dealt with this type of experiment before. In Section 12.4, we dealt with the mean of the paired differences represented by the parameter μ_D. In this section, we introduce two nonparametric techniques that test hypotheses in problems with the following characteristics.

1 The problem objective is to compare two populations.

2 The data are either ranked or quantitative (where the normality requirement necessary to perform the parametric test is unsatisfied).

3 The samples are matched pairs.

To extract all the potential information from a matched pairs experiment we must create the matched pairs differences. Recall that we did so when conducting the *t*-test and estimate of μ_D. We then calculated the mean and standard deviation of these differences and completed the test statistic and interval estimator. The first step in both nonparametric methods presented here is the same; compute the differences for each pair of observations. However, if the data are ranked we cannot perform any calculations on those differences because differences have no meaning.

To understand this point, consider comparing two populations of responses of people rating a product or service. The responses are "excellent," "good," "fair," and "poor." Recall that we can assign any numbering system as long as the order is maintained. The simplest system is 4-3-2-1. However, any other system such as 66-38-25-11 (a set of numbers randomly selected except for maintaining the order) is equally valid. Now suppose that in one matched pair the sample 1 response was "excellent" and the sample 2 response was "good." Calculating the matched pairs difference under the 4-3-2-1 system the difference is $4-3 = 1$. Using the 66-38-25-11 system, the difference is $66-38 = 28$. If we treat this and other differences as real numbers, we are likely to produce different results depending on which numbering system we used. Thus, we cannot use any method that uses the actual differences. However, we can use the sign of the differences. In fact, when the data are ranked that is the only method that is valid. That is, no matter what numbering system is employed we know that "excellent" is better than "good." In the 4-3-2-1 system the difference between "excellent" and "good" is $+1$. In the 66-38-25-11 system the difference is $+28$. If we ignore the magnitude of the number and only record the sign, the two numbering systems (and all other systems where the rank order is maintained) will produce exactly the same result.

As you will shortly discover the sign test only uses the sign of the differences. That's why it's called the sign test.

When the data are quantitative, however, differences have real meaning. Although we can use the sign test when the data are quantitative, doing so results in a loss of potentially useful information. For example, knowing that the difference in sales between two matched used car salespeople is 25 cars is much more informative than simply knowing that the first salesperson sold more cars than a second salesperson. As a result, when the data are quantitative but not normal we will use the Wilcoxon signed rank sum test, which incorporates not only the sign of the difference (hence the name), but the magnitude as well.

SIGN TEST

The **sign test** is employed in the following situations.

1 The problem objective is to compare two populations.

2 The data are ranked.

3 The experimental design is matched pairs.

Test Statistic

The sign test is quite simple. For each matched pair, we calculate the difference between the observation in sample 1 and the related observation in sample 2. We then count the number of positive differences and the number of negative differences. If the null hypothesis is true, we expect the number of positive differences to be approximately equal to the number of negative differences. Expressed another way, we expect the number of positive differences and the number of negative differences each to be approximately equal to half the total sample size. If either number is too large or too small, we reject the null hypothesis. By now you know that the determination of what is too large or too small comes from the sampling distribution of the test statistic. We will arbitrarily choose the test statistic to be the number of positive differences, which we denote x. The test statistic x is a binomial random variable, and under the null hypothesis, the binomial proportion is $p = .5$. Thus, the sign test is none other than the z-test of p first developed in Section 11.4.

Recall from Chapters 6 and 8 that x is binomially distributed and that, for sufficiently large n [$np \geq 5$ and $n(1 - p) \geq 5$], x is approximately normally distributed with mean $\mu = np$ and standard deviation $\sqrt{np(1 - p)}$. Thus, the standardized test statistic is

$$z = \frac{x - np}{\sqrt{np(1 - p)}}$$

The null hypothesis

H_0: The two population locations are the same

is equivalent to testing

H_0: $p = .5$

Therefore, the test statistic becomes

$$z = \frac{x - np}{\sqrt{np(1 - p)}} = \frac{x - .5n}{\sqrt{n(.5)(.5)}} = \frac{x - .5n}{.5\sqrt{n}}$$

The normal approximation of the binomial distribution is valid when $np \geq 5$ and $n(1 - p) \geq 5$. When $p = .5$,

$$np = n(.5) \geq 5$$

and

$$n(1 - p) = n(.5) \geq 5$$

implies that n must be greater than or equal to 10. Thus, this is one of the required conditions of the sign test. However, the quality of the inference with so small a sample size is poor. Larger sample sizes are recommended.

It is common practice in this type of test to eliminate the matched pairs of observations when the differences equal zero. Consequently, n equals the number of nonzero differences in the sample.

▼ EXAMPLE 16.4

In an experiment to determine which of two cars is perceived to have the more comfortable ride, 25 people rode (separately) in the back seat of an expensive European model and also in the back seat of a North American midsized car. Each of the 25 people was asked to rate the ride on the following 5-point scale.

$1 = $ Ride is very uncomfortable.
$2 = $ Ride is quite uncomfortable.
$3 = $ Ride is neither uncomfortable nor comfortable.
$4 = $ Ride is quite comfortable.
$5 = $ Ride is very comfortable.

The results are stored in file XM16-04 and are shown below. Do these data allow us to conclude at the 5% significance level that the European car is perceived to be more comfortable than the North American car?

Respondent	Comfort Rating of European Car	Comfort Rating of North American Car
1	4	5
2	2	1
3	5	4
4	3	2
5	2	1
6	5	3
7	1	3
8	4	2
9	4	2
10	2	2
11	3	2
12	4	3
13	2	1
14	3	4
15	2	1
16	4	3
17	2	1
18	4	3
19	5	4
20	3	1
21	4	2
22	3	3
23	3	4
24	5	2
25	2	3

Solution

IDENTIFY

The problem objective is to compare two populations of ranked data. Because the same 25 people rated both cars, we recognize the experimental design as matched pairs. The sign test is applied, with the following results.

H_0: The two population locations are the same

H_1: The location of population 1 (European car rating) is to the right of the location of population 2 (North American car rating)

Test statistic: $z = \dfrac{x - .5n}{.5\sqrt{n}}$

SOLVE

Rejection region: $z > z_\alpha = z_{.05} = 1.645$

To calculate the value of the test statistic, we calculate the paired differences and count the number of positive, negative, and zero differences. The differences are as follows.

$$-1,\ 1,\ 1,\ 1,\ 1,\ 2,\ -2,\ 2,\ 2,\ 0,\ 1,\ 1,\ 1,\ -1,\ 1,\ 1,\ 1,\ 1,\ 1,\ 1,\ 2,\ 2,\ 0,\ -1,\ 3,\ -1$$

There are 18 positive, 5 negative, and 2 zero differences. Thus, $x = 18$ and $n = 23$. The value of the test statistic is

$$z = \frac{x - .5n}{.5\sqrt{n}} = \frac{18 - .5(23)}{.5\sqrt{23}} = 2.71$$

p-value $= P(Z > 2.71) = .5 - .4966 = .0034$.

Excel Output for Example 16.4

	A	B	C
1	**Sign Test**		
2			
3	*Positive Differences = 18*		
4	*Negative Differences = 5*		
5	*Zero Differences = 2*		
6	*P-Value = 0.0053*		

The p-value .0053 is based on the actual distribution of the number of positive differences, which is binomial.

COMMANDS

1 Type or import the data into two adjacent columns.

2 Click **Tools, Data Analysis Plus,** and **Sign Test.**

3 Specify the **Input Range:.** Do not include the cells containing the variable names.

4 Click the appropriate alternative hypothesis. Click **OK.**

COMMANDS FOR EXAMPLE 16.4

Open file **XM16-04.**

A2:B26

The location of Population 1 is right of Population 2

Minitab Output for Example 16.4

Sign Test for Median

```
Sign test of median = 0.00000 versus  >  0.00000


                 N  Below  Equal  Above         P    Median
Diff            25      5      2     18    0.0053     1.000
```

Minitab prints the number of differences that are negative **(BELOW),** the number of zero differences **(EQUAL),** and the number of positive differences **(ABOVE).** The p-value .0053 is based on the actual distribution of the number of positive differences, which is binomial.

COMMANDS	COMMANDS FOR EXAMPLE 16.4
1 Type or import the data into two columns.	Open file **XM16-04.**
2 Create a new variable, the paired difference. Click **Calc and Calculator.** Specify the name of new variable.	**Diff** or **C3** **New–Aspirin** or **C1-C2**
3 Type the mathematical expression.	
4 Click **Stat, Nonparametrics,** and **1-Sample Sign . . . .**	
5 Specify the new variable.	**Diff** or **C3**
6 Select **Test median** and type **0.**	
7 Select one of **less than, not equal,** or **greater than.** Click **OK.**	greater than

INTERPRET

There is relatively strong evidence to indicate that people perceive the European car to provide a more comfortable ride than the North American car. There are, however, two aspects of the experiment that may detract from the conclusion that European cars provide a more comfortable ride. First, did the respondents know in which car they were riding? If so, they may have answered on their preconceived bias that European cars are more expensive and therefore better. If the subjects were blindfolded, we would be more secure in our conclusion. Second, was the order in which each subject rode the two cars varied? If all of the subjects rode the North American car first and the European car second, that may have influenced their ratings. The experiment should have been conducted so that the car each subject rode in first was randomly determined.

▲

CHECKING THE REQUIRED CONDITIONS

As we noted in Section 16.2, the sign test requires that the populations be identical in shape and spread. The histograms in Figures 16.7 and 16.8 confirm that these conditions are satisfied in this example. The other condition is that the sample size exceeds 10.

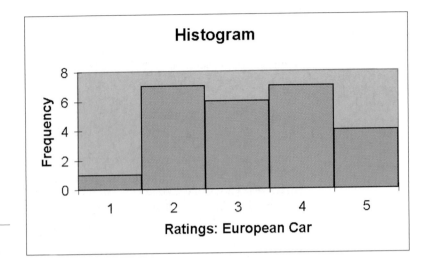

Figure 16.7

Histogram of ratings of
European car in Example 16.4

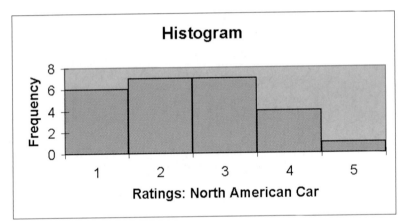

Figure 16.8

Histogram of ratings of North
American car in Example 16.4

Here are the factors that identify when to use the sign test.

Factors that Identify the Sign Test

1 Problem objective: compare two populations

2 Data type: ranked

3 Experimental design: matched pairs

WILCOXON SIGNED RANK SUM TEST FOR MATCHED PAIRS

The **Wilcoxon signed rank sum test for matched pairs** is used under the following circumstances.

1 The problem objective is to compare two populations.

2 The data are quantitative but not normally distributed.

3 The samples are matched pairs.

The Wilcoxon signed rank sum test is the nonparametric counterpart of the t-test of μ_D.

Because the data are quantitative, we can refer to the Wilcoxon signed rank sum test as a test of μ_D. However, to be consistent with the other nonparametric techniques and to avoid confusion, we will express the hypotheses to be tested in the same way as in Section 16.2.

Test Statistic

We begin by computing the paired differences $D = x_1 - x_2$. As we did in the sign test, we eliminate all differences where $D = 0$. Next we rank the absolute values of D where $1 = $ smallest value of $|D|$ and $n = $ largest value of $|D|$ and where $n = $ number of nonzero differences. (We average the ranks of tied observations.) The sum of the ranks of the positive differences (denoted T^+) and the sum of the ranks of the negative differences (denoted T^-) are then calculated. We arbitrarily select T^+, which we label T, as our test statistic.

For relatively small samples, which we define as $n \leq 30$, the critical values of T can be determined from Table 9 in Appendix B (reproduced below as Table 16.4). Note that n is the number of nonzero differences. This table lists values of T_L and T_U for sample sizes between 6 and 30. The values of T_L and T_U in part (a) of the table are such that

$$P(T \leq T_L) = P(T \geq T_U) = .025$$

Table 16.4   **Critical Values for the Wilcoxon Signed Rank Sum Test**

	(a) $\alpha = .025$ One-Tail $\alpha = .05$ Two-Tail		(b) $\alpha = .05$ One-Tail $\alpha = .10$ Two-Tail	
n	T_L	T_U	T_L	T_U
6	1	20	2	19
7	2	26	4	24
8	4	32	6	30
9	6	39	8	37
10	8	47	11	44
11	11	55	14	52
12	14	64	17	61
13	17	74	21	70
14	21	84	26	79
15	25	95	30	90
16	30	106	36	100
17	35	118	41	112
18	40	131	47	124
19	46	144	54	136
20	52	158	60	150
21	59	172	68	163
22	66	187	75	178
23	73	203	83	193
24	81	219	92	208
25	90	235	101	224
26	98	253	110	241
27	107	271	120	258
28	117	289	130	276
29	127	308	141	294
30	137	328	152	313

The values of T_L and T_U in part (b) of the table are such that

$$P(T \leq T_L) = P(T \geq T_U) = .05$$

Part (a) is used either in a two-tail test with $\alpha = .05$ or in a one-tail test with $\alpha = .025$. Part (b) is employed either in a two-tail test with $\alpha = .10$ or in a one-tail test with $\alpha = .05$.

For relatively large sample sizes (we will define this to mean $n > 30$), T is approximately normally distributed with mean

$$E(T) = \frac{n(n + 1)}{4}$$

and standard deviation

$$\sigma_T = \sqrt{\frac{n(n + 1)(2n + 1)}{24}}$$

Thus, the standardized test statistic is

$$z = \frac{T - E(T)}{\sigma_T}$$

▼ EXAMPLE 16.5

Traffic congestion on roads and highways costs industry billions of dollars annually as workers struggle to get to and from work. Several suggestions have been made about how to improve this situation, one of which is called *flextime,* which involves allowing workers to determine their own schedules (provided they work a full shift). Such workers will likely choose an arrival and departure time to avoid rush-hour traffic. In a preliminary experiment designed to investigate such a program, the general manager of a large company wanted to compare the times it took workers to travel from their homes to work at 8:00 A.M. with travel time under the flextime program. A random sample of 32 workers was selected. The employees recorded the time it took to arrive at work at 8:00 A.M. on Wednesday of one week. The following week, the same employees arrived at work at times of their own choosing. The travel time on Wednesday of that week was recorded. These results are stored in columns 1 (arrive at 8:00 A.M.) and 2 (flextime) in file XM16-05 and listed in the following table. Can we conclude at the 5% significance level that travel times under the flextime program are different from travel times to arrive at work at 8:00 A.M.?

WORKER	TRAVEL TIME: ARRIVAL AT 8:00 A.M.	TRAVEL TIME: FLEXTIME PROGRAM
1	34	31
2	35	31
3	43	43
4	46	44
5	16	15
6	26	28
7	68	63
8	38	39
9	61	63
10	52	54
11	68	65
12	13	12
13	69	71

(continued)

WORKER	TRAVEL TIME: ARRIVAL AT 8:00 A.M.	TRAVEL TIME: FLEXTIME PROGRAM
14	18	13
15	53	55
16	18	19
17	41	41
18	25	23
19	17	14
20	26	21
21	44	40
22	30	33
23	19	18
24	48	51
25	29	33
26	24	21
27	51	50
28	40	38
29	26	22
30	20	19
31	19	21
32	42	38

Solution

IDENTIFY

The objective is to compare two populations; the data are quantitative and were produced from a matched pairs experiment. If travel times are normally distributed, we should apply the t-test of μ_D. To judge whether the data are normal, we computed the paired differences and drew the histogram (actually Excel did). Figure 16.9 depicts this histogram. Apparently, the normal requirement is not satisfied, indicating that we should employ the Wilcoxon signed rank sum test.

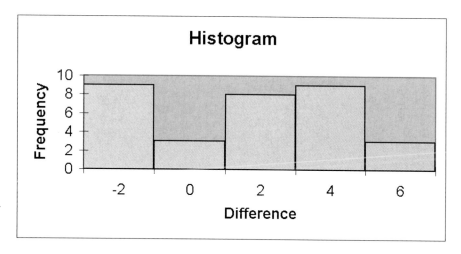

Figure 16.9

Histogram of the differences for Example 16.5

Because we want to know whether the two groups of times differ, we perform a two-tail test.

H_0: The two population locations are the same

H_1: The location of population 1 (current work schedule) is different from the location of population 2 (flextime program)

SOLVE

For each worker, we compute the difference between travel time with arrival at 8:00 A.M. and travel time under flextime.

WORKER	TRAVEL TIME: ARRIVAL AT 8:00 A.M.	TRAVEL TIME: FLEXTIME PROGRAM	DIFFERENCE	|DIFFERENCE|	RANK
1	34	31	3	3	21.0
2	35	31	4	4	27.0
3	43	44	−1	1	(4.5)
4	46	44	2	2	13.0
5	16	15	1	1	4.5
6	26	28	−2	2	(13.0)
7	68	63	5	5	31.0
8	38	39	−1	1	(4.5)
9	61	63	−2	2	(13.0)
10	52	54	−2	2	(13.0)
11	68	65	3	3	21.0
12	13	12	1	1	4.5
13	69	71	−2	2	(13.0)
14	18	13	5	5	31.0
15	53	55	−2	2	(13.0)
16	18	19	−1	1	(4.5)
17	41	38	3	3	21.0
18	25	23	2	2	13.0
19	17	14	3	3	21.0
20	26	21	5	5	31.0
21	44	40	4	4	27.0
22	30	33	−3	3	(21.0)
23	19	18	1	1	4.5
24	48	51	−3	3	(21.0)
25	29	33	−4	4	(27.0)
26	24	21	3	3	21.0
27	51	50	1	1	4.5
28	40	38	2	2	13.0
29	26	22	4	4	27.0
30	20	19	1	1	4.5
31	19	21	−2	2	(13.0)
32	42	38	4	4	27.0

The differences and the absolute values of the differences are calculated. We rank the absolute differences. (If there were any zero differences we would eliminate them before ranking the absolute differences.) Ties are resolved by calculating the averages. The ranks of the negative differences are placed in parentheses to facilitate the summing of the ranks. The rank sums of the positive and negative differences are

$$T^+ = 367.5 \quad \text{and} \quad T^- = 160.5$$

The test statistic is

$$z = \frac{T - E(T)}{\sigma_T}$$

where

$$T = T^+ = 367.5$$

$$E(T) = \frac{n(n + 1)}{4} = \frac{32(33)}{4} = 264$$

$$\sigma_T = \sqrt{\frac{n(n + 1)(2n + 1)}{24}} = \sqrt{\frac{32(33)(65)}{24}} = 53.48$$

Thus,

$$z = \frac{T - E(T)}{\sigma_T} = \frac{367.5 - 264}{53.48} = 1.94$$

The rejection region is

$$z > z_{\alpha/2} = z_{.025} = 1.96 \quad \text{or} \quad z < -z_{\alpha/2} = -1.96$$

p-value $= 2P(Z > 1.94) = 2(.5 - .4738) = .0524.$

Excel Output for Example 16.5

	A	B	C	D
1	**Wilcoxon Signed Rank Sum Test**			
2				
3	*Number of Nonzero Differences = 32*			
4	*T+ = 367.5*			
5	*T- = 160.5*			
6	*Large Sample Approximation*			
7	*Test Statistic Z = 1.935*			
8	*P-Value = 0.0529*			

The output includes the rank sums $T^+ = 367.5$ and $T^- = 160.5$. The test statistic is $z = 1.935$ with a p-value of .0529.

COMMANDS	COMMANDS FOR EXAMPLE 16.5
1 Type or import the data into two adjacent columns.	Open file **XM16-05**.
2 Click **Tools, Data Analysis Plus,** and **Wilcoxon Signed Rank Sum Test.**	
3 Specify the **Input Range:.** Do not include cells containing the variable names.	**A2:B33**
4 Click the appropriate alternative hypothesis. Click **OK.**	**The location of Population 1 differs from Population 2**

Minitab Output for Example 16.5

Wilcoxon Signed Rank Test

```
Test of median = 0.000000 versus median not = 0.000000

                N for    Wilcoxon              Estimated
          N    Test    Statistic        P      Median
Diff     32      32        367.5    0.054       1.000
```

The output includes the original sample size, the number of nonzero differences (**N for Test**), the value of T^+ (**Wilcoxon Statistic 367.5**), and the p-value (**0.054**).

COMMANDS

Follow the same steps as in the sign test. At step 4 click **Stat, Nonparametrics,** and **1-Sample Wilcoxon . . . .**

INTERPRET

There is not enough evidence to infer that flextime commutes are different from the commuting times under the current schedule. This conclusion may be due primarily to the way in which this experiment was performed. All of the drivers recorded their travel time with an 8:00 A.M. arrival on the first Wednesday and their flextime travel time on the second Wednesday. If the second day's traffic was heavier than usual, that may account for the conclusion reached. As we pointed out in Example 16.4, the order of schedules should have been randomly determined for each employee. In this way, the effect of varying traffic conditions could have been minimized.

▲

Here is how we recognize when to use the two techniques introduced in this section.

Factors that Identify the Sign Test

1 Problem objective: compare two populations

2 Data type: ranked

3 Experimental design: matched pairs

Factors that Identify the Wilcoxon Signed Rank Sum Test for Matched Pairs

1 Problem objective: compare two populations

2 Data type: quantitative

3 Distribution of differences: nonnormal

4 Experimental design: matched pairs

EXERCISES

16.12 If in a matched pairs experiment we find 30 negative, 5 zero, and 15 positive differences, perform the sign test to determine whether the two population locations differ. (Use a 5% significance level.)

16.13 Suppose that in a matched pairs experiment we find 28 positive differences, 7 zero differences, and 41 negative differences. Can we infer at the 10% significance level that the location of population 1 is to the left of the location of population 2?

16.14 A matched pairs experiment yielded the following results.

Positive differences: 18
Zero differences: 0
Negative differences: 12

Can we infer at the 5% significance level that the location of population 1 is to the right of the location of population 2?

16.15 Use the sign test on the following data, which are also stored in file XR16-15, to determine whether the location of population 1 is to the right of the location of population 2. (Use $\alpha = .01$.)

Pair:	1	2	3	4	5	6	7	8	9	10	11	12	13	14	15	16
1	5	3	4	2	3	4	3	5	4	3	4	5	4	5	3	2
2	3	2	4	3	3	1	3	4	2	5	1	2	2	3	1	2

16.16 Given the following statistics from a matched pairs experiment perform the Wilcoxon signed rank sum test to determine whether we can infer at the 5% significance level that the two population locations differ.

$$T^+ = 660 \quad T^- = 880 \quad n = 55$$

16.17 A matched pairs experiment produced the statistics below. Conduct a Wilcoxon signed rank sum test to determine whether the location of population 1 is to the right of the location of population 2. (Use $\alpha = .01$.)

$$T^+ = 3,457 \quad T^- = 2,429 \quad n = 108$$

16.18 Perform the Wilcoxon signed rank sum test for the following matched pairs to determine whether the two population locations differ. (Use $\alpha = .10$.)

Pair: 1   2   3 4 5   6
Sample 1: 9 12 13 8 7 10
Sample 2: 5 10 11 9 3   9

16.19 Perform the Wilcoxon signed rank sum test to determine whether the location of population 1 differs from the location of population 2 given the data below (also stored in file XR16-19). (Use $\alpha = .05$.)

Pair: 1   2   3   4   5   6
Sample 1: 18.2 14.1 24.5 11.9 9.5 12.1
Sample 2: 18.2 14.1 23.6 12.1 9.5 11.3

Pair: 7   8   9   10   11   12
Sample 1: 10.9 16.7 19.6 8.4 21.7 23.4
Sample 2:   9.7 17.6 19.4 8.1 21.9 21.6

16.20 In April 1989, NBC aired a 1-hour special program titled "Black Athletes—Fact and Fiction," which attempted to explain why African-Americans dominate American professional and amateur sports. Some of the people interviewed believe that the reasons are genetic, while others point to social and cultural factors. In one test reported on the program, 1,200 black and white children up to age 6 were tested for motor skill development. The researchers found that in 30 separate tests, black children outperformed white children in 15, while white children were superior in 3. What conclusions can be drawn at the 5% significance level from the results of the 30 tests?

The following exercises require the use of a computer and software. The answers may be calculated manually. See Appendix A for the sample statistics.

16.21 Suppose the housework study referred to in Exercise 16.7 was repeated with some changes. In the revised experiment, 60 women were asked 5 years ago and again this year how many hours of housework they perform weekly. The results are stored in file XR16-21. (Column 1 = woman, column 2 = hours of housework this year, and column 3 = hours of housework 5 years ago.) Can we conclude at the 1% significance level that women as a group are doing less housework now than 5 years ago?

16.22 At the height of the energy shortage during the 1970s, governments were actively seeking ways to persuade consumers to reduce their energy consumption. Among other efforts undertaken, several advertising campaigns were launched. To provide input on how to design effective advertising messages, a poll was taken in which people were asked how concerned they were about shortages of gasoline and electricity. There were four possible responses to the questions.

1 = not concerned at all
2 = not too concerned
3 = somewhat concerned
4 = very concerned

A poll of 150 individuals produced the results stored in file XR16-22 where column 1 = respondent, column 2 = concern about gasoline shortage, and column 3 = concern about electricity shortage. Do these data provide enough evidence at the 5% significance level to allow us to infer that concern about a gasoline shortage exceeded concern about an electricity shortage?

16.23 A locksmith is in the process of selecting a new key-cutting machine. If there is a difference in key-cutting speed between the two machines under consideration, he will purchase the faster one. If there is no difference, he will purchase the cheaper machine. The times (in seconds) required to cut each of the 24 most common types of keys are stored in columns 1 (key), 2 (machine 1) and 3 (machine 2, the cheaper one) of file XR16-23. If times are not normally distributed, what should he do? (Use $\alpha = .05$.)

16.24 A large sporting goods store located in Florida is planning a renovation that will result in an increase in the floor space for one department. The manager of the store has narrowed her choice about which department's floor space to increase to two possibilities: the tennis equipment department or the swimming accessories department. The manager would like to enlarge the tennis equipment department because she believes that this department improves the overall image of the store. She decides, however, that if the swimming accessories department can be shown to have higher gross sales, she will choose that department. She has collected each of the two departments' weekly gross sales data for the past 6 months; these are stored in columns 1 (week), 2 (tennis equipment sales), and 3 (swimming accessories sales) of file XR16-24. Which department should be enlarged? (Use $\alpha = .05$.) (Assume that sales are not normally distributed.)

16.25 Does the brand name of an ice cream affect consumers' perceptions of it? The marketing manager of a major dairy pondered this question. She decided to ask 60 randomly selected people to taste the same flavor of ice cream in two different dishes. The dishes contained exactly the same ice cream but were labeled differently. One was given a name that suggested that its maker was European and sophisticated; the other was given a name that implied that the product was domestic and inexpensive. The tasters were asked to rate each ice cream on a 10-point scale, where 1 = poor and 10 = excellent. The responses are stored in file XR16-25 (column 1 = respondent, column 2 = ratings for "European" ice cream; column 3 = ratings for "domestic" ice cream). Do the results allow the manager to conclude at the 10% significance level that the ice cream with the European label is preferred?

16.26 Do children feel less pain than adults? That question was addressed by nursing professors at the Universities of Alberta and Saskatchewan (reported in the *Toronto Star,* 14 June, 1991). Suppose that in a preliminary study, 50 eight-year-old children and their mothers were subjected to moderately painful pressure on their hands. Each was asked to rate the level of pain as very severe (4), severe (3), moderate (2), or weak (1). The data are stored in file XR16-26 using the codes in parentheses. (Column 1 = family, column 2 = responses from children; column 3 = responses from their mothers.) Can we conclude at the 5% significance level that children feel less pain than adults?

16.27 In a study to determine whether gender affects salary offers for graduating M.B.A. students, 25 pairs of students were selected. Each pair consisted of a male and a female student who had almost identical grade-point averages, courses taken, ages, and previous work experience. The highest salary offered to each student upon graduation was recorded and stored in columns 1 (pair), 2 (female offers) and 3 (male offers) of file XR16-27. An analysis of the data reveals that salary offers are not normally distributed. Is there sufficient evidence at the 5% significance level to allow us to conclude that the salary offers differ between men and women? (This exercise is identical to Exercise 12.85 except that the distribution of the data has been changed.)

16.28 Admissions officers at universities and colleges face the problem of comparing grades achieved at different high schools. As a step toward developing a more informed interpretation of such grades, an admissions officer at a large state university conducts the follow-ing experiment. The records of 100 students from the same local high school who just completed their first year at the university were selected. Each of these students was paired (according to average grade in the last year of high school) with a student from another local high school who also just completed the first year at the university. For each matched pair, the average letter grades [A (4), B (3), C (2), D (1), or F (0)] in the first year of university study were recorded. The results are stored in file XR16-28 (column 1 = pair, column 2 = grades of students from high school 1; column 3 = grades of students from high school 2). Do these results allow us to conclude that, in comparing two students with the same high school average (one from high school 1 and the other from high school 2), preference in admissions should be given to the student from high school 1? (Use a 5% significance level.)

16.29 Some movie studios believe that by adding sexually explicit scenes to the home video version of movies they can increase the movie's appeal and profitability (*The Wall Street Journal,* 14 October, 1988). A studio executive decided to test this belief. She organized a study that involved 40 movies that were rated PG-13. Versions of each movie were created by adding scenes that changed the rating to R. The two versions of the movies were then made available to rental shops. For each of the 40 pairs of movies, the total number of rentals in one major city during a 1-week period was recorded and stored in file XR16-29 (column 1 = movie, column 2 = rentals of PG-13 version; column 3 = rentals of R version). Do these data provide enough evidence at the 1% significance level to support the belief, assuming that the number of rentals is not normally distributed?

16.4 KRUSKAL–WALLIS TEST

In this section we introduce the first of two statistical procedures designed to compare two or more populations. The **Kruskal–Wallis test** is applied to problems with the following characteristics.

1 The problem objective is to compare two or more populations.

2 The data are either ranked or quantitative but nonnormal.

3 The samples are independent.

When the data are quantitative and normal we used the analysis of variance *F*-test presented in Chapter 14 to determine whether differences exist. When the data are not normal we will treat the data as if they were ranked and employ the Kruskal–Wallis test.

The null and alternative hypotheses for this test are similar to those we specified in the analysis of variance. Because the data are ranked or are treated as ranked, however, we test population locations instead of population means. In all applications of the Kruskal–Wallis test, the null and alternative hypotheses are

H_0: The locations of all k populations are the same

H_1: At least two population locations differ

Here, k represents the number of populations to be compared.

Test Statistic

The test statistic is calculated in a way that closely resembles the way in which the Wilcoxon rank sum test for independent samples was calculated. The first step is to rank all the observations. As before, $1 =$ smallest observation and $n =$ largest observation, where $n = n_1 + n_2 + \cdots + n_k$. In case of ties, average the ranks.

If the null hypothesis is true, the ranks should be evenly distributed among the k samples. The degree to which this is true is judged by calculating the rank sums (labeled $T_1, T_2, \ldots, T_k$). The last step is to calculate the test statistic, which is denoted H.

Test Statistic for the Kruskal–Wallis Test

$$H = \left[\frac{12}{n(n+1)} \sum_{j=1}^{k} \frac{T_j^2}{n_j} \right] - 3(n+1)$$

Although it is impossible to see from this formula, if the rank sums are similar, the test statistic will be small. As a result, a small value of H supports the null hypothesis. Conversely, if considerable differences exist among the rank sums, the test statistic will be large. To judge the value of H, we need to know its sampling distribution.

Sampling Distribution of the Test Statistic

The distribution of the test statistic can be derived in the same way we derived the sampling distribution of the test statistic in the Wilcoxon rank sum test. That is, we can list all possible combinations of ranks and their probabilities to yield the sampling distribution. A table of critical values can then be determined. However, this is only necessary for small sample sizes. For sample sizes greater than or equal to 5, the test statistic H is approximately chi-squared distributed with $k - 1$ degrees of freedom. Recall that we introduced the chi-squared distribution in Section 11.3 when we tested and estimated the population variance. If you did not cover that section or otherwise need a review of the chi-squared distribution, turn to page 365.

Rejection Region

As we noted above, large values of H are associated with different population locations. Consequently, we want to reject the null hypothesis if H is sufficiently large. Thus, the rejection region is

$$H > \chi^2_{\alpha, k-1}$$

Figure 16.10 describes this sampling distribution and the rejection region.

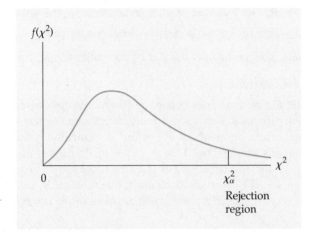

Figure 16.10

Sampling distribution of *H* and the rejection region

▼ **EXAMPLE 16.6**

The management of fast-food restaurants is extremely interested in knowing how their customers rate the quality of food and service and the cleanliness of the restaurants. Customers are given the opportunity to fill out customer comment cards similar to the one reproduced below. Suppose that one franchise wanted to compare how customers rate the three shifts (4:00 P.M. to midnight, midnight to 8:00 A.M., and 8:00 A.M. to 4:00 P.M.). In a preliminary study, 10 customer cards were randomly selected from each shift. The responses to the question concerning speed of service were stored in columns 1 to 3, respectively, in file XM16-06 (4 = excellent, 3 = good, 2 = fair, and 1 = poor), and are listed on the following page. Do these data provide sufficient evidence at the 5% significance level to indicate whether customers perceive the speed of service to be different among the three shifts?

CUSTOMER COMMENT CARD

Help Us To Serve You Better

Please complete this card and drop in our Comment Card Box or in any mailbox. Thank you.

Location (Stamp)

Date of Visit _____

Time: _____ am/pm

QUALITY	EXCELLENT	GOOD	FAIR	POOR
Quality of food	☐	☐	☐	☐
Value for money	☐	☐	☐	☐
Did you receive exactly what you ordered?	☐	☐	☐	☐

What did you order? _____

SERVICE	EXCELLENT	GOOD	FAIR	POOR
Speed of service	☐	☐	☐	☐
Courtesy of employees	☐	☐	☐	☐
Appearance of employees	☐	☐	☐	☐

CLEANLINESS				
Inside store	☐	☐	☐	☐
Outside store	☐	☐	☐	☐
Washrooms	☐	☐	☐	☐

Comments: _____

Name: _____
Address: _____
City: _____ Prov/State _____ P.C/Zip: _____
Phone No: _____

4:00 P.M. to Midnight	Midnight to 8:00 A.M.	8:00 A.M. to 4:00 P.M.
4	3	3
4	4	1
3	2	3
4	2	2
3	3	1
3	4	3
3	3	4
3	3	2
2	2	4
3	3	1

Solution

IDENTIFY

The problem objective is to compare three populations (the ratings of the three shifts), and the data are ranked. These two factors are sufficient to determine the use of the Kruskal–Wallis test. The complete test follows.

H_0: The locations of all three populations are the same

H_1: At least two population locations differ

Test statistic: $H = \left[\dfrac{12}{n(n+1)} \sum \dfrac{T_j^2}{n_j} \right] - 3(n+1)$

SOLVE

The data are ranked in the same way as we ranked the data in the Wilcoxon rank sum test. Ties are resolved by assigning the average rank. When all the data have been ranked, the rank sums are computed.

Sample 1 Rank		Sample 2 Rank		Sample 3 Rank	
4	27.0	3	16.5	3	16.5
4	27.0	4	27.0	1	2.0
3	16.5	2	6.5	3	16.5
4	27.0	2	6.5	2	6.5
3	16.5	3	16.5	1	2.0
3	16.5	4	27.0	3	16.5
3	16.5	3	16.5	4	27.0
3	16.5	3	16.5	2	6.5
2	6.5	2	6.5	4	27.0
3	16.5	3	16.5	1	2.0
	$T_1 = 186.5$		$T_2 = 156.0$		$T_3 = 122.5$

Rank Sums

The value of the test statistic is

$$H = \left[\frac{12}{n(n+1)} \sum \frac{T_j^2}{n_j} \right] - 3(n+1)$$

$$= \frac{12}{n(n+1)} \left(\frac{T_1^2}{n_1} + \frac{T_2^2}{n_2} + \frac{T_3^2}{n_3} \right) - 3(n+1)$$

$$= \frac{12}{30(30+1)} \left(\frac{186.5^2}{10} + \frac{156^2}{10} + \frac{122.5^2}{10} \right) - 3(30+1)$$

$$= 2.64$$

Rejection region:

$$H > \chi^2_{\alpha, k-1} = \chi^2_{.05,2} = 5.99147$$

Excel Output for Example 16.6

	A	B	C	D	E	F
1	**Kruskal Wallis Test**					
2	*Sample*	*RankSum*	*SampSize*			
3	1	186.5	10	*Test Statistic H = 2.6445*		
4	2	156	10	*P-Value = 0.2665*		
5	3	122.5	10			

COMMANDS

1 Type or import the data into *k* adjacent columns.
2 Click **Tools, Data Analysis Plus,** and **Kruskal-Wallis Test.**
3 Specify the **Input Range:**. Do not include cells containing the variable names.

COMMANDS FOR EXAMPLE 16.6

Open file **XM16-06.**

A2:C11

Minitab Output for Example 16.6

Kruskal-Wallis Test

LEVEL	NOBS	MEDIAN	AVE. RANK	Z VALUE
1	10	3.000	18.6	1.39
2	10	3.000	15.6	0.04
3	10	2.500	12.3	-1.43
OVERALL	30		15.5	

```
H = 2.64   d.f. = 2   p = 0.267
H = 3.01   d.f. = 2   p = 0.222 (adjusted for ties)
```

Minitab prints two sets of values; the actual value of H and its p-value and the test statistic and its p-value adjusted for ties. We ignore the latter.

COMMANDS

1 Type or import the data. The data must be stacked.
2 Click **Stat, Nonparametrics,** and **Kruskal-Wallis . . . .**
3 Type the name of the response variable.
4 Hit **tab** and type the name of the factor levels. Click **OK.**

COMMANDS FOR EXAMPLE 16.6

Open file **XM16-06.** The data are stacked in column 4, codes in column 5.

Service or **C4**

Shift or **C5**

| INTERPRET | There is not enough evidence to infer that a difference in speed of service exists among the three shifts. Management should assume that all three of the shifts are equally rated, and any action to improve service should be applied to all three shifts. Management should also bear in mind that the data were generated from a self-selecting sample. (See the story of the *Literary Digest* presented in Chapter 5.) |

▲

KRUSKAL–WALLIS TEST AND THE WILCOXON RANK SUM TEST

The Kruskal–Wallis test can be used to test for a difference between two populations. It will produce the same outcome as the two-tail Wilcoxon rank sum test. However, the Kruskal–Wallis test can only determine whether a difference exists. To determine whether one population is larger than another, we must apply the Wilcoxon rank sum test.

We complete this section with a review of how to recognize the use of the Kruskal–Wallis test.

> ### *Factors that Identify the Kruskal–Wallis Test*
>
> **1** Problem objective: compare two or more populations
>
> **2** Data type: ranked or quantitative but not normal
>
> **3** Experimental design: independent samples

EXERCISES

16.30 Conduct the Kruskal–Wallis test on the statistics below. Use a 5% significance level.

$T_1 = 984 \quad n_1 = 23$

$T_2 = 1,502 \quad n_2 = 36$

$T_3 = 1,430 \quad n_3 = 29$

16.31 From the following statistics test (with $\alpha = .01$) to determine whether the population locations differ.

$T_1 = 1,207 \quad n_1 = 25$

$T_2 = 1,088 \quad n_2 = 25$

$T_3 = 1,310 \quad n_3 = 25$

$T_4 = 1,445 \quad n_4 = 25$

16.32 Use the following statistics to determine whether there is enough statistical evidence at the 10% significance level to infer that the population locations differ.

$T_1 = 3,741 \quad n_1 = 47$

$T_2 = 1,610 \quad n_2 = 29$

$T_3 = 4,945 \quad n_3 = 67$

16.33 Use the Kruskal–Wallis test on the data in the following table to determine whether the population locations differ. (Use $\alpha = .05$.)

Sample 1: 27 33 18 29 41 52 75
Sample 2: 37 12 17 22 30
Sample 3: 19 12 33 41 28 18

16.34 Using the Kruskal–Wallis test, determine if there is enough evidence provided by the data in the accompanying table to enable us to infer that at least two population locations differ. (Use $\alpha = .05$.)

Sample 1: 25 15 20 22 23
Sample 2: 19 21 23 22 28
Sample 3: 27 25 22 29 28

16.35 Apply the Kruskal–Wallis test to determine if there is enough evidence at the 10% significance level to infer that at least two population locations differ, given the following data. (The data are stored in file XR16-35.)

Sample 1: 39 8 7 21 14 40 42 15
Sample 2: 31 43 50 57 54 46 26 29
Sample 3: 13 58 16 26 44 17 15 19
Sample 4: 50 51 55 28 57 37 41 37

The following exercises require the use of a computer and software. The answers may be calculated manually. See Appendix A for the sample statistics.

16.36 In an effort to determine whether differences exist among three methods of teaching statistics, a professor of business taught his course differently in each of three large sections. In the first section, he taught by lecturing; in the second, he taught by the case method; and in the third, he used a computer software package extensively. At the end of the semester, each student was asked to evaluate the course on a 7-point scale, where 1 = atrocious, 2 = poor, 3 = fair, 4 = average, 5 = good, 6 = very good, and 7 = excellent. From each section, the professor chose 25 evaluations at random. The data are in columns 1, 2, and 3 of file XR16-36. Is there evidence that differences in student satisfaction exist with respect to at least two of the three teaching methods? (Use α = .05.)

16.37 A consumer testing service is comparing the effectiveness of four different brands of drain cleaners. The experiment consists of using each product on 50 different clogged sinks and measuring the amount of time that elapses until each drain became unclogged. The recorded times, measured in minutes, are stored in columns 1 through 4 in file XR16-37.

a Which techniques should be considered as possible procedures to apply to determine if differences exist? What are the required conditions? How do you decide?

b If a statistical analysis has shown that the times are not normally distributed, can the service conclude at the 5% significance level that differences exist among the speeds at which the four brands perform?

16.38 During the last presidential campaign, the Gallup organization surveyed a random sample of 30 registered Democrats in January, another 30 in February, and yet another 30 in March. All 90 Democrats were asked to "rate the chances of the Democrats winning the presidential race in your state." The responses and their numerical codes were excellent (4), good (3), fair (2), and poor (1). The results of the surveys are stored in columns 1 to 3, respectively, in file XR16-38. Do these data allow us to infer at the 10% significance level that Democrats' ratings of their chances of winning the presidency changed over the 3-month period?

16.39 It is common practice in the advertising business to create several different advertisements and then ask a random sample of potential customers to rate the ads on several different dimensions. Suppose that an advertising firm developed four different ads for a new breakfast cereal and asked a sample of 400 shoppers to rate the believability of the advertisements. One hundred people viewed ad 1, another 100 viewed ad 2, another 100 saw ad 3, and another 100 saw ad 4. The ratings were very believable (4), quite believable (3), somewhat believable (2), and not believable at all (1). The responses are stored in columns 1 to 4, respectively, in file XR16-39. Can the firm's management conclude at the 1% significance level that differences exist in believability among the four ads?

16.5 FRIEDMAN TEST

This section introduces another statistical technique whose objective is to compare two or more populations of ranked or quantitative data. In Section 14.4, we presented the randomized block model of the analysis of variance. In this section, we present its nonparametric counterpart. The **Friedman test** is applied to problems with the following characteristics.

1 The problem objective is to compare two or more populations.

2 The data are either ranked or quantitative but not normal.

3 The data are generated from a randomized block experiment.

The null and alternative hypotheses are identical to the ones tested in the Kruskal–Wallis test. That is,

H_0: The locations of all k populations are the same

H_1: At least two population locations differ

Test Statistic

To calculate the test statistic, we first rank each observation within each block, where 1 = smallest observation and k = largest observation, averaging the ranks of ties.

Then we compute the rank sums, which we label $T_1, T_2, \ldots, T_k$. The test statistic is defined as follows. (Recall that b = number of blocks.)

Test Statistic for the Friedman Test

$$F_r = \left[\frac{12}{b(k)(k+1)} \sum_{j=1}^{k} T_j^2 \right] - 3b(k+1)$$

Sampling distribution of the test statistic

The test statistic is approximately chi-squared distributed with $k - 1$ degrees of freedom, provided that either k or b is greater than or equal to 5. As was the case with the Kruskal–Wallis test, we reject the null hypothesis when the test statistic, is large. Hence the rejection region is

$$F_r > \chi^2_{\alpha, k-1}$$

This test, like all the other nonparametric tests, requires that the populations being compared be identical in shape and spread.

▼ EXAMPLE 16.7

The personnel manager of a national accounting firm has been receiving complaints from senior managers about the quality of recent hirings. All new accountants are hired through a process whereby four managers interview the candidate and rate her or him on several dimensions, including academic credentials, previous work experience, and personal suitability. Each manager then summarizes the results and produces an evaluation of the candidate. There are five possibilities, which follow.

1 = The candidate is in the top 5% of applicants.
2 = The candidate is in the top 10% of applicants, but not in the top 5%.
3 = The candidate is in the top 25% of applicants, but not in the top 10%.
4 = The candidate is in the top 50% of applicants, but not in the top 25%.
5 = The candidate is in the bottom 50% of applicants.

The evaluations are then combined in making the final decision. The personnel manager believes that the quality problem is caused by the evaluation system. However, she needs to know whether there is general agreement or disagreement among the interviewing managers in their evaluations. To test for differences among the managers, she takes a random sample of the evaluations of eight applicants. The results are shown below and are stored in file XM16-07. What conclusions can the personnel manager draw from these data? Employ a 5% significance level.

	Manager			
Applicant	1	2	3	4
1	2	1	2	2
2	4	2	3	2
3	2	2	2	3
4	3	1	3	2
5	3	2	3	5
6	2	2	3	4
7	4	1	5	5
8	3	2	5	3

Solution

The problem objective is to compare the four populations of managers' evaluations, which we can see are ranked data. This experiment is identified as a randomized block design because the eight applicants were evaluated by all four managers. (The treatments are the managers, and the blocks are the applicants.) The appropriate statistical technique is the Friedman test. The null and alternative hypotheses are as follows.

H_0: The locations of all four populations are the same

H_1: At least two population locations differ

The test statistic is

$$F_r = \left[\frac{12}{b(k)(k+1)} \sum_{j=1}^{k} T_j^2 \right] - 3b(k+1)$$

which is chi-squared distributed with $k-1$ degrees of freedom.

The following table demonstrates how the ranks are assigned and the rank sums calculated. Notice how the ranks are assigned by moving across the rows (blocks) and the rank sums computed by adding down the columns (treatments).

			Manager					
Applicant	1	(Rank)	2	(Rank)	3	(Rank)	4	(Rank)
1	2	(3)	1	(1)	2	(3)	2	(3)
2	4	(4)	2	(1.5)	3	(3)	2	(1.5)
3	2	(2)	2	(2)	2	(2)	3	(4)
4	3	(3.5)	1	(1)	3	(3.5)	2	(2)
5	3	(2.5)	2	(1)	3	(2.5)	5	(4)
6	2	(1.5)	2	(1.5)	3	(3)	4	(4)
7	4	(2)	1	(1)	5	(3.5)	5	(3.5)
8	3	(2.5)	2	(1)	5	(4)	3	(2.5)
	$T_1 = 21$		$T_2 = 10$		$T_3 = 24.5$		$T_4 = 24.5$	

The value of the test statistic is

$$F_r = \left[\frac{12}{b(k)(k+1)} \sum_{j=1}^{k} T_j^2 \right] - 3b(k+1)$$

$$= \left[\frac{12}{8(4)(5)} (21^2 + 10^2 + 24.5^2 + 24.5^2) \right] - 3(8)(5)$$

$$= 10.61$$

The rejection region is

$$F_r > \chi^2_{\alpha, k-1} = \chi^2_{.05,3} = 7.81473$$

Excel Output for Example 16.7

	A	B	C	D	E	F	G
1	**Friedman Test**						
2	2	1	2	2	*Test Statistic Fr = 10.613*		
3	4	2	3	2	*P-Value = 0.014*		
4	2	2	2	3			
5	3	1	3	2			
6	3	2	3	5			
7	2	2	3	4			
8	4	1	5	5			
9	3	2	5	3			
10	*21*	*10*	*24.5*	*24.5*			

COMMANDS

1 Type or import the data into k adjacent columns.
2 Click **Tools, Data Analysis Plus,** and **Friedman Test.**
3 Specify the **Input Range:.** Do not include cells containing the variable names. Click **OK.**

COMMANDS FOR EXAMPLE 16.7

Open file **XM16-07**.

A2:D9

Minitab Output for Example 16.7

Friedman Test

```
Friedman test for Ratings by Manager blocked by Applicant

S = 10.61   DF = 3   P = 0.014
S = 12.86   DF = 3   P = 0.005 (adjusted for ties)

                        Est        Sum of
Manager       N       Median        Ranks
1             8       2.8750        21.0
2             8       2.0000        10.0
3             8       3.0000        24.5
4             8       3.1250        24.5

Grand median    =     2.7500
```

COMMANDS

1 Type or import the data in stacked format. The responses are stored in one column, the treatment codes are stored in another column, and the block codes are stored in a third column.
2 Click **Stat, Nonparametrics,** and **Friedman . . . .**
3 Type the name of the **Response:.**
4 Type the name of the **Treatment:.**
5 Type the name of the **Blocks:.** Click **OK.**

COMMANDS FOR EXAMPLE 16.7

Open file **XM16-07**. Stack all observations in column 5, the subscripts are put in column 6, and the block codes typed into column 7.

Ratings or **C5**
Manager or **C6**
Applicant or **C7**

INTERPRET   There appears to be sufficient evidence to indicate that the manager's evaluations differ. The personnel manager should attempt to determine why the evaluations differ. Is the problem the way in which the assessment is conducted, or is it that some managers are using different criteria? If it is the latter, those managers may need additional training.

THE FRIEDMAN TEST AND THE SIGN TEST

The relationship between the Friedman and sign tests is the same as the relationship between the Kruskal–Wallis and Wilcoxon rank sum tests. That is, we can use the Friedman test to determine whether two populations differ. The conclusion will be the same as that produced from the sign test. However, we can only use the Friedman test to determine whether a difference exists. If we want to determine whether one population is larger than another, we must use the sign test.

Here is a list of the factors that tell us when to use the Friedman test.

Factors that Identify the Friedman Test

1 Problem objective: compare two or more populations

2 Data type: ranked or quantitative but not normal

3 Experimental design: blocked samples

EXERCISES

16.40 Apply the Friedman test to the accompanying table of data to determine whether we can conclude that at least two population locations differ. (Use $\alpha = .10$.)

			Treatment	
Block	1	2	3	4
1	10	12	15	9
2	8	10	11	6
3	13	14	16	11
4	9	9	12	13
5	7	8	14	10

16.41 The following data were generated from a blocked experiment. Conduct a Friedman test to determine if at least two population locations differ. (Use $\alpha = .05$.)

		Treatment	
Block	1	2	3
1	7.3	6.9	8.4
2	8.2	7.0	7.3
3	5.7	6.0	8.1
4	6.1	6.5	9.1
5	5.9	6.1	8.0

16.42 Ten judges were asked to test the sensory quality of four different brands of orange juice. The judges assigned scores using a 5-point scale where 1 = bad, 2 = poor, 3 = average, 4 = good, and 5 = excellent.

The results are shown here and stored in file XR16-42. Can we conclude at the 5% significance level that there are differences in sensory quality among the four brands of orange juice?

		Orange juice brand		
Judge	1	2	3	4
1	3	5	4	3
2	2	3	5	4
3	4	4	3	4
4	3	4	5	2
5	2	4	4	3
6	4	5	5	3
7	3	3	4	4
8	2	3	3	3
9	4	3	5	4
10	2	4	5	3

16.43 The manager of a personnel company is in the process of examining her company's advertising programs. Currently, the company advertises in each of the three local newspapers for a wide variety of positions, including computer programmers, secretaries, and receptionists. The manager has decided that only one newspaper will be used if it can be determined that there are differences in the number of inquiries generated among the newspapers. The following experiment was performed. For 1 week (6 days), six different jobs were advertised in each of the three newspapers. The number of inquiries was counted, and the results appear in the accompanying table.

Job advertised	Newspaper		
	1	2	3
Receptionist	14	17	12
Systems analyst	8	9	6
Junior secretary	25	20	23
Computer programmer	12	15	10
Legal secretary	7	10	5
Office manager	5	9	4

a What techniques should be considered in reaching a decision? What are the required conditions? How do we determine whether the conditions are satisfied?

b Assuming that the data are not normally distributed, can we conclude at the 5% significance level that differences exist among the newspapers' abilities to attract potential employees?

The following exercises require the use of a computer and software. The answers may be calculated manually. See Appendix A for the sample statistics.

16.44 A well-known soft drink manufacturer has used the same secret recipe for its product since its introduction more than 100 years ago. In response to a decreasing market share, however, the president of the company is contemplating changing the recipe. He has developed two alternative recipes. In a preliminary study, he asked 20 people to taste the original recipe and the two new recipes. He asked each to evaluate the taste of the product on a 5-point scale, where 1 = awful, 2 = poor, 3 = fair, 4 = good, and 5 = wonderful. These data are stored in columns 1 (respondent number), 2 (original recipe), 3 (new recipe 1), and 4 (new recipe 2) in file XR16-44. The president decides that unless significant differences exist among evaluations of the products, he will not make any changes. Can we conclude at the 1% significance level that there are differences in the ratings of the three recipes?

16.45 The manager of a chain of electronic products retailers is trying to decide on a location for its newest store. After a thorough analysis, the choice has been narrowed to three possibilities. An important factor in the decision is the number of people passing each location. The number of people passing each location per

day was counted during 30 days. The data are stored in columns 1 (day number), 2 (site 1), 3 (site 2), and 4 (site 3) in file XR16-45.

a Which techniques should be considered to determine whether the locations differ? What are the required conditions? How do you select a technique?

b Can management conclude at the 1% significance level that there are differences in the numbers of people passing the three locations if the number of people passing each location is not normally distributed?

16.46 In recent years, lack of confidence in the Postal Service has led many companies to send all of their correspondence by private courier. A large company is in the process of selecting one of three possible couriers to act as its sole delivery method. To help in making the decision, an experiment was performed whereby letters were sent using each of the three couriers at 12 different times of the day to a delivery point across town. The number of minutes required for delivery was recorded and stored in file XR16-46 (columns 2 through 4 list the delivery times of couriers 1, 2, and 3, respectively, and column 1 contains codes representing the time of day). Can we conclude at the 10% significance level that there are differences in delivery times among the three couriers? An analysis of the data indicates that the delivery times are not normally distributed. (This exercise is identical to Exercise 14.26 except for the data.)

16.47 Many North Americans suffer from high levels of cholesterol, which can lead to heart attacks. For those with very high levels (over 280), doctors prescribe drugs to reduce cholesterol levels. A pharmaceutical company has recently developed three such drugs. To determine if any differences exist in their benefits, an experiment was organized. The company selected 25 groups of three men, each of whom had levels in excess of 280. In each group, the men were matched according to age and weight. The drugs were administered over a 2-month period, and the reduction in cholesterol was recorded. The data are stored in columns 2 to 4 of file XR16-47 (column 1 stores the code representing the group number). Do these results allow the company to conclude at the 5% significance level that differences exist among the three new drugs? (Assume that cholesterol reduction is not normally distributed.) (This exercise is identical to Exercise 14.29 except for the data.)

16.6 TESTING FOR NORMALITY

In Section 15.5 we presented the chi-squared test for normality. Because of the rule of five this procedure requires relatively large samples to ensure its validity. In this section we introduce a nonparametric test for normality that can be applied to any number of observations. In fact, there are two such tests. The first is called the

Kolmogorov–Smirnov (shortened to K-S for those who can't spell or pronounce the names of the Russian inventors of the test). The second method is the **Lilliefors test.** Both tests work similarly by comparing the actual and normal cumulative probabilities. The difference between them is that K-S assumes that we know the mean and standard deviation of the population, while Lilliefors requires us to compute the mean and standard deviation from the data. Because assuming knowledge of the population parameters is unrealistic, we describe and use only the Lilliefors test.

A cumulative distribution function is defined as

$$F(x) = P(X \leq x)$$

We encountered this function in Chapter 6 when we discussed the tables of the cumulative binomial and Poisson distributions (Tables 1 and 2, respectively, in Appendix B). In both cases, the tables provide values for

$$P(X \leq k) = \sum_{x=0}^{k} p(x)$$

for several values of k.

The sample cumulative distribution function, $S(x)$, is defined as the proportion of sample values that are less than or equal to x. To illustrate how $S(x)$ is computed, suppose that we have the following 10 observations.

110, 89, 102, 80, 93, 121, 108, 97, 105, 103

We begin by placing the values of x in ascending order, as follows.

80, 89, 93, 97, 102, 103, 105, 108, 110, 121

Since $x = 80$ is the smallest of the 10 values, the proportion of values of x that are less than or equal to 80 is

$$S(80) = 1/10 = .1$$

Similarly, two of the 10 values are less than or equal to 89 (namely, 80 and 89). Hence,

$$S(89) = 2/10 = .2$$

The remaining values of $S(x)$, each determined in a like manner, are as follows.

x	S(x)
80	.1
89	.2
93	.3
97	.4
102	.5
103	.6
105	.7
108	.8
109	.9
121	1.0

We want to test to determine whether these data were drawn from a normal population. The null and alternative hypotheses are

H_0: The data are normally distributed

H_1: The data are not normally distributed

As we've done repeatedly in hypothesis testing we assume that the null hypothesis is true. This assumption allows us to calculate the normal cumulative probabilities for the 10 values of x. To calculate any normal probabilities requires that we know the mean and standard deviation. In the Lilliefors test we must estimate the population parameters from the sample statistics. Thus, we must calculate $\bar{x}$ and s from the data. (In the K-S test we would employ the population mean and standard deviation after assuming we know them.)

From the data we find

$$\bar{x} = 100.8 \quad \text{and} \quad s = 11.62$$

Using these statistics as estimates of μ and σ, respectively, we calculate the cumulative distribution function, $F(x)$, as shown in the following table.

Calculation of the Normal Cumulative Probabilities

x	$F(x)$
80	$P(X \leq 80) = P\left(\dfrac{X - \mu}{\sigma} \leq \dfrac{80 - 100.8}{11.62}\right) = P(Z \leq -1.79) = .0367$
89	$P(X \leq 89) = P\left(\dfrac{X - \mu}{\sigma} \leq \dfrac{89 - 100.8}{11.62}\right) = P(Z \leq -1.02) = .1539$
93	$P(X \leq 93) = P\left(\dfrac{X - \mu}{\sigma} \leq \dfrac{93 - 100.8}{11.62}\right) = P(Z \leq -0.67) = .2514$
97	$P(X \leq 97) = P\left(\dfrac{X - \mu}{\sigma} \leq \dfrac{97 - 100.8}{11.62}\right) = P(Z \leq -0.32) = .3745$
102	$P(X \leq 102) = P\left(\dfrac{X - \mu}{\sigma} \leq \dfrac{102 - 100.8}{11.62}\right) = P(Z \leq 0.10) = .5398$
103	$P(X \leq 103) = P\left(\dfrac{X - \mu}{\sigma} \leq \dfrac{103 - 100.8}{11.62}\right) = P(Z \leq 0.19) = .5753$
105	$P(X \leq 105) = P\left(\dfrac{X - \mu}{\sigma} \leq \dfrac{105 - 100.8}{11.62}\right) = P(Z \leq 0.36) = .6406$
108	$P(X \leq 108) = P\left(\dfrac{X - \mu}{\sigma} \leq \dfrac{108 - 100.8}{11.62}\right) = P(Z \leq 0.62) = .7324$
110	$P(X \leq 110) = P\left(\dfrac{X - \mu}{\sigma} \leq \dfrac{110 - 100.8}{11.62}\right) = P(Z \leq 0.79) = .7852$
121	$P(X \leq 121) = P\left(\dfrac{X - \mu}{\sigma} \leq \dfrac{121 - 100.8}{11.62}\right) = P(Z \leq 1.74) = .9591$

If the null hypothesis is true the sample and normal cumulative probabilities should be similar. If the null hypothesis is false we expect $S(x)$ and $F(x)$ to differ for at least some of the values of x. We define the test statistic D as the largest absolute difference between $S(x)$ and $F(x)$. That is,

$$D = \max |F(x) - S(x)|$$

To calculate D, we find the absolute difference between the sample and normal cumulative probabilities for each x as shown on the next page.

x	F(x)	S(x)	|F(x) − S(x)|
80	.0367	.1	.0633
89	.1539	.2	.0461
93	.2514	.3	.0486
97	.3745	.4	.0255
102	.5398	.5	.0398
103	.5753	.6	.0247
105	.6406	.7	.0594
108	.7324	.8	.0674
110	.7852	.9	.1148
121	.9591	1.0	.0409

The largest absolute difference is $D = .1148$.

We judge this value in the same way we judge all test statistic values, by referring to the sampling distribution. In this test we compare D with the critical values listed in the Lilliefors table, exhibited in Table 10 in Appendix B.

The table is quite easy to use. Find the sample size down the left column and select a significance level. In this example if we choose $\alpha = .05$ the critical value is $D = .258$. This means the rejection region is

$$D > .258$$

We calculated $D = .1148$. Thus, D does not fall into the rejection region. Accordingly we do not reject the null hypothesis. As usual this does not mean that the null hypothesis is true. We simply conclude that there is not enough evidence to infer that the data are nonnormally distributed. In the absence of sufficient evidence of nonnormality we will employ a parametric test for quantitative data rather than a nonparametric one.

Let's apply the Lilliefors test to the data from Example 11.1. Recall that we applied the t-test of μ, which requires that the data be normally distributed. We test the hypotheses

H_0: The data are normally distributed

H_1: The data are not normally distributed

We'll conduct the test at the 5% significance level. From Table 10 we discover that the rejection region is

$$D > \frac{.886}{\sqrt{50}} = .125$$

SOLVE

Because of the amount of tedious calculations we will conduct this test by computer only.

Excel Output for the Lilliefors Test for Example 11.1

Only some of the printout is shown.

	A	B	C	D	E	F	G	H
1	Lilliefors Test							
2	Data	Ordered	S(x)	Z	F(x)	|S(x)-F(x)|		
3	505	373	0.02	-2.250488	0.012209	0.007791	*Lilliefors Test Statistic*	
4	400	400	0.04	-1.555098	0.0599614	0.0199614	*D = 0.074*	
5	499	405	0.06	-1.426322	0.0768878	0.0168878		
6	415	409	0.08	-1.323301	0.0928677	0.0128677		

The value of the test statistic is $D = .074$.

COMMANDS	COMMANDS FOR EXAMPLE 11.1
1 Type or import the data into one column.	Open file **XM11-01**.
2 Click **Tools, Data Analysis Plus,** and **Lilliefors Test.**	
3 Specify the input range. Do not include the cell containing the variable name. Click **OK.**	**A2:A51**

Minitab Output for the Lilliefors Test for Example 11.1

Normal Probability Plot

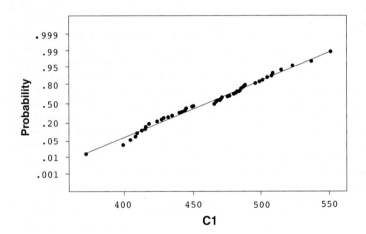

Minitab prints the normal probability plot, which is interpreted in the following way. If the data are normal the plot will appear as a straight line. The further the line is from linear, the more nonnormal the data. The printout includes $\bar{x}$ **(Average: 460.38),** s **(StDev: 38.8271),** and n **(N: 50),** as well as the test statistic. Minitab refers to this as the **Kolmogorov-Smirnov Normality Test.** However, since the test statistic is based on the sample mean and sample standard deviation, Minitab is actually conducting the Lilliefors test. Minitab's test statistic is $D = 0.077$ with an approximate p-value of .15.

COMMANDS	COMMANDS FOR EXAMPLE 11.1
1 Type or import the data into one column.	Open file **XM11-01**.
2 Click **Stat, Basic Statistics,** and **Normality Test . . . .**	
3 Specify the variable name.	**Packages** or **C1**
4 Use the cursor to select **Kolmogorov-Smirnov.** Click **OK.**	

INTERPRET

There is not enough evidence to infer that the data are nonnormal. The use of the t-test is valid.

EXERCISES

16.48 In performing a Lilliefors test with 100 observations we found $D = .0833$. What does this statistic tell you? (Use $\alpha = .10$.)

16.49 The value of the test statistic in a Lilliefors test is $D = .188$ based on a sample of 20 observations. What conclusion can you draw with $\alpha = .05$?

16.50 The following six observations were obtained. Can we infer with $\alpha = .10$ that the population from which we sampled is not normal?

8, 4, 14, 9, 6, 12

16.51 Ten observations were drawn from a population whose distribution is unknown. They are

93, 99, 90, 97, 17, 85, 86, 60, 93, 98

Can we infer at the 10% significance level that the distribution is not normal?

The following exercises require the use of a computer and software.

16.52 A random sample of 100 observations was drawn with the data stored in file XR16-52. Can we conclude at the 5% significance level that the population is not normal?

16.53 Test with $\alpha = .10$ to determine whether the 25 observations stored in file XR16-53 was taken from a nonnormal population.

16.54 Refer to Exercise 11.32. The t-test of μ required that the data be normally distributed. Is there evidence at the 5% significance level to infer that the normality requirement is not satisfied?

16.55 In Exercise 11.35 you applied the t-test of μ, which requires that the data be normally distributed. Use the Lilliefors test with $\alpha = .05$ to determine whether that test was appropriate.

16.56 In answering the question asked in Exercise 12.23, you performed the equal-variances t-test of $\mu_1 - \mu_2$, which requires that the populations be normal and the variances equal. In Exercise 12.54 you tested the latter requirement. Apply the Lilliefors test at the 5% significance level to check the normality requirement.

16.57 Refer to Exercise 12.30. If the data are not normal, which test should you use? Test to determine which procedure is appropriate. Use $\alpha = .10$.

16.58 Refer to Exercise 12.45.

a What statistical tests could be applied?
b What are the conditions for each?
c Test with $\alpha = .05$ to determine whether the technique you used in Exercise 12.45 was correct.

SUMMARY

Nonparametric statistical tests are applied to problems where the data are either ranked or quantitative but not normal. The Wilcoxon rank sum test is used to compare two populations of ranked or quantitative data when the data are generated from independent samples. The sign test is used to compare two populations of ranked data drawn from a matched pairs experiment. The Wilcoxon signed rank sum test is employed to compare two populations of nonnormal quantitative data taken from a matched pairs experiment. When the objective is to compare two or more populations of independently sampled ranked or quantitative nonnormal data the Kruskal–Wallis test is employed. The Friedman test is used instead of the Kruskal–Wallis test when the samples are blocked. The Lilliefors test allows us to determine whether there is enough statistical evidence to infer that a population is normal.

IMPORTANT TERMS

Nonparametric techniques   *576*
Population locations   *576*
Distribution-free statistics   *576*
Wilcoxon rank sum test for
    independent samples   *577*
Mann-Whitney test   *583*

Sign test   *590*
Wilcoxon signed rank sum test for
    matched pairs   *594*
Kruskal–Wallis test   *602*
Friedman test   *608*
Lilliefors test   *614*

SUPPLEMENTARY EXERCISES

The following exercises require the use of a computer and software.

16.59 In a study to determine which of two teaching methods is perceived to be better, two sections of an introductory marketing course were taught in different ways by the same professor. At the course's completion, each student rated the course on a boring/stimulating spectrum. In this process, 1 = very boring, 2 = somewhat boring, 3 = a little boring, 4 = neither boring nor stimulating, 5 = a little stimulating, 6 = somewhat stimulating, and 7 = very stimulating. The results are stored in columns 1 (section 1) and 2 (section 2) of file XR16-59. Can we conclude at the 5% significance level that the ratings of the two teaching methods differ?

16.60 The researchers at a large carpet manufacturer have been experimenting with a new dyeing process in hopes of reducing the streakiness that frequently occurs with the current process. As an experiment, 15 carpets are dyed using the new process, and another 15 are dyed using the existing method. Each carpet is rated on a 5-point scale of streakiness, where 5 = extremely streaky, 4 = quite streaky, 3 = somewhat streaky, 2 = a little streaky, 1 = not streaky at all. The results are stored in columns 1 (new process) and 2 (existing process) of file XR16-60. Is there enough evidence at the 10% significance level to infer that the new method is better?

16.61 Some of the researchers described in Exercise 16.60 felt that the color of the dye might be a factor. The experiment was rerun, using the new and current processes to dye carpets 15 different colors. For each color, both types of carpets were rated on the 5-point scale. These data are stored in columns 1 (color code) and 2 (new process rating) and 3 (existing process rating) of file XR16-61. Can we conclude at the 10% significance level that the new process is superior?

16.62 The editor of the student newspaper was in the process of making some major changes in the newspaper's layout. He was also contemplating changing the typeface of the print used. To help make a decision, he set up an experiment in which 20 individuals were asked to read three newspaper pages, with each page printed in a different typeface. If the reading speed differed, the typeface that was read fastest would be used. However, if there were not enough evidence to allow the editor to conclude that such differences exist, the current typeface would be continued. The times (in seconds) to completely read one page were recorded and stored in columns 1 through 4 of file XR16-62. We have determined that the times are not normally distributed. Determine the course of action the editor should fol-

low. (Use $\alpha = .01$.) (This exercise is identical to Exercise 14.62, except in this exercise, the data are not normally distributed.)

16.63 Large potential profits for pharmaceutical companies exist in the area of hair-growth drugs. The head chemist for a large pharmaceutical company is conducting experiments to determine which of two new drugs is more effective in growing hair among balding men. One experiment was conducted as follows. A total of 30 pairs of men—each pair of which was matched according to their degree of baldness—were selected. One man used drug A, and the other used drug B. After 10 weeks, the men's new hair growth was examined, and the new growth was judged using the following ratings.

0 = no growth
1 = some growth
2 = moderate growth

The results are stored in columns 1 to 3 of file XR16-63. (Column 1 identifies the man, column 2 = rating for drug A and column 3 = rating for drug B.) Do these data provide sufficient evidence at the 1% significance level that drug B is more effective?

16.64 Suppose that a precise measuring device for new hair growth has been developed and is used in the experiment described in Exercise 16.63. The percentages of new hair growth for the 30 pairs of men involved in the experiment are stored in the first two columns of file XR16-64. Column 2 stores the results from drug A and column 3 stores the results from drug B. Do these data allow the chemist to conclude at the 1% significance level that drug B is more effective? (Assume that the percentages of new growth are not normally distributed.)

16.65 The printing department of a publishing company wants to determine whether there are differences in durability among three types of book bindings. Twenty-five books with each type of binding were selected and placed in machines that continually open and close them. The number of openings and closings until the pages separate from the binding were recorded and are stored in file XR16-65.

a What techniques should be considered to determine whether differences exist among the types of bindings? What are the required conditions? How do you decide which technique to use?

b If we know that the number of openings and closings is not normally distributed, test to determine whether differences exist among the types of bindings. (Use $\alpha = .10$.)

16.66 In recent years, consumers have become more safety conscious, particularly about children's products. A manufacturer of children's pajamas is looking for material that is as nonflammable as possible. In an experiment to compare a new fabric with the kind now being used, 50 pieces of each kind were exposed to an open flame, and the number of seconds until the fabric burst into flames was recorded. The data are stored in columns 1 (new material) and 2 (old material) of file XR16-66. Because the new material is more expensive, the manufacturer will switch only if the new material can be shown to be better. What should the manufacturer do? (Use a 5% significance level and assume that times are not normal.)

16.67 Samuel's is a chain of family restaurants. Like many other service companies, Samuel's surveys its customers on a regular basis to monitor their opinions. Two questions (among others) asked in the survey are as follows.

A   While you were at Samuel's, did you find the service

  1 slow   2 moderate   3 fast
B   What day did you visit Samuel's?

The responses of a random sample of 269 customers are stored in file XR16-67. (Column 1 stores the responses on Sunday, column 2 contains the responses for Monday, etc.) Can the manager infer at the 5% significance level that there are differences in customer perceptions of the speed of service among the days of the week?

16.68 An advertising firm wants to determine the relative effectiveness of two recently produced commercials for a car dealership. An important attribute of such commercials is their believability. To judge this aspect of the commercials, 60 people were randomly selected. Each watched both commercials and then rated them on a 5-point scale where 1 = not believable, 2 = somewhat believable, 3 = moderately believable, 4 = quite believable, and 5 = very believable. The ratings are stored in columns 1 (respondent), 2 (commercial 1) and 3 (commercial 2) of file XR16-68. Do these data provide sufficient evidence at the 10% significance level to indicate that there are differences in believability between the two commercials?

16.69 Researchers at the U.S. National Institute of Aging in Bethesda, Maryland, have been studying hearing loss. They have hypothesized that as men age they will lose their hearing faster than comparatively aged women because many more men than women have worked at jobs where noise levels have been excessive. To test their beliefs, the researchers randomly selected one man and one woman aged 45, 46, 47, . . . , 78, 79, 80 and measured the percentage hearing loss for each person. The data are stored in columns 1 (age), 2 (men) and 3 (women) in ascending order of age in file XR16-69. Can we infer at the 5% significance level that men

lose more hearing than women if we assume that hearing loss is not normally distributed?

16.70 In a Gallup Poll this year, 200 people were asked "Do you feel that the newspaper you read most does a good job of presenting the news?" The same question was asked of another 200 people 10 years ago. The results of both surveys are stored in columns 1 (this year) and 2 (10 years ago) in file XR16-70. The possible responses were as follows.

3 = good job
2 = fair job
1 = not a good job

Do these data provide enough evidence at the 5% significance level to infer that people perceive newspapers as doing a better job 10 years ago than today?

16.71 The increasing number of traveling businesswomen represents a large potential clientele for the hotel industry. Many hotel chains have made changes designed to attract more women. To help direct these changes, a hotel chain commissioned a study to determine whether major differences exist between male and female business travelers. A total of 100 male and 100 female executives were questioned on a variety of topics, one of which was the number of trips they had taken in the previous 12 months. The data are stored in columns 1 (male) and 2 (female) in file XR16-71. We would like to know whether these data provide enough evidence to allow us to conclude at the 10% significance level that businesswomen and businessmen differ in the number of business trips taken per year. Conduct a test assuming that the number of trips is not normally distributed.

16.72 To examine the effect that a rough midterm test has on student evaluations of professors, a statistics professor had her class evaluate her teaching effectiveness before the midterm test. The questionnaire asked for opinions on a number of dimensions, but the last question is considered the most important. It is "How would you rate the overall performance of the instructor?" The possible responses are 1 = poor, 2 = fair, 3 = good, 4 = excellent. After a difficult test, the evaluation was redone. The evaluation scores before and after the test for each of the 40 students in the class are stored in file XR16-72 as follows.

Column 1: student number (1 to 40)
Column 2: evaluation score before the test
Column 3: evaluation score after the test

Do the data allow the professor to conclude at the 5% significance level that the results of the midterm negatively influence student opinion?

16.73 The town of Stratford, Ontario, is very much dependent upon the Shakespearean Festival it holds every summer for its financial well-being. Thousands of people visit Stratford to attend one or more Shakespearean plays and spend money in hotels, restaurants, and gift shops. As a consequence, any sign that the number of visitors will decrease in the future is cause for concern. Two years ago, a survey of 100 visitors asked how likely it was that they would return within the next 2 years. This year the survey was repeated with another 100 visitors. The likelihood of returning within 2 years was measured as

4 = very likely
3 = somewhat likely
2 = somewhat unlikely
1 = very unlikely

The data are stored in column 1 (survey results from two years ago) and column 2 (survey results from this year) in file XR16-73. Conduct whichever statistical procedures you deem necessary to determine whether the citizens of Stratford should be concerned about the results of the two surveys. Use $\alpha = .05$.

16.74 Scientists have been studying the effects of lead in children's blood, bones, and tissue for a number of years. It is known that lead reduces intelligence and can cause a variety of other problems. A study directed by Dr. Herman Needleman, a psychiatrist at the University of Pittsburgh Medical Center, examined some of these problems. Two hundred boys attending public schools in Pittsburgh were recruited. Each boy was categorized as having low or high levels of lead in their bones. Each boy was then assessed by his teachers on a 4-point scale (1 = low, 2 = moderate, 3 = high, and 4 = extreme) on degrees of aggression. These data are stored so that column 1 = low lead level, column 2 = high lead level, in file XR16-74. Is there evidence to infer that boys with high levels of lead are more aggressive than boys with low levels of lead? Use $\alpha = .05$.

16.75 How does gender affect teaching evaluations? Several researchers addressed this question over the past decade. (See "The Use and Abuse of Student Ratings of Professors" by Peter Seldin, published in the *Chronicle of Higher Education,* 2 July, 1993.) In one study several female and male professors in the same department with similar backgrounds were selected. A random sample of 100 female students was drawn. Each student evaluated a female professor and a male professor. A sample of 100 male students was drawn and each also evaluated a female professor and a male professor. The ratings were based on a four-point scale where 1 = poor, 2 = fair, 3 = good, and 4 = excellent. The evaluations are stored in file XR16-75 in the following way.

Column 1 = female student
Column 2 = female professor ratings
Column 3 = male professor ratings
Column 4 = male student
Column 5 = female professor ratings
Column 6 = male professor ratings

a Can we infer at the 5% significance level that female students rate female professors higher than they rate male professors?

b Can we infer at the 5% significance level that male students rate male professors higher than they rate female professors?

16.76 It is an unfortunate fact of life that the characteristics that one is born with play a critical role in later life. For example, race is a critical factor in almost all aspects of North American life. Height and weight also determine how friends, teachers, employers and customers will treat you. And now we may add physical attractiveness to this list. A recent study conducted by economists Jeff Biddle of Michigan State University and Daniel Hamermesh from the University of Texas followed the careers of students from a prestigious U.S. law school. A panel of independent raters examined the graduation yearbook photos of the students and rated their appearance as unattractive, neither attractive nor unattractive, or attractive. The annual incomes in thousands of dollars five years after graduation were recorded and stored in columns 1 to 3, respectively, in file XR16-76. Assuming that incomes are not normally distributed, can we infer at the 5% significance level that incomes of lawyers are affected by physical attractiveness?

16.77 According to a CNN news report broadcast on November 26, 1995, 9% of full-time workers telecommute. This means that they do not work in their employer's offices, but instead perform their work at home using a computer and modem. To ascertain whether such workers are more satisfied than their nontelecommuting counterparts, a study was undertaken. A random sample of telecommuters and regular office workers was taken. Each was asked how satisfied they were with their current employment. The responses (1 = very unsatisfied; 2 = somewhat unsatisfied; 3 = somewhat satisfied; 4 = very satisfied) are stored in columns 1 (telecommuters) and 2 (regular office workers). The data are stored in file XR16-77. Can we infer at the 10% significance level that telecommuters are more satisfied than regular office workers?

16.78 Can you become addicted to exercise? In a study conducted at the University of Wisconsin at Madison, a random sample of dedicated exercisers that usually work out every day was drawn. Each completed a questionnaire that gauged their mood on a 5-point scale, where 5 = very relaxed and happy, 4 = somewhat relaxed and happy, 3 = neutral feeling, 2 = tense and anxious, and 1 = very tense and anxious. The group was then instructed to abstain from all workouts for the next 3 days. Moreover, they were told to be as physically inactive as possible. Each day their mood was measured using the same questionnaire. The data are stored in file XR16-78. Column 1 stores the code identifying the respondent, and columns 2 through 5 store the measures of mood for the day before the experiment began and for the 3 days of the experiment, respectively. Can we infer at the 5% significance level that for each day the exercisers abstained from physical activity they were less happy than when they were exercising?

16.79 How does alcohol affect judgment? To provide some insight an experiment was conducted. A random sample of customers of an Ohio club was selected. Each respondent was asked to assess the attractiveness of members of the opposite sex who were in the club at the time. The assessment was to be made on a 5-point scale (1 = very unattractive, 2 = unattractive, 3 = neither attractive nor unattractive, 4 = attractive, and 5 = very attractive). The survey was conducted 3 hours before closing and again just before closing using another group of respondents. The data have been stored in file XR16-79. Column 1 contains the assessments 3 hours before closing, and column 2 stores the assessments made just before closing. Can we conclude that the assessments made just before closing are higher than those made 3 hours earlier? If so, what does this imply about the effects of alcohol on judgments? (The survey results were reported in the September 1997 edition of the *Report on Business*.)

CASE 16.1   Capitalization Ratios in the United States and Japan*

Firms raise funds to finance their operations by issuing debt to lenders and by issuing equity to shareholders. If the amount of debt employed by a firm is high relative to its amount of equity, the firm is said to have a high degree of financial leverage. One measure of a firm's leverage is its *capitalization ratio*—the ratio of the value of a firm's equity to the total value of its equity plus debt. The smaller a firm's capitalization ratio is, the more highly leveraged the firm is. The size of the capitalization ratio, however, depends on whether its computation is based on the (accounting) book value of equity or the market value of equity.

In a study comparing the leverage of American and Japanese firms, Michel and Shaked computed the capitalization ratios for a sample of American firms and for a sample of Japanese firms, using both book values and market values of equity. They observed that the shapes of the distributions of capitalization ratios for Japanese firms exhibited considerable negative skewness. Michel and Shaked were primarily interested in testing "the commonly held belief among Japanese businessmen, Japanese government officials, and the investment community worldwide that Japanese firms on average are more highly leveraged than their American counterparts."

From each of 10 industries, Michel and Shaked selected a sample of 13 American firms and 13 Japanese firms. The average book value-based capitalization ratios that were computed for each of the 10 industries, for 1981, are shown in Table 1. Table 2 presents similar information, using market value-based capitalization ratios. These data are stored in columns 1 to 4 of file C16-01.

Do the data allow us to infer that the belief that Japanese firms are more highly leveraged than their American counterparts in terms of both the book value and market value/based capitalization ratios is correct?

*Adapted from Allen Michel and Israel Shaked, "Japanese Leverage: Myth or Reality?" *Financial Analyst's Journal* 41 (1985): 61–67.

Table 1 Book Value-Based Capitalization Ratios

Industry	U.S.A.	Japan
1	.582	.484
2	.597	.435
3	.485	.435
4	.476	.393
5	.435	.353
6	.483	.288
7	.428	.288
8	.392	.182
9	.433	.174
10	.400	.140

Table 2 Market Value-Based Capitalization Ratios

Industry	U.S.A.	Japan
1	.734	.654
2	.625	.662
3	.452	.662
4	.499	.546
5	.414	.495
6	.458	.390
7	.372	.390
8	.388	.262
9	.438	.252
10	.275	.226

CASE 16.2   Bank of Commerce Customer Survey

The concepts and techniques of total quality management have spread to all industries. As a consequence, many firms regularly survey their customers to determine their opinion on a number of issues. The Bank of Commerce is one such company. Each year it undertakes a survey of customers to measure their attitudes about the various services offered by the bank. For example, it asks about the promptness of the service and the adequacy of operating hours. Additionally, the survey asks the following questions.

1 How would you rate the overall quality of service you receive from the Bank of Commerce as a whole?

2 How would you rate the overall quality of service at your branch of the Bank of Commerce?

The responses to these questions are rated

1 = extremely poor

2 = very poor

3 = poor

4 = fair

5 = good

6 = very good

7 = extremely good

As part of a more extensive analysis of the survey results, a manager took a random sample of 50 completed surveys at each of three branches. The data are stored in file C16-02 using the following format.

Column 1: Respondent number from Branch 1

Column 2: Response to question 1

Column 3: Response to question 2

Column 4: Respondent number from Branch 2

Column 5: Response to question 1

Column 6: Response to question 2

Column 7: Respondent number from Branch 3

Column 8: Response to question 1

Column 9: Response to question 2

The manager would like answers to two questions:

a Do customers at the three branches differ in their assessment of the quality of service at their branch?

b For each branch, do customers have a different opinion of their branch than of the Bank of Commerce as a whole?

Chapter **17**

Simple Linear

Regression and

Correlation

17.1 Introduction

17.2 Model

17.3 Estimating the Coefficients

17.4 Error Variable: Required Conditions

17.5 Assessing the Model

17.6 Finance Application: Market Model

17.7 Using the Regression Equation

17.8 Coefficients of Correlation

17.9 Regression Diagnostics—I

17.10 Summary

17.1 INTRODUCTION

This chapter is the first in a series of three in which the problem objective is to analyze the relationship among quantitative variables. **Regression analysis** is used to predict the value of one variable on the basis of other variables. This technique may be the most commonly used statistical procedure because, as you can easily appreciate, almost all companies and government institutions forecast variables such as product demand, interest rates, inflation rates, prices of raw materials, and labor costs.

The technique involves developing a mathematical equation that describes the relationship between the variable to be forecast, which is called the **dependent variable,** and variables that the statistician believes are related to the dependent variable. The dependent variable is denoted y, while the related variables are called **independent variables** and are denoted $x_1, x_2, \ldots, x_k$ (where k is the number of independent variables).

If we are interested only in determining *whether* a relationship exists, we employ correlation analysis. We have already introduced this technique. In Chapter 2, we presented the graphical method to describe the association between two quantitative variables—the scatter diagram. We introduced the coefficient of correlation and covariance in Chapter 4. We discussed correlation and covariance again in Chapter 6.

Because regression analysis involves a number of new techniques and concepts, we divided the presentation into three chapters. In this chapter, we present techniques that allow us to determine the relationship between only two variables. In Chapter 18, we expand our discussion to more than two variables, and in Chapter 19, we discuss how to build regression models.

Here are three examples of regression analysis.

Example 1 The product manager in charge of a particular brand of children's breakfast cereal would like to predict the demand for the cereal during the next year. In order to use regression analysis, she and her staff list the following variables as likely to affect sales.

Price of the product

Number of children 5 to 12 years of age (the target market)

Price of competitors' products

Effectiveness of advertising (as measured by advertising exposure)

Annual sales this year

Annual sales in previous years

Example 2 A gold speculator is considering a major purchase of gold bullion. He would like to forecast the price of gold 2 years from now (his planning horizon), using regression analysis. In preparation, he produces the following list of independent variables.

Interest rates

Inflation rate

Price of oil

Demand for gold jewelry

Demand for industrial and commercial gold

Dow Jones Industrial Average

Example 3 A real estate agent wants to more accurately predict the selling price of houses. She believes that the following variables affect the price of a house.

Size of the house (number of square feet)

Number of bedrooms

Frontage of the lot

Condition

Location

In each of these examples, the primary motive for using regression analysis is forecasting. Nonetheless, analyzing the relationship among variables can also be quite useful in managerial decision making. For instance, in the first application, the product manager may want to know how price is related to product demand so that a decision about a prospective change in pricing can be made.

Another application comes from the field of finance. The market model analyzes the relationship between the returns of a particular stock and the behavior of a stock index (such as the S&P 500 Index). Its function is not to predict the stock's price but to assess the risk of the stock versus the risk of the stock market in general. (See Section 17.6.)

Regardless of why regression analysis is performed, the next step in the technique is to develop a mathematical equation or model that accurately describes the nature of the relationship that exists between the dependent variable and the independent variables. This stage—which is only a small part of the total process—is described in the next section. In the ensuing sections of this chapter (and in Chapter 18), we will spend considerable time assessing and testing how well the model fits the actual data. Only when we're satisfied with the model do we use it to estimate and forecast.

17.2 MODEL

The job of developing a mathematical equation can be quite complex, because we need to have some idea about the nature of the relationship between each of the independent variables and the dependent variable. For example, the gold speculator mentioned in Example 2 needs to know how interest rates affect the price of gold. If he proposes a linear relationship, that may imply that as interest rates rise (or fall), the price of gold will rise or fall. A quadratic relationship may suggest that the price of gold will increase over a certain range of interest rates but will decrease over a different range. Perhaps certain combinations of values of interest rates and other independent variables influence the price in one way, while other combinations change it in other ways. The number of different mathematical models that could be proposed is virtually infinite.

You might have encountered various models in previous courses. For instance, the following represent relationships in the natural sciences.

$E = mc^2$, where E = Energy, m = Mass, and c = Speed of light

$F = ma$, where F = Force, m = Mass, and a = Acceleration

$S = at^2/2$, where S = Distance, t = Time, and a = Gravitational acceleration

In other business courses, you might have seen the following equations.

Profit = Revenue − Costs

Total cost = Fixed cost + (Variable cost × Number of units produced)

These are all examples of **deterministic models,** so named because—except for small measurement errors—such equations allow us to determine the value of the dependent variable (on the left side of the equation) from the value of the independent variables. In many practical applications of interest to us, deterministic models are unrealistic. For example, is it reasonable to believe that we can determine the selling price of a house solely on the basis of its size? Unquestionably, the size of a house affects its price, but many other variables (some of which may not be measurable) also influence price. What must be included in most practical models is a method to represent the randomness that is part of a real-life process. Such a model is called a **probabilistic model.**

To create a probabilistic model, we start with a deterministic model that approximates the relationship we want to model. We then add a random term that measures the error of the deterministic component. Suppose that in our earlier Example 3, the real estate agent knows that the cost of building a new house is about \$75 per square foot and that most lots sell for about \$25,000. The approximate selling price would be

$$y = 25,000 + 75x$$

where y = Selling price and x = Size of the house in square feet. A house of 2,000 square feet would therefore be estimated to sell for

$$y = 25,000 + 75(2,000) = 175,000$$

We know, however, that the selling price is not likely to be exactly \$175,000. Prices may actually range from \$100,000 to \$250,000. In other words, the deterministic model is not really suitable. To represent this situation properly, we should use the probabilistic model

$$y = 25,000 + 75x + \epsilon$$

where ϵ (the Greek letter *epsilon*) represents the random term (also called the error variable)—the difference between the actual selling price and the estimated price based on the size of the house. The random term thus accounts for all the variables, measurable and immeasurable, that are not part of the model. The value of ϵ will vary from one sale to the next, even if x remains constant. That is, houses of exactly the same size will sell for different prices because of differences in location and number of bedrooms and bathrooms, as well as other variables.

In the three chapters devoted to regression analysis, we will present only probabilistic models. Additionally, to simplify the presentation, all models will be linear. In this chapter, we restrict the number of independent variables to one. The model to be used in this chapter is called the **first-order linear model**—sometimes called the **simple linear regression model.**

First-Order Linear Model

$$y = \beta_0 + \beta_1 x + \epsilon$$

where

y = dependent variable

x = independent variable

β_0 = y-intercept

β_1 = slope of the line (defined as the ratio rise/run or change in y/change in x)

ϵ = error variable

Figure 17.1 depicts the deterministic component of the model.

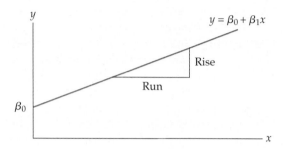

Figure 17.1

First-order linear model: deterministic component

The problem objective addressed by the model is to analyze the relationship between two variables, x and y, both of which must be quantitative. To define the relationship between x and y, we need to know the value of the coefficients of the linear model β_0 and β_1. However, these coefficients are population parameters, which are almost always unknown. In the next section, we discuss how these parameters are estimated.

17.3 ESTIMATING THE COEFFICIENTS

We estimate the parameters β_0 and β_1 in a way similar to the methods used to estimate all other parameters discussed in this book. We draw a random sample from the population of interest and calculate the sample statistics we need. Because β_0 and β_1 represent the coefficients of a straight line, their estimators are based on drawing a straight line through the sample data.

In Chapters 2 and 4 we introduced the descriptive methods employed to describe the relationship between two quantitative variables. We pointed out that we are particularly interested in determining whether a linear relationship exists. In Section 2.5 we introduced the **scatter diagram** from which we attempted to fit a straight line. We used the least squares method to draw the straight line that minimizes the sum of squared differences between the points and the line. The formulas, which were derived using calculus, are summarized below.

> **Calculation of b_0 and b_1**
>
> $$b_1 = \frac{\mathrm{cov}(X, Y)}{s_x^2}$$
> $$b_0 = \bar{y} - b_1\bar{x}$$

Statisticians have shown that b_0 and b_1 are unbiased estimators of β_0 and β_1, respectively. We will use the **least squares method** to produce the sample regression line

$$\hat{y} = b_0 + b_1 x$$

The following example illustrates how these coefficients are determined and interpreted.

Car dealers across North America use the "Red Book" to help them determine the value of used cars that their customers trade in when purchasing new cars. The book, which is published monthly, lists the trade-in values for all basic models of cars. It provides alternative values for each car model according to its condition and optional features. The values are determined on the basis of the average paid at recent used-car auctions. (These auctions are the source of supply for many used-car dealers.) However, the Red Book does not indicate the value determined by the odometer reading, despite the fact that a critical factor for used-car buyers is how far the car has been driven. To examine this issue, a used-car dealer randomly selected 100 three-year old Ford Tauruses that were sold at auction during the past month. Each car was in top condition and equipped with automatic transmission, AM/FM cassette tape player, and air conditioning. The dealer recorded the price and the number of miles on the odometer. These data are stored in file XM17-01; some of the data are listed below. The dealer wants to find the regression line.

Car	Odometer Reading	Auction Selling Price
1	37,388	$5,318
2	44,758	5,061
3	45,833	5,008
.	.	.
.	.	.
.	.	.
100	36,392	5,133

Solution

IDENTIFY

Notice that the problem objective is to analyze the relationship between two quantitative variables. Because we want to know how the odometer rating affects the selling price, we identify the former as the independent variable, which we label x, and the latter as the dependent variable, which we label y.

SOLVE

To determine the estimates of the coefficients, we must compute the sample means $\bar{x}$ and $\bar{y}$, the sample variance of x, s_x^2, and the sample covariance $\text{cov}(X,Y)$. They are

$$\bar{x} = \frac{\sum x_i}{n} = \frac{3,600,945}{100} = 36,009.45$$

$$\bar{y} = \frac{\sum y_i}{n} = \frac{541,141}{100} = 5,411.41$$

$$s_x^2 = \frac{\sum(x_i - \bar{x})^2}{n-1} = \frac{4,309,340,277}{99} = 43,528,690$$

$$\text{cov}(X, Y) = \frac{\sum(x_i - \bar{x})(y_i - \bar{y})}{n-1} = \frac{-134,269,298}{99} = -1,356,256$$

Using the last two statistics we find the slope coefficient.

$$b_1 = \frac{\text{cov}(X, Y)}{s_x^2} = \frac{-1,356,256}{43,528,690} = -.0312$$

We can determine the y-intercept coefficient from the slope and the sample means.

$$b_0 = \bar{y} - b_1\bar{x} = 5{,}411.41 - (-.0312)(36{,}009.45) = 6{,}533$$

The sample regression line is

$$\hat{y} = 6{,}533 - 0.0312x$$

The complete printouts are shown below. The printouts include more statistics than we need right now. However, we will be discussing the rest of the printouts later. We have also included the scatter diagrams, which is often a first step in the regression analysis. Notice that there does appear to be a straight-line relationship between the two variables.

Excel Output for Example 17.1

	A	B	C	D	E	F
1	SUMMARY OUTPUT					
2						
3	*Regression Statistics*					
4	Multiple R	0.8063				
5	R Square	0.6501				
6	Adjusted R Square	0.6466				
7	Standard Error	151.6				
8	Observations	100				
9						
10	ANOVA					
11		*df*	*SS*	*MS*	*F*	*Significance F*
12	Regression	1	4183528	4183528	182.1	0.0000
13	Residual	98	2251362	22973		
14	Total	99	6434890			
15						
16		*Coefficients*	*Standard Error*	*t Stat*	*P-value*	
17	Intercept	6533	84.51	77.31	0.0000	
18	Odometer	-0.0312	0.00231	-13.49	0.0000	

COMMANDS

1 Type or import the data into two adjacent columns.
2 Click **Tools, Data Analysis . . . ,** and **Regression.**
3 Specify **Input Y Range.**
4 Specify **Input X Range.** Click **OK.** Click **Labels** (if necessary).
5 To draw the scatter diagram click **Line Fit Plots** before clicking **OK.**

COMMANDS FOR EXAMPLE 17.1

Open file **XM17-01.**

B1:B101
A1:A101

(You can also draw the scatter diagram using the commands described in Chapter 2.)

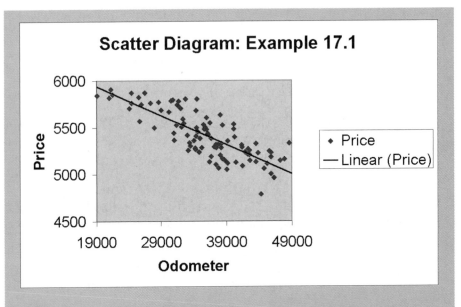

The scatter diagram will be drawn with the two axes starting at zero. This may cause the points to be bunched together leaving large blank spaces in the diagram. To modify the chart, proceed as follows.

6 Activate the chart by double-clicking anywhere within the boundaries of the box.

7 Double-click the Y-axis, click **Scale** (if necessary) and change the **Minimum, Maximum,** and/or **Major** and **Minor Units.** Click **OK.**

   4500 (Minimum) 6000 (Maximum) 500 (Major Units) 100 (Minor Units)

8 Repeat for the X-axis.

   19000 50000 10000 2000

Minitab Output for Example 17.1

Regression Analysis

```
The regression equation is
Price = 6533 - 0.0312  Odometer

Predictor        Coef        StDev           T         P
Constant      6533.38        84.51       77.31     0.000
Odometer    -0.031158      0.002309      -13.49     0.000

S = 151.6      R-Sq = 65.0%       R-Sq(adj) = 64.7%

Analysis of Variance

Source           DF          SS          MS         F         P
Regression        1     4183528     4183528    182.11     0.000
Residual Error   98     2251362      222973
Total            99     6434890
```

COMMANDS

1 Type or import the data into two columns.
2 Click **Stat, Regression,** and **Regression . . . .**
3 Type the name of the dependent **(Response)** variable.
4 Hit **tab,** and type the name of the independent **(Predictors)** variable. Click **OK.**

COMMANDS FOR EXAMPLE 17.1

Open file **XM17-01.**

Price or **C2**

Odometer or **C1**

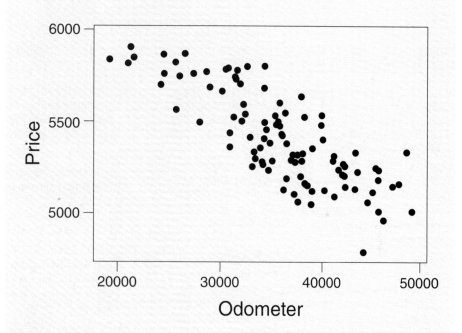

COMMANDS

1 Click **Stat, Regression,** and **Fitted Line Plot . . . .**
2 Type the name of the dependent variable **(Response [Y]).**
3 Use the cursor, and type the name of the independent variable **(Predictor [X]).**

COMMANDS FOR EXAMPLE 17.1

Price or **C2**

Odometer or **C1**

Alternatively, you can draw the scatter diagram using the commands described in Chapter 2.

INTERPRET

The slope coefficient b_1 is -0.0312, which means that for each additional mile on the odometer, the price decreases by an average of $0.0312 (3.12 cents).

The intercept is $b_0 = 6,533$. Technically, the intercept is the point at which the regression line and the y-axis intersect. This means that when $x = 0$ (i.e., the car was not driven at all) the selling price is $6,533. We might be tempted to interpret this number as the price of cars that have not been driven. However, in this case, the intercept is probably meaningless. Because our sample did not include any cars with zero miles on the odometer, we have no basis for interpreting b_0. As a general rule, we cannot determine the value of y for a value of x that is far outside the range of the sample values of x. In this example, the smallest and largest values of x are 19,057 and 49,223, respectively. Because $x = 0$ is not in this interval, we cannot safely interpret the value of y when $x = 0$.

In the sections that follow, we will return to this problem and the computer output to introduce other statistics associated with regression analysis.

▲

EXERCISES

Most of the exercises that follow were created to allow you to see how regression analysis is used to solve realistic problems. As a result, most feature a large number of observations. We anticipate that most students will solve these problems using a computer and statistical software. However, for students without these resources, we have computed the means, variances, and covariance that will permit them to complete the calculations manually. (See Appendix A.) We believe that it is pointless for students to compute the coefficients from the raw data except for several small-sample exercises that appeared in Chapter 4.

17.1 The term *regression* was originally used in 1885 by Sir Francis Galton in his analysis of the relationship between the heights of children and parents. He formulated the "law of universal regression," which specifies that "each peculiarity in a man is shared by his kinsmen, but on average in a less degree." (Evidently, people spoke this way in 1885.) In 1903 two statisticians, K. Pearson and A. Lee, took a random sample of 1,078 father–son pairs to examine Galton's law ("On the Laws of Inheritance in Man, I. Inheritance of Physical Characteristics," *Biometrika 2:* 457–62). Their sample regression line was

Son's height $= 33.73 + .516 \times$ Father's height

a Interpret the coefficients.
b What does the regression line tell you about the heights of sons of tall fathers?
c What does the regression line tell you about the heights of sons of short fathers?

17.2 Suppose that a statistician wanted to update the study described in Exercise 17.1. He collected data on 400 father–son pairs and stored the data in columns 1 (fathers' heights in inches) and 2 (sons' heights in inches) in file XR17-02.

a Determine the sample regression line.
b What does the value of b_0 tell you?
c What does the value of b_1 tell you?

17.3 Refer to Exercise 2.48. Determine the sample regression line that describes how mortgage rates affect the number of houses sold. What do the coefficients indicate about this relationship?

17.4 Refer to Exercise 2.46.

a Determine the sample regression line that depicts how the return on common stocks is affected by inflation.
b What does the value of b_0 tell you?
c What does the value of b_1 tell you?

17.5 Refer to Exercise 2.47. Find the sample regression line that describes how the monthly returns on the stock are affected by the return on the TSE. Discuss what the coefficients tell you about the relationship between the two variables.

17.6 In television's early years, most commercials were 60 seconds long. Now, however, commercials can be any length. The objective of commercials remains the same—to have as many viewers as possible remember the product in a favorable way and eventually buy it. In an experiment to determine how the length of a commercial affects people's memory of it, 60 randomly selected people were asked to watch a 1-hour television program. In the middle of the show, a commercial advertising a brand of toothpaste appeared. Some viewers watched a commercial that lasted for 20 seconds, others watched one that lasted for 24 seconds, 28 seconds, ..., 60 seconds. The essential content of the commercials was the same. After the show, each person was given a test to measure how much he or she remembered about the product. The commercial times and test scores (on a 30-point test) are stored in file XR17-06.

a Obtain a scatter diagram of the data to determine whether a linear model appears to be appropriate.
b Determine the least squares line.
c Interpret the coefficients.

17.7 After several semesters without much success, Pat Statsdud (a student in the lower quarter of a statistics course) decided to try to improve. Pat needed to know the secret of success for university and college students. After many hours of discussion with other, more successful, students, Pat postulated a rather radical theory: the longer one studied, the better one's grade. To test the theory, Pat took a random sample of 100 students in an economics course and asked each to report the average amount of time he or she studied economics and the final mark received. These data are stored in columns 1 (study time in hours) and 2 (final mark out of 100) in file XR17-07.

   a Determine the sample regression line.

   b Interpret the coefficients.

   c Is the sign of the slope logical? If the slope had had the opposite sign, what would that tell you?

17.9 The human resource manager of a telemarketing firm is concerned about the rapid turnover of the firm's telemarketers. It appears that many telemarketers do not work very long before quitting. There may be a number of reasons, including relatively low pay, personal unsuitability for the work, and the low probability of advancement. Because of the high cost of hiring and training new workers, the manager decided to examine the factors that influence workers to quit. He reviewed the work history of a random sample of 80 workers who quit in the last year and recorded the number of weeks on the job before quitting and the age of each worker when originally hired. There data are stored in file XR17-09 (column 1 contains the work period and column 2 contains the age).

   a Use a regression analysis to describe how the work period and age are related.

   b Briefly discuss what the coefficients tell you.

STATISTICS IN THE WORKPLACE

Human Resources Application

Human resource managers are responsible for a variety of tasks within organizations. As we pointed out in the introduction in Chapter 1, personnel/human resource managers are involved with recruiting new workers, determining which applicants are most suitable to hire, and in various aspects of monitoring the workforce, including absenteeism and worker turnover. For many firms, worker turnover is a costly problem. First, there is the cost of recruiting and attracting qualified workers. The firm must advertise vacant positions and make certain that applicants are judged properly. Second, the cost of training hirees can be high, particularly in technical areas. Third, new employees are often not as productive and efficient as experienced ones. Consequently, it is in the interests of the firm to attract and keep the best workers. Any information that the personnel manager can obtain is likely to be useful.

17.8 The growing interest in and use of the Internet has forced many companies into considering ways to sell their products on the web. Therefore it is of interest to these companies to determine who is using the web. A statistician undertook a study to determine how education and Internet use are connected. She took a random sample of 200 adults (20 years of age and older) and asked each to report the years of education they had completed and the number of hours of Internet use the previous week. These data are stored in columns 1 and 2 (education and Internet use, respectively) in file XR17-08.

   a Perform a regression analysis to describe how the two variables are related.

   b Interpret the coefficients.

17.10 The Trans-Alaska Pipeline System carries crude oil from Prudhoe Bay, on Alaska's North Slope, 800 miles to the port of Valdez, on the south coast of Alaska. The pipeline carries a mixture of different qualities of oil. Quality of oil is measured in API gravity degrees—the higher the degrees API, the higher the quality. Because the pipeline mixes oils of different degrees, shippers in Valdez receive oil of different quality than they purchased. To compensate shippers, a "Quality Bank" was established. The owners of the pipeline proposed compensating shippers 15 cents per barrel for every degree below the level to which the shippers agreed. However, a refinery near Fairbanks, which receives 26-degree oil and mixes it with 20-degree oil, objected to the proposal. It suggested a 3.09 to 5.35 cent differential. Because oil carriers are required to establish "just and reasonable" rates, a hearing before an administrative law judge was held. At the hearing, an expert hired by the shippers produced the table below to show the relationship between quality and price per barrel of Mideast oil. (The data are stored in file XR17-10.) Use regression analysis to determine the appropriate compensation.

Mideast oil degrees API	27.0	28.5	30.8	31.3	31.9	34.5	34.0
Price per barrel	12.02	12.04	12.32	12.27	12.49	12.70	12.80

Mideast oil degrees API	34.7	37.0	41.1	41.0	38.8	39.3
Price per barrel	13.00	13.00	13.17	13.19	13.22	13.27

Source: M. O. Finkelstein and B. Levin, *Statistics for Lawyers* (New York: Springer-Verlag, 1990), pp. 338–39.

17.11 All Canadians have government-funded health insurance, which pays for any medical care they require. However, when traveling out of the country, Canadians usually acquire supplementary health insurance to cover the difference between the costs incurred for emergency treatment and what the government program pays. In the United States this cost differential can be prohibitive. Until recently, private insurance companies (such as Blue Cross) charged everyone the same weekly rate, regardless of age. However, because of rising costs and the realization that older people frequently incur greater medical emergency expenses, insurers had to change their premium plans. They decided to offer rates that depend on the age of the customer. To help determine the new rates, one insurance company gathered data concerning the age and mean daily medical expenses of a random sample of 1,348 Canadians during the previous 12-month period. The data are stored in file XR17-11 (column 1 = age; column 2 = mean daily medical expense).

a Determine the sample regression line.
b Interpret the coefficients.
c What rate plan would you suggest?

17.12 The four C's—carats, cut, clarity, and color—determine the price of diamonds. Carats refer to the weight of the diamond. One carat equals .2 grams. An advertisement in a Singapore newspaper (*Straits Times,* 29 February, 1992) featured 48 ladies' diamond rings in which the stones varied in weight from .12 carats to .35 carats. The ad listed the weights of the stones together with the nonnegotiable price in Singapore dollars. These data are stored in columns 1 (weights) and 2 (price) in file XR17-12.

a Use regression analysis to determine how weight and price are related.
b What do the coefficients tell you?

17.4 ERROR VARIABLE: REQUIRED CONDITIONS

In the previous section, we described the least squares method of estimating the coefficients of the linear regression model. A critical part of this model is the **error variable** ϵ. In the next section, we will present an inferential method that determines whether there is a linear relationship. Later we will show how we use the regression equation to estimate and predict. For these methods to be valid, however, four requirement involving the probability distribution of the error variable must be satisfied.

Required Conditions for the Error Variable

1 The probability distribution of ϵ is normal.

2 The mean of the distribution is zero; that is, $E(\epsilon) = 0$.

3 The standard deviation of ϵ is σ_ϵ, which is a constant no matter what the value of x is.

4 The value of ϵ associated with any particular value of y is independent of ϵ associated with any other value of y.

Requirements 1, 2, and 3 can be interpreted in another way: For each value of x, y is a normally distributed random variable whose mean is

$$E(y) = \beta_0 + \beta_1 x$$

and whose standard deviation is σ_ϵ. Notice that the mean depends on x. The standard deviation, however, is not influenced by x, because it is a constant over all values of

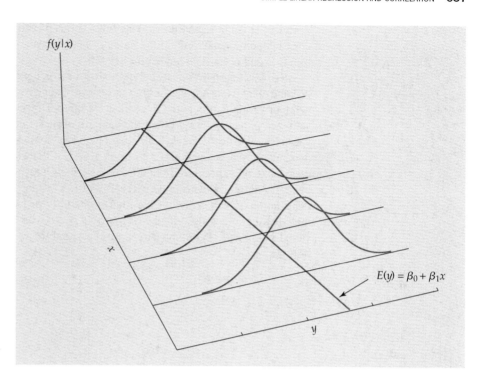

Figure 17.2

Distribution of *y* given *x*

x. Figure 17.2 depicts this interpretation. Notice that for each value of *x*, $E(y)$ changes, but the shape of the distribution of *Y* remains the same. That is, for each *x*, *y* is normally distributed with the same standard deviation.

In Section 17.9, we discuss how departures from these required conditions affect the regression analysis and how they are identified.

OBSERVATIONAL AND EXPERIMENTAL DATA

In Chapter 2 and again in Chapter 12 we described the difference between observational and experimental data. We pointed out that statisticians often design controlled experiments to enable them to interpret the results of their analyses more clearly than would be the case after conducting an observational study. Example 17.1 is an illustration of observational data. In that example we merely observed the odometer reading and auction selling price of 100 randomly selected cars.

In Exercise 17.6 experimental data were gathered through a controlled experiment. To determine the effect of the length of a television commercial on its viewers' memories of the product advertised, the statistician arranged for 60 television viewers to watch a commercial of differing lengths and then tested their memories of that commercial. Each viewer was randomly assigned a commercial length. The values of *x* ranged from 20 to 60 and were set by the statistician as part of the experiment. For each value of *x*, the distribution of the memory test scores is assumed to be normally distributed with a constant variance.

We can summarize the difference between the experiment described in Example 17.1 and the one described in Exercise 17.6. In Example 17.1 both the odometer reading and the auction selling price are random variables. We hypothesize that for each possible odometer reading, there is a theoretical population of auction selling prices that are normally distributed with a mean that is a linear function of the odometer reading and a standard deviation that is a constant. In Exercise 17.6 the length of commercial is not a random variable but a series of values selected by the statistician. For each commercial length, the memory test scores are required to be normally distributed with a constant standard deviation.

Regression analysis can be applied to data generated from either observational or controlled experiments. In both cases our objective is to determine how the independent variable affects the dependent variable. However, observational data can be analyzed in another way. When the data are observational both variables are random variables. We need not specify that one variable is independent and the other is dependent. We can simply determine *whether* the two variables are related. The equivalent of the required conditions described above is that the two variables are bivariate normally distributed. (Recall that in Chapter 6 we introduced the bivariate distribution, which describes the joint probability of two variables.) A bivariate normal distribution is described in Figure 17.3. As you can see, it is a three-dimensional bell curve. The dimensions are the variables x, y, and the joint density function $f(x, y)$.

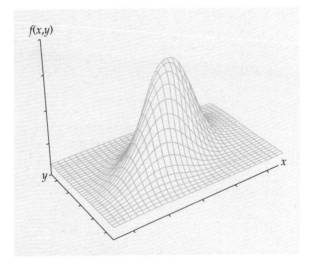

Figure 17.3

Bivariate normal distribution

In Section 17.8 we discuss the statistical technique that is used when both x and y are random variables and they are bivariate normally distributed. We also introduce a procedure applied when the normality requirement is not satisfied.

17.5 ASSESSING THE MODEL

The least squares method produces the best straight line. However, there may in fact be no relationship or perhaps a nonlinear (e.g., quadratic) relationship between the two variables. If so, the use of a linear model is likely to be impractical. Consequently, it is important for us to assess how well the linear model fits the data. If the fit is poor, we should discard the linear model and seek another one.

Several methods are used to evaluate the model. In this section, we present two statistics and one test procedure to determine whether a linear model should be employed. They are the standard error of estimate, the t-test of the slope, and the coefficient of determination. All of these methods are based on the sum of squares for error.

SUM OF SQUARES FOR ERROR

The least squares method is based on finding the coefficients that minimize the sum of squared differences between the points and the line defined by the coefficients. We can measure how well the straight line fits the data by calculating the value of the sum of squared differences. The difference between the points and the line are called **residuals.** That is,

$$\text{Residual} = y_i - \hat{y}_i$$

The residuals are the observed values of the error variable. Consequently, the minimized sum of squared differences is called the **sum of squares for error,** denoted SSE.

Sum of Squares for Error

$$SSE = \sum_{i=1}^{n} (y_i - \hat{y}_i)^2$$

The direct method of calculating SSE can be long and tedious. It requires that for each value of x we compute the value of $\hat{y}$. That is, for $i = 1$ to n,

$$\hat{y}_i = b_0 + b_1 x_i$$

For each point we then compute the difference between the actual value of y and the value calculated at the line, which is the residual. We square each residual and sum the squared values. Table 17.1 shows these calculations for the first three and last three cars in Example 17.1.

Table 17.1 **Calculation of SSE for Example 17.1**

Car i	Odometer Reading x_i	Auction Selling Price y_i	Regression* Equation $\hat{y}_i = 6533 - .0312x_i$	Residual $(y_i - \hat{y}_i)$	Squared $(y_i - \hat{y}_i)^2$
1	37388	5318	5368.46	−50.46	2545.96
2	44758	5061	5138.82	−77.82	6056.73
3	45833	5008	5105.33	−97.33	9473.21
.	.	.	.	.	.
.	.	.	.	.	.
.	.	.	.	.	.
98	33190	5259	5499.26	−240.26	57723.76
99	39196	5356	5312.12	43.88	1925.08
100	36392	5133	5399.49	−266.49	71017.24
				SSE =	2,251,362.47

*We used the actual (not the rounded) coefficients.

The sum of squares for error is 2,251,362.47. This statistic plays a role in every statistical technique that follows.

Both of our software packages report this statistic. To calculate SSE manually, a great deal of arithmetic is required. Fortunately, a shortcut is available. It uses the sample covariance and the sample variances.

> **Shortcut Calculation of SSE**
>
> $$SSE = (n - 1)\left\{ s_y^2 - \frac{[cov(X, Y)]^2}{s_x^2} \right\}$$
>
> where s_y^2 is the sample variance of variable y.

STANDARD ERROR OF ESTIMATE

In Section 17.4, we pointed out that the error variable ϵ is normally distributed with mean zero and standard deviation σ_ϵ. If σ_ϵ is large, some of the errors will be large, which implies that the model's fit is poor. If σ_ϵ is small, the errors tend to be close to the mean (which is zero) and, as a result, the model fits well. Hence, we could use σ_ϵ to measure the suitability of using a linear model. Unfortunately, σ_ϵ is a population parameter and, like most parameters, is unknown. We can, however, estimate σ_ϵ from the data. The estimate is based on SSE. The unbiased estimator of the variance of the error variable σ_ϵ^2 is

$$s_\epsilon^2 = \frac{SSE}{n - 2}$$

The square root of s_ϵ^2 is called the **standard error of estimate.**

> **Standard Error of Estimate**
>
> $$s_\epsilon = \sqrt{\frac{SSE}{n - 2}}$$

▼ **EXAMPLE 17.2**

SOLVE

Find the standard error of estimate for Example 17.1 and describe what it tells you about the model's fit.

Solution To compute the standard error of estimate, we need to compute SSE, which is computed from the sample variances and the covariance. We have already calculated the sample variance of x and the covariance. They are 43,528,690 and −1,356,256, respectively. The sample variance of y is

$$s_y^2 = \frac{\sum (y_i - \bar{y})^2}{n - 1} = \frac{6,434,890}{99} = 64,999$$

Thus,

$$SSE = (n - 1)\left\{ s_y^2 - \frac{[cov(X, Y)]^2}{s_x^2} \right\}$$

$$= (100 - 1)\left\{ (64,999) - \frac{(-1,356,256)^2}{43,528,690} \right\} = 2,251,363$$

and

$$s_\epsilon = \sqrt{\frac{\text{SSE}}{n-2}} = \sqrt{\frac{2,251,363}{98}} = 151.6$$

Excel Output for Example 17.2

Refer to page 631 to examine the Excel printout for Example 17.1. Excel reports the standard error of estimate as

Standard Error 151.6

Minitab Output for Example 17.2

Refer to page 632 to examine the Minitab printout for Example 17.1. Minitab reports the standard error of estimate simply as

S = 151.6

INTERPRET

The smallest value that s_ϵ can assume is zero, which occurs when SSE = 0, that is, when all the points fall on the regression line. Thus, when s_ϵ is small, the fit is excellent, and the linear model is likely to be an effective analytical and forecasting tool. If s_ϵ is large, the model is a poor one, and the statistician should improve it or discard it.

We judge the value of s_ϵ by comparing it to the values of the dependent variable y, or more specifically to the sample mean $\bar{y}$. In this example, because $s_\epsilon = 151.6$ and $\bar{y} = 5,411.4$, we would have to admit that the standard error of estimate is not very small. On the other hand, it is not a large number. Because there is no predefined upper limit on s_ϵ, it is difficult to assess the model in this way (except in cases where s_ϵ is obviously a small number). In general, the standard error of estimate cannot be used as an absolute measure of the model's utility.

Nonetheless, s_ϵ is useful in comparing models. If the statistician has several models from which to choose, the one with the smallest value of s_ϵ should generally be the one used. As you'll see, s_ϵ is also an important statistic in other procedures associated with regression analysis.

TESTING THE SLOPE

To understand this method of assessing the linear model, consider the consequences of applying the regression technique to two variables that are not at all linearly related. If we could observe the entire population and draw the regression line, we would observe the graph shown in Figure 17.4. The line is horizontal, which means that the value of y is unaffected by the value of x. Recall that a horizontal straight line has a slope of zero, that is, $\beta_1 = 0$.

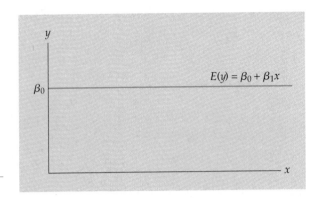

Figure 17.4

$\beta_1 = 0$

Because we rarely examine complete populations, the parameters are unknown. However, we can draw inferences about the population slope β_1 from the sample slope b_1.

The process of testing hypotheses about β_1 is identical to the process of testing any other parameter. We begin with the hypotheses. The null hypothesis specifies that there is no linear relationship, which means that the slope is zero. Thus, we specify

$$H_0: \beta_1 = 0$$

We can conduct one- or two-tail tests of β_1. Most often, we perform a two-tail test to determine whether there is sufficient evidence to infer that a linear relationship exists. We test

$$H_1: \beta_1 \neq 0$$

The test statistic is

$$t = \frac{b_1 - \beta_1}{s_{b_1}}$$

where s_{b_1} is the standard deviation of b_1 (also called the standard error of b_1). It is defined as

$$s_{b_1} = \frac{s_\epsilon}{\sqrt{(n-1)s_x^2}}$$

If the error variable is normally distributed, the test statistic is Student t distributed with $n - 2$ degrees of freedom.

▼ **EXAMPLE 17.3**

Test to determine whether there is enough evidence in Example 17.1 to infer that there is a linear relationship between the price and the odometer reading. Use a 5% significance level.

Solution   We test the hypotheses

IDENTIFY $H_0: \beta_1 = 0$
            $H_1: \beta_1 \neq 0$

If the null hypothesis is true no linear relationship exists. If the alternative hypothesis is true, some linear relationship exists between the two variables.

SOLVE

To compute the value of the test statistic we need b_1 and s_{b_1}. In Example 17.1 we found

$$b_1 = -.0312$$

and

$$s_x^2 = 43,528,690$$

Thus,

$$s_{b_1} = \frac{s_\epsilon}{\sqrt{(n-1)s_x^2}} = \frac{151.6}{\sqrt{(99)(43,528,690)}} = .00231$$

The value of the test statistic is

$$t = \frac{b_1 - \beta_1}{s_{b_1}} = \frac{-.0312 - 0}{.00231} = -13.49$$

The rejection region is

$$t > t_{\alpha/2,n-2} = t_{.025,98} \approx 1.984 \quad \text{or} \quad t < -t_{\alpha/2,n-2} \approx -1.984$$

Excel Output for Example 17.3

The output below was taken from the Excel output for Example 17.1 on page 631.

	A	B	C	D	E
16		Coefficients	Standard Error	t Stat	P-value
17	Intercept	6533	84.51	77.31	0.0000
18	Odometer	-0.0312	0.00231	-13.49	0.0000

The printout includes the standard deviation of b_1(**Standard Error**), the t-statistic (**t Stat**), and the two-tail p-value of the test (**P-value**). These values are .00231, -13.49, and 0.0000, respectively. Notice the printout includes a test for β_0. However, as we've pointed out before, interpreting the value of the y-intercept can lead to erroneous, if not ridiculous, conclusions. As a result, we ignore the test of β_0.

Minitab Output for Example 17.3

The output below was taken from the Minitab output for Example 17.1 on page 632.

```
Predictor        Coef          StDev           T          P
Constant      6533.38          84.51       77.31      0.000
Odometer     -0.031158       0.002309      -13.49      0.000
```

The printout includes the standard deviation of b_1 (**StDev**), the t-statistic (**T**), and the two-tail p-value of the test. These values are .002309, -13.49, and 0.000, respectively. Notice the printout includes a test for β_0. However, as we've pointed out before, interpreting the value of the y-intercept can lead to erroneous, if not ridiculous, conclusions. As a result, we ignore the test of β_0.

The value of the test statistic is $t = -13.49$, with a p-value of 0. There is overwhelming evidence to infer that a linear relationship exists. What this means is that the odometer reading does affect the auction selling price of the cars.

As was the case when we interpreted the y-intercept, the conclusion we draw here is valid only over the range of the values of the independent variable. That is, we can infer that there is a linear relationship between odometer reading and auction price for the 3-year-old Ford Tauruses whose odometer reading lies between 19,057 and 49,223 miles (the minimum and maximum values of x in the sample). Because we have no observations outside this range, we do not know how, or even whether, the two variables are related. This issue is particularly important to remember when we use the regression equation to estimate or forecast. (See Section 17.7.)

▲

COEFFICIENT OF DETERMINATION

The test of β_1 addresses only the question of whether there is enough evidence to infer that a linear relationship exists. In many cases, however, it is also useful to measure the strength of that linear relationship, particularly when we want to compare several different models. The statistic that performs this function is the coefficient of determination.

The **coefficient of determination,** denoted R^2, is computed in the following way.

Coefficient of Determination

$$R^2 = \frac{[\text{cov}(X, Y)]^2}{s_x^2 s_y^2}$$

With a little algebra, mathematicians can show that

$$R^2 = 1 - \frac{\text{SSE}}{\sum (y_i - \bar{y})^2}$$

The significance of this formula is based on the analysis of variance technique. In Chapter 14, we partitioned the total sum of squares into two sources of variation. Here, we begin the discussion by observing that the deviation between y_i and $\bar{y}$ can be decomposed into two parts. That is,

$$(y_i - \bar{y}) = (y_i - \hat{y}_i) + (\hat{y}_i - \bar{y})$$

This equation is represented graphically (for $i = 1$) in Figure 17.5.

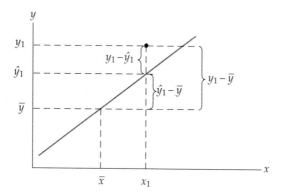

Figure 17.5

Analysis of the deviation

Now we ask, why are the values of y different from one another? In Example 17.1, we observe that the auction selling prices of the cars vary, and we'd like to explain why. From Figure 17.5, we see that part of the difference between y_i and $\bar{y}$ is the difference between $\hat{y}_i$ and $\bar{y}$, which is accounted for by the difference between x_i and $\bar{x}$. That is, some of the price variation is *explained* by the odometer reading. The other part of the difference between y_i and $\bar{y}$, however, is accounted for by the difference between y_i and $\hat{y}_i$. This difference is the residual, which to some degree reflects variables not otherwise represented by the model. (These variables likely include the local supply and demand for this type of used car, the color of the car, and other relatively small details.) As a result, we say that this part of the difference is *unexplained* by the odometer variation.

If we now square both sides of the equation, sum over all sample points, and perform some algebra, we produce

$$\sum (y_i - \bar{y})^2 = \sum (y_i - \hat{y}_i)^2 + \sum (\hat{y}_i - \bar{y})^2$$

The quantity on the left side of this equation is a measure of the variation in the dependent variable (selling price). The first quantity on the right side of the equation is SSE, and the second term is denoted SSR, for **sum of squares for regression.** We can rewrite the equation as

Variation in $y = $ SSE $+$ SSR

As we did in the analysis of variance, we partition the variation of y into two parts: SSE, which measures the amount of variation in y that remains unexplained; and SSR, which measures the amount of variation in y that is explained by the variation in the independent variable (odometer reading).

$$R^2 = 1 - \frac{\text{SSE}}{\sum (y_i - \bar{y})^2} = \frac{\sum (y_i - \bar{y})^2 - \text{SSE}}{\sum (y_i - \bar{y})^2} = \frac{\text{SSR}}{\sum (y_i - \bar{y})^2}$$

It follows that R^2 measures the proportion of the variation in y that is explained by the variation in x. Incidentally, the notation R^2 is derived from the fact that the coefficient of determination is the coefficient of correlation squared. Recall that we introduced the sample coefficient of correlation in Chapter 4 and labeled it r. (To be consistent with computer output, we capitalize r in the definition of the coefficient of determination.) We discuss the coefficient of correlation in Section 17.8.

▼ **EXAMPLE 17.4**

Find the coefficient of determination for Example 17.1 and describe what this statistic tell you about the regression model.

Solution

We have already calculated all the necessary components of this statistic. In Example 17.1 we found

$$\text{cov}(X,Y) = -1,356,256$$
$$s_x^2 = 43,528,690$$

and

$$s_y^2 = 64,999$$

Thus,

$$R^2 = \frac{[\text{cov}(X,Y)]^2}{s_x^2 \times s_y^2} = \frac{[-1,356,256]^2}{(43,528,690) \times (64,999)} = .6501$$

Excel Output for Example 17.4

Refer to page 631 to examine the Excel printout for Example 17.1. Excel reports the coefficient of determination as

R Square   .6501

Minitab Output for Example 17.4

Refer to page 632 to examine the Minitab printout for Example 17.1. Minitab reports the coefficient of determination as

R-sq   65.0%

Both Minitab and Excel print a second R^2 statistic called the *coefficient of determination adjusted for degrees of freedom.* We will define and describe this statistic in Chapter 18.

We found that R^2 is equal to 65%. This statistic tells us that 65% of the variation in the auction selling prices is explained by the variation in the odometer readings. The remaining 35% is unexplained. Unlike the value of a test statistic, the coefficient of determination does not have a critical value that enables us to draw conclusions. We know that the higher the value of R^2, the better the model fits the data. From the t-test of β_1 we know already that there is evidence of a linear relationship. The coefficient of determination merely supplies us with a measure of the strength of that relationship. As you will discover in the next chapter, when we improve the model, the value of R^2 increases.

▲

OTHER PARTS OF THE COMPUTER PRINTOUT

The last part of the printout shown on pages 631 to 632 relates to our discussion of the interpretation of the value of R^2, where its meaning is derived from the partitioning of the variation in y. The values of SSR and SSE are shown in an analysis of variance table similar to the tables introduced in Chapter 14. The general format of the table is shown below. The F-test performed in the ANOVA table will be explained in Chapter 18.

General Form of the ANOVA Table in the Simple Regression Model

Source	d.f.	Sums of Squares	Mean Squares	F-Value
Regression	1	SSR	MSR = SSR/1	F = MSR/MSE
Error	$n-2$	SSE	MSE = SSE/$(n-2)$	
Total	$n-1$	Variation in y		

Note: Excel calls the second source of variation "Residual."

DEVELOPING AN UNDERSTANDING OF STATISTICAL CONCEPTS

Once again, we encounter the concept of explained variation. We first discussed this concept in Chapter 12 when we introduced the matched pairs experiment, where that experiment was designed to reduce the variation among experimental units. This concept was extended in the analysis of variance, where we partitioned the total variation into two or more sources (depending on the model). And now in regression analysis, we use the concept to measure how the dependent variable is affected by the independent variable. We partition the variation of the dependent variable into two sources: the variation explained by the variation in the independent variable and the unexplained variation. The greater the explained variation, the better the model is. We often refer to the coefficient of determination as a measure of the *explanatory power* of the model.

CAUSE AND EFFECT RELATIONSHIP

A common mistake is made by many students when they attempt to interpret the results of a regression analysis when there is evidence of a linear relationship. They imply that changes in the independent variable *cause* changes in the dependent variable. It must be emphasized that we cannot infer a causal relationship from statistics alone. Any inference about the cause of the changes in the dependent variable must be justified by a reasonable theoretical relationship. For example, statistical tests established that the more one smoked, the greater the probability of developing lung cancer. However, this analysis did not prove that smoking causes lung cancer. It only demonstrated that smoking and lung cancer were somehow related. Only when medical investigations established the connection were scientists able to confidently declare that smoking causes lung cancer.

As another illustration, consider Example 17.1 where we showed that the odometer reading is linearly related to the auction price. While it seems reasonable to conclude that decreasing the odometer reading would cause the auction price to rise, this conclusion may not be entirely true. It is theoretically possible that the price is determined by the overall condition of the car and that the condition generally worsens when the car is driven longer. Another analysis would be needed to establish the veracity of this conclusion.

Be cautious about the use of the terms "explained variation" and "explanatory power of the model." Do not interpret the word "explained" to mean "caused." We say that coefficient of determination measures the amount of variation in y that is explained (not caused) by the variation in x. Thus, regression analysis can only show that a statistical relationship exists. We cannot infer that one variable causes another.

EXERCISES

The following exercises require the use of a computer and software. The answers may be calculated manually. See Appendix A for the sample statistics.

17.13 Describe what the required conditions mean in Exercise 17.2. Do these requirements seem reasonable?

17.14 If the required conditions are satisfied in Exercise 17.10, what can you say about the distribution of the price per barrel?

17.15 Assuming that the required conditions are satisfied in Exercise 17.11, what does this tell you about the distribution of mean daily expenses?

17.16 Refer to Exercise 17.2.

  a What is the standard error of estimate? Interpret its value.

  b Describe how well the heights of the fathers and sons are linearly related.

  c Are the heights of fathers and sons linearly related? Test using a 5% significance level.

17.17 Refer to Exercise 17.3. Apply the three methods of assessing the model to determine how well the linear model fits.

17.18 Refer to Exercise 17.4. Are the two variables linearly related? Conduct a test with a 10% significance level.

17.19 Refer to Exercise 17.5. Use two statistics to measure the strength of the linear association. What do these statistics tell you?

17.20 Refer to Exercise 17.6.

  a Determine the standard error of estimate and describe what this statistic tells you about the regression model.

  b Determine the coefficient of determination. What does this statistic tell you about how well the linear regression model fits?

  c Can we infer at the 5% significance level that the length of commercial and memory test score are linearly related?

17.21 Refer to Exercise 17.7.

  a Test at the 10% significance level to determine whether there is evidence of a linear relationship between study time and the final mark.

  b Determine the coefficient of determination. What does this statistic tell you about the regression line?

17.22 Refer to Exercise 17.8.

  a Determine the standard error of estimate, and describe what this statistic tells you about the regression line.

  b Can we conclude at the 1% significance level that educational level and Internet use are linearly related?

  c Determine the coefficient of determination and discuss what its value tell you about the two variables.

17.23 Refer to Exercise 17.9. Are work period and age linearly related? (Conduct a statistical test at the 5% significance level to decide.) If so, provide a statistic that measures the strength of the association.

17.24 Refer to Exercise 17.10. Use whatever statistics you think useful to describe the reliability of your suggested compensation plan.

17.25 Refer to Exercise 17.11. Use whatever statistics you think useful to describe the reliability of your insurance premium plan.

17.26 Refer to Exercise 17.12.

  a Determine the standard error of estimate and describe what this statistic tells you about the regression model.

  b Determine the coefficient of determination. What does this statistic tell you about how well the linear regression model fits?

  c Can we infer at the 5% significance level that the weight and price of the diamonds are linearly related?

17.27 An economist wanted to investigate the relationship between office rents and vacancy rates. Accordingly, he took a random sample of monthly office rents and the percentage of vacant office space in 30 different cities. The results were stored in file XR17-27 (column 1 = vacancy rates in percent and column 2 = monthly rents in dollars per square foot).

  a Determine the regression line.

  b Interpret the coefficients.

  c Can we conclude at the 5% significance level that higher vacancy rates result in lower rents?

STATISTICS IN THE WORKPLACE

Human Resources Application

In our introduction to human resources management in Chapter 1 we noted that the recruitment process at many firms involves tests to determine the suitability of candidates. The tests may be written to determine whether the applicant has sufficient knowledge in his or her area of expertise to perform well on the job. There may be oral tests to determine whether the applicant's personality matches the needs of the job. Manual or technical skills can be tested through a variety of physical tests. The test results contribute to the decision to hire. In some cases, the test result is the only criterion to hire. Consequently, it is vital to ensure that the test is a reliable predictor of job performance. If the tests are poor predictors, they should be discontinued. Statistical analyses allow personnel managers to examine the link between the test results and job performance.

d Measure how well the linear model fits the data. Discuss what this (these) measure(s) tells you.

17.28 Physicians have been recommending more exercise for their patients, particularly those who are overweight. One benefit of regular exercise appears to be a reduction in cholesterol, a substance associated with heart disease. To study the relationship more carefully, a physician took a random sample of 50 patients who do not exercise. She measured their cholesterol levels. She then started them on regular exercise programs. After 4 months, she asked each patient how many minutes per week (on average) he or she exercised and also measured their cholesterol levels. The results are stored in file XR17-28 (column 1 = weekly exercise in minutes; column 2 = cholesterol level before exercise program; column 3 = cholesterol level after exercise program).

a Determine the regression line that relates exercise time with cholesterol reduction.

b Interpret the coefficients.

c Can we conclude at the 5% significance level that the amount of exercise is linearly related to cholesterol reduction?

d Measure how well the linear model fits.

17.29 Although a large number of tasks in the computer industry are robotic, a number of operations require human workers. Some jobs require a great deal of dexterity to properly position components into place. A large North American computer maker routinely tests applicants for these jobs by giving a dexterity test that involves a number of intricate finger and hand movements. The tests are scored on a 100-point scale. Only those who have scored above 70 are hired. To determine whether the tests are valid predictors of job performance, the personnel manager drew a random sample of 45 workers who were hired 2 months ago. He recorded their test scores and the percentage of nondefective computers they produced in the last week. These data are stored in columns 1 and 2, respectively, in file XR17-29. Can the manager infer at the 10% significance level that the test is a valid predictor? That is, can he infer that higher test results are associated with higher percentages of nondefective units?

17.6 FINANCE APPLICATION: MARKET MODEL

In this section we describe one of the most important applications of simple linear regression. It is the well-known and applied **market model.** This model assumes that the rate of return on a stock is linearly related to the rate of return on the overall market. The mathematical description of the model is

$$R = \beta_0 + \beta_1 R_m + \epsilon$$

where R is the return on a particular stock and R_m is the return on some major stock index, such as the New York Stock Exchange Composite Index.

The coefficient β_1 is called the stock's **beta coefficient,** which measures how sensitive the stock's rate of return is to changes in the level of the overall market. For example, if β_1 is greater than 1, the stock's rate of return is more sensitive to changes in the level of the overall market than is the average stock. To illustrate, suppose that $\beta_1 = 2$. Then a 1% increase in the index results in an average increase of 2% in the stock's return. A 1% decrease in the index produces an average 2% decrease in the stock's return. Thus, a stock with a beta coefficient greater than 1 will tend to be more volatile than the market. A stock with a beta coefficient less than 1 will be less volatile.

A stock's beta is determined using the statistical tools described in this chapter. The regression analysis produces b_1, which is an estimate of a stock's beta. The coefficient of determination is also an important part of the financial-statistical analysis.

▼ **EXAMPLE 17.5**

The monthly rates of return for Northern Telecom stock (Nortel) and for the overall market over a 5-year period are stored in file XM17-05. [Column 1 stores the monthly percentage return for Northern Telecom; column 2 stores the monthly percentage return for all of the stocks on the Toronto Stock Exchange (TSE).] Estimate the market model and analyze the results.

Solution

A regression analysis was performed and the Excel and Minitab outputs are shown below.

Excel Output for Example 17.5

	A	B	C	D	E	F
1	SUMMARY OUTPUT					
2						
3	*Regression Statistics*					
4	Multiple R	0.5601				
5	R Square	0.3137				
6	Adjusted R Square	0.3019				
7	Standard Error	0.06312				
8	Observations	60				
9						
10	ANOVA					
11		*df*	*SS*	*MS*	*F*	*Significance F*
12	Regression	1	0.1056	0.1056	26.51	0.0000
13	Residual	58	0.2311	0.0040		
14	Total	59	0.3367			
15						
16		*Coefficients*	*Standard Error*	*t Stat*	*P-value*	
17	Intercept	0.0128	0.0082	1.56	0.1245	
18	TSE	0.8877	0.1724	5.15	0.0000	

Minitab Output for Example 17.5

Regression Analysis

The regression equation is
Nortel = 0.0128 + 0.888 TSE

Predictor	Coef	StDev	T	P
Constant	0.012818	0.008223	1.56	0.124
TSE	0.8877	0.1724	5.15	0.000

S = 0.06312   R-Sq = 31.4%   R-Sq(adj) = 30.2%

Analysis of Variance

Source	DF	SS	MS	F	P
Regression	1	0.10563	0.10563	26.51	0.000
Residual Error	58	0.23110	0.00398		
Total	59	0.33673			

INTERPRET

We can interpret the statistics provided in the printout in the same way we've been doing thus far in this chapter. However, we're particularly interested in the financial aspects of this procedure. In particular the financial analysis focuses on two statistics, b_1 and R^2.

The slope coefficient b_1 is a measure of the stock's **market-related** (or **systematic**) **risk** because it measures the volatility of the stock price that is related to the overall market volatility.

We note that the slope coefficient for Nortel is .8877. We interpret this to mean that in this sample for each 1% increase in the TSE return, the average increase in Nortel's return is .8877%.

The coefficient of determination measures the proportion of the total risk that is market related. In this case we see that 31.37% of Nortel's total risk is market related. That is, 31.37% of the variation in Nortel's returns is explained by the variation in the TSE's returns. The remaining 68.63% is the proportion of the risk that is associated with events specific to Nortel, rather than the market. A financial analyst (and most everyone else) calls this the **firm-specific** (or **nonsystematic**) **risk.** The firm-specific risk is attributable to variables and events not included in the market model, such as the effectiveness of Nortel's sales force and managers. This is the part of the risk that can be diversified away by creating a portfolio of stocks as discussed in Section 6.7. We cannot however, diversify the part of the risk that is market related.

When a portfolio has been created, we can estimate the beta of the portfolio by averaging the betas of the stocks that compose the portfolio. If an investor believes that the market is likely to rise, a portfolio with a beta coefficient greater than 1 is desirable. Risk-averse investors or ones who believe that the market will fall will seek out portfolios with betas of less than 1.

▲

EXERCISES

The following exercises require a computer and statistical software.

17.30 Apply the market model to the monthly returns of Intel and the Standard and Poor's Composite Index for the period January 1993 to December 1996, which are stored in columns 1 and 2, respectively, in file XR17-30.

  a What is the stock's beta and what does it tell you?
  b What is the coefficient of determination? What does this statistic indicate about the stock?

17.31 The monthly returns of Motorola and the Standard and Poor's Composite Index for the period January 1993 to December 1996 are stored in columns 1 and 2, respectively, in file XR17-31. Use the market model to compute the stock's beta and the coefficient of determination. What do these statistics tell you about the stock?

17.32 In columns 1 and 2 of file XR17-32 we have stored the monthly returns of General Motors and the Standard and Poor's Composite Index for the period January 1993 to December 1996.

  a What is the stock's beta and what does it tell you?

  b What is the coefficient of determination? What does this statistic indicate about the stock?

17.33 The monthly returns of Gillette and the Standard and Poor's Composite Index for the period January 1993 to December 1996 are stored in columns 1 and 2, respectively, in file XR17-33.

  a What is the stock's beta and what does it tell you?
  b What is the coefficient of determination? What does this statistic indicate about the stock?

17.34 Apply the market model to the monthly returns of General Electric and the Standard and Poor's Composite Index for the period January 1993 to December 1996, which are stored in columns 1 and 2, respectively. Briefly describe what the stock's beta and coefficient of determination tell you about the stock.

17.35 The monthly returns of Seagram and the Standard and Poor's Composite Index for the period January 1993 to December 1996 are stored in columns 1 and 2, respectively, in file XR17-35. Apply the market model to compute the stock's beta and the coefficient of determination. Briefly describe what each statistic tells you about the stock.

17.36 Use the market model to determine how the monthly returns of Coca Cola and the Standard and Poor's Composite Index are related. The returns for the period January 1993 to December 1996 are stored in columns 1 and 2, respectively, in file XR17-36.

    a What is the stock's beta and what does it tell you?

    b What is the coefficient of determination? What does this statistic indicate about the stock?

17.37 The monthly returns of McDonald's and the Standard and Poor's Composite Index for the period January

1993 to December 1996 are stored in columns 1 and 2, respectively, in file XR17-37. Apply the market model to compute the stock's beta and the coefficient of determination. Briefly describe what each statistic tells you about the stock.

17.38 Write a report describing the analyses conducted in Exercises 17.30 to 17.37. In your report discuss which stocks are the most sensitive and which the least sensitive to changes in the index. Which stock's risk can be diversified by creating an appropriate portfolio? Explain.

17.7 USING THE REGRESSION EQUATION

Using the techniques in Section 17.5, we can assess how well the linear model fits the data. If the model fits satisfactorily, we can use it to forecast and estimate values of the dependent variable. To illustrate, suppose that in Example 17.1, the used-car dealer wanted to predict the selling price of a 3-year-old Ford Taurus with 40,000 miles on the odometer. Using the regression equation, with $x = 40,000$, we get

$$\hat{y} = 6{,}533 - 0.0312x = 6{,}533 - 0.0312(40{,}000) = 5{,}285$$

Thus, the dealer would predict that the car would sell for $5,285.

By itself, however, this value does not provide any information about how closely the value will match the true selling price. To discover that information, we must use an interval. In fact, we can use one of two intervals: the prediction interval of a particular value of y or the interval estimate of the expected value of y.

PREDICTING THE PARTICULAR VALUE OF y FOR A GIVEN x

The first interval we present is used whenever we want to predict one particular value of the dependent variable, given a specific value of the independent variable. This interval, often called the **prediction interval,** is calculated as follows.

Prediction Interval

$$\hat{y} \pm t_{\alpha/2,n-2} s_\epsilon \sqrt{1 + \frac{1}{n} + \frac{(x_g - \bar{x})^2}{(n-1)s_x^2}}$$

where x_g is the given value of x and

$$\hat{y} = b_0 + b_1 x_g$$

ESTIMATING THE EXPECTED VALUE OF y FOR A GIVEN x

The conditions described in Section 17.4 imply that for a given value of x, there is a population of values of y whose mean is

$$E(y) = \beta_0 + \beta_1 x$$

To estimate the mean of y, given x, we would use the following interval.

Interval Estimator of the Expected Value of y

$$\hat{y} \pm t_{\alpha/2,n-2} s_\epsilon \sqrt{\frac{1}{n} + \frac{(x_g - \bar{x})^2}{(n-1)s_x^2}}$$

Unlike the formula for the prediction interval described above, this formula does not include the 1 under the square-root sign. As a result, the interval estimate of the expected value of y will be narrower than the prediction interval for the same given value of x and confidence level. This is because there is less error in estimating a mean value as opposed to predicting an individual value.

▼ **EXAMPLE 17.6**

a A used-car dealer is about to bid on a 3-year-old Ford Taurus equipped with automatic transmission, air conditioner, and AM/FM cassette tape player, and with 40,000 miles on the odometer. To help him decide how much to bid, he needs to predict the selling price.
b The used-car dealer mentioned in part (a) has an opportunity to bid on a lot of cars offered by a rental company. The rental company has 250 Ford Tauruses, all equipped with automatic transmission, air conditioning, and AM/FM cassette tape players. All of the cars in this lot have about 40,000 miles on the odometer. The dealer would like an estimate of the selling price of all the cars in the lot.

Solution

IDENTIFY

a The dealer would like to predict the selling price of a *single* car. Thus, he needs to employ the prediction interval

$$\hat{y} \pm t_{\alpha/2,n-2} s_\epsilon \sqrt{1 + \frac{1}{n} + \frac{(x_g - \bar{x})^2}{(n-1)s_x^2}}$$

b The dealer wants to determine the mean price of a large lot of cars, so he needs to calculate the interval estimate of the expected value.

$$\hat{y} \pm t_{\alpha/2,n-2} s_\epsilon \sqrt{\frac{1}{n} + \frac{(x_g - \bar{x})^2}{(n-1)s_x^2}}$$

Technically, this formula is used for infinitely large populations. However, we can interpret our problem as attempting to determine the average selling price of *all* Ford Tauruses equipped as described above, all with 40,000 miles on the odometer. The critical factor in part (b) is the need to estimate the mean price of a number of cars. We arbitrarily select a 95% confidence level.

SOLVE

From previous calculations, we have the following.

$$\hat{y} = 6,533 - 0.0312x = 6,533 - 0.0312(40,000) = 5,285$$
$$s_\epsilon = 151.6, \quad s_x^2 = 43,528,690, \quad \text{and} \quad \bar{x} = 36,009$$

From Table 4 in Appendix B, we find

$$t_{.025,98} \approx 1.984$$

a The 95% prediction interval is

$$\hat{y} \pm t_{\alpha/2,n-2} s_\epsilon \sqrt{1 + \frac{1}{n} + \frac{(x_g - \bar{x})^2}{(n - 1)s_x^2}}$$

$$= 5{,}285 \pm 1.984 \times 151.6 \sqrt{1 + \frac{1}{100} + \frac{(40{,}000 - 36{,}009)^2}{(100 - 1)(43{,}528{,}690)}}$$

$$= 5{,}285 \pm 303$$

The lower and upper limits of the prediction interval are 4,982 and 5,588, respectively.

b The 95% confidence interval estimate of the expected selling price is

$$\hat{y} \pm t_{\alpha/2,n-2} s_\epsilon \sqrt{\frac{1}{n} + \frac{(x_g - \bar{x})^2}{(n - 1)s_x^2}}$$

$$= 5{,}285 \pm 1.984 \times 151.6 \sqrt{\frac{1}{100} + \frac{(40{,}000 - 36{,}009)^2}{(100 - 1)(43{,}528{,}690)}}$$

$$= 5{,}285 \pm 35$$

The lower and upper limits of the interval estimate of the expected value are 5,250 and 5,320, respectively.

Excel Output for Example 17.6

	A	B	C	D
1	0.95	Prediction Interval		
2				
3	Predicted value =		5287.1	
4	Lower limit =		4984.2	
5	Upper limit =		5589.9	
6				
7	0.95	Confidence Interval Estimate		
8				
9	Lower limit =		5251.9	
10	Upper limit =		5322.3	

COMMANDS

1 Type or import the data into two columns.

2 Type the given value of x into any cell. We suggest the next available row in the column containing the independent variable.

3 Click **Tools, Data Analysis Plus,** and **Prediction Interval.**

4 Specify the input range of the dependent variable, the independent variable (Do not include cells containing the variable names.), the given value of x, and the confidence level. Click **OK.**

COMMANDS FOR EXAMPLE 17.6

Open file **XM17-01.**

40000 (in cell A102)

B2:B101
A2:A101
A102
.95

Minitab Output for Example 17.6

```
Predicted Values

      Fit  StDev Fit        95.0% CI            95.0% PI
   5287.1       17.7  (  5251.9,  5322.3) (  4984.2,  5589.9
```

The output includes the calculated value of y (**Fit**), the standard deviation of y (**Stdev.Fit**), which is

$$s_\epsilon = \sqrt{\frac{1}{n} + \frac{(x_g - \bar{x})^2}{(n-1)s_x^2}}$$

the 95% confidence interval estimate of the expected value of y (**95.0% CI**), and the 95% prediction interval (**95.0% PI**).

COMMANDS	COMMANDS FOR EXAMPLE 17.6
1 Proceed through the first four steps of regression analysis described on page 633. Do not click **OK.**	
2 Click **Options . . . .**	
3 Specify the given value(s) of x (**Prediction intervals for new observations**).	**40000**
4 Specify the **Confidence level**. Click **OK.**	**95**

INTERPRET

We predict that one car will sell for between $4,984.20 and $5,589.90. The average selling price of the population of 3-year-old Ford Tauruses is estimated to lie between $5,251.90 and $5,322.30. Because predicting the selling price of one car is more difficult than estimating the mean selling price of all similar cars, the prediction interval is wider than the interval estimate of the expected value.

THE EFFECT OF THE GIVEN VALUE OF x ON THE INTERVALS

If the two intervals were calculated for various values of x and graphed, Figure 17.6 would be produced. Notice that both intervals are represented by curved lines. This is due to the fact that the farther the given value of x is from $\bar{x}$, the greater the estimation error becomes. This factor is measured by

$$\frac{(x_g - \bar{x})^2}{(n-1)s_x^2}$$

which appears in both the prediction interval and the interval estimate.

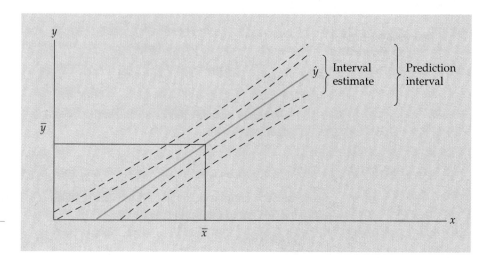

Figure 17.6

Interval estimates and
prediction intervals

EXERCISES

*The following exercises require the use of a computer and
software. The answers may be calculated manually. See Appendix A for the sample statistics.*

17.39 Briefly describe the difference between predicting a
value of *y* and estimating the expected value of *y*.

17.40 Refer to Exercise 17.2. A statistician wants to predict
the height of a man whose father is 72 inches tall.
What formula should be used? Produce such an interval using a confidence level of 99%.

17.41 Refer to Exercise 17.3. Predict with 95% confidence
the number of housing starts when the mortgage rate is
8%.

17.42 Refer to Exercise 17.6.

   a Predict with 95% confidence the memory test score
   of a viewer who watches a 36-second commercial.

   b Estimate with 95% confidence the mean memory
   test score of people who watch 36-second commercials.

17.43 Refer to Exercise 17.7.

   a Predict with 90% confidence the final mark of a student who studies for 25 hours.

   b Estimate with 90% confidence the average mark of
   all students who study for 25 hours.

17.44 Refer to Exercise 17.8 Estimate with 90% confidence
the mean amount of time spent on the Internet by people with 15 years of education.

17.45 Refer to Exercise 17.9. The company has just hired a
25 year-old telemarketer. Predict with 95% confidence
how long he will stay with the company.

17.46 Refer to Exercise 17.10. Predict with 90% confidence
the price of a barrel of oil if the API is 42.0.

17.47 Refer to Exercise 17.11.

   a Predict with 95% confidence the daily emergency
   medical expense of a 65-year-old Canadian.

   b Estimate with 95% confidence the mean daily emergency medical expense of all 65-year-old Canadians.

17.48 Refer to Exercise 17.12. Predict with 90% confidence
the price of a diamond that weighs .35 carats.

17.49 Refer to Exercise 17.27. Predict with 95% confidence
the monthly office rent in a city when the vacancy rate
is 10%.

17.50 Refer to Exercise 17.28.

   a Predict with 95% confidence the reduction in cholesterol level of an individual who plans to exercise
   for 300 minutes per week for a total of 4 months.

   b Suppose that an individual whose cholesterol level
   is 250 is planning to exercise for 250 minutes per
   week. Predict with 95% confidence his cholesterol
   level after 4 months.

17.8 COEFFICIENTS OF CORRELATION

In Section 17.5, we noted that the coefficient of determination is the coefficient of correlation squared. When we introduced the coefficient of correlation (also called the **Pearson coefficient of correlation**) in Chapter 4, we pointed out that it is used to measure the strength of linear association between two variables. Why then do we use the coefficient of determination as our measure of the regression model's fit? The answer: The coefficient of determination is a better measure than the coefficient of correlation because the values of R^2 can be interpreted precisely. That is, R^2 is defined as the proportion of the variation in y that is explained by the variation in x. Except for $r = -1$, 0, and 1, the coefficient of correlation cannot be interpreted. (When $r = -1$ or 1, every point falls on the regression line, and when $r = 0$, there is no linear pattern.) However, the coefficient of correlation can be useful in another way. We can use it to test for a relationship between two variables.

In cases where we're interested in determining *how* the independent variable affects the dependent variable, we estimate and test the linear regression model. The *t*-test of the slope presented in Section 17.5 allows us to determine whether a linear relationship actually exists. As we pointed out in Section 17.4, the statistical test requires that for each value of x, there exists a population of values of y that are normally distributed with a constant variance. This condition is required whether the data are experimental or observational.

In many circumstances we're interested in determining only *whether* a linear relationship exists and not the form of the relationship. When the data are observational and the two variables are bivariate normally distributed (see Section 17.4) we can calculate the coefficient of correlation and use it to test for linear association.

As we noted in Chapter 4, the population coefficient of correlation is denoted ρ (the Greek letter *rho*). Because ρ is a population parameter (which is almost always unknown), we must estimate its value from the sample data. Recall that the sample coefficient of correlation is defined as follows.

Sample Coefficient of Correlation

$$r = \frac{\text{cov}(X, Y)}{s_x s_y}$$

TESTING THE COEFFICIENT OF CORRELATION

When there is no linear relationship between the two variables $\rho = 0$. To determine whether we can infer that ρ is zero, we test the following hypotheses.

H_0: $\rho = 0$

H_1: $\rho \neq 0$

The test statistic is defined in the following way.*

---

*This test statistic is used only when testing $\rho = 0$. To test other values, another test statistic must be employed.

> ### Test Statistic for Testing $\rho = 0$
>
> $$t = r\sqrt{\frac{n-2}{1-r^2}}$$
>
> which is Student t distributed with $n - 2$ degrees of freedom, provided that the variables are bivariate normally distributed.

▼ **EXAMPLE 17.7**

Using the data in Example 17.1, test to determine whether we can infer that a linear relationship exists by testing the population correlation coefficient. Use a 5% significance level.

Solution   We test the hypotheses

$$H_0: \rho = 0$$
$$H_1: \rho \neq 0$$

SOLVE

The rejection region of the test is

$$t > t_{\alpha/2,n-2} = t_{.025,98} \approx 1.984 \qquad \text{or} \qquad t < -t_{.025,98} = -1.984$$

The value of r is calculated using the statistics already computed from earlier examples.

$$r = \frac{\text{cov}(X, Y)}{s_x s_y} = \frac{-1,356,256}{(6597.6)(254.9)} = -.806$$

The value of the test statistic is

$$t = r\sqrt{\frac{n-2}{1-r^2}} = (-.806)\sqrt{\frac{100-2}{1-(-.806)^2}} = -13.49$$

Excel Output for Example 17.7

	A	B	C
1		Odometer	Price
2	Odometer	1	
3	Price	-0.806	1

Excel prints the coefficient of correlation. The test can be completed manually.

COMMAND	COMMANDS FOR EXAMPLE 17.7
1 Type or import the data into two adjacent columns.	Open file **XM17-01**.
2 Click **Tools, Data Analysis . . .** , and **Correlation.**	
3 Specify the **Input Range.** Click **Labels in First Row** (if necessary). Click **OK.**	A1:B101

**Minitab Output
for Example 17.7**

Correlations (Pearson)

Correlation of Odometer and Price = 0.806, P-Value = 0.000

COMMANDS   COMMANDS FOR EXAMPLE 17.7

1 Type or import the data into two   Open file **XM17-01**.
columns.
2 Click **Stat, Basic Statistics,** and
Correlation . . . .
3 Type the variable names. Click **OK.**   **Price Odometer** or **C1 C2**

INTERPRET   There is overwhelming evidence to infer that the two variables are linearly related.

▲

If you review Example 17.3 where we tested the slope coefficient β_1, you will find
the same value of the test statistic, the same rejection region, and, of course, the same
conclusion as we produced earlier. This is not a coincidence; the two tests are identical. This should be no surprise, since data are the same and the objective is the same:
to determine whether two variables are linearly related. Hence, it is necessary to perform only one test, either the t-test of β_1 or the t-test of ρ. (We performed both tests
to show you that they are identical.)

SPEARMAN RANK CORRELATION COEFFICIENT

In the previous sections of this chapter, we have dealt only with quantitative variables and have assumed that all of the conditions for the validity of the hypothesis
tests and interval estimates have been met. In many situations, however, one or both
variables may be ranked; or if both variables are quantitative, the normality requirement may not be satisfied. In such cases, we measure and test to determine if a relationship exists by employing a nonparametric technique, the **Spearman rank correlation coefficient.**

The Spearman rank correlation coefficient is calculated like all of the previously
introduced nonparametric methods by first ranking the data. We then calculate the
Pearson correlation coefficient of the ranks.

The population Spearman correlation coefficient is labeled ρ_s, and the sample statistic used to estimate its value is labeled r_s.

> **Sample Spearman Rank Correlation Coefficient**
>
> $$r_s = \frac{\text{cov}(a, b)}{s_a s_b}$$
>
> where a and b are the ranks of the data.

We can test to determine if a relationship exists between the two variables. The
hypotheses to be tested are

$$H_0: \rho_s = 0$$
$$H_1: \rho_s \neq 0$$

(We also can conduct one-tail tests.) The test statistic is r_s. To determine whether the value of r_s is large enough to reject the null hypothesis, we refer to Table 11 in Appendix B, which lists the critical values of the test statistic for one-tail tests. To conduct a two-tail test, the value of α must be doubled. The table lists critical values for $\alpha =$ .005, .01, .025, and .05 and for $n = 5$ to 30. When n is greater than 30, r_s is approximately normally distributed with mean 0 and standard deviation $1/\sqrt{n-1}$. Thus, for $n > 30$, the test statistic is

$$z = \frac{r_s - 0}{1/\sqrt{n-1}} = r_s\sqrt{n-1}$$

Test Statistic for Testing $\rho_s = 0$ When $n > 30$

$$z = r_s\sqrt{n-1}$$

which is standard normally distributed.

▼ **EXAMPLE 17.8**

The production manager of a firm wants to examine the relationship between aptitude test scores given prior to hiring of production-line workers and performance ratings received by the employees three months after starting work. The results of the study would allow the firm to decide how much weight to give to these aptitude tests relative to other work-history information obtained, including references. The aptitude test results range from 0 to 100. The performance ratings are as follows.

1 = Employee has performed well below average.
2 = Employee has performed somewhat below average.
3 = Employee has performed at the average level.
4 = Employee has performed somewhat above average.
5 = Employee has performed well above average.

A random sample of 20 production workers yielded the results listed below and stored in columns 1 and 2 of file XM17-08. Can the firm's manager infer at the 5% significance level that aptitude test scores are correlated with performance rating?

Employee	Aptitude Test Score	Performance Rating
1	59	3
2	47	2
3	58	4
4	66	3
5	77	2
6	57	4
7	62	3
8	68	3
9	69	5
10	36	1
11	48	3

(continued)

Employee	Aptitude Test Score	Performance Rating
12	65	3
13	51	2
14	61	3
15	40	3
16	67	4
17	60	2
18	56	3
19	76	3
20	71	5

Solution

IDENTIFY

The problem objective is to analyze the relationship between two variables. The aptitude test score is quantitative, but the performance rating is ranked. We will treat the aptitude test score as if it is ranked and calculate the Spearman rank correlation coefficient.

To answer the question, we specify the hypotheses as

H_0: $\rho_s = 0$

H_1: $\rho_s \neq 0$

With $\alpha = .05$ and $n = 20$, the rejection region (from Table 11 in Appendix B) is

$r_s > .450$ or $r_s < -.450$

SOLVE

We rank each of the variables separately, averaging any ties that we encounter. The original data and ranks are as follows.

Employee	Aptitude Test Score	Rank (a)	Performance Rating	Rank (b)
1	59	9	3	10.5
2	47	3	2	3.5
3	58	8	4	17.0
4	66	14	3	10.5
5	77	20	2	3.5
6	57	7	4	17.0
7	62	12	3	10.5
8	68	16	3	10.5
9	69	17	5	19.5
10	36	1	1	1.0
11	48	4	3	10.5
12	65	13	3	10.5
13	51	5	2	3.5
14	61	11	3	10.5
15	40	2	3	10.5
16	67	15	4	17.0
17	60	10	2	3.5
18	56	6	3	10.5
19	76	19	3	10.5
20	71	18	5	19.5

We use the ranks (a) and (b) to compute the Pearson coefficient of correlation. We need to compute s_a, s_b, and cov(a,b). They are

$$s_a = 5.92$$

$$s_b = 5.50$$

$$\text{cov}(a, b) = 12.34$$

Thus,

$$r_s = \frac{\text{cov}(a,b)}{s_a\, s_b} = \frac{12.34}{(5.92)(5.50)} = .379$$

Excel Output for Example 17.8

	A	B	C
1	**Spearman Rank Correlation**		
2			
3	*Correlation Coefficient = 0.3792*		
4	*Test Statistic: Z = 1.653*		
5	*Two-tail P-Value = 0.0983*		

The Spearman coefficient of correlation is .379. Because $n < 30$, we ignore the other statistics.

COMMANDS	COMMANDS FOR EXAMPLE 17.8
1 Type or import the data into two adjacent columns	Open file **XM17-08.**
2 Click **Tools, Data Analysis Plus,** and **Spearman Rank Correlation.**	
3 Specify the **Input Range.** Do not include cells containing the variable names.	**A2:B21**

Minitab Output for Example 17.8

Correlations (Pearson)

```
Correlation of Rank Apt and Rank Perf = 0.379,
P-Value = 0.099
```

The original quantitative data were stored in columns 1 and 2. Minitab ranked each variable and stored the ranks in columns 3 and 4. The Pearson correlation coefficient of the ranks was found to be .379. Ignore the printed *p*-value.

COMMANDS	COMMANDS FOR EXAMPLE 17.8
1 Type or import the data into two columns.	Open file **XM17-08.**
2 Click **Manip** and **Rank . . . .**	
3 Type the name of the first variable (arbitrary choice).	**Aptitude** or **C1**
4 Hit **tab** and specify the column where the ranks are to be stored. Click **OK.**	**C3**

5 Click **Manip** and **Rank** and repeat step 2 for the second variable. Click **OK.**	Prfrmnce or **C2** **C4**
6 Click **Stat, Basic Statistics,** and **Correlation . . . .**	
7 Type the names of the ranked variables. Click **OK.**	**C3 C4**

INTERPRET

There is not enough evidence to believe that the aptitude test scores and performance ratings are related. This conclusion suggests that the aptitude test should be improved to better measure the knowledge and skill required by a production-line worker. If this proves impossible, the aptitude test should be discarded.

▲

EXERCISES

17.51 Given the following data

x	115	220	86	99	50	110
y	1.0	1.3	0.6	0.8	0.5	0.7

a Calculate the Pearson correlation coefficient, and test to determine whether we can infer that a linear relationship exists between the two variables. (Use $\alpha = .05$.)

b Calculate the Spearman rank correlation coefficient, and test to determine whether we can infer that a linear relationship exists between the two variables. (Use $\alpha = .05$.)

17.52 The weekly returns of two stocks are recorded for a 13-week period. These data are stored in file XR17-52 and listed below.

a Assuming that the returns are normally distributed, can we infer at the 5% significance level that the stocks are correlated?

b Assuming that the returns are not normally distributed, can we infer at the 5% significance level that the stocks are correlated?

Week	1	2	3	4	5	6	7	8	9	10	11	12	13
Stock 1	−7	−4	−7	−3	2	−10	−10	5	1	−4	2	6	−13
Stock 2	6	6	−4	9	3	−3	7	−3	4	7	9	5	−7

17.53 The general manager of an engineering firm wants to know if a draftsman's experience influences the quality of his work. She selects 24 draftsmen at random and records their years of work experience and their quality rating (as assessed by their supervisors). These data are stored in file XR17-53 (column 1 = work experience in years; column 2 = quality rating where 5 =

excellent; 4 = very good; 3 = average; 2 = fair; 1 = poor) and listed below. Can we infer from these data that years of work experience is a factor in determining the quality of work performed? Use $\alpha = .10$.

DRAFTSMAN	EXPERIENCE	RATING	DRAFTSMAN	EXPERIENCE	RATING
1	1	1	13	8	2
2	17	4	14	20	5
3	20	4	15	21	3
4	9	5	16	19	2
5	2	2	17	1	1
6	13	4	18	22	3
7	9	3	19	20	4
8	23	5	20	11	3
9	7	2	21	18	5
10	10	5	22	14	4
11	12	5	23	21	3
12	24	2	24	21	1

The following exercises require the use of a computer and software.

17.54 Refer to Exercise 17.6.

a Determine the coefficient of correlation.

b Test the coefficient of correlation to determine whether a linear relationship exists between the length of commercial and memory test score. Use $\alpha = .05$.

c Assume that the conditions for the test conducted in Exercise 17.6 are not met. Do the data allow us to conclude that the longer the commercial, the higher the memory test score will be?

17.55 Assume that the normality requirement in Exercise 17.7 is not met. Test to determine whether grade and study time are positively related.

17.56 Refer to Exercise 17.8.

  a Determine the coefficient of correlation.

  b Test the coefficient of correlation to determine whether a linear relationship exists between Internet use and education. Use $\alpha = .10$.

  c Assume that the conditions for the test conducted in Exercise 17.8 are not met. Do the data allow us to conclude that people with more education use the Internet more? Use $\alpha = .10$.

17.57 If the normality requirement in Exercise 17.9 has been violated, can we infer at the 5% significance level that age and work period are related?

17.58 Assume that the price and quality of the oil in Exercise 17.10 are not bivariate normally distributed. Conduct a

test (with $\alpha = .10$) to determine whether the higher prices are related to higher quality.

17.59 Refer to Exercise 17.11.

  a Determine the coefficient of correlation.

  b Test the coefficient of correlation to determine whether a linear relationship exists between age and average medical expense. Use $\alpha = .05$.

  c Assume that the normality requirement of the test conducted in Exercise 17.11 is not met. Do the data allow us to conclude at the 5% significance level that older Canadians incur higher medical expenses?

17.60 Refer to Exercise 17.12. If we assume that price and weight are not bivariate normally distributed can we infer that the two variables are related? Use $\alpha = .10$.

17.9 REGRESSION DIAGNOSTICS—I

In Section 17.4, we described the required conditions for the validity of regression analysis. Simply put, the error variable must be normally distributed with a constant variance, and the errors must be independent of each other. In this section, we show how to diagnose violations. Additionally, we discuss how to deal with observations that are unusually large or small. Such observations must be investigated to determine if an error was made in recording them.

RESIDUAL ANALYSIS

Most departures from required conditions can be diagnosed by examining the residuals, which we discussed in Section 17.5. Most computer packages allow you to output the values of the residuals and apply various graphical and statistical techniques to this variable.

We can also compute the standardized residuals. We standardize residuals in the same way we standardize all variables, by subtracting the mean and dividing by the standard deviation. The mean of the residuals is zero and because the standard deviation σ_ϵ is unknown, we must estimate its value. The simplest estimate is the standard error of estimate s_ϵ. Thus

$$\text{Standardized residuals for point } i = \frac{r_i}{s_\epsilon}$$

Excel calculates the standardized residuals by dividing the residuals by the standard deviation of the residuals. (The difference between the standard error of estimate and the standard deviation of the residuals is that in the formula of the former the denominator is $n - 2$, whereas in the formula for the latter, the denominator is $n - 1$.)

Part of the printout for Example 17.1 follows.

Excel Printout of Predicted Values, Residuals and Standardized Residuals for Example 17.1

	A	B	C	D
1	Observation	Predicted Price	Residuals	Standard Residuals
2	1	5368.46	-50.46	-0.3346
3	2	5138.82	-77.82	-0.5161
4	3	5105.33	-97.33	-0.6454
5	4	5571.79	223.21	1.4801
6	5	5545.53	238.47	1.5814
7				
8				
9				
10	96	5404.29	19.71	0.1307
11	97	5467.41	-184.41	-1.2229
12	98	5499.26	-240.26	-1.5932
13	99	5312.12	43.88	0.2910
14	100	5399.49	-266.49	-1.7672

COMMANDS

Proceed with the first 4 steps of regression analysis described on page 631. Before clicking **OK,** select **Residuals** and **Standardized Residuals.** The predicted values, residuals, and standardized residuals will be printed.

We can also standardize by computing the standard deviation of each residual. Mathematicians have determined that the standard deviation of the residual at point i is defined as follows.

Standard Deviation of the *i*th Residual

$$s_{r_i} = s_\epsilon \sqrt{1 - h_i}$$

where

$$h_i = \frac{1}{n} + \frac{(x_i - \bar{x})^2}{(n - 1)s_x^2}$$

The quantity h_i should look familiar; it was used in the formula for the prediction interval and the interval estimate of the expected value of y in Section 17.7. Minitab computes this version of the standardized residuals. Part of the printout for Example 17.1 follows.

Minitab Printout of Predicted Values, Residuals and Standardized Residuals for Example 17.1

Odometer	Price	FITS1	RESI1	SRES1
37388	5318	5368.46	-50.457	-0.33465
44758	5051	5138.82	-77.825	-0.52074
45833	5008	5105.33	-97.330	-0.65281
30862	5795	5571.79	223.207	1.48468
31705	5784	5545.53	238.473	1.58474
36238	5424	5404.29	19.711	0.13070
34212	5283	5467.41	-184.414	-1.22330
33190	5259	5499.26	-240.258	-1.59461
39196	5356	5312.12	43.876	0.29128
36392	5133	5399.49	-266.491	-1.76710

COMMANDS

Proceed with the first four steps of regression analysis as described on page 633. After specifying the **Response** and **Predictors**, click **Storage . . ., Fits, Residuals,** and **Standardized residuals.** The predicted values, residuals, and standardized residuals will be stored in the next three available columns.

An analysis of the residuals will allow us to determine if the error variable is non-normal, whether the error variance is constant, and whether the errors are independent. We begin with nonnormality.

NONNORMALITY

As we've done throughout this book, we check for normality by drawing the histogram of the residuals. Excel's version is shown below (Minitab's is similar). As you can see the histogram is bell shaped, leading us to believe that the error is normally distributed.

Excel Histogram of Residuals for Example 17.1

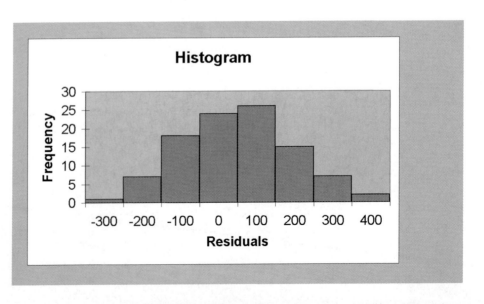

We also applied the Lilliefors test as well as the chi-squared test of normality both of whose outputs are exhibited below.

Excel Output of the Lilliefors Test of Residuals for Example 17.1

	A	B
1	**Lilliefors Test**	
2		
3	*Lilliefors Test Statistic*	
4	*D = 0.0584*	

Note: The critical value (at the 5% significance level) is $D = .0886$.

Excel Output of the Chi-Squared Test of Residuals for Example 17.1

	A	B	C	D
1	**Chi-Squared Test of Normality**			
2				
3	*Mean*	0.00		
4	*Standard deviation*	150.8		
5	*Observations*	100		
6				
7	**Intervals**	**Probability**	**Expected**	**Observed**
8	(z <= -1.5)	0.0668	6.68	6
9	(-1.5 < z <= -0.5)	0.2417	24.17	26
10	(-0.5 < z <= 0.5)	0.3829	38.29	37
11	(0.5 < z <= 1.5)	0.2417	24.17	25
12	(z > 1.5)	0.0668	6.68	6
13				
14				
15	*Chi-Squared Stat*	0.3487		
16	*P-Value*	0.8400		

Both tests do not allow us to infer that the error variable is not normally distributed.

HETEROSCEDASTICITY

The variance of the error variable σ_ϵ^2 is required to be constant. When this requirement is violated, the condition is called **heteroscedasticity.** (You can impress friends and relatives by using this term. If you can't pronounce it, try **homoscedasticity,** which refers to the condition where the requirement is satisfied.) One method of diagnosing heteroscedasticity is to plot the residuals against the predicted values of y. We then look for a change in the spread of the plotted points. Figure 17.7 describes such a situation. Notice that, in this illustration, σ_ϵ^2 appears to be small when $\hat{y}$ is small and large when $\hat{y}$ is large. Of course, many other patterns could be used to depict this problem.

Figure 17.8 illustrates a case in which σ_ϵ^2 is constant. As a result, there is no apparent change in the variation of the residuals.

Excel's plot of the residuals versus the predicted values of y for Example 17.1 is shown on the next page. There does appear to be a decrease in the variance for larger values of $\hat{y}$. However, it is far from clear that there is a problem here.

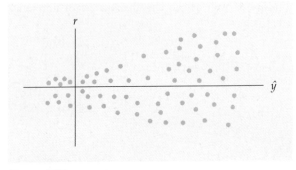

Figure 17.7

Plot of residuals depicting heteroscedasticity

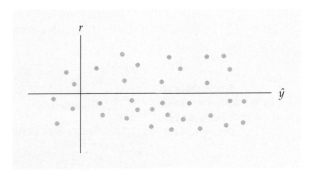

Figure 17.8

Plot of residuals depicting homoscedasticity

Excel Plot of Predicted Values Versus Residuals for Example 17.1

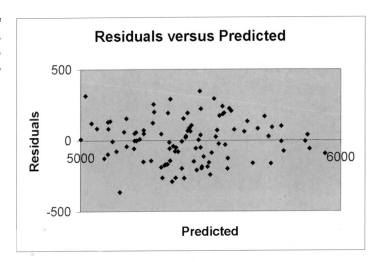

NONINDEPENDENCE OF THE ERROR VARIABLE

In Chapter 2, we briefly described the difference between cross-sectional and time series data. Cross-sectional data are observations made at approximately the same time, whereas a time series is a set of observations taken at successive points of time. The data in Example 17.1 are cross sectional because all of the prices and odometer readings were taken at about the same time. If we were to observe the auction price of cars every week for (say) a year, that would constitute a time series.

Condition 4 states that the values of the error variable are independent. When the data are time series, the errors often are correlated. Error terms that are correlated over time are said to be **autocorrelated** or **serially correlated.** For example, suppose that, in an analysis of the relationship between annual gross profits and some independent variable, we observe the gross profits for the years 1980 to 1999. The observed values of y are denoted $y_1, y_2, \ldots, y_{20}$, where y_1 is the gross profit for 1980, y_2 is the gross profit for 1981, and so on. If we label the residuals $r_1, r_2, \ldots, r_{20}$, then—if the independence requirement is satisfied—there should be no relationship among the residuals. However, if the residuals are related, it is likely that autocorrelation exists.

We can often detect autocorrelation by graphing the residuals against the time periods. If a pattern emerges, it is likely that the independence requirement is violated. Figures 17.9 (alternating positive and negative residuals) and 17.10 (increasing

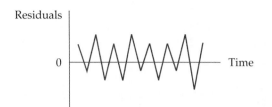

Figure 17.9

Plot of residuals versus time indicating autocorrelation
(alternating)

Figure 17.10

Plot of residuals versus time indicating autocorrelation
(increasing)

Figure 17.11

Plot of residuals versus time indicating independence

residuals) exhibit patterns indicating autocorrelation. (Notice that we joined the points
to make it easier to see the patterns.) Figure 17.11 shows no pattern (the residuals
appear to be randomly distributed over the time periods), and thus, likely represents
the occurrence of independent errors.

In Chapter 18, we introduce the Durbin–Watson test, which is another statistical
test to determine if one form of this problem is present.

We also describe a number of remedies to violations of the required conditions
in Chapter 18.

OUTLIERS

An outlier is an observation that is unusually small or unusually large. To illustrate,
consider Example 17.1, where the range of odometer readings was 19,057 to 49,223
miles. If we had observed a value of 5,000 miles, we would identify that point as an
outlier. There are several possibilities that we need to investigate.

1 There was an error in recording the value.

To detect an error we would check the point or points in question. In Example
17.1, we could check the car's odometer to determine if a mistake was made.
If so, we would correct it before proceeding with the regression analysis.

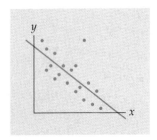

Figure 17.12

Scatter diagram with one outlier

2 The point should not have been included in the sample.

Occasionally, measurements are taken from experimental units that do not belong with the sample. We can check to ensure that the car with the 5,000-mile odometer reading was actually 3 years old. We should also investigate the possibility that the odometer was rolled back. In either case, the outlier should be discarded.

3 The observation was simply an unusually large or small value that belongs to the sample and that was recorded properly.

In this case we would do nothing to the outlier. It would be judged to be valid.

Outliers can be identified from the scatter diagram. Figure 17.12 depicts a scatter diagram with one outlier. The statistician should check to determine if the measurement was recorded accurately and whether the experimental unit should be included in the sample.

The standardized residuals also can be helpful in identifying outliers. Large absolute values of the standardized residuals should be thoroughly investigated. Minitab automatically reports standardized residuals that are less than -2 and greater than 2.

INFLUENTIAL OBSERVATIONS

Occasionally, in a regression analysis, one or more observations have a large influence on the statistics. Figure 17.13 describes such an observation and the resulting least squares line. If the point had not been included, the least squares line in Figure 17.14 would have been produced. Obviously, one point has had an enormous influence on the results. Influential points can be identified by the scatter diagram. The point may be an outlier and as such must be investigated thoroughly. Minitab also identifies influential observations.

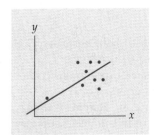

Figure 17.13

Scatter diagram with one influential observation

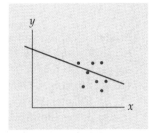

Figure 17.14

Scatter diagram without the influential observation

On page 632, we showed the Minitab output for Example 17.1. We intentionally omitted the last part of this output, but present it now. Minitab lists unusual observations, which consist of observations with large standardized residuals (marked R) and observations whose values of x give them a large influence (marked X). These are the points to be checked for accuracy and to ensure that the observations belong to the sample.

Minitab List of Unusual Observations

```
Unusual Observations
Obs     Odometer      Price     Fit     StDev    Fit Residual    St Resid
  8       19057      5845.0   5939.6    42.0         -94.6       -0.65 X
 14       34470      5805.0   5459.4    15.6         345.6        2.29 R
 19       48613      5333.0   5018.7    32.8         314.3        2.12 R
 63       21221      5911.0   5872.2    37.4          38.8        0.26 X
 74       20962      5820.0   5880.3    37.9         -60.3       -0.41 X
 78       44330      4787.0   5152.2    24.5        -365.2       -2.44 R
```

R denotes an observation with a large standardized residual.
X denotes an observation whose X value gives it large influence.

Points 14, 19, and 78 have standardized residuals that are greater than |2|, and so are judged to be unusual. Notice that points 8, 63, and 74 are identified as points that have a large influence. These three points are the three smallest odometer readings. Their removal would change the regression equation in a substantive way.

PROCEDURE FOR REGRESSION DIAGNOSTICS

The order of the material presented in this chapter is dictated by pedagogical requirements. Consequently, we presented the least squares method, methods of assessing the model's fit, predicting and estimating using the regression equation, coefficients of correlation, and finally, the regression diagnostics. In a practical application, the regression diagnostics would be conducted earlier in the process. It is appropriate to investigate violations of the required conditions when the model is assessed and before using the regression equation to predict and estimate. The following steps describe the entire process. (In Chapter 19, we will discuss model building, for which the following steps represent only a part of the entire procedure.)

1 Develop a model that has a theoretical basis. That is, for the dependent variable in question find an independent variable that you believe is linearly related to it.

2 Gather data for the two variables. Ideally, conduct a controlled experiment. If that is not possible, collect observational data.

3 Draw the scatter diagram to determine whether a linear model appears to be appropriate. Identify possible outliers.

4 Determine the regression equation.

5 Calculate the residuals and check the required conditions.
  Is the error variable nonnormal?
  Is the variance constant?
  Are the errors independent?
  Check the outliers and influential observations.

6 Assess the model's fit.
  Compute the standard error of estimate.
  Test to determine whether there is a linear relationship. (Test β_1 or ρ.)
  Compute the coefficient of determination.

7 If the model fits the data, use the regression equation to predict a particular value of the dependent variable and/or estimate its mean.

E X E R C I S E S

17.61 Given the following six points

x	−5	−2	0	3	4	7
y	15	9	7	6	4	1

   a Determine the regression equation.
   b Use the regression equation to determine the predicted values of y.
   c Use the predicted and actual values of y to calculate the residuals.
   d Compute the standardized residuals.
   e Identify possible outliers.

17.62 The observation of two variables was recorded as shown below.

x	1	2	3	4	5	6	7	8	9
y	5	28	17	14	27	33	39	26	30

   a Compute the regression equation.
   b Use the regression equation to determine the predicted values of y.
   c Use the predicted and actual values of y to calculate the residuals. Compute the standardized residuals.
   d Identify possible outliers.
   e Plot the residuals against the predicted values of y. Does the variance appear to be constant? Explain.

17.63 Each of the following pairs of values represents an actual value of y and a predicted value of y (based on a simple regression model). Graph the predicted values of y (on the horizontal axis) versus the residuals (on the vertical axis). In each case, determine from the graph whether the requirement that the variance of the error variable be constant is satisfied.

   a

y	155	112	163	130	143	182
	160	104	125	161	189	102
	142	149	180			

$\hat{y}$	143	108	180	133	146	193
	140	101	126	176	200	97
	145	151	158			

b

y	10	22	29	15	24
	13	17	23	11	27
	19	26	20	14	

$\hat{y}$	7	21	29	13	25
	16	19	22	14	27
	17	27	22	11	

c

y	46	40	53	60	56	62	44	49	52
	59	45	55	47	61	42	57	50	

$\hat{y}$	48	43	54	63	54	65	46	47	49
	56	41	53	44	57	45	62	51	

The following exercises require the use of a computer and software.

17.64 Refer to Exercise 17.6.

   a Determine the residuals and the standardized residuals.
   b Draw the histogram of the residuals. Does it appear that the errors are normally distributed? Explain.
   c Identify possible outliers.
   d Plot the residuals versus the predicted values of y. Does it appear that heteroscedasticity is a problem? Explain.

17.65 Refer to Exercise 17.7.

   a Does it appear that the errors are normally distributed? Explain.
   b Does it appear that heteroscedasticity is a problem? Explain.

17.66 Are the required conditions satisfied in Exercise 17.8?

17.67 Refer to Exercise 17.9.

   a Determine the residuals and the standardized residuals.
   b Draw the histogram of the residuals. Does it appear that the errors are normally distributed? Explain.
   c Identify possible outliers.
   d Plot the residuals versus the predicted values of y. Does it appear that heteroscedasticity is a problem? Explain.

17.68 Refer to Exercise 17.11. Are the required conditions satisfied?

17.10 SUMMARY

Simple linear regression and correlation are techniques for analyzing the relationship between two quantitative variables. Regression analysis assumes that the two variables are linearly related. The least squares method produces estimates of the intercept and the slope of the regression line. Considerable effort is expended in assessing how well the linear model fits the data. We calculate the standard error of estimate, which is an estimate of the standard deviation of the error variable. We test the slope to determine whether there is sufficient evidence of a linear relationship. The strength of the linear association is measured by the coefficient of determination. When the model provides a good fit, we can use it to predict the particular value and to estimate the expected value of the dependent variable. We can also use the Pearson correlation coefficient to measure and test the relationship between two normally distributed variables. The Spearman rank correlation coefficient analyzes the relationship between two variables, at least one of which is ranked. It can also be used when the variables are nonnormal. We completed this chapter with a discussion of how to diagnose violations of the required conditions.

IMPORTANT TERMS

Regression analysis   *626*
Dependent variable   *626*
Independent variable   *626*
Deterministic model   *628*
Probabilistic model   *628*
First-order linear model   *628*
Simple linear regression model   *628*
Scatter diagram   *629*
Least squares method   *629*
Error variable   *636*
Residuals   *664*
Sum of squares for error   *639*
Standard error of estimate   *640*
Coefficient of determination   *644*
Sum of squares for regression   *645*

Market model   *649*
Beta coefficient   *649*
Market-related (systematic) risk   *651*
Firm-specific (nonsystematic) risk   *651*
Prediction interval   *652*
Interval estimate of mean of *y*   *653*
Pearson coefficient of correlation   *657*
Spearman rank correlation coefficient   *659*
Heteroscedasticity   *667*
Homoscedasticity   *667*
Autocorrelation   *668*
Outlier   *669*
Influential observation   *670*

SUPPLEMENTARY EXERCISES

The following exercises require the use of a computer and software. The answers for Exercises 17.69 and 17.70 may be calculated manually. See Appendix A for the sample statistics.

17.69 The manager of Colonial Furniture has been reviewing weekly advertising expenditures. During the past 6 months all advertisements for the store have appeared in the local newspaper. The number of ads per week has varied from one to seven. The store's sales staff has been tracking the number of customers who enter the store each week. The number of ads and the number of customers per week for the past 26 weeks have been stored in the file XR17-69.

a Determine the sample regression line.
b Interpret the coefficients.
c Can the manager infer at the 5% significance level that the larger the number of ads, the larger the number of customers?
d Find and interpret the coefficient of determination.
e In your opinion, is it a worthwhile exercise to use the regression equation to predict the number of customers who will enter the store, given that Colonial intends to advertise five times in the newspaper? If so, find a 95% prediction interval. If not, explain why not.

17.70 The president of a company that manufactures car seats has been concerned about the number and cost of machine breakdowns. The problem is that the machines are old and becoming quite unreliable. However, the cost of replacing them is quite high, and the president is not certain that the cost can be made up in today's slow economy. To help make a decision about replacement, he gathered data about last month's costs for repairs and the ages (in months) of the plant's 20 welding machines. These data are stored in file XR17-70.

  a Find the sample regression line.

  b Interpret the coefficients.

  c Determine the coefficient of determination, and discuss what this statistic tells you.

  d Conduct a test at whatever significance level you deem suitable to determine whether the age of a machine and its monthly cost of repair are linearly related.

  e Is the fit of the simple linear model good enough to allow the president to predict the monthly repair cost of a welding machine that is 120 months old? If so, find a 95% prediction interval. If not, explain why not.

17.71 Several years ago, Coca-Cola attempted to change its 100-year-old recipe. One reason why the company's management felt this was necessary was competition from Pepsi Cola. Respondents of surveys of Pepsi drinkers indicated that they preferred Pepsi because it was sweeter than Coke. As part of the analysis that led to Coke's ill-fated move, the management of Coca-Cola performed extensive surveys wherein consumers tasted various versions of the new Coke. Suppose that a random sample of 200 cola drinkers was given versions of Coke with different amounts of sugar. After tasting the product, each drinker was asked to rate the taste quality. The possible responses were as follows.

5 = excellent   4 = good   3 = average   2 = fair
1 = poor

The responses and sugar content (percent by volume) of the version tasted are recorded in columns 1 and 2, respectively, of file XR17-71. Can management infer at the 5% significance level that sugar content affects drinkers' ratings of the cola?

17.72 An agronomist wanted to investigate the factors that determine crop yield. Accordingly, she undertook an experiment wherein a farm was divided into 30 one-acre plots. The amount of fertilizer applied to each plot was varied. Corn was then planted, and the amount of corn harvested at the end of the season was recorded. These data are stored in file XR17-72.

  a Find the sample regression line and interpret the coefficients.

  b Can the agronomist conclude at the 5% significance level that there is a linear relationship between the amount of fertilizer and the crop yield?

  c Find the coefficient of determination and interpret its value.

  d Does the simple linear model appear to be a useful tool in predicting crop yield from the amount of fertilizer applied? If so, produce a 95% prediction interval of the crop yield when 300 pounds of fertilizer are applied. If not, explain why not.

17.73 Auto manufacturers are required to test their vehicles for a variety of pollutants in the exhaust. The amount of pollutant varies even among identical vehicles, so that several vehicles must be tested. The engineer in charge of testing has collected data (in grams per kilometer driven) on the amount of two pollutants, carbon monoxide and nitrous oxide, for 50 identical vehicles. These data are stored in columns 1 and 2, respectively, in file XR17-73. The engineer believes the company can save money by testing for only one of the pollutants because the two pollutants are closely linked. That is, if a car is emitting a large amount of carbon monoxide it will also emit a large amount of nitrous oxide. Do the data support the engineer's belief?

17.74 It is doubtful that any sport collects more statistics than baseball. This surfeit of statistics allows fans to conduct a great variety of statistical analyses. For example, fans are always interested in determining which factors lead to successful teams. A statistician determined the team batting average and the team winning percentage for the 14 American League teams at the end of a recent season. We will assume that these data represent a random sample of the relationship between batting average and winning percentage for all time. These data are stored in file XR17-74.

  a Find the sample regression line and interpret the coefficients.

  b Find the standard error of estimate and describe what this statistic tells you.

  c Do these data provide sufficient evidence at the 5% significance level to conclude that higher team batting averages lead to higher winning percentages?

  d Find the coefficient of determination and interpret its value.

  e Predict with 90% confidence the winning percentage of a team whose batting average is .275.

17.75 In an effort to further analyze a baseball team's winning percentage, the statistician determined each team's earned run average (ERA). (An earned run average is the number of earned runs a baseball team gives up in an average nine-inning game.) These data, together with the team's winning percentage, are stored in file XR17-75.

a Find the sample regression line and interpret the coefficients.

b Find the standard error of estimate and describe what this statistic tells you.

c Do these data provide sufficient evidence with $\alpha = .05$ to conclude that lower earned run averages lead to higher winning percentages?

d Find the coefficient of determination and interpret its value.

e Predict with 90% confidence the winning percentage of a team whose ERA is 4.00.

17.76 In the last decade, society in general and the judicial system in particular have altered their opinions on the seriousness of drunken driving. In most jurisdictions, driving an automobile with a blood-alcohol level in excess of .08 is a felony. Because of a number of factors, it is difficult to provide guidelines on when it is safe for someone who has consumed alcohol to drive a car. In an experiment to examine the relationship between blood-alcohol level and the weight of a drinker, 50 men of varying weights were each given three beers to drink, and 1 hour later their blood-alcohol level was measured. These data are stored in file XR17-76.

a If we assume that the two variables are normally distributed, can we conclude that blood-alcohol level and weight are related? (Use a 5% significance level.)

b After examining the data, the statistician in charge of the experiment concluded that a regression analysis was invalid (because she determined that the error term was nonnormal). What conclusions can you draw from these data about the relationship between blood-alcohol level and weight? (Use a 5% significance level.)

17.77 One general belief held by observers of the business world is that taller men earn more money than shorter men. In a University of Pittsburgh study (reported in *The Wall Street Journal,* 30 December, 1986), 250 M.B.A. graduates, all about 30 years old, were polled and asked to report their height (in inches) and annual incomes (nearest $1,000). These data are stored in columns 1 and 2, respectively, in file XR17-77.

a Determine the sample regression line and interpret the coefficients.

b Do these data provide sufficient statistical evidence to infer at the 5% significance level that taller M.B.A.'s earn more money than shorter ones?

c Provide a measure of the strength of the linear relationship between income and height.

d Do you think this model is good enough to be used to estimate and predict income on the basis of height? If not, explain why not. If so, estimate with 95% confidence the mean income of all 6-foot men with M.B.A.'s and predict with 95% confidence the income of a man 5 feet 10 inches tall with an M.B.A.

17.78 Every year the U.S. Federal Trade Commission rates cigarette brands according to their levels of tar and nicotine, substances that are hazardous to smokers' health. Additionally, the commission includes the amount of carbon monoxide, which is a by-product of burning tobacco that seriously affects the heart. A random sample of 25 brands was taken. The data are stored in file XR17-78. Column 1 stores the brand name, column 2 stores the tar content in milligrams, column 3 holds the nicotine content in milligrams, column 4 contains the carbon monoxide in milligrams.

a Are the levels of tar and nicotine linearly related?

b Does the level of nicotine linearly affect the amount of carbon monoxide?

17.79 The analysis the human resources manager performed in Exercise 17.29 indicated that the dexterity test is not a predictor of job performance. However, before discontinuing the test he decided that the problem is that the statistical analysis was flawed in that it only examined the relationship between test score and job performance for those who scored well on the test. Recall that only those who scored above 70 were hired. Applicants who achieved scores below 70 were not hired. The manager decided to perform another statistical analysis. A sample of 50 job applicants who scored above 50 were hired, and as before the workers' performance was measured. The test scores and percentages of nondefective computers produced are stored in columns 1 and 2, respectively, in file XR17-79. On the basis of these data should the manager discontinue the dexterity tests?

CASE 17.1   Duxbury Press

The academic book business is different from most other businesses because of the way purchasing decisions are made. The customer, who is usually a student taking a university or college course, buys a specific book because the instructor of the course adopts (chooses to use) that book. Sales representatives of publishers sell their products by persuading instructors to adopt their books. Unfortunately, judging the quality of textbooks is not easy. To help with the decision process, sales representatives give free examination copies to instructors so that they can review the book and decide whether or not to adopt it. In many universities, several sections of the same course are taught, and book adoption committees meet to make the adoption decision.

Curt Hinrichs, an editor at Duxbury Press, was examining the latest sales data on the sales of three recently published statistics textbooks. He noted that the number of examination copies was quite large, which can be a serious problem, given the high cost of producing books. Duxbury distributes review copies only of the books or editions that came out in the current year. He wondered whether his sales representatives were giving away too many free books or perhaps not enough. The data that he is examining contain a code that identifies the sales representative (of which there are 78), the gross revenues from the sales of the statistics books, and the number of free copies given to professors by that representative. These data are stored in columns 1 to 3, respectively, of file C17-01. Curt would like to know whether there is a direct link between the number of free copies distributed and the gross revenues from new editions.

Perform an analysis to provide Curt with the information he needs.

CASE 17.2   Predicting University Grades from High School Grades*

Ontario High school students must complete a minimum of six Ontario Academic Credits (OACs) to gain admission to a university in the province. Most students take more than six OACs because universities take the average of the best six in deciding which students to admit. Most programs at universities require high school students to select certain courses. For example, science programs require two of chemistry, biology, and physics. Students applying to engineering must complete at least two mathematics OACs as well as physics. In recent years, one business program began an examination of all aspects of their program including the criteria used to admit students. Students are required to take English and calculus OACs, and the minimum high school average is about 85%. Strangely enough, even though students are required to complete English and calculus, the marks in these subjects are not included in the average unless they are in the top six courses in a student's transcript. To examine the issue, the registrar took a random sample of students who recently graduated with the B.B.A. (Bachelor of Business Administration) degree. He recorded the university GPA (range 0 to 12), the high school average based on the best six courses, and the high school average using English and calculus and the next four best marks. These data are stored in columns 1 to 3, respectively, in file C17-02.

   a   Is there a relationship between university grades and high school average using the best six OACs?

*The authors are grateful to Leslie Grauer for her help in gathering the data for this case.

b Is there a relationship between university grades and high school average using the best four OACs plus calculus and English?

c What should the university do about the information provided by this case?

CASE 17.3	**Insurance Compensation for Lost Revenues**

In July 1990, a rock-and-roll museum opened in Atlanta, Georgia. The museum was located in a large city block containing a variety of stores. In late July 1992, a fire that started in one of these stores burned the entire block, including the museum. Fortunately, the museum had taken out insurance to cover the cost of rebuilding as well as lost revenue. As a general rule, insurance companies base their payment on how well the company performed in the past. However, the owners of the museum argued that the revenues were increasing, and hence they are entitled to more money under their insurance plan. The argument was based on the revenues and attendance figures of an amusement park that was opened nearby, featuring rides and other similar attractions. The amusement park opened in December 1991. The two entertainment facilities were operating jointly during the last four weeks of 1991 and the first 28 weeks of 1992 (the point at which the fire destroyed the museum). In April 1995, the museum reopened with considerably more features than the original one.

The attendance for both facilities for December 1991 to October 1995 are listed in columns 1 (museum) and 2 (amusement park) in file C17-03. During the period when the museum was closed, the data show zero attendance.

The owners of the museum argue that the weekly attendance from the twenty-ninth week of 1992 to the sixteenth week of 1995 should be estimated using the most current data (seventeenth to forty-second week of 1995). The insurance company argues that the estimates should be based on the four weeks of 1991 and the 28 weeks of 1992, when both facilities were operating and before the museum reopened with more features than the original museum.

a Estimate the coefficients of the simple regression model based on the insurance company's argument. That is, use the attendance figures for the last four weeks in 1991 and the next 28 weeks in 1992 to estimate the coefficients. Then, use the model to calculate point predictions for the museum's weekly attendance figures when the museum was closed. Calculate the predicted total attendance.

b Repeat part (a) using the museum's argument. That is, use the attendance figures after the reopening in 1995 to estimate the regression coefficients and use the equation to predict the weekly attendance when the museum was closed. Calculate the total attendance that was lost because of the fire.

c In your opinion, which figure should be used to calculate how much the insurance company should award the museum? How should that compensation be determined?

*The case and the data are real. The names have been changed to preserve anonymity. The authors wish to thank Dr. Kevin Leonard for supplying the problem and the data.

Chapter 18

Multiple

Regression

18.1 Introduction

18.2 Model and Required Conditions

18.3 Estimating the Coefficients and Assessing the Model

18.4 Regression Diagnostics—II

18.5 Regression Diagnostics—III (Time Series)

18.6 Summary

18.1 INTRODUCTION

In the previous chapter, we employed the simple linear regression model to analyze how one quantitative variable (the dependent variable y) is affected by another quantitative variable (the independent variable x). The restriction of using only one independent variable was motivated by the need to simplify the introduction to regression analysis. Although there are a number of applications where we purposely develop a model with only one independent variable (see Section 17.6, for example), in general we prefer to include as many independent variables as can be shown to significantly affect the dependent variable. Arbitrarily limiting the number of independent variables also limits the usefulness of the model.

In this chapter, we allow for any number of independent variables. In so doing, we expect to develop models that fit the data better than would a simple linear regression model. We proceed in a manner similar to that in Chapter 17. We begin by describing the multiple regression model and listing the required conditions. We let the computer produce the required statistics and use them to assess the model's fit and diagnose violations of the required conditions. We employ the model by interpreting the coefficients, predicting the particular value of the dependent variable, and estimating its expected value.

18.2 MODEL AND REQUIRED CONDITIONS

We now assume that k independent variables are potentially related to the dependent variable. Thus, the model is represented by the following equation.

$$y = \beta_0 + \beta_1 x_1 + \beta_2 x_2 + \cdots + \beta_k x_k + \epsilon$$

where y is the dependent variable, $x_1, x_2, \ldots, x_k$ are the independent variables, β_0 $\beta_1, \ldots, \beta_k$ are the coefficients, and ϵ is the error variable. The independent variables may actually be functions of other variables. For example, we might define some of the independent variables as follows.

$$x_2 = x_1^2$$
$$x_5 = x_3 \cdot x_4$$
$$x_7 = \log(x_6)$$

In Chapter 19, we will discuss how and under what circumstances such functions can be used in regression analysis.

The error variable is retained because, even though we have included additional independent variables, deviations between predicted values of y and actual values of y will still occur. Incidentally, when there is more than one independent variable in the regression model, we refer to the graphical depiction of the equation as a **response surface** rather than as a straight line. Figure 18.1 depicts a scatter diagram of a response surface with $k = 2$. (When $k = 2$, the regression equation creates a **plane.**) Of course, whenever k is greater than 2, we can only imagine the response surface; we cannot draw it.

An important part of the regression analysis comprises several statistical techniques that evaluate how well the model fits the data. These techniques require the following conditions, which we introduced in the previous chapter.

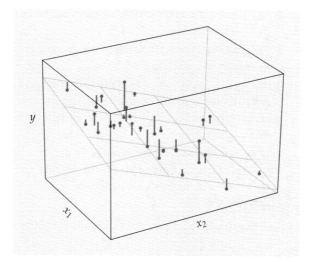

Figure 18.1

Scatter diagram and response surface with $k = 2$

Required Conditions for the Error Variable

1 The probability distribution of the error variable ϵ is normal.

2 The mean of the distribution is zero.

3 The standard deviation of ϵ is σ_ϵ, which is a constant.

4 The errors are independent.

In Section 17.8, we discussed how to recognize when the requirements are unsatisfied. Those same procedures can be used to detect violations of required conditions in the multiple regression model.

We now proceed as we did in Chapter 17; we discuss how the model's coefficients are estimated and how we assess the model's fit. However, there is one major difference between Chapters 17 and 18. In Chapter 17, we allowed for the possibility that some students will perform the calculations manually. The multiple regression model involves so many computations that it is virtually impossible to conduct the analysis without a computer. All analyses in this chapter will be performed by Excel and Minitab. Your job will be to interpret the output.

18.3 ESTIMATING THE COEFFICIENTS AND ASSESSING THE MODEL

The procedures introduced in Chapter 17 are extended to the multiple regression model. However, in Chapter 17, we discussed how to interpret the coefficients first, followed by a discussion of how to assess the model's fit. In practice, we reverse the process. That is, the first step is to determine how well the model fits. If the model's fit is poor, there is no point in a further analysis of the coefficients of that model. A much higher priority is assigned to the task of improving the model. We intend to discuss the art and science of model building in Chapter 19. In this chapter, we show how a regression analysis is performed. The steps we use are as follows.

1 Use a computer and software to generate the coefficients and the statistics used to assess the model.

2 Diagnose violations of required conditions. If there are problems, we attempt to remedy them.

3 Assess the model's fit. Three statistics that perform this function: the standard error of estimate, the coefficient of determination, and the F-test of the analysis of variance. The first two were introduced in Chapter 17, the third will be introduced here.

4 If we're satisfied with the model's fit and that the required conditions are met, we can attempt to interpret the coefficients and test them as we did in Chapter 17. We use the model to predict or estimate the expected value of the dependent variable.

We illustrate these techniques with the following example.

STATISTICS IN THE WORKPLACE

Operations Management Application

Location analysis is one operations management function. As we observed in Chapter 1, deciding where to locate a plant, warehouse, or retail outlet is a critical decision for any organization. A large number of variables must be considered in this decision problem. For example, a production facility must be located close to suppliers of raw resources and supplies, skilled labor, and transportation to customers. Retail outlets must consider the type and number of potential customers. In the following example we describe an application of regression analysis to find profitable locations for a motel chain.

▼ EXAMPLE 18.1*

La Quinta Motor Inns is a moderately priced chain of motor inns located across the United States. Its market is the frequent business traveler. The chain recently launched a campaign to increase market share by building new inns. The management of the chain is aware of the difficulty in choosing locations for new motels. Moreover, making decisions without adequate information often results in poor decisions. Consequently, they acquired data on 100 randomly selected inns belonging to La Quinta. The objective was to predict which sites are likely to be profitable.

To measure profitability, La Quinta used operating margin, which is that ratio of the sum of profit, depreciation, and interest expenses divided by total revenue. (Although occupancy is often used as measure of a motel's success, the statistician concluded that occupancy was too unstable, especially during economic turbulence.) The higher the operating margin, the greater the success of the inn. La Quinta defines profitable inns as those with an operating margin in excess of 50% and unprofitable ones with margins of less than 30%. After a discussion with a number of experienced managers La Quinta decided to select one or two independent variables from each of

*Adapted from Sheryl E. Kimes and James A. Fitzsimmons, "Selecting Profitable Hotel Sites at La Quinta Motor Inns," *Interfaces 20* (March–April 1990): 12–20.

these categories: competition, market awareness, demand generators, demographics, and physical. To measure the degree of competition, they determined the total number of motel and hotel rooms within 3 miles of each La Quinta inn. Market awareness was measured by the number of miles between the nearest competitor and the La Quinta inn. Two variables that represent sources of customers were chosen. The amount of office space and college and university enrollment in the surrounding community are demand generators. Both of these are measures of economic activity. A demographic variable that describes the community is the median household income. Finally, as a measure of the physical qualities of the location La Quinta chose the distance to the downtown core. These data are stored in file XM18-01, where column 1 stores the inn selected (INN), column 2 contains the operating margin (MARGIN in percent), and columns 3 through 8 (ROOMS, NEAREST in miles, OFFICE in thousands of square feet, COLLEGE enrollment in thousands, INCOME in $thousands, and DISTTWN in miles), respectively, store the six independent variables. Some of these data are shown below.

Conduct a regression analysis and analyze the results.

INN	MARGIN	ROOMS	NEAREST	OFFICE	COLLEGE	INCOME	DISTTWN
1	55.5	3,203	0.1	549	8	37	12.1
2	33.8	2,810	1.5	496	17.5	39	0.4
3	49	2,890	1.9	254	20	39	12.2
.	.	.	.	.	.	.	.
.	.	.	.	.	.	.	.
.	.	.	.	.	.	.	.
98	40	3,397	2.7	855	19.5	42	11.7
99	39.8	3,823	0.7	202	17	36	10
100	35.2	3,251	2.6	275	13	39	10.5

Solution   Excel and Minitab were used to perform the calculations, the results of which follow.

Excel Output for Example 18.1

	A	B	C	D	E	F
1	SUMMARY OUTPUT					
2						
3	*Regression Statistics*					
4	Multiple R	0.7246				
5	R Square	0.5251				
6	Adjusted R Square	0.4944				
7	Standard Error	5.51				
8	Observations	100				
9						
10	ANOVA					
11		*df*	*SS*	*MS*	*F*	*Significance F*
12	Regression	6	3123.8	520.6	17.14	0.0000
13	Residual	93	2825.6	30.4		
14	Total	99	5949.5			
15						
16		*Coefficients*	*Standard Error*	*t Stat*	*P-value*	
17	Intercept	72.45	7.89	9.18	0.0000	
18	ROOMS	-0.0076	0.0013	-6.07	0.0000	
19	NEAREST	-1.6462	0.6328	-2.60	0.0108	
20	OFFICE	0.0198	0.0034	5.80	0.0000	
21	COLLEGE	0.2118	0.1334	1.59	0.1159	
22	INCOME	-0.4131	0.1396	-2.96	0.0039	
23	DISTTWN	0.2253	0.1787	1.26	0.2107	

COMMANDS

1 Type or import the data into adjacent columns.
2 Click **Tools, Data Analysis ...** , and **Regression.**
3 Specify the **Input Y Range:.**
4 Specify the **Input X Range:.** Click **Labels** (if necessary). Click **OK.**

COMMANDS FOR EXAMPLE 18.1

Open file **XM18-01.**

B1:B101
C1:H101

Minitab Output for Example 18.1

Regression Analysis

```
The regression equation is
MARGIN = 72.5 - 0.00762 ROOMS - 1.65 NEAREST + 0.0198 OFFICE
+ 0.212 COLLEGE - 0.413 INCOME + 0.225 DISTTWN


Predictor        Coef         StDev           T         P
Constant       72.455         7.893        9.18     0.000
ROOMS       -0.007618      0.001255       -6.07     0.000
NEAREST       -1.6462        0.6328       -2.60     0.011
OFFICE       0.019766      0.003410        5.80     0.000
COLLEGE       0.2118        0.1334        1.59     0.116
INCOME       -0.4131        0.1396       -2.96     0.004
DISTTWN       0.2253        0.1787        1.26     0.211


S = 5.512      R-Sq = 52.5%      R-Sq(adj) = 49.4%

Analysis of Variance

Source          DF          SS           MS         F         P
Regression       6     3123.83       520.64     17.14     0.000
Residual Error  93     2825.63        30.38
Total           99     5949.46
```

COMMANDS

1 Type or import the data into adjacent columns.
2 Click **Stat, Regression,** and **Regression ....**
3 Specify the dependent variable **(Response:).**
4 Specify the independent variables **(Predictors:).** Click **OK.**

COMMANDS FOR EXAMPLE 18.1

Open file **XM18-01.**

MARGIN or **C2**

ROOMS NEAREST OFFICE COLLEGE INCOME DISTTWN or **C3-C8**

The regression model is estimated by

$$\text{MARGIN} = 72.5 - 0.0076 \text{ ROOMS} - 1.65 \text{ NEAREST} + 0.020 \text{ OFFICE} + 0.21 \text{ COLLEGE} - 0.41 \text{ INCOME} + 0.23 \text{ DISTTWN}$$

(Note that we have rounded the coefficients to ease the interpretation.)

We assess the model in three ways: the standard error of estimate, the coefficient of determination (both introduced in Chapter 17), and the *F*-test of the analysis of variance (presented below).

Standard Error of Estimate

Recall that σ_ϵ is the standard deviation of the error variable ϵ and that, because σ_ϵ is a population parameter, it is necessary to estimate its value by using s_ϵ. In multiple regression, the standard error of estimate is defined as follows.

Standard Error of Estimate

$$s_\epsilon = \sqrt{\frac{SSE}{n - k - 1}}$$

As we noted in Chapter 17, each of our software packages reports the standard error of estimate in a different way. Excel outputs s_ϵ for Example 18.1 as

Standard Error = 5.51

and Minitab outputs this value as

s = 5.512

Recall that we judge the magnitude of the standard error of estimate relative to the values of the dependent variable, and particularly to the mean of y. In this example, $\bar{y} = 45.739$ (not shown in printouts). It appears that the standard error of estimate is not particularly small.

Coefficient of Determination

Recall from Chapter 17 that the coefficient of determination is defined as

$$R^2 = 1 - \frac{SSE}{\sum(y_i - \bar{y})^2}$$

For Example 18.1, Excel prints

R Square = .5251

and Minitab outputs

R-Sq = 52.5%

This means that 52.51% of the variation in operating margin is explained by the six independent variables, while 47.49% remains unexplained.

Notice that Excel and Minitab print a second R^2 statistic, called the **coefficient of determination adjusted for degrees of freedom,** which has been adjusted to take into account the sample size and the number of independent variables. The rationale for this statistic is that, if the number of independent variables k is large relative to the sample size n, the unadjusted R^2 value may be unrealistically high. To understand this point, consider what would happen if the sample size is 2 in a simple linear regression model. The line will fit the data perfectly resulting in $R^2 = 1$ when, in fact, there may be no linear relationship. To avoid creating a false impression, the adjusted R^2 is often calculated. Its formula follows.

Coefficient of Determination Adjusted for Degrees of Freedom

$$\text{Adjusted } R^2 = 1 - \frac{SSE/(n - k - 1)}{\sum(y_i - \bar{y})^2/(n - 1)}$$

If n is considerably larger than k, the actual and adjusted R^2 values will be similar. But if SSE is quite different from zero and k is large compared to n, the actual and adjusted values of R^2 will differ substantially. If such differences exist, the analyst should be alerted to a potential problem in interpreting the coefficient of determination. In Example 18.1, the adjusted coefficient of determination is 49.44%, indicating that, no matter how we measure the coefficient of determination, the model's fit is moderately good.

Testing The Validity Of The Model

In the simple linear regression model, we tested the slope coefficient to determine whether sufficient evidence existed to allow us to conclude that there was a linear relationship between the independent variable and the dependent variable. However, because there is only one independent variable in that model, the t-test also tested to determine whether that model is valid. When there is more than one independent variable, we need another method to test the overall validity of the model. The technique is a version of the analysis of variance, which we introduced in Chapter 14.

To test the validity of the regression model, we specify the following hypotheses.

$$H_0: \beta_1 = \beta_2 = \cdots = \beta_k = 0$$

H_1: At least one β_i is not equal to zero.

If the null hypothesis is true, none of the independent variables $x_1, x_2, \ldots, x_k$ is linearly related to y, and therefore the model is useless. If at least one β_i is not equal to zero, the model does have some validity.

When we introduced the coefficient of determination in Chapter 17, we noted that the total variation in the dependent variable [measured by $\sum(y_i - \bar{y})^2$] can be decomposed into two parts: the explained variation (measured by SSR) and the unexplained variation (measured by SSE). That is,

Total Variation in y = SSR + SSE

Furthermore, we established that, if SSR is large relative to SSE, the coefficient of determination will be high—signifying a good model. On the other hand, if SSE is large, most of the variation will be unexplained, which indicates that the model provides a poor fit and consequently has little validity.

The test statistic is the same one we encountered in Section 14.2, where we tested for the equivalence of k population means. To judge whether SSR is large enough relative to SSE to allow us to infer that at least one coefficient is not equal to zero, we compute the ratio of the two mean squares. (Recall that the mean square is the sum of squares divided by its degrees of freedom; recall, too, that the ratio of two mean squares is F distributed, as long as the underlying population is normal—a required condition for this application.) The calculation of the test statistic is summarized in an analysis of variance (ANOVA) table, which in general appears as follows. The Excel and Minitab ANOVA tables are shown on the next page.

Analysis of Variance Table for Regression Analysis

Source of Variation	Degrees of Freedom	Sums of Squares	Mean Squares	F-Statistic
Regression	k	SSR	MSR = SSR/k	F = MSR/MSE
Residual	$n - k - 1$	SSE	MSE = SSE/$(n - k - 1)$	
Total	$n - 1$	$\sum(y_i - \bar{y})^2$		

Excel Analysis of Variance for Example 18.1

10	ANOVA					
11		df	SS	MS	F	Significance F
12	Regression	6	3123.8	520.6	17.14	0.0000
13	Residual	93	2825.6	30.4		
14	Total	99	5949.5			

Minitab Analysis of Variance for Example 18.1

```
Analysis of Variance

Source          DF        SS        MS        F        P
Regression       6    3123.83    520.64    17.14    0.000
Residual Error  93    2825.63     30.38
Total           99    5949.46
```

A large value of F indicates that most of the variation in y is explained by the regression equation and that the model is useful. A small value of F indicates that most of the variation in y is unexplained. The rejection region allows us to determine whether F is large enough to justify rejecting the null hypothesis. For this test, the rejection region is

$$F > F_{\alpha, k, n-k-1}$$

In Example 18.1, the rejection region (assuming $\alpha = .05$) is

$$F > F_{\alpha, k, n-k-1} = F_{05, 6, 93} \simeq 2.17$$

As you can see from the printout, $F = 17.14$. The printout also includes the p-value of the test, which is 0. Obviously, there is a great deal of evidence to infer that the model is valid.

F-Test, R^2, and $S\epsilon$

Although each assessment measurement offers a different perspective, all agree in their assessment of how well the model fits the data, because all are based on the sum of squares for error, SSE. The standard error of estimate is

$$s_\epsilon = \sqrt{\frac{\text{SSE}}{n - k - 1}}$$

and the coefficient of determination is

$$R^2 = 1 - \frac{\text{SSE}}{\sum(y_i - \bar{y})^2}$$

When the response surface hits every single point, SSE = 0. Hence $s_\epsilon = 0$, and $R^2 = 1$.

If the model provides a poor fit, we know that SSE will be large [its maximum value is $\sum(y_i - \bar{y})^2$], s_ϵ will be large, and [since SSE is close to $\sum(y_i - \bar{y})^2$] R^2 will be close to zero.

The F-statistic also depends on SSE. Specifically,

$$F = \frac{(\sum(y_i - \bar{y})^2 - \text{SSE})/k}{\text{SSE}/(n - k - 1)}$$

When SSE = 0,

$$F = \frac{\sum(y_i - \bar{y})^2/k}{0/(n - k - 1)}$$

which is infinitely large. When SSE is large, SSE is close to $\sum(y_i - \bar{y})^2$ and F is quite small.

The relationship among s_ϵ, R^2, and F is summarized in Table 18.1.

Table 18.1 **Relationship Among s_ϵ, R^2, and F**

SSE	s_ϵ	R^2	F	Assessment of Model
0	0	1	∞	Perfect
Small	Small	Close to 1	Large	Good
Large	Large	Close to 0	Small	Poor
$\sum(y_i - \bar{y})^2$	$\sqrt{\dfrac{\sum(y_i - \bar{y})^2}{n - k - 1}}^*$	0	0	Useless

*When n is large and k is small, this quantity is approximately equal to the standard deviation of y.

If we're satisfied that the model fits the data as well as possible, and that the required conditions are satisfied (see Section 18.4), we can interpret and test the individual coefficients and use the model to predict and estimate.

INTERPRET

The general form of the sample regression line is

$$\hat{y} = b_0 + b_1x_1 + b_2x_2 + \cdots + b_kx_k$$

In Example 18.1 $k = 6$, which is the number of independent variables analyzed in the model.

The intercept is $b_0 = 72.5$. This is the average operating margin when all of the independent variables are zero. As we observed in Chapter 17, it is often misleading to try to interpret this value, particularly if zero is outside the range of values of the independent variables (as is the case here).

The relationship between **MARGIN** and **ROOMS** is described by $b_1 = -.0076$. From this number we learn that in this model, for each additional room within 3 miles of a La Quinta inn, the operating margin decreases on average by .0076% (assuming that the other independent variables in this model are held constant). Changing the units we can interpret b_1 to say that for each additional 1,000 rooms the margin decreases by 7.6%.

The coefficient $b_2 = -1.65$ specifies that for each additional mile that the nearest competitor is to a La Quinta inn, the average operating margin decreases by 1.65% (assuming the constancy of the other independent variables).

The nature of the relationship between **ROOMS** and **MARGIN** and between **NEAREST** and **MARGIN** was expected. Obviously, more competitors closer to the inn will decrease the profitability of the inn.

The relationship between **OFFICE** and **MARGIN** is expressed by $b_3 = .02$. Because **OFFICE** is measured in thousands of square feet (of office space in the nearby community), we interpret this number as the average increase in operating margin for each additional thousand square feet of office space (keeping the other independent variables fixed). So, for every extra 100,000 square feet of office space the operating margin increases on average by 2%.

The relationship between **COLLEGE** and **MARGIN** is specified by $b_4 = .21$, which we interpret to mean that for each additional 1,000 students the average operating margin increases by .21% (when the other variables are constant).

Both **OFFICE** and **COLLEGE** produced positive coefficients indicating that these measures of economic activity are positively related to margin.

The relationship between **INCOME** and **MARGIN** is described by $b_5 = -.41$. For each additional $1,000 increase in median household income, the average operating margin *decreases* by .41% (holding all other variables constant). This result was unexpected. However, one interpretation of this result is that in more industrial areas the incomes tend to be lower. And, operating margins are higher in such communities.

The last variable in the model is **DISTTWN**. Its relationship with **MARGIN** is described by $b_6 = .23$. This tells us that for each additional mile to the downtown center, the operating margin increases on average by .23% (keeping the other independent variables constant).

Testing The Coefficients

In Chapter 17, we described how to test to determine whether there is sufficient evidence to infer that in the simple linear regression model x and y are linearly related. The null and alternative hypotheses were

$$H_0: \beta_1 = 0$$
$$H_1: \beta_1 \neq 0$$

The test statistic was

$$t = \frac{b_1 - \beta_1}{s_{b_1}}$$

which is Student t distributed with $n - 2$ degrees of freedom.

In the multiple regression model, we have more than one independent variable; for each such variable, we can test to determine if there is enough evidence of a linear relationship between it and the dependent variable.

Testing the Coefficients

$$H_0: \beta_i = 0$$
$$H_1: \beta_i \neq 0$$

(for $i = 1, 2, \ldots, k$); the test statistic is

$$t = \frac{b_i - \beta_i}{s_{b_i}}$$

which is Student t distributed with d.f. $= n - k - 1$.

To illustrate, we test each of the coefficients in the multiple regression model in Example 18.1. The tests that follow are performed just as all other tests in this book have been performed. We set up the null and alternative hypotheses, identify the test statistic, and use the computer to calculate the value of the test statistic and its p-value. For each independent variable, we test ($i = 1, 2, 3, 4, 5, 6$).

$$H_0: \beta_i = 0$$
$$H_1: \beta_i \neq 0$$

Refer to page 683 and examine the computer output for Example 18.1. The output includes the t-tests of β_i.

Test of β_1   Value of the test statistic: $t = -6.07$; p-value $= 0$.

There is evidence to infer that the number of motel and hotel rooms within 3 miles of the La Quinta inn and the operating margin are linearly related.

Test of β_2   Value of the test statistic: $t = -2.60$; p-value $= .0108$.

There is evidence to conclude that the distance to the nearest motel and the operating margin of the La Quinta inn are linearly related.

Test of β_3   Value of the test statistic: $t = 5.80$; p-value $= 0$.

This test allows us to infer that there is a linear relationship between the operating margin and the amount of office space around the inn.

Test of β_4   Value of the test statistic: $t = 1.59$; p-value $= .1159$.

From this statistical test we discover that there is no evidence of a linear relationship between college enrollment in the community around the inn and the operating margin.

Test of β_5   Value of the test statistic: $t = -2.96$; p-value $= .0039$.

There is overwhelming statistical evidence to indicate that the operating margin and the median household income are linearly related.

Test of β_6   Value of the test statistic: $t = 1.26$; p-value $= .2107$.

There is not enough evidence to infer the existence of a linear relationship between the distance to the downtown center and the operating margin of the La Quinta inn.

INTERPRET

We have discovered that in this model the number of hotel and motel rooms, distance to the nearest motel, amount of office space, and median household income are linearly related to the operating margin. Moreover, in this model we found no evidence to infer that college enrollment and distance to downtown center are linearly related to operating margin. The t-tests tell La Quinta's management that in choosing the site of a new motel they should look for locations where few other motels are present, where there is a great deal of office space, and where the surrounding households are relatively affluent.

A Cautionary Note About Interpreting The Results

Care should be taken when interpreting the results of this and other regression analyses. We might find that in one model there is enough evidence to conclude that a particular independent variable is linearly related to the dependent variable, but that in another model no such evidence exists. Consequently, whenever a particular t-test is *not* significant, we state that there is not enough evidence to infer that the independent and dependent variable are linearly related *in this model*. The implication is that another model may yield different conclusions.

Furthermore, if one or more of the required conditions are violated, the results may be invalid. In Section 17.9 we introduced the procedures that allow the statistician to examine the model's requirements. We will add to this discussion in Section 18.4. We also remind you that it is dangerous to extrapolate far outside the range of the observed values of the independent variables.

▲

t-TESTS AND THE ANALYSIS OF VARIANCE

The t-tests of the individual coefficients allow us to determine whether $\beta_i \neq 0$ (for $i = 1, 2, \ldots, k$), which tells us whether a linear relationship exists between x_i and y. There is a t-test for each independent variable. Consequently, the computer automatically performs k t-tests. (It actually conducts $k + 1$ t-tests, including the one for β_0, which we usually ignore.) The **F-test** in the analysis of variance combines these t-tests into a single test. That is, we test all the β_i at one time to determine if at least one of them is not equal to zero. The question naturally arises, why do we need the F-test if it is nothing more than the combination of the previously performed t-tests? Recall that we addressed this issue before. In Chapter 14, we pointed out that we can replace the analysis of variance by a series of t-tests of the difference between two means. However, by doing so we increase the probability of making a Type I error. That means that even when there is no linear relationship between each of the independent variables and the dependent variable, multiple t-tests will likely show some are significant. As a result, you will conclude erroneously that, since at least one β_i is not equal to zero, the model is valid. The F-test, on the other hand, is performed only once. Because the probability that a Type I error will occur in a single trial is equal to α, the chance of erroneously concluding that the model is valid is substantially less with the F-test than with multiple t-tests.

There is another reason why the F-test is superior to multiple t-tests. Because of a commonly occurring problem called *multicollinearity,* the t-tests may indicate that some independent variables are not linearly related to the dependent variable, when in fact they are. The problem of multicollinearity does not affect the F-test, nor does it inhibit us from developing a model that fits the data well. Multicollinearity is discussed in Section 18.4.

THE *F*-TEST AND THE *t*-TEST IN THE SIMPLE LINEAR REGRESSION MODEL

It is useful for you to know that we can use the F-test to test the validity of the simple linear regression model. However, this test is identical to the t-test of β_1. The t-test of β_1 in the simple linear regression model tells us whether that independent variable is linearly related to the dependent variable. However, because there is only one independent variable, the t-test of β_1 also tells us whether the model is useful, which is the purpose of the F-test.

The relationship between the t-test of β_1 and the F-test can be explained mathematically. Statisticians can show that if we square a t-statistic with ν degrees of freedom we produce an F-statistic with 1 and ν degrees of freedom. (We briefly discussed this relationship in Chapter 14.) To illustrate, consider Example 17.1 on pages 630. We found the t-statistic for β_1 to be -13.49, with degrees of freedom equal to 98 (d.f. $= n - 2 = 100 - 2 = 98$). The p-value was 0. The output included the analysis of variance table where $F = 182.11$ and p-value $= 0$. The t-statistic squared is $t^2 = (-13.49)^2 = 181.98$, which is approximately 182.11. (The difference is due to rounding errors.) Notice that the degrees of freedom of the F-statistic are 1 and 98. Thus, we can use either test to test the validity of the simple linear regression model.

USING THE REGRESSION EQUATION

As was the case with simple linear regression, we can use the multiple regression equation in two ways: We can produce the prediction interval for a particular value of y, and we can produce the interval estimate of the expected value of y. Like the other calculations associated with multiple regression, we call on the computer to do the work.

Suppose that in Example 18.1 a manager investigated a potential site for a La Quinta inn and found the following characteristics.

There are 3,815 rooms within 3 miles of the site and the closest other hotel or motel is 3.4 miles away. The amount of office space is 476,000 square feet. There is one college and one university nearby with a total enrollment of 24,500 students. From the census the manager learns that the median household income in the area (rounded to the nearest thousand) is $39,000. Finally the distance to the downtown center has been measured at 3.6 miles.

The manager wants to predict the operating margin if and when the inn is built.

As you discovered in the previous chapter both Excel and Minitab output the prediction interval for one inn and interval estimate of the expected (average) operating margin for all sites with the given variables.

The Excel and Minitab printouts are exhibited below.

Excel Prediction and Interval Estimate

	A	B	C	D
1	0.95	Prediction Interval		
2				
3	Predicted value =		37.09	
4	Lower limit =		25.40	
5	Upper limit =		48.79	
6				
7	0.95	Confidence Interval Estimate		
8				
9	Lower limit =		32.97	
10	Upper limit =		41.21	

COMMANDS

See the commands on page 654. In cells C102 to H102 we input the values **3815, 3.4, 476, 24.5, 39, 3.6,** respectively. We specified 95% confidence.

Minitab Prediction and Interval Estimate

```
Predicted Values

     Fit   StDev Fit        95.0% CI          95.0% PI
  37.091       2.076   ( 32.970, 41.213)   ( 25.395, 48.788)
```

COMMANDS

See the commands on page 655. We input the values **3815   3.4   476   24.5   39   3.6.** We specified 95% confidence.

INTERPRET

As you can see, we predict that the operating margin will fall between 25.40 and 48.79%. This interval is quite wide, confirming the need to have extremely well-fitting models to make accurate predictions. However, management defines a profitable inn as one with an operating margin greater than 50% and an unprofitable inn as one with an operating margin below 30%. As you can see, the entire prediction interval is below 50% and part of it is below 30%. The management of La Quinta will pass on this site.

The average operating margin of all sites that fit this category is estimated to be between 32.97 and 41.21%. We interpret this to mean that if we built inns on an infinite number of sites that have the characteristics described above, the average inn would not be profitable.

EXERCISES

Conduct all tests employing a 5% significance level.

18.1 A developer who specializes in summer cottage properties is considering purchasing a large tract of land adjoining a lake. The current owner of the tract has already subdivided the land into separate building lots and has prepared the lots by removing some of the trees. The developer wants to forecast the value of each lot. From previous experience, she knows that the most important factors affecting the price of the lot are size, number of mature trees, and distance to the lake. From a nearby area, she gathers the relevant data for 60 recently sold lots. These data are stored in file XR18-01. (Column 1 = price in thousands of dollars; column 2 = lot size in thousands of square feet; column 3 = number of mature trees; column 4 = distance to the lake in feet.) A multiple regression analysis was performed. The Excel and Minitab printouts are shown below.

	A	B	C	D	E	F
1	SUMMARY OUTPUT					
2						
3	*Regression Statistics*					
4	Multiple R	0.4924				
5	R Square	0.2425				
6	Adjusted R Square	0.2019				
7	Standard Error	40.24				
8	Observations	60				
9						
10	ANOVA					
11		*df*	*SS*	*MS*	*F*	*Significance F*
12	Regression	3	29030	9677	5.97	0.0013
13	Residual	56	90694	1620		
14	Total	59	119724			
15						
16		*Coefficients*	*Standard Error*	*t Stat*	*P-value*	
17	Intercept	51.39	23.52	2.19	0.0331	
18	Lot size	0.700	0.559	1.25	0.2156	
19	Trees	0.679	0.229	2.96	0.0045	
20	Distance	-0.378	0.195	-1.94	0.0577	

Regression Analysis

```
The regression equation is
Price = 51.4 + 0.700 Lot size + 0.679 Trees - 0.378 Distance

Predictor        Coef        StDev            T         P
Constant        51.39       23.52          2.19     0.033
Lot size       0.6999      0.5589          1.25     0.216
Trees          0.6788      0.2293          2.96     0.004
Distance      -0.3784      0.1952         -1.94     0.058

S = 40.24      R-Sq = 24.2%       R-Sq(adj) = 20.2%

Analysis of Variance

Source           DF           SS           MS         F         P
Regression        3        29030         9677      5.97     0.001
Residual Error   56        90694         1620
Total            59       119724
```

---

a What is the standard error of estimate? Interpret its value.

b What is the coefficient of determination? What does this statistic tell you?

c What is the coefficient of determination, adjusted for degrees of freedom? Why does this value differ from the coefficient of determination? What does this tell you about the model?

d Test the overall validity of the model. What does the *p*-value of the test statistic tell you?

e Interpret each of the coefficients.

f Test to determine whether each of the independent variables is linearly related to the price of the lot.

18.2 After analyzing the results of Exercise 17.7, Pat decided that a certain amount of studying could actually improve final grades. However, too much studying would not be warranted, since Pat's ambition (if that's what one could call it) was ultimately to graduate with the absolute minimum level of work. Pat was registered in a statistics course, which had only 3 weeks to go before the final exam, and where the final grade was determined in the following way.

Total mark = 20%(Assignment) + 30%(Midterm test) + 50% (Final Exam)

To determine how much work to do for the remaining 3 weeks, Pat needed to be able to predict the final exam mark on the basis of the assignment mark and the midterm mark. Pat's marks on these were 12/20 and 14/30, respectively. Accordingly, Pat undertook the following analysis. The final exam mark, assignment mark, and midterm test mark for 30 students who took the statistics course last year were collected. These data are stored in columns 1 to 3, respectively, in file XR18-02. A multiple regression analysis was performed using Excel and Minitab with the results following.

	A	B	C	D	E	F
1	SUMMARY OUTPUT					
2						
3	*Regression Statistics*					
4	Multiple R	0.8734				
5	R Square	0.7629				
6	Adjusted R Square	0.7453				
7	Standard Error	3.75				
8	Observations	30				
9						
10	ANOVA					
11		*df*	*SS*	*MS*	*F*	*Significance F*
12	Regression	2	1223.2	611.6	43.43	0.0000
13	Residual	27	380.2	14.1		
14	Total	29	1603.4			
15						
16		*Coefficients*	*Standard Error*	*t Stat*	*P-value*	
17	Intercept	13.01	3.53	3.69	0.0010	
18	Assignment	0.194	0.200	0.97	0.3417	
19	Midterm	1.112	0.122	9.12	0.0000	

Regression Analysis

```
The regression equation is
Final = 13.0 + 0.194 Assignment + 1.11 Midterm

Predictor        Coef         StDev           T         P
Constant       13.009        3.528         3.69     0.001
Assigme         0.1940       0.2004        0.97     0.342
Midterm         1.1121       0.1219        9.12     0.000

S = 3.752      R-Sq = 76.3%      R-Sq(adj) = 74.5%

Analysis of Variance

Source           DF           SS            MS         F         P
Regression        2        1223.18       611.59     43.43     0.000
Residual Error   27         380.18        14.08
Total            29        1603.37
```

a What is the standard error of estimate? Briefly describe how you interpret this statistic.

b What is the coefficient of determination? What does this statistic tell you?

c What is the coefficient of determination, adjusted for degrees of freedom? What do this statistic and the one alluded to in part (b) tell you about the model?

d Test the overall validity of the model. What does the p-value of the test statistic tell you?

e Interpret each of the coefficients.

f Can Pat infer from these results that the assignment mark is linearly related to the final grade?

g Can Pat infer from these results that the midterm mark is linearly related to the final grade?

18.3 The president of a company that manufactures drywall

wants to analyze the factors that affect demand for his product. Drywall is used to construct walls in houses and offices. Consequently, the president decides to develop a regression model in which the dependent variable is monthly sales of drywall (in hundreds of 4×8 sheets) and the independent variables are

> Number of building permits issued in the county
> Five-year mortgage rates (in percentage points)
> Vacancy rate in apartments (in percentage points)
> Vacancy rate in office buildings (in percentage points)

To estimate a multiple regression model, he took the monthly observations from the past 2 years. The data are stored in columns 1 to 5, respectively, in file XR18-03. A computer was used to produce the output below.

	A	B	C	D	E	F
1	SUMMARY OUTPUT					
2						
3	*Regression Statistics*					
4	Multiple R	0.9453				
5	R Square	0.8935				
6	Adjusted R Square	0.8711				
7	Standard Error	40.13				
8	Observations	24				
9						
10	ANOVA					
11		*df*	*SS*	*MS*	*F*	*Significance F*
12	Regression	4	256793	64198	39.86	0.0000
13	Residual	19	30602	1611		
14	Total	23	287395			
15						
16		*Coefficients*	*Standard Error*	*t Stat*	*P-value*	
17	Intercept	-111.8	134.3	-0.83	0.4155	
18	Permits	4.76	0.40	12.06	0.0000	
19	Mortgage	16.99	15.16	1.12	0.2764	
20	A Vacancy	-10.53	6.39	-1.65	0.1161	
21	O Vacancy	1.31	2.79	0.47	0.6446	

Regression Analysis

```
The regression equation is
Drywall = - 112 + 4.76 Permits + 17.0 Mortgage - 10.5 AVacancy + 1.31
Ovacancy

Predictor        Coef        StDev           T         P
Constant       -111.8        134.3       -0.83     0.416
Permits        4.7631       0.3950       12.06     0.000
Morgage         16.99        15.16        1.12     0.276
AVacancy      -10.528        6.394       -1.65     0.116
Ovacancy        1.308        2.791        0.47     0.645


S = 40.13       R-Sq = 89.4%       R-Sq(adj) = 87.1%


Analysis of Variance

Source            DF          SS           MS          F         P
Regression         4      256793        64198      39.86     0.000
Residual Error    19       30602         1611
Total             23      287395
```

a What is the standard error of estimate? Can you use this statistic to assess the model's fit? If so, how?

b What is the coefficient of determination and what does it tell you about the regression model?

c What is the coefficient of determination, adjusted for degrees of freedom? What do this statistic and the statistic referred to in part (b) tell you about how well this model fits the data?

d Test the overall validity of the model. What does the *p*-value of the test statistic tell you?

e Interpret each of the coefficients.

f Test to determine whether each of the independent variables is linearly related to drywall demand.

18.4 Suppose that the statistician who did the analysis described in Exercise 17.2 wanted to investigate other factors that determine heights. As part of the same study, she also recorded the heights of the mothers. These values are stored in column 3 of file XR18-04. (Columns 1 and 2 contain the data from Exercise 17.2.) The multiple regression printouts are shown below.

	A	B	C	D	E	F
1	SUMMARY OUTPUT					
2						
3	*Regression Statistics*					
4	Multiple R	0.5169				
5	R Square	0.2672				
6	Adjusted R Square	0.2635				
7	Standard Error	3.23				
8	Observations	400				
9						
10	ANOVA					
11		*df*	*SS*	*MS*	*F*	*Significance F*
12	Regression	2	1507.5	753.7	72.37	0.0000
13	Residual	397	4134.9	10.4		
14	Total	399	5642.4			
15						
16		*Coefficients*	*Standard Error*	*t Stat*	*P-value*	
17	Intercept	37.56	3.20	11.73	0.0000	
18	Father	0.4849	0.0412	11.78	0.0000	
19	Mother	-0.0229	0.0395	-0.58	0.5615	

Regression Analysis

```
The regression equation is
Son = 37.6 + 0.485 Father - 0.0229 Mother


Predictor        Coef         StDev           T          P
Constant       37.560         3.203       11.73      0.000
Father        0.48493       0.04118       11.78      0.000
Mother       -0.02292       0.03945       -0.58      0.562


S = 3.227        R-Sq = 26.7%       R-Sq(adj) = 26.3%


Analysis of Variance

Source            DF           SS            MS          F          P
Regression         2      1507.45        753.73      72.37      0.000
Residual Error   397      4134.94         10.42
Total            399      5642.40
```

STATISTICS IN THE WORKPLACE

Human Resources Application

In most firms the entire issue of compensation falls into the domain of the human resources manager. The manager must ensure that the method used to determine compensation contributes to the firm's objectives. Moreover, the firm needs to ensure that discrimination or bias of any kind is not a factor. Another function of the personnel manager is the development of severance packages for employees whose services are no longer needed because of downsizing or merger. The size and nature of severance is rarely part of any working agreement and must be determined by a variety of factors. Regression analysis is often useful in this area.

a What is the standard error of estimate and what does this statistic tell you?

b What is the coefficient of determination? What does this statistic tell you?

c What is the coefficient of determination, adjusted for degrees of freedom? What do this statistic and the one referred to in part (b) tell you about how well the model fits the data?

d Test the overall validity of the model. What does the test result tell you?

e Interpret each of the coefficients.

f Do these data allow the statistician to infer that the heights of the sons and the fathers are linearly related?

g Do these data allow the statistician to infer that the heights of the sons and the mothers are linearly related?

The following exercises require the use of a computer and statistical software.

18.5 When one company buys another company, it is not unusual that some workers are terminated. The severance benefits offered to the laid-off workers are often the subject of dispute. Suppose that the Laurier Company recently bought the Western Company and subsequently terminated 20 of Western's employees. As part of the buyout agreement, it was promised that the severance packages offered to the former Western employees would be equivalent to those offered to Laurier employees who had been terminated in the past year. Thirty-six-year-old Bill Smith, a Western employee for the past 10 years, earning $32,000 per year, was one of those let go. His severance package included an offer of 5 weeks of severance pay. Bill complained that this offer was less than that offered to Laurier's employees when they were laid off, in contravention of the buyout agreement. A statistician was called in to settle the dispute. The statistician was told that severance is determined by three factors: age, length of service with the company, and pay. To determine how generous the severance package had been, a random sample of 50 Laurier ex-employees was taken. For each, the following variables were recorded. (The data are stored in columns 1 to 4, respectively, of file XR18-05.)

> Number of weeks of severance pay
> Age of employee
> Number of years with the company
> Annual pay (in thousands of dollars)

a Determine the regression equation. Interpret the coefficients.

b Comment on how well the model fits the data.

c Do all of the independent variables belong in the equation? Explain.

d Are the required conditions satisfied? Explain.

e Perform an analysis to determine if Bill is correct in his assessment of the severance package.

18.6 The admissions officer of a university is trying to develop a formal system of deciding which students to admit to the university. She believes that determinants of success include the standard variables—high school grades and SAT scores. However, she also believes that students who have participated in extracurricular activities are more likely to succeed than those who have not. To investigate the issue, she randomly sampled 100 fourth-year students and recorded the following variables.

> GPA for the first 3 years at the university (range: 0 to 12)
> GPA from high school (range: 0 to 12)
> SAT score (range: 200 to 800)
> Number of hours on average spent per week in organized extracurricular activities in the last year of high school

The data are stored in columns 1 to 4 of file XR18-06.

a Develop a model that helps the admissions officer decide which students to admit, and use the computer to generate the usual statistics.

b What is the standard error of estimate? What does this statistic tell you?

c What is the coefficient of determination? Interpret its value.

d What is the coefficient of determination, adjusted for degrees of freedom? Interpret its value.

e Test the overall validity of the model. What does the *p*-value of the test statistic tell you?

f Interpret each of the coefficients.

g Test to determine whether each of the independent variables is linearly related to the dependent variable.

h Predict with 95% confidence the GPA for the first 3 years of university for a student whose high school GPA is 10, whose SAT score is 600, and who worked an average of 2 hours per week on organized extracurricular activities in the last year of high school.

i Estimate with 90% confidence the mean GPA for the first 3 years of university for all students whose high school GPA is 8, whose SAT score is 550, and who worked an average of 10 hours per week on organized extracurricular activities in the last year of high school.

18.7 The marketing manager for a chain of hardware stores needed more information about the effectiveness of the three types of advertising that the chain used. These are localized direct mailing (in which flyers describing sales and featured products are distributed to homes in the area surrounding a store), newspaper advertising, and local television advertisements. To determine which type is most effective, the manager collected 1 week's data from 25 randomly selected stores. For each store, the following variables were recorded.

> Weekly gross sales
> Weekly expenditures on direct mailing
> Weekly expenditures on newspaper advertising
> Weekly expenditures on television commercials

All variables were recorded in thousands of dollars and stored in columns 1 to 4, respectively, in file XR18-07.

a Find the regression equation.

b What are the coefficient of determination and the coefficient of determination, adjusted for degrees of freedom? What do these statistics tell you about the regression equation?

c What does the standard error of estimate tell you about the regression model?

d Test the overall validity of the model. What does the *p*-value of the test statistic tell you?

e Which independent variables are linearly related to weekly gross sales? Explain.

f Predict with 95% confidence next week's gross sales if a local store spent $800 on direct mailing, $1,200 on newspaper advertisements, and $2,000 on television commercials.

g Estimate with 95% confidence the mean weekly gross sales for all stores that spend $800 on direct mailing, $1,200 on newspaper advertising, and $2,000 on television commercials.

h Discuss the difference between the two intervals found in parts (f) and (g).

18.8 In an effort to explain to customers why their electricity bills have been so high lately, and how, specifically, they could save money by reducing the thermostat settings on both space heaters and water heaters, an electric utility company has collected total kilowatt consumption figures for last year's winter months, as well as thermostat settings on space and water heaters, for 100 homes. The data are stored in columns 1 (consumption), 2 (space heater thermostat setting), and 3 (water heater thermostat setting) of file XR18-08.

a Determine the regression equation.

b Determine the standard error of estimate and comment about what it tells you.

c Determine the coefficient of determination and comment about what it tells you.

d Test the validity of the model and describe what this test tells you.

e Predict with 95% confidence the electricity consumption of a house whose space heater thermostat is set at 70 and whose water heater thermostat is set at 130.

f Estimate with 95% confidence the average electricity consumption for houses whose space heater thermostat is set at 70 and whose water heater thermostat is set at 130.

18.9 In Exercise 17.27, a statistician examined the relationship between office rents and the city's office vacancy rate. The model appears to be quite poor. It was decided to add another variable that measures the state of the economy. The city's unemployment rate was chosen for this purpose. The data are stored in file XR18-09. Column 1 contains the rents, column 2 stores the vacancy rates (these data are identical to file XR17-27), and column 3 contains the unemployment rate in percent.

a Determine the regression equation.

b Determine the coefficient of determination and describe what this value means.

c Test the model's validity in explaining office rents.

d Determine which of the two independent variables is linearly related to rents.

e Predict with 95% confidence the office rent in a city whose vacancy rate is 10% and whose unemployment rate is 7%.

18.10 Exercise 17.8 analyzed the relationship between Internet use and education. In an effort to determine whether other variables affected Internet use another survey was performed. A random sample of two hundred adult Internet users was interviewed. Each person was asked to report his or her age and income. These data are stored in columns 1 (weekly Internet use in hours), 2 (age), and 3 (annual income in thousands of dollars) in file XR18-10.

    a Determine the regression equation.

    b Determine the coefficient of determination and describe what this value means.

    c Test the model's validity in explaining Internet use.

    d Predict with 90% confidence the Internet use for an individual who is 40 years old earning $60,000.

    e Estimate with 95% confidence the mean Internet use of all individuals who are 30 years old and who earn $35,000.

18.11 Refer to Exercise 18.1.

    a Predict with 90% confidence the selling price of a 40,000-square-foot lot that has 50 mature trees and is 25 feet from the lake.

    b Estimate with 90% confidence the average selling price of 50,000-square-foot lots that have 10 mature trees and are 75 feet from the lake.

18.12 Refer to Exercise 18.2.

    a Predict Pat's final exam mark with 95% confidence.

    b Predict Pat's final grade with 95% confidence.

18.13 Refer to Exercise 18.3. Predict next month's drywall sales with 95% confidence if the number of building permits is 50, the 5-year mortgage rate is 9.0%, and the vacancy rates are 3.6% in apartments and 14.3% in office buildings.

18.4 REGRESSION DIAGNOSTICS—II

In Section 17.9, we discussed how to determine whether the required conditions are unsatisfied. The same procedures can be used to diagnose problems in the multiple regression model. Here is a brief summary of the diagnostic procedure we described in Chapter 17.

Calculate the residuals and check the following.

1 Is the error variable nonnormal?

Draw the histogram of the residuals.

2 Is the error variance constant?

Plot the residuals versus the predicted values of y.

3 Are the errors independent (time-series data)?

Plot the residuals versus the time periods.

4 Are there observations that are inaccurate or do not belong to the target population?

Double-check the accuracy of outliers and influential observations.

If the error is nonnormal and/or the variance is not a constant, several remedies can be attempted. These are described at the end of this section.

Outliers and influential observations are checked by examining the data in question to ensure accuracy.

Nonindependence of a time series can sometimes be detected by graphing the residuals and the time periods and looking for evidence of autocorrelation. In Section 18.5, we introduce the **Durbin–Watson test,** which tests for one form of autocorrelation. We will offer a corrective measure for nonindependence.

There is another problem that is applicable to multiple regression models only. Multicollinearity is a condition wherein the independent variables are highly correlated. Multicollinearity distorts the t-tests of the coefficients, making it difficult to determine whether any of the independent variables are linearly related to the dependent variable. It also makes interpreting the coefficients problematic. We will discuss this condition and its remedy next.

MULTICOLLINEARITY

Multicollinearity (also called *collinearity* and *intercorrelation*) is a condition that exists when the independent variables are correlated with one another. The adverse effect of multicollinearity is that the estimated regression coefficients (b_1, b_2, etc.) tend to have large sampling variability. That is, the standard errors are large. Consequently, when the coefficients are tested, the *t*-statistics will be small, which infers that there is no linear relationship between the affected independent variables and the dependent variable. In some cases, this inference will be wrong. Fortunately, multicollinearity does not affect the *F*-test of the analysis of variance. We will illustrate the effects and remedy with the following example.

▼ **EXAMPLE 18.2**

A real estate agent wanted to develop a model to predict the selling price of a home. The agent believed that the most important variables in determining the price of a house are its size, number of bedrooms, and lot size. Accordingly, he took a random sample of 100 homes that recently sold and recorded the selling price, the number of bedrooms, the size (in square feet), and the lot size (in square feet). These data are stored in columns 1 through 4 of file XM18-02. Some of the data follow. Analyze the relationship among the four variables.

Price	Number of Bedrooms	House Size	Lot Size
$124,100	3	1,290	3,900
218,300	4	2,080	6,600
117,800	3	1,250	3,750
.	.	.	.
.	.	.	.
.	.	.	.
155,900	4	1,620	4,800

Solution   The proposed multiple regression model is

$$\text{PRICE} = \beta_0 + \beta_1 \text{ BEDROOMS} + \beta_2 \text{ H SIZE} + \beta_3 \text{ LOT SIZE} + \epsilon$$

The following regression output reveals that none of the independent variables is significantly related to the selling price. (The *t*-statistics are .33, 1.40, and −.26, respectively.) However, the *F*-test ($F = 40.73$ and *p*-value $= 0$) indicates that the complete model is valid. Moreover, the coefficient of determination is 56.0%, which tells us that the model's fit is good.

SOLVE

**Excel Output for
Example 18.2**

	A	B	C	D	E	F
1	SUMMARY OUTPUT					
2						
3	*Regression Statistics*					
4	Multiple R	0.7483				
5	R Square	0.5600				
6	Adjusted R Square	0.5462				
7	Standard Error	25023				
8	Observations	100				
9						
10	ANOVA					
11		*df*	*SS*	*MS*	*F*	*Significance F*
12	Regression	3	76501718347	25500572782	40.73	0.0000
13	Residual	96	60109046053	626135896		
14	Total	99	136610764400			
15						
16		*Coefficients*	*Standard Error*	*t Stat*	*P-value*	
17	Intercept	37718	14177	2.66	0.0091	
18	Bedrooms	2306	6994	0.33	0.7423	
19	H Size	74.30	52.98	1.40	0.1640	
20	Lot Size	-4.36	17.02	-0.26	0.7982	

**Minitab Output for
Example 18.2**

Regression Analysis

The regression equation is
Price = 37718 + 2306 Bedrooms + 74.3 H Size - 4.4 Lot Size

Predictor	Coef	StDev	T	P
Constant	37718	14177	2.66	0.009
Bedrooms	2306	6994	0.33	0.742
H Size	74.30	52.98	1.40	0.164
Lot Size	-4.36	17.02	-0.26	0.798

S = 25023   R-Sq = 56.0%   R-Sq(adj) = 54.6%

Analysis of Variance

Source	DF	SS	MS	F	P
Regression	3	76501718347	25500572782	40.73	0.000
Residual Error	96	60109046053	626135896		
Total	99	1.36611E+11			

If we run three simple regression models where the independent variable is (1) the number of bedrooms, (2) the house size, and (3) the lot size, the output below is produced. This result tells us that each of the independent variables is strongly related to selling price.

Excel Output for Example 18.2 (Simple Linear Regressions)

Regression of Price versus Bedrooms

	A	B	C	D	E	F
1	SUMMARY OUTPUT					
2						
3	*Regression Statistics*					
4	Multiple R	0.6454				
5	R Square	0.4166				
6	Adjusted R Square	0.4106				
7	Standard Error	28519				
8	Observations	100				
9						
10	ANOVA					
11		*df*	*SS*	*MS*	*F*	*Significance F*
12	Regression	1	56905922988	56905922988	69.97	0.0000
13	Residual	98	79704841412	813314708		
14	Total	99	136610764400			
15						
16		*Coefficients*	*Standard Error*	*t Stat*	*P-value*	
17	Intercept	25422	15642	1.625	0.1073	
18	Bedrooms	35439	4237	8.365	0.0000	

Regression of Price versus H-Size

	A	B	C	D	E	F
20	SUMMARY OUTPUT					
21						
22	*Regression Statistics*					
23	Multiple R	0.7478				
24	R Square	0.5591				
25	Adjusted R Square	0.5547				
26	Standard Error	24790				
27	Observations	100				
28						
29	ANOVA					
30		*df*	*SS*	*MS*	*F*	*Significance F*
31	Regression	1	76385713057	76385713057	124.30	0.0000
32	Residual	98	60225051343	614541340		
33	Total	99	136610764400			
34						
35		*Coefficients*	*Standard Error*	*t Stat*	*P-value*	
36	Intercept	40066	10521	3.81	0.0002	
37	H Size	64.20	5.76	11.15	0.0000	

Regression of Price versus Lot-Size

	A	B	C	D	E	F
39	SUMMARY OUTPUT					
40						
41	*Regression Statistics*					
42	Multiple R	0.7409				
43	R Square	0.5489				
44	Adjusted R Square	0.5443				
45	Standard Error	25077				
46	Observations	100				
47						
48	ANOVA					
49		*df*	*SS*	*MS*	*F*	*Significance F*
50	Regression	1	74984894543	74984894543	119.24	0.0000
51	Residual	98	61625869857	628835407		
52	Total	99	136610764400			
53						
54		*Coefficients*	*Standard Error*	*t Stat*	*P-value*	
55	Intercept	38940	10837	3.59	0.0005	
56	Lot Size	20.98	1.92	10.92	0.0000	

**Minitab Output for
Example 18.2 (Simple
Linear Regressions)**

Regression of Price versus Bedrooms
Regression Analysis

```
The regression equation is
Price = 25422 + 35439 Bedrooms


Predictor        Coef        StDev           T          P
Constant        25422        15642        1.63      0.107
Bedrooms        35439         4237        8.36      0.000


S = 28519       R-Sq = 41.7%      R-Sq(adj) = 41.1%


Analysis of Variance


Source          DF           SS          MS          F          P
Regression       1 56905922988 56905922988      69.97      0.000
Residual Error  98 79704841412   813314708
Total           99 1.36611E+11
```

Regression of Price versus H-Size
Regression Analysis

```
The regression equation is
Price = 40066 + 64.2 H Size


Predictor        Coef        StDev           T          P
Constant        40066        10521        3.81      0.000
H Size         64.203         5.759       11.15      0.000


S = 24790       R-Sq = 55.9%      R-Sq(adj) = 55.5%


Analysis of Variance


Source          DF           SS          MS          F          P
Regression       1 76385713057 76385713057     124.30      0.000
Residual Error  98 60225051343   614541340
Total           99 1.36611E+11
```

Regression of Price versus Lot-Size
Regression Analysis

```
The regression equation is
Price = 38940 + 21.0 Lot Size


Predictor        Coef        StDev           T          P
Constant        38940        10837        3.59      0.001
Lot Size       20.982         1.921       10.92      0.000


S = 25077       R-Sq = 54.9%      R-Sq(adj) = 54.4%


Analysis of Variance


Source          DF           SS          MS          F          P
Regression       1 74984894543 74984894543     119.24      0.000
Residual Error  98 61625869857   628835407
Total           99 1.36611E+11
```

The *t*-tests in the multiple regression model infer that no independent variable is a factor in determining the selling price. The three simple linear regression models contradict this conclusion. They tell us that the number of bedrooms, the house size, and the lot size are *all* linearly related to the price. How do we account for this contradiction? The answer is that the three independent variables are correlated with each other. It is reasonable to believe that larger houses have more bedrooms and are situated on larger lots, and that smaller houses have fewer bedrooms and are located on smaller lots. To confirm this belief, we computed the correlation among the three independent variables. The coefficient of correlation between number of bedrooms and house size is .846; the correlation between number of bedrooms and lot size is .837; the correlation between house size and lot size is .994. In the multiple regression model, multicollinearity affected the *t*-tests so that they inferred that none of the independent variables is linearly related to price when, in fact, all are.

Another problem caused by multicollinearity is the interpretation of the coefficients. We interpret the coefficients as measuring the change in the dependent variable when the corresponding independent variable increases by one unit while all the other independent variables are held constant. This interpretation may be impossible when the independent variables are highly correlated, because when the independent variable increases by one unit, some or all of the other independent variables will change. In the multiple regression model in this example, the coefficient of **BEDROOMS** is 2,306. Without multicollinearity we would interpret this coefficient to mean that for each additional bedroom the average price increases by $2,306, provided that the other variables are held constant. However, since **BEDROOMS** is correlated with **H SIZE** and **LOT SIZE**, it is impossible to increase **BEDROOMS** by 1 *and* hold the other variables constant.

This raises two important questions for the statistician. First, how do we recognize the problem when it occurs and, second, how do we avoid or correct it?

Multicollinearity exists in virtually all multiple regression models. In fact, finding two completely uncorrelated variables is rare. The problem becomes serious, however, only when two or more independent variables are highly correlated. Unfortunately, we do not have a critical value that indicates when the correlation between two independent variables is large enough to cause problems. To complicate the issue, multicollinearity also occurs when a combination of several independent variables is correlated with another independent variable or with a combination of other independent variables. Consequently, even with access to all of the correlation coefficients, determining when the multicollinearity problem has reached the serious stage may be extremely difficult. A good indicator of the problem is a large overall *F* but small *t* values.

Minimizing the effect of multicollinearity is often easier than correcting it. The statistician must try to include independent variables that are independent of each other. For example, the real estate agent wanted to include house size, the number of bedrooms, and the lot size, three variables that are clearly related. Rather than developing a model that uses all such variables, the statistician may choose to include only house size, plus several other variables that measure other aspects of a house's value.

Another alternative is to use a stepwise regression package. Forward stepwise regression brings independent variables into the equation one at a time. Only if an independent variable improves the model's fit is it included. If two variables are strongly correlated, the inclusion of one of them in the model makes the second one unnecessary. Backward stepwise regression starts with all the independent variables included in the equation and removes variables if they are not strongly related to the dependent variable. Because the stepwise technique excludes redundant variables, it minimizes multicollinearity. Stepwise regression is presented in Chapter 19.

▲

REMEDYING VIOLATIONS OF REQUIRED CONDITIONS

The most commonly used method to remedy nonnormality or heteroscedasticity is to transform the dependent variable. There are several points to note about this procedure. First, the actual form of the **transformation** depends on which condition is unsatisfied and on the specific nature of the violation. Because there are many different ways to violate the required conditions of the statistical techniques, the list of transformations given here is unavoidably incomplete. Second, these transformations can be useful in improving the model. That is, if the linear model appears to be quite poor, we often can improve the model's fit by transforming y. Third, many computer software systems allow us to make transformations quite easily. You might want to experiment to see the effect these transformations have on your statistical results.

Here is a brief list of the most commonly used transformations.

1 *Log Transformation:* $y' = \log y$ (provided $y > 0$). The log transformation is used when (a) the variance of the error variable increases as y increases or (b) the distribution of the error variable is positively skewed.

2 *Square Transformation:* $y' = y^2$. Use this transformation when (a) the variance is proportional to the expected value of y or (b) the distribution of the error variable is negatively skewed.

3 *Square-Root Transformation:* $y' = \sqrt{y}$ (provided that $y > 0$). The square-root transformation is helpful when the variance is proportional to the expected value of y.

4 *Reciprocal Transformation:* $y' = 1/y$. When the variance appears to significantly increase when y increases beyond some critical value, the reciprocal transformation is recommended.

The following example will illustrate how we diagnose a violation of the required condition, its consequences, and how we remedy the problem.

▼ **EXAMPLE 18.3**

A statistics professor wanted to know whether time limits on quizzes affected the marks on the quiz. Accordingly, he took a random sample of business statistics students and split them into five groups of 20 students each. All students took a quiz that involved simple manual calculations. Each group was given a different time limit. Group 1 was limited to 40 minutes; group 2, 45 minutes; group 3, 50 minutes; group 4, 55 minutes; and group 5, 60 minutes. The quizzes were marked (out of 40) and recorded in file XM18-03. (Column 1 stores the time limits, and column 2 stores the marks.) Conduct a complete regression analysis, including diagnostics.

Solution   The following regression model was postulated.

$$\text{MARK} = \beta_0 + \beta_1 \text{ TIME} + \epsilon$$

The Excel and Minitab outputs follow.

Excel Output for Example 18.3

	A	B	C	D	E	F
1	SUMMARY OUTPUT					
2						
3	*Regression Statistics*					
4	Multiple R	0.8625				
5	R Square	0.7440				
6	Adjusted R Square	0.7414				
7	Standard Error	2.30				
8	Observations	100				
9						
10	ANOVA					
11		*df*	*SS*	*MS*	*F*	*Significance F*
12	Regression	1	1512.5	1512.5	284.77	0.0000
13	Residual	98	520.5	5.31		
14	Total	99	2033.0			
15						
16		*Coefficients*	*Standard Error*	*t Stat*	*P-value*	
17	Intercept	-2.20	1.646	-1.34	0.1844	
18	Time	0.55	0.033	16.88	0.0000	

Minitab Output for Example 18.3

Regression Analysis

The regression equation is
Mark = - 2.20 + 0.550 Time

Predictor	Coef	StDev	T	P
Constant	-2.200	1.646	-1.34	0.184
Time	0.55000	0.03259	16.88	0.000

S = 2.305   R-Sq = 74.4%   R-Sq(adj) = 74.1%

Analysis of Variance

Source	DF	SS	MS	F	P
Regression	1	1512.5	1512.5	284.77	0.000
Residual Error	98	520.5	5.3		
Total	99	2033.0			

The regression equation is

MARK $= -2.2 + .55$ **TIME**

The standard error of estimate, the coefficient of determination, and the t-test of β_1 (and the F-test) all indicate a relatively good model. The residuals and the predicted values were calculated. The histogram of the residuals and the plot of the residuals versus the predicted values of y were produced by Excel and are exhibited next.

Histogram of Residuals in Example 18.3

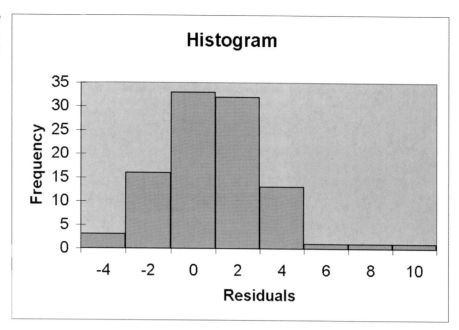

Plot of Residuals versus Predicted Values in Example 18.3

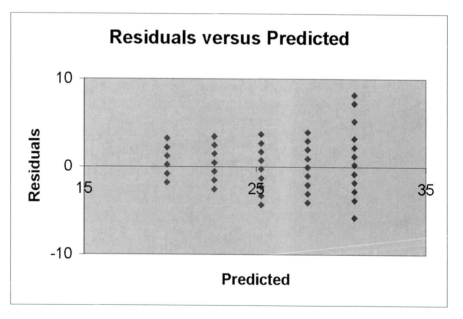

The error variable appears to be normal. However, the variance is clearly not constant; it increases as the predicted marks increase. The remedy we will apply is to transform the dependent variable. We will attempt the following two transformations.

1 $y' = \log_e(y)$ We will label the new variable **LOGMARK**.

2 $y' = 1/y$ We will label the new variable **1/MARK**.

Once again we use our software package to estimate the regression equation. The printouts follow.

**Excel Output for
Example 18.3
(LOGMARK)**

	A	B	C	D	E	F
1	SUMMARY OUTPUT					
2						
3	*Regression Statistics*					
4	Multiple R	0.8783				
5	R Square	0.7714				
6	Adjusted R Square	0.7691				
7	Standard Error	0.0844				
8	Observations	100				
9						
10	ANOVA					
11		*df*	*SS*	*MS*	*F*	*Significance F*
12	Regression	1	2.358	2.358	330.72	0.0000
13	Residual	98	0.699	0.0071		
14	Total	99	3.057			
15						
16		*Coefficients*	*Standard Error*	*t Stat*	*P-value*	
17	Intercept	2.130	0.0603	35.32	0.0000	
18	Time	0.0217	0.00119	18.19	0.0000	

**Minitab Output for
Example 18.3
(LOGMARK)**

Regression Analysis

The regression equation is
Logmark = 2.13 + 0.0217 Time

Predictor	Coef	StDev	T	P
Constant	2.12958	0.06030	35.32	0.000
Time	0.021716	0.001194	18.19	0.000

S = 0.08444   R-Sq = 77.1%   R-Sq(adj) = 76.9%

Analysis of Variance

Source	DF	SS	MS	F	P
Regression	1	2.3579	2.3579	330.72	0.000
Residual Error	98	0.6987	0.0071		
Total	99	3.0566			

**Histogram of Residuals
in Example 18.3
(LOGMARK)**

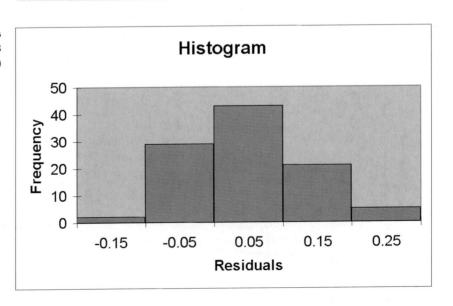

**Plot of Residuals Versus
Predicted Values in
Example 18.3
(LOGMARK)**

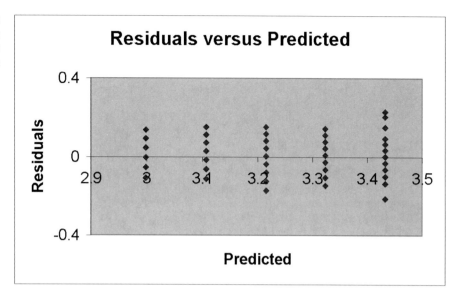

The histogram of the residuals indicates that the error variable may be normal. The plot of the residuals versus the predicted values of the dependent variable shows some change in the variance. However, the change is smaller than in the original model. Thus, the transformation has decreased the degree of heteroscedasticity.

**Excel Output for
Example 18.3 (1/MARK)**

	A	B	C	D	E	F
1	SUMMARY OUTPUT					
2						
3	*Regression Statistics*					
4	Multiple R	0.8820				
5	R Square	0.7779				
6	Adjusted R Square	0.7756				
7	Standard Error	0.00335				
8	Observations	100				
9						
10	ANOVA					
11		*df*	*SS*	*MS*	*F*	*Significance F*
12	Regression	1	0.00384	0.00384	343.21	0.0000
13	Residual	98	0.00110	0.000011		
14	Total	99	0.00494			
15						
16		*Coefficients*	*Standard Error*	*t Stat*	*P-value*	
17	Intercept	0.0846	0.00239	35.40	0.0000	
18	Time	-0.00088	0.000047	-18.53	0.0000	

Minitab Output for Example 18.3 (1/MARK)

Regression Analysis

```
The regression equation is
1/Mark = 0.0846 -0.000876 Time


Predictor        Coef       StDev           T         P
Constant      0.084574    0.002389       35.40     0.000
Time        -0.00087647  0.00004731     -18.53     0.000


S = 0.003345   R-Sq = 77.8%     R-Sq(adj) = 77.6%

Analysis of Variance

Source          DF         SS          MS          F         P
Regression       1     0.0038410   0.0038410    343.21     0.000
Residual Error  98     0.0010968   0.0000112
Total           99     0.0049377
```

Histogram of Residuals in Example 18.3 (1/MARK)

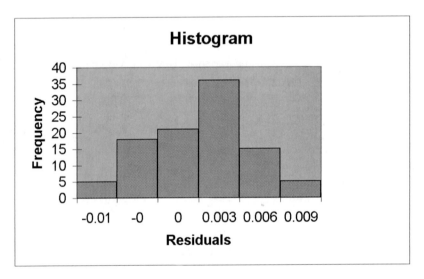

Plot of Residuals versus Predicted Values in Example 18.3 (1/MARK)

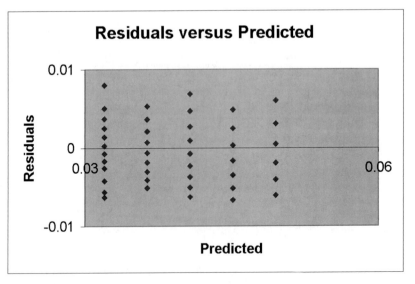

The problem of heteroscedasticity has been resolved. However, the error variable does not appear to be normal. Thus, the logarithmic transformation is judged to be superior.

By remedying a violation of the required condition, we have improved the fit. As you can see, both transformed dependent variable models have larger coefficients of determination and F-statistics. (Note that we cannot use the standard error of estimate to make the comparison because the dependent variables are different.)

In practice, statisticians often experiment with different transformations to determine which one works best. Ideally, we look for transformations where the required conditions are well satisfied and whose fit is best.

▲

EXERCISES

18.14 Refer to Exercise 18.1. The residuals and predicted values for the regression equation were determined. The histogram of the residuals and the graph of the residuals versus the predicted values are shown below.

a Does it appear that the normality requirement is violated? Explain.

b Is the error variable variance constant? Explain.

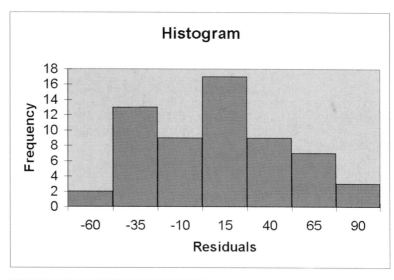

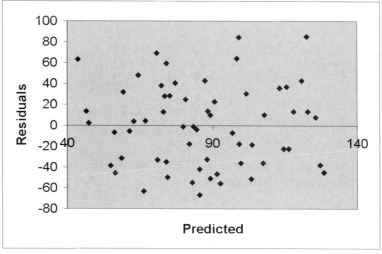

18.15 Refer to Exercise 18.1. The correlations for each pair of independent variables are shown below.

a What do these correlations tell you about the independent variables?

b What do these statistics tell you about the *t*-tests of the coefficients in the multiple regression model?

Pair of independent variables	Correlation
LOT-SIZE and **TREES**	.286
LOT-SIZE and **DISTANCE**	−.189
TREES and **DISTANCE**	.079

18.17 Refer to Exercise 18.2. The correlation between **AS SGNMNT** and **MIDTERM** is .104.

a What does this correlation tell you about the independent variables?

b What does it say about the *t*-tests of β_1 and β_2 in the multiple regression model?

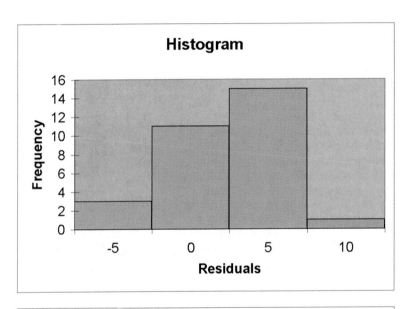

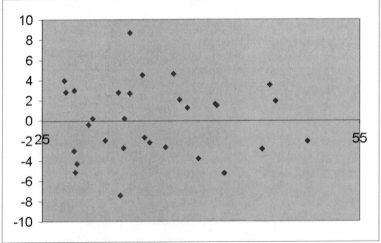

18.16 Refer to Exercise 18.2. The histogram of the residuals and the graph of the residuals and the predicted values are shown below.

a Does it appear that the normality requirement is violated? Explain.

b Is the error variable variance constant? Explain.

18.18 Refer to Exercise 18.4. The histogram of the residuals and the graph of the residuals and the predicted values follow.

a Does it appear that the normality requirement is violated? Explain.

b Is the error variable variance constant? Explain.

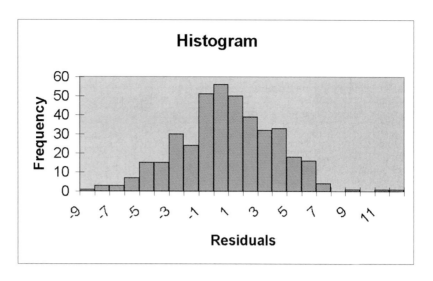

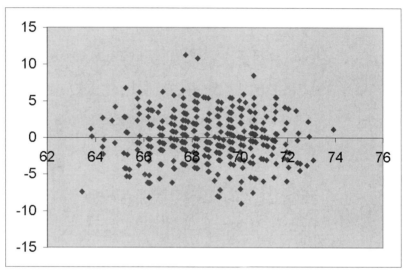

18.19 Refer to Exercise 18.4. The correlation between **FATHER** and **MOTHER** is .251.

    a What does this correlation tell you about the independent variables?

    b What does it say about the t-tests of β_1 and β_2 in the multiple regression model?

The following exercises require the use of a computer and statistical software.

18.20 The observations of variables y, x_1, and x_2 are stored in columns 1, 2, and 3, respectively, of file XR18-20.

    a Conduct a regression analysis of these data.

    b Calculate the residuals and standardized residuals. Identify any observations that should be checked.

    c Draw a histogram of the residuals. Is it likely that the normality requirement is violated?

    d Plot the residuals versus the predicted values of y. Is the variance of the error variable constant?

    e If heteroscedasticity exists, propose several possible remedies. Attempt each and report your findings.

18.21 The observations of variables y, x_1, and x_2 are stored in columns 1, 2, and 3, respectively, of file XR18-21.

    a Conduct a regression analysis of these data.

    b Calculate the residuals and standardized residuals. Identify the observations that should be checked for accuracy.

    c Draw a histogram of the residuals. Is it likely that the normality requirement is violated?

    d Plot the residuals versus the predicted values of y. Is the variance of the error variable constant?

    e If heteroscedasticity exists, propose several possible remedies. Attempt each and report your findings.

18.22 Refer to Exercise 17.70. Conduct an analysis of the residuals to determine whether any of the required conditions are violated. Identify any observations that should be checked for accuracy.

18.23 Determine whether there are violations of the required conditions in the regression model used in Exercise 17.77. Which, if any, observations should be checked to ensure that they were correctly recorded?

18.24 Determine whether the required conditions are satisfied in Exercise 17.79.

18.25 Refer to Exercise 18.5.

    a Is multicollinearity a problem? Explain.

    b Determine the residuals and predicted values using the regression equation.

    c Draw a histogram of the residuals. Does it appear that the error variable is normally distributed?

    d Plot the residuals (on the vertical axis) and the predicted values (on the horizontal axis). Is the variance of the error variable constant?

    e Identify observations that should be checked for accuracy.

18.26 Refer to Exercise 18.6.

    a Use whatever techniques you deem necessary to check the normality requirement and check for heteroscedasticity.

    b Is multicollinearity a problem? Explain.

    c Identify all observations that should be checked.

18.27 Refer to Exercise 18.7.

    a Use whatever techniques you deem necessary to check the normality requirement and check for heteroscedasticity.

    b Is multicollinearity a problem? Explain.

18.28 Refer to Exercise 18.8.

    a Determine whether the required conditions are satisfied.

    b Is multicollinearity a problem?

18.29 Refer to Exercise 18.9. Determine whether the required conditions are satisfied.

18.30 Determine whether the required conditions for the regression analysis conducted in Exercise 18.10 are satisfied.

18.5 REGRESSION DIAGNOSTICS—III (TIME SERIES)

In Chapter 17, we pointed out that, in general, we check to see if the errors are independent when the data constitute a times series—data gathered sequentially over a series of time periods. In Section 17.9, we described the graphical procedure for determining whether the required condition that the errors are independent is violated. We plot the residuals versus the time periods and look for patterns. In this section, we augment that procedure with the **Durbin–Watson test.**

DURBIN–WATSON TEST

The Durbin–Watson test allows the statistician to determine whether there is evidence of **first-order autocorrelation**—a condition in which a relationship exists between consecutive residuals r_i and r_{i-1}, where i is the time period. The Durbin–Watson statistic is defined as

$$d = \frac{\sum_{i=2}^{n}(r_i - r_{i-1})^2}{\sum_{i=1}^{n}r_i^2}$$

The range of the values of d is

$$0 \le d \le 4$$

where small values of d $(d < 2)$ indicate a positive first-order autocorrelation and large values of d $(d > 2)$ imply a negative first-order autocorrelation. Positive first-order autocorrelation is a common occurrence in business and economic time series. It occurs when consecutive residuals tend to be similar. In that case, $(r_i - r_{i-1})^2$ will be small, producing a small value for d. Negative first-order autocorrelation occurs when consecutive residuals differ widely. For example, if positive and negative residuals generally alternate, $(r_i - r_{i-1})^2$ will be large, and as a result, d will be greater than 2. Figures 18.2 and 18.3 depict positive autocorrelation, whereas Figure 18.4 illustrates negative autocorrelation. Notice that in Figure 18.2, the first residual is a small number; the second residual, also a small number, is somewhat larger; and that trend continues. In Figure 18.3, the first residual is large, and, in general, succeeding residuals decrease. In both figures, consecutive residuals are similar. In Figure 18.4, the first residual is a positive number, which is followed by a negative residual. The remaining residuals follow this pattern (with some exceptions). Consecutive residuals are quite different.

Table 12 in Appendix B is designed to test for positive first-order autocorrelation by providing values of d_L and d_U for a variety of values of n and k and for $\alpha = .01$ and $.05$.

The decision is made in the following way. If $d < d_L$, we conclude that there is enough evidence to show that positive first-order autocorrelation exists. If $d > d_U$,

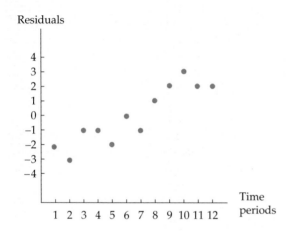

Figure 18.2

Positive first-order autocorrelation

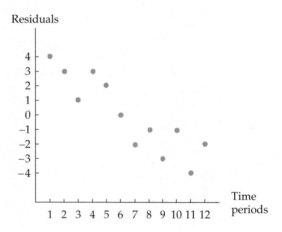

Figure 18.3

Positive first-order autocorrelation

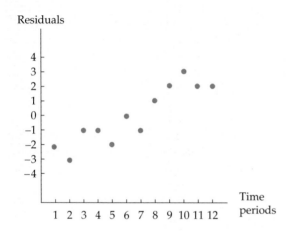

Figure 18.4

Negative first-order autocorrelation

we conclude that there is not enough evidence to show that positive first-order auto-correlation exists. And if $d_L \leq d \leq d_U$, the test is inconclusive. The recommended course of action when the test is inconclusive is to continue testing with more data until a conclusive decision can be made.

For example, to test for positive first-order autocorrelation with $n = 20$, $k = 3$, and $\alpha = .05$, we test the following hypotheses.

H_0: There is no first-order autocorrelation

H_1: There is positive first-order autocorrelation

The decision is made as follows.

If $d < d_L = 1.00$, reject the null hypothesis in favor of the alternative hypothesis.

If $d > d_U = 1.68$, do not reject the null hypothesis.

If $1.00 \leq d \leq 1.68$, the test is inconclusive.

To test for negative first-order autocorrelation, we change the critical values. If $d > 4 - d_L$, we conclude that negative first-order autocorrelation exists. If $d < 4 - d_U$, we conclude that there is not enough evidence to show that negative first-order autocorrelation exists. If $4 - d_U \leq d \leq 4 - d_L$, the test is inconclusive.

We can also test simply for first-order autocorrelation by combining the two one-tail tests. If $d < d_L$ or $d > 4 - d_L$, we conclude that autocorrelation exists. If $d_U \leq d \leq 4 - d_U$, we conclude that there is no evidence of autocorrelation. If $d_L \leq d \leq d_U$ or $4 - d_U \leq d \leq 4 - d_L$, the test is inconclusive The significance level will be 2α (where α is the one-tail significance level). Figure 18.5 describes the range of values of d and the conclusion for each interval.

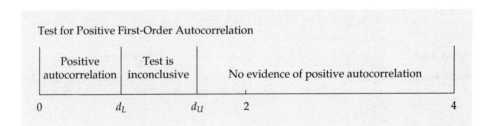

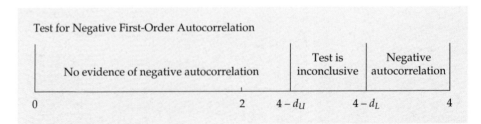

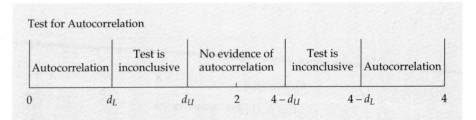

Figure 18.5

Durbin–Watson test

For time-series data, we add the Durbin–Watson test to our list of regression diagnostics. That is, we determine whether the error variable is normally distributed with constant variance (as we did in Section 18.4), we identify outliers and (if our software allows it) influential observations that should be verified, and we conduct the Durbin–Watson test.

▼ **EXAMPLE 18.4**

Christmas week is a critical period for most ski resorts. Because many students and adults are free from other obligations, they are able to spend several days indulging in their favorite pastime, skiing. A large proportion of gross revenue is earned during this period. A ski resort in Vermont wanted to determine the effect that weather had on their sales of lift tickets. The manager of the resort collected the number of lift tickets sold during Christmas week, the total snowfall (in inches), and the average temperature (in degrees Fahrenheit) for the past 20 years. These data are listed below and stored in columns 1 to 3, respectively, of file XM18-04. Develop the multiple regression model, and diagnose any violations of the required conditions.

Total Number of Tickets (TICKETS)	Total Snowfall (SNOWFALL)	Average Temperature (TEMPTURE)
6,835	19	11
7,870	15	−19
6,173	7	36
7,979	11	22
7,639	19	14
7,167	2	−20
8,094	21	39
9,903	19	27
9,788	18	26
9,557	20	16
9,784	19	−1
12,075	25	−9
9,128	3	37
9,047	17	−15
10,631	0	22
12,563	24	2
11,012	22	32
10,041	7	18
9,929	21	32
11,091	11	−15

Solution   We estimated the model

$$\text{TICKETS} = \beta_0 + \beta_1 \text{ SNOWFALL} + \beta_2 \text{ TEMPTURE} + \epsilon$$

The Excel and Minitab printouts follow.

	A	B	C	D	E	F
1	SUMMARY OUTPUT					
2						
3	*Regression Statistics*					
4	Multiple R	0.3465				
5	R Square	0.1200				
6	Adjusted R Square	0.0165				
7	Standard Error	1712				
8	Observations	20				
9						
10	ANOVA					
11		*df*	*SS*	*MS*	*F*	*Significance F*
12	Regression	2	6793798	3396899	1.16	0.3373
13	Residual	17	49807214	2929836		
14	Total	19	56601012			
15						
16		*Coefficients*	*Standard Error*	*t Stat*	*P-value*	
17	Intercept	8308	903.7	9.19	0.0000	
18	Snowfall	74.59	51.57	1.45	0.1663	
19	Temperature	-8.75	19.70	-0.44	0.6625	

Regression Analysis

```
The regression equation is
Tickets = 8308 + 74.6 Snowfall - 8.8 Tempture

Predictor        Coef        StDev            T          P
Constant       8308.0        903.7         9.19      0.000
Snowfall        74.59        51.57         1.45      0.166
Tempture        -8.75        19.70        -0.44      0.662


S = 1712        R-Sq = 12.0%       R-Sq(adj) = 1.7%


Analysis of Variance

Source           DF           SS            MS          F          P
Regression        2      6793798       3396899       1.16      0.337
Residual Error   17     49807214       2929836
Total            19     56601012
```

As you can see, the coefficient of determination is low ($R^2 = 12.0\%$ and adjusted $R^2 = 1.65\%$) and the p-value of the F-test is .3373, which indicates that the model is a poor one. We used Excel to determine the residuals and the predicted values. We then drew the histogram, plotted the residuals versus the predicted values of y, and plotted the residuals versus the time periods. (The observations constitute a time series because we observed the results from the past 20 years.)

Histogram of Residuals in Example 18.4

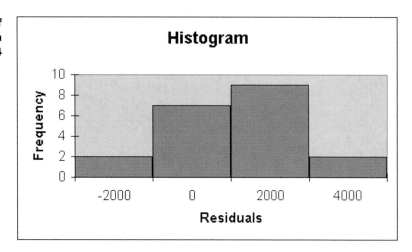

The histogram of the residuals indicates that the error variable may be normally distributed.

Plot of Residuals Versus Predicted Values of y in Example 18.4

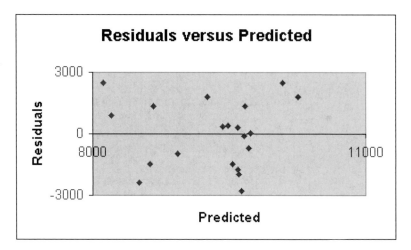

The graph of the residuals and predicted values seems to indicate that the variance of the error variable is constant.

Plot of Residuals Versus Time Periods in Example 18.4

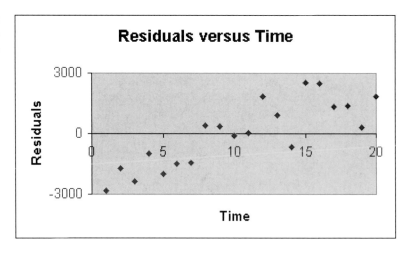

This graph reveals a serious problem. There is a strong relationship between consecutive values of the residuals, which indicates that the requirement that the errors are independent has been violated. To confirm this diagnosis, we instructed Excel and Mintab to calculate the Durbin–Watson statistic.

Excel
Durbin–Watson Statistic
for Example 18.4

	A	B	C
1	Durbin-Watson Statistic		
2			
3	d = 0.5931		

COMMANDS

Proceed through the usual steps to conduct a regression analysis and print the residuals (see page 684). Highlight the entire list of residuals and click **Tools, Data Analysis Plus,** and **Durbin-Watson Statistic.**

Minitab
Durbin–Watson Statistic
for Example 18.4

```
Durbin-Watson statistic = 0.59
```

COMMANDS

Follow steps 1 through 4 on page 684. Before clicking **OK,** click **Options ...** and **Durbin-Watson statistic.**

The critical values are determined by noting that $n = 20$ and $k = 2$ (there are two independent variables in the model). If we wish to test for positive first-order autocorrelation with $\alpha = .05$, we find in Table 12(a) in Appendix B

$d_L = 1.10$ and $d_U = 1.54$

The null and alternative hypotheses are

H_0: There is no first-order autocorrelation

H_1: There is positive first-order autocorrelation

The rejection region is $d < d_L = 1.10$. Since $d = .59$, we reject the null hypothesis and conclude that there is enough evidence to infer that positive first-order autocorrelation exists.

Autocorrelation usually indicates that the model has been misspecified. Specifically, we need to include one or more independent variables that have time-ordered effects on the dependent variable. The simplest such independent variable represents the time periods. To illustrate, we included a third independent variable that records the year since the data were gathered. Thus, TIME = 1, 2, ... , 20. The new model is

$$\text{TICKETS} = \beta_0 + \beta_1 \text{ SNOWFALL} + \beta_2 \text{ TEMPTURE} + \beta_3 \text{ TIME} + \epsilon$$

The results are shown on the following page.

Excel Output for Example 18.4 (Time Variable Included)

	A	B	C	D	E	F
1	SUMMARY OUTPUT					
2						
3	*Regression Statistics*					
4	Multiple R	0.8608				
5	R Square	0.7410				
6	Adjusted R Square	0.6924				
7	Standard Error	957.2				
8	Observations	20				
9						
10	ANOVA					
11		df	SS	MS	F	Significance F
12	Regression	3	41940217	13980072	15.26	0.0001
13	Residual	16	14660795	916300		
14	Total	19	56601012			
15						
16		Coefficients	Standard Error	t Stat	P-value	
17	Intercept	5966	631.3	9.450	0.0000	
18	Snowfall	70.18	28.85	2.433	0.0271	
19	Temperature	-9.23	11.02	-0.838	0.4145	
20	Time	230.0	37.13	6.193	0.0000	

Minitab Output for Example 18.4 (Time Variable Included)

Regression Analysis

The regression equation is
Tickets = 5966 + 70.2 Snowfall - 9.2 Tempture + 230 Time

Predictor	Coef	StDev	T	P
Constant	5965.6	631.3	9.45	0.000
Snowfall	70.18	28.85	2.43	0.027
Tempture	-9.23	11.02	-0.84	0.414
Time	229.97	37.13	6.19	0.000

S = 957.2   R-Sq = 74.1%   R-Sq(adj) = 69.2%

Analysis of Variance

Source	DF	SS	MS	F	P
Regression	3	41940217	13980072	15.26	0.000
Residual Error	16	14660795	916300		
Total	19	56601012			

As we did before, we calculate the residuals and conduct regression diagnostics using Excel. The results follow.

Histogram of Residuals in Example 18.4 (Time Variable Included)

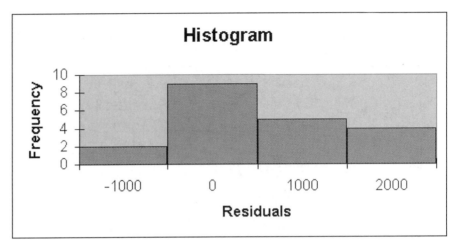

The histogram of the residuals indicates that the errors may be normally distributed.

Plot of Residuals Versus Predicted Values of y in Example 18.4 (Time Variable Included)

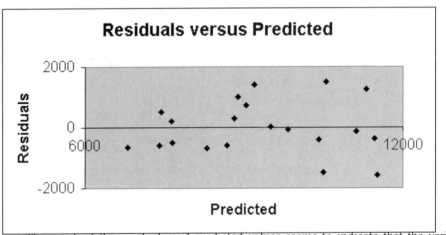

The graph of the residuals and predicted values seems to indicate that the variance of the error variable is constant.

Plot of Residuals Versus Time Periods in Example 18.4 (Time Variable Included)

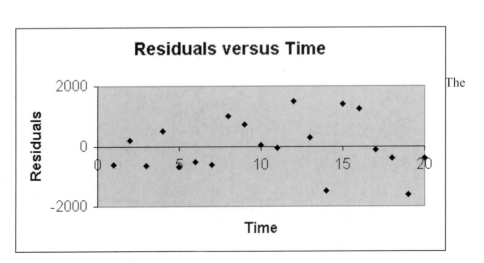

The

Durbin–Watson statistic is $d = 1.88$. From Table 12(a) in Appendix B, we find the critical values of the Durbin–Watson test. With $k = 3$ and $n = 20$, we find

$$d_L = 1.00 \text{ and } d_U = 1.68$$

Since $d > 1.68$, we conclude that there is not enough evidence to infer the presence of positive first-order autocorrelation.

Notice that the model is improved dramatically. The F-test tells us that the model is valid. The t-tests tell us that both the amount of snowfall and time are significantly linearly related to the number of lift tickets. This information could prove useful in advertising for the resort. For example, if there has been a recent snowfall, they could emphasize that in their advertising. If no new snow has fallen, they may emphasize their snow-making facilities.

▲

DEVELOPING AN UNDERSTANDING OF STATISTICAL CONCEPTS

Notice that the addition of the variable **TIME** explained a large proportion of the variation in the number of lift tickets sold. That is, the resort experienced a relatively steady increase in sales over the past 20 years. Once this variable was included in the model, the variable **SNOWFALL** became significant because it was able to explain some of the remaining variation in lift ticket sales. Without **TIME**, **SNOWFALL** and **TEMPTURE** were unable to explain a significant proportion of the variation in ticket sales. The graph of the residuals versus the time periods and the Durbin–Watson test enabled us to identify the problem and correct it. In overcoming the autocorrelation problem, we improved the model so that we identified **SNOWFALL** as an important variable in determining ticket sales. This result is quite common. Correcting a violation of a required condition will frequently improve the model.

EXERCISES

18.31 Given the following information, perform the Durbin–Watson test to determine whether first-order autocorrelation exists.

$n = 25$ $k = 5$ $\alpha = .10$ $d = .90$

18.32 Test the following hypotheses with $\alpha = .05$.

H_0: There is no first-order autocorrelation

H_1: There is positive first-order autocorrelation

$n = 50$ $k = 2$ $d = 1.38$

18.33 Test the following hypotheses with $\alpha = .02$.

H_0: There is no first-order autocorrelation

H_1: There is first-order autocorrelation

$n = 90$ $k = 5$ $d = 1.60$

18.34 Test the following hypotheses with $\alpha = .05$.

H_0: There is no first-order autocorrelation

H_1: There is negative first-order autocorrelation

$n = 33$ $k = 4$ $d = 2.25$

Exercises 18.35–18.37 and Exercises 18.41–18.43 require statistical software and a computer.

18.35 One hundred observations of variables y, x_1, and x_2 were taken over 100 consecutive time periods. The data are stored in the first three columns, respectively, of file XR18-35.

a Conduct a regression analysis of these data.

b Calculate the residuals and standardized residuals.

c Identify observations that should be checked.

d Draw the histogram of the residuals. Does it appear that the normality requirement is satisfied?

e Plot the residuals versus the predicted values of y. Is the error variance constant?

f Plot the residuals versus the time periods. Perform the Durbin–Watson test. Is there evidence of autocorrelation? Use $\alpha = .10$.

g If autocorrelation was detected in part (f), propose an alternative regression model to remedy the problem. Use the computer to generate the statistics associated with this model.

h Redo parts (a) through (f). Compare the two models.

18.36 Weekly sales of a company's product (y) and those of its main competitor (x) were recorded for one year. These data are stored in chronological order in columns 1 (company's sales) and 2 (competitor's sales) of file XR18-36.

a Conduct a regression analysis of these data.
b Calculate the residuals and standardized residuals.
c Identify observations that should be checked.
d Draw the histogram of the residuals. Does it appear that the normality requirement is satisfied?
e Plot the residuals versus the predicted values of y. Is the error variance constant?
f Plot the residuals versus the time periods. Perform the Durbin–Watson test. Is there evidence of autocorrelation? Use $\alpha = .10$.
g If autocorrelation was detected in part (f), propose an alternative regression model to remedy the problem. Use the computer to generate the statistics associated with this model.
h Redo parts (a) through (f). Compare the two models.

18.37 Observations of variables y, x_1, x_2, and x_3 were taken over 80 consecutive time periods. The data are stored in the first four columns, respectively, of file XR18-37.

a Conduct a regression analysis of these data.
b Calculate the residuals and standardized residuals.
c Identify observations that should be checked.
d Draw the histogram of the residuals. Does it appear that the normality requirement is satisfied?
e Plot the residuals versus the predicted values of y. Is the error variance constant?
f Plot the residuals versus the time periods. Perform the Durbin–Watson test. Is there evidence at the 10% significance level of autocorrelation?
g If autocorrelation was detected in part (f), propose an alternative regression model to remedy the problem. Use the computer to generate the statistics associated with this model.
h Redo parts (a) through (f). Compare the two models.

18.38 Refer to Exercise 18.3. The histogram of the residuals and the graph of the residuals and the predicted values are shown below.

a Does it appear that the normality requirement is violated? Explain.
b Is the error variable variance constant? Explain.

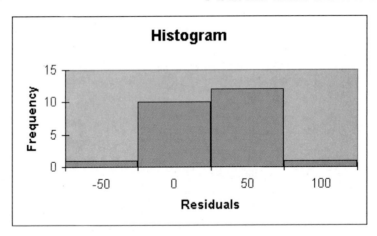

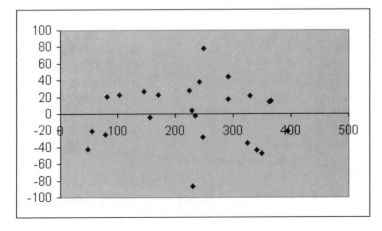

18.39 Refer to Exercise 18.3. The correlations for each pair of independent variables are shown below.

a What do these correlations tell you about the independent variables?

b Is it likely that the *t*-tests of the coefficients are meaningful? Explain.

Pair of independent variables	Correlation
PERMITS & **MORTGAGE**	.005
PERMITS & **A-VACNCY**	−.150
PERMITS & **O-VACNCY**	−.103
MORTGAGE & **A-VACNCY**	−.040
MORTGAGE & **O-VACNCY**	−.033
A-VACNCY & **O-VACNCY**	.065

18.40 Refer to Exercise 18.3. The Durbin–Watson statistic is $d = 1.75$. What does this statistic tell you about the regression model? Use $\alpha = .10$.

18.41 Refer to Exercise 17.69. Perform a complete regression diagnostic analysis of the simple regression model used in that exercise. That is, determine whether the error variable is normal with constant variance and whether the errors are independent. Identify any observations that should be checked for accuracy.

18.42 Refer to Example 17.5.

a Compute the residuals and the standardized residuals.

b Draw the histogram of the residuals. Does it appear that the normality requirement is satisfied?

c Are there observations that should be checked to ensure that they were recorded properly and whether they properly belong in the sample?

d Calculate the predicted values of the dependent variable, and plot them versus the residuals. Does it appear that the variance of the error variable is constant?

e Plot the residuals versus the time periods. Does it appear that the errors are not independent?

f Calculate the Durbin–Watson statistic and test (with $\alpha = .10$) to determine whether first-order autocorrelation exists.

18.43 The manager of a tire store in Minneapolis has been concerned with the high cost of inventory. The current policy is to stock all the snow tires that are predicted to sell over the entire winter at the beginning of the season (end of October). The manager can reduce inventory costs by having suppliers deliver snow tires regularly from October to February. However, he needs to be able to predict weekly sales to avoid stockouts that will ultimately lose sales. To help develop a forecasting model, he records the number of snow tires sold weekly during the last winter and the amount of snowfall (in inches) in each week. These data are stored in columns 1 and 2, respectively, in file XR18-43.

a Develop a regression model and use a software package to produce the statistics.

b Perform a complete diagnostic analysis to determine whether the required conditions are satisfied.

c If one or more conditions are unsatisfied, attempt to remedy the problem.

d Use whatever procedures you wish to assess how well the new model fits the data.

e Interpret and test each of the coefficients.

18.6 SUMMARY

The multiple regression model extends the model introduced in Chapter 17. The statistical concepts and techniques are similar to those presented in simple linear regression. We assess the model in three ways: standard error of estimate, the coefficient of determination (and the coefficient of determination adjusted for degrees of freedom), and the *F*-test of the analysis of variance. We can use the *t*-tests of the coefficients to determine whether each of the independent variables is linearly related to the dependent variable. As we did in Chapter 17, we showed how to diagnose violations of the required conditions and to identify other problems. Transformations were shown to be the best way of dealing with nonnormality and heteroscedasticity. We introduced multicollinearity and demonstrated its effect and its remedy. Finally, we presented the Durbin–Watson test to detect first-order autocorrelation.

IMPORTANT TERMS

Response surface *680*
Plane *680*
Coefficient of determination adjusted
    for degrees of freedom *685*
F-test *691*

Durbin–Watson test *699*
Multicollinearity *700*
Transformations *705*
First-order autocorrelation *714*

SUPPLEMENTARY EXERCISES

The following exercises require the use of a computer and statistical software.

18.44 An M.B.A. program that was started two decades ago wanted to analyze the factors that affect student performance. The dean of the School of Business decided to build a multiple regression model where the dependent variable is the M.B.A. grade point average (GPA) for each of 100 randomly selected M.B.A. students who graduated in the past 3 years. The independent variables are the undergraduate GPA, the Graduate Management Admissions Test score (GMAT), and the number of years of work experience prior to entering the program. These data are stored in columns 1 to 4, respectively, in file XR18-44.

   a Conduct a multiple regression analysis.
   b Briefly describe what the coefficients tell you.
   c Test to determine which independent variables affect the dependent variable. Use $\alpha = .01$.
   d Assess the model's fit.
   e Can we infer at the 1% significance level that the regression model is valid in analyzing the variables that affect M.B.A. GPA?
   f Predict with 95% confidence the M.B.A. GPA for an applicant whose undergraduate GPA is 8, GMAT score = 630, and who has worked for 5 years.

18.45 Refer to Exercise 18.44.

   a Determine whether any of the required conditions are violated.
   b Are the coefficients and *t*-tests of the coefficients affected by multicollinearity? Explain.

18.46 Supermarkets frequently price products such as bread and milk to attract customers to the store. A manager of a dairy that supplies milk to a supermarket wanted to know how sales of milk are affected by different prices. Consequently, she recorded the weekly sales of milk at one supermarket, the price of a quart of her company's brand (price A), and the price of a quart of her competitor's brand (price B). The data for the past 52 weeks are stored in columns 1 through 3, respectively, in file XR18-46.

   a Develop a regression model and use a software package to produce the statistics.
   b Assess how well the model fits the data.
   c Interpret each of the coefficients.
   d Can we infer at the 10% significance level that each of the independent variables is linearly related to the weekly sales of milk?
   e Test with $\alpha = .10$ to determine whether the model is valid.
   f Predict with 90% confidence the sales of milk when the company's price is 65 cents and the competitor's price is 45 cents.

18.47 Refer to Exercise 18.46.

   a Analyze the results and determine whether the required conditions are satisfied.
   b Is multicollinearity a problem that affects your answer in part (d)? Explain.

18.48 The general manager of the Cleveland Indians baseball team is in the process of determining which minor-league players to draft. He is aware that his team needs home-run hitters and would like to find a way to predict the number of home runs a player will hit. Being an astute statistician, he gathers a random sample of players and records the number of home runs each player hit in his first two full years as a major-league player, the number of home runs he hit in his last full year in the minor leagues, his age, and the number of years of professional baseball. These data are stored in columns 1 through 4, respectively, in file XR18-48.

   a Develop a regression model and use a software package to produce the statistics.
   b Interpret each of the coefficients.
   c How well does the model fit?
   d Test the model's validity at the 5% significance level.
   e Do each of the independent variables belong in the model? Test with a 5% significance level.
   f Predict with 95% confidence the number of home runs in the first 2 years of a player who is 25 years old, has played professional baseball for 7 years, and hit 22 home runs in his last year in the minor leagues.
   g Estimate with 95% confidence the expected number of home runs in the first 2 years of players who are 27 years old, have played professional baseball for 5 years, and hit 18 home runs in their last year in the minors.

18.49 Refer to Exercise 18.48.

   a Determine whether the required conditions are satisfied.
   b Is multicollinearity a problem? Could we have known about the multicollinearity before the model was created? Explain.

18.50 The agronomist referred to in Exercise 17.72 believed that the amount of rainfall as well as the amount of fertilizer used would affect the crop yield. She redid the experiment in the following way. Thirty greenhouses were rented. In each, the amount of fertilizer and the amount of water were varied. At the end of the growing season, the amount of corn was recorded with the data stored in file XR18-50 (column 1 = crop yield in kilograms; column 2 = amount of fertilizer applied in kilograms; column 3 = amount of water in liters per week).

a Determine the sample regression line, and interpret the coefficients.

b Do these data allow us to infer at the 5% significance level that there is a linear relationship between the amount of fertilizer and the crop yield?

c Do these data allow us to infer at the 5% significance level that there is a linear relationship between the amount of water and the crop yield?

d What can you say about the multiple regression model's fit?

e Predict the crop yield when 100 kilograms of fertilizer and 1,000 liters of water are applied. Use a confidence level of 95%.

18.51 Refer to Exercise 18.50. Perform a complete diagnostic analysis to determine whether the required conditions are satisfied. Which conditions, if any, are unsatisfied? Suggest a way to remedy the problem.

18.52 Regression analysis is often used in medical research to examine the variables that affect various biological processes. A study performed by medical scientists investigated nutritional effects on preweaning mouse pups. In the experiment, the amount of nutrients was varied by rearing the pups in different litter sizes. After 32 days, the body weight and brain weight (both measured in grams) were recorded. These data are stored in file XR18-52 (column 1 = brain weight; column 2 = litter size; column 3 = body weight).

a Conduct a multiple regression analysis where the dependent variable is the brain weight. Interpret the coefficients.

b Can we infer at the 5% significance level that there is a linear relationship between litter size and brain weight?

c Can we infer at the 5% significance level that there is a linear relationship between body weight and brain weight?

d What is the coefficient of determination, and what does it tell you about this model?

e Test the overall validity of the model. (Use a 5% significance level.)

f Predict with 95% confidence the brain weight of a mouse pup that came from a litter of 10 pups and whose body weight is 8 grams.

g Estimate with 95% confidence the mean weight of all mouse pups that came from litters of 6 pups and whose body weight is 7 grams.

Source: D. E. Matthews and V. T. Farewell, Using and Understanding Medical Statistics (Karger, 1988).

18.53 Refer to Exercise 18.52. Suppose that the experiment did not record the body weights of the mice.

a Conduct a simple linear regression analysis where the dependent variable is brain weight and the independent variable is litter size. Interpret the coefficients.

b Can we infer at the 5% significance level that there is a linear relationship between brain weight and litter size?

c What is the coefficient of determination, and what does it tell you about this model?

d Test the overall validity of the model with $\alpha = .05$. Compare the results of this test with the test performed in part (b).

e Predict with 95% confidence the brain weight of a mouse pup that came from a litter of 10 pups.

f Estimate with 95% confidence the mean weight of all mouse pups that came from litters of 6 pups.

18.54 The administrator of a school board in a large county was analyzing the average mathematics test scores in the schools under her control. She noticed that there were dramatic differences in scores among the schools. In an attempt to improve the scores of all the schools, she attempted to determine the factors that account for the differences. Accordingly, she took a random sample of 40 schools across the county and, for each, determined the mean test score last year, the percentage of teachers in each school who have at least one university degree in mathematics, the mean age, and the mean annual income of the mathematics teachers. These data are stored in columns 1 to 4, respectively, of file XR18-54.

a Conduct a regression analysis to develop the equation.

b Is the model valid in explaining the variation among schools? Explain.

c Are the required conditions satisfied? Explain.

d Is multicollinearity a problem? Explain.

e Interpret and test the coefficients (with $\alpha = .05$).

f Predict with 95% confidence the test score at a school where 50% of the mathematics teachers have mathematics degrees, the mean age is 43, and the mean annual income is $48,300.

18.55 Life insurance companies are keenly interested in predicting how long their customers will live, because their premiums and profitability depend on such numbers. An actuary for one insurance company gathered data for 100 recently deceased male customers. He recorded the age at death of the customer plus the ages at death of his mother and father, the mean ages at death of his grandmothers, and the mean ages at death of his grandfathers. These data are recorded in columns 1 to 5, respectively, of file XR18-55.

a Perform a multiple regression analysis on these data.

b Is the model likely to be useful in predicting men's longevity?

c Are the required conditions satisfied?

d Is multicollinearity a problem here?

e Interpret and test the coefficients. Use $\alpha = .05$.

f Predict with 95% confidence the longevity of a man whose parents lived to the age of 70, whose grandmothers averaged 80 years, and whose grandfathers averaged 75.

g Estimate with 95% confidence the mean longevity of men whose mothers lived to 75, whose fathers lived to 65, whose grandmothers averaged 85 years, and whose grandfathers averaged 75.

18.56 University students often complain that universities reward professors for research but not for teaching, and argue that professors react to this situation by devoting more time and energy to the publication of their findings and less time and energy to classroom activities. Professors counter that research and teaching go hand in hand; more research makes better teachers. A student organization at one university decided to investigate the issue. They randomly selected 50 economics professors employed by a multicampus university. The students recorded the salaries of the professors, their average teaching evaluations (on a 10-point scale), and the total number of journal articles published in their careers. These data are stored in columns 1 to 3, respectively, in file XR18-56. Perform a complete analysis (produce the regression equation, assess it, and diagnose it) and report your findings.

18.57 One of the critical factors that determine the success of a catalog store chain is the availability of products that consumers want to buy. If a store is sold out, future sales to that customer are less likely. Accordingly, delivery trucks operating from a central warehouse regularly resupply stores. In an analysis of a chain's operations, the general manager wanted to determine the factors that affected how long it took to unload delivery trucks. A random sample of 50 deliveries to one store was observed. The times (in minutes) to unload the truck, the total number of boxes, and the total weight (in hundreds of pounds) of the boxes were recorded and stored in file XR18-57.

a Determine the multiple regression equation.

b How well does the model fit the data? Explain.

c Are the required conditions satisfied?

d Is multicollinearity a problem?

e Interpret and test (with $\alpha = .05$) the coefficients. What does this analysis tell you?

f Produce a prediction interval for the amount of time needed to unload a truck with 100 boxes weighing 5,000 pounds. Use a 90% confidence level.

g Produce an interval estimate of the average amount of time needed to unload trucks with 100 boxes weighing 5,000 pounds. Use a 90% confidence level.

18.58 Lotteries have become important sources of revenue for governments. Many people have criticized lotteries, however, referring to them as a tax on the poor and uneducated. In an examination of the issue, a random sample of 100 adults was asked how much they spend on lottery tickets and was interviewed about various socioeconomic variables. The purpose of this study is to test the following beliefs.

1 Relatively uneducated people spend more on lotteries than do relatively educated people.

2 Older people buy more lottery tickets than younger people.

3 People with more children spend more on lotteries than people with fewer children.

4 Relatively poor people spend a greater proportion of their income on lotteries than relatively rich people.

The following data were stored in columns 1 to 5, respectively, of file XR18-58.

> Amount spent on lottery tickets as a percentage of total household income
> Number of years of education
> Age
> Number of children
> Personal income (in thousands of dollars)

a Develop the multiple regression equation.

b Is the complete model valid?

c Are the required conditions satisfied?

d Is multicollinearity a problem?

e Test each of the beliefs at the 5% significance level. What conclusions can you draw?

CASE 18.1   Duxbury Press Revisited

After performing the simple regression analysis of Case 17.1, Curt was disappointed with the results. The coefficient of determination was quite low, indicating a weak linear relationship. This suggested that the number of free copies is not an indicator of sales revenues. However, he was assured by all of the statistics authors that regression is a useful and commonly used tool. Consequently, Curt decided to improve the model by including additional variables that measure the ability of his representatives. He determined the number of years of experience and the total sales in dollars in the previous year. These data are stored in file C18-01 in the following way.

Column 1: code representing sales zone

Column 2: sales revenues from statistics books in 1993

Column 3: number of free copies

Column 4: years of experience

Column 5: sales revenues from statistics books in 1992

Include the additional variables in the model and discuss your findings.

CASE 18.2   Quebec Referendum Vote: Was There Electoral Fraud?*

As we described in Case 13.2 (page 476), Quebecers have been debating whether to separate from Canada and form an independent nation. A referendum was held on October 30, 1995, in which the people of Quebec voted not to separate. The vote was extremely close with the "No" side winning by only 52,448 votes. A large number of "No" votes was cast by the non-Francophone (Non-French speaking) people of Quebec, who make up about 20% of the population and who very much want to remain Canadians. The remaining 80% are Francophones, a majority of whom voted "Yes."

After the votes were counted, it became clear that the tallied vote was much closer than it should have been. Supporters of the "No" side charged that poll scrutineers, all of whom were appointed by the pro-separatist provincial government, rejected a disproportionate number of ballots in ridings where the percentage of "Yes" votes was low and where there are large numbers of Allophone (people whose first language is neither English nor French) and Anglophone (English-speaking) residents. (Electoral laws require that ballots that do not appear to be properly marked are to be rejected.) They were outraged that in a strong democracy like Canada votes would be rigged much like in many non-democratic countries around the world.

If, in ridings where there was a low percentage of "Yes" votes there was a high percentage of rejected ballots, this would be evidence of electoral fraud. Moreover, if in ridings where there were large percentages of Allophone and/or Anglophone voters, there were high percentages of rejected ballots, this too would constitute evidence of fraud on the part of the scrutineers and possibly the government.

In order to determine the veracity of the charges the following variables were recorded for each riding.

*This case is based on "Voting Irregularities in the 1995 Referendum on Quebec Sovereignty," Jason Cawley and Paul Sommers, *Chance,* Vol. 9, No. 4, Fall, 1996. We are grateful to Dr. Paul Sommers, Middlebury College, for his assistance in writing this case.

Riding number

Percentage of rejected ballots in referendum

Percentage of "Yes" votes

Percentage of Allophones

Percentage of Anglophones

These data are stored in columns 1 through 5, respectively, in file C18-02.

a   Perform an analysis to determine how the percentage of "yes" votes, Allophones, and Anglophones affects the percentage of rejected ballots.

b   Can we infer that electoral fraud took place? If so, how did it manifest itself?

CASE 18.3   **Quebec Referendum Vote: The Rebuttal**

Refer to Case 18.2. Government supporters acknowledged that the highest percentage of rejected ballots occurred in ridings where large numbers of Allophones live. Because the ballots were printed in English and French only, it is reasonable to believe that a greater number of voters would not be able to understand instructions and thus, inadvertently spoil their ballots. If they are right there should be a relationship between the percentages of rejected ballots in this referendum and in the previous provincial election held in 1994. Both variables are stored in columns 2 and 3, respectively, in file C18-03. (Column 1 stores the riding number.) What do these data tell you about the government's rebuttal?

Chapter 19

Model

Building

19.1 Introduction

19.2 Polynomial Models

19.3 Qualitative Independent Variables

19.4 Regression and the Analysis of Variance (Optional)

19.5 Stepwise Regression

19.6 Model Building

19.7 Human Resources Management Application: Pay Equity

19.8 Summary

19.1 INTRODUCTION

Chapters 17 and 18 introduced the techniques and concepts of regression analysis. We discussed how the model is developed, interpreted, assessed, and diagnosed for violations of required conditions. However, there is more to regression analysis. In this chapter, we demonstrate why this procedure is one of the most powerful and commonly used techniques in statistics. Regression analysis allows the statistician to use mathematical models to realistically describe relationships among variables.

In Section 19.2, we introduce models in which the relationship between the dependent variable and the independent variables may not be linear. Section 19.3 introduces indicator variables, which allow us to use qualitative independent variables. This leads to a wider discussion of models that connect regression analysis with the analysis of variance, a technique we presented in Chapter 14. In Section 19.5, we introduce stepwise regression, which enables the statistician to include the independent variables that yield the best fitting models. Section 19.6 discusses how to properly use regression analysis in building models. We close this chapter with an important human resources application, pay equity.

19.2 POLYNOMIAL MODELS

In Chapter 18, we introduced the multiple regression model.

$$y = \beta_0 + \beta_1 x_1 + \beta_2 x_2 + \cdots + \beta_k x_k + \epsilon$$

We included variables x_1, x_2, ... , and x_k because we believed that these variables were each linearly related to the dependent variable. In this section, we discuss models where the independent variables may be functions of a smaller number of *predictor* variables. The simplest form of this model is described below.

Polynomial Model with One Predictor Variable

$$y = \beta_0 + \beta_1 x + \beta_2 x^2 + \cdots + \beta_p x^p + \epsilon$$

Technically, this is a multiple regression model with p independent variables. However, all independent variables are based on only one variable, which we label the **predictor** variable. That is, $x_1 = x$, $x_2 = x^2$, ... , and $x_p = x^p$. In this model, p is the **order** of the equation. For reasons that we discuss later, we rarely propose a model whose order is greater than 3. However, it is worthwhile to devote individual attention to situations where $p = 1$, 2, and 3.

FIRST-ORDER MODEL

When $p = 1$, we have the now-familiar simple linear regression model introduced in Chapter 17.

$$y = \beta_0 + \beta_1 x + \epsilon$$

Obviously, this model is chosen when the statistician believes that there is a straight-line relationship between the dependent and independent variables over the range of the values of x.

SECOND-ORDER MODEL

With $p = 2$, the polynomial model is

$$y = \beta_0 + \beta_1 x + \beta_2 x^2 + \epsilon$$

When we plot x versus y, the graph is shaped like a parabola, as shown in Figures 19.1 and 19.2. The coefficient β_0 represents the intercept where the response surface strikes the y-axis. The signs of β_1 and β_2 control the position of the parabola relative to the y-axis. If $\beta_1 = 0$, for example, the parabola is symmetric and centered around $y = 0$. If β_1 and β_2 have the same sign, the parabola shifts to the left. If β_1 and β_2 have opposite signs, the parabola shifts to the right. The coefficient β_2 describes the curvature. If $\beta_2 = 0$, there is no curvature. If β_2 is negative, the graph is *concave* (as in Figure 19.1). If β_2 is positive, the graph is convex (as in Figure 19.2). The greater the absolute value of β_2, the greater the rate of curvature, as can be seen in Figure 19.3.

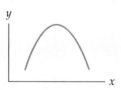
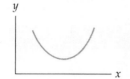
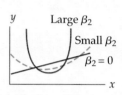

Figure 19.1

Second-order model with $\beta_2 < 0$

Figure 19.2

Second-order model with $\beta_2 > 0$

Figure 19.3

Second-order model with various values of β_2

THIRD-ORDER MODEL

By setting $p = 3$, we produce the third-order model

$$y = \beta_0 + \beta_1 x + \beta_2 x^2 + \beta_3 x^3 + \epsilon$$

Figures 19.4 and 19.5 depict this equation, whose curvature can change twice.

Figure 19.4

Third-order model with $\beta_3 < 0$

Figure 19.5

Third-order model with $\beta_3 > 0$

As you can see, when β_3 is negative, y is decreasing over the range of x, and when β_3 is positive, y increases. The other coefficients determine the position of the curvature changes and the point at which the curve intersects the y-axis.

The number of real-life applications of this model is quite small. Statisticians rarely encounter problems involving more than one curvature reversal. Therefore, we will not discuss any higher order models.

POLYNOMIAL MODELS WITH TWO PREDICTOR VARIABLES

If we believe that two predictor variables influence the dependent variable, we can use one of the following polynomial models. The general form of this model is rather cumbersome, so we will not show it. Instead we discuss several specific examples.

First-Order Model

The **first-order model** is represented by

$$y = \beta_0 + \beta_1 x_1 + \beta_2 x_2 + \epsilon$$

This model is used whenever the statistician believes that, on average, y is linearly related to each of x_1 and x_2 and the predictor variables do not interact. (Recall that we introduced interaction in Chapter 14.) This means that the effect of one predictor variable on y is independent of the value of the second predictor variable. For example, suppose that the sample regression line of the first-order model is

$$\hat{y} = 5 + 3x_1 + 4x_2$$

If we examine the relationship between y and x_1 for several values of x_2 (say, $x_2 = 1, 2,$ and 3), we produce the following equations.

x_2	$\hat{y} = 5 + 3x_1 + 4x_2$
1	$\hat{y} = 9 + 3x_1$
2	$\hat{y} = 13 + 3x_1$
3	$\hat{y} = 17 + 3x_1$

The only difference in the three equations is the intercept. (See Figure 19.6.) The coefficient of x_1 remains the same, which means that the effect of x_1 on y remains the same no matter what the value of x_2. (We could also have shown that the effect of x_2 on y remains the same no matter what the value of x_1.) As you can see from Figure 19.6, the first-order model with no interaction produces parallel straight lines.

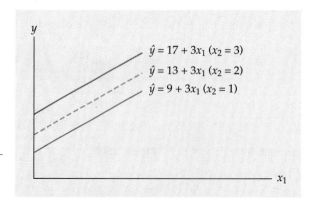

Figure 19.6

First-order model with two independent variables: no interaction

A statistician who thinks that the effect of one predictor variable on y is influenced by the other predictor variable can use the model described next.

First-Order Model with Two Predictor Variables and Interaction

Interaction means that the effect of x_1 on y is influenced by the value of x_2. (It also means that the effect of x_2 on y is influenced by x_1.)

First-Order Model with Interaction

$$y = \beta_0 + \beta_1 x_1 + \beta_2 x_2 + \beta_3 x_1 x_2 + \epsilon$$

Suppose that the sample regression line is

$$\hat{y} = 5 + 3x_1 + 4x_2 - 2x_1 x_2$$

If we examine the relationship between x_1 and y for $x_2 = 1, 2,$ and 3, we produce the following table of equations.

x_2	$\hat{y} = 5 + 3x_1 + 4x_2 - 2x_1 x_2$
1	$\hat{y} = 9 + x_1$
2	$\hat{y} = 13 - x_1$
3	$\hat{y} = 17 - 3x_1$

As you can see, not only is the intercept different, but the coefficient of x_1 also varies. Obviously, the effect of x_1 on y is influenced by the value of x_2. Figure 19.7 depicts these equations. The straight lines are clearly not parallel.

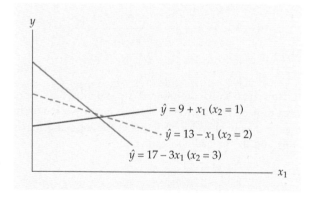

Figure 19.7

First-order model with interaction

Second-Order Model with Interaction

A statistician who believes that a quadratic relationship exists between y and each of x_1 and x_2 and that the predictor variables interact in their effect on y can use the following **second-order model.**

Second-Order Model with Interaction

$$y = \beta_0 + \beta_1 x_1 + \beta_2 x_2 + \beta_3 x_1^2 + \beta_4 x_2^2 + \beta_5 x_1 x_2 + \epsilon$$

Figures 19.8 and 19.9, respectively, depict this model without and with the interaction term.

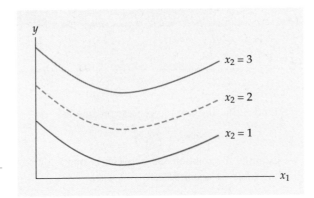

Figure 19.8

Second-order model without interaction ($\beta_5 = 0$)

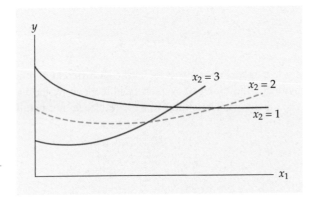

Figure 19.9

Second-order model with interaction

Now that we've introduced several different models, how do we know which model to use? The answer is that we employ a model based on our knowledge of the variables involved and then test that model using the statistical techniques presented in this and the preceding chapters.

▼ **EXAMPLE 19.1**

In trying to find new locations for their restaurants, fast-food restaurant chains like McDonald's and Wendy's usually consider a number of factors. Suppose that a statistician working for a fast-food restaurant chain has been asked to construct a regression model that will help identify new locations that are likely to be profitable. The statistician knows that this type of restaurant has, as its primary market, middle-income adults and their children, particularly those between the ages of 5 and 12. Which model should the statistician propose?

Solution   The dependent variable is gross revenue or net profit. The predictor variables will be mean annual household income and the mean age of children in the restaurant's neighborhood.

The relationship between the dependent variable and each predictor variable is probably quadratic. That is, members of relatively poor or relatively affluent households are less likely to eat at this chain's restaurants, since the restaurants attract mostly middle-income customers. Figure 19.10 depicts the hypothesized relationship.

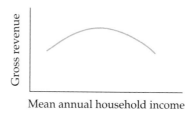

Figure 19.10

Relationship between annual
gross revenue and mean annual
household income

A similar relationship can be proposed for revenue and age. Neighborhoods where the mean age of children is either quite low or quite high will probably produce lower revenues than in similar areas where the mean age lies in the middle of the 5-to-12 range.

The question of whether or not to include the interaction term is more difficult to answer. When in doubt, it is probably best to include it. Thus, the model to be tested is

$$\text{REVENUE} = \beta_0 + \beta_1 \text{ INCOME} + \beta_2 \text{ AGE} + \beta_3 \text{ INCOME}^2 + \beta_4 \text{ AGE}^2 + \\ \beta_5 \text{ INCOME} \times \text{AGE} + \epsilon$$

▲

▼ EXAMPLE 19.2

To determine whether the second-order model with interaction is appropriate, the statistician in Example 19.1 selected 25 areas at random. Each area consists of approximately 5,000 households, as well as one of her employer's restaurants and one competing restaurant. The statistician recorded the previous year's annual gross sales, the mean annual household income, and the mean age of children (the latter two figures are available from the latest census); some of these data are listed in the accompanying table and stored in file XM19-02 (which also stores income², age², and income × age). What conclusions can be drawn from these data?

Area	Annual Gross Revenue (thousands of dollars) REVENUE	Mean Annual Household Income (thousands of dollars) INCOME	Mean Age of Children AGE
1	$1,128	$23.5	10.5
2	1,005	17.6	7.2
3	1,212	26.3	7.6
.	.	.	.
.	.	.	.
.	.	.	.
25	950	17.8	6.1

Solution From the following computer output, we determine that the value of the coefficient of determination (R^2) is 90.65%, which tells us that the model fits the data quite well. The value of the F-statistic is 36.86, which has a p-value of 0. This confirms that the model is valid.

SOLVE

**Excel Output for
Example 19.2**

	A	B	C	D	E	F
1	SUMMARY OUTPUT					
2						
3	*Regression Statistics*					
4	Multiple R	0.9521				
5	R Square	0.9065				
6	Adjusted R Square	0.8819				
7	Standard Error	44.70				
8	Observations	25				
9						
10	ANOVA					
11		*df*	*SS*	*MS*	*F*	*Significance F*
12	Regression	5	368140	73628	36.86	0.0000
13	Residual	19	37956	1998		
14	Total	24	406096			
15						
16		*Coefficients*	*Standard Error*	*t Stat*	*P-value*	
17	Intercept	-1134	320.0	-3.54	0.0022	
18	INCOME	173.2	28.20	6.14	0.0000	
19	AGE	23.55	32.23	0.73	0.4739	
20	INC sq	-3.726	0.542	-6.87	0.0000	
21	AGE sq	-3.869	1.179	-3.28	0.0039	
22	INC X AGE	1.967	0.944	2.08	0.0509	

**Minitab Output for
Example 19.2**

Regression Analysis

The regression equation is
REVENUE = - 1134 + 173 INCOME + 23.5 AGE - 3.73 INC sq - 3.87 AGE sq
          + 1.97 INC X AGE

Predictor	Coef	StDev	T	P
Constant	-1134.0	320.0	-3.54	0.002
INCOME	173.20	28.20	6.14	0.000
AGE	23.55	32.23	0.73	0.474
INC sq	-3.7261	0.5422	-6.87	0.000
AGE sq	-3.869	1.179	-3.28	0.004
INC X AG	1.9673	0.9441	2.08	0.051

S = 44.70   R-Sq = 90.7%   R-Sq(adj) = 88.2%

Analysis of Variance

Source	DF	SS	MS	F	P
Regression	5	368140	73628	36.86	0.000
Residual Error	19	37956	1998		
Total	24	406096			

Care must be taken when interpreting the t-tests of the coefficients in this type of model. Not surprisingly, each variable will be correlated with its square, and the interaction variable will be correlated with both of its components. As a consequence, multicollinearity distorts the t-tests of the coefficients in some cases, making it appear that some of the components should be eliminated from the model. In fact, in this example, Minitab warns (not shown) the statistician that multicollinearity is a problem.

As we noted in Chapter 18, we often determine the correlations among the independent variables to gauge the extent of multicollinearity. These calculations are also shown below. (Large correlations are set in bold type.) As you can see, **INCOME** and **AGE** are highly correlated with their respective squares and the interaction term. **AGE** and **INCOME**, however, are not correlated with each other, nor are they correlated with the other variable squared.

Correlations Between Pairs of Independent Variables

Pair	Correlation	Pair	Correlation
INCOME & AGE	.020	AGE & AGE^2	**.985**
INCOME & INCOME^2	**.994**	AGE & INCOME × AGE	**.886**
INCOME & AGE^2	−.042	INCOME^2 & AGE^2	−.099
INCOME & INCOME × AGE	.460	INCOME^2 & INCOME × AGE	.397
AGE & INCOME^2	−.045	AGE^2 & INCOME × AGE	**.840**

If the objective is to use the model to predict or estimate, we are not concerned about the multicollinearity. However, if we need to interpret and/or test each coefficient, the multicollinearity makes this impossible. Fortunately, we can transform the independent variables to reduce multicollinearity. We calculate the mean **INCOME** and mean **AGE**. They are

Mean **INCOME** = 24.2

Mean **AGE**   = 8.392

Then we define the following variables.

income = **INCOME** − 24.2

age   = **AGE** − 8.392

We then create the other variables in the polynomial model

$$\textbf{REVENUE} = \beta_0 + \beta_1 \text{ income} + \beta_2 \text{ age} + \beta_3 \text{ income}^2 + \beta_4 \text{ age}^2 + \beta_5 \text{ income} \times \text{age} + \epsilon$$

When we used the transformed data and determined the correlations we found the following.

Correlations Between Pairs of Transformed Independent Variables

Pair	Correlation	Pair	Correlation
income & age	.020	age & age^2	.401
income & income^2	−.173	age & income × age	−.372
income & age^2	−.312	income^2 & age^2	.096
income & income × age	−.614	income^2 & income × age	.168
age & income^2	−.612	age^2 & income × age	−.083

As you can see, the correlations between transformed independent variables are much smaller than the correlations between the original independent variables. Although we have not eliminated the problem completely, it appears that the correlations are small enough for us to interpret the coefficients and *t*-tests. When we performed the regression analysis using the transformed data, we produced the following. (Minitab did not issue a warning about this model.)

Excel Output for Example 19.2 (Transformed Variables)

	A	B	C	D	E	F
1	SUMMARY OUTPUT					
2						
3	*Regression Statistics*					
4	Multiple R	0.9521				
5	R Square	0.9065				
6	Adjusted R Square	0.8819				
7	Standard Error	44.70				
8	Observations	25				
9						
10	ANOVA					
11		*df*	*SS*	*MS*	*F*	*Significance F*
12	Regression	5	368140	73628	36.86	0.0000
13	Residual	19	37956	1998		
14	Total	24	406096			
15						
16		*Coefficients*	*Standard Error*	*t Stat*	*P-value*	
17	Intercept	1200	15.09	79.54	0.0000	
18	income	9.3678	2.7439	3.41	0.0029	
19	age	6.2255	5.4728	1.14	0.2695	
20	inc sq	-3.7261	0.5422	-6.87	0.0000	
21	age sq	-3.8687	1.1791	-3.28	0.0039	
22	inc X age	1.9673	0.9441	2.08	0.0509	

Minitab Output for Example 19.2 (Transformed Variables)

Regression Analysis

The regression equation is
REVENUE = 1200 + 9.37 income + 6.23 age - 3.73 inc sq - 3.87 age sq
          + 1.97 inc X age

Predictor	Coef	StDev	T	P
Constant	1200.07	15.09	79.54	0.000
income	9.368	2.744	3.41	0.003
age	6.225	5.473	1.14	0.269
inc sq	-3.7261	0.5422	-6.87	0.000
age sq	-3.869	1.179	-3.28	0.004
inc X ag	1.9673	0.9441	2.08	0.051

S = 44.70   R-Sq = 90.7%   R-Sq(adj) = 88.2%

Analysis of Variance

Source	DF	SS	MS	F	P
Regression	5	368140	73628	36.86	0.000
Residual Error	19	37956	1998		
Total	24	406096			

INTERPRET

Several statistics should be noted. First, the standard error of estimate, coefficient of determination, and F-statistics are identical. Thus, the model using the transformed variables and the model with the original variables fit the data equally well. Second, the coefficients of **INCOME** and **AGE** in the first model are different from the coefficients of **income** and **age** in the second model. The t-statistics also differ. However, the coefficients of $INCOME^2$, AGE^2, and $INCOME \times AGE$ are the same as the coefficients of $income^2$, age^2, and $income \times age$. Moreover, their t-statistics are the same.

Using the transformed data model we can perform the t-tests in the usual way. Thus, the independent variable **age** ($t = 1.14$ and p-value$= .269$) is not linearly related to **REVENUE**. The other independent variables are linearly related, although the interaction term is borderline (if we use a 5% significance level).

▲

EXERCISES

19.1 Graph y versus x_1 for $x_2 = 1, 2$, and 3, for each of the following equations.

a $y = 1 + 2x_1 + 4x_2$
b $y = 1 + 2x_1 + 4x_2 - x_1 x_2$

19.2 Graph y versus x_1 for $x_2 = 2, 4$, and 6, for each of the following equations.

a $y = 0.5 + 1x_1 - 0.7x_2 - 1.2x_1^2 + 1.5x_2^2$
b $y = 0.5 + 1x_1 - 0.7x_2 - 1.2x_1^2 + 1.5x_2^2 + 2x_1 x_2$

19.3 The general manager of a supermarket chain believes that sales of a product are influenced by the amount of space the product is allotted on shelves. If true, this would have great significance, because the more profitable items could be given more shelf space. The man-ager realizes that sales volume would likely increase with more space only up to a certain point. Beyond that point, sales would likely flatten and perhaps decrease (because customers often are dismayed by very large exhibits). To test his belief, the manager records the number of boxes of detergent sold during 1 week in 25 stores in the chain. For each store, he records the shelf space (in inches) allotted to the detergent. These data are stored in column 1 (sales) and column 2 (shelf space) in file XR19-03. The Excel and Minitab outputs for a second-order model are shown below.

a Write the equation that represents the model.
b Analyze either printout and discuss how well the model fits.

	A	B	C	D	E	F
1	SUMMARY OUTPUT					
2						
3	*Regression Statistics*					
4	Multiple R	0.6378				
5	R Square	0.4068				
6	Adjusted R Square	0.3528				
7	Standard Error	41.15				
8	Observations	25				
9						
10	ANOVA					
11		*df*	*SS*	*MS*	*F*	*Significance F*
12	Regression	2	25540	12770	7.54	0.0032
13	Residual	22	37248	1693		
14	Total	24	62788			
15						
16		*Coefficients*	*Standard Error*	*t Stat*	*P-value*	
17	Intercept	-109.0	97.24	-1.12	0.2744	
18	Space	33.09	8.59	3.85	0.0009	
19	Space sq	-0.666	0.177	-3.75	0.0011	

Regression Analysis

```
The regression equation is
Sales = - 109 + 33.1 Space - 0.666 Space sq

Predictor        Coef        StDev          T          P
Constant      -108.99        97.24      -1.12      0.274
Space          33.089        8.590       3.85      0.001
Space sq      -0.6655       0.1774      -3.75      0.001

S = 41.15        R-Sq = 40.7%        R-Sq(adj) = 35.3%

Analysis of Variance

Source             DF          SS          MS          F          P
Regression          2       25540       12770       7.54      0.003
Residual Error     22       37248        1693
Total              24       62788
```

S TATISTICS IN THE W ORKPLACE

Economics Application: Demand Curve

The law of supply and demand states that other things being equal, the higher the price of a product or service, the lower is the quantity demanded. The relationship between quantity and price is called a *demand curve*. Gen-

erally such a curve is modeled by a quadratic equation. To estimate the demand curve we measure the demand at several different prices and then employ regression analysis to calculate the coefficients of the model.

19.4 A fast-food restaurant chain whose menu features hamburgers and chicken sandwiches is about to add a fish sandwich to its menu. There was considerable debate among the executives about what the likely demand and what the appropriate price should be. A recently-hired economics graduate observed that the demand curve would reveal a great deal about the relationship between price and demand. She convinced the executives to conduct an experiment. A random sample of 20

restaurants was drawn. The restaurants were almost identical in terms of sales and in the demographics of the surrounding area. At each restaurant the fish sandwich was sold at a different price. The number of sandwiches sold over a seven-day period and the price were recorded and stored in columns 1 and 2, respectively in file XR19-04.

A second-order model was proposed and generated. The Excel and Minitab outputs follow.

	A	B	C	D	E	F
1	SUMMARY OUTPUT					
2						
3	*Regression Statistics*					
4	Multiple R	0.9862				
5	R Square	0.9726				
6	Adjusted R Square	0.9693				
7	Standard Error	5.96				
8	Observations	20				
9						
10	ANOVA					
11		*df*	*SS*	*MS*	*F*	*Significance F*
12	Regression	2	21374	10687	301.15	0.0000
13	Residual	17	603.3	35.5		
14	Total	19	21977			
15						
16		*Coefficients*	*Standard Error*	*t Stat*	*P-value*	
17	Intercept	766.9	37.40	20.50	0.0000	
18	Price	-359.1	34.19	-10.50	0.0000	
19	Price sq	64.55	7.58	8.52	0.0000	

Regression Analysis

```
The regression equation is
Sales = 767 - 359 Price + 64.5 Price sq

Predictor        Coef        StDev          T         P
Constant        766.91       37.40      20.50     0.000
Price          -359.10       34.19     -10.50     0.000
Price sq        64.547        7.576      8.52     0.000

S = 5.957      R-Sq = 97.3%     R-Sq(adj) = 96.9%

Analysis of Variance

Source           DF          SS         MS         F         P
Regression        2       21374      10687    301.15     0.000
Residual Error   17         603         35
Total            19       21977
```

a Describe how well the model fits.

b Calculate the point prediction for weekly sales when the price is $2.95.

19.5 A person starting a new job always takes a certain amount of time to adjust fully. In repetitive-task situations, such as those used in an assembly line, significant productivity gains can occur within a few days. In an experiment to study this phenomenon, the average amount of time required for a new employee to install electronic components in a computer was measured for her first 10 days. These data are shown below (and stored in file XR19-05).

Day	1	2	3	4	5	6	7	8	9	10
Mean times (minutes)	40	41	36	38	33	32	30	32	29	30

A second-order model was proposed. The computer outputs follow.

STATISTICS IN THE **W**ORKPLACE

Operations Management Application

A well-established phenomenon in operations management is the *learning curve,* which describes how quickly new workers learn to do their jobs. A number of mathematical models are used to describe the relationship between time on the job and productivity. Regression analysis allows the operations manager to select the appropriate model and use it to predict when workers achieve their highest level of productivity.

	A	B	C	D	E	F
1	SUMMARY OUTPUT					
2						
3	*Regression Statistics*					
4	Multiple R	0.9408				
5	R Square	0.8852				
6	Adjusted R Square	0.8524				
7	Standard Error	1.674				
8	Observations	10				
9						
10	ANOVA					
11		*df*	*SS*	*MS*	*F*	*Significance F*
12	Regression	2	151.3	75.64	26.98	0.0005
13	Residual	7	19.62	2.80		
14	Total	9	170.9			
15						
16		*Coefficients*	*Standard Error*	*t Stat*	*P-value*	
17	Intercept	43.73	1.969	22.21	0.0000	
18	Day	-2.49	0.822	-3.03	0.0191	
19	Day sq	0.106	0.0729	1.46	0.1889	

Regression Analysis

```
The regression equation is
Time = 43.7 - 2.49 Day + 0.106 Day sq

Predictor        Coef        StDev          T          P
Constant       43.733        1.969       22.21      0.000
Day           -2.4939       0.8225       -3.03      0.019
Day sq        0.10606      0.07287        1.46      0.189

S = 1.674       R-Sq = 88.5%      R-Sq(adj) = 85.2%

Analysis of Variance

Source           DF           SS           MS          F        P
Regression        2      151.276       75.638      26.98    0.001
Residual Error    7       19.624        2.803
Total             9      170.900
```

a Determine at the 5% significance level whether the model is valid.

b Describe how well the model fits.

The following exercises require a computer and statistical software. Conduct all statistical tests with a 5% significance level.

19.6 The dean of the School of Business described in Exercise 18.44 wanted to improve the regression model, which was developed to describe the relationship between M.B.A. GPA and undergraduate GPA, GMAT score, and years of work experience. The dean now believes that an interaction effect may exist between undergraduate GPA and the GMAT test score.

a Write the equation that describes the model.

b Use a computer to generate the regression statistics. Use whatever statistics you deem necessary to assess the model's fit. Is this model valid?

c Compare your results with those achieved in Exercise 18.44.

d Is there an interaction effect between undergraduate GPA and the GMAT score? Test at the 5% significance level.

19.7 The manager of the food concession at a major-league baseball stadium wanted to be able to predict the attendance of a game 24 hours in advance, in order to prepare the correct amount of food for sale. He believed that the two most important factors were the home team's winning percentage and the visiting team's winning percentages. To examine his beliefs, he collected the attendance figures, the home team's winning percentage, and the visiting team's winning percentage for 40 randomly selected games. These data are stored in columns 1 to 3 of file XR19-07.

a Conduct a regression analysis using a first-order model with interaction.

b Do these results indicate your model is valid in predicting attendance?

c Should the interaction term be included? Explain.

19.8 The manager of a large hotel on the Riviera in southern France wanted to forecast the monthly vacancy rate (as a percentage) during the peak season. After considering a long list of potential variables, she identified two variables that she believed were most closely related to the vacancy rate: the average daily temperature and the value of the currency in American dollars. She collected data for 25 months and stored them in file XR19-08.

a Perform a regression analysis using a first-order model with interaction.

b Perform a regression analysis using a second-order model with interaction.

c Which model fits better? Explain.

19.9 The coach and the general manager of a team in the National Hockey League are trying to decide what kinds of players to draft. To help in making their decision, they need to know which variables are most closely related to the goals differential—the difference between the number of goals their team scores and the number of goals scored by their team's opponents. (A positive differential means that their team wins, and a negative differential means a loss.) After some consideration, they decide that there are two important variables: the percentage of face-offs won and the penalty-minutes differential. The latter variable is the difference between the

number of penalty minutes assessed against their team and the number of penalty minutes assessed against their team's opponents. The data from 100 games are stored in file XR19-09.

a Perform a regression analysis using a first-order model with interaction.

b Is this model valid?

c Should the interaction term be included?

19.10 The production manager of a chemical plant wants to determine the roles that temperature and pressure play in the yield of a particular chemical produced at the plant. From past experience, she believes that when pressure is held constant, lower and higher temperatures tend to reduce the yield. When temperature is held constant, higher and lower pressures tend to increase the yield. She does not have any idea about how the yield is affected for various combinations of pressure and temperature. She observes 80 batches of the chemical in which the pressure and temperature were allowed to vary. These data are stored in file XR19-10 (column 1 = yield; column 2 = pressure; column 3 = temperature).

a Which model should be used? Explain.

b Conduct a regression analysis using the model you specified in part (a).

c Assess how well the model fits the data.

19.11 After examining the results of the regression analysis performed on the turnover rate and the age of the workers in Exercise 17.9, the personnel manager decided to redo the model by proposing a second-order model. Perform the necessary analysis and determine whether this model is better than the first-order model.

19.3 QUALITATIVE INDEPENDENT VARIABLES

When we introduced regression analysis, we pointed out that all the variables must be quantitative. But in many real-life cases, one or more independent variables are qualitative. For example, suppose that the used-car dealer in Example 17.1 believed that the color of a car is a factor in determining its auction price. Color is clearly a qualitative variable. If we assign numbers to each possible color, these numbers will be completely arbitrary, and using them in a regression model will usually be pointless. For example, if the dealer believes the colors that are most popular, white and silver, are likely to lead to higher prices than other colors, he may assign a code of 1 to white cars, a code of 2 to silver cars, and a code of 3 to all other colors. Columns 1 and 2 of file XM17-01A contain the auction price and the odometer reading (identical to file XM17-01). Column 3 includes codes identifying the color of the Ford Tauruses referred to in the original problem. If we now conduct a multiple regression analysis, the results below would be obtained.

**Excel Output for
Example 17.1 with
COLOR Variable**

	A	B	C	D	E	F
1	SUMMARY OUTPUT					
2						
3	*Regression Statistics*					
4	Multiple R	0.8095				
5	R Square	0.6552				
6	Adjusted R Square	0.6481				
7	Standard Error	151.2				
8	Observations	100				
9						
10	ANOVA					
11		*df*	*SS*	*MS*	*F*	*Significance F*
12	Regression	2	4216263	2108132	92.17	0.0000
13	Residual	97	2218627	22872		
14	Total	99	6434890			
15						
16		*Coefficients*	*Standard Error*	*t Stat*	*P-value*	
17	Intercept	6580	92.96	70.79	0.0000	
18	Odometer	-0.0313	0.0023	-13.56	0.0000	
19	Color	-21.67	18.11	-1.20	0.2345	

**Minitab Output for
Example 17.1 with
COLOR Variable**

Regression Analysis

```
The regression equation is
Price = 6580 - 0.0313 Odometer - 21.7 color

Predictor         Coef        StDev           T          P
Constant       6580.18        92.96       70.79      0.000
Odometer     -0.031278     0.002306      -13.56      0.000
Color          -21.67        18.11       -1.20      0.234


S = 151.2      R-Sq = 65.5%      R-Sq(adj) = 64.8%


Analysis of Variance

Source            DF          SS           MS          F          P
Regression         2     4216263      2108132      92.17      0.000
Residual Error    97     2218627        22872
Total             99     6434890
```

The regression equation is

PRICE $= 6,580 - .0313$ **ODOMETER** $- 21.7$ **COLOR**

Aside from the inclusion of the variable **COLOR**, this equation is very similar to the one we produced in the simple regression model (**PRICE** $= 6533 - 0.0312$ **ODOMETER**). An examination of the output above reveals that the variable representing color is not linearly related to price (t-statistic $= -1.20$, and p-value $= .2345$). There are two possible explanations for this result. First, there is no relationship between color and price. Second, color is a factor in determining the car's price, but the way in which the dealer assigned the codes to the colors made detection of that fact impossible. That is, the dealer treated the qualitative variable, color, as a quantitative variable. To further understand why we cannot use qualitative data in regression analysis, try to interpret the coefficient of **COLOR**. Such an effort is similar to attempting to interpret the mean of a sample of qualitative data. It is futile. Even though this effort failed, it is possible to include qualitative variables in the regression model. This is accomplished through the use of indicator variables.

An **indicator variable** (also called a **dummy variable**) is a variable that can assume either of only two values (usually 0 and 1), where one value represents the existence of a certain condition and the other value indicates that the condition does not hold. In this illustration we would create two indicator variables to represent the color of the car.

$$I_1 = 1 \text{ (if color is white)}$$
$$= 0 \text{ (if color is not white)}$$

and

$$I_2 = 1 \text{ (if color is silver)}$$
$$= 0 \text{ (if color is not silver)}$$

Notice that we need only two indicator variables to represent the three colors. A white car is represented by $I_1 = 1$ and $I_2 = 0$. A silver car is represented by $I_1 = 0$ and $I_2 = 1$. Because cars that are painted some other color are neither white nor silver, they are represented by $I_1 = 0$ and $I_2 = 0$. It should be apparent that we cannot have $I_1 = 1$ and $I_2 = 1$, as long as we assume that no Ford Taurus is two-toned.

The effect of using these two indicator variables is to create three equations, one for each of the three colors. As you're about to discover, we can use the equations to determine how the car's color affects its auction-selling price.

In general, to represent a qualitative variable with m categories, we must create $m - 1$ indicator variables.

INTERPRETING AND TESTING THE COEFFICIENTS OF INDICATOR VARIABLES

In columns 4 and 5 of file XM17-01A, we stored the values of I_1 and I_2. We then performed a multiple regression analysis using variables **ODOMETER**, I_1, and I_2. The printouts follow.

Excel Output for Example 17.1 with Two Indicator Variables

	A	B	C	D	E	F
1	SUMMARY OUTPUT					
2						
3	*Regression Statistics*					
4	Multiple R	0.8355				
5	R Square	0.6980				
6	Adjusted R Square	0.6886				
7	Standard Error	142.3				
8	Observations	100				
9						
10	ANOVA					
11		*df*	*SS*	*MS*	*F*	*Significance F*
12	Regression	3	4491749	1497250	73.97	0.0000
13	Residual	96	1943141	20241		
14	Total	99	6434890			
15						
16		*Coefficients*	*Standard Error*	*t Stat*	*P-value*	
17	Intercept	6350	92.17	68.90	0.0000	
18	Odometer	-0.0278	0.0024	-11.72	0.0000	
19	I1	45.24	34.08	1.33	0.1876	
20	I2	147.7	38.18	3.87	0.0002	

Minitab Output for Example 17.1 with Two Indicator Variables

Regression Analysis

The regression equation is
Price = 6350 - 0.0278 Odometer + 45.2 I1 + 148 I2

Predictor	Coef	StDev	T	P
Constant	6350.32	92.17	68.90	0.000
Odometer	-0.027770	0.002369	-11.72	0.000
I1	45.24	34.08	1.33	0.188
I2	147.74	38.18	3.87	0.000

S = 142.3   R-Sq = 69.8%   R-Sq(adj) = 68.9%

Analysis of Variance

Source	DF	SS	MS	F	P
Regression	3	4491749	1497250	73.97	0.000
Residual Error	96	1943141	20241		
Total	99	6434890			

The regression equation is

PRICE = $6,350 - .0278$ **ODOMETER** $+ 45.2\ I_1 + 148\ I_2$

The intercept (b_0) and the coefficient of **ODOMETER** (b_1) are interpreted in the usual manner. When **ODOMETER** $= I_1 = I_2 = 0$, the dependent variable **PRICE** equals 6,350. For each additional mile on the odometer, the auction price decreases, on average, by 2.78 cents. Now examine the remaining two coefficients.

$b_2 = 45.2$

$b_3 = 148$

These tell us that, in this sample, on average, a white car sells for $45.20 more than other colors and a silver car sells for $148 more than other colors. The reason both comparisons are made with other colors is that such cars are represented by $I_1 = I_2 = 0$. Thus, for a non-white and non-silver car, the equation becomes

PRICE $= b_0 + b_1$ **ODOMETER** $+ b_2(0) + b_3(0)$

which is

PRICE $= 6,350 - .0278$ **ODOMETER**

For a white car $(I_1 = 1$ and $I_2 = 0)$, the regression equation is

PRICE $= b_0 + b_1$ **ODOMETER** $+ b_2(1) + b_3(0)$

which is

PRICE $= 6,350 - .0278$ **ODOMETER** $+ 45.2 = 6,395.2 - .0278$ **ODOMETER**

Finally, for a silver car $(I_1 = 0$ and $I_2 = 1)$, the regression equation is

PRICE $= b_0 + b_1$ **ODOMETER** $+ b_2(0) + b_3(1)$

which simplifies to

PRICE $= 6,350 - .0278$ **ODOMETER** $+ 148 = 6,498 - .0278$ **ODOMETER**

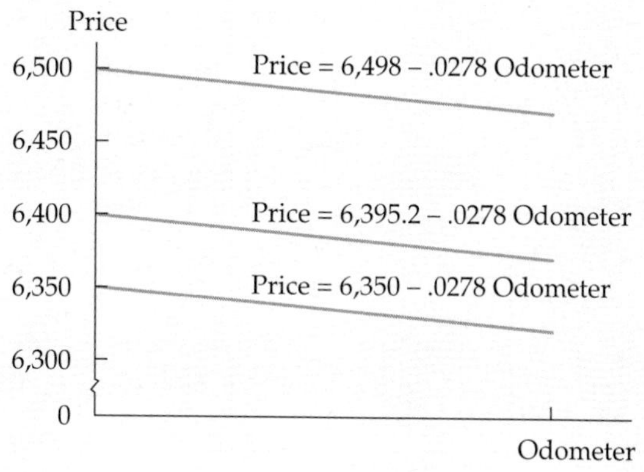

Figure 19.11

Price versus odometer for three colors

Figure 19.11 depicts the graph of **PRICE** versus **ODOMETER** for the three different color categories. Notice that the three lines are parallel (with slope $= b_1 = -.0278$), while the intercepts differ.

We can also perform the usual t-tests of β_2 and β_3; however, because the variables I_1 and I_2 represent different groups (the three color categories), these t-tests allow us to draw inferences about the differences in auction prices among the groups. The test of β_2 is conducted as follows.

$H_0: \beta_2 = 0$

$H_1: \beta_2 \neq 0$

Test statistic: $t = 1.33$ (p-value $= .1876$)

There is insufficient evidence to infer that white Tauruses sell for more or less than do nonwhite, nonsilver Tauruses. To determine if silver-colored Tauruses sell for a different price than other colors, we test

$H_0: \beta_3 = 0$

$H_1: \beta_3 \neq 0$

Test statistic: $t = 3.87$ (p-value $= .0002$)

We can conclude that there are differences in price between silver-colored Tauruses and the other category.

EXERCISES

19.12 Create and identify indicator variables to represent the following qualitative variables.

a religious affiliation (Catholic, Protestant, and others)

b working shift (8:00 A.M. to 4:00 P.M., 4:00 P.M. to 12:00 midnight, and 12:00 midnight to 8:00 A.M.

c Supervisor (Jack Jones, Mary Brown, George Fosse, and Elaine Smith)

19.13 In a study of computer applications, a survey asked which microcomputer a number of companies used. The following indicator variables were created.

$I_1 = 1$ (if IBM) $I_2 = 1$ (if Macintosh)

$ = 0$ (if not) $ = 0$ (if not)

What computer is being referred to by each of the following pairs of values?

a $I_1 = 0; I_2 = 1$ **b** $I_1 = 1; I_2 = 0$

c $I_1 = 0; I_2 = 0$

19.14 Suppose that in Exercise 18.44, the dean believed that the type of undergraduate degree also influenced the student's GPA as a graduate student. The most common undergraduate degrees of students attending the graduate school of business are B.B.A. (Business Administration), B.Eng., B.Sc., and B.A. Because the type of degree is a qualitative variable, the following three indicator variables were created.

$$I_1 = 1 \text{ (if degree is B.B.A.)}$$
$$= 0 \text{ (if not)}$$
$$I_2 = 1 \text{ (if degree is B.Eng.)}$$
$$= 0 \text{ (if not)}$$

$$I_3 = 1 \text{ (if degree is B.Sc.)}$$
$$= 0 \text{ (if not)}$$

The data for the 100 students are stored in columns 1 to 6 of file XR19-14. (Columns 1 to 4 are identical to columns 1 to 4 of file XR18-44.) The Excel and Minitab multiple regression analyses appear below.

	A	B	C	D	E	F
1	SUMMARY OUTPUT					
2						
3	*Regression Statistics*					
4	Multiple R	0.7469				
5	R Square	0.5578				
6	Adjusted R Square	0.5293				
7	Standard Error	0.7121				
8	Observations	100				
9						
10	ANOVA					
11		*df*	*SS*	*MS*	*F*	*Significance F*
12	Regression	6	59.50	9.916	19.55	0.0000
13	Residual	93	47.16	0.507		
14	Total	99	106.7			
15						
16		*Coefficients*	*Standard Error*	*t Stat*	*P-value*	
17	Intercept	0.5757	1.269	0.45	0.6512	
18	UnderGPA	0.0528	0.0999	0.53	0.5986	
19	GMAT	0.0108	0.0012	8.74	0.0000	
20	Work	0.0930	0.0208	4.46	0.0000	
21	I1	0.5285	0.1738	3.04	0.0031	
22	I2	0.6751	0.2203	3.06	0.0029	
23	I3	0.1136	0.2240	0.51	0.6134	

Regression Analysis

```
The regression equation is
MBA GPA = 0.58 + 0.0528 UnderGPA + 0.0108 GMAT + 0.0930 Work + 0.529 I1
          + 0.675 I2 + 0.114 I3

Predictor        Coef        StDev          T          P
Constant        0.576       1.269        0.45      0.651
UnderGPA        0.05276     0.09988      0.53      0.599
GMAT            0.010801    0.001235     8.74      0.000
Work            0.09304     0.02084      4.46      0.000
I1              0.5285      0.1738       3.04      0.003
I2              0.6751      0.2203       3.06      0.003
I3              0.1136      0.2240       0.51      0.613


S = 0.7121      R-Sq = 55.8%      R-Sq(adj) = 52.9%


Analysis of Variance

Source            DF          SS          MS          F          P
Regression         6      59.4963      9.9161      19.55      0.000
Residual Error    93      47.1599      0.5071
Total             99     106.6562
```

a Can we infer that, on average, the B.B.A. graduate outperforms the B.A. graduates?

b Can we conclude that, on average, the B. Eng. graduate performs better than the B.A. graduate?

c Can we infer that the average B.Sc. graduate outperforms the average B.A. graduate?

d Find the point prediction for graduate school GPA of a B.Eng. whose undergraduate GPA was 9.0, whose GMAT score was 700, and who has had 10 years of work experience.

e Repeat part (d) for a B.A. student.

19.15 Refer to Exercise 18.55, where a multiple regression analysis was performed to predict men's longevity based on the parents' and grandparents' longevity. Suppose that in addition to these data the actuary also recorded whether the man was a smoker (1 = yes and 0 = no). These data are stored in column 6 of file XR19-15. (Columns 1 to 5 are identical to columns 1 to 5 of file XR18-55.) A multiple regression analysis was performed with the printouts shown below.

a Compare the equation produced below to that produced in Exercise 18.55. Describe the differences.

b Does smoking affect length of life? Explain.

	A	B	C	D	E	F
1	SUMMARY OUTPUT					
2						
3	Regression Statistics					
4	Multiple R	0.8973				
5	R Square	0.8051				
6	Adjusted R Square	0.7947				
7	Standard Error	2.323				
8	Observations	100				
9						
10	ANOVA					
11		df	SS	MS	F	Significance F
12	Regression	5	2096	419.3	77.66	0.0000
13	Residual	94	507.5	5.398		
14	Total	99	2604			
15						
16		Coefficients	Standard Error	t Stat	P-value	
17	Intercept	23.57	5.978	3.94	0.0002	
18	Mother	0.3061	0.0542	5.65	0.0000	
19	Father	0.3030	0.0476	6.37	0.0000	
20	Gmothers	0.0316	0.0577	0.55	0.5853	
21	Gfathers	0.0778	0.0573	1.36	0.1777	
22	Smoker	-3.719	0.6691	-5.56	0.0000	

Regression Analysis

```
The regression equation is
Longvity = 23.6 + 0.306 Mother + 0.303 Father + 0.0316 Gmothers
         + 0.0778 Gfathers - 3.72 Smoker

Predictor        Coef        StDev           T          P
Constant       23.567       5.978        3.94      0.000
Mother        0.30612      0.05420        5.65      0.000
Father        0.30301      0.04758        6.37      0.000
Gmothers      0.03161      0.05772        0.55      0.585
Gfathers      0.07779      0.05729        1.36      0.178
Smoker        -3.7190       0.6691       -5.56      0.000


S = 2.323        R-Sq = 80.5%        R-Sq(adj) = 79.5%


Analysis of Variance

Source            DF          SS          MS          F          P
Regression         5     2096.30      419.26      77.66      0.000
Residual Error    94      507.46        5.40
Total             99     2603.76
```

19.16 The manager of an amusement park would like to be able to predict daily attendance, in order to develop more accurate plans about how much food to order and how many ride operators to hire. After some consideration, he decided that the following three factors are critical.

> Yesterday's attendance
> Weekday or weekend
> Predicted weather

He then took a random sample of 40 days. For each day, he recorded the attendance, the previous day's attendance, day of the week, and weather forecast. The first independent variable is quantitative, but the other two are qualitative. Accordingly, he created the following sets of indicator variables.

$I_1 = 1$ (if weekend)
$\quad = 0$ (if not)
$I_2 = 1$ (if mostly sunny is predicted)
$\quad = 0$ (if not)
$I_3 = 1$ (if rain is predicted)
$\quad = 0$ (if not)

These data are stored in file XR19-16. A multiple regression analysis was performed. The Excel and Minitab printouts are shown below.

a Is this model valid?
b Can we conclude that weather is a factor in determining attendance?
c Do these results provide sufficient evidence that weekend attendance is, on average, larger than weekday attendance?

	A	B	C	D	E	F
1	SUMMARY OUTPUT					
2						
3	*Regression Statistics*					
4	Multiple R	0.8368				
5	R Square	0.7002				
6	Adjusted R Square	0.6659				
7	Standard Error	810.8				
8	Observations	40				
9						
10	ANOVA					
11		*df*	*SS*	*MS*	*F*	*Significance F*
12	Regression	4	53729535	13432384	20.43	0.0000
13	Residual	35	23007438	657355		
14	Total	39	76736973			
15						
16		*Coefficients*	*Standard Error*	*t Stat*	*P-value*	
17	Intercept	3490	469.2	7.44	0.0000	
18	Yest Att	0.3685	0.0779	4.73	0.0000	
19	I1	1623	492.5	3.30	0.0023	
20	I2	733.5	394.4	1.86	0.0713	
21	I3	-765.5	484.7	-1.58	0.1232	

Regression Analysis

```
The regression equation is
Attendance = 3490 + 0.369 Yest Att + 1623 I1 + 733 I2 - 766 I3

Predictor        Coef        StDev           T         P
Constant       3490.5       469.2         7.44     0.000
Yest Att      0.36855     0.07789         4.73     0.000
I1             1623.1       492.5         3.30     0.002
I2              733.5       394.4         1.86     0.071
I3             -765.5       484.7        -1.58     0.123

S = 810.8       R-Sq = 70.0%       R-Sq(adj) = 66.6%

Analysis of Variance

Source          DF          SS            MS          F         P
Regression       4     53729535      13432384      20.43     0.000
Residual Error  35     23007438        657355
Total           39     76736973
```

The following exercises require a computer and statistical software.

19.17 Exercises 2.44 and 4.76 consider a firm's investigation into the relationship between direct labor cost and the number of units produced per batch by its sophisticated machines. In Exercise 4.76, you estimated the fixed labor cost and variable cost per unit in a batch. The accountant believes you can improve on your estimates by taking into account the fact that two different products are being produced, and runs producing batches of the more expensive product require longer setup and production time. Conduct a regression to improve on the previous results. Column 1 of file XR19-17 stores the labor costs, column 2 stores the number of units per batch, and column 3 stores a 1 to indicate an expensive batch and 0 otherwise.

  a Determine the regression equation using the indicator variable.

  b Use the equation to estimate the fixed labor cost and variable cost for each type of batch.

19.18 The real estate agent described in Example 18.2 has become so fascinated by the multiple regression technique that he decided to improve the model. Recall that the agent believed that the most important variables in determining the price of a house are its size, number of bedrooms, and lot size. He took a random sample of 100 houses that were recently sold and recorded the price of the house plus the other three variables. After some consideration, he decided that structure of the house was also a factor. There are four structures. They are two story, side split, back split, and ranch. Each house was classified. Three indicator variables were created. They are

$$I_1 = 1 \text{ (if two story)}$$
$$\quad = 0 \text{ (if not)}$$

$$I_2 = 1 \text{ (if side split)}$$
$$\quad = 0 \text{ (if not)}$$
$$I_3 = 1 \text{ (if back split)}$$
$$\quad = 0 \text{ (if not)}$$

Variables I_1, I_2, and I_3 are stored in columns 5, 6, and 7, respectively, in file XR19-18. (Columns 1 to 4 are identical to columns 1 to 4 of file XM18-02.)

  a Perform a multiple regression analysis, and compare your results with Example 18.2.

  b Interpret and test the coefficients of the indicator variables.

19.19 After reviewing the results of Exercises 17.9 and 19.11, the human resources manager tried one last time to improve the model. He recorded the gender of the worker where 1 = female and 0 = male. These codes were stored in column 3 of file XR19-19. Columns 1 and 2 are identical to those in file XR17-09. Can we infer at the 5% significance level that female telemarketers stay at their jobs longer than male telemarketers?

19.20 Recall Exercise 17.6 where a statistician analyzed the relationship between the length of a commercial and viewers' memory of the commercial's product. The experiment was repeated measuring the same two variables. However, in this experiment not only was the length varied but also the type of commercial. There were three types; humorous(1), musical(2), and serious(3). The memory test scores, lengths, and type of commercial (using the codes in parentheses) were recorded in columns 1 to 3 of file XR19-20.

  a Perform a regression analysis using the codes provided in the data file.

  b Can we infer that the memory test score is affected by the type of commercial? Test with $\alpha = .05$.

  c Create indicator variables to describe the type of commercial and perform another regression analysis.

d Repeat part (b) using the second model.

e Discuss the reasons for the differences between parts (b) and (d).

19.21 Refer to Exercise 18.57 where the amount of time to unload a truck was analyzed. The manager realized that another variable may affect unloading time, the time of day. He recorded the following codes: 1 = morning; 2 = early afternoon; 3 = late afternoon. These codes are stored in column 4 of file XR19-21. (Columns 1 to 3 are identical to columns 1 to 3 of file XR18-57).

a Run a regression using the codes for time of day.

b Create indicator variables to represent time of day. Perform a regression analysis with these new variables.

c Which model fits better? Explain.

d Does time of day affect the time to unload?

19.22 Profitable banks are ones that make good decisions on loan applications. Credit scoring is the statistical technique that helps banks make that decision. However, many branches overturn credit scoring recommendations, while other banks do not use the technique. In an attempt to determine the factors that affect loan decisions, a statistician surveyed 100 banks and recorded the percentage of bad loans (any loan that is not completely repaid), the average size of the loan, and whether a scorecard is used, and if so, whether scorecard recommendations are overturned more than 10% of the time. These results are stored in columns 1 (percentage good loans); 2 (average loan); and 3 (code 1 = no scorecard; 2 = scorecard overturned more than 10% of the time; 3 = scorecard overturned less than 10% of the time) in file XR19-22.

a Create indicator variables to represent the codes.

b Perform a regression analysis.

c How well does the model fit the data?

d Interpret and test the coefficients. What does this tell you?

e Predict with 95% confidence the percentage of bad loans for a bank whose average loan is $10,000 and which does not use a scorecard.

19.23 Refer to Exercise 17.70, where a simple linear regression model was used to analyze the relationship between welding machine breakdowns and the age of the machine. The analysis proved to be so useful to company management that they decided to expand the model to include other machines. Data were gathered for two other machines. These data as well as the original data are stored in file XR19-23 in the following way.

Column 1: Cost of repairs
Column 2: Age of machine
Column 3: Machine (1 = welding machine;
2 = lathe; 3 = stamping machine)

a Develop a multiple regression model.

b Interpret the coefficients.

c Can we conclude that welding machines cost more to repair than stamping machines?

19.24 Absenteeism is a serious employment problem in most countries. It is estimated that absenteeism reduces potential output by more than 10%. Two economists launched a research project to learn more about the problem. They randomly selected 100 organizations to participate in a 1-year study. For each organization, they recorded the average number of days absent per employee and several variables thought to affect absenteeism. File XR19-24 contains the following information.

Column 1: Average employee wage
Column 2: Percentage of part-time employees
Column 3: Percentage of unionized employees

STATISTICS IN THE WORKPLACE

Human Resources Application

Most aspects of workers' performance fall into the domain of the human resources/personnel department. An important performance measurement is the attendance record of each worker. Personnel managers need to know what factors are likely to influence a worker to be absent more frequently than the norm. This can enable the manager to determine whether someone should be hired in the first place. Once hired, the manager needs to be able to influence worker attitudes and performance.

Column 4: Availability of shiftwork
   (1 = yes; 0 = no)
Column 5: Union–management relationship
   (1 = good; 0 = not good)
Column 6: Average number of days absent per
   employee

a Conduct a regression analysis.
b Can we infer at the 5% significance level that the availability of shiftwork affects absenteeism?

c Is there enough evidence at the 5% significance level to infer that in organizations where the union–management relationship is good, absenteeism is lower?

(The authors are grateful to James Fong and Diana Mansour for developing this exercise. The data are based on M. Chadhurg and I. Ng, "Absenteeism Predictors," *Canadian Journal of Economics,* August 1992.)

19.4 REGRESSION AND THE ANALYSIS OF VARIANCE (OPTIONAL)

Consider a problem where the only independent variables are indicator variables representing one factor. As you are about to discover, we have already addressed the technique used to make inferences about this type of problem. It is the analysis of variance procedure introduced in Section 14.2. To illustrate, examine Example 14.1, which tested to determine whether differences in the weekly sales of liquid concentrate apple juice existed among three cities where the advertising approach varied. The data were stored in columns 1, 2, and 3 of file XM14-01. We now redo this problem using regression analysis. We begin by creating two indicator variables. Let

$$I_1 = 1 \text{ (if the sales figure came from City 1)}$$
$$= 0 \text{ (if not)}$$
$$I_2 = 1 \text{ (if the sales figure came from City 2)}$$
$$= 0 \text{ (if not)}$$

The stacked sales data and the values of variables I_1 and I_2 are stored in columns 1, 2, and 3 of file XM14-01A. We then conducted a multiple regression analysis with the resulting output reproduced below.

Excel Output for Example 14.1A

	A	B	C	D	E	F
1	SUMMARY OUTPUT					
2						
3	*Regression Statistics*					
4	Multiple R	0.3192				
5	R Square	0.1019				
6	Adjusted R Square	0.0704				
7	Standard Error	94.31				
8	Observations	60				
9						
10	ANOVA					
11		*df*	*SS*	*MS*	*F*	*Significance F*
12	Regression	2	57512	28756	3.23	0.0468
13	Residual	57	506984	8894		
14	Total	59	564496			
15						
16		*Coefficients*	*Standard Error*	*t Stat*	*P-value*	
17	Intercept	608.7	21.09	28.86	0.0000	
18	I1	-31.10	29.82	-1.04	0.3014	
19	I2	44.35	29.82	1.49	0.1425	

Regression Analysis

```
The regression equation is
Sales = 609 - 31.1 I1 + 44.4 I2

Predictor          Coef         StDev            T           P
Constant         608.65         21.09        28.86       0.000
I1               -31.10         29.82        -1.04       0.301
I2                44.35         29.89         1.49       0.143

S = 94.31        R-Sq = 10.2%       R-Sq(adj) = 7.0%

Analysis of Variance

Source            DF           SS            MS          F         P
Regression         2         57512         28756       3.23     0.047
Residual Error    57        506984          8894
Total             59        564496
```

Compare the analysis of variance table above with the one that was produced in Chapter 14. Despite the fact that two different techniques were used, the ANOVA tables are identical except for the names of the sources of variation. The degrees of freedom, sums of squares, mean squares, F-statistic, and p-value are the same. Obviously, so is the conclusion; there is sufficient evidence to infer that differences in sales among the cities exist.

This example illustrates an extremely important concept, particularly if you plan to take additional statistics courses or to use the analysis of variance technique. That is, that we can develop mathematical models to describe analysis of variance models. For example, consider the independent samples single-factor analysis of variance. Suppose that we wish to compare five treatment means. We would create four indicator variables (we pointed out that the number of indicator variables is one less than the number of groups to be compared) I_1, I_2, I_3, and I_4 (each equaling 0 or 1). The model we would propose is

$$y = \beta_0 + \beta_1 I_1 + \beta_2 I_2 + \beta_3 I_3 + \beta_4 I_4 + \epsilon$$

The analysis of variance portion of the output would include the value of the F-statistic, which tests the hypotheses

H_0: $\beta_1 = \beta_2 = \beta_3 = \beta_4 = 0$

H_1: At least one coefficient is not equal to zero

The null hypothesis infers that no differences exist, whereas the alternative hypothesis is interpreted to mean that some differences exist.

Because for each observation at most one of the indicator variables is equal to 1, we can express the model as

$$y = \beta_0 + \beta_i + \epsilon \text{ (for } i = 1, 2, 3 \text{ and } 4)$$

In this expression, β_0 is the mean of the fifth treatment, and $\beta_0 + \beta_i$ is the mean of the ith treatment. As a consequence, the model is usually expressed as

$$y = \mu_i + \epsilon$$

where μ_i is the mean of the ith treatment. The analysis of variance procedure tests the hypotheses

H_0: $\mu_1 = \mu_2 = \mu_3 = \mu_4 = \mu_5$

H_1: At least two means differ

Recall that these hypotheses are of the kind tested in Chapter 14.

Other models of the analysis of variance can easily be modeled and tested. We leave the task of teaching this concept to another textbook.

In Chapter 14, we showed that we can test for a difference between two means by using a model of the analysis of variance. Now we have shown that we can perform the analysis of variance using regression analysis. As a consequence, we can conduct almost all of the techniques used to test for differences in quantitative data by producing a mathematical model like those seen in this chapter. Figure 19.12 describes the relationship among the procedures that are applied to quantitative data. Thus, we can test for a difference between two means using a t-test, or the F-test of the analysis of variance, which in turn can be replaced by regression analysis. In Section 19.6, we discuss how models are built.

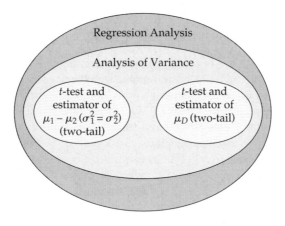

Figure 19.12

Relationship among tests of quantitative data

EXERCISES

The following exercises require a computer and statistical software.

19.25 Refer to Exercise 14.9.

    a Create indicator variables that represent the four high schools.

    b Write the multiple regression model's equation.

    c Perform a regression analysis. Compare your results with the results from the analysis of variance procedure.

19.26 Refer to Exercise 14.10.

    a Create indicator variables to represent the four IRS forms.

    b Write the equation representing the model.

    c Perform a multiple regression analysis, and compare the results with those in Exercise 14.10.

19.27 Refer to Exercise 14.11. Create indicator variables and perform a multiple regression analysis and compare the results with those in Exercise 14.11.

19.28 Refer to Exercise 14.12. Create indicator variables for the three departments, and perform a multiple regression analysis. Compare the results with those of Exercise 14.12.

19.5 STEPWISE REGRESSION

In Section 18.4 we introduced multicollinearity and described the problems it causes by distorting the t-tests of the coefficients. If one of the objectives of the regression analysis is to determine whether and how each independent variable affects the dependent variable, it is necessary to reduce the extent of multicollinearity.

As we discussed in Section 18.4, one of the ways to reduce multicollinearity is to include independent variables that appear to be uncorrelated with each other. A correlation matrix is usually produced to determine the correlation coefficients for each pair of variables. In many cases the correlation matrix will not be able to identify whether multicollinearity is a serious problem because there are many ways for variables to be related. For example, one variable may be a function of several other variables. Consequently, a correlation matrix may not reveal the problem. In this section, we introduce **stepwise regression,** a procedure that eliminates correlated independent variables.

Stepwise regression is an iterative procedure that adds and deletes one independent variable at a time. The decision to add or delete a variable is made on the basis of whether that variable improves the model. Minitab features this and related procedures. Excel does not. However, we created a macro for this purpose. Note that this macro is different from the ones you have encountered thus far in this book. Specific instructions for its use are provided in this section.

STEPWISE REGRESSION PROCEDURE

The procedure begins by computing the simple regression model for each independent variable. The independent variable with the largest F-statistic (which in a simple regression model is the t-statistic squared) or, equally, with the smallest p-value is chosen as the first entering variable. (Minitab uses the F-statistic, and the Excel macro can use either the F-statistic or the p-value.) The standard is usually set at $F = 4.0$, which is chosen because the significance level is about 5%. The standard may be changed in both Minitab and Excel. The standard is called the F-to-enter. If no independent variable exceeds the F-to-enter, the procedure ceases with no regression model produced. If at least one variable exceeds the standard, the procedure continues. It then considers whether the model would be improved by adding a second independent variable. It examines all such models to determine which is best and whether the F-statistic of the second variable (with the first variable already in the equation) is greater than the F-to-enter.

If two independent variables are highly correlated, only one of them will enter the equation. Once the first variable is included, the added explanatory power of the second variable will be minimal and its F-statistic will not be large enough to enter the model. In this way multicollinearity is reduced.

The procedure continues by deciding whether to add another independent variable at each step. The computer also checks to see if the inclusion of previously added variables is warranted. At each step the p-values of all variables are computed and compared to the F-to-remove. If a variable's F-statistic falls below this standard, it is removed from the equation.

These steps are repeated until no more variables are added or removed.

▼ **EXAMPLE 19.3**

In Exercise 17.75, we examined the relationship between a baseball team's winning percentage and its batting average. Exercise 17.76 looked at the relationship between the winning percentage and the earned run average. In an attempt to learn more about the variables that determine winning and losing, several more variables were recorded. Variables that are believed to be related to scoring runs are batting average, home runs, stolen bases, bases on balls received, and number of strikeouts. Variables related to runs allowed are earned runs, hits, errors, bases on balls allowed, and strikeouts of opposing players. The data from the American League for a recent season are stored in file XM19-03 and are listed below.

Table A shows, for example, that the Baltimore Orioles' winning percentage was .414 (actually 67 wins and 95 losses in the 162-game season); they scored a total of 686 runs and had a team batting average of .254 (1,421 hits in 5,604 at bats with 170 home runs, 50 stolen bases, 528 bases on balls, and 974 strikeouts. Table B exhibits defensive statistics. It shows, for example, that Orioles pitchers gave up a total of 796 runs, of which 743 were earned. (An unearned run is a run that is scored because of an error.) Pitchers allowed 1,534 hits, issued 504 bases on balls and struck out 868 opposing batters. The defense made 91 errors.

Table A   Offensive Statistics

Team	Winning %	Runs	Batting Average	Home Runs	Stolen Bases	Bases on Balls	Strikeouts
Baltimore	.414	686	.254	170	50	528	974
Boston	.519	731	.269	126	59	593	820
California	.500	653	.255	115	94	448	928
Chicago	.537	758	.262	139	134	610	896
Cleveland	.352	576	.254	79	84	449	888
Detroit	.519	817	.247	209	109	699	1,185
Kansas City	.506	727	.264	117	119	523	969
Milwaukee	.512	799	.271	116	106	556	802
Minnesota	.586	776	.280	140	107	526	747
New York	.438	674	.256	147	109	473	861
Oakland	.519	760	.248	159	151	642	981
Seattle	.512	702	.255	126	97	588	811
Texas	.525	829	.270	177	102	596	1,039
Toronto	.562	684	.257	133	148	499	1,043

Table B   Defensive Statistics

Team	Earned Runs	Runs	Hits	Errors	Bases on Balls	Strikeouts
Baltimore	796	743	1,534	91	504	868
Boston	712	642	1,405	116	530	999
California	649	591	1,351	102	543	990
Chicago	681	622	1,302	116	601	923
Cleveland	759	678	1,551	149	441	862
Detroit	794	726	1,570	104	593	739
Kansas City	722	639	1,473	125	529	1,004
Milwaukee	744	674	1,498	118	527	859
Minnesota	652	595	1,402	95	488	876
New York	777	709	1,510	133	506	936
Oakland	776	734	1,425	107	655	892
Seattle	674	616	1,387	110	628	1,003
Texas	814	734	1,486	134	662	1,022
Toronto	622	569	1,301	127	523	971

Source: Creative Statistics Company.

Perform an analysis to determine which variables affect a team's winning percentage.

Solution   Here is an example in which we cannot use all the recorded variables in a regression model that attempts to explain the variation in a team's winning percentage. There are two problems. First, when there are few observations relative to the number of variables, the model will almost always appear to fit well when if fact, it may not. Consider a simple regression model (one independent variable) with only three observations. It is likely that the regression equation will appear to fit well because two observations are needed to fit the model and only one observation is left over to compute the standard error. Consequently, R^2 will be high. However, there may be no linear relationship between the two variables. Thus, to enable us to assess how well each of the variables affects the winning percentage it is necessary to reduce the number of variables.

Second, it is likely that some of the independent variables are correlated either directly with each other or correlated with a combination of independent variables. As a result, it will be impossible to determine whether each independent variable is linearly related to the winning percentage.

In fact, the multiple regression model created by using all 12 independent variables was estimated (results shown below). The coefficient of determination was 98.67% (the adjusted coefficient of determination was 82.66%) and the standard error of estimate was quite small (0.0252), but the F-test was not significant (p-value = .3058) and no t-test was significant. (All p-values were greater than .4778.) These results are so contradictory that it is impossible to properly interpret the results. A large coefficient of determination and a small standard error of estimate indicate a good fit. However, the large p-values for the F-test and the t-tests indicate that the model is not valid and that none of the independent variables affect a team's winning percentage.

Excel Output for Example 19.3: Ordinary Multiple Regression

	A	B	C	D	E	F
1	SUMMARY OUTPUT					
2						
3	*Regression Statistics*					
4	Multiple R	0.9933				
5	R Square	0.9867				
6	Adjusted R Square	0.8266				
7	Standard Error	0.0252				
8	Observations	14				
9						
10	ANOVA					
11		*df*	*SS*	*MS*	*F*	*Significance F*
12	Regression	12	0.0471	0.0039	6.17	0.3058
13	Residual	1	0.00064	0.00064		
14	Total	13	0.0478			
15						
16		*Coefficients*	*Standard Error*	*t Stat*	*P-value*	
17	Intercept	-0.155	0.905	-0.17	0.8922	
18	Rns_Scrd	0.00056	0.00059	0.95	0.5148	
19	Team_BA	0.8632	3.102	0.28	0.8272	
20	Team_Hmr	0.00025	0.00059	0.42	0.7450	
21	Team_SB	0.00035	0.00058	0.60	0.6571	
22	Team_Wlk	0.00016	0.00028	0.57	0.6689	
23	Team_SO	0.00005	0.00014	0.40	0.7604	
24	Rns_Alw	-0.00189	0.00200	-0.95	0.5177	
25	Erns_Alw	0.00115	0.00179	0.64	0.6376	
26	Hits_Alw	0.00018	0.00033	0.56	0.6756	
27	Team_Ers	-0.00012	0.00036	-0.32	0.8011	
28	Wlk_Alw	0.00023	0.00021	1.07	0.4778	
29	SO	0.00017	0.00119	0.14	0.9105	

Minitab Output for Example 19.3: Ordinary Multiple Regression

Regression Analysis

```
The regression equation is
Win_Pct = - 0.155 +0.000558 Rns_Scrd + 0.86 Team_BA +0.000249 Team_Hmr
             +0.000348 Team_SB +0.000163 Team_Wlk +0.000054 Team_SO
             - 0.00189 Rns_Alw + 0.00115 Erns_Alw +00000183 Hits_Alw
             -0.000117 Team_Ers +0.000229 Wlk_Alw + 0.00017 SO


Predictor        Coef        StDev           T         P
Constant       -0.1547       0.9048       -0.17     0.892
Rns_Scrd      0.0005584    0.0005851        0.95     0.515
Team_BA         0.863         3.102         0.28     0.827
Team_Hmr      0.0002489    0.0005879        0.42     0.745
Team_SB       0.0003479    0.0005822        0.60     0.657
Team_Wlk      0.0001627    0.0002841        0.57     0.669
Team_SO       0.0000541    0.0001370        0.40     0.760
Rns_Alw       -0.001895     0.002003       -0.95     0.518
Erns_Alw       0.001145     0.001789        0.64     0.638
Hits_Alw      0.0001834    0.0003281        0.56     0.676
Team_Ers      -0.0001169   0.0003617       -0.32     0.801
Wlk_Alw       0.0002292    0.0002138        1.07     0.478
SO             0.000169     0.001195        0.14     0.910


S = 0.02524     R-Sq = 98.7%      R-Sq(adj) = 82.7%

Analysis of Variance

Source            DF          SS          MS         F        P
Regression        12     0.0471477   0.0039290      6.17    0.306
Residual Error     1     0.0006372   0.0006372
Total             13     0.0477849
```

We then conducted a stepwise regression analysis. The results are shown on the next page.

Excel Output for Example 19.3: Ordinary Stepwise Regression

	A	B	C	D	E	F	G
1	Results of stepwise regression						
2							
3	Step 1 - Entering variable: Rns_Scrd						
4							
5	Summary measures						
6		Multiple R	0.6792				
7		R-Square	0.4613				
8		Adj R-Square	0.4164				
9		StErr of Est	0.0463				
10							
11	ANOVA Table						
12		Source	df	SS	MS	F	p-value
13		Explained	1	0.0220	0.0220	10.2766	0.0076
14		Unexplained	12	0.0257	0.0021		
15							
16	Regression coefficients						
17			Coefficient	Std Err	t-value	p-value	
18		Constant	0.0716	0.1342	0.5336	0.6034	
19		Rns_Scrd	0.0006	0.0002	3.2057	0.0076	
20							
21	Step 2 - Entering variable: Rns_Alw						
22							
23	Summary measures			Change	% Change		
24		Multiple R	0.9678	0.2886	%42.5		
25		R-Square	0.9367	0.4754	%103.0		
26		Adj R-Square	0.9252	0.5088	%122.2		
27		StErr of Est	0.0166	-0.0297	-%64.2		
28							
29	ANOVA Table						
30		Source	df	SS	MS	F	p-value
31		Explained	2	0.0448	0.0224	81.3769	0.0000
32		Unexplained	11	0.0030	0.0003		
33							
34	Regression coefficients						
35			Coefficient	Std Err	t-value	p-value	
36		Constant	0.4624	0.0645	7.1704	0.0000	
37		Rns_Scrd	0.0007	0.0001	10.9019	0.0000	
38		Rns_Alw	-0.0007	0.0001	-9.0884	0.0000	

COMMANDS

1 Type or import the data according to the instructions below.
2 Click **Tools, Data Analysis Plus,** and **Stepwise Regression.**
3 Specify the dependent variable (**Response variable:**).
4 Specify the independent variables (**Explanatory variables:**).
5 Select the **Significance option.** Click **OK** to choose **p-values** as the criteria. Click **OK** to accept the default values for **p-to-enter** and **p-to-leave.**
6 Select the **scatterplots** you wish to see. Click **OK.**
7 Select the location of the output. Click **OK.**

COMMANDS FOR EXAMPLE 19.3

Open file **XM19-03.**

Win_Pct

Highlight the entire list.

Special Instructions For Stepwise Regression

Before beginning place the cursor somewhere in the data set. If you don't, you will be forced to close the macro and repeat.

The macro will ask about missing values. The data sets that are stored on the diskettes do not have missing values. Simply accept the default and proceed. However, if you have created your own data set that has missing values, click the box to erase the checkmark.

Instead of specifying the block coordinates of the data, you simply specify variable names for the dependent and the independent variables. The names must start with a letter or underscore. Do not use names that are the same as cell addresses (e.g., A2), R or C, or names consisting only of numbers (e.g., 55). Do not use symbols other than letters, numbers, and underscores.

The dependent variable must be quantitative. It cannot be an indicator (dummy) variable. You may use independent indicator variables.

You will be asked to specify the significance options, which refers to the way in which the stepwise regression decides which variables enter and which variables leave. Until you learn more about these choices we suggest that you accept the defaults.

The macro will draw several different plots. Specify the ones you want.

The output will be placed on the same worksheet as the data or on a different worksheet. If you choose the latter, the macro will ask you to name the worksheet.

Minitab Output for Example 19.3: Stepwise Regression

Stepwise Regression

```
F-to-Enter:       4.00     F-to-Remove:       4.00

Response is Win_Pct  on 12 predictors, with N =    14

       Step          1        2
Constant      0.07162  0.46240

Rns_Scrd      0.00059  0.00074
T-Value          3.21    10.90

Rns_Alw                -0.00069
T-Value                   -9.09

S              0.0463   0.0166
R-Sq            46.13    93.67
```

COMMANDS

COMMANDS FOR EXAMPLE 19.3

1 Type or import the data.

Open file **XM19-02**.

2 Click **Stat, Regression,** and **Stepwise.**

3 Specify the dependent variable (**Response:**).

Win_Pct or **C1**

4 Specify the independent variables (**Predictors:**).

C2-C13

5 To change the **F to enter** and/or **F to remove,** click **Options.** type the new values and click **OK.** Click **OK.**

INTERPRET

All one-independent-variable models are proposed, and the one that fits best is chosen. As you can see, in step 1 the variable **Rns_Scrd** was judged to be best. The model is

Win_Pct = .07162 + .0006 **Rns_Scrd**

Its standard error of estimate is .0463, and the coefficient of determination is 46.13%.

In step 2, each of the remaining independent variables is included in a two-variable model with **Rns_Scrd.** The best two-variable model is selected. Thus, **Rns_Alw** is included with **Rns_Scrd.** At the same time, the new F-statistic for **Rns_Scrd** is computed and compared to the F-to remove. Evidently it is large enough, and **Rns_Scrd** is retained. The regression equation is

Win_Pct = .4624 + .0007 **Rns_Scrd** − .0007 **Rns_Alw**

The standard error of estimate is .0166, and the coefficient of determination is 93.67%.

In step 3, the remaining independent variables are examined. All three-variable models (with **Rns_Scrd** and **Rns_Alw**) are tested. If the new independent variable's F-statistic is larger than the F-to-enter, that variable is added to the equation. In this example, the F-statisic of each of the remaining variables was not sufficiently large. No other variables were added to the model. This means that whatever explanatory power is provided by variables, such as the number of home runs a team hits or the number of stolen bases it allows, has already been factored into the model with the inclusion of the number of runs scored and the number of runs allowed.

For baseball fans this result is rather obvious (although it was probably not obvious until we pointed this out). The two most important variables in determining a team's winning percentage are the number of runs the team scores and the number of runs the team allows the opponents to score. We don't need sophisticated statistical methods to tell us that. However, stepwise regression could now be useful in identifying which offensive-related variables (Table A) are linearly related to the number of runs a team scores and which defensive variables (Table B) are linearly related to the number of runs a team gives up. (See Exercises 19.33 and 19.34.) In this way, a manager may be able to determine what characteristics of a team are most important in producing a winning team. This information could be most useful in deciding trades, drafts, and free agent signings.

▲

EXERCISES

The following exercises require the use of a computer and statistical software.

19.29 Refer to Exercise 18.5.

   a Use a stepwise regression procedure to produce the regression equation.

   b What differences are there between this printout and the one produced in Exercise 18.5?

19.30 Refer to Exercise 18.6.

   a Use a stepwise regression procedure to produce the regression equation.

   b What differences are there between this printout and the one produced in Exercise 18.6?

19.31 Refer to Exercise 18.7. Use a stepwise regression procedure to produce the regression equation. Why was

this result predictable from the analysis performed in Exercise 18.7?

19.32 Refer to Exercise 18.10. Use a stepwise regression procedure to produce the regression equation. Why were both independent variables included in the regression equation?

19.33 Refer to Example 19.3. Use stepwise regression to determine which offensive variables (Table A) are linearly related to the number of runs scored.

19.34 Refer to Example 19.3. Use stepwise regression to determine which defensive variables (Table B) are linearly related to the number of runs allowed.

19.6 MODEL BUILDING

At this point, we have described several different regression models. You now have the tools to describe several different nonlinear relationships in addition to the use of qualitative predictor variables. In this section, we describe how the statistician builds a model.

As we discussed in Chapter 19, regression analysis is used either to determine how one or more predictor variables affect a dependent variable or to predict the value of the dependent variable and estimate its expected value. Although the process differs between the two objectives, there are many similarities in the approach.

Here is the procedure that statisticians employ in the building of a model.

1 Identify the dependent variable. Clearly define the variable that you wish to analyze or predict. For example, if you want to forecast sales, decide whether it is to be the number of units sold, gross revenue, or perhaps net profits. Additionally, decide whether to forecast weekly, monthly, or annual figures.

2 List potential predictors. Using your knowledge of the dependent variable, produce a list of predictors that may be related to the dependent variable. Although we cannot establish a causal relationship, we should attempt to include predictor variables that cause changes in the dependent variable. Bear in mind the problems caused by multicollinearity and the cost of gathering, storing, and processing data. Be selective in your choices. It is best to use the fewest independent variables that produce a satisfactory model.

3 Gather the required observations for the potential models. A general rule is that there should be at least six observations for each independent variable used in the equation.

4 Identify several possible models. Once again, use your knowledge of the dependent variable and predictor variables to formulate a model. For example, if you believe that a predictor variable affects the dependent variable, but you are uncertain about the form of the relationship, formulate first-order and second-order models with and without interaction. It may be helpful to draw a scatter diagram of the dependent variable and each predictor variable to discover the nature of the relationship.

5 **Use statistical software to estimate the models.** Use ordinary or stepwise regression to determine which variables to include in the model. If the objective is to determine which predictor variables affect the dependent variable, you will need to ensure that multicollinearity is not a problem. If it is, attempt to reduce the number of independent variables.

6 **Determine whether the required conditions are satisfied.** If not, attempt to correct the problem. At this point, you may have several "equal" models to choose from.

7 **Use your judgment and the statistical output to select the best model.** This may be the most difficult part of the process. There may be a model that fits best, but another one may be a better predictor, and yet another may feature fewer variables and, thus, be easier to work with. Experience with regression helps. Taking another statistics course is likely to be your best strategy.

19.7 HUMAN RESOURCES MANAGEMENT APPLICATION: PAY EQUITY

In the history of North America there are many examples of racial, ethnic, and gender discrimination. In the last three decades, a number of endeavors have been designed to eliminate discriminatory practices and to right past wrongs. One of these efforts is pay equity, a program that attempts to correct discrimination in the way workers are paid. Our goal in this section is to describe the statistical component of the pay equity issue.

There are two forms of pay equity. The first is "equal pay for equal work." This form is relatively straightforward, arguing that if two individuals do the same job with similar qualifications and experience they should be paid the same. In many jurisdictions it is illegal to violate "equal pay for equal work." The second form is "equal pay for work of equal value." This form is controversial for several reasons including the use of subjectively assigned measures of qualifications and working conditions.

Regression analysis is employed extensively in pay-equity cases. However, the methodology used in equal pay for equal work cases differs from that for equal pay for work of equal value cases. The following example illustrates how statistical analyses can be utilized for the former.

▼ EXAMPLE 19.4

A large firm employing tens of thousands of workers has been accused of discriminating against its female managers. The accusation is based on a random sample of 100 managers. The mean annual salary of the 38 female managers is $76,189, while the mean annual salary of the 62 male managers is $97,832. A statistical test reveals that the t-test of the difference between two means yields a p-value of less than 1%, which provides overwhelming evidence that male managers are paid more than female managers. In rebuttal, the president of the firm points out that the company has a strict policy of equal pay for equal work and that the difference may be due to other variables. Accordingly, he found and recorded the number of years of education and the number of years of experience for each of the 100 managers in the sample. Also recorded are the salary and gender (0 = female and 1 = male). All the data are stored in file XM19-04. The president wanted to know whether a regression analysis would shed some light on the issue.

Solution

Using salary as the dependent variable, a multiple regression analysis was performed with the results shown below.

Excel Output for Example 19.4

	A	B	C	D	E	F
1	SUMMARY OUTPUT					
2						
3	*Regression Statistics*					
4	Multiple R	0.8326				
5	R Square	0.6932				
6	Adjusted R Square	0.6836				
7	Standard Error	16274				
8	Observations	100				
9						
10	ANOVA					
11		*df*	*SS*	*MS*	*F*	*Significance F*
12	Regression	3	57434095083	19144698361	72.29	0.0000
13	Residual	96	25424794888	264841613		
14	Total	99	82858889971			
15						
16		*Coefficients*	*Standard Error*	*t Stat*	*P-value*	
17	Intercept	-5835	16083	-0.36	0.7175	
18	Education	2119	1018	2.08	0.0401	
19	Experience	4099	317.2	12.92	0.0000	
20	Gender	1851	3703	0.50	0.6183	

Minitab Output for Example 19.4

Regression Analysis

The regression equation is
Salary = − 5835 + 2119 Education + 4099 Experience + 1851 Gender

Predictor	Coef	StDev	T	P
Constant	−5835	16083	−0.36	0.718
Educatio	2119	1018	2.08	0.040
Experien	4099.3	317.2	12.92	0.000
Gender	1851	3703	0.50	0.618

S = 16274   R-Sq = 69.3%   R-Sq(adj) = 68.4%

Analysis of Variance

Source	DF	SS	MS	F	P
Regression	3	57434095083	19144698361	72.29	0.000
Residual Error	96	25424794888	264841613		
Total	99	82858889971			

INTERPRET

The model fits quite well. The coefficient of determination is .6932, which tells the president that 69.32% of the variation in salaries is explained by the model. The F-statistic is 72.29, which has a p-value of 0. There is overwhelming evidence to infer that the model is valid.

The p-value of the t-tests to determine whether there is evidence of a linear relationship between salary and each of education, experience, and gender are .0401, 0, and .6183, respectively. Both the number of years of education and the number of years of experience are linearly related to salary. However, the t-test of the slope for gender tells us that there is no evidence of a difference between female and male managers. Thus, the result of the t-test of $\mu_1 - \mu_2$ alluded to in the question is contradicted. A further analysis of the data tells us that the discrepancy in salaries is due to the years of experience. In general, female managers have less experience and hence lower salaries.

▲

REGRESSION ANALYSIS FOR EQUAL PAY FOR WORK OF EQUAL VALUE CASES

Cases involving the issue of equal pay for work of equal value are much more difficult. The issue generally revolves around female-dominated and male-dominated jobs. The former refers to jobs that are generally held by women (e.g., secretaries) and the latter refers to jobs generally held by men (e.g., maintenance workers). Women's groups claim that male-dominated jobs are more highly paid. Here the issue is not underpaying women doing exactly the same job performed by men. Instead the issue is that women's jobs are undervalued. Thus, it is necessary to evaluate jobs.

There are several jurisdictions where pay equity for work of equal value laws apply. One such jurisdiction is the province of Manitoba. The Manitoba Pay Equity Act is mandatory in the province's civil service, crown corporations, hospitals, and universities. The act defines gender-dominated job classes as ones with at least 10 workers where at least 70% are of the same gender. The act requires that all such jobs be evaluated to determine whether female-dominated jobs are undervalued and underpaid compared to male-dominated jobs.

Although regression analysis is employed there are major differences between the technique described in Example 19.4 and the one used in this case. Rather than estimate a regression model that explains how several related variables affect pay, we need to develop a job evaluation system (JES). The system is used to assign a score to each job, which is then used as an independent variable in regression where pay is again the dependent variable. The regression analysis can be conducted in several ways. Using the male-dominated jobs only the simple linear regression equation can be estimated. The coefficients are then used to calculate the "correct" female-dominated job pay rates. The difference between the "correct" and the actual pay rates represents the degree of underpayment. Alternatively a regression analysis with both male- and female-dominated jobs can be employed. An indicator variable representing gender is included. The value of the indicator variable's coefficient represents the difference between male- and female-dominated jobs and the degree of underpayment. The following example illustrates the latter type of analysis, which was adapted from the province of Manitoba Pay Equity Act manuals that describe the law and how it is to be administered.

▼ **EXAMPLE 19.5**

In a university a total of eight jobs were identified as gender dominated. The female-dominated jobs are secretary, cleaner, and workers in the bookstore and cafeteria. The male-dominated jobs are gardener, security guard, maintenance worker, and technician. Perform a pay-equity analysis to determine whether and to what degree female-dominated jobs are undervalued and underpaid.

Solution   The hourly pay rates are as follows.

Job Categories	Pay Rate
Maintenance	13.55
Security	15.65
Gardener	13.80
Technician	19.90
Cleaner	11.85
Secretary	14.75
Bookstore	18.90
Cafeteria	13.30

After some consideration the following factors were selected as part of the job evaluation system.

Knowledge and training

Responsibility

Mental effort

Physical effort

Working conditions

Each factor is subjectively assigned a weight that reflects its importance. The weights (which must sum to one) are 25%, 23%, 22%, 15%, and 15%, respectively.

A score for each job is determined by assigning a value between 1 and 10 for each of the five factors and then multiplying by the weight. Smaller values represent less demanding requirements or better conditions. The male-dominated jobs are evaluated as follows.

Factors	Weight	Maintenance	Security	Gardener	Technician
Knowledge & training	0.25	1	2	3	9
Responsibility	0.23	2	7	1	7
Mental effort	0.22	2	3	1	8
Physical effort	0.15	7	1	6	4
Working conditions	0.15	7	4	8	1
Total score		3.25	3.52	3.30	6.37

As you can see the scores assigned to the maintenance workers and gardeners reflect relatively small demands on knowledge, training, and mental effort but high demands on physical effort and poor working conditions. The technician, on the other hand has excellent working conditions but requires a high level of knowledge and training.

The evaluations of the female-dominated jobs are as follows.

Factors	Weight	Cleaner	Secretary	Bookstore	Cafeteria
Knowledge & training	0.25	1	6	4	2
Responsibility	0.23	2	7	7	2
Mental effort	0.22	2	6	7	2
Physical effort	0.15	7	3	2	5
Working conditions	0.15	5	1	1	6
Total score		2.95	5.03	4.60	3.05

As was the case with the male-dominated jobs, the scores for the female-dominated jobs are based on a subjective assessment of the requirements and work that the jobs entail.

The score and an indicator variable are used as independent variables in a regression analysis with pay as the dependent variable.

The following data are used in the regression analysis.

Job Categories	Pay Rate	Score	Gender
Maintenance	13.55	3.25	1
Security	15.65	3.52	1
Gardener	13.80	3.30	1
Technician	19.90	6.37	1
Cleaner	11.85	2.95	0
Secretary	14.75	5.03	0
Bookstore	18.90	4.60	0
Cafeteria	13.30	3.05	0

where

$$\text{Gender} = 1 \text{ if male-dominated job}$$
$$= 0 \text{ if female-dominated job}$$

The results of the regression follow.

Excel Output for Example 19.5

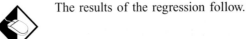

	A	B	C	D	E	F
1	SUMMARY OUTPUT					
2						
3	*Regression Statistics*					
4	Multiple R	0.8515				
5	R Square	0.7251				
6	Adjusted R Square	0.6152				
7	Standard Error	1.750				
8	Observations	8				
9						
10	ANOVA					
11		*df*	*SS*	*MS*	*F*	*Significance F*
12	Regression	2	40.39	20.19	6.59	0.0396
13	Residual	5	15.31	3.06		
14	Total	7	55.70			
15						
16		*Coefficients*	*Standard Error*	*t Stat*	*P-value*	
17	Intercept	7.145	2.309	3.10	0.0270	
18	Score	1.933	0.547	3.54	0.0166	
19	Gender	0.633	1.242	0.51	0.6318	

Minitab Output for Example 19.5

Regression Analysis

The regression equation is
Pay Rate = 7.15 + 1.93 Score + 0.63 Gender

Predictor	Coef	StDev	T	P
Constant	7.145	2.309	3.10	0.027
Score	1.9334	0.5468	3.54	0.017
Gender	0.633	1.242	0.51	0.632

S = 1.750   R-Sq = 72.5%   R-Sq(adj) = 61.5%

Analysis of Variance

Source	DF	SS	MS	F	P
Regression	2	40.388	20.194	6.59	0.040
Residual Error	5	15.310	3.062		
Total	7	55.699			

INTERPRET   We cannot apply the usual statistical inference because the eight observations represent the entire population under consideration. Instead we simply use the coefficients of interest. In this case we discover that male-dominated jobs are paid an average of .633 more than female-dominated jobs after adjusting for the value of each job. If we accept the validity of this analysis (see Exercises 19.36 and 19.37), we conclude that the holders of female-dominated jobs need to have their pay rates increased by 63 cents per hour.

▲

EXERCISES

19.35 Pay equity for men and women has been an ongoing source of conflict for a number of years in North America. Suppose that a statistician is investigating the factors that affect salary differences between male and female university professors. She believes that the following variables have some impact on a professor's salary.

> Number of years since first degree
> Highest degree = 1 (if highest degree is a Ph.D.)
>   = 0 (if highest degree is not a Ph.D.)
> Average score on teaching evaluations
> Number of articles published in refereed journals
> Gender = 1 (if professor is male)
>   = 0 (if professor is female)

A random sample of 100 university professors was taken and the data stored in file XR19-35.

> Column 1: Annual salary
> Column 2: Number of years since first degree

> Column 3: Highest degree
> Column 4: Mean score on teaching evaluation
> Column 5: Number of articles published
> Column 6: Gender

a Can the statistician conclude that the model is valid?
b Can the statistician conclude at the 5% significance level that male professors earn more than equally-qualified female professors?

An Excel spreadsheet, XM19-05.xls was created to perform the analysis described in Example 19.5. The jobs, pay rates, job scores, and the values of the indicator variable are shown at the bottom of the sheet. These data were used as inputs in the regression analysis. The worksheet is set up so that any change in the factor scores and/or weights automatically changes the job scores at the bottom of the page. A Minitab file, XM19-05.mpj, was also created. However, to change the total score you will have to recalculate column C7.

19.36 Change the weights in Example 19.5 for knowledge and training to 15% and for working conditions to

25%. What effect does this have on the conclusion? Briefly explain why the result was predictable.

19.37 Redo Example 19.5 by assigning your own values to each factor and to the weights. What conclusion did you reach?

19.38 Discuss how the factor values and weights affect the final result of Example 19.5. Explain the strengths and weaknesses of the statistical analysis.

19.8 SUMMARY

This chapter completes our discussion of the regression technique, which began in Chapter 17. We presented several additional models for predicting the value of one variable on the basis of other variables. Polynomial models with one and two independent variables were presented. We discussed how indicator variables allow us to use qualitative variables, and we showed how regression analysis is related to analysis of variance. To help choose the model that is best for our purposes, we introduced stepwise regression. We completed the chapter by providing some advice on how statisticians build models.

IMPORTANT TERMS

Polynomial model *732*

Predictor *732*

Order *732*

First-order model *732*

Second-order model *733*

Interaction *734*

Indicator (dummy) variable *747*

Stepwise regression *758*

SUPPLEMENTARY EXERCISES

The following exercises require the use of a computer and statistical software. Conduct all statistical tests at the 5% significance level.

19.39 Car designers have been experimenting with ways to improve gas mileage for many years. An important element in this research is the way in which a car's speed affects how quickly fuel is burned. Competitions whose objective is to drive the furthest on the smallest amount of gas have determined that low speeds and high speeds are inefficient. Designers would like to know which speed burns gas most efficiently. As an experiment, 50 identical cars are driven at different speeds and the gas mileage measured. These data are stored in columns 1 (gas mileage in miles per gallon) and 2 (speed in miles per hour), respectively, in file XR19-39.

  a Write the equation of the model that you think is appropriate.

  b Perform a regression analysis using your model.

  c How well does it fit?

19.40 The number of car accidents on a particular stretch of highway seems to be related to the number of vehicles that travel over it plus the speed at which they are traveling. A city alderman has decided to ask the county sheriff to provide him with statistics covering the last few years, with the intention of examining these data statistically so that he can (if possible) introduce new speed laws that will reduce traffic accidents. Using the number of accidents as the dependent variable, he obtains estimates of the number of cars passing along a stretch of road and their average speeds (in miles per hour). The observations for 60 randomly selected days are stored in columns 1 (number of accidents), 2 (number of cars), and 3 (average speed) in file XR19-40.

  a Which model should the alderman use? Explain.

  b Conduct a regression analysis using a first-order model with interaction.

  c Is the model valid?

19.41 Refer to Exercise 19.40.

  a Estimate a second-order model with interaction.

  b Is this model valid?

19.42 After analyzing whether the number of ads affected the number of customers, the manager in Exercise 17.69 decided to determine whether where he advertised made any difference. As a result, he reorganized the experiment. Each week he advertised several times per week, but in only one of the advertising media. He again recorded the weekly number of customers, the number of ads, and the location of that week's advertisement (1 = newspaper, 2 = radio, and 3 = television). These data are stored in columns 1 to 3, respectively, in file XR19-42.

a Create indicator variables to describe the advertising medium.

b Conduct a regression analysis. Test to determine whether the model is valid.

c Does the advertising medium make a difference? Explain.

19.43 A baseball fan has been collecting data from a newspaper on the various American League teams. She wants to explain each team's winning percentage as a function of its batting average and its earned run average plus an indicator variable for whether or not the team fired its manager within the last 12 months (code = 1 if it did and code = 0 if it did not). The data for 50 randomly selected teams playing during the last five seasons are stored in file XR19-43.

a Perform a regression analysis using a first-order model (no interaction).

b Do these data provide sufficient evidence that a team that fired its manager within the last 12 months wins less frequently than a team that did not fire its manager?

19.44 A growing segment of the textile industry in the United States is based on piecework, wherein workers are paid for each unit they produce, instead of receiving an hourly wage. The manager of one such company has observed that inexperienced workers perform quite poorly, but they usually improve quickly. However, very experienced workers do not perform as well as expected. Analysts attribute this phenomenon to boredom. More experienced workers grow weary of the monotonous work and become less productive. In an attempt to learn more about piecework labor, a statistician took a random sample of workers with varying years of experience and counted the number of units each produced in 8 hours. These data are stored in columns 1 (number of units) and 2 (years of experience) of file XR19-44.

a Write the equation of the model you think would fit.

b Perform a regression analysis using your model.

c Describe how well the model fits.

19.45 The maintenance of swimming pools is quite costly because of all the chlorine that is needed to keep the water clear and relatively free of germs. A chain of hotels (all with outdoor pools) seeking to reduce costs decided to analyze the factors that determine how much chlorine is needed. They commissioned a chemist to conduct an analysis. It is believed that the speed at which chlorine in a pool is depleted is dependent on the temperature of the water (higher temperature uses chlorine faster); pH level, which is a measure of the acidity of the water (pH ranges from 0 to 14, where 0 is very acidic and 14 is very alkaline; levels around 7.5 use the least chlorine); and weather (sunshine uses up chlorine). The chemist conducted the following experiment. The percentage of chlorine depletion during 8-hour days was recorded under varying conditions of pH level, water temperature, and weather conditions. These data are recorded in file XR19-45 in the following way.

Column 1: Percentage of chlorine depletion over 8 hours
Column 2: Temperature (degrees Fahrenheit)
Column 3: pH level
Column 4: 1 = mainly cloudy; 2 = sunny; 3 = partly sunny

a Write the equation of the model that you would suggest.

b Use regression analysis to estimate the model's coefficients.

c Test to determine whether the model is valid.

d Can we infer that higher temperatures deplete chlorine more quickly?

e Is there evidence to infer that the belief about the relationship between chlorine depletion and PH level is correct?

f Can we infer that weather is a factor in chlorine depletion?

CASE 19.1   Challenger Disaster

On January 28, 1986, the space shuttle *Challenger* exploded moments after takeoff, killing the eight astronauts aboard. The cause was O-ring failure, which produced a leak of fuel that was ignited by the rocket's engines. (The O-rings sealed the gaps between the parts of the solid rocket motors, preventing gas leaks.) The temperature at the Kennedy Space Center in Florida at liftoff was 31° F. Before the launch, several scientists had stated that the low temperatures would cause the O-rings to harden and ultimately leak. They argued that the launch should be delayed until the temperature increased. However, other scientists using Figure C19.1 pointed out that there appeared to be no relationship between the number of O-ring failures and temperature. As you can see, there is no indication that lower temperatures yield larger numbers of O-ring failures. On the basis of this figure and other arguments, the *Challenger* was launched to its disastrous end.

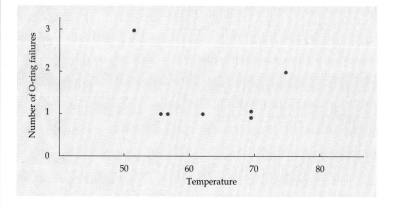

Figure C19.1

Incomplete scatter diagram of number of O-ring failures and temperature

Incredibly, the fateful decision was made with an incomplete graph. Figure C19.1 was created using only the launches where there was at least one O-ring failure. It omitted the 17 launches where there were no O-ring failures. Figure C19.2 was drawn with the missing data. It is obvious from Figure C19.2 that there is a relationship between temperature and the number of O-ring failures; the lower the temperature, the greater the number of O-ring failures.

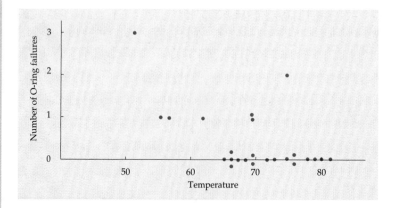

Figure C19.2

Scatter diagram of number of O-ring failures and temperature

The actual data for all 24 successful pre-Challenger flights are listed in columns 1 (temperature) and 2 (number of O-ring failures) in file C19-01. [Source: Volume 1, p. 145, *Report of the Presidential Commission on the Space Shuttle Challenger Accident* (1986).]

Develop two models that could be used to describe the relationship between temperature and number of O-ring failures. Use the one you judge to be better to predict with 95% confidence the number of O-ring failures when the temperature is 31° F.

CASE 19.2   **Track And Field Performance Forecasts***

There have been steady improvements in athletic performances in all sports. Olympic track and field events are an excellent example of this phenomenon. Over the past 50 years most track and field events have produced new Olympic games records. To examine this issue, a researcher recorded the winning performance in each Olympic games between 1948 and 1988 for each of the following events.

1 Men's 100-meter (seconds)

2 Women's 100-meter (seconds)

3 Men's 4X100 relay (seconds)

4 Women's 4X100 relay (seconds)

5 Men's 1500-meter (seconds)

6 Women's 1500-meter (seconds)

7 Men's high jump (inches)

8 Women's high jump (inches)

9 Men's long jump (feet)

10 Women's long jump (feet)

11 Men's javelin (feet)

12 Women's javelin (feet)

13 Men's shot-put (feet)

14 Women's shot-put (feet)

These data are stored in columns 1 through 14 of file C19-02. Column 15 contains the years: 1 = 1948; 2 = 1952; ... ; 11 = 1988.

For each event, develop a model that uses the year as an independent variable to forecast future performances. Use the models to predict the 1992 performances. Can we use the model to forecast when the fastest women's 100-meter race will be less than 10 seconds? Explain.

*The authors would like to thank Jim Beaudoin and Paul Weber for writing this case. The data were taken from *Sports Illustrated: 1992 Sports Almanac and Record Book.*

Chapter 20

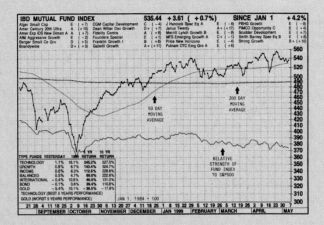

Time-Series

Analysis

and Forecasting

20.1 Introduction

20.2 Components of a Time Series

20.3 Smoothing Techniques

20.4 Trend Analysis

20.5 Measuring the Cyclical Effect

20.6 Measuring the Seasonal Effect

20.7 Introduction to Forecasting

20.8 Time-Series Forecasting with Exponential Smoothing

20.9 Time-Series Forecasting with Regression

20.10 Summary

20.1 INTRODUCTION

Any variable that is measured over time in sequential order is called a **time series.** Our objective in this chapter is to analyze time series in order to detect patterns that will enable us to forecast the future value of the time series. There is an almost unlimited number of such applications in management and economics. Some examples follow.

1 Governments want to know future values of interest rates, unemployment rates, and percentage increases in the cost of living.

2 Housing industry economists must forecast mortgage interest rates, demand for housing, and the cost of building materials.

3 Many companies attempt to predict the demand for their product and their share of the market.

4 Universities and colleges often try to forecast the number of students who will be applying for acceptance at post-secondary-school institutions.

As indicated above, forecasting is a common practice among business and government decision-makers. This chapter will focus on **time series forecasting,** which is forecasting that uses historical time series data to predict future values of variables such as sales or unemployment rates. This entire chapter may be thought of as an application tool both for economists and for managers in all functional areas of business, because forecasting is such a vital factor in decision-making in these areas.

For example, the starting point for aggregate production planning by operations managers is to forecast demand for the company's products. These forecasts will make use of economists' forecasts of macroeconomic variables (such as gross domestic product, disposable income, and housing starts) as well as the marketing managers' internal forecasts of their customers' future needs. Not only are these sales forecasts critical to production planning, but they are the key to accurate proforma (i.e. forecasted) financial statements, which are produced by the accounting and financial managers to assist in their planning for future financial needs such as borrowing. Likewise, the human resources department will find such forecasts of a company's growth prospects to be invaluable in their planning for future manpower requirements.

There are many different forecasting techniques. Some are based on developing a model that attempts to analyze the relationship between a dependent variable and one or more independent variables. We presented some of these methods in the chapters on regression analysis (Chapters 17 and 18). The forecasting methods to be discussed in this chapter are all based on time-series analysis. The first step is to analyze the components of a time series, which we discuss in the next section. In Sections 20.3 through 20.6, we deal with methods for detecting and measuring which components exist. After we uncover this information, we can develop forecasting tools. We will only scratch the surface of this topic. Our objective is to expose you to the concepts of forecasting and to introduce some of the simpler techniques. The level of this text precludes us from investigating more complicated methods.

20.2 COMPONENTS OF A TIME SERIES

A time series can consist of four different components, as described below.

Components of a Time Series
1 Long-term trend (T)
2 Cyclical effect (C)
3 Seasonal effect (S)
4 Random variation (R)

A **trend** (also known as a *secular trend*) is a long-term, relatively smooth pattern or direction exhibited by a series. Its duration is more than 1 year. For example, the population of the United States exhibited a trend of relatively steady growth from 147 million in 1948 to 258 million in 1993. (See Figure 20.1.)

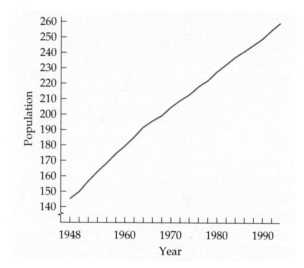

Figure 20.1

Population of the United States: 1948–1993

Source: Statistical Abstract of the United States.

The trend of a time series is not always linear. For example, Figure 20.2 describes U.S. beer consumption per person (over age 21) from 1970 to 1992. As you can see, per capita consumption grew between 1970 and 1980, leveled off, and then began decreasing. In Section 20.4, we discuss a model that fits this type of time series quite well.

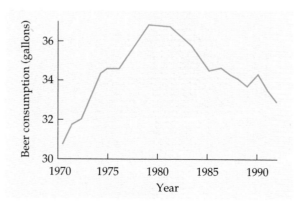

Figure 20.2

U.S. beer consumption per person over 21

Source: Standard and Poor's Industry Surveys.

A **cycle** is a wavelike pattern describing a long-term trend that is generally apparent over a number of years, resulting in a **cyclical effect.** By definition, it has a duration of more than 1 year. Examples of cycles include the well-known business cycles that record periods of economic recession and inflation, long-term product-demand cycles, and cycles in monetary and financial sectors.

Figure 20.3 displays a series of regular cycles. Unfortunately, in practice, cycles are seldom regular and often appear in combination with other components. The percentage change in U.S. domestic exports between 1970 and 1993 is depicted in Figure 20.4. This time series appears to exhibit three irregular cycles and a long-term decrease.

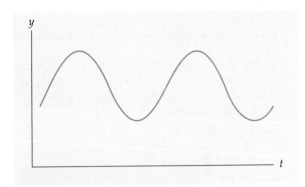

Figure 20.3

Cyclical variation in a time series

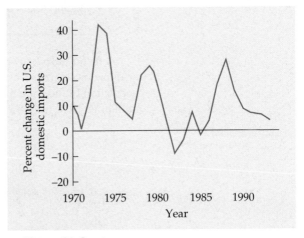

Figure 20.4

Percentage change in U.S. domestic imports
Source: Statistical Abstract of the United States.

Seasonal variations are like cycles, but they occur over short repetitive calendar periods and, by definition, have a duration of less than 1 year. The term "seasonal variation" may refer to the four traditional seasons or to systematic patterns that occur during the period of 1 week or even over the course of 1 day. Stock market prices, for example, often show highs and lows at particular times during the day.

An illustration of seasonal variation is provided in Figure 20.5, which graphs monthly U.S. traffic volume (in billions of miles). It is obvious from the graph that Americans drive more during the summer months than during the winter months.

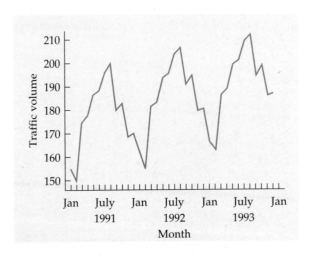

Figure 20.5

Traffic volume in billions of miles
Source: Standard & Poor's Industry Surveys.

Random variation comprises the irregular changes in a time series that are not caused by any other component. It tends to hide the existence of the other, more predictable components. Because random variation exists in almost all time series, one of the functions of this chapter is to present ways to remove the random variation, thereby allowing us to describe and measure the other components and, ultimately, to make accurate forecasts. If you examine Figures 20.1, 20.2, 20.4, and 20.5, you will detect some degree of random variation; because of it, even if we knew precisely about the other components, we would not be able to predict the time series with 100% confidence. If you've learned anything from the previous chapters in this book, you will recognize that this is not something new. Statisticians must always live with uncertainty.

TIME-SERIES MODELS

The time-series model is generally expressed either as an **additive model,** where the value of the time series at time t is specified as

$$y_t = T_t + C_t + S_t + R_t$$

or as a **multiplicative model,** where the value of the time series at time t is specified as

$$y_t = T_t \times C_t \times S_t \times R_t$$

Recall that the four components of the time-series model are long-term trend (T), cyclical effect (C), seasonal effect (S), and random variation (R).

Both models may be equally acceptable. However, it is frequently easier to understand the techniques associated with time-series analysis if we refer to the multiplicative model.

In the next four sections, we present ways of determining which components are present in a time series.

20.3 SMOOTHING TECHNIQUES

If we can determine which components actually exist in a time series, we can develop a better forecast. Unfortunately, the existence of the random variation component often hides the other components. One of the simplest ways of removing the random fluctuation is to smooth the time series. In this section, we describe two methods of doing this: *moving averages* and *exponential smoothing.*

MOVING AVERAGES

A **moving average** for a time period is the simple arithmetic average of the values in that time period and those close to it. For example, to compute the three-period moving average for any time period, we would sum the value of the time series in that time period, the value in the previous time period, and the value in the following time period and divide by 3. We calculate the three-period moving average for all time periods except the first and the last. To compute the five-period moving average, we average the value in that time period, the values in the two previous time periods, and the values in the two following time periods. We can choose any number of periods with which to calculate the moving averages.

▼ **EXAMPLE 20.1**

As part of an effort to forecast future gasoline sales, an operator of five independent gas stations recorded the quarterly gasoline sales (in thousands of gallons) for the past 4 years. These are shown in the accompanying table and stored in file XM20-01.

Time Period	Year	Quarter	Gasoline Sales (thousands of gallons)
1	1	1	39
2		2	37
3		3	61
4		4	58
5	2	1	18
6		2	56
7		3	82
8		4	27
9	3	1	41
10		2	69
11		3	49
12		4	66
13	4	1	54
14		2	42
15		3	90
16		4	66

Calculate the three-quarter and five-quarter moving averages. Then graph the quarterly sales and the moving averages.

Solution To compute the first three-quarter moving average, we group the gasoline sales in periods 1, 2, and 3, and then average them. Thus, the first moving average is

$$\frac{39 + 37 + 61}{3} = \frac{137}{3} = 45.7$$

The second moving average is calculated by dropping the first period's sales (39), adding the fourth period's sales (58), and then computing the new average. Thus, the second moving average is

$$\frac{37 + 61 + 58}{3} = \frac{156}{3} = 52.0$$

The process continues as shown in the following table. Similar calculations are made to produce the five-quarter moving averages (also shown in the table).

Time Period	Gasoline Sales	Three-Quarter Moving Average	Five-Quarter Moving Average
1	39	—	—
2	37	45.7	—
3	61	52.0	42.6
4	58	45.7	46.0
5	18	44.0	55.0
6	56	52.0	48.2
7	82	55.0	44.8
8	27	50.0	55.0

(continued)

Time Period	Gasoline Sales	Three-Quarter Moving Average	Five-Quarter Moving Average
9	41	45.7	53.6
10	69	53.0	50.4
11	49	61.3	55.8
12	66	56.3	56.0
13	54	54.0	60.2
14	42	62.0	63.6
15	90	66.0	—
16	66	—	—

Notice that we place the moving averages in the center of the group of values being averaged. It is for this reason that we prefer to use an odd number of periods in the moving averages. Later in this section, we discuss how to deal with an even number of periods.

Excel Output for Example 20.1

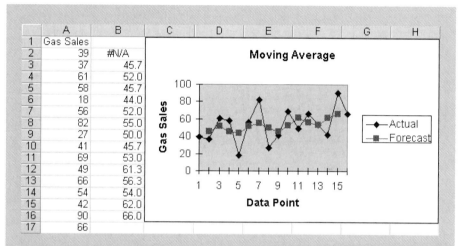

We show the printout for the 3-period moving average only. Notice that Excel places the moving averages in the third period of each group of three rather than in the center. The graph accompanying the table is drawn the same way. Command 7 below shows how to modify the Excel table (and hence the graph) so that the moving averages appear in the second period of each group.

COMMANDS	COMMANDS FOR EXAMPLE 20.1
1 Type or import the data into one column.	Open file **XM20-01.**
2 Click **Tools, Data Analysis . . . ,** and **Moving Average.**	
3 Specify the **Input Range.** Click **Labels** (if necessary).	A1:A17
4 Specify the number of periods (**Interval:**).	3
5 Specify the **Output Range.**	B2
6 Specify **Chart Output** if you want to graph the time series. Click **OK.**	

To modify the table (and hence the graph) so that the moving averages appear in the second period of each group, proceed as follows.

7 Use the left button on the mouse and click the first cell containing "N/A". Click the right button. Click (with the left button) **Delete.** Select **shift cells up.** Click **OK.**

Minitab Output for Example 20.1

Period	Sales	AVER1
1	39	*
2	37	45.6667
3	61	52.0000
4	58	45.6667
5	18	44.0000
6	56	52.0000
7	82	55.0000
8	27	50.0000
9	41	45.6667
10	69	53.0000
11	49	61.3333
12	66	56.3333
13	54	54.0000
14	42	62.0000
15	90	66.0000
16	66	*

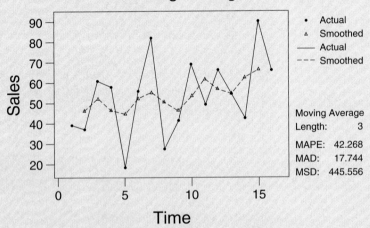

We show the output for the three-period moving average only. The table lists the original time series (sales) and the moving averages. Also included are three statistics (accuracy measures) that deal with another use for moving averages, forecasting, which we'll discuss later in this chapter. Minitab prints the graph of both the original time series and the moving averages.

COMMANDS	COMMANDS FOR EXAMPLE 20.1
1 Type or import the data into one column.	Open file **XM20-01.**
2 Click **Stat, Time Series,** and **Moving Average**	
3 Type the variable name.	**Sales** or **C1**
4 Type the number of periods (**MA length**):	**3**
5 Click **Center the moving averages.**	
6 Click **Results** . . . , **Plot smoothed vs. actual,** and **Summary table.** Click **OK.**	
7 Click **Storage** . . . and **Moving Averages.** Click **OK.**	

INTERPRET

To see how the moving averages remove some of the random variation, examine Figures 20.6 and 20.7. Figure 20.6 depicts the quarterly gasoline sales. Discerning any of the time-series components is difficult because of the large amount of random variation. Now consider the three-quarter moving average in Figure 20.7. You should be able to detect the seasonal pattern that exhibits peaks in the third quarter of each year (periods 3, 7, 11, and 15) and valleys in the first quarter of the year (periods 5, 9, and 13). There is also a small but discernible long-term trend of increasing sales.

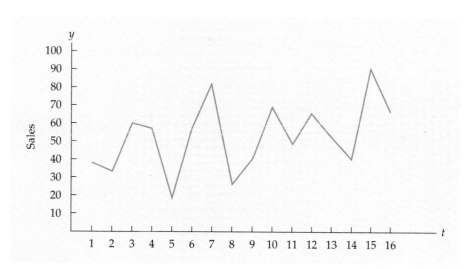

Figure 20.6

Quarterly gasoline sales

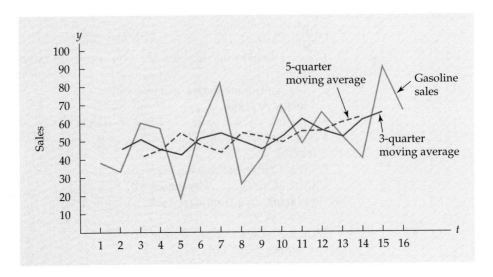

Figure 20.7

Quarterly gasoline sales and the three-quarter and five-quarter moving averages

Notice also in Figure 20.7 that the five-quarter moving average produces more smoothing than the three-quarter moving average. In general, the longer the time period over which we average, the smoother the series becomes. Unfortunately, in this case we've smoothed too much—the seasonal pattern is no longer apparent in the five-quarter moving average. All we can see is the long-term trend. It is important to realize that our objective is to smooth the time series sufficiently to remove the random variation and to reveal the other components (trend, cycle, and/or season) present. With too little smoothing, the random variation disguises the real pattern. With too much smoothing, however, some or all of the other effects may be eliminated along with the random variation.

▲

CENTERED MOVING AVERAGES

Using an even number of periods to calculate the moving averages presents a problem about where to place the moving averages in a graph or table. For example, suppose that we calculate the four-period moving average of the following time series.

Period	Time Series
1	15
2	27
3	20
4	14
5	25
6	11

The first moving average is

$$\frac{15 + 27 + 20 + 14}{4} = 19.0$$

However, because this value represents time periods 1, 2, 3, and 4, we must place it between periods 2 and 3. The next moving average is

$$\frac{27 + 20 + 14 + 25}{4} = 21.5$$

and it must be placed between periods 3 and 4. The moving average that falls between periods 4 and 5 is

$$\frac{20 + 14 + 25 + 11}{4} = 17.5$$

Having the moving averages fall between the time periods causes various problems, including graphing difficulty. Centering the moving averages corrects the problem. We do this by computing the two-period moving average of the moving averages. Thus, the centered moving average for period 3 is

$$\frac{19.0 + 21.5}{2} = 20.25$$

The centered moving average for period 4 is

$$\frac{21.5 + 17.5}{2} = 19.50$$

The following table summarizes these results.

Period	Time Series	Four-Period Moving Average	Four-Period Centered Moving Average
1	15		—
		—	
2	27		—
		19.0	
3	20		20.25
		21.5	
4	14		19.50
		17.5	
5	25		—
		—	
6	11		—

Minitab centers the moving averages on command. Excel does not center the moving averages. We will now describe how to center the moving averages in Excel and how to deal with an even number of periods.

Excel Instructions for Centered Moving Averages

Excel places the moving average in the last of the periods being averaged. You can use **Cut** and **Paste** to move the averages to the center of the periods. However, the graph will remain unchanged. If the number of periods is an even number, compute a two-period moving average of the moving averages. For the illustration shown on page 786, proceed as follows. (Excel requires a minimum of four time-series values to perform the calculations. For reasons explained below, we added a seventh observation, 18, to column A.)

1 Store the data in column A.
2 Click **Tools, Data Analysis ...**, and **Moving Average.**
3 Specify the input range **A1:A7** and the number of periods **4**.
4 Specify the output range **B1**. Click **OK.** Cells **B1**, **B2**, and **B3** will show **#NA**. The four-period moving averages will be stored in **B4** to **B7**.
5 Click **Tools, Data Analysis ...**, and **Moving Average.**
6 Specify the input range as **B4:B7** and the number of periods as **2**. Incidentally, had we not added a seventh observation to column A, there would be only three moving averages in column B and Excel would not proceed.
7 Specify the output range as **C2**. Click **OK.** The centered moving averages will be stored in column C in the appropriate locations.

EXPONENTIAL SMOOTHING

Two drawbacks are associated with the moving average method of smoothing time series. First, we do not have moving averages for the first and last sets of time periods. If the time series has few observations, the missing values can represent an important loss of information. Second, the moving average "forgets" most of the previous time-series values. For example, in the five-month moving average described in Example 20.1, the average for month 4 reflects months 2, 3, 4, 5, and 6 but is not affected by month 1. Similarly, the moving average for month 5 forgets months 1 and 2. Both of these problems are addressed by **exponential smoothing.**

Exponentially Smoothed Time Series

$$S_t = wy_t + (1 - w)S_{t-1} \qquad (\text{for } t \geq 2)$$

where

S_t = exponentially smoothed time series at time t

y_t = time series at time t

S_{t-1} = exponentially smoothed time series at time $t - 1$

w = smoothing constant, where $0 \leq w \leq 1$

We begin by setting

$$S_1 = y_1$$

Then

$$S_2 = wy_2 + (1 - w)S_1$$
$$= wy_2 + (1 - w)y_1$$
$$S_3 = wy_3 + (1 - w)S_2$$
$$= wy_3 + (1 - w)[wy_2 + (1 - w)y_1]$$
$$= wy_3 + w(1 - w)y_2 + (1 - w)^2 y_1$$

and so on. In general, we have

$$S_t = wy_t + w(1 - w)y_{t-1} + w(1 - w)^2 y_{t-2} + \cdots + (1 - w)^{t-1} y_1$$

This formula states that the smoothed time series in period t depends on all the previous observations of the time series.

The smoothing constant w is chosen on the basis of how much smoothing is required. A small value of w produces a great deal of smoothing. A large value for w results in very little smoothing. Figure 20.8 depicts a time series and two exponentially smoothed series with $w = .1$ and $w = .5$.

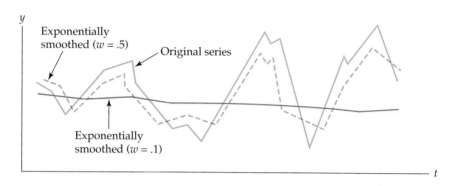

Figure 20.8

Original time series and two exponentially smoothed series

▼ **EXAMPLE 20.2**

Apply the exponential smoothing technique with $w = .2$ and $w = .7$ to the data in Example 20.1, and graph the results.

Solution   The exponentially smoothed values are calculated from the formula

$$S_t = wy_t + (1 - w)S_{t-1}$$

The results with $w = .2$ and $w = .7$ are shown in the following table.

Time Period	Gasoline Sales	Exponentially Smoothed Sales (with $w = .2$)	Exponentially Smoothed Sales (with $w = .7$)
1	39	39.0	39.0
2	37	38.6	37.6
3	61	43.1	54.0
4	58	46.1	56.8
5	18	40.5	29.6
6	56	43.6	48.1
7	82	51.2	71.8
8	27	46.4	40.4
9	41	45.3	40.8
10	69	50.1	60.6
11	49	49.8	52.5
12	66	53.1	61.9
13	54	53.3	56.4
14	42	51.0	46.3
15	90	58.8	76.9
16	66	60.2	69.3

**Excel Output for
Example 20.2**

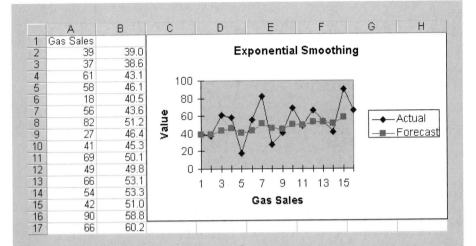

	A	B
1	Gas Sales	
2	39	39.0
3	37	38.6
4	61	43.1
5	58	46.1
6	18	40.5
7	56	43.6
8	82	51.2
9	27	46.4
10	41	45.3
11	69	50.1
12	49	49.8
13	66	53.1
14	54	53.3
15	42	51.0
16	90	58.8
17	66	60.2

We show the output for $w = .2$ (damping factor $= .8$) only. This printout is similar to the one produced to show moving averages. Notice that Excel places the smoothed values one period later than the way we calculated them above, which we rectify using Commands 7 and 8 below. The graph cannot be changed.

COMMANDS

1 Type or import the data into one column.
2 Click **Tools, Data Analysis . . .** , and **Exponential Smoothing.**
3 Specify the **Input Range.** Click **Labels** (if necessary).
4 Hit **tab,** and type the value of the **Damping factor,** which is $1 - w$.
5 Specify the **Output Range:.**
6 Specify **Chart Output** if you want a graph. Click **OK.**

COMMANDS FOR EXAMPLE 20.2

Open file **XM20-01.**

A1:A17

.8

B2

To modify the table so that the smoothed values appear the way we calculated them by hand, proceed as follows.

7 Use the left button on the mouse and click the cell containing "N/A". Click the right button. Click (with the left button) **Delete.** Select **shift cells up.** Click **OK.**
8 Click the cell containing the last smoothed value displayed (here 58.8) and drag it to the cell below to reveal the final smoothed value (here 60.2).

Minitab Output for Example 20.2

Single Exponential Smoothing

```
Data        Sales
Length      16.0000
NMissing    0

Smoothing Constant
Alpha: 0.2

Accuracy Measures
MAPE:  34.068
MAD:   15.643
MSD:   398.443
```

Row	Time	Sales	Smooth	Predict	Error
1	1	39	39.0000	39.0000	0.0000
2	2	37	38.6000	39.0000	-2.0000
3	3	61	43.0800	38.6000	22.4000
4	4	58	46.0640	43.0800	14.9200
5	5	18	40.4512	46.0640	-28.0640
6	6	56	43.5610	40.4512	15.5488
7	7	82	51.2488	43.5610	38.4390
8	8	27	46.3990	51.2488	-24.2488
9	9	41	45.3192	46.3990	-5.3990
10	10	69	50.0554	45.3192	23.6808
11	11	49	49.8443	50.0554	-1.0554
12	12	66	53.0754	49.8443	16.1557
13	13	54	53.2603	53.0754	0.9246
14	14	42	51.0083	53.2603	-11.2603
15	15	90	58.8066	51.0083	38.9917
16	16	66	60.2453	58.8066	7.1934

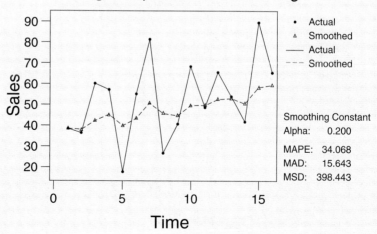

Single Exponential Smoothing

Smoothing Constant
Alpha: 0.200

MAPE: 34.068
MAD: 15.643
MSD: 398.443

We show the printout for $w = .2$. (Minitab calls the smoothing constant alpha.) The printout for exponential smoothing is similar to that of moving averages.

COMMANDS	COMMANDS FOR EXAMPLE 20.2
1 Type or import the data into one column.	Open file **XM20-01**.
2 Click **Stats, Time Series,** and **Single Exp Smoothing . . . .**	
3 Type the variable name.	**Sales** or **C1**
4 Specify **Weight to Use in Smoothing, Use** and type the value of **w.**	**.2**
5 Click **Options . . . , Plot smoothed vs. actual,** and **Summary table.**	
6 **Set initial smoothed value** at **1.** (That is, **Use average of first 1 observations.**) Click **OK.**	
7 Click **Storage . . .** and **Smoothed data.** Click **OK.**	

INTERPRET

Figure 20.9 depicts the graph of the original time series and the exponentially smoothed series. As you can see, $w = .7$ results in very little smoothing, whereas $w = .2$ results in perhaps too much smoothing. In both smoothed time series, it is difficult to discern the seasonal pattern that we detected by using moving averages. A different value of w (perhaps $w = .5$) would be likely to produce more satisfactory results.

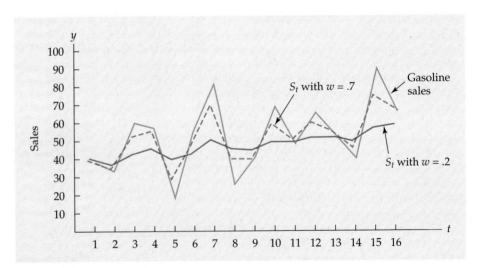

Figure 20.9

Quarterly gasoline sales and exponentially smoothed sales with $w = .2$ and $w = .7$

Moving averages and exponential smoothing are relatively crude methods of removing the random variation in order to discover the existence of other components. In the next three sections, we attempt to measure these components more precisely.

So far, we have used exponential smoothing only to smooth a time series in order to better detect the components of the series. Using exponential smoothing for forecasting will be discussed in Section 20.8.

EXERCISES

20.1 For the following time series, compute the 3-period moving averages.

Period t	y_t	Period t	y_t
1	48	7	43
2	41	8	52
3	37	9	60
4	32	10	48
5	36	11	41
6	31	12	30

20.2 For Exercise 20.1, compute the 5-period moving averages.

20.3 For Exercises 20.1 and 20.2, graph the time series and the two moving averages.

20.4 For the following time series, compute the 3-period moving averages.

Period t	y_t	Period t	y_t
1	16	7	24
2	22	8	29
3	19	9	21
4	24	10	23
5	30	11	19
6	26	12	15

20.5 For Exercise 20.4, compute the 5-period moving averages.

20.6 For Exercises 20.4 and 20.5, graph the time series and the two moving averages.

20.7 Apply exponential smoothing with $w = .1$ to help detect the components of the following time series.

Period t	y_t	Period t	y_t
1	12	6	16
2	18	7	25
3	16	8	21
4	24	9	23
5	17	10	14

20.8 Repeat Exercise 20.7 with $w = .8$.

20.9 For Exercises 20.7 and 20.8, draw the time series and the two sets of exponentially smoothed values. Does there appear to be a trend component in the times series?

20.10 Apply exponential smoothing with $w = .1$ to help detect the components of the following time series.

Period t	y_t	Period t	y_t
1	38	6	48
2	43	7	50
3	42	8	49
4	45	9	46
5	46	10	45

20.11 Repeat Exercise 20.10 with $w = .8$.

20.12 For Exercises 20.10 and 20.11, draw the time series and the two sets of exponentially smoothed values. Does there appear to be a trend component in the times series?

20.13 The daily sales figures below have been recorded in a medium-size merchandising firm. (They are also stored in column 1 of file XR20-13.)

a Compute the 3-day moving averages.
b Plot the series and the moving averages on a graph.
c Does there appear to be a seasonal (weekly) pattern?

	Week			
Day	1	2	3	4
Monday	43	51	40	64
Tuesday	45	41	57	58
Wednesday	22	37	30	33
Thursday	25	22	33	38
Friday	31	25	37	25

20.14 For Exercise 20.13, compute the 5-day moving averages, and superimpose these on the same graph. Does this help you answer part (c) of Exercise 20.13?

20.15 The quarterly sales of a department store chain were recorded for the years 1996–1999. They are listed below and stored in column 1 of file XR20-15.

Year	Quarter	Sales (millions of dollars)
1996	1	18
	2	33
	3	25
	4	41
1997	1	22
	2	20
	3	36
	4	33
1998	1	27
	2	38
	3	44
	4	52
1999	1	31
	2	26
	3	29
	4	45

a Calculate the four-quarter centered moving averages.
b Graph the time series and the moving averages.
c What can you conclude from your time-series smoothing?

20.16 Repeat Exercise 20.15, using exponential smoothing with $w = .4$.

20.17 Repeat Exercise 20.15, using exponential smoothing with $w = .8$.

20.4 TREND ANALYSIS

In the previous section, we described how smoothing a time series can give us a clearer picture of which components are present. In order to forecast, however, we often need more precise measurements of trend, cyclical effects, and seasonal effects. In this section, we discuss methods that allow us to describe trend. In subsequent sections, we consider how to measure the cyclical and seasonal effects.

As we pointed out before, a trend can be linear or nonlinear and, indeed, can take on a whole host of other functional forms, some of which we will discuss. The easiest way of isolating the long-term trend is by regression analysis, where the independent variable is time. If we believe that the long-term trend is essentially linear, we will use the following **linear model.**

Linear Model for Long-Term Trend

$$y = \beta_0 + \beta_1 t + \epsilon$$

where t is the time period.

Although various nonlinear models are available, we will consider only one: the second-order polynomial model described in Chapter 19.

If we think that the time series is nonlinear with one change in slope, the second-order polynomial or **quadratic model** may be best.

Quadratic Model for Long-Term Trend

$$y = \beta_0 + \beta_1 t + \beta_2 t^2 + \epsilon$$

Figure 20.10

Quadratic model

Figure 20.10 depicts one form of the quadratic model. This form might apply, for example, to a new product that has experienced a rapid early growth rate followed by the inevitable leveling off.

▼ **EXAMPLE 20.3**

Annual sales (in millions of dollars) for a pharmaceutical company have been recorded for the 10 years from 1990 to 1999. These data are shown in the accompanying table and stored in file XM20-03.

Year	Sales (millions of dollars)	Year	Sales (millions of dollars)
1990	18.0	1995	21.1
1991	19.4	1996	23.5
1992	18.0	1997	23.2
1993	19.9	1998	20.4
1994	19.3	1999	24.4

The management of the company believes that the trend over this period is basically linear. Use regression analysis to measure the trend.

Solution   Although this technique can be performed manually, realistic applications use the computer exclusively. So will we.

We can use the regression techniques introduced in Chapters 17 and 18. To do so, we must store the values of t (and t^2 for the quadratic model). It is easier (though not necessary) to change the times from years 1990 through 1999 to time periods 1 through 10. When that is done, our software packages are used to estimate the model, resulting in the following output. Minitab also can perform the trend analysis directly from the time series, which is the method we use below.

Excel Output for Example 20.3

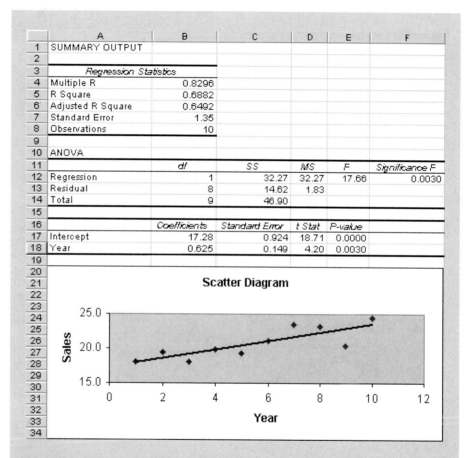

The regression equation is

$$\hat{y} = 17.28 + .625t, \text{ where } t = 1, 2, \ldots, 10$$

The value of R^2 is $= .6882$, which indicates a relatively good fit. It is important to realize that, because of the possible presence of cyclical and seasonal effects and because of random variation, we do not usually expect a very good fit. Remember that we're measuring only the trend in this analysis and not any other components.

Minitab Output for Example 20.3

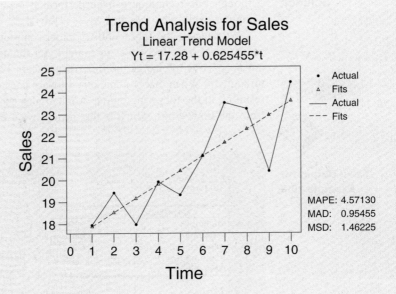

The fitted trend equation is

$$\hat{y}_t = 17.28 + .625t$$

Minitab's summary table (not shown) lists the original time series, the fitted values, and the differences between the two (which Minitab calls "detrend").

COMMANDS	COMMANDS FOR EXAMPLE 20.3
1 Type or import the data into one column.	Open file **XM20-03**.
2 Click **Stat, Time Series,** and **Trend Analysis . . . .**	
3 Type the variable name.	**Sales** or **C1**
4 Use the cursor to select **Linear** model.	
5 Click **Options . . . ,** and use the cursor to specify **Display plot** and **Summary table.** (If you wish to see the original time series, the fitted values, and the differences between the two—which Minitab calls detrend—click **Summary table and results table.** Click **OK** twice.	

INTERPRET

The time series is shown graphically in Figure 20.11. The regression trend line is superimposed on the graph: It shows a clear upward trend to the right.

One of the purposes of isolating the trend, as we suggested before, is to use it for forecasting. For example, we could use it for forecasting 1 year in advance— through 2000 ($t = 11$). From our trend equation, we get

$$\hat{y} = 17.28 + .625t = 17.28 + .625(11) = 24.16$$

This value, however, represents the forecast based only on trend. If we believe that a cyclical pattern also exists, we should incorporate that into the forecast as well.

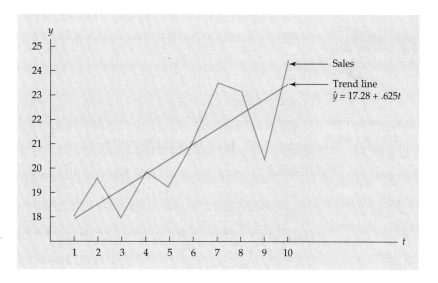

Figure 20.11

Time series and trend line for Example 20.3

▲

After years of advertising the negative health effects of cigarette smoking, we have seen a downturn in smoking. The following table lists the average number of cigarettes smoked per year by Americans 18 years and older. (These data are stored in file XM20-04.) Use an appropriate regression model to determine the long-term trend.

Year	Cigarette Consumption (per capita, 18 years and older)	Year	Cigarette Consumption (per capita, 18 years and older)
1955	3,675	1975	4,152
1956	3,718	1976	4,110
1957	3,762	1977	4,044
1958	3,892	1978	3,935
1959	4,066	1979	3,936
1960	4,197	1980	3,914
1961	4,284	1981	3,849
1962	4,305	1982	3,631
1963	4,327	1983	3,566
1964	4,240	1984	3,501
1965	4,280	1985	3,435
1966	4,284	1986	3,370
1967	4,282	1987	3,240
1968	4,240	1988	3,109
1969	4,110	1989	3,022
1970	4,066	1990	2,935
1971	4,068	1991	2,870
1972	4,153	1992	2,761
1973	4,197	1993	2,718
1974	4,175	1994	2,696

Source: Standard & Poor's Industry Reports.

Solution   An examination of the data reveals that between 1955 and 1963, cigarette consumption rose steadily and has declined somewhat erratically since then. The pattern suggests that a quadratic model might be best. The model

$$y = \beta_0 + \beta_1 t + \beta_2 t^2 + \epsilon$$

was estimated with the following results. (Time periods were coded so that $t = 1$ represents 1955 and $t = 40$ represents 1994.) Before performing a regression to estimate this quadratic model, remember to set up a column for values of t and a column for values of t^2.

Excel Output for
Example 20.4

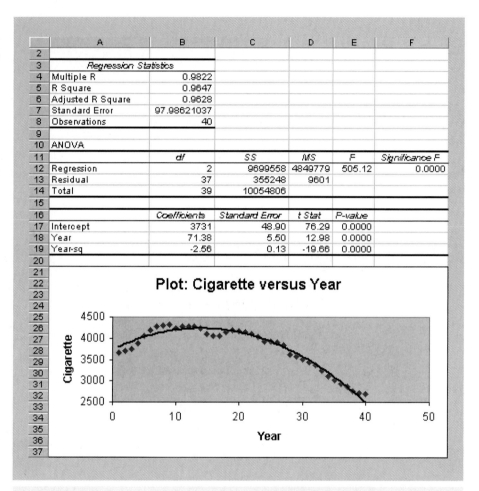

	A	B	C	D	E	F
2						
3	*Regression Statistics*					
4	Multiple R	0.9822				
5	R Square	0.9647				
6	Adjusted R Square	0.9628				
7	Standard Error	97.98621037				
8	Observations	40				
9						
10	ANOVA					
11		*df*	*SS*	*MS*	*F*	*Significance F*
12	Regression	2	9699558	4849779	505.12	0.0000
13	Residual	37	355248	9601		
14	Total	39	10054806			
15						
16		*Coefficients*	*Standard Error*	*t Stat*	*P-value*	
17	Intercept	3731	48.90	76.29	0.0000	
18	Year	71.38	5.50	12.98	0.0000	
19	Year-sq	-2.56	0.13	-19.66	0.0000	

Plot: Cigarette versus Year

Minitab Output for
Example 20.4

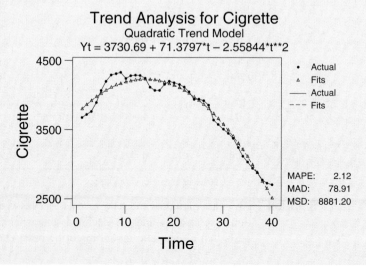

Trend Analysis for Cigrette
Quadratic Trend Model
$Yt = 3730.69 + 71.3797*t - 2.55844*t**2$

MAPE: 2.12
MAD: 78.91
MSD: 8881.20

The fitted trend line is

$$\hat{y}_t = 3,731 + 71.38t - 2.56t^2$$

COMMANDS

Use the commands described above to solve Example 20.3, but specify the **Quadratic** model.

All of the statistics ($R^2 = .9647$; $F = 505.12$; p-value $= 0$) indicate that the quadratic model fits the data quite well. Thus, the trend is measured by

$$\hat{y} = 3,731 + 71.38t - 2.56t^2$$

Figure 20.12 depicts the time series and the quadratic equation.

To forecast the per capita number of cigarettes to be smoked in 1995, we use the regression equation with $t = 41$. Thus,

$$\hat{y} = 3,731 + 71.4t - 2.56t^2 = 3,731 + 71.4(41) - 2.56(41)^2 = 2,355$$

Using only the trend line, we predict that the per capita cigarette consumption in 1995 will be 2,355 cigarettes.

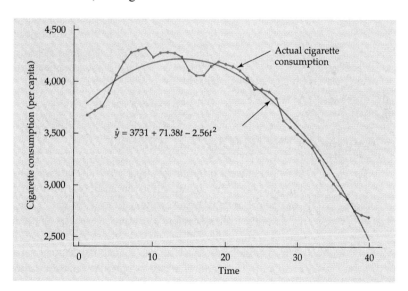

Figure 20.12

Time series and quadratic trend for Example 20.4

EXERCISES

20.18 Plot the following time series. Would the linear or quadratic model fit better? (The data are stored in file XR20-18.)

Time period	y	Time period	y
1	.5	5	4.1
2	.6	6	6.9
3	1.3	7	10.8
4	2.7	8	19.2

20.19 Plot the following time series to determine which of the trend models appears to fit better. (The data are also stored in file XR20-19.)

Time period	y	Time period	y
1	55	6	39
2	57	7	41
3	53	8	33
4	49	9	28
5	47	10	20

20.20 For Exercise 20.18, use the regression technique to calculate the linear trend line and the quadratic trend line. Which line fits better?

20.21 For Exercise 20.19, use the regression technique to calculate the linear trend line and the quadratic trend line. Which line fits better?

20.22 Enrollment in institutions of higher education has grown phenomenally in the post-war years. Forecasting this enrollment pattern, however, has been difficult. As a preliminary step, various attempts have been made to improve our understanding of the historical trend. One particular example consists of historical data on post-secondary enrollment in one midwestern state over the years 1990–2000. These data are shown in the accompanying table and stored in file XR20-22.

Year	FTE* enrollment (thousands)	Year	FTE* enrollment (thousands)
1990	185	1996	240
1991	188	1997	252
1992	192	1998	260
1993	198	1999	266
1994	210	2000	270
1995	225		

*Full-time equivalent.

a Plot the time series.
b Which trend model appears to fit better? Explain.

20.23 a Use regression analysis to calculate the linear and quadratic trend lines for Exercise 20.22.

b Which line fits the time series better? Explain.
c Forecast the FTE enrollment for 2001 and 2002.

20.24 Exports are an important component of the exchange rate and, domestically, are an important indicator of employment and profitability in certain industries. The value of merchandise exports, in particular, seems to have increased dramatically over the 20 years from 1973 through 1993, as the accompanying table suggests. (Data are stored in file XR20-24.)

Year	t	Exports (billions of dollars)	Year	t	Exports (billions of dollars)
1973	1	70.8	1984	12	217.9
1974	2	98.1	1985	13	213.1
1975	3	107.7	1986	14	217.3
1976	4	115.2	1987	15	254.1
1977	5	121.2	1988	16	322.4
1978	6	143.7	1989	17	363.8
1979	7	181.9	1990	18	393.6
1980	8	220.6	1991	19	421.7
1981	9	233.7	1992	20	448.2
1982	10	212.3	1993	21	464.8
1983	11	200.5			

a Plot the time series.
b Which trend model is likely to fit best? Explain.

20.25 Use regression analysis to compute the linear and quadratic trend lines for Exercise 20.24. Which line fits better? Explain.

20.5 MEASURING THE CYCLICAL EFFECT

The fundamental difference between cyclical and seasonal variations is the length of the time period under consideration. In addition, however, seasonal effects are considered to be predictable, whereas **cyclical effects** (except in the case of certain well-known economic and business cycles) are often viewed as unpredictable—varying in both duration and amplitude and not necessarily even repetitive. Nevertheless, cycles need to be isolated, and the measure we use to identify cyclical variation is the percentage of trend.

The **percentage of trend** is calculated in the following way.

1 Determine the trend line (by regression).
2 For each time period, compute the trend value $\hat{y}$.
3 The percentage of trend is $(y/\hat{y}) \times 100$.

▼ **EXAMPLE 20.5**

The annual demand for energy in the United States is affected by various factors, including price, availability, and the state of the economy. To help analyze the changes that have taken place and to develop a prediction, the annual total consumption for the United States (measured in quadrillions of BTUs) was recorded for the period 1970–1993. These data are shown in the following table and stored in file XM20-05. Assuming a linear trend, calculate the percentage of trend for each year.

Year	Time Period	Annual Energy Consumption	Year	Time Period	Annual Energy Consumption
1970	1	66.4	1982	13	70.8
1971	2	69.7	1983	14	70.5
1972	3	72.2	1984	15	74.1
1973	4	74.3	1985	16	74.0
1974	5	72.5	1986	17	74.3
1975	6	70.6	1987	18	76.9
1976	7	74.4	1988	19	80.2
1977	8	76.3	1989	20	81.3
1978	9	78.1	1990	21	81.3
1979	10	78.9	1991	22	81.1
1980	11	76.0	1992	23	82.4
1981	12	74.0	1993	24	84.0

Source: Statistical Abstract of the United States.

Solution

Excel Output for Example 20.5

We use our software packages to do the computations. The arithmetic is too time-consuming to perform manually.

	A Consume	B Time	C Predicted	D PoT
1				
2	66.4	1	69.80	95.13
3	69.7	2	70.30	99.14
4	72.2	3	70.81	101.97
5	74.3	4	71.31	104.20
6	72.5	5	71.81	100.96
7	70.6	6	72.31	97.63
8	74.4	7	72.81	102.18
9	76.3	8	73.32	104.07
10	78.1	9	73.82	105.80
11	78.9	10	74.32	106.16
12	76.0	11	74.82	101.57
13	74.0	12	75.32	98.24
14	70.8	13	75.83	93.37
15	70.5	14	76.33	92.36
16	74.1	15	76.83	96.45
17	74.0	16	77.33	95.69
18	74.3	17	77.83	95.46
19	76.9	18	78.34	98.17
20	80.2	19	78.84	101.73
21	81.3	20	79.34	102.47
22	81.3	21	79.84	101.83
23	81.1	22	80.34	100.94
24	82.4	23	80.85	101.92
25	84.0	24	81.35	103.26

COMMANDS

1 Type or import the data. For the linear model, store the values of t in a second column. For the quadratic model, store values of t and t^2 in two additional columns.

2 Click **Tools, Data Analysis ...**, and **Regression.**

3 Specify the **Input Y Range** (time series) and the **Input X Range** (t for the linear model and t and t^2 for the quadratic model). Click **Labels** (if necessary).

4 Specify the output range and click **OK.**

5 In column C, calculate the predicted values of y using the regression equation computed in steps 2, 3, and 4.

6 In column D, calculate the percentage of trend.

7 Plot the data. (See page 804.)

COMMANDS FOR EXAMPLE 20.5

Open file **XM20-05.**

A1:A25
B1:B25

=69.3 + .502*B1

=100*A1/C1

The regression equation is

$$\hat{y} = 69.3 + .502t$$

The percentage of trend values are listed in column D.

Minitab Output for Example 20.5

Row	Consume	Time	FITS1	PoT
1	66.4	1	69.8283	95.090
2	69.7	2	70.3299	99.104
3	72.2	3	70.8314	101.932
4	74.3	4	71.3329	104.160
5	72.5	5	71.8344	100.927
6	70.6	6	72.3359	97.600
7	74.4	7	72.8375	102.145
8	76.3	8	73.3390	104.037
9	78.1	9	73.8405	105.769
10	78.9	10	74.3420	106.131
11	76.0	11	74.8436	101.545
12	74.0	12	75.3451	98.215
13	70.8	13	75.8466	93.346
14	70.5	14	76.3481	92.340
15	74.1	15	76.8496	96.422
16	74.0	16	77.3512	95.668
17	74.3	17	77.8527	95.437
18	76.9	18	78.3542	98.144
19	80.2	19	78.8557	101.705
20	81.3	20	79.3572	102.448
21	81.3	21	79.8588	101.805
22	81.1	22	80.3603	100.920
23	82.4	23	80.8618	101.902
24	84.0	24	81.3633	103.241

COMMANDS	COMMANDS FOR EXAMPLE 20.5
1 Type or import the data. For the linear model, store the values of t in a second column. For the quadratic model, store values of t and t_2 in two additional columns.	Open file **XM20-05**.
2 Click **Stat, Regression,** and **Regression . . . .**	
3 Type the name of the dependent variable **(Response),** hit **tab,** and type the name of the independent variables **(Predictors).**	**Consume** or **C1** **Time** or **C2**
4 Use the cursor to specify **Fits.** Click **OK.** The fitted values are stored in the next available column (**C3** for a linear model and **C4** for a quadratic model). The percentage of trend will be calculated and stored in the next column.	
5 Click **Calc** and **Mathematical Expressions . . . .**	
6 Type the name of the variable **(percentage of trend),** hit **tab** twice, and type the equation for percentage of trend.	**Trend** or **C4** **100*Consume/FITS1** or **100*C1/C3**
7 Click **OK** and print the results.	
8 To plot the percentage of trend, click **Graph** and **Time series plot . . . .** Type the variable name. Click **OK.**	**C4**

INTERPRET   Figure 20.13 describes the time series and the trend line. The percentage of trend represents the amount by which the actual energy consumption lies above or below the line. Figure 20.14 shows another way of depicting these values; the trend line appears as the 100% line.

The problem we face in trying to interpret Figure 20.14 is that of distinguishing between random variation and a cyclical pattern. If there appears to be a random collection of percentage of trend values above and below the 100% line, we could conclude that its cause is random and not cyclical. However, if we see alternating groups of percentage of trend values above and below the 100% line and the patterns are regular, we would confidently identify the cyclical effect. In Figure 20.14, there appears to be a cyclical pattern, although it is not very regular. This example highlights the major problem of forecasting time series that possess a cyclical component: The cyclical effect is often quite clearly present but too irregular to forecast with any degree of accuracy. Forecasting methods for this type of problem are available, but they are too advanced for our use. We will be satisfied with simply identifying and measuring the cyclical component of time series.

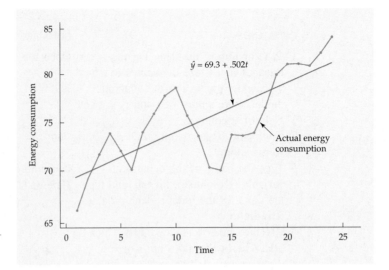

Figure 20.13

Time series and trend line for Example 20.5

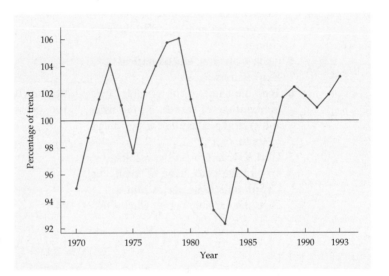

Figure 20.14

Percentage of trend for Example 20.5

EXERCISES

20.26 Consider the time series shown in the following table and stored in file XR20-26.

Time period	y	Time period	y
1	30	9	41
2	27	10	38
3	24	11	43
4	21	12	36
5	23	13	29
6	27	14	24
7	33	15	20
8	38	16	18

a Calculate the percentage of trend for each time period.

b Plot the percentage of trend.
c Describe the cyclical effect (if there is one).

20.27 The time series shown in the following table is also stored in file XR20-27.

Time period	y	Time period	y
1	6	7	20
2	11	8	22
3	21	9	18
4	17	10	17
5	27	11	12
6	23	12	15

a Plot the time series.

b Calculate the percentage of trend.
c Plot the percentage of trend.
d Describe the cyclical effect (if there is one).

20.28 As a preliminary step in forecasting future values, a large mail-order retail outlet has recorded the sales figures shown in the accompanying table. (The data are also stored in file XR20-28.)

Year	Sales (millions of dollars)	Year	Sales (millions of dollars)
1980	6.7	1991	18.1
1981	7.4	1992	16.0
1982	8.5	1993	11.2
1983	11.2	1994	14.8
1984	12.5	1995	15.2
1985	10.7	1996	14.1
1986	11.9	1997	12.2
1987	11.4	1998	15.7
1988	9.8	1999	14.1
1989	11.5	2000	17.9
1990	14.2		

a Plot the time series.
b Compute the percentage of trend.
c Plot the percentage of trend.
d Describe the cyclical effect (if there is one).

20.29 One interesting phenomenon of the past several decades is the extent to which certain classes of assets have kept up with inflation while certain others have not. In terms of nominal interest rates, domestic corporate bond yields in the United States have assumed the values shown in the accompanying table (and stored in file XR20-29) over the years from 1971 to 1993.

Year	t	Domestic corporate bond yields (%)
1971	1	7.85
1972	2	7.59
1973	3	7.89
1974	4	9.42
1975	5	9.51
1976	6	8.59
1977	7	8.20
1978	8	8.98
1979	9	10.05
1980	10	12.77
1981	11	15.48
1982	12	14.68
1983	13	12.25
1984	14	13.37

Year	t	Domestic corporate bond yields (%)
1985	15	11.75
1986	16	9.23
1987	17	9.69
1988	18	9.96
1989	19	9.55
1990	20	9.84
1991	21	9.05
1992	22	8.33
1993	23	7.34

a Plot the time series.
b Calculate the percentage of trend.
c Plot the percentage of trend. Does there appear to be a cyclical effect? Describe it (if there is one).

20.30 In terms of nominal rates of return, long-term government bond returns in Canada have assumed the values shown in the accompanying table (and stored in file XR20-30) over the years from 1971 to 1993.

Year	t	Long-term government bond returns (%)
1971	1	11.55
1972	2	1.11
1973	3	1.71
1974	4	−1.69
1975	5	2.82
1976	6	19.02
1977	7	5.97
1978	8	1.29
1979	9	−2.62
1980	10	2.06
1981	11	−3.02
1982	12	42.98
1983	13	9.60
1984	14	15.09
1985	15	25.26
1986	16	17.54
1987	17	0.45
1988	18	10.45
1989	19	16.29
1990	20	3.34
1991	21	24.43
1992	22	13.07
1993	23	22.88

a Plot the time series.
b Calculate the percentage of trend.
c Plot the percentage of trend.
d Does there appear to be a cyclical effect? If so, describe it.

(continued)

20.6 MEASURING THE SEASONAL EFFECT

Seasonal variation may occur within a year or within an even shorter time interval, such as a month, week, or day. To measure the seasonal effect, we construct **seasonal indexes,** which attempt to gauge the degree to which the seasons differ from one another. One requirement for this method is that we have a time series sufficiently long to allow us to observe the variable over several seasons. For example, if our seasons are the quarters of a year, we need to observe the time series for at least 4 years. If the seasons are the days of the week, our time series should be observed for no less than a month. The seasonal indexes are computed in the following way.

1 Remove the effect of seasonal and random variation. This can be accomplished in one of two ways.

We could calculate moving averages by setting the number of periods in the moving average equal to the number of types of seasons. For example, if the seasons represent quarters, the moving averages should be calculated on the basis of four quarters. The effect of moving averages is seen in the multiplicative model of time series.

$$y_t = T_t \times C_t \times S_t \times R_t$$

The moving averages remove S_t and R_t, leaving

$$MA_t = T_t \times C_t$$

By taking the ratio of the time series divided by the moving average, we obtain

$$\frac{y_t}{MA_t} = \frac{T_t \times C_t \times S_t \times R_t}{T_t \times C_t} = S_t \times R_t$$

The second method, which is easier to apply with the computer, employs regression analysis. If the time series is not cyclical, we can represent it by

$$y_t = T_t \times S_t \times R_t$$

Because the regression line $\hat{y}_t = \beta_0 + \beta_1 t$ represents trend, it follows that the time series divided by the predicted values produces

$$\frac{y_t}{\hat{y}_t} = S_t \times R_t$$

Thus, the two methods measure seasonal and random variation, and yield similar results. Because we generally deal with time series with no cyclical effect, we shall use this method to compute the seasonal indexes.

2 For each type of season, calculate the average of the ratios in step 1. This procedure removes most (although we can seldom remove all) of the random variation. The average is a measure of the seasonal differences.

3 The seasonal indexes are the average ratios from step 2 adjusted to ensure that the average seasonal index is 1.

▼ EXAMPLE 20.6

The tourist industry is subject to enormous seasonal variation. A hotel in Bermuda has recorded its occupancy rate for each quarter over a 5-year period. These data are shown in the following table and stored in file XM20-06.

Calculate the seasonal indexes for each quarter in order to measure seasonal variation.

Year	Quarter	Occupancy Rate	Year	Quarter	Occupancy Rate
1995	1	.561	1998	1	.622
	2	.702		2	.708
	3	.800		3	.806
	4	.568		4	.632
1996	1	.575	1999	1	.665
	2	.738		2	.835
	3	.868		3	.873
	4	.605		4	.670
1997	1	.594			
	2	.738			
	3	.729			
	4	.600			

Solution

Because of the large amount of arithmetic required to produce seasonal indexes, we will use the computer exclusively.

Excel Output for Example 20.6

We performed a regression analysis with y = occupancy rate and t = time period 1, 2, ..., 20. Excel produced the equation

$$\hat{y} = .639368 + .005246t$$

Excel was instructed to calculate $\hat{y}$ for each value of t and compute the ratio $y/\hat{y}$. We collected the ratios associated with each quarter and computed the averages as shown below.

Year		Quarter			
	1	2	3	4	Total
1995	.871	1.081	1.222	.861	
1996	.864	1.101	1.284	.888	
1997	.866	1.067	1.046	.855	
1998	.879	.994	1.123	.874	
1999	.913	1.138	1.182	.901	
Average	.878	1.076	1.171	.875	4.000
Index	.878	1.076	1.171	.875	4.000

COMMANDS

1 Type or import the data (time series in column A, the time periods t = 1, 2, ..., in column B, and the codes identifying the seasons in column C).
2 Click **Tools, Data Analysis ...**, and **Regression.**
3 Specify the **Input Y Range** (time series) and the **Input X Range** (time periods). Click **Labels** (if necessary).
4 Specify the output range, and click **OK.**

COMMANDS FOR EXAMPLE 20.6

Open file **XM20-06.**

A1:A21
B1:B21

5 In column D, calculate the predicted values of y using the regression equation computed in steps 2, 3, and 4.	=.639368+.005246*B1
6 In column E, calculate the ratio of the time series divided by the predicted values.	=A1/D1

Complete the rest of the calculations manually. Collect the ratios for each season, calculate the average, and adjust the averages if necessary to produce the seasonal indexes. [It would be necessary to adjust, or normalize, the averages if they didn't sum to 4, the number of quarters. If the averages had totaled 4.1, for example, we would multiply each average by (4/4.1) to obtain the seasonal indexes.]

Minitab Output for Example 20.6

```
Trend Line Equation


Yt = 0.639368 + 5.25E-03*t



Seasonal Indices

Period    Index

    1     0.877012
    2      1.08008
    3      1.17723
    4     0.865681
```

The output includes the trend line equation, the seasonal indexes, and several measures of how well the model fits the data.

COMMANDS	COMMANDS FOR EXAMPLE 20.6
1 Type or import the data into one column.	Open file **XM20-06**.
2 Click **Stat, Time Series,** and **Decomposition . . . .**	
3 Type the name of the variable.	**Rate** or **C1**
4 Hit **tab,** and type the number of periods (**Seasonal length**).	**4**
5 Use the cursor to select **Multiplicative** model and **Trend plus seasonal** model components.	
6 Use the cursor to specify which season the first observation applies to.	**1**
7 Click **Options . . . ,** and specify **Summary table** (if you only want the seasonal indexes) or **Summary table and results table** (if you want more details). Use the cursor to specify whether you want plots of the results. Click **OK** twice.	

The seasonal indexes tell us that, on average, the occupancy rates in the first and fourth quarters are below the annual average, and the occupancy rates in the second and third quarters are above the annual average. That is, we expect the occupancy rate in the first quarter to be 12.2% (100% $-$ 87.8%) below the annual rate. The second and third quarters' rates are expected to be 7.6% and 17.1%, respectively, above the annual rate. The fourth quarter's rate is 12.5% below the annual rate.

Figure 20.15 depicts the time series and the regression line for this example.

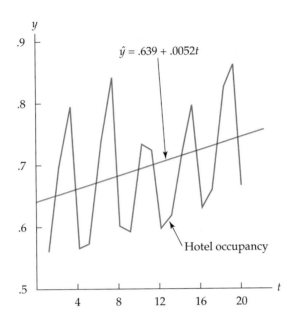

Figure 20.15

Time series and trend line for Example 20.6

DESEASONALIZING A TIME SERIES

One application of seasonal indexes is to remove the seasonal effects of a time series. The process is called **deseasonalizing** a time series. The result is called a **seasonally adjusted** time series. Often this allows the statistician to more easily compare the time series across seasons. For example, the unemployment rate varies according to the season. During the winter months, unemployment usually rises, and it falls in the spring and summer. To determine whether unemployment has increased or decreased from the previous month, we frequently deseasonalize the data.

The process is quite simple. After computing the seasonal indexes, we *divide the time series by the seasonal indexes*. To illustrate, we have deseasonalized the occupancy rates in Example 20.6 (using the seasonal indexes produced by Excel). The seasonally adjusted rates are shown in the table below.

Year	Quarter	Seasonal Index	Occupancy Rate	Seasonally Adjusted Occupancy Rate
1995	1	.878	.561	.639
	2	1.076	.702	.652
	3	1.171	.800	.683
	4	.875	.568	.649
1996	1	.878	.575	.655
	2	1.076	.738	.686
	3	1.171	.868	.741
	4	.875	.605	.691
1997	1	.878	.594	.677
	2	1.076	.738	.686
	3	1.171	.729	.623
	4	.875	.600	.686
1998	1	.878	.622	.708
	2	1.076	.708	.658
	3	1.171	.806	.688
	4	.875	.632	.722
1999	1	.878	.665	.757
	2	1.076	.835	.776
	3	1.171	.873	.746
	4	.875	.670	.766

By removing the seasonality, we can see when there has been a "real" increase in the occupancy rate. This enables the statistician to examine the factors that produced the higher rate. We can also more easily see that there has been an increase in the occupancy rate over the 5-year period.

In Section 20.9, we present a forecasting technique that uses the seasonal indexes in another way.

EXERCISES

20.31 For the following time series, compute the 5-day moving averages to remove the seasonal and random variation. (The times series is stored in file XR20-31.)

Day	Week 1	2	3	4
Monday	12	11	14	17
Tuesday	18	17	16	21
Wednesday	16	19	16	20
Thursday	25	24	28	24
Friday	31	27	25	32

20.32 For Exercise 20.31, calculate the seasonal (daily) indexes.

20.33 The regression trend line for Exercise 20.31 is

$$\hat{y} = 16.8 + .366t \quad (t = 1, 2, \ldots, 20)$$

Calculate the seasonal indexes, based on this regression trend line.

20.34 Given the following time series (stored in file XR20-34), compute the seasonal (quarterly) indexes, using the 4-quarter centered moving averages.

Quarter	Year 1	2	3	4	5
1	55	41	43	36	50
2	44	38	39	32	25
3	46	37	39	30	24
4	39	30	35	25	22

20.35 The regression trend line for Exercise 20.34 is

$$\hat{y} = 47.7 - 1.06t \quad (t = 1, 2, \ldots, 20)$$

Calculate the seasonal indexes, based on this trend line.

20.36 The quarterly earnings of a large soft-drink company have been recorded for the years 1996–1999. These data (in millions of dollars) are shown in the accompanying table and stored in file XR20-36.

Quarter	1996	1997	1998	1999
1	52	57	60	66
2	67	75	77	82
3	85	90	94	98
4	54	61	63	67

Year (header above)

Using an appropriate moving average, measure the quarterly variation by computing the seasonal (quarterly) indexes.

20.37 For Exercise 20.36, the linear trend line calculated by regression analysis is

$$\hat{y} = 61.7 + 1.18t \quad (t = 1, 2, \ldots, 16)$$

Calculate the seasonal indexes, using this trend line.

20.38 Cable TV subscriptions over the past few years have been growing dramatically, although sometimes somewhat erratically. In one southwestern state, the data shown in the accompanying table were observed and stored in file XR20-38.

Year	Quarter	Cable subscribers (1,000s)	Year	Quarter	Cable subscribers (1,000s)
1994	1	184	1997	1	236
	2	173		2	219
	3	160		3	211
	4	189		4	272
1995	1	191	1998	1	280
	2	185		2	261
	3	184		3	275
	4	200		4	322
1996	1	205	1999	1	331
	2	192		2	301
	3	200		3	306
	4	229		4	351

a Plot the time series.
b Calculate the 4-quarter centered moving averages.
c Compute the seasonal (quarterly) indexes.

20.39 The linear trend line (from regression analysis) for Exercise 20.38 is

$$\hat{y} = 143 + 7.42t$$

Calculate the seasonal indexes, using this trend line.

20.40 The owner of a pizzeria wants to forecast the number of pizzas she will sell each day. She records the number sold daily during the past 4 weeks. These data are shown in the accompanying table and stored in file XR20-40.

Day	1	2	3	4
Sunday	240	221	235	219
Monday	85	80	86	91
Tuesday	93	75	74	102
Wednesday	106	121	100	89
Thursday	125	110	117	105
Friday	188	202	205	192
Saturday	314	386	402	377

Week (header above)

Calculate the seasonal (daily) indexes, using a seven-day moving average.

20.41 The linear trend line (from regression analysis) for Exercise 20.40 is

$$\hat{y} = 145 + 1.66t$$

Calculate the seasonal indexes, using this trend line.

20.42 A manufacturer of ski equipment is in the process of reviewing his accounts receivable. He has noticed that there appears to be a seasonal pattern. Accounts receivable increase in the winter months and decrease during the summer. The quarterly accounts receivable (in millions of dollars) for the years 1996–1999 are shown in the accompanying table. (The data are also stored in file XR20-42.)

Quarter	1996	1997	1998	1999
1	106	115	114	121
2	92	100	105	111
3	65	73	79	82
4	121	135	140	163

Year (header above)

To measure the seasonal variation, compute the seasonal (quarterly) indexes based on the regression trend line, which was calculated as

$$\hat{y} = 90.4 + 2.02t \quad (t = 1, 2, \ldots, 16)$$

20.7 INTRODUCTION TO FORECASTING

As we've noted before, many different forecasting methods are available. One of the factors we consider in choosing among them is the type of component that makes up the time series we're attempting to forecast. Even then, however, we have a variety of techniques from which to choose. One way of deciding which method to use is to select the technique that results in the greatest forecast accuracy. The two most commonly used measures of forecast accuracy are the **mean absolute deviation (MAD)** and the **sum of squares for forecast error (SSE).** These are defined as follows.

Mean Absolute Deviation

$$\text{MAD} = \frac{\sum_{t=1}^{n} |y_t - F_t|}{n}$$

where

y_t = actual value of the time series at time t

F_t = forecast value at time t

n = number of time periods

Sum of Squares for Forecast Error

$$\text{SSE} = \sum_{i=1}^{n} (y_t - F_t)^2$$

MAD averages the absolute differences between the actual values and the forecast values; SSE squares these differences. Which measure to use in judging forecast accuracy depends on the circumstances. If avoiding large errors is extremely important, SSE should be used, because it penalizes large deviations more heavily than does MAD. Otherwise, use MAD.

It is probably best to use some of the observations of the time series to develop several competing forecasting models and then forecast for the remaining time periods. Afterward, we can compute either MAD or SSE for the latter period. For example, if we have 5 years of monthly observations, we can use the first 4 years to develop the forecasting techniques and then use them to forecast the fifth year. Since we know the actual values in the fifth year, we can choose the technique that results in the most accurate forecast.

▼ **EXAMPLE 20.7**

Annual data from 1968 to 1995 were used to develop three different forecasting models. Each model was used to forecast the time series for 1996, 1997, 1998, and 1999. The forecasted and actual values for these years are shown in the accompanying table. Use MAD and SSE to determine which model performed best.

		Forecast Value Using Model		
Year	Actual Value of y	1	2	3
1996	129	136	118	130
1997	142	148	141	146
1998	156	150	158	170
1999	183	175	163	180

Solution   For model 1, we have

$$\text{MAD} = \frac{|129 - 136| + |142 - 148| + |156 - 150| + |183 - 175|}{4}$$

$$= \frac{7 + 6 + 6 + 8}{4} = 6.75$$

$$\text{SSE} = (129 - 136)^2 + (142 - 148)^2 + (156 - 150)^2 + (183 - 175)^2$$
$$= 49 + 36 + 36 + 64 = 185$$

For model 2, we compute

$$\text{MAD} = \frac{|129 - 118| + |142 - 141| + |156 - 158| + |183 - 163|}{4}$$

$$= \frac{11 + 1 + 2 + 20}{4} = 8.5$$

$$\text{SSE} = (129 - 118)^2 + (142 - 141)^2 + (156 - 158)^2 + (183 - 163)^2$$
$$= 121 + 1 + 4 + 400 = 526$$

The measures of forecast accuracy for model 3 are

$$\text{MAD} = \frac{|129 - 130| + |142 - 146| + |156 - 170| + |183 - 180|}{4}$$

$$= \frac{1 + 4 + 14 + 3}{4} = 5.5$$

$$\text{SSE} = (129 - 130)^2 + (142 - 146)^2 + (156 - 170)^2 + (183 - 180)^2$$
$$= 1 + 16 + 196 + 9 = 222$$

Model 2 is inferior to both models 1 and 3, no matter how we measure forecast accuracy. Using MAD, model 3 is best, but using SSE, model 1 is the most accurate. The choice between model 1 and model 3 should be made on the basis of whether we prefer a model that consistently produces moderately accurate forecasts (model 1) or one whose forecasts come quite close to most actual values but miss badly in a small number of time periods (model 3).

▲

EXERCISES

20.43 For the actual values and forecast values of a time series shown in the following table, calculate MAD and SSE.

Forecast Value F_t	Actual Value y_t
173	166
186	179
192	195
211	214
223	220

20.44 Two forecasting models were used to predict the future values of a time series. These are shown in the accompanying table, together with the actual values.

Forecast Value F_t		Actual Value y_t
Model 1	Model 2	
7.5	6.3	6.0
6.3	6.7	6.6
5.4	7.1	7.3
8.2	7.5	9.4

Compute MAD and SSE for each model to determine which was more accurate.

20.45 Calculate MAD and SSE for the forecasts that follow.

Forecast Value F_t	Actual Value y_t
63	57
72	60
86	70
71	75
60	70

20.46 Three forecasting techniques were used to predict the values of a time series. These values are given in the table below. Compute MAD and SSE for each technique to determine which was most accurate.

Forecast Value F_t			Actual Value y_t
Technique 1	Technique 2	Technique 3	
21	22	17	19
27	24	20	24
29	26	25	28
31	28	31	32
35	30	39	38

20.8 TIME-SERIES FORECASTING WITH EXPONENTIAL SMOOTHING

In Section 20.3, we presented smoothing techniques whose function is to reduce random fluctuation, enabling us to identify the time-series components. One of these methods, exponential smoothing, can also be used in forecasting. Recall the exponential smoothing formula

$$S_t = wy_t + (1 - w)S_{t-1}$$

where the choice of the smoothing constant w determines the degree of smoothing. A value of w close to 1 results in very little smoothing, whereas a value of w close to zero results in a great deal of smoothing.

When a time series exhibits a gradual trend and no evidence of cyclical effects or seasonal effects, exponential smoothing can be a useful way of forecasting. Suppose that t represents the current time period and we've computed the smoothed value S_t. This value is then the forecasted value at time $t + 1$. That is,

$$F_{t+1} = S_t$$

If we wish, we can forecast two or three or any number of time periods into the future.

$$F_{t+2} = S_t \quad \text{or} \quad F_{t+3} = S_t$$

It must be understood that the accuracy of the forecast decreases rapidly for predictions of the time series more than one period into the future. However, as long as we're dealing with a time series that possesses no cyclical or seasonal effect, we can produce reasonably accurate forecasts for the next period.

▼ **EXAMPLE 20.8**

The annual United States consumption of distilled spirits (in millions of 9-liter cases) for the years 1960 to 1993 is listed in the accompanying table (and stored in file XM20-08). Use exponential smoothing to forecast 1994 consumption.

Year	Consumption	Year	Consumption	Year	Consumption
1960	99	1972	164	1984	179
1961	102	1973	171	1985	176
1962	106	1974	175	1986	169
1963	108	1975	178	1987	159
1964	113	1976	179	1988	157
1965	124	1977	181	1989	155
1966	129	1978	184	1990	156
1967	136	1979	187	1991	151
1968	144	1980	189	1992	146
1969	152	1981	188	1993	144
1970	158	1982	184		
1971	159	1983	182		

Source: Standard & Poor's Industry Reports.

Solution

SOLVE

A plot of the time series (see Figure 20.16) reveals a gradual increase up until 1980 and a gradual decrease since then. There is no cyclical pattern. As a consequence, exponential smoothing is an appropriate forecasting method. There does not appear to be a great deal of random variation. As a consequence, we choose $w = .8$, which results in very little smoothing.

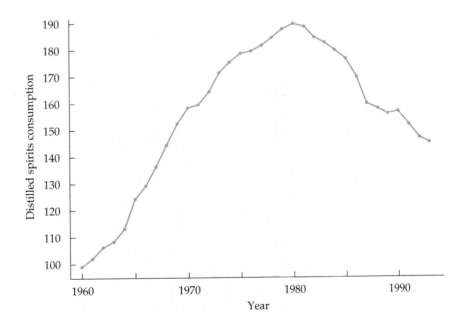

Figure 20.16

Time series for Example 20.8

The graphs of the time series and of the smoothed values will therefore be almost coincident, as you can see from the computer output below. The smoothed values (shown in the computer output) are obtained from the formula

$$S_t = wy_t + (1 - w)S_{t-1} \quad \text{(with } w = .8\text{)}$$

Since $F_{t+1} = S_t$, the forecast for 1994 ($t = 35$) is given by

$$F_{1994} = F_{35} = S_{34} = 144.639$$

Excel Output for Example 20.8

	A	B
1	Consumption	
2	99	99.00
3	102	101.40
4	106	105.08
5	108	107.42
6	113	111.88
7	124	121.58
8	129	127.52
9	136	134.30
10	144	142.06
11	152	150.01
12	158	156.40
13	159	158.48
14	164	162.90
15	171	169.38
16	175	173.88
17	178	177.18
18	179	178.64
19	181	180.53
20	184	183.31
21	187	186.26
22	189	188.45
23	188	188.09
24	184	184.82
25	182	182.56
26	179	179.71
27	176	176.74
28	169	170.55
29	159	161.31
30	157	157.86
31	155	155.57
32	156	155.91
33	151	151.98
34	146	147.20
35	144	144.64

Excel treats the smoothed values as forecasts. Thus, the last smoothed value, 147.20, in the table produced by Excel (which differs slightly from the table shown here), is actually the forecast for period 34. The forecast for period 35 must be completed manually. Thus,

$$F_{1994} = .8(144) + .2(147.20) = 144.64$$

In Section 20.3, where we presented exponential smoothing as a process to detect the components of a time series, we pointed out that Excel places the smoothed values in the next period. We showed in Example 20.2 (page 790) how to modify the Excel table so that the smoothed values appear in the same period. We also showed how to reveal the final smoothed value (here 144.64).

This modified Excel table is the one shown here. Each smoothed value in this table represents the forecast for the next period. For example, the last smoothed value, 144.64, is the forecast for period 35.

Minitab Output for Example 20.8

Single Exponential Smoothing

Data	Consumption
Length	34.0000
NMissing	0

Smoothing Constant
Alpha: 0.8

Accuracy Measures
MAPE: 3.3035
MAD: 4.9246
MSD: 33.4065

Row	Time	Consumption	Smooth	Predict	Error
1	1	99	99.000	99.000	0.0000
2	2	102	101.400	99.000	3.0000
3	3	106	105.080	101.400	4.6000
4	4	108	107.416	105.080	2.9200
5	5	113	111.883	107.416	5.5840
6	6	124	121.577	111.883	12.1168
7	7	129	127.515	121.577	7.4234
8	8	136	134.303	127.515	8.4847
9	9	144	142.061	134.303	9.6969
10	10	152	150.012	142.061	9.9394
11	11	158	156.402	150.012	7.9879
12	12	159	158.480	156.402	2.5976
13	13	164	162.896	158.480	5.5195
14	14	171	169.379	162.896	8.1039
15	15	175	173.876	169.379	5.6208
16	16	178	177.175	173.876	4.1242
17	17	179	178.635	177.175	1.8248
18	18	181	180.527	178.635	2.3650
19	19	184	183.305	180.527	3.4730
20	20	187	186.261	183.305	3.6946
21	21	189	188.452	186.261	2.7389
22	22	188	188.090	188.452	-0.4522
23	23	184	184.818	188.090	-4.0904
24	24	182	182.564	184.818	-2.8181
25	25	179	179.713	182.564	-3.5636
26	26	176	176.743	179.713	-3.7127
27	27	169	170.549	176.743	-7.7425
28	28	159	161.310	170.549	-11.5485
29	29	157	157.862	161.310	-4.3097
30	30	155	155.572	157.862	-2.8619
31	31	156	155.914	155.572	0.4276
32	32	151	151.983	155.914	-4.9145
33	33	146	147.197	151.983	-5.9829
34	34	144	144.639	147.197	-3.1966

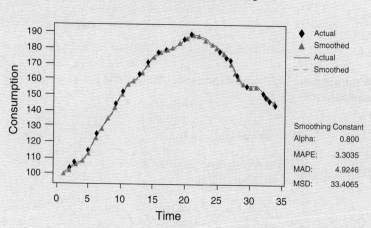

Single Exponential Smoothing

Smoothing Constant	
Alpha:	0.800
MAPE:	3.3035
MAD:	4.9246
MSD:	33.4065

As we pointed out in Section 20.3, where we introduced exponential smoothing as a technique employed to detect the components of a time series, Minitab also applies exponential smoothing to forecast. In the table above, Minitab printed the original time series in the third column and the smoothed values in the fourth column. If our interest is to detect components, we're only interested in column 4 of the table. However, notice that the fifth column uses the smoothed values to forecast one period in advance. For example, the second smoothed value, 101.4, is the prediction for the third year. The actual value in year 3 is 106. In column 6, Minitab outputs the error, which is the difference between the actual value and the prediction: $106 - 101.4 = 4.6$. At the top of the printout, Minitab computed three measures of accuracy. These are

MAPE: mean absolute percentage error

MAD: mean absolute deviation

MSD: mean squared deviation, which is defined as SSE/n

At the bottom of the printout is S_{34} ($= 144.639$), which is the forecast for the 35th year. That is, $F_{35} = 144.639$.

EXERCISES

20.47 Use exponential smoothing, with $w = .6$, to forecast the next value of the time series that follows.

t	y	t	y
1	23	4	27
2	18	5	24
3	26	6	22

20.48 Use the exponential smoothing technique, with $w = .3$, to forecast the value of the following time series at time $t = 8$.

t	y	t	y
1	12	5	15
2	20	6	11
3	16	7	14
4	19		

20.49 Use the given time series for the years 1991–1996 to develop forecasts for 1997–1999, with the following values.

a $w = .3$ **b** $w = .6$ **c** $w = .7$

Year	y	Year	y
1991	110	1995	126
1992	103	1996	115
1993	111		
1994	117		

20.50 For the data in Exercise 20.49, compare each of the three sets of forecasts with the actual values for 1997–1999 given in the accompanying table, and compute the MAD for each model. Which model is best?

Year	y
1997	120
1998	115
1999	127

20.51 Continue using the forecasting model that you determined was best in Exercise 20.50 to forecast the time-series value for 2000.

20.52 Retail sales in durable goods are an important indicator of overall economic activity. Sales in durable goods from 1980 to 1994 are shown in the accompanying table and stored in file XR20-52. Use exponential smoothing, with $w = .7$, to forecast sales for 1995.

Year	Durable goods sales (billions of dollars)	Year	Durable goods sales (billions of dollars)
1980	299	1988	629
1981	325	1989	657
1982	336	1990	669
1983	391	1991	650
1984	454	1992	704
1985	498	1993	778
1986	541	1994	881
1987	576		

Source: Statistical Abstract of the United States.

20.53 The increased awareness among consumers of the health effects of cigarettes is expected to have an adverse impact on the tobacco industry. To help analyze the problem, a tobacco industry executive wants to forecast future production of cigarettes. The production amounts for the period 1981–1992 are shown in the accompanying table and stored in file XR20-53. Because of the relatively small changes that have taken place, it was decided to use exponential smoothing. Forecast the 1993 cigarette production, using a smoothing constant of $w = .5$.

Year	Cigarette production (billions)	Year	Cigarette production (billions)
1981	744	1987	689
1982	694	1988	698
1983	667	1989	677
1984	669	1990	710
1985	665	1991	695
1986	658	1992	719

Source: Statistical Abstract of the United States.

20.54 An important measure of a nation's manufacturing activity is earnings as a percentage of value added, which is calculated by dividing total nominal earnings of employees by the nominal value added. This shows labor's share of income generated in the manufacturing sector. U.S. earnings as a percentage of value added for the years 1976 to 1993 are shown in the accompanying table and stored in file XR20-54. Use exponential smoothing, with $w = .7$, to forecast earnings for 1994.

Year	Earnings as a percentage of value added	Year	Earnings as a percentage of value added
1976	41.7	1985	39.7
1977	41.4	1986	38.8
1978	41.3	1987	36.8
1979	39.9	1988	30.6
1980	40.9	1989	35.4
1981	40.8	1990	35.6
1982	41.4	1991	35.5
1983	40.0	1992	35.3
1984	39.1	1993	35.7

Source: Statistical Abstract of the United States.

20.9 TIME-SERIES FORECASTING WITH REGRESSION

Regression analysis has been applied to various problems. It was used in Chapter 17 to analyze the relationship between two variables, and it was used in Chapter 18 to analyze how a dependent variable is influenced by a group of independent variables. In those chapters, regression analysis was used to predict the value of the dependent variable. In this section, we again want to use regression techniques, but now the independent variable or variables will be measures of time. The simplest application would be a time series in which the only component (in addition to random variation, which is always present) is a linear trend. In that case, the model

$$y = \beta_0 + \beta_1 t + \epsilon$$

would likely provide excellent forecasts. However, we can take this basic model and augment it so that it can be used in other situations.

There are two ways to use regression analysis to forecast time series whose components are trend and seasonal effect. The first involves using the seasonal indexes developed in Section 20.6. The second involves using indicator variables, which were introduced in Section 19.3.

FORECASTING WITH SEASONAL INDEXES

The seasonal indexes measure the season-to-season variation. If we combine these indexes with a forecast of the trend, we produce the following formula.

> **Forecast of Trend and Seasonality**
>
> $$F_t = [\hat{\beta}_0 + \hat{\beta}_1 t] \cdot SI_t$$
>
> where
>
> F_t = forecast for period t
>
> SI_t = seasonal index for period t

The process we use to forecast with seasonal indexes is as follows.

1 Use simple linear regression to find the trend line

$$\hat{y} = \hat{\beta}_0 + \hat{\beta}_1 t$$

2 Use the trend line to calculate the seasonal indexes.

3 For the future time period t, find the trend value $\hat{y}_t$.

4 Multiply the trend value $\hat{y}_t$ by the seasonal index for the season to forecast.

$$F_t = \hat{y} \times SI_t$$

▼ **EXAMPLE 20.9**

Recall that in Example 20.6 we computed the seasonal (quarterly) indexes for the hotel occupancy rates. Compute the linear trend line and use the seasonal indexes to forecast each quarter's occupancy rate for 2000.

Solution   The trend line that was calculated from the quarterly data for 1995–1999 is

$$\hat{y} = .639 + .00525t$$

For $t = 21, 22, 23,$ and 24, we find the following trend values.

Year	Quarter	t	Trend Value $\hat{y}_t = .639 + .00525t$
2000	1	21	.749
	2	22	.755
	3	23	.760
	4	24	.765

We now multiply the trend values by the seasonal indexes (computed from the trend line rather than from moving averages). Thus, the seasonalized forecasts are as follows.

Year	Quarter	Trend Value $\hat{y}_t$	Seasonal Index	Forecast $F_t = \hat{y}_t \cdot SI_t$
2000	1	.749	.878	.658
	2	.755	1.076	.812
	3	.760	1.171	.890
	4	.765	.875	.670

Thus, we forecast that the quarterly occupancy rates during 2000 will be .658, .812, .890, and .670.

▲

▼ EXAMPLE 20.10

At the end of 1993, a major builder of residential houses in the northeastern United States wanted to predict the number of housing units to be started in 1994. This information would be extremely useful in determining a variety of variables, including housing demand, availability of labor, and the prices of building materials. To help develop an accurate forecasting model, researchers collected information on the number of housing starts for the previous 60 months (1989–1993). These numbers (in thousands of units) are shown in the accompanying table (and stored in file XM20-10). Forecast the housing starts for the 12 months of 1994.

Housing Starts in the Northeast United States (in thousands)

Year	Jan.	Feb.	Mar.	Apr.	May	Jun.	Jul.	Aug.	Sep.	Oct.	Nov.	Dec.
1989	15.3	8.8	12.2	19.9	17.5	17.9	19.6	14.5	14.4	16.4	14.8	7.2
1990	10.0	9.1	10.0	12.5	12.6	11.2	12.0	12.4	8.7	14.4	12.4	6.0
1991	4.9	3.8	7.3	9.4	11.6	14.2	11.2	11.4	9.1	12.0	9.7	8.3
1992	8.7	6.4	9.5	12.0	11.7	12.8	12.2	10.4	11.4	12.0	9.6	9.8
1993	6.9	5.6	6.8	10.9	11.3	13.9	12.7	12.2	13.2	11.8	11.7	9.3

Source: Standard & Poor's Industry Surveys.

Solution The data display a very clear seasonal pattern, as might be expected since much construction activity ceases during the winter months. Operating under the assumption that there is little cyclical variation, we chose to determine the seasonal indexes for 1989–1993 by using linear regression.

Our software packages produced the following regression equation.

$$\hat{y} = 13.3 - .0657t$$

As we did in Example 20.6, we computed the values of $\hat{y}$ (for $t = 1, 2, \ldots, 60$) and the ratios $y/\hat{y}$, from which we calculated the seasonal (monthly) indexes. They are

Month	Seasonal Index	Month	Seasonal Index
January	.775	July	1.201
February	.579	August	1.094
March	.791	September	1.035
April	1.121	October	1.204
May	1.134	November	1.061
June	1.244	December	.763

Finally, we employ the regression equation to compute $\hat{y}_t$ for the next 12 months ($t = 61, 62, \ldots, 72$) and multiply these values by the seasonal indexes. The table below summarizes these computations.

Year	Month	Time Period	Seasonal Index	Trend Value $\hat{y}_t = 13.3 - .0657t$	Forecast $F_t = \hat{y}_t \cdot SI_t$
1994	January	61	.775	9.29	7.20
	February	62	.579	9.23	5.34
	March	63	.791	9.16	7.25
	April	64	1.121	9.10	10.20
	May	65	1.134	9.03	10.24
	June	66	1.244	8.96	11.15
	July	67	1.201	8.90	10.69
	August	68	1.094	8.83	9.66
	September	69	1.035	8.77	9.07
	October	70	1.204	8.70	10.48
	November	71	1.061	8.64	9.16
	December	72	.763	8.57	6.54

Figure 20.17 depicts the time series, the trend line, and the forecasted values.

When we examine the actual 1994 monthly housing starts, we see that the forecasts are not very accurate. Table 20.1 offers a comparison of the forecasted and actual housing starts for 1994. Compare these numbers with Table 20.2, which exhibits the results of the same model when used to forecast 1986 housing starts. (See the first edition of this book, pages 518–520.) Notice how accurate the 1986 predictions were. The question arises: Why are the 1994 forecasts so inaccurate?

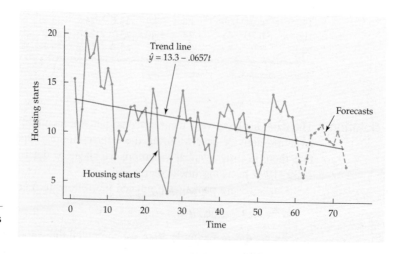

Figure 20.17

Time series, trend, and forecasts for Example 20.10

It is easy to see why the model worked so poorly in predicting 1994 housing starts. The economy was in a deep recession in the late 1980s and early 1990s. As a result, there is a distinct downward trend prior to 1992. However, 1992 marked the end of the recession, whereupon the downward trend stalled, and housing starts increased in 1994. Because the forecasts are based on a continuation of the trend and seasonality, any changes in the existing pattern result in poor forecasts. As you can see, the forecasted values match the actual values in their seasonality. The change in the trend, however, resulted in our forecasted values being consistently too low (except January). Thus, when using a forecasting model such as this one, care must be taken to consider whether major factors, such as the state of the economy, can be expected to change the future direction of the trend.

Table 20.1 **Forecasted and Actual Housing Starts in 1994**

Month	Forecast F_t	Actual Housing Starts
January	7.20	4.9
February	5.34	5.8
March	7.25	9.5
April	10.20	14.0
May	10.24	13.5
June	11.15	15.1
July	10.69	12.3
August	9.66	14.9
September	9.07	11.9
October	10.48	12.2
November	9.16	14.3
December	6.54	9.6

Source: Standard & Poor's Industry Surveys, 1995.

Table 20.2 **Forecasted and Actual Housing Starts in 1986**

Month	Forecast F_t	Actual Housing Starts
January	9.5	14.1
February	10.8	12.3
March	19.1	20.6
April	24.9	29.3
May	28.2	27.5
June	29.5	27.5
July	31.3	28.1
August	31.8	34.0
September	30.2	29.1
October	28.9	27.2
November	26.1	21.7
December	18.2	19.1

▲

FORECASTING SEASONAL TIME SERIES WITH INDICATOR VARIABLES

As an alternative to calculating and using seasonal indexes to measure the seasonal variations, we can use indicator variables. For example, if the seasons are the quarters of a year, the multiple regression model

$$y = \beta_0 + \beta_1 t + \beta_2 Q_1 + \beta_3 Q_2 + \beta_4 Q_3 + \epsilon$$

can be used where

$$t = \text{time period}$$
$$Q_1 = 1 \text{ (if quarter 1)}$$
$$= 0 \text{ (if not)}$$
$$Q_2 = 1 \text{ (if quarter 2)}$$
$$= 0 \text{ (if not)}$$
$$Q_3 = 1 \text{ (if quarter 3)}$$
$$= 0 \text{ (if not)}$$

Thus, for each time period, the **indicator variables** Q_1, Q_2, and Q_3 would be used to represent the quarters. The coefficients β_0, β_1, β_3, and β_4 would be estimated in the usual way, and the regression equation would be used to predict future values.

Notice that for the fourth quarter, the three indicator variables are all equal to zero, and we are simply left with

$$y = \beta_0 + \beta_1 t + \epsilon$$

▼ EXAMPLE 20.11

Use indicator variables and regression analysis to forecast hotel occupancy in 2000, using the data in Example 20.6. (The data are stored in file XM20-11, which stores the values of y, t, Q_1, Q_2, and Q_3 in columns 1 through 5, respectively.)

Solution   Because the seasons are the quarters of the year, we begin by creating indicator variables Q_1, Q_2, and Q_3 as described earlier. Thus,

$$Q_1 = 1, Q_2 = 0, Q_3 = 0$$

represents an observation in quarter 1;

$$Q_1 = 0, Q_2 = 1, Q_3 = 0$$

identifies the second-quarter measurement;

$$Q_1 = 0, Q_2 = 0, Q_3 = 1$$

represents the third quarter; and

$$Q_1 = 0, Q_2 = 0, Q_3 = 0$$

represents the fourth quarter.

The model to be estimated is

$$y = \beta_0 + \beta_1 t + \beta_2 Q_1 + \beta_3 Q_2 + \beta_4 Q_3 + \epsilon$$

SOLVE   The data in file XM20-11 were input, and the following computer output was produced.

**Excel Output for
Example 20.11**

	A	B	C	D	E	F	G
1	SUMMARY OUTPUT						
2							
3	*Regression Statistics*						
4	Multiple R	0.9430					
5	R Square	0.8893					
6	Adjusted R Square	0.8598					
7	Standard Error	0.0381					
8	Observations	20					
9							
10	ANOVA						
11		*df*	*SS*	*MS*	*F*	*Significance F*	
12	Regression	4	0.175	0.0436	30.122	0.0000	
13	Residual	15	0.0217	0.0014			
14	Total	19	0.196				
15							
16		*Coefficients*	*Standard Error*	*t Stat*	*P-value*		
17	Intercept	0.555	0.0248	22.35	0.0000		
18	Time	0.00504	0.0015	3.35	0.0044		
19	Q1	0.00351	0.0245	0.14	0.8879		
20	Q2	0.139	0.0243	5.74	0.0000		
21	Q3	0.205	0.0241	8.51	0.0000		

**Minitab Output for
Example 20.11**

```
The regression equation is
Rate = 0.555 + 0.00504 t + 0.0035 Q1 + 0.139 Q2 + 0.205 Q3


Predictor        Coef         StDev       t-ratio          P
Constant      0.55455       0.02481         22.35      0.000
t             0.005038      0.001504         3.35      0.004
Q1            0.00351       0.02449          0.14      0.888
Q2            0.13927       0.02426          5.74      0.000
Q3            0.20524       0.02412          8.51      0.000


S = 0.03806     R-Sq = 88.9%      R-Sq(adj) = 86.0%


Analysis of Variance

SOURCE         DF          SS            MS            F          P
Regression      4     0.174531      0.043633        30.12      0.000
Error          15     0.021728      0.001449
Total          19     0.196259
```

INTERPRET

The values $F = 30.12$ (p-value $= 0$) and $R^2 = 88.9\%$ indicate that the model's fit to the data is very good. The t-value for Q_1 (.14) and its p-value (.888) tell us that there is no significant difference in occupancy rates between quarters 1 and 4. The t-values for Q_2 and Q_3 (5.74 and 8.51, respectively) and their p-values (both 0) provide enough evidence to allow us to conclude that the occupancy rates in quarters 2 and 3 differ significantly from those in quarter 4.

The model's fit appears to be reasonable, so we can use it to forecast the 2000 quarterly occupancy rates, as shown in the accompanying table.

					Forecast
Quarter	t	Q_1	Q_2	Q_3	$\hat{y} = .555 + .00504t + .00351Q_1 + .139Q_2 + .205Q_3$
1	21	1	0	0	.664
2	22	0	1	0	.805
3	23	0	0	1	.876
4	24	0	0	0	.675

These forecasts are quite similar to those produced by using seasonal indexes in Example 20.9.

▲

AUTOREGRESSIVE MODEL

Recall that one of the requirements for the use of regression analysis is that the errors be independent of one another. In Chapter 19, we developed a test for first-order auto-correlation, called the Durbin–Watson test. While the existence of strong autocorrelation tends to destroy the validity of regression analysis, it also provides an opportunity to produce accurate forecasts. If we believe that there is a correlation between consecutive residuals, then the **autoregressive model**

$$y_t = \beta_0 + \beta_1 y_{t-1} + \epsilon$$

can be helpful in forecasting future values of y. The model specifies that consecutive values of the time series are correlated (which follows from the conclusion that the residuals are correlated). We estimate β_0 and β_1 by least squares and then use the equation to forecast.

▼ **EXAMPLE 20.12**

The Consumer Price Index (CPI) is used as a general measure of inflation. It is an important measure because a high rate of inflation often influences governments to take some corrective action. The table that follows lists the annual percentage increase in the CPI from 1951 through 1993.

Year	Percent Increase in CPI	Year	Percent Increase in CPI	Year	Percent Increase in CPI
1951	7.9	1966	2.9	1980	13.5
1952	2.2	1967	2.9	1981	10.4
1953	0.8	1968	4.2	1982	6.1
1954	0.5	1969	5.4	1983	3.2
1955	−0.4	1970	5.9	1984	4.3
1956	1.5	1971	4.3	1985	3.6
1957	3.6	1972	3.3	1986	1.9
1958	2.7	1973	6.2	1987	3.6
1959	0.8	1974	11.0	1988	4.1
1960	1.6	1975	9.1	1989	4.8
1961	1.0	1976	5.8	1990	5.4
1962	1.1	1977	6.5	1991	4.2
1963	1.2	1978	7.7	1992	3.0
1964	1.3	1979	11.3	1993	3.0
1965	1.7				

Source: Statistical Abstract of the United States.

In an attempt to forecast this value on the basis of time alone, we estimated the model as

$$\hat{y} = 2.14 + .0984t$$

We found that $R^2 = 15.0\%$ (indicating a poor model), but more important, we found the Durbin–Watson statistic to be $d = .47$, which indicates a strong autocorrelation. Because of this condition, an autoregressive model appears to be a desirable technique. Estimate the autoregressive model, and forecast the increase in the CPI in 1994. (File XM20-12 stores the CPI increase for years 1952 to 1993 in column 1. Column 2 contains the CPI increase for years 1951 to 1992.)

Solution The model to be estimated is

$$y_t = \beta_0 + \beta_1 y_{t-1} + \epsilon$$

where y_t = increase in the CPI in year t and y_{t-1} = increase in the CPI in year $t - 1$.

Excel Output for Example 20.12

	A	B	C	D	E	F	G
1	SUMMARY OUTPUT						
2							
3		*Regression Statistics*					
4	Multiple R	0.7979					
5	R Square	0.6366					
6	Adjusted R Square	0.6275					
7	Standard Error	1.94					
8	Observations	42					
9							
10	ANOVA						
11		*df*	*SS*	*MS*	*F*	*Significance F*	
12	Regression	1	264.6	264.6	70.06	0.0000	
13	Residual	40	151.1	3.78			
14	Total	41	415.7				
15							
16		*Coefficients*	*Standard Error*	*t Stat*	*P-value*		
17	Intercept	0.807	0.506	1.59	0.1188		
18	CPI-t-1	0.787	0.0940	8.37	0.0000		

Minitab Output for Example 20.12

```
The regression equation is
CPI-t = 0.807 + 0.787 CPI-t-1

Predictor        Coef        StDev      t-ratio         P
Constant       0.8066      0.5061         1.59     0.119
CPI-t-1       0.78705     0.09403         8.37     0.000

S = 1.943        R-Sq = 63.7%      R-Sq(adj) = 62.7%

Analysis of Variance

SOURCE         DF          SS           MS          F         P
Regression      1      264.60       264.60      70.06     0.000
Error          40      151.07         3.78
Total          41      415.66
```

INTERPRET   The forecast for 1994 is

$$\hat{y}_{1994} = .807 + .787y_{1993} = .807 + .787(3.0) = 3.2$$

The autoregressive model predicts that in 1994 the CPI should increase by 3.2%.

▲

EXERCISES

20.55 The following trend line and seasonal indexes were computed from 10 years of quarterly observations.

$$\hat{y} = 150 + 3t$$

Quarter	SI
1	.7
2	1.2
3	1.5
4	.6

Forecast the next four values.

20.56 The following trend line and seasonal indexes were computed from 4 weeks of daily observations.

$$\hat{y} = 120 + 2.3t$$

Day	SI
Sunday	1.5
Monday	.4
Tuesday	.5
Wednesday	.6
Thursday	.7
Friday	1.4
Saturday	1.9

Forecast the seven values for the next week.

20.57 The following trend line and seasonal indexes were computed from 6 years of quarterly observations.

$$\hat{y} = 2,000 + 80t - 2t^2$$

Quarter	SI
1	.6
2	.9
3	1.1
4	1.4

Forecast the four quarterly values for next year.

20.58 Regression analysis with $t = 1$ to 96 was used to develop the following forecast equation.

$$\hat{y} = 220 + 6.5t + 1.3Q_1 - 1.6Q_2 - 1.3Q_3$$

where

$$Q_i = 1 \text{ (if quarter } i\text{)} \quad (i = 1, 2, 3)$$
$$\quad = 0 \text{ (otherwise)}$$

Forecast the next four values.

20.59 Daily observations for 52 weeks (5 days per week) have produced the following regression model.

$$\hat{y} = 1,500 + 250t - 20D_1 + 10D_2 + 20D_3$$
$$\quad + 50D_4$$
$$(t = 1, 2, \ldots, 260)$$

where

$$D_1 = 1 \text{ (if Monday)} \qquad D_3 = 1 \text{ (if Wednesday)}$$
$$\quad = 0 \text{ (otherwise)} \qquad \quad = 0 \text{ (otherwise)}$$
$$D_2 = 1 \text{ (if Tuesday)} \qquad D_4 = 1 \text{ (if Thursday)}$$
$$\quad = 0 \text{ (otherwise)} \qquad \quad = 0 \text{ (otherwise)}$$

Forecast the next week.

20.60 A daily newspaper wanted to forecast 2-day revenues from its classified ads section. The revenues (in thousands of dollars) were recorded for the past 104 weeks. From these data, the regression equation was computed. Forecast the 2-day revenues for the next week. (Note that the newspaper appears 6 days per week.)

$$\hat{y} = 2,550 + .05t - 205D_1 - 60D_2$$
$$(t = 1, 2, \ldots, 312)$$

where

$$D_1 = 1 \text{ (if Monday or Tuesday)}$$
$$\quad = 0 \text{ (otherwise)}$$
$$D_2 = 1 \text{ (if Wednesday or Thursday)}$$
$$\quad = 0 \text{ (otherwise)}$$

20.61 Use the following autoregressive model to forecast the next value of the time series if the last observed value is 65.

$$\hat{y}_t = 625 - 1.3y_{t-1}$$

20.62 The following autoregressive model was developed.

$$\hat{y}_t = 155 + 21y_{t-1}$$

Forecast the next value of the time series if the last observation was 11.

20.63 The following autoregressive model was produced from the time series in Exercise 20.38.

$$\hat{y}_t = 0.2 + 1.03y_{t-1}$$

Forecast the number of cable subscribers in the first quarter of 2000.

20.64 Refer to Exercises 20.36 and 20.37. Forecast the quarterly earnings for 2000.

20.65 For Exercises 20.38 and 20.39, forecast the number of cable subscribers over the next eight quarters.

20.66 Refer to Exercise 20.38. Develop a regression model, using indicator variables to represent quarters, to forecast the number of cable subscribers over the next eight quarters.

20.67 Refer to Exercises 20.40 and 20.41. Forecast the number of pizzas sold daily for the next two weeks.

20.68 The seasonal indexes for the time series of revenues in Exercise 20.31 were calculated in Exercise 20.33. Use these indexes to forecast the revenues for Monday through Friday of week 5.

20.69 Total retail sales are an important indicator of overall economic activity. They, in turn, are affected by people's perceptions of the economy and especially by prevailing interest rates and financing availability. Sales are said to exhibit considerable seasonal variability. Consider the data in the accompanying table (data also stored in file XR20-69).

a Using regression analysis, compute the seasonal (monthly) indexes.

b Forecast the monthly total retail sales for 1994.

Total retail sales (millions of dollars)

	Jan.	Feb.	Mar.	Apr.	May	June
1989	136,557	134,340	134,621	136,593	136,336	135,900
1990	139,968	138,674	138,616	138,071	137,487	138,199
1991	131,812	134,059	135,861	135,172	135,578	136,178
1992	137,185	138,204	137,457	137,204	137,648	137,651
1993	144,157	143,076	141,655	144,029	145,291	145,892

	July	Aug.	Sept.	Oct.	Nov.	Dec.
1989	136,720	139,407	138,450	136,667	137,843	137,934
1990	138,347	137,995	137,792	136,511	136,541	134,536
1991	135,870	135,091	135,517	134,694	134,318	134,688
1992	137,940	139,020	140,019	142,272	142,362	143,945
1993	146,685	147,392	147,609	149,739	150,675	152,566

Source: U.S. Department of Commerce, Bureau of Economic Analysis, Survey of Current Business (1994).

20.10 SUMMARY

In this chapter, we discussed the classical time series and its decomposition into long-term trend and cyclical, seasonal, and random variation. Moving averages and exponential smoothing were used to remove some of the random fluctuation, enabling us to identify the time series' other components. The long-term trend was measured more scientifically by one of two regression models—linear and quadratic. The cyclical and seasonal effects are more clearly detected through calculation of percentage of trend and seasonal indexes.

When the components of a time series are identified, we can select one of many available methods to forecast the time series. When there is no or very little trend or cyclical and seasonal variation, exponential smoothing is recommended. When trend and seasonality are present, we can use regression analysis with seasonal indexes or indicator variables to make predictions. We can also use the autoregressive model.

IMPORTANT TERMS

Time series *778*
Trend *779*
Cyclical effect *780*
Seasonal variation *780*
Random variation *781*
Additive model *781*
Multiplicative model *781*
Smoothing *781*
Moving average *781*
Exponential smoothing *788*
Linear model *794*

Quadratic model *794*
Percentage of trend *800*
Seasonal indexes *805*
Deseasonalizing *809*
Seasonally adjusted *809*
Mean absolute deviation
  (MAD) *812*
Sum of squares for forecast error
  (SSE) *812*
Indicator variables *824*
Autoregressive model *826*

SUPPLEMENTARY EXERCISES

20.70 The cost of health care in the United States has been increasing rapidly. The accompanying table lists annual per capita national health expenditures for 1970–1993. (The data are also stored in file XR20-70.)

Year	t	Per capita national health expenditures ($)	Year	t	Per capita national health expenditures ($)
1970	1	346	1982	13	2,369
1971	2	379	1983	14	1,490
1972	3	421	1984	15	1,620
1973	4	464	1985	16	1,761
1974	5	521	1986	17	1,871
1975	6	591	1987	18	2,013
1976	7	671	1988	19	2,214
1977	8	755	1989	20	2,433
1978	9	838	1990	21	2,686
1979	10	937	1991	22	2,882
1980	11	1,068	1992	23	3,094
1981	12	1,227	1993	24	3,299

Source: Statistical Abstract of the United States.

a Plot the time series.
b Compute the percentage of trend.

20.71 The number of hospital beds is a function of various factors, including medical costs, population age, and economic conditions. The number of beds available in the United States between 1980 and 1993 is recorded in the accompanying table (and stored in file XR20-71).

Year	Number of hospital beds (1,000s)	Year	Number of hospital beds (1,000s)
1980	1,365	1987	1,261
1981	1,362	1988	1,241
1982	1,360	1989	1,224
1983	1,350	1990	1,211
1984	1,339	1991	1,197
1985	1,309	1992	1,174
1986	1,283	1993	1,158

Source: Statistical Abstract of the United States.

Use exponential smoothing, with $w = .4$, to forecast the number of hospital beds available in 1994.

20.72 An important measure of a country's economic health is the difference between the value of its exports and value of its imports. This quantity is sometimes called the resource balance. Canada's resource balance for the 15 years from 1978–1992 is shown below. (The data are also stored in file XR20-72.)

Year	Resource balance (billions of dollars)	Year	Resource balance (billions of dollars)
1978	10.25	1986	9.17
1979	5.56	1987	4.91
1980	3.70	1988	−0.67
1981	−0.09	1989	−9.42
1982	13.38	1990	−6.12
1983	11.94	1991	−9.74
1984	14.63	1992	−7.31
1985	12.46		

Source: World Tables (1994).

Use exponential smoothing, with $w = .4$, to forecast the 1993 figure.

Exercises 20.73 through 20.78 are based on the following problem.

The revenues (in millions of dollars) of a chain of ice cream stores are listed for each quarter during the years 1995–1999 in the accompanying table and in file XM20-73.

Quarter	Year				
	1995	1996	1997	1998	1999
1	16	14	17	18	21
2	25	27	31	29	30
3	31	32	40	45	52
4	24	23	27	24	32

20.73 Plot the time series.

20.74 Discuss why exponential smoothing is not recommended as a forecasting method in this case.

20.75 Calculate the four-quarter centered moving averages, and plot these values.

20.76 Use the moving averages computed in Exercise 20.75 to calculate the seasonal (quarterly) indexes.

20.77 Use regression analysis to develop the trend line.

20.78 Using the trend line and seasonal indexes calculated in Exercises 20.76 and 20.77, forecast revenues for the four quarters of 2000.

Exercises 20.79 through 20.84 are based on the following problem.

The monthly unemployment rate in Canada typically displays a great deal of seasonal variation, partly because of the country's climate. This factor plays an important role when governments attempt to forecast unemployment. The monthly unemployment rates for

1990–1993 are listed in the accompanying table and stored in file XR20-79.

Month	Year			
	1990	1991	1992	1993
January	7.7	9.7	10.5	11.0
February	7.6	10.2	10.7	10.8
March	7.2	10.5	11.2	11.0
April	7.3	10.2	11.1	11.4
May	7.7	10.3	11.2	11.4
June	7.6	10.5	11.6	11.3
July	8.0	10.5	11.6	11.6
August	8.4	10.6	11.6	11.3
September	8.5	10.2	11.4	11.2
October	8.9	10.3	11.3	11.1
November	9.1	10.3	11.8	11.0
December	9.3	10.3	11.5	11.2

Source: Canadian Economic Observer, Statistics Canada, 1994.

20.79 Plot the time series. Would the linear or quadratic model fit better?

20.80 Compute the seasonal (monthly) indexes using a quadratic regression model.

20.81 Using the quadratic trend line and seasonal indexes calculated in Exercise 20.80, forecast the monthly unemployment rates for 1994.

20.82 Develop a multiple regression model, using indicator variables to represent the months, to forecast the 1994 monthly unemployment rates.

20.83 The regression line referred to in Exercise 20.81 produced a Durbin–Watson statistic of $d = .47$. Develop an autoregressive model to forecast the 1994 monthly unemployment rates.

20.84 The actual 1994 unemployment rates were as follows.

1994 Unemployment Rates											
J	F	M	A	M	J	J	A	S	O	N	D
11.4	11.0	10.6	11.0	10.6	10.3	10.2	10.3	10.0	10.0	9.6	9.6

Source: Canadian Economic Observer, Statistics Canada, Jan. 1995.

Calculate MAD and SSE for each of the forecasts in Exercises 20.81, 20.82, and 20.83. Which forecasting model is most accurate?

Chapter 21

Statistical

Process

Control

21.1 Introduction

21.2 Process Variation

21.3 Control Charts for Variables: $\bar{X}$ and S Charts

21.4 Control Charts for Variables: $\bar{x}$ and R Charts (Optional)

21.5 Control Chart for Attributes: p Chart

21.6 Summary

21.1 INTRODUCTION

In the introduction to operations management in Chapter 1 we pointed out that operations managers are responsible for developing and maintaining the production processes that deliver quality products and services. In Section 14.6 (Taguchi Methods) we briefly introduced a statistical procedure that is used to investigate sources of variation and determine ways to reduce that variation. The goal is to select the methods, materials, machines, and personnel (manpower) that combine to yield the production process that features the smallest amount of variation at a reasonable cost. Once the production process is operating it is necessary to monitor it constantly to ensure that it functions the way it was designed. The statistical methods we are about to introduce are the most common application of statistics. At any point in time there are literally thousands of firms applying these methods. This chapter deals with the subject of **statistical process control** or **SPC** (formerly called **quality control**). Using terminology employed throughout this book we may refer to this entire chapter as an "Operations Management Application."

Statistical process control refers to a form of hypothesis testing that is employed extensively in industry to monitor the quality of a firm's products and services. In the last few years, quality has become much more important to North American companies. It is easy to see why. In many industries, foreign countries have been able to produce goods that are more reliable and less costly than their North American counterparts. A critical factor in this phenomenon is the extensive use of statistical process control.

There are two general approaches to the management of quality. The first approach is to produce the product and, at the completion of the production process, inspect the unit to determine whether it conforms to specifications; if it doesn't, it is either scrapped or repaired. This approach has several drawbacks. Foremost among them is that it is costly to produce defective products regardless of whether they are later scrapped or fixed. Additionally, 100% inspection is not 100% effective. Also, mass inspection takes action on the product, not the process. As such, it *detects* defects but does not *prevent* them. In recent years, this approach has been employed by a decreasing number of companies. Instead, many firms have adopted the **prevention approach.** Using the concepts of hypothesis testing, statisticians concentrate on the production process. Rather than inspect the product, we inspect the process to determine when the process starts producing units that do not conform to specifications. This allows us to correct the production process before it creates a large number of defective products.

In the next section, we discuss the problem of process variation and why it is often the key to the management of quality. We also introduce the concept and logic of control charts and show why they work. In the rest of the chapter, we introduce four specific control charts.

21.2 PROCESS VARIATION

The key to understanding SPC is understanding that all production processes result in variation; that is, no product is exactly the same as another. You can see for yourself that this is true by weighing, for example, two boxes of breakfast cereal that are each supposed to weigh 16 ounces. Not only will they not weigh exactly 16 ounces, but they will not even have equal weights. All products exhibit some degree of variation. There are two sources of variation. **Chance variation** is caused by a number of randomly occurring events that are part of the production process and that in general cannot be reduced without changing the process. In effect, chance variation was built into the product when the production process was first set up, perhaps as a result of a statistical analysis that attempted to minimize but not necessarily eliminate such variation (see Section 14.6). **Assignable variation** is caused by specific events or factors that are frequently temporary and that can usually be identified and eliminated. To illustrate, consider a paint company that produces and sells paint in 1-gallon cans. The cans are filled by an automatic valve that regulates the amount of paint in each can. The designers of the valve acknowledge that there will be some variation in the amount of paint even when the valve is working as it was designed to do. This is chance variation. Occasionally the valve will malfunction, causing the amount of variation in the amounts delivered to each can to increase significantly. This increase is the assignable variation.

Perhaps the best way to understand what is happening is to consider the volume of paint in each can as a random variable. If the only sources of variation are caused by chance, then each can's volume is drawn from identical distributions. That is, each distribution has the same shape, mean, and standard deviation as depicted in Figure 21.1. Under such circumstances the production process is said to be **under control.** In recognition of the fact that variation in output will occur even when the process is under control and operating properly, most processes are designed so that their products will fall within designated **specification limits** or "specs.". For example, the process that fills the paint cans may be designed so that the cans contain between .98 and 1.02 gallons.

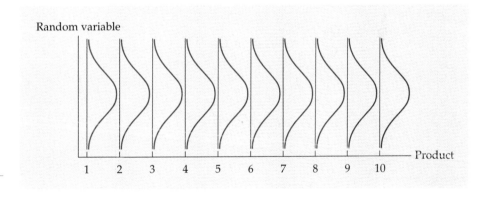

Figure 21.1

Identical process distributions

Inevitably, some event or combination of factors in a production process will cause the process distribution to change. When it does, the process is said to be **out of control.** There are several possible ways for the process to go out of control. Here is a list of the most commonly occurring possibilities and their likely assignable causes.

1 Level shift   This is a change in the mean of the process distribution. Assignable causes include machine breakdown, new machine and/or operator, or a change in the environment. In the paint-can illustration, a temperature or humidity change may affect the density of the paint, resulting in less paint in each can. Figure 21.2 depicts a decrease in the process mean level of paint.

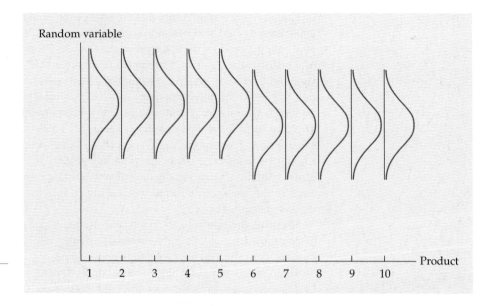

Figure 21.2

Level shift: change in process distribution mean

2   Instability   This is the name we apply to the process when the standard deviation increases. (As we discuss later, a decrease in the standard deviation is desirable.) This may be caused by a machine in need of repair, defective materials, wear of tools, or an incompetent operator. Suppose, for example, that a part in the valve that controls the amount of paint wears down, causing greater variation than normal. Figure 21.3 describes the process distributions in this example.

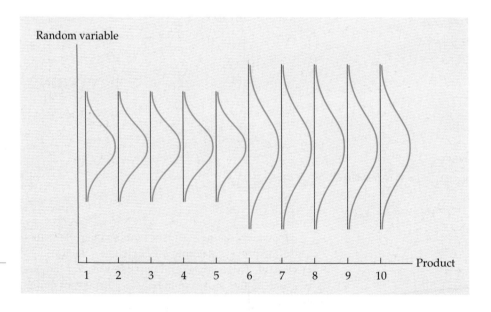

Figure 21.3

Instability: increase in process distribution standard deviation

3   Trend   When there is a slow, steady shift (either up or down) in the process distribution mean, the result is a trend. This is frequently the result of less-than-regular maintenance, operator fatigue, residue or dirt buildup, or gradual loss of lubricant. If the paint-control valve becomes increasingly clogged, we would expect to see a steady decrease in the amount of paint delivered. Figure 21.4 describes this effect.

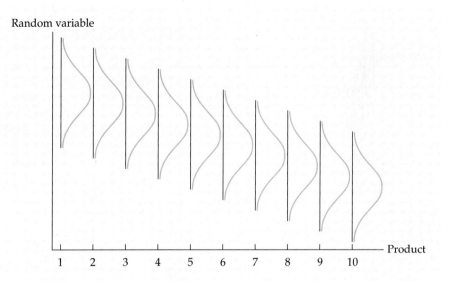

Figure 21.4

Trend: steady change in process distribution mean

4 Cycle   This is a repeated series of small observations followed by large observations. Likely assignable causes include environmental changes, worn parts, or operator fatigue. If there are changes in the voltage in the electricity that runs the machines in the paint-can example, we might see series of overfilled cans and series of underfilled cans. See Figure 21.5.

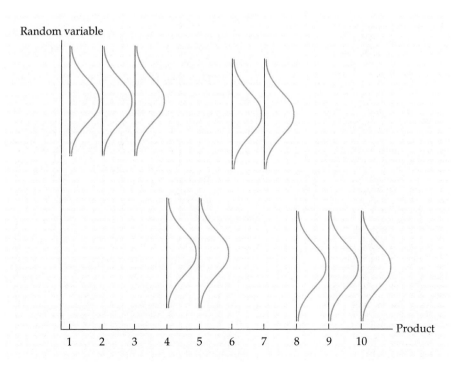

Figure 21.5

Cycle: large and small observations

The key to quality is to detect when the process goes out of control so that we can correct the malfunction and restore control of the process. The control chart is the statistical method that we use to detect problems.

CONTROL CHARTS

A *control chart* is a plot of statistics over time. For example, an $\bar{x}$ chart plots a series of sample means taken over a period of time. Each control chart contains a **center-line** and *control limits*. (See Figure 21.6.) The control limit above the centerline is called the **upper control limit** and that below the centerline is called the **lower control limit.** If, when the sample statistics are plotted, all points are randomly distributed between the control limits, we conclude that the process is under control. If the points are not randomly distributed between the control limits, we conclude that the process is out of control.

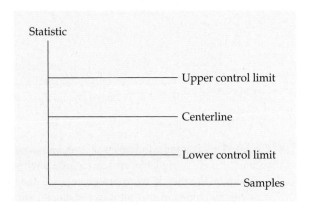

Figure 21.6

Control chart

To illustrate the logic of control charts, let us suppose that in the paint-can example described earlier, we want to determine whether the central location of the distribution has changed from one period to another. We will draw our conclusion from an $\bar{x}$ chart. For the moment, let us assume that we know the mean μ and standard deviation σ of the process when it is under control. We can construct the $\bar{x}$ chart, as shown in Figure 21.7. The chart is drawn so that the vertical axis plots the values of $\bar{x}$ that will be calculated and the horizontal axis tracks the samples in the order in which they are drawn. The centerline is the value of μ. The control limits are set at three standard deviations from the centerline. Because the standard deviation of $\bar{x}$ (the statistic we intend to track in this chart) is $\sigma/\sqrt{n}$, we define the control limits as follows.

$$\text{Lower control limit} = \mu - 3\frac{\sigma}{\sqrt{n}}$$

$$\text{Upper control limit} = \mu + 3\frac{\sigma}{\sqrt{n}}$$

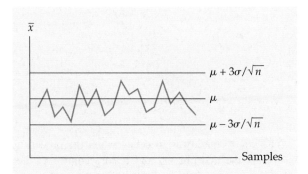

Figure 21.7

$\bar{x}$ chart: μ and σ known

After we've constructed the control chart by drawing the centerline and control limits, we use it to plot the sample means, which are joined to make it easier to interpret. The principles underlying control charts are identical to the principles of hypothesis testing. The null and alternative hypotheses are

H_0: The process is under control

H_1: The process is out of control

For an $\bar{x}$ chart, the test statistic is the sample mean $\bar{x}$. However, because we're dealing with a dynamic process rather than a fixed population, we test a series of sample means. That is, we compute the mean for each of a continuing series of samples taken over time. For each series of samples, we want to determine whether there is sufficient evidence to infer that the process mean has changed. We reject the null hypothesis if at any time the sample mean falls outside the control limits. It is logical to ask why we use 3 standard deviations and not 2 or 1.96 or 1.645, as we did when we tested hypotheses about a population mean in Chapter 10. The answer lies in the way in which all tests are conducted. Because test conclusions are based on sample data, there are two possible errors. In SPC, a Type I error occurs if we conclude that the process is out of control when in fact it is not. The error can be quite expensive, because the production process must be stopped and the causes of the variation found and repaired. Consequently, we want the probability of a Type I error to be small. With control limits set at 3 standard deviations from the mean, the probability of a Type I error is $\alpha = P(|z| > 3) = .0026$. A small value of α results in a relatively large value of the probability of a Type II error. This means that, for each sample, we are less likely to recognize when the process goes out of control. However, because we will be performing a series of tests (one for each sample), we will eventually discover that the process is out of control and take steps to rectify the problem.

Suppose that in order to test the production process that fills 1-gallon paint cans, we choose to take a sample of size 4 every hour. Let us also assume that we know the mean and standard deviation of the process distribution of the amount of paint when the process is under control, say, $\mu = 1.01$ and $\sigma = .02$. (This means that when the valve is working the way it was designed, the amount of paint put into each can is a random variable whose mean is 1.01 gallons and whose standard deviation is .02 gallons.) Thus,

$$\text{Centerline} = \mu = 1.01$$
$$\text{Lower control limit} = \mu - 3\sigma/\sqrt{n} = 1.01 - 3(.02)/\sqrt{4} = 1.01 - .03 = .98$$
$$\text{Upper control limit} = \mu + 3\sigma/\sqrt{n} = 1.01 + 3(.02)/\sqrt{4} = 1.01 + .03 = 1.04$$

Figure 21.8 depicts a situation in which the first 15 samples were taken when the process was under control. However, after the 15th sample was drawn, the process went out of control and produced sample means outside the control limits. We conclude that the process distribution has changed, because the data display variability beyond that predicted for a process with the specified mean and standard deviation. This means that the variation is assignable, and that the cause needs to be identified and corrected.

As we stated above, SPC is a slightly different form of hypothesis testing. The concept is the same but there are differences that you should be aware of. The most important difference is that when we tested means and proportions in Chapters 10 and 11, we were dealing with fixed but unknown parameters of populations. For instance, in Example 10.1 the population we dealt with was the account balances of the department store customers. The population mean balance was a constant value that we

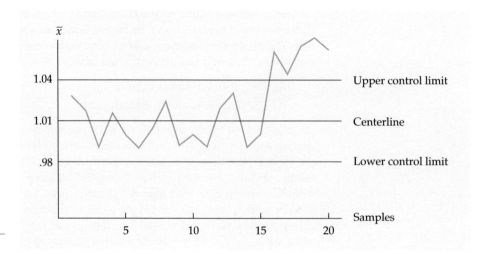

Figure 21.8

x̄ chart: process out of control

simply did not know. The purpose of the test was to determine if there was enough statistical evidence to allow us to infer that the mean balance was greater than $170. So we took one sample and based the decision on the sample mean. When dealing with a production process, it's important to realize that the *process distribution* itself is *variable.* That is, at any time, the process distribution of the amount of paint fill may change if the valve malfunctions. Consequently, we do not simply take one sample and make the decision. Instead, we plot a number of statistics over time in the control chart. Simply put, in Chapters 10 through 19, we assumed static population distributions with fixed but unknown parameters and in this chapter, we assume a dynamic process distribution with parameters subject to possible shifts.

In our demonstration of the logic of control charts, we resorted to traditional methods of presenting inferential methods; we assumed that the process parameters were known. When the parameters are unknown, we estimate their values from the sample data. In the next three sections, we discuss how to construct and use control charts in more realistic situations.

In Sections 21.3 and 21.4, we present control charts when the data are quantitative. In the context of statistical process control, we call these **control charts for variables.** Section 21.5 demonstrates the use of control charts that record whether a unit is defective or nondefective. These are called **control charts for attributes.**

21.3 CONTROL CHARTS FOR VARIABLES: x̄ AND S CHARTS

There are several ways to judge whether a change in the process distribution has occurred when the data are quantitative. To determine whether the distribution means have changed, we employ the x̄ **chart.** To determine whether the process distribution standard deviation has changed, we use the S (which stands for standard deviation) chart or the R (which stands for range) chart.

Note that throughout this textbook we have used the sample standard deviation to estimate the population standard deviation. However, for a variety of reasons, SPC frequently employs the range instead of the standard deviation. This is primarily because computing the range is simpler than computing the standard deviation. Because many practitioners conduct SPC performing calculations by hand (with the assistance of a calculator), they select the computationally simple range as the method to estimate the process standard deviation. In this section, we will introduce control charts that feature the sample standard deviation. In Section 21.4, we employ the sample range to construct our charts.

$\bar{x}$ CHART

As we explained above, if we know the mean and standard deviation of the process distribution, we can compute the centerline and control limits. However, it is unrealistic to believe that the mean and standard deviation of the process distribution are known. Thus, in order to construct the $\bar{x}$ chart, we need to estimate the relevant parameters from the data.

We begin by drawing samples when the process is under control. We discuss later how to determine that the process is under control. For each sample, we compute the mean and the standard deviation. The estimator of the mean of the distribution is the mean of the sample means (denoted $\bar{\bar{x}}$)

$$\bar{\bar{x}} = \frac{\sum_{j=1}^{k} \bar{x}_j}{k}$$

where $\bar{x}_j$ is the mean of the jth sample and there are k samples.

To estimate the standard deviation of the process distribution, we calculate the sample variance s_j^2 for each sample. We then compute the pooled standard deviation,* which we denote S and define as

$$S = \sqrt{\frac{\sum_{j=1}^{k} s_j^2}{k}}$$

In the previous section, where we assumed that the process distribution mean and variance were known, the centerline and control limits were defined as

$$\text{Centerline} = \mu$$
$$\text{Lower control limit} = \mu - 3\sigma/\sqrt{n}$$
$$\text{Upper control limit} = \mu + 3\sigma/\sqrt{n}$$

Since the values of μ and σ are unknown, we must use the sample data to estimate them. The estimator of μ is $\bar{\bar{x}}$ and the estimator of σ is S. Therefore the centerline and control limits are

Centerline and Control Limits for $\bar{x}$ Chart
$\text{Centerline} = \bar{\bar{x}}$
$\text{Lower control limit} = \bar{\bar{x}} - 3S/\sqrt{n}$
$\text{Upper control limit} = \bar{\bar{x}} + 3S/\sqrt{n}$

---

*This formula requires that the sample size be the same for all samples, a condition that is satisfied throughout this chapter.

▼ **EXAMPLE 21.1***

Lear Seating of Kitchener, Ontario, manufactures seats for Chrysler, Ford, and General Motors cars. Several years ago, Lear instituted statistical process control, which has resulted in improved quality and lower costs. One of the components of a front-seat cushion is a wire spring, produced from 4-mm (millimeter) steel wire. A machine is employed to bend the wire so that the spring's length is 500 mm. If the springs are longer than 500 mm, they will loosen and eventually fall out. If they are too short, they won't easily fit into position. (In fact, in the past, when there was a relatively large number of short springs, workers incurred arm and hand injuries when attempting to install the springs.) To determine if the process is under control, random samples of four springs are taken every two hours. The last 25 samples are shown in Table 21.1 (and stored in file XM21-01). Construct an $\bar{x}$ chart from these data.

Table 21.1 **25 Samples of Springs for Example 21.1**

Sample				
1	501.02	501.65	504.34	501.10
2	499.80	498.89	499.47	497.90
3	497.12	498.35	500.34	499.33
4	500.68	501.39	499.74	500.41
5	495.87	500.92	498.00	499.44
6	497.89	499.22	502.10	500.03
7	497.24	501.04	498.74	503.51
8	501.22	504.53	499.06	505.37
9	499.15	501.11	497.96	502.39
10	498.90	505.99	500.05	499.33
11	497.38	497.80	497.57	500.72
12	499.70	500.99	501.35	496.48
13	501.44	500.46	502.07	500.50
14	498.26	495.54	495.21	501.27
15	497.57	497.00	500.32	501.22
16	500.95	502.07	500.60	500.44
17	499.70	500.56	501.18	502.36
18	501.57	502.09	501.18	504.98
19	504.20	500.92	500.02	501.71
20	498.61	499.63	498.68	501.84
21	499.05	501.82	500.67	497.36
22	497.85	494.08	501.79	501.95
23	501.08	503.12	503.06	503.56
24	500.75	501.18	501.09	502.88
25	502.03	501.44	502.76	503.79

Solution The means and standard deviations for each sample were computed and listed in Table 21.2. We then calculated the mean of the means and the pooled standard deviation. These statistics are as follows.

$$\bar{\bar{x}} = 500.380$$
$$S = 1.956$$

---

*The authors are grateful to Pat Bourke, Barry Cress, Kevin Lewis, and Brial Riehl of Lear Seating Ltd. for their assistance in writing this example and several exercises.

Table 21.2 **Means and Standard Deviations of Samples in Example 21.1**

Sample					$\bar{x}_j$	s_j
1	501.02	501.65	504.34	501.10	502.027	1.56689
2	499.80	498.89	499.47	497.90	499.015	0.83309
3	497.12	498.35	500.34	499.33	498.785	1.37556
4	500.68	501.39	499.74	500.41	500.555	0.68268
5	495.87	500.92	498.00	499.44	498.557	2.15204
6	497.89	499.22	502.10	500.03	499.810	1.76323
7	497.24	501.04	498.74	503.51	500.133	2.74085
8	501.22	504.53	499.06	505.37	502.545	2.93381
9	499.15	501.11	497.96	502.39	500.152	1.97782
10	498.90	505.99	500.05	499.33	501.068	3.31578
11	497.38	497.80	497.57	500.72	498.367	1.57771
12	499.70	500.99	501.35	496.48	499.630	2.21625
13	501.44	500.46	502.07	500.50	501.117	0.77994
14	498.26	495.54	495.21	501.27	497.570	2.81996
15	497.57	497.00	500.32	501.22	499.027	2.05853
16	500.95	502.07	500.60	500.44	501.015	0.73487
17	499.70	500.56	501.18	502.36	500.950	1.11886
18	501.57	502.09	501.18	504.98	502.455	1.72412
19	504.20	500.92	500.02	501.71	501.712	1.79633
20	498.61	499.63	498.68	501.84	499.690	1.50694
21	499.05	501.82	500.67	497.36	499.725	1.94345
22	497.85	494.08	501.79	501.95	498.918	3.74115
23	501.08	503.12	503.06	503.56	502.705	1.10603
24	500.75	501.18	501.09	502.88	501.475	0.95480
25	502.03	501.44	502.76	503.79	502.505	1.01261

Thus, the centerline and control limits are

$$\text{Centerline} = \bar{\bar{x}} = 500.380$$
$$\text{Lower control limit} = \bar{\bar{x}} - 3S/\sqrt{n} = 500.380 - 3(1.956)/\sqrt{4} = 497.446$$
$$\text{Upper control limit} = \bar{\bar{x}} + 3S/\sqrt{n} = 500.380 + 3(1.956)/\sqrt{4} = 503.314$$

SOLVE

The centerline and control limits are drawn and the sample means plotted in the order in which they occurred. To examine the chart, see the Excel or Minitab printout below.

Excel Output for Example 21.1

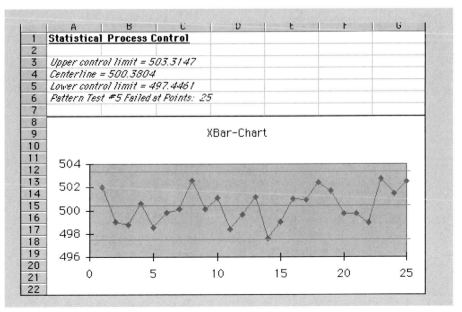

We will discuss pattern tests following this example.

COMMANDS	COMMANDS FOR EXAMPLE 21.1
1 Type or import the data into one column.	Open file **XM21-01.**
2 Click **Tools, Data Analysis Plus,** and **Statistical Process Control.**	
3 Specify the block coordinates of the data. Do not include cell containing variable names.	**A2:A101**
4 Click **XBAR Chart.**	
5 Specify the sample size.	**4**
6 Click **S** (to estimate σ, the process standard deviation).	

Minitab Output for Example 21.1

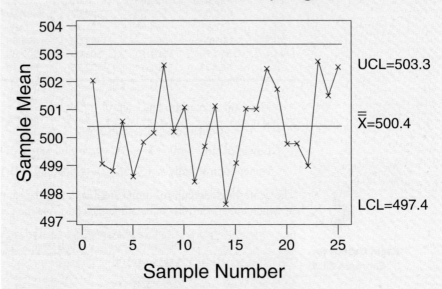

X-bar Chart for Springs

COMMANDS	COMMANDS FOR EXAMPLE 21.1
1 Type or import the data into one column.	Open file **XM21-01.**
2 Click **Stat, Control Charts,** and **Xbar. . . .**	
3 Specify **Data are arranged as Single column:** and type the variable name.	**Springs** or **C1**
4 Type the **Subgroup size:**	**4**
5 Click **Estimate . . .** and **Pooled standard deviation.**	
6 Click **OK.**	

INTERPRET

As you can see, no point lies outside the control limits. We conclude from this fact that the variation in the lengths of the springs is caused by chance. That is, there is not enough evidence to infer that the process is out of control. No remedial action is called for.

We stress that statistical process control allows us to detect assignable variation only. In this example, we determined that the process is under control, which means that there are no detectable sources of assignable variation. However, this does not mean that the process is a good one. It may well be that the production process yields a large proportion of defective units because the amount of chance variation is large. Recall that in Chapter 14, we noted that chance variation decreases product quality and increases costs. If the costs of producing defective units is high because of large chance variation, we can only improve quality and reduce costs by changing the process itself.

▲

PATTERN TESTS TO DETERMINE WHEN THE PROCESS IS OUT OF CONTROL

When we tested hypotheses in the other parts of this book, we used only one sample statistic to make a decision. However, in statistical process control, the decision is made from a series of sample statistics. In the $\bar{x}$ chart we make the decision after plotting at least 25 sample means. As a result, we can develop tests that are based on the pattern the sample means make when plotted. To describe them, we need to divide the $\bar{x}$ chart between the control limits into six zones, as shown in Figure 21.9. The C zones represent the area within one standard deviation of the centerline. The B zones are the regions between one and two standard deviations from the centerline. The spaces between two and three standard deviations from the centerline are defined as A zones.

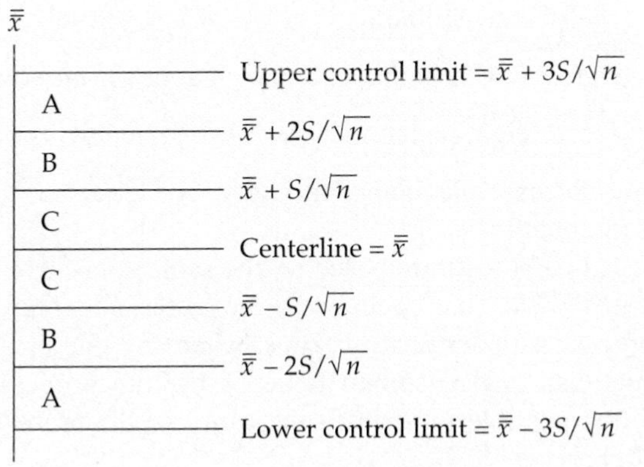

Figure 21.9

Zones of $\bar{x}$ charts

The width of the zones is 1 standard deviation of $\bar{x}$, which is estimated as $S/\sqrt{n}$. In Example 21.1, the width of each zone is $S/\sqrt{n} = 1.956/\sqrt{4} = .978$. Figure 21.10 describes the centerline, control limits, and zones for Example 21.1.

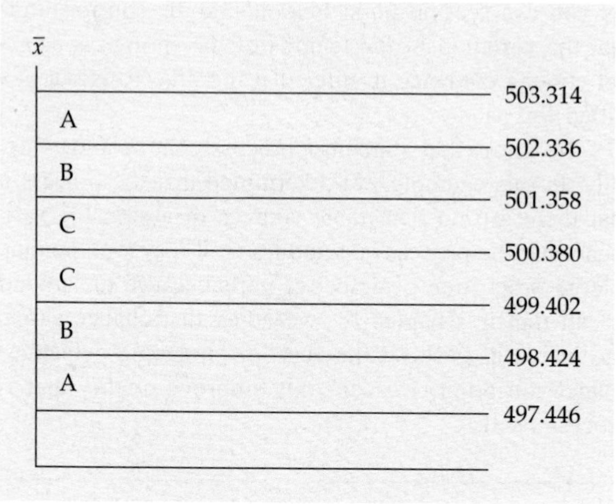

Figure 21.10

Zones for $\bar{x}$ chart: Example 21.1

Several pattern tests can be applied. Below we list eight tests that are conducted by Minitab (and by the Excel macro we created).

Test 1: one point beyond zone A. This is the method discussed above, where we conclude that the process is out of control if any point is outside the control limits.

Test 2: nine points in a row in zone C or beyond (on the same side of the centerline).

Test 3: six increasing or six decreasing points in a row.

Test 4: fourteen points in a row alternating up and down.

Test 5: two out of three points in a row in zone A or beyond (on the same side of the centerline).

Test 6: four out of five points in a row in zone B or beyond (on the same side of the centerline).

Test 7: fifteen points in a row in zone C (on both sides of the centerline).

Test 8: eight points in a row beyond zone C (on both sides of the centerline).

In the examples shown in Figure 21.11, each of the eight tests indicates a process out of control.

All eight tests are based on the same concepts used to test hypotheses throughout this book. That is, any of these patterns is a rare event, unlikely to occur when a process is under control. Thus, when any one of these patterns is recognized, the statistician has reason to believe that the process is out of control. In fact, it is often possible to identify the cause of the problem from the pattern in the control chart.

Figure 21.12 depicts the zones and the means for Example 21.1. After a thorough examination, we discover that points 23 and 25 are in zone A above the centerline. Thus, we conclude that the process went out of control at point 25. A technician would be called in to correct the problem.

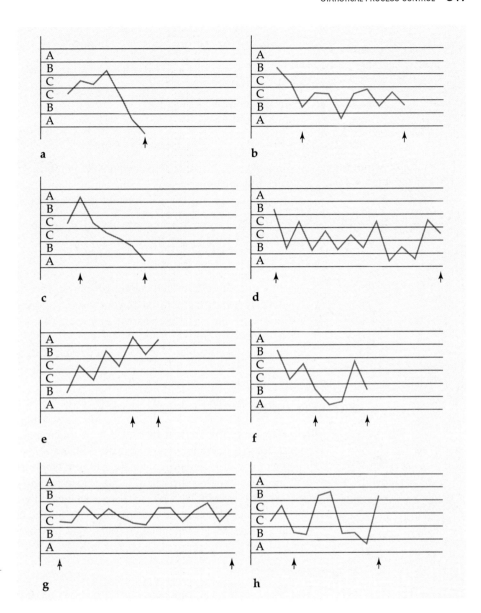

Figure 21.11

Examples of patterns indicating process out of control

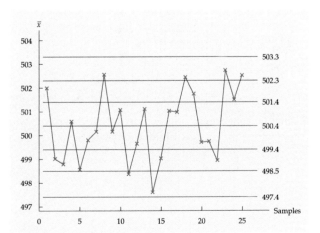

Figure 21.12

$\bar{x}$ chart with zones: Example 21.1

Excel Pattern Test Results: Example 21.1

Excel automatically performs all eight tests. It reported the following.

	A	B	C	D	E	F	G	H	I
1	Pattern Test #5 Failed at Points: 25								
2									
3									
4									

Minitab Pattern Test Results: Example 21.1

Minitab has the capability to conduct all eight tests and report when any of them indicate that the process is out of control. For Example 21.1, Minitab printed the following when it was commanded to conduct the pattern tests.

> TEST 5. Two of 3 points in a row in zone A or beyond (on one side of CL). Test Failed at points: 25

COMMANDS

Before clicking **OK** on the commands above, use the cursor to select **Tests . . .** and **Perform all eight tests.** If you wish to apply specific tests, instead click **Choose specific tests to perform** and select the one(s) you want. To draw the zones, click **S Limits . . .** and type **1 2 3** in the **Sigma limit positions:** box (the number of standard deviations of $\bar{x}$ from the centerline). Click **OK.**

PATTERN TESTS IN PRACTICE

There appears to be a great deal of disagreement among statisticians with regard to pattern tests. Some authors and statistical software packages apply eight tests while others employ a different number. In addition, some statisticians apply pattern tests to $\bar{x}$ charts, but not to other charts. Rather than joining the debate with our own opinions, we will use Minitab's rules. There are eight pattern tests for $\bar{x}$ charts, no pattern tests for S and R charts, and four pattern tests for the chart presented in Section 21.5 (p charts). The same rule applies to our Excel macros.

S CHARTS

The **S chart** graphs sample standard deviations to determine if the process distribution standard deviation has changed. The format is similar to that of the $\bar{x}$ chart: there is a centerline and control limits. However, the formulas for the centerline and control limits are more complicated than those for the $\bar{x}$ chart. Consequently, we will not display the formulas; instead we will let the computer do all the work.

▼ EXAMPLE 21.2

Using the data provided in Example 21.1, determine whether there is evidence to indicate that the process distribution standard deviation has changed over the period when the samples were taken.

Solution

Excel Output for Example 21.2

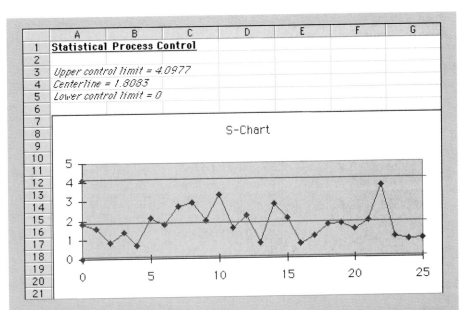

The centerline and control limits are functions of S, which we found to be 1.956 (in Example 21.1).

COMMANDS	COMMANDS FOR EXAMPLE 21.2
1 Type or import the data into one column.	Open file **XM21-01**.
2 Click **Tools, Data Analysis Plus,** and **Statistical Process Control.**	
3 Specify the block coordinates of the data. Do not include cell containing variable name.	A2:A101
4 Click **S Chart.**	
5 Specify the sample size.	4

Minitab Output for Example 21.2

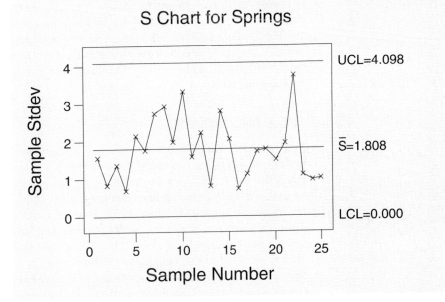

The centerline and control limits are functions of S, which we found to be 1.956 (in Example 21.1). The centerline is denoted $\overline{S}$ and is equal to 1.808.

COMMANDS	COMMANDS FOR EXAMPLE 21.2
1 Type or import the data into one column.	Open file **XM21-01**.
2 Click **Stat, Control Charts,** and **S. . . .**	
3 Specify **Data are arranged as Single column:** and type the variable name.	**Springs** or **C1**
4 Type the **Subgroup size:**.	**4**
5 Click **Estimate . . .** and **Pooled standard deviation.**	
6 Click **OK.**	

INTERPRET

There are no points outside the control limits. Because we do not apply any of the pattern tests, we conclude that there is no evidence to believe that the standard deviation has changed over this period.

▲

GOOD NEWS AND BAD NEWS ABOUT S CHARTS

In analyzing the S charts, we would conclude that the process distribution has changed if we observe points outside the control limits. Obviously, points above the upper control limit indicate that the process standard deviation has increased—an undesirable situation. Points below the lower control limit also indicate that the process standard deviation has changed. However, cases in which the standard deviation has decreased are welcome occurrences because reducing the variation generally leads to improvements in quality. The operations manager should investigate cases where the sample standard deviations or ranges are small to determine the factors that produced such results. The objective is to determine if permanent improvements in the production process can be made. Care must be exercised in cases where the S chart reveals a *decrease* in the standard deviation, since this is often caused by improper sampling.

USING THE $\overline{x}$ AND S CHARTS

In this section, we have introduced $\overline{x}$ and S charts as separate procedures. In actual practice, however, the two charts must be drawn and assessed together. The reason for this is that the $\overline{x}$ chart uses S to calculate the control limits and zone boundaries. Consequently, if the S chart indicates that the process is out of control, the value of S will not lead to an accurate estimate of the standard deviation of the process distribution. The usual procedure is to draw the S chart first. If it indicates that the process is under control, we then draw the $\overline{x}$ chart. If the $\overline{x}$ chart also indicates that the process is under control, we are then in a position to use both charts to maintain control. If either chart shows that the process was out of control at some time during the creation of the charts, we can detect and fix the problem, then redraw the charts with new data.

We can often diagnose the problem from the patterns exhibited in the control charts. For example, a level shift is easily detected from the $\bar{x}$ chart shown in Figure 21.13. Figure 21.14 describes an $\bar{x}$ chart where a trend has occurred. Cycles are also detected from $\bar{x}$ charts. (See Figure 21.15.) Instability is diagnosed from the S chart as shown in Figure 21.16. A knowledgeable operations manager would be capable of determining the problem and needed repairs from these charts.

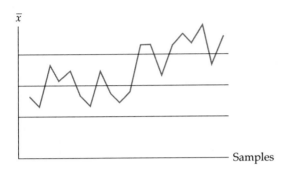

Figure 21.13

$\bar{x}$ chart: level shift

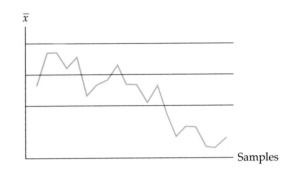

Figure 21.14

$\bar{x}$ chart: trend

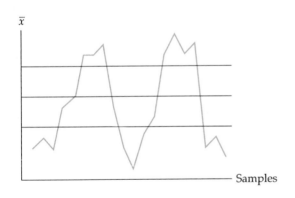

Figure 21.15

$\bar{x}$ chart: cycle

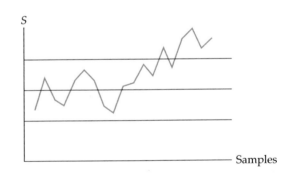

Figure 21.16

S chart: instability

DEVELOPING AN UNDERSTANDING OF STATISTICAL CONCEPTS

The concepts that underlie statistical process control are the same as the fundamental principles of hypothesis testing. That is, statistics that are not consistent with the null hypothesis lead us to reject the null hypothesis. However, there are two critical differences between SPC and hypothesis testing. First, in SPC we test processes rather than parameters of populations. That is, we test to determine whether there is evidence that the process distribution has changed. Second, in SPC we test a series of statistics taken over time. From a pedagogical point of view, there is another fundamental difference. Most students of statistics have difficulty identifying the correct hypothesis-testing procedure to employ. However, SPC applications tend to be rather uncomplicated. We use control charts for variables (as in this and the next section) to determine whether the process is under control when the product produced must be measured quantitatively. Identifying the correct technique is seldom difficult and thus does not require technique-identification skills developed throughout this book.

EXERCISES

21.1 Given the following statistics drawn from 30 samples of size 4, calculate the centerline and control limits for the $\bar{x}$ chart.

$$\bar{\bar{x}} = 453.6 \quad S = 12.5$$

21.2 The mean of the sample means and the pooled standard deviation of 40 samples of size 9 taken from a production process under control are shown below. Compute the centerline, control limits, and zone boundaries for the $\bar{x}$ chart.

$$\bar{\bar{x}} = 181.1 \quad S = 11.0$$

21.3 Twenty-five samples of size 4 were taken from a production process. The sample means are listed below. The mean of the sample means and the pooled standard deviation are

$$\bar{\bar{x}} = 13.3 \quad S = 3.8$$

Sample	1	2	3	4	5	6	7
$\bar{x}_j$	14.5	10.3	17.0	9.4	13.2	9.3	17.1

Sample	8	9	10	11	12	13
$\bar{x}_j$	5.5	5.3	16.3	10.5	11.5	8.8

Sample	14	15	16	17	18	19
$\bar{x}_j$	12.6	10.5	16.3	8.7	9.4	11.4

Sample	20	21	22	23	24	25
$\bar{x}_j$	17.6	20.5	21.1	16.3	18.5	20.9

    a Find the centerline and control limits for the $\bar{x}$ chart.
    b Plot the sample means on the $\bar{x}$ chart.
    c Is the process under control? Explain.

The following exercises require a computer and statistical software.

21.4 Thirty samples of size 4 were drawn from a production process. The data were stored in file XR21-04.

    a Construct an S chart.
    b Construct an $\bar{x}$ chart.
    c Do the charts allow you to conclude that the process is under control?
    d If the process went out of control, which of the following is the likely cause: level shift, instability, trend, or cycle?

21.5 The fence of a saw is set so that it automatically cuts 2-by-4s into 96-inch lengths needed to produce prefabricated homes. To ensure that the lumber is cut properly, three pieces of wood are measured after each 100 cuts

are made. The measurements in inches for the last 40 samples are stored in file XR21-05.

    a Do these data indicate that the process is out of control?
    b If so, when did it go out of control? What is the likely cause: level shift, instability, trend, or cycle?
    c Speculate on how the problem could be corrected.

21.6 An Arc Extinguishing Unit (A.E.U.) is used in the high-voltage electrical industry to eliminate the occurrence of electrical flash from one live 25,000-volt switch contact to another. A small but important component of an A.E.U. is a nonconductive sliding bearing called a (ST-90811) pin guide. The dimensional accuracy of this pin guide is critical to the overall operation of the A.E.U. If any one of its dimensions is "out of spec" (specification), the part will bind within the A.E.U., causing failure. This would cause the complete destruction of both the A.E.U. and the 25,000-volt switch contacts, resulting in a power blackout. A pin guide has a square shape with a circular hole in the center, as shown below with its specified dimensions and tolerance limits.

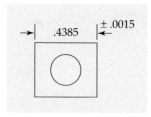

Due to the critical nature of the dimensions of the pin guide, statistical process control is used during long production runs to check that the production process is under control. Suppose that samples of five pin guides are drawn every hour. The results of the last 25 samples are stored in file XR21-06. Do these data allow the technician to conclude that the process is out of control?

21.7 KW Paints is a company that manufactures various kinds of paints and sells them in 1- and 4-liter cans. The cans are filled on an assembly line with an automatic valve regulating the amount of paint. If the cans are overfilled, paint and money will be wasted. If the cans are underfilled, customers will complain. To ensure that the proper amount of paint goes into each can, statistical process control is used. Every hour five cans are opened, and the volume of paint is measured. The results from the last 30 hours from the 1-liter production line are stored in file XR21-07. To avoid rounding errors, we recorded the volumes (in millimeters) after subtracting 1,000. Thus, the file contains the amounts of overfill and underfill. Draw the $\bar{x}$ and S charts to determine if the process is under control.

21.8 Lear Seating of Kitchener, Ontario, produces seats for Cadillacs and other GM cars and trucks. The Cadillac seat includes a part called the EK headrest. The frame of the headrest is made from steel rods. A machine is used to bend the rod into a U-shape described as shown. The width is critical; if it is too wide or too narrow, it will not fit into the holes drilled into the seat frame. The

process is checked by drawing samples of size 3 every 2 hours. The last 20 samples are stored in file XR21-08.

a What do these data tell you about the process?
b If it went out of control, at what sample did this occur?
c What is the likely assignable cause?

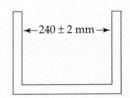

EK Headrest Frame

21.4 CONTROL CHARTS FOR VARIABLES: $\bar{x}$ AND R CHARTS (Optional)

As you have already seen, we can use the sample variances to estimate the process distribution standard deviation. For technicians who perform the analysis by hand, the calculation of sample variances is relatively time consuming. Moreover, the formulas that convert S to the centerline and the control limits are complicated. As a consequence, many companies prefer to estimate the process standard deviation by computing the sample ranges. This change affects the creation of the $\bar{x}$ chart and how we test to see if the process standard deviation has changed.

Recall that the range is the difference between the largest and smallest observations in a sample. As a first step in estimating the process standard deviation, we calculate the range for each sample and the mean of the sample ranges (denoted $\bar{R}$).

$$\bar{R} = \frac{\sum_{j=1}^{k} R_j}{k}$$

where R_j is the range of the jth sample.

Mathematicians have developed methods that produce estimates of the standard deviation that are based on the sample range. We estimate the process standard deviation by $\bar{R}/d_2$, where d_2 is a constant that depends on the sample size. Table 13 in Appendix B lists the values of d_2 (as well as other constants required in statistical process control) for sample sizes between 2 and 25. Thus,

$$\text{Lower control limit} = \bar{\bar{x}} - \frac{3(\bar{R}/d_2)}{\sqrt{n}}$$

$$\text{Upper control limit} = \bar{\bar{x}} + \frac{3(\bar{R}/d_2)}{\sqrt{n}}$$

We can simplify the control limits by letting

$$A_2 = \frac{3}{d_2\sqrt{n}}$$

where the values of A_2 are also listed in Table 13 in Appendix B. Using A_2, we can rewrite the control limits.

> ### Centerline and Control Limits for the $\bar{x}$ Chart: Using the Sample Ranges
>
> $$\text{Centerline} = \bar{\bar{x}}$$
> $$\text{Lower control limit} = \bar{\bar{x}} - A_2\bar{R}$$
> $$\text{Upper control limit} = \bar{\bar{x}} + A_2\bar{R}$$

▼ EXAMPLE 21.3

Repeat Example 21.1, using the sample ranges instead of the sample standard deviations.

Solution

SOLVE

Table 21.3 lists the samples, the sample means, and the sample ranges. From these statistics, we find

$$\bar{\bar{x}} = 500.380 \quad \text{and} \quad \bar{R} = 3.934$$

The centerline is drawn at $\bar{\bar{x}} = 500.380$. From Table 13 in Appendix B, we find that with $n = 4$, $A_2 = .729$. The control limits are

$$\text{Lower control limit} = \bar{\bar{x}} - A_2\bar{R} = 500.380 - .729(3.934) = 497.512$$
$$\text{Upper control limit} = \bar{\bar{x}} + A_2\bar{R} = 500.380 + .729(3.934) = 503.248$$

To conduct the pattern tests, we need to determine the width of the zones. The simplest way to do this is to note that the difference between the upper control limit and the centerline is 3 standard deviations of $\bar{x}$. Thus,

$$\text{Width of zones} = \frac{503.248 - 500.380}{3} = .956$$

See the computer output below to examine this $\bar{x}$ chart. No mean lies outside the control limits. However, we can see that two out of three points (points 23, 24, and 25) lie in zone A above the centerline.

Table 21.3   Means and Ranges of Samples in Example 21.1

Sample					$\bar{x}_j$	R_j
1	501.02	501.65	504.34	501.10	502.027	3.32
2	499.80	498.89	499.47	497.90	499.015	1.90
3	497.12	498.35	500.34	499.33	498.785	3.22
4	500.68	501.39	499.74	500.41	500.555	1.65
5	495.87	500.92	498.00	499.44	498.557	5.05
6	497.89	499.22	502.10	500.03	499.810	4.21
7	497.24	501.04	498.74	503.51	500.133	6.27
8	501.22	504.53	499.06	505.37	502.545	6.31
9	499.15	501.11	497.96	502.39	500.152	4.43
10	498.90	505.99	500.05	499.33	501.068	7.09
11	497.38	497.80	497.57	500.72	498.367	3.34
12	499.70	500.99	501.35	496.48	499.630	4.87
13	501.44	500.46	502.07	500.50	501.117	1.61
14	498.26	495.54	495.21	501.27	497.570	6.06
15	497.57	497.00	500.32	501.22	499.027	4.22

(continued)

Sample					$\bar{x}_j$	R_j
16	500.95	502.07	500.60	500.44	501.015	1.63
17	499.70	500.56	501.18	502.36	500.950	2.66
18	501.57	502.09	501.18	504.98	502.455	3.80
19	504.20	500.92	500.02	501.71	501.712	4.18
20	498.61	499.63	498.68	501.84	499.690	3.23
21	499.05	501.82	500.67	497.36	499.725	4.46
22	497.85	494.08	501.79	501.95	498.918	7.87
23	501.08	503.12	503.06	503.56	502.705	2.48
24	500.75	501.18	501.09	502.88	503.475	2.13
25	502.03	501.44	502.76	503.79	502.505	2.35

Excel Output for Example 21.3

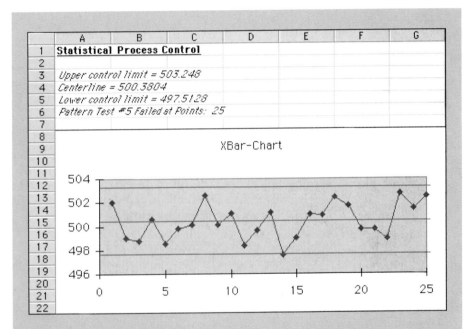

The centerline is 500.3804 and the lower and upper control limits are 497.5128 and 503.248, respectively. No point lies outside the control limits. Once again, the data fail test 5 at points 23, 24, and 25.

COMMANDS

Follow the instructions provided in Example 21.1, except click **R** instead of **S** (to estimate σ).

Minitab Output for Example 21.3

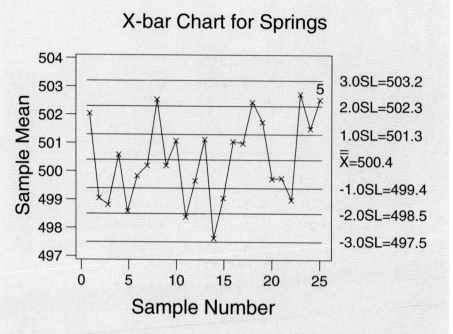

The centerline is 500.4 and the lower and upper control limits are 497.5 and 503.2, respectively. No point lies outside the control limits. Once again, the data fail test 5 at points 23, 24, and 25. Minitab announces this result by placing a "5" at sample 25 on the chart.

COMMANDS

Follow the instructions provided in Example 21.1, except specify **Rbar** instead of **Pooled standard deviation.**

INTERPRET

Because we used the sample ranges instead of the sample standard deviations, the control limits differed (only slightly) from those computed in Example 21.1. However, the results are the same. We discover that the process went out of control at point 25. The production process would be stopped and corrective action taken.

▲

R CHARTS

In general, if we use the sample ranges to help create the $\bar{x}$ chart, we use the *R* **chart,** which graphs sample ranges, to determine when and if the process distribution standard deviation changes. The format is similar to that of the $\bar{x}$ and *S* charts. The centerline is the mean of the ranges $\bar{R}$. As was the case with the $\bar{x}$ chart, we need an estimate of the standard deviation of the ranges. We estimate that standard deviation with

$$d_3 \frac{\bar{R}}{d_2}$$

where d_3 is another constant provided by Table 13 in Appendix B. The control limits are as follows.

$$\text{Lower control limit} = \overline{R} - 3d_3\frac{\overline{R}}{d_2} = \overline{R}\left(1 - \frac{3d_3}{d_2}\right)$$

$$\text{Upper control limit} = \overline{R} + 3d_3\frac{\overline{R}}{d_2} = \overline{R}\left(1 + \frac{3d_3}{d_2}\right)$$

We simplify these formulas by letting

$$D_3 = 1 - \frac{3d_3}{d_2}$$

$$D_4 = 1 + \frac{3d_3}{d_2}$$

Values for D_3 and D_4 are provided in Table 13 in Appendix B for $n = 2$ to 25. For n less than or equal to 6, D_3 is actually negative. However, since a negative control limit is meaningless, the values of D_3 in Table 13 for n less than or equal to 6 are reported as zero.

Centerline and Control Limits for *R* Chart

$$\text{Centerline} = \overline{R}$$
$$\text{Lower control limit} = D_3\overline{R}$$
$$\text{Upper control limit} = D_4\overline{R}$$

▼ **EXAMPLE 21.4**

Using the data from Example 21.1, construct the R chart.

Solution

SOLVE

In Example 21.3, we found $\overline{R} = 3.934$. To calculate the control limits, we find in Table 13 in Appendix B that with $n = 4$, $D_3 = 0$, and $D_4 = 2.282$. Thus,

$$\text{Centerline} = \overline{R} = 3.934$$
$$\text{Lower control limit} = D_3\overline{R} = 0(3.934) = 0$$
$$\text{Upper control limit} = D_4\overline{R} = 2.282(3.934) = 8.977$$

See computer output below to examine the R chart.

**Excel Output for
Example 21.4**

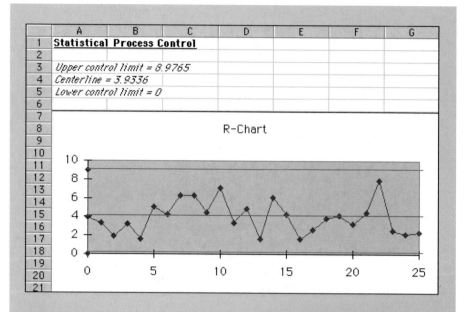

COMMANDS

1 Type or import the data into one
  column.
2 Click **Tools, Data Analysis Plus,** and
  Statistical Process Control.
3 Specify the block coordinates of the
  data. Do not include cell containing
  the variable name.
4 Click **R Chart.**
5 Specify the sample size.

COMMANDS FOR EXAMPLE 21.4

Open file **XM21-01.**

A2:A101

4

**Minitab Output for
Example 21.4**

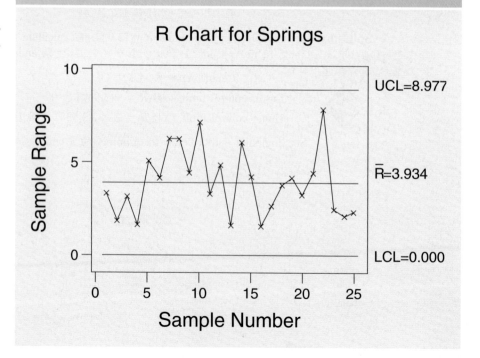

COMMANDS	COMMANDS FOR EXAMPLE 21.4
	Open file **XM21-01**.
1 Type or import the data into one column.	
2 Click **Stat, Control Charts,** and **R. . . .**	
3 Specify **Data are arranged as Single column:** and type the variable name.	**Springs** or **C1**
4 Type the **Subgroup size:**.	**4**
5 Click **Estimate . . .** and **Rbar.**	
6 Click **OK.**	

INTERPRET

The R chart indicates that the process distribution standard deviation is unchanged. However, we discovered that the process mean has been altered. Thus, after we've repaired the machine we start anew. We draw more samples and create the $\bar{x}$ and S (or R) charts. When both charts show that the process is under control, we then use them to maintain control.

Note the similarity between centerline and control limits of the $\bar{x}$ chart using R and the $\bar{x}$ chart using S. Obviously the two methods of estimating σ are quite similar. This is confirmed by examining the R chart and the S chart. The two charts are almost identical yielding the same conclusion.

▲

EXERCISES

21.9 The following statistics were calculated from 30 samples of size 4.

$$\bar{\bar{x}} = 175.6 \quad \bar{R} = 11.8$$

Calculate the following.

a The centerline and control limits for the $\bar{x}$ chart

b The boundaries of the zones for the $\bar{x}$ chart

c The centerline and control limits for the R chart

21.10 The means of the sample means and sample ranges of 40 samples of size 9 taken from a process under control are $\bar{\bar{x}} = 27.3$ and $\bar{R} = 6.1$.

a Calculate the centerline and control limits for the $\bar{x}$ chart.

b Calculate the zone boundaries for the $\bar{x}$ chart.

c Calculate the centerline and control limits for the R chart.

21.11 The mean of the sample ranges of 50 samples of size 10 taken from a process under control is $\bar{R} = 5.89$. Calculate the centerline and control limits for the R chart.

21.12 Twenty-five samples of size $n = 4$ were drawn. For each sample, the mean and range were computed as follows.

a Draw the R chart.

b Draw the $\bar{x}$ chart.

c Does it appear that the process is under control?

Sample	1	2	3	4	5	6	7
$\bar{x}_j$	19	22	18	16	18	19	21
R_j	7	11	6	18	5	10	7

Sample	8	9	10	11	12	13
$\bar{x}_j$	23	13	18	23	19	2
R_j	7	6	12	8	12	24

Sample	14	15	16	17	18	19
$\bar{x}_j$	26	12	20	22	24	17
R_j	11	13	16	7	20	11

Sample	20	21	22	23	24	25
$\bar{x}_j$	12	26	15	24	27	13
R_j	13	10	6	14	20	18

21.13 Twenty samples of size $n = 6$ were drawn. For each sample, the mean and range were computed as follows.

a Draw the R chart.

b Draw the $\bar{x}$ chart.

c Does it appear that the process is under control?

Sample	1	2	3	4	5	6	7	8	9	10
$\bar{x}_j$	28.6	26.4	26.8	25.9	27.5	27.9	27.0	28.3	29.1	27.9
R_j	7.3	6.2	5.9	6.3	7.3	7.9	6.0	5.8	7.1	6.8

Sample	11	12	13	14	15	16	17	18	19	20
$\bar{x}_j$	29.3	25.9	26.7	27.1	26.9	28.7	28.5	27.7	27.8	28.2
R_j	7.2	4.3	5.0	7.5	7.9	8.1	7.1	8.6	9.4	8.4

21.14 Plastic pipe is used in almost all new homes; it is used in sinks and toilets. If the pipes are too wide or too narrow, they will not connect properly with other pieces of pipe. A manufacturer of 3-inch-diameter pipes employs statistical process control to maintain the quality of its products. The sampling plan is to draw a sample of three 10-foot-long pipes every hour and measure the diameters. Twenty hours ago, the production process was shut down for repairs. The results of the 20 samples taken since then are shown in the accompanying table and stored in file XR21-14. Draw the R and $\bar{x}$ charts. Has the process gone out of control? If so, when?

Sample				$\bar{x}$	R_j
1	3.059	3.002	3.006	3.02233	.057
2	2.980	3.065	3.007	3.01733	.085
3	2.916	3.065	2.959	2.98000	.149
4	2.988	3.020	3.030	3.01267	.042
5	2.986	3.037	3.007	3.01000	.051
6	2.911	2.918	2.938	2.92233	.027
7	2.947	2.977	2.986	2.97000	.039
8	3.025	2.947	2.989	2.98700	.078

(continued)

Sample				$\bar{x}$	R_j
9	2.939	3.040	3.040	3.00633	.101
10	2.959	3.023	3.037	3.00633	.078
11	3.002	2.910	2.999	2.97033	.092
12	2.966	2.977	2.922	2.95500	.055
13	2.948	3.008	2.934	2.96333	.074
14	3.000	2.950	2.968	2.97267	.050
15	2.964	2.989	3.070	3.00767	.106
16	3.025	3.017	2.960	3.00067	.065
17	2.996	3.015	2.963	2.99133	.052
18	2.981	2.977	3.067	3.00833	.090
19	3.037	2.935	2.990	2.98733	.102
20	3.011	3.021	2.945	2.99233	.076
				$\bar{\bar{x}} = 2.98992$	$\bar{R} = .07345$

The following exercises require the use of a computer and statistical software.

21.15 Refer to Exercise 21.5.

   a Draw the R chart.
   b Draw the $\bar{x}$ chart (using the sample ranges to estimate the process standard deviation).
   c Is the process under control?

21.16 Refer to Exercise 21.6. Using the R and $\bar{x}$ charts, determine if the process is under control.

21.17 Refer to Exercise 21.7. Using the R and $\bar{x}$ charts, determine if the process is under control.

21.18 Refer to Exercise 21.8. Use the R and $\bar{x}$ charts to discover whether the process appears to be under control.

21.5 CONTROL CHART FOR ATTRIBUTES: p CHART

In this section, we introduce a control chart that is used to monitor a process whose results are categorized as either defective or nondefective. We construct a **p chart** to track the proportion of defective units in a series of samples.

p CHART

We draw the p chart in a way similar to the construction of the $\bar{x}$ chart. We draw samples of size n from the process at a minimum of 25 time periods. For each sample, we calculate the sample proportion of defective units, which we label $\hat{p}_j$. We then compute the mean of the sample proportions, which is labeled $\bar{p}$. That is

$$\bar{p} = \frac{\sum_{j=1}^{k} \hat{p}_j}{k}$$

The centerline and control limits are defined as follows.

Centerline and Control Limits for the p Chart

$$\text{Centerline} = \bar{p}$$

$$\text{Lower control limit} = \bar{p} - 3\sqrt{\frac{\bar{p}(1 - \bar{p})}{n}}$$

$$\text{Upper control limit} = \bar{p} + 3\sqrt{\frac{\bar{p}(1 - \bar{p})}{n}}$$

If the lower control limit is negative, set it equal to zero.

PATTERN TESTS

As we did in the sections above, we use Minitab's pattern tests. Minitab performs only tests 1 to 4, which are as follows.

Test 1: one point beyond zone A.

Test 2: nine points in a row in zone C or beyond (on the same side of the centerline).

Test 3: six increasing or six decreasing points in a row.

Test 4: fourteen points in a row alternating up and down.

▼ **EXAMPLE 21.5**

A company that produces 3.5-inch computer disks has been receiving complaints from its customers about the large number of disks that will not store data properly. Company management has decided to institute statistical process control in order to remedy the problem. Every hour, a random sample of 200 disks is taken, and each disk is tested to determine whether it is defective. The results of the first 40 hours are shown in the accompanying table and stored in file XM21-05. Using these data, draw a p chart to monitor the production process. Was the process out of control when the sample results were generated?

Sample	Number of Defectives	Sample	Number of Defectives	Sample	Number of Defectives
1	19	15	18	29	10
2	5	16	20	30	18
3	16	17	13	31	15
4	20	18	6	32	16
5	6	19	8	33	5
6	12	20	3	34	14
7	18	21	8	35	3
8	6	22	7	36	10
9	13	23	4	37	19
10	15	24	19	38	13
11	10	25	3	39	19
12	6	26	19	49	9
13	7	27	9		
14	10	28	10		

Solution

For each sample, we compute the proportion of defective disks and calculate the mean sample proportion. We find $\bar{p} = .05762$. Thus,

$$\text{Centerline} = \bar{p} = .05762$$

$$\text{Lower control limit} = \bar{p} - 3\sqrt{\frac{\bar{p}(1-\bar{p})}{n}}$$

$$= .05762 - 3\sqrt{\frac{(.05762)(1-.05762)}{200}} = .008188$$

$$\text{Upper control limit} = \bar{p} + 3\sqrt{\frac{\bar{p}(1-\bar{p})}{n}}$$

$$= .05762 + 3\sqrt{\frac{(.05762)(1-.05762)}{200}} = .1071$$

Since

$$\sqrt{\frac{\bar{p}(1-\bar{p})}{n}} = \sqrt{\frac{(.05762)(1-.05762)}{200}} = .01648$$

the boundaries of the zones are as follows.

Zone C: $.05762 \pm .01648 = (.04114, .0741)$

Zone B: $.05762 \pm 2(.01648) = (.02467, .09057)$

Zone A: $.05762 \pm 3(.01648) = (.008188, .1071)$

The output below exhibits this p chart.

Excel Output for Example 21.5

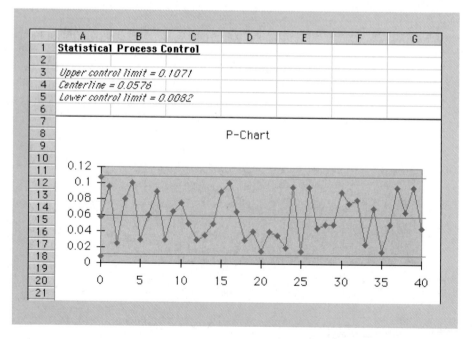

COMMANDS	COMMANDS FOR EXAMPLE 21.5
1 Type or import the data into one column.	Open file **XM21-05**.
2 Click **Tools, Data Analysis Plus,** and **Statistical Process Control.**	
3 Specify the block coordinates of the data. Do not include cell containing the variable name.	**A2:A41**
4 Click **P Chart.**	
5 Specify the sample size.	**200**

Minitab Output for Example 21.5

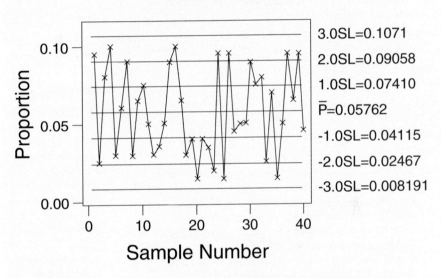

P Chart for Disks

3.0SL=0.1071
2.0SL=0.09058
1.0SL=0.07410
$\bar{P}$=0.05762
-1.0SL=0.04115
-2.0SL=0.02467
-3.0SL=0.008191

COMMANDS	COMMANDS FOR EXAMPLE 21.5
1 Type or import the data into one column.	Open file **XM21-05**.
2 Click **Stat, Control Charts,** and **P. . . .**	
3 Type the **Variable name.**	**Disks** or **C1**
4 Type the **Subgroup size:**	**200**
5 Specify **Perform all four tests.**	
6 To draw the zones click **S Limits . . .** and type **1 2 3** Click **OK.**	

INTERPRET None of the points lies outside the control limits (test 1), and the other test results are negative. There is no evidence to infer that the process is out of control. ▲

The comment we made about R charts is also valid for p charts. That is, sample proportions that are less than the lower control limit indicate a change in the process that we would like to make permanent. We need to investigate the reasons for such a change just as vigorously as we investigate the causes of large proportions of defects.

EXERCISES

21.19 To ensure that a manufacturing process is under control, 40 samples of size 1,000 were drawn and the number of defectives in each sample was counted. The mean sample proportion was 0.035. Compute the centerline and control limits for the p chart.

21.20 Random samples of 200 widgets were taken on an assembly line every hour for the past 25 hours. The number of defective widgets is shown in the accompanying table and stored in file XR21-20. Are there any points beyond the control limits? If so, what do they tell you about the production process?

Sample	1	2	3	4	5	6	7
No. of defectives	3	5	3	2	2	11	12

Sample	8	9	10	11	12	13
No. of defectives	6	7	5	0	7	8

Sample	14	15	16	17	18	19
No. of defectives	2	10	6	4	2	10

Sample	20	21	22	23	24	25
No. of defectives	5	4	11	10	13	14

21.21 Raytheon of Canada Limited produces printed circuit boards (PCBs), which involve a number of soldering operations. At the end of the process, the PCBs are tested to determine if they work properly. There are several causes of PCB failure. Possible causes include bad flux, improper heating, and impurities. A reject rate of less than 0.80% is considered acceptable. Statistical process control is used by Raytheon to constantly check quality. Every hour, 500 PCBs are tested. The number of defective PCBs for the past 25 hours is shown in the accompanying table and stored in file XR21-21. Draw a p chart and apply the pattern tests to determine if the process is under control.

Sample	1	2	3	4	5	6	7
No. of defectives	3	1	2	2	1	2	3

Sample	8	9	10	11	12	13
No. of defectives	3	3	2	3	0	0

Sample	14	15	16	17	18	19
No. of defectives	0	2	0	0	2	4

Sample	20	21	22	23	24	25
No. of defectives	1	1	1	4	1	3

21.22 A plant produces 10,000 cordless telephones daily. A random sample of 1000 telephones is inspected each day. After 30 days, the following number of defectives was found. (The data are also stored in file XR21-22.) Construct a p chart to determine if the process is out of control.

Sample	1	2	3	4	5	6
No. of defectives	5	0	4	3	0	3

Sample	7	8	9	10	11	12
No. of defectives	1	1	5	0	2	1

Sample	13	14	15	16	17	18
No. of defectives	6	0	3	0	5	5

Sample	19	20	21	22	23	24
No. of defectives	8	5	0	1	9	6

Sample	25	26	27	28	29	30
No. of defectives	11	6	6	4	5	10

21.23 The Woodsworth Publishing Company produces millions of books containing hundreds of millions of pages each year. To ensure the quality of the printed page, Woodsworth uses statistical process control. In each production run, 1,000 pages are randomly inspected. The examiners look for print clarity and whether the material is properly centered on the page. The number of defective pages in the last 40 production runs is listed in the accompanying table and stored in file XR21-23. Draw the p chart. Using the pattern tests, can we conclude that the production process is under control?

Sample	Number of defective pages	Sample	Number of defective pages	Sample	Number of defective pages
1	11	15	18	29	21
2	9	16	19	30	17
3	17	17	17	31	20
4	19	18	15	32	17
5	15	19	7	33	17
6	15	20	16	34	18
7	18	21	17	35	23
8	21	22	22	36	29
9	18	23	12	37	24
10	6	24	12	38	27
11	27	25	12	39	23
12	14	26	16	40	21
13	7	27	12		
14	18	28	9		

21.6 SUMMARY

In this chapter, we introduced statistical process control and explained how it contributes to the maintenance of quality. We discussed how control charts detect changes in the process distribution and introduced the $\bar{x}$ chart, S chart, R chart, and p chart.

IMPORTANT TERMS

Statistical process control (SPC) *834*

Quality control *834*

Prevention approach *834*

Chance variation *834*

Assignable variation *835*

Under control *835*

Specification limits *835*

Out of control *835*

Centerline *838*

Upper and lower control limits *838*

Control charts for variables *840*

Control chart for attributes *840*

$\bar{x}$ chart *840*

S chart *848*

R chart *856*

p chart *860*

SUPPLEMENTARY EXERCISES

The following exercises require the use of a computer and statistical software.

21.24 The degree to which nuts and bolts are tightened in numerous places on a car is often important. For example, in Toyota cars, a nut holds the rear signal light. If the nut is not tightened sufficiently, it will loosen and fall off; if it is too tight, the light may break. The nut is tightened with a torque wrench with a set clutch. The target torque is 8 kgf/cm (kilogram-force per centimeter) with a tolerance of 2 kgf/cm (7 to 9 kgf/cm). Statistical process control is employed to constantly check the process. Random samples of size 4 are drawn after every 200 nuts are tightened. The data from the last 25 samples are stored in file XR21-24. (The authors are grateful to Ted Couves for contributing this exercise.)

 a Determine if the process is under control.

 b If it is out of control, identify when this occurred and the likely cause.

21.25 A company that manufactures batteries employs statistical process control to ensure that its product functions properly. The sampling plan for the D-cell batteries calls for samples of 500 batteries to be taken and tested. The number of defective batteries in the last 30 samples is stored in file XR21-25. Determine whether the process is under control.

21.26 The seats for the F-150 series Ford trucks are manufactured by Lear Seating. The frames must be 1,496 mm wide with a tolerance of 3 mm. Frames that are wider than 1,497.5 mm or narrower than 1,494.5 mm result in assembly problems, because seat cushions and/or other parts won't fit. The process is tested by drawing random samples of five frames every two hours. The last 25 samples are stored in file XR21-26. What can we conclude from these data?

21.27 A courier delivery company advertises that it guarantees delivery by noon the following day. The statistical process control plan calls for sampling 2,000 deliveries each day to ensure that the advertisement is reasonable. The number of late deliveries for the last 30 days is stored in file XR21-27. What can we conclude from these data?

21.28 Long Manufacturing produces heat exchangers, primarily for the automotive industry. One such product, a transmission oil cooler, is used in the cooling of bus transmissions. It is composed of a series of copper tubes that are soldered into a header. The header must have a diameter of 4.984 inches with a tolerance of .006 inches. Oversize headers result in an inability to assemble the components. Undersize headers result in fluid mixing and possible failure of the device. For every 100 headers produced, the operations manager draws a sample of size 4. The data from the last 25 samples are stored in file XR21-28. What can we conclude from these data?

21.29 Refer to Exercise 21.28. Nuts and bolts are used in the assembly of the transmission oil coolers. They are supposed to be tightened by a torque wrench to 7 foot-pounds with a tolerance of 2 foot-pounds. To test the process, three nuts are tested every three hours. The results for the last 75 hours are stored in file XR21-29. Does it appear that the process is under control?

21.30 Optical scanners are used in all large supermarkets to speed the checkout process. Whenever the scanner fails to read the bar code on the product, the cashier is required to manually punch the code into the register. Obviously, unreadable bar codes slow the checkout process. Statistical process control is used to determine whether the scanner is working properly. Once a day at each checkout counter, a sample of 500 scans is taken and the number of times the scanner is unable to read the bar code is determined. (The sampling process is performed automatically by the cash register.) The results for one checkout counter for the past 25 days are stored in file XR21-30.

a Draw the appropriate control chart(s).

b Does it appear that the process went out of control? If so, identify when this happened and suggest several possible explanations for the cause.

21.31 Almost all computer hardware and software producers offer a toll-free telephone number to solve problems associated with their product. The ability to work quickly to resolve difficulties is critical. One software maker's policy is that all calls must be answered by a software consultant within 120 seconds. (All calls are initially answered by computer and the caller is put on hold until a consultant attends to the caller.) To help maintain the quality of the service, four calls per day are monitored. The amount of time before the consul-

tant responds to the caller is recorded. The record of the last 30 days is stored in file XR21-31.

a Draw the appropriate control chart(s).

b Does it appear that the process went out of control? If so, when did this happen, and what are the likely causes and remedies?

21.32 Motor oil is packaged and sold in plastic bottles. The bottles are often handled quite roughly, either in delivery to the stores (bottles are packed in boxes, which are stacked to conserve truck space), in the stores themselves, or by the consumer. The bottles must be hardy enough to withstand this treatment without leaking. Before leaving the plant, the bottles undergo statistical process control procedures. Five out of every 10,000 bottles are sampled. The burst strength (the pressure required to burst the bottle) is measured in pounds per square inch (psi). The process is designed to produce bottles that can withstand up to 800 psi. The burst strengths of the last 30 samples are stored in file XR21-32.

a Draw the appropriate control chart(s).

b Does it appear that the process went out of control? If so, when did this happen, and what are the likely causes and remedies?

Chapter 22

Statistical

Inference:

Conclusion

22.1 Introduction

22.2 Identifying the Correct Technique: Summary of Statistical Inference

22.3 The Last Word

22.1 INTRODUCTION

You now have been introduced to about 35 statistical techniques. If you are like most students, you probably understand statistical inference and are capable of interpreting computer output. However, at this point you may not be confident that you can apply statistical techniques in real life. The main problem is that it is difficult to ascertain which statistical procedure to apply. In this chapter, we attempt to calm your fears. We begin by displaying the flowchart that allows statisticians to determine the appropriate technique to apply. As we did in Chapter 13, we provide a guide detailing the test statistics, interval estimators, and required conditions. The flowchart is augmented by an Excel macro that performs the same function. It is described on the next page.

The guide and flowchart apply to the procedures presented in Chapters 11 through 19. We have omitted time-series analysis and forecasting (Chapter 20) and statistical process control (Chapter 21) because the use of these techniques tends to be quite obvious and they represent a different kind of inference.

Use the flowchart and guide to determine how each of the exercises and cases is to be addressed. Because these exercises and cases were drawn from a wide variety of applications and require the use of many of the methods introduced in this book, they provide the same kind of challenge faced by real statisticians. By attempting to solve these problems, you will be getting a realistic exposure to statistical applications. Incidentally, this also provides practice in the approach required to succeed in a statistics course examination.

22.2 IDENTIFYING THE CORRECT TECHNIQUE: SUMMARY OF STATISTICAL INFERENCE

A list of the inferential techniques that are applied in describing populations, comparing populations, and analyzing relationships among variables follows. We have not included the two tests for normality (Lilliefors and chi-squared test) and Bartlett's test. All three are investigative statistical procedures employed to help identify the statistical method to use to solve a problem or to check a required condition.

LIST OF STATISTICAL METHODS INTRODUCED IN CHAPTERS 11–19

t-Test and estimator of μ

Chi-squared-test and estimator of σ^2

z-Test and estimator of p

t-Test and estimator of $\mu_1 - \mu_2$ (equal-variances formulas)

t-Test and estimator of $\mu_1 - \mu_2$ (unequal-variances formulas)

t-Test and estimator of μ_D

F-test and estimator of σ_1^2/σ_2^2

z-Test (cases 1 and 2) and estimator of $p_1 - p_2$

Wilcoxon rank sum test for independent samples

Sign test

Wilcoxon signed rank sum test for matched pairs

F-test of the analysis of variance: independent samples

F-tests of the analysis of variance: independent samples—two factors

F-tests of the analysis of variance: randomized blocks

LSD multiple comparison method

Tukey's multiple comparison method

Kruskal–Wallis test

Friedman test

Chi-squared goodness-of-fit test

Chi-squared test of a contingency table

Simple linear regression and correlation

Spearman rank correlation

Multiple regression

The following techniques were introduced in Chapters 20 and 21. These techniques are used in analyzing and forecasting time series and production processes.

Time-series analysis and forecasting

Moving averages

Exponential smoothing

Trend analysis

Measuring cyclical effects

Measuring seasonal effects

Statistical process control

Control charts for variables

Control charts for attributes

Figure 22.1 depicts the flowchart used to identify which technique to employ to solve any problem where we must draw an inference about a population from a sample (except for investigative techniques, time-series analysis, forecasting, and statistical process control). All techniques introduced in Chapters 11 through 19 are shown here and in Table 22.1.

We have also created an Excel macro that asks the questions that appear in the flowchart. When you supply the answers, Excel identifies the technique. Simply click **Tools, Data Analysis Plus,** and **Technique Identification** and follow instructions.

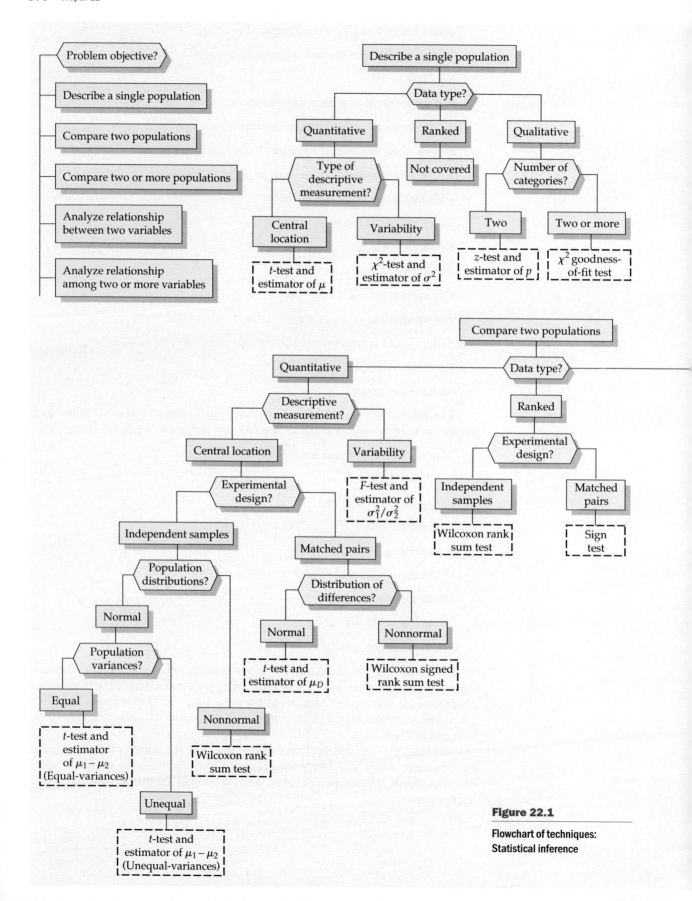

Figure 22.1

Flowchart of techniques:
Statistical inference

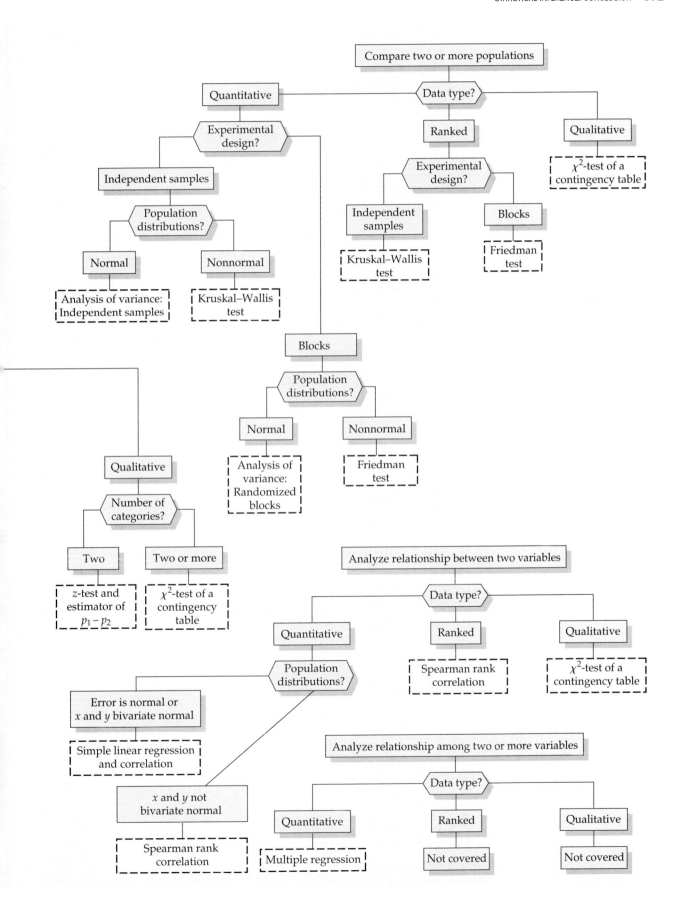

Table 22.1   Summary of Statistical Inference Techniques: Chapters 11 through 19

Problem objective: Describe a single population.
Data type: Quantitative
Descriptive measurement: Central location
Parameter: μ

Test statistic: $t = \dfrac{\bar{x} - \mu}{s/\sqrt{n}}$

Interval Estimator: $\bar{x} \pm t_{\alpha/2}\dfrac{s}{\sqrt{n}}$

Required condition: Population is normal.
Descriptive measurement: Variability
Parameter: σ^2

Test statistic: $\chi^2 = \dfrac{(n-1)s^2}{\sigma^2}$

Interval estimator: LCL $= \dfrac{(n-1)s^2}{\chi^2_{\alpha/2}}$ UCL $= \dfrac{(n-1)s^2}{\chi^2_{1-\alpha/2}}$

Required condition: Population is normal.
Data type: Qualitative
Number of categories: Two
Parameter: p

Test statistic: $z = \dfrac{\hat{p} - p}{\sqrt{p(1-p)/n}}$

Interval estimator: $\hat{p} \pm z_{\alpha/2}\sqrt{\dfrac{\hat{p}(1-\hat{p})}{n}}$

Required condition: $np \geq 5$ and $n(1-p) \geq 5$ (for test)
$n\hat{p} \geq 5$ and $n(1-\hat{p}) \geq 5$ (for estimate)
Number of categories: Two or more
Parameters: $p_1, p_2, \ldots, p_k$

Test statistic: $\chi^2 = \displaystyle\sum_{i=1}^{k} \dfrac{(f_i - e_i)^2}{e_i}$

Required condition: $e_i \geq 5$
Problem objective: Compare two populations.
Data type: Quantitative
Descriptive measurement: Central location
Experimental design: Independent samples
Population variances: $\sigma_1^2 = \sigma_2^2$
Parameter: $\mu_1 - \mu_2$

Test statistic: $t = \dfrac{(\bar{x}_1 - \bar{x}_2) - (\mu_1 - \mu_2)}{\sqrt{s_p^2\left(\dfrac{1}{n_1} + \dfrac{1}{n_2}\right)}}$

Interval estimator: $(\bar{x}_1 - \bar{x}_2) \pm t_{\alpha/2}\sqrt{s_p^2\left(\dfrac{1}{n_1} + \dfrac{1}{n_2}\right)}$

Required condition: Populations are normal.
If populations are nonnormal, apply Wilcoxon rank sum test for independent samples.
Population variances: $\sigma_1^2 \neq \sigma_2^2$
Parameter: $\mu_1 - \mu_2$

Test statistic: $t = \dfrac{(\bar{x}_1 - \bar{x}_2) - (\mu_1 - \mu_2)}{\sqrt{\dfrac{s_1^2}{n_1} + \dfrac{s_2^2}{n_2}}}$

d.f. $= \dfrac{(s_1^2/n_1 + s_2^2/n_2)^2}{\left(\dfrac{(s_1^2/n_1)^2}{n_1 - 1} + \dfrac{(s_2^2/n_2)^2}{n_2 - 1}\right)}$

Interval estimator: $(\bar{x}_1 - \bar{x}_2) \pm t_{\alpha/2}\sqrt{\dfrac{s_1^2}{n_1} + \dfrac{s_2^2}{n_2}}$

Required condition: Populations are normal.
Experimental design: Matched pairs
Parameter: μ_D

Test statistic: $t = \dfrac{\bar{x}_D - \mu_D}{s_D/\sqrt{n_D}}$

Interval estimator: $\bar{x}_D \pm t_{\alpha/2}\dfrac{s_D}{\sqrt{n_D}}$

Required condition: Differences are normal.

If differences are nonnormal, apply Wilcoxon signed rank sum test for matched pairs.

Nonparametric technique: Wilcoxon signed rank sum test for matched pairs.

Test statistic: $z = \dfrac{T - E(T)}{\sigma_T}$

Required condition: Populations are identical in shape and spread.

Descriptive measurement: Variability

Parameter: σ_1^2/σ_2^2

Test statistic: $F = s_1^2/s_2^2$

Interval estimator: $\text{LCL} = \left(\dfrac{s_1^2}{s_2^2}\right)\dfrac{1}{F_{\alpha/2,\nu_1\nu_2}}$ $\text{UCL} = \left(\dfrac{s_1^2}{s_2^2}\right)F_{\alpha/2,\nu_2\nu_1}$

Required condition: Populations are normal.

Data type: Ranked

Experimental design: Independent samples

Nonparametric technique: Wilcoxon rank sum test for independent samples

Test statistic: $z = \dfrac{T - E(T)}{\sigma_T}$

Required condition: Populations are identical in shape and spread.

Experimental design: Matched pairs

Nonparametric technique: Sign test

Test statistic: $z = \dfrac{x - .5n}{.5\sqrt{n}}$

Required condition: Populations are identical in shape and spread.

Data type: Qualitative

Number of categories: Two

Parameter: $p_1 - p_2$

Test statistic:

Case 1: $H_0: (p_1 - p_2) = 0$

$z = \dfrac{(\hat{p}_1 - \hat{p}_2)}{\sqrt{\hat{p}(1 - \hat{p})\left(\dfrac{1}{n_1} + \dfrac{1}{n_2}\right)}}$

Case 2: $H_0: (p_1 - p_2) = D$ $(D \neq 0)$

$z = \dfrac{(\hat{p}_1 - \hat{p}_2) - (p_1 - p_2)}{\sqrt{\dfrac{\hat{p}_1(1 - \hat{p}_1)}{n_1} + \dfrac{\hat{p}_2(1 - \hat{p}_2)}{n_2}}}$

Interval estimator: $(\hat{p}_1 - \hat{p}_2) \pm z_{\alpha/2}\sqrt{\dfrac{\hat{p}(1 - \hat{p}_1)}{n_1} + \dfrac{\hat{p}_2(1 - \hat{p}_2)}{n_2}}$

Required conditions: $n_1\hat{p}_1$, $n_1(1 - \hat{p}_1)$, $n_2\hat{p}_2$, and $n_2(1 - \hat{p}_2) \geq 5$

Number of categories: Two or more

Statistical technique: Chi-squared test of a contingency table

Test statistic: $\chi^2 = \displaystyle\sum_{i=1}^{k} \dfrac{(f_i - e_i)^2}{e_i}$

Required condition: $e_i \geq 5$

Problem objective: Compare two or more populations.

Data type: Quantitative

Experimental design: Independent samples (1 and 2 factors)

Parameters: $\mu_1, \mu_2, \ldots, \mu_k$

Test statistic: $F = \dfrac{\text{MST}}{\text{MSE}}$

Required conditions: Populations are normal with equal variances. If populations are nonnormal, apply Kruskal–Wallis test.

Experimental design: Randomized blocks

Parameters: $\mu_1, \mu_2, \ldots, \mu_k$

Test statistic: $F = \dfrac{\text{MST}}{\text{MSE}}$

Required conditions: Populations are normal with equal variances. If populations are nonnormal, apply Friedman test.

Data type: Ranked

    Experimental design: Independent samples

    Nonparametric technique: Kruskal–Wallis test

    Test statistic: $H = \left[\dfrac{12}{n(n+1)} \sum_{j=1}^{k} \dfrac{T_j^2}{n_j} \right] - 3(n+1)$

    Required condition: Populations are identical in shape and spread and $n_j \geq 5$.

    Experimental design: Randomized blocks

    Nonparametric technique: Friedman Test

    Test statistic: $F_r = \left[\dfrac{12}{b(k)(k+1)} \sum_{j=1}^{k} T_j^2 \right] - 3b(k+1)$

    Required condition: Populations are identical in shape and spread and b or $k \geq 5$.

Data type: Qualitative

    Statistical technique: Chi-squared test of a contingency table

    Test statistic: $\chi^2 = \sum_{i=1}^{k} \dfrac{(f_i - e_i)^2}{e_i}$

    Required condition: $e_i \geq 5$

Problem objective: Analyze the relationship between two variables.

Data type: Quantitative

    Parameters: β_0, β_1 (simple linear regression)

    Test statistic: $t = \dfrac{b_1 - \beta_1}{s_{b_1}}$

    Interval estimator: $\hat{y} \pm t_{\alpha/2}\, s_\epsilon \sqrt{\dfrac{1}{n} + \dfrac{(x_g - \bar{x})^2}{(n-1)s_x^2}}$

    Prediction interval: $\hat{y} \pm t_{\alpha/2}\, s_\epsilon \sqrt{1 + \dfrac{1}{n} + \dfrac{(x_g - \bar{x})^2}{(n-1)s_x^2}}$

    Required conditions: ϵ is normally distributed with mean zero and standard deviation σ_ϵ; ϵ values are independent.

    To test whether two bivariate normally distributed variables are linearly related:

    Parameter: ρ

    Test statistic: $t = r\sqrt{\dfrac{(n-2)}{1-r^2}}$

    If x and y are not bivariate normally distributed, apply Spearman rank correlation coefficient test.

Data type: Ranked

    Statistical technique: Spearman rank correlation coefficient test

    Parameter: ρ_s

    Test statistic: $z = r_s\sqrt{n-1}$

    Required condition: none

Data type: Qualitative

    Statistical technique: Chi-squared test of a contingency table

    Test statistic: $\chi^2 = \sum_{i=1}^{k} \dfrac{(f_i - e_i)^2}{e_i}$

    Required condition: $e_i \geq 5$

Problem objective: Analyze the relationship among two or more variables.

Data type: Quantitative

    β_0, β_1, β_2, ... , β_k (multiple regression)

    Test statistics: $t = \dfrac{b_i - \beta_i}{s_{b_i}}$ $(i = 1, 2, \ldots, k)$

    $F = \dfrac{\text{MSR}}{\text{MSE}}$

    Required conditions: ϵ is normally distributed with mean zero and standard deviation σ_ϵ; ϵ values are independent.

We illustrate the use of the guide and flowchart with the following cases.

CASE 22.1   Do Banks Discriminate Against Women Business Owners?—1*

Increasingly, more women are becoming owners of small businesses. However, questions concerning how they are treated by banks and other financial institutions have been raised by women's groups. Banks are particularly important to small businesses, since studies show that bank financing represents about one-quarter of total debt, and that for medium-sized businesses the proportion rises to approximately one-half. If women's requests for loans are rejected more frequently than are men's requests, or if women must pay higher interest charges than men do, women have cause for complaint. Banks might then be subject to criminal as well as civil suits. To examine this issue, a research project was launched.

The researchers surveyed a total of 1,165 business owners, of which 115 were women. The percentage of women in the sample, 9.9%, compares favorably with other sources that indicate that women own about 10% of established small businesses. The survey asked a series of questions to men and women business owners who applied for loans during the previous month. It also determined the nature of the business, its size, and its age. Additionally, the owners were asked about their experiences in dealing with banks. The questions asked in the survey included the following.

1 What is the gender of the owner?

   1 female   2 male

2 Was the loan approved?

   1 no   2 yes

3 If it was approved, what interest rate did you get? (How much above the prime rate was your rate?)

Of the 115 women who asked for a loan, 14 were turned down. A total of 98 men who asked for a loan were rejected. The rates above prime for all loans that were granted were recorded. These data are stored in columns 1 (rates paid by women) and 2 (rates paid by men) in file C22-01.

What do these data disclose about possible gender bias by the banks?

Solution

IDENTIFY

The problem objective is to compare two populations: small businesses owned by women and by men. We can compare them in two ways: whether their loan applications are denied; and for loans granted, how much above prime they pay in interest. Whether the loans are approved is a qualitative variable. There are two possible "values" of this variable: "approve the loan" and "don't approve the loan." The appropriate technique is the z-test of $p_1 - p_2$.

To test whether gender bias exists, we test to determine if the proportions of loans denied is greater for women (p_1) than for men (p_2).

$$H_0: p_1 - p_2 = 0$$
$$H_1: p_1 - p_2 > 0$$

This is an application of the Case 1 test procedure. Thus, the test statistic is

$$z = \frac{(\hat{p}_1 - \hat{p}_2)}{\sqrt{\hat{p}(1 - \hat{p})\left(\dfrac{1}{n} + \dfrac{1}{n_2}\right)}}$$

Both Excel and Minitab can calculate this statistic from the number of loans denied and the sample sizes.

*Adapted from A. L. Riding and C. S. Swift, "Giving Credit Where It's Due: Women Business Owners and Canadian Financial Institutions," Carleton University Working Paper Series WPS 89-07, 1989.

**Excel Output of the
Difference Between
Two Proportions**

	A	B	C	D	E	F
1	z-Test of the Difference Between Two Proportions (Case 1)					
2						
3	Sample 1					
4	Sample proportion	0.1217				
5	Sample size	115				
6						
7	Sample 2					
8	Sample proportion	0.0933				
9	Sample size	1050				
10						
11	z Stat	0.9810				
12	Two-tail p-value	0.3266				

The one-tail p-value is .3266/2 = .1633.

**Minitab Output of the
Difference Between
Two Proportions**

```
Sample        X         N     Sample P
1            14        115    0.121739
2            98       1050    0.093333

Estimate for p(1) - p(2):  0.0284058
95% CI for p(1) - p(2):  (-0.0338927, 0.0907043)
Test for p(1) - p(2) = 0 (vs > 0):  Z = 0.98  P-Value = 0.163
```

The interest rate is a quantitative variable, the descriptive measurement is central location, and the samples are independent. A preliminary analysis reveals that the amount above prime may be normally distributed. The histograms (shown below) are bell-shaped. Moreover, both the Lilliefors test and the chi-squared test for normality (not shown) can be interpreted to not reject the hypothesis of normality. The F-test of $\sigma_1^2 \neq \sigma_2^2$ (shown on p. 878) indicates that there is not enough evidence to believe that the population variances are unequal. Putting all these factors together gives us the equal-variances t-test of $\mu_1 - \mu_2$.

**Excel Histogram of
Points Above Prime:
Women's Loans**

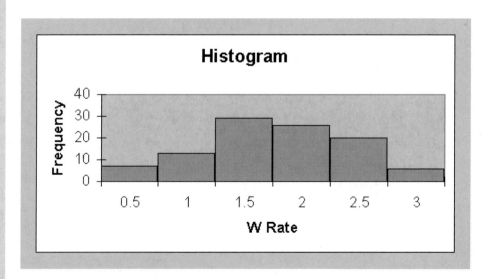

Excel Histogram of Points Above Prime: Men's Loans

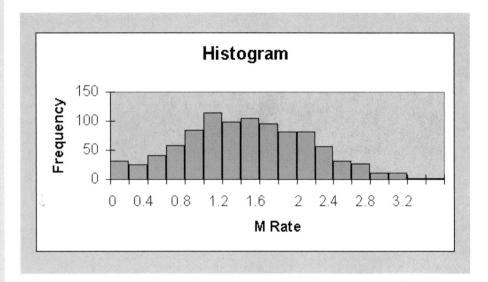

Minitab Histogram of Points Above Prime: Women's Loans

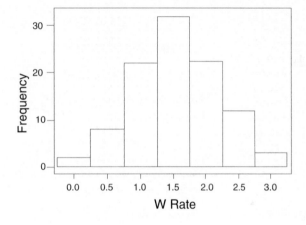

Minitab Histogram of Points Above Prime: Men's Loans

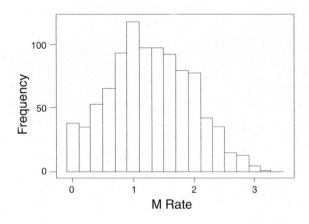

Excel Output of *F*-Test of the Ratio of Two Variances: Points Above Prime of Women's and Men's Loans

	A	B	C
1	F-Test Two-Sample for Variances		
2			
3		W Rate	M Rate
4	Mean	1.545	1.278
5	Variance	0.405	0.446
6	Observations	101	952
7	df	100	951
8	F	0.91	
9	P(F<=f) one-tail	0.28	
10	F Critical one-tail	0.7713	

The two-tail *p*-value is 2 × .2784 = .5568.

Minitab Output of *F*-Test of the Ratio of Two Variances: Points Above Prime of Women's and Men's Loans

Homogeneity of Variance

```
F-Test (normal distribution)

Test Statistic:  1.099
P-Value       :  0.557
```

For loans granted, we need to know whether there is evidence that women's rates (μ_1) are greater than men's rates (μ_2).

$H_0: \mu_1 - \mu_2 = 0$

$H_1: \mu_1 - \mu_2 > 0$

The test statistic is

$$t = \frac{(\bar{x}_1 - \bar{x}_2) - (\mu_1 - \mu_2)}{\sqrt{s_p^2\left(\frac{1}{n_1} + \frac{1}{n_2}\right)}}$$

We employ our software packages to produce the following printouts.

SOLVE

Excel Output for the Test of the Difference between Two Means: Points Above Prime

	A	B	C
1	t-Test: Two-Sample Assuming Equal Variances		
2			
3		W Rate	M Rate
4	Mean	1.55	1.28
5	Variance	0.405	0.446
6	Observations	101	952
7	Pooled Variance	0.442	
8	Hypothesized Mean Difference	0	
9	df	1051	
10	t Stat	3.85	
11	P(T<=t) one-tail	0.0001	
12	t Critical one-tail	1.646	
13	P(T<=t) two-tail	0.0001	
14	t Critical two-tail	1.962	

Minitab Output for the Test of the Difference between Two Means: Points Above Prime

Two Sample T-Test and Confidence Interval

```
Two sample T for W Rate vs M Rate

              N      Mean     StDev    SE Mean
W Rate      101     1.545     0.637     0.063
M Rate      952     1.278     0.668     0.022


95% CI for mu W Rate - mu M Rate: ( 0.131,  0.404)
T-Test mu W Rate = mu M Rate (vs >) : T = 3.85   P = 0.0001 DF = 1051
Both use pooled StDev = 0.665
```

INTERPRET

There is not enough evidence to show that women's loan requests are denied more frequently than men's. However, there is overwhelming evidence to infer that the mean rate of women's loans is greater than that for men. There appears to be evidence of gender bias by banks.

CASE 22.2   **Do Banks Discriminate Against Women Business Owners?—II***

To help explain the apparent discrimination against women documented in Case 22.1, researchers performed further analyses. In the original study, the following pieces of information were gathered for each company.

1 form of business:

   a proprietorship

   b partnership

   c corporation

---

*Adapted from A. L. Riding and C. S. Swift, "Giving Credit Where It's Due: Women Business Owners and Canadian Financial Institutions," Carleton University Working Paper Series WPS 89-07, 1989.

2 annual gross sales

3 age of the firm

These data, together with the data from Case 22.1, are stored in file C22-02 in the following way.

Column 1: Rates above prime paid by women

Column 2: Type of women's business (1 = proprietorship; 2 = partnership; 3 = corporation)

Column 3: Annual gross sales of women's businesses (in thousands of dollars)

Column 4: Age of women's businesses

Column 5: Rates above prime paid by men

Column 6: Type of men's business (1 = proprietorship; 2 = partnership; 3 = corporation)

Column 7: Annual gross sales of men's businesses (in thousands of dollars)

Column 8: Age of men's businesses

What do these data tell you about the alleged discrimination against women by banks?

Solution

We are looking for additional reasons to account for the results obtained from Case 22.1. Specifically, we would like to know whether there is a relationship between annual gross sales and interest rates and between age of firm and interest rates. If there are such relationships, we need to know whether men's businesses are older and have higher gross sales. If so, the apparent gender bias shown in Case 22.1 may be explained by banks' legitimate desire to grant favorable terms to more established businesses with higher sales. We can use the data about the type of business to determine whether banks view certain types of businesses more favorably than others, and if men's businesses tend to be of the types favored by banks. Before we can discuss the consequences of such findings, we need to conduct several tests. We will identify the technique to apply by asking specific questions.

1 Do banks grant lower interest rates to businesses with higher sales?

2 Do banks grant lower interest rates to older businesses?

IDENTIFY

For each question, we wish to analyze the relationship between two quantitative variables. An analysis (not shown) indicates that the data are bivariate normally distributed. Thus, the appropriate technique is simple linear regression and correlation. Because we want to discover whether a relationship exists (and not the mathematical form of the relationship), we will calculate and test the coefficient of correlation. For each pair of variables, we want to know whether the relationship is negative. We test

$H_0: \rho = 0$

$H_1: \rho < 0$

The test statistic is $t = r\sqrt{\dfrac{(n-2)}{1-r^2}}$

The rejection region is $t < -t_{.05,1051} = -1.645$

	A	B	C
1		*Rates*	*Sales*
2	Rates	1	
3	Sales	-0.269966	1

	A	B	C
1		*Rates*	*Age*
2	Rates	1	
3	Age	-0.191472	1

Correlations (Pearson)

Correlation of Rates and Sales = -0.270, P-Value = 0.0000

Correlations (Pearson)

Correlation of Rates and Age = -0.191, P-Value = 0.0000

The values of the test statistics are calculated below.

Interest rates and annual gross sales:

$$\text{Test statistic: } t = r\sqrt{\frac{(n-2)}{1-r^2}} = -.270\sqrt{\frac{(1{,}053-2)}{1-(-.270)^2}} = -9.09$$

Interest rates and age:

$$\text{Test statistic: } t = r\sqrt{\frac{(n-2)}{1-r^2}} = -.191\sqrt{\frac{(1{,}053-2)}{1-(-.191)^2}} = -6.31$$

There is overwhelming statistical evidence to infer that banks grant lower rates to older businesses and business with higher sales.

This result presents two additional questions.

3 Do women's businesses have lower gross sales than men's businesses?

4 Are women's businesses younger than men's businesses?

The problem objective is to compare two populations of quantitative data. Using a similar analysis to that employed in Case 22.1, we discover that the appropriate technique for each question is the t-test of $\mu_1 - \mu_2$. For both questions, we test the following hypotheses (where μ_1 equals the mean (annual gross sales and age) of women's businesses and μ_2 equals the mean (annual gross sales and age) of men's businesses).

$$H_0: \mu_1 - \mu_2 = 0$$
$$H_1: \mu_1 - \mu_2 < 0$$

SOLVE

Excel Output of the Test of the Difference Between Two Means: Sales

	A	B	C
1	t-Test: Two-Sample Assuming Equal Variances		
2			
3		W Sales	M Sales
4	Mean	552	1183
5	Variance	60133	128618
6	Observations	101	952
7	Pooled Variance	122102	
8	Hypothesized Mean Difference	0	
9	df	1051	
10	t Stat	-17.27	
11	P(T<=t) one-tail	0.0000	
12	t Critical one-tail	1.646	
13	P(T<=t) two-tail	0.0000	
14	t Critical two-tail	1.962	

Excel Output of the Test of the Difference Between Two Means: Age

	A	B	C
1	t-Test: Two-Sample Assuming Equal Variances		
2			
3		W Age	M Age
4	Mean	9.24	12.58
5	Variance	15.98	27.05
6	Observations	101	952
7	Pooled Variance	26.00	
8	Hypothesized Mean Difference	0	
9	df	1051	
10	t Stat	-6.261	
11	P(T<=t) one-tail	0.0000	
12	t Critical one-tail	1.646	
13	P(T<=t) two-tail	0.0000	
14	t Critical two-tail	1.962	

Minitab Output of the Test of the Difference Between Two Means: Sales

Two Sample T-Test and Confidence Interval

Two sample T for W Sales vs M Sales

	N	Mean	StDev	SE Mean
W Sales	101	552	245	24
M Sales	952	1183	359	12

95% CI for mu W Sales – mu M Sales: (–703, –560)
T-Test mu W Sales = mu M Sales (vs <): T = –17.27 P = 0.0000 DF = 1051
Both use Pooled StDev = 349

Minitab Output of the Test of the Difference Between Two Means: Age

Two Sample T-Test and Confidence Interval

```
Two sample T for W Age vs M Age

              N      Mean     StDev    SE Mean
W Age        101      9.24     4.00      0.40
M Age        952     12.58     5.20      0.17

95% CI for mu W Age - mu M Age:  ( -4.39,  -2.29)
T-Test mu W Age = mu M Age (vs <) : T = -6.26  P = 0.0000  DF = 1051
Both use Pooled StDev = 5.10
```

INTERPRET

There is very strong statistical evidence to infer that men own businesses that are older than women's and that men's businesses have larger gross sales than women's. This result is not surprising, since only in the last 25 years have women become involved in full-time work in large numbers. Up until about 1975 ownership of businesses had been a male domain. Moreover, more established businesses tend to have higher gross sales.

There is one more factor that may explain the outcome of Case 22.1. It is the type of business.

5 Do the data allow us to infer that certain types of businesses have different rates of interest?

IDENTIFY

There are three populations of quantitative data to compare: interest rates for proprietorships, for partnerships, and for corporations. The appropriate technique is the single-factor independent samples analysis of variance. (We can show that the required conditions are satisfied.)

$H_0: \mu_1 = \mu_2 = \mu_3$

H_1: At least two means differ

SOLVE

Excel Output of the Analysis of Variance of Points Above Prime Among the Three Types of Businesses

	A	B	C	D	E	F
1	Anova: Single Factor					
2						
3	SUMMARY					
4	*Groups*	Count	Sum	Average	Variance	
5	Proprietorship	193	273.4	1.417	0.411	
6	Partnership	86	104.2	1.211	0.467	
7	Corporation	774	994.9	1.285	0.451	
8						
9						
10	ANOVA					
11	*Source of Variation*	SS	df	MS	F	P-value
12	Between Groups	3.455	2	1.728	3.88	0.0209
13	Within Groups	467.4	1050	0.445		
14						
15	Total	470.9	1052			

Minitab Output of the Analysis of Variance of Points Above Prime Among the Three Types of Businesses

One-way Analysis of Variance

```
Analysis of Variance for Rates
Source      DF        SS         MS         F         P
Bus          2      3.455     1.728      3.88     0.021
Error     1050    467.434     0.445
Total     1052    470.889
                                    Individual 95% CIs For Mean
                                    Based on Pooled StDev
Level       N       Mean      StDev    -+---------+---------+---------+-----
1          193    1.4166     0.6415                            (--------*--------)
2           86    1.2114     0.6830    (-----------*-----------)
3          774    1.2853     0.6717                 (---*---)
                                       -+---------+---------+---------+-----
Pooled StDev =  0.6672                1.08      1.20      1.32      1.44
```

INTERPRET

The statistical analysis reveals that there are differences in rates among the three types of businesses.

Finally, we need to know whether men and women own different types of businesses.

6 Is there a relationship between gender and business type?

IDENTIFY

The problem objective is to analyze the relationship between two qualitative variables, gender and business type. The appropriate method is the chi-squared test of a contingency table.

H_0: The two variables are independent

H_1: The two variables are dependent

The test statistic is $\chi^2 = \sum\limits_{i=1}^{k} \dfrac{(f_i - e_i)^2}{e_i}$

SOLVE

Excel Output of the Chi-squared Test of a Contingency Table of Business Type and Gender

	A	B	C	D
1	**Contingency Table**			
2		*1*	*2*	*Total*
3	*1*	31	162	193
4	*2*	10	76	86
5	*3*	60	714	774
6	*Total*	101	952	*1053*
7	*Test Statistic CHI-Squared = 12.7504*			
8	*P-Value = 0.0017*			

Minitab Output of the Chi-squared Test of a Contingency Table of Business Type and Gender

Tabulated Statistics

```
Rows: Bus       Columns: Gender

              1          2        All
1            31        162        193
2            10         76         86
3            60        714        774
All         101        952       1053


Chi-Square = 12.750, DF = 2, P-Value = 0.002


    Cell Contents --
                 Count
```

INTERPRET

There is a relationship between gender and type of business. The proportion of women's businesses in this study is 9.6%. From the contingency table, you can see that the proportion of proprietorships owned by women is $31/193 = 16.1\%$. From the analysis of variance printout, we discover that, on average, proprietorships pay the highest interest rates. Apparently, women own businesses that banks view as riskier, resulting in higher rates of interest.

INTERPRETING THE RESULTS OF CASES 22.1 AND 22.2

Cases 22.1 and 22.2 present statisticians with real challenges. The results of the cases are contradictory. One case presents evidence of bias and the other provides evidence to suggest that the apparent bias is actually attributable to other factors. Results such as these have led less-than-competent observers to state that one can prove anything with statistics. Although there are often several different interpretations of data based on different analyses, we can perform further analyses to arrive at the truth. Consider how we can resolve the apparent contradictions in Cases 22.1 and 22.2. It is necessary to consider carefully which data and techniques we should use. You will encounter our answer eventually.

22.3 THE LAST WORD

We have come to the end of the journey that began with the words "Statistics is a way to get information from data." You will shortly write the final examination in your statistics course. (We assume that readers of this book are taking a statistics course and not just reading it for fun.) If you believe that this event will be the point where you and statistics part company, you could not be more wrong. In the world into which you are about to graduate, the potential applications of statistical techniques are virtually limitless. However, if you are unable or unwilling to employ statistics, you cannot consider yourself to be competent. Can you imagine a marketing manager who does not fully understand marketing concepts and techniques? Can an accountant who knows little about accounting principles do his or her job? Similarly, you cannot be a competent decision maker without a comprehension of statistical concepts and techniques.

In our experience, we have come across far too many people who display an astonishing ignorance of probability and statistics. In some cases, this is displayed in the way they gamble. (Talk to people in a casino in Las Vegas or Atlantic City and discover how many believe in the law of averages; see how many of them lose money.) We have seen managers who regularly make decisions involving millions of dollars who don't understand the fundamental principles that should govern the way decisions are made. The worst may be the managers who have access to vast amounts of information no further away than the nearest computer but don't know how to get it or even that it is there.

This raises the question, "What statistical concepts and techniques will you need for your life after the final exam?" We don't expect students to remember the formulas (or computer commands) that calculate the interval estimates or test statistics. (Statistics reference books are available for that purpose.) However, you must know what you can and cannot do with statistical techniques. You must remember a number of important principles that were covered in this book. To assist you, we have selected the 12 most important concepts and listed them. They are drawn from the "Developing an Understanding of Statistical Concepts" subsections that are scattered throughout the book. We hope that they prove useful to you.

Twelve Statistical Concepts You Need For Life After The Statistics Final Exam

1 Statistical techniques are methods that convert data into information. Descriptive techniques describe and summarize; inferential techniques allow us to make estimates and draw conclusions about populations from samples.

2 We need a large number of techniques because there are numerous objectives and types of data. There are three types of data: quantitative (real numbers), qualitative (categories), and ranked (ratings). Each combination of data type and objective requires specific techniques.

3 We gather data by various sampling plans. However, the validity of any statistical outcome is dependent on the validity of the sampling. "Garbage in/garbage out" very much applies in statistics.

4 The sampling distribution is the source of statistical inference. The interval estimator and the test statistic are derived directly from the sampling distribution. All inferences are actually probability statements based on the sampling distribution.

5 All tests of hypotheses are conducted similarly. We assume that the null hypothesis is true. We then compute the value of the test statistic. If the difference between what we have observed (and calculated) and what we expect to observe is too large, we reject the null hypothesis. The standard that decides what is "too large" is determined by the probability of a Type I error.

6 In any test of hypothesis (and in most decisions) there are two possible errors, Type I and Type II errors. The relationship between the probability of these errors helps us decide where to set the standard. If we set the standard so high that the probability of a Type I error is very small, we increase the probability of a Type II error. A procedure designed to decrease the probability of a Type II error must have a relatively large probability of a Type I error.

7 We can improve the exactitude of an interval estimator or decrease the probability of a Type II error by increasing the sample size. More data means more information, which results in narrower intervals or lower probabilities of making mistakes, which produces better decisions.

8 The sampling distributions that are used for quantitative data are the Student t and the F. These distributions are related so that the various techniques for quantitative data are themselves related. We can use the analysis of variance in place of the t-test of two means. We can use regression analysis with indicator variables in place of the analysis of variance. We often build a model to represent relationships among quantitative variables, including indicator variables.

9 In analyzing quantitative data, we attempt to explain as much of the variation as possible. By doing so, we can learn a great deal about whether populations differ and what variables affect the response (dependent) variable.

10 The techniques used on qualitative data require that we count the number of times each category occurs. The counts are then used to compute statistics. The sampling distributions we use for qualitative data are the z (standard normal) and the chi-squared distributions. These distributions are related, which also describes the relationship among the techniques.

11 The techniques used on ranked data are based on a ranking procedure. Statisticians call these techniques nonparametric. Because the requirements for the use of nonparametric techniques are less than those for a parametric procedure, we often use nonparametric techniques in place of parametric ones when the required conditions for the parametric test are not satisfied. To ensure the validity of a statistical technique, we must check the required conditions.

12 We can obtain data through experimentation or by observation. Observational data lend themselves to several conflicting interpretations. Data gathered by an experiment are more likely to lead to a definitive interpretation. In addition to designing experiments, statisticians can also select particular sample sizes to produce the accuracy and confidence they desire.

We believe that these concepts will serve you well in reading and understanding reports that use statistics. They will also allow you to exploit fully the sets of data that you will encounter in your professional life and apply the appropriate statistical technique that converts the data into information. In so doing, you will be a better decision maker.

EXERCISES

Most of the following exercises require the use of a computer and statistical software. All students should at least attempt to identify the techniques required to answer the questions. Students with the necessary resources should produce the answers and check the required conditions.

22.1 Mutual funds minimize risks by diversifying the investments they make. There are mutual funds that specialize in particular types of investments. For example, the TD Precious Metal Mutual Fund buys shares in gold mining companies. The value of this mutual fund depends on a number of factors related to the companies in which the fund invests as well as on the price of gold. To investigate the relationship between the value of the fund and the price of gold, an M.B.A. student gathered the daily fund price and the daily price of gold for a 28-day period. These data are stored in columns 1 and 2, respectively, of file XR22-01. Can we infer from these data that there is a positive linear relationship between the value of the fund and the price of gold? (*The authors are grateful to Jim Wheat for writing this exercise.*)

22.2 Scientists at the Genetics and IVF Institute, a private fertility center in Virginia, announced the development of a new technique that allows parents to choose the sex of their baby before conception. A group of women who wanted their babies to be female were impregnated using the new technology. Of the 17 resulting babies, 15 were girls. Does this provide sufficient evidence to infer that the new technology does affect the sex of the baby?

22.3 The widespread use of salt on roads in Canada and the northern United States during the winter and acid precipitation throughout the year combine to cause rust on cars. Car manufacturers and other companies offer rust-proofing services to help purchasers preserve the value of their cars. A consumer protection agency decides to determine whether there are any differences between the rust protection provided by automobile manufacturers and that provided by two competing types of rust-proofing services. As an experiment, 60 identical new cars are selected. Of these, 20 are rust-proofed by the manufacturer. Another 20 are rust-proofed using a method that applies a liquid to critical areas of the car. The liquid hardens, forming a (supposedly) lifetime bond with the metal. The last 20 are treated with oil and are re-treated every 12 months. The cars are then driven under similar conditions in a Minnesota city. The number of months until the first rust appears is recorded and stored in columns 1 to 3, respectively, in file XR22-03. Is there sufficient evidence to conclude that at least one rust-proofing method is different from the others?

22.4 In the door-to-door selling of vacuum cleaners, various factors influence sales. The Birk Vacuum Cleaner Company considers its sales pitch and overall package to be extremely important. As a result, it often thinks of new ways to sell its product. Because the company's management dreams up so many new sales pitches each year, there is a two-stage testing process. In stage 1, a new plan is tested with a relatively small sample. If there is sufficient evidence that the plan increases sales, a second, considerably larger, test is undertaken. The statistical test is performed so that there is only a 1% chance of concluding that the new pitch is successful in increasing sales when it actually does not increase sales. In a stage 1 test to determine if the inclusion of a "free" 10-year service contract increases sales, 100 sales representatives were selected at random from the company's list of several thousand. The monthly sales of these representatives were recorded for 1 month prior to use of the new sales pitch and for 1 month after its introduction. The results are stored in file XR22-04. Should the company proceed to stage 2?

22.5 Two drugs are used to treat heart attack victims. Streptokinase, which has been available since 1959, costs about $460. The second drug is t-PA, a genetically engineered product that sells for about $2,900. Both Streptokinase and t-PA work by opening the arteries and dissolving blood clots, which are the cause of heart attacks. Several previous studies have failed to reveal any differences between the effects of the two drugs. Consequently, in many countries where health care is funded by governments, physicians are required to use the less expensive Streptokinase. However, t-PA's maker, Genentech Inc., contended that in the earlier studies showing no difference between the two drugs, their drug was not used in the right way. Genentech decided to sponsor a more thorough experiment. The experiment was organized in 15 countries, including the United States and Canada, and involved a total of 41,000 patients. In this study, t-PA was given to patients in 90 minutes instead of 3 hours as in previous trials. Half of the sample of 41,000 patients were treated by a rapid injection of t-PA with intravenous heparin, while the other half received Streptokinase along with heparin. The number of deaths in each sample was recorded. A total of 1,497 patients treated with Streptokinase died, while 1,292 patients who received t-PA died.

a Can we infer that t-PA is better than Streptokinase in preventing deaths?

b Estimate with 95% confidence the cost per life saved by using t-PA.

22.6 A small but important part of a university library's budget is the amount collected in fines on overdue books. Last year, a library collected $75,652.75 in fine payments; however, the head librarian suspects that some employees are not bothering to collect the fines on overdue books. In an effort to learn more about the situation, she asked a sample of 400 students (out of a total student population of 50,000) how many books they had returned late to the library in the previous 12 months. They were also asked how many days overdue the books had been. The results indicated that the total number of days overdue ranged from 0 to 55 days. The number of days overdue was stored in file XR22-06.

a Estimate with 95% confidence the average number of days overdue for all 50,000 students at the university.

b If the fine is 25 cents per day, estimate the amount that should be collected annually. Should the librarian conclude that not all the fines were collected?

22.7 The practice of therapeutic touch is used in hospitals all over the world and is taught in some medical and nursing schools. In this therapy, trained practitioners manipulate something that they call the "human energy field." The manipulation is carried out without actually touching the patient's body. Practitioners claim that anyone can be trained to feel this energy field. Some researchers say that no reliable evidence exists showing that this technique actually heals patients. James Randi, a professional magician who is also known as a skeptic of some types of alternative medicine, has tried for years to test the practice of therapeutic touch. So far, only one practitioner has agreed to submit to his test, and she did no better than chance in detecting the energy field. Emily Rosa, an 11-year-old Colorado girl working on a science fair project was more successful in recruiting trained therapists. For her experiment, Emily placed a screen between a practitioner's eyes and hands, and then held her own hand over one of the practitioner's hands. If the human energy field can be felt, then practitioners should be able to identify which of their hands Emily held hers over. Emily conducted 280 tests with the 21 subjects. The results of these tests are stored in file XR22-07 where 2 = correct location and 1 = incorrect location. What can we infer about touch therapy from these data?

22.8 Alcohol abuse is a serious problem in this country. To examine whether age is a factor in determining who drinks alcohol, the Gallup organization polled 1,054 adults and asked each, "Do you ever use alcoholic beverages such as liquor, wine, or beer?" Respondents were also asked to report their age category. The data are stored in file XR22-08. (Column 1 records age category: 1 = 18–29, 2 = 30–49, 3 = 50 and over; column 2 records whether the person uses alcohol: 2 = yes and 1 = no.) Can we infer that differences exist among the age categories with respect to alcohol use?

22.9 Despite the increase in the number of working women, it appears that women continue to perform most of the household functions such as cooking and cleaning. Two researchers from the University of Arizona undertook a study to examine how much housework teenagers are performing. The researchers were particularly interested in the differences between boys and girls and between the children of parents where the mother did not go out to work and where both parents worked outside the home. A random sample of teenagers was selected. Each teenager reported the number of hours of housework he or she performs in an average week (column 1) their gender (column 2: 1 = female and 2 = male), and whether the mother works inside or outside the home (column 3: 1 = inside and 2 = outside).

a Can we conclude that teenage girls do more housework than teenage boys?

b Can we infer that children whose mothers work outside the home do more housework than children whose mothers work inside the home?

22.10 One of the ways in which advertisers measure the value of television commercials is by telephone surveys conducted shortly after commercials are aired. Respondents who watched a certain television station at a given time period during the commercial appeared are asked if they can recall the name of the product in the commercial. Suppose an advertiser wants to compare the recall proportions of two commercials. The first commercial is relatively inexpensive. A second commercial shown a week later is quite expensive to produce. The advertiser decides that the second com-

mercial is viable only if its recall proportion is more than 15% higher than the recall proportion of the first commercial. Two surveys of 500 television viewers each were conducted after each commercial was aired. Each person was asked whether he or she remembered the product name. The results are stored in columns 1 (commercial 1) and 2 (commercial 2) (2 = remembered the product name and 1 = did not remember the product name) in file XR22-10. Can we infer that the second commercial is viable?

22.11 A professor has noted that the exam results of students who write their exams at 1:00 appear to be better than the marks of students who write their exams at 4:00. He forms the belief that the difference is caused by energy levels that are affected by the timing of the most recent meal. In other words, eating a meal before the exam will produce higher grades. To test this belief, he randomly selects 100 students to write a test at 12:30. Half the class is provided lunch and the other half are deprived of lunch. The test scores are recorded in columns 1 (test score of those who had lunch) and 2 (test scores of those with no lunch) in file XR22-11. Do the data support the professor's belief?

22.12 Refer to Exercise 22.11. The professor would like to know whether the type of meal affects test scores. He randomly selects 200 students; 50 are fed a lunch of pizza, another are fed tuna sandwiches, another 50 are fed hamburgers, and the remaining 50 eat a salad for lunch. The test scores are stored on columns 1 through 4, respectively in file XR22-12. Do these data indicate that the type of meal affects test scores?

22.13 How consistent are professional athletes? Do they perform at about the same level year-in and year-out, or do they have great seasons interspersed with bad ones? To answer these questions for hockey players, an M.B.A. student randomly selected 50 National Hockey League players who played in the 1992–1993 and 1993–1994 seasons. For each player, he recorded the average points per game and their plus/minus scores. (Plus/minus scores measure the number of goals their teams score minus the number of goals the opposing team scores while that player is on the ice.) These data are stored in file XR22-13 in the following way.

Column 1: Player

Column 2: 1993–1994 points per game

Column 3: 1992–1993 points per game

Column 4: 1993–1994 plus/minus

Column 5: 1992–1993 plus/minus

Can we conclude from these data that players are inconsistent from one year to the next in terms of points per game and their plus/minus ratio? *(The authors are grateful to Gordon Barnett for writing this exercise.)*

22.14 Professional athletes in North America are paid very well for their ability to play games that amateurs play for fun. To determine the factors that influence a team to pay a hockey player's salary, an M.B.A. student randomly selected 50 hockey players who played in the 1992–1993 and 1993–1994 seasons. He recorded their salaries at the end of the 1993–1994 season as well as a number of performance measures in the previous two seasons. The following data were recorded in file XR22-14.

>   Columns 1 and 2: Games played in 1992–1993 and 1993–1994
>
>   Columns 3 and 4: Goals scored in 1992–1993 and 1993–1994
>
>   Columns 5 and 6: Assists recorded in 1992–1993 and 1993–1994
>
>   Columns 7 and 8: Plus/minus score in 1992–1993 and 1993–1994
>
>   Columns 9 and 10: Penalty minutes served in 1992–1993 and 1993–1994
>
>   Column 11: Salary in U.S. Dollars

(Plus/minus is the number of goals scored by his team minus the number of goals scored by the opposing team while the player is on the ice.)

Develop a model that analyzes the relationship between salary and the performance measures. Describe your findings. *(The authors wish to thank Gordon Barnett for writing this exercise.)*

22.15 Winter is the influenza season in North America. Each winter thousands of elderly and sick people die from the flu and its attendant complications. Consequently, many elderly people receive flu shots in the fall. It has generally been accepted that young healthy North Americans need not receive flu shots because although many contract the disease, few die from it. However, there are economic consequences. Sick days cost both the employee and employer. A study published in the *New England Journal of Medicine* reported the results of an experiment to determine whether it is useful for young healthy people to take flu shots. A random sample of working adults was selected. Half received a flu shot in November; the other half received a placebo. The number of sick days over the next 6-month period were recorded in columns 1 (flu shot) and 2 (placebo). Columns 3 (flu shot) and 4 (placebo) contain the number of visits to the doctor. All the data are in file XR22-15.

a Can we conclude that the number of sick days is less for those who take flu shots?

b Can we conclude that those who take flu shots visit their doctors less frequently?

22.16 Sales of a product may depend on its placement in a store. Cigarette manufacturers frequently offer discounts to retailers who display their products more prominently than competing brands. To examine this phenomenon more carefully, a cigarette manufacturer (with the assistance of a national chain of restaurants) planned the following experiment. In 20 restaurants, the manufacturer's brand was displayed behind the cashier's counter with all the other brands (this was called position 1). In another 20 restaurants, the brand was placed separately but close to the other brands (position 2). In a third group of 20 restaurants, the cigarettes were placed in a special display next to the cash register (position 3). The number of cartons sold during 1 week at each restaurant was recorded and is stored in columns 1, 2, and 3, respectively, in file XR22-16. Is there sufficient evidence to infer that sales of cigarettes differ according to placement? Comment on the policy of offering discounts to the retailer for displaying their product more prominently.

22.17 After a recent study, researchers reported on the effects of folic acid on the occurrence of spina bifida—a birth defect in which there is incomplete formation of the spine. A sample of 2,000 women who gave birth to children with spina bifida was recruited. Prior to attempting to get pregnant again, half the sample were given regular doses of folic acid, and the other half were given a placebo. After 18 months, there were 1,209 births. The number of births and the number of children born with spina bifida are shown. Determine whether we can infer that folic acid reduces the incidence of spina bifida?

	Group taking folic acid	Group taking placebos
Number of births	597	612
Number of children born with spina bifida	6	21

22.18 The image of the U.S. Postal Service has suffered in recent years. One reason may be the perception that postal workers are rude in their dealings with the public. In an effort to improve its image, the Postal Service is contemplating the introduction of public relations seminars for all of its inside workers. Because of the substantial costs involved, the Postal Service decided to institute the seminars only if there is more than a 25% reduction in the number of written customer complaints about personnel who took the seminars. As a trial, the employees of 30 large postal centers attended the seminar. The monthly average number of complaints per center (for all centers) was 640 before the trial. The number of complaints in the 30 centers is stored in file XR22-18. Can we conclude that the seminars should be instituted?

22.19 Discrimination in hiring has been illegal for a number of years. It is illegal to discriminate against any person on the basis of race, sex, or religion. It is also illegal to discriminate because of a person's handicap if it in no way prevents that person from performing that job. In recent years, the definition of "handicap" has widened. Several people have successfully sued companies because they were denied employment for no other reason than that the applicant was overweight. A study was conducted to examine attitudes toward overweight people. The experiment involved showing a number of subjects a videotape of an applicant being interviewed for a job. Prior to the interview, the subject was given a description of the job. Following the interview, the subject was asked to score the applicant in terms of how well the applicant was suited for the job. The score was out of 100, where higher scores described greater suitability. The same procedure was repeated for each subject. However, the sex and weight (average and overweight) of the applicant varied. The results are stored in file XR22-19 using the following format.

Column 1: Score for average weight males

Column 2: Score for overweight males

Column 3: Score for average weight females

Column 4: Score for overweight females

Can we infer that differences in scores are affected by gender, weight, or some interaction between gender and weight?

22.20 The Scholastic Aptitude Test (SAT), which is organized by the Educational Testing Service (ETS), is important to high school students seeking admission to colleges and universities throughout the United States. A number of companies offer courses to prepare students for the SAT. The Stanley H. Kaplan Educational Center claims that its students gain on average, more than 110 points by taking its course. ETS, however, insists that preparatory courses can improve a score by no more than 40 points. (The minimum and maximum scores of the SAT are 400 and 1,600, respectively.) Suppose a random sample of 40 students wrote the exam, then took the Kaplan preparatory course, and then wrote the exam again. The results of both tests are stored in columns 1 (after Kaplan) and 2 (before Kaplan) of file XR22-20.

a Do these data provide sufficient evidence to refute the ETS claim?

b Do these data provide sufficient evidence to refute Kaplan's claim?

22.21 It is generally believed that salespeople who are paid on a commission basis outperform salespeople who are paid a fixed salary. Some management consultants argue, however, that in certain industries the fixed-salary salesperson may sell more because the consumer will feel less sales pressure and respond to the salesperson less as an antagonist. In an experiment to study this, a random sample of 180 salespeople from a retail clothing chain was selected. Of these, 90 salespeople were paid a fixed salary, and the remaining 90 were paid a commission on each sale. The total dollar amount of 1 month's sales for each was recorded and stored in columns 1 (fixed salary) and 2 (commission) in file XR22-21. Can we conclude that commission salespeople outperform fixed-salary salespeople?

22.22 Obesity among children in North America is said to be at near-epidemic proportions. Some experts blame television for the problem, citing the statistic that children watch on average about 26 hours per week. During this time, children are not engaged in any physical activity, which results in weight gains. However, the problem may be compounded by a reduction in metabolic rate. In an experiment to address this issue (The study results were published in the February 1993 issue of the medical journal *Pediatrics*.), scientists from Memphis State University and the University of Tennessee at Memphis took a random sample of 223 children aged 8 to 12, 41 of whom were obese. Each child's metabolic rate (the amount of calories burned per hour) was measured while at rest and also measured while the child watched a television program ("The Wonder Years"). The differences between the two rates were recorded and are stored in file XR22-22. (Column 1 contains the numbers representing the decrease in metabolic rate and column 2 codes the children: 1 = obese and 2 = nonobese.)

a Do these data allow us to conclude that there is a decrease in metabolism when children watch television?

b Can we conclude that the decrease in metabolism while watching television is greater among obese children?

22.23 The game of Scrabble is one of the oldest and most popular board games. It is played all over the world and there is even an annual world championship competition. The game is played by forming words and placing them on the board to obtain the maximum number of points. It is generally believed that a large vocabulary is the only skill required to be successful. However, there is a strategic element to the game that suggests that mathematical skills are just as necessary. To determine which skills are most in demand, a statistician recruited a random sample of fourth-year university English and mathematics majors, and asked them to play the game. A total of 500 games were played by different pairs of English and mathematics majors. The scores in each game are stored in file XR22-23 (column 1: English major scores; column 2: Mathematics major scores).

a Can we conclude that mathematics majors win more frequently than do English majors?

b Do these data allow us to infer that scores, obtained by English majors are greater than those for mathematics majors?

c Why are the results of parts (a) and (b) not the same?

(The authors would like to thank Scott Bergen for his assistance in writing this exercise.)

22.24 The cost of workplace injuries is high for the individual worker, the company, and for society. It is in everyone's interests to rehabilitate the injured worker as quickly as possible. A statistician working for an insurance company has investigated the problem. He believes that a major determinant in how quickly a worker returns to his or her job after sustaining an injury is the physical condition. To help determine whether he is on the right track, he organized an experiment. He took a random sample of male and female workers who were injured in the last year. He recorded their gender, their physical condition, and the number of working days until they returned to their job. These data are stored in file XR22-24 in the following way. Columns 1 and 2 store the number of working days until return to work for men and women, respectively. In each column the first 25 observations relate to those who are physically fit, the next 25 rows relate to individuals who are moderately fit, and the last 25 observations are for those who are in poor physical shape. Can we infer that differences in return times are affected by gender, physical fitness, or some interaction between gender and physical fitness?

22.25 Some psychologists believe that there are at least three different personality types: type A is the aggressive workaholic; type B is the relaxed underachiever; type C displays various characteristics of types A and B. The personnel manager of a large insurance company believes that, among life insurance salespersons, there are equal numbers of all three personality types and that their degree of satisfaction and sales ability are not influenced by personality type. In a survey of 150 randomly selected salespersons, she determined the type of personality, measured their job satisfaction on a seven-point scale (where 1 = very dissatisfied and 7 = very satisfied), and determined the total amount of life insurance sold by each during the previous year. The results are stored in file XR22-25 using the following format.

Column 1: Personality type (A = 1; B = 2; C = 3)

Column 2: Job satisfaction

Column 3: Total amount of life insurance sold (in hundreds of thousands of dollars)

Test all three of the personnel manager's beliefs. That is, test to determine whether there is enough evidence to justify the following conclusions.

i The proportions of each personality type are different.

ii The job satisfaction measures for each personality type are different.

iii The life insurance sales for each personality type are different.

22.26 Simco Inc. is a manufacturer that purchased a new piece of equipment designed to reduce costs. After several months of operation, the results were quite unsatisfactory. The operations manager believes that the problem lies with the machine's operators, who were unable to master the required skills. It was decided to establish a training program to upgrade the skills of those workers with the greatest likelihood of success. To do so, the company needed to know which skills are most needed to run the machine. Experts identified six such skills. They are dexterity, attention to detail, teamwork skills, mathematical ability, problem-solving skills, and technical knowledge. To examine the issue, a random sample of workers was drawn. Workers were measured on each of the six skills through a series of paper-and-pencil tests and through supervisor ratings. Additionally, each worker received a score on the quality of his or her actual work on the machine. These data are stored in columns 1 through 7 of file XR22-26. (Columns 1 to 6 are the scores on the skills tests and column 7 stores the quality-of-work scores.) Identify the skills that affect the quality of work. *(We are grateful to Scott Bergen for writing this exercise.)*

22.27 The high cost of medical care makes it imperative that hospitals operate efficiently and effectively. As part of a larger study, patients leaving a hospital were surveyed. They were asked how satisfied they were with the treatment they received. The responses were recorded with a measure of the degree of severity of their illness (as determined by the admitting physician) and the length of stay. These data are recorded in file XR22-27 in the following way.

Column 1: Satisfaction level (1 = very unsatisfied; 2 = somewhat unsatisfied; 3 = neither satisfied nor dissatisfied; 4 = somewhat satisfied; 5 = very satisfied)

Column 2: Severity of illness (1 = least severe and 10 = most severe)

Column 3: Number of days in hospital

a Is the satisfaction level affected by the severity of illness?

b Is the satisfaction level higher for patients who stay for shorter periods of time?

22.28 Since germs have been discovered parents have been telling their children to wash their hands. Common sense tells us that this should help minimize the spread of infectious diseases and lead to better health. A study reported in the *University of California at Berkeley Wellness Letter* (Volume 13, Issue 6, March 1997) may confirm the advice our parents gave us. A study in Michigan tracked a random sample of children some of whom washed their hands four or more times during the school day. The number of sick days due to colds and flu and the number of sick days due to stomach illness were recorded for the past year and stored in file XR22-28. Column 1 contains a code representing whether the child washed his or her hands four or more times per school day (1) or not (2). Column 2 stores the number of sick days due to cold and flu, and column 3 contains the number of sick days due to stomach illness.

a Do these data allow us to infer that a child who washed his or her hands four or more times during the school day will have fewer sick days due to cold and flu than other children?

b Repeat part (a) for sick days due to stomach illness.

22.29 The experiment to determine the effect of taking a preparatory course to improve SAT scores in Exercise 22.20 was criticized by other statisticians. They argued that the first test would provide a valuable learning experience that would produce a higher test score from the second exam even without the preparatory course. Consequently, another experiment was performed. Forty students wrote the SAT without taking any preparatory course. At the next scheduled exam (3 months later), these same students took the exam again (again with no preparatory course). The scores for both exams are stored in columns 1 (first test scores), and 2 (second test scores) in file XR22-29. Can we infer that repeating the SAT produces higher exam scores even without a preparatory course?

22.30 In recent years, North Americans have experienced flooding in various parts of the continent. In an effort to develop flood-forecasting tools, scientists wanted to determine the relationship between river flows and precipitation and evaporation. In one study, scientists gathered annual data for the total discharge of water on the Grand River at Galt, Ontario. They also recorded precipitation (snow and rain) and a measure of potential evaporation (which is a function of temperature, humidity, and wind) for each year between 1914 and 1980 around Galt. These data are stored in columns 1 (potential evaporation), 2 (precipitation in millimeters), and 3 (river flow in cubic decimeters) in file XR22-30. It is generally believed that flow and precipitation should be positively related and flow and potential evaporation should be negatively related. Do the data confirm the scientists' beliefs? (*This exercise*

was prepared by Lynette Snelgrove. The data are from The Impact of Climate Change on the Water in the Grand River Basin, Ontario, *Department of Geography Publication Series No. 40, University of Waterloo.*)

22.31 Betting on the results of National Football League games is a popular North American activity. In many states and provinces, it is legal to do so provided that wagers are made through the government-authorized betting organization. In the province of Ontario, Pro-Line serves that function. Bettors can choose any team on which to wager, and Pro-Line sets the odds, which determine the winning payoffs. It is also possible to bet that in any game a tie will be the result. (A tie is defined as a game in which the winning margin is three or fewer points. A win occurs when the winning margin is greater than three.) To assist bettors, Pro-Line lists the favorite for each game and predicts the point spread between the two teams. To judge how well Pro-Line predicts outcomes, the Creative Statistics Company tracked the results of the 1993 season. It recorded whether a team was favored by three or fewer points (1); 3.5 to 7 points (2); 7.5 to 11 points (3); or 11.5 or more points (4). It also recorded whether the favored team won (1); lost (2); or tied (3). These data are recorded in columns 1 (Pro-Line's predictions) and 2 (game results) in file XR22-31. Can we conclude at the 5% significance level that Pro-Line's forecasts are useful for bettors?

22.32 At the completion of repair work at one of a chain of automotive centers, customers are asked to fill out the following form.

Tell us what you think.

Are you satisfied?	Good	Fair	Poor
1 Quality of work performed			
2 Fairness of price			
3 Explanation of work and guarantee			
4 Checkout process			
5 Will return in future			
6 Comments?			

A random sample of 134 responses was drawn. The results were recorded in file XR22-32. The responses to questions 1 through 4 (1 = poor; 2 = fair; 3 = good) are stored in columns 1 through 4, respectively. Responses to question 5 (2 = yes; 1 = no) are stored in column 5. If a positive comment was made, 1 is recorded in column 6, 2 if a negative comment was made, and 3 if no comment was made.

Can we infer at the 5% significance level that those who say they will return assess each category higher than those who will not return?

22.33 Refer to Exercise 22.32. Is there sufficient evidence at the 5% significance level to infer that those who make positive comments, negative comments, and no comments differ in their assessment of each category?

22.34 Refer to Exercise 22.32. Suppose that 100 responses from each of three stores in the chain are recorded in file XR22-33 using the format below.

>   Columns 1 to 6: Responses to questions 1 to 5 plus comments code
>
>   Column 7: Code representing stores 1, 2, and 3

Can we conclude at the 5% significance level that differences exist among the three stores?

22.35 Several years ago we heard about the "Mommy Track," the phenomenon of women being underpaid in the corporate world because of what is seen as their divided loyalties between home and office. There may also be a "Daddy Differential." The "Daddy Differential" refers to the situation where men whose wives stay at home earn more than men whose wives work. It is argued that the differential occurs because bosses reward their male employees if they come from "traditional families." Linda Stroh of Loyola University of Chicago studied a random sample of 348 male managers employed by 20 Fortune 500 companies. Each manager reported whether his wife stayed at home to care for their children or worked outside the home, and his annual income. The incomes (in thousands of dollars) are stored in file XR22-35. The incomes of the managers whose wives stays at home are stored in column 1. Column 2 contains the incomes of managers whose wives work outside the home.

a Can we conclude at the 5% significance level that men whose wives stay at home earn more than men whose wives work outside the home?

b If your answer in part (a) is affirmative, does this establish a case for discrimination? Can you think of another cause-and-effect scenario? Explain.

22.36 A popular game of chance is craps, which uses two dice. The "shooter" rolls both dice, winning on the first roll if he throws a 7 or 11, and losing if he rolls 2, 3, or 12. If he rolls any other number, he continues to roll the dice until he repeats the number and wins, or throws a 7 and loses. Elementary rules of probability allow even students of probability and statistics to calculate the probability of winning and losing. These probabilities are based on the probability distribution of the total of two fair dice. They are as follows.

Total	2	3	4	5	6	7
Probability	1/36	2/36	3/36	4/36	5/36	6/36

Total	8	9	10	11	12
Probability	5/36	4/36	3/36	2/36	1/36

A professor of statistics suspects that the dice are not fairly balanced and records each of 1,000 throws. These data are stored in file XR22-36.

a Do these data allow us to infer at the 10% significance level that the dice are not fair?

b Can we conclude at the 10% significance level that the dice are set up so that the probability of 7 is less than 6/36?

22.37 A programmer for a small software company has almost completed the company's newest network program. He just finished the user interface and was about to perform a routine backup. As a rule, a backup is performed once a day to guard against power, hardware, or software failure. Once the backup has started, the information is unavailable until the backup is completed. The amount of time that the program takes to complete the backup is critical. For systems that are in constant use, a portion of time must be set aside to back up files, during which work on that system ceases. The company has developed three different systems of backing up files that are basically equivalent in memory usage. However, because time is critical, the company wanted to determine whether differences existed in the amount of time taken for each to work. A programmer randomly selected 26 different programs at random and backed up each of them using the three backing systems. The amount of time taken for each was recorded (in minutes) and stored in columns 1 to 3 of file XR22-37. (The rows represent the 26 different programs.) Can we infer at the 5% significance level that the backup times differ among the three systems? *(The authors are grateful to James Pong and Diana Mansour and the Ortech Company for their assistance in this exercise.)*

22.38 There are enormous differences between health care systems in the United States and Canada. In a study to examine one dimension of these differences, 300 heart attack victims in each country were randomly selected. (Results of the study conducted by Dr. Daniel Mark of Duke University Medical Center, Dr. David Naylor of Sunnybrook Hospital in Toronto, and Dr. Paul Armstrong of the University of Alberta were published in the *Toronto Sun,* 27 October, 1994.) Each patient was asked the following questions regarding the effect of his or her treatment.

1 How many days did it take you to return to work?

2 Do you still have chest pain? (This question was asked 1 month, 6 months, and 12 months after the patients' heart attacks.)

The responses are stored in file XR22-38 in the following way.

>   Column 1: Code representing nationality: 1 = U.S.; 2 = Canada
>
>   Column 2: Responses to question 1
>
>   Column 3: Responses to question 2—1 month after heart attack: 2 = yes; 1 = no

Column 4: Responses to question 2—6 months after heart attack: 2 = yes; 1 = no

Column 5: Responses to question 2—12 months after heart attack: 2 = yes; 1 = no

Can we conclude at the 5% significance level that recovery is faster in the United States?

22.39 As all baseball fans know, first base is the only base that the base runner may overrun. At second and third base the runner may be tagged out if he runs past them. Consequently, on close plays at second and third base, the runner will slide, enabling him to stop at the base. In recent years, however, several players have chosen to slide headfirst when approaching first base, claiming that this is faster than simply running over the base. In an experiment to test this claim, the 25 players on one National League team were recruited. Each player ran to first base with and without sliding, and the times to reach the base were recorded. These data are stored in columns 1 (player), 2 (no slide), and 3 (slide) in file XR22-39. Can we conclude at the 5% significance level that sliding is slower than not sliding?

22.40 Du Pont is always looking for new ways to improve their products and reduce costs. Researchers in the Teflon coatings laboratory recently uncovered a compound that degrades into two potentially salable products, which were labeled C and Y. The research team carried out several experiments to determine the factors that affect the production of C and Y. In particular, they examined how the temperature and flow rate determined the percentage yield of each component. The higher the temperature and flow rate, the more expensive the production becomes. However, this may be offset by greater yields. The experiment used three different flow rates (5, 35, and 80 milliliters per minute) and two temperature (360°C and 400°C). The experiment was repeated several times for each combination of flow rate and temperature. The percentage yields were recorded and stored in file XR22-40 using the following format.

Column 1: Percent yield of C

Column 2: Percent yield of Y

Column 3: Flow rate

Column 4: Temperature

Do the data allow us to conclude at the 5% significance level that for each of C and Y

a flow rate affects yield?

b temperature affects yield?

c particular interactions of flow rate and temperature affect yields?

(The authors are grateful to James Fong and Diana Mansour for creating this exercise.)

22.41 How does mental outlook affect a person's health? The answer to this question may allow physicians to care more effectively for their patients. In an experiment to examine the relationship between attitude and physical health, Dr. Daniel Mark, a heart specialist at Duke University, studied 1,719 men and women who recently had undergone a heart catheterization, a procedure that checks for clogged arteries. Patients undergo this procedure when heart disease results in chest pain. All of the patients in the experiment were in about the same condition. In interviews, 14% of the patients doubted that they would recover sufficiently to resume their daily routines. Dr. Mark identified these individuals as pessimists; the others were (by default) optimists. After 1 year, Dr. Mark recorded how any patients were still alive. The data are stored in columns 1 (1 = optimist, 2 = pessimist) and 2 (2 = alive, 1 = dead) in file XR22-41. Do these data allow us to infer at the 5% significance level that pessimists are less likely to survive than optimists with similar physical ailments?

22.42 Can music make you smarter? If so, which kind of music works best? Two University of California at Irvine professors addressed these questions (as reported on "Dateline" in September 1994). A random sample of 135 students was given tests that measured the ability to reason. One-third of the students was then put in a room where rock and roll music was played. A second group of 45 students was placed in a room and listened to music composed by Mozart. The last group was placed in a room where no music was played. The students then took another test. The differences (second test score minus first test score) were recorded and stored in columns 1 to 3, respectively, in file XR22-42. Can we infer that the type of music affects test results?

22.43 As a follow-up to the experiment described in Exercise 22.42, the students again were placed in their chosen rooms. After leaving their rooms, the students waited 10 minutes before being tested. The differences (third test score minus first test score) were recorded and stored in file XR22-43 (using the same format as in file XR22-42). Does it appear that the effects of the music wear off after 10 minutes?

22.44 A study in the journal *Neurology* reported that ibuprofen (sold commercially as Motrin, Advil, and Nuprin) may slow or even prevent the progression of Alzheimer's disease. The study was based on a sample of 1,500 volunteers of varying ages who kept detailed records of what medications they took. Researchers at the Johns Hopkins School of Public Health noticed that those who had taken ibuprofen for at least 2 years showed a 60% lower risk of getting Alzheimer's. Aspirin had a smaller effect and acetaminophen (the main ingredient in Tylenol) had no effect. Further analysis revealed that almost all of those who taken ibuprofen for at least 2 years did so to relieve the symptoms of arthritis. Assuming that the 60% reduction in the risk of Alzheimer's seen in the sample is statistically significant, can we infer that taking ibuprofen regularly will reduce the incidence of Alzheimer's? Suggest another way to interpret the results that do not lead to the conclusion about the relationship between ibuprofen and Alzheimer's.

22.45 Researchers in both the business world and the academic world often treat college students as representative of the adult population. This practice reduces sampling costs enormously, but its effectiveness is open to question. An experiment was performed to determine the suitability of using student surrogates in research. The study used two groups of people.

1 The first consisted of 60 adults (18 years of age or older) chosen so that they represented by age and occupation the adult population of a Midwestern state.

2 The second consisted of 60 students enrolled in an introductory marketing course at a public university.

The experiment involved showing each group a 60-second television commercial advertising a financial institution. Each respondent was asked to assess the commercial's believability. The responses were recorded as follows.

4 Very believable
3 Somewhat believable
2 Not very believable
1 Not at all believable

These data are stored in columns 1 and 2, respectively in file XR22-45.

a Can we infer that there are differences among the two groups of respondents? Test at the 5% significance level.

b What conclusions can you draw regarding the suitability of using students as surrogates in marketing research?

[Adapted from R. Kesevan, D. G. Anderson, and O. Mascarenhas, "Students as Surrogates in Advertising Research," Developments in Marketing Science, 7 *(1984): 438–41.]*

22.46 The battle between customers and car dealerships is

often intense. Customers want the lowest price and dealers want to extract as much money as possible. One source of conflict is the trade-in car. Most dealers will offer a relatively low trade-in in anticipation of negotiating the final package. In an effort to determine how dealers operate, a consumer organization undertook an experiment. Seventy-two individuals were recruited. Each solicited an offer on "their" 5-year-old Ford Taurus. The exact same car was used throughout the experiment. The only variables were the age and gender of the "owner." The ages were categorized as (1) young, (2) middle, and (3) senior. The cash offers are stored in columns 1 and 2 in file XR22-46. Column 1 stores the data for female owners and column 2 contains the offers made to male owners. The first twelve rows in both columns represent the offers made to young people, the next twelve rows represent the middle group, and the last twelve rows represent the elderly owners.

Do the data allow us to conclude that either age, gender, or some interaction affects offers?

22.47 After studying the results of the analyses performed in Cases 18.2 and 18.3 a statistician observed that one needed to determine the amount of increase or decrease in the percentage of rejected ballots between the referendum and the 1994 provincial election, and how the change relates to whether the majority voted "Yes" or "No." Accordingly, the statistician recorded the percentage of rejected ballots in the referendum, the percentage of rejected ballots in the 1994 provincial election, and whether the riding majority voted "Yes" (1) or "No" (2). These data are stored in columns 2, 3, and 4, respectively in file XR22-47. (Column 1 contains the riding number.)

a Can we infer from these results that in ridings with a majority of "No" votes, there was an increase in the percentage of rejected ballots?

b Can we infer that in ridings with a majority "Yes" vote that there was a decrease in the percentage of rejected ballots?

22.48 Repeat Case 22.1, assuming that interest rates are not normally distributed.

22.49 Repeat Case 22.2, assuming that interest rates, annual gross sales, and age of businesses are not normally distributed.

| CASE 22.3 | **Ambulance and Fire Department Response Interval Study*** |

Every year, thousands of people die of heart attacks partly because of delays while waiting for emergency medical care to arrive. One form of heart attack is ventricular fibrillation rhythm, which is treated by a defibrillator. However, immediate medical attention is critical. In general, if a patient receives treatment within 8 minutes, he or she if very likely to survive. It is estimated that the probability of survival is reduced by 7–10% for each minute thereafter that defibrillation is delayed.

The region in the Ambulance and Fire Department Response Interval Study is composed of the three cities of Cambridge, Waterloo, and Kitchener. Each city has a fire department, and the region has a 911 emergency telephone system. When a medical-related call is received by the Police Dispatch Center, it is relayed to the Central Ambulance Communication Center (CACC). The CACC dispatches both the ambulance and the fire department to certain calls that match one of several criteria indicating the need for fire department personnel. Two ambulance services cover the region: the Cambridge Memorial Hospital Ambulance Service and the Kitchener-Waterloo Regional Ambulance Service.

Currently, all defibrillation is performed by ambulance personnel sent to the patient after a 911 call. A city counselor recently suggested that, since the fire department has more centers, it is likely that fire department personnel could arrive at the scene more quickly than ambulance personnel. A study was undertaken to determine whether fire department personnel should be trained in the use of defibrillators and sent to treat ventricular fibrillation rhythm.

Between March 1, 1994, and August 31, 1994, all calls that involved both ambulance and fire department personnel were monitored. The times for each service to arrive at the scene were recorded and stored in file C22-03, using the format below.

Column 1: Call number for Cambridge calls

Column 2: Time in minutes for the ambulance to arrive

Column 3: Time for fire truck to arrive

Column 4: Call number for Kitchener calls

Column 5: Time in minutes for the ambulance to arrive

Column 6: Time for fire truck to arrive

Column 7: Call number for Waterloo calls

Column 8: Time in minutes for the ambulance to arrive

Column 9: Time for fire truck to arrive

It has been decided that the training of fire department personnel is warranted only if it can be shown that a fire truck arrives at the scene on average more than 1 minute sooner than an ambulance and that the frequency of arrival within 8 minutes is greater for the fire department.

What conclusions can be drawn from the data?

*The authors are grateful to Bruce Jermyn for supplying this case. The data are real. However, the sample size was reduced to ease disk-storage problems.

Case 22.4   Underpricing in Initial Public Offerings[*]

When a company offers its common shares to the public for the first time, the process is referred to as the company's initial public offering (IPO). The company retains an investment banker to establish the price at which the shares will be sold initially. If the price is set too high, there will be insufficient demand to sell all the shares. On the other hand, if the shares are underpriced, the company will receive less money for its shares than the maximum possible.

Studies concerning IPOs in the United States indicate that, on average, "IPOs tend to be underpriced by 11 to 18%." Studies concerning IPOs in Canada, using pre-1970 data, "reported an average degree of underpricing in excess of 40%." The evidence of excessive underpricing has caused the Canadian government to consider direct intervention in the capital markets to reduce this underpricing and thereby encourage entrepreneurs to raise capital through public offerings.

Researchers have suggested that, before the government decides to intervene, it should consider the results of their underpricing study using more recent data. A financial analyst took a sample of 100 Canadian IPOs issued during a recent 12-year period. For each IPO, he computed (for three time intervals) the values of the following underpricing measures.

U_{jt} = the percentage of underpricing of the jth IPO measured from $t = 0$ to day t of public trading (for $t = 1, 35$)

The value of U_{jt} is essentially the percentage price appreciation of the jth IPO, measured from $t = 0$ to day t of public trading. Thus, underpricing is indicated by positive values of U_{jt}.

The observations for $t = 1, 3$, and 5 are stored in columns 1, 2, and 3, respectively, in file C22-04. The government is interested in knowing if there is evidence of (a positive percentage of) underpricing and, also, if this percentage exceeds 5%, in which case the degree of underpricing would be sufficiently high to allow traders to profit from it even after paying brokerage commissions. What conclusions might the government draw from this study?

CASE 22.5   PC Magazine Survey[†]

In general, consumers of personal computers are not particularly brand conscious. Most people decide which brand of computer to buy on the basis of price and features. However, brand-name manufacturers are attempting to win back customers by providing a number of services and high-quality products. To examine whether personal computer users perceive differences among manufacturers, a marketing research consultant undertook a survey of PC users. He asked a random sample of Apple, Compaq, Dell, IBM, and Packard-Bell owners several questions.

The questions and possible responses follow.

Did you ever call the computer manufacturer to help with a problem?

[*]Adapted from Vijay M. Jog and Allan L. Riding, "Underpricing in Canadian IPOs," *Financial Analysts' Journal* (Nov.–Dec. 1987): 48–55.
[†]The authors are grateful to Alex Eliadis and David Jones for their help in this case. The case is based on an actual survey conducted by Willard Shullman for *PC Magazine*.

The following questions were asked only of those who answered "yes."

1 How long approximately (in seconds) did it take to reach a technician?

2 How long approximately (in minutes) did it take to solve the problem?

3 Rate the quality of the technical support.

1 = poor; 2 = fair; 3 = average; 4 = good; 5 = excellent

4 Would you recommend this brand of computer to a friend?

2 = yes; 1 = no

The results are stored in file C22-05. Columns 1 through 4 store the responses to questions 1 to 4, respectively. Column 5 identifies the computer brand (1 = Apple; 2 = Compaq; 3 = Dell; 4 = IBM; 5 = Packard-Bell). For each question, can we infer that differences among the brands exist?

CASE 22.6   **WLU Graduate Survey***

Every year, the graduates of Wilfrid Laurier University are surveyed to determine their employment status and annual income. The university offers undergraduate degrees in arts and music, business administration, and science, as well as several master's degrees. The survey asked a random sample of 1994 graduates the following questions.

1 With which degree did you graduate?

1 Arts and music
2 Business administration—nonaccounting
3 Business administration—accounting
4 Science
5 Master's

2 What is your current employment status?

1 Completing additional education
2 Employed
3 Other
4 Unemployed

3 If you are employed, what is your annual income?

The data are stored in columns 1 to 7 in file C22-06 in the following way.

Column 1: Degree

Column 2: Employment status

Columns 3–7: Income for those employed with degrees in arts and music, business (nonaccounting), business (accounting), science, and master's, respectively.

High school students who are about to choose a university program would like to know the following information.

a Are there differences in the employment status among the five groups of graduates?

b Are there differences in income among the five groups of graduates?

*Source: "Wilfrid Laurier 1994 Graduate Survey Report" as printed in the *Atrium*, 8 (November 1995).

c   Among business administration graduates, is there a difference in income between accounting and nonaccounting graduates?

CASE 22.7   Evaluation of a New Antidepressant Drug

Clinical depression afflicts many people and costs businesses billions of dollars. Fortunately, several drugs are available that effectively treat this disease. Pharmaceutical companies are constantly experimenting to develop new and better drugs. Statistical techniques are used to determine whether and to what degree the new drug is better and whether there are certain people in whom the drug appears to be more effective. Suppose that a random sample of men and women who suffer from moderate depression are given a new antidepressant. Each person is asked to rate its effectiveness by filling out the form below. The form asks people to assess the drug after 7 and 14 days, because antidepressants usually take several days to take effect. Similar drugs often have different effects on men and women. Consequently, the gender of the patient was recorded. Also recorded is whether the patient suffered from the most common side effect, headaches.

To evaluate your experience with this medication, place a check mark to show how you have felt since you began taking it.

	After Therapy (Day)	
	7	14
1 Very much worse		
2 Much worse		
3 A little worse		
4 No change		
5 A little better		
6 Much better		
7 Very much better		

The responses are stored in file C22-07 in the following way.

Columns 1 and 2: Evaluations for days 7 and 14 for women

Columns 3 and 4: Evaluations for days 7 and 14 for men

Column 5: Headaches among women (2 = yes; 1 = no)

Column 6: Headaches among men (2 = yes; 1 = no)

The company wants answers to the following questions.

a   Among female patients, is there improvement between days 7 and 14?

b   Among male patients, is there improvement between days 7 and 14?

c   Does the frequency of headaches differ between men and women?

CASE 22.8   Nutrition Education Programs*

Nutrition education programs, which teach their clients how to lose weight or reduce cholesterol levels through better eating patterns, have been growing in popularity. The nurse in charge of one such program at a local hospital wanted to know whether the programs actually work. A random sample of 33 clients who attended a nutrition education program for those with elevated cholesterol levels was drawn. The study recorded the weight, cholesterol levels, total dietary fat intake per average day, total dietary cholesterol intake per average day, and percent of daily calories from fat. These data were gathered both before and 3 months after the program. The researchers also determined the gender, age, and height of the clients.

The data are stored in file C22-08 in the following way.

Column 1: Gender (1 = female; 2 = male)

Column 2: Age

Column 3: Height (in meters)

Columns 4 and 5: Weight, before and after (in kilograms)

Columns 6 and 7: Cholesterol level, before and after

Columns 8 and 9: Total dietary fat intake per average day, before and after
(in grams)

Columns 10 and 11: Dietary cholesterol intake per average day, before and after
(in milligrams)

Columns 12 and 13: Percent daily calories from fat, before and after

The nurse would like the following information.

a In terms of each of weight, cholesterol level, fat intake, cholesterol intake, and calories from fat, is the program a success?

b Does gender affect the amount of reduction in each of weight, cholesterol level, fat intake, cholesterol intake, and calories from fat?

c Does age affect the amount of reduction in weight, cholesterol level, fat intake, cholesterol intake, and calories from fat cholesterol?

CASE 22.9   Do Banks Discriminate Against Women Business Owners?—III

A statistician made a final effort to determine whether banks discriminate against women business owners because of their gender. For each of the women business owners who had received a loan, she attempted to find a male business owner whose characteristics closely matched. The matching was done on the basis of type of business (proprietorship, partnership, or corporation), gross sales, and age of company. A match was made when the type of business was the same, the gross sales were within $10,000 of each other, and the ages were within 1 year of each other. The interest rates (points above prime) for each pair are recorded in columns 1 (matched pair), 2 (women's rates), and 3 (men's rates) in file C22-09. What do these data tell you? Is this analysis definitive? Explain.

*The authors would like to thank Karen Cavrag for writing this case.

Appendix A
Data File Sample Statistics

Chapter 9

9.21 $\bar{x}=252.38$
9.22 $\bar{x}=1810.16$
9.23 $\bar{x}=12.10$
9.24 $\bar{x}=10.21$
9.25 $\bar{x}=.5096$
9.26 $\bar{x}=26.81$
9.37 $\bar{x}=19.28$
9.38 $\bar{x}=15.00$
9.39 $\bar{x}=261.00$
9.41 $\bar{x}=22.84$
9.42 $\bar{x}=14.98$
9.44 $\bar{x}=411.30$

Chapter 10

10.37 $\bar{x}=5065$
10.38 $\bar{x}=29,120$
10.39 $\bar{x}=569$
10.40 $\bar{x}=10.50$
10.41 $\bar{x}=19.13$
10.58 $\bar{x}=-1.2$
10.59 $\bar{x}=55.8$
10.60 $\bar{x}=5.04$
10.61 $\bar{x}=19.39$
10.62 $\bar{x}=105.7$
10.63 $\bar{x}=17.55$

Chapter 11

11.28 $\bar{x}=22.6$; $s=3.42$; $n=25$
11.29 $\bar{x}=101.77$; $s=9.99$; $n=75$
11.30 $\bar{x}=7.15$; $s=1.65$; $n=200$
11.31 $\bar{x}=8.02$; $s=.04$; $n=50$
11.32 $\bar{x}=24.19$; $s=13.42$; $n=100$
11.33 $\bar{x}=5.87$; $s=1.02$; $n=50$
11.34 $\bar{x}=62.9$; $s=5.16$; $n=30$
11.35 $\bar{x}=2.12$; $s=.374$; $n=100$
11.46 $s^2=270.58$
11.48 $s^2=22.56$
11.49 $s^2=174.47$
11.68 $n(1)=71$; $n(2)=329$
11.69 $n(1)=57$; $n(2)=35$; $n(3)=4$; $n(4)=4$
11.70 $n(1)=226$; $n(2)=195$; $n(3)=106$; $n(4)=328$; $n(5)=1145$
11.71 $n(1)=355$; $n(2)=32$
11.72 $\bar{x}=31.95$; $s=7.19$
11.73 $n(1)=312$; $n(2)=144$; $n(3)=225$
11.74 $\bar{x}=57.79$; $s=6.58$

11.75 $s^2=27.47$
11.76 $n(1)=232$; $n(2)=268$
11.77 $\bar{x}=71.88$; $s=10.03$
11.78 $\bar{x}=117.54$; $s=50.24$
11.79 $n(1)=92$; $n(2)=158$
11.80 $\bar{x}=6.91$; $s=.226$
11.81 $\bar{x}=6.35$; $s=2.16$
11.82 $\bar{x}=5.79$; $s=2.86$
11.83 $n(1)=24$; $n(2)=48$
11.84 $s^2=6.52$
11.85 $n(1)=86$; $n(2)=9$; $n(3)=5$
11.86 $\bar{x}=1.1$; $s=.98$
11.87 $\bar{x}=9.16$; $s=2.64$
11.89 $n(1)=508$; $n(2)=92$
11.90 $\bar{x}=3.61$; $s=.400$
Case 11.1 $\bar{x}=1.316$; $s=1.1147$
Case 11.3 $n(1)=226$; $n(2)=7$; $n(3)=16$

Chapter 12

12.19 $\bar{x}_1=50.80$; $s_1=9.42$; $n_1=125$; $\bar{x}_2=53.93$; $s_2=10.49$; $n_2=95$
12.20 $\bar{x}_1=246.80$; $s_1=28.80$; $n_1=100$; $\bar{x}_2=239.66$; $s_2=11.57$; $n_2=150$
12.21 $\bar{x}_1=44.58$; $s_1=59.16$; $n_1=40$; $\bar{x}_2=62.75$; $s_2=52.26$; $n_2=40$
12.22 $\bar{x}_1=122.9$; $s_1=38.38$; $n_1=60$; $\bar{x}_2=134.38$; $s_2=11.77$; $n_2=50$
12.23 $\bar{x}_1=36.93$; $s_1=4.23$; $n_1=15$; $\bar{x}_2=31.36$; $s_2=3.35$; $n_2=25$
12.24 $\bar{x}_1=39.46$; $s_1=12.96$; $n_1=48$; $\bar{x}_2=43.81$; $s_2=11.95$; $n_2=48$
12.25 $\bar{x}_1=10.23$; $s_1=2.87$; $n_1=100$; $\bar{x}_2=9.66$; $s_2=2.89$; $n_2=100$
12.26 $\bar{x}_1=115.5$; $s_1=21.68$; $n_1=30$; $\bar{x}_2=109.4$; $s_2=22.36$; $n_2=30$
12.27 $\bar{x}_1=13.52$; $s_1=2.40$; $n_1=25$; $\bar{x}_2=9.92$; $s_2=3.63$; $n_2=25$
12.28 $\bar{x}_1=58.99$; $s_1=30.77$; $n_1=250$; $\bar{x}_2=52.96$; $s_2=43.32$; $n_2=250$
12.29 $\bar{x}_1=74.71$; $s_1=24.02$; $n_1=24$; $\bar{x}_2=52.5$; $s_2=9.04$; $n_2=16$
12.30 $\bar{x}_1=5.02$; $s_1=1.39$; $n_1=200$; $\bar{x}_2=7.80$; $s_2=3.09$; $n_2=200$
12.44 $\bar{x}_D=-1.05$; $s_D=2.58$; $n_D=20$
12.45 $\bar{x}_D=19.75$; $s_D=30.63$; $n_D=40$
12.46 $\bar{x}_D=-3.47$; $s_D=10.04$; $n_D=50$
12.52 $s_1^2=76.50$; $n_1=50$; $s_2^2=129.09$; $n_2=50$

12.57 $s_1^2=.0261$; $n_1=52$; $s_2^2=.0875$; $n_2=52$
12.58 $s_1^2=3.35$; $n_1=100$; $s_2^2=10.95$; $n_2=100$
12.74 $n_1(1)=301$; $n_1(2)=699$; $n_2(1)=156$; $n_2(2)=444$
12.75 $n_1(1)=268$; $n_1(2)=232$; $n_2(1)=311$; $n_2(2)=189$
12.76 $n_1(1)=37$; $n_1(2)=19$; $n_2(1)=119$; $n_2(2)=25$
12.77 $n_1(1)=152$; $n_1(2)=248$; $n_2(1)=240$; $n_2(2)=260$
12.78 $\bar{x}_1=10.01$; $s_1=4.43$; $n_1=120$; $\bar{x}_2=9.12$; $s_2=4.45$; $n_2=120$
12.79 $\bar{x}_1=5;746$; $s_1=409$; $n_1=15$; $\bar{x}_2=5,372$; $s_2=441$; $n_2=24$
12.80

Size	Uninsulated	Insulated
1251	504	452
1395	550	474
1525	571	524
1604	608	542
1703	622	557
1844	620	557
1986	682	619
2002	699	641
2095	741	670
2158	855	800
2233	900	838
2320	912	850
2461	1043	990
2573	1123	1103
2804	1203	1155

12.81 $n_1(1)=234$; $n_1(2)=257$; $n_2(1)=218$; $n_2(2)=272$
12.82 $n_1(1)=106$; $n_1(2)=221$; $n_2(1)=94$; $n_2(2)=288$

12.83

Time	Gender	Income
15	2	1
40	2	2
10	1	1
120	1	2
30	1	1
25	1	2
50	1	2
35	1	1
30	2	1
120	2	2
30	1	1
40	2	1
60	1	2
90	2	2
30	1	1
20	2	1
25	1	2
45	2	1
80	2	1
45	2	2
100	1	2
40	2	1
0	1	1
25	1	1
30	2	1
45	1	2
20	2	1
90	2	2
60	1	2
45	2	1
30	1	2
45	1	1
60	2	2
25	2	2
50	2	2
50	2	1
25	1	2
30	1	1
20	1	2
45	2	1

12.84 $\bar{x}_1=32.42$; $s_1=6.08$; $n_1=200$; $\bar{x}_2=33.72$; $s_2=6.75$; $n_2=200$

12.85

Female	Male
71	72
55	60
68	70
61	63
62	61
54	49
44	48
49	47
42	40
55	53
67	69
69	72
69	71
71	71
47	48
68	72
48	53
49	50
62	54
42	46
42	44
47	50
47	47
57	58
46	42

12.86 $n_1(1)=222$; $n_1(2)=171$; $n_2(1)=248$; $n_2(2)=137$

12.87

A-Units	A-Defects	B-Units	B-Defects
247	10	219	12
242	13	218	4
250	3	205	12
233	10	216	17
241	11	222	23
244	11	216	14
252	11	218	15
236	14	197	4
244	19	217	18
255	14	205	15
229	11	210	6
255	16	219	11
250	12	207	14
252	16	227	18
235	8	208	4
225	8	207	14
233	7	223	10
243	11	203	7
238	22	228	24
232	4	215	17
237	5	213	22
247	11	211	16
247	10	214	17
221	8	236	18

12.89

Day	DC-Before	DC-After	DS-Before	DS-After	CS-Before	CS-After
1	195	173	319	317	307	287
2	194	204	347	331	393	390
3	146	153	306	301	407	394
4	186	184	316	306	352	314
5	178	168	324	318	337	308
6	146	145	339	340	445	419
7	161	141	272	248	440	429
8	190	185	285	284	357	320
9	162	157	312	284	389	354
10	154	154	346	325	410	398
11	153	163	266	268	314	270
12	172	175	309	282	359	339
13	174	170	315	268	425	380
14	141	145	258	262	310	272

12.90 20-year-old men: $\bar{x}=125.7$; $s=5.65$; $n=26$
40-year-old men: $\bar{x}=129.9$; $s=5.65$; $n=24$
20-year-old women: $\bar{x}=134.0$; $s=6.01$; $n=26$
40-year-old women: $\bar{x}=141.1$; $s=6.28$; $n=24$
12.91 $n_1(1)=94$; $n_1(2)=38$; $n_2(1)=846$; $n_2(2)=212$
12.92 $\bar{x}_1=1246$; $s_1=154.3$; $n_1=25$; $\bar{x}_2=1916$; $s_2=256.1$; $n_2=25$
12.93 $\bar{x}_1=69,933$; $s_1=7959.8$; $n_1=89$; $\bar{x}_2=48,246$; $s_2=10,079.1$; $n_2=61$
12.94 $n_1(1)=13$; $n_1(2)=237$; $n_2(1)=20$; $n_2(2)=230$
12.95 Weights: $\bar{x}_1=1.038$; $s_1=.1118$; $n_1=59$; $\bar{x}_2=.9804$; $s_2=.0951$; $n_2=109$
Heights: $\bar{x}_1=.953$; $s_1=.1010$; $n_1=59$; $\bar{x}_2=1.004$; $s_2=.0089$; $n_2=109$
12.96 $\bar{x}_1=41.09$; $s_1=9.03$; $n_1=100$; $\bar{x}_2=42.67$; $s_2=8.17$; $n_2=100$
12.97 $\bar{x}_1=44.79$; $s_1=8.23$; $n_1=100$; $\bar{x}_2=66.98$; $s_2=13.94$; $n_2=100$
Case 12.3 $\bar{x}_1=2.081$; $s_1=1.185$; $n_1=296$; $\bar{x}_2=2.125$; $s_2=1.1539$; $n_2=24$; $\bar{x}_3=2.7593$; $s_3=1.045$; $n_3=54$; $\bar{x}_4=2.2190$; $s_4=1.2100$; $n_4=210$; $\bar{x}_5=2.000$; $s_5=1.1339$; $n_5=15$; $\bar{x}_6=2.280$; $s_6=1.0310$; $n_6=50$

Chapter 14

14.7 $\bar{x}_1=19.64$; $s_1=6.8$; $n_1=25$; $\bar{x}_2=23.32$; $s_2=6.44$; $n_2=25$; $\bar{x}_3=19.4$; $s_3=5.99$; $n_3=25$
14.8 $\bar{x}_1=52.4$; $s_1=15.60$; $n_1=10$; $\bar{x}_2=55.0$; $s_2=11.92$; $n_2=21$; $\bar{x}_3=36.25$; $s_3=15.71$; $n_3=16$; $\bar{x}_4=53.65$; $s_4=13.18$; $n_4=20$; $\bar{x}_5=47.5$; $s_5=16.37$; $n_5=18$
14.9 $\bar{x}_1=68.83$; $s_1=7.23$; $n_1=20$; $\bar{x}_2=65.08$; $s_2=6.11$; $n_2=26$; $\bar{x}_3=62.01$; $s_3=7.97$; $n_3=16$; $\bar{x}_4=64.64$; $s_4=7.54$; $n_4=19$
14.10 $\bar{x}_1=90.17$; $s_1=31.49$; $n_1=30$; $\bar{x}_2=95.77$; $s_2=30.01$; $n_2=30$; $\bar{x}_3=106.83$; $s_3=30.47$; $n_3=30$; $\bar{x}_4=111.17$; $s_4=31.99$; $n_4=30$
14.11 $\bar{x}_1=162.40$; $s_1=34.87$; $n_1=25$; $\bar{x}_2=185.64$; $s_2=41.47$; $n_2=25$; $\bar{x}_3=155.80$; $s_3=34.13$; $n_3=25$; $\bar{x}_4=182.60$; $s_4=40.72$; $n_4=25$; $\bar{x}_5=178.80$; $s_5=34.00$; $n_5=25$
14.12 $\bar{x}_1=5.81$; $s_1=2.49$; $n_1=100$; $\bar{x}_2=5.30$; $s_2=2.01$; $n_2=100$; $\bar{x}_3=5.33$; $s_3=1.97$; $n_3=100$
14.13 $\bar{x}_1=551.50$; $s_1=52.36$; $n_1=20$; $\bar{x}_2=576.75$; $s_2=51.39$; $n_2=20$; $\bar{x}_3=559.45$; $s_3=55.94$; $n_3=20$
14.16 $\bar{x}_1=153.60$; $s_1=25.58$; $n_1=20$; $\bar{x}_2=151.50$; $s_2=30.40$; $n_2=20$; $\bar{x}_3=133.25$; $s_3=25.04$; $n_3=20$
14.22 SST=151.27; SSB=7396.30; SSE=195.40; SS(Total)=7742.97

14.23 SST=2126.51; SSB=35,300.00; SSE=6642.24; SS(Total)=44068.75
14.24 SST=11.025; SSB=51.475; SSE=63.475; SS(Total)=125.975
14.25 SST=7131.03; SSB=177,464.60; SSE=1098.30; SS(Total)=185693.93
14.26 SST=204.22; SSB=1150.22; SSE=495.11; SS(Total)=1849.56
14.27 SST=4206.09; SSB=126842.60; SSE=5763.66; SS(Total)=136812.35
14.28 SST=10.26; SSB=3020.30; SSE=226.71; SS(Total)=3257.27
14.29 SST=97.69; SSB=3122.99; SSE=996.81; SS(Total)=4217.48
14.52 $\bar{x}_1=61.6$; $s_1=8.97$; $n_1=10$; $\bar{x}_2=57.3$; $s_2=8.39$; $n_2=10$; $\bar{x}_3=61.8$; $s_3=4.71$; $n_3=10$; $\bar{x}_4=51.8$; $s_4=8.68$; $n_4=10$
14.53 $\bar{x}_1=53.17$; $s_1=13.95$; $n_1=30$; $\bar{x}_2=49.37$; $s_2=12.35$; $n_2=30$; $\bar{x}_3=44.33$; $s_3=11.40$; $n_3=30$

Chapter 15

15.7 $n(1)=28$; $n(2)=17$; $n(3)=19$; $n(4)=17$; $n(5)=19$
15.8 $n(1)=41$; $n(2)=107$; $n(3)=66$; $n(4)=19$
15.9 $n(1)=114$; $n(2)=92$; $n(3)=84$; $n(4)=101$; $n(5)=107$; $n(6)=102$
15.10 $n(1)=11$; $n(2)=32$; $n(3)=62$; $n(4)=29$; $n(5)=16$
15.11 $n(1)=8$; $n(2)=4$; $n(3)=3$; $n(4)=8$; $n(5)=2$
15.12 $n(1)=159$; $n(2)=28$; $n(3)=47$; $n(4)=16$
15.13 $n(1)=36$; $n(2)=58$; $n(3)=74$; $n(4)=29$

15.14 $n(1)=408$; $n(2)=571$; $n(3)=221$
15.15 $n(1)=19$; $n(2)=23$; $n(3)=14$; $n(4)=194$
15.24 $n(1,1)=50$; $n(1,2)=15$; $n(1,3)=8$; $n(2,1)=11$; $n(2,2)=42$; $n(2,3)=25$
15.25 $n(1,1)=60$; $n(1,2)=31$; $n(1,3)=12$; $n(2,1)=65$; $n(2,2)=53$; $n(2,3)=13$
15.26 $n(1,1)=33$; $n(1,2)=24$; $n(1,3)=19$; $n(2,1)=23$; $n(2,2)=17$; $n(2,3)=26$; $n(3,1)=16$; $n(3,2)=27$; $n(3,3)=46$; $n(4,1)=14$; $n(4,2)=38$; $n(4,3)=57$
15.27 $n(1,1)=65$; $n(1,2)=64$; $n(2,1)=39$; $n(2,2)=48$
15.28 $n(1,1)=34$; $n(1,2)=23$; $n(2,1)=251$; $n(2,2)=212$; $n(3,1)=159$; $n(3,2)=248$; $n(4,1)=16$; $n(4,2)=57$
15.29 $n(1,1)=46$; $n(1,2)=24$; $n(2,1)=37$; $n(2,2)=52$; $n(3,1)=10$; $n(3,2)=12$; $n(4,1)=7$; $n(4,2)=12$
15.30 $n(1,1)=51$; $n(1,2)=8$; $n(1,3)=5$; $n(1,4)=11$; $n(2,1)=24$; $n(2,2)=14$; $n(2,3)=12$; $n(2,4)=8$; $n(3,1)=26$; $n(3,2)=9$; $n(3,3)=19$; $n(3,4)=8$
15.42 $n_1(1)=116$; $n_1(2)=119$; $n_1(3)=29$; $n_1(4)=52$; $n_1(5)=48$; $n_1(6)=16$; $n_1(7)=26$; $n_1(8)=24$; $n_1(9)=70$; $n_2(1)=122$; $n_2(2)=92$; $n_2(3)=58$; $n_2(4)=39$; $n_2(5)=34$; $n_2(6)=33$; $n_2(7)=29$; $n_2(8)=21$; $n_2(9)=72$
15.43 $n(1,1)=104$; $n(1,2)=125$; $n(1,3)=32$; $n(1,4)=49$; $n(2,1)=14$; $n(2,2)=17$; $n(2,3)=5$; $n(2,4)=9$
15.44 $n(1,1)=4$; $n(1,2)=21$; $n(1,3)=31$; $n(1,4)=14$; $n(2,1)=27$; $n(2,2)=32$; $n(2,3)=18$; $n(2,4)=2$; $n(3,1)=1$; $n(3,2)=20$; $n(3,3)=42$; $n(3,4)=22$; $n(4,1)=10$; $n(4,2)=44$; $n(4,3)=22$; $n(4,4)=3$

15.45

Number	Frequency	Number	Frequency	Number	Frequency
1	5	18	7	34	5
2	6	19	5	35	8
3	7	20	10	36	12
4	5	21	6	37	5
5	3	22	5	38	8
6	5	23	2	39	4
7	12	24	8	40	6
8	8	25	5	41	9
9	8	26	8	42	9
10	5	27	5	43	8
11	6	28	6	44	5
12	7	29	8	45	5
13	9	30	6	46	2
14	3	31	6	47	6
15	5	32	4	48	10
16	4	33	6	49	6
17	9				

15.46 $n(1,1)=18$; $n(1,2)=41$; $n(1,3)=32$; $n(1,4)=20$; $n(1,5)=4$; $n(2,1)=6$; $n(2,2)=16$; $n(2,3)=40$; $n(2,4)=21$; $n(2,5)=7$

15.47 $n(0)=8$; $n(1)=35$; $n(2)=57$; $n(3)=69$; $n(4)=28$; $n(5)=3$

15.48 $n(1,1)=29$; $n(1,2)=1$; $n(2,1)=10$; $n(2,2)=7$; $n(3,2)=9$; $n(3,3)=14$

15.49 $n(1,1)=26$; $n(1,2)=4$; $n(2,1)=9$; $n(2,2)=8$; $n(3,1)=9$; $n(3,3)=14$

15.50 $n(1,1)=36$; $n(1,2)=4$; $n(1,3)=30$; $n(1,4)=8$; $n(2,1)=63$; $n(2,2)=7$; $n(2,3)=73$; $n(2,4)=10$; $n(3,1)=29$; $n(3,2)=164$; $n(3,3)=23$; $n(3,4)=43$; $n(4,1)=58$; $n(4,2)=49$; $n(4,3)=41$; $n(4,4)=55$

Chapter 16

16.6 $T_1=797$; $n_1=30$; $T_2=1033$; $n_2=30$

16.7 $T_1=3368$; $n_1=58$; $T_2=4135$; $n_2=64$

16.8 $T_1=10,691$; $n_1=100$; $T_2=9409$; $n_2=100$

16.9 $T_1=2810$; $n_1=50$; $T_2=2240$; $n_2=50$

16.10 $T_1=383.5$; $n_1=15$; $T_2=436.5$; $n_2=25$

16.11 $T_1=439.5$; $n_1=20$; $T_2=380.5$; $n_2=20$

16.21 $T^+=103.5$; $T^-=1492.5$; $n=56$

16.22 $T^+=3302.5$; $T^-=1548.5$; $n=98$

16.23 $T^+=40.5$; $T^-=235.5$; $n=23$

16.24 $T^+=111$; $T^-=240$; $n=26$

16.25 $n(\text{positive})=32$; $n(\text{negative})=12$

16.26 $n(\text{positive})=5$; $n(\text{negative})=15$

16.27 $T^+=190$; $T^-=135$; $n=25$

16.28 $n(\text{positive})=32$; $n(\text{negative})=16$

16.29 $T^+=48$; $T^-=732$; $n=39$

16.36 $T_1=767.5$; $n_1=25$; $T_2=917$; $n_2=25$; $T_3=1165.5$; $n_3=25$

16.37 $T_1=4180$; $n_1=50$; $T_2=5262$; $n_2=50$; $T_3=5653$; $n_3=50$; $T_4=5005$; $n_4=50$

16.38 $T_1=1504.5$; $n_1=30$; $T_2=1366$; $n_2=30$; $T_3=1224.5$; $n_3=30$

16.39 $T_1=21,246$; $n_1=100$; $T_2=19,784$; $n_2=100$; $T_3=20,976$; $n_3=100$; $T_4=18,194$; $n_4=100$

16.44 $T_1=33$; $T_2=39.5$; $T_3=47.5$

16.45 $T_1=46$; $T_2=72$; $T_3=62$

16.46 $T_1=22.5$; $T_2=19.5$; $T_3=18$

16.47 $T_1=68.5$; $T_2=70.5$; $T_3=41$

Chapter 17

17.2 Fathers: $\bar{x}=67.14$; $s^2=16.43$
Sons: $\bar{y}=68.70$; $s^2=14.14$; $\text{cov}(X,Y)=7.87$

17.3 Rates: $\bar{x}=8.95$; $s^2=1.07$
Stats: $\bar{y}=11,218.17$; $s^2=4,325,254$; $\text{cov}(X,Y)=-1286.82$

17.4 CPI: $\bar{x}=5.09$; $s^2=11.49$
Returns: $\bar{y}=11.08$; $s^2=254.96$; $\text{cov}(X,Y)=-2.67$

17.5 Index: $\bar{x}=.75$; $s^2=10.86$
ABX: $\bar{y}=3.89$; $s^2=77.92$; $\text{cov}(X,Y)=14.39$

17.6 Length: $\bar{x}=38.0$; $s^2=193.90$
Test: $\bar{y}=13.8$; $s^2=47.96$; $\text{cov}(X,Y)=51.86$

17.7 Time: $\bar{x}=27.95$; $s^2=82.01$
Mark: $\bar{y}=74.06$; $s^2=363.94$; $\text{cov}(X,Y)=153.95$

17.8 Education: $\bar{x}=11.04$; $s^2=3.90$
Internet: $\bar{y}=6.67$; $s^2=22.16$; $\text{cov}(X,Y)=3.08$

17.9 Age: $\bar{x}=37.28$; $s^2=55.11$
Job: $\bar{y}=26.28$; $s^2=4.00$; $\text{cov}(X,Y)=-6.44$

17.10 Degrees: $\bar{x}=34.61$; $s^2=21.39$
Price: $\bar{y}=12.73$; $s^2=.209$; $\text{cov}(X,Y)=2.03$

17.11 Age: $\bar{x}=56.00$; $s^2=228.26$
Expense: $\bar{y}=6.67$; $s^2=179.88$; $\text{cov}(X,Y)=51.53$

17.12 Weight: $\bar{x}=.204$; $s^2=.003225$
Price: $\bar{y}=500.1$; $s^2=45,643$; $\text{cov}(X,Y)=12.00$

17.27 Vacancy: $\bar{x}=11.33$; $s^2=35.47$
Rent: $\bar{y}=17.20$; $s^2=11.24$; $\text{cov}(X,Y)=-10.78$

17.28 Exercise: $\bar{x}=283.14$; $s^2=13,641$
Reduction: $\bar{y}=27.80$; $s^2=221.43$; $\text{cov}(X,Y)=1240.6$

17.29 Test: $\bar{x}=79.47$; $s^2=16.07$
Nondefective: $\bar{y}=93.89$; $s^2=1.28$; $\text{cov}(X,Y)=.826$

17.69 Ads: $\bar{x}=4.12$; $s^2=3.47$
Customers: $\bar{y}=384.81$; $s^2=18,552.08$; $\text{cov}(X,Y)=74.02$

17.70 Age: $\bar{x}=113.35$; $s^2=378.77$
Repair: $\bar{y}=395.21$; $s^2=4094.79$; $\text{cov}(X,Y)=936.82$

Appendix B

Tables

Table 1

Binomial Probabilities

Tabulated values are $P(X \le k) = \sum_{x=0}^{k} p(x)$. (Values are rounded to three decimal places.)

$n = 5$

k								p							
	.01	.05	.10	.20	.25	.30	.40	.50	.60	.70	.75	.80	.90	.95	.99
0	.951	.774	.590	.328	.237	.168	.078	.031	.010	.002	.001	.000	.000	.000	.000
1	.999	.977	.919	.737	.633	.528	.337	.187	.087	.031	.016	.007	.000	.000	.000
2	1.000	.999	.991	.942	.896	.837	.683	.500	.317	.163	.104	.058	.009	.001	.000
3	1.000	1.000	1.000	.993	.984	.969	.913	.812	.663	.472	.367	.263	.081	.023	.001
4	1.000	1.000	1.000	1.000	.999	.998	.990	.969	.922	.832	.763	.672	.410	.226	.049

$n = 6$

k								p							
	.01	.05	.10	.20	.25	.30	.40	.50	.60	.70	.75	.80	.90	.95	.99
0	.941	.735	.531	.262	.178	.118	.047	.016	.004	.001	.000	.000	.000	.000	.000
1	.999	.967	.886	.655	.534	.420	.233	.109	.041	.011	.005	.002	.000	.000	.000
2	1.000	.998	.984	.901	.831	.744	.544	.344	.179	.070	.038	.017	.001	.000	.000
3	1.000	1.000	.999	.983	.962	.930	.821	.656	.456	.256	.169	.099	.016	.002	.000
4	1.000	1.000	1.000	.998	.995	.989	.959	.891	.767	.580	.466	.345	.114	.033	.001
5	1.000	1.000	1.000	1.000	1.000	.999	.996	.984	.953	.882	.822	.738	.469	.265	.059

$n = 7$

k								p							
	.01	.05	.10	.20	.25	.30	.40	.50	.60	.70	.75	.80	.90	.95	.99
0	.932	.698	.478	.210	.133	.082	.028	.008	.002	.000	.000	.000	.000	.000	.000
1	.998	.956	.850	.577	.445	.329	.159	.063	.019	.004	.001	.000	.000	.000	.000
2	1.000	.996	.974	.852	.756	.647	.420	.227	.096	.029	.013	.005	.000	.000	.000
3	1.000	1.000	.997	.967	.929	.874	.710	.500	.290	.126	.071	.033	.003	.000	.000
4	1.000	1.000	1.000	.995	.987	.971	.904	.773	.580	.353	.244	.148	.026	.004	.000
5	1.000	1.000	1.000	1.000	.999	.996	.981	.937	.841	.671	.555	.423	.150	.044	.002
6	1.000	1.000	1.000	1.000	1.000	1.000	.998	.992	.972	.918	.867	.790	.522	.302	.068

Table 1

continued

n = 8

k								p							
	.01	.05	.10	.20	.25	.30	.40	.50	.60	.70	.75	.80	.90	.95	.99
0	.923	.663	.430	.168	.100	.058	.017	.004	.001	.000	.000	.000	.000	.000	.000
1	.997	.943	.813	.503	.367	.255	.106	.035	.009	.001	.000	.000	.000	.000	.000
2	1.000	.994	.962	.797	.679	.552	.315	.145	.050	.011	.004	.001	.000	.000	.000
3	1.000	1.000	.995	.944	.886	.806	.594	.363	.174	.058	.027	.010	.000	.000	.000
4	1.000	1.000	1.000	.990	.973	.942	.826	.637	.406	.194	.114	.056	.005	.000	.000
5	1.000	1.000	1.000	.999	.996	.989	.950	.855	.685	.448	.321	.203	.038	.006	.000
6	1.000	1.000	1.000	1.000	1.000	.999	.991	.965	.894	.745	.633	.497	.187	.057	.003
7	1.000	1.000	1.000	1.000	1.000	1.000	.999	.996	.983	.942	.900	.832	.570	.337	.077

n = 9

k								p							
	.01	.05	.10	.20	.25	.30	.40	.50	.60	.70	.75	.80	.90	.95	.99
0	.914	.630	.387	.134	.075	.040	.010	.002	.000	.000	.000	.000	.000	.000	.000
1	.997	.929	.775	.436	.300	.196	.071	.020	.004	.000	.000	.000	.000	.000	.000
2	1.000	.992	.947	.738	.601	.463	.232	.090	.025	.004	.001	.000	.000	.000	.000
3	1.000	.999	.992	.914	.834	.730	.483	.254	.099	.025	.010	.003	.000	.000	.000
4	1.000	1.000	.999	.980	.951	.901	.733	.500	.267	.099	.049	.020	.001	.000	.000
5	1.000	1.000	1.000	.997	.990	.975	.901	.746	.517	.270	.166	.086	.008	.001	.000
6	1.000	1.000	1.000	1.000	.999	.996	.975	.910	.768	.537	.399	.262	.053	.008	.000
7	1.000	1.000	1.000	1.000	1.000	1.000	.996	.980	.929	.804	.700	.564	.225	.071	.003
8	1.000	1.000	1.000	1.000	1.000	1.000	1.000	.998	.990	.960	.925	.866	.613	.370	.086

Table 1

continued

n = 10

k	.01	.05	.10	.20	.25	.30	.40	.50	.60	.70	.75	.80	.90	.95	.99
													p		
0	.904	.599	.349	.107	.056	.028	.006	.001	.000	.000	.000	.000	.000	.000	.000
1	.996	.914	.736	.376	.244	.149	.046	.011	.002	.000	.000	.000	.000	.000	.000
2	1.000	.988	.930	.678	.526	.383	.167	.055	.012	.002	.000	.000	.000	.000	.000
3	1.000	.999	.987	.879	.776	.650	.382	.172	.055	.011	.004	.001	.000	.000	.000
4	1.000	1.000	.998	.967	.922	.850	.633	.377	.166	.047	.020	.006	.000	.000	.000
5	1.000	1.000	1.000	.994	.980	.953	.834	.623	.367	.150	.078	.033	.002	.000	.000
6	1.000	1.000	1.000	.999	.996	.989	.945	.828	.618	.350	.224	.121	.013	.001	.000
7	1.000	1.000	1.000	1.000	1.000	.998	.988	.945	.833	.617	.474	.322	.070	.012	.000
8	1.000	1.000	1.000	1.000	1.000	1.000	.998	.989	.954	.851	.756	.624	.264	.086	.004
9	1.000	1.000	1.000	1.000	1.000	1.000	1.000	.999	.994	.972	.944	.893	.651	.401	.096

n = 15

k	.01	.05	.10	.20	.25	.30	.40	.50	.60	.70	.75	.80	.90	.95	.99
													p		
0	.860	.463	.206	.035	.013	.005	.000	.000	.000	.000	.000	.000	.000	.000	.000
1	.990	.829	.549	.167	.080	.035	.005	.000	.000	.000	.000	.000	.000	.000	.000
2	1.000	.964	.816	.398	.236	.127	.027	.004	.000	.000	.000	.000	.000	.000	.000
3	1.000	.995	.944	.648	.461	.297	.091	.018	.002	.000	.000	.000	.000	.000	.000
4	1.000	.999	.987	.836	.686	.515	.217	.059	.009	.001	.000	.000	.000	.000	.000
5	1.000	1.000	.998	.939	.852	.722	.403	.151	.034	.004	.001	.000	.000	.000	.000
6	1.000	1.000	1.000	.982	.943	.869	.610	.304	.095	.015	.004	.001	.000	.000	.000
7	1.000	1.000	1.000	.996	.983	.950	.787	.500	.213	.050	.017	.004	.000	.000	.000
8	1.000	1.000	1.000	.999	.996	.985	.905	.696	.390	.131	.057	.018	.000	.000	.000
9	1.000	1.000	1.000	1.000	.999	.996	.966	.849	.597	.278	.148	.061	.002	.000	.000
10	1.000	1.000	1.000	1.000	1.000	.999	.991	.941	.783	.485	.314	.164	.013	.001	.000
11	1.000	1.000	1.000	1.000	1.000	1.000	.998	.982	.909	.703	.539	.352	.056	.005	.000
12	1.000	1.000	1.000	1.000	1.000	1.000	1.000	.996	.973	.873	.764	.602	.184	.036	.000
13	1.000	1.000	1.000	1.000	1.000	1.000	1.000	1.000	.995	.965	.920	.833	.451	.171	.010
14	1.000	1.000	1.000	1.000	1.000	1.000	1.000	1.000	1.000	.995	.987	.965	.794	.537	.140

Table 1

continued

$n = 20$

k	.01	.05	.10	.20	.25	.30	.40	.50	.60	.70	.75	.80	.90	.95	.99
0	.818	.358	.122	.012	.003	.001	.000	.000	.000	.000	.000	.000	.000	.000	.000
1	.983	.736	.392	.069	.024	.008	.001	.000	.000	.000	.000	.000	.000	.000	.000
2	.999	.925	.677	.206	.091	.035	.004	.000	.000	.000	.000	.000	.000	.000	.000
3	1.000	.984	.867	.411	.225	.107	.016	.001	.000	.000	.000	.000	.000	.000	.000
4	1.000	.997	.957	.630	.415	.238	.051	.006	.000	.000	.000	.000	.000	.000	.000
5	1.000	1.000	.989	.804	.617	.416	.126	.021	.002	.000	.000	.000	.000	.000	.000
6	1.000	1.000	.998	.913	.786	.608	.250	.058	.006	.000	.000	.000	.000	.000	.000
7	1.000	1.000	1.000	.968	.898	.772	.416	.132	.021	.001	.000	.000	.000	.000	.000
8	1.000	1.000	1.000	.990	.959	.887	.596	.252	.057	.005	.001	.000	.000	.000	.000
9	1.000	1.000	1.000	.997	.986	.952	.755	.412	.128	.017	.004	.001	.000	.000	.000
10	1.000	1.000	1.000	.999	.996	.983	.872	.588	.245	.048	.014	.003	.000	.000	.000
11	1.000	1.000	1.000	1.000	.999	.995	.943	.748	.404	.113	.041	.010	.000	.000	.000
12	1.000	1.000	1.000	1.000	1.000	.999	.979	.868	.584	.228	.102	.032	.000	.000	.000
13	1.000	1.000	1.000	1.000	1.000	1.000	.994	.942	.750	.392	.214	.087	.002	.000	.000
14	1.000	1.000	1.000	1.000	1.000	1.000	.998	.979	.874	.584	.383	.196	.011	.000	.000
15	1.000	1.000	1.000	1.000	1.000	1.000	1.000	.994	.949	.762	.585	.370	.043	.003	.000
16	1.000	1.000	1.000	1.000	1.000	1.000	1.000	.999	.984	.893	.775	.589	.133	.016	.000
17	1.000	1.000	1.000	1.000	1.000	1.000	1.000	1.000	.996	.965	.909	.794	.323	.075	.001
18	1.000	1.000	1.000	1.000	1.000	1.000	1.000	1.000	.999	.992	.976	.931	.608	.264	.017
19	1.000	1.000	1.000	1.000	1.000	1.000	1.000	1.000	1.000	.999	.997	.988	.878	.642	.182

Table 1

continued

$n = 25$

k								p							
	.01	.05	.10	.20	.25	.30	.40	.50	.60	.70	.75	.80	.90	.95	.99
0	.778	.277	.072	.004	.001	.000	.000	.000	.000	.000	.000	.000	.000	.000	.000
1	.974	.642	.271	.027	.007	.002	.000	.000	.000	.000	.000	.000	.000	.000	.000
2	.998	.873	.537	.098	.032	.009	.000	.000	.000	.000	.000	.000	.000	.000	.000
3	1.000	.966	.764	.234	.096	.033	.002	.000	.000	.000	.000	.000	.000	.000	.000
4	1.000	.993	.902	.421	.214	.090	.009	.000	.000	.000	.000	.000	.000	.000	.000
5	1.000	.999	.967	.617	.378	.193	.029	.002	.000	.000	.000	.000	.000	.000	.000
6	1.000	1.000	.991	.780	.561	.341	.074	.007	.000	.000	.000	.000	.000	.000	.000
7	1.000	1.000	.998	.891	.727	.512	.154	.022	.001	.000	.000	.000	.000	.000	.000
8	1.000	1.000	1.000	.953	.851	.677	.274	.054	.004	.000	.000	.000	.000	.000	.000
9	1.000	1.000	1.000	.983	.929	.811	.425	.115	.013	.000	.000	.000	.000	.000	.000
10	1.000	1.000	1.000	.994	.970	.902	.586	.212	.034	.002	.000	.000	.000	.000	.000
11	1.000	1.000	1.000	.998	.989	.956	.732	.345	.078	.006	.001	.000	.000	.000	.000
12	1.000	1.000	1.000	1.000	.997	.983	.846	.500	.154	.017	.003	.000	.000	.000	.000
13	1.000	1.000	1.000	1.000	.999	.994	.922	.655	.268	.044	.011	.002	.000	.000	.000
14	1.000	1.000	1.000	1.000	1.000	.998	.966	.788	.414	.098	.030	.006	.000	.000	.000
15	1.000	1.000	1.000	1.000	1.000	1.000	.987	.885	.575	.189	.071	.017	.000	.000	.000
16	1.000	1.000	1.000	1.000	1.000	1.000	.996	.946	.726	.323	.149	.047	.000	.000	.000
17	1.000	1.000	1.000	1.000	1.000	1.000	.999	.978	.846	.488	.273	.109	.002	.000	.000
18	1.000	1.000	1.000	1.000	1.000	1.000	1.000	.993	.926	.659	.439	.220	.009	.000	.000
19	1.000	1.000	1.000	1.000	1.000	1.000	1.000	.998	.971	.807	.622	.383	.033	.001	.000
20	1.000	1.000	1.000	1.000	1.000	1.000	1.000	1.000	.991	.910	.786	.579	.098	.007	.000
21	1.000	1.000	1.000	1.000	1.000	1.000	1.000	1.000	.998	.967	.904	.766	.236	.034	.000
22	1.000	1.000	1.000	1.000	1.000	1.000	1.000	1.000	1.000	.991	.968	.902	.463	.127	.002
23	1.000	1.000	1.000	1.000	1.000	1.000	1.000	1.000	1.000	.998	.993	.973	.729	.358	.026
24	1.000	1.000	1.000	1.000	1.000	1.000	1.000	1.000	1.000	1.000	.999	.996	.928	.723	.222

Table 2

Poisson Probabilities

Tabulated values are $P(X \le k) = \sum_{x=0}^{k} p(x)$. (Values are rounded to three decimal places.)

k	.10	.20	.30	.40	.50	1.0	1.5	2.0	2.5	3.0	3.5	4.0	4.5	5.0	5.5	6.0
0	.905	.819	.741	.670	.607	.368	.223	.135	.082	.050	.030	.018	.011	.007	.004	.002
1	.995	.982	.963	.938	.910	.736	.558	.406	.287	.199	.136	.092	.061	.040	.027	.017
2	1.000	.999	.996	.992	.986	.920	.809	.677	.544	.423	.321	.238	.174	.125	.088	.062
3	1.000	1.000	1.000	.999	.998	.981	.934	.857	.758	.647	.537	.433	.342	.265	.202	.151
4	1.000	1.000	1.000	1.000	1.000	.996	.981	.947	.891	.815	.725	.629	.532	.440	.358	.285
5						.999	.996	.983	.958	.916	.858	.785	.703	.616	.529	.446
6						1.000	.999	.995	.986	.966	.935	.889	.831	.762	.686	.606
7							1.000	.999	.996	.988	.973	.949	.913	.867	.809	.744
8								1.000	.999	.996	.990	.979	.960	.932	.894	.847
9									1.000	.999	.997	.992	.983	.968	.946	.916
10										1.000	.999	.997	.993	.986	.975	.957
11											1.000	.999	.998	.995	.989	.980
12												1.000	.999	.998	.996	.991
13													1.000	.999	.998	.996
14														1.000	.999	.999
15															1.000	.999
16																1.000
17																
18																
19																
20																

Table 2

continued

k	6.5	7.0	7.5	8.0	8.5	9.0	μ 9.5	10	11	12	13	14	15
0	.002	.001	.001	.000	.000	.000	.000	.000	.000	.000	.000	.000	.000
1	.011	.007	.005	.003	.002	.001	.001	.000	.000	.000	.000	.000	.000
2	.043	.030	.020	.014	.009	.006	.004	.003	.001	.001	.000	.000	.000
3	.112	.082	.059	.042	.030	.021	.015	.010	.005	.002	.001	.000	.000
4	.224	.173	.132	.100	.074	.055	.040	.029	.015	.008	.004	.002	.001
5	.369	.301	.241	.191	.150	.116	.089	.067	.038	.020	.011	.006	.003
6	.527	.450	.378	.313	.256	.207	.165	.130	.079	.046	.026	.014	.008
7	.673	.599	.525	.453	.386	.324	.269	.220	.143	.090	.054	.032	.018
8	.792	.729	.662	.593	.523	.456	.392	.333	.232	.155	.100	.062	.037
9	.877	.830	.776	.717	.653	.587	.522	.458	.341	.242	.166	.109	.070
10	.933	.901	.862	.816	.763	.706	.645	.583	.460	.347	.252	.176	.118
11	.966	.947	.921	.888	.849	.803	.752	.697	.579	.462	.353	.260	.185
12	.984	.973	.957	.936	.909	.876	.836	.792	.689	.576	.463	.358	.268
13	.993	.987	.978	.966	.949	.926	.898	.864	.781	.682	.573	.464	.363
14	.997	.994	.990	.983	.973	.959	.940	.917	.854	.772	.675	.570	.466
15	.999	.998	.995	.992	.986	.978	.967	.951	.907	.844	.764	.669	.568
16	1.000	.999	.998	.996	.993	.989	.982	.973	.944	.899	.835	.756	.664
17		1.000	.999	.998	.997	.995	.991	.986	.968	.937	.890	.827	.749
18			1.000	.999	.999	.998	.996	.993	.982	.963	.930	.883	.819
19				1.000	.999	.999	.998	.997	.991	.979	.957	.923	.875
20					1.000	1.000	.999	.998	.995	.988	.975	.952	.917
21							1.000	.999	.998	.994	.986	.971	.947
22								1.000	.999	.997	.992	.983	.967
23									1.000	.999	.996	.991	.981
24										.999	.998	.995	.989
25										1.000	.999	.997	.994
26											1.000	.999	.997
27												.999	.998
28												1.000	.999
29													1.000

Table 3

Normal Curve Areas   — no error

(handwritten: ← measures 0 – z the left side / numbers could be – negative / 1.25)

z	.00	.01	.02	.03	.04	.05	.06	.07	.08	.09
0.0	.0000	.0040	.0080	.0120	.0160	.0199	.0239	.0279	.0319	.0359
0.1	.0398	.0438	.0478	.0517	.0557	.0596	.0636	.0675	.0714	.0753
0.2	.0793	.0832	.0871	.0910	.0948	.0987	.1026	.1064	.1103	.1141
0.3	.1179	.1217	.1255	.1293	.1331	.1368	.1406	.1443	.1480	.1517
0.4	.1554	.1591	.1628	.1664	.1700	.1736	.1772	.1808	.1844	.1879
0.5	.1915	.1950	.1985	.2019	.2054	.2088	.2123	.2157	.2190	.2224
0.6	.2257	.2291	.2324	.2357	.2389	.2422	.2454	.2486	.2517	.2549
0.7	.2580	.2611	.2642	.2673	.2704	.2734	.2764	.2794	.2823	.2852
0.8	.2881	.2910	.2939	.2967	.2995	.3023	.3051	.3078	.3106	.3133
0.9	.3159	.3186	.3212	.3238	.3264	.3289	.3315	.3340	.3365	.3389
1.0	.3413	.3438	.3461	.3485	.3508	.3531	.3554	.3577	.3599	.3621
1.1	.3643	.3665	.3686	.3708	.3729	.3749	.3770	.3790	.3810	.3830
1.2	.3849	.3869	.3888	.3907	.3925	.3944	.3962	.3980	.3997	.4015
1.3	.4032	.4049	.4066	.4082	.4099	.4115	.4131	.4147	.4162	.4177
1.4	.4192	.4207	.4222	.4236	.4251	.4265	.4279	.4292	.4306	.4319
1.5	.4332	.4345	.4357	.4370	.4382	.4394	.4406	.4418	.4429	.4441
1.6	.4452	.4463	.4474	.4484	.4495	.4505	.4515	.4525	.4535	.4545
1.7	.4554	.4564	.4573	.4582	.4591	.4599	.4608	.4616	.4625	.4633
1.8	.4641	.4649	.4656	.4664	.4671	.4678	.4686	.4693	.4699	.4706
1.9	.4713	.4719	.4726	.4732	.4738	.4744	.4750	.4756	.4761	.4767
2.0	.4772	.4778	.4783	.4788	.4793	.4798	.4803	.4808	.4812	.4817
2.1	.4821	.4826	.4830	.4834	.4838	.4842	.4846	.4850	.4854	.4857
2.2	.4861	.4864	.4868	.4871	.4875	.4878	.4881	.4884	.4887	.4890
2.3	.4893	.4896	.4898	.4901	.4904	.4906	.4909	.4911	.4913	.4916
2.4	.4918	.4920	.4922	.4925	.4927	.4929	.4931	.4932	.4934	.4936
2.5	.4938	.4940	.4941	.4943	.4945	.4946	.4948	.4949	.4951	.4952
2.6	.4953	.4955	.4956	.4957	.4959	.4960	.4961	.4962	.4963	.4964
2.7	.4965	.4966	.4967	.4968	.4969	.4970	.4971	.4972	.4973	.4974
2.8	.4974	.4975	.4976	.4977	.4977	.4978	.4979	.4979	.4980	.4981
2.9	.4981	.4982	.4982	.4983	.4984	.4984	.4985	.4985	.4986	.4986
3.0	.4987	.4987	.4987	.4988	.4988	.4989	.4989	.4989	.4990	.4990

SOURCE: Abridged from Table 1 of A. Hald, *Statistical Tables and Formulas* (New York: Wiley & Sons, Inc.), 1952. Reproduced by permission of A. Hald and the publisher, John Wiley & Sons, Inc.

Table 4

Critical Values of t

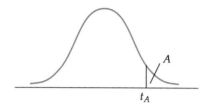

DEGREES OF FREEDOM	$t_{.100}$	$t_{.050}$	$t_{.025}$	$t_{.010}$	$t_{.005}$	DEGREES OF FREEDOM	$t_{.100}$	$t_{.050}$	$t_{.025}$	$t_{.010}$	$t_{.005}$
1	3.078	6.314	12.706	31.821	63.657	24	1.318	1.711	2.064	2.492	2.797
2	1.886	2.920	4.303	6.965	9.925	25	1.316	1.708	2.060	2.485	2.787
3	1.638	2.353	3.182	4.541	5.841	26	1.315	1.706	2.056	2.479	2.779
4	1.533	2.132	2.776	3.747	4.604	27	1.314	1.703	2.052	2.473	2.771
5	1.476	2.015	2.571	3.365	4.032	28	1.313	1.701	2.048	2.467	2.763
6	1.440	1.943	2.447	3.143	3.707	29	1.311	1.699	2.045	2.462	2.756
7	1.415	1.895	2.365	2.998	3.499	30	1.310	1.697	2.042	2.457	2.750
8	1.397	1.860	2.306	2.896	3.355	35	1.306	1.690	2.030	2.438	2.724
9	1.383	1.833	2.262	2.821	3.250	40	1.303	1.684	2.021	2.423	2.705
10	1.372	1.812	2.228	2.764	3.169	45	1.301	1.679	2.014	2.412	2.690
11	1.363	1.796	2.201	2.718	3.106	50	1.299	1.676	2.009	2.403	2.678
12	1.356	1.782	2.179	2.681	3.055	60	1.296	1.671	2.000	2.390	2.660
13	1.350	1.771	2.160	2.650	3.012	70	1.294	1.667	1.994	2.381	2.648
14	1.345	1.761	2.145	2.624	2.977	80	1.292	1.664	1.990	2.374	2.639
15	1.341	1.753	2.131	2.602	2.947	90	1.291	1.662	1.987	2.369	2.632
16	1.337	1.746	2.120	2.583	2.921	100	1.290	1.660	1.984	2.364	2.626
17	1.333	1.740	2.110	2.567	2.898	120	1.289	1.658	1.980	2.358	2.617
18	1.330	1.734	2.101	2.552	2.878	140	1.288	1.656	1.977	2.353	2.611
19	1.328	1.729	2.093	2.539	2.861	160	1.287	1.654	1.975	2.350	2.607
20	1.325	1.725	2.086	2.528	2.845	180	1.286	1.653	1.973	2.347	2.603
21	1.323	1.721	2.080	2.518	2.831	200	1.286	1.653	1.972	2.345	2.601
22	1.321	1.717	2.074	2.508	2.819	∞	1.282	1.645	1.960	2.326	2.576
23	1.319	1.714	2.069	2.500	2.807						

SOURCE: From M. Merrington, "Table of Percentage Points of the t-Distribution," *Biometrika* 32 (1941): 300. Reproduced by permission of the Biometrika Trustees.

Table 5

Critical Values of χ^2

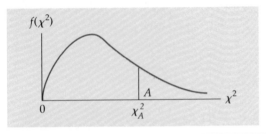

DEGREES OF FREEDOM	$\chi^2_{.995}$	$\chi^2_{.990}$	$\chi^2_{.975}$	$\chi^2_{.950}$	$\chi^2_{.900}$	$\chi^2_{.100}$	$\chi^2_{.050}$	$\chi^2_{.025}$	$\chi^2_{.010}$	$\chi^2_{.005}$
1	0.0000393	0.0001571	0.0009821	0.0039321	0.0157908	2.70554	3.84146	5.02389	6.63490	7.87944
2	0.0100251	0.0201007	0.0506356	0.102587	0.210720	4.60517	5.99147	7.37776	9.21034	10.5966
3	0.0717212	0.114832	0.215795	0.351846	0.584375	6.25139	7.81473	9.34840	11.3449	12.8381
4	0.206990	0.297110	0.484419	0.710721	1.063623	7.77944	9.48773	11.1433	13.2767	14.8602
5	0.411740	0.554300	0.831211	1.145476	1.61031	9.23635	11.0705	12.8325	15.0863	16.7496
6	0.675727	0.872085	1.237347	1.63539	2.20413	10.6446	12.5916	14.4494	16.8119	18.5476
7	0.989265	1.239043	1.68987	2.16735	2.83311	12.0170	14.0671	16.0128	18.4753	20.2777
8	1.344419	1.646482	2.17973	2.73264	3.48954	13.3616	15.5073	17.5346	20.0902	21.9550
9	1.734926	2.087912	2.70039	3.32511	4.16816	14.6837	16.9190	19.0228	21.6660	23.5893
10	2.15585	2.55821	3.24697	3.94030	4.86518	15.9871	18.3070	20.4831	23.2093	25.1882
11	2.60321	3.05347	3.81575	4.57481	5.57779	17.2750	19.6751	21.9200	24.7250	26.7569
12	3.07382	3.57056	4.40379	5.22603	6.30380	18.5494	21.0261	23.3367	26.2170	28.2995
13	3.56503	4.10691	5.00874	5.89186	7.04150	19.8119	22.3621	24.7356	27.6883	29.8194
14	4.07468	4.66043	5.62872	6.57063	7.78953	21.0642	23.6848	26.1190	29.1413	31.3193
15	4.60094	5.22935	6.26214	7.26094	8.54675	22.3072	24.9958	27.4884	30.5779	32.8013
16	5.14224	5.81221	6.90766	7.96164	9.31223	23.5418	26.2962	28.8454	31.9999	34.2672
17	5.69724	6.40776	7.56418	8.67176	10.0852	24.7690	27.5871	30.1910	33.4087	35.7185
18	6.26481	7.01491	8.23075	9.39046	10.8649	25.9894	28.8693	31.5264	34.8053	37.1564
19	6.84398	7.63273	8.90655	10.1170	11.6509	27.2036	30.1435	32.8523	36.1908	38.5822
20	7.43386	8.26040	9.59083	10.8508	12.4426	28.4120	31.4104	34.1696	37.5662	39.9968
21	8.03366	8.89720	10.28293	11.5913	13.2396	29.6151	32.6705	35.4789	38.9321	41.4010
22	8.64272	9.54249	10.9823	12.3380	14.0415	30.8133	33.9244	36.7807	40.2894	42.7956
23	9.26042	10.19567	11.6885	13.0905	14.8479	32.0069	35.1725	38.0757	41.6384	44.1813
24	9.88623	10.8564	12.4011	13.8484	15.6587	33.1963	36.4151	39.3641	42.9798	45.5585
25	10.5197	11.5240	13.1197	14.6114	16.4734	34.3816	37.6525	40.6465	44.3141	46.9278
26	11.1603	12.1981	13.8439	15.3791	17.2919	35.5631	38.8852	41.9232	45.6417	48.2899
27	11.8076	12.8786	14.5733	16.1513	18.1138	36.7412	40.1133	43.1944	46.9630	49.6449
28	12.4613	13.5648	15.3079	16.9279	18.9392	37.9159	41.3372	44.4607	48.2782	50.9933
29	13.1211	14.2565	16.0471	17.7083	19.7677	39.0875	42.5569	45.7222	49.5879	52.3356
30	13.7867	14.9535	16.7908	18.4926	20.5992	40.2560	43.7729	46.9792	50.8922	53.6720
40	20.7065	22.1643	24.4331	26.5093	29.0505	51.8050	55.7585	59.3417	63.6907	66.7659
50	27.9907	29.7067	32.3574	34.7642	37.6886	63.1671	67.5048	71.4202	76.1539	79.4900
60	35.5346	37.4848	40.4817	43.1879	46.4589	74.3970	79.0819	83.2976	88.3794	91.9517
70	43.2752	45.4418	48.7576	51.7393	55.3290	85.5271	90.5312	95.0231	100.425	104.215
80	51.1720	53.5400	57.1532	60.3915	64.2778	96.5782	101.879	106.629	112.329	116.321
90	59.1963	61.7541	65.6466	69.1260	73.2912	107.565	113.145	118.136	124.116	128.299
100	67.3276	70.0648	74.2219	77.9295	82.3581	118.498	124.342	129.561	135.807	140.169

SOURCE: From C. M. Thompson, "Tables of the Percentage Points of the χ^2-Distribution," *Biometrika* 32 (1941): 188–89. Reproduced by permission of the Biometrika Trustees.

Table 6(a)

Percentage Points of the F Distribution, A = .05

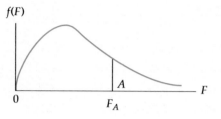

ν_2 \ ν_1	NUMERATOR DEGREES OF FREEDOM								
	1	2	3	4	5	6	7	8	9
1	161.4	199.5	215.7	224.6	230.2	234.0	236.8	238.9	240.5
2	18.51	19.00	19.16	19.25	19.30	19.33	19.35	19.37	19.38
3	10.13	9.55	9.28	9.12	9.01	8.94	8.89	8.85	8.81
4	7.71	6.94	6.59	6.39	6.26	6.16	6.09	6.04	6.00
5	6.61	5.79	5.41	5.19	5.05	4.95	4.88	4.82	4.77
6	5.99	5.14	4.76	4.53	4.39	4.28	4.21	4.15	4.10
7	5.59	4.74	4.35	4.12	3.97	3.87	3.79	3.73	3.68
8	5.32	4.46	4.07	3.84	3.69	3.58	3.50	3.44	3.39
9	5.12	4.26	3.86	3.63	3.48	3.37	3.29	3.23	3.18
10	4.96	4.10	3.71	3.48	3.33	3.22	3.14	3.07	3.02
11	4.84	3.98	3.59	3.36	3.20	3.09	3.01	2.95	2.90
12	4.75	3.89	3.49	3.26	3.11	3.00	2.91	2.85	2.80
13	4.67	3.81	3.41	3.18	3.03	2.92	2.83	2.77	2.71
14	4.60	3.74	3.34	3.11	2.96	2.85	2.76	2.70	2.65
15	4.54	3.68	3.29	3.06	2.90	2.79	2.71	2.64	2.59
16	4.49	3.63	3.24	3.01	2.85	2.74	2.66	2.59	2.54
17	4.45	3.59	3.20	2.96	2.81	2.70	2.61	2.55	2.49
18	4.41	3.55	3.16	2.93	2.77	2.66	2.58	2.51	2.46
19	4.38	3.52	3.13	2.90	2.74	2.63	2.54	2.48	2.42
20	4.35	3.49	3.10	2.87	2.71	2.60	2.51	2.45	2.39
21	4.32	3.47	3.07	2.84	2.68	2.57	2.49	2.42	2.37
22	4.30	3.44	3.05	2.82	2.66	2.55	2.46	2.40	2.34
23	4.28	3.42	3.03	2.80	2.64	2.53	2.44	2.37	2.32
24	4.26	3.40	3.01	2.78	2.62	2.51	2.42	2.36	2.30
25	4.24	3.39	2.99	2.76	2.60	2.49	2.40	2.34	2.28
26	4.23	3.37	2.98	2.74	2.59	2.47	2.39	2.32	2.27
27	4.21	3.35	2.96	2.73	2.57	2.46	2.37	2.31	2.25
28	4.20	3.34	2.95	2.71	2.56	2.45	2.36	2.29	2.24
29	4.18	3.33	2.93	2.70	2.55	2.43	2.35	2.28	2.22
30	4.17	3.32	2.92	2.69	2.53	2.42	2.33	2.27	2.21
40	4.08	3.23	2.84	2.61	2.45	2.34	2.25	2.18	2.12
60	4.00	3.15	2.76	2.53	2.37	2.25	2.17	2.10	2.04
120	3.92	3.07	2.68	2.45	2.29	2.17	2.09	2.02	1.96
∞	3.84	3.00	2.60	2.37	2.21	2.10	2.01	1.94	1.88

SOURCE: From M. Merrington and C. M. Thompson, "Tables of Percentage Points of the Inverted Beta (F)-Distribution," *Biometrika* 33 (1943): 73–88. Reproduced by permission of the Biometrika Trustees.

Table 6(a)

continued

ν_2 \ ν_1	NUMERATOR DEGREES OF FREEDOM									
	10	12	15	20	24	30	40	60	120	∞
1	241.9	243.9	245.9	248.0	249.1	250.1	251.1	252.2	253.3	254.3
2	19.40	19.41	19.43	19.45	19.45	19.46	19.47	19.48	19.49	19.50
3	8.79	8.74	8.70	8.66	8.64	8.62	8.59	8.57	8.55	8.53
4	5.96	5.91	5.86	5.80	5.77	5.75	5.72	5.69	5.66	5.63
5	4.74	4.68	4.62	4.56	4.53	4.50	4.46	4.43	4.40	4.36
6	4.06	4.00	3.94	3.87	3.84	3.81	3.77	3.74	3.70	3.67
7	3.64	3.57	3.51	3.44	3.41	3.38	3.34	3.30	3.27	3.23
8	3.35	3.28	3.22	3.15	3.12	3.08	3.04	3.01	2.97	2.93
9	3.14	3.07	3.01	2.94	2.90	2.86	2.83	2.79	2.75	2.71
10	2.98	2.91	2.85	2.77	2.74	2.70	2.66	2.62	2.58	2.54
11	2.85	2.79	2.72	2.65	2.61	2.57	2.53	2.49	2.45	2.40
12	2.75	2.69	2.62	2.54	2.51	2.47	2.43	2.38	2.34	2.30
13	2.67	2.60	2.53	2.46	2.42	2.38	2.34	2.30	2.25	2.21
14	2.60	2.53	2.46	2.39	2.35	2.31	2.27	2.22	2.18	2.13
15	2.54	2.48	2.40	2.33	2.29	2.25	2.20	2.16	2.11	2.07
16	2.49	2.42	2.35	2.28	2.24	2.19	2.15	2.11	2.06	2.01
17	2.45	2.38	2.31	2.23	2.19	2.15	2.10	2.06	2.01	1.96
18	2.41	2.34	2.27	2.19	2.15	2.11	2.06	2.02	1.97	1.92
19	2.38	2.31	2.23	2.16	2.11	2.07	2.03	1.98	1.93	1.88
20	2.35	2.28	2.20	2.12	2.08	2.04	1.99	1.95	1.90	1.84
21	2.32	2.25	2.18	2.10	2.05	2.01	1.96	1.92	1.87	1.81
22	2.30	2.23	2.15	2.07	2.03	1.98	1.94	1.89	1.84	1.78
23	2.27	2.20	2.13	2.05	2.01	1.96	1.91	1.86	1.81	1.76
24	2.25	2.18	2.11	2.03	1.98	1.94	1.89	1.84	1.79	1.73
25	2.24	2.16	2.09	2.01	1.96	1.92	1.87	1.82	1.77	1.71
26	2.22	2.15	2.07	1.99	1.95	1.90	1.85	1.80	1.75	1.69
27	2.20	2.13	2.06	1.97	1.93	1.88	1.84	1.79	1.73	1.67
28	2.19	2.12	2.04	1.96	1.91	1.87	1.82	1.77	1.71	1.65
29	2.18	2.10	2.03	1.94	1.90	1.85	1.81	1.75	1.70	1.64
30	2.16	2.09	2.01	1.93	1.89	1.84	1.79	1.74	1.68	1.62
40	2.08	2.00	1.92	1.84	1.79	1.74	1.69	1.64	1.58	1.51
60	1.99	1.92	1.84	1.75	1.70	1.65	1.59	1.53	1.47	1.39
120	1.91	1.83	1.75	1.66	1.61	1.55	1.50	1.43	1.35	1.25
∞	1.83	1.75	1.67	1.57	1.52	1.46	1.39	1.32	1.22	1.00

DENOMINATOR DEGREES OF FREEDOM

Table 6(b)

Percentage Points of the F Distribution, A = .025

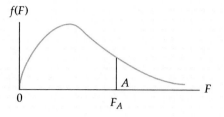

v_2 \ v_1	NUMERATOR DEGREES OF FREEDOM								
	1	**2**	**3**	**4**	**5**	**6**	**7**	**8**	**9**
1	647.8	799.5	864.2	899.6	921.8	937.1	948.2	956.7	963.3
2	38.51	39.00	39.17	39.25	39.30	39.33	39.36	39.37	39.39
3	17.44	16.04	15.44	15.10	14.88	14.73	14.62	14.54	14.47
4	12.22	10.65	9.98	9.60	9.36	9.20	9.07	8.98	8.90
5	10.01	8.43	7.76	7.39	7.15	6.98	6.85	6.76	6.68
6	8.81	7.26	6.60	6.23	5.99	5.82	5.70	5.60	5.52
7	8.07	6.54	5.89	5.52	5.29	5.12	4.99	4.90	4.82
8	7.57	6.06	5.42	5.05	4.82	4.65	4.53	4.43	4.36
9	7.21	5.71	5.08	4.72	4.48	4.32	4.20	4.10	4.03
10	6.94	5.46	4.83	4.47	4.24	4.07	3.95	3.85	3.78
11	6.72	5.26	4.63	4.28	4.04	3.88	3.76	3.66	3.59
12	6.55	5.10	4.47	4.12	3.89	3.73	3.61	3.51	3.44
13	6.41	4.97	4.35	4.00	3.77	3.60	3.48	3.39	3.31
14	6.30	4.86	4.24	3.89	3.66	3.50	3.38	3.29	3.21
15	6.20	4.77	4.15	3.80	3.58	3.41	3.29	3.20	3.12
16	6.12	4.69	4.08	3.73	3.50	3.34	3.22	3.12	3.05
17	6.04	4.62	4.01	3.66	3.44	3.28	3.16	3.06	2.98
18	5.98	4.56	3.95	3.61	3.38	3.22	3.10	3.01	2.93
19	5.92	4.51	3.90	3.56	3.33	3.17	3.05	2.96	2.88
20	5.87	4.46	3.86	3.51	3.29	3.13	3.01	2.91	2.84
21	5.83	4.42	3.82	3.48	3.25	3.09	2.97	2.87	2.80
22	5.79	4.38	3.78	3.44	3.22	3.05	2.93	2.84	2.76
23	5.75	4.35	3.75	3.41	3.18	3.02	2.90	2.81	2.73
24	5.72	4.32	3.72	3.38	3.15	2.99	2.87	2.78	2.70
25	5.69	4.29	3.69	3.35	3.13	2.97	2.85	2.75	2.68
26	5.66	4.27	3.67	3.33	3.10	2.94	2.82	2.73	2.65
27	5.63	4.24	3.65	3.31	3.08	2.92	2.80	2.71	2.63
28	5.61	4.22	3.63	3.29	3.06	2.90	2.78	2.69	2.61
29	5.59	4.20	3.61	3.27	3.04	2.88	2.76	2.67	2.59
30	5.57	4.18	3.59	3.25	3.03	2.87	2.75	2.65	2.57
40	5.42	4.05	3.46	3.13	2.90	2.74	2.62	2.53	2.45
60	5.29	3.93	3.34	3.01	2.79	2.63	2.51	2.41	2.33
120	5.15	3.80	3.23	2.89	2.67	2.52	2.39	2.30	2.22
∞	5.02	3.69	3.12	2.79	2.57	2.41	2.29	2.19	2.11

DENOMINATOR DEGREES OF FREEDOM (vertical label for v_2 column)

SOURCE: From M. Merrington and C. M. Thompson, "Tables of Percentage Points of the Inverted Beta (F)-Distribution," *Biometrika* 33 (1943): 73–88. Reproduced by permission of the Biometrika Trustees.

Table 6(b)

continued

ν_2 \ ν_1	NUMERATOR DEGREES OF FREEDOM									
	10	12	15	20	24	30	40	60	120	∞
1	968.6	976.7	984.9	993.1	997.2	1,001	1,006	1,010	1,014	1,018
2	39.40	39.41	39.43	39.45	39.46	39.46	39.47	39.48	39.49	39.50
3	14.42	14.34	14.25	14.17	14.12	14.08	14.04	13.99	13.95	13.90
4	8.84	8.75	8.66	8.56	8.51	8.46	8.41	8.36	8.31	8.26
5	6.62	6.52	6.43	6.33	6.28	6.23	6.18	6.12	6.07	6.02
6	5.46	5.37	5.27	5.17	5.12	5.07	5.01	4.96	4.90	4.85
7	4.76	4.67	4.57	4.47	4.42	4.36	4.31	4.25	4.20	4.14
8	4.30	4.20	4.10	4.00	3.95	3.89	3.84	3.78	3.73	3.67
9	3.96	3.87	3.77	3.67	3.61	3.56	3.51	3.45	3.39	3.33
10	3.72	3.62	3.52	3.42	3.37	3.31	3.26	3.20	3.14	3.08
11	3.53	3.43	3.33	3.23	3.17	3.12	3.06	3.00	2.94	2.88
12	3.37	3.28	3.18	3.07	3.02	2.96	2.91	2.85	2.79	2.72
13	3.25	3.15	3.05	2.95	2.89	2.84	2.78	2.72	2.66	2.60
14	3.15	3.05	2.95	2.84	2.79	2.73	2.67	2.61	2.55	2.49
15	3.06	2.96	2.86	2.76	2.70	2.64	2.59	2.52	2.46	2.40
16	2.99	2.89	2.79	2.68	2.63	2.57	2.51	2.45	2.38	2.32
17	2.92	2.82	2.72	2.62	2.56	2.50	2.44	2.38	2.32	2.25
18	2.87	2.77	2.67	2.56	2.50	2.44	2.38	2.32	2.26	2.19
19	2.82	2.72	2.62	2.51	2.45	2.39	2.33	2.27	2.20	2.13
20	2.77	2.68	2.57	2.46	2.41	2.35	2.29	2.22	2.16	2.09
21	2.73	2.64	2.53	2.42	2.37	2.31	2.25	2.18	2.11	2.04
22	2.70	2.60	2.50	2.39	2.33	2.27	2.21	2.14	2.08	2.00
23	2.67	2.57	2.47	2.36	2.30	2.24	2.18	2.11	2.04	1.97
24	2.64	2.54	2.44	2.33	2.27	2.21	2.15	2.08	2.01	1.94
25	2.61	2.51	2.41	2.30	2.24	2.18	2.12	2.05	1.98	1.91
26	2.59	2.49	2.39	2.28	2.22	2.16	2.09	2.03	1.95	1.88
27	2.57	2.47	2.36	2.25	2.19	2.13	2.07	2.00	1.93	1.85
28	2.55	2.45	2.34	2.23	2.17	2.11	2.05	1.98	1.91	1.83
29	2.53	2.43	2.32	2.21	2.15	2.09	2.03	1.96	1.89	1.81
30	2.51	2.41	2.31	2.20	2.14	2.07	2.01	1.94	1.87	1.79
40	2.39	2.29	2.18	2.07	2.01	1.94	1.88	1.80	1.72	1.64
60	2.27	2.17	2.06	1.94	1.88	1.82	1.74	1.67	1.58	1.48
120	2.16	2.05	1.94	1.82	1.76	1.69	1.61	1.53	1.43	1.31
∞	2.05	1.94	1.83	1.71	1.64	1.57	1.48	1.39	1.27	1.00

DENOMINATOR DEGREES OF FREEDOM

Table 6(c)

Percentage Points of the *F* Distribution, *A* = .01

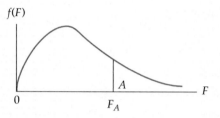

ν_2 \ ν_1	1	2	3	4	5	6	7	8	9
				NUMERATOR DEGREES OF FREEDOM					
1	4,052	4,999.5	5,403	5,625	5,764	5,859	5,928	5,982	6,022
2	98.50	99.00	99.17	99.25	99.30	99.33	99.36	99.37	99.39
3	34.12	30.82	29.46	28.71	28.24	27.91	27.67	27.49	27.35
4	21.20	18.00	16.69	15.98	15.52	15.21	14.98	14.80	14.66
5	16.26	13.27	12.06	11.39	10.97	10.67	10.46	10.29	10.16
6	13.75	10.92	9.78	9.15	8.75	8.47	8.26	8.10	7.98
7	12.25	9.55	8.45	7.85	7.46	7.19	6.99	6.84	6.72
8	11.26	8.65	7.59	7.01	6.63	6.37	6.18	6.03	5.91
9	10.56	8.02	6.99	6.42	6.06	5.80	5.61	5.47	5.35
10	10.04	7.56	6.55	5.99	5.64	5.39	5.20	5.06	4.94
11	9.65	7.21	6.22	5.67	5.32	5.07	4.89	4.74	4.63
12	9.33	6.93	5.95	5.41	5.06	4.82	4.64	4.50	4.39
13	9.07	6.70	5.74	5.21	4.86	4.62	4.44	4.30	4.19
14	8.86	6.51	5.56	5.04	4.69	4.46	4.28	4.14	4.03
15	8.68	6.36	5.42	4.89	4.56	4.32	4.14	4.00	3.89
16	8.53	6.23	5.29	4.77	4.44	4.20	4.03	3.89	3.78
17	8.40	6.11	5.18	4.67	4.34	4.10	3.93	3.79	3.68
18	8.29	6.01	5.09	4.58	4.25	4.01	3.84	3.71	3.60
19	8.18	5.93	5.01	4.50	4.17	3.94	3.77	3.63	3.52
20	8.10	5.85	4.94	4.43	4.10	3.87	3.70	3.56	3.46
21	8.02	5.78	4.87	4.37	4.04	3.81	3.64	3.51	3.40
22	7.95	5.72	4.82	4.31	3.99	3.76	3.59	3.45	3.35
23	7.88	5.66	4.76	4.26	3.94	3.71	3.54	3.41	3.30
24	7.82	5.61	4.72	4.22	3.90	3.67	3.50	3.36	3.26
25	7.77	5.57	4.68	4.18	3.85	3.63	3.46	3.32	3.22
26	7.72	5.53	4.64	4.14	3.82	3.59	3.42	3.29	3.18
27	7.68	5.49	4.60	4.11	3.78	3.56	3.39	3.26	3.15
28	7.64	5.45	4.57	4.07	3.75	3.53	3.36	3.23	3.12
29	7.60	5.42	4.54	4.04	3.73	3.50	3.33	3.20	3.09
30	7.56	5.39	4.51	4.02	3.70	3.47	3.30	3.17	3.07
40	7.31	5.18	4.31	3.83	3.51	3.29	3.12	2.99	2.89
60	7.08	4.98	4.13	3.65	3.34	3.12	2.95	2.82	2.72
120	6.85	4.79	3.95	3.48	3.17	2.96	2.79	2.66	2.56
∞	6.63	4.61	3.78	3.32	3.02	2.80	2.64	2.51	2.41

DENOMINATOR DEGREES OF FREEDOM

SOURCE: From M. Merrington and C. M. Thompson, "Tables of Percentage Points of the Inverted Beta (*F*)-Distribution," *Biometrika* 33 (1943): 73–88. Reproduced by permission of the Biometrika Trustees.

Table 6(c)

continued

ν_2	NUMERATOR DEGREES OF FREEDOM ν_1									
	10	12	15	20	24	30	40	60	120	∞
1	6,056	6,106	6,157	6,209	6,235	6,261	6,287	6,313	6,339	6,366
2	99.40	99.42	99.43	99.45	99.46	99.47	99.47	99.48	99.49	99.50
3	27.23	27.05	26.87	26.69	26.60	26.50	26.41	26.32	26.22	26.13
4	14.55	14.37	14.20	14.02	13.93	13.84	13.75	13.65	13.56	13.46
5	10.05	9.89	9.72	9.55	9.47	9.38	9.29	9.20	9.11	9.02
6	7.87	7.72	7.56	7.40	7.31	7.23	7.14	7.06	6.97	6.88
7	6.62	6.47	6.31	6.16	6.07	5.99	5.91	5.82	5.74	5.65
8	5.81	5.67	5.52	5.36	5.28	5.20	5.12	5.03	4.95	4.86
9	5.26	5.11	4.96	4.81	4.73	4.65	4.57	4.48	4.40	4.31
10	4.85	4.71	4.56	4.41	4.33	4.25	4.17	4.08	4.00	3.91
11	4.54	4.40	4.25	4.10	4.02	3.94	3.86	3.78	3.69	3.60
12	4.30	4.16	4.01	3.86	3.78	3.70	3.62	3.54	3.45	3.36
13	4.10	3.96	3.82	3.66	3.59	3.51	3.43	3.34	3.25	3.17
14	3.94	3.80	3.66	3.51	3.43	3.35	3.27	3.18	3.09	3.00
15	3.80	3.67	3.52	3.37	3.29	3.21	3.13	3.05	2.96	2.87
16	3.69	3.55	3.41	3.26	3.18	3.10	3.02	2.93	2.84	2.75
17	3.59	3.46	3.31	3.16	3.08	3.00	2.92	2.83	2.75	2.65
18	3.51	3.37	3.23	3.08	3.00	2.92	2.84	2.75	2.66	2.57
19	3.43	3.30	3.15	3.00	2.92	2.84	2.76	2.67	2.58	2.49
20	3.37	3.23	3.09	2.94	2.86	2.78	2.69	2.61	2.52	2.42
21	3.31	3.17	3.03	2.88	2.80	2.72	2.64	2.55	2.46	2.36
22	3.26	3.12	2.98	2.83	2.75	2.67	2.58	2.50	2.40	2.31
23	3.21	3.07	2.93	2.78	2.70	2.62	2.54	2.45	2.35	2.26
24	3.17	3.03	2.89	2.74	2.66	2.58	2.49	2.40	2.31	2.21
25	3.13	2.99	2.85	2.70	2.62	2.54	2.45	2.36	2.27	2.17
26	3.09	2.96	2.81	2.66	2.58	2.50	2.42	2.33	2.23	2.13
27	3.06	2.93	2.78	2.63	2.55	2.47	2.38	2.29	2.20	2.10
28	3.03	2.90	2.75	2.60	2.52	2.44	2.35	2.26	2.17	2.06
29	3.00	2.87	2.73	2.57	2.49	2.41	2.33	2.23	2.14	2.03
30	2.98	2.84	2.70	2.55	2.47	2.39	2.30	2.21	2.11	2.01
40	2.80	2.66	2.52	2.37	2.29	2.20	2.11	2.02	1.92	1.80
60	2.63	2.50	2.35	2.20	2.12	2.03	1.94	1.84	1.73	1.60
120	2.47	2.34	2.19	2.03	1.95	1.86	1.76	1.66	1.53	1.38
∞	2.32	2.18	2.04	1.88	1.79	1.70	1.59	1.47	1.32	1.00

DENOMINATOR DEGREES OF FREEDOM

Table 7(a)

Percentage Points of the Studentized Range $q_\alpha(k, \nu)$, $\alpha = .05$

ν	2	3	4	5	6	7	8	9	10	11	12	13	14	15	16	17	18	19	20
1	18.0	27.0	32.8	37.1	40.4	43.1	45.4	47.4	49.1	50.6	52.0	53.2	54.3	55.4	56.3	57.2	58.0	58.8	59.6
2	6.08	8.33	9.80	10.9	11.7	12.4	13.0	13.5	14.0	14.4	14.7	15.1	15.4	15.7	15.9	16.1	16.4	16.6	16.8
3	4.50	5.91	6.82	7.50	8.04	8.48	8.85	9.18	9.46	9.72	9.95	10.2	10.3	10.5	10.7	10.8	11.0	11.1	11.2
4	3.93	5.04	5.76	6.29	6.71	7.05	7.35	7.60	7.83	8.03	8.21	8.37	8.52	8.66	8.79	8.91	9.03	9.13	9.23
5	3.64	4.60	5.22	5.67	6.03	6.33	6.58	6.80	6.99	7.17	7.32	7.47	7.60	7.72	7.83	7.93	8.03	8.12	8.21
6	3.46	4.34	4.90	5.30	5.63	5.90	6.12	6.32	6.49	6.65	6.79	6.92	7.03	7.14	7.24	7.34	7.43	7.51	7.59
7	3.34	4.16	4.68	5.06	5.36	5.61	5.82	6.00	6.16	6.30	6.43	6.55	6.66	6.76	6.85	6.94	7.02	7.10	7.17
8	3.26	4.04	4.53	4.89	5.17	5.40	5.60	5.77	5.92	6.05	6.18	6.29	6.39	6.48	6.57	6.65	6.73	6.80	6.87
9	3.20	3.95	4.41	4.76	5.02	5.24	5.43	5.59	5.74	5.87	5.98	6.09	6.19	6.28	6.36	6.44	6.51	6.58	6.64
10	3.15	3.88	4.33	4.65	4.91	5.12	5.30	5.46	5.60	5.72	5.83	5.93	6.03	6.11	6.19	6.27	6.34	6.40	6.47
11	3.11	3.82	4.26	4.57	4.82	5.03	5.20	5.35	5.49	5.61	5.71	5.81	5.90	5.98	6.06	6.13	6.20	6.27	6.33
12	3.08	3.77	4.20	4.51	4.75	4.95	5.12	5.27	5.39	5.51	5.61	5.71	5.80	5.88	5.95	6.02	6.09	6.15	6.21
13	3.06	3.73	4.15	4.45	4.69	4.88	5.05	5.19	5.32	5.43	5.53	5.63	5.71	5.79	5.86	5.93	5.99	6.05	6.11
14	3.03	3.70	4.11	4.41	4.64	4.83	4.99	5.13	5.25	5.36	5.46	5.55	5.64	5.71	5.79	5.85	5.91	5.97	6.03
15	3.01	3.67	4.08	4.37	4.59	4.78	4.94	5.08	5.20	5.31	5.40	5.49	5.57	5.65	5.72	5.78	5.85	5.90	5.96
16	3.00	3.65	4.05	4.33	4.56	4.74	4.90	5.03	5.15	5.26	5.35	5.44	5.52	5.59	5.66	5.73	5.79	5.84	5.90
17	2.98	3.63	4.02	4.30	4.52	4.70	4.86	4.99	5.11	5.21	5.31	5.39	5.47	5.54	5.61	5.67	5.73	5.79	5.84
18	2.97	3.61	4.00	4.28	4.49	4.67	4.82	4.96	5.07	5.17	5.27	5.35	5.43	5.50	5.57	5.63	5.69	5.74	5.79
19	2.96	3.59	3.98	4.25	4.47	4.65	4.79	4.92	5.04	5.14	5.23	5.31	5.39	5.46	5.53	5.59	5.65	5.70	5.75
20	2.95	3.58	3.96	4.23	4.45	4.62	4.77	4.90	5.01	5.11	5.20	5.28	5.36	5.43	5.49	5.55	5.61	5.66	5.71
24	2.92	3.53	3.90	4.17	4.37	4.54	4.68	4.81	4.92	5.01	5.10	5.18	5.25	5.32	5.38	5.44	5.49	5.55	5.59
30	2.89	3.49	3.85	4.10	4.30	4.46	4.60	4.72	4.82	4.92	5.00	5.08	5.15	5.21	5.27	5.33	5.38	5.43	5.47
40	2.86	3.44	3.79	4.04	4.23	4.39	4.52	4.63	4.73	4.82	4.90	4.98	5.04	5.11	5.16	5.22	5.27	5.31	5.36
60	2.83	3.40	3.74	3.98	4.16	4.31	4.44	4.55	4.65	4.73	4.81	4.88	4.94	5.00	5.06	5.11	5.15	5.20	5.24
120	2.80	3.36	3.68	3.92	4.10	4.24	4.36	4.47	4.56	4.64	4.71	4.78	4.84	4.90	4.95	5.00	5.04	5.09	5.13
∞	2.77	3.31	3.63	3.86	4.03	4.17	4.29	4.39	4.47	4.55	4.62	4.68	4.74	4.80	4.85	4.89	4.93	4.97	5.01

Table 7(b)

Percentage Points of the Studentized Range $q_\alpha(k, v)$, $\alpha = .01$

v										k									
	2	3	4	5	6	7	8	9	10	11	12	13	14	15	16	17	18	19	20
1	90.0	135	164	186	202	216	227	237	246	253	260	266	272	277	282	286	290	294	298
2	14.0	19.0	22.3	24.7	26.6	28.2	29.5	30.7	31.7	32.6	33.4	34.1	34.8	35.4	36.0	36.5	37.0	37.5	37.9
3	8.26	10.6	12.2	13.3	14.2	15.0	15.6	16.2	16.7	17.1	17.5	17.9	18.2	18.5	18.8	19.1	19.3	19.5	19.8
4	6.51	8.12	9.17	9.96	10.6	11.1	11.5	11.9	12.3	12.6	12.8	13.1	13.3	13.5	13.7	13.9	14.1	14.2	14.4
5	5.70	6.97	7.80	8.42	8.91	9.32	9.67	9.97	10.2	10.5	10.7	10.9	11.1	11.2	11.4	11.6	11.7	11.8	11.9
6	5.24	6.33	7.03	7.56	7.97	8.32	8.61	8.87	9.10	9.30	9.49	9.65	9.81	9.95	10.1	10.2	10.3	10.4	10.5
7	4.95	5.92	6.54	7.01	7.37	7.68	7.94	8.17	8.37	8.55	8.71	8.86	9.00	9.12	9.24	9.35	9.46	9.55	9.65
8	4.74	5.63	6.20	6.63	6.96	7.24	7.47	7.68	7.87	8.03	8.18	8.31	8.44	8.55	8.66	8.76	8.85	8.94	9.03
9	4.60	5.43	5.96	6.35	6.66	6.91	7.13	7.32	7.49	7.65	7.78	7.91	8.03	8.13	8.23	8.32	8.41	8.49	8.57
10	4.48	5.27	5.77	6.14	6.43	6.67	6.87	7.05	7.21	7.36	7.48	7.60	7.71	7.81	7.91	7.99	8.07	8.15	8.22
11	4.39	5.14	5.62	5.97	6.25	6.48	6.67	6.84	6.99	7.13	7.25	7.36	7.46	7.56	7.65	7.73	7.81	7.88	7.95
12	4.32	5.04	5.50	5.84	6.10	6.32	6.51	6.67	6.81	6.94	7.06	7.17	7.26	7.36	7.44	7.52	7.59	7.66	7.73
13	4.26	4.96	5.40	5.73	5.98	6.19	6.37	6.53	6.67	6.79	6.90	7.01	7.10	7.19	7.27	7.34	7.42	7.48	7.55
14	4.21	4.89	5.32	5.63	5.88	6.08	6.26	6.41	6.54	6.66	6.77	6.87	6.96	7.05	7.12	7.20	7.27	7.33	7.39
15	4.17	4.83	5.25	5.56	5.80	5.99	6.16	6.31	6.44	6.55	6.66	6.76	6.84	6.93	7.00	7.07	7.14	7.20	7.26
16	4.13	4.78	5.19	5.49	5.72	5.92	6.08	6.22	6.35	6.46	6.56	6.66	6.74	6.82	6.90	6.97	7.03	7.09	7.15
17	4.10	4.74	5.14	5.43	5.66	5.85	6.01	6.15	6.27	6.38	6.48	6.57	6.66	6.73	6.80	6.87	6.94	7.00	7.05
18	4.07	4.70	5.09	5.38	5.60	5.79	5.94	6.08	6.20	6.31	6.41	6.50	6.58	6.65	6.72	6.79	6.85	6.91	6.96
19	4.05	4.67	5.05	5.33	5.55	5.73	5.89	6.02	6.14	6.25	6.34	6.43	6.51	6.58	6.65	6.72	6.78	6.84	6.89
20	4.02	4.64	5.02	5.29	5.51	5.69	5.84	5.97	6.09	6.19	6.29	6.37	6.45	6.52	6.59	6.65	6.71	6.76	6.82
24	3.96	4.54	4.91	5.17	5.37	5.54	5.69	5.81	5.92	6.02	6.11	6.19	6.26	6.33	6.39	6.45	6.51	6.56	6.61
30	3.89	4.45	4.80	5.05	5.24	5.40	5.54	5.65	5.76	5.85	5.93	6.01	6.08	6.14	6.20	6.26	6.31	6.36	6.41
40	3.82	4.37	4.70	4.93	5.11	5.27	5.39	5.50	5.60	5.69	5.77	5.84	5.90	5.96	6.02	6.07	6.12	6.17	6.21
60	3.76	4.28	4.60	4.82	4.99	5.13	5.25	5.36	5.45	5.53	5.60	5.67	5.73	5.79	5.84	5.89	5.93	5.98	6.02
120	3.70	4.20	4.50	4.71	4.87	5.01	5.12	5.21	5.30	5.38	5.44	5.51	5.56	5.61	5.66	5.71	5.75	5.79	5.83
∞	3.64	4.12	4.40	4.60	4.76	4.88	4.99	5.08	5.16	5.23	5.29	5.35	5.40	5.45	5.49	5.54	5.57	5.61	5.65

SOURCE: From E. S. Pearson and H. O. Hartley, *Biometrika Tables for Statisticians*, 1: 176–77. Reproduced by permission of the Biometrika Trustees.

Table 8   Critical Values of the Wilcoxon Rank Sum Test for Independent Samples

(a) α = .025 one-tail; α = .05 two-tail

n_2	n_1 = 3 T_L	T_U	4 T_L	T_U	5 T_L	T_U	6 T_L	T_U	7 T_L	T_U	8 T_L	T_U	9 T_L	T_U	10 T_L	T_U
4	6	18	11	25	17	33	23	43	31	53	40	64	50	76	61	89
5	6	21	12	28	18	37	25	47	33	58	42	70	52	83	64	96
6	7	23	12	32	19	41	26	52	35	63	44	76	55	89	66	104
7	7	26	13	35	20	45	28	56	37	68	47	81	58	95	70	110
8	8	28	14	38	21	49	29	61	39	73	49	87	60	102	73	117
9	8	31	15	41	22	53	31	65	41	78	51	93	63	108	76	124
10	9	33	16	44	24	56	32	70	43	83	54	98	66	114	79	131

(b) α = .05 one-tail; α = .10 two-tail

n_2	n_1 = 3 T_L	T_U	4 T_L	T_U	5 T_L	T_U	6 T_L	T_U	7 T_L	T_U	8 T_L	T_U	9 T_L	T_U	10 T_L	T_U
3	6	15	11	21	16	29	23	37	31	46	39	57	49	68	60	80
4	7	17	12	24	18	32	25	41	33	51	42	62	52	74	63	87
5	7	20	13	27	19	36	26	46	35	56	45	67	55	80	66	94
6	8	22	14	30	20	40	28	50	37	61	47	73	57	87	69	101
7	9	24	15	33	22	43	30	54	39	66	49	79	60	93	73	107
8	9	27	16	36	24	46	32	58	41	71	52	84	63	99	76	114
9	10	29	17	39	25	50	33	63	43	76	54	90	66	105	79	121
10	11	31	18	42	26	54	35	67	46	80	57	95	69	111	83	127

SOURCE: From F. Wilcoxon and R.A. Wilcox, "Some Rapid Approximate Statistical Procedures" (1964), p. 28. Reproduced with the permission of American Cyanamid Company.

Table 9

Critical Values for the Wilcoxon Signed Rank Sum Test for the Matched Pairs Experiment	(a) $\alpha = .025$ one-tail $\alpha = .05$ two-tail			(b) $\alpha = .05$ one-tail $\alpha = .10$ two-tail	
n	T_L	T_U		T_L	T_U
6	1	20		2	19
7	2	26		4	24
8	4	32		6	30
9	6	39		8	37
10	8	47		11	44
11	11	55		14	52
12	14	64		17	61
13	17	74		21	70
14	21	84		26	79
15	25	95		30	90
16	30	106		36	100
17	35	118		41	112
18	40	131		47	124
19	46	144		54	136
20	52	158		60	150
21	59	172		68	163
22	66	187		75	178
23	73	203		83	193
24	81	219		92	208
25	90	235		101	224
26	98	253		110	241
27	107	271		120	258
28	117	289		130	276
29	127	308		141	294
30	137	328		152	313

Table 10 Critical Values of the Lilliefors Test

SAMPLE SIZE n	SIGNIFICANCE LEVEL α				
	.20	**.15**	**.10**	**.05**	**.01**
4	.300	.319	.352	.381	.417
5	.285	.299	.315	.337	.405
6	.265	.277	.294	.319	.364
7	.247	.258	.276	.300	.348
8	.233	.244	.261	.285	.331
9	.223	.233	.249	.271	.311
10	.215	.224	.239	.258	.294
11	.206	.217	.230	.249	.284
12	.199	.212	.223	.242	.275
13	.190	.202	.214	.234	.268
14	.183	.194	.207	.227	.261
15	.177	.187	.201	.220	.257
16	.173	.182	.195	.213	.250
17	.169	.177	.189	.206	.245
18	.166	.173	.184	.200	.239
19	.163	.169	.179	.195	.235
20	.160	.166	.174	.190	.231
25	.142	.147	.158	.173	.200
30	.131	.136	.144	.161	.187
Over 30	$\dfrac{.736}{\sqrt{n}}$	$\dfrac{.768}{\sqrt{n}}$	$\dfrac{.805}{\sqrt{n}}$	$\dfrac{.886}{\sqrt{n}}$	$\dfrac{1.031}{\sqrt{n}}$

SOURCE: From H. W. Lilliefors, "On the Kolmogorov–Smirnov Test for Normality with Mean and Variance Unknown," *Journal of the American Statistical Association* 62(1967): 399–402. As adapted by Conover, *Practical Nonparametric Statistics* (New York: John Wiley, 1971), p. 398. Reprinted by permission of John Wiley & Sons, Inc., and the American Statistical Association.

Table 11

Critical Values of the Spearman Rank Correlation Coefficient

The α values correspond to a one-tail test of $H_0: \rho_s = 0$. The value should be doubled for two-tail tests.

n	$\alpha = .05$	$\alpha = .025$	$\alpha = .01$	$\alpha = .005$
5	.900	—	—	—
6	.829	.886	.943	—
7	.714	.786	.893	—
8	.643	.738	.833	.881
9	.600	.683	.783	.833
10	.564	.648	.745	.794
11	.523	.623	.736	.818
12	.497	.591	.703	.780
13	.475	.566	.673	.745
14	.457	.545	.646	.716
15	.441	.525	.623	.689
16	.425	.507	.601	.666
17	.412	.490	.582	.645
18	.399	.476	.564	.625
19	.388	.462	.549	.608
20	.377	.450	.534	.591
21	.368	.438	.521	.576
22	.359	.428	.508	.562
23	.351	.418	.496	.549
24	.343	.409	.485	.537
25	.336	.400	.475	.526
26	.329	.392	.465	.515
27	.323	.385	.456	.505
28	.317	.377	.448	.496
29	.311	.370	.440	.487
30	.305	.364	.432	.478

SOURCE: From E. G. Olds, "Distribution of Sums of Squares of Rank Differences for Small Samples," *Annals of Mathematical Statistics* 9 (1938). Reproduced with the permission of the Institute of Mathematical Statistics.

Table 12(a)

Critical Values for the Durbin–Watson d Statistic, $\alpha = .05$

n	$k = 1$ d_L	d_U	$k = 2$ d_L	d_U	$k = 3$ d_L	d_U	$k = 4$ d_L	d_U	$k = 5$ d_L	d_U
15	1.08	1.36	.95	1.54	.82	1.75	.69	1.97	.56	2.21
16	1.10	1.37	.98	1.54	.86	1.73	.74	1.93	.62	2.15
17	1.13	1.38	1.02	1.54	.90	1.71	.78	1.90	.67	2.10
18	1.16	1.39	1.05	1.53	.93	1.69	.82	1.87	.71	2.06
19	1.18	1.40	1.08	1.53	.97	1.68	.86	1.85	.75	2.02
20	1.20	1.41	1.10	1.54	1.00	1.68	.90	1.83	.79	1.99
21	1.22	1.42	1.13	1.54	1.03	1.67	.93	1.81	.83	1.96
22	1.24	1.43	1.15	1.54	1.05	1.66	.96	1.80	.86	1.94
23	1.26	1.44	1.17	1.54	1.08	1.66	.99	1.79	.90	1.92
24	1.27	1.45	1.19	1.55	1.10	1.66	1.01	1.78	.93	1.90
25	1.29	1.45	1.21	1.55	1.12	1.66	1.04	1.77	.95	1.89
26	1.30	1.46	1.22	1.55	1.14	1.65	1.06	1.76	.98	1.88
27	1.32	1.47	1.24	1.56	1.16	1.65	1.08	1.76	1.01	1.86
28	1.33	1.48	1.26	1.56	1.18	1.65	1.10	1.75	1.03	1.85
29	1.34	1.48	1.27	1.56	1.20	1.65	1.12	1.74	1.05	1.84
30	1.35	1.49	1.28	1.57	1.21	1.65	1.14	1.74	1.07	1.83
31	1.36	1.50	1.30	1.57	1.23	1.65	1.16	1.74	1.09	1.83
32	1.37	1.50	1.31	1.57	1.24	1.65	1.18	1.73	1.11	1.82
33	1.38	1.51	1.32	1.58	1.26	1.65	1.19	1.73	1.13	1.81
34	1.39	1.51	1.33	1.58	1.27	1.65	1.21	1.73	1.15	1.81
35	1.40	1.52	1.34	1.58	1.28	1.65	1.22	1.73	1.16	1.80
36	1.41	1.52	1.35	1.59	1.29	1.65	1.24	1.73	1.18	1.80
37	1.42	1.53	1.36	1.59	1.31	1.66	1.25	1.72	1.19	1.80
38	1.43	1.54	1.37	1.59	1.32	1.66	1.26	1.72	1.21	1.79
39	1.43	1.54	1.38	1.60	1.33	1.66	1.27	1.72	1.22	1.79
40	1.44	1.54	1.39	1.60	1.34	1.66	1.29	1.72	1.23	1.79
45	1.48	1.57	1.43	1.62	1.38	1.67	1.34	1.72	1.29	1.78
50	1.50	1.59	1.46	1.63	1.42	1.67	1.38	1.72	1.34	1.77
55	1.53	1.60	1.49	1.64	1.45	1.68	1.41	1.72	1.38	1.77
60	1.55	1.62	1.51	1.65	1.48	1.69	1.44	1.73	1.41	1.77
65	1.57	1.63	1.54	1.66	1.50	1.70	1.47	1.73	1.44	1.77
70	1.58	1.64	1.55	1.67	1.52	1.70	1.49	1.74	1.46	1.77
75	1.60	1.65	1.57	1.68	1.54	1.71	1.51	1.74	1.49	1.77
80	1.61	1.66	1.59	1.69	1.56	1.72	1.53	1.74	1.51	1.77
85	1.62	1.67	1.60	1.70	1.57	1.72	1.55	1.75	1.52	1.77
90	1.63	1.68	1.61	1.70	1.59	1.73	1.57	1.75	1.54	1.78
95	1.64	1.69	1.62	1.71	1.60	1.73	1.58	1.75	1.56	1.78
100	1.65	1.69	1.63	1.72	1.61	1.74	1.59	1.76	1.57	1.78

SOURCE: From J. Durbin and G. S. Watson, "Testing for Serial Correlation in Least Squares Regression, II," *Biometrika* 30 (1951): 159–78. Reproduced by permission of the Biometrika Trustees.

Table 12(b)

Critical Values for the Durbin–Watson d Statistic, $\alpha = .01$

n	$k = 1$ d_L	d_U	$k = 2$ d_L	d_U	$k = 3$ d_L	d_U	$k = 4$ d_L	d_U	$k = 5$ d_L	d_U
15	.81	1.07	.70	1.25	.59	1.46	.49	1.70	.39	1.96
16	.84	1.09	.74	1.25	.63	1.44	.53	1.66	.44	1.90
17	.87	1.10	.77	1.25	.67	1.43	.57	1.63	.48	1.85
18	.90	1.12	.80	1.26	.71	1.42	.61	1.60	.52	1.80
19	.93	1.13	.83	1.26	.74	1.41	.65	1.58	.56	1.77
20	.95	1.15	.86	1.27	.77	1.41	.68	1.57	.60	1.74
21	.97	1.16	.89	1.27	.80	1.41	.72	1.55	.63	1.71
22	1.00	1.17	.91	1.28	.83	1.40	.75	1.54	.66	1.69
23	1.02	1.19	.94	1.29	.86	1.40	.77	1.53	.70	1.67
24	1.04	1.20	.96	1.30	.88	1.41	.80	1.53	.72	1.66
25	1.05	1.21	.98	1.30	.90	1.41	.83	1.52	.75	1.65
26	1.07	1.22	1.00	1.31	.93	1.41	.85	1.52	.78	1.64
27	1.09	1.23	1.02	1.32	.95	1.41	.88	1.51	.81	1.63
28	1.10	1.24	1.04	1.32	.97	1.41	.90	1.51	.83	1.62
29	1.12	1.25	1.05	1.33	.99	1.42	.92	1.51	.85	1.61
30	1.13	1.26	1.07	1.34	1.01	1.42	.94	1.51	.88	1.61
31	1.15	1.27	1.08	1.34	1.02	1.42	.96	1.51	.90	1.60
32	1.16	1.28	1.10	1.35	1.04	1.43	.98	1.51	.92	1.60
33	1.17	1.29	1.11	1.36	1.05	1.43	1.00	1.51	.94	1.59
34	1.18	1.30	1.13	1.36	1.07	1.43	1.01	1.51	.95	1.59
35	1.19	1.31	1.14	1.37	1.08	1.44	1.03	1.51	.97	1.59
36	1.21	1.32	1.15	1.38	1.10	1.44	1.04	1.51	.99	1.59
37	1.22	1.32	1.16	1.38	1.11	1.45	1.06	1.51	1.00	1.59
38	1.23	1.33	1.18	1.39	1.12	1.45	1.07	1.52	1.02	1.58
39	1.24	1.34	1.19	1.39	1.14	1.45	1.09	1.52	1.03	1.58
40	1.25	1.34	1.20	1.40	1.15	1.46	1.10	1.52	1.05	1.58
45	1.29	1.38	1.24	1.42	1.20	1.48	1.16	1.53	1.11	1.58
50	1.32	1.40	1.28	1.45	1.24	1.49	1.20	1.54	1.16	1.59
55	1.36	1.43	1.32	1.47	1.28	1.51	1.25	1.55	1.21	1.59
60	1.38	1.45	1.35	1.48	1.32	1.52	1.28	1.56	1.25	1.60
65	1.41	1.47	1.38	1.50	1.35	1.53	1.31	1.57	1.28	1.61
70	1.43	1.49	1.40	1.52	1.37	1.55	1.34	1.58	1.31	1.61
75	1.45	1.50	1.42	1.53	1.39	1.56	1.37	1.59	1.34	1.62
80	1.47	1.52	1.44	1.54	1.42	1.57	1.39	1.60	1.36	1.62
85	1.48	1.53	1.46	1.55	1.43	1.58	1.41	1.60	1.39	1.63
90	1.50	1.54	1.47	1.56	1.45	1.59	1.43	1.61	1.41	1.64
95	1.51	1.55	1.49	1.57	1.47	1.60	1.45	1.62	1.42	1.64
100	1.52	1.56	1.50	1.58	1.48	1.60	1.46	1.63	1.44	1.65

Table 13

Control Chart Constants

SAMPLE SIZE n	A_2	d_2	d_3	D_3	D_4
2	1.880	1.128	.853	.000	3.267
3	1.023	1.693	.888	.000	2.575
4	.729	2.059	.880	.000	2.282
5	.577	2.326	.864	.000	2.115
6	.483	2.534	.848	.000	2.004
7	.419	2.704	.833	.076	1.924
8	.373	2.847	.820	.136	1.864
9	.337	2.970	.808	.184	1.816
10	.308	3.078	.797	.223	1.777
11	.285	3.173	.787	.256	1.744
12	.266	3.258	.778	.284	1.716
13	.249	3.336	.770	.308	1.692
14	.235	3.407	.762	.329	1.671
15	.223	3.472	.755	.348	1.652
16	.212	3.532	.749	.364	1.636
17	.203	3.588	.743	.379	1.621
18	.194	3.640	.738	.392	1.608
19	.187	3.689	.733	.404	1.596
20	.180	3.735	.729	.414	1.586
21	.173	3.778	.724	.425	1.575
22	.167	3.819	.720	.434	1.566
23	.162	3.858	.716	.443	1.557
24	.157	3.895	.712	.452	1.548
25	.153	3.931	.709	.459	1.541

SOURCE: From E. S. Pearson, "The Percentage Limits for the Distribution of Range in Samples from a Normal Population," *Biometrika* 24 (1932): 416. Reproduced by permission of the Biometrika Trustees.

Appendix C

Answers to Selected Even-Numbered Exercises

All answers have been double-checked for accuracy. However, we cannot be absolutely certain that no errors remain. Students should not automatically assume that answers that don't match the ones below are wrong. When and if we discover mistakes we will post corrected answers on our web page. (See page 16 for the address.) If you find any errors please e-mail the authors (address on web page). We will be happy to acknowledge you with the discovery.

Chapter 1

1.4 a the complete production run **b** 1,000 chips **c** proportion of the production run that is defective **d** proportion of sample chips that are defective (7.5%) **e** parameter **f** statistic **g** Because the sample proportion is less than 10%, we can conclude that the claim is true.
1.6 a Flip the coin 100 times and count the number of heads and tails. **b** outcomes of flips **c** outcomes of the 100 flips **d** proportion of heads **e** proportion of heads in the 100 flips

Chapter 2

2.2 a quantitative **b** qualitative **c** ranked **d** quantitative
2.4 a quantitative **b** qualitative **c** qualitative **d** ranked **e** quantitative
2.6 a quantitative **b** ranked **c** qualitative **d** quantitative **e** ranked
2.8 g .533; .467
2.14 The distribution is approximately bell shaped and unimodal, with the modal class consisting of incomes between $25,000 and $30,000.
2.16 a 48.67% **b** 61.34%
2.18 b 27.0% **c** 16.5%
2.22 b bimodal **c** Mortgage rates were less than 9% until 1968, and greater than 9% after 1968.
2.24 c yes
2.34 a qualitative in each column
2.38 a qualitative in both columns
2.42 b There is a positive linear relationship between electrical power cost and hours of machine usage.

2.44 b There is a positive linear relationship between labor costs and number of units per batch.
2.46 b There is no linear relationship between stock returns and inflation rates from 1960 to 1994. **c** It does not appear that stocks provide a good hedge against inflation.
2.48 b There is a negative linear relationship between mortgage rates and number of homes sold over this period.
2.50 a quantitative in columns 1 and 4; qualitative in columns 2, 3, and 5
2.52 a quantitative
2.66 b There is no linear relationship (or at best, a very weak negative linear relationship) between bond returns and inflation rates from 1960 to 1994. **c** It does not appear that bonds provide a good hedge against inflation.

Chapter 4

4.2 mean $= 1.417$; median $= 1$; modes $= -3, 0,$ and 4
4.4 mode
4.8 a 5.85; 5; 5
4.10 $43.59; $26.91; $0.00
4.12 $28,015.50; $28,250
4.14 a 6.17; 5; 5
4.16 a 12.2% **b** 12.98% **c** $1995.10 **d** 12.98%
4.18 no
4.20 15; 19; 35.56; 5.96
4.22 $-.14$; 5.81; 2.41
4.24 a 9; 10; 3.16 **b** 0; 4; 2 **c** 6; 4; 2 **d** 5; 0; 0
4.26 a 46.5; 6.82 **b** 6.5; 2.55 **c** 174.5; 13.21
4.30 mean; standard deviation
4.32 a 10.2; -4.5; 13.65; 4.75; 30.7; 34.1; 21.3; 7.95; .09; 20.95 **b** 14% **c** 12.63% **d** Fund A, Portfolio, Fund B (lowest return and risk)
4.34 a 2.9571; 1.7196
4.36 a 47.83; 44; 52.7, 48; 65.355, 55.5 **b** 103, 176.25, 13.28; 128, 385.72, 19.64; 176, 890.68, 29.84
4.38 a Would expect American Barrick to have the higher mean return and standard deviation, because it has higher volatility

(risk) than the index.
4.40 a (62, 76); (55, 83); (48, 90) **b** approx. 340; approx. 475; virtually all 500
4.42 a .04; .20; **b** approx. .20
4.44 a approx. 68%; virtually 100% **b** approx. 32%; **c** approx. .975
4.46 a 6,743.42; 82.12 **b** approx. 59.5
4.48 a at least 750; at least 889 **b** approx. 950; virtually all 1,000
4.50 first (lower) quartile; second quartile or median; third (upper) quartile
4.52

	Q_1	Q_3
a stocks	$-.42\%$	25.07%
b bonds	.45%	10.45%

4.54 a The distribution is skewed to the right. **b** Fewer than 25% of incomes are greater than $48,000. **c** $46,000 - 23,000 = $23,000 **d** The middle 50% of incomes are between $23,000 and $46,000.
4.56 interquartile range $Q_3 - Q_1$
An outlier is an extreme observation: more than $1.5(1QR)$ from the box.
4.58 b $Q_1 = 2$; $Q_2 = 7$; $Q_3 = 15.75$ **c** The distribution is highly skewed to the right and has two outliers: 54 and 52.
4.62 a $\bar{x} \cong 32.8$; $s^2 \cong 230.34$ **b** $s^2 \cong 256$
4.64 a $\bar{x} \cong 21.33$; $s^2 \cong 163.77$ **b** $s^2 \cong 100$
4.66 a $\bar{x} \cong 35.56$ mpg; $s \cong 4.68$ mpg
4.68 $\hat{y} = -5.356 + 3.399x$
4.70 b $\hat{y} = .273 + .0048x$ **c** $cov(X,Y) = 15.69$; $r = .938$; strong positive relationship
4.72 b $r = .32$ **c** weak relationship
4.74 a $cov(X,Y) = 215.5$; $r = .95$ There is a strong positive linear relationship between X and Y. **b** $\hat{y} = 404.8 + 62.37x$ **c** fixed cost $= 404.80; variable cost $= 62.37 per 1,000 hours
4.76 a $cov(X,Y) = 170.7$; $r = .77$ There is a moderately strong positive relationship between X and Y. **b** $\hat{y} = 315.5 + 3.3x$ **c** fixed cost $= 315.50; variable cost $= 3.30/unit
4.78 b $y = 3.64 + .267x$ **c** For each additional second of commercial, the memory test score increases by an average of .267.

$, Y) = -2.67$; $r = -.05$
y weak negative relationship
ck returns and inflation. **c** no
$-.60$; There is a moderate negative
ship between house sales and
mortgage rates.

4.84 a $\mu = 3.17$; median = 4.5; $\sigma = 6.23$
b $Q_3 = 7.5$; $Q_1 = 0$
4.86 b 100% fall into (4.6, 29.4) **c** only very roughly mound shaped **d** interval; actual; empirical rule (10.8, 23.2); .64; .68; (4.6, 29.4); 1.00; .95
4.88 a $\bar{x} = 47.6$ **b** $s^2 = 115.42$ **c** $s = 10.74$
4.92 b = 1.56 today, down from 3.36
4.94 a

	$\bar{x}$	s
1	7.28	29.35
2	9.44	3.40
3	8.52	8.59
4	8.8	4.2
5	13.42	19.48

b Fund 2 is better than funds 1, 3, and 4 because it has higher average return and lower risk. The choice betweeen funds 2 and 5 depends on the level of risk you prefer.
4.100 a $\text{cov}(X, Y) = -28.94$; $r = -0.91$
b There is a strong negative relationship between house sales and mortgage rates.
4.102 a 35.8; 26.9; 22.5; 28.1; 21.7; 10.4; 18.6 **b** 23.4% **c** 23.2%
d $1,440,958 **e** 25.9%; above average growth rate

Chapter 6

6.4 b $S = \{0, 1, 2, 3, 4\}$ **c** 36/80; 28/80; 12/80; 2/80; 2/80 **d** relative frequency **e** .05
6.6 a 28/75; 7/25; 26/75; 43/75; 32/75 **b** 47/75
6.8 a 1/13 **b** 1/13 **c** yes
6.10 .20
6.12 a 67/125 **b** 41/125 **c** no **d** no
6.14 12/44
6.16 a .125 **b** .325 **c** .375 **d** .875
6.18 a .24 **b** .66 **c** .2
6.20 a $(.99999)^4$ **b** $1 - (.99999)^4 - (.00001)^4$ **c** independence of failures
6.22 a 39% **b** 100%
6.24 a .16 **b** .84 **c** .36
6.26 a 42/90
6.28 a .7 **b** .18
6.30 a 3,600 **b** .41 **c** .34 **d** .805
6.32 .526
6.34 a .6981 **b** .9542
6.36 a all numbers in [o, m], where m is the maximum number of miles possible from one tank **b** theoretically uncountable, but can only measure countable number **c** continuous
6.38 a .5 **b** .8 **c** .7 **d** .2 **e** 0 **f** .9

6.40 Tables (a) and (b) are not valid.
6.42 a

x	0	1	2	3
p(x)	⅛	⅜	⅜	⅛

6.44 a .72 **b** .71 **c** .02
6.46 a

x	0	1	2	3
p(x)	.512	.384	.096	.008

c .104
6.48 a 2.0; 1.0 **b** yes
6.50 a 15.75; 33.1875 **b** 60; 531
6.52 a 8.5; 45.25 **b** 117.5; 587.5
6.54 a up to $18 **b** $55.46
6.56 $500 in cash
6.62 a 950; 322,500 **b** 475; 80,626
6.64 medium ($338 million)
6.66 $p(x,y) = p(x) \cdot p(y)$ for all (x,y)
6.68 a

x	0	1	2
p(x)	.7	.2	.1

y	0	1	2
p(y)	.6	.3	.1

b yes **c** .3
d

x + y	0	1	2	3	4
p(x + y)	.42	.33	.19	.05	.01

e .20 **f** 0
6.70 a 17%; 21.16(%)² **b** portfolio
6.72 portfolio: 14.5; 29.95; It depends on your desired level of risk.
6.74 a Motorola: .020; .0071 Coke: .021; .0017 **b** .00028 **c** .0208; .0015
6.76 a 10 **b** 15 **c** 15 **d** 1 **e** 1
6.78 a .1488 **b** .2461 **c** .3151
6.80 a .0512 **b** .3241 **c** .3115
6.82 a .127 **b** .131 **c** .147 **d** .688 **e** 0 **f** .046
6.84 a .250 **b** .078 **c** .014
6.86 a 0 **b** .058 **c** .665 **d** .328
6.88

x	p(x)
0	.970299
1	.029403
2	.000297
3	.000001

6.90 a .015 **b** .558 **c** .594
6.92 a .616 **b** .176 **c** .238
6.96 a .277; .365; .231 **b** $\mu = 1.25$; .287; .358; .235
6.98 .036
6.100 a .265 **b** .456 **c** .125
6.102 a .122 **b** .687
6.104 a .004 **b** The claim is probably false.

6.106 a 2/36 **b** 10/36 **c** 6/36 **d** 5/36 **e** 18/36 **f** 10/36
6.108 a .71 **b** .16 **c** 55/180
6.110 a .78 **b** .22 **c** .35 **d** 21/78 **e** 14/22 **f** 8/22 **g** 8/65 **h** 0 **i** 1 **j** .57
6.112 a .000027 **b** .084681 **c** .087327
6.114 a .8 **b** .6 **c** .375
6.116 a $(.015)(.05)(.1)^6$ **b** $1-(.6)^6-6(.1)^5(.9)$
6.118 a $P(A) = 5/15$; $P(B) = 4/15$; $P(C) = 3/15$ **b** 3/15
6.120 You should be indifferent.
6.122 a 4.4; 2.42 **b** 25.2 **c** 95.8 **d** 20.2; 7.26
6.124 a $85,000 **b** $629,504
6.126 a 16%; 6.73% **b** stock, combination, real estate
6.128 a .016 **b** .012 **c** .874 **d** .245 **e** .545 **f** .505
6.130 a .677 **b** .165 **c** .323 **d** .866
6.132 a .096 **b** .994
6.134 $89.20
6.136 a .837 **b** .999 **c** .45
6.138 a .163 **b** .181 **c** .180

Chapter 7

7.2 c .8 **d** 0 **e** .5
7.4 a .25 **c** .58
7.6 a .0446 **b** .8289 **c** .025 **d** .9925 **e** .0823 **f** .8123
7.8 a 2.575 **b** 2.33 **c** 1.645
7.10 a .25 **b** -1.25 **c** -1.875 **d** 1.75 **e** -2.25 **f** -1.625
7.12 a .0062 **b** 38,420
7.14 a .0475 **b** .3830 **c** .9901 **d** $2,902,000
7.16 a .9544 **b** .1587
7.18 a 10 **b** 7796
7.20 a .7340; .3783 **b** 96
7.22 a 1.15 **b** .9693 **c** .1762
7.26 a .1353 **b** .0183 **c** .6321 **d** .5507
7.28 a .0025 **b** .999994 **c** .0497 **d** 0
7.30 a .8892
7.32 b .865; .982 **c** .05 **d** .05
7.34 a .3679 **b** highly skewed to right **c** .095 **d** .035 **e** .095; same
7.36 a .0505 **b** .1059 **c** .6985 **d** .7439
7.38 6.082 ounces
7.40 .2912
7.42 a .6703 **b** .3679 **c** .8647

Chapter 8

8.2 $\bar{X}$ is approximately normal, with mean 40 and standard deviation 1.2.
8.4 a .1587 **b** .2199 **c** .0228
8.6 a .2347 **b** .4435 **c** .5328
8.8 We can answer part (c) and possibly part (b). We cannot answer part (a).
8.10 .3085
8.12 a .2514 **b** .0681 **c** .0010

8.14 The professor needs to know the mean and standard deviation of the weights of the population of people who use the elevator, and that the distribution is not extremely nonnormal.

8.16 a binomial: .134; normal approximation: .1378 **b** binomial: .910; normal approximation: .9049 **c** binomial: .956; normal approximation: .9599

8.18 a binomial: .7635; normal approximation: .7611 **b** binomial: .8578; normal approximation: .8577 **c** binomial: 0.8582; normal approximation: .8577 **d** binomial: .2160; normal approximation: .2177 **e** binomial: .0239; normal approximation: .0241

8.20 0.0250

8.22 0.0035

8.24 0.1151; the claim is possible.

8.26 0; the commercial is likely dishonest.

8.28 0.0033

8.30 a 0.6331 **b** 0.7794

8.32 0.9875

Chapter 9

9.10 125 ± 3.29 or LCL = 121.71, UCL = 128.29

9.12 125 ± 1.96 or LCL = 123.04, UCL = 126.96

9.14 125 ± 7.84 or LCL = 117.16, UCL = 132.84

9.18 22 ± 1.29 or LCL = 20.71, UCL = 23.29

9.20 43.75 ± 6.93 or LCL = 36.82, UCL = 50.68

9.22 1810.16 ± 98 or LCL = 1712.16, UCL = 1908.16

9.24 $10.21 \pm .57$ or LCL = 9.64, UCL = 10.78

9.26 $26.81 \pm .36$ or LCL = 26.45, UCL = 27.17

9.28 $n = 384$

9.30 a 100 ± 5 or LCL = 95, UCL = 105 **b** The sample size was selected to produce this interval estimate.

9.32 100.00 ± 2.00 or LCL = 98.00, UCL = 102.00

9.34 $n = 2,148$

9.36 $n = 1,082$

9.38 $15.00 \pm .59$ or LCL = 14.41, UCL = 15.59

9.40 $n = 216$

9.42 $14.98 \pm .31$ or LCL = 14.67, UCL = 15.29

9.44 411.30 ± 4.9 or LCL = 406.40, UCL = 416.20

Chapter 10

10.2 H_0: You are able to complete the Ph.D.

H_1: You are unable to complete the Ph.D.

Type I error: You miss out on having a life of fame, fortune and happiness because you did not complete the Ph.D.

Type II error: You waste 5 years of your life in a futile attempt to achieve the Ph.D. The Type I error is more costly.

10.4 H_0: The return on the risky investment wil be positive.

H_1: The return on the risky investment will be negative.

Type I error: Suffer a large opportunity loss but no real cost.

Type II error: Suffer a large loss.

Both errors are costly.

10.6 The exercise refers to the two O.J. Simpson trials. The trials produced different verdicts because of the different definitions of "sufficient evidence of guilt."

10.8 $z = .60$, p-value = .2743; do not reject the null hypothesis.

10.10 $z = 0$, p-value = 1; do not reject the null hypothesis.

10.12 $z = 1.33$, p-value = .9082; do not reject the null hypothesis.

10.14 $z = 1.00$, p-value = .1587. There is not enough evidence to infer that the mean amount of television watched by all young adult men is greater than 60 minutes.

10.16 $z = 2.83$, p-value = .0023. There is enough evidence to infer that the mean amount of television watched by all young adult men is greater than 60 minutes.

10.18 $z = .71$, p-value = .2389. There is not enough evidence to infer that the mean amount of television watched by all young adult men is greater than 60 minutes.

10.20 a z increases **b** z increases **c** z increases

10.22 $z = -1.88$, p-value = .0301. There is enough evidence to infer that the average student spent less than the recommended amount of time studying statistics.

10.24 $z = -4.24$, p-value = 0. There is overwhelming evidence to infer that the average student spent less than the recommended amount of time studying statistics.

10.26 $z = -5.30$, p-value = 0. There is overwhelming evidence to infer that the average student spent less than the recommended amount of time studying statistics.

10.28 a p-value decreases **b** p-value decreases **c** p-value decreases

10.30 a $z = -2.50$, p-value = .0062 **b** $z = -.50$, p-value = .3085 **c** $z = -2.50$, p-value = .0062

10.32 $z = -1.41$, p-value = .0793 There is not enough evidence to infer that the population mean is less than 160.

10.34 $z = 1.87$, p-value = .0614 There is enough evidence to infer that the population mean is not equal to 25.

10.36 $z = 2.00$, p-value = .0456 There is enough evidence to infer that the population mean diameter is not equal to .50.

10.38 $z = -2.06$, p-value = .0197 There is enough evidence to infer that the president is correct.

10.40 $z = 1.91$, p-value = .0281. There is enough evidence to infer that the article's hypothesis is correct.

10.42 $\beta = 0$

10.44 $\beta = .7357$

10.48 $\beta = .0038$

10.50 $\mu = 900$: $\beta = .0012$

$\mu = 940$: $\beta = .1492$

$\mu = 980$: $\beta = .8300$

$\mu = 1020$: $\beta = .8300$

$\mu = 1060$: $\beta = .1492$

$\mu = 1100$: $\beta = .0012$

10.54 The probability of a Type II error increases when the sample size decreases.

10.56 $z = 2.46$, p-value = .9931. There is not enough evidence to infer that the system will not be effective. We reached a different conclusion because we asked a different question.

10.58 $z = -1.70$, p-value = .0446. There is enough evidence to infer that the equipment is effective.

10.60 $z = 4.90$, p-value = .0. There is enough evidence to infer that the expert is right.

10.62 $z = 3.00$, p-value = .0013. There is enough evidence to infer that the site is acceptable.

For all exercises in Chapters 11, 12, 13, and 22 that are accompanied by data files with qualitative data, our answers are based on defining "success" as the highest coded value. For example, in most of these exercises, the qualitative data are stored as 1s and 2s. Our solutions define 2 = success. The p-values for the t-statistics and the χ^2-statistics were computed by Excel. The p-values of the z-statistics were calculated manually,

Chapter 11

11.2 510 ± 24.8 or LCL = 485.2, UCL = 534.8

11.4 510 ± 56.8 or LCL = 453.2, UCL = 566.8

11.6 510 ± 29.6 or LCL = 480.4, UCL = 539.6

11.8 a the interval widens **b** the interval widens **c** the interval widens

11.10 $t = 1.05$, p-value = .1597. There is not enough evidence to infer that the population mean is greater than 20.

11.12 $t = 2.68$, p-value $= .0074$. There is enough evidence to infer that the population mean is greater than 20.

11.14 $t = .50$, p-value $= .3125$. There is not enough evidence to infer that the population mean is greater than 20.

11.16 a The t-statistic decreases and the p-value increases. **b** The t-statistic decreases and the p-value increases. **c** The t-statistic increases and the p-value decreases.

11.18 50 ± 9.30 or LCL $= 40.70$, UCL $= 59.30$

11.20 $t = -1.41$, p-value $= .1001$. There is not enough evidence to infer that the population mean is less than 100.

11.22 The standard normal distribution is narrower than the Student t distribution. Hence, the same value of the test statistic produces different p-values.

11.24 $15,500 \pm 517.6$ or LCL $= 14,982.4$, UCL $= 16,017.6$

11.26 4.91 ± 1.59 or LCL $= 3.32$, UCL $= 6.50$

11.28 a 22.6 ± 1.41 or LCL $= 21.19$, UCL $= 24.01$ **b** $t = 3.80$, p-value $= .0004$. There is enough evidence to infer that the population mean is greater than 20. **c** The population is required to be normal. The condition appears not to be satisfied.

11.30 $7.15 \pm .23$ or LCL $= 6.92$, UCL $= 7.38$

11.32 $t = 3.12$, p-value $= .0012$. There is enough evidence to infer that the doctor's claim is true.

11.34 a 62.90 ± 1.93 or LCL $= 60.97$, UCL $= 64.83$ **b** Prices are required to be normally distributed. The condition appears to be satisfied.

11.36 $\chi^2 = 72.6$, p-value $= .0427$. There is sufficient evidence to infer that the variance is not equal to 300.

11.38 $\chi^2 = 39.2$, p-value $= .1596$. There is not sufficient evidence to infer that the variance is less than 100.

11.40 $\chi^2 = 27.84$, p-value $= .2669$. There is not sufficient evidence to infer that the variance is greater than 50.

11.42 $\chi^2 = 6.79$, p-value $= .2545$. There is not sufficient evidence to infer that the variance is less than 500.

11.44 LCL $= .219$, UCL $= 2.07$

11.46 $\chi^2 = 25.98$, p-value $= .7088$. There is not sufficient evidence to infer that the variance is not equal to 250.

11.48 $\chi^2 = 305.81$, p-value $= .0044$. There is enough evidence to infer that the variance is greater than 18.

11.50 $.48 \pm .044$ or LCL $= .436$, UCL $= .524$

11.52 $.48 \pm .031$ or LCL $= .449$, UCL $= .511$

11.54 $.10 \pm .026$ or LCL $= .074$, UCL $= .126$

11.56 $.84 \pm .025$ or LCL $= .815$, UCL $= .865$

11.58 $z = 1.80$, p-value $= .0359$. There is enough evidence to infer that the proportion is greater than .50.

11.60 p-value $= .0694$

11.62 a $.5 \pm .03$ or LCL $= .47$, UCL $= .53$ **b** Yes, the sample size was selected to produce this result.

11.64 $n = 564$

11.66 a $.92 \pm .019$ or LCL $= .901$, UCL $= .939$ **b** The interval is narrower than the one specified. **c** Although the cost is higher than necessary the interval is more accurate and hence we have more information.

11.68 $z = 1.13$, p-value $= .1292$. There is not enough evidence to infer that the claim is true.

11.70 $.098 \pm .013$ or LCL $= .085$, UCL $= .111$

11.72 a $t = 3.04$, p-value $= .0015$. There is enough evidence to infer that the candidate is correct. **b** 31.95 ± 1.27 or LCL $= 30.68$, UCL $= 33.22$ **c** The costs are required to be normally distributed, a condition that appears to be satisfied.

11.74 $t = -1.64$, p-value $= .0569$. There is not enough evidence to infer that the supplier's assertion is correct.

11.76 $z = 1.61$, p-value $= .0537$. There is not enough evidence to infer that the Republican candidate will win.

11.78 117.54 ± 9.35 or LCL $= 108.19$, UCL $= 126.89$

11.80 a 6.91, $\pm .069$ or LCL $= 6.841$, UCL $= 6.979$ **b** Times are required to be normally distributed. The condition is satisfied. **c** $t = -3.48$, p-value $= .0004$. There is enough evidence to infer that the average postal worker spends less than 7 hours per day working.

11.82 $5.79 \pm .678$ or LCL $= 5.112$, UCL $= 6.468$

11.84 $\chi^2 = 161.4$, p-value $= .0001$. There is enough evidence to infer that the number of springs requiring rework will be unacceptably large.

11.86 $1.10 \pm .163$ or LCL $= .937$, UCL $= 1.263$

11.88 $n = 2401$

11.90 Number of cars: $t = .46$, p-value $= .3351$. There is not enough evidence to infer that the employee is stealing by lying about the number of cars.
Amount of time: $t = 6.90$, p-value $= 0$. There is enough evidence to infer that the employee is stealing by lying about the amount of time.

For all exercises in Chapter 12, 13, and 22 we employed the F-test of two variances at the 5% significance level to decide which one of the equal-variances or unequal-variances t-test and estimator of the difference between two means to use to solve this type of problem. Additionally, for exercises that compare two populations and are accompanied by data files, our answers were derived by defining the sample from population 1 as the data stored in the first column (often column A in Excel and column 1 in Minitab). The data stored in the second column represent the sample from population 2. Paired differences were defined as the difference between the variable in the first column minus the variable in the second column. The hypotheses and test conclusions and the interval estimators were answered using these rules. For exercises involving qualitative data files, see the note before Chapter 11.

Chapter 12

12.2 a $t = .69$, p-value $= .4941$. There is not enough evidence to infer that the population means differ. **b** 55 ± 160.49 or LCL $= -105.49$, UCL $= 215.49$

12.4 a $t = 2.78$, p-value $= .0060$. There is enough evidence to infer that the population means differ. **b** 55 ± 39.01 or LCL $= 15.99$, UCL $= 94.01$

12.6 a $t = 1.94$, p-value $= .0280$. There is enough evidence to infer that μ_1 is greater than μ_2. **b** 3 ± 2.58 or LCL $= .42$, UCL $= 5.58$

12.8 The t-statistic decreases and the interval widens.

12.10 The t-statistic increases and the interval narrows.

12.12 a $t = -.81$, p-value $= .2117$. There is not enough evidence to infer that μ_1 is less than μ_2. **b** -79 ± 197.41 or LCL $= -276.41$, UCL $= 118.41$

12.14 a $t = -2.31$, p-value $= .0118$. There is enough evidence to infer that μ_1 is less than μ_2. **b** -79 ± 68.09 or LCL $= -147.09$, UCL $= -10.91$

12.16 a $t = -2.26$, p-value $= .0147$. There is enough evidence to infer that μ_1 is less than μ_2. **b** -113 ± 101 or LCL $= -214$, UCL $= -12$

12.18 The farther $\bar{x}_1$ is from $\bar{x}_2$ the more negative the t-statistic. The width of the interval is not affected by increasing or decreasing $\bar{x}_1$.

12.20 a $t = 2.36$, p-value $= .0101$. There is enough evidence to infer that μ_1 is greater than μ_2. **b** 7.14 ± 5.03 or LCL $= 2.11$, UCL $= 12.17$ **c** The variables are required to be normally distributed with unequal variances. **d** The histograms are bell shaped and the sample variances are quite dissimilar.

12.22 a $t = -2.20$, p-value $= .0156$. There is enough evidence to infer that μ_1 is less than μ_2.

12.24 a $t = -1.71$, p-value $= .0452$. There is enough evidence to infer that taking vitamin and mineral supplements daily increases the body's immune system.

12.26 $t = 1.07$, p-value $= .1440$. There is not enough evidence to retain supplier A.

12.28 a $t = 1.79$, p-value $= .0737$. There is not enough evidence to infer that a difference exists between the two groups. **b** 6.03 ± 6.60 or LCL $= -.57$, UCL $= 12.63$ **c** The histogram of the times for the 35-to-50 age group is not bell shaped. The sample size may be large enough to overcome this violation of the required condition. The sample variances are dissimilar.

12.30 a $t = -11.61$, p-value $= 0$. There is enough evidence to infer that unsuccessful firms waste more time than successful ones. **b** $-2.78 \pm .47$ or LCL $= -3.25$, UCL $= -2.31$; Unsuccessful firms waste between 2.31 and 3.25 hours per week more than successful firms.

12.32 1. Tastee is actually better in that babies gain weight faster with this product. 2. Mothers who choose Tastee are better mothers and the babies of better mothers gain weight faster.

12.34 a The data were taken from people who either chose to smoke or chose not to smoke. No one assigned them to their group. **b** It is possible that people who choose to smoke are more prone to cancer. **c** In a controlled experiment the scientist would command a random sample of people to smoke and another random sample not to smoke.

12.36 $t = -1.90$, p-value $= .0898$. There is enough evidence to infer that the two population means differ.

12.38 a $t = 1.16$, p-value $= .2581$. There is not enough evidence to infer that the population means differ. **b** 9.58 ± 17.12 or LCL $= -7.54$, UCL $= 26.70$ **c** $t = 7.25$, p-value $= 0$. There is enough evidence to infer that the population means differ. **d** 9.42 ± 2.86 or LCL $= 6.56$, UCL $= 12.28$ **e** The matched pairs experiment produced a larger t-statistic and a narrower interval.

12.40 a $t = 2.10$, p-value $= .0474$. There is enough evidence to infer that the population means differ. **b** 8.92 ± 8.81 or LCL $= .11$, UCL $= 17.73$ **c** $t = 1.68$,

p-value $= .1208$. There is not enough evidence to infer that the population means differ. **d** 9.08 ± 11.89 or LCL $= -2.81$, UCL $= 20.97$ **e** The matched pairs experiment produced a smaller t-statistic and a wider interval.

12.42 a $t = -2.02$, p-value $= .0344$. There is enough evidence to infer that the new fertilizer is more effective. **b** -2.08 ± 2.27 or LCL $= -4.35$, UCL $= .19$ **c** The paired differences are required to be normally distributed. **d** The histogram is somewhat bell shaped. **e** The data are experimental because the statistician randomly assigned each plot to be fertilized by the current or new fertilizer. **f** The independent samples experiment would likely be better.

12.44 $t = -1.82$, p-value $= .0851$. There is not enough evidence to infer that tips for waiters and waitresses differ.

12.46 $t = -2.44$, p-value $= .0091$. There is enough evidence to infer that the new drug is effective.

12.48 LCL $= .239$ or UCL $= 1.05$

12.50 $F = .262$, p-value $= .0914$. There is enough evidence to infer that the population variances differ.

12.52 $F = .593$, p-value $= .0350$. There is not enough evidence to infer that the variance of population 1 is less than the variance of population 2.

12.54 $F = 1.595$, p-value $= .3050$. There is not enough evidence to infer that the population variances differ. The equal-variances t-test of $\mu_1 - \mu_2$ was the correct procedure to use in Exercise 12.23.

12.56 $F = .203$, p-value $= 0$. There is enough evidence to infer that the population variances differ. The unequal-variances t-test of $\mu_1 - \mu_2$ was the correct procedure to use in Exercise 12.30.

12.58 $F = .306$, p-value $= 0$. There is enough evidence to infer that the variances in service times differ between the two tellers.

12.60 p-value $= .3898$

12.62 $z = 1.72$, p-value $= .0856$. There is enough evidence to infer that the population proportions differ. $.06 \pm .0683$ or LCL $= -.0083$, UCL $= .1283$

12.64 $z = 2.07$, p-value $= .0193$. There is enough evidence to infer that the population proportion 1 is greater than population proportion 2 by more than 5%.

12.66 $z = -1.63$, p-value $= .0515$. There is enough evidence to infer that population proportion 1 is less than population proportion 2.

12.68 $z = -1.14$, p-value $= .1272$. There is not enough evidence to infer that

population proportion 1 is less than population proportion 2. $-.04006 \pm .0687$ or LCL $= -.1087$, UCL $= .0287$

12.70 $z = .71$, p-value $= .2384$. There is not enough evidence to infer that Hismanal's claim is false.

12.72 $z = -2.85$, p-value $= .0022$. There is enough evidence to infer that management should adopt process 1.

12.74 a $z = -1.76$, p-value $= .0788$. There is not enough evidence to infer that population proportions differ. **b** $-.0410 \pm .0594$ or LCL $= -.1004$, UCL $= .0184$

12.76 a $z = 2.54$, p-value $= .0055$. There is enough evidence to infer that smokers have a higher incidence of heart disease than nonsmokers. **b** $.1657 \pm .1163$ or LCL $= .0494$, UCL $= .2820$

12.78 $t = 1.56$, p-value $= .1204$. There is not enough evidence to infer that oat bran differs from other cereals in terms of cholesterol reduction.

12.80 a $t = 16.92$, p-value $= 0$. There is enough evidence to infer that heating costs are lower for insulated houses. **b** 57.40 ± 7.28 or LCL $= 50.12$, UCL $= 64.68$ **c** The differences are required to be normally distributed.

12.82 $z = -2.30$, p-value $= .0106$. There is enough evidence to infer that seatbelt usage increased over the last year.

12.84 a $t = -2.03$, p-value $= .0218$. There is enough evidence to infer that housing cost as a percentage of income has increased during the last 5 years. **b** The equal-variances t-test of $\mu_1 - \mu_2$ requires that the population variances be equal and the variables normally distributed. We conduct the F-test of $\sigma_1^2/$ to test the first requirement and draw the histograms to check the second.

$F = .811$, p-value $= .1404$. There is not enough evidence to infer that the population variances differ. (This test must be conducted by computer because the F-table is not precise.) The histograms appear to be bell shaped.

12.86 $z = 2.26$, p-value $= .0119$. There is enough evidence to infer that Americans have grown more distrustful of television and newspaper reporting during the last 3 years.

12.88 $z = -4.28$, p-value $= 0$. There is enough evidence to infer that the defective rates differ.

12.90 a $t = 2.62$, p-value $= .0059$. There is enough evidence to infer that 40-year-old men have more iron in their blood than do 20-year-old men. **b** $t = 4.08$, p-value $= .0001$. There is enough evidence to infer that 40-year-old women have more iron in their blood than do 20-year-old women.

12.92 $t = -11.21$, p-value $= 0$. There is enough evidence to infer that the mean number of words written by students allotted a small space is less than that for students allotted a large space.

12.94 $z = 1.26$, p-value $= .1037$. There is enough evidence to infer that the new company is better.

12.96 $t = -1.30$, p-value $= .0979$. There is not enough evidence to infer that Avalon owners are older than Tercel buyers.

Chapter 13

13.2 a z-test of $p_1 - p_2$ (case 1): $z = 2.83$, p-value $= .0024$. There is overwhelming evidence to infer that customers who see the ad are more likely to make a purchase than those who do not see the ad. **b** Equal-variances t-test of $\mu_1 - \mu_2$: $t = .90$, p-value $= .1853$. There is no evidence to infer that customers who see the ad and make a purchase spend more than whose who do not see the ad and make a purchase. **c** z-estimator of p: We estimate that between 34.23% and 52.50% of all customers who see the ad will make a purchase. **d** t-estimator of μ: We estimate that the mean amount spent by customers who see the ad and make a purchase lies between \$90.22 and \$104.55.

13.4 a z-test of p: $z = 1.54$, p-value $= .0619$. There is no (or at best, weak) evidence to infer that the spokesperson's claim is true. **b** z-test of $p_1 - p_2$ (case 1): $z = 3.02$, p-value $= .0013$. There is overwhelming evidence to infer that Priority Mail delivers letters within 2 days more frequently than does ordinary mail.

13.6 speeds: Equal-variances t-test of $\mu_1 - \mu_2$: $t = 1.07$, p-value $= .1424$. There is no evidence to infer that speed bumps reduce speeds.
Proper stops: Equal-variances t-test of $\mu_1 - \mu_2$: $t = -.84$, p-value $= .2021$. There is no evidence to infer that speed bumps increase the number of proper stops.

13.8 t-test of μ_D: $t = 3.73$, p-value $= .0002$. There is overwhelming evidence to infer that the law discourages bicycle use.

13.10 t-test of μ: $t = .96$, p-value $= .1711$. There is no evidence to infer that the franchiser should build on this site.

13.12 z-test of p: $z = 1.02$, p-value $= .1548$. There is no evidence to conclude that more Americans eat their spaghetti by winding on a fork than by cutting the strands.

13.14 Unequal-variances t-test of $\mu_1 - \mu_2$: $t = 14.06$, p-value $= 0$. There is

overwhelming evidence to infer that quitting smoking results in weight gains.

13.16 Equal-variances t-tests of $\mu_1 - \mu_2$:
Memory: $t = 3.27$, p-value $= .0008$
Reasoning: $t = 4.11$, p-value $= 0$
Reaction time: $t = -.58$, p-value $= .5637$
Vocabulary: $t = 1.25$, p-value $= .2163$
There is overwhelming evidence to indicate that bridge players score higher on memory and reasoning tests. There is no evidence to infer a difference in reaction time and vocabulary.

13.18 t-estimator of μ: On average, each copier is estimated to require between .2043 and .4357 service calls in the first year. Total number of service calls: LCL $=$ $1000(.2043) = 204.3$, UCL $= 1000(.4357)$ $= 435.7$. It is estimated that the company's copiers will require between 204 and 436 service calls in the first year.

13.20 Unequal-variances t-test of $\mu_1 - \mu_2$: $t = -3.27$, p-value $= .0011$. There is overwhelming evidence to support the professor's theory.

13.22 a z-test of p: $z = 1.74$, p-value $=$ $.0406$. There is evidence to indicate that the campaign will increase home delivery sales. **b** z-test of p: $z = 1.07$, p-value $= .1417$. There is no evidence to conclude that the campaign will be successful.

Chapter 14

14.4 ANOVA table

Source	Degrees of Freedom	Sums of Squares	Mean Squares	F
Treatments	2	365.8	182.9	4.27
Error	32	1370.5	42.8	
Total	34	1736.3		

14.6 $F = 5.51$. There is enough evidence to infer that the population means differ.

14.8 a $F = 4.75$, p-value $= .0017$. There is enough evidence to infer that the population means differ. **b** The populations are requried to be normally distributed with equal variances. **c** The histograms are bell shaped and the sample variances are similar.

14.10 a $F = 2.94$, p-value $= .0363$. There is enough evidence to infer that there are differences among the completion times of the four income tax forms. **b** The times for each form must be normally distributed with the same variance. **c** The histograms are approximately bell shaped and the sample variances are similar.

14.14 a $F = 13.95$, p-value $= 0$. There is sufficient evidence to conclude that the leaf sizes differ among the three groups. **b** $F =$ 101.47, p-value $= 0$. There is sufficient evidence to infer that the amounts of nicotine differ among the three groups.

c The claim is false.

14.16 $F = 3.41$, p-value $= .0400$. There is enough evidence to infer that sales will vary according to price.

14.18 a $F = 16.50$. There is enough evidence to infer that the treatment means differ. **b** $F = 4.00$. There is enough evidence to infer that the block means differ.

14.20 a $F = 1.75$. There is not enough evidence to infer that the treatment means differ. **b** $F = 2.70$. There is not enough evidence to infer that the block means differ.

14.22 $F = 6.97$, p-value $= .0057$. There is enough evidence to conclude that the treatment means differ.

14.24 $F = 3.30$, p-value $= .0851$. There is not enough evidence to conclude that waiters and waitresses get different amounts of tips. This is the same answer (and p-value) as we produced in Exercise 12.44.

14.26 a $F = 4.54$, p-value $= .0224$. There is enough evidence to conclude that there are differences in delivery times among the couriers. **b** $F = 4.65$, p-value $= .0011$. There is enough evidence to indicate that there are differences among the times of day, which tells us that this experimental design is recommended.

14.28 a $F = .86$, p-value $= .4313$. There is no evidence to conclude that there are differences in sales ability among the holders of the three degrees. **b** $F = 26.64$, p-value $= 0$. There is sufficient evidence to indicate that there are differences among the blocks of students. The independent samples design would not be recommended. **c** The commissions for each type of degree are required to be normally distributed with same variance.

14.30 a $F = 5.85$. There is enough evidence to conclude that differences exist among the levels of factor A. **b** $F = 7.20$. There is enough evidence to conclude that differences exist among the levels of factor B. **c** $F = 9.50$. There is enough evidence to conclude that factors A and B interact.

14.32 a $F = .52$. There is not enough evidence to conclude that factors A and B interact. **b** $F = 9.99$. There is enough evidence to conclude that differences exist among the levels of factor A. **c** $F = .04$. There is not enough evidence to conclude that differences exist among the levels of factor B.

14.34 a There are two factors—class configuration and time. **b** The response variable is the number of times students ask and answer questions. **c** There are two levels of class configuration and three levels of time. **d** Test for interaction: $F = 12.28$, *p*-value = .0002. There is enough evidence to conclude that the class configuration and time interact. Thus, there are combinations of the two factors that produce better results.

14.36 a Factor A (columns) is the form and factor B (samples) is the income group. **b** The response variable is the completion time. **c** There are $a = 4$ forms and $b = 3$ income groups. **d** $F = 2.56$, *p*-value = .0586. There is not enough evidence to conclude that differences exist among the forms. **e** $F = 4.11$, *p*-value = .0190. There is enough evidence to conclude that differences exist among the three income groups. **f** Test for interaction. **g** $F = 1.04$, *p*-value = .4030. There is no evidence to conclude that forms and income groups interact. Thus, we conclude that there are differences among income groups only.

14.38 a The *p*-values for devices, alloys, and interaction are .0775, .5798, and .7584, respectively. There are no sources of variation.

14.40 LSD = 24.53; μ_2 differs from μ_1 and μ_3.

14.42 $\omega = 29.53$; μ_2 and μ_3 differ.

14.44 LSD = 22.30; μ_1 and μ_5, μ_2 and μ_4, μ_3 and μ_4, and μ_4 and μ_5 differ.

14.46 μ_1 and μ_3 differ.

14.48 $\omega = 20.83$. μ_1 and μ_4 differ.

14.50 $\omega = 29.16$. μ_2 and μ_3 differ.

14.52 a $F = 3.56$, *p*-value = .0236. There is enough evidence to infer that differences exist among the flares with respect to burning times. **b** LSD = 9.85; μ_3 and μ_4 differ. **c** $\omega = 9.45$; μ_1 and μ_4 and μ_3 and μ_4 differ.

14.54 $B = .38$. There is no evidence to infer that the population variances differ.

14.56 $B = 1.56$, *p*-value = .6692. There is no evidence to infer that the population variances differ.

14.58 $B = 1.89$, *p*-value = .7561. There is no evidence to infer that the population variances differ.

14.60 $B = .15$, *p*-value = .9281. There is no evidence to infer that the population variances differ.

14.62 $F = 13.79$, *p*-value = 0. There is sufficient evidence to conclude that the reading speeds differ among the four typefaces. The typeface that was read the fastest should be used.

14.64 a $F = 7.67$, *p*-value = .0001. There is sufficient evidence to infer that the differences in productivity exist among the four groups of companies. **b** $\omega = .48$; μ_1 differs from μ_2, μ_3, and μ_4. Companies that offered extensive training have productivity levels different from the other companies.

14.66 a Factor A (columns) is the faculty. The levels are business, engineering, arts, and science. Factor B (samples) is the rank. The levels are professor, associate professor, assistant professor, and lecturer. **b** $F = .61$, *p*-value = .6109. There is not enough evidence to conclude that differences exist among the ranks. **c** $F = 4.49$, *p*-value = .0064. There is enough evidence to conclude that differences exist among the faculties. **d** Test for interaction. **e** $F = 3.04$, *p*-value = .0044. There is evidence to conclude that ranks and faculties interact. There are certain combinations of ranks and faculties that work harder than others.

14.68 a $F = 5.12$, *p*-value = .0006. There is enough evidence to infer that the bumpers differ in their reaction to low-speed collisions. **b** LSD = 64.25; μ_3 differs from μ_2 and μ_4.

14.70 $F = 11.79$, *p*-value = 0. There is enough evidence to infer that typing speeds differ among the six groups of students.

14.72 a $F = 136.58$, *p*-value = 0. There is sufficient evidence to infer that differences exist among the effects of the three teaching approaches. **b** $\omega = .75$. All three means differ from one another. From the sample means we may infer that the pure method is best, followed by embedded, and by whole-language.

14.74 a $F = 9.17$, *p*-value = 0. There is enough evidence to infer that there are differences in changes to the TSE depending on the loss the previous day.

Chapter 15

15.2 $\chi^2 = 7.00$, *p*-value = .1359. There is not enough evidence to infer that at least one p_i is not equal to its specified value.

15.4 χ^2 decreases and its *p*-value increases.

15.6 $\chi^2 = 9.96$, *p*-value = .0189. There is enough evidence to infer that at least one p_i is not equal to it specified value.

15.8 $\chi^2 = 6.85$, *p*-value = .0769. There is not enough evidence to infer that at least one p_i is not equal to its specified value.

15.10 $\chi^2 = 14.07$, *p*-value = .0071. There is enough evidence to infer that grades are distributed differently from grades in the past.

15.12 $\chi^2 = 33.85$, *p*-value = 0. There is enough evidence to infer that the aging schedule has changed.

15.14 $\chi^2 = 6.35$, *p*-value = .0419. There is enough evidence to infer that voter support has changed since the election.

15.16 $\chi^2 = 19.10$, *p*-value = 0. There is enough evidence to infer that the two variables are dependent.

15.18 $\chi^2 = 4.77$, *p*-value = .0289. There is enough evidence to infer that the two classifications L and M are dependent.

15.20 $\chi^2 = 4.40$, *p*-value = .1110. There is not enough evidence to infer that the two classifications R and C are dependent.

15.22 $\chi^2 = 2.35$, *p*-value = .3087. There is not enough evidence to infer that there are differences in quality among the three shifts.

15.24 $\chi^2 = 46.37$, *p*-value = 0. There is enough evidence to infer that commercials viewed during happy television programs have a different effect than those viewed during sad television programs.

15.26 $\chi^2 = 31.48$, *p*-value = 0. There is enough evidence to infer that the antismoking campaign has reason to be concerned.

15.28 $\chi^2 = 41.76$, *p*-value = 0. There is enough evidence to infer that the amount of education is a factor in determining whether a smoker will quit.

15.30 $\chi^2 = 20.89$, *p*-value = .0019. There is enough evidence to infer that there are differences in teaching approach among the four types of degrees. The editor can design books and sales campaigns based on the distribution of degrees.

15.32 $\chi^2 = 9.87$, *p*-value = .0017. There is enough evidence to infer that the data are not normally distributed.

15.34 $\chi^2 = 1.07$, *p*-value = .5855. There is no evidence to infer that weight of discarded newspaper is not normally distributed.

15.36 $\chi^2 = 1.14$, *p*-value = .2853. There is no evidence to infer that the matched pairs difference in Exercise 12.46 is not normally distributed.

15.38 $\chi^2 = 19.71$, *p*-value = 0. There is enough evidence to infer that the return rates differ among the different inducements.

15.40 $\chi^2 = 5.41$, *p*-value = .2478. There is no evidence to infer that there is a relationship between the days an employee is absent and the shift on which the employee works.

15.42 a $\chi^2 = 23.81$, *p*-value = .0025. There is enough evidence to infer that North Americans changed their favorite sport between 1985 and 1993. **b** $z = 2.09$, *p*-value = .0364. There is enough evidence to infer that the popularity of baseball has changed.

15.44 $\chi^2 = 86.62$, *p*-value = 0. There is enough evidence to infer that educational level affects the way adults read the newspaper.

15.46 $\chi^2 = 15.88$, p-value $= .0032$. There is enough evidence to infer that there are differences in RRSP positions among the five income brackets.

15.48 $\chi^2 = 20.99$, p-value $= 0$. There is enough evidence to infer that the research findings are related to whether the research is funded by drug companies.

15.50 $\chi^2 = 274.62$, p-value $= 0$. There is enough evidence to infer that the readership of the four daily newspapers differs in terms of the occupation of their readers.

Chapter 16

The exercises that are accompanied by data files have been solved by the Excel macros. Minitab users should note that when ties exist Minitab computes two p-values for the Wilcoxon rank sum test, the Kruskal–Wallis test, and the Friedman test. The first p-value is calculated using the exact sampling distribution (as opposed to the approximate sampling distribution used by Excel) and the second makes an adjustment for ties. Both p-values may differ from the Excel p-values calculated below.

16.2 $z = 1.66$, p-value $= .0485$. There is not enough evidence to infer that the location of population 1 is to the right of the location of population 2.

16.4 $T = 19$. There is enough evidence to infer that the location of population 1 is to the left of the location of population 2.

16.6 $z = -1.74$, p-value $= .0409$. There is enough evidence to infer that companies that provide exercise programs should be given discounts.

16.8 $z = 1.57$, p-value $= .0582$. There is enough evidence to infer that public support decreased during the last year.

16.10 $z = 2.12$, p-value $= .0170$. There is enough evidence to infer that Tastee baby food is better.

16.12 $z = -2.24$, p-value $= .0250$. There is enough evidence to infer that the population locations differ.

16.14 $z = 1.10$, p-value $= .1357$. There is not enough evidence to infer that the location of population 1 is to the right of the location of population 2.

16.16 $z = -.92$, p-value $= .3576$. There is not enough evidence to infer that the population locations differ.

16.18 $T = 19.5$. There is enough evidence to infer that the population locations differ.

16.20 $z = 2.83$, p-value $= .0046$. There is enough evidence to infer that black and white children up to the age of 6 differ in motor skill devleopment.

16.22 $z = 2.22$, p-value $= .0132$. There is enough evidence to infer that concern about a gasoline shortage exceeded concern about an electricity shortage.

16.24 $z = -1.64$, p-value $= .0505$. There is not enough evidence to infer that the swimming department has higher sales.

16.26 $z = -2.24$, p-value $= .0125$. There is enough evidence to infer that children feel less pain than adults.

16.28 $z = 2.31$, p-value $= .0104$. There is enough evidence to infer that preference in admissions should be given to the student from high school 1.

16.30 $H = 1.56$, p-value $= .4589$. There is not enough evidence to conclude that the population locations differ.

16.32 $H = 6.30$, p-value $= .0429$. There is enough evidence to conclude that the population locations differ.

16.34 $H = 4.46$, p-value $= .1075$. There is not enough evidence to conclude that the population locations differ.

16.36 $H = 6.81$, p-value $= .0333$. There is enough evidence to conclude that there are differences in student satisfaction among the three teaching methods.

16.38 $H = 1.91$, p-value $= .3839$. There is not enough evidence to infer that the Democrats' ratings of their winning the presidency changed over the 3-month period.

16.40 $F_r = 7.74$, p-value $= .0517$. There is enough evidence to conclude that at least two population locations differ.

16.42 $F_r = 9.42$, p-value $= .0242$. There is enough evidence to conclude that there are differences in sensory quality among the four brands of orange juice.

16.44 $F_r = 5.28$, p-value $= .0715$. There is not enough evidence to infer that there are differences in the ratings of the three recipes.

16.46 $F_r = 2.63$, p-value $= .2691$. There is not enough evidence to infer that there are differences in delivery times among the three couriers.

16.48 $D = .0833$. There is enough evidence to infer that the data are not normally distributed.

16.50 $D = .1507$. There is not enough evidence to infer that the data are not normally distributed.

16.52 $D = .0829$. There is not enough evidence to infer that the data are not normally distributed.

16.54 $D = .0571$. There is not enough evidence to infer that the normality requirement is not satisfied.

16.56 Tastee baby food: $D = .1195$. There

is not enough evidence to infer that the weight gain with Tastee is not normal. Competitor's baby food: $D = .1524$. There is not enough evidence to infer that the weight gain with the competitor's product is not normal.

16.58 a Statisticians can apply the t-test or the Wilcoxon signed rank sum test. **b** The t-test of μ_D requires that the matched pairs differences be normally distributed. The Wilcoxon signed rank sum test requires nonnormality of matched pairs differences. **c** $D = .0540$. There is not enough evidence to infer that the normality requirement is not satisfied. The test was appropriate.

16.60 $z = -1.04$, p-value $= .1499$. There is not enough evidence to conclude that the new method is better.

16.62 $F_r = 12.83$, p-value $= .0016$. There is enough evidence to conclude that differences in reading speeds exist among the three typefaces. Use the best one.

16.64 $T = 36$. There is enough evidence to indicate that drug B is more effective.

16.66 $z = 1.53$, p-value $= .0630$. There is not enough evidence to indicate that the manufacturer should switch to the new material.

16.68 $x = 16$, $n = 39$, p-value $= .3368$. There is no evidence to indicate that there are differences in believability between the two commercials.

16.70 $z = -2.23$, p-value $= .0130$. There is enough evidence to indicate that the people perceive newspapers as doing a better job 10 years ago.

16.72 $x = 19$, $n = 24$, p-value $= .0033$. There is sufficient evidence to indicate that the results of the midterm negatively influence student opinion.

16.74 $z = -2.43$, p-value $= .0075$. There is enough evidence to infer that boys with high levels of lead are more aggressive than boys with low levels of lead.

16.76 $H = 42.59$, p-value $= 0$. There is enough evidence to conclude that incomes of lawyers are affected by physical attractiveness.

16.78 Day 1: $x = 67$, $n = 67$, p-value $= 0$. There is enough evidence to conclude that exercisers are less happy after 1 day of not exercising than when they were exercising. Day 2: $x = 59$, $n = 59$, p-value $= 0$. There is enough evidence to conclude that exercisers are less happy after 2 days of not exercising than when they were exercising. Day 3: $x = 35$, $n = 35$, p-value $= 0$. There is enough evidence to conclude that exercisers are less happy after 3 days of not exercising than when they were exercising.

Chapter 17

Both Excel and manual calculations produced the answers below. They may differ from yours because of rounding.

17.2 a $\hat{y} = 36.54 + .479x$ **b** Nothing **c** For each additional inch of father's height, the son's height increases on average by .479 inch.

17.4 a $\hat{y} = 12.26 - .233x$ **b** Nothing **c** For each additional 1% increase in CPI, the average annual return decreases by .233%.

17.6 b $\hat{y} = 3.64 + .267x$ **c** $b_1 = .267$; for each additional second of commercial, the memory test score increases, on average by .267. $b_0 = 3.64$ is the y-intercept.

17.8 a $\hat{y} = -2.03 + .788x$ **b** $b_1 = .788$; for each additional year of education, Internet use increases, on average by .788 hour. $b_0 = -2.03$ is the y-intercept.

17.10 $\hat{y} = 9.44 + .0949x$; the appropriate compensation is 9.49 cents per degree API.

17.12 a $\hat{y} = -259.6 + 3721x$ **b** $b_1 = 3721$; for each additional carat of weight, the price increases, on average by \$3721. $b_0 = -259.6$ cannot be interpreted.

17.14 It is normally distributed with constant variance and a mean that is a linear function of the quality of the oil.

17.16 a $s_\epsilon = 3.22$ **b** $R^2 = .2666$ **c** $t = 12.04$. There is enough evidence to infer that the heights of sons and fathers are linearly related.

17.18 $t = -.28$. There is not enough evidence to infer that the stock's returns and the CPI are linearly related.

17.20 a $s_\epsilon = 5.89$ **b** $R^2 = .2892$ **c** $t = 4.85$. There is enough evidence to infer that the length of the commercial and memory test scores are linearly related.

17.22 a $s_\epsilon = 4.45$ **b** $t = 4.94$. There is enough evidence to infer that educational level and Internet use are linearly related. **c** $R^2 = .1098$

17.24 $s_\epsilon = .134$, $t = 11.35$. There is enough evidence to infer that oil quality and price are linearly related. $R^2 = .9218$

17.26 a $s_\epsilon = 31.83$ **b** $R^2 = .9783$ **c** $t = 45.51$. There is enough evidence to infer that the price and weight of diamonds are linearly related.

17.28 a $\hat{y} = 2.05 + .0909x$ **b** $b_1 = .0909$; for each additional minute of exercise, cholesterol is reduced, on average by .0909. $b_0 = 2.05$ cannot be interpreted. **c** $t = 7.05$. There is enough evidence to infer that exercise and cholesterol reduction are linearly related. **d** $R^2 = .5095$

17.30 a Intel's beta is 1.47, which means that Intel's stock is more volatile than the market. **b** The coefficient of determination is .1480; 14.80% of the total risk is market

related. The remaining 85.20% of the total risk is associated specifically with Intel.

17.32 a General Motors' beta is .843. GM's stock is less volatile than the market. **b** The coefficient of determination is .1280; 12.80% of the total risk is market related. The remaining 87.20% is associated specifically with events and actions at General Motors.

17.34 General Electric's beta is 1.09, which means that GE's stock is more volatile than the market. The coefficient of determination is .4049. Thus, 40.49% of the total risk is market related. The remaining 59.51% is associated specifically with General Electric.

17.36 a Coca Cola's beta is .506, which means its stock is less volatile than the market. **b** The coefficient of determination is .0962, which means that only 9.62% of the total risk is market related. The remaining 90.38% of the total risk is associated specifically with Coca Cola.

17.40 62.52, 79.40

17.42 a 1.38, 25.15 **b** 11.73, 14.80

17.44 8.62, 10.96

17.46 13.16, 13.70

17.48 985.14, 1100.33

17.50 a 7.95, 50.72 **b** Prediction interval for reduction: 3.39, 46.18. Prediction interval for cholesterol level after exercise: 203.82, 246.61

17.52 a $r = .323$, $t = 1.13$. There is no evidence to infer that the returns on the two stocks are correlated. **b** $r_s = .225$. There is not enough evidence to infer that the returns on the two stocks are correlated.

17.54 a $r = .5378$ **b** $t = 4.86$, p-value = 0. There is sufficient evidence to infer that length of commercial and memory test score are linearly related. **c** $r_s = .546$, $z = 4.19$, p-value = 0. There is sufficient evidence to infer that length of commercial and memory test score are linearly related.

17.56 a $r = .3308$ **b** $t = 4.93$, p-value = 0. There is sufficient evidence to infer that education and Internet use are linearly related. **c** $r_s = .3657$, $z = 5.16$, p-value = 0. There is sufficient evidence to infer that education and Internet use are linearly related.

17.58 $r_s = .9381$. There is sufficient evidence to infer that higher quality oil is associated with higher prices.

17.60 $r_s = .9656$, $z = 6.62$, p-value = 0. There is enough evidence to conclude that the price and the weight of diamonds are linearly related.

17.62 a $\hat{y} = 11.25 + 2.62x$ **d** There are no outliers. **e** The sample size may be too small to ascertain. However, the variance appears to be constant.

17.64 b It appears that the errors are normally distributed. **c** Observations 18, 25,

53, and 59 have s
absolute value ex
ticity does not ap
17.66 The histo
that the errors ar
The plot of the r
indicates some c
17.68 The histo
The plot of residuals versus predicted exhibits a clear picture of heteroscedasticity.

17.70 a $\hat{y} = 114.85 + 2.47x$ **b** $b_1 = 2.47$; for each additional month of age repair costs increase, on average by \$2.47. $b_0 = 114.85$; this statistic is the y-intercept. **c** $R^2 = .5659$; 56.59% of the variation in repair is explained by the variation in age. **d** $t = 4.84$, p-value = .0001. There is enough evidence to infer that repair costs and age are linearly related. **e** LCL = \$318.12, UCL = \$505.18

17.72 a $\hat{y} = 60.50 + .0606x$. The slope is .0606, which tells us that for each additional unit of fertilizer, corn yield increases on average by .0606. The y-intercept is 60.50, which has no real meaning. **b** $t = 1.04$, p-value = .3072. There is no evidence of a linear relationship between amount of fertilizer and corn yield. **c** $R^2 = .0372$; 3.72% of the variation in corn yield is explained by the variation in amounts of fertilizer. **d** The model is too poor to be used to predict.

17.74 a $\hat{y} = -.227 + 2.794x$. The slope is 2.794. For each one point increase in batting average, the team's winning percentage increases on average by 2.794 points. **b** $s_\epsilon = .0567$. This statistic is large relative to the average winning percentage, .500. The model is poor. **c** $t = 1.69$, p-value = .0580. There is not enough evidence to infer a positive linear relationship between team batting average and winning percentage. **d** $R^2 = .1931$; 19.31% of the variation in winning percentage is explained by the variation in team batting average. **e** .4283, .6549.

17.76 a $r = .4177$, $t = 3.19$, p-value Excel = .0025. There is sufficient evidence to infer that weight and blood-alcohol level are linearly related. **b** $r_s = .3702$, $z = 2.59$, p-value = .0096. There is sufficient evidence to infer that weight and blood-alcohol level are linearly related.

17.78 a $r = .9766$, $t = 21.78$, p-value = 0. There is enough evidence to infer that levels of tar and nicotine are linearly related. **b** $r = .9259$, $t = 11.76$, p-value = 0. There is enough evidence to infer that levels of nicotine and carbon monoxide are linearly related.

Chapter 18

18.2 a $s_\epsilon = 3.75$; this statistic is an estimate of the standard deviation of the error variable.

.7629; 76.29% of the variation in marks is explained by the model. **c** R^2 (adjusted) = .7453. It differs from R^2 because it includes an adjustment for the number of independent variables. **d** $F = 43.43$, p-value = 0. There is sufficient evidence to infer that the model is valid.
e $t = .97$, p-value = .3417. There is no evidence to conclude that the final mark and assignment mark are linearly related. **f** $t = 9.12$, p-value = 0. There is sufficient evidence to conclude that the final mark and midterm mark are linearly related.
18.4 a $s_\epsilon = 3.23$; this statistic is an estimate of the standard deviation of the error variable **b** $R^2 = .2672$; 26.72% of the variation in heights is explained by the model. **c** R^2 (adjusted) = .2635. It differs from R^2 because it includes an adjustment for the number of independent variables. **d** $F = 72.37$, p-value = 0. There is sufficient evidence to infer that the model is valid. **f** $t = 11.78$, p-value = 0. There is sufficient evidence to conclude that the heights of fathers and their sons are linearly related. **g** $t = -.58$, p-value = .5615. There is no evidence to infer that the heights of mothers and their sons are linearly related.
18.6 a $\hat{y} = .72 + .611$ HS GPA + .0027 SAT + .0463 Activities **b** $s_\epsilon = 2.03$; this statistic is an estimate of the standard deviation of the error variable. **c** $R^2 = .2882$; 28.82% of the variation in 3-year GPA is explained by the model. **d** R^2 (adjusted) = .2600. It differs from R^2 because it includes an adjustment for the number of independent variables. **e** $F = 12.96$, p-value = 0. There is sufficient evidence to infer that the model is valid. **f** HS GPA: $b_1 = .611$; for each unit increase in high school GPA, the 3-year university GPA increases on average by .611. SAT: $b_2 = .0027$; for each one point increase in SAT, the 3-year university GPA increases on average by .0027. Activities: $b_3 = .0463$; for each additional hour of extracurricular activities, the 3-year university GPA increases on average by .0463. **g** HS GPA: $t = 6.06$, p-value = 0. SAT: $t = .94$, p-value = .3482 Activities: $t = .72$, p-value = .4270. Only high school GPA is linearly related to the 3-year university GPA. **h** 4.45, 12 (maximum) **i** 6.90, 8.22
18.8 a $\hat{y} = 577 + 90.6$Space + 9.66Water **b** $s_\epsilon = 213.7$; this statistic is an estimate of the standard deviation of the error variable. **c** $R^2 = .7081$; 70.81% of the variation in electricity consumption is explained by the model. **d** $F = 117.64$, p-value = 0. There is sufficient evidence to infer that the model is valid. **e** 7748, 8,601. **f** 8,127, 8,222.
18.10 a $\hat{y} = 13.03 - .279$Age + .0938Income **b** $R^2 = .1985$; 19.85% of the

variation in Internet use is explained by the model. **c** $F = 24.39$, p-value = 0. There is sufficient evidence to infer that the model is valid. **d** .55, 14.44 **e** 6.27, 9.61
18.12 a 23, 38.8 **b** 49, 64.8
18.14 a The histogram is approximately bell shaped. **b** The variance of the error variable appears to be constant.
18.16 a The histogram is approximately bell shaped. **b** The variance of the error variable appears to be constant.
18.18 a The histogram is approximately bell shaped. **b** The variance of the error variable appears to be constant.
18.20 b Observations 63, 81, 82, and 97 **c** The histogram is bell shaped. **d** The variance of the error grows as the predicted value increases. **e** Let $y' = \log y$ or $1/y$. Neither transformation is effective.
18.22 The histogram is not bell shaped, the variance of the error variable appears to be constant, and there are no outliers.
18.24 The variance of the error variable decreases as the predicted value increases. The histogram is negatively skewed.
18.26 a The variance of the error variable appears to be constant and the histogram is bell shaped. **b** Multicollinearity does not appear to be a problem. **c** Observation 91
18.28 a The variance of the error variable appears to be constant and the histogram is bell shaped. **b** Multicollinearity does not appear to be a problem.
18.30 The variance of the error variable is not constant and the histogram is negatively skewed.
18.32 There is evidence that positive first-order autocorrelation exists.
18.34 There is no evidence that negative first-order autocorrelation exists.
18.36 a $\hat{y} = 2260 + .423x$ **c** Observation 4 **d** The histogram is bell shaped. **e** The variance of the error variable appears to be constant. **f** $d = .7859$. There is evidence of autocorrelation. **g** $y = \beta_0 + \beta_1 x + \beta_2 t + \epsilon$; $\hat{y} = 446.2 + 1.10x + 38.92t$ **h** The second model fits better.
18.38 a The histogram is bell shaped. **b** The variance of the error variable appears to be constant.
18.40 The test is inconclusive.
18.42 b The histogram is bell shaped. **c** Check observations 1, 11, 25, 28, and 46. **d** The variance of the error variable appears to be constant **e** The errors appear to be independent. **f** $d = 1.9547$. There is no evidence of first-order autocorrelation.
18.44 a $\hat{y} = .530 + .0824$UnderGPA .0109GMAT + .0928Work **b** $b_1 = .0824$; for each additional point increase in undergraduate GPA the MBA GPA increases on average by .0824. $b_2 = .0109$; for each

unit increase in GMAT the MBA GPA increases on average by .0109. $b_3 = .0928$; for each additional year of work the MBA GPA increases on average by .0928. $b_0 = .530$; this is the y-intercept. **c** UnderGPA: $t = .78$, p-value = .4359. There is no evidence of a linear relationship between undergraduate GPA and MBA GPA. GMAT: $t = 8.50$, p-value = 0. There is sufficient evidence of a linear relationship between GMAT and MBA GPA. Work: $t = 4.22$, p-value = 0. There is sufficient evidence of a linear relationship between work and MBA GPA. **d** $s_\epsilon = .7541$, $R^2 = .4881$. The model fits moderately well. **e** $F = 30.52$, p-value = 0. There's sufficient evidence to support the model's validity. **f** 6.96, 10.10
18.46 a $\hat{y} = 3719 - 46.77$Price A + 58.52Price B **b** $s_\epsilon = 558.7$, $R^2 = .4933$. The model fits moderately well. **c** $b_1 = -46.77$; for each additional one cent increase in the company's price sales decrease on average by 46.77. $b_2 = 58.52$; for each one cent increase in the competitor's price sales increase by 58.52. $b_0 = 3719$; this is the y-intercept. **d** Price A: $t = -4.32$, p-value = .0001. There is enough evidence to conclude that the company's price and sales are linearly related. Price B: $t = 5.59$, p-value = 0. There is enough evidence to conclude that the competitor's price and company sales are linearly related. **e** $F = 23.85$, p-value = 0. There's sufficient evidence to support the model's validity. **f** 2341, 4284
18.48 a $\hat{y} = -1.97 + .666$MinorHR + .136Age + 1.18YearsPro **b** $b_1 = .666$; for each additional minor league home run, the number of major league home runs increases on average by .666. $b_2 = .136$; for each additional year of age the number of major league home runs increases on average by .136. $b_3 = 1.18$; for each additional year as a professional, the number of major league home runs increases by 1.18. **c** $s_\epsilon = 6.99$, $R^2 = .3511$. The model fits moderately well. **d** $F = 22.01$, p-value = 0. There's sufficient evidence to support the model's validity. **e** MinorHR: $t = 7.64$, p-value = 0. Age: $t = .26$, p-value = .7961. YearsPro: $t = 1.75$, p-value = .0819. **f** 9.86, 38.76 **g** 14.66, 24.47
18.50 a $\hat{y} = 195 + .123$Fertilizer + .0248Water **b** $t = 1.66$, p-value = .1088. There is not enough evidence to infer that amount of fertilizer and yield are linearly related. **c** $t = 4.06$, p-value = .0004. There is enough evidence to infer that amount of water and yield are linearly related. **d** $s_\epsilon = 57.29$, $R^2 = .4157$. The model fits moderately well. **e** 104.7, 359.2
18.52 a $\hat{y} = .178 + .0067$Lsize + .0243Bdywght **b** $t = 2.14$, p-value = .0475.

There is enough evidence to conclude that litter size and brain weight are linearly related. **c** $t = 3.59$, p-value $= .0023$. There is enough evidence to conclude that body weight and brain weight are linearly related. **d** $R^2 = .6505$; 65.05% of the variation in brain weight is explained by the model. **e** $F = 15.82$, p-value $= .0001$. There is sufficient evidence to conclude that the model is valid. **f** .407, .472 **g** .367, .410

18.54 a $\hat{y} = 35.7 + .247$MathDgr $+ .245$Age $+ .133$Income **b** $F = 6.66$, p-value $= .0011$. There is enough evidence to infer that the model is valid. **c** The error variable appears to be normal with constant variance. **d** Age and Income are correlated, which likely affects the t-tests. **e** MathDgr: $b_1 = .247$; for each one percentage point increase in the percentage of teachers with math degrees the mean test score increases on average by .247. $t = 3.54$, p-value $= .0011$. There is evidence of a linear relationship between the percentage of teachers with math degrees and mean test scores. Age: $b_2 = .245$; for each additional year of average age of teachers the mean test score increases on average by .245. $t = 1.32$, p-value $= .1945$. There is not enough evidence of a linear relationship between the mean age of teachers and mean test scores. Income: $b_3 = .133$; for each additional thousand dollars of income of math teachers the mean test score increases on average by .133. $t = .87$, p-value $= .3889$. There is no evidence of a linear relationship between teachers' incomes and mean test scores. **f** 49.01, 81.02

18.56 a $\hat{y} = 47.77 + .776$Evaluation $+ 1.06$Articles, $s_\epsilon = 7.01$, $R^2 = .7209$. The model fits moderately well. $F = 60.70$, p-value $= 0$. There is sufficient evidence to conclude that the model is valid. The error appears to be normally distributed with constant variance. Evaluation and Articles are correlated making the t-tests misleading.

18.58 a $\hat{y} = 11.91 - .430$Education $+ .0292$Age $+ .0934$Children $- .0745$Income **b** $F = 18.17$, p-value $= 0$. There is sufficient evidence to conclude that the model is valid. **c** The histogram of the residuals is approximately bell shaped but the variance may not be constant. **d** The correlation between Education and Income may distort these t-tests. **e 1.** $t = -3.26$, p-value $= .0008$. **2.** $t = 1.16$, p-value $= .1251$ **3.** $t = .42$, p-value $= .3390$ **4.** $t = -2.69$, p-value $= .0043$. Beliefs 1 and 4 appear to be true.

Chapter 19

19.4 a $s_\epsilon = 5.96$, $R^2 = .9726$: The model fits well. **b** 269.3

19.6 a MBA GPA $= \beta_0 + \beta_1$ UnderGPA $+ \beta_2$ GMAT $+ \beta_3$ Work $+ \beta_4$ UnderGPA $\times$

GMAT $+ \epsilon$ **b** $s_\epsilon = .756$ and $R^2 = .4908$. The model's fit is poor. $F = 22.89$, p-value $= 0$. The model is valid. **c** Exercise 18.44: $s_\epsilon = .754$ and $R^2 = .4881$.

19.8 a $\hat{y} = 260.7 - 3.32$Temperature $- 164.3$Currency, $+ 3.64$Temperature $\times$ Currency $s_\epsilon = 5.20$, $R^2 = .8566$, $F = 41.83$, p-value $= 0$. **b** $\hat{y} = 274.8 - 1.72$Temperature $- 828.6$Currency $- .0024$Temperature$^2 + 2054$Currency$^2 - .870$Temperature $\times$ Currency, $s_\epsilon = 5.27$, $R^2 = .8671$, $F = 24.80$, p-value $= 0$. **c** The first-order model has a slightly smaller standard error of estimate.

19.10 a Second-order model with interaction **b** $\hat{y} = 74,462 + 14.4$Pressure $- 613.3$Temperature $- .0159$Pressure$^2 + 1.23$Temperature$^2 + .0381$Pressure $\times$ Temperature **c** $s_\epsilon = 512.2$, $R^2 = .6872$, $F = 32.52$, p-value $= 0$.

19.12 a $I_1 = 1$, if Catholic, $I_1 = 0$, otherwise $I_2 = 1$, if Protestant, $I_2 = 0$, otherwise **b** $I_1 = 1$, if 8:00 a.m.–4:00 p.m, $I_1 = 0$, otherwise $I_2 = 1$, if 4:00 p.m.–12 midnight, $I_2 = 0$, otherwise **c** $I_1 = 1$, if Jack Jones, $I_1 = 0$, otherwise $I_2 = 1$, if Mary Brown, $I_2 = 0$, otherwise $I_3 = 1$, if George Fosse, $I_3 = 0$, otherwise

19.14 a $t = 3.04$, p-value $= .0016$. There is enough evidence to infer that the BBA graduate outperforms the BA graduate **b** $t = 3.06$, p-value $= .0015$. There is enough evidence to infer that the BEng graduate outperforms the BA graduate **c** $t = .51$, p-value $= .3067$. There is not enough evidence to infer that the BSc graduate outperforms the BA graduate **d** 10.22 **e** 9.54

19.16 a $F = 20.43$, p-value $= 0$. There is enough evidence to support the model's validity. **b** I_2: $t = 1.86$, p-value $= .0713$. I_3: $t = -1.58$, p-value $= .1232$. There is not enough evidence to conclude that weather is a factor. **c** $t = 3.30$, p-value $= .0012$. There is enough evidence to conclude that weekend attendance is, on average, larger than weekday attendance.

19.18 a $\hat{y} = 29,217 - 938$Bedrooms $+ 79.9$Hsize $- 5.07$Lsize $+ 20,487 I_1 + 12,795 I_2 + 19,512 I_3$. Example 18.2: $\hat{y} = 37,718 + 2306$Bedrooms $+ 74.3$Hsize $- 4.36$Lsize **b** I_1: $b_4 = 20,487$; in this sample the average two-story house sells for $20,487 more than the average ranch house. $t = 2.93$, p-value $= .0043$. There is enough evidence to infer that two-story houses sell for a different amount than ranch houses. I_2: $b_5 = 12,795$; in this sample the average side-split house sells for $12,795 more than the average ranch house. $t = 1.76$, p-value $= .0812$. There is not enough evidence to infer that side-split houses sell for a different amount than ranch

houses. I_3: $b_6 = 19,512$; in this sample the average back-split houses sell for $19,512 more than the average ranch house. $t = 2.45$, p-value $= .0162$. There is enough evidence to infer that back-split houses sell for a different amount than ranch houses.

19.20 a $\hat{y} = 7.02 + .250$Length $- 1.35$Type **b** $t = -1.43$, p-value $= .1589$. There is no evidence to conclude that the type of commercial affects memory test scores. **c** $I_1 = 1$ if type 1, $I_1 = 0$ otherwise $I_2 = 1$ if type 2, $I_2 = 0$ otherwise **d** $\hat{y} = 2.53 + .223$Length $+ 2.91 I_1 + 5.50 I_2$; I_1: $t = 1.61$, p-value $= .1130$; I_2: $t = 3.01$, p-value $= .0039$. There is enough evidence to infer that the type of commercial affects memory test scores. **e** The first model attempted to treat a qualitative variable as if it were quantitative.

19.22 a $I_1 = 1$ if no scorecard, $I_1 = 0$ otherwise $I_2 = 1$ if scorecard overturned more than 10%, $I_2 = 0$ otherwise **b** $\hat{y} = 4.65 + .00012$LoanSize $+ 4.08 I_1 + 10.2 I_2$ **c** $s_\epsilon = 4.20$, $R^2 = .5327$; the model fits moderately well. **d** Loan size: $b_1 = .00012$; for each additional dollar of loan the default rate in the sample increases on average by .00012. $t = .83$, p-value $= .4084$. There is no evidence to infer that default rate and loan size are linearly related. I_1: $b_2 = 4.08$; in the sample the average default rate for banks with no scorecard is 4.08% higher than banks with scorecards. $t = 3.57$, p-value $= .0006$. There is sufficient evidence to infer that the default rate at banks with no scorecard is different from the default rate at banks with scorecards that overturn less than 10%. I_2: $b_3 = 10.2$; in the sample the average default rate for banks that overturn more than 10% is 10.2% higher than banks with scorecards that overturn less than 10%. $t = 10.08$, p-value $= 0$. There is sufficient evidence to infer that the default rate at banks that overturn more than 10% is different from the default rate at banks with scorecards that overturn less than 10%. **e** 1.62, 25.36

19.24 $\hat{y} = 10.26 - .0002$Wage $- .1069$PctPT $+ .0599$PctU $+ 1.56$AvShift $- 2.64$U-MRel **b** $t = 3.11$, p-value $= .0025$. There is enough evidence to infer that the availability of shiftwork affects absenteeism. **c** $t = -5.36$, p-value $= 0$. There is enough evidence to conclude that in organizations where union–management relations are good absenteeism is lower.

19.26 a $I_1 = 1$ if form 1, $I_1 = 0$ otherwise $I_2 = 1$ if form 2, I_2

= 0 otherwise

$I_3 = 1$ if form 3, I_3

= 0 otherwise

b Time $= \beta_0 + \beta_1 I_1 + \beta_2 I_2 + \beta_3 I_3 + \epsilon$ **c** F = 2.94, p-value = .0363. This is the same result as we produced in Exercise 14.10.

19.28 a $I_1 = 1$ if English department, $I_1 = 0$ otherwise

$I_2 = 1$ if Mathematics department, $I_2 = 0$ otherwise

b $F = 1.73$, p-value = .1783

19.30 a $\hat{y} = 2.410 + .611$HSGPA **b** In Exercise 18.6 the regression equation included SAT and Activities.

19.32 The result is the same as that achieved in Example 18.10 because both independent variables were shown to be linearly related to the dependent variable.

19.34 $\hat{y} = -72.06 + .896$Erns_Alw + $.406$SO + $.1096$Hits_Alw. Only earned runs allowed, strikeouts, and hits allowed were related to runs scored by opponents.

19.36 Gender: $b_2 = -.039$ in this application female-dominated jobs are higher paid than male-dominated jobs.

19.40 a First-order model with interaction **b** $\hat{y} = 641 - 64.2$Cars $- 10.6$Speed + 1.08Cars$\times$Speed **c** $F = 54.14$, p-value = 0. There is sufficient evidence to infer that the model is valid.

19.42 a $I_1 = 1$ if ad was in newspaper

$I_1 = 0$ otherwise

$I_2 = 1$ if ad was on radio

$I_2 = 0$ otherwise

b $F = 2.33$, p-value = .1023. There is not enough evidence to infer that the model is valid. **c** In part (b) we showed that the model is not statistically valid which allows us to infer that none of the independent variables are linearly related to the number of customers.

19.44 a Units $= \beta_0 + \beta_1$ Years $+ \beta_2$ Years^2 + ϵ **b** $\hat{y} = 331.2 + 21.45$Years $-$ $.848$Years^2 **c** $s_\epsilon = 87.98$ and $R^2 = .1893$. The model fits poorly.

Chapter 20

20.2

Period	Five-Period Moving Average
1	—
2	—
3	38.8
4	35.4
5	35.8
6	38.8
7	44.4
8	46.8
9	48.8
10	46.2
11	—
12	—

20.4

Period	Three-Period Moving Average
1	—
2	19.00
3	21.67
4	24.33
5	26.67
6	26.67
7	26.33
8	24.67
9	24.33
10	21.00
11	19.00
12	—

20.8

Period	S_t
1	12
2	16.80
3	16.16
4	22.43
5	18.09
6	16.42
7	23.28
8	21.46
9	22.69
10	15.74

20.10

Period	S_t
1	38
2	38.5
3	38.85
4	39.47
5	40.12
6	40.91
7	41.82
8	42.53
9	42.88
10	43.09

20.14

Period	Five-Day Moving Average
1	—
2	—
3	33.2
4	34.8
5	34.0
6	37.0
7	36.4
8	35.2
9	33.0
10	36.2
11	34.8
12	37.0
13	39.4
14	44.2
15	44.4
16	45.0
17	46.0
18	43.6
19	—
20	—

20.16

Period	S_t
1	18.0
2	24.0
3	24.4
4	31.0
5	27.4
6	24.5
7	29.1
8	30.6
9	29.2
10	32.7
11	37.2
12	43.1
13	38.3
14	33.4
15	31.6
16	37.0

20.26 a

Period	Percentage of Trend
1	101.3
2	91.2
3	81.1
4	71.0
5	77.8
6	91.4
7	111.8
8	128.8
9	139.0
10	128.9
11	145.9
12	122.2
13	98.5
14	81.6
15	68.0
16	61.2

20.28

Period	Percentage of Trend
1	76.7
2	81.1
3	89.3
4	113.1
5	121.5
6	100.2
7	107.5
8	99.5
9	82.7
10	94.0
11	112.5
12	139.1
13	119.4
14	81.3
15	104.4
16	104.4
17	94.3
18	79.6
19	99.8
20	87.5
21	108.5

20.32

Day	Seasonal Index
Monday	.671
Tuesday	.865
Wednesday	.855
Thursday	1.260
Friday	1.349

20.34

Quarter	Seasonal Index
1	1.193
2	.956
3	.993
4	.859

20.36

Quarter	Seasonal Index
1	.839
2	1.057
3	1.275
4	.829

20.38

Quarter	Seasonal Index
1	1.055
2	.956
3	.930
4	1.059

20.40

Day	Seasonal Index
Sunday	1.336
Monday	.511
Tuesday	.499
Wednesday	.616
Thursday	.698
Friday	1.175
Saturday	2.165

20.42

Quarter	Seasonal Index
1	1.094
2	.958
3	.688
4	1.260

20.44 Model 1: MAD = 1.225, SSE = 7.39; Model 2: MAD = .625, SSE = 3.75
20.46 Tech. 1: MAD = 2.0, SSE = 24; Tech. 2: MAD = 3.4, SSE = 93; Tech. 3: MAD = 2.2, SSE = 31
20.48 14.2
20.50 MAD = 5.5, 4.87, 4.9 for ω = .3, .6, .7, respectively
20.52 842.1
20.54 35.6
20.56 280.1; 75.6; 95.7; 116.2; 137.1; 277.5; 381.0
20.58 851.8; 855.4; 862.2; 870.0
20.60 Mon., Tue.: 2501.5; Wed., Thur.: 2647; Fri., Sat.: 2707.5

20.62 386
20.64 1: 68.60; 2: 87.75; 3: 106.83; 4: 71.05
20.68 16.5; 22.2; 21.8; 31.0; 35.2
20.70

Period	Percentage of Trend
1	−1696.1
2	350.9
3	178.1
4	127.2
5	105.6
6	95.1
7	89.5
8	86.0
9	83.2
10	82.5
11	84.5
12	88.1
13	90.0
14	90.4
15	91.2
16	92.4
17	92.0
18	93.1
19	96.6
20	100.6
21	105.4
22	107.7
23	110.3
24	112.5

20.72 −6.335
20.76 1: .636; 2: 1.041; 3: 1.398; 4: .925
20.78 1: 22.980; 2: 37.938; 3: 52.036; 4: 34.142
20.80 Jan 1.012; Feb 1.007; Mar 1.004; Apr .994; May 1.000; Jun .999; Jul 1.008; Aug 1.007; Sep .986; Oct .989; Nov .997; Dec .995

Chapter 21

21.2 170.1, 173.77, 177.43, 181.1, 184.77, 188.43, 192.1
21.4 c No **d** level shift
21.6 c The process is under control
21.8 The process went out of control at sample 19 ($\bar{x}$ chart).
21.10 a & b 25.25, 25.93, 26.62, 27.30, 27.99, 28.67, 29.36 **c** 1.12, 6.10, 11.08
21.12 a 0, 11.68, 26.65 **b** 10.25, 18.76, 27.27 **c** The process went out of contrtol at sample 13 ($\bar{x}$ chart).
21.14 The process is under control.
21.16 The process is under control.
21.18 The process went out of control at sample 19 ($\bar{x}$ chart).

21.20 The process went out of control at sample 25.

21.24 The process went out of control at sample 21 (S chart).

21.26 The process went out of control at sample 23 (S chart).

21.28 The process is under control.

21.30 The process went out of control at sample 24.

21.32 The process went out of control at sample 29 ($\bar{x}$ chart).

Chapter 22

In all exercises involving comparing two or more populations of quantitative data and analyzing the relationship between two quantitative variables, we applied the chi-squared test for normality at the 5% significance level to determine whether to apply a parametric or nonparametric test. See the notes that appear before Chapters 11, 12, and 16.

22.2 z-test of p: $z = 3.15$, p-value $= .0016$. There is overwhelming evidence to conclude that the new technology affects the sex of the baby.

22.4 t-test of μ_D: $t = -2.29$, p-value $= .0121$. There is not enough evidence at the 1% significance level to conclude that company should proceed to stage 2.

22.6 a t-estimator of μ: LCL $= 6.40$, UCL $= 7.77$ **b** LCL $= \$80,031$, UCL $= \$97,156$

22.8 χ^2-test of a contingency table: $\chi^2 = 25.03$, p-value $= 0$. There is overwhelming evidence to infer that differences exist among the age categories with respect to alcohol use.

22.10 z-test of $p_1 - p_2$ (case 2): $z = -2.28$, p-value $= .0114$. There is evidence to indicate that the second commercial is viable.

22.12 Analysis of variance, single-factor independent samples design: $F = 1.37$, p-value $= .2543$. There is no evidence to infer that the type of meal affects test scores.

22.14 Multiple regression, test of coefficients (high degree of multicollinearity—stepwise regression used). The only independent variables that are linearly related to salary are assists in 1992–93 ($t = 2.79$, p-value $= .0076$) and goals in 1992–93 ($t = 2.78$, p-value $= .0077$). It appears that players' salaries are most strongly related to the number of goals and the number of assists in the previous season.

22.16 Analysis of variance, single-factor independent samples design: $F = 1.09$, p-value $= .3441$. There is no evidence to infer that sales of cigarettes differ according to placement.

22.18 t-test of μ: $t = -1.31$, p-value $= .0994$. There is little evidence to conclude that the seminars should be instituted.

22.20 t-tests of μ_D **a** $t = 2.98$, p-value $= .0024$. There is enough evidence to conclude that the ETS claim is false. **b** $t = -3.39$, p-value $= .0008$. There is enough evidence to conclude that the Kaplan claim is also false.

22.22 t-test of μ: $t = 20.61$, p-value $= 0$. There is overwhelming evidence to infer that there is a decrease in metabolism when children watch television. **b** Wilcoxon rank sum test: $z = 3.10$, p-value $= .0010$. There is enough evidence to conclude that the decrease in metabolism is greater among obese children.

22.24 Analysis of variance, two-factor design: test for interaction: $F = 1.66$, p-value $= .1935$. There is no evidence of interaction. Test for gender: $F = 3.77$, p-value $= .0541$. There is weak evidence of a difference between men and women. Test for fitness: $F = 39.97$, p-value $= 0$. There is overwhelming evidence of differences among the three levels of fitness.

22.26 Multiple regression t-tests of the coefficients: Only problem-solving skill ($t = 6.27$, p-value $= 0$) and technical knowledge ($t = 11.24$, p-value $= 0$) are linearly related to quality.

22.28 a Equal-variances t-test of $\mu_1 - \mu_2$: $t = -3.71$, p-value $= .0001$. There is enough evidence to infer that children who wash their hands four or more times per day have fewer sick days due to cold and flu. **b** Wilcoxon rank sum test: $z = -6.03$, p-value $= 0$. There is enough evidence to infer that children who wash their hands four or more times per day have fewer sick days due to stomach illness.

22.30 Multiple regression t-tests of the coefficients: Neither potential evaporation ($t = 1.36$, p-value $= .177$) nor precipitation ($t = .98$, p-value $= .329$) appears to be related to flow.

22.32 Wilcoxon rank sum tests

Question 1: $z = -4.95$, p-value $= 0$. There is overwhelming evidence to infer that customers who say they will return assess quality of work higher than customers who do not plan to return.

Question 2: $z = -1.56$, p-value $= .0589$. There is weak evidence to infer that customers who say they will return assess fairness of price higher than customers who do not plan to return.

Question 3: $z = -.56$, p-value $= .2888$. There is no evidence to infer that customers who say they will return assess explanation of work and guarantee higher than customers who do not plan to return.

Question 4: $z = -1.65$, p-value $= .0490$. There is evidence to infer that customers who say they will return assess the checkout process higher than customers who do not plan to return.

22.34 Questions 1 to 4: Kruskal–Wallis tests

Question 1: $H = 2.63$, p-value $= .2678$. There is no evidence to conclude that there are differences in the assessment of quality of work performed among the three stores.

Question 2: $H = 5.25$, p-value $= .0723$. There is no evidence to conclude that there are differences in the assessment of fairness of price among the three stores.

Question 3: $H = .37$, p-value $= .8304$. There is no evidence to conclude that there are differences in the assessment of explanation of work and guarantee among the three stores.

Question 4: $H = 1.25$, p-value $= .5341$. There is no evidence to conclude that there are differences in the assessment of the checkout process among the three stores.

Question 5 and comments: χ^2-test of a contingency table

Question 5: $\chi^2 = 2.48$, p-value $= .2897$. There is no evidence to conclude that differences exist among the three stores with respect to whether the customer will return in the future.

Comments: $\chi^2 = 30.98$, p-value $= 0$. There is overwhelming evidence to conclude that differences exist among the three stores with respect to customer comments.

22.36 a χ^2 goodness-of-fit test: $\chi^2 = 9.40$, p-value $= .4943$. There is no evidence to indicate that the dice are not fairly balanced. **b** z-test of p: $z = -.48$, p-value $= .3152$. There is no evidence to infer that the dice are set up so that the probability of 7 is less than 6/36.

22.38 Question 1: Equal-variances t-test of $\mu_1 - \mu_2$: $t = -4.00$, p-value $= 0$. There is enough evidence to indicate that recovery is faster in the United States.

Question 2: z-tests of $p_1 - p_2$ (case 1)

1 month after heart attack: $z = -1.55$, p-value $= .0609$. There is no (or at best, weak) evidence to infer that recovery is faster in the United States.

6 months after heart attack: $z = .43$, p-value $= .6646$. There is no evidence to infer that recovery is faster in the United States.

12 months after heart attack: $z = .26$, p-value $= .6016$. There is no evidence to infer that recovery is faster in the United States.

22.40 b Analysis of variance, two-factor design

Product C: Test for interaction: $F = 1.03$, p-value $= .3628$. There is no evidence of interaction.

Test for flow: $F = 3.69$, p-value $= .0315$. There is evidence to infer that there are differences in yield among the three flows.

Test for temperature: $F = 14.06$, p-value $= .0004$. There is evidence to infer that there are differences in yield between the two temperatures.

Product Y: Test for interaction: $F = 14.03$, p-value $= 0$. There is enough evidence to conclude that temperature and flow interact to affect product yield.

22.42 Analysis of variance single-factor, independent samples design: $F = 34.35$, p-value $= 0$. There is enough evidence to conclude that the type of music affects test results.

22.44 The data are observational. There may be a link between arthritis and Alzheimer's disease that explains the statistical result.

22.46 Analysis of variance, two-factor design: Test for interaction: $F = .72$, p-value $= .4927$. There is no evidence of interaction. Test for age: $F = 6.37$, p-value $= .0030$. There is enough evidence to conclude that age affects offers.

Test for gender: $F = 7.98$, p-value $= .0062$. There is enough evidence to conclude that gender affects offers.

22.48 Wilcoxon rank sum test: $z = 3.83$, p-value $= .0001$. There is enough evidence to conclude that women pay higher rates of interest than men.

22.49 Relationship between interest rates and sales: Spearman rank correlation coefficient test: $r_s = -.2629$, $z = -8.53$, p-value $= 0$. There is overwhelming evidence to infer that interest rates and sales are linearly related.

Relationship between interest rates and ages: Spearman rank correlation coefficient test: $r_s = -.1853$, $z = -6.01$, p-value $= 0$. There is overwhelming evidence to infer that interest rates and age of business are linearly related.

Difference between sales: Wilcoxon rank sum tests: $z = -14.09$, p-value $= 0$. There is overwhelming evidence to conclude that businesses owned by women have lower sales than businesses owned by men.

Difference between ages: Wilcoxon rank sum tests: $z = -6.26$, p-value $= 0$. There is overwhelming evidence to conclude that businesses owned by men are older than businesses owned by women.

Interest rates among the three types of businesses: Kruskal–Wallis test: $H = 7.22$, p-value $= .0270$. There is enough evidence to conclude that there are differences in interest rates among the three types of business.

Credits

Index

A

Acceptance sampling, 223
Accounting, 12, 13
Addition rule, 178, 179
Additive model, 781
Adjusted R^2, 685
Advertising, 56
Aggregate production planning, 11, 12
Alternative hypothesis, 313, 340, 341
Analysis of variance (ANOVA), 479–542
  Bartlett's test, 533, 534
  Bonferroni adjustment, 528
  Fisher's LSD method, 526, 527
  fixed vs. random-effects models, 499
  independent samples/blocks, 498
  multiple comparisons, 526–533
  operations management application, 521–525
  randomized block design, 499–507
  regression analysis, and, 755–757
  single-factor ANOVA, 481–497
  single-factor vs. multifactor models, 498
  Tukey's multiple comparison method, 528, 529
  two-factor ANOVA, 507–521
Analysis of variance (ANOVA) table, 487
ANOVA. *See* Analysis of variance (ANOVA)
ANOVA table, 487
Approximate mean/variance for grouped data, 124
Approximate sampling distribution of sampling proportion, 279
Aptitude test, 96
Arithmetic mean, 90–93
Assignable variation, 835
Association. *See* Measures of association
Audit Sampling Guide, 162
Auditing, 161, 162
Autocorrelation, 668, 669

B

Backordering, 12
Balanced, 509
Bar charts, 48–51
Bartlett's test, 533, 534
Bayes theorem, 183
Bayesian decision analysis, 183
Beta coefficient, 649
Between-treatments variation, 483
Bias, 161
Billings, Josh, 386
Bimodal, 33
Binomial distributions, 209–219
  binomial tables, 214, 215
  Excel, 217
  Minitab, 218
  Poisson distribution, and, 222, 223
Binomial probability distribution, 210
Binomial random variable, 210
Binomial tables, 214, 215
Bivariate distribution, 200–205
Bonferroni adjustment, 528
Bourke, Pat, 842n
Box-and-whisker plot, 119
Box plots, 39, 119–123
Branding, 9
Brando, Marlon, 387
Business cycles, 780

C

Capital budgeting, 7
Capital structure, 8
Cases
  accounting course exemptions, 456
  ambulance/fire department response interval study, 897
  antidepressant drug, evaluation of, 900
  bank discrimination against women owners, 875, 879, 901
  Bank of Commerce customer survey, 623
  baseball (bunting), 233
  Bombardier Inc., 66
  Bonanza International, 455
  Canadian federal budget, 87
  capitalization ratios, 622
  Challenger disaster, 774
  code of professional ethics, effects of, 570
  Duxbury Press, 676, 729
  financial planning, effects of, 540
  host selling/announcer commercials, 476
  insurance compensation for lost revenues, 677
  IPOs, 898
  Let's Make a Deal, 231
  market timing, 231
  multinational firms (diversification strategy), 541
  North American Free Trade Agreement, 67
  nutrition education programs, 901
  Pacific salmon catches, 66
  PC Magazine survey, 898
  Pepsi's exclusivity agreement with a university, 391, 392
  Quebec referendum vote, 729, 730
  Quebec separation, 476
  speciality advertising recall, 454
  sports betting (intermediate results), 569
  stock market returns (death of key executives), 475
  stock market, probabilities theory, 232
  stock return distributions, 571
  track and field performance forecasts, 775
  uninsured motorists, 392
  university grades (predicting, from high school grades), 676
  Wilfred Laurier University graduate survey, 899
Centered moving averages, 786–788
Centerline, 838
Central limit theorem, 266
Central location. *See* Measures of central location
Chance variation, 834

Chartjunk, 77
Chase strategy, 11
Chebyshev, Pavroty, 115
Chebyshev's theorem, 115, 116
Chi-squared distribution, 364–372
Chi-squared goodness-of-fit test, 544–551
Chi-squared statistic, 364
Chi-squared test of a contingency table, 551–560
Choosing the correct statistical technique, 342–344, 462–466
Class relative frequency, 30
Classes, 25
Classical approach, 168
Cluster sampling, 159
Coefficient of correlation
  Pearson, 128, 657, 673
  population, 128
  sample, 128
  Spearman rank correlation coefficient, 659–664
  testing, 657–659
Coefficient of determination
  multiple regression, 685, 686
  simple linear regression, 644–646
Coefficient of determination adjusted for degrees of freedom, 685
Coefficient of variation, 110, 111
Collinearity, 700
Comparison of two populations, 393–459
  difference between two means (independent sample), 395–412
  difference between two means (matched pairs experiment), 414–425
  difference between two population proportions, 434–445
  market segmentation, 447–449
  observational/experimental data, 413, 414
  ratio of two variances, 425–434
Comparisonwise Type I error rate, 527
Complement, 171
Complement rule, 178
Complete factorial experiment, 509
Completely randomized design, 490
Computer programs. See Excel, Minitab
Computer simulation. See Simulation experiments
Concepts (statistical), 886, 887
Conditional probability, 173–176, 200, 201
Confidence interval estimator of expected value of y, 653
Confidence level, 7, 290

Consistency, 288
Contingency (cross-classification) table, 551
Continuity correction factor, 277
Continuous probability distributions, 235–260
  exponential distribution, 254–257
  normal distribution, 240–254
  probability density function, 237
  uniform distribution, 238, 239
Continuous random variable, 187
Control charts, 838–840
Control charts for attributes, 860–864
Control charts for variables, 840–860
Control limits, 838
Correlation, 128
Covariance, 126–128, 203, 204
CPM, 12, 252
CRC Standard Management Tables, 155
Cress, Barry, 842n
Cross-classification table, 551
Cross-sectional data, 22
Cumulative relative frequency, 34
Cycle, 780, 837
Cyclical effect, 800–805

D
Data
  cross-sectional, 22
  defined, 19
  experimental, 413, 414
  observational, 413, 414
  primary, 148
  published, 148, 149
  qualitative, 19
  quantitative, 19
  ranked, 20, 21
  secondary, 149
  time-series, 22
Data Analysis, CD-ROM (inside back cover)
Data collection
  observational/experimental studies, 149, 150
  published data, 148, 149
  surveys, 150–152
Deciles, 118
Degrees of freedom (d.f.), 349, 361
Dependent events, 174
Dependent variable, 56, 626
Description of single population. See Single population
Descriptive methods. See Graphical descriptive techniques, Numerical descriptive measures
Descriptive statistics, 18
Deseasonalizing, 809, 810

Deterministic model, 628
Dexterity test, 96
Discrete probability distribution, 188, 189
Discrete random variable, 187
Distribution-free statistics, 576. See also Nonparametric techniques
Diversification, 204
DJIA, 82, 83
Dollar unit sampling (DUS), 162
Dot plots, 38
Dow Jones Industrial Average (DJIA), 82, 83
Dummy variable, 747
Durbin-Watson test, 714–723
DUS, 162

E
Economics, 14
Empirical Rule, 113–115
Equal pay for equal work, 766
Equal pay for work of equal value, 766–771
Equal-variances test statistic and interval estimator, 397
Error variable, 636
Estimate, 152, 286
Estimation, 285–309
  consistency, 288
  interval estimators, 286
  point estimators, 286
  population mean/population standard deviation known, 289–302
  relative efficiency, 288
  sample size, 302–304
  simulation experiments, 305–308
  unbiasedness, 287
  width of interval, 300, 301
Event, 168
Excel, 69. See also Minitab
  autoregressive model, 827
  bar chart, 49
  Bartlett's test, 534
  beta, 338, 339
  binomial distribution/inference about proportion, 383
  binomial probabilities, 217
  Bonferroni adjustment, 530
  box plot, 121, 122
  centered moving averages, 787, 788
  chi-squared estimate of variance, 371
  chi-squared goodness-of-fit test, 547, 548
  chi-squared test of a contingency table, 555
  chi-squared test of normality, 565

chi-squared test of variance, 369
complete factorial experiment, 509, 516, 517
correlation, 131
correlation of coefficient, 658
counting, 547
covariance, 130
cumulative frequency distribution, 35
cyclical effects, 801, 802
data analysis, 69
data retrieval, 69
Durbin-Watson test, 718, 720, 721
equal-variance t-test, 469
estimate of ratio of two variances, 433
exponential probabilities, 257
exponential smoothing, 790
F test, 430, 433, 468
Fisher's LSD method, 530
flowchart of techniques, 869
forecasting (exponential smoothing), 816
forecasting (regression analysis), 825, 827
Friedman test, 611
histogram, 27–30
inference about population proportion, 376, 379
Kruskal-Wallis test, 606
Lilliefors test, 616
Lilliefors test for residuals, 667
macros, 69
manipulating data, 458
market segmentation, 448, 449
matched pairs experiment, 415, 418
mean difference, 420
measures of central location, 97
missing data, 380
moving average, 783, 787
multicollinearity, 701
multiple regression, 683, 687, 692
95% confidence interval estimate, 295, 296
normal probabilities, 250
ogive, 35
P-Chart, 862, 863
p-value of test, 323
pattern test, 848
pay equity, 767, 770
pie chart, 46, 47
Poisson probabilities, 222
polynomial models, 738, 740
population mean (population standard deviation unknown), 356, 357, 359
prediction interval, 654
probability of Type II error, 339

quartiles, 121
R Chart, 858
random numbers, 155, 156
randomized block design ANOVA, 502, 505
recoding data, 381
regression analysis, 136
residuals/standardized residuals, 665
S chart, 849
scatter diagram, 58
seasonal effect, 807, 808
sign test, 592
simple linear regression, 631
simulation (sampling distribution), 273–275
single-factor ANOVA, 489, 494
slope, 643
Spearman rank coefficient, 662
standard error of estimate, 641
stepwise regression, 762, 763
t-estimate of 2 means, 402, 470
t-test (two samples), 400, 405
test of hypothesis about $P_1 - P_2$, 439, 442, 444
Toolpak, 69
transformations, 706, 708, 709
trend analysis, 795, 798
Tukey's method, 530
two-factor ANOVA, 509, 516, 517, 524, 542
Wilcoxon rank sum test, 583, 586
Wilcoxon signed rank sum test, 599
X-bar chart, 843, 844, 855
z-test of difference between two proportions, 467
Exhaustive, 167
Expected frequency, 546
Expected value, 192, 193
Experimental data, 413, 414, 637
Experimental study, 150
Experimental unit, 483
Experimentwise Type I error rate, 527
Exponential distribution, 254–257
Exponential random variable, 254
Exponential smoothing, 788–793, 814–819

F

F distribution, 426–434
F statistic, 426
F-to-enter, 758
F-to-remove, 758
Facility layout, 11
Factor, 480
Factorial experiments, 507
Feasibility study, 10

Fences, 120n
Financial accounting, 13
Financial management, 7, 8
Firm-specific (nonsystematic) risk, 651
First-order autocorrelation, 714, 715
First-order linear model, 628. *See also* Simple linear regression
First-order model, 732, 734, 735
Fisher's least significant difference (LSD) method, 526, 527
Fitted line, 132
Fixed-effects, 499
Forecasting, 811–828
    autoregressive model, 826–828
    exponential smoothing, 814–819
    MAD, 812
    regression analysis, 819–828
    SSE, 812
Form design, 11
4–3–2–1 system, 589
Fractional factorial experiments, 525
Frequency distribution, 25
Frequency histogram, 26–30
Friedman test, 608–612
Functional design, 10
Functional organization, 7

G

Gaber, Brian, 161n
Gallup Poll, 150
Geometric mean, 99, 100
Goalpost syndrome, 521, 522
Goodness-of-fit test, 544–551
Gosset, William S., 349, 353
Graphical deception, 81–86
Graphical descriptive techniques, 17–88
    bar charts, 48–51
    box plots, 39
    captions, 82, 83
    dot plots, 38
    frequency distribution, 25
    graphical deception, 81–86
    graphical excellence, 74–81
    histograms, 26–30
    least squares line, 59
    line charts, 51–53
    ogives, 34, 35
    pie charts, 44–48, 51
    relative frequency histograms, 30, 31
    scatter diagrams, 55–59
    stem-and-leaf displays, 35–38
    time-series chart, 51
Graphical excellence, 74–81
Grauer, Leslie, 676n

H

Harris Survey, 150
Hearn, Chick, 386
Heteroscedasticity, 667
Histograms
 bell-shaped, 33, 34
 frequency, 26–30
 modal classes, 33
 relative frequency, 30, 31
 skewness, 32
 symmetry, 32
Homoscedasticity, 667
Human resources management, 13
Hypothesis testing, 311–346
 alternative hypothesis, 313, 340, 341
 conclusions, 324
 critical concepts, 313, 314
 interval estimator, 330, 331
 null hypothesis, 313
 one-tail test, 325–327
 p-value method, 318–322
 population mean/population standard
  deviation known, 315
 power of a test, 338–340
 probability of Type II error, 333–337
 rejection region method, 315–317
 sample size, 337, 338
 setting up the alternative hypothesis,
  340, 341
 specification of hypotheses, 325
 standardized test statistic, 317, 318
 statistical process control, contrasted,
  852, 853
 test statistic, 314
 two-tail test, 327–330
 Type I error, 313
 Type II error, 313, 333–337

I

Important concepts, 886, 887
Independence samples
 difference between two means,
  395–412
 matched pairs experiment, compared,
  420, 421
 single-factor ANOVA, 481–497
 two-factor ANOVA, 507–521
 Wilcoxon rank sum test, 577–589
Independent events, 174
Independent random variables, 202
Independent variable, 626
Indicator variables, 747, 824
Inference
 background, 282, 283
 difference between two means
  (independent sample), 395–412

difference between two means
 (matched pairs experiment),
 414–425
difference between two population
 proportions, 434–445
flowchart of techniques, 870, 871
population mean/population standard
 deviation unknown, 349–363
population proportion, 373–386
population variance, 363–373
ratio of two variances, 425–434
review, 462–466, 868–874
sampling distribution, and, 269–271
single population, 347–392
Influential observations, 670
Information systems, 14
Instability, 836
Interaction, 734–736
Intercorrelation, 700
Interquartile range (IQR), 119
Interval estimator, 286
Interval estimator of μ, 290
Interval scale, 19
Inventory models, 12
Investment management, 8
Investment portfolio diversification,
 205–209
IQR, 119

J

Jermyn, Bruce, 897n
Job evaluation system, 768
Joint distribution, 200–205
Joint probability, 200

K

K-S test, 614
Kennedy, John, 79
Kolmogorov-Smirnov normality test,
 614, 617
Kruskal-Wallis test, 602–607

L

Landon, Alfred, 153
Law of averages, 386, 387
Law of large numbers, 386
Laws of expected value, 193
Laws of variance, 196
LCL, 290
Lead time, 252
Leaf, 35
Least squares line, 59, 132
Least squares method, 131–135,
 629–634
Leonard, Kevin, 677n
Level, 480

Level shift, 835
Lewis, Kevin, 842n
Lilliefors test, 614–617
Line charts, 51–53
Linear model, 794
Linear relationship, 57
Literary Digest poll, 153
Location analysis, 11
Log transformation, 705
Logistics, 11
Long-distance telephone services, 24
Lower confidence limit (LCL), 290
Lower control limit, 838
LSD, 526, 527

M

Macroeconomics, 14
MAD, 812
Managerial accounting, 12, 13
Manitoba Pay Equity Act, 768
Mann-Whitney test, 583, 586
Marginal probability, 200, 201
Market model, 8, 649–652
Market-related (systematic) risk, 651
Market segmentation, 9, 447–449
Marketing management, 9
Marketing mix, 9, 10
Markowitz, Harry, 205
Mass marketing, 9
Matched pairs experiment
 inference about difference between
  two means, 414–425
 sign test, 590–594
 Wilcoxon rank sum test, 594–600
Mathematical derivations, 343, 344
Mean
 arithmetic, 90–93
 geometric, 99, 100
Mean absolute deviation (MAD), 812
Mean of a population, 91
Mean of a sample, 91
Mean of binomial random variable, 215
Mean of the population of difference,
 417
Mean square for treatments, 486
Mean squares, 486
Mean value, 192
Measures of association, 126–139
 coefficient of correlation, 128
 covariance, 126–128
 least squares method, 131–135
Measures of central location, 90–102
 arithmetic mean, 90–93
 comparing the measures, 94–96
 geometric mean, 99, 100
 median, 93

mode, 94
symmetrical/skewed, 95
Measures of relative standing, 117–119
Measures of variability, 102–113
  coefficient of variation, 110, 111
  range, 103, 104
  standard deviation, 107
  variance, 104–107
Median, 93
Method of least squares, 59
Microeconomics, 14
Microsoft Excel. *See* Excel
Minitab, 70–72. *See also* Excel
  autoregressive model, 827
  bar chart, 50
  Bartlett's test, 535
  binomial distribution (inference about
    proportion), 384
  binomial probabilities, 218
  box plots, 122
  chi-square test, 556
  chi-squared goodness-of-fit test, 573
  chi-squared test for normality, 573,
    574
  chi-squared test for residuals, 667
  commands, 70, 71
  correlations, 131, 659
  covariance, 131
  cyclical effects, 802, 803
  data input, 71
  dialog boxes, 71
  difference between two proportions,
    439, 442, 444, 467
  Durbin-Watson test, 718, 720, 721
  equal-variances *t*-test, 469
  exponential probabilities, 257
  exponential smoothing, 791, 792
  F test, 431, 469
  Fisher's LSD method, 532
  forecasting (exponential smoothing),
    817
  forecasting (regression analysis), 825,
    827
  Friedman test, 611
  histogram, 28–30
  importing data, 71
  inference about population
    proportion, 377, 379
  Kolmogorov-Smirnov normality test,
    617
  Kruskal-Wallis test, 606
  Lilliefors test, 617
  manipulating data, 459
  Mann-Whitney test, 583, 586
  market segmentation, 449
  matched pairs experiment, 415, 419

mean difference, 420
measures of central location, 98
menus/tools, 70
missing data, 380
moving average, 784, 785
multicollinearity, 701
multiple regression, 684, 687, 692
95% confidence interval estimate,
  296, 297
normal probabilities, 250
outliers (unusual observations)?, 671
p chart, 863
p-value of test, 323, 324
pattern tests, 848, 861
pay equity, 767, 771
Pearson correlation coefficient, 659,
  662
pie chart, 47
Poisson probabilities, 222
polynomial models, 738, 740
power of the test, 339, 340
prediction interval, 655
projects/worksheets, 71
R chart, 858, 859
random numbers, 156, 157
randomized block design ANOVA, 503
recoding data, 381
regression analysis, 136
releases, 72
residuals/standardized residuals, 666
S chart, 849, 850
scatter diagram, 58, 59
seasonal effect, 808
sign test, 593
simple linear regression, 632, 633
simulation (sampling distribution),
  274, 275
single-factor ANOVA, 490
slope, 643
stacked data, 459
standard error of estimate, 641
stem-and-leaf displays, 36–38
stepwise regression, 763, 764
t confidence intervals, 360
t-test of mean, 357
transformations, 706, 708, 709
trend analysis, 796, 798
Tukey's method, 531
two sample *t*-test, 400, 402, 406
two-way ANOVA, 517, 524
web site, 72
Wilcoxon signed rank test, 599
windows, 70
X-bar chart, 844, 856
z-test, 323, 324
Missing data, 380

Modal class, 33, 98
Mode, 94
Model building, 765, 766
Modern portfolio theory (MPT), 205
Moving averages, 781–788
MSE, 486
MST, 486
Multicollinearity, 691, 701
Multifactor, 498
Multimodal, 33
Multinomial experiment, 544, 545
Multiple regression, 679–730. *See also*
  Regression analysis, Simple
  linear regression
  coefficient of determination, 685, 686
  Durbin-Watson test, 714–723
  estimating coefficients/assessing
    model, 681–699
  F-test, 691
  first-order autocorrelation, 714
  multicollinearity, 700
  regression diagnostics, 699–725
  required conditions for error variable,
    681
  standard error of estimate, 685
  t-test, 690, 691
  testing the coefficients, 689, 690
  testing validity of model, 686–689
  transformations, 705
Multiplication rule, 179
Multiplicative model, 781
Mutually exclusive, 167

N

Negative first-order autocorrelation,
  714, 715
Negative linear relationship, 57
Negatively skewed, 32, 33, 95
Nielsen ratings, 153
Nightline phone-in show, 154
95% confidence interval estimator of μ,
  291
Nodes, 170
Nominal scale, 19
Nonlinear relationship, 57
Nonparametric techniques, 576–624
  Friedman test, 608–612
  Kruskal-Wallis test, 602–607
  Lilliefors test, 614–617
  Mann-Whitney test, 583, 586
  sign test, 590–594
  Spearman rank correlation coefficient,
    659–663
  test for normality, 613–617
  Wilcoxon rank sum test for
    independent samples, 577–589

Nonparametric techniques, *continued*
  Wilcoxon rank sum test for matched
    pairs, 594–600
Nonresponse error, 161
Nonsampling error, 161, 162
Nonsystematic risk, 651
Normal approximation of the binomial
    distribution, 276–279
Normal distribution, 240–254
Normal random variable, 241
Null hypothesis, 313
Numerical descriptive measures,
    89–146
  arithmetic mean, 90–93
  Chebyshev's theorem, 115, 116
  coefficient of correlation, 128
  coefficient of variation, 110, 111
  covariance, 126–128
  empirical rule, 113–115
  geometric mean, 99, 100
  measures of relative standing,
    117–119
  median, 93
  mode, 94
  range, 103, 104
  standard deviation, 107
  variance, 104–107

O

Observational data, 413, 414, 637
Observational study, 149
Ogive, 34, 35
One-sided interval estimators, 331
One-tail test, 325–327
One-way ANOVA, 481–497
Open-ended class, 31
Operations management, 10–12
Opportunity costs, 14
Order, 732
Ordinal scale, 20, 21
Origin, 171
Orthogonal arrays, 525
Out of control, 835–837
Outliers, 120, 123, 669, 670
Oy vey, 154

P

p chart, 860–863
p-value method, 318–322
p-value of a test, 319
Parameter, 6
Partitioning of the sum of squares, 488
Pattern tests, 845–848, 861
Pay equity, 766–771
Pearson coefficient of correlation, 128,
    657, 673

Percentage of trend, 800
Percentile, 118
Personal interview, 151
PERT, 12, 252
Pie charts, 44–48, 51
Plane, 680
Point estimator, 286
Poisson distribution, 162, 219–223
Poisson experiment, 219
Poisson random variable, 220
Polynomial models, 732–745
Pooled proportion estimate, 436
Pooled variance estimate, 397
Population, 6
Population coefficient of correlation,
    128
Population coefficient of variation, 110
Population covariance, 126
Population locations, 576
Population mean, 91
Population standard deviation, 107
Population variance, 105
Portfolio diversification, 205–209
Portfolio performance measurement,
    108
Positive first-order autocorrelation, 714,
    715
Positive linear relationship, 57
Positive relationship, 57
Positively skewed, 32, 33, 95
Posterior probabilities, 182
Power of a test, 338–340
PPS, 162
Prediction interval, 652–656
Predictor, 732
Preliminary design, 10
Prevention approach, 834
Pricing, 9
Primary data, 148
Prior probabilities, 182
Probabilistic model, 628
Probability, 165–234
  addition rule, 178, 179
  classical approach, 168
  complement rule, 178
  conditional, 173–176, 200, 201
  definition, 168
  joint, 200
  marginal, 200, 201
  multiplication rule, 179
  posterior, 182
  prior, 182
  relative frequency, and, 189, 190
  relative frequency approach, 168
  requirements, 169
  subjective approach, 168

Type II error, of, 333–337
Probability density function, 237
Probability distribution, 187
  binomial, 210
  binomial experiment, of, 212
  bivariate, 200, 201
  continuous. *See* Continuous
    probability distributions
  discrete, 188, 189
  Poisson random variables, of, 220
Probability of an event, 169
Probability proportionate to size (PPS),
    162
Probability trees, 170, 171, 180–183
Problem objectives, 343, 344
Process planning, 11
Process variation, 834–840
Product design, 10, 11
Production design, 11
Project management, 12
Published data, 148, 149
Publisher's home page, 15

Q

Quadratic model, 794
Qualitative data, 19, 21, 342. *See also*
    Tests for qualitative data
Quality control, 834. *See also* Statistical
    process control (SPC)
Quantitative data, 19, 21, 343
Quartile, 118
Questionnaire design, 151
Queuing, 12

R

R chart, 856–859
R^2, 644
Random-effects, 499
Random experiment, 166, 167
Random numbers, 155–157
Random variable, 186
Random variation, 781
Randomized block design, 498
Range, 103, 104
Range approximation, 115
Ranked data, 20, 21, 342
Rate of return, 100n
Reagan, Ronald, 79
Reciprocal transformation, 705
Recoding date, 381
Regression analysis, 626
  analysis of variance, and, 755–757
  forecasting, and, 819–828
  indicator variables, 747
  linear regression. *See* Simple linear
    regression

model building, 765, 766
multiple regression. *See* Multiple regression
pay equity, and, 766–771
polynomial models, 732–745
qualitative independent variables, 745–755
stepwise regression, 758–765
Regression line, 132
Rejection region, 316
Rejection region method, 315–317
Relative efficiency, 288
Relative frequency histograms, 30, 31
Relative frequency approach, 168
Relative frequency distribution, 30
Relative standing, 117–119
Repeated measures design, 498
Replicate, 509
Research hypothesis, 313
Residual analysis, 664–667
Residuals, 134, 639
Response surface, 680
Response variable, 483
Responses, 483
Reverse conditional probability, 183
Riehl, Brial, 842n
Robust, 353
Roosevelt, Franklin D., 153
Rule of five, 548, 557

S

S chart, 846–851
Sample, 6
Sample coefficient of correlation, 128
Sample coefficient of variation, 110
Sample covariance, 126
Sample mean, 91
Sample size, 159
  estimation of a proportion, 381–383
  estimation, and, 302–304
  probability of Type II error, and, 337, 338
Sample size to estimate mean, 303
Sample space, 167
Sample standard deviation, 107
Sample variance, 106
Sampled population, 153
Sampling, 152–162
  auditing, and, 161, 162
  cluster, 159
  errors, 160, 161
  Literary Digest poll, 153
  Nielsen ratings, 153
  Nightline phone-in show, 154
  sample size, 159
  simple random, 154–157

stratified random, 157–159
Sampling distribution of difference between two means, 280–282
Sampling distribution of the mean, 262–273
Sampling distributions, 261–284
  approximate sampling distribution of sampling proportion, 279
  central limit theorem, 266
  computer simulation, 273–276
  inference, and, 269–271
  normal approximation of binomial, 276–279
  sampling distribution of difference between two means, 280–282
  sampling distribution of the mean, 262–273
Sampling error, 160
Scatter diagrams, 55–59, 629
Seasonal effect, 805–811
Seasonal indexes, 805
Seasonal variation, 780
Seasonally adjusted, 809
Seaver, Tom, 387
Second-order model, 733, 735, 736
Secondary data, 149
Secular trend, 779
Selection bias, 161
Self-administered questionnaire, 151
Self-elected samples, 153
Serially correlated, 668
Shape of a distribution, 140
Sign test, 590–594
Significance level, 7, 318
Simple event, 167
Simple linear regression, 625–677. *See also* Multiple regression, Regression analysis
  autocorrelation, 668, 669
  cause and effect relationship, 647, 648
  coefficient of determination, 644–646
  coefficients of correlation, 657–654
  confidence interval estimator of expected value of *y*, 653
  error variable, 636
  finance application (market model), 649–652
  heteroscedasticity, 667
  influential observations, 670
  least squares method, 629–634
  observational/experimental data, 637, 638
  outliers, 669, 670
  prediction interval, 652–656
  regression diagnostics, 664–671
  residual analysis, 664–667

slope, 641, 642
Spearman rank correlation coefficient, 659–663
standard error of estimate, 640, 641
sum of squares for error, 639
Simple random sample, 154–157
Simulation experiments
  estimation, 305–308
  sampling distributions, 273–276
Single population, 347–392
  law of averages, 386, 387
  population mean/population standard deviation unknown, 349–363
  population proportion, 373–386
  population variance, 363–373
Single-factor ANOVA, 481–497
66–38–25–11 system, 589
Skewness, 32, 33, 95
SLOP, 154
Smoothing techniques, 781–793
Software programs. *See* Excel, Minitab
SPC. *See* Statistical process control (SPC)
Spearman rank correlation coefficient, 659–663
Specification limits, 835
Square-root transformation, 705
Square transformation, 705
SS(Total), 488, 489
SSB, 499, 500
SSE
  sum of squares for error, 134, 484, 639
  sum of squares for forecast error, 812
SSR, 645
SST, 483, 484
Standard deviation, 107, 195
Standard deviation of *i*th residual, 665
Standard error of estimate, 640, 641, 685
Standard error of the mean, 267
Standard normal distribution, 242
Standard normal random distribution, 242, 243
Standardized test statistic, 317, 318
Statistic, 6
Statistical Abstract of the United States, The, 149
Statistical applications in business, 7–14
Statistical concepts, 886, 887
Statistical inference, 6. *See also* Inference
Statistical process control (SPC), 833–866
  control charts, 838–840
  control charts for attributes, 860–864

Statistical process control (SPC),
    continued
  control charts for variables, 840–860
  estimate process standard deviation by
      computing range, 853, 854
  hypothesis testing, contrasted, 852,
      853
  out of control, 835–837
  p chart, 860–863
  pattern tests, 845–848, 861
  process variation, 834–840
  R chart, 856–859
  S chart, 846–851
  $\bar{x}$ chart, 840–845, 850, 851, 853–856
Statistical techniques, 342–344,
    462–466
Statistics Canada, 148
Stem, 35
Stem-and-leaf displays, 35–38
Stepwise regression, 758–765
Stock and bond valuation, 8
Stratified random sample, 157–159
Student t distribution, 349–354
Subjective approach, 168
Sum of squares for blocks (SSB), 499,
    500
Sum of squares for error (SSE), 134,
    484, 639
Sum of squares for forecast error (SSE),
    812
Sum of squares for regression (SSR),
    645
Sum of squares for treatments (SST),
    483, 484
Sum of two random variables, 202
Summation notation, 144–146
Surveys, 150–152
Symmetry, 32
Systematic risk, 651

T

t-statistic, 349
Taguchi, Genichi, 521
Taguchi loss function, 521, 522
Target marketing, 9
Target population, 153
Telephone interview, 151
Test for normality
  chi-squared test, 562–565
  Kolmogorov-Smirnov test, 614

Lilliefors test, 614–617
Test marketing, 9
Test statistic, 314
Tests for qualitative data, 543–574
  chi-squared goodness-of-fit test,
      544–551
  chi-squared test for normality,
      562–565
  chi-squared test of a contingency
      table, 551–560
  z-test of p, 373–386
  z-test of $p_1 - p_2$, 434–445
Third-order model, 733
Time series, 778, 779
Time-series analysis, 777–831
  centered moving averages, 786–788
  components of a time series,
      779–781
  cyclical effect, 800–805
  deseasonalizing, 809, 810
  exponential smoothing, 788–793,
      814–819
  forecasting, 811–828. *See also*
      Forecasting
  moving averages, 781–788
  seasonal effect, 805–811
  seasonally adjusted, 809
  smoothing techniques, 781–793
  time-series models, 781
  trend analysis, 794–800
  uses, 778
Time-series chart, 51
Time-series data, 22
Time-series forecasting, 778. *See also*
    Forecasting
Time-series models, 781
Tolerance, 521
Total sum of squares [SS(Total)], 488,
    489
Transformation, 705
Treatment means, 480
Trend, 779, 836
Trend analysis, 794–800
Tukey, John, 35
Tukey's multiple comparison method,
    528, 529
Two-factor, 498
Two-factor ANOVA, 507–521
Two populations. *See* Comparison of
    two populations

Two-tail test, 327–330
Two-way classification, 509
Type I error, 313
Type II error, 313, 333–337

U

UCL, 290
Unbiased estimator, 287
Unconditional probability, 173
Under control, 835
Unequal-variances test statistic and
    interval estimator, 397, 398
Uniform distribution, 238, 239
Unimodal, 33
United States Bureau of the Census, 148
Upper confidence limit (UCL), 290
Upper control limit, 838

V

Variability, 103. *See also* Measures of
    variability
Variable, 18
Variance, 104–107, 193–197
Variance of a population, 105
Variance of a sample, 106
Variance of binomial random variable,
    215
Venn diagram, 172

W

Web page for book, 15
Width of interval, 300, 301
Wilcoxon rank sum test for independent
    samples, 577–589
Wilcoxon rank sum test for matched
    pairs, 594–600
Within-treatments variation, 484
Working capital management, 8

X

X-bar, $\bar{x}$ chart, 840–845, 850, 851,
    853–856
χ^2-statistic, 364

Z

z-test and estimator of p, 373–386
z-test and estimator of $p_1 - p_2$, 434–445